The SAGE Handbook of

Social Geographies

The SAGE
Handbook of

Social Geographies

Edited by
Susan J. Smith
Rachel Pain
Sallie A. Marston
and John Paul Jones III

Los Angeles | London | New Delhi
Singapore | Washington DC

First published 2010

SAGE Publications Ltd
1 Oliver's Yard
55 City Road
London EC1Y 1SP

SAGE Publications Inc.
2455 Teller Road
Thousand Oaks, California 91320

SAGE Publications India Pvt Ltd
B1/I 1, Mohan Cooperative Industrial Area
Mathura Road, Post Bag 7
New Delhi 110 044

SAGE Publications Asia-Pacific Pte Ltd
33 Pekin Street # 02-01
Far East Square, Singapore 048763

Library of Congress Control Number: 2009923580

British Library Cataloguing in Publication data

A catalogue record for this book is available from the British Library

ISBN 978-1-4129-3559-3

Typeset by Glyph International, Bangalore, India
Printed by MPG Books Groups, Bodmin, Cornwall
Printed on paper from sustainable resources

Contents

Contributors

Gavin Andrews received an undergraduate degree in human geography from Lampeter University in 1992 and a PhD in medical/health geography from University of Nottingham in 1997. Formerly a Lecturer, Senior Lecturer and Reader in Health Studies in the UK, in 2001 Gavin was appointed as Associate Professor at the Faculty of Nursing, University of Toronto and since 2006 has been Chair and Full Professor at McMaster University. His research contributes to three fields of health-geographic inquiry – 'the geography of health care organizations and work'; 'the geography of aging' and 'the geography of complementary medicine'. He recently co-edited three books: *Ageing and Place: Perspectives, Policy, Practice* (Routledge, 2005), *Sociology of Ageing: a Reader* (Rawat, 2008) and *Primary Health Care: People, Practice, Place* (Ashgate, 2009). He is the North American Editor *for International Journal of Older People Nursing*, and Associate Editor, *Journal of Applied Gerontology*.

Nicola Ansell is Reader in Human Geography in the Centre for Human Geography at Brunel University. Her research has focused on the geographies of children and youth in contexts of social and cultural change in southern Africa. She is the author of *Children, Youth and Development* (Routledge, 2005). Her current research addresses the impacts of AIDS on young people's livelihoods and future food security in Malawi and Lesotho.

Leela Bakshi is a volunteer trustee with Spectrum LGBT community forum in Brighton and Hove, and a volunteer researcher with the Count Me In Too project which examines contemporary LGBT lives in Brighton and Hove. This chapter is her first involvement in academic writing, and she is now contributing to writing a book exploring themes and learning from the project.

Clive Barnett is Reader in Human Geography at The Open University, Milton Keynes, UK. His research focuses on the geographies of democracy and public life. He is author of *Culture and Democracy* (Edinburgh University Press, 2003), Globalizing Responsibility (with Paul Cloke, Nick Clarke, and Alice Malpass, Wiley-Blackwell, 2010), co-editor of *Spaces of Democracy* (with Murray Low, Sage, 2004), *Geographies of Globalisation* (with Jennifer Robinson and Gillian Rose, Sage, 2008), *Extending Hospitality* (with Mustafa Dikeç and Nigel Clark, Edinburgh University Press, 2009), and *Rethinking the Public* (with Nick Mahony and Janet Newman, Policy Press, 2010).

Paul Bennett spent 9 years as Lecturer in Economic Geography at the University of Edinburgh. His research has explored the relationships between poor health and financial exclusion in the life insurance sector, including the implications of new genetic technologies, as well as the positive role insurance might play in the governance of corporate environmental standards. He is also interested in European economic and social policies, particularly in relation to the shipping sector, where he has investigated the tensions between competition law and environmental goals, between state-aid law and the provision of publicly-owned transport services, and between competitiveness and labour-standards. Paul is currently a Senior Researcher at the Scottish Government in Edinburgh.

Kathryn Besio is an Associate Professor of Geography at the University of Hawai'i at Hilo. She is a social-cultural geographer, and is interested in how the violent and messy legacies of colonialisms manifest in material inequalities and class, gender and ethnic privilege. She has also been told that she is 'obsessed' with issues of representation and how that informs research practice. This has led to a number of publications on autoethnography. Currently, she is researching 'Local' and local food on the island of Hawai'i, and the intersections between plantation and industrial agriculture, small scale agriculture, home gardens and Hawai'i Regional Cuisine.

Kath Browne works at the University of Brighton and has been lead researcher for the Count Me In Too research project since its inception in 2005. In 2007 Kath was awarded the Gill Memorial Award from the Royal Geographical Society recognizing geographical research in young researchers who have shown great potential. Kath co-edited the publication of *Geographies of Sexualities: Theory, Practices and Politics* with Jason Lim and Gavin Brown. In addition to the *Count Me In Too* book, she is currently working on two books, *Queer Methods and Methodologies,* co-edited with Catherine J. Nash (due 2010) and *Queer Spiritual Spaces,* with Sally Munt and Andrew Yip (due 2010). She has written over 30 academic publications and numerous community reports and is a trustee of Pride in Brighton and Hove.

David B. Clarke is Professor of Human Geography and Director of the Centre for Urban Theory at Swansea University/Prifysgol Abertawe. His research focuses on urbanism and social theory, poststructuralism, consumerism, the media, and film. He is the author of *The Consumer Society and the Postmodern City* (Routledge, 2003), editor of *The Cinematic City* (Routledge, 1997), and co-editor of *The Consumption Reader* (Routledge, 2003) and, most recently, *Jean Baudrillard: Fatal Theories* (Routledge, 2009).

Joyce Davidson is Associate Professor of Geography, cross-appointed with Women's Studies, at Queen's University, Canada. Following the publication of *Phobic Geographies* (Ashgate, 2003), Davidson developed a research and teaching program focused around health, embodiment and emotion. She has published in sociology and philosophy as well as geography journals, and is co-author of *Subjectivities, Knowledges and Feminist Geographies* (Rowman and Littlefield, 2002). Davidson's current research examines virtual reality therapies for autism spectrum and anxiety disorders. Organizer of the first (Lancaster, 2002) and second (Queen's, 2006, with Laura Cameron), Interdisciplinary Conference on Emotional Geographies, Davidson has also co-edited special issues and books on this subject, including: *Gender, Place and Culture* (with Liz Bondi, 2004, 11:3), *Social and Cultural Geography* (with Christine Milligan, 2004, 5:4), *Emotional Geographies* (with Liz Bondi and Mick Smith, Ashgate, 2005), and *Emotion, Place and Culture* (with Mick Smith, Laura Cameron and Liz Bondi, Ashgate, 2009). Davidson is lead and founding editor of the new Elsevier journal, *Emotion, Space and Society.*

Michael L. Dorn is Assistant Professor of Urban Education and Coordinator of the Disability Studies Program at Temple University. He is a cultural and health geographer with additional research interests in historical geography, the history of science and medicine, and disability studies. A key contributor to debates around research traditions and perspectives in medical and health geography, Mike has also encouraged the expansion of interest in disability topics beyond the focus on institutionalization and deinstitutionalization. Current research concerns the history of geographic thought in the Atlantic world, the historic and contemporary geopolitics of disability, and community-based service learning and community development in the Anglophone Caribbean. His book project examines the place of medical geographic ideas in the formation of American regional identities, linking early conjectures and projections of Ohio Valley as a region for European settlement and civilization into the larger body of scholarship on the Atlantic World.

Nancy Ettlinger is an Associate Professor of Geography at the Ohio State University. As a critical human geographer, she is interested in the relation between individuals and larger-scale phenomena (firms, institutions, societal projects), and in developing an interconnected view of social, political, economic, and cultural processes. Specific issues of interest include: the social, political, and cultural dimensions of production and consumption, culture as a lens through which to view all industries (not just a specific subset), and how and why the 'non-economic' figures in competitive dis/advantage; based on a critique of existing systems, the conditions under which competitiveness and social well being might converge; how the everyday economy figures in the urban landscape of uneven development; how we might draw insights from economic theory, while reconfiguring it, to merge economic with social and political goals; the implications of different interpretations of 'democracy' and how democracy/ies dis/connect with the everyday economy; how everyday citizens are governed and enrolled in societal projects (e.g. neoliberalism), the possibilities for constructive change, and the relation between subjectivity and change.

Nicholas R. Fyfe is Professor of Human Geography at the University of Dundee and Director of the Scottish Institute for Policing Research. His main research interests are in the fields of crime, criminal justice and policing but he has also worked on issues relating to activism, 'the shadow state' and voluntary sector. He undertook pioneering work on witness protection arrangements for those involved in serious and organized crime investigations and has written widely on the nature and impact of witness intimidation. His current research looks at the role of activism in the delivery of community safety, the nature of civility, and the policing of wildlife crime. In addition to contributing to academic debates, he has also worked closely with the policy community and has held several public appointments, including being a Special Advisor to the Scottish Parliament's Justice Committee.

Michael Hillman is an environmental geographer and Senior Lecturer in Environmental Policy and Management at Manchester Metropolitan University in the UK. He is a Fellow of the Royal Geographical Society / Institute of British Geographers and member of the Institute of Australian Geographers. He has an academic and professional background in trade unions, community development and environmental science in Australia, based in Sydney and Newcastle. His doctoral work and subsequent publications have focused on interdisciplinary approaches to environmental management, in particular integration of the biophysical and social dimensions of river rehabilitation. His work has emphasized the application of social and environmental justice in this field.

Peter Hopkins is a Senior Lecturer in Social Geography in the School of Geography, Politics and Sociology, Newcastle University, England, UK. He is a social geographer whose research interests focus upon a diverse range of social and spatial inequalities in contemporary Britain, including: critical perspectives on young people's geographies; urban geographies of race, racism and ethnicity; and geographies of religion. His work tends to be informed by qualitative research and draws upon debates within feminist social and urban geographies. Recent publications have appeared in *Area, ACME, Children's Geographies and Progress in Human Geography*. He is author of *The issue of masculine identities for British Muslims after 9/11* (Edwin Mellen) and co-editor of *Geographies of Muslim identities* (Ashgate), *Muslims in Britain* (Edinburgh University Press).

Richard Howitt is Professor of Human Geography in the Department of Environment and geography at Macquarie University, Sydney. His research is concerned with the interplay of social and environmental justice, particularly in relation to Indigenous rights. His book *Rethinking Resource Management* (Routledge, 2001) advocated deep integration of social, environmental and economic dimensions of justice into natural resource management systems. His teaching and applied research focuses on social impact assessment, corporate strategy, Indigenous rights, regional planning, social theory, human rights and resource and environmental policy. He received the Australian Award for University Teaching (Social Science) in 1999 and became Fellow of the Institute of Australian Geographers in 2004.

Robin Kearns is Professor of Geography at the University of Auckland and a ministerial appointment to New Zealand's National Health Committee. He has expertise in a range of qualitative methods and has applied these over the past two decades, principally in studies of health services and health determinants. His work is informed by a social justice vantage point and he has contributed to key debates theorizing the role of place in health geography. Robin's interests are increasingly shifting from health to wellbeing and current research projects include: investigating the effects of large-scale residential developments on coastal experience; the links between neighbourhood design and physical activity (especially for children); home maintenance issues for older people; and the place of activism in influencing urban change.

Carla C. Keirns is Assistant Professor of Preventive Medicine, Medicine and History at Stony Brook University, USA. She is a physician, historian, and health services research whose work is concerned with the contemporary and historical impact of chronic disease on individuals, communities, and societies. Her current research is concerned with the social context of asthma, hypertension and diabetes. Recent publications address changing trends in morbidity and mortality within and between societies, raising question about both overmedicalization and lack of access to health care, and the social resources fundamental to good health. Her book on the history of asthma in the United States will be published next year by the Johns Hopkins University Press.

Sara Kindon is a social geographer at Victoria University of Wellington, Aotearoa, New Zealand, where she teaches in the human geography and development studies programmes. Sara's research focuses on questions around how research can be democratised to effect social change and she currently works with a range of youth, refugee and indigenous partners in Wellington and the central north island. She has written extensively about the role of participatory action research within social geography both individually and as part of the collectives, mrs kinpaisby and mrs c kinpaisby-hill. She is also completing her doctorate, which explores aspects of her own power, complicity and desire within a participatory video research project with a group of Maaori over the past 10 years.

Audrey Kobayashi is Professor of Geography and Queen's Research Chair at Queen's University, Kingston. She teaches geographies of anti-racism and citizenship. Her published work spans a broad range of human rights issues including immigration, legal geographies, community activism, anti-racism, gender, and disability. She is currently involved in two major university-community research alliances, one to work with municipalities and volunteer groups to develop infrastructure for immigrant integration and anti-racism in second-tier cities; the other to work with Canadian disability organizations on disability policy development and implementation.

Hille Koskela is an Academy Research Fellow in the Department of Social Policy, University of Helsinki, Finland. She is also an Adjunct Professor in urban geography. Her research interests include women's fear of violence in cities, urban security politics, culture of fear, video surveillance and the politics of control, the emotional experience of being watched, and most recently, webcams as voluntary visual representations on the Internet. Currently she is conducting a research project analyzing the connection between visual surveillance and voluntary visual representation of the self and examining how webcams expose cultural tensions surrounding conceptions of visibility, agency and power.

Mei-Po Kwan is Distinguished Professor of Social and Behavioral Sciences at the Ohio State University (Columbus, USA), Belle van Zuylen Chair at Utrecht University (the Netherlands), and Adjunct Professor of Epidemiology and Biostatistics at Case Western Reserve University (Cleveland, USA). She is currently Editor of the Annals of the Association of American Geographers and Associate Editor of Geographical Analysis. She received the UCGIS Research Award from the University Consortium for Geographic Information Science (UCGIS) and the Edward L. Ullman Award from the Transportation Geography Specialty Group of the Association of American Geographers. Her research interests include research method; geographies of gender, race, and religion; information and communication technologies; geographic information science and systems; and feminist perspectives on geospatial technologies.

Arthur Law is coordinator of Spectrum LGBT Community Forum in Brighton & Hove, which provides development support to local LGBT communities and facilitates and supports strategic work related to LGBT needs, bringing together stakeholders from local statutory, voluntary and community, and LGBT sectors. He has been active in a number of local LGBT groups and services and in equalities campaigns spanning 25 years. Arthur has been involved in the planning and delivery of key local LGBT research projects Critical Tolerance (1996), Project Zorro (1998), Count Me In (2000) as well as Count Me In Too (2007).

Jennifer Lea is a human geographer with interests in bodies and practice, health and the therapeutic. Her PhD research was concerned with the practices of massage and yoga, and she is also interested in complementary and alternative medicines and their significance in contemporary culture. She is currently researching the historical and current geographies of therapeutic spaces in Scotland. She has worked at the University of Glasgow and Lancaster University. Her most recent publications are in *Geoforum* and *Body and Society*.

Sarah de Leeuw is an assistant professor in the Northern Medical Program at the University of Northern British Columbia, the Faculty of Medicine at the University of British Columbia. She is a cultural-historical geographer whose work focuses on the sociospatial marginalization of Indigenous peoples and on historic and contemporary colonialism as a determinant of Indigenous people's health. For over a decade she has worked on issues of social justice with feminist and Indigenous organizations, including work with inmates in women's prisons and national aboriginal health organizations in Canada. Recent publications address interactions between Indigenous patients and the medical system, the linkages between governmental policies and ill-health in Aboriginal communities, and the discursivities of 'Indianness' in neocolonial contexts.

Roger Lee is professor of geography at Queen Mary, University of London. He is an economic geographer who argues that there can be no such thing as economies, only economic geographies. A recent unexpected encounter with an early publication (from 1974) made him realize that he had spent more than 40 years of his career just repeating the same arguments around the ways in which the materially integrated nature of, and socially constructed, directed and assessed relations of value in economic geographies remain crucially significant to geographies of social justice and rights. His work has focused primarily on the ways in which these social relations of value are shaped within social life and on the role of money and finance within economic geographies. It has ranged from the ultra-localized to the most geographically extensive. He is managing editor of *Progress in Human Geography* and a former editor of *Transactions of the Institute of British Geographers*.

Brian J. Marks is a PhD candidate and lecturer of Geography at the University of Arizona. A political ecologist and economic geographer, his present research project is on shrimp farming and fisheries in the Mississippi and Mekong Deltas, specifically production practices and environmental outcomes, the household economies of producers, conflict and collaboration in regional commodity chains, and the potential for international cooperation for higher prices. His research interests also encompass the application of political ecology to wetland and estuarine environments and the diffusion of crops and farming systems to the Lower Mississippi Valley through the Columbian Exchange.

Sallie A. Marston is a Professor in the Department of Geography and Regional Development at the University of Arizona. Her work is located at the intersection of socio-spatial theory and the state, particularly with respect to how identities related to the state, are made, remade and transformed in the intimate spaces of everyday life. Professor Marston's main empirical questions have attended to: who has access to certain spaces and how access is negotiated through state policies, practices and rules. Her current collaborative research project focuses on the development of a socio-spatial theoretical and methodological framework – the site ontology – which is an event-space that is a differentiated and differentiating singularity.

Richard Mitchell is Professor of Health and Environment the department of Public Health and Health Policy, University of Glasgow. He leads the department's Social and Environmental Public Health Research theme. Originally trained as a geographer and then as an epidemiologist, Richard now blends these two perspectives in his research on the state, growth and causes of health inequalities. He is particularly interested in how social and physical environments interact to produce health and how they can improve population health and reduce inequalities. Recent publications have included attempts to find and examine areas in the UK where population health appears resilient in the face of economic adversity, a demonstration that health inequalities are narrower in areas with plenty of green space and an examination of gender inequalities in deaths from alcohol-related causes.

Don Mitchell is a Distinguished Professor of Geography in the Maxwell School at Syracuse University. He teaches and conducts research on the geographies of labor, landscape, homelessness, public space, Marxism and theories of culture. With Lynn Staeheli he is the author of *The People's Property? Power, Politics and the Public* (2008) and is currently at work with Lynn on a new project on democracy and public life in the United States and United Kingdom, as well as a study of the historical geography of the post-World War II *bracero* 'guest worker' program in California, an edited collection on the globalization of homelessness (with Jurgen von Mahs), and a textbook on the cultural landscape (with Carrie Breitbach).

Rachel Pain is a social geographer at Durham University in the UK, where she is involved in teaching, research and community engagement. Rachel's key interests lie in social justice, social inequalities and social transformations. Feminist and participatory theory and practice inform much of her research on fear, violence and community safety; emotions and geopolitics; the wellbeing and safekeeping of young refugees; gender, youth, old age and intergenerational relations; and participatory geographies, politics, theory and activism. She is co-author of *Introducing Social Geographies* (Arnold, 2001), and co-editor of *Connecting People, Participation and Place: Participatory Action Research Approaches and Methods* (Routledge, 2008) and *Fear: Critical Geopolitics and Everyday Life* (Ashgate, 2008).

John Paul Jones III is Professor of Geography and Director of the School of Geography and Development at the University of Arizona. He has a longstanding interest in social and cultural theory as it pertains to geographic thought and methodology. Much of his work has examined the linkages between spatial theory and poststructuralist theories of identity and representation. His work on explanation in human geography has placed special emphasis on the concepts of contingency, scale, epistemology, and ontology. Selected substantive projects include the geographic dimensions of the feminization of poverty in the U.S., the epistemology of whiteness in the U.S. and Mexico, and the globalization of civil society organizations in Oaxaca, Mexico. He is currently collaborating on a research project that examines the spatial ontologies and epistemologies underwriting environmental and public health responses to the management of mosquitoes in southern Arizona.

Linda Peake is Professor in the Department of Social Science and the School of Women's Studies and previous Director of the Centre for Feminist Research at York University, Toronto, Canada. She is a feminist geographer whose work spans social, political and urban geography, and the prior editor of the journal *Gender, Place and Culture*. She has interests in issues of transnational feminist praxis, feminist methodologies, whiteness and racism, and the formation of gendered subjectivities in the urban global south. She has worked on these and other issues for nearly two decades with the Guyanese women's organization, Red Thread, as well as conducting empirical research in Canada and the United States.

Jeff Popke is an Associate Professor in the Department of Geography at East Carolina University. His work has explored the ways in which social theory, and in particular theories of ethics and responsibility, can contribute to geographical scholarship and also help to shed light on contemporary processes of social and spatial change. He has carried out fieldwork in South Africa, Mexico and the United States, and is currently investigating the relationships between neoliberal restructuring and transnational migration in rural Mexico and North Carolina.

Amy Ross is Associate Professor of Geography at the University of Georgia and an affiliate faculty member in Women's Studies and Latin American and Caribbean Studies. Her work focuses on human rights and wrongs; impunity and accountability; trauma and truth; institutions of truth/justice; and genocide. Dr Ross studies massive violence in local, national and international arenas in order to illuminate the inter-relationship between the production of space and power. She has conducted research in Guatemala, El Salvador, Chile, Peru, South

Africa, Uganda, the Democratic Republic of the Congo. Her current research project focuses on the International Criminal Court in The Hague.

Paul Robbins is Professor of Geography and Regional Development at the Univeristy of Arizona. His research centers on the relationships between individuals (homeowners, hunters, professional foresters), environmental actors (lawns, elk, mesquite trees), and the institutions that connect them, seeking to explain human environmental practices and knowledges, the influence non-humans have on human behavior and organization, and the implications these interactions hold for ecosystem health, local community, and social justice. Past projects have examined chemical use in the suburban United States, elk management in Montana, forest product collection in New England, and wolf conservation in India.

Lynn A. Staeheli is Ogilvie Professor of Human Geography at the University of Edinburgh. Her work is at the intersections of urban, political, social and feminist geographies. She has contributed to theoretical debates on democracy, citizenship, justice, and care; empirical work has examined various issues related to community activism, the voluntary sector, public space, immigration, security, and the intersections between gender, race and religion. Recent publications include articles in *Political Geography, Antipode, Global Networks, Society and Space, Social and Cultural Geography*, and *Citizenship Studies*. She is co-author with Don Mitchell of *The People's Property? Power, Politics, and the Public* (Routledge, 2008).

Fiona Smith is based at Brunel University where she is senior lecturer in the Centre for Human Geography and Director of the Out of School Childcare Research Unit. Fiona is a social geographer with a particular interest in gender, childcare services and children's geographies. Over the last 15 years she has carried out a large number of externally funded research projects, aimed at both academics and policy makers/practitioners. She is currently carrying out research for two UK Government Departments, exploring children's views of paid work, parental employment and living on benefits and mapping the ways young people spend their time out of school. This work will ensure the views of young people are presented to policy makers currently working on the Extended Schools Agenda in the UK.

Susan J. Smith is Mistress of Girton College, Cambridge. She was previously Professor of Geography and a Director of the Institute of Advanced Studies at Durham University, and before that held the Ogilvie Chair of Geography at the University of Edinburgh. She is a social geographer whose work is concerned with injustice and inequality of all kinds. In a career spanning more than twenty years, she has contributed to debates on citizenship and social policy, the problems of racism and gender inequality, the indignity of victimization and fear of crime, and the intractable link between housing and health. Her current research is concerned with the cultural economy and material geographies of the housing economy. Recent publications address the interplay of home prices, mortgage debt and financial risk, profiling in particular the uneasy encounter between markets dynamics and an ethic of care.

Marv Waterstone is a faculty member in the Department of Geography and Regional Development at the University of Arizona, and most of his work (research, writing, and teaching) is aimed at understanding and promoting progressive social change. Much of his work has been focused on these matters for 25 years. He is currently in the process of working through a number of grounded cases that examine the construction, maintenance, and sometimes, subversion of the common sense in several facets of everyday life. One recent example of this work is a new book, *Geographic Thought: A Praxis Perspective*, which he co-edited with a George Henderson from the University of Minnesota, published by Routledge in October 2008.

Katie D. Willis is Reader in Development Geography at Royal Holloway, University of London. Her research interests lie in the areas of transnationalism, migration, gender and health, with a particular focus on East Asia and Latin America. She has published widely on these issues, including the edited volumes *State/Nation/Transnation: Perspectives on Transnationalism in the Asia-Pacific* (Routledge, 2004 with Brenda Yeoh) and *Gender and Migration* (Edward Elgar, 2000, edited with Brenda Yeoh). She is editor of *Geoforum* and *International Development Planning Review*.

Keith Woodward is Assistant Professor of Geography at the University of Wisconsin-Madison. His research explores intersections of affect, politics and ontology as means for developing new understandings of social movements, political change, direct action and autonomous organization. He is also the co-author of a series of papers devoted to `site ontology' that, among other things, reconsider the relation between scale, space and politics in human geography..

Introduction: Situating Social Geographies

Susan J. Smith, Rachel Pain, Sallie A. Marston and John Paul Jones III

The label 'social geography' is more than a century old. As evidenced in correspondence, French geographer Élisée Reclus appears to have coined the term around 1895 (Dunbar, 1977). He wrote about it in the early drafts and final versions of his six-volume work *L'Homme et la Terre (Man and the Earth)*, which was published posthumously in 1905 (see also Kropotkin, 1902). Concerned with the way space mediates the production and reproduction of key social divides – such as class, race, gender, age, sexuality and disability – social geography eventually became broadly established as 'the study of social relations and the spatial structures that underpin those relations' (Jackson, 2000b: 753). Within that broad rubric, different authors have approached the subject in a variety of ways: Jackson and Smith (1984) set out its philosophical underpinnings; Cater and Jones (1989) opt for a focus on social problems; Valentine (2001) concentrates on the many scales of inclusion, exclusion and identity; Pain et al. (2001), like Ley (1983) and Knox (2000), explore the production of inequality; and Panelli (2004) turns attention, theoretically and empirically, to the many facets of difference. Social geographies can be specialized – as in Peach's (1975) version of 'spatial sociology'; but they can also be so wide-ranging as to subsume the whole of human geography, as evidenced in the several edited collections that profile the eclecticism of the subject (see, for example, Eyles, 1986; Pacione, 1987; Hamnett, 1996).

Like every other part of geography, social geographies have changed with the times: methodological signatures have shifted, and intellectual fortunes have waxed and waned, as topics that once seemed cutting-edge turn out to be mundane. In recent years, moreover, the volatility of politics and economy has unsettled existing intellectual traditions, demanding a radical overhaul of nearly every way of knowing and being; and social geographies are not exempt. Successive 'turns' to culture, politics, environment and economy have, indeed, frequently eclipsed geographers' identification with the social. During the 1990s, for example, there was a sense that human geographers had become so caught up in the circulation of discourses and the instability of representations that they were unable to recognize the material practices sustaining social exclusion. In response, Smith (1993), Gregson (1995) and Peach (2002) all – in their different ways – expressed concern that social geographers' radical commitment to tackling oppression, inequality and poverty was weakening. More recently, in a world where culture merges with nature, humanity is wired to technology, genetics blur into experience, and the human and non-human form complex material and affective assemblages, even the idea of 'the social' seems less persuasive than it once was.

At the start of the twenty-first century, the 'social' has certainly begun to be articulated in new (and renewed) ways. For example, alongside a resurgence of concern for social justice, 'the social' has been reframed to express more directly the materiality of social life (Gregson, 2003); social geographies have begun to build capacity for more moral, caring and politically aware research (Cloke, 2002); and the subject has been reinvigorated by ideas, drawn from philosophers such as Deleuze, Guattari and Latour, which have prompted geographers interested in non-representational theory to interpret 'the social' in quite different ways. In short, understandings of the social have, on the one hand, splintered (creating both tensions and complementarities in the subject), but on the other hand, they have also become more nuanced and (often) increasingly relevant (Del Casino and Marston, 2006).

Questions of relevance, in particular, have acquired a new urgency as critiques of globalization and neoliberalism have called for practical action from inside as well as outside the academy. While combining research and activism has been a longstanding interest for a minority of social geographers, an editorial published in *Area* by Kitchin and Hubbard (1999) marked a sea-change of interest in this aspect of the subdiscipline (see also Fuller and Kitchin, 2004; Pain, 2003; Kindon et al., 2007). One result is that, across a wide range of contexts, inclusive, participatory action research in social geography is gaining momentum in a bid to develop fully collaborative research, publication and intervention, in partnership with those who have traditionally been the 'subjects' of research.

There is, of course, no singular history or unified trajectory for the subject: social geographies, like all forms of knowledge and knowing, are diverse. Notably, there is a 'geography of social geography'. The generalizations above, and indeed those which follow, refer especially to the Anglo-American geographies about which this handbook has most to say. But it is important to recognize that, beyond the Anglo-American realms and which seem still to marginalize the geographies that are produced elsewhere and other ways of approaching the subject are taking centre stage. These are, as might be expected, highly diverse (Kitchin, 2007). Particularly exciting are developments in the Antipodes, where attempts to integrate various indigenous perspectives into geographical scholarship present a fundamental challenge to ideas rooted in the 'global north' (Kearns and Panelli, 2007; Kindon and Latham, 2002; Panelli, 2008). In some parts of Europe, in contrast, social geographies are barely visible: a poor relation to economic or cultural geographies (see Garcia-Ramón et al., 2007, on Spain); And where they do thrive they often lack the critical edge that is so much their hallmark elsewhere (see, for example, Musterd and de Pater, 2007, on Holland; Timár, 2007, on Hungary). These multiple social geographies reflect both national traditions and the intellectual and political trajectories of individual authors. As Kitchin's (2007) collection shows, they all contribute in valuable ways to the patchwork of social geographies whose whole – we will now argue – adds up to much more than the sum of its parts. Importantly, while the Handbook that follows is mainly written by Anglo-American social geographers for an English-reading audience, it also draws from wider traditions which are altering what social geographies are and redefining who these geographies are for (see, for example, in this volume, Kobayashi and de Leeuw (Chapter 4), and Kindon and others (Section 23)).

MOTIVATIONS

Scholarship self-consciously labelled 'social geography' may be radical or conservative, life changing or mundane, engagingly relevant, comprehensively bland or uniquely quirky. It is above all diverse, covering many topics, embracing a mix of methods, rooted in a variety of places and practised in different, multiple, ways. Hence the title: a *Handbook of Social Geographies*. But why collect so many snippets of such a wide-ranging subject into a single volume? It is certainly not the desire to revive, define or narrate a particular vision or version of social geography that inspired this work. The time when defining what is and is not appropriate for scholars to research has long passed. So too has the space for positioning the social 'turn' as a means of, for example, reconstituting geography as a social science, or placing social problems at the heart of the subject, or creating any singular role for academic geography. Compiling a historiography of social geography might have been an interesting option, but more compelling was a sense of the urgency – and timeliness – expressed by colleagues and authors for considering what social geography might *become*. So, this collection is, above all, a commentary on what social geographers can do for the projects of social science in general and for the conduct of geography in particular.

To this end, it is worth remembering that, in the past, social geographies often gained their momentum by exploring a wide range of specialist subjects, all of which are inspired, first, by a pressing interest in how the social world works, and second by a common respect for the power of geography – of arrangements in time and space – in accounting for this (Buttimer, 1968). Social geographers might, then, have specialist knowledge about the laws against discrimination, but their underlying aim will be to provide new interpretations of, say, residential segregation or the spaces of citizenship. Similarly, social geographers might know a lot about the interweaving of genetic, behavioural and environmental precursors of disease, but in disentangling these factors, their aim is to account for the enduring link between place and health. One of the key achievements of social geography over the years has, indeed, been to speak powerfully to the policies and practices that have made experiencing different kinds of spaces – at home, at work, in cities, in rural communities, in schools, hospitals and prisons – so divided and unequal.

The challenge for the 21st century is that these issues – of exclusion, inequality and welfare – not only persist but have tended to become both entrenched and unexceptional. A series of successive human and environmental catastrophes has prompted a crisis of justice, politics and ethics, demanding a radical overhaul of nearly every way of knowing and being. For geography, the disciplinary practicalities of this are compounded by the extent to which traditional appeals to space, either in its own right or in its entanglements with time, have been far too successful. No discipline escaped the 'spatial turn' into the new millennium, and since then, time has similarly repositioned itself at the centre of the social stage. Geography's perpetual identity crisis is back on the agenda, callously stripping away a once-neat spatio-temporal container from the 'selection of different things' whose coherence it formerly secured. Human geography in general and social geography in particular have merged into other subject specialisms; disciplinary space is fractured, its role fragmented across a new intellectual division of labour.

The editors and authors in this Handbook offer some thoughts about what comes next by using social geography as a prism, refracting a subfield whose specialisms were once linked by a common concern with 'space and place' into a spectrum of approaches whose central theme is that of 'making connections'. This focus on connectivity (across space, place, sites, situations and positionings) combines the varieties of social geographies into an outward-looking enterprise whose momentum comes from forging connections, crossing intellectual horizons and being committed to making a difference. The remainder of this essay amplifies this point.

We begin by offering some ***reflections*** on the rich archive assembled in the name of social geography. This archive is not presented as a systematic historiography but rather as a commentary on a series of foundational propositions – around society and space, social inequality and welfare, ethics, morality and justice, and methodological diversity – that have intruded insistently into the lexicon of social geography for at least a hundred years. Sifting through the debris of days long gone, we present a selection of themes which, far from being locked in the past, speak actively to the future.

The second section of this introduction turns attention more squarely onto the ***connections*** scholars now trace between social geographies, on the one hand, and the subject matter of geography's other subfields, indeed of the varied specialisms of social science as a whole, on the other. By profiling four nodes in this web of connectivity – social–nature, social–economic, social–political and social–cultural – we suggest that social geographies today are, above all, about the possibilities and limitations of relatedness; about the spaces of creativity forged 'in between' established approaches and ideas. These, at least, are the kinds of social geographies that run through this collection, as the authors explore the construction, production and practice of ideas that reach across old boundaries, seek out new alliances and perhaps help create a new kind of world.

Finally, the third section of this overview essay concludes with some ***projections*** – a taste of the sections comprising the five parts of the handbook, which, far from representing a stylized account of 'progress' in social geography, are very much about the multiple lines of flight that are now poised to materialize. Each of these sections has a short editorial introduction of its own, which immediately prefaces the chapters concerned. The discussion here is therefore intended simply to give a flavour of what is to come as we – the editors, and the 37 other authors who have contributed to this work – attempt to capture, perhaps create, the shape of the future. To that end, we offer a passing comment on the changing landscapes of difference and diversity, the intercalation of economy and society, the vexed question of well-being, the urgency of revisiting social justice, and the challenge of actually *doing* social geographies.

REFLECTIONS

It is always tempting to cling to the idea that disciplines and their constituencies 'progress'; that knowledge is cumulative; that what we know now (and how we learn about it) must be somehow better – more refined, ethically improved, more fitted to the times – than anything that has gone before. And it would be worrying if there were not some grain of truth in the progressive thesis. But the history of ideas is a fractured, even murky, affair. As writings, reputations, careers and fashions come and go, great ideas often do displace mediocrity, and enduring truths can nudge passing fashions out of the limelight; but, equally, things of value are lost, trivia have a habit of taking centre stage, average ideas are too often stripped from old contexts and made to look new, and some of the least inspiring themes can be surprisingly sticky. Turning to the past is, therefore, anything but straightforward. Yet the central themes of this book owe a considerable debt to earlier generations, and it is worth attending to these sources not just as historical documents, but also to consider what lessons they hold for today. In this section we consider four enduring and important foundations for social geography – themes that have come to define the subfield as a distinct enterprise within and beyond geography.

First we address the truism that social geography has always been committed to – well – ***the idea of the social***. Initially, as we see below, this meant documenting the structures and processes that connect societies with space and thereby infuse the different modes of engagement and avoidance among people. Increasingly, as the essays that follow show, it is about exploring the social and emotional content of relations that tie people to the elements of nature and to the object-world of things.

Second, there is a longstanding pre-occupation among social geographers (much more so, ironically, than among economic geographers) with the ***hard edge of inequality and the uneven experience of welfare***. Whether to its credit or not (and it has been criticized for this), social geography has tended to be associated with a multi-dimensional view of inequality: with a vision of social structure in which income does not map directly onto class, and where class is not the only axis of inclusion; but where, nevertheless, all relations are power filled, and where inequalities, which may be shifting, are always systematic and are enacted through the medium of space.

Third, enlarging on this, social geography has always been ***a moral enterprise***, characterized above all by a drive for the principles and practicalities of justice. Some of this work has focused primarily on critique: on 'simply' trying to understand how unequal the world might be, and aiming to document the extent and experience of injustice. Increasingly, however, social geographies are drawn into a normative 'turn' in social research, and there is growing interest not only in how things are, but also in what they should become.

Finally, social geographies have acquired ***a reputation for methodological eclecticism***. In the past, this may have been cast as a weakness: a failure to grasp the importance of theory; a tendency to lapse into unthinking empiricism. But more recently this eclecticism is being positioned as a strength: not just because mixed methods are coming into their own, but because of the space this opens up for a wider range of tactics of encounter, partnership and activism. The methods of social geography are increasingly geared to enhancing its practical relevance and exploiting its normative leanings.

Society and space together

First, then, social geography has always been committed to integrating 'the social' with 'the spatial'. This seems like an obvious point, given the combination of terms that identify 'social geography' as a distinct subfield. But connecting society and space is not that simple: the materialities and concepts registered by these terms have seen considerable theoretical disruption over the past century. Society, for its part, was often the taken-for-granted empirical description of the characteristics of a population, typically demarcated by national, linguistic, environmental or other boundaries (Vidal de la Blache, 1911; see Buttimer, 1971). As the residual of cultural traits, and particularly when constrained by national and sub-national boundaries in data collection, characteristics of 'the social' were often reduced to demographic data on birth rates, death rates, 'racial' composition, sex ratios, age structure and the like (Hettner, 1977; Trewartha, 1953).

Under the theoretical influences of modern sociology, however, the study of society in social geography took both an institutional and a relational 'turn' in the post-war era. On the one hand, society became increasingly distinguished from culture through a focus on institutions like the family, the school and the workplace. On the other hand, a concentration on social relations between people, rather than simple descriptions of their socio-demographic characteristics, led to a more interesting set of questions regarding the status of the individual within society (Giddens, 1984), including her or his relationship to social structures and to the institutions that embed and perpetuate them. All of these orientations led sociologists in particular to amass a large body of theory orientated around the concept of 'stratification' – the study of the differential allocation of and access to resources, including power, among different social groups. 'Society' was further differentiated – destabilized is perhaps a better descriptor – by the social constructivist approaches developed in the 1980s and 1990s (see Jackson and Penrose, 1993; S.J. Smith, 1989).

Like the idea of the social, the concept of geography also had its unfurlings. Early on, 'space' was reduced to topographical or climatological regions that underwrote sweeping approximations of cultural and social differences (see 'Social/Nature' below). This view of containerized space fits well with the undifferentiated view of society, as national and subnational boundaries were convenient demarcations for simplifying the collection of data on populations and enabling the cartographic description of spatial variations. Against the backdrop of the 'quantitative revolution' of the 1960s, however, social geographers came to embrace the mapping and analysis of spatial variations, using what for many were the new tools of statistics – with factor analysis and regression leading the way. Social geographic research during this period focused on the geography of poverty (Morrill and Wohlenberg, 1971), social inequality (D. Smith, 1973), residential differentiation (Murdie, 1969), ghetto formation (H.M. Rose, 1971), residential relocation (Brown and Moore, 1970) and migration (Roseman, 1977), among other topics. Central, and controversial, questions in these studies were the nature and direction of spatial correlates: how did racial distributions relate to spatial patterns of poverty, for example? Whether or not the quantitative 'spatial sociologies' inspired by such questions could ever yield a definitive answer – could measures of the intensity of segregation or the extent of isolation say anything about the degree of 'choice' or 'constraint' structured into residential patterns, for example – geographers made an important empirical contribution as they experimented with different techniques, sought cross-contextual validation of findings, and engaged with mainstream theories in sociology, economics and political science in formulating their hypotheses (see Del Casino and Jones III, 2007).

It was not until the rise of dialectical spatiality in the mid-to-late 1970s (Harvey, 1973; Soja, 1980; Massey, 1984; McDowell, 1983; S.J. Smith, 1984) that geographers began to conceptualize new approaches to linking society and space: not a space in which social characteristics are mapped and relations unfold *on space*, but a geography that is integral to and formed by those characteristics and relations. An overview of this shift is given in S.J. Smith (1999, 2005). The more contemporary view – which drew in large measure on interpretations of Henri Lefebvre's 'production of space' (1991, originally 1974) – holds that social and spatial relations are co-determinate. Thus, for example, a social relation such as patriarchy cannot be described or analyzed outside of the segregated spaces of the home, which in traditional architecture has tended to separate and thereby reinforce the gendered character of different social and work activities (Hayden, 1984). Likewise, a city's geography – its spatial distributions of homes, day-care facilities and workspaces – can produce a triple-day, a constrained time-geography that adds commuting to a workday already burdened by the time spent in production and social reproduction (England, 1993; Hanson and Pratt, 1995; Preston and McLafferty, 1993). Not that these relations and spatialities are uncontested: indeed, older patriarchies are challenged by modern housing designs, and by partners who do their share of coordinating the demands of social reproduction. But, under the dialectical view, any shift in social relations requires some sort of spatial reorganization, some new form of *socio-spatial* practice that brings into being new possibilities, including new social spaces.

This conjoined emphasis on space and society finds adherents in other social disciplines, especially in sociology following Giddens (1984), with stratification scholars undertaking what amounts to a spatial 'turn' (Gans, 2002; Gieryn, 2000; Lobao, 1993, 2004; Tickamyer, 2000). As a recent book aimed at integrating contemporary stratification theory with theories of space, scale and place proclaims: 'Increasingly, sociologists view geographic space alongside race, class, gender, age and sexuality as an important source of differential access to resources and opportunities …' (Lobao et al., 2007: 3). This is, perhaps encouragingly, very similar to definitions of social geography written as much as a decade before, and it is a reminder of the extent to which the sub-fields of human geography can be a catalyst, as well as a crucible, for cross-disciplinary and intra-disciplinary engagement.

Social inequality and welfare

When social geography emerged at the turn of the twentieth century, it was during a period of popular political ferment and revolutionary hope in Europe and the Americas and in response to a myth about the inevitability of 'progress'. It was in this context that Élysée Reclus, who was pivotal to the emerging field, wrote *L'Homme et la Terre*. In effect this means that the first comprehensive statement about social geography was aimed at opposing all forms of domination of people and nature (Clark and Martin, 2004). Reclus attempted to synthesize social theory, social and environmental geography and anarchism, in order to 'help humanity discover its meaning as a historical being and as an aspect of the earth's larger processes of self-realization' and to demonstrate that 'the discovery of these truths about ourselves can also help us to act consciously and responsibly as part of a developing human community and a developing earth community' (Clark and Martin, 2004: 3). In light of this, it is particularly interesting to note, as Dunbar (1977) has pointed out, that in nineteenth century France 'socialist' and 'social' were synonymous terms and that, from its first appearance as a distinct concept, social geography was, within a larger discipline, the orientation most committed to understanding and addressing social ills.

This mantle has subsequently been worn by a number of key figures who might be thought of as social geographers. While it is fair to say that social geography has been dominated by scholars arranged from the centre to the Left of the political spectrum, it is pointless to look for political agreement, because there is little to find (although there is, as we later suggest, scope to build productive alliances around morality and ethics across diverse socialist, feminist and anti-racist research agendas). What is important here is the extent to which social geography – whatever its politics – has been concerned with the multi-dimensionality of inequality, whether forged through the spatial relations of production (income and class), embedded in patterns of distribution (the provision and consumption of education, health care, housing, and financial services, as well as the acquisition of commodities and experiences), or ingrained in the structures of participation (the entitlements and obligations of citizenship).

Inevitably, handling these many dimensions of inequality means that, at some times, in some places, and among some authors, certain themes have been privileged over others. There is, for example, a rich archive of research focusing on *either* race, *or* gender, *or* sexuality, *or* religion, *or* age, *or* health, *or* disability. Whether for practical reasons, or for heuristic purposes, or to make an important political point, there has been a tendency to separate out different axes of oppression; and these enduring markers of inequality (race, gender, class, age and disability) continue to be interrogated in this collection. Amongst other things, this orientation reflects and extends a tradition that has always been interested in the intersection of social structures with income or class, but which equally has resisted the temptation to reduce everything to these financial markers.

In practice, of course, most scholars also recognize that even the most entrenched and enduring markers of difference (which are both symbols of identification and principles of inclusion of exclusion) are not separate. All social relations are gendered, *and* racialized, *and* about ability/disability, *and* structured by age, *and* mediated by income and class, and so on. The challenge is to ask whether and when the many categories of social life should be held together, and to establish when, where and why it might be appropriate to focus on one of them and not another. It is particularly important to grasp the first as well as the second element of this challenge, at a time when the systematic, overlapping and interacting character of different styles of discrimination and exclusion tends – partly through a valid concern to recognize qualities of difference and expressions of diversity – to be fragmented and dispersed. So the editors and authors of this collection seek explicitly to recognize and address the splintering of social life, not only embracing the extent to which difference and inequality are multidimensional, but grasping the significance of their intersectionality and engaging in an ongoing struggle to recognize and confront the complex *disequalizing* practices embedded in struggles for welfare and wellbeing.

One of the things the diverse social structurings of human life share is, of course, the fact that they are mediated by geography. Space and place (as materials and as metaphors) have accordingly been powerful routes into a better understanding of just how inequality works. David Smith recognized this in the early 1970s when he coined the much-quoted phrase 'Who gets what, where and how?' (Smith 1973, 1977). The core of the question is plucked from the heart of moral philosophy, but Smith's attempt to operationalize it in geography drew attention to the distributional inequalities that inspired a generation of 'welfare geographies'. This achieved a number of important things, two of which merit particular attention.

First, the broad focus on 'who gets what' underlined the extent to which societies are structured not just by markets, incomes and employments, but also by inequalities in entitlements to, and the materials of, welfare. That is, while some of the key divides that have preoccupied social geography can be accounted for with reference to the workings of economy, this is only true to the extent that economies are structured, tempered and divided by a politics of welfare. Race-making works, and gender divisions and other inequalities are reproduced through the interaction and interconnection of labour markets, housing systems, educational structures and welfare transfers: none of these is entirely reducible to the other; each demands interrogation. Recognizing this inspired a generation of research on welfare geography which, amongst other things, pointed to the merits of distributing goods and services according to need rather than ability to pay (see Smith and Easterlow (2004) for a critique and reaffirmation of this tradition). And when welfare states came under attack from the political Right this tradition, in turn, informed a new wave of critical research on geographies of welfare restructuring, whose momentum was established well before the label 'neo-liberalism' gained the notoriety it has today.

Second, this work on welfare geographies helped identify the challenge of promoting well-being as a goal that is separate from (if related to) poverty, and which requires its own research agenda. This was part of a rallying cry for a shift from medical to health geographies (Kearns and Moon 2002), and it sowed the seeds of a new interest in geographies of well-being and contentment, which is taken up in this volume.

Ethics, morality and justice

A third thread that binds the history and geography of socio-geographical research is the positioning of such scholarship as part of an ethical and moral enterprise. The subdiscipline has always been characterized by a drive for justice, through strands of work that carry a strong sense both of morality (what is wrong or right with the world) and of ethics (what our responsibilities toward others are). Such scholarship is concerned above all to employ moral and ethical sensibilities to question the relevance of geography in the pursuit of fairness and equity (see, for example, Cloke, 2002; Proctor and Smith, 1999; D. Smith, 2000).

The impulse for this comes from several overlapping directions, all of them radical geographies in the sense of wanting to break with complacency and to use both practice and critique to create a better world. This commitment was, in a sense, institutionalized though the establishment of *Antipode: a Radical Journal of Geography* in 1969 at Clark University in the USA. At first, this journal reflected the era's Marxist and socialist geographical critiques of capitalist societies and their inequitable class relations (e.g. Harvey, 1973; Peet, 1977). Later feminist geographers exposed the inequalities in gender relations that also underpin cultures, societies and spaces (e.g. Hanson and Monk 1982; McDowell 1983); such work also helped strengthen understandings of the everyday experiential dimensions of inequality, forcing a shift of attention from power-wielders to various forms of resistance to power in social life (see Pain et al., 2001; Panelli, 2004; Valentine, 2001). More recently, anti-racist, postcolonial and indigenous geographies have questioned the whiteness and imperialism that remain ingrained within the discipline, preserving and recreating spaces of racist and neo-imperialist oppression (Blunt and Rose, 1994; Kobayashi and Peake, 2000; Shaw et al., 2006). And now there is a growing interest among radical geographers in working between the boundaries of feminist, postcolonial and anti-racist geographies, exploring their intersections with sexualities, age and (dis)ability. These various related leanings – which have, arguably, become mainstream in critical/radical social geography scholarship – have common ground in being drawn towards a new 'normative turn' in academia, acknowledging and forefronting the goals of equality, justice and human rights. This ongoing encounter between radical geographies and normative theory is, significantly, profiled in a recent volume of *Antipode* (Olson and Sayer, 2009).

This encounter is important because, whilst much of the history of (radical) social geography has been about diagnozing what is wrong and establishing what scholarship is against, arguably we have had less to say about what social geography is *for*. This is of course an overstatement, but it is certainly the case that disagreements over the roots of key problems, arguments over desirable ends, and debates on the most appropriate or workable means of achieving them, have made normative theorizing (imaging, debating and practising how the world *should* be) difficult and, to an extent, unpopular. What is exciting, however, is the growing possibility of a convergence of interest across domains of radical, moral and ethical geographies in the idea and practice of an ethics of care. S.J. Smith (2005), for example, points to a possible alliance of socialist idealism with critical feminism in the drive to place care at the centre of social and welfare policies, extending this even into the heart of the marketplace. In the same way, Clark et al. (2007) draw attention to the ethical dimensions of consumption which are changing the way goods are produced and sold. In ways too numerous to list here, the centrality of care-giving and receiving to all of human life – to the constitution of the social – is now widely recognized and is beginning to occupy centre stage in accounts of society and social geography.

On the one hand, this has prompted a rethink of the quality of social relations in the spaces of homes, institutions and national jurisdictions. This quest to construct more care-full spaces has brought together scholars interested in informal care (highlighting in particular its gendered character through, for example, the idea of 'caringscapes' (McKie et al., 2002)), in the institutionalization of an ethic of care, within and beyond social policy, and in the challenge of putting the principle of caring into practice in every sphere of life. On the other hand, this interest in an ethic of care has drawn attention to a new kind of social geography, prompting scholars to wrestle with the question: what are our human responsibilities not just for those nearby (with whom our interdependence is readily recognizable) but also for *distant* others (those who are geographically removed from our direct experience) who are the victims of exploitation, abuse, repression or violence? How *far*, asks David Smith (1998, 2000), can and should we care Barnett (2005) offers a helpful philosophical and theoretical comment on possible answers, while Gerhardt (2008) illustrates the urgent practicalities of this with respect to the genocide in Darfur, Sudan. This growing body of work is attempting to engage issues in moral philosophy and social theory, and to develop a concept, practice and ethics of care which recognizes the embeddedness of human life within complex webs of geographically varying norms and values.

It is around issues of justice and fairness that social geography is, perhaps, at its most practically engaged. In seeking to use social geographic research as a way into questions of justice, some use their work to try to inform policy, locally, nationally or even internationally; some provide support for the specific redistributive objectives which their lay collaborators are working towards; others use the knowledge produced to motivate through their writing, dissemination and teaching. As recent debates about 'public geographies' have suggested (Hawkins et al., forthcoming; Fuller, 2008), geographers as a whole could be much better at influencing public debates and shaping what goes on outside the academy. Though this potential is not yet fully realized, there is no question that many social geographers continue to be engaged with struggles for a better world.

Methodological diversity

Finally, as befits such a rich and varied history, social geographies are methodologically diverse, and have generally sustained this diversity even as technological innovation or intellectional fashion favour some elements of the methodological toolkit over others. Empirics have always been of fundamental importance here: a longstanding tradition of fieldwork accompanied the early development of the sub-discipline, and all kinds of fieldwork remain popular today. Quantification has always been of interest, though the technical skills required to use quantitative methods wisely and effectively remain unevenly spread. Qualitative research of all kinds has proved increasingly popular, and, not surprisingly for a lexicon that spans interviews, encounter, textual interpretation, historical analysis, visual practices, action research and much, much more, these approaches have, together, been a hallmark of social geography for the past fifteen years. It is, nevertheless, possible to think of this methodological diversity as embracing perhaps four major 'shifts' over the past half century; it may even be fair to characterize these shifts as 'progressive' in some way.

The first significant turn was to a positivist epistemology from the 1960s onwards. During this 'quantitative revolution' the assumptions of pure science (such as generalizability and law-building) were applied to the study of social problems, underpinned by a belief that this would allow geographers to make significant contributions to progressive social change. This kind of hope had long characterized empirical social science, especially in Europe where turn-of-the-twentieth-century social reformists such as William Booth placed great faith in the power of numbers to resolve the problem of what to do politically about poverty. By the 1960s, however, the possibility of using new and rapidly developing survey, statistical and computational methods to add precision, confidence and authority to the process gave new impetus to this quest (Billinge et al., 1984; S.J. Smith, 1986). At the same time, quantitative methods were seen as a unifying force for geography as the discipline moved through one of its many identity crises. For a mix of reasons, therefore, the quantitative tradition became, and in certain parts of the sub-discipline remains, extremely popular. Before too long, however, these approaches were critiqued: first, because their application too often proved inconclusive; second, for their failure to identify the deeper causes of social inequalities; and finally, because of the unreasonable claim that quantitative, 'scientific' researchers might be thought of as neutral, objective 'disinterested observers' whose findings were especially authoritative (see Mercer, 1984; Rose, 1993). It was this 'value-free' myth that radical approaches, including Marxist and feminist geographies, quickly began to challenge (Blunt and Wills, 2000) as a critical tradition displaced the claims of inductivism on social geographers' imaginations.

However, positivism and its spinoffs have a long and diverse history (Hoggart et al., 2002), and dismissing their many epistemological or methodological manifestations on these grounds alone is too simple. Recently, some have argued for a return to quantitative methods on the grounds that they may – as their early practitioners had hoped – be useful for challenging inequality simply because they are the tools most widely acceptable to politicians and policy-makers (Mattingly and Falconer-Al-Hindi, 1995); others seek to increase the validity and purchase of quantitative techniques by using them alongside qualitative methods (McKendrick 1999); some distinguish quantitative methods from positivist approaches (see Kwan in Chapter 26) or uncouple quantitative approaches from masculinist versions of science by challenging the quantitative/qualitative dualism itself (Lawson, 1995). In short, quantitative social geography is alive, well, and could do more for us in the future than it has in the past.

The empirical tradition in social geography was preserved by a second 'turn', this time towards qualitative methods, in the early 1980s. This had its origins in the advent of humanistic geography (see Ley, 1974; Tuan, 1976) which itself arose in response to positivism, challenging deterministic explanations and eschewing the idea of researchers as independent or value-free. Qualitative research, in contrast, focuses on direct engagement with the meaning and interpretation of complex social and spatial relations; it uses inductive theory emergently and reflexively, attaching value to logical or substantive, rather than statistical, significance, and using detailed case studies or extensive interviews to illustrate the breadth and depth of human experience. Qualitative methods may initially have been as implicated as the 'quantitative revolution' in the inherent masculinism of the discipline – a masculinism powerfully exposed by Gillian Rose (1993) in her book on the gender of geography. But these qualitative tools were well suited to the conceptual and political aims of feminist geographers, who used them to give voice to social groups frequently marginalized in and through academic research, and to turn attention to questions of ethics and positionality (McDowell, 1992; Women and Geography Study Group, 1997). This feminist critique of who social geographers are – and of the impact of their work on researchers' own social identities, working methods, theories and other outcomes – is one echoed in anti-racist and postcolonial research (Driver, 1992; Kobayashi, 1994; Sidaway, 1992).

Through the 1980s and 1990s, qualitative research became the new orthodoxy across the discipline (Crang, 2002), though it did not always realize the political potential that some feminist geographers had hoped for. So, despite the rich seam of qualitative work that continues to infuse social geographies, such approaches have sometimes been criticized for their lack of rigour and limited validity (Martin and Sunley, 2001), and for being self-referential rather than effecting change for respondents or having wider policy impacts (Pain and Kindon, 2007). That qualitative methods were also associated with an increasingly disparate 'cultural' frame also drew them into critiques of a sometimes introverted, esoteric style of knowing (Peach, 2002). The lesson here is that no method inherently has more political potential than any other, and all methodologies demand and deserve rigorous application.

The third shift of interest for the practice of social geographies is the 'non-representational' turn of the last decade, which has steered the methodological emphasis away from meaning and interpretation and toward theories of everyday practice (Thrift, 1997, 2004). In contrast to these earlier reflective approaches, non-representational social geographies require methods of investigation that hinge on bodily engagement: on affective and material relationships and practices which do not mirror or mine the empirical world but rather experience, enact, perform and create it (e.g., Kraftl and Adey, 2008). Like all innovations, the practicalities are much debated. Geographers such as Bondi (2005), Thien (2005) and Tolia-Kelly (2006), for example, have questioned some non-representational approaches, suggesting that they can, paradoxically, *distance* emotion and embodiment from scholarship and the public arena whilst begging important questions about authority and who is speaking for whom (for a response, see Woodward and Lea in Chapter 6).

Nevertheless, by revisiting an earlier engagement with pragmatism (S.J. Smith, 1984) and combining it with other philosophies of encounter (as described in Smith, 2001), non-representational geographies achieve at least two very important methodological goals. First, by emphasizing the way knowledge is acquired and produced through whole bodies, these approaches challenge the dominance of the visual in the creation of geographical knowledge, turning attention to what can be known through the domains of sound, smell and touch (see Crang, 2003; Dewsbury et al., 2002; Smith, 1994; Thrift, 2002). Second, by identifying the perfomativity of the world – recognizing that it has constantly to be made – these methods of encounter open up the possibility that the future can, through practical acts, be made differently (just as it can also deliberately be kept the same).

The salience of human agency, and the prospect of research and writing actually having effects, are themes which can be traced across at least forty years of social geography. If there is a fourth shift currently under way, however, it is towards a growing suite of increasingly empowering action epistemologies. Recently, calls encouraging wider participation in human geography research have become louder. This is not about recruiting research subjects more carefully or inclusively (though this is important); it refers rather to forging research partnerships, pursuing joint research with activists and engaging in critical policy research that seeks to radically change agendas (e.g. Fuller and Kitchin, 2004; Kindon et al., 2007; Pain, 2003; Elwood, 2006a, 2006b). These debates around the wider ethics and politics of research have in some ways served to put methods into perspective. The argument is that however well-honed are traditional methods and forms of analysis, they all operate within the same tight epistemological frame: knowledge production by academics for academics. In an attempt to break free of this, social geographers have led the turn to participatory methods involving joint knowledge production with 'the researched' (Kindon et al., 2007), which is discussed in detail in Section 5 of the Handbook. This turn is firmly underpinned by feminist theory and practice, and while it is a difficult endeavour which is open to criticism (see Cooke and Kothari, 2001; Kesby, 2007), embrace it does the early ideals of feminist research and harness some strengths of qualitative approaches that have not always been realized in social geographical practice (see Kindon et al., 2007).

None of these shifts can be analyzed separately from the shape of the theoretical knowledge that their advocates produce and want to see. So this mix of methods and approaches continues to develop, sometimes in tension and sometimes as productive collisions (Brown and Knopp, 2008), but always by way of an eclecticism, and a mix of methods, that is now being positioned as a strength. We return to these issues in the final section of the book.

CONNECTIONS

The *Handbook of Social Geographies* is at first glance, and by its very title, about the multiplicity of approaches to appreciating and conducting social life. By definition, then, it is not intended to cover everything that might be construed as social geography: some areas are missing by accident (a question of who is able to deliver what, when) and others by design. In fact, this collection was originally offered as a 'compendium' of social geography; a *selection* of different things in a single container; a bringing-together of core elements and new directions in a diverse but identifiable substantive field of enquiry. Rather than attempting to be comprehensive then this compendium-handbook is a work of connectivity. Instead of imagining social geography to be a coherent set of ideas and approaches that – at different times and places – 'relate to', overlap with or even merge into other subdisciplines (as for example in the celebrated alliance of social and cultural geography), we imagine the subject as existing *only* in and through the connections it inhabits. Social geography – like any other subdiscipline – is an experience of forging links, embracing tensions, and engaging in the uneasy alliances that the unfolding of knowledge demands. Four of these close encounters – the articulations of social/nature, social/economic, social/political and social/cultural – run through the entire volume, and we introduce them below.

Social/nature

The relationship between human life and the natural environment is more than a piece of connective tissue that complicates social geography: for many it has been and continues to be the defining pillar of geography itself (Glacken, 1967; Turner, 2002). With roots in natural histories, travel diaries, and the founding of the modern university, the modern human–environment tradition came to flourish in the nineteenth and early twentieth centuries in the UK and continental Europe under the sway of geographers like Reclus, Kroptkin and Vidal, introduced earlier, as well as A.J. Herbertson, Alexander von Humboldt, Carl Ritter, Friedrich Ratzel and Ferdinand von Richthofen. In the US the tradition took hold through the work of naturalist George Perkins Marsh, historian Frederick Jackson Turner, and geographers Ellen Churchill Semple, William Morris Davis and Ellsworth Huntington. The diversity amongst these authors notwithstanding – they varied greatly in terms of their commitment to field investigation, empirical detail and teleological design – they held in common an analytic approach focused on the scientific explanation of human–environment relationships. Yet, within that general rubric, history has recorded numerous approaches to theorizing the direction and force of the causal arrows.

The 'determinist influence'

We can point famously to one such approach, that of environmental determinism, wherein the characteristics and forces of natural environments were seen to stand in a direct and exogenously causal relationship with those of their resident populations. In drawing variously on Darwinian, Lamarckian and Spencerian evolutionary traditions, the determinists were to select their causal language from different points along a continuum defined by strict deterministic 'controls' on the one hand to weaker 'influences' on the other. What united them was their use of environment to explain a diverse array of perceived social differences among population groups, including whether they were pantheistic or monotheistic, sedentary or nomadic, slovenly or energetic, civilized or barbaric, inventive or unimaginative, gay or melancholic, analytic or sensual, peaceful or unruly, irascible or agreeable (Livingstone, 1992). In spite of determinism's scientific pretensions, the number of hypothesized arrows could prove too complicated to verify empirically, as is demonstrated in this quote from Ellen Churchill Semple:

> The physical environment of a people consists of all the natural conditions to which they have been subjected, not merely a part. Geography admits no single blanket theory. The slow historical development of the Russian folk has been due to many geographic causes – to excess of cold and deficiency of rain, an outskirt location on the Asiatic border of Europe exposed to the attacks of nomadic hordes, a meager and, for the most part, ice-bound coast which was slowly acquired, an undiversified surface, a lack of segregated regions where an infant civilization might be cradled, and a vast area of unfenced plains wherein the national energies spread out thin and dissipated themselves (1911: 14).

It was not just that a few of the foundations of contemporary social geography – notably social difference and diversity – were bulldozed by such banalities: determinism as it was often practised was also methodologically flawed, led by a strategy of empirical affirmation rather than falsification. Thus, even in the face of the counter-claim that some social characteristics might not be the product of, say, climate but of yet another social factor, explanations could be found to redouble on the environment, as in this defence of determinism by Semple:

> Even so astute a geographer as Strabo, though he recognizes the influence of geographic isolation in differentiating dialects and customs in Greece, ascribes some national characteristics to the nature of the country, especially to its climate, and the others to education and institutions. He thinks that the nature of their respective lands had nothing to do with making the Athenians cultured, the Spartans and Thebans ignorant. ... But here arise the questions, how far custom and education in their turn depend upon environment; to what degree natural conditions, molding economic and political development, may through them fundamentally affect social customs, education, culture, and the dominant intellectual capacity of a people (Semple, 1911: 22–23).

Breaking the chains of nature

Not that environment always ruled with the heavy fist or backdoor logics that Semple identified. Vidal (1899), in establishing the French tradition, put forth the concept of 'possibilism' to describe the limits and potentials set by the environment. He argued that how people respond to these depends on their traditional ways of living (*genre de vie*), a concept he employed not only to point to culture, institutions, technologies, etc., as operative agents of society, but also to open the door to different interpretations of the environment, presaging later concepts such as environmental perception. Similarly, in the UK, the influential town planner Patrick Geddes told geographers that:

> ... while circumstances modify man [*sic*], and that in mind as well as body, man, especially as he rises in material civilization, seems to escape from the grasp of environment, and to react, and that more and more deeply, upon nature, at length, as he develops his ideas and systematizes his ideals into the philosophy of religion of his place and time, he affirms his superiority to fate, his moral responsibility and independence; his escape from slavery to nature into an increasing mastership (Geddes, 1898; as quoted in Livingstone, 1992: 274–5).

Years later, once the reaction against determinism was in full swing, the president of the Association of American Geographers, Harlan H. Barrows, argued on behalf of a holistic 'human ecology' of 'mutual relations' that presupposed no directionality between the forces of society or environment. Barrows's programmatic injunction (1923) did not prove to be much of a rallying point outside of the Chicago School of Environmental Geography from which he wrote, but it was nonetheless important to Gilbert White, who, along with his students, carried on Barrows's torch for many decades (Burton et al., 1978). In addition to asking questions based on the reversal of the causal arrow, they also were noteworthy for their attention to the policy implications of their work (White, 1972) and for their groundbreaking studies in environmental perception (Saarinen, 1969).

A second environmental tradition in the US was anchored by Carl Sauer, who firmly rejected determinism in his seminal piece, 'The morphology of landscape', in 1925. He and his adherents went on to fashion a cultural geography that documented the 'destructive exploitation' of earth at the hands of 'man' (Mikesell, 1978; Thomas, 1956). Sauer disapprovingly witnessed these transformations throughout his life, as the 'medium' in his famous injunction – 'Culture is the agent, the natural area is the medium, the cultural landscape is the result' (1925, 46) – receded into yet another urban centre, industrial development or sprawling suburb. To be sure, even when he wrote 'Morphology' it might have been difficult to have found a 'natural' landscape composed of unmodified climates, landforms, water bodies and vegetation. Sauerian approaches to the environment have been accused of having a conservative bias – of being backward-looking, rural-favouring and unscientific. But the research is noteworthy for a number of reasons: for a historical approach centred on both socio-cultural and environmental change and adaptation; for situating technology in a mediative role between society and environment; and for detailed field studies that traced the origins and diffusions of both material culture and environmental practices.

A related approach to the environment, cultural ecology, developed out of expeditions by anthropologists and geographers in the 1950s and 1960s. With time, the term was widely adopted by those cultural geographers whose work focused on the environment. More analytic than the individualistic and particularistic tradition it supplanted, cultural ecology was noteworthy for merging ecology with systems analysis, giving 'ecosystems' that included both the environment and the institutions and practices of human society. Its adherents tended to pay rigorous attention to the flows of energy and materials in these systems. Nature and society are, in this view, not 'separate entities or opposing forces, but rather interlocking components of a system' (Mikesell, 1978: 7–8). Most cultural ecologists – Karl Butzer, Billie Lee Turner II and Peter Vayda among them – retained with their predecessors a critical eye toward development, including a disdain for rampant consumerism, unbridled economic growth and unflinching faith in technocratic solutions to environmental problems. But beyond this, explanation tended to wither, for most held an aversion to deeper, structural explanations, particularly those offered by political economy. This, in turn, opened doors to another subfield, political ecology, where we find a resurgent converzation involving topics of interest to social geographers. Operating with a more vigorous commitment to theory that situates the use and destruction of the environment within larger socio-economic, political and cultural-discursive contexts, political ecologists are attentive to both social difference and the ways that capital, the state, and other institutions socially 'construct' and materially 'produce' natures (Robbins, 2004). Since the 1990s political ecology has been the subfield to turn to for: understandings of environmental conflict written in terms of race, class and gender; critiques of conservation schemes and participatory development practices by considering the inevitable exclusions they embed; and discourse analyses of various environmental and social narratives (wilderness, Gaia, development, progress, etc.) at play in making bits of nature the object of environmental management strategies (Williems-Braun, 1997).

Tracing a long arc through this historiography, we see the following picture emerge. First, for the environmental determinists 'the social' was the explandum, and not a very active or differentiated one at that. For complicated historical reasons, including the fact that many early modern geographers were trained in the natural sciences, researchers spent more of their efforts examining the active and variegated environmental drivers than the complications of the social responses. As a result, as Platt (1948) points out, determinists ignored extensive counter-evidence showing that the social characteristics of a people could vary greatly within the same environment. Nor were determinists capable of explaining why people hold on to certain habits long after they have changed their environments.

Second, following the obituaries of determinism written by Geddes, Vidal, Barrows, Sauer and others, there developed in social geography a profound suspicion of nature altogether. To cross the boundary of nature–society in the post-determinism era, one might risk being reminded of an embarrassing geographical period, particularly in terms of the discipline's treatment of race in its service to colonialism and imperialism (see Peet, 1984; Livingstone, 1992; Dwyer, 1997). Most social geographers at this time adopted the spatial-chorological view, which stressed integrative areal study and spatial variations (Turner, 2002) and which was readily adaptable to questions of inequality, social welfare and justice (e.g., D. Smith, 1973) – and, it turned out, largely without the need for environmental backup. So, as discussed elsewhere here, social geographers of the mid-century and beyond went out exploring other connections, such as those of culture, politics and economy. While a general mid-century neglect of nature in human geography played out differently across the subfields, the recoil was particularly acute in social geography, where studies of urban social environments predominated. It wasn't until political ecology came along – with its tools of Marxism, feminism and postcolonialism – that critical social geographers could safely engage the environment without fear of being tarnished as determinists.

Retheorizing the social with nature

And, for some, just in time. For, as many have noted, theorists of the human–environment connection now face some very tricky objects, as capital and technology combine to produce a hundred hybrid forms of new social/natures (Haraway, 1991; Whatmore, 2002). No longer separated by a dash ('–'), these are bits of social/nature that disrupt attempts at clean classification: the state-managed forest, the genetically modified tomato, the beloved family dog with his microchip implant. Even the designer baby (Fukuyama, 2002) is trotted out as a millennial example of troubling new forms of life and technology.

But while these hybrid forms might give pause, it is not the loss of their 'essential character' that troubles the nature–society divide. It is, instead, how they point to the work that has gone into preserving the polarities that now seem in need of negotiation. As Latour writes:

> Critical explanation always began from the poles and headed toward the middle, which was first the separation point and then the conjunction point for opposing resources. ... In this way, the middle was simultaneously maintained and abolished, recognized and denied, specified and silenced. ... How? ... By conceiving every hybrid as a mixture of two pure forms (1993; quoted in Whatmore, 2002: 2).

As Sarah Whatmore (2002) notes, the challenge today is to destabilize these seemingly pure forms by de-centring what has long been sacrosanct: social agency itself. This move posits a world beyond – or perhaps before – the nature–society dualism. As Braun puts it:

> It is precisely to avoid such unintentional returns to the 'human itself' that many scholars in the social sciences and humanities – geographers included – have turned to philosophers such as Spinoza, Bergson, Deleuze, and Serres (see Whatmore, 2002). What these writers offer is an understanding of bodies, including 'human' bodies, as always already an effect of their composition in and through their relations with the world. In this sense, the human has no essence, and never did, but is rather understood as an 'in-folding' of the world, an effect of ongoing and ceaseless ontological play (Harrison, 2000). The human, then, was 'post' from the beginning (Braun, 2004: 1354).

To speak, therefore, of a post-human geography (Castree and Nash, 2004) is to deconstruct the nature–society binary. This requires us to put nature 'under erasure' (i.e., 'display', following Derrida, 1976), for nature has always been the key resource for propping up the social, and yet it is a Nature that can never be – *a priori*, primordial, beyond construction. Only through this constitutive other has 'the social' been secured. In particular, for Derrida (2003) the persistent gap between nature and society has everything to do with the nature that is animal. Braun (2004), drawing on Derrida's animal–human deconstruction in his discussion of Badmington's post-human thesis (2004), elaborates on this point:

> Without this distinction, humanism has no foundation. Derrida shows this fundamental anthropology at work across the spectrum of Western philosophy – in Descartes, Freud, Heidegger, and Lacan, among others – in order to reveal not only how the space of the 'human' is differentially produced, but also how the 'properly human' comes to be defined within, and is dependent upon, this system of difference. Derrida gives us a neologism – *animot* – that brilliantly captures his point. The word phonetically singularizes the plural for animal (*animaux*) and combines it with the word for 'word' (*mots*), thereby calling attention to the habit of rolling all animal species into one, producing an undifferentiated 'other' against which the 'human' can be juxtaposed and defined. This animal-word at once founds and grounds humanism. ... Of course, Derrida goes on to explain that this 'fundamental anthropology' deconstructs itself. Humanism's founding difference – the differentiation of human from animal – is, ultimately, unstable; a supplement is always required to fix the difference ([the commonly invoked 'specifically' human skills of]

language, reason, tool-making), yet each and every supplement is inadequate to the task (Braun, 2004: 1352–3, brackets added).

Yet, in concluding, it should be emphasized that, however much one might welcome a post-human social geography, this does not mean that we can dispense with a political analysis attentive to invocations of 'the human' or 'the social' (Castree and Nash, 2006). Just as Don Mitchell (1995) warned us to be wary when the term 'culture' was being wielded, so too must we be suspicious of daily encounters with a nature-reinforced 'society' (see also Joseph, 2002, on 'community'). Even if Margaret Thatcher did turn out to be serendipitously prescient in her claim that 'there is no such thing as society', this does not mean that 'the social' has not been nor will not remain a contested discourse, an object of politics. If anything, Thatcher herself only substantiates the point.

Social/economy

Social geographies are often rooted in everyday life, focusing attention on the relationships and behaviours that elaborate the ordinary world. Not surprisingly, this point of departure rarely sits easily with the atomistic, individuated, ostensibly rational 'economic men' whose stylized behaviours still drive empirical economics; nor has it resonated with the ostensibly separate spheres of economy and society that are ingrained in an intellectual division of labour and materialized in the institutional arrangements of governance. But the latter is easier to live with than the former, and social geography has *de facto* tended to be about social, not economic, life. Yet the isolation of 'the economic' is rarely maintained in practice, and to the extent that it is, this begs the question of how economic essentials have *been made* to prevail in certain kinds of settings or encounters. So it is not surprising that a shift of scholarly interest from high theory to situated practices, spanning nearly two decades, has come to recognize two key truths. First, that there is more to economy than economics: indeed, that 'economics has failed by neglecting to develop a theory of real markets and their multiple modes of functioning' (Callon, 1998). Second, and equally, that 'the economy is ordinary; it is an integral part of everyday life. … Not only are economies inescapably social, societies are inescapably economic' (Lee, 2006). Together, these observations encapsulate a sea-change in the study of both economy and society, recognizing that the projects are linked and their scope interdisciplinary. Critically for this handbook, it is now clear that progress in accounting for economies and economics can no longer be dominated by economists; it is a challenge for us all.

Nevertheless, it is surprising how long it has taken a range of disciplines (other than economics) fully to embrace the challenge of understanding what economies consist of and how 'the economy' works. It is, for example, striking how few references to economic geography appear in the Journal of Social and Cultural Geography – a publication whose mission since the turn of the millennium has been 'to report on the role of space, place and culture in relation to social issues, cultural politics, aspects of daily life, cultural commodities, consumption, identity and community, and historical legacies'. Economy is, to be sure, an aspect of daily life and an element of consumption studies, but that is at best implicit in the mix of papers published in this journal. A similar picture emerges from the limited reference made to social geography in the *Journal of Economic Geography*, a publication established in 2001 as an attempt to 'redefine and reinvigorate the intersection between economics and geography'. Notably there is no statement about connecting economic geography with the rest of the discipline, and although some contributors clearly are engaged in this task, the majority of works testify to a still-entrenched division of roles between economic geography on the one hand and social and cultural geographies on the other.

Arguably, a more obvious place to look for rapprochement across this specific subdisciplinary divide is *Tijdschrift voor Economishe en Sociale Geografie*. Dating from 1967, this is the one English language journal in geography to contain the words 'economic' and 'social' in its title. Its mission statement however makes more of the connection between Anglo-American and Continental human geographies than of integrating social and economic affairs: searches on key words bring up very little overlap in this latter respect. On the other hand, perhaps signalling changes that are already in train, the online journal *Social Geography* (first published in 2005) includes amongst its 'topical fields' the words 'labour', 'production' and 'consumption'. In fact, the very first article in the series is effectively an assessment of social geography's take on economy (Van Wezemael, 2005).

It would be a mistake, particularly in light of recent trends, to overstate the extent of the social–economic divide in geography. There have always been individuals and institutions committed to bridge-building: that, after all, is part of the geographical imagination. And a concern with political economy (a critique of how whole economies are managed) is of course at the heart of many areas of human geography. It is, nevertheless, worth pausing to consider why, and with what consequences, the analytical line between economy and society has, so often, been so sharply drawn. More importantly, it seems timely to attend to a host of recent attempts, within and beyond geography, to recognize the economy in society and to work with the sociality of economy.

Economy and society

In an engaging essay entitled 'Capturing markets from the economists', Don Slater (2002) observes that 'The division between economic and socio-cultural analysis constitutes a kind of deep structure of modern Western thought' (p. 59). This division of intellectual labour is sometimes attributed to the so-called 'Parsons' pact' – a deal that enabled the expansion of sociology, and cemented the isolationism of economics, during the early twentieth century. Commenting on this division of territory, David Stark (2000) tells how, as Talcott Parsons put his grand design for sociology into practice, there was only one discipline he was not prepared to take on, and that was economics. Basically, says Stark, 'Parsons made a pact: in my gloss – you, economists, study value; we, sociologists, will study values. You will have claim on the economy. We will study the social relations in which economies are embedded' (p. 1).

More structural explanations for the divorce of society from economy are forwarded by Anderson (2003), who argues that the exclusion of democratic and civil society from the realm of economy is a requirement of the capitalist condition; and by S.J. Smith (2005), who recognizes the essentialization of markets to be both a condition of, and an explanation for, the weakly developed ethic of care in modern political democracies. Such authors imply that, while the separation of economy and society may have been a condition through which disciplines (and subdisciplines) developed in one way rather than another, more critically still, the split has been necessary for economics, economies and welfare states to function as they do.

Both these explanations – for a division of intellectual labour and a separation of real-world activity – help to account for the divorce of social from economic geographies; for the creation of subdisciplines whose subject matter and approaches have, until recently, been almost completely distinct. In this longstanding separation of roles, social geography tends to occupy one of four positions. All these positions are caricatures, of course; and all accommodate some quite excellent ideas and contributions. But they do add up to a tendency not just to privilege the social (a move that might be ethically appealing), but also to represent social life as if it were not an economic affair (a position that is ontologically unsustainable).

First, there are social geographies that take particular economic conditions as given: either as a benign backdrop against which social life works; or as machine that structures the social world. On the one hand this underpins social geography's much-criticized tendency to assign too much agency to individuals, as if residential patterns, flows of migration and so on are a product only of similarity and dissimilarity in the characteristics of who people choose to live, work and socialize with. On the other hand it produces a kind of determinism in which economic processes map onto social outcomes, producing systems of stratification which are expressed as social geographies, through processes of (essentially economic) categorization which its incumbents are powerless to control.

Second, there are many rich empirical studies in social geography which attend to all kinds of social and cultural processes yet choose not to document, or comment on, their economic content. Think, for example, of a large body of work on consumption which profiles all kinds of tastes, qualities, identities and behaviours, yet scarcely mentions how much it costs to produce, buy and sell the goods concerned. Consider equally a fascinating body of work on domestic interiors that, for its many fine achievements, glosses over the financial costs of key objects and materials and pays only passing attention to how such expenditures are funded. Even work on that staple of social geography – residential segregation – has until recently had surprisingly little to say about (for example) the fundamentals of housing market dynamics (of course there are important exceptions; see, for example, the work of Steve Holloway and Elvin Wyly and the papers collected in Smith and Searle, (in press)).

Third, social geography embraces a strong welfare tradition, which – although intimately concerned with the financial edge of inequality – is generally more interested in how best to *suspend* the price mechanism (with, for example, needs-based systems of allocation) than in the finer detail of how markets, price determination, valuation, credit scoring, and so on, work. Welfare geography has, as a consequence, generally contributed (albeit in some very important ways) to a line of thinking which divides states from markets and assigns the former a role in 'mending' the latter by compensating in cash or kind for widening inequalities (see Smith and Easterlow (2004) for an overview and critique of this position). The result is that much more is known about 'states' than about the economies they manage; more is known about social exclusion from the economy than about the entanglement of social and economic affairs that is a condition of human life. And even though the challenge of matching welfare resources to individual and collective needs, funding and delivering formal and informal care, and promoting well-being demands sensitivity to economic themes, work in this vein has rarely been central to mainstream social geographies.

Finally, social geographies – multiple though they are – have been strangely silent on themes that might reasonably be located at the heart of the enterprise. In recent years, the sociology of work, for example, has been tackled mainly (though magnificently) by a handful of (generally feminist) geographers. The economics of domestic labour – the cost and content of housework – have an even lower profile. And the consumption of financial services – mortgages, insurances, banking, personal loans and so on – is woefully under-researched for a subdiscipline concerned with the consumption (though rarely the cost) of virtually every other imaginable product or object. Again, there are exceptions: in the UK, Elaine Kempson and colleagues at Bristol University, together with Andrew Leyshon and colleagues at Nottingham University, have made important contributions in the area of personal financial services, financial capability and an understanding of 'financial ecologies'. The message nevertheless is that, as an interdisciplinary effort to unpack the sociality (the materiality, the relationality and the emotional content) of key economic ideas (markets, prices, information, calculation) gathers speed, the social geographies inherent in this cry out for greater attention.

The division of geographical labour into which social geographies have hitherto been so neatly cast may be enduring, but the indication already is that old boundaries are being transgressed, indeed erased, by a rethink of what constitutes economy, as well as by a shift this demands in the understanding of society. Whatever it was that split social geographies apart from their inherent economies, there is an impulse now for their reconnection, and evidence that this process is seriously under way. This is the product of a concerted effort across a range of disciplines – sociology, anthropology, politics, psychology and geography – to open up the 'black boxes' of economy, recognizing the ontological impossibility, and epistemological undesirability, of an oddly enduring (if practically unsustainable) intellectual rift.

A cultural turn

Perhaps the most general case made in recent years for expanding the sociological significance of economics (as a practice), and of economies and their constituent elements (as socio-technical asemablages), has been dubbed 'cultural economy'. This label is broad, but it marks the extension of an interdisciplinary 'cultural turn' into the area that has resisted it most: economics. Geographers have played a role here, not least by gathering key works into influential interdisciplinary those edited by DuGay and Pryke, (2002), Amin and Thrift (2004), and Pryke and DuGay (eds) (2007). These collections capture the idea 'that something called "culture" is both somehow critical to understanding what is happening to, as well as to practically intervening in, contemporary organizational and economic life' (DuGay and Pryke, 2002: 1). Such approaches are thus concerned with 'the social and cultural relations that go to make up what we conventionally term the economic' (Amin and Thrift, 2004: xviii). In a series of fine-grained empirical examples, the authors in collections like these show what is to be gained by recognizing that 'economy' is constituted through a myriad of social, emotional, political, material and symbolic activities and arrangements – events and relationships that are not 'additional to' economic affairs, but inherent within them (see Woodward and Lea, Chapter 6). This moreover has been true throughout history, even though the way economic agents operate may itself have changed in recent years, recognizing – and exploiting – the extent to which cultural themes underpin the organization of work, the contents of products, styles of consumption and modes of circulation.

The idea of cultural economy has been an exciting one for geography. On the one hand, it has attracted the attention of a very large cultural geography constituency to the salience of the economic themes which in practice infuse every nook and cranny of life's meanings and materials. On the other hand, it has appealed to a cross-section of economic geographers, particularly those whose work is concerned with beliefs, behaviours and outcomes, which simply defy conventional economic understanding. But it has not been an entirely comfortable ride, for at least three reasons. First, the turn to cultural economy in geography has been troubled by a charge of 'vague theory and thin empirics' which – to be fair – is not without foundation. But at the same time it is also a charge that overlooks the many opportunities which have been seized to bring the 'close dialogue' of qualitative encounter into dialogue with the stylized facts of economics (see Clark, 1998). Second, cultural economy perspectives have tended to alight most readily on the cultural content of economic entities, and on the imprint or exercise of these cultural economies on wider societies. That is, they have sometimes acquired a deterministic flavour, focusing on the way economic ambitions are culturally imposed; how products are represented; or how consumers are 'captured'. For example, the four essays comprising a section on 'the economy of passions' in the *Cultural Economy* reader (Amin and Thrift, 2004) mainly tackle the way emotions can be cynically manipulated for economic gain. Finally, it is arguable that a preoccupation with the meanings, representations and discourses of economy means that the project of cultural economy has not yet gone far enough to advance understandings of the sociality or materiality of economic life. As Al James (2006, 2007) has shown in his discussions of the methods and substance of research on cultural economy, there is considerable scope both to mend and to build the interdisciplinary bridges that cultural economy appeals to, and to develop this approach in innovative and important ways. We point equally the additional possibility that some elements of this project might fruitfully be 'wired in' to the more connected social geographies that inspire the form and contents of this Handbook.

The special case of 'social economy'

Curiously, the most obvious label for this new connectivity – social economy – has acquired a rather specialized, albeit entirely apt, meaning, in which the prefix 'social' signals a welfare role. That is, the social economy *sensu stricto* works to an unconventional bottom line – one that may not even be drawn up with reference to measures of credit or cash. Local currency systems, for example, are an element of the social economy. These include local exchange trading schemes or systems (LETS), time-dollars and other initiatives which are based on the (usually localized) informal exchange of goods and services whose values are determined in a variety of ways and exchanged using local currencies (see Lee et al., 2004). LETS, for example, create 'alternative' economies, usually among participants who are wholly or partly financially excluded (unemployed, retired, unable to work regular hours, and so on). They have also been shown to have a social dimension which, in some cases, exceeds their subsistence role, for example where participants accumulate credits but fail to spend them – as if this 'capital' were an indicator of their value to the community.

More recently, social economy has come to refer to a broader sweep of benevolent economic activities: strategies 'that privilege meeting social (and environmental) needs before profit maximization, through the involvement of disadvantaged communities in the production or consumption of socially useful goods and services' (Amin, 2008: 1). Diverse in form and variable in content, it is tempting to set this social economy alongside the many varieties of capitalism that currently co-exist, and define it into social geography. Certainly this provides an appealing analytical starting point and an obvious inroad into the economy for social geographers. But the concern is that the institutions and practices of social economy may not be one of many; instead, they may be distinctive in one important way, as the socially inflected Other to a 'real' economy, which is the dominant economy, inherently riddled with inequality and geared only to profit.

In a helpful overview of the field, Hudson (2008) implies, that social economy is indeed Other to the mainstream in at least two ways: as a safety net, supporting those who are not adequately served by markets; and as an 'alternative' economic space, which may be detached from the wider economy but is perhaps preferred on ethical grounds and might be more enjoyable. Only Hudson's third vision of social economy – as a space of transformation which could be at the leading edge of a real shift in the way economies (and economics) function – engages with a vision of social economy as a more mainstream affair. This last version, connects up with the ideas of Gibson-Graham whose website on alternative economies (www.communityeconomies.org) shows how this transformative role is not a minority exercise but a part of a wider internationally based, feminist-inspired reworking of what economies are and whom they are for.

Most commentators on the social economy – whether this label is used narrowly, or more generally – are at pains to stress that society and economy are inextricably entwined: that the institutions and individuals of one are at the same time the agents of the other. But there is nevertheless a divide in the literature between approaches designed specifically to explore the institutions of social economy (which are in a sense part of the welfare state) and those that recognize that societies – even with their existing structures of inequality, changing hierarchies of need, entrenched welfare ideals and variable ethics of care – are always and inherently economic (e.g. Boyer, 2003). By profiling social economy in this second sense, this Handbook contributes to the efforts of those who now seek to bridge a gap in the geographical literature between those distinctive sets of practices and institutions that constitute the social economy, on the one hand, and the multiple meanings and materials that constitute a passionate, if slippery, but very broadly based cultural economy, on the other. In doing so it engages mainly with the third of the social-economy projects listed above – it is about excavating the content and shaping the potential of highly diverse 'economic societies'.

Economic society

The province of 'the economy' has expanded in recent years as states have retreated and families have changed their form: neither informal provision nor state support now offer the first port of call for providers, or for those in need, of goods, services, resources or care. It is alongside this expansion of a particular (some might call it neo-liberal) style of economic geography that the role of economy in society and the sociality of economy come under scrutiny. The term 'social economy' may usefully describe either 'alternative economies' or state interventions to stimulate markets in underserved areas, but social geographers also need a vocabulary for their work on how 'the economy' is itself an intrinsically social affair. Two aspects of life in economic societies are particularly important.

First, there is the truism that 'the economy' is embedded in the routine of everyday life: it is *ordinary*. This point is forcefully made by Roger Lee (2006), who examines 'the business' of making a living. His point is that the constitution of social life is itself an economic enterprise, just as the economy is a social affair. There is no separate sphere; living economy is about all the myriad entanglements of value, sentiment, meanings, materials, exchange and interchange that constitute the sociality of human life. To be sure, the ordinary economy is diverse, multiple and heterogeneous; but above all it *is* ubiquitous: 'and, in this light, alternative economies are a contradiction in terms' (Lee, 2006: 422). Economics, like societies, like politics, exist everywhere and in everything.

Second, there is the question of what to do with this ubiquitous co-existence of social/economy. To an extent, 'simply' demonstrating it and taking it seriously is itself an exercise in critical activism. This is at the heart of the Gibson–Graham collaboration which set out to reclaim the economy from its singular, capitalist space, recovering the heterogeneity that the capitalist economy subdues or denies, and constituting through this an arena of myriad economic practices and activism: 'a whirlwind of inventions and interventions'. Their project is not to create an 'alternative economy' but to show that what is generally labelled 'the economy' is a small part of a much more diverse, interlocking means of producing, exchanging and distributing values. It is the sectors of activity which are currently 'submerged' beneath the tip of the conventional economic iceberg that Gibson-Graham look to, as a route to establishing a 'radically heterogeneous economy' which signals a transition to post-capitalism (Gibson-Graham 1996, 2006). Smith (2005) makes a related point, arguing that even the 'conventional' elements of what has been constituted as a singular capitalist space are in practice far more diverse than they seem. The iceberg has no singular 'tip'. Drawing from the work of Elizabeth Grosz, Smith's point is that even at the zenith of a capitalist order, economic life is constituted through 'a thousand tiny markets' whose ethic is not given but made and whose geography might be different. From this perspective 'the diversity of actually existing markets and the multitude of normative ideas and practices that are, or could be, built into them, is not just a new economic geography, or a social curiosity: it is a far-reaching political resource' (Smith, 2005: 17).

By these varied routes, social geography is one of many disciplines now contributing to a paradigm shift at the interface of economy and society, emphasizing the social and power-filled character of economic mechanisms and ideas: valorising their diversity and complexity, their sensitivity to context, their passions as well as their 'rationality', and their part in the social construction and performance of everyday life. There is, in short, an ordinariness and a heterogeneity in economy, whose social geographies have still to be fully excavated. Such ideas may be illustrated in studies of labour markets, financial markets, small businesses or multinational firms; however, more accessible points of departure for those engaged with themes central to social geography may be found in recent research on housing markets, consumption and everyday life. By whatever tactics and examples, this all means that the division between social and economic geography, like the division between economics and sociology, which has been one of the most enduring in modern thought, simply cannot last. Politics, if nothing else, will see to that.

Social/political

If we take social geography to be the study of social practices in space, then – as we have already seen in discussions of social/nature and social/economy – it is impossible to divorce the social from the political in any attempt to interrogate it. As Henri Lefebvre (1991) remarked, any action in space is always already politically fraught and all politics is an effort to remake space. As such, the social and the political (and the context within which they occur) constitute a nexus upon which all of human life proceeds and must, accordingly, be considered in tandem. The co-constitution of social and political geography is hardly surprising as, within the larger realm of the social sciences, formerly un-breachable disciplinary boundaries are also themselves being sundered. Within geography itself, the connections between the social and the political are becoming increasingly recognized, appreciated, theorised and investigated. What is perhaps surprising is the fact that social and political geography have actually, for a very long time already, been relationally conceptualized and those connections have been severed and sutured many times over the course of the development of the discipline and across different national traditions. Indeed, the contemporary critical/radical origins of social geography can be traced not to the political unrest of the 1960s – where it is often located in short-sighted historiographies – but back further still to the anarchist traditions of nineteenth century geographers Pyotr Kropotkin and Élisée Reclus.

Early social and political geographies

Predictably, social geography, social science and sociology share overlaps in their development. Sociology as a disciplining frame for producing knowledge emerged in the mid-late nineteenth century, first in Europe and later in the US and the UK. Early on, sociology and the classical theorists of sociology understood the purview of their discipline as a response to modernity and modernization and the challenges of social disintegration and exploitation that accompanied them. While not always considering themselves to be sociologists, Marx, Weber, Durkheim, Tonnies, Pareto and Simmel, among others, formulated classical social theories that were foundational to the development of social science and sociology. Dunbar (1977) has argued that there is ample documentary evidence to indicate that the appearance of the concept of social geography was part of a larger intellectual movement that produced both social science as a multifaceted approach to human life and sociology as a more narrow disciplinary formulation. He places the origin of this movement – one that entrained social geography in its wake – in the early 1880s with the Le Play school of French sociology. The Le Playists, students of Frédéric Le Play, were interested in the relevance of environment and industrialization to poverty and destitution. They saw these problems as tractable and rejected the readily available Marxist critique of capitalism and dialectical materialism because it was considered too abstract to actually solve them. Instead, they championed the social survey as a way of understanding place, work and family, and thereby offering reforms to address the dislocating effects of urbanization and industrialization upon them.

Early social science's and sociology's concern for understanding the particularities of place helped to produce conceptual frames such as Frédéric Ratzel's 'anthropogeography' and Paul Vidal de la Blache's 'human geography', along with the Le Playists' 'social geography'. Yet, while Reclus was also employing the term social geography around this time, his application of it questioned these prevailing framings that tended to be descriptions or catalogues of the people and places threatened by the gathering forces of modernization and instead employed the concept to reflect upon a more relevant and politicized social geography that was attentive to 'class struggle, the search for equilibrium, and the sovereign decision of the individual' (Dunbar, 1977: 17). It was thus with Reclus that the circulating approaches to people and places were deferred from objectivity's conventional standards of the time, and toward social geographic study as a deeply political act.

Interestingly, while a different area of geography – political geography – was at the time focused on geopolitics and empire, social geography, in contrast, emerged with a focus on much more localized political questions that revolved around environments – broadly understood – and the people, plants, animals and landscapes that constituted them. As such, the internationally focused 'geopolitics' of Friedrich Ratzel (and later Halford Mackinder) was rejected by Reclus and Kropotkin, who very deliberately aligned themselves with a socialist/anarchist commitment to political change that focused on people in places and not on the more abstract concepts of territories, populations, frontiers and states. French geographer Yves Lacoste argues that the emergence of social geography as a concept – as an organic, rooted political orientation – was an 'epistemological turning point' in the history of the discipline. Before its appearance, geography had been a foundational component of the state apparatus: a tool of colonialism and imperialism with maps as its most powerful object (see Clark and Martin, 2004: 61). But with the anarchist geographers' more political and situated formulation of social geography, the discipline and its practitioners became a force that could be turned against the state and capital. Disappointingly, the influence of anarchist and socialist thought on social geography in particular and the discipline more widely did not persist with any vigour into the early twentieth century. While the renowned activist town planner Patrick Geddes promoted some of Reclus's and Kropotkin's ideas about social geography in the UK, and though some British geographers subscribed to them for a while (Meller, 1993), by the 1920s the lure of natural-science approaches to geographic questions had begun to be felt. There and elsewhere the sharp political orientation of social geography became blunted in favour of a more 'objective' social geography (Livingstone, 1992).

The exclusion of radical thinkers from the academy produced a similar trajectory in the post-World War I social science community in the US. In a fascinating assessment of the period, David Sibley (1995) shows how the political orientation of social geography and sociology was crowded out by the scientific orientation of sociology, which, when understood as a science, was distinctly different from social service or social work. He compares the writings and practices of the Chicago School of Sociology, especially founder Robert Park (1864–1944) and Ernest Burgess (1886–1966), to those of the early twentieth century African-American urban theorist and activist W.E.B. Dubois (1868–1963) and Jane Addams (1860–1935), a Chicago social theorist, organizer and founder of the Settlement Movement and co-founder of Hull House. Through a close reading of a wide set of texts, Sibley shows how Park and Burgess largely ignored the engaged, socially relevant work of Dubois and Addams. While the latter two produced some of the most detailed and perceptive ethnographic and social survey studies on the emerging capitalist city in the

US – particularly with respect to the impacts of exclusion, exploitation and deprivation around race, income, gender and ethnicity – their work was devalued by the intellectually ascendant Chicago School practitioners because it was regarded as descriptive (not analytically consistent with natural science models) and politically motivated, and therefore scientifically suspect. Addams was explicitly radical in her politics and used the research she and her colleagues conducted through Hull House and the Chicago School of Social Service Administration to challenge the state and capital with respect to issues of immigration, women's rights, child labour, war and housing. Dubois's social surveys unambiguously identified racism as the force behind housing deprivation and economic disparity. Moreover, both Dubois and Addams recognized the inextricability of theory and practice, whereas Park was adamant that theory should remain aloof from political practice. Sibley argues that because the Chicago School of Sociology was able to maintain control over the urban canon for five decades, the work of neither of these more politically motivated researchers was able to challenge its intellectual hegemony in an increasingly conservative and nationalist period. In the absence of a foothold for either critical sociology or the socio-political geography of Reclus, it wasn't until the late 1960s and early 1970s that the work of the anarchist geographers was rediscovered and yoked to a newly radical social geography; Addams and Dubois had to wait a few more decades for their work to attract similar attention among social geographers.

The 1960s and the return to the political

There is no way to overstate the significance of the political events of 1968 on the discipline of geography generally and social geography in particular. That year was the peak of an international protest movement that stretched across the 1960s through to the end of the Vietnam War in 1975. Student protests in Europe, the UK, the US; the popular support for Che Guevara in Latin America; Fidel Castro's newly socialist Cuba; international circulation of Mao Zedong's *The Little Red Book*; and scores of anti-colonial independence struggles across the globe – most prominently the one led by Ho Chi Minh in Vietnam – were all components of new political engagements that sparked a renewal in social geography. This period produced a re-radicalization of the subfield that was felt across a range of national fronts. Within human geography, liberal responses to state power, inequality and racism eventually came to be superseded, initially by a rediscovery of the anarchist roots of social geography, and then by a growing adherence to Marxism as the intellectual and political touchstone. David Harvey's *Social Justice and the City* (1973) exquisitely exemplifies this transformation and stands as the most significant marker of the revolution that occurred in social geography, as the discipline became thoroughly politicized following an extensive commitment to scientific objectivity that had characterized most research during the previous two decades.

The history of this complex period in human geography has yet to be satisfactorily written. It is important, nonetheless, to provide some sense of the key influences on the progressive political identity which came to characterize social geography during this period and which continues to greatly influence it today. The 1968 revolutionary events were very much founded on complex theorizations of the relationship between state, society and space, and social geography participated in a similar re-visioning. Reflecting on the student strikes in Paris in 1968, philosophers and social theorists such as Louis Althusser and Nicos Poulantzas attempted to make sense of those events by developing theories of the state that could account for its complex structure and function, as well as its relationship to capitalist domination. Althusser (1971), through careful and extensive reading of Marx's works, moved beyond the classical accounts of the violence of the Repressive State Apparatus (RSA) and its manifestation in the police, the military, the courts, the prisons, the government, etc., to more subtle aspects of state power that operate ideologically to deploy and reproduce the 'rules of the established order'. Building on Gramsci's (1971) concept of hegemony, Althusser theorized that the Ideological State Apparatus (ISA) operates and is institutionalized in the more private sphere of social life: the school, the family, the arts, television, radio, etc. His structuralism quite clearly delineates the role of the state in shaping state subjects through the spatial contexts of both (public) repressive forces and (private) ideological ones. Poulantzas's contribution to state theory during this period was to argue against the instrumentalist interpretation – that the state was an 'instrument of the bourgeoisie' – by insisting that although the state is relatively autonomous from the capitalist class, it functions to ensure the smooth operation of capitalist society and therefore benefits the capitalist class. Following in this tradition, later state theorists such as Bob Jessop (1990) explored the porous border between the state and capital, posing the former as an ensemble of social relations that is dialectically related to the latter. His state–society theory proved attractive to many political geographers, but it was the more poststructuralist, subject-oriented theory of power put forth by Ernesto Laclau and Chantal Mouffe (1985) that gained wider purchase among social and cultural geographers, some of whom used the theory to explore the spatial dimensions of subject formation (e.g., Natter and Jones, 1997).

Contemporary inter-connections

The contemporary landscape of social and political geography continues to make central the nexus of people, power and place. It also offers opportunities for change. The transformations that have occurred in political geographers' embrace of the social in the last several years, particularly the focus on the materiality of state practice (Kuus, 2007a, b; Koefoed and Simonsen, 2007; Marston, 2004; Mountz, 2004), have been enabled by explicit attention to the production of political subjects through a social process that is always spatial. For example, Joe Painter's concept of 'prosaic states' (2006) contends that everyday life is 'permeated with stateness' such that the only way we can understand or approach the state is through the effects that it has on social practice. Painter maintains that the state – a political concept *par excellence* – can be approached only through the influence it exerts on our daily lives: eating, sleeping, shopping, working, dying, marrying, having sex, and the list goes on. Moreover, the impact of the state, when understood in these terms, is seen to be geographically explicit; that is, it varies from one space to another and from place to place so that its reach is uneven and irregular. Another example is Anna Secor's work on biopolitics in Turkey (2006, 2007), in which she exposes the state as a social relation that unfolds in myriad ways. She looks in particular at how subjectivity is founded in state sovereignty – showing how the 'idea of the state' circulates in the daily lives of Turkish citizens, disrupting any fixed boundary between state and society and pointing, instead, to 'the everyday state'. Though fragmented and multiple, the state coheres in everyday life through 'the resonance (between sites, agents, rationalities, and techniques) that is discursively produced through the circulation and arrest of people, documents, information, money, and influence' (2007: 49).

Secor and Painter's work, as well as that of a growing number of other political-cum-social geographers, underscores the impossibility of understanding the state without taking 'the social' into account. If we wish to understand the workings of nationalism, for instance, we must approach it through the social practices that constitute it; if we wish to understand geopolitics, we must recognize that it is embodied in mundane as well as contentious social relationships. As Sara Smith argues, the tense geopolitical standoff between India and Pakistan is manifested in intimate bodily practices about marriage and procreation among and between different ethnic groups in India (2009).

While the deliberate juxtaposing of political and social geographic framings is intellectually interesting, these innovative approaches do much more than stimulate new ways of seeing connections. Particularly in the more activist-oriented work of geographers and others, they enable us to imagine and enact alternative ways of challenging power, domination and exploitation by revealing that the state is not something 'out there', institutionally inaccessible, but is rather an 'effect' (Mitchell, 1999) that is materially negotiable and resistible precisely through its inherence in daily practices. Notably, it is in recent discussions of the value of community as a response to state power that a return to the work of the early anarchist geographers, particularly Kropotkin, can be traced (Day, 2005). Organized around the logic of affinity, drawn in part from Kropotkin's concept of mutual aid, the possibility of rejecting hegemonic state relations is facilitated by organizing alternative social spaces that reject racist, sexist, classist, homophobic, ageist, able-ist, capitalist and other forms of exclusionary politics and embrace instead spaces of becoming where forms of association exist that are neither dependent on capital nor authoritarian. It means, in short, rejecting the state as the starting point of radical social change and turning instead to non-revolutionary *and* non-reformist forms of social organization that are non-hierarchical, non-universalizing and non-coercive, and are based on shared ethico-political commitments to progressive practices. Richard Day calls these alternatives 'affinity-based practices'. Undertaken by those 'who are striving to recover, establish or enhance their ability to determine the conditions of their own existence, while allowing and encouraging others to do the same' (2005: 13), they are effecting an explicitly social as opposed to merely political revolution, in the tradition of Kropotkin and Reclus as well as other early anarchists such as William Godwin and Gustav Landauer.

Social/cultural

The intersection of social with cultural geography is perhaps the most well worn connection of all those contained in the handbook. As a result, while the three intersections we have discussed so far seem fresh and lively, profiling the relationships between social and cultural geography might feel a little jaded. Furthermore, while social/cultural may be the most obvious zone of integration to look to – though it is in fact no more 'natural' than any of the other connections – the nexus of social and cultural geography has provoked heated debate, especially in Anglo-American geography where it has formed a catalyst for the discipline's recurring self-analysis. In continental Europe, by contrast, there are places where the social and cultural never parted ways, remaining indistinguishable parts of the same endeavour (see Simonsen, 2007, on Denmark; Paasi, 2007, on Finland) and jurisdictions where they form oppositional poles (see Chivallon, 2007, on France).

This is not the place to review the many histories of social and cultural geography – their discontinuities and entanglements – which now pepper the literature. What is of interest here is that these histories have become 'stylized' in ways which might constructively be challenged. This stylization generally talks, first, of a time when the two approaches were separated and unevenly examined (with the social dominating the cultural), then of a period in which they came briefly together, before, finally, a period in which roles were reversed, so that the cultural now dominates the social. There is also a geographical account in which social geography's European roots were spliced onto quantitative US social science to form a style of 'spatial sociology' that was set apart from North American cultural geography, rooted as it was in the material landscapes of American anthropology. Meanwhile, UK social geography was transformed by the humanistic traditions of British anthropology and British cultural studies, whose vocabulary rarely included the word 'social' but whose engagement with shared meanings and powerful representations opened a whole new world for social geographers to explore.

However the story is told, the result is a certain disgruntlement: worries that social geography has lost its identity; concerns that cultural geography has no real commitment to recognizing or challenging inequality and injustice (see Gregson, 1995); calls for rapprochement around renewed sensitivity to materialism in cultural studies and social research (Jackson, 2000a); and so on. The fact of this handbook suggests that predictions of social geography's dissolution are premature (see also Pain, 2003); but our larger point is that there have always been multiple and overlapping accounts of the 'social' and the 'cultural' in geography, and it is among these folds that the most productive ideas emerge.

The social and cultural – a re-assemblage?

Despite speculation and counter-claims, notwithstanding disciplinary tensions, and acknowledging their uneven profiles, the fact is that in geography (and more generally) the social and cultural have always been intrinsically linked. Rather than telling this story 'in the round' – a tale that can be recovered relatively easily from a burgeoning literature – we have opted to conclude this overview of social geography's connectivity by illustrating the intimate entanglement of social and cultural affairs through an example from just one area of research, the social geographies of fear. This is just one of many possible narratives, and it sketches rather than details the contours of research. Fear is an apt example, however, not just because it is an emotive topic which is perhaps impossible to pin down, but also because it is at once individual and collective, discursive and experiential, material and imaginary, embodied and emplaced; the 'feared' and the 'fearful' have complex and overlapping subject positions and spatial lives (Day, 1999). That fear is open to vastly different definitions, interpretations, ontological and epistemological positions has, indeed, made for a rich vein of research on its spatialities.

The earliest work on fear among geographers is best encapsulated in David Ley's (1974) exploration of ethnic segregation in 'the black inner city'. This was embraced as a work of urban social geography, but was very different to those on offer at the time, tackling issues of uncertainty, violence and fear among residents through ethnography. Ley adopted some conventional spatial mapping approaches, but he also dealt with representations of the neighbourhood, foreshadowing one of cultural geography's staple concerns. Indeed, the book's pluralistic but predominantly humanistic approach to the social world, along with its underlying concern to document the inequalities and injustices its subjects faced, nicely positions it between 'social' and 'cultural' geographies (in refreshing contrast to the positivist spatial studies of both segregation and crime that predominated at the time). It might in fact be seen as the epitome of social–cultural geography, illustrating the indivisibility of these human conditions.

Yi Fu Tuan's (1979) work on landscapes of fear was more centrally concerned with understanding the experience of emotion itself, and has always been regarded as a work of cultural geography. Tuan chronicled the nature of human fear and its placement in landscapes, including the immaterial and intangible; he explored fear of ethereal as well as more concrete threats, and drew attention to what would now be labelled discourses of fear, charting their origins and effects. Tuan was less concerned with fear as a societal issue and has been criticized for failing to identify that Western populations have in fact little materially to fear in comparison with those in poorer parts of the world (Sonnenfeld, 1981). Yet there are key ways in which this was also a work of social geography, with its emphasis on shared meanings and the sociality of fear.

Pain (1997), Smith (1986) and Valentine (1989, 1992), in their work on the racialization and gendering of fear, spoke powerfully to a growing sociological interest in the emotional structuring of inequality, noting the impact this has on the material conditions of everyday life for women and people of colour. These approaches sit quite centrally in the sphere of social geographies. But in comparison to the work on these themes employing spatial science/GIS in the 1980s and 1990s, these were much more qualitative cultural takes, focusing on discourses, images and ideas about fear as well as first-hand experiences of violence. And while some spatial science is rightly criticized for turning subjective experiences into objectivized patterns, others have found ways to use technologies such as geovisualization productively to augment intensive research into highly personal issues of emotion (see Kwan, 2008, on Muslim women's fears in the US). The social in social/cultural is again contextual and relational: the one constituting the other.

There are many other examples of the interleaving, and relationality, of ideas about the social and the cultural, the meanings and the materials of fear. Equally there is a literature invoking these ideas in reaction to simplistic or essentialized accounts of what fears are and how they are produced. Scholars of planning and architecture such as Oscar Newman (1972) and Alice Coleman (1985), for example, promoted the idea (especially popular with policy makers) that built environments directly affect crime and fear, and that they can therefore be remedied by changing those environments, making them more protective. In response to ideas like this, Gilling (1997: 186) showed how such interventions simply reinforced 'mutual suspicion and a profoundly anti-communitarian fortress mentality', while others – for example, Koskela (1997) – drew attention to the enabling possibilities of behavioural and emotional qualities like boldness, and still others concentrate on the emancipatory potential of hope (Wright, 2008). Once again, then, it is the intersectionality of the social and cultural rather than their separate effects that is most apparent.

This continues to be so in more recent times as fear, and studies of it, have experienced a renaissance in light of the war on terror and other pressing geopolitical issues (Gregory and Pred, 2007; Pain and Smith, 2008). In this new literature, the resurrection of a masculinist geopolitics setting the 'West' once again opposite 'the rest' is countered by a new generation of place-based researchers (see also Dowler and Sharp, 2001; Hyndman, 2003; Pain, 2009), as well as by a return to classic oppositions to the growing militarization of public space, such as that elegantly revealed in Davis's (1992) social history of segregation, fear and the distribution of wealth and power in Los Angeles.

So, while it is tempting to see an explosion of interest in emotional geographies (see, for example, Anderson and Smith, 2001; Davidson et al., 2005) as the new domain of cultural rather than social geography, this is really just one element of a wider engagement with hope, fear, anxiety and contentment that has permeated the co-development of social and cultural research over at least four decades. There is no linear history of social 'versus' cultural geography, or of one perspective extinguishing the other. Without denying tensions which are worth exploring, the bigger picture is that these approaches are each part of a kaleidoscope of understanding of social and cultural emotional geographies. Social-cultural geographies are together part of the wider project of excavating the materials and meanings of life. Rather than debating where the cultural ends and the social begins, time may be better spent pondering other schisms: for example, around our purposes and involvement in knowledge production; and our engagements in ethics, politics, relevance and epistemology.

PROJECTIONS

Having entered a space where relationships with, and even among, things may be as interesting as relationships among people, no one has a monopoly on defining or engaging with the complexity of the social world. Likewise, in a setting where the workings of 'economy' are no longer taken for granted, where 'markets' are as much about subjective encounters as financial affairs, social geography is forced to recognize that what was once of marginal interest – supply, demand, cost and value, for example – now occupies a central place. And at a time when researchers engaged with policy are no longer thought to be sullying their hands by reproducing power structures that are unchanging and unchallengeable, nothing short of a paradigm shift of relevance is in train. The *Handbook of Social Geographies* is designed to reflect all this: to reconsider and redirect the cutting edge of a long-established, frequently revised and currently revived subfield; to engage with the way a map of established territory has burst into new 'lines of flight'.

So what, to this end, does the Handbook contain? As noted earlier, it does not contain a little of everything; it is not a dictionary, an encyclopaedia, a systematic text or an exhaustive review. It is a selective excursion into the depths and across the breadth of a changeable, vibrant field of study. Consistent with an emphasis on connections rather than legacies, on trajectories rather then origins, we have invited contributions which show how different debates – whose influence may have waxed and waned in the past – are moving on. Neither we, the editors, nor the authors have tried to be definitive. Rather the collection is eclectic and exploratory, tracking the past to an extent, but with a preference for debating what the subject, and the world it is getting to know, might become. To that end, the volume is organized around five thematic hubs that are anchored in social geography; these are inspired by, but not neatly contained in, the subdisciplinary connectivities outlined above. Each section has its own editor, and each has its own editorial overview, providing a summary of, and commentary on, the individual chapters. Broadly, however, the shape of the social geographies that follow looks something like this.

The first section is concerned with a longstanding core interest among social geographers with questions of ***difference and diversity***. This builds upon enduring ideas about the structuring of social relations. It examines the ruptures and rifts, continuities and connections around race, gender, age, health and disability, bodies and affectual relations; and it uses the postsocial 'turn' to reconsider the way some key geographies of inequality are made and sustained.

This section examines the social relations of difference, a keystone of social geography. The opening chapters consider the role of geography in placing and reproducing 'traditional' social divisions around race/gender/age/disability/nation. All of these markers make some reference to the 'naturalness' of difference – often under the banner of 'diversity' – and contrast those appeals to the claims of social constructivism, anti-essentialism, and geographies of relation. The injustices these essentialized axes produce help explain why, during the late twentieth century, social geography was part of a critical, and remarkably successful, attempt to undermine appeals to nature in accounts of social difference. Authors of these early chapters explore what is at stake theoretically and politically now that these appeals to essential differences are no longer possible.

The section's chapters also explore the turn to other 'post-social' axes of difference that have recently unsettled old ideas about categories and identities. They therefore consider newer divides – around genetic geographies, non-human animals, technologies and preconscious affectivities – that not only question the theoretical demarcation of 'the social' from its Others, but also point to the role of such an analytic in reproducing inequalities formed through the traditional axes of gender, race, etc. In marking these new directions, these chapters clarify the encounter between social constructionism and new materialisms in shaping the social geography of social inequality. They tell the story of how social geography has responded to calls to embrace 'nature', to recognize the salience of the object world, and to take the post-human realm seriously.

The second section of the Handbook is about the inseparability of ***economy and society***, and about the contribution of social geography – alongside other areas of social research – to the development of concepts and ideas that have previously been the domain of economy and economists. As we have already seen, the division between social and economic geography, like the division between economics and sociology, is one of the most enduring in modern thought. No social commentator denies that there is a material, and therefore economic, edge to the inequalities that divide the world, but the economic mechanisms which underpin these – money, markets, prices, costs, calculation – have too often been taken for granted rather than subjected to debate. Confronting this challenge, the essays in this section draw attention to the sociality, subjectivity, emotional qualities and placement of money, markets, price and value, recognizing the importance of examples drawn from home, work and services, from production, consumption and exchange. These authors recognize that because 'the economy' now dominates so many areas of life – attending to needs as well as wants, delivering basics as well as distributing surplus – much more work is required to excavate its social and cultural content and to draw out its political relevance. This task could be addressed through discussions about labour markets, financial markets, small businesses or multinational firms; however, the section also works with ideas that are traditionally more central to social geography, such as consumption and everyday life.

Section three hinges around ***geographies of wellbeing***. The aim here is to draw together, and find links between, the many aspects of material and emotional wellbeing and distress, which are documented in the literature. This section builds from a foundation of work on the spaces of fear, anxiety and disease towards newer concerns with geographies of health, resilience and contentment. Perhaps the two key dimensions of wellbeing hinge around safekeeping and health. Each is impaired by the patterning of risks and vulnerabilities, and these in turn underpin geographies of emotional and material harm. On the other hand, safety and positive health, or wellbeing, are both promoted by key sets of (material and psycho-social) resources, which not only work directly to keep people well and safe but also build up resilience to harmful circumstances and events. This section considers both sides of the coin. It documents geographies of risk, fear and victimization, as well as geographies of personal and community safety. It is concerned with the patterning of health inequalities and with geographies of disability, but it also taps into the emotional, and affective, geographies of resilience, contentment and hope as it considers the impact of inequalities in wealth and power on material and psychosocial wellbeing.

The fourth section focuses on ***geographies of social justice***. The question of who gets what, where and why has, for years, formed a core concern for social geography. The neoliberal environment, however, encasing both global and local concerns over the last 25 years, has set the competitive individualism of markets against a co-operative or relational ethics of care, such that the latter has been confined to the voluntarism of families or the residual sphere of social policy. Social geography, nevertheless, has always held onto the argument that things could and should be different, and this concern with the possibilities and practicalities of normative theory is what connects the ideas in this section.

Where a subdiscipline is so engaged with inequality as something which is made rather than pre-given, we might expect a concern with how things should and could be different. This section is about the idea and practice of a more inclusive, just, ethical, caring society; and about the role which social geographers could have in forging it. Concern with social justice in geography intersects with various other disciplines but most especially with moral and political philosophy. Since David Harvey's pathbreaking 1973 book, *Social Justice and the City*, geographers have attempted to grapple with the spatial implications of moral and political questions and especially with how value is determined and the just distribution of value in society. But such a construction, based as it is upon distributive questions, fails to appreciate that social injustice is the result of differential access to power and resources and not merely about the distributional outcomes of valuation. For instance, access to justice and the rights that inhere within the social and political category of citizenship are more complicated than the distribution of access to citizenship itself.

This fourth section traverses the history and contemporary terrain of social justice in geography, recognizing the many different ways in which the term has been problematized. We address the ideal of morality and ethics with respect to justice as well as the tension that exists between liberal notions of social justice and feminist reconceptualization of it around an 'ethic of care'. We also address the intersections of social justice and environmental justice and more recent attempts to develop a meta-ethics of justice for the discipline. Finally, we explore various justice- and rights- based struggles for both the capacity to become and act and to have equal access to the political, social and cultural resources that constitute worlds.

Reflecting this interest in practice and practical engagement, the handbook ends with a fifth section containing a set of commentaries on methods and ethics: on what is implied in ***doing social geography***. This is not a systematic overview of the 'how to' of research: there are plenty of volumes now devoted to methodology. It is rather about the entanglement of research with practicalities, moralities and politics. It is about the possibilities for, and limits to, activism. Doing social geography has always been about practice and practical engagement – it is one area of geography where the 'doing' has always been bound into the 'knowing'. It is, indeed, social geographers who have begun to respond to calls for more grounded research and theory across the discipline, and who have tied the achievements of a sometimes too detached 'cultural turn' into pressing concerns about welfare and inequality. This makes social geography well placed to address key questions, which are currently resurfacing across social science, about the relevance of academic research and its relationship with policy and other forms of intervention.

This section covers different ways of engaging with the world outside social geography. It encourages readers to link practical research strategies with wider theories of research and its political, ethical and institutional contexts. The contributors offer personal accounts which reflect how they have negotiated these issues in their own research practice. The editorial commentary draws these themes together and provides some thought-provoking observations on the conduct of social geographical research in the twenty-first century.

THE SHAPE OF SOCIAL GEOGRAPHY

To restate: it is obvious, even in a volume of this scale and size, that we cannot hope to present a comprehensive picture of a subject as longstanding or as wide ranging as social geography. Nor can we claim to have done justice to the many vibrant social geographies that are currently in play. We are conscious of some glaring gaps, just as we are inspired by so much of what has been written. What we have tried to convey above all in this collection is a sense of the energy, diversity, relevance and curiosity that drives the work of social geographers today. The essays contain a flavour of what matters, a glimpse of where the cutting edge lies, a brush with the most dangerous territory, and a signal of what is still to come. This is not a geography of everything for anyone; but hopefully it contains something of value for geographers generally, for social scientists in the wider community, and for social geographers in particular.

REFERENCES

Althusser, L. (1971) 'Ideology and ideological state apparatuses (notes toward an investigation)', in *Lenin and Philosophy and Other Essays*, translated by B. Brewster. New York: Monthly Review Press. pp. 127–86.

Amin, A. (2008) Extraordinarily ordinary. Working in the social economy. In review.

Amin, A. and Thrift, N. (eds) (2004) *Cultural Economy: a Reader*. Oxford: Blackwell.

Anderson, J. (2003) 'American hegemony after 11 September: allies, rivals and contradictions', *Geopolitics*, 8: 35–60.

Anderson, K. and Smith, S.J. (2001) Editorial: 'Emotional geographies', *Transactions of the Institute of British Geographers*, 26 (1): 7–10.

Badmington, N. (2004) 'Mapping posthumanism', *Environment and Planning A*, 36: 1344–51.

Barnett, C. (2005) 'Ways of relating: hospitality and the acknowledgement of otherness', *Progress in Human Geography*, 29: 5–21.

Barrows, H.H. (1923) 'Geography as human ecology', *Annals of the Association of American Geographers*, 13 (1): 1–14.

Billinge, M., Gregory, D.J. and Martin, R. (1984) *Recollections of a Revolution*. London: Macmillan.

Blunt, A. and Rose, G. (1994) *Writing Women and Space: Colonial and Postcolonial Geographies.* New York: Guilford.

Blunt, A. and Wills, J. (2000) *Dissident Geographies: an Introduction to Radical Ideas and Practice*. Harlow: Longman.

Bondi, L. (2005) 'Making connections and thinking through emotions: between geography and psychotherapy', *Transactions of the Institute of British Geographers*, 30 (4): 433–48.

Boyer, K. (2003) 'At work, at home? New geographies of work and care-giving under welfare reform in the US', *Space and Polity*, 7: 75–86.

Braun, B. (2004) 'Modalities of posthumanism', *Environment and Planning A*, 36: 1352–55.

Brown, L.A. and Moore, E. (1970) 'The intra-urban migration process: a perspective', *Geografiska Annaler, Series B*, 52 (1): 1–13.

Brown, M. and Knopp, L. (2008) 'Queering the map: the productive tensions of colliding epistemologies', *Annals of the Association of American Geographers*, 98: 1–19.

Burton, I., Kates, R.W. and White, G.F. (1978) *The Environment as Hazard*. New York: Oxford University Press.

Buttimer, A. (1968) 'Social geography', *International Encyclopedia of the Social Sciences*, 6: 134–45.

Buttimer, A. (1971) *Society and Mileu in the French Geographic Tradition*. Chicago: Rand McNally.

Callon, M. (1998) 'Introduction: the embeddedness of economic markets in economics', in M. Callon (ed.), *The Laws of the Markets*. Oxford: Blackwell. pp. 1–57.

Castree, N. and Nash, C. (2004) 'Introduction: posthumanism in question', *Environment and Planning A*, 36: 1341–43.

Castree, N. and Nash, C. (2006) 'Posthuman geographies', *Social and Cultural Geography*, 7 (4): 501–4.

Cater, J. and Jones, T. (1989) *Social Geography*. London: Edward Arnold.

Chivallon, C. (2007) 'A vision of social and cultural geography in France', in R. Kitchin (ed.), *Mapping Worlds: International Perspectives on Social and Cultural Geographies*. Abingdon: Routledge. pp. 21–38.

Clark, G. (1998) 'Stylized facts and close dialogue: methodology in economic geography', *Annals of the Association of American Geographers*, 88: 73–87.

Clark, J.R. and Martin, C. (2004) *Anarchy, Geography, Modernity: The Radical Social Thought of Élisée Reclus*. Lanham, MD: Lexington Books.

Clarke, N., Barnett, C., Cloke, P. and Malpass, A. (2007) 'The political rationalities of fair-trade consumption in the United Kingdom', *Politics and Society*, 35: 583–607.

Cloke, P. (2002) 'Deliver us from evil? Prospects for living ethically and acting politically in human geography', *Progress in Human Geography*, 26 (5): 587–604.

Coleman, A. (1985) *Utopia on Trial*. London: Hilary Shipman.

Cooke, B. and Kothari, U. (eds) (2001) *Participation: the New Tyranny?* London: Zed Books.

Crang, M. (2002) 'Qualitative methods: the new orthodoxy?', *Progress in Human Geography*, 26: 647–55.

Crang, M. (2003) 'Qualitative methods: touchy, feely, look-see?', *Progress in Human Geography*, 27 (4): 494–504.

Davidson, J., Bondi, L. and Smith, M. (2005) *Emotional Geographies*. Aldershot: Ashgate.

Davis, M. (1992) *City of Quartz: Excavating the Future of Los Angeles*. New York: Vintage.

Day, K. (1999) 'Embassies and sancturaries: women's experiences of race and fear in public space', *Environment and Planning D: Society and Space*, 17: 307–12.

Day, R.J.F. (2005) *Gramsci is Dead: Anarchist Currents in the Newest Social Movements*. London: Pluto Press.

Del Casino, V.J. and Jones, J.P. III (2007) 'Space for social inequality researchers: a view from geography', in L.M. Lobao, G. Hooks and A.R. Tickamyer (eds), *The Sociology of Spatial Inequality*. Albany: SUNY Press. pp. 233–51.

Del Casino, V.J. and Marston S.A. (2006) 'Social geography in the United States: everywhere and nowhere', *Social and Cultural Geography*, 7 (6): 995–1008.

Derrida, J. (1976) *Of Grammatology*, translated by G.C. Spivak. Baltimore: Johns Hopkins University Press.

Derrida, J. (2003) 'And say the animal responded?', in C. Wolfe (ed.), *Zoontologies: The Question of the Animal*. Minneapolis: University of Minnesota Press. pp. 121–46.

Dewsbury, D., Harrison, P., Rose, M. and Wylie, J. (2002) 'Enacting Geographies', *Geoforum*, 33: 437–40.

Dowler, L. and Sharp, J. (2001) 'A feminist geopolitics?' *Space and Polity*, 5: 165–76.

Driver, P. (1992) 'Geography's empire: histories of geographical empire', *Environment and Planning D: Society and Space*, 10: 23–40.

DuGay, P. and Pryke, M. (eds) (2002) *Cultural Economy*. London: Sage.

Dunbar, G.S. (1977) 'Some early occurrences of the term "social geography"', *Scottish Geographical Journal*, 93 (1): 15–20.

Dwyer, O.J. (1997) 'Geographical research about African Americans: a survey of journals, 1911–1995', *The Professional Geographer*, 49 (4): 441–51.

Elwood, S. (2006a) 'Beyond cooptation or resistance: urban spatial politics, community organizations, and GIS-based spatial narratives', *Annals of the Association of American Geographers*, 96: 323–41.

Elwood, S. (2006b) 'Negotiating knowledge production: the everyday inclusions, exclusions, and contradictions of participatory GIS research', *The Professional Geographer*, 58: 197–208.

England, K.V.L. (1993) 'Suburban pink collar ghettos: the spatial entrapment of women?', *Annals of the Association of American Geographers*, 83: 225–42.

Eyles, J. (ed.) (1986) *Social Geography in International Perspective*. London: Rowman and Littlefield.

Fukuyama, F. (2002) *Our Posthuman Future: Consequences of the Biotechnology Revolution*. New York: Picador.

Fuller, D. (2008) 'Public geographies 1: Taking stock', *Progress in Human Geography*, 32 (6): 834–44.

Fuller, D. and Kitchin, R. (eds) (2004) *Radical Theory, Critical Praxis: Making a Difference Beyond the Academy?* Praxis E-Press available at http://www.praxis-epress.org/rtcp/contents.html.

Gans, H. (2002) 'The sociology of space: a use-centered view,' *City and Community*, 1: 329–39.

Garcia-Ramón, M.D., Albet, A. and Zusman, P. (2007) Recent developments in social and cultural geography in Spain, in R. Kitchin (ed.), *Mapping Worlds: International Perspectives on Social and Cultural Geographies*. Abingdon: Routledge. pp. 39–52.

Gerhardt, H. (2008) 'Geopolitics, ethics, and the evangelicals' commitment to Sudan', *Environment and Planning D: Society and Space*, 26: 911–28.

Gibson-Graham, J.K. (1996) *The End of Capitalism (as we knew it): A Feminist Critique of Political Economy*. Oxford, UK, and Cambridge, USA: Blackwell.

Gibson-Graham, J.K. (2006) *A Postcapitalist Politics*. Minneapolis: University of Minnesota Press.

Giddens, A. (1984) *The Constitution of Society*. Berkeley: University of California Press.

Gieryn, T.F. (2000) 'A space for place in sociology', *Annual Review of Sociology*, 26: 463–96.

Gilling, D. (1997) *Crime Prevention*. London: UCL Press.

Glacken, C. (1967) *Traces on the Rhodian Shore: Nature and Culture in Western Thought from Ancient Times to the End of the Eighteenth Century*. Berkeley: University of California Press.

Gramsci, A. (1971) 'State and civil society,' in *Selections from the Prison Notebooks*. New York: International Publishers. pp. 257–76.

Gregory, D. and Pred, A. (2007) *Violent Geographies: Fear, Terror and Political Violence*. London: Routledge.

Gregson, N. (1995) 'And now it's all consumption!', *Progress in Human Geography*, 19 (1): 135–41.

Gregson, N. (2003) 'Reclaiming "the social" in social and cultural geography', in K. Anderson, M. Domosh, S. Pile and N. Thrift (eds), *Handbook of Cultural Geography*. London: Sage. pp. 43–57.

Hamnett, C. (1996) *Social Geography: A Reader*. London: Edward Arnold.

Hanson, S. and Monk, J. (1982) 'On not excluding half the human in geography', *Professional Geographer*, 34 (1): 11–23.

Hanson, S. and Pratt, G. (1995) *Gender, Work and Space*. New York: Routledge.

Haraway, D. (1991) *Simians, Cyborgs and Women: The Reinvention of Nature*. New York: Routledge.

Harrison, P. (2000) 'Making sense: embodiment and the sensibilities of the everyday', *Environment and Planning D: Society and Space*, 18: 497–517.

Harvey, D. (1973) *Social Justice and the City*. London: Edward Arnold.

Hawkins, H., Sacks, S., Cook, I., Rawling, E., Griffiths, H., Swift, D., Evans, J., Rothnie, G., Wilson, J., Williams, A., Feenay, K., Gordon, L., Prescott, H., Murphy, C., Allen, D., Mitchell, T., Wheeldon, R., Roberts, M., Robinson, G., Flaxman, P., Fuller, D., Lovell, T. et al. (forthcoming) 'Organic public geographies: "making the connection"', *Antipode*.

Hayden, D. (1984) *Redesigning the American Dream: Gender, Housing and Family Life*. New York: W.W. Norton.

Hettner, A. (1977) *Allgemeine Geographie des Menschen*. Darmstadt: Wissenschaftliche Buchgesellschaft.

Hoggart, K., Lees, L. and Davies, A. (2002) *Research in Human Geography*. London: Edward Arnold.

Hudson, R. (2008) 'Life on the edge. Navigating the competitive tensions between the "social" and the "economic" in the social economy and its relations to the mainstream'. Paper presented to the seminar *Changing cultures of competitiveness: Global production and labour relations*. Manchester (July).

Hyndman, J. (2003) Beyond either/or: a feminist analysis of September 11th, *ACME*, 2: 1–13.

Jackson, P. (2000a) 'Rematerializing social and cultural geography', *Social and Cultural Geography*, 1: 9–14.

Jackson, P. (2000b) 'Social geography', in R.J. Johnston, D. Gregory, G. Pratt, and M. Watts (eds), *Dictionary of Human Geography*. Oxford: Blackwell. pp. 753–54.

Jackson, P. and Penrose, J. (1993) 'Introduction: placing "race" and nation,' in P. Jackson and J. Penrose (eds), *Constructions of Race, Place and Nation*. Minneapolis: University of Minnesota Press. pp. 1–23.

Jackson, P. and Smith, S.J. (1984) *Exploring Social Geography*. London: Allen and Unwin.

James, A. (2006) 'Critical moments in the production of "rigorous" and "relevant" cultural economic geographies', *Progress in Human Geography*, 30: 289–308.

James, A. (2007) 'Demystifying the role of culture in innovative regional economies', *Regional Studies*, 39: 1197–1216.

Joseph, M. (2002) *Against the Romance of Community*. Minneapolis: University of Minnesota Press.

Jessop, B. (1990) *State Theory: Putting States in their Place*. Pennsylvania, PA: Pennsylvania State University Press.

Kearns, R. and Moon, G. (2002) 'From medical to health geography: novelty, place and theory after a decade of change', *Progress in Human Geography*, 26: 605–25.

Kearns, R. and Panelli, R. (2007) 'Directions to enlarge our worlds? Social and cultural geography in New Zealand', in R. Kitchin (ed.), *Mapping Worlds: International Perspectives on Social and Cultural Geographies*. Abingdon: Routledge. pp. 263–74.

Kesby, M. (2007) 'Spatializing participatory approaches: geography's contribution to a mature debate', *Environment and Planning A*, 39 (12): 2813–31.

Kindon, S. and Latham A. (2002) 'From mitigation to negotiation: ethics and the geographic imagination in Aotearoa New Zealand', *New Zealand Geographer*, 58: 14–22.

Kindon, S. Pain, R. and Kesby, M. (2007) *Connecting People, Participation and Place: Participatory Action Research Approaches and Methods*. Abingdon: Routledge.

Kitchin, R. (2007) *Mapping Worlds: International Perspectives on Social and Cultural Geographies*. Abingdon: Routledge.

Kitchin, R.M. and Hubbard, P.J. (1999) Editorial: 'Research, action and "critical" geographies', *Area*, 31: 195–8.

Knox, P. (2000) *Urban Social Geography*. London: Longman.

Kobayashi, A. (1994) 'Coloring the field: gender, "race", and the politics of fieldwork', *The Professional Geographer*, 46: 73–80.

Kobayashi, A. and Peake, L. (2000) 'Racism out of place: thoughts on whiteness and an anti-racist geography in the new millennium', *Annals of the Association of American Geographers*, 90 (2): 392–403.

Koefoed, L. and Simonsen, K. (2007) 'The price of goodness: everyday national narratives in Denmark', *Antipode*, 39 (2): 310–30.

Koskela, H. (1997) '"Bold walk and breakings": women's spatial confidence versus fear of violence', *Gender, Place and Culture*, 4 (3): 301–19.

Kraftl, P. and Adey, P. (2008) 'Architecture/affect/dwelling', *Annals of the Association of American Geographers*, 98: 213–31.

Kropotkin, P. (1902) *Mutual Aid: A Factor of Evolution* (The Project Etext of *Mutual Aid*). (http://www.gutenberg.org/dirs/etext03/mtlad10.txt) accessed 29 February 2008.

Kuus, M. (2007a) 'Ubiquitous identities and elusive subjects: puzzles from Central Europe', *Transactions of the Institute of British Geographers,* 31 (1): 90–101.

Kuus, M. (2007b) 'Love, peace and NATO: imperial subject-making in Central Europe', *Antipode*, 39 (2): 269–90.

Kwan, M. (2008) 'From oral histories to visual narratives: re-presenting the post-September 11 experiences of the Muslim women in the USA', *Social and Cultural Geography,* 9 (6): 653–69.

Laclau, E. and Mouffe, C. (1985) *Hegemony and Socialist Strategy*. New York: Verso.

Latour, B. (1993) *We Have Never been Modern*. Translated by C. Porter. Cambridge: Harvard University Press.

Lawson, V. (1995) 'The politics of difference: examining the quantitative/qualitative dualism in post-structuralist feminist research', *The Professional Geographer*, 47 (4): 449–57.

Lee, R. (2006) 'The ordinary economy: tangled up in values and geography', *Transactions, Instititute of British Geographers*, NS 31: 413–32.

Lee, R., Leyshon, A., Aldridge, T., Tooke, J., Williams, C. and Thrift, N. (2004) 'Making geographies and histories? Constructing local circuits of value', *Environment and Planning D: Society and Space*, 22: 595–647.

Lefebvre, H. (1991) *The Production of Space*. Translated by D. Nicholson-Smith. Oxford: Basil Blackwell.

Ley, D. (1974) *The Black Inner City as Frontier Outpost*. Washington D.C.: Association of American Geographers, monograph series no. 7.

Ley, D. (1983) *A Social Geography of the City*. New York: Harper and Row.

Livingstone, D. (1992) *The Geographical Tradition*. Oxford: Blackwell.

Lobao, L.M. (1993) 'Renewed significance of space in social research: implications for labor market studies', in J. Singelmann and F.A. Deseran (eds), *Inequalities in Labor Market Areas*. Boulder: Westview Press. pp. 11–31.

Lobao, L.M. (2004) 'Continuity and change in place stratification: spatial inequality and middle-range territorial units', *Rural Sociology*, 61: 77–102.

Lobao, L.M., Hooks, G. and Tickamyer, A.R. (2007) 'Introduction: advancing the sociology of inequality', in L.M. Lobao, G. Hooks and A.R. Tickamyer (eds), *The Sociology of Spatial Inequality*. Albany: SUNY Press. pp. 1–25.

McDowell, L. (1983) 'Towards an understanding of the gender division of urban space', *Environment and Planning D: Society and Space*, 1 (1): 59–72.

McDowell, L. (1992) 'Doing gender: feminism, feminists and research methods in human geography', *Transactions of the Institute of British Geographers*, New Series, 17 (4): 399–416.

McKendrick, J.H. (1999) 'Multi-method research: an introduction to its application in population geography', *The Professional Geographer,* 51 (1): 40–50.

McKie, L., Gregory, S. and Bowlby, A. (2002) 'Shadow times: the temporal and spatial frameworks and experiences of caring and working', *Sociology*, 36: 897–924.

Marston, S.A. (2004) 'State, culture, space: uneven developments in political geography', *Political Geography*, 23 (1): 1–16.

Martin, R. and Sunley, P. (2001) 'Rethinking the "Economic" in Economic Geography: broadening our vision or losing our focus?', *Antipode*, 33 (2): 148–61.

Massey, D. (1984) *Spatial Divisions of Labor: Social Structures and the Geography of Production*. New York: Methuen.

Mattingly, D. and Falconer-Al-Hindi, K, (1995) 'Should women count? A context for the debate', *The Professional Geographer,* 47: 427–35.

Meller, H. (1993) *Patrick Geddes: Social Evolutionist and City Planner*. London: Routledge.

Mercer, D. (1984) 'Unmasking technocratic geography', in M. Billinge, D.J. Gregory and R. Martin (eds), *Recollections of a Revolution*. London: Macmillan,153–99.

Mikesell, M. (1978) 'Tradition and innovation in cultural geography', *Annals of the Association of American Geographers*, 68 (1): 1–16.

Mitchell, D. (1995) 'There's no such thing as culture: towards a reconsideration of the idea of culture in geography', *Transactions of the Institute of British Geographers*, 20 (1): 102–16.

Mitchell, T. (1999) 'Society, economy, and the state effect', in G. Steinmetz (ed.), *State/Culture: State-Formation after the Cultural Turn*. Ithaca: Cornell University Press. pp. 76–97.

Morrill, D. and E. Wohlenberg (1971) *The Geography of Poverty in the United States*. New York: McGraw-Hill.

Mountz, Alison (2004) 'Embodying the nation-state: Canada's response to human smuggling', *Political Geography*, 23 (3): 323–45.

Murdie, R.A. (1969) *Factorial Ecology of Metropolitan Toronto, 1951–1961: An Essay on the Social Geography of the City*. Chicago: University of Chicago Department of Geography.

Musterd, S. and de Pater, B. (2007) 'Eclectic and pragmatic: the colours of Dutch social and cultural geography', in R. Kitchin (ed.), *Mapping Worlds: International Perspectives on Social and Cultural Geographies.* Abingdon: Routledge. pp. 53–68.

Natter, W. and Jones, J.P. III (1997) 'Identity, space and other uncertainties', in G. Benko and U. Strohmayer (eds), *Space and Social Theory: Interpreting Modernity and Postmodernity*. Oxford: Blackwell. pp. 141–61.

Newman, O. (1972) *Defensible Space*. New York: Macmillan.

Olson, E. and Sayer, A. (2009) 'Radical geography and its critical standpoints: embracing the normative', *Antipode*, 41: 180–98.

Paasi, A. (2007) 'Between national and international pressures: contextualizing the progress of Finnish social and cultural geography', in R. Kitchin (ed.), *Mapping Worlds: International Perspectives on Social and Cultural Geographies*. Abingdon: Routledge. pp. 191–214.

Pacione, M. (ed.) (1987) *Social Geography: Progress and Prospect*. London: Croom Helm.

Pain, R.H. (1997) 'Social geographies of women's fear of crime', *Transactions of the Institute of British Geographers*, 22 (2): 231–44.

Pain, R. (2003) 'Social geography: on action-orientated research', *Progress in Human Geography*, 27 (5): 677–85.

Pain, R. (2009) 'Globalized fear: towards an emotional geopolitics', *Progress in Human Geography*,

Pain, R. and Kindon, S. (2007) 'Participatory geographies', *Environment and Planning A,* 39: 2807–12.

Pain, R. and Smith, S.J. (2008) *Fear: Critical Geopolitics and Everyday Life*. Aldershot: Ashgate.

Pain, R., Barke, M., Gough, J., Fuller, D. MacFarlane, R. and Mowl, G. (2001) *Introducing Social Geographies*. London: Arnold.

Painter, J. (2006) 'Prosaic geographies of stateness', *Political Geography*, 25 (7): 752–74.

Panelli, R. (2004) *Social Geographies: From Difference to Action*. London: Sage.

Panelli, R. (2008) 'Social geographies: encounters with indigenous and more-than-White/Anglo geographies', *Progress in Human Geography,* 32: 801–11.

Peach, C. (ed.) (1975) *Urban Social Segregation*. London and New York: Longman.

Peach, C. (2002) 'Social geography: new religions and ethnoburbs – contrasts with cultural geography', *Progress in Human Geography,* 26 (2): 252–60.

Peet, R. (1977) *Radical Geography*. Chicago: Maaroufa Press.

Peet, R. (1984) 'The social origins of environmental determinism', *Annals of the Association of American Geographers,* 75 (3): 309–33.

Platt, R.S. (1948) 'Environmentalism versus geography', *American Journal of Sociology,* 53 (5): 351–58.

Preston, V. and McLafferty, S. (1993) 'Gender differences in commuting at suburban and central locations', *Canadian Journal of Regional Science,* 16 (2): 237–59.

Proctor, J.D. and Smith, D.M. (eds) (1999) *Geography and Ethics: Journeys in a Moral Terrain*. London: Routledge.

Pryke, M. and DuGay, P. (2007) 'Take an issue: cultural economy and finance', *Economy and Society*, 36: 339–54.

Robbins, P.F. (2004) *Political Ecology: A Critical Introduction*. Oxford: Basil Blackwell.

Rose, G. (1993) *Feminism and Geography: The Limits of Geographical Knowledge*. London: Polity Press.

Rose, H.M. (1971) *The Black Ghetto: A Spatial Behaviorial Perspective*. New York: McGraw-Hill.

Roseman, C.C. (1977) *Changing Migration Patterns within the United States*. Washington, DC: Association of American Geographers.

Saarinen, T.F. (1969) *Perception of Environment*. Washington, DC: Association of American Geographers.

Sauer, C.O. (1925) 'The morphology of landscape', *University of California Publications in Geography,* 2 (2): 19–54.

Secor, Anna (2006) 'An unrecognizable condition has arrived: law, violence and the state of exception in Turkey', in Derek Gregory and Allan Pred (eds), *Violent Geographies: Fear, Terror, and Political Violence*. New York: Routledge. pp. 37–53.

Secor, Anna (2007) 'Between longing and despair: state, space and subjectivity in Turkey', *Environment and Planning D: Society and Space,* 25: 33–52.

Semple, E.C. (1911) *Influences of Geographic Environment*. New York: Henry Holt.

Shaw, W.S., Herman, R.D.K. and Dobbs, G.R. (2006) 'Encountering indigeneity: re-imagining and decolonizing geography', *Geografiska Annaler,* 88B: 267–76.

Sibley, D. (1995) *Geographies of Exclusion*. London: Routledge.

Sidaway, J.D. (1992) 'In other worlds: on the politics of research by "First World" geographers in the "Third World"', *Area,* 24 (4): 403.

Simonsen, K. (2007) 'On being "in-between": social and cultural geography in Denmark', in R. Kitchin (ed.), *Mapping Worlds: International Perspectives on Social and Cultural Geographies.* Abingdon: Routledge. pp. 7–20.

Slater, D. (2002) 'Capturing markets from the economists', in P. Du Gay and M. Pryke (eds), *Cultural Economy*. London: Sage. pp. 59–77.

Smith, D. (1973) *The Geography of Social Well-Being in the United States: An Introduction to Territorial Social Indicators*. New York: McGraw-Hill.

Smith, D. (1977) *Human Geography: A Welfare Approach*. London: Edward Arnold.

Smith, D. (1998) 'How far should we care? On the spatial scope of beneficence', *Progress in Human Geography*, 22: 15–38.

Smith, D. (2000) *Moral Geographies: Ethics in a World of Difference*. Edinburgh: Edinburgh University Press.

Smith, N. (1984) *Uneven Development: Nature, Capital and the Production of Space*. Oxford: Blackwell.

Smith, S.J. (1984) 'Practising humanistic geography, *Annals of the Association of American Geographers,* 74: 353–74.

Smith, S.J. (1986) *Crime, Space and Society*. Cambridge: Cambridge University Press.

Smith, S.J. (1989) *The Politics of 'Race' and Residence*. Cambridge: Polity Press.

Smith S.J. (1993) 'Social landscapes: continuity and change', in R. Johnston (ed), *A Changing World: A Changing Discipline?* Oxford: Blackwell.

Smith, S.J. (1994) 'Soundscape', *Area*, 26: 232–40.

Smith, S.J. (1999, revised 2005) 'Society-space', in P. Cloke, P. Crang and M. Goodwin (eds), *Introducing Human Geographies* (1st and 2nd editions). London: Edward Arnold.

Smith, S.J. (2001) 'Doing qualitative research: from interpretation to action', in M. Limb and C. Dwyer (eds), *Qualitative Methodologies for Geographers*. London: Edward Arnold.

Smith, S.J. (2005) 'States, markets and an ethic of care', *Political Geography,* 24: 1–20.

Smith, S.J. (2008) 'Owner occupation living with a hybrid of money and materials', *Environment and Planning A*, 40: 520–35.

Smith, S.J. and Easterlow, D. (2004) 'The problem with welfare' in D. Smith and R. Lee (eds), *Geographies and Moralities*. Oxford: Blackwell.

Smith, S.H. (2009) 'The domestication of geopolitics: Buddhist-Muslim conflict and the politics of marriage and the body in Ladakh, India', *Geopolitics*, 14 (2):1–22.

Smith, S. J. and Searle, B. A. (eds) (in press) *The Blackwell Companion to the Economics of Housing. The Housing Wealth of Nations*. Wiley-Blackwell.

Soja, E. (1980) 'The socio-spatial dialectic', *Annals of the Association of American Geographers*, 70 (2): 207–25.

Sonneneld, J. (1981) 'Review of Tuan's landscapes of fear', *Annals of the Association of American Geographers*, 71 (4): 594–6.

Stark, D. (2000) *For a Sociology of Worth*. Working Paper Series, Center on Organizational Innovations, Columbia University. Available online at www.col.columbia.edu/pdf/stark_fsw.pdf

Thien, D. (2005) 'After or beyond feeling? A consideration of affect and emotion in geography', *Area*, 37 (4): 450–56.

Thomas, W.M. (ed.) (1956) *Man's Role in Changing the Face of the Earth*. Chicago: University of Chicago Press.

Thrift, N. (1997) 'The still point: resistance, expressive embodiment and dance', in S. Pile and M. Keith (eds), *Geographies of Resistance*. London: Routledge.

Thrift, N. (2002) 'The future of geography', *Geoforum*, 33: 291–8.

Thrift, N. (2004) 'Intensities of feeling: towards a spatial politics of affect', *Geografiska Annaler, Series B: Human Geography*, 86 (1): 57–78.

Tickamyer, A. (2000) 'Space matters! Spatial inequality in future sociology', *Contemporary Sociology*, 29: 805–13.

Timár, J. (2007) 'The transformation of social and cultural geography during the transition period (1989 to present time) in Hungary', in R. Kitchin (ed), *Mapping Worlds: International Perspectives on Social and Cultural Geographies*. Abingdon: Routledge. pp. 305–24.

Tolia-Kelly, D.P. (2006) 'Affect – an ethnocentric encounter? Exploring the "universalist" imperative of emotional/affective geographies', *Area*, 38 (2): 213–17.

Trewartha, G. (1953) 'A case for population geography', *Annals of the Association of American Geographers*, 43 (2): 71–97.

Tuan, Y.F. (1976) 'Humanistic geography', *Annals of the Association of American Geographers*, 66 (2): 266–76.

Tuan, Y.F. (1979) *Landscapes of Fear*. New York: Pantheon.

Turner, B.L. II (2002) 'Contested identities: human-environment geography and disciplinary implications in a restructuring academy', *Annals of the Association of American Geographers*, 92 (1): 52–74.

Valentine, G. (1989) 'The geography of women's fear', *Area*, 21 (4): 385–90.

Valentine, G. (1992) 'Images of danger: women's sources of information about the spatial distribution of male violence', *Area*, 24 (1): 22–9.

Valentine, G. (2001) *Social Geographies: Space and Society*. London: Prentice Hall.,

Van Wezemael, J.E. (2005) 'Contributions to economical geography-making', *Social Geography: Discussions*, 1: 1–23.

Vidal de la Blache, P. (1899) 'Leçon d'ouverture du cours de géographie', *Annales de Géographie*, 8: 97–109.

Vidal de la Blache, P. (1911) 'Les genres de vie dans la géographie humaine', *Annales de Géographie*, 20 (111,112): 193–212, 289–304.

Whatmore, S. (2002) *Hybrid Geographies: Natures, Cultures, Spaces*. London: Sage.

White, G.F. (1972) 'Geography and public policy', *The Professional Geographer*, 24 (2): 101–4.

Willems-Braun, B. (1997) 'Buried epistemologies: the politics of nature in (post)colonial British Columbia', *Annals of the Association of American Geographers*, 87 (3): 3–31.

Women and Geography Study Group (1997) *Feminist Geographies: Explorations in Diversity and Difference*. Harlow: Addison Wesley Longman.

Wright, S. (2008) 'Practising hope: learning from social movement strategies in the Philippines', in R. Pain and S.J. Smith (eds), *Fear: Critical Geopolitics and Everyday Life*. Aldershot: Ashgate.

SECTION 1

Difference and Diversity

Edited by
John Paul Jones III

Introduction: Social Geographies of Difference

John Paul Jones III

This section of the Handbook assembles seven chapters that chart the distinctiveness of social geography's commitment to difference and diversity. They cover an array of axes of difference, including gender, race, sexuality, disability, nation, age and indigeneity. The authors examine these positionalities in terms of intersectionality, commonality and socio-spatial conflict. Though generally sympathetic to constructivist accounts of the subject, all in one way or another engage the materiality of identity, in some instances doing so by calling upon the more-than-representational and the post-human. Before I summarize the central arguments of the papers with an eye to their theoretical contributions, I first offer a few words of context regarding social geography's take on difference.

UNSETTLING IDENTITY

A central problem in social geography is how to sort out the relations between identity, on the one hand, and space, on the other, particularly in terms of how their interplay affects the well-being of people and the prospects of the places they inhabit and move through. In an old but still valuable formulation, we might encapsulate the central moments of this problem by asking with David Smith (1974) the question of 'who gets what, where?' Geographers have worked on the empirical specificities of his question for decades, but at the same time social and spatial theory has reworked how we understand both identity and space (the 'who' and the 'where'). The so-called 'spatial turn' is well covered elsewhere (Soja, 1996; Smith et al., this volume); here I say a few words about the unsettling of identity, which is the hallmark of social science's attention to difference and diversity.

Although attention to difference has a long history in social theory, it was the theoretical upheavals of the 1970s that truly destabilized Identity – that turned our lenses away from older notions of naturalized or 'essentialized' diversity around timeless and spaceless innate characteristics, to socially constructed differences that were malleable across context, tenuously stitched together from the raw materials of discourse and practice (Dixon and Jones, 2006). This shift in thinking is more than high theory; it has also underwritten a remarkable methodological upheaval. For when identities are conceived in terms of 'essences', then difference can be said to follow straightforwardly from long-held social categories and the means to measure them (e.g., the census). Not getting difference 'right' in this instance usually requires only some fine tuning of the categorical distinctions (e.g., black, homosexual, male), but the underlying centrality of centers is maintained. In contrast, anti-essentialist approaches require interpretative, qualitative study of the fluidities of difference and ethnographic attention to the context of their fluctuations. This is one reason for the sea-change in methods in geography over the past thirty years.

While the shift from essentialism to anti-essentialism has roots in political theory and philosophy, as well as in literary theory and cultural studies, most important have been the cross-cutting contributions of feminist theorists. Early moves to theorize difference were made by socialist/Marxist and radical feminists of the 1970s, whose theories of patriarchy complicated traditional class analysis and led to debates on the intersectionality of class and gender that would dominate discussions of social ontology for years (see Walby, 1990). In geography, these issues came to a head in a widely read debate between radical and socialist feminists in the pages of *Antipode* (see Foord and Gregson, 1986; Gregson and Foord, 1987; Knopp and Lauria, 1987; McDowell, 1986).

What these theorists and their successors – the 'dual-systems' theorists – shared was a strongly materialist perspective on social relations; what they had not grappled with was the emergence of the poststructuralist subject, a category first popularized in political theory through the discursive analytic of Ernesto Laclau and Chantal Mouffe (1985). Their book, *Hegemony and Socialist Strategy*, drew attention to the construction of categories of difference out of pure alterity: temporary stabilizations (or 'nodal points') of identification are produced in a process of exclusion that is central to category-making. As a result, no identity can ever claim the mantle of a positive center:

> The constitutive outside is a relational process by which the outside – or 'Other' – of any category is actively at work on both sides of the constructed boundary, and is thus always leaving its trace within the category. Thus, what may appear to be a self-enclosed category maintained by boundaries is found in fact to unavoidably contain the marks of inscription left by the outside from which it seemingly has been separated. As Derrida has shown through the work of deconstruction ... the outside of any category is already found to be resident within, permeating the category from the *inside* through its traceable presence-in-absence within the category (Natter and Jones, 1997: 146; emphasis in original).

Roughly coinciding with Laclau's and Mouffe's destabilization of the subject was the invention of the 'feminist standpoint' (Harding, 1986; Hartsock, 1985) – a rejoinder of sorts that acknowledges the epistemological dimensions of identity (e.g., Haraway's 'situated knowledges', 1991) but retains a strong political-economic analysis. The key to the standpoint is the Marxist recognition that social positionality is not given but is produced through the material practices of human labor; and, while we may not be able to reconcile different world views, surely it is those whose experiences include oppression and exploitation who will be able to produce the clearest insights into the actual functioning of the world.

This argument was both specified and seized upon by feminists of color (Anzaldúa, 1987; Collins, 1990; hooks, 1984, 1989, 1991; Moraga and Anzaldúa, 1983), and indeed interest in standpoint theory coincided with the proliferation of difference *within* feminism – offering a much needed correction to its mainstream 'white liberal' bias. At the same time, increasing fragmentation of the gendered subject prompted some to question whether there was any experience broad enough to secure a common political position (Butler and Scott, 1992; also see Spivak, 1988, on 'strategic essentialism' and

Harvey, 1996, on 'militant particularism'). Increasingly from the mid-1980s onward, theorists of many persuasions clashed over how best to theorize and mobilize difference, in part through their sometimes uneasy engagements at the intersection of feminism and postmodernism (Hennessy, 1993; Nicholson, 1990), and in part through more sympathetic writings that deconstructed difference (often through the 'constitutive outside') from Global South, transnational, post-colonial and queer perspectives (e.g., Bhabha, 1994; Gilroy, 1993; Grewal and Kaplan, 1994; Morrison, 1992; Sedgwick, 1990). A key intervention in these debates was Butler's (1990, 1993) theory of performativity. Like Laclau and Mouffe, she drew on a discursive analysis (aided also by psychoanalysis) to claim that identities do not come to us as given but are produced through interpretive grids maintained by iteration and citation, out of which subjects produce and subvert meaning. Though accused by some of idealism, for Butler the materiality of the body is not outside performativity; quite the contrary, it is central to it.

Finally, for the unconvinced – for those who continue to point to the primacy of experience in asserting identity – historian Joan Scott issued this caution:

> When experience is taken as the origin of knowledge, the vision of the individual subject (the person who had the experience or the [social scientist] who recounts it) becomes the bedrock of evidence on which explanation is built. Questions about the constructed nature of experience, about how subjects are constituted as different in the first place, about how one's vision is structured – about language (or discourse) and history – are left aside. The evidence of experience then becomes evidence for the fact of difference, rather than a way of exploring how difference is established, how it operates, how and in what ways it constitutes subjects who see and act in the world (Scott, 1991: 777; brackets added).

Having offered an abbreviated cut through essentialist and anti-essentialist takes on identity and difference, I now want to make a few observations about this conceptual map in regard to social geography.

First, I think it is fair to say that while most geographers would seem to accept the anti-essentialist thesis, there have been some tensions. Harvey's famous foray (1989) into the matter led to reactions (Deutsche, 1991; Massey, 1991; also Harvey, 1996) that mirror to some extent the debate around postmodernism's 'death of the subject' and the felt imperative to ground political mobilization (as mentioned above). Looking back, these tensions in geography appear to have two tributaries: (a) the differences between class and gender analyses found in Marxist and feminist geography; and (b) the clash over discourse and materiality in geography, at least some of which is responsible for the cleavages between social and cultural geography. A lot of the unease seems to be waning now (see Smith et al.'s introduction to this volume), but geographers' use of anti-essentialism can still be a bit clunky. In particular, there is a tendency for us to grant nodding assent to constructivism while at the same deploying social categories as if they in themselves accounted for the phenomena being studied. When we do this, we fail to heed the lessons of the anti-essentialist critique. Put slightly differently, Joan Scott was right: we need to make difference the explandum, the dependent variable rather than the 'evidence on which explanation is built'.

Second, it should not surprise us to know that, with a few exceptions (Friedman, 1998; Kirby, 1996), most 'deconstructions' of identity undertaken outside the discipline of geography have failed to build a compelling account for space in the construction of subjectivity. Fortunately, geographers can point to a number of efforts to produce spatial 'correctives' to a-spatial difference theories. I am thinking here of Clive Barnett (2005) and Jeffrey Popke (2003) on ethics, subjectivity and hospitality; Michael Brown (2000) on Sedgwick's epistemology of the closet; Nicki Gregson and Gillian Rose (2000) on Butler's performativity; Peter Jackson and Jan Penrose (1995) on the geographies of 'race' and nation; Natter and Jones (1997) on Derrida's constitutive outside; Anna Secor (2004) on theories of citizenship; David Sibley (1995) on object relations theory; Ed Soja (1996) on Bhabha's hybridity; and Gill Valentine (2007) on intersectionality; among others. Yet, in spite of these contributions, some of our work continues to deploy a simplistic geography that is almost stage-like in its relation to identity: 'here you are in this place; there you are, a bit different, in that other place'. Geography, however, has a lot more to offer to identity theory than the idea that spatial contexts affect how we perform or even 'experience' our identities. Subjectivity is much more spatial than that: it inhales and exhales space. It has a spatial ontology *and* a spatial epistemology (Dwyer and Jones, 2000). And it never rests; subjectivity is:

> constantly circulating in sites, extending itself, offering itself up as explanation or cause for any number of different relations, recommending the way forward, canvassing for converts and new members. Subjectivity is the solipsistic cartographer, the drunken salesman, the restless busybody that must resolve every relation within its purview to its own context or else declare it null and void (Woodward, et al., 2008: 16).

Finally, I think it is important that social geographers embrace and help configure new theoretical developments that, at first glance, might appear to lie outside the traditional purview of identity, space and well-being. In particular, those three moments – which I used to open this chapter – are just as relevant to affect and non-representational theory (Woodward and Lea, this volume) and to the post-human (Robbins and Marks, this volume) as they are to the distinctions between essentialist and anti-essentialist accounts of the subject. In fact, I see both as a further extension of the second point above: non-representational theory and post-human geographies are part of the larger spatio-material register for producing identity; paying attention to them can extend our analyses in ways that we overlooked when writing in the 1990s. The former points us to domains beyond or before the representational, where, it can be argued, a great deal of identity-making takes place (Thrift, 2008). The second populates the social with nature, both deconstructing the human and offering insights into how we maintain its boundaries (Anderson, 2006; Whatmore, 2002). A good example of both can be found in Paul Robbins's book, *Lawn People* (2007), which provides a reading of the masculine, self-disciplining middle-class subject who is caught between the soft gaze of the neighbors and the seasonal productivity of turfgrass. He dutifully applies the chemicals, waters the ground, and mows the result, all repeated in a cycle that solidifies his positionality as a master of nature, when if anything he is a slave to it. Robbins's work suggests that the 'trace of the Other' that buttresses the identification of the Midwestern home owner is not simply the uncooperative neighbor who lets his grass go to seed, but the very stuff of the grass itself.

CHAPTER SUMMARIES

Linda Peake's examination of gender, 'race' and sexuality kicks off this section. It is fitting that we begin with her paper, for these three axes of identity have been the most important ones in defining the theoretical approaches to difference within social geography. They have also been the ones in which – next to class relations in both social and economic geography – we find the greatest contributions to our understanding of the 'difference that space makes' in the sphere of the social. And, not least, these are three large areas of analysis with a significant empirical record.

In her strongly geographic accounting of these relations, Peake considers how each moved from static, empirical, and biologically grounded conceptions of difference to ones that are dynamic, discursive, and constructed. She begins with gender, and in her account of that evolution she addresses not only the transition from biology to constructivism but also the more subtle distinctions within constructivist accounts that variously engage embodiment. She then details the development of space and sexuality, paying close attention to the rise of queer studies in geography and its relationship with feminist geography.

Race too is shown to have essentialist origins that are overturned through poststructuralist critiques, and these are followed by studies that chart the material and epistemological coordinates of whiteness.

Peake then goes on to consider more explicitly the intersection of gender, sexuality and race. For her, intersectionality is more than simple social simultaneity or connection: it refers to intersections that are 'bound up in spatialities … [for] social differences, however tightly or loosely bound together, always come into being through interactions in specific places'. The geographies of intersectionality include being in or out of place depending on the intersection of specific social axes; the differentials of travel through public and private space; and the space-power that not only excludes but also creates the settings for resistance. She exemplifies this discussion of different spatial effects with an adapted excerpt from her work with Alissa Trotz on Afro-Guyanese men and women; it shows how masculinity/femininity, 'race', and sexuality intersect in the spaces of the community and home.

Finally, Peake examines the ontological status of 'the social' in response to critiques by critical social and cultural geographers whose work has taken a post-human turn in the wake of the deconstruction of the nature–society and human–animal binaries (see Smith et al.'s introduction, this volume; also Robbins and Marks, this volume). She notes that 'humans are no longer being regarded as separate from and having control over nature and machines. … their interfaces are coming under scrutiny as different and new assemblages of people, things and matter come into being, calling into question how we can "unlearn" this construct of the "human" (as always-already human) and how non-human entities also come to be'. Peake extends this argument by developing the point that gender, race, and sexuality are – of all the social categories – probably the ones best suited to complicate nature, that is, to provide deeper insights into the post-human turn in social geography. And from this vantage point she concludes by asking us to direct our social geographies of difference to 'other' ways of knowing, forms of knowledge production informed by non-Western ontologies and epistemologies.

In the next entry, Rachel Pain and Peter Hopkins take up the relationality of age in a chapter that offers an analysis of the literature on aging and a plan for moving forward. They begin on a theme they will return to throughout: the importance of looking beyond either children or the aged in a more comprehensive approach to the relationally constructed lifecourse. As they put it:

> Our argument is that – paradoxically, when the very study of children and younger people is one demarcated by age – this attention does not always encompass issues *of age*. … despite the dominant social constructivist perspective of such work, it quite rarely rejects the category it works within. Further, although there is much work about children, and a little less about younger people, geographies of people in other age groups are scarce. Studies of old age in social geography are present, but nowhere near as fashionable as work on childhood, and have a tendency to be conceptually and methodologically mundane, preoccupied with old age as a social problem rather than a problematised identity.

Interestingly, this fashionable endpoint view that favors children and the aged has parallels in other areas of social geography where the emphasis has traditionally been on the non-hegemonic 'other': women over men (and masculinity); 'raced' peoples over European whites, homosexuals over heterosexuals, and so on. In response, Pain and Hopkins develop a holistic and relational view of the geographies of age.

They first review four approaches to the geography of age: 'accepting age as a biological or chronological given; forwarding age as socially constructed; retheorising the body, and interrogating being/becoming'. Their review shows how each approach has further destabilized age as a social category: how socio-cultural differences in aging have provided evidence against the biological model; how some scholars augment discursive analyses with those centered on the physical body; and how concepts of agency and resistance have come to be associated with different age groups.

Pain and Hopkins then offer three concepts of value to producing a relational perspective on aging: intergenerationality, intersectionality and the lifecourse. The first draws attention to the relations among individuals and groups across generations, in family situations and elsewhere, thereby adding new contextual layers to otherwise static categories such as childhood and old age. The second draws attention to how age intersects with other axes of identity, connections that, as with Peake, are not the same across different spaces or sets of experience. Finally, their lifecourse approach implies a connection across the aging process, based on the 'recognition that, rather than following fixed and predictable life stages, we live in dynamic and varied lifecourses which have, themselves, differently situated meanings'. Lifecourse analysis is about transitions, including the different identities that are taken on over time and across distinct spaces of social experience. These open up the category of age in ways consistent with other deconstructive approaches to identity in the wake of the anti-essentialist turn; Pain and Hopkins note that multiple, fracturing, and dissident age identities can be found in a diverse array of examples, including the infantilized adult, the youthful retiree, and the child sex worker. Each suggests lines of research focusing on identities that transgress traditional expectations.

Michael Dorn and Carla Keirns begin their chapter with a cautionary note about lingering residues of essentialism in disability studies: 'Definitions of disability are the product of bio-political efforts to render a legible social order. ... Social geographers, while expressing their intentions to critically examine the power-laden constructions that produce such designations – usually in search of new social imaginaries – nevertheless too often adopt as given the analytic distinctions of medical, social and political authorities'. In the face of this contradiction, the authors offer an analysis of the history of disability, disability studies, and disability activism, showing their interconnected if not parallel unfolding with the histories of both health science and modern citizenship.

Their focus is the 54 million disabled-designated population in the US, but the analyses are applicable anywhere and are suggestive of the need for comparative work. Dorn and Keirns first raise the issue of citizenship and disability, a theme they will return to at various points in the narrative. Though often overlooked as an intersecting process, both citizenship and disability are formed through exclusionary processes, and in the case of immigration policy they work hand in hand.

Dorn and Keirns trace a long arc through the literatures on the social geographies of disability, mental illness, and deinstitutionalization, and while they do not question the political motives of the authors under review, they note tendencies toward objectification and victimization consistent with dependency formulations: 'As disability rights activists remind us, they would not need "accommodations" if planning for workplaces, housing, health care, schools, and other public and private spaces followed the principles of universal design, imagining a range of human variation in sight, mobility, and sensation ...'. In subsequent sections, Dorn and Keirns examine: the distinctions between disability designations driven by medical and social administrative agencies; the emergence, out of the medical geographies of the seventeenth, eighteenth, and nineteenth centuries, of disability as a distinct social category; and the rise of formal systems of disability care alongside the growth of modern industries, modern welfare states, and patriotic calls to care for infirm soldiers and their families.

Dorn and Keirns offer a particularly strong political message at the end of their chapter, relevant to both social geographers and activists. More so than most of the authors in this section, they are suspicious regarding the political implications of constructivist accounts:

> Contextual accounts of disability point to its 'social construction' and find parallels in the contemporary

study of other identity categories. For those who subscribe to the social model, disability may be considered yet another category of otherness, akin to race, class, gender, or nationality, posing intriguing possibilities for exploring their intersection in individual and group experiences. Yet disability remains as well – more than many of these other group markers – an acceptable tool in social discourse for discrediting marginalized groups more generally. And although discussions of 'intersectionality' have become popular in critical race theory, feminist studies, queer theory and disability studies, popular conceptions of, and academic theorizing on, disability is still largely divorced from rubrics that are given center stage.

They end by critiquing celebratory accounts of new technologies for and discourses of mobility that only serve to highlight the continued inaccessibility of huge areas of social life – from housing and education to leisure and transportation.

Audrey Kobayashi's and Sarah de Leeuw's chapter on the social geographies of racialization begins with the story of the Cherokee Nation, which in 2007 expelled the descendants of former African slaves in the US South from their list of qualifying members of the indigenous tribe. Following the end of the US Civil War, the Nation signed a treaty granting citizenship to their emancipated slaves; the move was an attempt to swell the numbers of Cherokee and to thereby increase land allocations from the US government. All members of slave descent, regardless of their lineage, were designated as Cherokee Freedmen. In a controversial referendum in 2007, the Nation's members voted to expel the Freedmen. As the authors summarize the issues, 'Cherokee leaders opposed to disenfranchisement argue that citizenship in the Cherokee Nation must never rest on blood quantum traits while those in favor of disenfranchising the Freedmen argue that indigenous governments, like other governments and nations, must have the right to decide who is and who is not granted citizenship'.

For Kobayashi and de Leeuw, this story highlights the complex nature of difference in the aftermath of colonialism. Illustrating a little studied aspect of the process of 'double colonialism', the fact that both indigenous and diasporic peoples are subjects of European people's racialization processes, it sets up contrasts between the indigenous peoples whose lands were taken – and who were themselves often displaced – and those who were moved, forcefully or not, as colonialism played out in slavery, indentured labor, and transnational 'voluntary' labor. In describing these colliding social geographies, they draw from various countries, including Canada, the US, Australia, Aotearoa/New Zealand, and Fiji. These and other cases have led to increased calls for justice from among the world's 370 million indigenous peoples. Their contemporary struggles are focused on halting land expropriation by white and diasporic settlers, securing access to historic resources, attaining full rights to both 'modern' and 'traditional' forms of citizenship and self-determination, and preserving language and culture in the face of a white-washed multiculturalism and an ever-expanding consumer capitalism.

And though some racialized diasporic and indigenous peoples have used global proclamations and new technologies to forge important transnational linkages, there remain significant tensions. As Kobayashi and de Leeuw point out, one's position as a raced Other in relation to a white center does not necessarily provide the basis for solidarity. Instead, 'It makes a difference whether Otherness occurs *at a distance* from the metropole within a colonial context, as shown in Said's original work; *in place* in colonial contexts, as has occurred in the subordination of most indigenous peoples; or through the creation of *diasporic* or transnational communities of difference, as represented by most of the large non-white migrant groups today'. In concluding, Kobayashi and de Leeuw dismiss citizenship claims based on abstract territorial formulations: e.g., 'Who was here first?'. Nor are they convinced that universalist accounts, such as those based on class or 'blackness', will produce solidarities across different groups. They believe, rather, that relational thinking about identity needs to be combined with analyses of the *actual spatial conditions* in which people live. In these real territorial engagements are the seeds for understanding conflicts and working collectively toward justice.

The section then turns to a chapter by Katie Willis on 'social collisions', a term that captures what can happen when individuals and groups come together to contest – or collide over – space. Importantly, she rejects the presumption that conflict is the only outcome to expect in the face of encounters in social 'contact zones': 'rather than being inherently destructive or conflictual, the coming together of diverse individuals can sometimes have productive outcomes. In addition, interactions may be for a short period of time, or they may be an on-going process'. Underlying these contingencies are the facts that identities are not predetermined in advance of their immersion in concrete spatial settings, and that while identities and spaces co-determine one another in mutual relation, they do so in open-ended, rather than fixed, ways. Within this context, one needs to consider 'the internal heterogeneity of groups, the time or placing of the encounter, the importance of … intersectionality, and how the encounters themselves provide opportunities for reflexivity that can result in a hardening of group boundaries, or a chance for greater engagement and understanding'.

Willis begins with a review of segregation studies in geography, which she qualifies politically, theoretically, and methodologically: such studies tended to unquestioningly project difference onto an assumed white center; they failed to recognize both internal differences and the socio-historical specificities attending immigration streams (e.g., Chicago in the 1920s); and they relied on macro-level variables, as if these could provide clues to causalities rooted at the level of experience. She then goes on to consider several key moments in the study of socio-spatial interactions under the rubric of anti-essentialist theories of identity, including efforts to pay greater attention to internal differences in groups, the fits and starts associated with the concepts of multiculturalism and cosmopolitanism, and the insights gained from contemporary work on transnationalism.

A section on the outcomes of collisions, progressive and otherwise, follows. Willis discusses both flashpoints of conflict, such as have occurred around 'race'/ethnicity and gay pride marches, and efforts to contest social discrimination through activism – usually the occupation of public spaces. She also notes how social change can emerge in particular contexts in which differences are negotiated or made the basis for collective action.

In the final sections of her paper, Willis discusses the embodied nature of social contact, including not only bodily co-presence in space but also how 'interactions are based on embodied sensual experiences', including smell and hearing. Efforts to understand this aspect of social interaction are part of a larger move to rematerialize social geography, and at the same time they point to efforts to better understand the role of mundane and everyday encounters among different groups of people. Willis concludes her essay with five suggestions for future work: greater attention to comparative analysis through multi-site ethnography; increased work on the *interactions* between less powerful groups (e.g., 'racial' minorities) and hegemonic ones (e.g., whites), rather than a narrow focus on one or the other; additional research on the role of emotions in social collisions; new efforts to place 'hospitality' within the theoretical frame of identity and space; and greater integration of local ethnographic studies with the geopolitical force fields that structure immigration policies and the relations between nations.

Keith Woodward and Jennifer Lea begin their chapter on affect with the film classic, *Modern Times* (1936), where a young Charlie Chaplin tries to keep up with the assembly line. With startling, arm-waving dramatic effects, the film's gears, clocks, and human labor depict an assemblage of affective relations. Drawing on Chaplin's recollection of the movie's inspiration, Woodward and Lea write: '… changing developments in capitalist production announce the birth of relations that initiate and synthesize new correspondences between bodily, psychic and social trauma. To signal the emergence of a new class of workers in this context is to announce the arrival of new kinds of bodies, the products of changing relations of exertion and stress relative to increasingly rationalized and intense production speeds'. Woodward and Lea go on to show how affective force relations add a new layer of analysis to existing political economies of capitalist production.

The chapter proceeds by providing a Spinozist account of affect, one with touchstones to a number of central concerns in social geography: '*Affect is the medium through which bodies sustain and transform each other*, and as such, *it is fundamentally social: a materialist account of bodily association*' (emphasis in original). From this, Woodward and Lea identify four domains of rethinking social geography: a shift, both theoretical and methodological, from epistemology to ontology; a de-privileging of the human 'as the reservoir of agency in the world'; attention to the complexity of social materiality; and a focus on doing and becoming rather than being.

The authors then illustrate the value of affect theory for extending social geographic studies of identity theory. They offer an immanent ethics of doing that contrasts with transcendental moralities of what should be done: 'a "body", as a conjunction of whatever bits of materiality (blocs of matter) have gathered into relations of moving, affecting, and being affected *together*, must discover what good(s) – if any – might be determined by virtue of its situation'. This active sense of ethics is the result of a moving and mutable social – what they call the 'bodymap' – which leads them to a theory of affective power. In it, power is immanent to affective relations among bodies, not through the fixities of identities or forms, but through the forces that emerge in the situation. This theory pivots on a number of body tendencies often overlooked in studies of identity: thoughts, recollections, emotions, and perceptions; habits, pre-cognitions, performances, and enactments; visceral reactions, sensorial pleasures and dissonance, pain and comfort.

Finally, Woodward and Lea come back to the workers in *Modern Times*. Joining together Marx and affect, they note that: 'The grotesque genius of capitalism lies in its appropriation of the most immediate of affective contexts, making our own capacities for initiating forceful relations – our ability to work – seem strange and unfamiliar. Channeling our affectivities into processes that contribute paradoxically to our own disempowerment, capitalism simultaneously reframes the resultant commodity as that which offers the gift of empowerment, here in the form of a supplement to practices of consumption'. This move shows that, far from being apolitical, affect theory has the potential to enhance political economic analysis, and with that, to contribute to the achievement of justice that lies at the heart of social geography.

In the concluding chapter, Paul Robbins and Brian Marks use the Deleuzean concept of assemblage to gather together lines of developing inquiry in the area of post-human geography. They begin their paper with a story about a 2000 vote over commercial hunting in the Rocky Mountain state of Montana. Part of the ballot result hinged on the state's elk population. The animal's disdain for confinement and its susceptibility to chronic wasting disease, a highly infectious product of neural proteins called prions, helped to change the social map of property relations in Montana, creating unheard-of alliances between working-class hunters and national environmental groups. The elk and its proteins are part of the social assemblage, a 'world constituted by more-than-human actors, joined in a cat's cradle of physically grasping relationships, threaded through a fun house of representations'.

Robbins and Marks survey the developments of the post-human turn in human geography, one that relies on an attentiveness to the participation, labor, productions, and constituting powers of objects of nature – from trees, gardens, and lawns to mosquitoes, bears, and dogs. They identify the potentials and the elisions in what has been identified as a 'rematerialization' of human geography following the constructivist and discursive turn associated with poststructuralist cultural geography. The lines of connection here involve renewed attention to built environments and bits of nature, and new attention to human/non-human bodies. Less an epochal 'post-ing' than the recovery of an always existing ontological condition, a world of interacting objects, bodies, and actors requires the relational and geographical perspective of social geography, but in the process both 'social' and 'natural' become 'unstable modifiers'. Attuned to differences in how this area of research has developed, Robbins and Marks use the umbrella of 'assemblage geographies' to provide some direction to what has yet to fully jell in terms of theoretical coherence, methodological specificity, and narrative strategy.

Robbins and Marks go on to produce a table of assemblage theories, organized by key thinkers and their conceptual–analytic strategies: Bruno Latour's symmetrical form, focused on quasi-objects; Donna Haraway's intimate form, focused on companion species; Karl Marx's metabolic form, focused on circulation and metabolism; and Timothy Mitchell's genealogical form, focused on epistemic things. Each approach is found to have distinct explanatory principles and favored styles of narrative (paradoxical vs. reflexive vs. tragic vs. ironic). The authors draw from case studies in the current post-human literature – covering sewer lines, gardens, elm trees, and 'mad cow' disease – to illustrate emblematic features of each approach and to suggest questions they tend to leave unanswered. In combination, each approach shows how, in the authors' terms, the 'field of causality' in social geography is populated 'with new and troubling actors', as well as how 'social relations are more-than-social and more than extensions of the social into other locations'. They caution us, finally, to not accept these complications as an excuse for sloppiness in our examinations of a post-human, post-social world. More than ever, the new ontological combinations and epistemological ruptures of the post-human require us to adopt a methodology sensitive to the complexity of causality and a narrative style that clarifies rather than obfuscates those findings.

REFERENCES

Anderson, K. (2006) *Race and the Crisis of Humanism*. London: Routledge.

Anzaldúa, G. (1987) *Boderlands/La Frontera: The New Mestiza*. San Francisco: Aunt Lute Books.

Barnett, C. (2005) 'Ways of relating: hospitality and the acknowledgement of otherness', *Progress in Human Geography,* 29: 5–21.

Bhabha, H. (1994) *The Location of Culture*. London: Routledge.

Brown, M. (2000) *Closet Space: Geographies of Metaphor from the Body to the Globe*. London: Routledge.

Butler, J. (1990) *Gender Trouble: Feminism and the Subversion of Identity*. London: Routledge.

Butler, J. (1993) *Bodies that Matter: On the Discursive Limits of Sex*. London: Routledge.

Butler, J. and Scott, J.W. (eds) (1992) *Feminists Theorize the Political*. London: Routledge.

Collins, P.H. (1990) *Black Feminist Thought*. London: Routledge.

Deutsche, R. (1991) 'Boys town', *Environment and Planning D: Society and Space*, 9: 5–30.

Dixon, D.P. and Jones III, J.P. (2006) 'Feminist geographies of difference, relation, and construction', in G. Valentine and S. Aitken (eds), *Philosophies, People, Places and Practices: An Introduction to Approaches in Human Geography*. Thousand Oaks: Sage. pp. 42–56.

Dwyer, O. and Jones III, J.P. (2000) 'White socio-spatial epistemologies', *Social and Cultural Geography*, 1: 209–22.

Foord, J. and Gregson, N. (1986) 'Patriarchy: towards a reconceptualization', *Antipode,* 18: 186–211.

Friedman, S.S. (1998) *Mappings: Feminism and the Cultural Geographies of Encounter*. Princeton: Princeton University Press.

Gilroy, P. (1993) *The Black Atlantic: Modernity and Double-Consciousness*. Cambridge, MA: Harvard University Press.

Gregson, N. and Foord, J. (1987) 'Patriarchy: comments on critics', *Antipode*, 19: 371–5.

Gregson, N. and Rose, G. (2000) 'Taking Butler elsewhere: performativities, spatialities and subjectivities', *Environment and Planning D: Society and Space*, 18: 433–52.

Grewal, I. and Kaplan, C. (eds) (1994) *Scattered Hegemonies: Postmodernity and Transnational*

Feminist Practices. Minneapolis: University of Minnesota Press.
Haraway, D. (1991) *Simians, Cyborgs, and Women*. London: Routledge.
Harding, S. (1986) *The Science Question in Feminism*. Ithaca: Cornell University Press.
Hartsock, N. (1985) *Money, Sex and Power*. Evanston: Northwestern University Press.
Harvey, D. (1989) *The Condition of Postmodernity: An Enquiry into the Origins of Cultural Change*. Oxford: Blackwell.
Harvey, D. (1996) *Justice, Nature and the Geography of Difference*. Oxford: Blackwell.
Hennessy, R. (1993) *Materialist Feminism and the Politics of Discourse*. London: Routledge.
hooks, b. (1984) *Feminist Theory: From Margin to Center*. Boston: South End Press.
hooks, b. (1989) *Talking Back: Thinking Feminist, Thinking Black*. Boston: South End Press.
hooks, b. (1991) *Yearning: Race, Gender and Cultural Politics*. Boston: South End Press.
Jackson, P. and Penrose, J. (1995) 'Introduction: placing "race" and "nation"', in P. Jackson and J. Penrose (eds), *Constructions of Race, Place and Nation*. Minneapolis: University of Minnesota Press. pp. 1–23.
Kirby, K. (1996) *Indifferent Boundaries: Spatial Concepts of Subjectivity*. New York: Guilford.
Knopp, L. and Lauria, M. (1987) 'Gender relations and social relations', *Antipode*, 19: 48–53.
Laclau, E. and Mouffe, C. (1985) *Hegemony and Socialist Strategy*. London: Verso.
McDowell, L. (1986) 'Beyond patriarchy: a class-based explanation of women's subordination', *Antipode*, 18: 311–21.
Massey, D. (1991) 'Flexible sexism', *Environment and Planning D: Society and Space*, 9: 31–57.
Moraga, C. and Anzaldúa, G. (eds) (1983) *This Bridge Called my Back: Writings by Radical Women of Color*. New York: Kitchen Table Press.
Morrison, T. (1992) *Playing in the Dark: Whiteness and the Literary Imagination*. Cambridge, MA: Harvard University Press.
Natter, W. and Jones III, J.P. (1997) 'Identity, space, and other uncertainties', in G. Benko and U. Strohmayer (eds), *Space and Social Theory: Geographical Interpretations of Postmodernity*. Oxford: Blackwell. pp. 141–61.
Nicholson, L.J. (ed.) (1990) *Feminism/Postmodernism*. London: Routledge.
Popke, E.J. (2003) 'Poststructuralist ethics: subjectivity, responsibility, and the space of community', *Progress in Human Geography*, 27: 298–316.
Robbins, P. (2007) *Lawn People: How Grasses, Weeds and Chemicals Make Us Who We Are*. Philadelphia: Temple University Press.
Scott, J. (1991) 'The evidence of experience', *Critical Inquiry*, 17: 773–97.
Secor, A. (2004) '"There is an Istanbul that belongs to me": citizenship, space and identity in the city', *Annals of the Association of American Geographers*, 94: 352–68.
Sedgwick, E. (1990) *The Epistemology of the Closet*. Berkeley: University of California Press.
Sibley, D. (1995) *Geographies of Exclusion*. London: Routledge.
Smith, D.M. (1974) 'Who gets what, where, and how: a welfare focus for human geography', *Geography*, 4: 289–97.
Soja, E. (1996) *Thirdspace: Journeys to Los Angeles and Other Real-and-Imagined Places*. Oxford: Blackwell.
Spivak, G.C. (1988) *In Other Worlds: Essays in Cultural Politics*. New York: Routledge.
Thrift, N. (2008) *Non-Representational Theory: Space/Politics/Affect*. London: Routledge.
Valentine, G. (2007) 'Theorizing and researching intersectionality: a challenge for feminist geography', *The Professional Geographer*, 59: 10–21.
Walby, S. (1990) *Theorizing Patriarchy*. Oxford: Basil Blackwell.
Whatmore, S. (2002) *Hybrid Geographies: Natures, Cultures, Spaces*. London: Sage.
Woodward, K., Marston, S. and Jones III, J.P. (2008) 'On autonomous spaces', paper presented at the conference *Spaces of Democracy*, California State University, Long Beach, August 5, 2008.

1

Gender, Race, Sexuality

Linda Peake

INTRODUCTION

Gender, race and sexuality are pervasive constructions – all three are discursive and material forces, globally recognized public markers of social difference – but they are also elusive, fictional regulations that are constituted relationally through (mostly) routine embodied encounters in specific times and places.[1] They are terms we feel we can easily understand, because they are often so closely linked with personal identity and embodiment. But they are also mercurial terms; just when we think we have a grasp of them, they shift shape and their apparent solidity and stability dissipate, leaving seemingly new traces with each new context and encounter. And just as one analytical framing of gender, race or sexuality becomes established, critique of the assumptions associated with particular ways of knowing, of representing and of naming begins, revealing our understanding(s) to be partial, unpersuasive even. This is to say that our understanding of gender, race and sexuality, and of the ways in which they are socially produced, is laden with knowledges and politics that are particular to time and location. Currently, there appears to be a desire among social geographers to bring both the local and global, the material and discursive, to their analyses, in order to attach geographic and historical specificity to these contested categories of difference. It is this insistence on thinking spatially and contextually about these analytical abstractions that has marked out the approach of social geographers to studies of gender, race and sexuality, albeit through differing stylizations of the social and the spatial.

Arguably, thinking about space has been more explicit and flexible than thinking around the social. In the late twentieth century the search for rational and knowable socio-spatial patterns was abandoned as critiques grew of the dominant modernist Cartesian conceptualization of space as a container or static backdrop, and everyday life, or as Thrift (2003: 103) would style it 'rhythms of being', came to be conceived as co-constitutively occurring in a variety of spaces – physical, material, symbolic, visual, technological – in a dialectic of flows and permanences. Amongst social geographers, whether space is understood, or not, in terms of scalar constructions (Smith, 2000a; Marston, 2000; Marston et al., 2005), rhizomatic spaces of inbetweeness (Deleuze and Guattari, 1988; Flusty, 2004), submarine geographies (Glissant, 1992; McKittrick and Woods, 2007), networks (Thrift 1996; Whatmore, 2002), or 'more-fluid-constructions-that-as-yet-have-no-name' (Rose, 1996), there is still general agreement that space is relational and constitutive, that there are no innocent views of stasis or movement, stickiness or fluidity, and that to imagine space is to think about power.

There is less agreement, though, about what is called upon when geographers speak of the 'social'.[2] Indeed, until recently, there has been surprisingly little discussion of the ontological constitution of the social. Most commonly there has been an almost implicit understanding that the social is defined by lack; it is the soft underbelly left over when the state, the economic and the political, and increasingly the cultural, have been claimed and correspondingly carved off for specialist sub-disciplinary study. More recently, ascertaining what constitutes the social has been couched in terms dominated by radical and Marxist Anglo-American geographers about the nature of the relationship between social and cultural geography (Smith, 2000b; Gregson, 2003). Neil Smith (2000b), among others, is wary of the rising star of cultural geography; it has resulted in the fickle fans of social geography being seduced by sexy discursive constructions of difference and identities and abandoning the stodgy terrains of subjugation, deprivation, oppression and dispossession, causing social geography to wane in the wings.[3] According to Nicky Gregson (2003), this scenario regarding the demise of social geography is too simplistic to take seriously. Far from being abandoned, social geography, she maintains, has been reconfigured, specifically in the following ways: a concern with individuals at the expense of collectivities; increasing attention being paid to the bodily and, in particular, to individual bodies; a focus on the social that appears to refer to little more than inclusion/ exclusion and marginalization; and a paucity of efforts to locate the social within the economic.

I find the narrowly framed nature of this discussion – of viewing the social solely through the lens of the cultural – difficult to defend. Notwithstanding that it concerns itself only with the state of affairs in Anglo-American geography, it also has implications for what we think the social is and how we know it. Gender, sexuality and race traditionally have been coded in binary yet simultaneously hierarchical ways: public/culture/mind/reason/active/global versus private/nature/body/emotion/passive/local. But since the early 1990s there has been an increasing emphasis on seeing the social in more complex relational terms of intricate interdependencies. Concepts of assemblages, imbroglios, circulations, networks and metabolisms are increasingly coming to replace binary tropes (Shillington, 2007; Robbins and Marks, this volume). Many social geographers are now calling for a wider frame of reference, one that conceptualizes the social less in structural terms and recognizes it in terms of fluidity, of mobility and of inter-connections, and specifically one that can incorporate the so-called natural world. So Pred (1998), among others, argues that instead of social relations we should think of natural-social-cultural relations (see also Robbins and Marks, this volume). And while ontological understandings of what constitutes the boundaries of the social, of what is inside and outside it, are being challenged, so are the epistemologies through which we come to know the social relations and identities that comprise the social. Of particular concern to many social geographers is that sexuality, race and gender are still primarily being viewed through white and Anglo-American eyes. Thus, how social geographers understand the concepts of race, sexuality and gender is not only a question of differing theoretical positions but also one of where we (literally and figuratively) see social geography from (Harvey, 2000).

While constructions of gender, race and sexuality, given their mercurial natures and 'always-in-a-state-of-becomingness', cannot be separated out from each other, in this chapter I attempt to trace the ways social geographers have analyzed each of these concepts and some of the current ways they are being mobilized, before turning to the ways in which social geographers have addressed the intersectionality of these constructions. The remainder of the chapter examines the implications of both the increasing interest in the relations between the social and the natural and the need to broaden our epistemological horizons with regard to the ways in which social geographers study gender, race and sexuality. The first decade of the 21st century is indeed a disconcerting, anxiety-provoking and yet potentially exciting time to be writing about gender, race and sexuality. While many 'certainties' and established differences, such as sexualized divides, are being challenged, new distinctions, such as human/animal/machine interfaces, are emerging. New issues have also arisen – global environmental change, Islamaphobia, geographies of emotions and affect – while many established ones – social divisions of labour, class divides, racism, poverty and violence – refuse to disappear.

GENDER

Apart from class, gender is the social relation of power that has been most addressed by social geographers. Studies date back to the early 1970s when there was already a surprisingly eclectic range of studies, although it was a field that was quickly to become dominated by feminist analyses. At least three different trajectories of study can be recognized. What Thrift (2003: 96) refers to as 'empirical constructions of space' were very visible. Obviously there were (and still are) attempts to simply describe and map the differential geographies of men and women, registering their disparate access to services, employment and facilities (Caris, 1978; Mazey and Lee, 1983; WGSG, 1981, 1983). Secondly, there were studies of the status and position of women within the discipline (Zelinsky, 1973; Rubin, 1979). Thirdly, and perhaps most fruitful, were studies that initially explored sexual differences but quickly moved on to studying gendered differences. Initially, such studies introduced the concept of gender roles – that men's and women's roles are separate but complimentary – into social geography, with the seminal work being Jacqui Tivers's (1978) study of mothers' access to childcare in London, England. It was, however, feminist geographers working in the long-established field of Marxist urban social geography, critiquing models of the city that associated women with the suburbs and men with the world of employment (Burnett, 1973; Breughel, 1973; Mackenzie, 1984), that was to establish the study of gender relations. Indeed, in the Anglo-American world studies of gender came to be dominated in the 1980s by socialist feminist analyses that focused on understanding women's labour as central not only to the reproduction of the labour force but also to the functioning of everyday urban life (WGSG, 1984).[4] The 1980s were a productive period of study for feminist geographers, who made contributions to a wide range of studies of gender in both the urban global North (Mackenzie, 1980; Bowlby et al., 1982; Wekerle, 1984; Little et al., 1988) and the global South (Momsen and Townsend, 1987; Brydon and Chant, 1989).

A small dent was made into the stranglehold that socialist feminism had on feminist work by the so-called patriarchy debate in *Antipode,* which developed in response to an article by Foord and Gregson (1986) (see McDowell, 1986; Johnson, 1987; Gier and Walton, 1987), but it was not until a concern emerged with gendered identities, as opposed to gendered relations, that studies of gender began to admit alternative theoretical constructions.[5] The late 1980s was a period of intense creativity in intellectual thought in the Western academy, and over the space of a few years feminists were radically recasting their ideas about gender (Bondi, 1990; McDowell, 1991). Throughout the 1990s the cultural turn in geography, entwined with the post-structuralist concept of difference, led to the discarding of the notion of a coherent, bounded, autonomous and independent identity – the subject of earlier analyses – that was capable of self-determination and progress, in favour of a socially constructed category defined by the constitutive outside. The earlier distinction between gender as socially created, resting upon the biological distinction of sex, was abandoned, creating room for research that highlighted how gendered subjectivities, far from being based on a stable content, were produced, performed, destabilized and redrawn in complex ways, drawing meaning from routine interactions with others in specific historical and geographical contexts. These realizations had, by the late 1980s, opened up a range of studies by social geographers on multiple constructions of both femininities (Laurie et al., 1999) and masculinities (Jackson, 1991).

The erasure of distinctions between sex and gender also opened the space for that which brought them together, the body. That bodies are sites of performance in their own right rather than simply surfaces for discursive inscription (Butler, 1990) led to a burgeoning interest in bodily gendered geographies: 'An interest in the corporeal – the flesh – and of thinking through the body developed alongside an understanding that the body is not only the primary site of identity but also the place, the site, of the individual' (McKittrick and Peake, 2005: 48). Moss and Dyck (1999: 389) define corporeal space as that 'where the discursive and the material are synchronous'; but embodied approaches to human subjectivity are not just about prioritizing the corporeal, rather they speak to the social and spatial construction of embodied identities (Jackson, 2003). Gregson (2003) for one, as mentioned earlier, is wary of the recent focus on the scale of the bodily and its attendant geographies of '"everyday" landscapes, places and institutions' (2003: 46). Such a focus, she argues, is less likely to relate to questions of inequalities than is one on the scale of the neighbourhood or the urban and is also more likely to centre on individual experiences of exclusion and inclusion than on the varied 'sociality/ies of particular embodiments' (Gregson, 2003: 46). That a focus on the scale of the body is likely to be suggestive of a social that has more to do with the politics of difference than of inequality is also a concern of McKittrick, who berates social geographies for emphasizing the body 'as the only relevant black geographic scale' (McKittrick and Woods 2007: 7). McKittrick's (2006) work on the black female body links it specifically to its materialities – to how it is understood by the weaving together of social relations, especially those based on use and exchange.

Indeed, it is now almost *de rigueur* to differentiate between studies of social geographies of the body versus embodied social geography (Moss and Dyck, 2003). While the former can describe bodily experiences of environments and bodily activities in specific places, it is arguably the latter and its interest with embodiment that has been of more interest to social geographers. Embodiment not only locates bodies within the discursive and material environments that constitute them, it is also concerned with 'constructing knowledge that theorizes *from* bodies, privileging the *material* ways in which bodies are constituted, experienced and represented' (Moss and Dyck, 2003: 60). In their studies of embodiment, social geographers have shown how bodily activities are (self) regulated, producing bodies that are constantly under surveillance either by the self or society. Substantive areas of concern have been the performativity of bodies (Longhurst, 2001), labouring bodies (McDowell and Court, 1994), disabled bodies (Chouinard, 1999), fat bodies (A. Mitchell, 2006), clothed bodies (Colls, 2006), pregnant bodies (Longhurst, 2007) and sexualized bodies (Oswin, 2007).

Currently, social geographies of gender reveal three trajectories. Studies of embodiment, for example, are beginning to challenge the adult-centredness of social geographies of gender. Children's bodies are starting to enter the frame both in terms of those working on bodies and embodiment and those who focus on children's and young people's geographies (Costello and Duncan, 2006; Colls and Evans, 2008). There have also been studies of the masculinist practices of the mapping of emotions and feelings onto the bodies of women, questioning the exclusion of emotion from the realm of embodiment, and thus introducing the study of affect and emotional geographies into this field (Bondi, 2005; Len and Woodward, this volume).[6] Finally, there have been systematic attempts to dislodge the Anglo-American hegemony of such studies (see, for example, Garcia-Ramon and Monk, 2007).

SEXUALITY

It was in the late 1970s that sexuality studies in geography first started to emerge, with informal meetings of gay and lesbian geographers at the annual conferences of the Association of American Geographers as well as a few published studies by gay geographers (Ketteringham, 1979; Winters, 1979). In the early 1980s the positivism that underlay these early studies began to be challenged, using insights from feminism and political economy approaches (see especially the work of Bob McNee (1984) and Larry Knopp (Lauria and Knopp, 1985)). In a similar manner to the way in which gender studies emerged (partially) from critiques of exclusively class-based analyses of the urban, sexuality studies in social geography in the late 1980s began to earnestly address the role of gay men in processes of gentrification in cities in the United States (Lauria and Knopp, 1985). These studies were soon to be followed in the early 1990s by the first studies of lesbian urban social geographies (Adler and Brenner, 1992), marked in particular by the pioneering work of Gill Valentine (1993a, b, c).[7] Throughout the 1990s a number of studies emerged that detailed lesbian and gay geographies, almost without exception in the global North, with studies on access to housing, including gentrification (Peake, 1993), gay and lesbian residential and commercial spaces (Binnie, 1995), social networks (Rothenberg, 1995), identity formation (Bell, 1991) and sexual practices (Binnie, 1997). Increasing dissatisfaction with the exclusive focus on homosexuality also led to the emergence of studies of social geographies of heterosexualities, which began to cohere into a field broadly defined as sexuality and space (Elder et al., 2003; Knopp, 2007), legitimized, at least in North America, in 1996, by the emergence of the Sexuality and Space Specialty Group of the AAG.

By the mid 1990s there had been an explosion of sexuality studies in geography that were 'theoretically anti-structuralist, anti-modernist and very self-consciously queer' (Brown and Knopp, 2003: 315). Queer geographers were challenging the fixity and certainties that accompany so many dominant ontologies of space and place as well as identifying themselves as more closely aligned with queer geographies and distanced from feminist geographies. Tensions have arisen, with some claiming feminism has not always been a welcoming place for queer geographers (Bell 1997; Binnie and Valentine, 1999) and with others pointing out, for example, the ability of some white gay men to benefit from heteropatriarchies (Nast, 2004). Yet, as Knopp (2007) makes clear, queer studies and feminism, despite the fact that both are internally theoretically and politically diverse, have much in common. Indeed, queer studies have benefited from feminist geographers' interest in (the destabilizing of) gender and sexual relations at a variety of scales from the body to the global, as well as from feminist critiques of the authority of science and its claims to 'objectivity' and 'truth', and while feminist geographers have tended to be less influenced by queer studies, there have been notable exceptions, such as Gibson-Graham's (1996) efforts to queer economic geographies of capitalism. Needless to say, the degree of commonality or difference depends on place – where one is writing from and in which language, where one can see from – with some geographers claiming to being unable to differentiate between the interests and practices of feminist and queer scholars in their part of the world (Johnston and Longhurst, 2008).

Notwithstanding these tensions and overlaps between feminist and queer geographies, it is probably the latter that have done most to question the relations between gender, sex and sexuality and to open upto study a world of multiple genders and sexualities. Most recently, queer geographers, with their interests in sexuality as the social process that allows for the expression of desire, have expressed dissatisfaction with the limited and essentialized (and Westernized) nature of the categorization of sexualities. They have emphasized the fluid, unstable and ambiguous nature of sexual identities and their associated spatialities and have tended, according to Knopp (2007: 49), to move away from '... reified phenomena such as "gay gentrification" and "gay neighborhoods" (which also tended to be celebrated) to understanding more fluid, ambiguous and contingently sexualized spatialities such as circuits and fields', leading to studies of the cultural politics of sexuality, of queer performativity, and of the examination of archetypal constructs such as the closet (Bell and Valentine, 1995; Ingram et al., 1997). Brown's (2000) study of the closet refers to it not just as a metaphor but as a 'spatial practice of power-knowledge' that encompasses the scales of the body, the city, the national and the global and in which the closet 'is not always a disempowered, abject artifact, but can also be a setting for creative, ingenious and transformative sexual, cultural and political resistances to heteronormativity' (Brown and Knopp, 2003: 315). Queer geographies have also moved away from their initial urban focus to investigate queer rural geographies (Phillips et al., 2000; Vanderbeck, 2006), racialized queer geographies (Nast, 2004; Puar, 2006), global-scale studies of sexualities (Oswin, 2007) and queer cyberspace (Wincapaw, 2000). Although queer social geographers have been successful in opening up the category of sexuality, this has been uneven; there are still very few investigations into the lives of transgendered, transexual or bisexual people (but see Doan, 2007). There is also dissension among so-called queer geographers as to what constitutes queer work (Oswin, 2008). And in their recent review of sexuality studies in cultural geography, Brown and Knopp (2003: 318) remark that sexuality studies are still marginal in geography because the discipline's 'traditional corpus has been largely untouched by a queer sensibility'.

Perhaps a more optimistic interpretation of the study of sexuality and of its somewhat embattled relationship to gender is offered by Richardson's (2007: 464) recent work on what she refers to as the 'patterned fluidity' between them. She proposes a specifically geographical metaphor for a way of working through their tensions:

> I propose ... a metaphor to (re)imagine the relationship between gender and sexuality: that of the shoreline, a boundary in motion between land and sea. Moreover, this is a boundary that far from being self contained is extensive and informed by the hinterlands that shape and shift it. But which is sea and which is land? In most theoretical accounts, gender is understood as having greater fixity than sexuality, which is regarded as more fluid and capable of reconfiguration. ... On this basis, we can think of the two hinterlands that frame the shoreline, the land and the sea, as gender and sexuality respectively. Where they intersect, the relationship between them, constitutes the shoreline. This is a dynamic relationship, affected by both local and global conditions (micro and macro climates) in which land and sea bleed into each other and are inter-related (they shape each other), but are also distinguishable. ... The relationship between gender and sexuality is not free floating, but like shoreline construction has patterns to its fluidity. ... It enables the recognition of both the possibility of the fluid interplay between gender and sexuality, and that there exists structure and materiality as well as socially and culturally meaningful 'sexual and gender stories' ... that give the subject social coherence and intelligibility (Richardson, 2007: 470).

While this dialectical construction – that of the land and sea – is new to queer theorists it is one that theorists of race have long explored (a point I return to later in the chapter).

RACE

Empirical studies of race (understood as a biological concept) by human geographers precede those of gender and sexuality, starting in the early twentieth century with studies of the effects of tropical climates on white skin (Woodruff, 1905; Trewartha, 1926). In their ostensible concern with skin colour these studies built upon the work of the Enlightenment geographer Immanuel Kant. Kobayashi, among others, points out that Kant was the first geographer to discuss race; he surmized that skin colour was the result of distance from the equator 'and that those of darker skin colour were possessed of inferior moral, social and intellectual qualities' (Kobayashi, 2003: 544). Indeed, the Enlightenment view of race has been a fundamental part of Western understanding of what it is to be human; Enlightenment-racialized knowledge, through which white people were viewed as morally superior and further from nature than non-whites, underpinned the European colonial project (Kobayashi, 2003). Certainly, Bonnett (2000a, b) attributes these early studies to anxieties about the decline of the British Empire and a crisis of whiteness characterized by a profound sense of vulnerability, rooted not only in the threat of miscegenation but also in the realization that World War I made clear the impossibility of an international white solidarity, especially across class divides. For social geographers the subsequent combination of the decline of the paradigm of environmental determinism, the predominance of white male geographers at the helm of European and American geography, and the growth of scientific human geography, meant that nearly half a century was to pass until they were to again ask questions about race.

The early 1970s was a period marked by eclecticism, and three separate and divergent strands of studies of race have been recognized (Kobayashi, 2003). Empirical studies of spatial patterns of inequality experienced by African-Americans were initially undertaken by the African-American geographer Harold Rose (1970) and later taken up by Joe Darden (1988) and others (see also Dwyer, 1997). A second stream, the study of race and racism, was conducted by white radical (mostly Marxist) geographers publishing in the journal *Antipode*. They were largely concerned with the conditions of life in urban ghettoes in the United States and in the developing world (Blaut, 1974; Bunge, 1971; Harvey, 1972; Smith, 1974). But as Kobayashi (2003: 548) points out, 'both approaches involve constituting people as problems, rather than seeking direct engagement with their lives; and neither approach involves enhancing the power to change people's lives' (but cf. Blaut, 1993). While empirical studies in the United States measuring spatial patterns of inequality have continued (see, for example, Holloway and Wyly, 2002), Marxist concerns have largely turned away from racism, reducing race to an effect of class. A third trajectory was carved out by Anglo-American humanistic geographers interested in the everyday lives of racialized ethnic communities (Peach, 1975; Ley, 1974; Jackson and Smith, 1981), an approach that was eventually to lead to the new cultural geography. It was, however, the critical turn in geography from the late 1980s onwards that was to lead to a convergence of interests among these disparate approaches in the recognition of race, like gender and sexuality, as a social construction, charged through with power lines, social meanings and identities. As Kobayashi contends:

> The idea of 'race' has allowed the construction of the raced body according to historically, culturally and place-based sets of meanings. Thus the term 'racialization' refers to the process by which somatic characteristics (which *may* be phenotypical or genotypical) have been made to go beyond themselves to designate the socially inscribed values and the attributes of racialized bodies. The bodies are the results of normative vision, constituted by the eye of the most powerful viewer. Such values determine how those bodies will be used, as slaves, as racialized labour, or, in the case of 'white' bodies, in positions of power (2003: 549).

Over the last two decades the influence of feminist, post-structuralist and post-colonial scholars, especially Frantz Fanon and Edward Said, combined with the development of critical race theory and Black Studies, has produced a slow but consistent growth of interest in issues of race, and increasingly anti-racism, by social geographers. Within this literature I would recognize a number of interconnected strands. In particular, as in studies of gender and sexuality, the focus, for some, has been turning from one on marginalized groups, of people of colour, to whiteness (i.e., to those in positions of power who are able to perpetuate the study of race and racialized categories). Whiteness can be understood:

> as an historically and geographically specific social construct that has been accorded a privileged position at the centre of racialized and embodied systems of social stratification and differentiation. Its contextual specificity indicates though that whiteness is never a stable bodily signifier; rather, the social meanings it conveys are always contingent. But this is not to deny that it has real effects on people's lives – white skin privilege is the other side of racism – and it is invariably deployed to augment oppressive relations of power (Peake, 2009).

Bonnett (2000a, b), more than any other geographer, has attempted to develop a comprehensive historical and geographical analysis of whiteness. His concern has been to show 'the history of whiteness became racialized is also the history of how groups previously identified as white (such as the Chinese) began to call themselves something else and how Europeans began to believe that they were the world's only true whites' (Bonnett and Nayak, 2003: 309). Social geographers have now contributed to a wide range of studies of whiteness, including whiteness as epistemology (Dwyer and Jones, 2000), historical geographies of whiteness (Delaney, 1998), the role of whiteness in discourses of nation (Radcliffe, 1999), whiteness and the production of racialized landscapes (Peake and Ray, 2001; Schein, 2006), embodied whiteness (Winders et al., 2005), and processes of social change in white identities (Pulido, 2002). Recent work (Vanderbeck, 2006) has also looked at contestations of whiteness from within, particularly how notions of gender and sexuality feature strongly in contestations over what constitutes hegemonic or 'appropriate' whiteness, including how certain regional constructions of whiteness have come to be feminized and (homo)sexualized in particular ways.

Studies of whiteness have also been controversial, though, for their tendency to reproduce that which they seek to deconstruct, calling for some (including Bonnett) to focus attention instead on anti-racism. Indeed, for many geographers of colour engaging in political action and social change is prioritized: 'to put it simply, anti-racist geography is about caring about the conditions of life for specific living individuals, more than it is about theorizing "race"' (Kobayashi, 2003: 551). This concern with specific people has encroached into the discipline itself, with a number of social geographers of colour commenting on the racism present in academic institutions as well as in the practices and subject matter of geography itself (Pulido, 2002; see the theme issue of *Gender, Place and Culture,* Vol. 13 (1)).

Theorizing race still plays an important role in the work of many social geographers, albeit in differing ways. One new strand of work to emerge (that predates September 11th 2001) engages with the intersection between race and religion, focusing in particular on how young Muslim men and women construct their identities (Dwyer, 1999, 1998; Hopkins, 2007; Phillips, 2006; Secor, 2002). Also, in the late twentieth century, there was an emergence of black geographies that went beyond representing blackness as 'measureable, knowable and indicative of dispossession' (McKittrick, 2006: 14). Although empirical studies documenting the daily conditions of life in African-Canadian (Mensah, 2002) and African-American (Darden, 1988) communities continue, there have also been attempts to develop non-essentialized accounts of black geographies (Woods, 1998; McKittrick, 2006; McKittrick and Woods, 2007). As McKittrick opines:

> Finding and recognizing black geographies is difficult, not only because socio-spatial denial, objectification, and capitalist value systems render them invisible, but also because the places and spaces of blackness are adversely shaped by the basic rules of traditional geographies. Prevailing geographic rules have a stake in the ghettoization of difference and/or the systemic concealment of physical locations that map this difference. ... Thus the production of black spaces in the diaspora is tied

> to locations that were and are explicitly produced in conjunction with race, racism, captivity and economic profit. Traditional geographies did, and arguably still do, *require* black displacement, black placelessness, black labour, and a black population that submissively stays 'in place'(2006: 8–9).

At the same time, calls for the transcendence of race have come from post-race theorists, such as Paul Gilroy (2000), who argue for a 'post-racial humanism'. While they agree that processes of racialization (through which categories of race are constructed) and racism (the outcome of acceptance of racial categories) are discursive and material realities, race is not and serves only to divide people, thus having no useful purpose, particularly in terms of liberty and global humanism. But if the cultural reality of race is to be dismissed, then what is it about race that exists? Indeed, the denial of race is also a strategy of the new racism, in which racism is expressed in carefully coded messages about cultural differences rather than in crudely overt themes about biologically distinct races.[8] Hence arguments for the denial of post-racial humanism are emerging from proponents of the 'material turn' taking place in the social sciences. They argue that there is increasing recognition that social construction *per se* is not enough to understand the machinations of race and that the materiality of racial categories has been disavowed. Physical differences, even if only superficial, do exist and race, it is claimed, may best be understood as 'culturally embedded phenotype' (Saldanha, 2006: 20).

INTERSECTIONALITY, PLACE AND SPACE

How have social geographers, many of them working in more than one of these fields, of gender, sexuality and race, made sense of their connections, their intersectionality? As early as the 1970s and throughout the 1980s many social geographers, heavily influenced by socialist and Marxist analyses, were *de facto* also incorporating class into their analyses. With the cultural turn of the early 1990s and a proliferation of theoretical approaches, class, for many, was no longer *the* benchmark against which intersectionality was gauged. The limitations of privileging one system of inequality – capitalism – over others – patriarchy, racism, homophobia – became subject to intense debate (Harvey, 1989; Massey, 1991). Critiques of studies of intersectionality came, for example, from both white and non-white feminists who objected to approaches in which identities were 'added on' to each other, commonly referred to the 'mix and stir' approach. Women of colour in particular explained that race could not simply be added onto a presumed stable white base (Combahee River Collective, 1977; Hill Collins, 1990), as if these dimensions were totally separate and additive as opposed to being formed in relation to each other and experienced bodily often in non-distinguishable ways.

Critiques of studies of intersectionality by social geographers, however, had an additional focus, namely, that most studies by social geographers have usually restricted their analyses to only two dimensions of subjectivity (Valentine, 2007). However, there is not a total lack of empirical work on the 'full implications' of subjectivities, although most relate to the global South and have therefore not received the same degree of attention that they would have if conducted in the global North (see, for example, Radcliffe, 1993, 2006; Katz, 2004; Peake and Trotz, 1999). One such case study of the formation of intersectionalities is outlined below.

While this study speaks to the specific relationship between heterosexuality and Afro-Guyanese working class gendered and racialized identities in relation to national belonging, it does not speak to such connections among Indo-Guyanese or Amerindian people in Guyana, or anywhere else. Indeed, the utility of researching foundationalist notions of identities, outside of geographical and historical contexts, has long been eschewed by social geographers.

Constructing working-class, Afro-Guyanese masculinities and femininities in Guyana (adapted from Peake and Trotz, 1999)

Starting from the premise that masculinities and femininities are not given but are historically produced via struggle and consent, we interviewed 140 working-class Afro-Guyanese men and women in the interior mining town of Linden, Guyana, to explore current articulations of gender – as constituent dimensions of racialized working-class identities – revealing the centrality of (hetero)sexuality to their construction. Our concern was to examine the effects of economic changes in the town over several decades from being a one industry (bauxite mining) town with high levels of male employment and remuneration to one in which the majority of the population is living below the poverty line. Within this current context of economic immiseration, what ruptures and continuities are visible in the ways sexuality and gender have come to be articulated and contested? What expectations about appropriate behavior for themselves and the opposite sex do men and women now have? And how are gendered norms and practices regarding appropriate behavior being reconciled in a situation whereby women are increasingly being forced to join the labour force at a rate which exceeds that previously known in the community?

Norms of what constitutes success are themselves contingent and mediated by social and economic conditions; they are discursive resources that transform, and themselves are transformed by, the behavioral practices they represent. Williams (1996b) claims appropriate modes of class behavior require a balance between egalitarian ('living good' with one's neighbours) and hierarchical (increasing access to material resources or 'betterment') values and that these are blended in men and women in a way that is consistent with, and representative of, their racialized identities. Our interviews revealed that, in addition to motherhood and a desire for 'betterment', women's ability to acquire a man was a further hallmark of the successful woman. This norm was expressed through the axiom that women should have a man (at whatever cost), the ultimate degradation in such a patriarchal community being to live without sexual contact with a man.

If motherhood, material success and sexual gratification were signifiers of the successful Afro-Guyanese working-class woman, what were the gendered norms laid out for masculinity? Masculine ideals of 'betterment' were expressed through exonerating the values of hard work and material advancement while avoiding any boasting about, or flaunting of, wealth. Younger men (including those up to their mid-30s or so) also have to build up reputations, which they do by 'liming' outside the home and relating to other men their 'acts of strength', such as the fathering of children and engagement in hard work. A sense of independence was also integral to conceptions of Afro-Guyanese working-class masculinity, expressed through freedom of movement and a degree of detachment from the ties of family. Indeed, Afro-Guyanese masculinities are defined and contested in public places that are sites of male socialization. In these spaces masculinities are continually reinforced to prevent men from being stigmatized as what they are not, i.e., anti-men (a local colloquialism for being homosexual). Liming, the occupation of public space usually centered on recreational drinking, allows 'true' Afro-Guyanese men to develop their masculine reputations and keep on showing women, other men and themselves that they are masculine. Men's visibility in the lime makes clear they are not spending all their time working, neither are they in the home under a woman's thumb. Liming not only establishes their independence from women and difference from Indo-Guyanese men, but also confirms them as men who have money to spend (with and on other men) and provides a space in which they can relate their sexual adventures to other men, thereby corroborating their heterosexuality.

In practice, dimensions of masculinity and femininity were defined in opposition, yet also as complementary, to each other; gendered relations were realised through men and women both attempting to 'live good' and achieve 'betterment', yet also with men attempting to retain their patriarchal privileges and women their distance from such subordinating practices. As a result there was a wide range of behavior displayed in individual relationships as well as contradictory behavior by individuals as they attempted to live out their identities within a dialectic of norms and practices. Intimate relations between women and men, especially younger men and women, were structured by men's deep suspicion and distrust of women, even misogyny, fuelled by fears of being cuckolded. Relationships were virtually contracts based on sexual acts of exchange (see also Miller, 1994: 175–176; Williams, 1991); otherwise gender relations had few other avenues of expression and were synonymous with the expression of a tightly circumscribed heterosexuality, the boundaries of conventional masculinities and femininities being policed by homophobia. The centrality of heterosexual relations to Afro-Guyanese working-class masculinity was expressed through men's fear of 'getting blow' (adultery), while a lack of interest in men by women was interpreted as a woman's inability to succeed in life (infertility being regarded as a curse). Overwhelmingly, among both men and women, there were feelings of disgust pleasure, and abhorrence towards homosexuals and lesbians, who were castigated for having sex purely for their own interests rather than for procreation and the reproduction of the ethnic group, and were described in terms of intense hatred, such as 'nastiness', 'wickedness', 'abnormality', being 'cursed' or 'sick'.

Although to differing degrees, women would tolerate male infidelity as long as they and their children did not financially suffer as a result. A further source of tension derived from the rigid gendered division of labour in the household that proved resistant to women's increasing employment responsibilities outside the home. Although women felt men did not do their 'fair' share of housework, they were reluctant to question the division of tasks within the home. To do so would transgress the foundation of their sexual and gendered identities; too much immersion in housework would deprive men of their masculinity and run the risk of turning them into homosexuals. As one woman commented:

> I don't feel a boy child should be, you know, his time should be occupied in the kitchen. I feel dat does change dem up.... It get a boy right behind us you know, he grow with his grandmother and constant doing housework and ah mean they say his mind does really cause it. He is a faggot right now (Susan, age 28).

That the erasure of masculinity takes place when men occupy women's spaces and supposedly adopt women's identities is a process that is not only well known and avoided, it is also one that is learned from an early age. As one mother commented on the differential access boys and girls had to public space:

> Guys don't have respect for little girls [teenagers] and if dey see yuh go certain place they want to tek dey eyes and pass yuh. So I don't allow her to stay out late. But de boy I would give him more privilege, he got to be a tough man in de street (Marilyn, age 36).

Men and women attempt to transverse the gap between norms that emphasize working-class respectability combined with a middle-class orientation and the lived reality of relationships by the policing of each other's sexuality. The decline in male employment and increase in female employment, with their material consequences, have had a limited impact on these norms. That a lack of changes in behavioral practices has been accommodated to ensure the continuity of norms speaks to the latter's threading together by the hegemony of heterosexuality. This has proven not only to tie women and men together in their mutual desires for the social reproduction of 'Afro-Guyaneseness' but also to limit the potentially divisive consequences of economic and social changes, although it has also prevented transformations in one area of woman's life – such as increasing engagement in income-generating activities – leading to improvements in other areas of their daily lives, such as men's participation in housework. Thus are current practices of masculinity and femininity among the Afro-Guyanese working class, and the (hetero)sexualized meanings underpinning them, part of the ongoing process of participating in the struggle for national inclusion in relation to social, economic and sexual opportunities on their own terms.

Social geographers, perhaps more than others, have shown how intersectionalities are bound up in spatialities, that social differences, however tightly or loosely bound together, always come into being through interactions in specific places.[9] As the above case study shows, space and identities are co-produced; the places people occupy – the space of the lime, the kitchen – are constitutive of identities, and spaces are given meaning through the social practices of the groups that repeatedly occupy them. As many social geographers have pointed out, how identities are produced, circulated and transformed within these spatialities through the division of continuous territory into 'insides' and 'outsides' facilitates the categorization of groups into 'us v. them' arrangements (Natter and Jones, 1997; Cresswell, 1996). And, as Valentine states:

> When individual identities are 'done' differently in particular temporal moments they rub up against, and so expose, these dominant spatial orderings that define who is in place/out of place, who belongs and who does not, [as well as exposing] the ways that power operates in and through particular spaces to systematically (re)produce particular inequalities (2007: 19).

Most recent discussions by social geographers of being in and out of place, and of who is allowed to be there at all, center around critiques of the work of the theorist Georgio Agamben (1998). His interest in the figure of the *Homo sacer*, the male figure who is excluded, and theories of differential inclusion or displacement, are based on how certain territories are exempted from 'normal' laws and how the people trapped within them are treated in a differential manner based on the state's power over this space. However, feminist critiques (Sanchez, 2004; K. Mitchell, 2006; Pratt, 2005; Secor, 2006) emphasize that the concept of displacement 'implies both a prior "placement" in citizenship/humanity and the possibility of return to that privileged status' (Mitchell, 2006: 99). As feminist academics have long acknowledged, there are categories of women who by virtue of their 'mobile and nomadic condition' (K. Mitchell, 2006: 99) are always already out of place and that, while for some the possibility of return is possible, for others it is not. The flaneur and the prostitute, two paradigmatic figures of women in urban public space that are capable of inducing anxiety and moral panic, illustrate how the ability to negotiate space is constrained by some female-gendered identities. Women have, however, reclaimed spaces from which they have been excluded – all-male clubs, 'Bring back the Night' marches – and they create their own spaces from nunneries to battered women's shelters to all-women festivals. Queer folk have also reclaimed their own spaces, from gay neighbourhoods to queer spaces of performativity, while non-white communities have also asserted their rights to be, to return, and to occupy space. Subjectivities can and do perform and produce spaces differently and not always routinely, invisibly or quietly.

While intersectionality (of race, gender and sexuality) has allowed social geographers to develop deep understandings of the ways in which social constructions have played out in the configuration of local, national and global social formations and subjectivities, it is only recently that they have begun to question how an understanding of the historical context of the formation of subjectivities has led to the questioning of the very humanness of the subject. Arguably, the context for understanding the evolution of thinking about subjectivity was born out of Europe's 1492 invasion of the Caribbean, the crucible of modernity, leading Slater (2003: 422) to support the contention of the Argentinian philosopher Enrique Dussel (1995) that 'the Spanish *conquisto* (or *vinco*), i.e., I conquer, must be given historical and ontological priority over the Cartesian *cogito, ergo sum* (I am thinking, therefore I exist) as the first determination of the subject of modernity'. By definition, 'to conquer' not only implies to overcome other humans but also to acquire their lands and seas and their contents, that is, their natures. Conceptualizing the social in ways that focus not only on a 'biocentric' mode of thinking but also on understanding the intrinsic connections between humans and natures – in other words, questioning the ontological construction of the social – has now come to dominate theoretical reasoning by social geographers in the West.

GENDER, SEXUALITY, RACE AND NATURE

While nature has long been a central theme of geographical enquiry, social geographers have been at the forefront of the recent interrogations into its ontological status.[10] Going beyond nature/society dualisms has taken social geographers into debates about different ways of understanding the networks through which humans and non-human phenomena intertwine and the hybrid spaces in which these operate. It is perhaps in the study of what has been called 'post-humanism' that the ways in which these dimensions are being rethought is most advanced in social geography. Kay Anderson states:

> Post-humanism, as a philosophical framework, is a disparate body of ideas calling into ontological question the meaning and integrity of 'the human'. ... [Key texts] argue in different ways, humanity is not an essence, but a shifting mode of being. Try thinking carefully about how you would define 'human' and it soon becomes clear that 'humanness' is neither given in any *absolute* human/animal contrast, nor in any objective *fact* of separation from what western people often think of as their interior animality – their instincts, and all those non putatively non-rational bodily impulses. Conceived as an entity entangled with rather than separated from nature, 'the human' is problematized in relation to societal/technological change and the assumptions of a long tradition of western humanism. ... Questioning the meaning and limits of 'the human' has intensified in recent years in the context of contemporary advances in medical, reproductive and information technologies. (2007: 2).

Anderson and other social geographers are tuning in to a way of thinking in which human life is intimately tied up with and connected to diverse natures, to other non-human living and nonliving entities. These entanglements of culture and nature, or assemblage geographies (see Robbins and Marks, this volume), have had profound effects on the ways in which social geographers approach the foundational figure of the human subject. Humans are no longer being regarded as separate from and having control over nature (and machines). Increasingly, their interfaces are coming under scrutiny as different and new assemblages of people, things and matter come into being, calling into question how we can 'unlearn' this construct of the 'human' (as always, already human) and how non-human entities also come to be (Haraway, 1997), thus having to take into account more than human interactions and relations, or what David Harvey (2000: 208) calls 'species being'. Areas of study to emerge from the framing of post-humanism include those on socio-materialities of nature and the recognition that the natural has order, purpose and meaning (Cronon, 1995); hybrid geographies, in which the complexity of species barriers is explored (Whatmore, 2002); actor–network theories (FitzSimmons and Goodman, 1998; Kaika and Syngedouw, 2000); the field of animal geographies (Wolch and Emel, 1998: Philo and Wilbert, 2000); questioning of the concept of scale (Marston et al., 2005); and the emergence of the study of the socio-cultural politics of race and nature (Kobayashi, 2003; Anderson, 2007; McKittrick and Woods, 2007). These lines of study have also opened up the ethics of attempts to transcend dualistic ways of thinking, moving from an essentializing framing of 'us v. other' to one of 'non-appropriating openness' (Whatmore 2002: 203).

These questionings of the ontological dimensions of the social are revealing of the ways in which the categories of race, sexuality and gender have been produced. While for some the post-human invokes anxieties 'about the erosion of the ideal human subject' (Castree and Nash, 2006: 501), for others it is to be celebrated – humanism has always involved hierarchies in which the categories of gender, race and sexuality have been used to place some humans as closer to nature than others. However, while there have been numerous studies of gender – particularly of femininities – in relation to nature, very few relate gender to post-humanism, and studies by queer social geographers appear to be almost non-existent, leading Brown and Knopp (2003: 321) to ask: 'how might the closeting of queer desire in western societies discipline men's and women's constructions and uses of nature? In the context of "non-western" cultures, we might ask why it is that so many people who in the west might be considered "queer" are ascribed special status as spiritual naturists (for example, the berdache of some native North American cultures)'. Rather, social geographers have turned to studies of race to illustrate how both nature and humans have been constructed through processes of colonialism and imperialism.

Perhaps the most important recent study that successfully marries the study of post-humanism to critical race theory is that by Kay Anderson (2007). Her argument, that classical humanness has assumed that the humanness of 'the human' lies in its separateness from the non-human and nature, has two dimensions. First is the notion of 'the human' as separate from the sphere in which it exists – nature/the environment – and non-human animals. Second, humanness, especially as it came to be conceived in Christian thought and in the Enlightenment, is understood as being able to transcend its corporeal nature, which is thought of as animal-like and which resides within humans (Anderson, 2007: 8). In other words, nature is both exteriorized and interiorized. It is this latter aspect of the interiorization of nature that Anderson forcefully claims has been missing from critical race analyses of the emergence of race and racism. Her study of the Australian aborigine, who was historically perceived as having little interest in settled cultivation, problematized the view that humans were moving out of nature and thus the view of humanness itself. She claims it was in the mid-nineteenth century that intellectual anxieties about human exception, provoked by Darwin's notion of evolutionism, reached a crisis point and provoked a revision of the monogenist world view. Consequently, the notion of race lost its fluidity as a marker of difference and became constituted as one in which distinct groups were recognized and identified on the basis of biological categories of race, determined by their degree of separation from nature. But this concept of humanism, based on racialized divides, has been fraught with anxieties and, as Bonnett (2000b) has shown, has also, in Europe at least, increasingly been constructed through a discourse of whiteness that reached a crisis in the period 1890–1930.

That constructions of whiteness, and of emasculated masculinism and subjugated femininity, pervade the 'social/natural' is not only the purview of post-humanist scholars of social geography.[11] This has long been known by radical black intellectuals who have not only engaged with a revisioned humanism but also with conceptions of space.[12] Recent developments in the studies of black geographies have led to the reinterrogation of these works. McKittrick and Woods (2007), for example, have examined the work of the Caribbean philosopher Edouard Glissant (1989; Dash, 1995; Britton, 1999), who draws on notions of rhizomatic space, to question ways in which whiteness limits geographical imaginaries of the social. That nature–culture coalesces, Glissant argues, is underwritten by a non-white and violent human bodily history that has seeped into the land and the sea. In his conceptualization of 'submarine geographies', Glissant (1989) denotes the rhizome as an image of the in-between. The rhizome is not a negation of the root/rootedness but a hybrid modification of it, an affirmation of relational dynamics, of the tension between written and oral cultures that is often signified by the sea, the black Atlantic. Most recently the notion of the black Atlantic, with its 'rhizomorphal, fractal structure' (Gilroy, 1993: 4), is that of an interactional space of cultural exchange.[13] McKittrick and Woods (2007) draw attention to the ways in which the black Atlantic can illuminate the study of social geographies. They outline their understanding of submarine geographies as:

> The storm-torn bodies, those thrown overboard and forgotten, and the many other narratives and experiences that are violently and/ or uncomfortably situated within the geography of reason [and which] have produced what Edouard Glissant calls 'submarine roots': a network of branches, cultures and relations that position black geographies and the oceanic history of diaspora as integral to and entwining with – rather than outside – what has been called 'coloniality's persistence'.

Submarine geographies can enhance the study of the social by drawing to the centre marginalized subjects, such as refugees and displaced peoples. This spatial framework can also illuminate networks, such as transnational ties, that overlay the established grids and subjects of the modern world, those of bounded nation states and their citizens. As such, submarine geographies expand non-humanist questionings of the ontology of the social in that they address ways in which nature incorporates the 'sea'. But they do more. With their attention to forgotten subjects they also question how we know the social. It is to such epistemological concerns that I now turn.

GENDER, SEXUALITY, RACE AND THE SOCIAL PRODUCTION OF KNOWLEDGE

The silences in social geography about the work of numerous non-white theorists, the latent hostilities between some feminist and queer theorists, and the persistent ability of male theorists to prioritize the work of other men to that of, say, feminists, is indicative of deep divisions in academic productions of knowledge. Fields of interest develop in isolation from each other, world regions are still studied separately, and theory is often representative of a supposedly unmarked and unlocated realm (Yeung, 2001) that in fact is 'profoundly tagged by its production in the dominant Anglo-American "heartland" of graduate schools, research funds and publication outlets' (Robinson, 2003: 400). The geographical imaginary, continues Robinson, is firmly embedded in the global hegemony of Western scholarship with a continuing marginalization of knowledge not identified as white and Anglo-American in social geography.[14] The implications for how we understand race, gender and sexuality are profound.

The production and circulation of academic knowledge and practices, however, are being subjected to incursions from those who are attempting to decentre, or 'provincialize' (Chakrabarty, 2000) Anglo-American social geography. A critical mass of social geographers is investigating alternative sites and processes of knowledge production, attempting to broaden the epistemological realms of their field. Slater (2003), for example, argues for the need for respectful and critical dialogue with non-Western ways of doing and knowing, citing the example of combining liberal, representational Western notions of democracy with non-Western, such as indigenous, forms of democratic practice. And Howitt and Suchet-Pearson (2003), with reference to their work in Australia with indigenous peoples, state that cross-cultural understandings rely on being open to the creation of meanings and difference. Drawing on the indigenous concept of the Dreaming, they claim social geographers have yet to go beyond Eurocentric assumptions and ways of understanding and that we have not yet engaged with the metaphysical scale of the infinite:

> although indigenous peoples' sense of place is often glossed as exemplifying a localized world view, the Dreaming offers a scale metaphor which encompasses the infinite within the immediate. It mediates relationships across time and space at vast scales, while retaining embodiment that is concrete, local and specific. ... In the Dreaming, there is an ethical narrative that establishes a very different relationship between the here-and-now of places and the wider narrative of distant horizons of space, time and social and environmental order (Howitt and Suchet-Pearson, 2003: 561).

Similarly, as mentioned earlier, Harvey (2000: 254) argues that our ability to create new geographies is hampered or enabled by three aspects of our intellectual engagements: where we can see geography from; how far we can see; and where we can learn geography from. It is through such situated engagement, rather than monologue, that social geographers have the opportunity to further develop understandings of race, sexuality and gender through alternative ways of thinking or dreaming about our futures in ways that consciously desire difference (McKittrick and Peake, 2005).

CONCLUSION

As I said in my introduction, there is a mercurial nature to our understandings of concepts of race, sexuality and gender. Such knowledge can keep spreading out, but to where, to what ends, to what purpose? Neither gender, race nor sexuality are universal concepts, yet the desire to assume that they are is so strongly embedded (and so strongly rewarded) in Western societies, and in many non-Western societies, that these categories are very much taken for granted. Indeed, essentialist conceptions of race, gender and sexuality are considered the norm by millions of people around the globe; the foundational figure of the human subject is alive and doing well. Even when literally confronted with non-hegemonic subjectivities, ones that cannot be visually known and appraised according to dominant categories (male/female; black/white/Asian; heterosexual), the fluidity of boundaries is rarely questioned and people are shoehorned instead into already existing familiar categories.

Social geographers have critiqued such understandings through a reliance on the locatedness of material and discursive realities. In a desire to avoid reinforcing and recentering essentialist concepts and practices, they have outlined how many domains of social life are being transfigured through technologies of surveillance and globalization, creating new networks, new sites of transactions and new social interactions. In particular, understandings of how we live in increasingly networked assemblages of 'beings' has led to studies of the unravelling of the Cartesian dualism between humans and nature and the recognition that humans are ontologically constituted out of relations with both humans and non-humans. For many, though, the social still centres on the materiality of human social life, its organization and its reproduction, its examination of inequalities and its attention to redistributional politics, and its focus on significant lines of social differentiation. And many more still see only through a white Anglophone lens. Moving away from the totalizing categories of Western discourses and engaging with non-Western local knowledges would not only help to dismantle *a priori* categories but could also help undo dominant constructions of race, sexuality and gender that hide from view more humane and just ways of organizing the world.

NOTES

1 After agreeing to write this chapter I wondered whether the holy trinity of gender, race and class of the 20th century had come to be replaced in the 21st with more culturally inflected concerns with identities, subjectivities and difference. I was somewhat perturbed by the lack of reference to class. How could one of the most oppressive categories of differencing ever to be addressed by social geographers not be specifically mentioned? Of course, this chapter does not have a monopoly over these concerns and the editors felt that class was already strongly represented throughout the book.

2 Invariably the social has encompassed the realms of both the private and the public, with social geographers embracing studies of the body and embodiment, the family (children, youths and parenting), the household, the home, the community, the neighbourhood, civil society, the social sectors of housing, health, welfare and education, subsistence, and the spheres of social policy, social reproduction and social justice.

3 Tongue in cheek aside, this divide is one that has much resonance outside the discipline of Geography. Both non-white and white feminists, for example, have critiqued the cultural turn in the social sciences that has replaced class-based notions of oppression with references to difference (hooks, 2006; Fraser, 1997).

4 Recently, McDowell (2006) has pointed out how outdated this body of work feels, given that women's labour is no longer thought of as essential for the maintenance and reproduction of cities, being replaced by fast food outlets, dog walkers, meal delivery services, Internet shopping, eldercare, nannies and so on. It should be noted, however, that this replacement is much less true for working-class households as well as for the vast majority of those in the global South.

5 Accounts already exist of the ways in which gender has been analyzed by feminist geographers. McDowell (1993a, b), for example, recognizes three phases in terms of the ways in which gender has been conceptualized: feminist empiricism, standpoint feminism and postmodern feminism. More recently, Bondi and Davidson (2003) order their review around four phases of Western feminism: concerns with equality (most readily associated with liberal feminism); women's autonomy (associated with radical and lesbian feminisms); differences (associated with anti-racist feminism); and deconstruction (associated with post-structuralist and post-colonial feminists). In both accounts there is an underlying narrative of progression and of a reliance on English-language ways of knowing (the term gender does not translate easily into other languages, not even other linguistically related European languages such as French and Spanish; see Garcia-Ramon et al., 2006). For excellent reviews of the development of the study of gender in geography see the journal *Progress in Human Geography*.

6 Affect 'point[s] to something which is non-individual, an impersonal force resulting from [an] encounter, an ordering in the relations between bodies which results in an increase or decrease in the potential to act' (Thrift, 2003: 104). As such, it refers to an emotional state – love, hope, fear, anger – without any specific reference to an object (such as love of one's neighbour or hope for peace), indicating that it is a non-representational mode of thought.

7 Jacquelyn Beyer, a lesbian geographer at the University of Colorado–Colorado Springs, did present a paper on lesbian geographies based on a survey of women geographers – 'Geography of women's spaces: a press report' – in 1985 but did not publish any of her results.

8 'The new racist argument goes as follows: racism is no longer acceptable in modern society; to talk about racism is therefore to make an accusation of behaviour that goes against social norms; those

who talk about racism therefore seek either to cause trouble or to displace the blame for a given social condition from some other cause, such as culture or poverty'. (Kobayashi and Peake, 2007: 173).

9 Even if those places are 'unseeable'. See, for example, Ruth Wilson Gilmore (2007) on prisons.

10 Not least, current anxieties about nature arise from the many signifiers – global warming, species extinction, genetic modification – of the 'end of nature'.

11 Documenting conditions under Caribbean slavery, Hilary Beckles describes how:

> ... the black male was denied what was familiar, and his masculine impulses targeted by surveillance systems that directed the nature of everyday life. Black masculinities, then, were politicized within the context of white patriarchal ideological representations. In social relations, the black male and his offspring were fed, clothed and sheltered by white men whose hegemonic ideology determined that being 'kept' and 'kept down' were symbolic of submissive inferiority, and gendered feminization (1996: 4).

12 Such as Frantz Fanon, Edouard Glissant, C.L.R. James, W.E.B. Du Bois, James Baldwin, Frederick Douglass, Richard Wright, Ralph Ellison, Wilson Harris and Sylvia Winter.

13 Unlike Said, who stated that '[E]verything about human history is rooted in the earth' (1993: 5).

14 As McKittrick notes, 'The black subject and black communities are rarely given any formal academic geographic relevancy, whether in terms of a black way of interpreting the world, analyses of black places, a black politics of location or black senses of place as *mutual* to other forms of understanding, politicizing and mapping the world' (2006: 9–10).

REFERENCES

Adler, S. and Brenner, J. (1992) 'Gender and space: lesbians and gay men in the city', *International Journal of Urban and Regional Research*, 16 (1): 24–34.

Agamben, G. (1998) *Homo Sacer: Sovereign Power and Bare Life*, trans. D. Heller-Roazen. Stanford: Stanford University Press.

Anderson, K. (2007) *Race and the Crisis of Humanism*. London: Routledge.

Beckles, H. (1989) *A History of Barbados: From Amerindian to Settlement to Nation State*. Oxford: Clarendon Press.

Bell, D. (1991) 'Insignificant others: lesbian and gay geographies', *Area*, 23: 323–9.

Bell, D. (1997) 'Fucking geography, again', in K. Browne, J. Lim, and G. Brown (eds), *Geographies of Sexualities: Theories, Practices and Politics*. Aldershot: Ashgate. pp. 81–86.

Bell, D. and Valentine, G. (eds) (1995) *Mapping Desire: Geographies of Sexuality*. London: Routledge.

Binnie, J. (1995) 'Trading places: consumption, sexuality and the production of queer space', in D. Bell and G. Valentine (eds), *Mapping Desires: Geographies of Sexuality*. New York: Routledge. pp. 182–99.

Binnie, J. (1997) 'Coming out of geography: towards a queer epistemology', *Environment and Planning D: Society and Space*, 15: 223–37.

Binnie, J. and Valentine, G. (1999) 'Geographies of sexuality – a review of progress', *Progress in Human Geography*, 23: 175–87.

Blaut, J.M. (1974) 'The ghetto as an internal neo-colony', *Antipode*, 6 (1): 37–41.

Blaut, J.M. (1993) *The Colonizer's Model of the World: Geographical Diffusionism and Eurocentric History*. New York: Guilford.

Bondi, L. (1990) 'Progress in geography and gender: feminism and difference', *Progress in Human Geography*, 14 (3): 438–45.

Bondi, L. (2005) 'Making connections and thinking through emotions: between geography and psychotherapy', *Transactions of the Institute of British Geographers*, 30: 433–48.

Bondi, L. and Davidson, J. (2003) 'Troubling the place of gender', in K. Anderson, M. Domosh, S. Pile and N. Thrift (eds), *Handbook of Cultural Geography*. London: Sage. pp. 325–44.

Bonnett, A. (2000a) 'The first crisis of whiteness', *History Today*, 50 (12): 38–40.

Bonnett, A. (2000b) *White Identities: Historical and International Perspectives*. Harlow: Prentice Hall.

Bonnett, A. and Nayak, A. (2003) 'Cultural geographies of racialization: the territory of race', in K. Anderson, M. Domosh, S. Pile and N. Thrift (eds), *Handbook of Cultural Geography*. London: Sage. pp. 300–12.

Bowlby, S., Foord, J. and Mackenzie, S. (1982) 'Feminism and geography', *Area*, 14: 19–25.

Breughel, I. (1973) 'Cities, women and social class: a comment', *Antipode*, 5 (3): 62–3.

Britton, C. (1999) *Edouard Glissant and Postcolonial Theory: Strategies of Language and Resistance*. Charlottestown: University Press of Virginia.

Brown, M. (2000) *Closet Space: Geographies of Metaphor from the Body to the Globe*. London: Routledge.

Brown, M. and Knopp, L. (2003) 'Queer cultural geographies: we're here! We're queer! We're over there, too!', in K. Anderson, M. Domosh, S. Pile and N. Thrift (eds), *Handbook of Cultural Geography*. London: Sage. pp. 313–24.

Brydon, L. and Chant, S. (eds) (1989) *Women in the Third World: Gender Issues in Rural and Urban Areas*. London: Edward Elgar.

Bunge, W. Jr. (1971) *Fitzgerald: Geography of a Revolution*. Cambridge, UK: Cambridge University Press.

Burnett, P. (1973) 'Social change, the status of women and models of city form and development', *Antipode*, 5 (3): 57–62.

Butler, J. (1990) *Gender Trouble: Feminism and the Subversion of Identity*. New York and London: Routledge.

Combahee River Collective (1977) 'A black feminist statement', reprinted in Linda Nicolson (ed.) (1997), *The Second Wave: A Reader in Feminist Theory*. New York: Routledge.

Caris, S. (1978) 'Geographic perspectives on women: a review', *Transition: Quarterly Journal of the Socially and Ecologically Responsible Geographers,* 8 (1): 10–14.

Castree, N. and Nash, C. (2006) 'Editorial: posthuman geographies', *Social and Cultural Geography,* 7 (4): 501–04.

Chakrabarty, D. (2000) *Provincializing Europe: Postcolonial Thought and Historical Difference*. Princeton: Princeton University Press.

Chouinard, V. (1999) 'Body politics: disabled women's activism in Canada and beyond', in R. Butler and H. Parr (eds), *Mind and Body Spaces: Geographies of Illness, Impairment and Disability.* London: Routledge. pp. 269–94.

Colls, R. (2006) 'Outsize/outside: bodily bignesses and the emotional experiences of British women shopping for clothes', *Gender, Place and Culture,* 13 (5): 529–45.

Colls, R. and Evans, B. (2008) 'Embodying responsibility: children's health and supermarket initiatives', *Environment and Planning A.* 40 (3): 615–31.

Costello, L. and Duncan, D. (2006) 'The "evidence" of sex, the "truth" of gender: shaping children's bodies', *Children's Geographies,* 4: 157–72.

Cresswell, T. (1996) *In Place/Out of Place: Geography, Ideology and Transgression.* Minneapolis: University of Minnesota Press.

Cronon, W. (ed.) (1995) *Uncommon Ground: Toward Reinventing Nature.* New York: W.W. Norton.

Darden, J. (1988) 'Blacks and other racial minorities: the significance of colour in inequality', *Conference on Comparative Ethnicity: The Conference Papers, June 1988.* California: University of Los Angeles.

Dash, J.M. (1995) *Edouard Glissant.* Cambridge: Cambridge University Press.

Delaney, D. (1998) *Race, Place, and the Law, 1836–1948.* Austin: University of Texas Press.

Deleuze, G. and Guattari, F. (1988) *A Thousand Plateaus: Capitalism and Schizophrenia,* trans. B. Massumi. London: Athlone.

Doan, P. (2007) 'Queers in the American city: transgendered perceptions of urban space', *Gender, Place and Culture,* 14 (1): 57–74.

Dussel, E. (1995) *The Invention of the Americas: Eclipse of 'the Other' and the Myth of Modernity,* trans. Michael D. Barber. New York: Continuum.

Dwyer, C. (1998) 'Contested identities: challenging dominant representations of young British Muslim women', in T. Skelton and G. Valentine (eds), *Cool Places: Geographies of Youth Cultures.* London and New York: Routledge. pp. 50–65.

Dwyer, C. (1999) 'Veiled meanings: young British Muslim women and the negotiation of differences', *Gender, Place and Culture,* 6 (1): 5–26.

Dwyer, Owen J. (1997) 'Geograpical research about African Americans: a survey of journals, 1911–1995'. *Professional Geographer,* 49 (4): 441–51.

Dwyer, O. and Jones III, J.P. (2000) 'White socio-spatial epistemology', *Social and Cultural Geography,* 1 (2): 209–22.

Elder, G., Knopp, L. and Nast, H. (2003) 'Sexuality and space' in G. Gaile and C. Willmot (eds), *Geography in America at the Dawn of the 21st Century.* Oxford: Oxford University Press. pp. 200–08.

Fitzsimmons, M. and Goodman, D. (1998) 'Incorporating nature: environmental narratives and the reproduction of food', in

B. Braun and N. Castree (eds), *Remaking Reality: Nature at the Millennium*. London: Routledge. pp. 194–220.

Flusty, S. (2004) *De-Coca-Colonization: Making the Globe from the Inside Out*. New York: Routledge.

Foord, J. and Gregson, N. (1986) 'Patriarchy: towards a reconceptualization', *Antipode*, 18 (2): 186–211.

Fraser, N. (1997) *Justice Interruptus: Critical Reflections on the Post-Colonial Condition*. New York: Routledge.

Garcia-Ramon, M.D. and Monk, J. (2007) 'Feminist geographies around the world', *Belgeo*, 3.

Garcia-Ramon, M.D., Simonsen, K. and Vaiou, D. (2006) 'Guest editorial: does Anglophone hegemony permeate *Gender, Place and Culture?*', *Gender, Place and Culture*, 13 (1): 1–5.

Gibson-Graham, J.K. (1996) *The End of Capitalism (as we knew it): A Feminist Critique of Political Economy*. Cambridge: Blackwell.

Gier, J. and Walton, J. (1987) 'Some problems with reconceptualizing patriarchy', *Antipode*, 19 (1): 54–8.

Gilmore, R.W. (2007) *Golden Gulag: Prisons, Surplus, Crisis and Opposition in Globalizing California*. Berkeley: University of California Press.

Gilroy, P. (1993) *The Black Atlantic: Modernity and Double Consciousness*. London: Verso.

Gilroy, P. (2000) *Against Race: Imagining Political Culture Beyond the Colour Line*. Cambridge: Harvard University Press.

Glissant, E. (1989) *Caribbean Discourse: Selected Essays*, trans. J.M. Dash. Charlottesville: Caraf Books/University Press of Virginia.

Gregson, N. (2003) 'Reclaiming "the social" in social and cultural geography', in K. Anderson, M. Domosh, S. Pile and N. Thrift (eds), *Handbook of Cultural Geography*. London: Sage. pp. 43–57.

Haraway, D. (1997) *Modest_Witness @ Second_Millenium: FemaleMan©_Meets_ Oncomouse™*. London: Routledge.

Harvey, D. (1972) 'Revolutionary and counter revolutionary theory in geography and the problem of ghetto formation', *Antipode*, 4 (2): 1–13.

Harvey, D. (1989) *The Condition of Postmodernity*. Oxford: Blackwell.

Harvey, D. (2000) *Spaces of Hope*. Oxford: Blackwell.

Hill Collins, P. (1990) *Black Feminist Thought: Knowledge, Consciousness, and the Politics of Empowerment*. Boston: Unwin Hyman.

Holloway, S. and Wyly, E. (2002) 'The disappearance of race in mortgage lending,' *Economic Geography*, 78 (2): 129–69.

hooks, B. (2006) *Homegrown: Engaged Cultural Criticism*. Cambridge, MA: South End Press.

Hopkins, Peter E. (2007) 'Young people, masculinities, religion and race: new social geographies', *Progress in Human Geography*, 31 (2), 163–77.

Howitt, R. and Suchet-Pearson, S. (2003) 'Contested cultural landscapes', in K. Anderson, M. Domosh, S. Pile and N. Thrift (eds), *Handbook of Cultural Geography*. London: Sage. pp. 557–69.

Ingram, G.B., Bouthillette, A.M. and Retter, Y. (eds) (1997) *Queers in Space: Communities, Public Spaces and Sites of Resistance*. Seattle: Bay Press.

Jackson, P. (1991) 'The cultural politics of masculinity: towards a social geography', *Transactions of the Institute of British Geographers*, 16 (2): 199–213.

Jackson, P. (2003) 'Introduction', in K. Anderson, M. Domosh, S. Pile and N. Thrift (eds), *Handbook of Cultural Geography*. London: Sage. pp. 37–42.

Jackson, P. and Smith, S.J. (eds) (1981) 'Introduction', in *Social Interaction and Ethnic Segregation*. Institute of British Geographers Special Publication 12. London: Academic.

Johnson, L. (1987) '(Un)Realist perspectives: patriarchy and feminist challenges in geography', *Antipode*, 19 (2): 210–15.

Johnston, L. and Longhurst, R. (2008) 'Queer(ing) geographies "down under": some notes on sexuality and space in Australasia', *Australian Geographer*, 39 (3): 247–57.

Kaika, M. and Syngedouw, E. (2000) 'Fetishizing the modern city: the phantasmagoria of urban technological networks', *International Journal of Urban and Regional Research*, 24 (1): 120–38.

Katz, C. (2004) *Growing up Global: Economic Restructuring and Children's Everyday Lives*. Minneapolis, MN: University of Minnesota Press.

Ketteringham, W. (1979) 'Gay public space and the urban landscape', paper presented at the Annual Meeting of the Association of American Geographers.

Knopp, L. (2007) 'On the relationship between queer and feminist geographies', *The Professional Geographer,* 59 (1): 47–55.

Kobayashi, A. (2003) 'The construction of geographical knowledge: racialization, spatialization', in K. Anderson, M. Domosh, S. Pile and N. Thrift (eds), *Handbook of Cultural Geography.* London: Sage. pp. 544–56.

Kobayashi, A. and Peake, L. (2007) 'Racism in place: another look at shock, horror and racialization', in P. Moss and K. Falconer Al-Hindi (eds), *Feminisms in Geography: Rethinking space, place and knowledges.* Lanham, MD: Rowman and Littlefield. pp. 171–78.

Lauria, M. and Knopp, L. (1985) 'Towards an analysis of the role of gay communities in the urban renaissance', *Urban Geography,* 6 (2): 152–69.

Laurie, N., Dwyer, C., Holloway, S. and Smith, F. (eds) (1999) *Geographies of New Femininities.* London: Longman.

Ley, D. (1974) *The Black Inner City as Frontier Outpost: Images and Behaviour of a Philadelphia Neighborhood.* Washington, DC: Association of American Geographers.

Little, J., Peake, L. and Richardson, P. (eds) (1988) *Women in Cities: Gender and the Urban Environment.* Basingstoke: Macmillan.

Longhurst, R. (2001) *Bodies: Exploring Fluid Boundaries.* London: Routledge.

Longhurst, R. (2007) *Maternities: Gender, Bodies, Space.* London and New York: Routledge.

McDowell, L. (1986) 'Beyond patriarchy: a class-based explanation of women's subordination', *Antipode,* 18 (3): 311–21.

McDowell, L. (1991) 'Deconstruction and feminist theory in geography', *Geoforum,* 22 (2): 123–33.

McDowell, L. (1993a) 'Space, place and gender relations: 1, feminist empiricism and the goegraphy of social relations', *Progress in Human Geography,* 17 (2): 157–79.

McDowell, L. (1993b) 'Space, place and gender relations: 2, identity, difference, feminist geometries and geographies', *Progress in Human Geography,* 17 (3): 305–18.

McDowell, L. (2006) 'Reconfigurations of gender and class relations: class differences, class condescension and the changing place of class relations', *Antipode,* 38 (4): 825–50.

McDowell, L. and Court, G. (1994) 'Performing work: bodily representations in merchant banks', *Environment and Planning D: Society and Space,* 12: 727–50.

Mackenzie, S. (1980) 'Women's place–women's space', *Area,* 12: 47–49.

Mackenzie, S. (1984) 'Editorial introduction', *Antipode,* 16 (3): 3-10.

McKittrick, K. (2006) *Demonic Grounds: Black Women and the Cartographies of Struggle.* Minneapolis, MN: Minnesota Press.

McKittrick, K. and Peake, L. (2005) 'What difference does "difference" mean to geography?', in N. Castree, A. Rogers and D. Sherman (eds), *Questioning Geography: Essays on a Contested Discipline.* Oxford: Blackwell. pp. 39–54.

McKittrick, K. and Woods, C. (eds) (2007) *Black Geographies and the Politics of Place.* Toronto: Between the Lines and Cambridge, MA: South End Press.

McNee, B. (1984) 'If you are squeamish…', *East Lakes Geographer,* 19: 16–27.

Marston, S. (2000) 'The social construction of scale', *Progress in Human Geography,* 24 (2): 219–42.

Marston, S., Jones III, J.P. and Woodward, K. (2005) 'Human geography without scale', *Transactions of the Institute of British Geographers,* 30: 416–32.

Massey, D. (1991) 'Flexible Sexism', *Environment and Planning D: Society and Space,* 9: 31–57.

Mazey, E. and Lee, D. (1983) *Her Space, Her Place: A Geography of Women.* Washington, DC.: Association of American Geographers.

Mensah, J. (2002) *Black Canadians: History, Experiences, Social Conditions.* Halifax: Fernwood.

Miller, D. (1994) *Modernity, an Ethnographic Approach: Dualism and Mass Consumption in Trinidad.* Oxford: Berg.

Mitchell, A. (2006) *Corporeographies of Size: Fat Women in Urban Space.* PhD Dissertation, York University, Toronto.

Mitchell, K. (2006) 'Geographies of identity: the new exceptionalism', *Progress in Human Geography,* 30 (1): 95–106.

Mohammad, R. (2001) '"Insiders" and/or "outsiders": positionality, theory and praxis', in M. Limb and C. Dwyer (eds), *Qualitative Methodologies for Geographers: Issues and Debates.* London: Edward Arnold. pp. 101–20.

Momsen, J. and Townsend, J. (eds) (1987) *Geography of Gender in the Third World.* London: Hutchinson.

Moss, P. and Dyck, I. (1999) 'Body, corporeal space and legitimating chronic illness: women diagnosed with ME', *Antipode,* 31 (4): 372–97.

Moss, P. and Dyck, I. (2003) 'Embodying social geography', in K. Anderson, M. Domosh, S. Pile and N. Thrift (eds), *Handbook of Cultural Geography.* London: Sage. pp. 58–73.

Nast, H. (2004) 'Queer patriarchies, queer racisms, international', *Antipode,* 34 (5): 874–909.

Natter, W. and Jones III, J.P. (1997) 'Identity, space, and other uncertainties', in G. Benko and U. Strohmayer (eds), *Space and Social Theory. Interpreting Modernity and Postmodernity.* Oxford: Blackwell. pp. 141–61.

Oswin, Natalie (2007) 'The end of queer as we knew it: globalization and the making of a gay friendly South Africa', *Gender, Place and Culture,* 14 (1): 93–110.

Oswin, N. (2008) 'Critical geographies and the uses of sexuality: deconstructing queer space', *Progress in Human Geography,* 32: 89–103.

Peach, C. (1975) *Urban Social Segregation.* London: Longman.

Peake, L. (1993) '"Race" and sexuality: challenging the patriarchal structuring of urban social space?', *Environment and Planning: Society and Space D*, 11: 415–32.

Peake, L. (2009) 'Whiteness', in R. Kitchin and N. Thrift (eds), *The International Encyclopedia of Human Geography.* London: Elsevier.

Peake, L. and Ray, B. (2001) 'Racializing the Canadian landscape: whiteness, uneven geographies, and social justice', *The Canadian Geographer,* 45 (1): 180–86.

Peake, L. and Trotz, A. (1999) *Gender, Ethnicity and Place: Women and Identity in Guyana.* London: Routledge.

Phillips, D. (2006) 'Parallel lives? Challenging discourses of British Muslim self-segregation', *Environment and Planning D: Society and Space,* 24 (1): 25–40.

Phillips, R., Watt, D. and Shuttleton, D. (2000) *De-centring Sexualities: Politics and Representations Beyond the Metropolis.* London: Routledge.

Philo, C. and Wilbert, C. (2000) *Animal Spaces, Beastly Places: New Geographies of Human–Animal Relations*. London: Routledge.

Pratt, G. (2005) 'Abandoned women and spaces of the exception', *Antipode,* 37 (5): 1052–78.

Pred, A. (1998) 'The nature of de-naturalized consumption', in B. Braun and N. Castree (eds), *Remaking Reality: Nature at the Millenium.* London: Routledge. pp. 150–68.

Puar, J. (2006) 'Mapping US homonormativities', *Gender, Place and Culture,* 13 (1): 67–88.

Pulido, L. (2002) 'Reflections on a white discipline', *The Professional Geographer,* 54: 42–9.

Radcliffe, S. (1993) 'Women's place/el lugar de las mujeres: Latin America and the politics of gender identity', in M. Keith and S. Pile (eds), *Place and the Politics of Identity.* New York: Routledge. pp. 102–16.

Radcliffe, S. (1999) 'Embodying national identities: Mestizo men and White women in Ecuadorian racial-national imaginaries', *Transactions of the Institute of British Geographers,* 24: 213–25.

Radcliffe, S. (2006) 'Development and geography: gendered subjects in development processes and interventions', *Progress in Human Geography,* 30 (4): 524–32.

Richardson, D. (2007) 'Patterned fluidities: (re) imagining the relationship between gender and sexuality', *Sociology,* 41 (3): 457–74.

Robinson, J. (2003) 'Introduction', in K. Anderson, M. Domosh, S. Pile and N. Thrift (eds), *Handbook of Cultural Geography.* London: Sage. pp. 399–404.

Rose, G. (1996) 'As if the mirrors had bled: masculine dwelling, masculinist theory and feminist masquerade', in N. Duncan (ed.), *BodySpace: Destabilizing Geographies of Gender and Sexuality.* London: Routledge.

Rose, H.M. (1970) 'The development of an urban subsystem: the case of the Negro ghetto', *Annals of the Association of American Geographers,* 60: 1–17.

Rose, N. (1999) *The Powers of Freedom.* Cambridge, UK: Cambridge University Press.

Rothenberg, T.Y. (1995) '"And she told two friends": lesbians creating urban social space', in D. Bell and G. Valentine (eds), *Mapping Desire: Geographies of Sexuality*. London: Routledge. pp. 165–81.

Rubin, B. (1979) 'Women in geography revisited: present status, new options', *The Professional Geographer,* 31 (2): 125–34.

Said, E. (1993) *Culture and Imperialism*. London: Chatto and Windus.

Saldanha, A. (2006) 'Reontologizing race: the machinic geography of phenotype', *Environment and Planning D: Society and Space,* 24: 9–24.

Sanchez, L. (2004) 'The global e-rotic subject, the ban, and the prostitute-free zone: sex work and the theory of differential exclusion', *Environment and Planning D: Society and Space,* 22: 861–83.

Schein, R. (ed) (2006) *Landscapes of Race in the United States*. New York: Routledge.

Secor, A. (2002) 'The veil and urban space in Istanbul: women's dress, mobility and Islamic knowledge', *Gender, Place and Culture,* 9 (1): 5–22.

Secor, A. (2006) '"An unrecognizable condition has arrived": law, violence, and the state of exception in Turkey', in D. Gregory and A. Pred (eds), *Spaces of Political Violence*. London and New York: Routledge.

Shillington, Laura (2007) *Complex Ecologies and Cityspaces: Social–ecological Networks in Urban Agriculture, Managua, Nicaragua*. PhD Dissertation, York University, Toronto.

Slater, David (2003) 'Beyond Euro-Americanism: democracy and post-colonialism', in K. Anderson, M. Domosh, S. Pile and N. Thrift (eds), *Handbook of Cultural Geography*. London: Sage. pp. 420–32.

Smith, D. (1974) 'Geography, racial inequality and affirmative action', *Antipode,* 6 (2): 34–41.

Smith, N. (2000a) 'Scale', in R.J. Johnston et al. (eds), *The Dictionary of Human Geography* (fourth edition). Cambridge, MA: Blackwell, pp. 724–7.

Smith, N. (2000b) 'Socializing culture, radicalizing the social', *Social and Cultural Geography,* 1: 25–28.

Thrift, N. (1996) *Spatial Formations*. Thousand Oaks, CA: Sage.

Thrift, N. (2003) 'Space: the fundamental stuff of human geography', in S. Holloway, S. Rice and G. Valentine (eds), *Key Concepts in Geography*. London: Sage. pp. 95–108.

Tivers, J. (1978) 'How the other half lives: the geographical study of women', *Area,* 10: 302–6.

Trewartha, G. (1926) 'Recent thoughts on the problem of white acclimatization in the wet tropics', *Geographical Review,* 16: 467–78.

Valentine, G. (1993a) 'Desperately seeking Susan: a geography of lesbian friendships', *Area*, 25: 109–16.

Valentine, G. (1993b) '(Hetero)Sexing space: lesbian perceptions and experiences of everyday spaces', *Environment and Planning D: Society and Space,* 11 (4): 395–413.

Valentine, G. (1993c) 'Negotiating and managing multiple sexual identities: lesbian time–space strategies', *Transactions of the Institute of British Geographers,* 18 (2): 237–48.

Valentine, G. (2007) 'Theorizing and researching intersectionality: a challenge for feminist geography', *The Professional Geographer,* 59 (1): 10–21.

Vanderbeck, R. (2006) 'Vermont and the imaginative geographies of American Whiteness', *Annals of the Association of American Geographers,* 96 (3): 641–59.

Wekerle, G. (1984) 'A woman's place is in the city', *Antipode,* 16 (3): 11–20.

Whatmore, S. (2002) *Hybrid Geographies: Natures, Cultures, Spaces*. London: Sage.

Williams, B. (1991) *Stains on my Name, War in my Veins: Guyana and the Politics of Cultural Struggle*. Durham, NC: Duke University Press.

Williams, B. (1996a) 'Introduction: mannish women and gender after the act', in B. Williams (ed.), *Women out of Place: the Gender of Agency and the Race of Nationality*. London: Routledge.

Williams, B. (1996b) 'A race of men, a class of women: nation, ethnicity, gender, and domesticity among Afro-Guyanese', in B. Williams (ed.), *Women out of Place: the Gender of Agency and the Race of Nationality*. London: Routledge.

Wincapaw, C. (2000) 'The virtual spaces of lesbian and bisexual women's electronic mailing lists', *Journal of Lesbian Studies,* 4: 45–59.

Winders, J., Jones, J.P. and Higgins, M.J. (2005) 'Making Güueras: selling white identities on late night Mexican television', *Gender, Place and Culture,* 12 (1): 71–93.

Winters, C. (1979) 'The social identity of evolving neighborhoods', *Landscape,* 23: 8–14.

Wolch, J. and Emel, J. (eds) (1998) *Animal Geographies: Place, Politics and Identity in the Nature–Culture Borderlands.* London: Verso.

Women and Geography Study Group, Institute of British Geographers (IBG) (1981) *Perspectives on Feminism and Geography.* Papers presented at a meeting of the IBG, Reading University, 26 September.

Women and Geography Study Group, IBG (1983) *Meeting of the Minds?: Feminism and Modes of Geographic Thought.* Papers presented at a meeting of the IBG, Reading University, 14 May.

Women and Geography Study Group, IBG (1984) *Geography and Gender: An Introduction to Feminist Geography.* London: Hutchinson.

Woodruff, C. (1905) *The Effects of Tropical Light on White Men.* New York: Reman.

Woods, C. (1998) *Development Arrested: Regional Planning in the Mississippi Delta.* New York: Verso.

Yeung, H.W.C. (2001) 'Redressing the geographical bias in social science knowledge', *Environment and Planning A,* 33 (1): 2–9.

Zelinsky, W. (1973) 'The strange case of the missing female geographer', *The Professional Geographer,* 25 (2): 101–05.

2

Social Geographies of Age and Ageism

Rachel Pain and Peter Hopkins

INTRODUCTION: GEOGRAPHIES OF AGE

Age occupies an uneasy position alongside other markers of difference. It is at once a very obvious source of difference between people and their geographies, given the age-related rights, responsibilities and roles that – though their form varies – mark every culture around the world. It is also a source of commonality as well as divergence: almost all of us can expect to move from childhood, through adolescence and early adulthood into middle and old age.[1] In terms of everyday geographies, age provides both the least segregation (as people of all ages mix together in families and certain public spaces) and the most visible and pervasive segregation (in terms of who occupies which space and what it is acceptable for them to do there). Yet age is mundane. For the most part, it does not engender impassioned enthusiasm among geographers seeking to understand and explore the complexity of the social world. This ambivalence mirrors attitudes in Western societies more generally, where issues around age discrimination do not generally provoke the same outrage as those of race or disability. And while there is talk of intersectionality being increasingly important in discussions of identity, social scientists seem much quicker to scrutinise and prioritise *other* markers of difference than to interrogate the multiple effects of age. In short, while it is routinely added to identity checklists alongside gender, race, class and disability as traditional foci of interest in difference, there has been surprisingly little curiosity about *age* amongst social geographers. This chapter investigates why this is, and forwards an alternative agenda in which geographies of age become a central concern.

All this is not to say that the geographies of *particular* ages or age groups have not been the subject of considerable focus. In particular, there has been an explosion of research into the geographies of childhood in recent years, moving rapidly from a position in the early 1990s where children were described as marginalised within the discipline

(James, 1990), to forming a solid sub-disciplinary area with its own journal, research groups, conferences, and debates over theories and methods (e.g. Aitken, 2001; Holloway and Valentine, 2000b; Skelton and Valentine, 1998; Vanderbeck, 2008). We are not questioning this focus in itself, which was long overdue, and indeed we have both contributed to the body of knowledge on younger people's geographies ourselves (e.g. Hopkins, 2004; Pain, 2006). Our argument is that – paradoxically, when the very study of children and younger people is one demarcated by age – this attention does not always encompass issues *of age*. What we mean by this is that despite the dominant social constructivist perspective of such work, it quite rarely rejects the category it works within. Further, although there is much work about children, and a little less about younger people, geographies of people in other age groups are scarce. Studies of old age in social geography are present, but nowhere near as fashionable as work on childhood, and have a tendency to be conceptually and methodologically mundane, preoccupied with old age as a social problem rather than a problematised identity. This is despite the contradictory propensity for ideas about space and place to be well established in those other disciplines that have an interest in gerontology (Andrews et al., 2007). The literatures on early adulthood and middle age, meanwhile, are almost completely absent (Biggs, 2007; Maxey, 2009): at these times of life, age appears to become irrelevant. And there are very few examples of work that focuses on age in an holistic way, examining the ways in which it shapes all human social geographies materially, emotionally, discursively or relationally.

Why might this be? If we look at the various ways in which geographers have approached other issues of difference (many of which are represented elsewhere in this section), a pattern is clear: early research tended to focus on the non-hegemonic, the exotic, the 'other'. Research on gender in geography before the 1990s largely concerned women as its subject (Women and Geography Study Group, 1997), work on sexuality focused on sexualities at the margins rather than heterosexualities (Hubbard, 2000), and, as Alastair Bonnett (1997: 194) observed a decade ago, there has been 'a perversely intense focus upon the marginal subject-groups constituted within the Western and imperial imagination. The White centre of that imagination has not been discussed'. Yet, when it comes to age, geographers still ignore the centre, focusing disproportionately on the social–chronological margins and rarely connecting them directly. Children, it seems from scanning recent geographical work, are far more fashionable, appealing and rewarding as research subjects. Pressing questions have been raised recently about the limited and consensual nature of children's geographies as a sub-discipline (Horton and Kraftl, 2006; Vanderbeck, 2008), and we have asked elsewhere why this intense fascination with mapping younger lives, this stark but rarely mentioned fetishisation of difference, is so extensive (Hopkins and Pain, 2007).

The problem is not that geographers have ignored the situated, fluid and contested nature of age. Some of the earliest geographical studies of childhood problematised the common association of qualities, capacities, roles and life experiences with fixed chronological age groups (James, 1990; Winchester, 1991). This conceptual mainstay has been developed over the last fifteen years in different fields (e.g. Katz, 1993; Panelli, 2002; Valentine, 1996). Critical geographies of older people's lives are far patchier, but here too 'old age' has been viewed as culturally variable and underpinned by a range of social and economic processes, lived experiences and spatial practices (e.g. Harper, 1997a; Harper and Laws, 1995; Laws, 1994; Mansvelt, 1997; Pain et al., 2000). The widely accepted basis for understanding age as fluid, connected and spatialised, then, is in place in social geographical scholarship.

But still, age has been given a fixity which belies the suggestion of cultural variance and fluidity. And beyond the academic arena, the focus on the very young and very old – but no one else – as *aged* holds currency too. (We mean this in the sense that black and ethnic minority groups are commonly perceived in Western societies to be *raced*, but white people are not – see Bonnett, 2000). We can see this in widespread discourses about older and younger people as well as in their material experiences, in policy responses, and in the ways they are drawn into wider moral and material panics about wealth, welfare and crime (Pain et al., 2001).

In this chapter, our aim is to develop and forward a more holistic and relational view of geographies of age. This reflects a significant recent shift among a small group of geographers (e.g. Hopkins and Pain, 2007; Kesby, 2007; Maxey, 2009; Pain et al., 2001; Rawlins, 2006; Vanderbeck, 2007) who have begun to identify the importance of the age relations between people in different 'age groups', explore points and spaces of similarity as well as difference between people of different ages, and discuss more explicitly the pervasive geographies of ageism, prejudice and inequality. Issues of justice are key to our analysis. We argue that, in the case of age, there are complex relations of power operating that – while they can be analysed in terms of age, and are often resisted and reworked – operate in different ways to produce and shore up difference, and often injustice, for some of the most marginalised people in Western societies.

First, we review four existing conceptual approaches to childhood and old age that can be identified between social geography and the wider social science literatures. These are: accepting age as a biological or chronological given; forwarding age as socially constructed; retheorising the body; and interrogating being/becoming. We then investigate the recent relational turn in more detail, promoting an holistic approach to 'age' in geography which counterposes the ghettoisation of work on childhood and old age. We identify three conceptual tools – intergenerationality, intersectionality and lifecourse – which enable these relational frameworks of age. Following this, we turn our attention to wider literatures where we suggest that the performance, messiness and 'queering' (Kesby, 2007) of age identities might potentially provide exciting lines of enquiry for geographical research. The expansion of analysis of age through a relational lens allows us to interrogate some of the changing geographies of age in the twenty-first century. We examine the core theme of ageism, arguing for a new approach to age that is beyond 'the social' if we are to appreciate in a more holistic way these changing geographies and unlock the potential of geographical research to tackle ageism. Here, we pay some attention to issues of method and epistemology, including consideration of the positionalities of geographers of age.

THINKING ABOUT LANDSCAPES OF AGE: FRAMEWORKS AND APPROACHES

In this section, we discuss some of the most popular conceptual frameworks through which social geographers have worked with 'age'. We draw examples from geographies of childhood and old age. Because the literature is largely restricted to these age groups at present, our consideration in this section is equally limited: but later in the paper we reflect on the geographies of other age groups. Although the separateness of analysis of children's and older people's lives in the social sciences is marked, there is cross-applicability between many approaches, as we discuss below. Further, while we waymark the development of these approaches over time, all are present too in recent work on the landscapes of age. Moreover, each set of understandings is politically constructed itself, containing assumptions about how we know about age which are products of particular times and spaces (see Peake, Chapter 1 of this volume). Many geographers, it seems, have unintentionally pursued concretising and delimiting understandings of 'older people' or 'children' through their focus. Paradoxically, this conflicts with what we are learning about the fluidity and relatedness of aged people's spatial lives.

Accepting age as a biological or chronological given

> The rise of scientific gerontology with its focus on the aged body and its discourses of senescence has been a key element in the constitution of old age in the modern period. It is through such expert systems of power-knowledge that the lives of older people have been regulated, ordered, known, and disciplined (Twigg, 2003: 65).

The earliest and most enduring approaches to geographical research on age rarely articulated what we label here as its conceptual basis. Early on, children and older people both constituted populations which had been largely ignored by geographers. In the 1970s, as social geography surged as a sub-discipline, it was older people who first became the subject of attention. A raft of studies involved tacit, though not necessarily explicit, acceptance that physiological, psychological or emotional limitations necessarily constrain the autonomy and opportunities of the very old, or else create the need for younger and middle-aged adults to control them (see Warnes, 1981, 1990). The effect has been that unequal patterns of life chances and conditions between age groups are naturalised and not questioned in the same way that geographers have since criticised analyses of differences of gender, race and (dis)ability. Roles, activities and differences determined by chronological age were not questioned.

For social geographical research, acceptance of this notion of age meant that age was taken as given and uncontested; research may have highlighted patterns of social life and especially its problems (for example, due to poorly planned environments or uneven service provision), but rarely challenged or disrupted notions about age or considered the possibility that it might be spatially constituted itself. The project of mapping difference is, of course, where many social geographies of identity began. It can, of course, be theoretically sophisticated and politically empowering (see Brown and Knopp, 2008), and from the late 1970s and early 1980s onwards radical work on social identities became identifiable in Anglo-American geography that raised awareness of the structural disadvantage of particular groups. However, with a very few exceptions (e.g. Bunge, 1973), work on age did not enjoy this radical critique. A wealth of empirical contributions about older and young people's lives has not necessarily formed or challenged age-neutral work. Indeed, this tendency is still identifiable, with the age range of research targets often stipulated as though this gives the reader more knowledge about them. In the meantime, however, shifts elsewhere in how children and older people are conceptualised have had more catalytic and profound effects on geographies of age.

Forwarding age as socially constructed

The geographies of both children and older people benefited from early humanistic work that, while they were quite isolated as bodies of scholarship, began to map out the relations between aged people and place in ways that forefronted the cultural sensitivity and diversity of age (e.g. Hart, 1979; Rowles, 1978). However, it was the growing popularity of social constructivism from the 1980s onwards that decisively disrupted biological or chronological accounts, offering a polar opposite way of conceptualising age. 'Social' age holds that it is beliefs and attitudes about age, expressed through legislature, cultural forms and behaviour, that construct identities and govern people's social and spatial lives (Bytheway, 1995). Various limits are imposed and reinscribed, such as beginning and ending education, getting married, undertaking family living arrangements, becoming criminally responsible and so on. Perhaps the most important of these is who is allowed to participate in the cash economy as a worker. It is the cultural specificity and geography of these limits that alerts us to their constructed nature. This shift from seeing age and lifecourse stages as socially constructed categories rather than independent variables means that space and place gain significance (Harper and Laws, 1995; Katz and Monk, 1993) – people have different access to and experiences of places on the grounds of their age, and spaces associated with certain age groups influence who uses them and how (Pain et al., 2001).

Early work on childhood as being socially constructed tended to situate children as passive in the face of social forces; for example, the socialisation thesis set out the ways in which children learn to be first children and then adults, their identities fluid but essentially shaped by others. More recently the onus has shifted to focusing on children's own agency and capacities to influence the socio-spatial world (Holloway and Valentine, 2000a, b). Such work arises from the new social studies of childhood, 'an ontological interrogation of terms such as child and childhood, highlighting the extent to which these terms are socially, culturally and politically constructed' (Maxey, 2009); arguably not so new, given earlier work such as Roger Hart's (1979). This work has shown that these 'natural' concepts vary widely over time and space, and asserts that children are competent social actors who exercise agency to change their environments and conditions.

For old age, there has been no cohesive interdisciplinary body of work. However, social gerontologists have forwarded social constructivist notions of old age, questioning the nature of 'old age' and even positioning it as a cultural artefact (e.g. Featherstone and Wernick, 1995). Others have placed emphasis on social discrimination and ageism as centrally important (Biggs, 1993; Bytheway, 1995; Cole, 1992). In time, more critical work on old age in human geography developed which took this body of scholarship on board, working through the ways in which spatial formations interplay with old-age identities (see Andrews and Phillips, 2005; Harper and Laws, 1995; Mansvelt, 1997; McHugh, 2003; Pain et al., 2000). The late Glenda Laws had significant influence in turning geographies of old age around; she contended that '*where* we are says a lot about who we are … aged identities are not only the product of particular spatialities but … they also constitute spaces and places' (Laws, 1997: 93), and her research provided some of the most engaging conceptual development and empirical support.

Within and across scales, cultural constructions of 'old age' and 'childhood' exist which are varied and contradictory (see Katz and Monk, 1993). For example, Valentine (1996) has discussed how parents simultaneously voice concerns about their own 'innocent' children's safety and the dangerous, 'out of control' children of other people. Kevin McHugh (2003) explores Cole's (1992) notion of bipolar ageism that older people are subject to: the pressures created by simultaneous and dualistic discourses of decline and elixir. Because of these variations, Bytheway (1995) has suggested that 'age' can be spoken about only in *relative* rather than *absolute* terms. Some suggest giving up the language of age altogether, as even to talk about older people and children is to identify them as groups with common experiences, and imply that these experiences are shaped by a 'master identity' of age.

Such perspectives on childhood and old age have a considerable amount in common. Both address groups occupying ends of the lifecourse, whose opportunities and geographies are profoundly shaped by their economic dependence and discourses around physical and social vulnerability (Pain et al., 2001). Both older people and children are subject to ageism, which constructs stereotypes, assumptions and 'aged' spaces and places. There is a tendency too in wider society (mirrored in academic work) for children and older people to be portrayed in terms of 'crises' that threaten the security or well-being of others. For at least a century, recurrent moral panics or crises have been constructed around youth subcultures, particularly those in which working-class boys are involved (Pearson, 1983). The most longstanding of these concerns is around crime and disorder, but younger people are frequently scapegoats for a range of problems including underage sex, alcohol and drug use, educational underachievement, unemployment, and simply their unwanted presence in public space. Most recently a spate of health concerns, especially obesity, have added to moral panics about childhood (Colls and Evans, 2008). Older people, too, are increasingly portrayed in terms of a 'crisis' in what Katz (1992) has called an alarmist demography. The ageing of Western populations is predominantly presented as a threat to the rest of society, posing financial burdens on the welfare state in the provision of pensions, health and social care for these growing proportions of older people, with growing intergenerational conflict forecast as a result. So the socially constructed and marginal positions of older and younger people are fundamentally linked; and yet, until very recently, this relationship has not been explicitly analysed in geography (Vanderbeck, 2007).

Retheorising the body

It is increasingly argued that to understand social identity we must comprehend the social and physical as intertwined; the body has re-emerged as an important site implicated in the constitution, living and reworking of identities. Like women, ethnic and sexual minorities, older people are embodied or defined by physical characteristics (Featherstone and Wernick, 1995). In particular, in Western societies, ageing bodies tend to be identified with physical and mental decline, closeness to death, economic and physical dependency and social isolation (Biggs, 1993; Bytheway, 1995; Featherstone and Wernick, 1995). Paradoxically, while social and geographical gerontology have reproduced assumptions about the biological fixedness of ageing, they have been very slow to tackle the ageing body explicitly (Twigg, 2003). Nonetheless, since the 1990s a small body of work has argued that the identities of old age available to older people are held to be fracturing and multiplying as a feature of postmodernity, and that age has performative aspects; through presenting and representing the body in certain ways, identities shift (Featherstone and Hepworth, 1989; Featherstone and Wernick, 1995). Other intersecting social identities, and particularly gender, affect the social and cultural constitution of the ageing body (Twigg, 2003). Sarah Harper has asserted both the role of space in these performances and the role of the ageing body in the peripheralisation of older people into discrete locations (Harper, 1997a). Drawing on the feminist work of Grosz (1993), the ageing body is inscribed with social and cultural messages through various processes of labelling and representation (Harper, 1997a, b; Laws, 1995). Harper (1997b: 183) suggests that notions about the physical body, especially its finality, have become replaced by the cultural notion of frailty; the idea that death and decline can be controlled, 'somehow transcended by science'. Thus old age is no longer seen as inevitable, but as a separate stage of life. For those older people who are not seen to deal successfully with this frailty, it serves to distance their ageing bodies and, as a consequence, to distance all 'older people' from other stages of life and the spaces associated with them. Building on this framework, Mowl et al. (2000) have argued that ageist discourses centred on the body affect older men's and women's use of the homespace and its meaning to them, while Laws (1994, 1995) and McHugh (2000, 2003) have interrogated how constructions of ageing bodies produce the spaces of segregated housing and retirement communities. Katz (2000) has suggested that bodily activity has become an overarching, unquestioned indicator of well-being in modern Western constructions of older age – a discourse of 'active' ageing which is reproduced in older people's own, highly spatialised, accounts (see Mowl et al., 2000).

The place of the body is also significant in research with children and younger people: the contested bodies of children and younger people are increasingly evident in the ways that youthful bodies are governed and controlled, and provided with access to particular locations, institutional contexts and social settings (Colls and Horschelmann, forthcoming; Gagen, 2000). Important work has offered a series of critiques of the ways in which children's bodies are being governed through health, well-being and anti-obesity discourses (Evans, 2006; Colls and Evans, 2008; Hopkins, 2008). Research on the social geographies of clubbing has shown how snap judgements about age made at the club door, based on appearance, have implications for younger people's experiences of a night out (Malbon, 2000). Hill et al. (2006) are amongst those who have challenged the stereotypical assumption that younger people are a threat when occupying the public spaces of the street, instead highlighting the corporeal strategy of hanging around with friends in order to protect themselves. Research with asylum-seeking younger people has also shown that, because their age is not always documented, some younger people have to endure age assessments in order to determine their placement in either children's or adults' services, which can have important consequences (Crawley, 2004; Hopkins and Hill, forthcoming).

Interrogating being/becoming: competency, agency and resistance

Interest has grown in the ways that people actively create and resist particular age identities through their use of space and place (see Pain et al., 2001; Valentine, 2004). Recent perspectives within children's geographies and the new social studies of childhood emphasise two key and related notions: first, that children are capable and competent social actors; and second, that children are 'beings' rather than in an incomplete process of 'becoming' adults (Qvortrup, 2005). Within the social geographies of childhood in recent years, much research has sought to support this notion of children as competent agents in their own lives and worlds, who should be recognised as such and offered greater equality of opportunity in wider society as well as through research.

Several geographers have recently asked questions about the pervasiveness (perhaps even hegemony) of this notion in what Vanderbeck (2008) considers the overly polite, consensual subdiscipline of children's geographies. He raises wider moral and philosophical questions about the lack of willingness to integrate considerations of parents' agency and control, and how this might be balanced with that of children. Elsewhere, he demonstrates the value of exploring the complex forms of agency over children's lives deployed by social welfare organisations (Vanderbeck, 2008). Ansell (2009) also critiques the 'liberal concept of agency' as construed in the new social studies of childhood literature, suggesting it has led to a diversion of attention away from other important issues of power that structure children's lives and spaces. She highlights recent work by Kesby et al. (2006) and Holt (2006), amongst others, who are suggesting reconceptualisations of agency. As Kesby et al. (2006) suggest, there is no reductionist choice between seeing children as social becomings and competent agents in their own right – instead, like adults, children can be seen as both at the same time.

Such debates about agency are clearly not just of theoretical interest. Vanderbeck (2008) outlines some of the pressing political questions and dilemmas that arise from different standpoints on agency. While the mainstreamed view of children's agency is by no means universal (Skelton, 2007), it has simultaneously seeped into policy-making across the world (see also Maxey, 2009). Skelton (2007) critically appraises the related and widespread assumption among children's geographers that one positive way of respecting and enabling children's agency is to provide greater opportunities for participation in formal decision-making structures (e.g. Hart, 1992; Matthews and Limb, 1999). Reflecting more general disillusionment among left scholars with participatory development (Cooke and Kothari, 2001), Skelton shows how children's 'participation' in decision-making can serve to disenchant and disenfranchise younger people. While the rhetoric of UNICEF is on children as the future, containing hopes, dreams and potential which they can realise through participation, Skelton notes that many children – especially the most vulnerable – want and need their present-day problems and issues to be addressed, and argues it is the responsibility of adults to do this.

In the literature on old age in human geography, there has not seemed the same urgency for asserting older people's agency, competency or resistance to ageist discourses (for an exception see Pain et al., 2000), or debates over what it means for them to be neoliberal subjects cast in particular changing social and economic reproductive forms. Instead, where agency and empowerment are discussed, it has tended to be an implicitly Anglo-American view where agency is equated with successful adaptation to the 'challenges' of ageing (Wray, 2004). Wray's work with older women from different cultural and ethnic backgrounds, exploring agency and empowerment, highlights the salience of context to their different readings; for example, the importance of spirituality and relational links with family and friends to older women as they pursue control over their lives. A small number of social gerontologists have also developed Foucauldian notions of power and governance in their work (e.g. Biggs and Powell, 2000; Tulle and Mooney, 2002), giving primary importance to the ways in which ageing processes become regulated by the state and cultural norms and how, in the face of this, older people conduct themselves and establish empowered (or disempowered) senses of self. For Tulle and Mooney (2002), resisting the older body is limited, as older people's strategies for resistance cannot avoid them engaging with – and having a sense of – themselves as old. Thus (and this is a proposition that has not been widely taken up) research on age might seek a more nuanced and theoretically informed understanding of agency and resistance that transgresses normative narratives of physical and social competence (after Tulle and Mooney, 2002).

In the same vein, compared with work on children, there have been far fewer calls for older people's participation in research in order to shape the agendas and influence the outcomes of social geographical research (for an exception see Ziegler, 2007), although in the voluntary sector this principle and the accompanying processes are well developed (e.g. HelpAge International, 2002). Moreover, there has been no questioning by social geographers of the forms of younger and middle-aged adults' agency, at least not through a lens of age. Other factors such as class, profession, geography, political position at different scales, gender, race and so on tend to be held as important in affecting the capital and power available to adults and the ways in which they deploy them. Equally, we would suggest, age *is* a key unspoken dimension to middle adults' relative experiences; and these intersections are essential in thinking not just about the potential for agency of people of any age, but whether and how they unlock and utilise it.

FOR RELATIONAL GEOGRAPHIES OF AGE

All these perspectives (above) are influential and important in enriching understanding, but there have been few crossovers between work on older people and children, or insight drawn from each other. Moreover, as we have noted, there is silence on the 'invisible middle years' (Maxey, 2009). In common with Larch Maxey, we have called for a relational approach to geographies of age (Hopkins and Pain, 2007) which might connect these various concerns of interdisciplinary work on children and older people, and extend these various themes and approaches to bring the experiences of those in between into a more holistic analysis. Here, we highlight and illustrate three concepts that can help in this project of scoping the wider landscapes of age, rather than merely charting the manifestations of spatial processes for particular groups: intergenerationality, intersectionality and lifecourse. Social geographers have recently begun to work with these concepts in their work on age; in enabling us to think about age relationally, they broaden the narrow focus of much research to date on the very young and very old.

Intergenerationality

In recent years there has been a growing focus on generations across the social sciences (Edmunds and Turner, 2002a, b). Generations, conceptualised as biological, psychological and/or historical/cultural phenomena (Biggs, 2007), are considered by some as being a more appropriate division than chronological age for defining and examining experiences at different life stages. Moreover, there is increasing interest in the relations between generational groups, or intergenerationality. Here, it is the interactions between generations – themselves products of particular times, spaces and cultures – that have significant effects on a whole range of social issues, from wealth to health, from public space to meanings of the home (see, for example, Antonucci et al., 2007; Costanzo and Hoy, 2007; Walker, 1996). Vanderbeck (2007) has argued for the centrality of intergenerational geographies: the many ways in which space facilitates or limits intergenerational contact, knowledge, conflict or cohesion (see also Pain, 2005).

For the social geographies of identity, an emphasis on intergenerationality suggests that individuals' and groups' sense of themselves and others is partly on the basis of generational difference or sameness. This entails more than, for example, acknowledging that what it is to be a child is affected by people of other age groups. It also suggests that identities of children and others are produced *through* interactions with other age/generational groups and are in a constant state of flux. Therefore, children and childhood interact with others in family and community settings and so are *more than* children alone; studying them in context adds new layers to understanding (Hopkins and Pain, 2007, 2008). Thus intergenerationality helps to dismantle rigid categories such as childhood and old age, exposing their porosity and cultural specificity while being open to the same critiques.

Geographers have begun to examine these at a range of scales and sites, from detailed local outcomes through to global processes. First, intergenerational relations are played out nationally: dire warnings about the impacts of global age profiles mean that the 'intergenerational contract' within nation states tends to be seen in very negative terms, although a critical literature is developing which contests this discourse (see Harper, 2005; S. Katz, 1992). Issues of social identity among and between generational groups at macro levels have also seen some critical attention outside of geography (e.g. Edmunds and Turner, 2002a, b; Kerns, 2003), including work on pensions and the 'cost' of different generations to others (Walker, 1996). Local cultural differences within their global contexts have proven of interest to geographers focusing on generational patterns and change over time (Chant and McIlwaine, 1998; C. Katz, 1993, 2004). A number of investigations into young people's use of urban spaces have raised, though not fully explored, issues of intergenerational conflict (Skelton, 2000; Matthews et al., 2000, Pain, 2003; Tucker, 2003). While there are differences and shifts in the nature of intergenerationality across these scales, it has tended to be constituted in terms of crisis, conflict and fearfulness, rather than ambivalence, cohesion or hope. Strangely, geographers have showed little interest in family relations (see Duncan and Smith, 2002), but examinations of intergenerational family practices have begun recently, for example on fathering (Aitken, 2000, 2005; Hopkins, 2006b), mothering (Holloway, 1998, 1999), and parents' and children's everyday practices in contesting the use of space (McKendrick, 1997; Valentine, 2004; Valentine and Holloway, 2001). Focusing on family consumption practices, Rawlins (2006) has shown the complex ways in which mothers influence their daughters' fashion choices in the home, school and community, while Valentine et al. (2008) have investigated the impacts of changing intergenerational relations on drinking practices. The emotional aspects of relationships between teenagers and their grandparents have been explored recently by Ross et al. (2005), while Mann (2007) sets out an agenda for research on grandfatherhood in the context of age and masculinity. Hopkins' (2006b) research on the relationships between young Muslim men and their parents identified respect for the hard-working nature of their parents' generation, and in so doing challenged the notion of generational conflict within ethnic minority communities. Young and Ansell's (2003) account of families affected by HIV/AIDS in southern Africa identifies the complexities of intergenerational relations when traditional family structures are disrupted.

The majority of this work has explored issues of intergenerational difference, transmission, continuity and change, sometimes obliquely. Taken together, it is clear that intergenerationality is a powerful mode of explanation to be considered alongside others, and there are many promising avenues for expanding conceptual and empirical work in social geography. Horton and Kraftl (2008) recently questioned exactly what work intergenerationality does: are generations more than another item on a checklist of social identities? There is indeed much work across the social sciences on intergenerationality which goes no further than description, but we have argued for the power of these relational aspects of people's lives in shaping material and discursive geographies at different scales (Hopkins and Pain, 2008).

Intersectionality

Our second suggestion for advancing relational understandings of age is that social geographers might make better use of the concept of intersectionality. Everything that we have said about intergenerationality above (and lifecourse below) is contingent upon context, and understanding the landscapes and lives of aged people must involve the range of other identities and processes including gender, race, ethnicity, sexuality, (dis)ability, religion and so on. Geographers have not always used intersectionality effectively, either focusing too narrowly on one particular identity 'box' or favouring a few over others (see Wray, 2003 on ethnicity, gender and age). In contrast, intersectionality is suggestive of 'the relationships among multiple dimensions and modailities of social relations and subject formations' (McCall, 2005: 1771). The term is normally credited to Crenshaw (1993), who employed intersectionality to analyse the various ways in which gender and race influence the multi-dimensional nature of Black women's employment experiences. As she observed, her intention was:

> to illustrate that many of the experiences Black women face are not subsumed within the traditional boundaries of race or gender discrimination as these boundaries are currently understood, and that the intersection of racism and sexism factors into Black women's lives in ways that cannot be captured wholly by looking at the race or gender dimensions of those experiences separately (Crenshaw, 1993: 1244).

Intersectionality has been pursued primarily by feminist social scientists who find the concept 'foregrounds a richer and more complex ontology than approaches that attempt to reduce people to one category at a time' and 'indicates that fruitful knowledge production must treat social positions as relational. ... [intersectionality] is thus useful as a handy catchall phrase that aims to make visible the multiple positioning that constitutes everyday life and the power relations that are central to it' (Phoenix and Pattynama, 2006: 87). The focus of an approach informed by intersectionality upon social relations, subject formations and power inequalities therefore lends itself to advancing understandings about social landscapes of age. A key issue for exploration here concerns the ways in which geographies, landscapes and experiences of age change, transform or remain the same as they intersect and interact with other markers of social and cultural difference, in different places and times. Furthermore, certain social identities and places may be transformed or may take on different meanings and associations as a result of assumptions made about the aged bodies occupying them.

For example, Dwyer's (1999) work has drawn attention to the ways in which religious, ethnic and gendered identities intersect with age in the experiences of young Muslim women in the West. She highlights the ways in which young women's everyday identities are influenced by ethnicised and religious discourses. Thomas (2005) explores how younger women reinscribe social differences of race and class through their use of public space. McDowell's (2003) research demonstrates how class, masculinity and place intersect with understandings of work to create particular experiences for working-class young men in the UK. Here, a series of intersectional influences on the young men – their performance of their masculine identities, their locality and class-based expectations and their familial experiences and outlooks – all combine to determine their employment prospects and future trajectories. Pain et al. (2000) have explored the ways in which old age intersects with other identities to shape older people's spatial experiences, for example how gender, class and ability inform constructions of bodies and homespaces as 'old' (Mowl et al., 2000).

Lifecourse

Thirdly, greater attention to lifecourses (rather than fixed life stages) is relevant to relational geographies of age. A lifecourse approach involves recognition that, rather than following fixed and predictable life stages, we live dynamic and varied lifecourses which have, themselves, differently situated meanings (Hopkins and Pain, 2007). As Hockey and James (2003: 5) describe it, the term lifecourse has 'been adopted as a way of envisaging the passage of a lifetime less as the mechanical turning of a wheel and more as the unpredictable flow of river'.

Research which has adopted this approach often draws on experiences across the lifecourse to make sense of current-day patterns and conditions, particularly for older people's lives. For example, while the geography of fear of crime is often measured through surveys that gather 'snapshot' data about people's present circumstances, it is often underlain by individuals' experiences much earlier in life, as well as changes over time to local environments and social structures (Pain, 1995). Much research has also focused upon times and spaces of transition, especially younger people's transitions to adulthood. This body of work has largely been concerned with education and the economy, focusing on the move from school to full-time permanent employment, the tensions and struggles associated with this transition, and the ways in which this lifecourse change has altered dramatically in nature over the last few decades (e.g. Jones, 2002; Bynner, 2001). An important contribution of social geography here has been the ways in which younger working-class men seek to maintain 'domestic conformity' and 'working class respectability' (McDowell, 2002: 115) whilst also managing their increasingly fragile transition into the adult labour market. Winchester et al. (1999)

carried out a study of 'Schoolies Week' on the Australian Gold Coast, a week that school leavers spend away from home and school which is often regarded as a rite of passage from youth to adulthood. Geography is significant, as the week occurs in a highly constrained period of space and time, and involves ritualised and transgressive bodily experiences. The spatial context is significant, as physical separation from their homes and places of the everyday allows these younger people to detach themselves and transform their identities into something new; younger people can do what they want without being accountable to parental or school supervision. It therefore represents an important rite of passage on their journey to adulthood.

There are many other transitions and lifecourse experiences that people face in their negotiations of everyday life, and these offer fruitful avenues for research on social geographies of age. Despite the fetishisation of childhood we have identified, transitions from nursery/kindergarten to primary/elementary school, primary/elementary to high school, and from school to college or university have received scant attention from geographers. A fifteen-year longitudinal study of school leavers' transitions to adulthood in Canada identified a range of influences, including social class, gender and external structures (Andres and Adamuti-Trache, 2008). And, as Peter Hopkins identifies,

> A young person's life course trajectory towards adulthood often involves negotiating a range of transitions: school to college/university to work; parental home to shared accommodation with peers to their own home; child of a family to partnership/cohabitation to partner with children; 'pocket money' income to part-time work/temporary income to full salary; and general economic dependence through semi-dependence to full independence (Jones, 2002: 2; see also Hill and Tisdall, 1997) (Hopkins, 2006a: 240–41).

Later lifecourse transitions tend to have been overlooked (Hopkins and Pain, 2007; though see Teather, 1999). Examples, which may provide rich seams of understanding into the use and meaning of everyday uses of space, senses of self and aged identities, include the transition to and meaning of 'middle age'; transitions to unemployment, redundancy or part-time work; the transition to becoming a parent; and the experience of children leaving home. Bytheway (2005) identifies a number of important transitions for older people, including grandparenthood, birthdays, adjusting to life on a pension, to life without a partner, to life in a smaller, more manageable home, or to receiving care services – times of change that bring societal ageism more clearly into focus.

Summary

So relationality does not just pose interesting questions about age, but marks a fundamental change in the way we approach and think about it. Fionagh Thomson (2007: 207–8) has recently critiqued the 'metanarrative of "children" that is based on the polarised, fixed and separated identities of child and adult'. Instead, she calls for 'hybrid, intersubjective theories of identity, that recognise the interplay between social structural influences and an individual's own agency/reflexivity'. We support this call for more sophisticated conceptual dealings with age among geographers. In particular, we suggest that if we think about and work with age as being produced in the interactions between different people – employing some of these ideas and themes around intergenerationality, intersectionality and lifecourse in support – then it becomes more difficult to continue to talk about the geographies of children, older people or anyone else in isolation.

EXPERIENCING LANDSCAPES OF AGE: SETTINGS, ENCOUNTERS AND PRACTICES

A relational approach to the study of age opens up for analysis a range of important subjects that have not to date received much attention from geographers. These include the settings and encounters of age identities, discourses and practices. Our aim is not to encourage age-neutral or 'ageless' accounts (see Andrews, 1999), but is rather to pursue a more holistic purchase on age: we feel that research that starts between or outside of the usual categories of old or young is likely to make the most radical leaps in understanding.

We make two suggestions for future social geographical work on age, building on our suggestions for relational geographies: firstly, the development of critical geographies of ageism in order to raise and contest issues of justice across the lifecourse; and secondly, more hybridised explorations of age identities that focus on those that appear fractured or dissident. We also track some recent innovations in methodological and epistemological approaches to geographies of age which can help to enable these kinds of enquiry.

Ageism and everyday life: equity and justice

Despite the explosion of interest in younger people in recent years and in their social and political status, geographers have been strangely quiet about ageism (see Maxey, 2009; Pain et al., 2001). If we view ageism as culturally prescribed sets of norms which may apply to people across the lifecourse, it then becomes clearly linked to the framework of relational age outlined above. Bill Bytheway, a social gerontologist, is one of the most radical writers on ageism (Bytheway, 1995, 2002, 2005). He employs an understanding of the lifecourse as composed of stages that may not have clear beginnings and ends, nor be experienced in the same ways by people sharing chronological age. Rather, different 'ages' such as childhood, middle age or older age are culturally constructed and articulated, and ageism may affect people at any stage. Such fluid constructions – and their potential implications for conceptualising and critiquing 'old age' – have been criticised by Andrews (1999) and Gibson (2000) for asserting 'agelessness': relegating or denying that older age is a bodily and materially separate stage of life. In rejoinder, Bytheway (2000) has denied that his conception of ageism involves agelessness, and has reasserted his original desire to see gerontologists question the label 'older age' far more. As Cole (1992) and Biggs (1993) outline, ageism may have diverse and contradictory forms, but to acknowledge that is not to lose sight of its fundamental relationship with power. Employing a Foucauldian understanding of power as complex, emergent and fluid (see Sharp et al., 2000) sits well with this assertion about age relations.

So ageism, perhaps more so than other forms of oppressive practice, cannot simply be described as being practised by one social group and suffered by another. Ageism constitutes a set of situated practices, in that it both marks space and comes into being in particular spaces (Pain et al., 2000). Practices which label, include and exclude may be exercised by and between older and younger people. Given that ageism, racism and sexism are mutually constructive, rather than separate, forms of oppression which interplay and intersect (Arber and Ginn, 1995; Dressel et al., 1997), ageism is best conceptualised as intergenerational, intersectional and as a phenomenon that occurs over the lifecourse: it is a situated discourse and material practice that is centrally important in forming and binding together the relational geographies of age.

To date, geographers' work on age has mostly involved either positivist studies of need and service provision (especially for older people) or cultural accounts which emphasise everyday experience and ideologies around certain age groups (especially younger people). Yet these geographies might be politicised, we would argue, rather more: the politics of age have been quiet compared to those of gender, race and sexuality amongst geographers interested in inequality and injustice (see for exceptions Ruddick, 2007; Ansell, 2009; Ansell and Smith, Chapter 15 of this volume). There are many live political issues with important policy ramifications surrounding ageism (see Maxey, 2009; Vanderbeck, 2008). Ageism is manifested in spatial segregation at different scales which are seldom questioned, such as formal age bars on spaces of work, education and leisure; in spaces of representation and communication such as the media and internet; in homespaces (family homes, care homes, sheltered housing and so on); through changing cultural traditions of social reproduction; and in public space, expressed through planning and behaviour. Kevin McHugh's work (2000, 2003) explores the importance of place in understanding images and scripts involved in discourses of 'successful ageing' and 'anti-ageing' which, he argues, have arisen in Western societies as alternatives to discourses of decline, but which are equally ageist. His work explores how these play out in the promotion of Sun Belt retirement communities in the USA (see also Laws, 1995).

Such explorations of ageism, its production and effect at different sites and scales, must situate social relations in particular spatial or historical contexts (see Laws, 1994). For example, Pain et al. (2000) draw contemporary changes such as the spatial and social restructuring of employment, shifts in social demography, and increased social and economic polarisation into their discussion of the changing meaning and experience of old age in north-east England. Such work might also view the various ways in which these processes are scaled, where scales are interconnecting and simultaneous. While we should be aware of the limits of too closely focused local work, as exists in profusion in children's geographies (Ansell, 2009), we should also bear in mind strategies for 'scale-jumping' to establish causality in the wider social and political spheres while remaining accountable to the ground (Cahill et al., 2007; Fine et al., 2007).

Fracturing, contesting and queering age identities

The longstanding project of including minority voices in social geography is not just about communicating and representing oppression, but about challenging oppression; presenting positive discourses, resistance and hopefulness (hooks, 1994; Thomson, 2007). So we should exercise caution over which categories and stereotypes we reproduce through our research. If age identities are made through space, then there are always opportunities for resisting and recasting them (Pain et al., 2000, 2001) and for considering how they change over time. Our argument here is that opening up more relational geographies of age supports ideas about multiple, fracturing and dissident age identities.

The postmodern turn of 1990s social science led to an interest in what appeared to be diversifying identities of old age available to older people (Featherstone and Hepworth, 1989). We would suggest that geographers are well placed to pursue analyses of the performance, messiness or 'queering' (Kesby, 2007) of age identities, to identify their spatial and temporal contextualisation, and to question their wider causation as well as their novelty in particular places and historical points. Meyrowitz's (1984) classic thesis on the role of television in blurring distinctions between adults and children has raised many other questions about the muddying of culturally prescribed roles and behaviours at different ages. Many of these issues have been ignored by geographers – for example, the idea of an emergent rather than sudden transition to adulthood, with a growing number of younger people in their twenties and thirties living at home with their parent(s) as a result of not being able to afford to buy a house, and the ways in which this influences their aged behaviours. This also applies to the infantilisation of adulthood in certain cultural spaces, and the implications of play and playfulness for adults as well as children. The growing and contested notion of lifelong education; the youthful retiree; the existence of child workers, child carers and child sex workers – all of these contain lines for research about the experiences of people who transgress traditional expectations associated with their aged identities, and offer much potential for invigorating geographies of age.

Geographical work which has a bearing on these questions to date includes work with unaccompanied asylum-seeking children in the UK who, due to a lack of certification associated with their age, may be regarded as adults and placed in adult services due to assumptions being made on the basis of their physical deportment, facial hair and general sense of maturity. They may also have taken on adult roles of work, care and decision-making from a younger age (Hopkins and Hill, 2006). Outside the West, children often take on household and family responsibilities from a younger age, and are often very competent at a variety of activities and tasks that children in the global North would not be accustomed to (Ansell, 2005). Such apparent breaks with standard ideas about childhood are often, of course, closely influenced by other norms such as those around gender roles. For example, in Western societies it is more important for women to resist the bodily manifestations of old age than men (Mowl et al., 2000), with the impetus to look and act young increasingly becoming a part of cultural codes that are always emplaced and embodied (McHugh, 2003). We might add to this focus on the body a call for emotional geographies of age that chime with the prominence that emotions are receiving elsewhere in the discipline (see Davidson et al., 2005; Koskela, this volume, Chapter 17; and Woodward and Lea, this volume, Chapter 6); see for example Grenier's (2006) work on women's emotions around being 'frail' in old age.

Moreover, there is increasingly room for people to 'play' with age, adopting social and sexual lifestyles and behaviours that would not have been acceptable a century ago (or at least, would not have been as public). Aside from this, we need to bear in mind the enduring effect of ageism, especially as it intersects with gender, poverty and race, on the availability of such breakout identities to the most marginalised people. Thus it is possible to see resisting or queering age as itself sometimes structured by forms of privilege. While the diversity and hybridity of age forms that are now apparent might seem to represent a kaleidoscopic fracturing of identities in a postmodern era, historical and geographical surveys of age identities are more likely to suggest that there is less linear change than interrupted continuity. Where age is changing, it is often one part of assemblages of wider change in economic and social geographies. There is a need to connect the economic and the social in constituting identity (see Smith et al., Introduction in this volume) – including, for social geographies of age, the effect of retirement, pensions and the changing welfare state not just in affecting life chances and living conditions for different ages, but in actively shaping aged identities and the ways in which people are able to respond to or resist them. Our suggestion is that these should be understood within a framework which privileges issues of justice and equity.

Researching landscapes of age

A number of methods are especially useful for drawing out the relational aspects of geographies of age. For example, oral histories enable a lifecourse perspective on ageing (Andrews et al., 2007), while Kesby (2007: 195) has written of the potential for creative, playful and childish methods to 'prove a powerful, if "queer" method for participants of all ages to research and re-imagine the worlds they inhabit'. Intergenerational practice, well established in the community development arena, provides an exciting approach for action research which draws together people of different ages to work with and through difference and similarity (Pain, 2005). Further, research that is participatory and seeks to co-produce knowledge – in sharing ownership of research questions, design, data collection, analysis and dissemination – can enrich scholarship with the ideas, priorities, perspectives, analyses and theories of people who are differently aged to ourselves (Hopkins and Pain, 2007).

Ageism in the way that geographers have tended to approach and represent children and older people in their research (see Pain, 1997; Sibley, 1991) is compounded by the selection of tightly bounded age groups for study (Bytheway, 2005; Grenier, 2006). This may result in the reproduction of norms and stereotypes about age, or it may produce age as important or primary when it is not (Thomson, 2007). Allowing respondents to self-select according to criteria other than biological or chronological age (e.g. Bytheway, 2005) might offer more relational and intersubjective analyses of issues of age. Researcher positionalities, while considered more recently in children's geographies (see the special issue edited by Kesby, 2007), have been downplayed in research with people in other age groups. Yet, critical debates around positionalities linked to the organisation of society by gender, class and race have been taken on board within social geography, but a wider consideration of how age plays into this is lacking. It may be that geographers' own age (as, predominantly, young or middle adults) partly explains their penchant for aged geographies only of 'others' (see related arguments in gerontology, for example Featherstone and Wernick, 1995). It is not a question of which of gender, class, race, nationality, age and so on have primacy in explaining the socio-spatial world; rather, the task is to draw out how they intersect in different ways in particular situations and contexts. As Grenier (2006) argues, age and generation are not always important in shaping social issues or the research experience, and drawing ideas about intersectionality into research practice can sensitise us (and our participants) to what it is that shapes our interactions.

CONCLUSION

We have argued for a relational approach to geographies of age that first connects, and might ultimately get beyond, current interest in childhood and old age. Intergenerationality, intersectionality and lifecourse are crucial concepts in forging these relational geographies. We have suggested that geographers might make useful contributions to changing identities of age, linking these to wider processes of social, economic and spatial change. At the same time, we have argued for greater emphasis on inequality, ageism and social justice, across the lifecourse and between scales, and have supported recent calls for studying the relation of detailed local outcomes to global processes. Ultimately, we need an approach that goes beyond 'the social' if we are to appreciate age in a more holistic way and use our research as a resource to chart and tackle ageism. Moving beyond the project of representing the voices of aged people at the two extremes of the lifecourse is well overdue; the challenge for developing more innovative and invigorated approaches to landscapes of age is to de-exoticise, de-fetishise and de-colonise research encounters, through reconstructing and working from categories that are meaningful to those involved.

NOTE

1 In this paper we use the terms childhood, youth, middle age (or early and middle adulthood) and old age as loose descriptors for life stages that are fluid rather than fixed. We use the terms older people, younger people, middle-aged (or younger and middle) adults, and children, to describe people generally recognised to share similarities at particular life stages. We use these terms to locate our arguments within existing scholarship and cultural discourses, but we recognise a need to improve on or even surpass them. When we refer to aged people we mean everyone.

REFERENCES

Aitken, S. (2000) 'Fathering and faltering: "Sorry, but you don't have the necessary accoutrements"', *Environment and Planning A*, 32: 581–98.

Aitken, S.C. (2001) *Geographies of Young People: the Morally Contested Spaces of Identity*. London: Routledge.

Aitken, S. (2005) 'The awkward spaces of fathering', in B. Van Hoven and K. Horschelmann (eds), *Spaces of Masculinities*. London: Routledge. pp. 222–36.

Andres, L. and Adamuti-Trache, A. (2008) 'Life-course transitions, social class, and gender: a 15-year perspective of the lived lives of Canadian young adults', *Journal of Youth Studies,* 11 (2): 115–45.

Andrews, G.J. and Phillips, D.R. (2005) *Ageing and Place: Perspectives, Policy, Practice*. London: Routledge.

Andrews, G.J., Cutchin, M., MacCracken, K., Phillips, D.R. and Wiles, J. (2007) 'Geographical gerontology: the constitution of a discipline', *Social Science and Medicine*, 65: 151–68.

Andrews, M. (1999) 'The seductiveness of agelessness', *Ageing and Society* 19 (3): 301–18.

Andrews et al. oral histories.

Ansell, N. (2005) *Children, Youth and Development.* London: Routledge.

Ansell, N. (2009) 'Childhood and the politics of scale: descaling children's geographies?', *Progress in Human Geography,* 33 (2): 190–209.

Antonucci, T.C., Jackson, J.S. and Biggs, S. (2007) 'Intergenerational relations: theory, research, and policy', *Journal of Social Issues*, 63 (4): 679–93.

Arber, S. and Ginn, J. (1995) *Connecting Gender and Ageing: A Sociological Approach*. Buckingham: Open University Press.

Biggs, S. (1993) *Understanding Ageing: Images, Attitudes and Professional Practice*. Buckingham: Open University Press.

Biggs, S. (2007) 'Thinking about generations: conceptual positions and policy implications', *Journal of Social Issues,* 63 (4): 695–711.

Biggs, S. and Powell, J.L. (2000) 'Surveillance and elder abuse: the rationalities and technologies of community care', *Journal of Contemporary Health*, 8 (2): 43–8.

Bonnett, A. (1997) 'Geography, 'race' and Whiteness: invisible traditions and current challenges', *Area*, 29: 193–9.

Bonnett, A. (2000) *White Identities*. Harlow: Prentice Hall.

Brown, M. and Knopp, L. (2008) 'Queering the map: the productive tensions of colliding epistemologies', *Annals of the Association of American Geographers*, 98 (1): 40–58.

Bunge, W. (1973) 'The point of reproduction: a second front', *Antipode,* 9: 60–76.

Bynner, J. (2001) 'British youth transitions in comparative perspective', *Journal of Youth Studies,* 4: 5–23.

Bytheway, B. (1995) *Ageism*. Buckingham: Open University Press.

Bytheway, B. (2000) 'Youthfulness and agelessness: a comment', *Ageing and Society*, 20 (6): 781–789.

Bytheway, B. (2002) 'Positioning gerontology in an ageist world', in L. Andersson (ed.), *Cultural Gerontology*. Greenwood Publishing Group. pp. 59–76.

Bytheway, B. (2005) 'Ageism and age categorization', *Journal of Social Issues*, 61 (2): 361–74.

Cahill, C. Sultana, F. and Pain, R. (2007) 'Participatory ethics: politics, practices, institutions', *ACME: an International E-Journal for Critical Geographies*, 6 (3): 304–18.

Chant, S. and McIlwaine, C. (1998) *Three Generations, Two Genders, One World: Women and Men in a Changing Century*. London: Zed Books.

Cole, T.R. (1992) *The Journey of Life: a Cultural History of Ageing in America*. Cambridge: Cambridge University Press.

Colls, R. and Evans, B. (2008) 'Embodying responsibility: children's health and supermarket initiatives', *Environment and Planning A*, 40 (3): 615–31.

Colls, R. and Horschelmann, K. (forthcoming) *Contested Bodies of Childhood and Youth.* London: Palgrave.

Cooke, B. and Kothari, U. (eds) (2001) *Participation the New Tyranny?* London: Zed Books.

Costanzo, P.R. and Hoy, M.B. (2007) 'Intergenerational relations: themes, prospects and possibilities', *Journal of Social Issues*, 63 (4): 885–902.

Crawley, H. (2004) *Working with Children and Young People subject to Immigration Control: Guidelines for Best Practice*. London: ILPA.

Crenshaw, Kimberle (1993) 'Mapping the margins: intersectionality, identity politics, and violence against women of color', *Stanford Law Review,* 43: 1241–76.

Dressel, P., Minkler, M. and Yen, I. (1997) 'Gender, race, class, and aging: advances and opportunities', *International Journal of Health Services*, 27 (4): 579–600.

Duncan, Simon and Smith, D.P. (2002) 'Geographies of family formations: spatial differences and gender cultures in Britain', *Transactions of the Institute of British Geographers*, 27 (4): 471–93.

Dwyer, C. (1999) 'Contradictions of community: questions of identity for young British Muslim women', *Environment and Planning A*, 31 (1): 53–68.

Edmunds, J. and Turner, B.S. (2002a) *Generational Consciousness, Narrative, and Politics*. Lanham: Rowman and Littlefield.

Edmunds, J. and Turner, B.S. (2002b) *Generations, Culture and Society*. Buckingham: Oxford University Press.

Evans, B. (2006) '"Gluttony or sloth": critical geographies of bodies and morality in (anti) obesity policy', *Area*, 38: 259–67.

Featherstone, M. and Hepworth, M. (1989) 'Ageing and old age: reflections on the post-modern life course', in B. Bytheway, T. Keil, P. Allatt and A. Bryman (eds), *Becoming and Being Old: Sociological Approaches to Later Life*. London: Sage. pp. 143–57.

Featherstone, M. and Wernick, A. (eds) (1995) *Images of Aging: Cultural Representations of Later Life*. London: Routledge.

Fine, Michelle, Tuck, Eve and Zeller-Berkman, Sarah (2007) 'Do you believe in Geneva?', in N. Denzin, L. T. Smith and Y. Lincoln (eds), *Handbook of Critical and Indigenous Knowledges*. Beverley Hills: Sage.

Gagen, E. (2000) 'Playing the part: performing gender in America's playgrounds' in S.L. Holloway and G. Valentine (eds), *Children's Geographies: Playing, Living, Learning*. London: Routledge. pp. 213–29.

Gibson, H.B. (2000) 'It keeps us young', *Ageing and Society,* 20 (6): 773–9.

Grenier, A. (2006) 'The distinction between being and feeling frail: exploring emotional experiences in health and social care', *Journal of Social Work Practice*, 20 (3): 299–313.

Grosz, E. (1993) 'Bodies and knowledges: feminism and the crisis of reason', in L. Alcoff and E. Potter (eds), *Feminist Epistemologies*. London: Routledge.

Harper, S. (1997a) 'Contesting later life' in P. Cloke and J. Little (eds), *Contested Countryside Cultures.* London: Routledge. pp. 189–96.

Harper, S. (1997b) 'Constructing later life/ constructing the body: some thoughts from feminist theory' in A. Jamieson, S. Harper and C. Victor (eds), *Critical Approaches to Ageing and Later Life.* Buckingham: Open University Press. pp. 160–74.

Harper, S. (2005) *Ageing Societies*. London: Hodder.

Harper, S. and Laws, G. (1995) 'Rethinking the geography of ageing', *Progress in Human Geography*, 19 (2): 199–221.

Hart, R. (1979) *Children's Experience of Place*. New York: Irvington.

Hart, R. (1992) 'Children's participation: from tokenism to citizenship'. Innocenti Essay no. 4, UNICEF, Florence, Italy.

HelpAge International (2002) *Participatory Research with Older People: a Sourcebook*. http://www.helpage.org/research/pla/plamiddle.html

Hill, M. and Tisdall, K. (1997) *Children and Society*. Essex: Pearson Education.

Hill, M., Turner, K., Walker, M., Stafford, A. and Seaman, P. (2006) 'Children's perspectives on social exclusion and resilience in disadvantaged urban communities', in K.M. Tisdall, J.M. Davis, M. Hill and A. Prout (eds), *Children, Young People and Social Inclusion: Participation for What*? Bristol: Policy Press. pp. 39–56.

Hockey, J. and James, A. (2003) *Social Identities Across the Life Course*. New York: Palgrave Macmillan.

Holloway, S.L. (1998) '"She lets me go out once a week": mothers' strategies for obtaining personal time and space', *Area,* 30 (4): 321–30.

Holloway, S.L. (1999) 'Reproducing motherhood', in N. Laurie, C. Dwyer, S. Holloway and F. Smith, *Geographies of New Femininities*. Harlow: Longman.

Holloway, S. and Valentine, G. (2000a) 'Spatiality and the new social studies of childhood', *Sociology*, 34: 763–83.

Holloway, S. and Valentine, G. (2000b) *Children's Geographies: Playing, Living, Learning*. London: Routledge.

Holt, L. (2006) 'Exploring "other" childhoods through quantitative secondary analyses of large scale surveys: opportunities and challenges for children's geographies', *Children's Geographies*, 4 (2): 143–56.

hooks, b. (1994) *Teaching to Transgress: Education as the Practice of Freedom*. New York: Routledge.

Hopkins, Peter (2004) 'Young Muslim men in Scotland: inclusions and exclusions', *Children's Geographies*, 2 (2): 257–72.

Hopkins, P.E. (2006a) 'Youth transitions and going to university: the perceptions of students attending a geography summer school access programme', *Area*, 38 (3): 240–7.

Hopkins, P.E. (2006b) 'Youthful Muslim masculinities: gender and generational relations', *Transactions of the Institute of British Geographers*, 31 (3): 337–52.

Hopkins, P. (2008) 'Critical geographies of body size', *Geography Compass*, 2 (6): 2111–26.

Hopkins, P. and Pain, R. (2007) 'Geographies of age: thinking relationally', *Area*, 39 (3): 287–94.

Hopkins, P. and Pain, R. (2008) 'Is there more to life? Relationalities in here and out there', *Area*, 40 (2): 289–92.

Hopkins, P. and Hill, M. (2006) 'This is a Good Place to Live and Think about the Future': *The Needs and Experiences of Unaccompanied Asylum Seeking Children and Young People in Scotland.* Glasgow: Scottish Refugee Council.

Hopkins, P. and Hill, M. (forthcoming) 'Contested bodies of asylum-seeking children', in K. Horschelmann and R. Colls (eds), *Contested Bodies of Childhood and Youth.* London: Palgrave.

Horton, J. and Kraftl, P. (2006) 'Not just growing up, but *going on*: materials, spacings, bodies, situations', *Chidren's Geographies*, 4 (3): 259–76.

Horton, J. and Kraftl, P. (2008) 'Commentary: reflections on geographies of age', *Area*, 40 (2): 284–88.

Hubbard, P.J. (2000) 'Desire/disgust: moral geographies of heterosexuality', *Progress in Human Geography*, 24 (2): 191–217.

James, A. (1990) 'Is there a place for children in geography?', *Area,* 22 (3): 278–83.

Jones, G. (2002) *The Youth Divide: Diverging Paths to Adulthood*. York: Joseph Rowntree Foundation.

Katz, C. (1993) 'Growing girls/closing circles: limits on the spaces of knowing in rural Sudan and US cities', in C. Katz and J. Monk, *Full Circles: Geographies of Women over the Lifecourse*. London: Routledge. pp. 88–106.

Katz, C. (2004) *Growing up Global: Economic Restructuring and Children's Everyday Lives.* Minnesota: University of Minnesota Press.

Katz, C. and Monk, J. (1993) *Full Circles: Geographies of Women over the Lifecourse.* London: Routledge.

Katz, S. (1992) 'Alarmist demography: power, knowledge and the elderly population', *Journal of Aging Studies*, 6 (3): 203–25.

Katz, S. (2000) 'Busy bodies: activity, aging, and the management of everyday life', *Journal of Aging Studies*, 14 (2): 135–52.

Kerns, M. (2003) 'Post-solidarity and postmodern intergenerational relationships', *The Gerontologist*, 43: 252.

Kesby, M. (2007) 'Methodological insights on and from Children's Geographies', *Children's Geographies*, 5 (3): 193–205.

Kesby, M. Gwanzura-Ottemoller, F. and Chizororo, M. (2006) 'Theorising *other*, "other childhoods": issues emerging from work on HIV in urban and rural Zimbabwe', *Chidren's Geographies*, 4 (2): 185–202.

Laws, G. (1994) 'Aging, contested meanings, and the built environment', *Environment and Planning A*, 26: 1787–802.

Laws, G. (1995) 'Theorizing ageism: lessons from postmodernism and feminism', *The Gerontologist*, 35, 112–18.

Laws, G. (1997) 'Spatiality and age relations', in A. Jamieson, S. Harper, and C. Victor (eds), *Critical Approaches to Ageing and Later.* Buckingham: Open University Press. pp. 90–100.

McCall, Leslie, (2005) 'The complexity of intersectionality', *Signs: Journal of Women in Culture and Society*, 30 (3): 1771–800.

McDowell, L. (2002) 'Masculine discourses and dissonances: strutting "Lads", protest masculinity, and domestic respectability', *Environment and Planning D: Society and Space*, 20 (1): 97–119.

McDowell, L. (2003) *Redundant Masculinities: Employment Change and White Working Class Youth*. Oxford: Blackwell.

McHugh, K.E. (2000) 'The "ageless self"? Emplacement of identities in Sun Belt retirement communities', *Journal of Aging Studies*, 14 (1): 103–15.

McHugh, K.E. (2003) 'Three faces of ageism: society, image and place', *Ageing and Society*, 23: 165–85.

McKendrick, J. (1997) 'Regulating children's street life: a case study of everyday politics in the neighbourhood'. SPA Working Paper 39, School of Geography, University of Manchester.

Malbon, B. (2000) Clubbing: *Dancing, Ecstasy and Vitality*. London: Routledge.
Mann, R. (2007) 'Out of the shadows? Grandfatherhood, age and masculinities', *Journal of Aging Studies*, 21: 281–91.
Mansvelt, J. (1997) 'Working at leisure: critical geographies of ageing', *Area*, 29 (4): 289–98.
Matthews, H. and Limb, M. (1999) 'Defining *an* agenda for the geography of children: review and prospect', *Progress in Human Geography*, 23 (1): 61–90.
Matthews, H., Limb, M. and Taylor, M. (2000) 'The street as "thirdspace"', in S.L. Holloway and G. Valentine (eds), *Children's Geographies: Playing, Living, Learning*. London: Routledge. pp. 63–79.
Maxey, L. (2009) 'Ageism and geographies of age', in R. Kitchin and N. Thrift (eds), *International Encyclopaedia of Human Geography*. Oxford: Elsevier.
Meyrowitz, J. (1984) 'The adult child and the child-like adult', *Daedalus*, 113 (3): 19–48.
Mowl, G., Pain, R. and Talbot, C. (2000) 'The ageing body and the homespace', *Area*, 32: 2.
Pain, R.H. (1995) 'Local contexts and the fear of crime: elderly people in north east England', *Northern Economic Review*, 24: 96–111.
Pain, R.H. (1997) '"Old age" and ageism in urban research: the case of fear of crime', *International Journal of Urban and Regional Research*, 21 (1): 117–28.
Pain, R. (2003) 'Youth, age and the representation of fear', *Capital and Class*, 60: 151–71.
Pain, R. (2005) *Intergenerational relations and practice in the development of sustainable communities*. Report to Office of the Deputy Prime Minister, London.
Pain, R. (2006) 'Paranoid parenting? Rematerialising risk and fear for children', *Social and Cultural Geography*, 7 (2): 221–43.
Pain, R., Barke, M., Gough, J., Fuller, D., MacFarlane, R. and Mowl, G. (2001) *Introducing Social Geographies*. London: Arnold.
Pain, R., Mowl, G. and Talbor, C. (2000) 'Difference and the negotiation of "old age"', *Environment and Planning D: Society and Space*, 18 (3): 377–94.
Panelli, R. (2002) 'Young rural lives: strategies beyond diversity', *Journal of Rural Studies*, 18: 113–22.
Pearson, G. (1983) *Hooligan: a History of Respectable Fears*. London: Macmillan.
Phoenix, Anne and Pattynama, Pamela (2006) 'Editorial: intersectionality', *European Journal of Women's Studies*, 13 (3): 187–92.
Qvortrup, J. (2005) 'Varieties of childhood', in J. Qvortrup (ed.), *Studies in Modern Childhood: Society, Agency, Culture*. London: Palgrave Macmillan. pp. 1–20.
Rawlins, Emma (2006) 'Mother knows best? Intergenerational notions of fashion and identity', *Children's Geographies*, 4 (3): 359–77.
Ross, N., Hill, M., Sweeting, H. and Cunningham-Burley, S. (2005) *Grandparents and Teen Grandchildren: Exploring Intergenerational Relationships*. Edinburgh: CRFR.
Rowles, G. (1978) *Prisoners of Space? Exploring the Geographical Experience of Older People*. Boulder, CO: Westview Press.
Ruddick, S. (2007) 'At the horizons of the subject: neo-liberalism, neo-conservatism and the rights of the child. Part One: from "knowing" fetus to "confused" child', *Gender, Place and Culture*, 14 (5): 513–26.
Sharp, J., Routledge, P., Philo, C. and Paddison, R. (2000) *Entanglements of Power: Geographies of Domination and Resistance*. London: Routledge.
Sibley, D. (1991) 'Children's geographies: some problems of representation', *Area,* 23 (3): 269–70.
Skelton, T. (2000) '"Nothing to do, nowhere to go?": teenage girls and "public" space in the Rhondda Valleys, South Wales', in S.L. Holloway and G. Valentine (eds), *Children's Geographies: Playing, Living, Learning.* London: Routledge. pp. 80–99.
Skelton, T. (2007) 'Children, young people, UNICEF and participation', *Children's Geographies,* 5 (1 & 2): 165–81.
Skelton, T. and Valentine, G. (1998) *Cool Places: Geographies of Youth Cultures*. London: Routledge.
Teather, E.K. (1999) *Embodied Geographies: Spaces, Bodies and Rites of Passage*. London: Routledge.
Thomas, M. (2005) 'Girls, consumption space and the contradictions of hanging out in the city', *Social and Cultural Geography,* 6 (4): 587–605.
Thomson, F. (2007) 'Are methodologies for children keeping them in their place?', *Children's Geographies*, 5 (3): 207–18.

Tucker, F. (2003) 'Sameness or difference? exploring girls' use of recreational space', *Children's Geographies*, 1 (1): 111–24.

Tulle, E. and Mooney, E. (2002) 'Moving to "age-appropriate" housing: government and self in later life', *Sociology*, 36: 685.

Twigg, J. (2003) 'The body, gender, and age: feminist insights in social gerontology', *Journal of Aging Studies*, 18: 59–73.

Valentine, G. (1996) 'Angels and devils: moral landscapes of childhood', *Environment and Planning D: Society and Space*, 14: 581–99.

Valentine, G. (2004) *Public Space and the Culture of Childhood*. Aldershot: Ashgate.

Valentine, G. and Holloway, S. (2001) 'On-line dangers? Geographies of parents' fears for children's safety in cyberspace', *Professional Geographer*, 53 (1): 71–83.

Valentine, G., Holloway, S.L., Jayne, M. and Knell, C. (2008) 'Drinking places: young people and drinking cultures in rural environments', *Journal of Rural Studies,* 24 (1): 28–40.

Vanderbeck, R. (2007) 'Intergenerational geographies: age relations, segregation and reengagements', *Geography Compass*, 1: 200–21.

Vanderbeck, R. (2008) 'Reaching critical mass? Theory, politics, and the culture of debate in children's geographies', *Area,* 40 (3): 393–400.

Vanderbeck, R. (forthcoming) 'Gypsy–Traveller young people and the spaces of social welfare: a critical ethnography', *ACME: an International e-journal of Critical Geographies*.

Walker, A. (1996) *The New Generational Contract: Intergenerational Relations, Old Age and Welfare*. London: UCL Press.

Warnes, A.M. (1981) 'Towards a geographical contribution to gerontology', *Progress in Human Geography*, 5: 317–41.

Warnes, A.M. (1990) 'Geographical questions in gerontology: needed directions for research', *Progress in Human Geography,* 14: 24–56.

Winchester, H. (1991) 'The geography of children', *Area,* 23 (4): 357–60.

Winchester, Hilary, McGuirk, P.M., Pauline, M. and Everett, Kathryn (1999) 'Schoolies week as a rite of passage: a study of celebration and control', in E. Kenworthy Teather (ed.), *Embodied Geographies: Spaces, Bodies and Rites of Passage*. London: Routledge. pp. 59–77.

Women and Geography Study Group (1997) *Feminist Geographies: Explorations in Diversity and Difference*. Harlow: Addison Wesley.

Wray, S. (2003) 'Connecting ethnicity, ageing and agency', *Sociological Research Online*, 8: 4.

Wray, S. (2004) 'What constitutes agency and empowerment for women in later life?', *The Sociological Review*, 52 (1): 22–38.

Young, L. and Ansell, N. (2003) 'Fluid households, complex families: the impacts of children's migration as a response to HIV/AIDS in southern Africa', *The Professional Geographer,* 55 (4): 464–79.

Ziegler, F. (2007) 'Getting around: reporting research findings of a study into daily mobility and social exclusion with older people in County Durham, UK', Durham: Age Concern Durham County.

3

Disability, Health and Citizenship

Michael L. Dorn and Carla C. Keirns

INTRODUCTION

Contemporary geographies of disability adopt a variety of methods and perspectives, from phenomenological accounts of places as perceived by people with sensory impairments, to geospatial analyses of enabling and disabling environments, to explorations of citizenship and exclusion based on bodily variation. This work has debts to long traditions in medical geography (disease patterns) and health care geography (health service distribution), but expands its purview on the basis of attention to the perspectives and lived experiences of people with disabilities.

Emerging from the deinstitutionalization and disability rights movements of the 1960s and 1970s, the first generation of work in disability geography presented the history and consequences of these movements, often with explicit goals of fostering human freedom. Empirical studies of the spatial distribution of people with mobility impairments, deafness, blindness and mental illness have a shared genealogy, leading back to efforts to document the location, housing, and service needs of the newly deinstitutionalized. Building on this early groundwork, recent scholars have explored ways in which images of disability have been used to justify discriminatory immigration and employment regulations, and other forms of social exclusion frequently cued by social cleavages organized around race, class, and gender.

Definitions of disability are the product of bio-political efforts to render a legible social order. Classification as 'able-bodied' determines an individual's experience in family life, schooling and work just as surely as other social categories that define the responsibilities of individuals, groups, and society at large. Social geographers, while expressing their intentions to critically examine the power-laden constructions that produce such designations – usually in search of new social imaginaries – nevertheless too often adopt as given the analytic distinctions of medical, social and political authorities. In the face of such contradictions, the history of science, medicine and technology can offer significant insight into the shifting construction of, and response to, disabled populations, and into the variety of ways in which relations between anomalous bodies and their social environments have been conceived.

In this chapter, we consider the creation of disability identities, the changing social uses and meanings of these categories, and conclude by considering some of the challenges and alternative narratives as we consider the meaning of 'disability' in the twenty-first century. Examining professional geographers' contributions to disability rights, citizenship and the 'social model' of disability, we find that that much remains obscured behind the frame. What is needed, then, is a step away from the professional geography of disability to its geosophy (Wright, 1947) – the spatial knowledge of disability, as constructed by statisticians, social surveyors, and institution-builders and activists.

The construction and contestation of geographic knowledge on disability will be discussed in a roughly chronological sequence, starting with the administrative categories for disability emerging with the industrial revolution. In the late nineteenth and early twentieth centuries, public health surveillance activities expanded from their traditional focus on infectious and epidemic diseases to include chronic and occupational diseases. This trend was accelerated in the early twentieth century with recognition of hazardous chemicals in the workplace and the roles of disability and injury in absenteeism. The recording of congenital and childhood disorders in the population and the burden of occupational disabilities drew increased attention during the worldwide economic depression of the 1930s. Thereafter there arose a new legitimacy of disability under the welfare states of the 1950s to 1970s, though always with a distinction between those whose impairments were congenital or arose from work, warfare, or some other experience. Finally, we turn to questions of disability as identity; here we consider emergent spatialities of disability, given current trends towards economic liberalism and globalization.

DISABILITY RIGHTS, CITIZENSHIP, AND THE 'SOCIAL MODEL' OF DISABILITY

Disability is a social category ripe for exclusionary practices. These are, however, often examined through the micro spaces of mobility: through streets and neighborhoods, for example. Less frequently is disability linked to the larger spaces of citizenship – this is certainly true in comparison with race and indigeneity. And it is also true that scholars of citizenship have long overlooked disability and chronic illness. Yet both play a fundamental role in the nation-building process. The creation of a national body politic requires a means of adjudicating claims for inclusion, and determining the responsibilities of citizens to the state and each other (Craddock and Dorn, 2001). Central to the construction of citizenship are a number of signifiers for 'otherness', including gender, race, literacy and property ownership. Yet, as Allison Carey (2003: 423) has noted, many of these distinctions would lose their power over time: '… it became increasingly difficult to exclude on the basis of race and class, due to both legal and medical justifications [but] few people criticized the restriction of rights for people with intellectual and mental disabilities.' Successful claims of women and African Americans to positive inclusion have rested upon each group's ability to gain popular and legal acceptance for their 'non-disabled status' (Baynton, 1997). The concomitant restrictions upon those marked with 'disability' went far beyond the commonly noted restriction against the immigration of those deemed 'incompetent', 'defective' or 'dependent' (Dorr, 2003; Richards, 2004). Within the national territory, micro-practices of power distinguished between legitimate and illegitimate forms of movement, from conspicuous begging to flat feet, and excluded a range of individuals from membership in the social body on the basis of variations in strength, sensation or movement that rendered them unable to support themselves financially (Davenport, 1915; Cresswell, 2006; Linker, 2007; Schweik, 2007).

One of the major innovations to emerge from the Anglo-American Disability Rights Movement is the distinction between the social model and the medical model of disability. Simply being able to conceive of an alternative to individualizing medicalization was a radical achievement, bound up in a liberatory conception of space and a vision of human interdependence. In the book *Disability Politics*, Jane Campbell and Mike Oliver (1996) trace the origins of the social model of disability to the ideological entrepreneurship of Paul Hunt. In 1972, Hunt wrote to the editor of the Manchester Guardian: 'Sir, Severely physically handicapped people find themselves in isolated unsuitable institutions where their views are ignored and they are subject to authoritarian and often cruel regimes. I am proposing the formation of a consumer group to put forward nationally the views of actual and potential residents of these successors to the Workhouse. Yours faithfully, Paul Hunt.' The Union of the Physically Impaired Against Segregation (UPIAS) was founded in response to his initial rallying cry, on the model of many other civil rights, women's rights and patients' rights groups of the time, but with its own in-your-face definition of the 'disability problem': 'Disability: The disadvantage or restriction of activity caused by a contemporary social organization which takes no or little account of people who have physical impairments and thus excludes them from the mainstream of social activity' (Oliver, 1990: 11). This turn of the lens was an opening not only for sociologists such as Mike Oliver and Victor Finkelstein, but also for the emerging field of urban social geography.

Anne Buttimer (1993) and Felix Driver (1988) have traced the genealogy of social geography back to enlightenment humanists and the rise of moral statistics of the mid-nineteenth century. Although measurements of human conformation and capacity had contributed to enlightenment anatomy and natural history, and mid-nineteenth century moral statistics had led to the promotion of physical norms and the diffusion of county mental deficiency asylums, one can argue that 'disability' was not identified as a discrete topic in social geographic inquiry until the 1960s. Even then, geographers held this population at arms length, as 'defectives', 'dependents' and bearers of discrete diagnoses.

Disability became an explicit focus of geographic analysis in its own right during the 1970s as social geographers applied economic and ecological models to patterns of urban residence and the implications of policy change (Giggs, 1973; Ley, 1974; Wolpert et al., 1972). This was part of a broader movement toward more 'relevant' work in the social sciences (Eyles, 1977). Disability as a planning issue was a matter of finding the correct geographical fix. Urban social geographers tracked the implications of the nationwide campaign against institutional models of care, culminating in the closure of state mental hospitals and the establishment of community mental health centers. For reviews of this literature see Dorn (1994), Park et al. (1998), Philo (1997a, 2005), and Wolch and Philo (2000).

Urban social geographers reported and critiqued the social imaginary that drove deinstitutionalization, documenting the relocation in physical and social space from impersonal institutions to communities whose geographies of housing, employment, transportation and health services turned out to be inadequate to the task of community integration. Some argued for the delivery of a required training curriculum in signage and geographic wayfinding to intellectually disabled residents before their release (Golledge et al., 1979). A group previously fixed in spaces of totalizing social control was welcomed back into the fabric of American urban life, only to find that restrictions on movement continued to operate in housing, transportation and employment, albeit at a different scale. From Julian Wolpert's perspective the presumed incompetence of this population was merely reinforced by an '...ever-increasing and ever-more-demanding technology and institutional structure. ... For marginal citizens and marginal areas, extraordinary remedies are targeted not to the structural change that would make mainstream participation possible but to making participation unnecessary' (Wolpert, 1980: 397). The resultant patterns of inner-city service dependency were mapped and dubbed the 'public city' (Dear, 1980; Wolch, 1979).

In these studies of deinstitutionalization, homelessness, and modern topographies of illness, social geographers contributed to the construction of disability as a public problem (Gusfield, 1981). In doing so, they conceived of disabled people, particularly ex-hospital residents, as victims of objectifying attitudes and discourses. No doubt this construct was relevant to the populations they tracked under the blanket category of 'service dependency'. Yet the product of so much effort to understand the continued urban concentration of this population was the image of an 'asylum without walls', inner-city bastions of relative tolerance surrounded by high walls of suburban ignorance and intolerance of difference (Taylor, 1988; Law and Gleeson, 1998). Historians of the suburbanization process have argued that the disabled, poor, and racial minorities were intentionally excluded, sometimes through restrictive covenants, but more frequently through a failure to make provision for public transportation, affordable housing, and medical and social services (Hirsch, 1983; Jackson, 1985). Yet disability outside of the planner's slick-sided surface of urban intolerance appears to have been literally 'off the map' of social geographic analysis at the time. Due consideration needs to be given, however, to geographies of physical and sensory disability emerging in student master's theses and dissertations (Perle, 1969; Hill, 1986; Cook, 1991; Dorn, 1994; Gleeson, 1993; Kruse, 2001), in concert with the growing visibility of physically disabled people in schools, workplaces and urban landscapes, and with new legal mandates based on individual rights and modeled on legislation barring discrimination based on race and gender. This work became more prominent with the passage of the Americans with Disabilities Act and the emergence of critical disability studies in the United Kingdom.

In the 1998 National Organization on Disability/Harris survey, respondents with disabilities reported that their hopes of employment had gone largely unmet. That this remains the case seventeen years after the passage of the Americans with Disabilities Act is a commentary on the continuing power of medical and governmental frameworks and economic arrangements to fix identities at the level of the individual and close out opportunities. The ADA, narrowed by succeeding Supreme Court decisions, has proven ineffective in advancing the wellbeing of this class, which is deemed to have been uniquely disadvantaged and marginalized in areas such as employment and access to affordable housing (Burgdorf and Burgdorf, 1975; Krieger, 2003). In part this has been the result of enforcement mechanisms that relied on the power and political acumen of the individual, requiring individual lawsuits rather than proactive regulatory compliance actions.

Activists and observers have come to recognize crucial limitations with the social model of disability and its offspring, the minority model (Hahn, 1988), both because of the variability and liminality of disabled states and because of its link with dependency and claims on social resources. One of the problems encountered when claims to citizenship and rights are based on status as a discrete and uniquely disadvantaged minority is the question of whether disabled people are seeking the negative right not to be discriminated against or the positive right that others make accommodations to their needs (Switzer, 2003). This framework of negative rights – the right to be left alone – and positive rights for social provision is itself contested in the case of disability. As disability rights activists remind us, they would not need 'accommodations' if planning for workplaces, housing, health care, schools and other public and private spaces followed the principles of universal design, imagining a range of human variation in sight, mobility and sensation that is seen both across the population and across the lifecourse (as people lose sensory abilities with aging). Conversely, court challenges to the Americans with Disabilities Act in the United States have demonstrated the difficulties of defining disability as an immutable personal characteristic: if a hearing aid, glasses, or a wheelchair can restore normal functioning, the US Supreme Court has ruled that the individual is no longer disabled for purposes of the Americans with Disabilities Act, regardless of the Act's stipulation of protection for those perceived as having disabilities (Krieger, 2003).

This recent history of disability rights in the US gives scholars of disability studies and disability geographers reason to pause and reflect. Since the late 1960s a social approach to disability has been advanced, devoted to protecting the rights of the country's largest minority group (with an estimated 54 million 'members'). These legal protections have in turn been undercut by a series of Supreme Court decisions that limit the reach of the ADA and doubt the integrity of the disability experience. In concert with the broader movement, geographers have all too often trafficked in simplistic understandings of exclusion/inclusion, actively forgetting the essentially political and economic nature of disability constructs. Exclusionary practices were never of one piece, and the fight for inclusion in Caribbean societies will look far different than barrier removal in an American city or wealthy suburb, which will differ as well from inclusion in Western Europe.

The remainder of this chapter will explore the relationships of disability to larger social categories and social movements in the creation of nation states, the rise of social welfare movements and programs, and the ways in which disability has been theorized and ignored in work in the geography of health, illness and health care services. Disability constructs are tied up in nation-building practices and space – economic transformations as much as they are practices of medical treatment and planning practice. When disability is taken as central to the analysis, familiar geographies of health, disease, public health and surveillance look different. By the last quarter of the twentieth century, features such as landscape, architecture, transportation and differential access to social services come to the fore.

BUREAUCRACY AND THE ADMINISTRATIVE DETERMINATION OF DISABILITY

Standards for disability classification have become commonplaces of medical discourse, and have been accepted as such by the general population, but their origins lay just as much in bureaucratic enterprises charged with addressing workforce and welfare policies. While diseases and injuries, defined and diagnosed by physicians and other health care providers, form the basis for most determinations of disability, defining a person as 'able-bodied' or 'disabled' is typically a more administrative or legalistic process. The goals of this process are usually to determine whether a person is entitled to specific services such as special education, transportation services, health care, housing subsidies and cash payments. The administrative determination is divorced from the medical because it is the laws, codes, insurance contracts and budgets of welfare agencies that determine who receives what kinds of benefits. Medical certification serves the moral purpose of drawing a bright line between those offered publicly or privately financed benefits, on the one hand, and the 'malingerers' who are not entitled to assistance with the needs of life, on the other hand. But the medical categories of specific diseases and injuries do not map directly onto the administrative categories of temporarily, permanently, partially or completely disabled, as defined by governments and insurance companies. Furthermore, whether a particular injury or medical condition interferes with social functioning depends on a person's social role and the available support and accommodations. Both the medical and administrative criteria serve as changing realities, with boundaries redrawn on the basis of scientific, economic and political considerations. As a result, the designation of disability is often provisional, permeable and contested.

In the past 25 years, however, both of these professionally defined hierarchies have been challenged by legislation, litigation and protest movements, while part-time and informal employment arrangements have left more individuals outside the protection of even these imperfect systems (Wilton, 2004a, b; Wilton and Schuer, 2006). Studies of stigmatization have demonstrated the ways in which bodily difference has been linked to social marginalization (Giggs and Smith, 1988; Sibley, 1995). Disability activists and advocates have challenged established social practices, such as segregation of those with bodily variations into separate schools, nursing homes, and other kinds of institutions, building a movement for inclusive housing, education and other services within community settings (Laws, 1994; Dorn, 1998; Chouinard, 1999; Fleischer and Zames, 2001; Kitchin and Wilton, 2003).

These determinations of ability, disability, bodily normality and difference derive from distinct fields of theory and practice in the late nineteenth and early twentieth centuries. In concert with the growth of national statistics, the rise of the welfare state, and cultural anxieties about physical fitness of individuals and nations, disability became increasingly categorized, bounded and moralized. The normal body became a cultural ideal and an administrative reality, with specific measurements and physical capacities (Davis, 1997). In order to understand the challenge of recent rights-based and person-centered changes, one first has to understand the origins of this vision of the normative body. There are many perspectives from which one might tell this story of geographic knowledge, or geosophy: from the bird's eye of asylum provision and economic labor market theory on the one hand, to the grounded experience of people, with all of their infirmities and strengths, on the other. For the sake of brevity our analysis is more attentive to the bird's-eye view of the statistician, the epidemiologist and the policy analyst as they frame our understanding of these communities and their potentialities. Disability requires the act of identification; laden with cultural and political significance, its contribution to geographic knowledge is too easily overlooked. Bodies are made to carry meanings at a variety of levels; these meanings may be understood as the outcome of symbolic struggle across social fields invested with multiple projects (Schatzki, 2002).

GEOGRAPHIES OF PUBLIC HEALTH AND NATIONAL FITNESS

Geographic theorizing on health and disease enjoys a distinguished historical career, drawing on the classic accounts of Thucydides, Herodotus and Hippocrates. Epidemics of plague, cholera and yellow fever that circled the world from the fourteenth to the nineteenth centuries increased the salience of synthesizing medical geographies for physicians, politicians, and the general public, and inspired collaborations between growing communities of physicians, statisticians and cartographers (Jordanova, 1997; Barrett, 2000). More recently, scholars in history, geography and regional studies have made the case that disease surveillance and prevention projects were critical to the colonization of Africa, Asia and Latin America by Europeans, both through technologies designed to protect European bodies in the tropics and ideologies of racial superiority that provided the political and moral discourses to justify the enterprise (Curtin, 1989; Anderson, 2006; Driver and Martins, 2005; Moran, 2007). From the perspective of population health, disability appeared as a flaw in need of remediation at the very least, excision and removal if possible.

Technologies of surveillance were developed by states to track their populations and understand their characteristics, first to explore epidemics, as in the 'Bills of Mortality' issued in London during the plague years of the 1660s, then routine registration of births and deaths, and later to characterize the frequency of mental illness, blindness, deafness, amputation, and other physical characteristics of the social body (Eyler, 1979; Graunt, 1676). But even from the beginning these tallies of bodily difference became linked to questions of the fitness of individuals and populations, concern for the health of populations, and arguments about race and immigration. The 1840 US census demonstrated the political uses of statistics in linking stigmatized categories, when a Southern senator in charge of the compilation of the census reported that nearly all free African-Americans in the northern states were insane (Grob, 1978). These efforts to quantify illness and disability in populations accelerated in nineteenth-century surveys of British workers and the establishment of workers' insurance in Germany under Bismarck in the last decades of the nineteenth century (Hamlin, 1998; Riley, 1997; Stone, 1984).

Records of early almshouses and hospitals offer historical geographers and social historians useful raw material from which to construct a more fine-grained view of lives spent on the economic margins of industrializing cities (Gleeson, 1999; Newman, 2003). A street-level view can be found in the work of nineteenth-century statisticians who undertook rudimentary spatial analysis and argued for the expansion or the dispersal of hospitals for the custodial care of the vagrant, the errant and the feeble (Driver, 1993; Park, 1995; Philo, 1995; Radford and Park, 1995). The health and evolutionary fitness of national populations became a cultural concern across Europe and the United States at the beginning of the twentieth century, and with it a fear of disability and a conflation of mental and physical weakness with racial others (Tyner, 1999; Irving, 2000; Jordan, 1992; Linker, 2007). In the United States these eugenic ideas combined with anti-immigrant sentiment in a program of medical inspection to prevent the migration of individuals with contagious diseases, as well as those felt to be likely to become a burden on the state. Medical inspection programs to isolate cases of blinding trachoma, tuberculosis, deaf-muteness and 'mental defects' of all sorts led some families to choose between immigration to better material circumstances or the abandonment of family members, whether elderly or with real or perceived disabilities (Baynton, 2005; Fairchild, 2003; Kraut, 1994; Richards, 2004).

A new enthusiasm for medical geography emerged during the interwar period as national competitiveness was increasingly framed in terms of overall population health. Seeking to contribute to this effort, social scientists fought under the banner of 'social medicine' against the narrowing of perspective encouraged by germ theory (Anderson, 1996; Porter, 1997). Internationalist in perspective, the founders of the Johns Hopkins University Institute of the History of Medicine each offered their own visions for a comparative medical geography, visions shared with scholars at the Yale School of Public Health, Harvard Medical School, and the health committees of the League of Nations. Fielding Hudson Garrison employed the term 'geomedicine', Henry Sigerist 'historical-geographical pathology', each from contemporary German usage. Historian of public health Elizabeth Fee (1989: 133) notes: 'With his usual ambitious scope, Sigerist … proposed an international journal for historic-geographic pathology, a series of monographs on the history and geography of the different diseases, and an atlas that would show the distribution of disease in time and space.' Efforts to improve population health necessarily required attentiveness to the architecture and infrastructure of the state and the economy. Fighting the increasing burden of chronic disease and disability would require different approaches to the traditional containment strategies employed against epidemics.

An example of this turn to public health appeared in Connecticut in the 1930s. The state developed its own cancer registry under the leading public health theorist and activist C.E.A. Winslow (Fairchild et al., 2007: 121). Finding alarming rates of cancer in New Haven, 'Winslow and his colleagues mounted a comprehensive program … including public education campaigns and new cancer clinics'. Winslow explained this expanded role accordingly: '… public health which in its early days was an engineering science and has now become also a medical science must expand until it is in addition a social science'

(Winslow, 1945 : 196, cited in Terris, 1998: 140). Winslow also wrote extensively on occupational health questions, and in 1921 was asked by the National Safety Council to prepare a report on sandblasting and the danger of the lung disease silicosis in foundries. Unwilling to see his observations buried in response to demands from industry, Winslow eventually secured publication for his full results in a German periodical (Markowitz, 1998: 155–6). Winslow's colleague at Yale University, George Rosen, devoted an entire monograph to a 'medical and social interpretation' of miner's disease (1943) as well as providing the documentation of the conjoined histories of medical geography and medical police (1953a, b). During this time, the place of physicians in the workplace remained one of certifying ability to work and excluding those with chronic illnesses and disabilities, rather than identifying and reporting workplace exposures that might cause physical and mental hardship. One can find this role repeated around the colonial world to ironic effect, as when the men of Botswana were subjected to thorough physical examinations before being allowed to work in the South African mines, from which many would in turn acquire tuberculosis and miners' lung diseases (Livingstone, 2005; Packard, 1989).

Acquired disabilities among the working-age and elderly populations have been a major component of national surveys and vital statistics for the past half century. Starting in 1957, in the United States the National Health Interview Survey's door-to-door surveys were more interested in determining the number of days of work lost to sickness and the use of medical services than the particular infirmities that caused either (Wilder, 1963). Similar surveys have been central to planning for the needs of populations, particularly for planning health care and social welfare services, with a focus on rehabilitation and returning citizens to remunerative work. This focus on wage-labor has frequently meant that social supports are arranged for vocational rehabilitation, with lower priority given to those who work in domestic, informal, and unpaid settings, or who are not expected to work for wages at all.

Knowledge of the circumstances of the 'crippled child' in the city grew out of the application of social survey methods by community organizations. While the focus of New York's Crippled Children's Driving Fund in the first decade of the twentieth century was the prevalence of tuberculosis, after the major epidemic in 1916 polio became 'central to successful initiatives to identify, track, and guide crippled children to services' (Fairchild et al., 2007: 145). Fraternal organizations, long involved in establishing orphanages and hospitals, pushed for systematic notification of new cases of polio and speedier linkage to social, economic and medical services. During the Depression of the 1930s, officials in Britain and the United States recognized that the fate of children was ultimately a public responsibility (Dunham, 1940). The surveillance of birth defects took on increased importance in the 1960s and 1970s as countries sought to lower infant mortality and improve services for disabled children (Naylor et al., 1974; Watkins et al., 1996). The US Standard Birth Certificate was revised in 1978 to ease the reporting of birth defects and complications by moving from a three-inch box, in which the physician was to report any problems at birth, to a checklist of dozens of boxes covering medical risk factors for the pregnancy, including maternal tobacco use, obstetric procedures, complications of labor and delivery, abnormal conditions at birth and congenital anomalies (US Department of Health and Human Services, 1982: technical appendix, 4–4). Increased ease of reporting led to dramatic increases in reported birth defects after the revised certificate was adopted (Dundon et al., 1983). Drawing on comparable information provided by British district medical officers, geographers Andrew Lovett and Anthony Gatrell (1988) were able to review the geography of spina bifida at the national scale, demonstrating the impact that maternal screenings (in many cases resulting in abortion) were having on the prevalence of the condition amongst children.

Such research provocatively suggests how practices for identifying potentially disabling conditions can impact the human ecology of regions. Yet, from the perspective of the wheelchair user or the Braille reader, modern public health can appear largely irrelevant, since its services, whether assuring clean water, campaigns for injury prevention, or epidemiologic analysis, are aimed at maintaining population health and preventing disability rather than dealing with the needs of those already living with disabilities. Instead of public health systems, people with disabilities are much more likely to deal with: social welfare agencies, which are the gatekeepers to disability payments and health insurance; rehabilitation agencies housed within Departments of Labor, which may control access to workplace support and educational assistance; or housing agencies and advocacy organizations, which can help find and sometimes pay for accessible housing.

REHABILITATION, INDUSTRIALIZATION, AND THE WELFARE STATE

Disability is entwined with the history of industrialization, the nature of the social contract between citizens and their governments, and the relations between the first and third worlds in a globalizing economy. Materialist histories of disability suggest that medieval community life and non-Western societies offered a variety of social roles for members with mental and physical impairments (Gleeson, 1999; Philo, 1997b; Scheer and Groce, 1988). While life for those whose bodies differed from cultural norms was hardly idyllic in preindustrial societies, starting in the 1800s the industrial revolution ushered in an era of standardization in time, space, and human organization which excluded or marginalized people who were blind, deaf, had limited strength or mobility, or who otherwise did not meet social and employer expectations (Fairchild, 1981; Jureidini and White, 2000; Nugent, 1983; Thompson, 1967). In addition, these new industries, with their heavy machinery, rapid assembly lines and novel industrial processes, posed new risks to workers, moving many from the able-bodied to the disabled ranks at much younger ages than workers had been used to (Derickson, 1998; Rosner and Markowitz, 1991; Sellers, 1997; Zelizer, 1985). For illustration, in nineteenth-century railroad work, how many fingers one had was a key part of one's resumé for certain jobs, particularly for those rail workers who linked the cars together. In a classic case of Catch 22, if you had all of your fingers then you must not have had much experience; if you had lost too many you must be clumsy (Aldrich, 2006; Licht, 1983).

The modern welfare state had its ideological beginnings in this period, partly harnessed to the intense fears workers had about their own and their family's poverty if or when they were to become disabled. In Bismarck's Germany, where modern occupational accident protection was born, insurance was used to buy worker loyalties to the state, and in other countries labor unions used it to rally demonstrations and inspire solidarity (Berkowitz and Fox, 1989; Eghigian, 2000; Riley, 1997; Sigerist, 1943; Yelin, 1992).

Modern armies, with their production of disabled soldiers, widows and orphans, were also forced to provide for the casualties of their campaigns. Funding and policies around disability pensions and service provision waxed and waned (Blanck and Millender, 2000; Resch, 1999). Pensions for widows and orphans were awarded after the United States Revolutionary War (1776–1783) and the US Civil War (1861–1865), but in most countries disability pensions and services waited until the first decades of the twentieth century, with World War I as an important turning point. Social provision for disabled soldiers, workers, and their dependents came to be accepted as a moral and contractual responsibility, while those who had been born with disabilities that limited their participation in education and work roles had a much more precarious place in social hierarchies, sometimes raised up as the noble and worthy benefactors of charity (especially for those who where blind, deaf and/or mobility impaired). At other times people with disabilities were targeted for police brutality and institutionalization or criticized as placing a burden on the body politic, under banners of degeneration theory, eugenics and genetic fitness.

The challenges of provision for the disabled and elderly also served as part of the inspiration for a period of retirement, a concept relatively unknown until the first decades of the twentieth century. The great corporations of the nineteenth century, including railroads and power companies, as well as civil service bureaucracies, often allowed supervisors to protect their more unproductive workers from job termination – in a way, an early version of the Fordist social contract. Ultimately, business and government leaders concluded that the only way that these workers could be peacefully moved out of their sinecures was by creating a dignified form of support for them outside of work: the first retirement pensions (Graebner, 1980).

In the past few decades the welfare state that protected its members has been challenged by political movements, economic pressures, transnational migration and neoliberal economic and social policies. While workers have sought to better working conditions and wages in the first world, employers have sought to move work to regions whose populations are thought to be less demanding and cheaper to employ, leading to dramatic shifts in living standards, expectations, and toxic exposures (Athanasiou, 1996; Kim, 2000; Rogers et al., 2000). At the same time, most third-world populations have undergone health transitions from a predominant burden of acute and infectious diseases to one of chronic diseases and disabilities, similar to the health transitions seen in first-world countries in the early decades of the twentieth century (Murray and Lopez, 1996). Even as critiques abound of the system of industrial capitalism bounded by nation-states and their complementary welfare systems, globalization is undermining the labor union contracts and tax revenues that underwrote some protections for workers in the case of illness or misfortune. What will replace these social welfare provisions in the new global labor market is far from certain.

DISABILITY IDENTITY IN CONTEMPORARY SOCIETY

As this chapter has shown, rather than remaining a fixed expression of medicalized characteristics, disability expression and intensity varies according to particular socio-spatial and historical circumstances. Contextual accounts of disability point to its 'social construction' and find parallels in the contemporary study of other identity categories. For those who subscribe to the social model, disability may be considered yet another category of otherness, akin to race, class, gender or nationality, posing intriguing possibilities for exploring their intersection in individual and group experiences. Yet disability remains as well – more than many of these other group markers – an acceptable tool in social discourse for discrediting marginalized groups more generally. And although discussions of 'intersectionality' have become popular in critical race theory, feminist studies, queer theory and disability studies, popular conceptions of, and academic theorizing on, disability is still largely divorced from rubrics that are given center stage: gender, race, sexuality, nationality (Davis, 2006; Frye et al., 2008). As Irving Kenneth Zola (1993) and Lennard Davis (2001) note, disability may well be different from many other identities in that it necessarily subjects people to increased moral scrutiny, more like alternative sexual identity than even race or gender. In particular, divisions between benefits that are considered earned (i.e., linked to work) and those that are bestowed as charity have often marked quite different levels of support, particularly in the United States (Vaughn, 2003). Comparisons of the social provisions made for a child born blind and a manual worker who is injured on the job highlight many of these problematics, and demonstrate links between disability, employment, and the welfare state. Because disability has always been a problematic category, tied into questions of individual responsibility and social provision, work by geographers, sociologists and historians can help us evaluate these contemporary political disputes. Meanwhile, the very real experience of people with multiple disabilities will further complicate social scientists' frameworks.

Bodies are made to represent and feel differently in different cultural vernaculars (Guerts, 2002; Halliburton, 2005; Scarry, 1985; Zola, 1983). In light of this, consider the stark choices being offered in contemporary Western societies. On the one hand, we find with the development of prosthetic technologies that Western society has shifted from a recognition that the external appearance of normality will suffice, leaving the internal subjectivity alone, to the sense in today's configuration of identity politics that appearance *is all there is*, that by changing the affective connectivity of the surface we in fact modify the essence of the person (Elliott, 2003). This could well represent a triumph of physicalist norms and of affective motility over emotional depth (Thien, 2005). On the other hand, as we are entering an era where post-human dreams and genetic fantasies have new currency, we may in fact be gaining broader familiarity with, and acceptance of, disability: 'for Garland-Thomson, within the context of contemporary US capitalism, disability is now "chic" as evidenced in various advertising campaigns that feature sexualized disabled bodies' (Sothern, 2007: 144). Matthew Sothern asks us to further consider the ways that new imagery of disability and sexuality is harnessed to a 'project of self-governance that scarcely challenges contemporary structures of neoliberalism' while privileging heteronormativity. The repressed has returned to the urban mediascape, but at whose bidding? New geographies of disability emerge from this recognition that the environment (in the Hippocratic sense, and in the sense of space-time compression and network connection) fully enters into and cooperates in the constitution of disability at the level of the individual and the body politic. These new geographies of disability may also inform the way we think about other identity categories (Davis, 2001).

If, as British materialist historians tell us, disability as we know it is a product of the fundamental division of labor and citizenship that accompanied the onset of capitalism and rise of the nation-state (see Finkelstein, 1980), then where do we find ourselves now that the nation-state has been undercut by multinational corporations and globalized social movements? Rights to movement and citizenship have become a keyword for political and population geographers, and major funders of geographic research are now concerned with population flows and circular migrations. Yet geographers' analyses of disability have continued to exhibit a 'sedentarist metaphysics' (Cresswell, 2006), privileging presence and place over lines of flight and movement. Humanistic accounts in health and social geography tend to focus on the residential situations of disabled people. Studies of mentally disabled populations still point back to the static backdrop of the institution even though, as Metzel and Walker (2001) note, it never housed the majority of this population. An emerging literature on the experience of mental illness, attending to the importance of gardening, performance, and play, serves as a counterpoint to this sedentarist metaphysics in post-institutional geographies (Küppers, 2004; Parr, 2007; Tuntiya, 2007). Perhaps because of a long-standing queasiness towards bringing the acting body into these studies, all too few geographers offer personalized accounts that start with *genres of movement* rather than stasis (but see Dorn, 1998; Hansen and Philo, 2007; also Golfus and Simpson, 1994).

Just as traveling cultures are celebrated as hybrid and flexible, and body theorists, ethicists and anthropologists are heralding the arrival of 'post-humanism', one may ask whether the first decades of the twenty-first century might be a period of 'post-disability'. If we follow the line of argument of many disability theorists that the production of disability is part and parcel with the emergence of nation-states and the defining of nation-citizens, then the narrative of the weakened nation-state in the era of footloose capitalism and globalization would suggest the disappearance of disability as a discrete identity, to be replaced by recasting 'dependency', along with the social welfare provisions and benefits that defined it, as 'connectivity' within a complex field of disabling propensities and compensations (Gibson, 2006). While changes in the national and world political economy, driven by technology, create new enablements and new disablements, we find ourselves laboring under a bureaucratic apparatus of assigned identity that is out of step with the newly emerging genetic and post-human geographies of the present. New configurations of the space-economy create new opportunities and yet cannot simply erase identities that were, and are, shaped under different codes.

The ideology of 'universal design' feeds this dream of accommodating a wider range of consumers, and yet runs up against the reality that advanced capitalist accumulation also thrives on more specialized consumption. All too often, disabled people experience a shadow citizenship and entitlement, excluded from opportunities for participation and from the development of fluid identities, relegated instead to 'legal peripheries or places in which law as discursively represented and law as lived are fundamentally at odds' (Chouinard, 2001: 187). Disabled people are not offered equal access to public accommodations and are then blamed for their occupancy of consumption cul-de-sacs. Consider, for example, the market in rehabilitation goods as discussed by Hughes et al. (2005). Assistive technologies may well enhance the lives and mobility of disabled people, but all too often their design is informed by the medical model rather than by the expectation of mainstream socialization and accommodation. The success of state-of-the-art technologies, such as Dean Kamen's IBOT wheelchair and advanced augmentative communication devices, depends, in part, upon the continued inaccessibility of broad spheres of mainstream consumption, including housing, education and transportation (Stobie, 1994).

Disabled people in the United States, like the Canadian women interviewed by Chouinard (1999) and young people interviewed by Hughes et al. (2005), are frustrated by the widening gap between the rhetoric of policy makers and their own experiences of 'denied access'. In a society where segments of the disability community are the focus of a multi-million dollar industry involving 'health care and medical professions; hospitals; therapy businesses and home care agencies; assisted care facilities; the pharmaceutical, medical supply and technology industries and insurance companies; architects, law practices, banks and accounting firms specializing in disability; government and lobby groups; politicians; and last, the consumer' (Albrecht, 1992, as cited in Hughes et al., 2005: 10), the privileging of mobile and nomadic identities as disability liberation seems premature.

A PATH FORWARD?

Looking at contemporary social organization through disability foregrounds tensions inherent in consumerism, nationalism and globalization, demonstrating how physical norms still serve to define group membership. Ultimately, accommodation for human differences begs profound questions: Are we predominantly citizens, workers, or consumers, and how are the conflicts between these roles to be resolved? What do we owe to our fellow humans in terms of employment and material assistance to participate fully in society? Disability highlights important differences in cultural values, between individual-centered societies that provide, through informal caregiving and workers' insurance, societies that value social solidarity and public provision for the people with disabilities through charity, and societies that take the next step, advocating full inclusion in schooling and work as the right of every citizen, and providing the means to achieve it. In considering these questions, geographers allied to the 'meta-institutional formation' (Snyder and Mitchell, 2006: 203) known as disability studies will be called upon to help re-examine taken-for-granted belief and practice, and cooperate with disabled people themselves in forging new responses. But, as Imrie and Edwards (2007) suggest, these alliances are themselves complicated by the exclusive nature of academic disciplines and competing standards against which expertise and excellence are measured. True diversity in subjectivities, institutional orientations and worldviews is absolutely essential in this field if disability geographers are to engage constructively in these debates and push forward on the long march towards social justice.[1]

The survey presented here suggests several paths for further research. Kruse's master's thesis (2001) takes as its starting point the intriguing difference between the bird's-eye view of scientific geography and the more minute and mobile geographies of little people. But the vast social spaces and historical geographies of disability activism remain largely unexplored. Geographers, after Tyner (1999), have demonstrated their eagerness to explore the geopolitics of wartime eugenics. But what of the more mundane public health practices of diagnosis, reporting and 'preventing disability' that continually reshape the bodyscape? Researchers at the Dartmouth School of Medicine have explored the regional variations in the usage and effectiveness of certain medical procedures (Baicker et al., 2005). But how effective are disability movements in impacting these practices? Finally, there is a rich tradition of social geographers employing their tools of the trade in pursuing concrete projects of social justice. New handheld devices and internet applications offer the possibility of constructing communities of difference that link sites of production and consumption in intriguing new ways (Gilbert and Masucci, 2005). And yet we might do well to 'mind the gap' between the affirmation of difference that we find in movement-driven spaces of liberation and the residuum of solutions to the disability problem that have been reached too quickly or that were begun with inspiration, only to be allowed to wither and congeal.

Some have suggested that parallel strategies for empowerment and change have emerged from the mental health activist/consumers and physical disability/independent living consumer movements. If so, then how? Geographers have explored mental health issues as well as physical accessibility, and should have more to say in these matters. Disability scholars in the field need to develop strategies and find funding to work cooperatively in pursuing questions such as these – taking us beyond the either/or of public policy vs. disability studies, to consider the both/and of coalition-building and place-changing.

NOTE

1 Those interested in joining these conversations are invited to join the GEOGABLE electronic discussion list, hosted by the Computing Center at the University of Kentucky. Subscription information is available on the website of the Disability Specialty Group of the Association of American Geographers, or at http://isc.temple.edu/neighbor/service.

REFERENCES

Albrecht, Gary L. (1992) *The Disability Business: Rehabilitation in America.* Newbury Park: Sage.

Aldrich, Mark (2006) *Death Rode the Rails: American railroad accidents and safety, 1828–1965.* Baltimore, MD: Johns Hopkins University Press.

Anderson, Warwick (1996) 'Disease, race, and empire', *Bulletin of the History of Medicine,* 70: 62–7.

Anderson, Warwick (2006) *Colonial Pathologies: American tropical medicine, race, and hygiene in the Philippines*. Durham: Duke University Press.

Athanasiou, Tom (1996) *Divided Planet: The ecology of rich and poor*. Boston: Little, Brown.

Baicker, Katherine, Chandra, Amitabh and Skinner, Jonathan (2005) 'Geographic variation in health care and the problem of measuring racial disparities', *Perspectives in Biology and Medicine*, 48: S42–S53.

Barrett, Frank A. (2000) *Disease and Geography: The history of an idea*. Toronto: York University, Atkinson College.

Baynton, Douglas C. (1997) 'Disability: A useful category of historical analysis', *Disability Studies Quarterly*, 17: 81–7.

Baynton, Douglas C. (2005) 'Defectives in the land: Disability and American immigration policy, 1882–1924', *Journal of American Ethnic History*, 24: 31–44.

Berkowitz, Edward and Fox, Daniel M. (1989) 'The politics of social security expansion: Social Security Disability Insurance, 1935–1986', *Journal of Policy History*, 1: 233–60.

Blanck, Peter and Millender, Michael (2000) 'Before Disability Civil Rights: Civil War pensions and the politics of disability in America', *Alabama Law Review,* 52: 1–50.

Burgdorf, Marcia Pearce and Burgdorf, Robert (1975) 'A history of unequal treatment: The qualifications of handicapped persons as a "suspect class" under the equal protection clause', *Santa Clara Lawyer*, 15: 855–910.

Buttimer, Anne (1993) *Geography and the Human Spirit*. Baltimore: Johns Hopkins University Press.

Campbell, Jane and Oliver, Mike (1996) *Disability Politics: Understanding our past, changing our future*. London: Routledge.

Carey, Allison C. (2003) 'Beyond the medical model: A reconsideration of "feeblemindedness", citizenship, and eugenic restrictions', *Disability and Society,* 18: 411–30.

Chouinard, Vera (1999) 'Body politics: Disabled women's activism in Canada and beyond' in R. Butler and H. Parr (eds), *Mind and Body Spaces: Geographies of illness, impairment and disability*. London and New York: Routledge. pp. 269–94.

Chouinard, Vera (2001) 'Legal peripheries: Struggles over Disabled Canadian's places in law, society and space,' *The Canadian Geographer*, 45: 187–192.

Cook, Ian (1991) 'Drowning in see-world?', Critical ethnographies of blindness', PhD dissertation, University of Kentucky, Lexington, KY.

Craddock, Susan and Dorn, Michael L. (2001) 'Nationbuilding: Gender, race, and medical discourse', *Journal of Historical Geography,* 27: 313–18.

Cresswell, Tim (2006) *On the Move: Mobility and the modern Western world*. New York: Routledge.

Curtin, Philip D. (1989) *Death by Migration: Europe's Encounter with the Tropical World in the Nineteenth Century*. Cambridge, UK: Cambridge University Press.

Davenport, Charles B. (1915) *Nomadism, or the Wandering Impulse, with Special Reference to Heredity, Inheritance of Temperament*. Washington, DC: Carnegie Institution of Washington.

Davis, Lennard (1997) 'Constructing normalcy: The bell curve, the novel, and the invention of the disabled body in the nineteenth century', in L. Davis (ed.), *The Disability Studies Reader*. London: Routledge. pp. 9–28.

Davis, Lennard (2001) 'Identity politics, disability, and culture', in G.L. Albrecht, K.D. Seelman and M. Bury (eds), *Handbook of Disability Studies*. Thousand Oaks, CA: Sage. pp. 535–45.

Davis, Lennard (2006) 'Preface to the second edition', in L. Davis (ed.), *The Disability Studies Reader*. London: Routledge. pp. xiii–xiv.

Dear, Michael J. (1980) 'The public city', in W.A.V. Clark and E.G. Moore (eds), *Residential Mobility and Public Policy*. Beverly Hills: Sage. pp. 219–41.

Derickson, Alan (1998) *Black Lung: Anatomy of a public health disaster*. Ithaca, NY: Cornell University Press.

Dorn, Michael L. (1994) 'Disability as spatial dissidence: A cultural geography of the stigmatized body', MS thesis, Pennsylvania State University, University Park, PA.

Dorn, Michael L. (1998) 'Beyond nomadism: the travel narratives of a "cripple"', in H. Nast and S. Pile (eds), *Places Through the Body*. New York: Routledge. pp. 183–206

Dorr, Lisa Lindquist (2003) 'Arm in arm: Gender, eugenics, and Virginia's Racial Integrity Acts of the 1920s', *Journal of Women's History*, 11: 143–66.

Driver, Felix (1988) 'Moral geographies: social science and the urban environment in mid-nineteenth century England', *Transactions of the Institute of British Geographers*, 13: 275–87.

Driver, Felix (1993) *Power and Pauperism: The workhouse system, 1834–1884*. Cambridge, UK: Cambridge University Press.

Driver, Felix and Martins, Luciana (2005) *Tropical Visions in an Age of Empire*. Chicago: University of Chicago Press.

Dundon, M.L., Gay, G.A. and George, J.L. (1983) 'The 1978 revision of the U.S. standard certificates', *Vital and Health Statistic*, 4 (23): 1–58.

Dunham, Arthur (1940) 'The development of child welfare programs', *Annals of the American Academy of Political and Social Sciences*, 212: 216–22.

Eghigian, Greg (2000) *Making Security Social: Disability, insurance, and the birth of the social entitlement state in Germany*. Ann Arbor: University of Michigan Press.

Elliott, Carl (2003) *Better Than Well: American medicine meets the American dream*. New York: W.W. Norton.

Eyler, John M (1979) *Victorian Social Medicine: The ideas and methods of William Farr*. Baltimore and London: Johns Hopkins University Press.

Eyles, John (1977) 'After the relevance debate: The teaching of social geography', *Journal of Geography in Higher Education*, 1: 3–12.

Fairchild, Amy L. (2003) *Science at the Borders: Immigrant medical inspection and the shaping of the modern industrial labor force*. Baltimore: Johns Hopkins University Press.

Fairchild, Amy L., Bayer, Ronald, Colgrove, James Keith and Daniel Wolfe (2007) *Searching Eyes: Privacy, the state, and disease surveillance in America*. Berkeley: University of California Press.

Fairchild, Audrey B. Davis (1981) 'Life insurance and physical examination: A chapter in the rise of American medical technology', *Bulletin of the History of Medicine*, 55: 392–406.

Fee, Elizabeth (1989) 'Henry E. Sigerist: From the social production of disease to medical management and scientific socialism', *The Milbank Quarterly*, 67: 127–50.

Finkelstein, Vic. (1980) *Attitudes and Disabled People*. New York: World Rehabilitation Fund.

Fleischer, Doris Z. and Frieda Zames (2001) *The Disability Rights Movement: From charity to confrontation*. Philadelphia, PA: Temple University Press.

Frye, Victoria, Putnam, Sara and O'Campo, Patricia (2008) 'Whither gender in urban health?', *Health and Place*, 14: 616–22.

Gibson, Barbara E. (2006) 'Disability, connectivity and transgressing the autonomous body', *Journal of Medical Humanities*, 27: 187–96.

Giggs, John A. (1973) 'The distribution of schizophrenics in Nottingham', *Transactions of the Institute of British Geographers*, 59: 55–76.

Giggs, John A. and Smith, Christopher J. (1988) *Location and Stigma: Contemporary perspectives on mental health and mental health care*. London and Boston: Allen & Unwin.

Gilbert, Melissa R. and Masucci, Michele M. (2005) 'Research directions for information and communication technology and society in geography', *Geoforum*, 36: 277–9.

Gleeson, Brendan (1993) 'Second nature: The socio-spatial production of disability', PhD dissertation. University of Melbourne, Australia.

Gleeson, Brendan (1999) *Geographies of Disability*, London and New York: Routledge.

Golfus, Billie and Simpson, David E. (1994) *When Billy Broke his Head ... and Other Tales of Wonder*. Boston, MA: Fanlight Productions.

Golledge, Reginald G., Parnicky, J.J. and Rayner, J.N. (1979) 'An experimental design for assessing the spatial competence of mildly retarded populations', *Social Science and Medicine*, 13D: 292–5.

Graebner, William (1980) *A History of Retirement: The meaning and function of an American Institution, 1885–1978*. New Haven, CT: Yale University Press.

Graunt, John (1676) *Natural and Political Observations, mentioned in a following index, and made upon the bills of mortality*. London: John Martyn.

Grob, Gerald N. (1978) *Edward Jarvis and the Medical World of Nineteenth-century America*. Knoxville: University of Tennessee Press.

Guerts, Kathryn Linn (2002) *Culture and the Senses: Bodily ways of knowing in an*

African community. Berkeley: University of California Press.
Gusfield, Joseph R. (1981) *The Culture of Public Problems: Drinking-driving and the symbolic order*. Chicago: University of Chicago Press.
Hahn, Harlan (1988) 'The politics of physical differences: Disability and discrimination', *Journal of Social Issues*, 44: 39–47.
Halliburton, Murphy (2005) '"Just about some spirits": The erosion of spirit possession and the rise of "tension" in south India', *Medical Anthropology*, 24: 111–44.
Hamlin, Christopher (1998) *Public Health and Social Justice in the Age of Chadwick: Britain, 1800–1854*. New York: Cambridge University Press.
Hansen, Nancy and Philo, Chris (2007) 'The normality of doing things differently: Bodies, spaces and disability geography', *Tijdschrift voor Economische en Sociale Geografie*, 98: 493–506.
Hill, Miriam Helen (1986) 'The nonvisual life-world: A comparative phenomenology of blindness', PhD dissertation, Kent State University, Kent, OH.
Hirsch, Arnold R. (1983) *Making the Second Ghetto: Race and housing in Chicago, 1940–1960*. Cambridge, UK: Cambridge University Press.
Hughes, Bill, Russell, Rachel and Paterson, Kevin (2005) 'Nothing to be had "off the peg": consumption, identity and the immobilization of young disabled people', *Disability and Society*, 20: 3–17.
Imrie, Rob and Edwards, Claire (2007) 'The geographies of disability: Reflections on the development of a sub-discipline', *Geography Compass*, 1: 623–40.
Irving, Katrina (2000) *Immigrant Mothers: Narratives of race and maternity, 1890–1925*. Urbana: University of Illinois Press.
Jackson, Kenneth T. (1985) *Crabgrass Frontier: The suburbanization of America*. New York: Oxford University Press.
Jordan, Thomas E. (1992) *The Degeneracy Crisis and Victorian Youth*. Albany: State University of New York Press.
Jordanova, Ludmilla J. (1997) 'Earth science and environmental medicine: The synthesis of the late Enlightenment', in L.J. Jordanova and R.S. Porter (eds), *Images of the Earth: Essays in the history of the environmental sciences.* Oxford: printed by the Alden Press for the British Society for the History of Science. pp. 127–51
Jureidini, Ray and White, Kevin (2000) 'Life insurance, the medical examination and cultural values', *Journal of Historical Sociology*, 13: 190–214.
Kim, Jim Yong (2000) *Dying for Growth: Global inequality and the health of the poor*. Monroe, ME: Common Courage Press.
Kitchin, Rob and Wilton, Robert D. (2003) 'Disability activism and the politics of scale', *The Canadian Geographer*, 47: 97–115.
Kraut, Alan M. (1994) *Silent Travelers: Germs, genes, and the 'immigrant menace'*. New York, NY: Basic Books.
Krieger, Linda Hamilton (2003) *Backlash against the ADA: Reinterpreting disability rights*. Ann Arbor: University of Michigan Press.
Kruse, Robert J., II (2001) 'Social spaces of little people', MA thesis, Kent State University, Kent, OH.
Küppers, Petra (2004) *Disability and Contemporary Performance: Bodies on edge*. New York: Routledge.
Law, Robin and Gleeson, Brendan J. (1998) 'Another landscape of despair? Charting the "service-dependent ghetto" in Dunedin', *New Zealand Geographer*, 54: 27–36.
Laws, Glenda (1994) 'Oppression, knowledge, and the built environment', *Political Geography*, 13: 7–32.
Ley, David (1974) *Community Participation and the Spatial Order of the City*. Vancouver: Tantalus Research.
Licht, Walter (1983) *Working for the Railroads: The organization of work in the nineteenth century*. Princeton, NJ: Princeton University Press.
Linker, Beth (2007) 'Feet for fighting: Locating disability and social medicine in First World War America', *Social History of Medicine*, 20: 91–109.
Livingstone, Julie (2005) *Debility and the Moral Imagination in Botswana*. Bloomington: Indiana University Press.
Lovett, Andrew A. and Gatrell, Anthony C. (1988) 'The geography of spina bifida in England and Wales', *Transactions of the Institute of British Geographers*, 13: 288–302.
Markowitz, Gerald (1998) 'Commentary [C.-E. A. Winslow]', *Journal of Public Health Policy*, 19: 154–9.

Metzel, Deborah S. and Walker, Pamela M. (2001) 'The illusion of inclusion: Geographies of the lives of people with developmental disabilities in the United States', *Disability Studies Quarterly*, 21. Retrieved June 19, 2008. http://www.dsq-sds.org/_articles_pdf/2001/Fall/dsq_2001_Fall_13.pdf

Moran, Michelle Therese (2007) *Colonizing Leprosy: Imperialism and the politics of public health in the United States*. Chapel Hill: University of North Carolina Press.

Murray, Christopher J.L. and Lopez, Alan D. (1996) *The Global Burden of Disease: A comprehensive assessment of mortality and disability from diseases, injuries, and risk factors in 1990 and projected to 2020*. Cambridge, MA: Harvard University Press.

National Organization on Disability (1998) *The 1998 N.O.D. / Harris Survey of Americans with Disabilities*. Washington, D.C.: Author.

Naylor, A., Eaton, A.P., Aplin, E.R. and Eska, B. (1974) 'Birth certificate revision and reporting of congenital malformations', *American Journal of Public Health*, 64 (8): 786–91.

Newman, Simon P. (2003) *Embodied History: The lives of the poor in early Philadelphia*. Philadelphia: University of Pennsylvania Press.

Nugent, Angela (1983) 'Fit for work: The introduction of physical examinations in industry', *Bulletin of the History of Medicine*, 57: 578–95.

Oliver, Mike (1990) *The Politics of Disablement: A sociological approach*. New York: St Martin's Press.

Packard, Randall M. (1989) *White Plague, Black Labor: Tuberculosis and the political economy of health and disease in South Africa*. Berkeley: University of California Press.

Park, Deborah C. (1995) 'An imprisoned text: Reading the Canadian mental handicap asylum', PhD dissertation, York University, Toronto.

Park, Deborah C., Radford, John and Vickers, Michael (1998) 'Disability studies in human geography', *Progress in Human Geography*, 22: 208–33.

Parr, Hester (2007) 'Mental health, nature work, and social inclusion', *Environment and Planning D: Society and Space*, 31: 537–61.

Perle, Edward D. (1969) 'Urban mobility needs of the handicapped: An exploration', PhD dissertation, University of Pittsburgh, Pittsburgh, PA.

Philo, Chris (1995) 'Journey to asylum: A medical–geographical idea in historical context', *Journal of Historical Geography*, 21: 148–68.

Philo, Chris (1997a) 'Across the water: Reviewing geographical studies of asylums and other mental health facilities', *Health and Place*, 3: 73–89.

Philo, Chris (1997b) 'The "chaotic spaces" of medieval madness: Thoughts on the English and Welsh experience', in M. Teich, R. Porter and B. Gustafsson (eds), *Nature and Society in Historical Context*. Cambridge: Cambridge University Press. pp. 51–90.

Philo, Chris (2005) 'The geography of mental health: An established field?', *Current Opinion in Psychiatry*, 18: 585–91.

Porter, Dorothy (1997) 'Introduction', in Dorothy Porter (ed.), *Social Medicine and Medical Sociology in the Twentieth Century*. Atlanta GA: Editions Rodopi. pp. 1–32.

Radford, John P. and Park, Deborah C. (1995) 'The eugenic legacy', *Journal of Developmental Disabilities*, 4: 63–74.

Resch, John Phillips (1999) *Suffering Soldiers: Revolutionary War veterans, moral sentiment, and political culture in the early republic*. Amherst: University of Massachusetts Press.

Richards, Penny L. (2004) 'Points of entry: Disability and the historical geography of immigration', *Disability Studies Quarterly*, 24.

Riley, James C. (1997) *Sick, not Dead: The health of British workingmen during the mortality decline*. Baltimore, MD: Johns Hopkins University Press.

Rogers, Richard G., Hummer, Robert A. and Nam, Charles B. (2000) *Living and Dying in the USA: Behavioral, health, and social differentials of adult mortality*. San Diego, CA: Academic Press.

Rosen, George (1943) *The History of Miners' Diseases: A medical and social interpretation*. New York: Schuman's.

Rosen, George (1953a) 'Cameralism and the concept of medical police', *Bulletin of the History of Medicine*, 27: 21–42.

Rosen, George (1953b) 'Leonhard Ludwig Finke and the first medical geography', in E.A. Underwood (ed.), *Science, Medicine and History: Essays on the evolution of scientific thought and medical practice*. London: Oxford University Press. pp. 186–9.

Rosner, David and Markowitz, Gerald E. (1991) *Deadly Dust: Silicosis and the politics of occupational disease in twentieth-century America*. Princeton, NJ: Princeton University Press.

Scarry, Elaine (1985) *The Body in Pain: The making and unmaking of the world*. New York: Oxford University Press.

Schatzki, Theodore R. (2002) *The Site of the Social: A philosophical account of the constitution of social life and change*. University Park, PA: Pennsylvania State University Press.

Scheer, Jessica and Groce, Nora (1988) 'Impairment as a human constant: Cross-cultural and historical perspectives on variation', *Journal of Social Issues*, 44: 23–37.

Schweik, Susan (2007) 'Begging the question: Disability, mendicancy, speech and the law', *Narrative*, 15: 58–70.

Sellers, Christopher C. (1997) *Hazards of the Job: From industrial disease to environmental health science*. Chapel Hill: University of North Carolina Press.

Sibley, David (1995) *Geographies of Exclusion*. New York: Routledge.

Sigerist, Henry E. (1943) 'From Bismarck to Beveridge: Developments and trends in social security legislation', *Bulletin of the History of Medicine*, 13: 365–88.

Snyder, Sharon L. and Mitchell, David T. (2006) *Cultural Locations of Disability*. Chicago: University of Chicago Press.

Sothern, Matthew (2007) 'You could truly be yourself if you just weren't you: Sexuality, disabled body space, and the (neo)liberal politics of self-help', *Environment and Planning D: Society and Space*, 25: 144–59.

Stobie, Jamie (1994) *'Freedom Machines'*. Harriman, New York: New Day Films.

Stone, Debra A. (1984) *'The Disabled State'*. Philadelphia, PA: Temple University Press.

Switzer, Jacqueline Vaughn (2003) *Disabled Rights: American disability policy and the fight for equality*. Washington, DC: Georgetown University Press.

Taylor, S. Martin (1988) 'Community reactions to deinstitutionalization', in C. Smith and J. Giggs (eds), *Location and Stigma: Contemporary perspectives on mental health and mental health care*. Boston, MA: Unwin Hyman. pp. 224–45.

Terris, Milton (1998) 'C.-E.A. Winslow: Scientist, activist, and theoretician of the American Public Health Movement throughout the first half of the twentieth century', *Journal of Public Health Policy*, 19: 135–46.

Thien, Deborah (2005) 'After or beyond feeling? A consideration of affect and emotion in geography', *Area*, 37: 450–6.

Thompson, E.P. (1967) 'Time, work-discipline, and industrial capitalism', *Past and Present*, 38: 56–97.

Tuntiya, Nana (2007) 'Free-air treatment for mental patients: The deinstitutionalization debate of the nineteenth century', *Sociological Perspectives*, 50: 469–88.

Tyner, James A. (1999) 'The geopolitics of eugenics and the exclusion of Philippine immigrants from the United States', *Geographical Review*, 89: 54–73.

US Department of Health and Human Services (1982) *Vital Statistics of the United States 1978, Volume I – Natality*. Washington, DC: By author.

Vaughn, Jacqueline (2003) *Disabled Rights: American disability policy and the fight for equality*. Washington, DC: Georgetown University Press.

Watkins, M.L., Edmonds, L., McClearn, L.A., Mullins, L., Mulinare, J. and Khoury, M. (1996) 'The surveillance of birth defects: The usefulness of the revised US standard birth certificate', *American Journal of Public Health*, 86: 731–34.

Wilder, C.S. (1963) 'Acute conditions, incidence and associated disability (United States–July 1961–June 1962)', Report No. 1, Series 10, Data from the National Health Interview Survey. Hyattsville, MD: National Center for Health Statistics. (PHS) 1000. PB-281659. PC A04 MF A01. Available online at http://www.cdc.gov/nchs/products/pubs/pubd/series/ser.htm#sr10

Wilton, Robert D. (2004a) 'From flexibility to accommodation?, Disabled people and the reinvention of paid work', *Transactions of the Institute of British Geographers*, 29: 420–32.

Wilton, Robert D. (2004b) 'More responsibility, less control: Psychiatric survivors and welfare state restructuring', *Disability and Society*, 19: 371–85.

Wilton, Robert D. and Schuer, S. (2006) 'Towards socio-spatial inclusion? Disabled people, neoliberalism and the contemporary labour market', *Area*, 38: 186–95.

Winslow, C.-E. A. (1945) 'Changing challenges of public health', *American Journal of Public Health*, 35: 191–98.

Wolch, Jennifer R. (1979) 'Residential location of the provision of human services: Some directions for geographic research', *Professional Geographer*, 31: 271–7.

Wolch, Jennifer R. and Philo, Chris (2000) 'From distributions of deviance to definitions of difference: Past and future mental health geographies', *Health and Place*, 6: 137–57.

Wolpert, Julian (1980) 'The dignity of risk', *Transactions of the Institute of British Geographers*, 5: 391–410.

Wolpert, Julian, Mumphrey, A. and Seley, J. (1972) 'Metropolitan neighborhoods: Participation and conflict over change', in Association of American Geographers, *Commission on College Geography, Resource Paper No. 16*. Washington, DC.

Wright, John K. (1947) 'Terrae incognitae: The place of the imagination in geography', *Journal of Historical Geography*, 37: 1–15.

Yelin, Edward H. (1992) *Disability and the Displaced Worker*. New Brunswick, NJ: Rutgers University Press.

Zelizer, Viviana A. Rotman (1985) *Pricing the Priceless Child: The changing social value of children*. New York: Basic Books.

Zola, Irving Kenneth (1983) 'Pathways to the doctor – From person to patient', *Social Science and Medicine*, 7: 677–89.

Zola, Irving Kenneth (1993) 'The sleeping giant in our midst: Redefining "persons with disabilities"', in L.O. Gostin and H.A. Beyer (eds), *Implementing the Americans with Disabilities Act: Rights and responsibilities of all Americans*. Baltimore: Paul H. Brooks. pp. xvii-xx.

4

Colonialism and the Tensioned Landscapes of Indigeneity

Audrey Kobayashi and Sarah de Leeuw

In a 2007 interview with *USA Today*, Native American activist Lynn Hart gave personal voice to a complex issue: 'When I go to the [Indian] reservation, people see me as black. When I walk among blacks, they see me as Indian' (quoted in Hatton, 2007). Hart's words capture a deep tension between indigenous peoples and other racialized minorities, illustrating the many complex identity issues experienced by people who are multiply-othered within contemporary, globalized white settler colonial geographies. Hart was commenting on the Cherokee Freedmen debate, which was of such importance that the *New York Times* (2007: A22) dedicated an entire editorial to the issue. The controversy revolved around blood lines, genealogy, identity, self-determination, and historical claims to race and ethnicity. The Cherokee Freedmen came into being after the Civil War. Cherokee peoples had for millennia kept slaves, a tradition that did not abate with the arrival of African slaves during the 17th century. After the Civil War, in an effort to secure tribal sovereignty as a distinct nation within America and with significant input from the federal government of the United States, the Cherokee people in 1866 signed a treaty granting Cherokee citizenship to emancipated slaves who had previously been owned by Cherokee peoples. Shortly thereafter, for the purposes of fixing resource obligations to citizens of the Cherokee Nation, the government began to enumerate all Cherokee citizens, including Freedmen (Ray, 2006).

In a profoundly divisive move in keeping with colonial efforts to minimize responsibility to indigenous or displaced slaves, census lists were compiled throughout the 1890s as a means to establish levels of government responsibility to members of the Cherokee Nation. The so-called 'Dawes Roll'[1] enumerated Cherokee citizens on the basis of a percentage of Indian ancestry. All citizens of slave decent were listed as Freedmen, whatever their Cherokee lineage may have been, while predominantly non-black citizens were listed as being Cherokee by 'blood'. This colonially imposed distinction has led to troubling contemporary schisms, including efforts by the Cherokee Nation to revoke the citizenship of all Freedmen members under the proposition that, as descendants of slaves, they are not Cherokee people. While disenfranchisement was ruled illegal in 2006 by the Cherokee National Tribal Court, a special referendum authorizing revocation of the Freedmen's status was approved by members in 2007. In response, the Congressional Black Caucus has called for funding to the Cherokee Nation to be cut off. The disenfranchised Cherokee Freedmen, along with many members of the Cherokee Nation, are petitioning the Cherokee Tribal Government and the Federal Courts with arguments of racial discrimination. Cherokee leaders opposed to disenfranchisement argue that citizenship in the Cherokee Nation must never rest upon blood quantum traits while those in favor of disenfranchising the Freedmen argue that indigenous governments, like other governments and nations, must have the right to decide who is and who is not granted citizenship within their boundaries. The Cherokee Freedmen controversy illustrates the immense complexities of relationships between indigenous and diasporic peoples, both of whom are racialized and marginalized within colonial settler societies. These complex relationships play out across multiple places and require nuanced and sensitive methods of understanding and investigation, particularly in reference to colonial geographies.

Colonialism has produced two distinct and often conflicting forms of geographic displacement. In colonized societies, it has usurped the land and resources of indigenous peoples in places, with widespread and widely acknowledged consequences that continue to the present day. In many places, especially in white settler societies, it has also resulted in large-scale movements of migrant labor imported to carry out subordinate work in conditions that range from slavery that began throughout the Americas during the 17th century, to indentured labor throughout those parts of the world where plantation or natural resource extraction economies were established, to the creation of large diasporic and transnational labor forces in today's advanced capitalist economies. The results of both processes have been extensively studied and theorized by geographers and other social scientists; but rather little attention has been paid to the contradictions and conflicts that may result from these two different historical geographies.

In many parts of the world, social geographies of displacement have developed simultaneously and dramatically, and often in close spatial proximity. Throughout the Caribbean, for example, indigenous populations were wiped out by disease and genocide at the same time that massive movements of plantation workers, first as slaves from Africa and later as indentured workers from South and East Asia, were established in large numbers. In North America, laborers, particularly from China, were brought by the thousands to do the dangerous work of driving the transcontinental railway lines through the mountains at the same time that local indigenous peoples were being violently subdued and relocated to reservations. In contemporary white settler societies, the number of non-white labor migrants (both documented and undocumented) working in the lowest-paid positions has reached unprecedented numbers and proportions, especially but not only in large cities, while indigenous peoples live in deep poverty, especially but not only in marginal rural areas.

Both indigenous and migratory displaced peoples share the experience of racialization in a colonial context, although the range of experiences and geographical conditions of racialization is vast and complex. Yet both broadly defined groups create fiduciary, legal, demographic and political contention for nation-states and individual citizens of those states, particularly in claims for reconciliation and redress (Gooder and Jacobs, 2000). Additionally, while all bear the scars of colonialism, the conflicts between indigenous and racialized migrant peoples across their respective historical geographies can produce multiple tensions across three major pairings: 1) those between all racialized groups and white Eurocolonial settler populations; 2) between indigenous peoples and predominantly white Eurocolonial peoples;

and 3) between indigenous peoples and non-white, non-indigenous peoples. Colonial and postcolonial landscapes are thus fraught with competing claims to power, many of which come into stark relief when viewed through a social geographic lens of multiple othernesses and difference. Such a lens highlights the political, strategic and socially constructed (and contested) nature of identity claims. A lens of multiple otherness serves to illustrate the ontological and material nature of social positionings. Contemporary relationships between indigenous peoples and Others therefore provide compelling examples of negotiations and collisions between identity and politics, power, and inequality, positioned across a broad social geographical spectrum.

Such conflicts are more compelling given the degree to which anti-oppression and anti-racism politics have increased in recent times, both locally and internationally. Indigenous peoples around the world are increasingly becoming organized and mobilized through an international movement for 'indigenism' (Niezen, 2000). International anti-racist organizations, including, for example, the movement for slavery reparations (one of the most controversial anti-racist initiatives), span many nations in their quest to redress racialization as a global phenomenon. In localized struggles, indigenous voices and perspectives also often come into direct conflict with the everyday lives of non-indigenous peoples. This is certainly the case given the resurgence of indigenous peoples' demands for redress for cultural and material losses associated with colonization and colonial practices.

In this chapter we explore the social geography of citizenship, nationality and claims to nationhood, race, access to resources, identity, and the politics of difference and sameness as each of these themes is manifest in often competing and difficult relations between indigenous and non-indigenous peoples. Over the past two decades human geography has, first through the cultural turn and then through the responding ontological turn, taken a number of directions with reference to questions of race, difference, matrices of power and politics and, more recently, the rights of indigenous and diasporic peoples. We provide an overview of discussions about social geographies of sameness and difference. We then move to indigeneity, a topic that has received relatively little attention from social geographers. We stress the importance of the writings of indigenous peoples, many of whom point out the risks associated with homogenous categorizations of vastly different peoples. Next we explore some of the racialized conflicts between indigenous peoples and Others, an even more neglected topic of social geography. We conclude our discussion with thoughts about future new directions in research about the social geographies of difference, how geographic methods may account for questions of multiple otherness, the social relationships among the people who ultimately embody otherness, and the possibilities for a more robust and rejuvenated social geography premised in part on understanding the complex relationships between indigenous and non-indigenous peoples.

RACIALIZATION, IDENTITY, AND SOCIAL GEOGRAPHIES OF DIFFERENCE

Although precise definitions of social geography have, over the years, become more and more mutable, the subdiscipline might be understood as focusing on the spatiality of social conditions; social geographers tend also to be motivated by concerns about issues of social (in)justice and political (in)equality (Smith, 2000). Themes of difference, particularly when differences are situated within constructions of gender, race, class and, more recently, sexual orientation, and mobility or disability, are often the focus of study by social geographers (e.g., Peake and Shein, 2000; Anderson, 2001; Browne, 2007).

Social geography became a strong force in Britain, the United States and Canada through the 1970s, fueled primarily by the qualitative revolution and a growing Marxist social consciousness in the academy (Smith, 2000). By the late 1980s, however, radical and critical geographers, including feminist geographers, had become heavily invested in questions of culture and the cultural. Theories of difference in human geography have received their most expansive discussion in the umbrella of cultural geography, because the 'cultural turn' focused on the discursive process of representation through which human identities are constructed. Nevertheless, by placing great emphasis on the socially constitutive and socially constructed nature of the world, the cultural turn drew criticism from feminist, Marxist and antiracist geographers who observed the danger of reducing everything to the realm of the discursive, the semiotic, the constructed, or the 'immaterial' (Domosh 2005). Although it is now widely accepted through human geography that difference and sameness are both socially constructed and material, an uneasy tension nonetheless persists between social and cultural geography. Many have tried to address the tension by reinvigorating the politics of geography's cultural turn on the one hand, and, on the other, addressing cultural considerations within studies of the social without reducing the social to an immaterial cultural expression (Smith, 2000; Pain and Bailey, 2004). Perhaps somewhat ironically from a social geography perspective, many critical cultural geographers argued that this reduction negated considerations of social justice and political action by erasing realities of power and difference between diverse subjects across multiple places and times.

Despite these criticisms, geography's cultural turn drastically altered the contours of the discipline and social geography as a subdiscipline experienced a diminishment while cultural geography experienced sustained growth. By the onset of the 21st century, and in great part on account of continual and creative efforts to reinvent 'the critical edge of scholarship' (Smith, 2000: 26), aspects of cultural geography had increasingly transformed into a politicized sphere of inquiry. Part of that politicization, as borne out in the literature, arose from cultural geography's increased reconnection with social geography, the result of which was (and is) an overall rematerialization of human geography. These disciplinary evolutions have been summarized as transformations 'from the material to the immaterial and back again' (Pain and Bailey, 2004) and have more recently, with reference to questions of race, been considered, albeit thinly, by human geographers (Saldanha, 2006).

We take issue, however, with the depiction of theory by some geographers as 'material' and 'immaterial'. The wide range of studies that call themselves 'cultural studies', and the poststructuralist movement in general, are firmly grounded in historical materialism through the work of scholars such as Raymond Williams, Edward Said and Michel Foucault. In the emphasis on discursive acts that marked the 1990s, however, cultural geographers did tend to place much greater stress on questions of representation, without necessarily making it clear that acts of representation are also often acts of political struggle involving a commitment to activism. In this contemporary moment of 'back again', social geography is again positioned to ask questions about social (in)justice and (in)equality, particularly as they are spatially experienced. Of particular concern are questions of embodied difference, including questions of race and racialization, in which indigenous peoples are beginning to appear more prominently.

That racial typologies are a wholly imagined, antiquated, and problematic means of differentiating between humans has achieved broad and multidisciplinary agreement. There remains, however, the persistent and challenging reality that such classifications continue to play out in our everyday lives (Saldanha, 2006), with problematic outcomes for people who, according to what Gyatri Spivak identifies as the politics of chromatics (social divisions of people based on skin color), are cast outside a visual spectrum of whiteness (see McClintock, 1995). 'Race' might thus be understood as 'a social construction, not a biological essence, but a result of discursive, and thoroughly material – and human – social process [whereby] the material and the ideological … are not separate, nor are they alternative, but rather two dimensions of human action, ontologically inseparable' (Kobayashi and Peake, 1994; 2000: 393.). Racialization is 'therefore the processes by which racialized groups are identified, given stereotypical characteristics, and coerced into specific social/spatial segregation. … It is one of the most enduring and fundamental means of organizing society' (Kobayashi and Peake, 2000: 393). As such, a consideration of the process of racialization is fundamental to social geography.

Although race and racialization remain enduring means of producing striated and hierarchical social spaces, it would be a mistake either to think that the practices of racialization are produced homogeneously or to assume that racialization uniformly affects all racialized bodies. Instead, in order to understand social constructions of race and processes of racialization, particularly as they unfold across different geographies and are embodied by varied subjects, it is useful to recognize the deep differences between people who nonetheless share experiences of being racialized. Recognition of different subjects who share some experiences as othered bodies is well considered, especially as those differences are also articulated through markers of gender, class, ability, or sexual orientation (Pratt and Hanson, 1994).

It is also imperative to consider internal differences among peoples who might self-identify as sharing the experience of being racialized because of a common ethnic heritage. Although understanding distributions of Chinese Canadians across a city such as Vancouver must account for the production of racialized subjects in relation to specific places such as Chinatown (Anderson, 1991), the social distribution might be more fully understood when theorized in tandem with class, family connections, or even sexual orientation. Such an approach avoids reductionism by moving beyond the privileging of 'Chineseness' when considering how racialized peoples experience and live in the cities and places experienced as home. Although immigrants from Bangladesh to Britain may share some common social experiences of segregation and ghettoization circumscribed by a racialized status dictated by white British citizens (Peach, 1996), some members within the racialized group may experience more acute senses of that segregation based on gender. This difference might lead in turn to feelings of identity-affinity that supersede racialized identity and rest instead on identifying first and foremost as a man, woman, or transgendered person. Identity, then, hinges on a complex and multivalent set of material and ideological factors. Race is certainly a prominent lens through which to understand people's experience of self as social beings and their spatial expressions of identity but, like other socially constructed markers, race cannot meaningfully be understood in isolation from other factors. If there exist multiple differences between subjects already marked as different on the basis of processes of racialization, a question arises about the inter- and intra-relationships of differently racialized peoples. What is surprising about the social geography literature is that, having addressed the complicated intersection of race and other forms of social identity, rather little has been said about the intersections of different kinds of race. Relations between indigenous and non-indigenous peoples, particularly when the non-indigenous peoples are also non-white racialized bodies, have much to offer our understanding of social geographies of difference.

THE SOCIAL GEOGRAPHIES OF INDIGENEITY AND INDIGENOUS PEOPLES

Indigenous peoples have for a long time figured in the research of human geographers. The nature of that research and the assumptions and methods behind it, however, have shifted significantly through the 20th century and into the 21st century. Much of the transformation of geographic research involving indigenous peoples has occurred in conjunction with broader disciplinary developments that politicized the practices of scholarly research, recognized questions of power and identity in the production of knowledge, and insisted upon feminist and anti-racist programs of research within and outside the discipline (Driver, 1992; Domosh, 1997; Katz, 1992; Kobayashi and Peake, 2000). Through most of the 20th century, if it considered them at all, geographic research was inclined to conflate indigenous peoples and the natural environment, perpetuating ideals of the 'noble savage' living in spiritually attuned communities understood both biologically and culturally to be authentic and unmediated primordial outcomes of wild, untamed lands. Geographic research in the humanistic tradition looked idealistically to indigenous societies as exemplars of the spiritually elevated, representing possible elixirs to the ills of a modern world, which included fast-paced, citified, suburbanized, soulless, non-indigenous societies living at odds with their surrounding natural landscapes (e.g., Bunske, 2004; Tuan, 1971; Sauer, 1975; Sack, 1986).

Critics of early work concerning indigenous peoples charged that the research was essentialist and simplistic. Much of this criticism was anchored in a growing deployment of post-structuralism, the tenets of which demanded a destabilization of fixed notions of identity and emphasized the recursive relationship between subjects constructing their own identity and colonial ascriptions. Antiracist, postcolonial and feminist geographers have observed that the production of research, particularly about socially marginalized and racialized peoples, is a political act in and of itself, often with outcomes that perpetuate the marginalization of the subjects upon whom the research is focused. As such claims have taken hold within the discipline, geography's project has turned to recognizing configurations of power that have situated indigenous peoples spatially in specific ways, and to understanding the various social, cultural, economic and political means by which their experiences are organized (e.g., Jacobs, 1996). The focus has been strongly on colonial discourses that have produced indigenous imaginaries among Eurocolonists, thereby justifying colonization of land and territory, as well as on the dynamic ways in which indigenous people inhabit, produce, and respond to multiple places, including the urban environment (e.g., Clayton, 2000; Peters, 2000; Braun, 2002; Harris, 2002; Razack, 2002). In short, by destabilizing fixed and essentialized assumptions, geographic inquiry moved towards a much more complex and nuanced understanding of indigenous peoples, their identities, and their relationships to and with other indigenous and non-indigenous peoples (Willems-Braun, 1997; Sparke 1998). By drawing upon these new trajectories and, importantly, by challenging essentialist assumptions, we challenge the ontological status of indigeneity as well as that of whiteness.

As the discipline has shifted, so has the language about indigenous peoples. Nomenclature pertaining to indigenous peoples has become a site of significant discussion, signaling the increased politicization of naming practices linked to identity, the reclamation of voices dispossessed by colonialism, and the highly variable and often fragmented circumstances of groups of people who might all identify as indigenous to an area. Around the world, indigenous peoples are repatriating names of which they were stripped under colonial rule (Retzlaff, 2005). For instance, the indigenous peoples of northern Europe and Scandinavia, once called by the settler term Laplanders, are now known as Sami. In Mexico, peoples such as the Zapatistas are distinguishing themselves as Mayans. Peoples once called Aborigines in Australia have reconfigured references to themselves to be known as Aboriginal Australians broadly and, more specifically, by names of individual lineages (the Noongar in southern Western Australia or the

Anangu in northern South Australia and neighboring parts of Western Australia). In both Canada and the United States, the ubiquitous term 'Indian' has given way to terms that recognize differences in culture, geography, and status. First Nations, Native American, Aboriginal, Métis or Inuit have displaced the term Indian, although these broader categories do not account for cultural specificity; here, indigenous peoples argue for the names of their particular cultures or nations. The Haida live on the northwest coast of Canada and the Tohono O'odham reside in the southwestern United States (Arizona) and northwestern Mexico. Globally, indigenous peoples have politicized their oftentimes marginalized socioeconomic status by referring to themselves as Fourth World Peoples, while the term First Peoples is also circulating within global contexts such as that of the United Nations. In short, as Taiaiake Alfred (1999, 2007) of the Kanien'kehaka (Mohawk) Nation asserts, indigenous peoples embody all, if not more, of the sociocultural complexities embodied by non-indigenous peoples while sharing a common experience of being colonized.

Despite the increasing complexity of naming practices, which signal an intensified effort to establish sovereign social and cultural identities separate from settler-colonial peoples, there remain difficulties in delineating a specific set of traits or characteristics that define or demarcate exactly what it means to be an indigenous person. These difficulties exist both internally and externally for indigenous communities. In some countries, including Australia, Aotearoa/New Zealand and Canada, settler-colonial governments continue to play a role in defining indigeneity. In Canada, for instance, the national constitution recognizes indigenous or aboriginal peoples (First Nations, Inuit and Métis) as having differential rights, including the rights to access unique services or to be consulted about land uses and resource allocations in some jurisdictions. Such rights stem directly from their status as first inhabitants of their respective territories. The federal government, however, retains jurisdictional power over defining who does and who does not meet the criteria that give the right to be an indigenous person, thereby externally bestowing upon a people their claim to an identity. The example of the Cherokee Freedmen, in contrast, evokes the tensions *within* an indigenous nation over identity rights.

The United Nations Permanent Forum on Indigenous Issues (UNPFII, no date) defines indigenous peoples as 'those which, having a historical continuity with pre-invasion and pre-colonial societies that developed on their territories, consider themselves distinct from other sectors of the societies now prevailing in those territories, or parts of them' (Cobo, 1986). UNPFII identifies some 370 million people in seventy nations as indigenous. The United Nations *Declaration on the Rights of Indigenous People* (adopted by the General Assembly on 13 September 2007 with four nations – Australia, Canada, Aotearoa/New Zealand and the United States – voting against) does not define indigeneity as such, but takes as given that indigenous peoples have been deprived of rights, lands and resources as a result of colonialism. It also explicitly recognizes the international movement, and the right, of indigenous peoples to reclaim what they have lost. This international definition, then, does not rely on essentialized or primordial definitions, but on the active engagement between colonizer and colonized in the negotiation of human rights.

For social geographers who work with indigenous issues, challenges arise from questioning essentialized and reductionist characterizations while simultaneously acknowledging that very real differences in social, economic and cultural factors continue to structure the lives of indigenous peoples *vis-à-vis* non-indigenous peoples. While there is an increasing effort to unfix biologically anchored categorizations of peoples, there is also a desire to politicize the unjust and unequal positions of the world's most marginalized (e.g., Nettleton et al., 2007). Additionally, much geographic work concerning indigenous peoples draws, at least in part, on pathbreaking works developed by postcolonial theorists Homi Bhabha, Edward Said and Gyatri Spivak, whose writings often focus upon geographies from which British and French colonial presences have departed (Gilmartin and Berg, 2007). The fundamental incongruity of using these theories and models is that many indigenous peoples in Pacific Island nations, in North and South America, and in Aotearoa/New Zealand and Australia, understand themselves as still living under colonial occupation, particularly in regions where territory was never ceded, where the settler-colonial presence remains, and where the right to sovereignty and self-determination is still denied by a colonial infrastructure (Yazzie, 1996; Fletcher, 2005). In this sense, discussions of (post)coloniality – at least in terms of a settler presence and land occupation – cannot be unproblematically superimposed from one place to another or upon peoples in differently colonized landscapes.

For indigenous peoples themselves, definitions of identity are equally complex. Many argue unique and/or traditional relationships with ecology and land (Battiste, 2000; Battiste and Youngblood-Henderson, 2000). Stemming from this relationship they articulate distinctive ways of knowing and being that manifest in languages, cultural representations, spiritual practices and social structures. Many connect indigeneity with a lineage to the first inhabitants of an area, while others link their identities to being colonized peoples (Smith, 1999). Indigenous peoples themselves recognize the many challenges of identity. An increasingly globalized and urbanizing world is leading to the wide hybridization of peoples for whom identity claims based on a specific lineage become difficult. Linking identity to nature and ecology has proven problematic in the past and often continues to elicit in non-indigenous peoples an understanding of indigenous cultures as quaint and unidimensional, best understood through cultural performances and relic landscapes (Alfred and Lowe, 2006). Additionally, no culture is static; identity claims based on essentialized notions of tradition run the risk of supporting regressive, externally imposed, policies or social positioning. Finally, different indigenous peoples and communities can have overlapping land, resource, and cultural claims, sometimes leading to competing claims concerning 'authentic' indigeneity and corresponding rights (Sterritt et al., 1998). Despite their broad differences, however, many indigenous peoples agree at least in part that their sense of indigeneity is captured in Māori scholar Linda Tuhiwai Smith's (1999) assertion that what makes a person indigenous is that they have no *other* homeland, other than that which they occupy, to which they might return or which might be (re)claimed. Taking into account the complexities of identity, it is safe to say that place and geography are significant factors in the ways that indigenous peoples define and understand themselves. Their identity is not only a matter or cultural recognition, but of citizenship (De Costa, 2006).

All definitions of indigeneity are relational. As Castree (2004: 153) points out, the term has only arisen in the post-World War II era through the recognition of the effects of colonialism and is based on the recognition that indigenous peoples have 'had to reckon with the influence of "non-indigenous" peoples past and present. As anthropologists Cleveland and Murray ([et al.], 1997: 479) argue, "indigenous peoples must be understood in terms of their interaction with the modern world"'. Those interactions need to take into account not only a colonial past but a globalized and still colonial present.

Issues of identity, and the characteristics that allow some and not others to claim indigeneity, ultimately play out on the ground in material ways. Tense relationships between white Eurocolonial settlers and indigenous peoples present some of the clearest examples of competing claims, particularly in relation to land and territory. In efforts to legitimate and secure claims to land in

Australia, white Eurocolonial settlers have formulated complex arguments about their own indigenous connection with place (Perera, 1996; see also Nash, 2002). In Canada, land claims and demands for self-government have been tested in the country's highest courts, have resulted in blockades of railways and highways, have motivated contentious referendums around which tremendous social tensions have arisen, and have even resulted in small pop-culture industries spawning bumper stickers, T-shirts, caps and posters with competing slogans like 'One Country, One People, One Law' or 'Canada, You're home on Native land' (Blomley, 1996; Wood, 2003; Rossiter and Wood, 2005). No such tongue-in-cheek quips are relevant, however, where armed standoffs have occurred, with sometimes tragic results when indigenous peoples have stood their ground. The results have been so tragic that Amnesty International called for a public inquiry into the Ipperwash Provincial Park confrontation during which police shot and killed Dudley George, an unarmed indigenous man occupying land claimed to be sacred ground (Amnesty International Canada, 2006). For seventy-eight days between July and September of 1990, thousands of Mohawk people clashed with members of the Royal Canadian Mounted Police and the Canadian Armed Forces over territory the Mohawk Nation claimed as unceded land. Three deaths were attributed to the standoff and relationships between all involved have, by many accounts, never healed (York and Pindera, 1991).

In contrast to stand-off situations, the development in recent years of what is now termed 'indigenism' represents a movement to use the international political forum to forge transnational coalitions of indigenous peoples, linking experiences of colonialism across geographic boundaries. As Niezen (2000: 120–21) notes:

> The indigenous peoples' movement has arisen out of the shared experience of marginalized groups facing the negative impacts of resource extraction and economic modernization and, as Benedict Kingsbury sagely notes, to the social convergence and homogenization these ambitions tend to bring about (1998: 421). Indigenous identity has also grown largely out of successful nationalisms themselves; international legislative bodies of states have provided the conceptual origins and practical focus of indigenous identity. With little public awareness, and with the obvious terminology little up to this point, an international movement has led to an important new 'ism'.

The indigenism movement has supported a large number of high-profile actions that have brought the concerns of indigenous people to world attention, capitalizing upon coalition politics. In 1990, led by Grand Chief Matthew Coon Come and assisted by a range of other indigenous groups and environmental groups, James Bay Cree and Inuit canoeists paddled from Ottawa to New York City, approaching the United Nations along the Hudson River, not far from the protective eye of the Statue of Liberty. The strategic significance of this act was not lost on cosmopolitan New Yorkers (Scudder, 2005: 206–7). To cite another example, in its effort to repatriate farmland from structures established during colonization, the *Movimento Sem Terra* (MST) or Landless Peoples' Movement in Brazil, which is one of the strongest social movements in South America, often aligns itself with indigenous voices and interests (Kenrick and Lewis, 2004). According to Ramos (1998), in countries where indigenous peoples make up extremely small percentages of the total population (about 2 percent in Brazil), indigenism provides the basis for effective social action by mobilizing across broad coalitions that include religious and lay groups, NGOs, and rights activists, to mediate the tension between ethnic pluralism and national homogeneity. In the context of the UN convention, such issues are increasingly being taken up across borders (Lawlor, 2003).

The expansion of indigenism as a global movement has not been without criticism, including charges that the very concept of 'indigenousness' is porous and is deployed overly strategically, leading to essentialism (Bowen, 2000). This issue is likely to become more contentious as, in the wake of the UN agreement, indigenous claims are pressed throughout the world. Nonetheless, the efforts of indigenism to re-scale the geography of oppression by forging links across identities, and to cast these issues into the international arena through the use of international courts as well as transnational social movements, may provide a partial way out of the essentialism that has long characterized more local expressions of rights. We take up this issue again below.

The potential for globalization to create a common cause of indigenism is of course deeply ironic given that it was colonialism that gave rise in the first place to the very globalizing tendencies against which indigenous peoples are struggling. As Sarah Radcliffe (2007) and others have pointed out recently, although the effects of colonialism are by no means a thing of the past, indigenous issues are intricately bound up with other major issues as globalization lumbers on through its neoliberal phase. For example, Radcliffe (2007: 386) shows that 'in the anti-terror geographies of fear, commentators perceive a clear tie between armed groups and activist ethnic groups, identifying a homology between Islamic fundamentalism and Latin American [indigenous activism]' which pulls indigenous activists into the 'axis of evil'. Similar cases occurred in Canada and Australia when attempts to include indigenous protests under post-9/11 anti-terrorist legislation drew wide popular protest. Such orchestration of issues that are seen as countering neoliberal definitions of democracy and development are as significant today as they were in earlier historical phases of international development. Nonetheless, if the conditions that make up the neoliberal agenda are homologous, so too are the possibilities for international indigenous solidarity in a postdevelopment context, as 'transnational activism has become a tool for Latin American indigenous political organization and a key shaper of state restructuring' (Radcliffe, 2007: 3; see also Radcliffe, 2001).

To stress the point that indigenous rights need to be understood not simply as relics of a colonial past but as ongoing expressions of globalization, other geographers have also shown that the relationship between indigenous rights and neoliberalism is complex and often contradictory. It frequently involves forging new political alliances that include multiethnic groups, environmental groups, Christian organizations and established NGOs (Radcliffe, 2007: 393; see also Brysk, 2000; Warren and Jackson, 2002 ; Andolina et al., 2005; Radcliffe and Laurie, 2006; Cupples et al., 2007), all of which are concerned with advancing the agenda of post-development. However, as Walker et al. (2007) have also recently pointed out with respect to the Zoque struggle for development in Chimalapas, Mexico, such unholy alliances do not always represent a progressive transcendence of former colonial relations, but may redeploy uneven power relations in a postdevelopment context.

All the examples cited above illustrate the clear tensions between indigenous and non-indigenous, white Eurocolonial peoples, which may be born of colonialism but have very urgent social implications in the present. They also point to the ongoing construction of indigenous issues in relation to larger questions of globalization, and to the countervailing potential for indigenous groups to forge common cause across the very colonial terrain upon which their oppression has been written. The examples lack, however, a more nuanced illustration of tensions *between* peoples who are racially othered in reference to white colonial subjects.

CONNECTIONS AND CLASHES ON THE MARGINS: RELATIONSHIPS BETWEEN RACIALIZED SETTLER-IMMIGRANTS AND INDIGENOUS PEOPLES

Strong historic alliances, often articulated against white settler colonialism, exist between indigenous and other racialized peoples. Many of these alliances arose in the mid- and late-20th century as outcomes of the civil rights movement, expanding and strengthening social movements, and an increased global consciousness about racism and inequities between white and not-white subjects around the world. Indigenous authors in North America, including Vine Deloria and Harold Cardinal, published indigenous manifestos and treatises on indigenous liberation contemporaneously with anti-colonial texts such as *The Wretched of the Earth* by Franz Fanon (Cardinal, 1969; Deloria, 1969). Calls by Māori in Aotearoa/New Zealand for self-determination, culture and language revitalization and land repatriation arose in concert with global anti-racist movements (Maclellan, no date; Maaka and Fleras, 2005). The US-based American Indian Movement (AIM) and the Canadian-based National Indian Council (NIC) and National Indian Brotherhood (NIB) all came into being during the 1960s, concurrently with other civil rights activities including Martin Luther King's March on Washington. Additional alliances between indigenous and racialized people grew in the contexts of other social movements, including the feminist movement and the trade-unionist movement. Since the 1960s, a few alliances have succeeded and more have failed (Pulido, 2007). Certainly, many connections can be made between the experiences of indigenous peoples and those of other racialized subjects, particularly when those racialized subjects have themselves lived as colonized peoples or have experienced, as indigenous peoples do, the realities of racism and white hegemony. There are differences, though, in the social positions of indigenous peoples and other racialized peoples. These differences can and have become tense and difficult, particularly in relation to land claims, self-determination and resource allocation.

In 1990, at the height of debates about identity politics, a feminist publishing collective (Press Gang Publishers) in Vancouver, Canada, brought together for discussion and collaboration a group of women understood to represent identities in polar opposite to white, patriarchal and heterosexual norms (Maracle et al., 1990). The group consisted of First Nations women, Japanese- and Indo-Canadian women, lesbian identified women, and some women who identified as multiply-othered across these categorizations. The initial goal of the project was collaboration among the women for the purpose of articulating a unified and cohesive stance against oppressive normative hegemonies. The final outcome, however, was radically different. Lee Maracle, a First Nations woman of Cree and Salish descent, voiced frustration about conflating indigenous issues and the issues facing other racialized women in the group. Maracle's principal objection appeared to be located in colonization: she and her family had their lands and cultures stolen from them by settler immigrants, included among whom were people who, she acknowledged, faced racism from white Eurocolonial settlers. This discriminatory reality did not, according to Maracle, diminish the role of racialized peoples in displacing indigenous peoples from unceded lands and territory, even if those people or their ancestors had themselves been displaced from their own indigenous lands across the seas. In other words, racialized difference, or the position of Other in reference to whiteness, does not in itself result in seamless connections between groups of peoples.

Tension between differently othered peoples can be seen particularly in negotiations of urban environments. In Australia and Canada, Pacific seaboard cities have seen increasing migration from Asian Pacific countries, resulting in an ever-increasing heterogeneity of urban spaces and resultant changes in housing and land-use patterns (Anderson, 2000). In both countries, spatial negotiations can no longer be understood as contradictory encounters between indigenous peoples and Eurocolonial settlers. Particularly in cities, relationships unfold across and beyond categories of indigenous/white-settler/racialized immigrant. Conflicts over real estate provide clear examples of tensions between variously racialized Others. In the Vancouver area, two separate cases have seen

First Nations refuse to extend long-term leases on cottage property and lucrative waterfront condominium properties. Other cases have seen First Nations given title over valuable tracts of land. Many of the potentially displaced residents were recent immigrants to Canada, a status that was of little or no interest to the First Nations reclaiming the territory (Simpson, 2004; Cernetig, 2007). In some cases in British Columbia, the tensions were so violent that homeowners burned the houses they had built on the property leased to them by First Nations. Multiculturalism has been actively deployed in efforts to smooth out such social contusions arising when new (im)migrants move into spaces previously guarded and understood as belonging to non-indigenous white Eurocolonists (Mitchell, 1993; Anderson, 2000).

The application of these narratives by government bodies and other structures of power, however, have been met with significant criticism by both indigenous and non-white, non-indigenous peoples. Generally, discourses of multiculturalism focus on the performativity of cultural traits – for instance food, dances, and artistic expressions – deemed authentic yet acceptable to the sensibilities of those invested in maintaining power (Eurocolonial settlers) within the nation-state. Multiculturalism thus provides a framework in which racialized difference can be recognized while ensuring both that difference remains non-political and pacified and that a sense of sameness is imposed upon all those who are not-White. Indigenous peoples, though, have actively resisted inclusion into narratives of multiculturalism; most multicultural narratives have also not made effort to envelop indigeneity. In Canada, in a clear rejection of multicultural narratives based on constitutional recognition, the Assembly of First Nations (2003) asserts First Nations as a founding party of Canada, alongside the British and the French, and actively distances itself from comparisons with more recent, racialized, immigrant peoples. Tensions thus persist between two groups of marginalized people.

Indigenous peoples of Pacific Island Nations (Fiji, Guam, Hawaii, Papua New Guinea, etc.) also articulate particular tensions with non-Eurocolonial peoples. These are examples of plantation societies in which indigenous peoples have been severely diminished, while larger numbers of transplanted laborers have been put in place to work under indentured circumstances. In Fiji, in particular, the colonial positioning of indentured South Asian labour against indigenous Pacific Islanders has resulted in a contemporary society structured along both ethnic and class lines, which many anthropologists (see Jayawardena, 1983) held up as a shining example of peaceful ethnic coexistence until the elections of 1987 erupted in partisan violence. As recent analysts have pointed out, however, it would be a mistake to interpret the tension in Fiji as simply a clash of indigenous and non-indigenous cultures that are a relic of colonialism. The situation needs to be understood both in terms of a colonial legacy and contemporary globalization processes that layer new dimensions upon older colonial patterns (White, 2001). Situations such as that in Fiji and other Pacific islands are given an additional ironic twist when it is recognized that one aspect of recent globalization is the rapid growth of the tourism industry, including travelers from former colonial nations in Asia, who are neither settlers nor citizens.

In Aoteoroa/New Zealand the colonial past is managed in ways that contain many potential conflicts. New Zealanders are rightfully proud of having achieved a society organized along bicultural lines that gives official status to both Māori and Pākēha peoples, both of whom are recognized as having come from afar. Their prior claim gives Māori the designation of indigenous, along with many of the social disadvantages of colonized indigenous peoples the world over. Largely in an attempt to address the lack of social opportunities in their homeland, however, many have emigrated, especially to Australia, where it is estimated that there are 73,000 Māori. The number living in Australia is expected to exceed the number in Aotearoa/New Zealand by 2020. In Australia, however, their marginal conditions are often overlooked in a context where they are immigrants (Kiwis) compared to indigenous Australians (Hohepa and Jenkins, 1995; Hamer 2008; Te Ara, nod.). Meanwhile, the number of non-Pākēha immigrants to New Zealand is increasing. Pacific Islanders, who make up an increasing population of the largest city, Auckland, arguably have the most underprivileged socioeconomic conditions of all citizens of Aotearoa/New Zealand. Their conditions have given rise to a specific government department devoted to 'social and economic prosperity for Pacific peoples' (New Zealand Ministry of Pacific Island Affairs, no date). Furthermore, as the number of immigrants from East Asia and Africa increases, so do the instances of racism against the doubly othered (neither Māori nor Pākēha), in a context in which there is very little institutional attention to issues of racism (Bedford, 2004; Guerin et al., 2004; Kobayashi, 2009).

The effects of colonialism are thus multiple and layered. As many of the former indigenous populations of the world – particularly those originating in Asia and Africa but, increasingly, indigenous peoples of South and Meso-America – become more and more diasporic, in many places the indigenous population is rapidly decreasing as a percentage of the whole population, partly as a result of the effects of immigration. This situation has prompted some indigenous scholars to speak about their own processes of 'double colonialism' (Trask, 1999), which occur when Eurocolonial institutions, many of which retain power over land and government in colonized nations, are joined by new (im)migrants to the region. Those new immigrants may be socioeconomically marginalized themselves. As some of the above cases illustrate, they may also have come from colonial situations where they are themselves indigenous. Nevertheless, they may also occupy spaces that indigenous peoples claim as unceded territory. The result is a social geography of conflict that needs to be understood as pluralistic and nuanced, and that requires small-scale considerations about the social geographies of race, racism and racialization, as well as large-scale considerations about questions of identity, belonging and citizenship.

NOT INDIGENOUS, NOT WHITE: ETHNICITY, CITIZENSHIP, AND SOCIAL CONSTRUCTIONS OF OTHERNESS

Edward Said's classic works (1978, 1993) on the construction of the Oriental Other through colonialism are widely cited to explain the discursive practice of racialization, but it should be emphasized that Said's writings refer *almost entirely to racialization of the indigenous*, specifically in the Middle East. Scholars who miss this point when applying Said's analysis across the full spectrum of racialization also miss the irony involved in considering contradictions that may arise in relationships between the indigenous and the non-white, non-indigenous, in colonial settings, especially when such conflicts arise because colonialism has treated them so differently. Most non-indigenous racialized groups in contemporary society have been displaced by two distinctive types of racialization, that of plantation and that of transplantation. While millions of the world's people have seen their traditional landscapes, and their labor, transform in situ under colonial regimes, many of those same millions have been transplanted through forced movement of slavery, the semi-forced movement of indentured labor, or the contemporary movement of labor migrants and refugees within neoliberal economic regimes.

Perhaps because this disconnect within Saidian analyses has been little noticed, scholars have had much to say about the construction of the Other, but have had much less to say about the geographical variations of such constructions. It makes a difference whether Otherness occurs *at a distance* from the metropole within a colonial context, as shown in Said's original work; *in place* in colonial contexts, as has occurred in the subordination of most indigenous peoples; or through the creation of *diasporic* or transnational communities of difference, as represented by most of the large non-white migrant groups today. These differences are profoundly geographical, in that they represent spatial variations in the process of racialization that need to be understood both historically and in place. It makes a difference, in other words, whether Indian laborers have become part of the production of tea or cotton in India, or moved to coffee plantations in Kenya or sugar plantations in the Caribbean. It makes a difference whether African people have become labor for the mining industry in Africa, or been moved to cotton plantations in the southern US, from whence their descendants have come to people inner cities throughout America. These differences are crucial, therefore, to our argument.

Globalization and international migration, starting with the slave trade in the 16th century and continuing through the formation of significant diasporic and transnational communities today, have resulted in the re-positioning of people who may have once been considered 'indigenous' colonial subjects within white societies, including those in Europe, those in white settler nations, as well as those in colonial plantation societies throughout the Caribbean and the Pacific. They are, in effect, doubly colonized.

Franz Fanon spatialized Said's notion of the Oriental Other by recognizing – as Said never did – the colonial violence inherent in the social geographical *condition* of blackness. Colonial positioning fragments; it disembodies, disconnecting the black body from its place in the world, as Fanon's (1967: 112) most famous passage captures so well:

> In the train I was given not one but two, three places. ... I existed triply: I occupied space. I moved toward the other ... and the evanescent other, hostile but not opaque, transparent, not there, disappeared. Nausea. ... completely dislocated, unable to be abroad with the other, the white man, who unmercifully imprisoned me, I took myself far off from my own presence, far indeed, and made myself an object. What else could it be for me but an amputation, an excision, a hemorrhage that spattered my whole body with black blood?

The social geography of racialized bodies is the geography of complete dislocation. Like indigeneity, migration and the formation of transnational communities have challenged modernist notions of exclusive citizenship and universalist notions of human rights by virtue of the fact that they are premised upon the denial of universal human rights. The problem of specifying citizenship rights in increasingly pluralist societies is well known, of course, although the solutions remain partial and tend to be framed in the normative terms of the political philosopher rather than according to the actual experiences of those who are marginalized through multiple displacements.

In summarizing this literature, Isin and Wood (1999) point out that liberal approaches based on a politics of recognition, such as that of Charles Taylor (1989, 1994) leave no room to challenge the cultural hegemony of the dominant group. Scholars who have attempted to take account of differential rights claims and diverse forms of minority identity, most notable of whom is Will Kymlicka (1995, 2001; see also Pearson, 2002), have similarly failed to go beyond a normative understanding of dominant culture. Kymlicka's work is especially important for our purposes because he is one of the few scholars to recognize the potential contradictions between rights claims of indigenous and diasporic communities, which he distinguishes on the grounds that only the first are attached to territory.[2] For both types of citizenship claims, he upholds the liberal principle that group rights depend upon the ability of the individual to exercise the right to group identity.

Kymlicka has been widely criticized for two reasons: first, because in differentiating between types of rights claims (which in itself accords with our own argument) he also creates a hierarchy of rights claims (Parekh, 1997), privileging indigenous claims over those of other racialized minorities precisely because they involve territory. Iris Young (1997) criticizes Kymlicka because she believes that he fails to recognize that difference, the basis for multiculturalism, constitutes a range of potential experiences, all of which need to be situated according to their own conditions. To do otherwise is not only to create a hierarchy of rights but also ultimately to normalize the dominant group.

Many are tempted to privilege the claims of indigenous peoples because 'they were here first'. To do so, however, is to give in to the notion that it is claim to, or possession of, territory that gives people rights, rather than the right to identity, dignity and adequate resources that gives people claims. To privilege claims to territory is itself a very colonial act that has many times paralyzed those on the left who struggle to name the basis on which human rights should be afforded. Such privileging also fails to recognize the global context in which different forms of dispossession are connected. The dispossession of South Asians from their traditional lands and their wholesale movement to plantations in the South Pacific or the Caribbean are related processes, just as the creation of black slave societies in the Americas is related to the dispossession of Africa. As Paul Gilroy (1993) has shown, slavery was from the beginning a transnational practice that has undergone a series of significant transnational transformations since. Gilroy introduces two kinds of 'double consciousness': one, the need to consider the marginal experiences of black slaves as part of Atlantic history at the same time that their experiences are considered in their own right; and two, the need to consider contemporary conditions in their own right at the same time as the colonial history that produced them, as well as all those who by virtue of the 'irreducible sign of their common racial subordination' are designated as Other. To engage such a double consciousness, and to expand upon it to multiple consciousnesses, is also to engage the contradictions of the present.

Such an engagement in double and multiple consciousnesses would then not privilege territory as a particular spatial basis for rights, at least not in any simplistic sense. Instead, it would recognize the myriad and layered ways in which territorial claims are relational, set both within colonialism's original transnational project of territory claiming and within contemporary circumstances through which people displaced by different forms of colonialism are also related.

What difference might such an approach mean? One of the reasons that political philosophers have had difficulty is that they have relied upon forms of governance, rather than social formation, to explain the provision of rights. Forms of governance rely – perhaps rightly – upon highly normative ideals that specify the *possible* spatial relationships under which human beings might live. Liberal political philosophies are especially relevant here because they specify the potential rights of the individual, seldom going so far as to ensure the acquisition of such rights. The result, as has been shown over and over again in land claims cases, can be a disembodied concept of territory rather than one of inhabited places.

Social geographers, on the other hand, have the means and the inclination to study the *actual* spatial conditions under which people live. To do so is more than simply to counterbalance the theoretical with the empirical. It is to recognize that the act of spatializing human relationships is itself an act of creating and defining social justice and the potential for subsequent social change. Colonialism is not simply an application of particular notions of law and territory; it is an active positioning of people on a massive scale. The conflicts that occur in a variety of international contexts between indigeneity and multiculturalism represent not simply ideological debates, but active territorial engagements. Social geographers have the potential both to understand the dynamics of those engagements and to recognize the ways in which each territorial act creates new potential conflicts. They also have the potential, however, to suggest that such conflicts can be overcome through new ideas about the meaning of territory and territorial claims. To make this suggestion, however, we must also acknowledge the irony that by merely suggesting new meanings of territory we are ourselves engaging in the re-placement, or re-spatialization, of the colonial experience.

We are *not* suggesting that territorially based claims should be nullified. What we are suggesting is that such claims must be made on the basis of multiple movements between considerations of claims in their own right, and recognition of the relationship between different forms of colonial dispossession, often on a transnational basis. Such recognition would also take into account the contradictions that are fundamental to colonialism. In other words, it would recognize the possibility of rights claims not on some essential notion of either blackness or indigeneity, or on an essentialized concept of space as territory, but on the basis of the socially constructed conditions under which particular forms of difference are lived. Indigenous claims, in this sense, would follow what Macklem (2001: 32) calls an 'appropriate distributive principle' rather than one that has the potential of privileging one form of rights over another.

For social geographers, the challenge is to take seriously the specific ways in which dispossession has occurred spatially, on the ground, without at the same time privileging or essentializing the very ground upon which contemporary rights are negotiated. This is not an easy challenge. Our argument challenges all those, such as the Cherokee, who continue to use essentialism strategically to overcome the oppression of their own past without providing any means of overcoming the oppression of the Freedmen. At the same time, however, it suggests that to address the dilemma of the Freedmen is not necessarily an abrogation of the naming rights of the Cherokee if the colonial experiences of both are considered.

FUTURE DIFFERENCE: CONSIDERING NEW RESEARCH TRAJECTORIES ABOUT INDIGENEITY AND RACIALIZATION IN SOCIAL GEOGRAPHY

It is one thing to make the academic claim that racialization is not a homogeneous process and that we need to take account of the varied forms of colonialism, the varied social geographies, and the varied forms of identity formation that mark differentially racialized groups. That claim is now well established by geographers and other social scientists. It is a challenge of a different order of magnitude, however, to be able to respond to differential racialization with a concept of differential citizenship.

Much of the struggle to address the issues that we bring up here will occur on the ground, in the actual social, geographical conditions under which people live their lives, struggle for justice, affirm identities, and establish social relations. For David Harvey (1996) those conditions need to be ameliorated by an appeal to a universal concept of justice and erasure of the structural conditions, particularly those of class, that create inequality. He writes that 'struggles to bring a particular kind of discourse about justice into a hegemonic position have then to be seen as part of a broader struggle over ideological hegemony between conflicting groups in society' (361). As a result:

> Respect for identity and 'otherness' must be tempered by the recognition that though all others may be others, 'some are more other than others' and that in any society certain principles of exclusion have to operate. How this exclusion shall be gauged is embedded in the first instance in a universality condition which prevents groups from imposing their will oppressively on others. ... The 'epistemology that can tell the difference' between significant and insignificant differences or 'othernesses' is one which can understand the social processes of construction of situatedness, places, otherness, difference, political identity and the like.

We agree wholeheartedly with Harvey's contention that we need to situate difference.

Indeed, as we have stated repeatedly, it is in the situation of difference, and the differently situated, that we find tensions across the social landscape. In everyday social relations, however, the tension between a politics of difference and a politics of solidarity is fraught. Iris Young (1989) takes David Harvey (1996) to task for asking too much of the politics of class solidarity as a basis for solving such tensions. Indeed, it is precisely because of the situatedness of colonial oppression that class differences – as well as those of indigeneity, race and gender – take different forms and therefore risk coming into conflict. We know, of course, that class, like race, is largely a product of colonialism. Jim Blaut (1992) had one word for it: fourteen ninety-two. But both Blaut's universality explanation and Harvey's universalist solidarity run the risk of reducing anti-oppression struggles to struggles over class positioning, as though the products of colonialism were one-dimensional. As Young states:

> The claim of justice ... carries embedded in it the notion that we are together, socially bound to one another, whether we like it or not. Being together, we aim to resolve our differences by negotiation instead of just fighting. ... In my view it is a grave mistake to rest appeals to justice on perceptions of similarity, because it invites us to deny that we have obligations to those whom we perceive as different. I think it is better to rest appeals to justice on recognition that we are objectively together even though we may not see ourselves in community (Young, 1989: 41).

Young's appeal could perhaps be put to the Cherokee and the Freedmen, in hopes that they may see common cause because the differences that divide them were created by colonialism; but they may also see that the way to overcome the tension will not be in a simple choice between annihilating difference (making everyone Cherokee) on the one hand, or, on the other, allowing one difference to trump the other. A multidimensional issue requires a multidimensional analysis and solution. Although we do not pretend to have *the* solution, we do believe that as social geographers we have the means to recast notions of difference and sameness as they are lived out in ever-shifting social relations, and in so doing to remake the very ground upon which we walk.

NOTES

1 In 1887 the US Federal Government General Allotment Act, referred to widely as the Dawes Act, set forth to allocate 160-acre parcels of land to individual Native Americans on the basis of a blood quantum definition of who was Indian and who was not. In 1899 the Dawes Commission began to enumerate the Cherokee Nation and, by 1906, the Dawes Rolls were complete: individuals were listed as Cherokees by blood, Cherokee Freedmen, and intermarried whites. Everyone else was excluded (Sturm, 1998, 2002).

2 Kymlicka also recognizes the rights claims of a third group, those who inhabit sub-national territories such as Quebec. Although this is an important issue, it lies outside of the scope of this chapter.

REFERENCES

Alfred, T. (1999) *Peace, Power, Righteousness: An Indigenous Manifesto.* Don Mills, Ontario: Oxford University Press.

Alfred, T. (2007). 'Pathways to an ethics of struggle', in *Canadian Dimension: Special Feature – Indian Country: Art, Politics, and Resistance.* 41(1): 35–9.

Alfred, T. and Lowe, L. (2006). 'Warrior societies in contemporary indigenous communities', *Upping the Anti: A Journal of Theory and Action*, 2: 82–102.

Amnesty International Canada (July 28, 2006) *Indigenous Peoples, Land Rights and the Justice System: Making Human Rights A Priority.* Canada: Amnesty International English Branch. (accessed February 2007). http://www.amnesty.ca/themes/resources/ipperwash/ai_submissions_ipperwash.pdf

Anderson, C.A. (2001). 'Claiming disability in the field of geography: Access, recognition and integration', *Social and Cultural Geography*, 2 (1): 87–93.

Anderson, K. (1991) *Vancouver's Chinatown: Racial Discourse in Canada, 1875–1980.* Montreal and Buffalo: McGill-Queen's University Press.

Anderson, K. (2000) 'Thinking post-nationally: Dialogue across multicultural, indigenous and settler spaces', *Annals, Association of American Geographers,* 90 (2): 381–391.

Andolina, R., Laurie, N. and Radcliffe, S.A. (2005) 'Development and culture: Transnational identity making in Bolivia', *Political Geography,* 24 (6): 678–702.

Assembly of First Nations (2003) *Charter of the Assembly of First Nations*. http://www.afn.ca/article.asp?id=57 (accessed February 2008).

Battiste, M. (ed.) (2000) *Reclaiming Indigenous Voice and Vision*. Vancouver: UBC Press.

Battiste, M. and Youngblood-Henderson, J.S. (2000) *Protecting Indigenous Knowledge and Heritage: A Global Challenge*. Saskatoon, Canada: Purich.

Bedford, Richard (2004) 'International migration, identity and development in Oceania: A synthesis of ideas, in D. Massey and J. Taylor (eds), *International Migration: Prospects and Policies in a Global Market*. New York: Oxford University Press. pp.230–58.

Blaut, James (1992) 'Fourteen ninety-two', *Political Geography,* 11 (4): 355–85.

Blomley, N.K. (1996) '"Shut the Province down": First Nations' blockades in British Columbia', *B.C. Studies,* 3: 5–35.

Bowen, J.R. (2000) 'Should we have a universal concept of "Indigenous Peoples' Rights"?: Ethnicity and essentialism in the twenty-first century', *Anthropology Today,* 16 (4): 12–16.

Braun, B. (2002) 'Colonialism's afterlife: Vision and visuality on the Northwest Coast', *Cultural Geographies*, 9: 202–47.

Browne, K. (2007) 'Lesbian geographies', *Social and Cultural Geography*, 8 (1): 1–7.

Brysk, A. (2000) *From Tribal Village to Global Village: Indian Rights and International Relations in Latin America.* Stanford, CA: Stanford University Press.

Bunkse, Edmunds Valdemars (2004) *Geography and the Art of Life.* Boston: MIT Press.

Cardinal, Harold (1969) *The Unjust Society: The Tragedy of Canada's Indians*. Edmonton: M.G. Hurtig.

Castree, Noel (2004) 'Differential geographies: place, indigenous rights, and "local" resources', *Political Geography*, 23: 133–67.

Cernetig, M. (2007) 'Musqueam stand to make it rich on real estate', *The Vancouver Sun*, 26 November: A3.

Clayton, D. (2000) *Islands of Truth: The Imperial Fashioning of Vancouver Island*. Vancouver: UBC Press.

Cleveland, David A., Murray, Stephen C., Alcorn, Janis B., Brush, Stephen B., Dove, Michael R., Downes, David R., Duvick, Donald N., Fowler, Cary, Gupta, Anil K., Kothari, Ashish and Richards, Paul (1997) 'The world's crop genetic resources and the rights of indigenous farmers', *Current Anthropology*, 38 (4): 477–515.

Cobo, José R. Martinez (1986) *Study of the problem of discrimination against indigenous peoples*, Vol. V. UN doc E/CN.4/Sub.2/1986/7/Add.4.

Cupples, Julie, Glynn, Kevin and Larios, Irving (2007) 'Hybrid cultures of postdevelopment: The struggle for popular hegemony in rural Nicaragua', *Annals of the Association of American Geographers*, 97 (4): 786–801.

De Costa, Ravi (2006) 'Identity, authority, and the moral worlds of indigenous petitions', *Comparative Study of Society and History,* 48 (3): 689–98.

Deloria Jr, V. (1969) *Custer Died for Your Sins: An Indian Manifesto*. New York: Macmillan.

Domosh, M. (1997). 'Geography and gender: The personal and the political', *Progress in Human Geography*, 21 (1): 81–7.

Domosh, M. (2005) 'An uneasy alliance? Tracing the relationships between cultural and feminist geographies', *Social Geography,* 1: 37–41.

Driver, F. (1992) 'Geography's empire: histories of geographical knowledge', *Environment and Planning D. Society and Space*, 10 (1): 23–40.

Fanon, F. (1967) *Black Skin, White Masks*, trans. Charles Lam Markmann. New York: Grove Press.

Fletcher, M.L.M. (2005) 'The insidious colonialism of the conqueror: The federal government in modern tribal affairs', *Washington University Journal of Law and Policy*, 19: 273–312.

Gilmartin, M. and Berg, L. (2007) 'Locating postcolonialism: Commentary', *Area*, 39 (1): 120–24.

Gilroy, Paul (1993) *The Black Atlantic: Modernity and Double Consciousness*. New York: Verso.

Gooder, H. and Jacobs, J.M. (2000) 'On the border of the unsayable: The apology in postcolonizing Australia', *Interventions: International Journal of Postcolonial Studies*, 2 (2): 229–47.

Guerin, B., Guerin, P.B., Diiriye, R.O. and Abdi, A. (2004) 'Living in a close community:

The everyday life of Somali refugees', *Network: Journal of the Australian College of Community Psychologists*, 16: 7–17.

Hamer, Paul (2008) 'Living and dying in the lucky country', *New Zealand Herald*, 12 February. http://www.nzherald.co.nz/section/466/story.cfm?c_id=466&objectid=10491857&pnum=0 (accessed 15 February 2008).

Harris, C. (2002) *Making Native Space: Colonialism, Resistance, and Reserves in British Columbia*. Vancouver: UBC Press.

Harvey, David (1996) *Justice, Nature, and the Politics of Difference*. Oxford: Blackwell.

Hatton, L. (2007) '"Black" Cherokees fight for heritage', *USA Today*, 12 October: 09A.

Hohepa , M. and Jenkins, K. (1995) Te Ao Tuhi – Māori literacy: A consequence of racism?, in J. Collins (ed.), *Contemporary Racism in Australia, Canada and New Zealand*. Selected papers from the Conference on Racism, Aboriginality, Ethnicity and Gender, University of Technology, Sydney, Australia, December 9–11, 1993. Sydney: Faculty of Business, University of Technology.

Isen, Engin and Wood, Patricia K. (1999). Citizenship and Identity. London: Sage.

Jacobs, J.M. (1996) *Edge of Empire: Postcolonialism and the City*. New York and London: Routledge.

Jayawardena, Chandra (1983) 'Culture and ethnicity in Guyana and Fiji', *Man*, 15: 430–50.

Katz, C. (1992) 'All the world is staged: intellectuals and the projects of ethnography', *Environment and Planning D: Society and Space*, 10 (5): 495–510.

Kenrick, J. and Lewis, J. (2004) 'Indigenous peoples' rights and the politics of the term "Indigenous"', *Anthropology Today*, 20 (2): 4–9.

Kingsbury, Benedict (1998). '"Indigenous peoples" in international law: a constructivist approach to Asian controversy', American Journal of International Law 92 (3): 414–57.

Kobayashi, Audrey (2009) '"Here we go again:" Christchurch's anti-racism rally as a discursive crisis', Julie Cupples (ed.), special issue, *The New Zealand Geographer,* 65: 59–72.

Kobayashi, Audrey and Linda Peake (1994) 'Un-natural discourse: "Race" and gender in geography', *Gender, Place and Culture,* 1 (2): 225–44.

Kobayashi, Audrey and Peake, Linda (2000) 'Racism out of place: Thoughts on whiteness and an antiracist geography in the new millennium', *Annals of the Association of American Geographers*, 90 (2): 392–403.

Kymlicka, Will (1995) *Multicultural Citizenship: A Liberal Theory of Minority Rights.* Oxford, New York: Clarendon Press.

Kymlicka, Will (2001) *Politics in the Vernacular: Nationalism, Multiculturalism and Citizenship.* Oxford, New York: Clarendon Press.

Lawlor, Mary (2003) 'Indigenous internationalism: native rights and the UN', *Comparative American Studies: An International Journal*, 1 (3): 351–69.

Maaka, R. and Fleras, A. (2005) *The Politics of Indigeneity: Challenging the State in Canada and Aotearoa New Zealand*. Dunedin, NZ: University of Otago Press.

McClintock, A. (1995) *Imperial Leather: Race, Gender and Sexuality in the Colonial Contest*. New York: Routledge.

Macklem, Patrick (2001). *Indigenous Difference and the Constitution of Canada.* Toronto: University of Toronto Press.

Maclellan, N. (n.d.). *Indigenous Peoples in the Pacific and the World Conference on Racism*. The Pacific Concerns Resource Centre Inc. (PCRC). http://www.tebtebba.org/tebtebba_files/summit/wcar/ippacific.html (accessed November 2007).

Maracle, L. with Warlland, B. and Marlatt, D. (1990) *Telling It: Women and Languages Across Cultures*. Vancouver: Press Gang Publishers.

Mitchell, K. (1993) 'Multiculturalism, or the united colours of capitalism?', *Antipode*, 25 (4): 263–94.

Nash, C. (2002) 'Genealogical identities', *Environment and Planning D: Society and Space*, 20: 27–52.

Nettleton, C., Napolitano, D.A. and Stephens, C. (2007) *An Overview of Current Knowledge of the Social Determinants of Indigenous Health*. Commissioned by the World Health Organization (WHO) for the Symposium on the Social Determinants of Indigenous Health. Adelaide, Australia: World Health Organization.

New York Times, The (2007) 'An unjust expulsion: editorial', *The New York Times*, 8 March: A22(L).

New Zealand Ministry of Pacific Island Affairs (n.d.) *Social and economic prosperity for Pacific peoples*. http://www.minpac.govt.nz/ (accessed 15 February 2008).

Niezen, Ronald (2000) 'Recognizing indigenism: Canadian unity and the international movement of indigenous peoples', *Society for the International Study of Society and History*, 42 (1): 119–48.

Pain, R. and Bailey, C. (2004) 'British social and cultural geography: Beyond turns and dualisms?', *Social and Cultural Geography*, 5 (1): 319–29.

Parekh, B. (1997) 'Dilemmas of a multicultural theory of citizenship', *Constellations*, 4 (1): 54–62.

Peach, C. (1996) 'Does Britian have ghettos?', *Transactions of the Institute of British Geographers*, 21 (1): 216–35.

Peake, L. and Shein, R.H. (2000) 'Racing geography into the new millennium: Studies of race and North American geographies', *Social and Cultural Geography*, 1 (2): 133–42.

Pearson, David (2002) 'Theorizing citizenship in British settler societies', *Ethnic and Racial Studies*, 25 (6): 988–1012.

Perera, S. (1996) 'Claiming Truganini: Australian national narratives in the year of indigenous peoples', *Cultural Studies*, 10 (3): 393–412.

Peters, E. (2000) 'Aboriginal people and Canadian geography: a review of the recent literature', *The Canadian Geographer*, 44 (1): 44–55.

Pratt, G. and Hanson, S. (1994) 'Geography and the construction of difference', *Gender, Place and Culture*, 1 (1): 5–29.

Pulido, L. (2007). *Black, Brown, Yellow and Left; Radical Activism in Los Angeles*. Los Angeles: University of California Press.

Radcliffe, S.A. (2001) 'Development, the state, and transnational political connections: State formation and networks in Latin America', *Global Networks*, 1 (1): 19–36.

Radcliffe, Sarah A. (2007) 'Latin American indigenous geographies of fear: living in the shadow of racism, lack of development, and antiterror measures', *Annals of the Association of American Geographers*, 97 (2): 385–97.

Radcliffe, S.A. and Laurie, Nina (2006) 'Indigenous groups, culturally appropriate development and the socio-spatial fix of Andean development', *Society and Space*, 24 (2): 231–48.

Ramos, Alcida Rita (1998) *Indigenism: Ethnic Politics in Brazil*. Madison: University of Wisconsin Press.

Rata, Elizabeth (2001) 'The indigenization of ethnicity', in R. Prozniak and A. Durlik (eds), *Places and Politics in an Age of Globalization*. Lanham, MD: Rowman and Littlefield. pp. 167–92.

Ray, S.A. (2006) 'A race or a nation? Cherokee national identity and the status of Freedmen's descendents', *The Berkley Electronic Press*: bePress Legal Series. http://law.bepress.com/expresso/eps/1570 (accessed February 2008).

Razack, S. (2002) 'When place becomes Race: Introduction', in Sherene Razac (ed.), *Race, Space and the Law: Unmapping a White Settler Society*. Toronto: Between the Lines. pp.1–21.

Retzlaff, S. (2005) 'What's in a name? The politics of labelling and native identity contructions', *The Canadian Journal of Native Studies*, 25 (2): 609–26.

Rossiter, David and Wood, Patricia K. (2005) 'Fantastic topographies: Neo-liberal responses to aboriginal land claims in British Columbia', *The Canadian Geographer*, 49 (4): 352–66.

Sack, R. (1986) *Human Territoriality: Its Theory and History*. New York: Cambridge University Press.

Said, Edward (1978) *Orientalism*. New York: Vintage Books.

Said, Edward (1993) *Culture and Imperialism*. New York: Vintage Books.

Saldanha, Arun (2006) 'Reontologising race: The mechanic geography of phenotype', *Environment and Planning D: Society and Space*, 24: 9–24.

Sauer, C. (1975) *Man in Nature: America before the Days of the White Men. A First Book in Geography*. New York: Scribners.

Scudder, Thayer (2005) *The Future of Large Dams: Dealing with the Social, Environmental and Political Costs*. London: Earthscan.

Simpson, S. (2004) 'A vision in the land facing the sea', *The Vancouver Sun*, 28 February: B2.

Smith, L.T. (1999) *Decolonizing Methodologies: Research and Indigenous Peoples*. New York: Zed Books.

Smith, N. (2000) 'Socializing culture, radicalizing the social', *Social & Cultural Geography*, 1 (1): 25–8.

Sparke, Matthew (1998) 'A map that roared and an original atlas: Canada, cartography, and the narration of nation', *Annals of the Association of American Geographers*, 88 (3): 463–95.

Sterritt, N.J., Marsden, S., Galois, R., Grant, P. and Overstall, R. (1998) *Tribal Boundaries in the Nass Watershed*. Vancouver: UBC Press.

Sturm, C.D. (1998) 'Blood politics, racial classification, and Cherokee National identity', *The American Indian Quarterly*, 22 (1–2): 230–42.

Sturm, C.D. (2002) *Blood Politics: Race, Culture, and Identity in the Cherokee Nation of Oklahoma*. Berkeley: University of California Press.

Taylor, Charles. (1989). Sources of the Self: The Making of the Modern Identity. Cambridge, MA: Harvard University Press.

Taylor, Charles. (2004) Modern Social Imaginaries. Durham: Duke University Press

Te Ara (n.d.) *The Encyclopedia of New Zealand*. Māori overseas. http://www.teara.govt.nz/NewZealanders/MaoriNewZealanders/MaoriOverseas/3/en (accessed 15 February 2008).

Trask, H.K. (1999) *From a Native Daughter: Colonialism and Sovereignty in Hawai'i*. Honolulu: University of Hawaii Press.

Tuan, Yi-Fu (1971) *Man and Nature*. Washington, DC: Association of American Geographers. Resource paper #10.

United Nations Permanent Forum on Indigenous Issues (n.d.) 'About UNPFII and a brief history of indigenous peoples and the international system'. Online publication available at: http://www.un.org/esa/socdev/unpfii/en/history.html (last accessed 8 February 2008)

Walker, David, Jones III, John Paul, Roberts, Susan M. and Fröhling, Oliver R. (2007) 'When participation meets empowerment: The WWF and the politics of invitation in the Chimalapas, Mexico', *Annals of the Association of American Geographers*, 97 (2): 423–44.

Warren, Kay B. and Jackson, Jean E. (eds) (2002) *Indigenous movements, self-representation, and the state in Latin America*. Austin: University of Texas Press.

White, Geoffrey, M. (2001) 'Natives and nations: Identity formation in post-colonial Melanesia', in Roxann Prozniak and Arif Durlik (eds), *Places and Politics in an Age of Globalization*. Lanham, MD: Rowman and Littlefield. pp. 139–66.

Willems-Braun, Bruce (1997) 'Buried epistemologies: The politics of nature in (post) colonial British Columbia', *Annals of the Association of American Geographers*, 87 (1): 3–31.

Wood, P.K. (2003) 'A road runs through it: Aboriginal citizenship at the edge of urban development', *Citizenship Studies*, special issue on Aboriginal Citizenship, 7 (4): 463–79.

Yazzie, R. (1996) 'Indigenous peoples and postcolonial colonialism', in M. Battiste (ed.), *Reclaiming Indigenous Voice and Vision*. Vancouver: UBC Press. pp.39–50.

York, Geoffrey and Pindera, Loreen (1991) *People of the Pines*. Boston: Little Brown.

Young, Iris Marion (1989) 'Polity and group difference: A critique of the ideal of universal citizenship', *Ethics*, 99 (2): 250–74.

Young, Iris Marion (1997) 'A multicultural continuum: A critique of Will Kymlicka's ethnic–nation dichotomy', *Constellations*, 4 (1): 48–53.

5

Social Collisions

Katie D. Willis

INTRODUCTION

> The next world war, if there is one, will be a war between civilizations (Huntington, 1993: 39).

The coming together of socially distinct groups is often represented as violent and negative – Huntington's dire prognostication of the consequences of 'West' meeting 'Non-West' demonstrates the point in an extreme form. Contrary to such representations, however, encounters of difference need not have destructive outcomes. Social geographers have been among those who have sought to examine such encounters from a range of different perspectives. Such work has often been at the heart of what social geography is about: the ways in which the occupation and use of space is fought over, negotiated or challenged, as well as the processes through which space itself is socially constructed through these tensions (Lefebvre, 1991).

Contestations over space may result from what particular spaces materially contain, such as access to prized natural resources. More broadly, however, space is fought over (usually figuratively rather than actually) because the ability to control and shape it both reflects and is constitutive of power (Keith and Pile, 1993). As Brown (2000: 3) writes: 'spatiality is already part and parcel of power/knowledge'. Since resistance or challenge to territorial dominance is always possible, control over space is never total. But powerful groups may occupy and control spaces through practices of exclusion which seek to enforce barriers to entry, or through policing strategies which regulate forms of behaviour in those spaces.

'Social collisions' are the result of change, usually (although not always) through the spatial mobility of at least one of the groups involved. This results in an encounter in a specific space, creating possibilities for tension and conflict. This may be because one group is viewed as 'invading' the space of another group and thus being 'out of place' (Cresswell, 1996), or because both groups are claiming territory which was previously understood or constructed as 'unclaimed'.

The colonial encounter is often presented as an extreme form of social collision – one where very different social groups found themselves occupying the same space. Pratt (1992: 7) uses the concept of a 'contact zone' to refer to that particular moment, describing the term as 'an attempt to invoke the spatial and temporal co-presence of subjects previously separated by geographic and historical junctures, and whose trajectories now intersect'. Subjects meet in contact zones not only as individuals, but as persons belonging to particular social groupings that shape the outcome of the encounter. The concept of a 'contact zone' can also be drawn upon to discuss contemporary meetings between groups divided along particular social axes.

Simple representations of 'social collisions' fail to recognize, however, the complexities of such situations. As this chapter will outline, work on the encounters between social groups has increasingly engaged with diversity: the internal heterogeneity of groups, the timing or placing of the encounter, the importance of recognizing intersectionality, and how the encounters themselves provide opportunities for reflexivity that can result in a hardening of group boundaries or, alternatively, a chance for greater engagement and mutual understanding. The challenge within this work is to continue to highlight the importance of the 'social' and the way in which power is exercised along different axes, which, although their character changes over time and space, still produce and reinforce exclusion and marginalization.

In this chapter, after outlining some of the earlier work on social collisions in urban space, I go on to discuss work which has increasingly recognized the possibility that, rather than being inherently destructive or conflictual, the coming together of diverse individuals can sometimes have productive outcomes. In addition, interactions may be for a short period of time, or they may be an ongoing process. The meetings may also be rather mundane and 'everyday', or they may be very dramatic. As Sibley (1995: xiii) says, '[I]t is a truism that space is contested but relatively trivial conflicts can provide clues about power relations and the role of space in social control'. Thus, part of the chapter deals with the contrasts between what could be termed 'flashpoints' in temporal and spatial terms, and the more everyday encounters through which members of different groups construct and experience their identities through engagements with 'the Other'. Such work also considers the sensory nature of social collision; where not only particular visual or spoken interactions result from or create social difference, but where noise or smells may also contribute to the differences which collide in certain spaces.

Research has also highlighted how the nature of the space within which encounters take place will both shape and be shaped by the events. While social collisions are, in theory, possible in all spaces, it is in urban areas where engagement with diversity has been the most common (Young, 1990), and thus where social geographers have tended to focus their work (Jacobs and Fincher, 1998). This attention to the urban sphere will be obvious from this chapter, which draws heavily on research in these spaces, although rural engagements will also be mentioned.

Finally, although ethnicity/race has often been the main way in which social geographers have considered the meetings between different groups, it is important to identify the potential for creative or destructive outcomes from the coming together of groups divided by other forms of difference, such as class or sexuality. The ways in which these different groups are able to exercise power help shape the outcomes of these encounters.

This chapter is divided into five further sections. The first, on 'segregation', deals with early research on the ways in which the coming together of different groups results in spatial segregation. The next section considers how diversity and anti-essentialism has been dealt with in social geographical research, with a focus on the practices associated with cosmopolitanism and transnationalism. The chapter then considers particular flashpoints in both temporal and spatial terms, before going on to look at the ways in which the meetings between different groups are usually very mundane and everyday in quality. Finally, there is some consideration of possible future directions in geographical research about the coming together of different groups.

SEGREGATION

Much early work by social geographers focused on how social difference was inscribed on urban space through processes of residential segregation, particularly with reference to race or ethnicity. Thus, spatial segregation both reflected and minimized the potential social collisions, which were deemed as inevitable with the spatial and temporal co-presence of contrasting groups. This chimed with prevailing ideas of spatial distance and social distance being mutually reinforcing. Such segregation in the built environment reflected and reinscribed power relations (Sibley, 1995).

In the context of immigration, work in North America and Western Europe focused on processes of assimilation and acculturation, arguing that ethnic residential segregation would decline over time as immigrant groups adapted to their new environment (see, for example, Peach, 1975; Peach et al., 1981). In the US, such work clearly fitted with the wider political discourse around a 'melting pot' and the US as a 'society of immigrants', and drew on the pioneering work of the Chicago School of Sociology (Park et al., 1925).

Residential segregation was often presented as reflecting both a positive choice by the immigrant group and an outcome of fear and hostility. As newcomers, immigrants wanted to live in an environment which would provide social support and assistance in adapting to new ways of living. They thus stayed close to co-ethnic groups. Such behaviours also reflected the fear of potential or actual hostility on the part of the 'host' population; living with other immigrants from the same part of the world provided physical security and protection. In addition, research focused on ideas around 'tipping points' in residential neighbourhoods, where once a particular level of ethnic minority residents had been reached, a rapid exodus of the existing population (sometimes termed 'white flight') ensued (Glaster, 1990; Schwab and Marsh, 1980).

The nature of this research meant a focus on macro-level data, with a significant use of quantitative measures such as segregation indices. These measures were usually based on census information and used census tracts as the units of analysis. This meant a reliance on the categories used by census offices and the questions asked in the census. For example, in relation to work on race and immigration into England and Wales in the 1960s and 1970s, Jones highlights 'no question is asked [in the census] on skin colour or ethnic origin' (1978: 515), so place-of-birth information was used. While there was some attempt to consider the actual life contexts and experiences of immigrant and ethnic minority groups, in most such research it was assumed that causality could be modelled and assessed using macro-level socio-economic and demographic variables.

This approach to analyzing, theorizing and understanding spatial outcomes of social difference in relation to immigration has received significant criticism. As Holloway (2000: 201) suggests, the theories developed through the lens of the US experience in the late nineteenth and early twentieth centuries have inappropriately universalized the specific social and political contexts of migration at that particular time and place. There is, for example, a need to consider the internal heterogeneity of immigrant groups, as well as the manner in which distinct structural processes shaped the residential decisions of urban residents (Jackson, 1987). Even today, as Ellis and Wright (1998) argue, the use of the term 'balkanization' to describe the continued ethnic separation in the US implies that these spatial patterns are reflections of choice on the part of 'minority' groups, rather than outcomes of much more complex processes.

During the 1980s, these more critical approaches to examining immigration and urban racial segregation developed significantly. Rather than focusing on the immigrant Other as the 'problem' who had to conform to the supposedly 'natural' host culture and way of life, researchers turned their attention to questions of racism, both overt and institutional (see, for example, Smith, 1987, on English government housing policy; Hirsch, 1983, on housing policy in Chicago; Holloway, 2000, on mortgage availability for African-American home-buyers). Such processes reinforced and deepened patterns of racial segregation (whether between immigrant and non-immigrant groups or between ethnically distinct non-immigrant groups).

While research on encounters between different ethnic groups has increasingly recognized the complexities of such meetings (see the following section and Kobayashi and de Leeuw, Chapter 4 of this volume), it is also important to acknowledge and examine how the binaries of 'them' and 'us', particularly along immigration status lines, are mobilized and experienced. Examples include the propositions reducing illegal immigrant access to social services in California in the 1990s (Liu, 2000) or the construction of immigrants, particularly illegal ones, as a threat needing control (Mains, 2000). Similarly, marginalized groups have mobilized to present a united front against hostility and discrimination (see Pulido, 2007). In such situations, the collisions between different groups (albeit internally divided) are played out in particular political spaces: the polling booth, the border post, or the street, in the case of demonstrations.

In other contexts, the status of immigrants has meant that a very different set of processes has operated in relation to social collisions. As noted in the introductory section, colonialism involved very extreme forms of encounter in terms of the social distance between the parties involved. Colonial encounters resulted in the 'newcomers' imposing their ways of life on the 'native' population, albeit with differing outcomes. For present-day highly-skilled expatriate workers, the distinction between themselves and the bulk of the population is usually clear, in both class and ethnicity terms. For such migrant populations, the residential exclusivity of particular enclaves or compounds is viewed not as a temporary measure en route to assimilation, but rather as a permanent way of life (Gordon, 2008). Such patterns are viewed as part of the spatial outcomes of changing economies in the world's global cities (Sassen, 2001).

Similarly, governments may encourage such separateness, or at least not promote assimilation. For example, the Singaporean government, while committed to policies of multiculturalism and ethnic residential mixing for 'Singaporeans', adopts a different approach when encouraging 'foreign talent' to the island state. This can lead to feelings of resentment on the part of the Singaporean population (Ho, 2006). In some countries, most notably China and some Middle Eastern states, foreigners are limited to particular residential enclaves or compounds.

Finally, before moving onto a discussion of how social geographers have developed their research to go beyond simple binaries and their associated expectations of social tensions and conflicts between different groups, it is important to recognize the existence of other axes of social difference which may result in conflict when groups encounter each other. In urban spaces, two key dimensions have been class/socioeconomic status and sexuality.

First, the operation of urban housing and land markets has meant that economically privileged households have been able to choose where they want to live, leaving poorer households to find accommodation in the remaining spaces of the city. As with ethnicity/race, segregation patterns and the extent and character of cross-class encounters are determined by the more powerful group. In some cases such encounters are made even less likely through the development of 'gated communities' (Alvarez-Rivadulla, 2007; Mycoo, 2006; Pow, 2007; Vesselinov et al., 2007), although there are some exceptions (Lemanski, 2006). Additionally, processes of 'gentrification' have become part of a 'global urban strategy' (Smith, 2002) in which the language of 'urban regeneration' or 'urban renewal' used by governments or private developers hides the dimensions of class power underpinning such changes. 'Gentrification' invariably involves the displacement of existing low-income residents or their exclusion from plans to reinvigorate city centre districts experiencing depopulation (see, for example, Keith and Pile, 1993, on the regeneration of the London Docklands). Working-class populations are rarely included in the groups 'to be allowed back into the city' (Smith, 2002: 445). Gentrification is therefore a key process in creating opportunities for class-based social collisions, but it may also lead to new forms of segregation and boundary drawing which makes actual engagements across class lines much rarer.

Second, as the research on gays and lesbians makes clear, the city is also a site of sexual segregation. As was true with research into other social axes, the use of binary distinctions in the study of urban sexual spaces was not uncommon. This was not just a reflection of theoretical conceptualizations of how difference was inscribed on the ground, but also a response to the very real feelings and experiences of marginality held by gay men and lesbians in many parts of the world. As with work on immigrants and ethnic minority groups, the presence of 'gay districts' in certain cities, particularly in the global North, was interpreted as the outcome of a positive desire for 'sexual minorities' to live and socialize together, but also a response to wider experiences of discrimination and fears of homophobia (Bell and Valentine, 1995; Castells, 1983; Nash, 2006; Podmore, 2006).

Michael Brown (2000) uses 'the closet' as a way of interrogating the ways in which space is constitutive of social relations, in this case between heterosexual and homosexual populations. 'The closet' is a place of concealment which, Brown argues, can be everywhere but hidden. He considers the spatialities of the closet at a range of scales – from the space of the individual body to the globe. For example, in a chapter co-written with Paul Boyle, he highlights how the US and UK censuses render gay people invisible, thus producing the closet in national space. In another chapter on the urban spaces of Auckland, New Zealand, the invisibility of gay social venues is used to demonstrate how the closet is actively produced in response to heteronormativity. Brown's work clearly shows that social collisions come in many forms and may result in absences or silences rather than in the more obvious or explicit claiming of space.

Social collisions as outlined in this section refer to the meeting of two or more internally homogenous groups. Residential segregation is one particular spatial outcome of this sort of encounter, which in this sense of the term may or may not involve an actual bodily encounter, but rather a coming together in urban space. While social geographers have built on this earlier work, recognizing both the complexity of such encounters and the ways in which broader economic, social and political conditions frame them, it is vital to continue to examine the very real ways in which binary forms of identification can lead to very real forms of discrimination, exclusion and violence.

RECOGNIZING DIVERSITY: MOVING BEYOND ESSENTIALISM

In this section I move on to discuss how social geographers have sought to bring diversity into their work, going beyond the relatively fixed categorization of groups in relation to one dimension of difference – gender, ethnicity, race, sexuality or class, for example. Here we find two general critiques. One is based on social geography's growing engagement with the concept of intersectionality (Valentine, 2007; also Peake, Chapter 1 of this volume), whereby the interacting and mutual constituting effects of different identity positions are examined. Clearly, it is important to recognize the multiplicity of identities in urban space. As Natter and Jones (1997: 144) warn, however, the presence of proliferating and intersecting axes of identity does not in itself constitute a critical stance toward the original social categories; rather, it 'merely reinscribes a new system of boundaries around increasingly differentiated subjects' (also see Oswin, 2008, for a critique of work on the geographies of sexuality in this context). Another approach adopted by social geographers seeking to challenge essentialist forms of identity is to understand them as relational, and therefore the result of 'always contingent and incomplete processes rather than determined outcomes' (Keith and Pile, 1993: 34). Thus, identities and the nature of social encounters are framed by the particular temporal and spatial dimensions of the meeting. The spatial outcomes of such meetings are framed by the exercise of power but cannot be 'read off' from particular preordained social categories.

Diversity of groups

In relation to immigration, constructions of a collision between 'immigrants' and 'non-immigrants' have been challenged with a significant amount of research that highlights different experiences of a range of immigrant groups coming into different locations (Mitchell, 1997; Winders, 2006). As highlighted in the earlier discussion of highly skilled expatriate workers, for some migrant groups the official welcome is very different from that for the unskilled, or for refugees or illegal migrants. This is typically the case for economically wealthy migrants who are viewed as making a significant contribution to the host economy, as outlined in Ong's (1999) work on 'flexible citizenship', as well as other research on the 'overseas Chinese' (Ley, 2003).

Among less wealthy migrants, concepts of social distance, for example around language or religion, may be used to explain government policy, or wider attitudes to immigrant groups. Stiell and England's work (1997) on domestic servants immigrating to Canada demonstrates very effectively how language, ethnicity and education shape the experiences of encounter between immigrant workers and their largely White employers. White English women with internationally recognized childcare qualifications find themselves treated, or being able to demand treatment, as equals, compared with other migrants, particularly those from the Caribbean and the Philippines.

Nationality and gender are two axes among multiple differences that have proven important in studies of the category of 'immigrant'. Some of this research has tended to present women as either victims or beneficiaries of the migration process, but much of it has provided more nuanced insights into the ways in which gendered immigration policies (Fincher, 1997; Kofman, 2000; Walton-Roberts, 2004), social networks (Salaff and Greve, 2004) and job opportunities (Kofman and Raghuram, 2006) result in varied immigration experiences – all of which can vary by region of origin. Jones-Correa (1998) highlights the ways in which Latin American immigrants to New York draw on different resources and conceptions of their new status to deal with their novel environment. 'Social collision' for many of the men resulted in a decrease in workplace status, leading them to participate in immigrant political networks to gain respect. Alternatively, many women used their existing social networks, as well as engagement with welfare services, to carve out a niche for themselves and their families. Other researchers have drawn attention to the potential collisions between individuals who are viewed as having the same ethnicity but fall on different sides of the immigration divide. In particular, this work has focused on the relations between Latino populations in the US who were either born in the US or who have legal immigrant status, and more recent illegal immigrants (Ochoa, 2004; Zavella, 2000). In some cases (see, for example, Pulido, 2007), these tensions have been played out with Mexican-Americans being involved in protests against illegal immigration. Such examples demonstrate the limits of using an essentialist idea of shared ethnicity as a way of understanding encounters between different groups.

Multiculturalism and cosmopolitanism

Recognition of the diversity of groups went some way in developing a more nuanced approach to the study of encounters between different migrant and non-migrant groups. There is, however, an increasing awareness of the multiplicity of interactions between groups, including how the blurred nature of group boundaries affects social interactions. This research has drawn from and developed concepts such as multiculturalism and cosmopolitanism. In particular, research has sought to question the more celebratory ways in which such concepts are mobilized, particularly for political ends.

The concept of 'multiculturalism' highlights or promotes the coexistence, mutual respect and understanding of different cultural or ethnic groups in one location, perhaps a city or a town. A discourse of people being 'different but equal' is a key dimension. In contrast, 'cosmopolitanism' implies a similar kind of cultural diversity, but encompasses a celebration of the ability of individuals to operate across group divides and 'a willingness to engage with the Other' (Hannerz, 1996: 103; see also Hannerz, 1990). It has often been used as a way of promoting a particular image, especially as part of gentrification processes in urban areas (Young et al., 2006).

While the notion of a 'cosmopolitan' space implies difference, inclusion and boundary crossing, what social geographers have highlighted is that the notion of 'cosmopolitan', or spaces of cosmopolitanism, are in fact exclusionary, promoting particular visions of urban space that rely on certain forms of cultural capital. These tend to favour people from privileged socio-economic groups, thereby reproducing existing structures of power and influence (Ley, 2004; Yeoh, 2004). In the context of their work in Manchester, UK, Young et al. highlight how 'the figure of the cosmopolitan produces an "other" who is defined by their not possessing the "correct" attitude or type of difference' (2006: 1705). In this case, the high end nature of consumption spaces produced as part of 'cosmopolitanism' limits participation by low-income groups, while the homeless and other marginal groups are explicitly excluded.

Kothari (2008) challenges the association of cosmopolitan attitudes and behaviours with elite and economically rich populations with her study of Bangladeshi and Senegalese male street traders in Barcelona. In order to succeed in their occupations as illegal or informal traders, these men have had to become very adaptable to a range of cultural environments, knowing among other things how to engage customers of different nationalities, which stock to choose and how to negotiate Spanish bureaucracy and the police system. The ability to operate in a range of environments with very different people clearly places them in a category that could be called 'cosmopolitan'. While in some cases these practices may be part of what Kothari calls 'strategic cosmopolitanism', which is adopted at particular times to meet certain livelihood requirements, these social skills could also survive and morph into new forms of identification.

Transnationalism

Linked to approaches to migration which highlight how social collisions may result in outcomes other than conflict, the spatial dynamics of transnationalism have also led to new ways of examining encounters across national borders. In particular, transnational practices have added further challenges to the earlier expectations of migrant assimilation to a homogenous host culture (Stodolska and Santos, 2006). An interesting dimension of transnationalism, which has been the focus of increasing research, is the experiences of second-generation migrants who have 'returned' to the homeland of their parents or grandparents. Such movements have provided new forms of social collision which are often unexpected from the point of view of the 'return migrant' whose emotional attachments and self-identifications appear to be linked to their parental home. For example, Christou (2006) discusses the experiences of Greeks who were born overseas 'returning' to Greece and confronting the recognition that while they may be 'Greek', their outlook on life and their expectations have been framed by their lives elsewhere. A similar jolt of recognition is experienced by Chinese Singaporeans working in China (Yeoh and Willis, 2005).

Such research has also highlighted the disappointments of those who migrate to resolve feelings of being 'out of place' or marginalized elsewhere. Once again, migrants bring different experiences and are viewed by 'host' populations through that lens and the particular histories of that location. Potter and Phillips (2008), in their work on Bajan-Brits returning or going to live in Barbados, describe how racism they experienced in the UK, where they were part of an ethnic minority group, was also found in Barbados where they were part of a Black majority. The racism was of a different form, but the privileging of whiter skin and particular ways of speaking meant that these Bajan-Brits had to continue negotiating their ways through the maze of locally constructed social difference. Examples such as these show how identities are not fixed or pre-given, but are made through social encounters.

Work on transnationalism has also helped challenge the assumptions that migration from the Global South to the Global North produces a particular form of clash between 'modernity' and 'tradition'. In relation to earlier work on immigration and assimilation, although the terms 'traditional' and 'modern' were often not used, the implicit assumption was that migrants from economically poorer countries would eventually adapt to 'modern' ways of living. The increasing ability of some groups to move backwards and forwards across international borders, as well as rapid economic growth in some parts of the Global South, has meant that previously accepted patterns of encounter have changed. These patterns are drawn out in work by Walton-Roberts and Pratt (2005), who use the example of an upper-middle-class Indian family which moves between India and Canada. Finally, the cultural practices of earlier migrants may have ossified, leaving more recent migrants from the same places bemused by their compatriots' activities.

SOCIO-SPATIAL COLLISIONS: PROGRESSIVE AND OTHERWISE

As the previous discussions show, the relational and contingent nature of identity and group affiliation requires an understanding of how particular forms of difference are both mobilized and experienced. And, in the absence of essentialist identities, perhaps we should not be too surprised to find that 'social collisions' can take many forms. Indeed, cooperation across lines of difference has been another area of social geographic research and provides examples of positive and progressive outcomes, rather than purely discriminatory or conflictual ones. Such cooperation is not, however, without its difficulties, as all groups involved have to negotiate ways of managing difference.

Heather Merrill's work (2006) on the anti-racist organization Alma Mater in Turin, Italy, is an excellent example of the dynamics of social alliance in the face of multiple religious, national and class differences. Alma Mater seeks to provide economic and social support for immigrant women in the context of a city with a long history of class- and feminist-based politics, but with escalating anti-immigrant feelings. Disputes within the organization reflect broader societal fractures, particularly across class lines, both within particular immigrant groups and between immigrant women and the Italian women involved in the group. On a larger scale, particular historical junctures may provide opportunities for more formal political alliances. An example of this in the US is the 'Rainbow Coalition', which formed around Jesse Jackson's bid for the presidential nomination for the Democratic Party in the 1980s (Rogers, 1990). Such moments may be historically fleeting, but again represent ways of coming together without conflict, with multiple parties working for greater understanding and a more progressive politics.

Social geographers have also been involved in trying to forge progressive partnerships in their research, particularly through an increasing focus on participatory methods and what has been termed 'participatory action research' (PAR). This involves researchers facilitating and supporting members of marginalized groups to set the research agenda, provide their insights into the problems they identify, and suggest solutions (Cahill, 2007; Kraftl and Horton, 2007). As with all forms of alliance, the subconscious exercise of power based on pre-existing hierarchies is often very difficult to overcome, and in a research context, external pressures from funding agencies or universities are an additional obstacle (Pain and Francis, 2003).

In terms of a more aggressive and conflictual concept of 'social collision', it is important to look at particular flashpoints, both in temporal and social terms. Such flashpoints usually occur in public space. As McCann (1999: 179) discusses in the context of racial segregation in Lexington, Kentucky: 'Contemporary public spaces are designed to keep the frequency of uncomfortable encounters to a minimum and to maintain a rigid power relation between Whites and people of color when such encounters do take place, while at the same time maintaining a veneer of unity and homogeneity'. Such uneasy coexistence can be threatened, as in the case of Lexington when the death of a young African-American man during a police raid led to protests and demonstrations in the usually White-dominated downtown area (see also Dwyer and Jones III, 2000).

Research has highlighted how the activities of supposedly marginalized groups can challenge the way that power is inscribed in urban spaces. This may be intentional, for example through parades, or it could be less conscious. Work on different types of parade has been used to demonstrate the agency of marginalized groups and to show their ability to make their presence felt through the occupation of spaces from which they are usually excluded, or are tolerated only if they follow certain behavioural norms. In some cases, such events may generate tensions and actual conflict, either between participants and observers (see for example O'Reilly and Crutcher, 2006 on the policing of a gay pride march in New Orleans), or between would-be participants and organizers, as with New York City's St Patrick's Day parade, whose organizers regularly excluded a local Irish lesbian and gay organization (Marston, 2002). The meanings and experiences of such cultural events may also change over time. For example, the Notting Hill Carnival in West London was originally established to celebrate Caribbean (and particularly Trinidadian) culture and identity in a city where racism and discrimination were common.

Similar processes have been examined in the context of leisure spaces. For example, research in Singapore and Hong Kong (Law, 2002; Yeoh and Huang, 1998) has shown how immigrant low-skilled workers occupy certain spaces in the city during their leisure time, transforming the previously highly regulated spaces of Statue Square, Hong Kong and Lucky Plaza, Singapore, among others, into new forms of social space. Such occupation of space brings out the ways in which individuals who are often framed purely as 'immigrants' or in terms restricted to their occupations – 'domestic servants' or 'construction workers' – are able to mobilize other forms of identity, particularly along lines of nationality. Such actions are rarely overt strategies to challenge and claim space by marginalized groups, but, as Law says, in the context of Filipino domestic workers in Statue Square, Hong Kong: 'While this collective feeling of "our place" may not fall within the classic understanding of resistance, it does help to create an alternative public sphere/space for self-expression' (2002: 1637).

Research on young people and their use of public space has also illuminated tensions and conflicts. Sibley (1995: xii) argues that the presence of unaccompanied young people in shopping malls 'necessarily constitutes deviance', because they are viewed as not acting as consumers within the capitalist, regulated space of the mall. Conflicts involving young people may be a result of security guards removing them from the premises, or may be due to other mall users, or residents, feeling threatened by the presence of young people (Vanderbeck and Johnson, 2000).

Shifts in the urban fabric may also provide moments of tension and direct confrontation between different groups. The move in many cities in both the Global North and South to promote the city as a location for investment has led to the proposed clearance of low-income housing and processes of gentrification (see the special issue of *Environment and Planning A*, 2007). Such activities are clear examples of a collision between social groups, along socio-economic lines but also often along ethnic or racial lines (He and Wu, 2007). The confrontations represent not only the meeting of different social groups, but also how broader structures of power (e.g., city governments) work to favour particular sectors of society (see also Smith, 2002, on urban regeneration). Research on homelessness policies also reveals how particular urban spaces are 'cleansed' of undesirables as part of city regeneration strategies (Mitchell, 1995).

EMBODIMENT AND EVERYDAY ENCOUNTERS

While the importance of social differences and the spatial structuring of social worlds has been vital in understanding the encounters between different groups in particular times and places, social geographers have also been mindful of the way these interactions – progressive or not – are based on embodied sensual experiences. As with work on transnationalism and cosmopolitanism, this work overlaps with that which may be termed 'cultural geography', and has been part of a growing tide of work aimed at 'rematerialising social and cultural geography' (Jackson, 2000). Social collisions are often physical encounters between bodies which are marked and understood as different; research has, however, also highlighted the way that other senses, particularly smell and hearing, have been implicated in experiencing difference and creating tensions. While extreme encounters may occur at flashpoint moments or locations, most encounters are more mundane, yet may either reinforce feelings of difference or increase the potential for cooperation and collaboration (see Amin, 2002, on the importance of everyday encounters in urban space).

The focus on the everyday and the mundane as a way of understanding social collisions is vital because so many forms of exclusion are taken for granted by the dominant group(s). Often, it is only when there is a build-up of tension to the point that a particular conflict or controversy erupts that the impacts of marginalization become apparent to the powerful. By considering the 'oddness of the ordinary' (Sibley, 1995: xv) – how social differences are experienced and managed on an everyday basis – we can glean insights into social collisions on a larger scale (Smith, 2001).

Many of these sorts of collisions are urban-dependent. As Thrift (2005: 140) states, 'urban experiences are the result of juxtapositions which are, in some sense, dysfunctional, which jar, scrape and rend'. Research is increasingly focusing on interrogating these experiences through an examination of the mundane. However, the majority of this work has dealt with more privileged groups, in particular 'transnational elites' and expatriates. This has been a response to some of the earlier work on these groups that presented them as 'placeless' because of their location within the workings of transnational capital (Sklair, 2001). But, as Ley (2004) and others have demonstrated, there is a need to recognize the grounded nature of transnationalism, especially the everyday practices of leisure and work that are created through social interactions in particular spaces (Conradson and Latham, 2005).

These interactions are usually face to face and visual difference is thus a key part of the process. However, difference can also be marked through other senses, such as the way people speak, or particular smells. Naylor and Ryan (2002) discuss tensions in South London around the expansion of the London Fazl mosque. Among the issues that were highlighted by local residents was the question of noise, most notably the call to prayer and the use of loudspeakers during services (see also Valentine, 2008).

Research on everyday encounters has benefited from ethnographic approaches, although more formal interviews remain important methods in some cases. A participant observation approach is not new in studies of social encounters in the city (Ley, 1974, and see Jackson, 1985, for a summary), but the recognition of how everyday processes construct broader understandings of social difference has brought it to the fore. Similarly, the 'emotional turn' in human geography (Anderson and Smith, 2001) has also required a rethinking of the ways in which social geographers go about researching particular themes or questions. This is very different from the quantitative research which dominated social segregation research in the past and which still has an important role to play in examining the nature of social engagement.

NEW DIRECTIONS

Given the very dynamic nature of social geographical work on migration, gentrification and social engagement in the city, trying to suggest new avenues of research or possible methodological directions is fraught with difficulties. There are, however, some emerging areas within human geography that offer useful starting points for further work on social collisions.

First, given the importance of spatial and temporal context for framing particular social encounters, the use of more multi-sited research would help contribute to an understanding of how particular groups are constructed and interact within and across very different political, economic and cultural environments. George Marcus (1995) calls for the adoption of 'multi-sited ethnography' within anthropology as a way not just of providing comparisons between sites, but of actually developing an understanding of how flows of people, things or ideas operate and the grounded experiences which result from these flows.

Second, research on social collisions has often been focused on the 'less powerful', whether that be ethnic minority communities, immigrants, gay men and lesbians or working-class urban residents (see also Pain and Hopkins, Chapter 2 of this volume). Such a focus has commonly been aimed at highlighting inequalities and injustices, but it has also reinforced ideas of difference which privilege and leave uncontested the 'powerful'. By challenging the supposed 'norm', we arguably gain equal insights into the power dynamics of marginalization and difference construction. Examples include the work of Bonnett (2000), who studies 'whiteness', and Hubbard (2000), who highlights the constructed nature of heterosexuality. However, very little research on social collisions involves work across a range of participants. The focus instead has tended to remain on one particular group and the way in which its experiences are constructed and understood in relation to an 'other' – which typically remains silent. As collisions inherently involve more than one party, engagement across the divide by researchers could be very productive.

A third area of possible future research draws on the rapidly emerging field of geographical work relating to emotions (Anderson and Smith, 2001). Examining the emotional experiences of social collision could help extend our understandings of such encounters, going beyond obvious material outcomes such as displacement or exclusion. Feelings of anger, joy, sadness, despair or hope, for example, may come from social encounters and will in turn help constitute particular identities. These may be viewed as progressive and contribute to Amin's (2002) vision of positive and harmonious urban relations. Alternatively, negative emotions of resentment and anger may entrench existing divisions, creating the conditions for violent collisions.

Fourth, recent work on hospitality and the ethics of engagement could contribute a great deal to research on social collisions. Barnett (2005: 16) argues, drawing on Derrida, that 'hospitality' requires borders or boundaries between individuals and groups: '[t]hresholds are the very scenes for the drama of responsiveness, hospitality and responsibility'. Boundaries are necessary because hospitality is predicated on the arrival of strangers into spaces controlled by others. Barnett holds that it is not only boundaries that are important for hospitality, but also the recognition of the nature of 'the stranger' (whether a person or group) whose presence inscribes difference. He concludes by calling for a hospitality based on a process of acknowledging otherness. Popke (2007: 516) draws a similar conclusion in calling for an openness 'to different ways of doing and being', thus potentially contributing to new ways of engaging with non-essentialist but politically progressive forms of theorizing social collision.

Finally, social collisions may be created or exacerbated by changing geopolitical processes. Geographical research which is mindful of how relations between existing social groups may be transformed by larger-scale events is key in developing understandings of the contingent nature of identity. For example, Phillips (2006) discusses the rising Islamaphobia experienced by British Muslims in the post-September 11th 2001 world. Government immigration policies, such as EU agreements with North African nations regarding the detention of illegal immigrants or the processing of immigrant applications, are also creating new spaces of exclusion without a physical collision between groups. Future research engaging with these shifting geopolitical landscapes is vital if progressive and ethical policies and possibilities are to emerge.

REFERENCES

Alvarez-Rivadulla, M.J. (2007) 'Golden ghettos: gated communities and class residential segregation in Montevideo, Uruguay', *Environment and Planning A*, 39: 47–63.

Amin, A. (2002) 'Ethnicity and the multicultural city: Living with diversity', *Environment and Planning A*, 34: 959–80.

Anderson, K. and Smith, S. (2001) 'Editorial: emotional geographies', *Transactions of the Institute of British Geographers*, 26: 7–10.

Barnett, C. (2005) 'Ways of relating: hospitality and the acknowledgment of otherness', *Progress in Human Geography*, 29: 5–21.

Bell, D. and Valentine, G. (eds) (1995) *Mapping Desire: Geographies of Sexualities*. London: Routledge.

Bonnett, A. (2000) *White Identities: International Perspectives*. Harlow: Pearson.

Brown, M.P. (2000) *Closet Space: Geographies of Metaphor from the Body to the Globe.* London: Routledge.

Cahill, C. (2007) 'The personal is political: Developing new subjectivities through participatory action research', *Gender, Place and Culture*, 14: 267–92.

Castells, M. (1983) *The City and the Grassroots: A Cross-Cultural Theory of Urban Social Movements*. London: Arnold.

Christou, A. (2006) 'Crossing boundaries – ethnicizing employment – gendering labor: gender, ethnicity and social networks in return migration', *Social & Cultural Geography*, 7: 87–102.

Conradson, D. and Latham, A. (2005) 'Transnational urbanism: Attending to everyday practices and mobilities', *Journal of Ethnic and Migration Studies*, 31: 227–33.

Cresswell, T. (1996) *In Place/Out of Place: Geography, Ideology and Transgression*. Minneapolis: University of Minnesota Press.

Dwyer, O.J. and Jones III, J.P. (2000) 'White socio-spatial epistemology', *Social & Cultural Geography*, 1: 209–22.

Ellis, M. and Wright, R. (1998) 'The balkanization metaphor in the analysis of US immigration', *Annals of the Association of American Geographers*, 88: 686–98.

Environment and Planning A (2007) Special issue on gentrification. 39 (1).

Fincher, R. (1997) 'Gender, age and ethnicity in immigration for an Australian nation', *Environment and Planning A*, 29: 217–36.

Glaster, G.C. (1990) 'White flight from racially integrated neighbourhoods in the 1970s: The Cleveland experience', *Urban Studies*, 27: 385–99.

Gordon, L. (2008) 'The Shell Ladies' project: Making and remaking home', in A. Coles and A.-M. Fechter (eds), *Gender and Family Among Transnational Professionals*. London: Routledge. pp. 21–39.

Hannerz, U. (1990) 'Cosmopolitans and locals in world culture', in M. Featherstone (ed.), *Global Culture: Nationalism, Globalization and Modernity*. London: Sage. pp. 237–51.

Hannerz, U. (1996) *Transnational Connections: Culture, People, Places*. London: Routledge.

He, S.J. and Wu, F. (2007) 'Socio-spatial impacts of property-led redevelopment on China's urban neighbourhoods', *Cities*, 24: 194–208.

Hirsch, A. (1983) *Making the Second Ghetto: Race and Housing in Chicago, 1940–1960*. Cambridge: Cambridge University Press.

Ho, E. (2006) 'Negotiating belonging and perceptions of citizenship in a transnational world: Singapore, a cosmopolis?', *Social & Cultural Geography*, 7: 385–401.

Holloway, S.R. (2000) 'Identity, contingency and the urban geography of "race"', *Social & Cultural Geography*, 1: 197–208.

Hubbard, P. (2000) 'Desire/disgust: mapping the moral contours of heterosexuality', *Progress in Human Geography*, 24: 191–217.

Huntington, S. (1993) 'The clash of civilizations?', *Foreign Affairs*, 72: 22–49.

Jackson, P. (1985) 'Urban ethnography', *Progress in Human Geography*, 9: 157–76.

Jackson, P. (1987) 'The idea of "race" and the geography of racism', in P. Jackson (ed.), *Race and Racism*. London: Allen & Unwin. pp. 3–21.

Jackson, P. (2000) 'Rematerialising social and cultural geography', *Social and Cultural Geography*, 1: 9–14.

Jacobs, J. and Fincher, R. (eds) (1998) *Cities of Difference*. London: Guilford Press.

Jones, P.N. (1978) 'The distribution and diffusion of the coloured population of England and Wales', *Transactions of the Institute of British Geographers*, 3: 515–32.

Jones-Correa, M. (1998) 'Different paths: Gender, immigration and political participation', *International Migration Review*, 32: 326–49.

Keith, M. and Pile, S. (1993) 'Introduction, Part 1: The politics of place ...', in M. Keith and S. Pile (eds), *Place and the Politics of Identity*. London: Routledge. pp.1–21.

Kofman, E. (2000) 'The invisibility of female skilled migrants and gender relations in studies of skilled migration in Europe', *International Journal of Population Geography*, 6: 45–59.

Kofman, E. and Raghuram, P. (2006) 'Gender and global labour migrations: Incorporating skilled workers', *Antipode*, 38: 282–302.

Kothari, U. (2008) 'Global peddlers and local networks: migrant cosmopolitanisms', *Environment and Planning D: Society and Space*, 26: 500–16.

Kraftl, P. and Horton, J. (2007) '"The health event": Everyday, affective politics of participation', *Geoforum*, 38: 1012–27.

Law, L. (2002) 'Defying disappearance: cosmopolitan public spaces in Hong Kong', *Urban Studies*, 39: 1625–45.

Lefebvre, H. (1991) *The Production of Space*. Oxford: Basil Blackwell.

Lemanski, C. (2006) 'Spaces of exclusivity or connection? Linkages between a gated community and its poorer neighbour in a Cape Town Master Plan Development', *Urban Studies*, 43: 397–420.

Ley, D. (1974) *The Black Inner City as Frontier Outpost: Images and Behavior of a Philadelphia Neighborhood*. Washington, DC: Association of American Geographers.

Ley, D. (2003) 'Seeking Homo Economicus: the Canadian state and the strange story of the Business Immigration Program', *Annals of the Association of American Geographers*, 93: 426–41.

Ley, D. (2004) 'Transnational spaces and everyday lives', *Transactions of the Institute of British Geographers*, 29: 151–64.

Liu, L.Y. (2000) 'The place of immigration in studies of geography and race', *Social & Cultural Geography*, 1: 169–82.

McCann, E.J. (1999) 'Race, protest and public space: contextualizing Lefebvre in the US city', *Antipode*, 31: 163–84.
Mains, S. (2000) 'An anatomy of race and immigration politics in California', *Social & Cultural Geography*, 1: 143–54.
Marcus, G. (1995) 'Ethnography in/of the world system: the emergence of multi-sited ethnography', *Annual Review of Anthropology*, 24: 95–117.
Marston, S. (2002) 'Making a difference: conflict over Irish identity in the New York City St. Patrick's Day parade', *Political Geography*, 21: 373–92.
Merrill, H. (2006) *An Alliance of Women: Immigration and the Politics of Race*. Minneapolis: University of Minnesota Press.
Mitchell, D. (1995) 'The end of public space? People's Park, definitions of public, and democracy', *Annals of the Association of American Geographers*, 85: 108–33.
Mitchell, K. (1997) 'Transnational discourse: bringing geography back in', *Antipode*, 29: 101–14.
Mycoo, M. (2006) 'The retreat of the upper and middle classes to gated communities in the poststructural adjustment era: the case of Trinidad', *Environment and Planning A*, 38: 131–48.
Nash, C.J. (2006) 'Toronto's gay village (1969–1982): Plotting the politics of gay identity', *Canadian Geographer*, 50: 1–16.
Natter, W. and Jones III, J.P. (1997) 'Identity, space and other uncertainties', in G. Benko and U. Strohmayer (eds), *Space and Social Theory: Interpreting Modernity and Postmodernity*. Oxford: Blackwell. pp. 141–61.
Naylor, S. and Ryan, J.R. (2002) 'The mosque in the suburbs: negotiating religion and ethnicity in South London', *Social & Cultural Geography*, 3: 39–59.
Ochoa, G.L. (2004) *Becoming Neighbors in a Mexican American Community: Power, Conflict and Solidarity*. Austin: University of Texas Press.
Ong, A. (1999) *Flexible Citizenship: The Cultural Logics of Transnationality*. Durham: Duke University Press.
O'Reilly, K. and Crutcher, M. (2006) 'Parallel politics: the spatial power of New Orleans' Labor Day parades', *Social & Cultural Geography*, 7: 245–65.
Oswin, N. (2008) 'Critical geographies and the uses of sexuality: deconstructing queer space', *Progress in Human Geography*, 32: 89–103.
Pain, R. and Francis, P. (2003) 'Reflections on participatory research', *Area*, 35: 46–54.
Park, R., Burgess, E. and McKenzie, R. (1925) *The City*. Chicago: University of Chicago Press.
Peach, C. (ed.) (1975) *Urban Social Segregation*. London: Longman.
Peach, C., Robinson, V. and Smith, S. (eds) (1981) *Ethnic Segregation in Cities*. London: Croom Helm.
Phillips, D. (2006) 'Parallel lives? Challenging discourses of British Muslim self-segregation', *Environment and Planning D: Society and Space*, 24: 25–40.
Podmore, J.A. (2006) 'Gone "underground"? Lesbian visibility and the consolidation of queer space in Montreal', *Social and Cultural Geography*, 7: 595–625.
Popke, J. (2007) 'Geography and ethics: spaces of cosmopolitan responsibility', *Progress in Human Geography*, 31: 509–18.
Potter, R. and Phillips, J. (2008) '"The past is still right here in the present": second-generation Bajan-Brit transnational migrants' views on issues relating to race and colour class', *Environment and Planning D: Society and Space*. DOI.10.1068/d80j, 26 (1): 123–45.
Pow, C.-P. (2007) 'Securing the "civilised enclaves": gated communities and the moral geographies of exclusion in (post-)socialist Shanghai', *Urban Studies*, 44: 1539–58.
Pratt, M.L. (1992) *Imperial Eyes: Travel Writing and Transculturation*. London: Routledge.
Pulido, L. (2007) 'A day without immigrants: The racial and class politics of immigrant exclusion', *Antipode*, 39: 1–7.
Rogers, A. (1990) 'Towards a geography of the Rainbow Coalition, 1983–89', *Environment and Planning D: Society and Space*, 8: 409–26.
Salaff, J. and Greve, A. (2004) 'Can women's social networks migrate?', *Women's Studies International Forum*, 27: 149–62.
Sassen, S. (2001) *The Global City*. Princeton, NJ: Princeton University Press.
Schwab, W. and Marsh, E. (1980) 'The tipping point model: prediction of change and racial composition of Cleveland, Ohio neighbourhoods, 1940–1970', *Environment and Planning A*, 12: 385–98.

Sibley, D. (1995) *Geographies of Exclusion: Society and Difference in the West*. London: Routledge.

Sklair, L. (2001) *The Transnational Capitalist Class*. Oxford: Blackwell.

Smith, M.P. (2001) *Transnational Urbanism: Locating Globalization*. Oxford: Blackwell.

Smith, N. (2002) 'New globalism, new urbanism: gentrification as global urban strategy', *Antipode*, 34: 427–49.

Smith, S. (1987) 'Residential segregation: A geography of English racism?', in P. Jackson (ed.), *Race and Racism*. London: Allen & Unwin. pp. 25–49.

Stiell, B. and England, K. (1997) 'Domestic distinctions: constructing difference among paid domestic workers in Toronto', *Gender, Place and Culture*, 4: 339–59.

Stodolska, M. and Santos, C.A. (2006) '"You must think of *Familia*": the everyday lives of Mexican migrants in destination communities', *Social & Cultural Geography*, 7: 627–47.

Thrift, N. (2005) 'But malice aforethought: Cities and the natural history of hatred', *Transactions of the Institute of British Geographers*, 30: 133–50.

Valentine, G. (2007) 'Theorizing and researching intersectionality: A challenge for intersectionality', *Professional Geographer*, 59: 10–21.

Valentine, G. (2008) 'Living with difference: reflections on geographies of encounter', *Progress in Human Geography*, 32: 323–37.

Vanderbeck, R.M. and Johnson, J.H. (2000) '"That's the only place where you can hang out": urban young people and the space of the mall', *Urban Studies*, 21: 5–25.

Vesselinov, E., Cazessus, M. and Falk, W. (2007) 'Gated communities and spatial inequality', *Journal of Urban Affairs*, 29: 109–27.

Walton-Roberts, M. (2004) 'Rescaling citizenship: gendering Canadian immigration policy', *Political Geography*, 23: 265–81.

Walton-Roberts, M. and Pratt, G. (2005) 'Mobile modernities: A South Asian family negotiates immigration, gender and class in Canada', *Gender, Place and Culture*, 12: 173–95.

Winders, J. (2006) '"New Americans" in a "New-South" city? Immigrant and refugee politics in the Music City', *Social & Cultural Geography*, 7: 421–35.

Yeoh, B. (2004) 'Cosmopolitanism and its exclusions in Singapore', *Urban Studies*, 41: 2431–45.

Yeoh, B. and Huang, S. (1998) 'Negotiating public space: strategies and styles of migrant female domestic workers in Singapore', *Urban Studies*, 35: 583–602.

Yeoh, B. and Willis, K. (2005) 'Singaporean and British transmigrants in China and the cultural politics of "contact zones"', *Journal of Ethnic and Migration Studies*, 31(2): 269–85.

Young, C., Diep, M. and Drabble, S. (2006) 'Living with difference? The "cosmopolitan city" and urban reimaging in Manchester, UK', *Urban Studies*, 43: 1687–1714.

Young, I.M. (1990) *Justice and the Politics of Difference*. Princeton, NJ: Princeton University Press.

Zavella, P. (2000) 'Latinos in the USA: changing socio-economic patterns', *Social & Cultural Geography*, 1: 155–67.

6

Geographies of Affect

Keith Woodward and Jennifer Lea

There is a famous opening sequence from *Modern Times* (1936) that could easily be mistaken for a fragment of light-hearted, capitalist porn. Charlie Chaplin stands at the assembly line, an unnamed worker in an unidentified Fordist factory, tightening bolts on the passing pieces of an unrecognizable commodity that we will see neither completed nor consumed. Instead, we bear witness to an economy of forces – the physical exchange of energies exerted and resisted between objects – enfolding the worker with the bits of the material world he repeatedly affects: those objects he builds. Chaplin's dramatic variations in workspeed – struggling to keep pace with production – lay bare the conspiracy between commodity and conveyor belt, work and widget, drawing and directing these affective relations into specific, oriented routines, ultimately delimiting and exhausting the labouring body's capacity to act. As the line speeds up, he is damned to chase after it, exerting more energy more quickly with more intensity on more matter. If he sneezes, he falls behind. If his arms tire or he looks away, his hand may fall under the hammer of the neighbouring worker. The *regulated assembly line*, with its *exacting speeds* and the *determinate interactions* of its objects, channels certain amounts of energy, at a certain orientation, exerted repetitively, by the same muscles enacting the same movements over and over and over again. And even when Chaplin momentarily escapes this tireless belt of frenzied production for a quick run to the toilet, his strained body still reiterates the jerky, diagrammatic movements of his specific labour, arms wrenching bolts that are no longer there, gestures building widgets from out of thin air.

Chaplin's factory paints a pared-down portrait of the dynamic politics of force relations that assemble a materialist study of affect. The production machine, feeding upon the energies of the worker (what Marx (1976: 273) would call realized 'labour-power'), actualizes a circuit of forces wherein working bodies affect materiality, transforming and assembling it in determinate ways, at precise speeds, imbuing the resulting product with its specific value – all conditioned by exactingly segmented durations, enabling a surplus of value to appear seemingly from nowhere. For geographers working in the wake of their own radicalization and in the midst of that movement's critical offspring, the exploitative drama of capitalist production has long been a familiar story. It is a tale frequently told from econocentric and spatiocentric perspectives that, although it would be a serious error to dismiss them, occupy privileged spots bought too often at the price of marginalizing other significant regimes of exploitation. One of the most frequently overlooked – both in terms of critique and mobilization – has been the political dimension of affect. In this regard, and by way of contrast to those more familiar analyses, consider Chaplin's description of his inspiration behind *Modern Times*:

> I remembered an interview I had with a bright young reporter on the New York *World*. Hearing that I was visiting Detroit, he had told me of the factory-belt system there – a harrowing story of big industry luring healthy young men off the farms who, after four or five years at the belt system, became nervous wrecks (Chaplin, 1966: 377).

Here, changing developments in capitalist production announce the birth of relations that initiate and systematize new correspondences between bodily, psychic and social trauma. To signal the emergence of a new class of workers in this context is to announce the arrival of new kinds of bodies, the products of changing relations of exertion and stress relative to increasingly rationalized and intense production speeds. It is true, these corporeal changes arise from the drive for capital accumulation that is granted such a pivotal position in classic Marxist critique, but, as Marx himself well knew, this is not the only plane in which these complex relations of exploitation find purchase. Upon the material plane – that regime enabling the possibility for labouring, affecting, or exerting force to become the *doings* from which one finds oneself alienated – Chaplin's assemblage of work, thought and the social invokes a set of mutually *affecting* force relations that add crucial analytic perspectives on the violence of capitalist production.

In the grander scheme of things, all of social life is awash in relations of affect; capitalism's devastating historical impact has merely been to channel these in specific directions. We will return to the particular connections between affect, labour and exploitation later in this chapter, but first we step back to trace the roots and developments in the growing revaluation of affect in social theory and social science, illustrating its contribution as a fundamental and thoroughly practical mechanism for holding together materialist accounts of the 'nature' of 'the social'. With reference to 'geographies of affect' (see for example Anderson, 2005, 2006, 2007; Lim, 2007; Lorimer, 2008; McCormack, 2003; Thrift, 2004), we assess how recent theorizations of affect intersect with social geographies, inviting perspectives that think beyond many current critical conventions.[1] We draw upon Spinozo–Deleuzian approaches to consider the new perspectives that affect offers on ethics, the complexity of social life, the place and enactment of power, the circulation and articulation of difference, and the politics of grounded material relations. In addition to asking how affect dynamically shapes our understandings of 'the social' and opens up seemingly new areas for future debate and deliberation, we endeavour to be sensitive to – and, at times, cautious of – the theoretical implications of envisioning the world in this way. Thus, by way of conclusion, we consider some of the possible futures opened up by affect studies as well as several of its traps and snares.

UNDERSTANDING AFFECT

How you approach affect depends very much upon how you position yourself relative to a number of heavy philosophical questions regarding the nature of the mind, the body and the material universe: 1) Are your 'mind' and your 'thoughts' fundamentally different 'kinds of things' than your material body? Are you a single, enclosed individual – a subject – who intends and is responsible for the actions extending from your body? *Or*, 2) is the mind in-*corp*-orated, sharing a continuous materiality with the body, while still being granted its own special capacities by virtue of the uniqueness of its specific form of material orientation? Could subjectivity quite literally be an afterthought, a cognitive reflex used for re-orienting and recontextualizing events that – at the time of their occurrence – assembled unwieldy, collective movements in which part of 'your' body played only a fragmentary role? While the latter series of questions is asked from the perspective of affect, the former patently downplays it, placing the mind (*via* 'rational agency') solely in the director's chair, *transcending* the 'base materialism' of bodily relations, an active, immaterial consciousness directing a passive, material body. Under this 'dualist' conceptualization, the mind controls and manipulates an otherwise inert body so as to extend conscious will into the world. We have Descartes to thank (or blame, as many did in the 20th century) for developing this portrait of mind–body dualism, one that became so pervasive in Western culture that many still uncritically naturalize its hypotheses. A pivotal outcome of this schema was the production of a privileged spot for Reason that, as a result and at every turn, downplayed the status of feelings and doings.[2]

The granting of such vaunted heights to rational faculties has more recently met with a number of critical responses eager to reassert the significance other forms of 'embodied thinking' such as affect:

> The ideal of Descartes is actually that of theoretical and intellectual knowledge which is a sort of dispassionate grasp of mathematical being and in which there is no place either for feelings or passions. Whence this idea, peculiar to all intellectualism, that affectivity in general is something inferior and could not as such belong to the pure essence of thought. Whence, finally, the hypothesis to the effect that the deterioration of pure thought into affectivity, while it cannot find its principle in the essence of this thought, necessarily stems from the interference in it of a foreign element, viz. the body (Henry, 1975: 140–41).

Although bodily affects, sensations and knowledges have often been historically remaindered, shrugged off as left-over traces of un-reasonable noise, their current theoretical uptake asserts the centrality of their dynamic contributions to the (re)production of everyday life (e.g., Berlant, 2000; Butler, 1997; Cvetkovich, 2003; Lingis, 2000; Sedgwick, 2003; Tomkins, 1995). There are innumerable merits in the growing and divergent approaches to their study, many of which have yet to see much exploration inside of geography. However, for the sake of brevity and consistency, the following discussion draws upon the interpretation of affects that has seen the most uptake within the discipline: the reading developed by Spinoza (2000) in his *Ethics* and its many 'reinterpretations' in contemporary theory (Balibar, 1998; Deleuze, 1988c, 1990; Deleuze and Guattari, 1987; Macherey, 1998; Massumi, 2002; Negri, 1991). The Spinozist perspective presents affect as part of an ontology of material force relations unfolding between bodies, whereby each 'exerts a causal effect' and is 'constantly impinged upon by others' (Gatens and Lloyd 1999: 13), fostering 'a basic sociality which is inseparable from the understanding of … individuality' (1999: 14). These active modes of relation create continuous aggregations and dissipations of complex bodies: interactive variations in relative movements and speeds correspond to a series of 'affections of the body by which the body's power of acting is increased or diminished, helped or hindered' (Spinoza, 2000: 164).[3] For Spinoza, a body tends almost invariably to be a dividual, that is, divisible into a collection of smaller, interacting bodies: the 'body is moved in various ways in accordance with the diversity of the nature of the bodies which move it, and, on the other hand … different bodies are moved in various ways by one and the same body' (2000: 127). Affect is the driving force in the collectivization and singularization of bodies and thus its *concept* is central to thinking bodily composibility and relationality. Here, the counter-Cartesian implication is that 'doings' are de-linked from a presupposed subject-agent and rediscovered through the broad regime of bodies of every size and complexity, situated within a variety of physical and material contexts and articulated via modes of relatedness to other individuals and groupings.

Reinterpreting Spinoza through the biosemiotic theory of Jakob von Uexküll, Deleuze (1988c: 125, 1993: 92; Deleuze and Guattari 1987: 257) co-opts the field ethology[4] to develop such a situated study of affects and percepts, giving them a generative and contextualizing role in the relation between a body and its *Umwelt*, or 'subjective environment'. This seemingly weird marriage of philosophy and science reframes a body's surroundings quite literally and is a collection of unfolding, localized, interacting force relations with which it constantly participates. Here, the '[p]owers of acting and capacities for being affected are partly determined by the circumstances in which a being finds itself' (Gatens and Lloyd 1999: 101), and therefore this participatory situatedness is at once both constructive and constrictive, enabling and delimiting the actions of associating bodies. Continuously immersed in these formative processes, bodies are mapped as the actualization of their mobile forces – the 'affects that occupy a body at each moment' (Deleuze 1988c: 127). A key outcome of this always changing, context-rich analytic is that it exercises predefinitions of bodies based upon 'functions ... species or Genus characteristics' in favour of, instead, counting a body's affects (see Deleuze and Guattari, 1987: 257) and considering its often novel organizations and doings.

These studies provide new (and renewed) perspectives for describing the social, foregrounding those forces through which bodies bind and separate, attract and repel, and which thereby engender increases or decreases in their collective capacities to act. *Affect is the medium through which bodies sustain and transform each other*, and, as such, *it is fundamentally social: a materialist account of bodily association.* In this regard, we recognize four critical domains that its study offers to rethinking the doing of social geography:

1. *Affect has epistemological and ontological consequences, orienting thought and practice towards dynamic processes often passed over in structuralist and categorical accounts of the social.* Contemporary epistemology asserts that we can neither engage in research under the assumption that there is a world 'out there' to explain, nor presume that there is a social composed of pre-formed, cataloguable individuals or entities.[5] By highlighting the continuous formation of the world as an infinite series of bodily enactments, affect *ontologically and materially* recontextualizes relations by hoisting them out of knowledge regimes and resituating them within the contexts of being and becoming. This joins a body of approaches antithetical to the 'Euro-American method' in which the 'bias is against process and in favour of product' (Law, 2004: 152).

2. *Affect de-privileges the human as the reservoir of agency in the world, instead founding action upon a series of bodies-in-moving-relation that incorporates both the human and the 'more-than-human' (e.g., inhuman forces and non-human animals and objects).* Del Casino and Marston (2006) suggest that such a 'post-human' turn challenges 'the integrity of social geography in the US', offering a theoretical and empirical moment that will continue to push the boundaries of how geographers theorize socio-spatial relations ... geographers in the US are rigorously and critically 'opening up' epistemological and ontological theorizations of various spaces and questioning the boundedness of the 'human' and the 'social' in the context of everyday geographies in ways that we are only just beginning to understand (2006: 1004).

   Affect's accounts of social production, becoming, and the taking-place of life – all processually enacted through coagulations of the human, inhuman, more than human, and non-human – allow us to re-interrogate the very 'subject' of the social[6] and thereby to problematize the human as a self-explanatory unit of analysis. As a result, the social becomes a complex of registers, crossing through and binding together, 'for example, the nervous system, hormones, hands, love letters, screens, crowds, money' (Anderson and Harrison, 2006: 334; see also Philo, 2009).

3. *Affect contributes and bears witness to the complexity and multidimensionality of sociality and materiality.* Philo notes that 'society is not a singular entity, undifferentiated from one place to the next, and that scholars – not just geographers, but all informed intellectuals – should think in terms of many societies in the plural' (Philo 2009: 702). Affect is a crucial component for assemblage-based understandings of the social, challenging

assertions of the self-evidentness of the 'static physicality' of the material (Anderson and Tolia-Kelly, 2004) that often found constricted readings of the social rooted in anthropocentric or even speciest preconceptions. Instead, '[s]ocial fabrics and practices are not locked in to rational or predictable logics' (Lorimer, 2008: 3), but rather re-invent association, relation and inclusion through each emerging collectivity.

4 *Studies of affect elucidate a material world animated by continuous doings.* Because some associations cohere and persist (such that we take them as concrete and permanent), one's focus is always at risk of shifting from what matter does to what (the essence of) the material is. The affective register arranges the social as a symphony of interacting bodies, inspiring pragmatic, grounded inquiries into how materialities are created through practice, how matter enrols bodies, and, more generally, what differences the realm of affect-imbued materiality makes in how we live. As such, it makes considerable ethical and political claims upon us, reminding us that we are always participants – sometimes unwillingly, sometimes unknowingly – in the continuous unmaking and remaking of the world.

THE ETHICS OF THE SOCIAL

Ethics is often popularly approached as a concept interchangeable with notions of 'morals' or 'morality' (see Smith, 1997, 2000). This is a variation on more classical discussions of ethics, which concerned the possibilities open to 'doing' ('what *can* be done?') in contrast to moral valuation of actions ('what *should* be done?'). This distinction has had a fundamental influence upon contemporary theorizations of practice, several of which have effectively suggested that presupposing the transcendental givenness of moral dictates in all action results in the 'replacement of specific acts of thinking with a representation that castrates thought of its vital power' (Goodchild, 1997: 42). In this sense, there remains a potentially reductive manoeuvre hidden in the transition from speculation regarding the sheer variety of possible doings open to a body to the valuation and privileging of a narrowed band of that spectrum in terms of 'good' and 'bad' doings. Much of the history of Western thought – as Nietzsche (1998) and Foucault (1978) have explained – subsumes questions of possibility under imperatives (handed down from God, the State or Hegel) to do the *good* or the *right* thing, often serving as a pre-emptive judgement-cut on the variety of potential bodily doings. Theories of affect, on the other hand, inhabit part of an alternative strain in Western thought that resists efforts to separate valuation from the materialities it endeavours to describe by effectively disconnecting ethical assessment from any set of predetermined moralizing injunctions. Spinozist formulations in particular eschew such transcendental value maps, offering a materialist challenge to systemic pronouncements that would endeavour to curtail or contain the consideration of bodily capabilities prior to an actual appearance of a living, doing body. As a theory of immanent ethics, and in keeping with a rejection of essentialist constructions of identity, it contests the equally essentialist predetermination of doings based upon the *a priori* presupposition of certain *kinds* of bodies. Instead, a 'body', as a conjunction of whatever bits of materiality (blocks of matter) have gathered into relations of moving, affecting, and being affected *together*, must discover what good(s) – if any – might be determined by virtue of its situation. Here, this means nothing more than 'good for sustaining the consistency of the assemblage' which accompanies the joy found in the articulation of as many capacities as possible that inhere through its specific relation (Spinoza, 2000: 194). Exploring these is no easy task, given how mired we are in daily routine, in bureaucratic institutions, in repetitive labour practices, and in banal consumption regimes. Foregrounding multiple-bodied doings sets the stage for onto-ethical speculation: acknowledging the potential complexity of interactions impacts thought, setting the ground for retheorizing – again and again – the types and ways that bodies and things can exist in the world. Spinoza's influence is felt acutely, for example, in that spectrum of thinkers who embrace anti-essentialism and anti-fascism, and who theoretically and practically seek out alternative forms of thinking and being in the world. Implicit and explicit affective concerns are recognizable in radical and critical feminisms of organization and embodiment (Butler, 1997; Dark Star Collective, 2002; Sedgwick, 2003), collective militancy in contemporary activism (Collectivo Situationes, 2007: 75–79), alternative living and alternative economies (Crimethinc, 2003; Gibson-Graham, 2006; Sitrin, 2006), green and food movements (Bové and Dufour, 2005; Shiva, 2000, 2002), DIY culture (The Trapese Collective, 2007), autonomy (Negri, 1999; Graeber, 2004), dynamic political organizing and resistance practices (Graeber, 2007; Milburn, 2004; Notes from Nowhere, 2003; Woodward, forthcoming), and countless other regimes where doings initiate rethinkings and reformulations of the critical practices that can go into living a life. As social geographers, we need look no further than Bové's *Confédération Paysanne* and the deconstruction of the localized sites of capitalist accumulation – their dismantling of a McDonald's in Millau – to recognize that the potentiality for action is realized most intensely at the intersection of aggregation and movement (Bové, 2001).

But how can we move on to considering worlds of doings when we are asked at the same time to discard so many of our strongly held understandings about the doers – the *whos* and the *whats* – whose reasoned choosing is so often said to *precede* an action? The project devoted to answering this question is still very much a work-in-progress within geography and without. In early investigations (see for example Anderson, 2005, 2006, 2007; McCormack, 2003, 2007; Wylie, 2002, 2005), ethics is detailed and enframed within the dynamic contexts of relational practices that seem to push any notion of centred agency into the background. Instead, everything participating in the composition of the real materiality of the world *associates* in any number of complex relations at once. From this monist perspective, the totality of what happens to be enfolded into affective relation in a given site simultaneously and auto-affectively operates as part of the *conditions* for that site's composition or destruction (Woodward forthcoming). The challenge to geographers of affect, then, is not so much to search far and wide for an ideal, exemplary relation to pin down, disentangle and disassociate with theoretical-surgical instruments as it is to struggle to animate the multiplicity of relations that necessarily go into the make-up of any given relation.

Consider, by way of contrast, the attempts of Social Darwinists to naturalize already existing social inequalities through theoretical works that sutured naïve realism to morality. From a competitive, individualistic reading of evolutionary struggles for survival there arise forms of economic liberalism that rate particular positions of power and accumulation as merely the result of the successful endeavours of an individual agent *against* the violent and dissonant workings of other individuals. Here, practices of exploitation and exclusion court their own legitimation and perpetuation through existent social differences taken as the irresistible articulations of natural sorting mechanisms. However, the perspective of affects rails against such tautological and exculpatory givenness: the capacity to negatively affect (assault, exploit and enslave) a body of individuals is enabled by the presence of conditions or constraints (guns, laws and chains) that pre-empt and delimit that group's ability to affect the world (to enact, express and liberate itself). It is with this in mind that Kropotkin reversed such dangerous appeals to evolutionary theory, cautioning that Darwin had

> pointed out how, in numberless animal societies, the struggle between separate individuals for the means of existence disappears, how *struggle* is replaced by *co-operation,* and how that substitution results in the development of intellectual and

> moral faculties which secure to the species the best conditions for survival (Kropotkin, 2006: 2 original emphasis).

Collective participation in survival ('mutual aid') is grounded in part in the recognition of the trans-individual nature of affectivity and has three crucial implications for thinking about the intersections between ethics, affect and social life: firstly, it recognizes a correlation between the emergence of the working social body and the complicated series of affective force relations unfolding between – and thus aggregating and disaggregating, or *associating* and *dissociating* – bodies. Individualistic accounts of the social tend to pass over the complex unevenness of privilege and access in a given situation that help solidify the conditions through which individuals become more or less affective. There is no simple exchange economy of affects that could clarify lines of division between actants, as they are only ever at work amidst any number of other circulating, enabling and disabling forces. Secondly, Kropotkin's account presents an alternative for conceiving the centrality of affect by explaining not simply the *em*bodied, but the *trans*-bodied nature of collective doings and cooperative practices. With this in mind we might say that affect studies provide us with a geo-sociology of matter as much as it does a materialist geo-sociology.

Finally, Kropotkin's theory of mutual aid further clarifies Spinoza's portrait of a body as an affective collectivity. Not the teleological outcome of aggregation – wherein some evolutionary goal of the collective is conceived and attained – the body is rather the gathering of mutualizing force relations that begin to work together in specific ways, their regular practices and processes transforming through routinization and variation in the environment. The affective and participatory co-tendencies of this multitude of bodies can thus be said to be indicative of a 'social body' characterized not by any formal, nominal, classed or categorized system, but rather by the question of ethics itself. The social becomes conditioned by its own situated localizations, the specific doings-together of bodies distributed like a series of freckles across a biologist's nose. Affect announces a social ethics of interrelation and interconnection, and as such it signals an ontological–political linkage between ethics and the social, where to frame a question in terms of one is literally and immediately to invoke the other. The pragmatic politicality of questions such as Lenin's (1988) and Kropotkin's (1995) 'What is to be done?' (see Woodward, forthcoming) invokes a constantly changing and mutable social (or, more precisely, *any number of socials*), where bodies constantly participate in collections of different doings with a number of different bodies. This in turn means that affect presents constant challenges to what the social *is*, opening itself to sites that invite new types of practices and new types of aggregations.[7] In this sense, its study highlights surprising processes and movements of social *change* instead of simply repackaging dated, formalist notions of social categorization and hierarchical coherence.

Here the crossovers between affective social geographies and contemporary radical thought (in particular where it continues to present challenges to capitalist and statist hegemonies, and to normative and fascistic social constructs) become particularly pronounced. A key tenet of many strands of contemporary anti- and alter-globalization movements involves rethinking what it means – both conceptually and practically – to live a life by seeking out alternative strategies for developing economic and social relations. In part, this clearly means inventing and negotiating nuanced or different affective relations and practices in defiance of pervasive capitalist organization (Gibson-Graham 2006) and its pervasive and banal spread of affect-commodities; but, even more, it means reconsidering the conditions for radical practice. Graeber, for example, offers that we might

> stop thinking about revolution as a thing – 'the' revolution, the great cataclysmic break – and instead ask 'what is revolutionary action?' We could then suggest: revolutionary action is any

> collective action which rejects, and therefore confronts, some form of power or domination and in doing so, reconstitutes social relations – even within the collectivity – in that light (Graeber, 2004: 45).

It is not (or *not only*) the predetermined revolutionary project (as outcome-directed practice and projection) but the continuous collective formulation of the social that maintains openness to the potentiality for yet still further reformulations of the social. However, while we find this to be a promising and hopeful step in the direction of theorizing a revolutionary and affective life, we recognize that liberation can only ever offer a fraction of the picture. Short of providing an account of negative and oppressive force relations cutting across so many dimensions of contemporary social life, accounts of affect run the risk of painting too simplified and rosy a portrait of social change, seeming critically naïve with regard to the broad array of violent crises that mark the contemporary sociopolitical moment. It is for this reason that we turn to the complex and conflicted role of power in social life that is introduced and enabled by affect.

THE POWER TO ACT

Echoing Spinoza, McCormack notes that 'the affective power of a body is understood in terms of its capacity to form relations with other bodies' (2007: 367). We suggested above that this can be either productive ('joyful') – when two bodies combine to form a 'more powerful whole' (Deleuze, 1988c: 19) and the regime of possible activities available is thereby increased – or inhibitive ('sad') – when the encounter results in the decomposition of one body, 'destroying the cohesion of its parts' (Deleuze, 1988c: 19) and diminishing its ability to act. The affects taking hold of a body at a particular moment detail a cartography of processes, charting numerous potential performances rather than realizing categorically pre-formed or 'inherent' competencies (see Deleuze and Guattari, 1987: 13). This bodymap is a moving picture of relationality – a creative process with regard to both its relative terms and the orientations their relatings initiate – and thus it can be apprehended only in those specifically connected actualizations of the present, not as a general figure or being. As Grosz explains, the body is

> not an organic totality which is capable of the wholesale expression of subjectivity, a welling up of the subject's emotions, attitudes, beliefs or experiences, but is itself an assemblage of organs, processes, pleasures, passions, activities, behaviours, linked by fine lines and unpredictable networks to other elements, segments and assemblages (1994: 120).

For the affective body, a key concern turns upon the possibility of empowering itself by increasing its number of interacting forces, its abilities and its engaged doings.

The relationship between affect and empowerment is made explicit in Deleuze's interpretation of Foucault, where, much like the reading of ethics discussed above, 'power' elides associations with moral categories, being rather the material relation existing between forces: the *character* of interacting forces is power (Deleuze, 1988b: 71–3). The linkage between force and affect is clarified through consideration of the ways that power is oriented or directed by interacting forces: 'power does not pass through forms but only through forces ... through particular *points* which on each occasion mark the application of a force, the action or reaction of a force in relation to others, that is to say an affect like "a state of power that is always local and unstable"' (Deleuze, 1988b: 73). Consider, for example, the excitingly productive readings of power that undergird notions of 'popular empowerment' in movements organized through collective action, where participatory politics is characterized by the relatively collabourative operation of forceful bodies (much as it is in Kropotkin's naturalized theory of mutual aid, above). Exposing the impracticality and uncertainty of politicalities dangling (always just out of reach) from transcendently prescriptive origins, corporeally assembled, collective engagements give rise to empowerment by being 'orientated toward the organization of social encounters so as to encourage useful and composable relationships' (Hardt, 1993: 110). Attendant to such organizations, the practical and theoretical marriage of thought and affect helps form the basis for the ability to actively intervene in political futures by learning how to facilitate joyful encounters. For Spinoza:

> repeated [joyful] encounters … leave traces in the body which, though initially ideas in the imagination, later become the basis for the formation of common notions … [that] represent the hinge which connects the imagination and joyful passions to reason and adequate knowledge (Gatens and Lloyd, 1999: 104–5).

Through a pedagogy of 'becoming active', learning cumulatively and socially to pursue those encounters or relations that increase affective capacity reflects a political practice geared toward productively engaging and enlisting the dynamic materialities of an unfolding, changing world.

However, this does not suggest that such aggregations and knowledges could ever emerge from or gesture toward any imaginary, friction-free regime of absolute freedom of thought or action. The power emerging from relations of force is always conditioned by the situatedness of their localized interactions (Jones et al., 2007; Marston et al., 2005; Woodward et al., 2007), which, particularly within more systemic engagements such as political participation, will always incorporate zones of limitation – even self-limitation (Balibar, 1998: 31) – operating in concert with its many enablements. This in many ways restrictive conditioning insists that attention be addressed to what happens when individuals become routinized into 'sad' encounters, states that are less affect*ive*, more affect*ed*. What materialities might invoke situations characterized by a decrease in powers to act or by states of disempowerment, for example through bodily configurations associated with addiction or illness, or through more 'structural' violences, obvious in everything from the ever-dwindling availability of social amenities and housing for the poor to the gross over-representation of percentages of raced subjects trapped within the prison industrial complex? In this regard, Tolia-Kelly (2006) and Lorimer (2008), among others, point to a considerable gap between considerations of contemporary political issues and discussions in geography of corresponding 'sad' affective relations that reduce the capacity of a body to act:

> [t]hose people anxious that non-representational theory should care more about mattering more … will know that the spectrum of emotions, passions and conditions felt in social life is by no means exhausted. … Lest anyone forget, the emotionally charged, performing body is not an ecstatic subject *tout court*. What of anger, disgust, hatred, horror, stress, isolation, alienation, fear, terror, dread, decay, loss, denial? … [F]or the likes of Mitchell … they are expressed and endured daily as self-defining realities in the destructive, debilitating, destabilizing, and devastating landscapes that he has charged cultural geographers with being culpably uninterested in (Lorimer, 2005: 90).

The worry is that such neglect has resulted in affective geographies that invoke 'pure, blank spaces of social encounter offered up as open-ended, experimental arenas for the forging of a revisionist, expressive ethics of affect' (Lorimer, 2008: 6) through which historical memory and relations of power no longer make a material difference. Indeed, much work still needs to be done in examining how and what kind of difference is produced in affective relations understood to be almost *of necessity* uneven (after all, *to affect* implies that something else *be affected*): how do these inequalities persist and how are individuals and groups variously constrained and captured in situations through which they become stripped of access and autonomy?

There are two critical areas in the study of political disempowerment that have developed within social theory over the course of the past several decades. These can, we suspect, set affect studies off on a series of future studies. First, affect theorists would benefit from seeking out inventive strategies for engaging situations (and their attendant studies) within which systemic injustices and inequalities distribute forces and blockages amongst the social field in ways that make collectivization and empowerment difficult, which systematically disempower groups of bodies by excessively delimiting their capacities for affecting the world, or that even violently repress specific groups. This is to say, essentially, the production of a set of bodies identified specifically for the accumulation of violent, oppressive, systemically organized affects and for an intense and simultaneous restriction of its own affectivity. Observe, for example, within the past several centuries of ongoing Western imperialism, the countless attempts to create 'sciences' of difference as a means for legitimating race- and gender-based violence and exploitation (Davis, 1998; Fanon, 1967; hooks, 1990; Malcolm X, 1999).

Second, and in addition to relations that turn upon systemic, *external* forces, are a series of studies devoted to understanding the traitorous phenomenon of oppression turned inward upon oneself. Examining the ways that institutions and their associated knowledges engender routinized practices that simultaneously constrain the affective capacities of their practitioner – best exemplified in Foucault's exploration of disciplinary power and the production of the 'docile body' – this work serves as a model for analysing the complex political implications of the sad affects. Rather than being a relation that simply constrains a body's forces, Foucault explains that 'Discipline increases the forces of the body (in economic terms of utility) and diminishes these same forces (in political terms of obedience). In short, it dissociates power from the body' (1977: 138). Thus, 'He [sic] who is subjected to a field of visibility, and who knows it, assumes responsibility for the constraints of power; he makes them play spontaneously upon himself; he inscribes in himself the power relation in which he simultaneously plays both roles; he becomes the principle of his own subjection' (1977: 202–3). An affect theorist from his earliest works, Foucault here offers contemporary thinkers a number of crucial theoretical routes for de-linking affect and empowerment from naïvely ecstatic associations between capacities-to-do and the agent-author of those doings. By contrast, his work makes clear that the production of sad affects extends even into our very capacities to act. In this way Foucault's overwhelming subtext is a continuous caution against might be called 'naïve affectivity' or 'naïve doings': though seemingly enabling because they indicate routes of doing, practices are always capable of delimiting a body's general affectivity. To recognize how having a capacity to affect the world in certain ways can so suddenly and easily become oppressive and delimiting for a body, we need look no further than old factory management strategies that forced workers to compete against each other by putting in longer hours for less money. Such conditions are compounded today in sweatshops, where the piece rate system – payment calculated according to the number of objects produced – infinitely multiplies the oppurtunities for self-exploitation available to the worker (Louie, 2001: 34).

Before turning to such examples in more detail below, we note that while one must remain on constant guard against its being co-opted and exploited, there remains much within 'the power to compose compatible relations with others' (Gatens and Lloyd, 1999: 106) that offers hope for the future:

> the potential of Spinoza's philosophy is to articulate an embodied ethical and political theory appropriate to different kinds of individuals, the different kinds of polities in which they dwell, and the different modalities of self-understanding which they express; and it does so without recourse to transcendent, universal norms by which to judge such individuals, associations and understandings. This is not to say, however, that one cannot make judgements or comparisons at all. However, such evaluations will be based on immanent norms and on the virtue or power of an individual, or community of individuals (1999: 106–7).

The singularity and specificity of affective situatedness shores itself up against the dangerous and indifferent waters of universal evenness, gesturing towards 'the political nature of affect and the infinite complexities of affect itself' in relation to the 'context of power geometries that shape our social world … thus require[ing] an engagement with the political fact of different bodies having different affective capacities' (Tolia-Kelly, 2006: 213). Bodies are 'affected *differently* depending on their own unique composition' and while the 'body retains traces of the changes brought about through interactions with other bodies', at the same time our imagination 'will reflect the diverse ways in which bodies are affected by particular experiences' (Williams, 2007: 355). Movements of bodily differentiation (the continual figuration and refiguration through individuated *and* collective action) give rise to different, (dis)connective affective configurations, countless firings and rearticulations of mind–body continua, and ever-changing localized histories of embodied relatedness; discussions of the implications of these areas for geography are still in the early stages and require much further research.[8]

FOLDS OF IDENTITY

As much as affect is 'routed' by existing power relations and the political–material fact of different bodies, it is also implicated in the production of the conditions of possibility that enable such differences. There is a multidirectional relationship between affect and 'power geometries' such that both are as much participants in the maintenance of exclusion and exploitation as they are enablers of inclusion and association. Social differences require sustained *performance* and, as such, have affective power in themselves. This compels us to interrogate the enrolment of affect in the localized, material (re)production of categories whose ordering functions build social relations and identities that 'capture, codify and control virtualities' (Lazzarato, 2006: 174). Massumi offers a particularly vehement critique of categorical understandings of the social that rely upon such a 'cultural freeze frame' of the identity grid: an 'oppositional framework of culturally constructed significations: male versus female, black versus white, gay versus straight and so on' (2002: 2).[9] For him, the rigorous divisions and rigid boxes demarcating a narrow typology of subjects do reductive, representational violence to the complex enactments of identities 'on the ground'. While such criticisms are sometimes quizzically interpreted as a call to liberate oneself from all categories through the performative affirmation of spontaneous, contingent disidentification, they more importantly call attention to the pervasive violence and oppression borne up by naïve insistence upon the absolute reality of the formal identity types.[10]

At the same time that imposing constructed subject positions serves to predefine and delimit bodies, 'pinning [them] to the grid' and allowing little 'potential for change' (Massumi, 2002: 2–3), affect studies shine lights into precognitive regimes of practice wherein circumscribed and normativized constructs become entrenched in the everyday, material relations of bodies. For example, heteronormative structures require 'performative repetition, institutionalization, discipline and policing' (Lim, 2007: 94) to shore them up, but these lines of disciplinarity are not simply concerned with producing a 'kind' of body or sexuality. To institute and sustain specific oppressive practices, affective relations are stabilized and regularized, so that otherwise 'eruptive' forces of multiplicity are captured on a routinized basis. Lazzarato argues that social categories are 'literally carved out from the multiplicity of activities, crystallizing possible interactions in the form of a dualism' (2006: 174–5; see also Natter and Jones, 1997). Still, while such categories present sequences or logics scripting the body's organizations and orientations, they are incapable of initiating any such action by themselves. Affect, on the other hand, is always the expression of specific, unfolding actions and, as such, illustrates the potential for differentiation even in the enactment of these categories, troubling the tendency to use identity and its social and cultural coordinates to fold the individual into a neat package. Identity attempts to describe a complex assemblage of different *tendencies* in thought, emotion, affect and experience, but inevitably falls short through the production of a delimited catalogue of ideal types. At the same time, while bodies are restlessly subjected to these formal concepts, they are simply not very good at sustaining them: their continuous, situated doings, inevitably – often indiscernibly and even in spite of themselves – 'extend the frameworks which attempt to contain them, [and] seep beyond their domains of control' (Grosz, 1994: xi). Differences are not accountable to the existence of *a priori* sociological categories; rather, they are expressions of how 'organisms connect to their environment and establish uneven relationships amongst each other' (Saldanha, 2006: 22). Given this, interrogating how social categories are nevertheless taken up as virtual memories in bodies (see Connolly, 2002) is an attempt to shed light upon the complex processes contributing to their maintenance within thought, cognition, precognition, habit and perception.

Approaching identity categories through the register of affects emphasizes enactments in the context of the visceral immediacy of bodily encounters. Edbauer reminds us that 'our encounters with bodies … *impinge* upon us before we have the chance to respond through the grid of the symbolic' (2004: 14). Thus affective and emotive reactions (e.g., shame, disgust, embarrassment) can be emphasized within social geographies of encounter and interrogated in the context of their reappropriation within representation, being reconfigured and reconstituted in the process. As Lim explains with regard to homophobia:

> An event of homophobic harassment on a city street, for example, feeds into the field of potential affects. The visceral dimension of trauma gathers in the body to be encountered again in new circumstances as a trigger to feeling and action. The event of harassment comes to resonate with certain situations that the person who suffers such harassment might find themselves in at a later date. Although impossible to predict in advance, there are many aspects of the latter encounter that might resonate with the former: markers of place, the tone of voice of somebody shouting, an ordering of events, a small gesture, glare or facial expression. Such resonation enters the process of selection of how to affect and be affected by other bodies (2007: 102).

The enaction of racism, bigotry and homophobia, while drawing upon a broad range of representational and identitarian constructs, finds its sedimentation through the cooptation and operationalization of affective registers and virtual memory in social sites. In this regard, the perspective of affect enables us to ask: how are homophobic responses learnt, habitualized and acculturated on the body? How does the body enact, experience and remember these modes of hurt, conserving such events as '"tendencies" to act out particular refrains of movement and expression when encountering circumstances that resonate with past events' (Lim, 2007: 101)? And crucially, what are the circumstances that might facilitate and make possible different responses? These questions draw upon a key understanding: the social, rather than consisting merely of a series of orders that we must, each of us, carefully police and tend to lest we dissolve into chaos, is extra- or more-than-cognitive. Never merely the result of our concentrated efforts, it is the materialization of associations in which we always find ourselves already immersed, already producing *us*. Even in my own body: I am a complex of interacting bodies, *I instantiate the social.* Politically, this calls to attention the numerous oppressions in which we take part merely by redeploying, by helping along, by not intercepting and, in general, by enabling the perpetuation and routinization of serialized forces that exploit and disempower other bodies.

Because its analytic is concerned with arrangements of *forces* and *bodies* rather than identities, a political reading of affect further exposes the arbitrariness of the categorical divisions serving as the legitimation for forms of *non*-human exploitation and experimentation that have long existed in the collusions of science with capitalism and the military industrial complex. Animal experimentation, abuse and consumption are all marked by a long history of poorly regulated, underpublicized and violent force relations, the necessity of which frequently stretches the gamut from the dubious, to the ridiculous, to the downright sadistic (Singer, 1995). The heavily Cartesian speciesism serving as justification for this regime of exploitation is directly related to the numerous other political violences based upon the construction of identity differences (Elstein, 2003; Sztybel, 2006), with rationales for the experimental use particularly dependent upon strange contextualizations of bodies as similar-but-different in relation to the human. Here, a legitimation system of resonance/dissonance with the human is propped up through logics of scientific/moral valuation: animals must be similar enough that results can be contextualized relative to the human (assuming the given experiment even has a human context), but different enough that we can condone the subjection of hundreds of thousands of feeling bodies every year to intense, perpetual suffering (Haraway, 2008; Lawlor, 2007).

Speciesism supposedly enables an identitarian *dis*association of the experimenter from the experimented-upon; however, from the perspective of affect, the relations of force and association in the laboratory (or any violent) relation form a continuum between the body of the scientist and that of the experimental subject. What is perhaps most telling in this regard is the way that many of the rationales for laboratory research on non-human animals often develop out of the context of interhuman relations. Take for example Harlow and Soumi's famous experiments on 'inducing depression by "allowing baby monkeys to attach to cloth surrogate mothers who could become monsters"' (Singer, 1995: 33). These monster-mothers were designed to shake violently, to eject 'high-pressure compressed air', and finally, in the case of the 'porcupine mother', to 'eject sharp brass spikes all over the ventral surface of its body' that would repeatedly impale the frightened, clinging infant (quoted in Singer, 1995: 33). As is so often the case, the experiments were centrally concerned with conflicted dimensions of affect, testing whether the infant monkeys would continue to return to these surrogates despite exposure to increasingly violent and painful forces. While such experiments are centrally concerned with affective relations – frequently taking their bearings from any number of anthropocentric contexts – experimenters insert constructions of identity (e.g., human versus animal) so as to transcend the affective violences and grotesqueries they enact. Rather, this sequence of relations – from the scientist to the surrogate to the infant – constitutes its own social relation. The picture painted by affect raises important questions about social relations, not just in terms of our doings or self-repressions, but about the *ways we go about doing* and how we select and legitimize such processes. Thinking from the viewpoint of the forceful assemblage of interacting bodies challenges and even reframes many of the relations we are often inclined to take for granted or normal, lending further political dimensions, for example, to the presence of armed police at protests, the nature of private property, the chemical manipulation of food products, and so on. Likewise, this calls upon us to ask what we are doing when we participate or consume in ways that bear up exploitative relations such as animal experimentation: we reduce animals to pain machines, surfaces upon which we test just how intensely they will be affected before they exhaust themselves or expire. Finally, the focus on ethics and power in affect studies calls attention to the *use* of bodies for comfort or enjoyment and, importantly, to the variety of structures and systems – or circuits and routines – that enable and normalize such relations.

THE POLITICS OF AFFECT

Marx's interpretation of the creation of surplus value through the alienation of workers from their own doings is riddled with reflections upon power and force, and provides one of the most thorough attempts since Spinoza to link affect directly to politics. The early Marx (1978) famously naturalizes labour, essentializing the connection between the human capacity for initiating focused, material transformations and the supposedly passive natural world that is thereby affected. While he later revises this schema and retreats from its humanistic overtones, interacting human and non-human force relations nevertheless remain a foundational component of his critiques of social relations under capitalism. Consider, for example, the 'aim of the application of machinery' in production, where the reproduction of human force exertion by the non-human object becomes the source of labour's gradual devaluation:

> Like every other instrument for increasing the productivity of labour, machinery is intended to cheapen commodities and, by shortening the part of the working day in which the worker works for himself, to lengthen the other part, the part he gives to the capitalist for nothing. The machine is a means for producing surplus value (Marx, 1976: 492).

As speed and force play an ever more pivotal role in capitalist accumulation, the blurry lines between the human–machine interface are increasingly exploited through the manipulation of their aggregative affects, so as to channel their realization into controlled forms of production.[11]

Within the framework of recent ontological debates (Deleuze, 1988a, 1994; Badiou, 2005, 2006; Mullarkey, 2006; Toscano, 2006), we might describe Marx's hard materialist interpretation of force relations as *actualist* rather than *virtualist*. His immediate political concerns lay less with the *potentiality* of force relations and their statistically distributed *capacities* to affect, than with the ways that their realizations and articulations become delimited and conditioned through specific situations articulated in the material world. Drawing upon this distinction, one of Marx's greatest contributions describes capitalism's tendency to capture these otherwise anexact (and thus non-representable) forces constituting everyday labour and to enlist them in systems of abstract (representative) value for the realization of profits:

> The worker … sells labour as a simple, predetermined exchange value, determined by a previous process – he sells labour itself as *objectified labour;* i.e. he sells labour only in so far as its equivalent is already measured, given; capital buys it as living labour, as the general productive force of wealth; activity which increases wealth. It is clear, therefore, that the worker cannot become *rich* in this exchange, since, in exchange for his labour capacity as a fixed, available magnitude, he surrenders his creative *power,* like Essau his birthright for a mess of pottage. Rather, he necessarily impoverishes himself … because the creative power of his labour establishes itself as the power of capital, as an *alien power* confronting him. He *divests* himself of labour as the force productive of wealth; capital appropriates it, as such. … Thus the productivity of his labour, his labour in general, in so far as it is not a *capacity* but a motion, *real* labour, comes to confront the worker as an *alien power;* capital, inversely, realizes itself through the *appropriation of alien power* (Marx, 1973: 307, original emphasis).

Capitalist relations of production violently resituate (or, to be more precise, *corner*) worker affectivity, disjointing and distinguishing it from bodily capacities (i.e., its purchase-ability is coextensive with its alienation). The grotesque genius of capitalism lies in its appropriation of the most immediate of affective contexts, making our own capacities for initiating forceful relations – our ability to work – seem strange and unfamiliar. Channelling our affectivities into processes that contribute paradoxically to our own disempowerment, capitalism simultaneously reframes the resultant commodity as that which offers the gift of empowerment, here in the form of a supplement to practices of consumption.

Today, this cooptation of force relations is so foundational to everyday, Western social relations that any theory of affect that does not take seriously the radical anti-capitalism it necessitates is either badly confused or a very dangerous project indeed. Recently, engagements between Marx and affect have begun to plumb the growing volume of capitalist relations unfolding away from the factory, paying considerable attention especially to the commodification of enjoyment and comfort in the booming service sectors and of the collection and management of information in communication and technological industries (Berardi and Fuller, 2001; Hardt, 1999; Hardt and Negri, 2000, 2004; Harney, 2005; Lazzarato, 1996, 2004, 2007; Marazzi, 2004; Read, 2002, 2003; Toscano, 2004, 2007). In contrast to earlier modes of capitalist production, where forces were enlisted for the production of an ostensibly singular and contained material commodity – something to be purchased and owned and used up, never secreted away – the object of contemporary production and consumption is increasingly '"immaterial labour," that is, labour that creates immaterial products, such as knowledge, information, communication, a relationship, or emotional response' (Hardt and Negri, 2004: 108). Affect remains at the heart of this transformation, but it is no longer realized simply in the material trace of exhausted workers, having expelled the last of their energies into cheap commodities (though it is *still* that, as well). Today, *affect itself* has become objectified for consumption:

> Unlike emotions, which are mental phenomena, affects refer equally to body and mind. In fact, affects, such as joy and sadness, reveal the present state of life in the entire organism, expressing a certain state of the body along with a certain mode of thinking. Affective labour, then, is labour that produces or manipulates affects such as a feeling of ease, well-being, satisfaction, excitement, or passion. One can recognize affective labour, for example, in the work of legal assistants, flight attendants, and fast food workers ... (Hardt and Negri, 2004: 108).

In agreement with feminist reassessments of the value and typologies of labour (Fortunati, 1995), theories of immaterial labour highlight the ways that the reproduction of social life itself has become a key site for the appropriation of affect, reframing even the smallest details of everyday life in terms of labour and consumption: 'Socialist feminist scholars have described this affective labour using terms such as *kin work*, *caring labour*, and *maternal work*. ... Affective labour is biopolitical in that it directly produces social relationship and form of life' (Hardt and Negri, 2004: 110, original emphasis). Despite some reservations about the 'workerism' inhering in such an account (Katsiaficas, 2006: 223), the production of affects is seated at the heart of contemporary capitalism: a sign that the reification and measurement of affect through value has came to be taken as a thing in itself, a commodity, a widget. And yet, by virtue of its very status *as affect*, such labour is already conditioned by its own cultural devaluation:

> Affective labour includes all forms of labour that produce and circulate states of being, feelings of well-being, desire, ease, and passion. ... At the bottom of the ladder of affective labour thus is a sector of the workforce (primarily female) that is not socialized in the sense of trained or invested with skills ... [instead,] there is 'zero degree sociality': the simple capacities to care, communicate, and interact ... .[It] is itself historically produced through the constitution of certain activities – such as caring for children and housework as 'natural,' and it is for this reason that such relations prove ripe for exploitation (Read, 2003: 128).

Key to these new regimes of cheap labour is their long history of givenness and devaluation within regimes of social reproduction. Much as it was in the past, 'Immaterial labour is often off the clock: It is not measured by the workday or week but by the "project." The irregularity of work, and with it the irregularity of pay, becomes an aspect of control and exploitation. Immaterial labour is not opposed to proletarianization ... rather, it is inseparable from the transformation of the very conditions of proletarianization' (Read, 2003: 128).

While affective labour has become a key commodity in those sites where wealthy individuals from the Global North do their consuming, touring and relaxing, factory-based exploitation has not at all receded, but has worsened exponentially. Within the contexts of maquiladoras and sweatshops, the appropriation of production-based affectivity colludes with increasingly deplorable labour conditions, subjecting the worker not only to a situation in which exhaustion becomes a way of life, but also to one in which the body becomes a material fold of – and is often disabled by – the substances her labour transforms. One sweatshop worker explains:

> Many of my friends develop pain and illnesses related to their work. ... They have to move their hands in the same motion over and over again so that some women have very sore hands and shoulders and back pains. They have to sit for a long time and many develop bad circulation and hemmorrhoids. The dust in some of the factories is so thick you can see it in the air and you develop allergies. So sometimes we wore masks we made by ourselves. Otherwise, we'd be sneezing all the time. When I went home from work sometimes, when I would blow my nose, the colors of the fabrics I worked with that day would appear on my Kleenex. I've heard of some women who have had lung and breathing problems because of having worked in garment and manufacturing for so long (Louie, 2001: 36–7).

Much like the processes from *Modern Times* that opened this chapter, we witness – still! – the slow erosion of bodily capacities through the routinization of its affects, the creation of localized disabilities through the body's endlessly repeated labours. Creating crippling circuits of auto-delimitation, the force relations assembled by the maquiladora and the sweatshop generate an environment poisoned by the very practices of production of those who work in it and who in turn grow increasingly ill ingesting the toxic materiality that they daily manipulate. Adding insult to injury, workers are often compelled to compete for their positions through piece rate systems that force them to work exorbitantly long hours seven days per week. From the perspective of affect, capitalism's ouroboric systematicity appears even more nightmarish: forever enlisting the materialities that sit at its limits, consuming itself, perpetually falling forward into, without ever reaching, its own exhaustion. In this seemingly endless struggle against the depletion of bodily forces – one carried out through the continuous *appropriation* of those forces – capitalism's relation to the worker is a battle over finitudes unravelling beneath the sign of death. While the inexhaustible versatility of capitalistic hunger seems incapable of finding a regime of force that it cannot exploit, for the theorist of affect the trace of such modes of exploitation remain constant: at its limit, the exhausted body of the worker becomes a corpse.

CONCLUSION

Affects occupy a central position in the continuous production of the social. Consistent with their immanent character, the multiple paths they potentially open for geographic study depend at every turn upon the numerous worlds they help coax into the light, the new and strange questions they invite us to ask, and the problems – problems unconditioned by solutions we have already at hand (Deleuze, 1994) – that they continue to announce. This is not to suggest that the work done thus far, particularly the exciting analyses concerning affect within cultural geography, have not already set us moving in many positive directions. Much of this research is making great strides in challenging our conceptualizations of the relations between identity and politics, humans and non-humans, and experience and materiality. It remains helpful for inquiries into the social, particularly with regard to its insistence upon de-linking any necessary relation between forces of association and overdetermined notions of value and judgment. In their place, studies of affect ask questions about the potentialities open to bodies engaged in continuous relations of force: What relations might exist for enabling and even increasing a body's affectivities? How might one go about inventing and sustaining them? To what degree might systems or relations that constrict a body's affectivity be escaped or avoided?

Such questions – which can only ever be answered within the specificities of their particular contexts – highlight a further, related concern that should attend any effort to wed studies of affect to topics of relevance. Such work must pay close attention to how it carries out its selection and framing of contexts for rethinking exploitation and difference. Given the overtly anti-fascist and counter-institutional tendencies present in much of the initial, grounding thought in affect (Nietzsche, 1998; Spinoza, 2000), and within its more recent articulations (Deleuze and Guattari, 1983; Freud, 1961; Reich, 1973; Szasz, 1988), geographers of affect should keenly seek out projects and avenues that offer grounds for critical and political thought at the same time that they open the door for participation in efforts to make positive social and political change. As we have tried to suggest above, theorizing affect requires an almost metaphysical approach to the complexities of social difference, a position that benefits from the sheer variety of subjects it makes available for consideration but, at the same time, one that must acknowledge the risks that come with not granting its objects of study a deeply committed seriousness. If it is to gain a stronger sense of gravity, it seems that affect studies *must* learn to prioritize and critically engage the countless relations of exploitation and difference that variously and violently scar contemporary social life. To do otherwise, to merely 'apply' affect to such issues – *using* sites of oppression to exemplify a concept or prove a theoretical point – is an unfit engagement with social science and the basest of cynicisms.

Still, in numerous ways, affect studies are never limited to such violences, populating the diverse orientations of the various social lives in which we find ourselves immersed day after day. As a formal subfield, the social geography of affect does not yet exist, and, in pretending that it does, we have engaged in a kind of speculative or subjunctive theorizing, drawing together strange analytic bedfellows from within and without geography. Key to our proposition for such a subfield is the suggestion – we think one that is implicit in the social dimensions of affect – that at its centre should reside the insistent affirmation of a portrait of social life that is collectivist and that, when it is working well, expresses anti-exclusivist, anti-exploitative and anti-fascist trajectories. Insofar as it gestures toward political theories, affect is decidedly anarchocommunistic. However, we recognize, given the perpetual situatedness of affect, that such politicalities stop short of naïve or utopian promises. Between coming together and falling apart, we find ourselves intertwining in the continuous contexts of our own traumas: no affective relation is friction free, but neither does this constitute an absolute limit for the emergent possibilities of the situation. At every turn we are invited to shift our footing, even if only slightly, gradually: a situated movement, like an affirmation that paradoxically makes it possible to opt for desire even while we find ourselves struggling against positions that keep us caged like rats.

NOTES

1 The relatively recent incorporation of theories of affect in geography has thus far been overwhelmingly cultural. This is doubtless an effect of the humanities having a larger, more stratified readership within cultural geographies than has been heretofore extant with social geographies: many of the key early studies of affect (excluding those having originated from philosophy departments) originated in manuscripts that signalled clear linkages to cultural studies (see Sedgwick and Frank, 1995; Massumi, 1995; Berlant, 2000; Cvetkovich, 2003).

2 However, in spite of the Cartesian tendency to dismiss the importance of affects, he nevertheless endeavoured to retain them as a strictly human capacity. This manoeuvre effectively strips animals of sentience, relegating what would otherwise appear to be expressions of feeling (pain, pleasure) to the status of a squeaky machine. This line of thinking helped usher in and rationalize an era of unbridled and gruesome animal experimentation in Western science. The vivisections and commodity and weapons testing that continue today, the subjection of bodies to any number of strange, violent and often unnecessary forces – frequently unto death – usually seeks justification through related logics (Cavalieri, 2006: 60–61).

3 Here Spinoza goes on to explain that 'at the same time the ideas of these affections' are equally restrained or enabled, thereby asserting a direct connection between matters of bodily affects and affection and the production of thought (Spinoza, 2000: 164).

4 The science of ethology – a subfield of biology – studies animal behaviour from the perspective of differing physiologies and the sensory worlds, rather

than from the anthropocentric perspectives employing analyses grounded in the context of human behaviours and lifeworlds. Deleuze borrows von Uexküll's famous example of a blood-sucking tick to illustrate the 'machinalist' (Kull, 2001: 6) explanation of the relation between an organism and its specific environment: 'define this body by three affects: the first has to do with light (climb to the top of a branch); the second is olfactive (let yourself fall onto the mammal that passes beneath the branch); and the third is thermal (seek the area without fur, the warmest spot)' (Deleuze, 1988c: 124–5). Naturally, the affects and percepts involved in thinking through relations involving humans are much more complex than in this simple organism.

5 This obviously has consequences for the methods we use, as they play a part in performing the world into being.

6 This has been problematic for some geographers who suggest that affect is a 'move to get after or beyond humanity in all our diversity' (Thien, 2005: 453), with the human acting as a 'limitation, an anchor, literally a drag' (2005: 452). We disagree with Thien's suggestion that affect is 'technocratic and distancing' (2005: 453; and see responses by McCormack, 2006, and Anderson and Harrison, 2006). Theories of affect offer precisely the empirical focus and theoretical vocabulary to negotiate the terrain of the human without predrawing its contours or foreclosing it within singular or privileged registers such as the rational or the emotional.

7 Kropotkin's political interests are particularly invested in this second element, as he notes in regard to Wallace's description of the evolutionary 'divergence of characters': 'in forming new habits, moving to new abodes, and taking to new sorts of food. … In all such cases there will be no extermination, even no competition – the new adaptation being *a relief from competition, if it ever existed* …' (Kropotkin, 2006: 53). Just as the 'survivor' of Social Darwinism in all actuality functions as a kind of affective parasite within the restrictive conditions and relations of a specific social site, Kropotkin suggests that practices aimed at changing the social conditions in which we find ourselves immersed can open new venues for affectivity.

8 Further, there have arisen some early cautionary notes regarding reductivism from within affect studies and related fields. Simonsen suggests that their concepts potentially install 'into analysis an extensive *indifference* between the countless objects of the world (human and nonhuman), subsequently ending up portraying them as potentially all the same' (2004: 1335). Similarly, Rose and Wylie suggest that the relational turn in geography potentially effects 'ontological overflattening' in which 'every point, every object, is accorded an equal weight and value (for example, bees, pubs, pigs, humans, moon … or jungles, slums, buildings, archives, streets). All equally cede to the primacy of the relational and the connective' (2006: 477). Indeed, it is *analytically* possible to draw such conclusions and it remains important to rehearse these cautions against sloppy theorizing. However, proper examples of such indifference or overflattening are as hard to find as they are to imagine, as it would become, of necessity, impossible to speak of *anything* (and thus differentiate it) after insisting upon such a system. Still, it seems equally likely that the typologies of valuation that such critics would like to retain have much more to do with epistemological than with ontological concerns.

9 It is important to note that Massumi's characterization here underemphasizes the complexity with which identity theorists grapple. Still, the critical practice that maps individuals onto a grid is incapable of seeing the fine-grained ways in which identities are fluid and momentary crystallizations of the 'swarms of difference' in the world.

10 For further discussion of the complicated relation between spontaneity and representation, see Woodward (forthcoming b).

11 As can be imagined, this picture is even further complicated when considered in cases of production involving 'non-human workers' (see Robbins and Marks, Chapter 7 of this volume).

REFERENCES

Anderson, B. (2005) 'Practices of judgment and domestic geographies of affect', *Social & Cultural Geography*, 6: 645–60.

Anderson, B. (2006) 'Becoming and being hopeful: Towards a theory of affect', *Environment and Planning D: Society and Space*, 24: 733–52.

Anderson, B. (2007) 'Hope for nanotechnology: Anticipatory knowledge and governance of affect', *Area*, 19: 156–65.

Anderson, B. and Harrison, P. (2006) 'Questioning affect and emotion', *Area*, 38: 333–5.

Anderson, B. and Tolia-Kelly, D. (2004) 'Matter(s) in social and cultural geography', *Geoforum*, 35: 669–74.

Badiou, A. (2005) *Being and Event*, trans. O. Feltham, New York: Continuum.

Badiou, A. (2006) *Logiques des Mondes*. Paris: Éditions du Seuil.

Balibar, E. (1998) *Spinoza and Politics*, trans. P. Snowdon. New York: Verso.

Berardi, F., 'Bifo' and Fuller, M. (2001) The factory of unhappiness. *www.nettime.org*.

<http://www.nettime.org/Lists-Archives/nettime-l-0106/msg00033.html>
Berlant, L. (ed.) (2000) *Intimacy*. Chicago: University of Chicago Press.
Bové, J. (2001) 'A farmer's international?', *New Left Review* 12: 89–101.
Bové, J. and Dufour, F. (2005) *Food for the Future: Agriculture for a Global Age*. Malden, MA: Polity Press.
Butler, J. (1997) *The Psychic Life of Power*. Stanford, CA: Stanford University Press.
Cavalieri, P. (2006) 'The animal debate: A reexamination', in P. Singer (ed.), *In Defense of Animals: The Second Wave*. Oxford: Blackwell. pp. 54–68.
Chaplin, C. (1966) *My Autobiography*. Harmondsworth, Middlesex: Penguin.
Collectivo Situationes (2007) 'Something more on research militancy: Footnotes on preceedures and (in)decisions', in S. Shukaitis and D. Graeber with E. Biddle (eds), *Constituent Imagination: Militant Investigations//Collective Theorization*. Oakland, CA: AK Press. pp. 73–93.
Connolly, W. (2002) *Neuropolitics: Thinking, Culture, Speed*. Minneapolis: University of Minnesota Press.
Crimethinc (2003) *Off the Map*. Olympia: Crimethinc.
Cvetkovich, A. (2003) *An Archive of Feelings: Trauma, Sexuality, and Lesbian Public Cultures*. Durham: Duke University Press.
Dark Star Collective (2002) *Quiet Rumours: An Anarcha-Feminist Reader*. Edinburgh: AK Press.
Davis, A.Y. (1998) *The Angela Y. Davis Reader*. Malden, MA: Blackwell.
Del Casino, V. and Marston, S. (2006) 'Social geography in the United States: everywhere and nowhere', *Social and Cultural Geography,* 7 (6): 995–1009.
Deleuze, G. (1988a) *Bergsonism*, trans. H. Tomlinson and B. Habberjam. New York: Zone Books.
Deleuze, G. (1988b) *Foucault*, trans. S. Hand. Minneapolis: University of Minnesota Press.
Deleuze, G. (1988c) *Spinoza: Practical Philosophy,* trans. R. Hurley. San Francisco: City Lights Books.
Deleuze, G. (1990) *Expressionism in Philosophy: Spinoza*, trans. M. Joughin. New York: Zone Books.
Deleuze, G. (1993) *The Fold: Leibniz and the Baroque,* trans. T. Conley. Minneapolis: University of Minnesota Press.
Deleuze, G. (1994) *Difference and Repetition,* trans. P. Patton. New York: Columbia University Press.
Deleuze, G. and Guattari, F. (1983) *Anti-Oedipus: Capitalism and Schizophrenia, vol. 1*, trans. R. Hurley, M. Seem and H.R. Lane. Minneapolis: University of Minnesota Press.
Deleuze, G. and Guattari, F. (1987) *A thousand Plateaus: Capitalism and Schizophrenia, vol. 2*, trans. B. Massumi. Minneapolis: University of Minnesota Press.
Edbauer, J. (2004) 'Executive overspill: Affective bodies, intensity, and Bush-in-relation', *Postmodern Culture,* 15 (1). <http://www3.iath.virginia.edu/pmc/text-only/issue.904/15.1edbauer.txt>
Elstein, D. (2003) 'Species as a social construction: Is species morally relevant?', *Animal Liberation Philosophy and Policy Journal*, 1 (1). <http://www.cala-online.org/Journal/Journal_Articles_download/Issue_1/Elstein.PDF>.
Fanon, F. (1967) *Black Skin, White Masks,* trans. C.L. Markmann. New York: Grove Press.
Fortunati, L. (1995) *The Arcane of Reproduction: Housework, Prostitution, Labour and Capital*, trans. H. Creek, J. Fleming, ed. Brooklyn, NY: Autonomedia.
Foucault, M. (1977) *Discipline and Punish: The Birth of the Prison.* trans. A. Sheridan. New York: Random House.
Foucault, M. (1978) *The History of Sexuality, vol. 1: An Introduction,* trans. R. Hurley. New York: Random House.
Freud, S. (1961) *Civilization and its Discontents*, trans. J. Strachey. New York: W.W. Norton.
Gatens, M. and Lloyd, G. (1999) *Collective Imaginings: Spinoza, Past and Present*. New York: Routledge.
Gibson-Graham, J.K. (2006) *A Postcapitalist Politics*. Minneapolis: University of Minnesota Press.
Goodchild, P. (1997) 'Deleuzian ethics', *Theory, Culture and Society,* 14 (2): 39–50.
Graeber, D. (2004) *Fragments of an Anarchist Anthropology*. Chicago: Prickly Paradigm Press.
Graeber, D. (2007) *Possibilities: Essays on Hierarchy, Rebellion, and Desire.* Oakland, CA: AK Press.

Grosz, E. (1994) *Volatile Bodies: Towards a Corporeal Feminism*. Bloomington, IN: Indiana University Press.
Haraway, D. (2008) *When Species Meet*. Minneapolis: University of Minnesota Press.
Hardt, M. (1993) *Gilles Deleuze: an Apprenticeship in Philosophy*. Minneapolis: University of Minnesota Press.
Hardt, M. (1999) 'Affective labour', *Boundary 2*, 26 (2): 89–100.
Hardt, M. and Negri, A. (2000) *Empire*. Cambridge, MA: Harvard University Press.
Hardt, M. and Negri, A. (2004) *Multitude*. New York: Penguin.
Harney, S. (2005) 'Why is management a cliché?', *Critical Perspectives on Accounting*, 16: 579–91.
Henry, M. (1975) *Philosophy and the Phenomenology of the Body*, trans. G. Etzkorn. The Hague: Nijhoff.
hooks, B. (1990) *Yearning: Race, Gender, and Cultural Politics*. Boston, MA: South End Press.
Jones III, J.P., Woodward, K. and Marston, S.A. (2007) 'Situating flatness', *Transactions of the Institute of British Geographers*, 32: 264–76.
Katsiaficas, G. (2006) *The Subversion of Politics*. Oakland, CA: AK Press.
Kropotkin, P. (1995) 'What is to be done?', in M.S. Shatz (ed.), *The Conquest of Bread and Other Writings*. Cambridge: Cambridge University Press. pp. 257–9.
Kropotkin, P. (2006) *Mutual Aid*. Mineola, NY: Dover.
Kull, K. (2001) 'Jakob von Uexküll: An introduction', *Semiotica*, 134: 1–59.
Law, J. (2004) *After Method: Mess in Social Science Research*. London: Routledge.
Lawlor, L. (2007) *This is not Sufficient: An Essay on Animality and Human Nature in Derrida*. New York: Columbia University Press.
Lazzarato, M. (1996) 'Immaterial labour', in P. Virno and M. Hardt (eds), *Radical Thought in Italy*. Minneapolis: University of Minnesota Press. pp. 133–47.
Lazzarato, M. (2004) 'From capital-labour to capital-life', *Ephemera*, 4 (3): 187–208.
Lazzarato, M. (2006) 'The concepts of life and the living in the societies of control', in M. Fuglsang and B. Sorensen (eds), *Deleuze and the Social*. Edinburgh: Edinburgh University Press. pp. 171–90.
Lazzarato, M. (2007) 'Machines to crystallize time: Bergson', *Theory, Culture & Society*, 24 (6): 93–122.
Lenin, V.I. (1988) *What Is to be Done*? trans. J. Fineberg, G. Hanna and R. Service. London: Penguin.
Lim, J. (2007) 'Queer critique and the politics of affect', in K. Browne, J. Lim and G. Brown (eds), *Geographies of Sexualities: Theory, Practices and Politics*. Aldershot: Ashgate. pp. 53–68.
Lingis, A. (2000) *Dangerous Emotions*. Berkeley, CA: University of California Press.
Lorimer, H. (2005) 'Cultural geography: the busyness of being "more-than-representational"', *Progress in Human Geography*, 29 (1): 83–94.
Lorimer, H. (2008) 'Cultural geography: non-representational conditions and concerns', *Progress in Human Geography*, 32(4): 551–9.
Louie, M. (2001) *Sweatshop Warriors: Immigrant Women Workers Take on the Global Factory*. Cambridge: South End Press.
McCormack, D. (2003) 'An event of geographical ethics in spaces of affect', *Transactions of the Institute of British Geographers*, 28 (4): 488–507.
McCormack, D. (2006) 'For the love of pipes and cables: A response to Deborah Thien', *Area*, 38 (3): 330–32.
McCormack, D. (2007) 'Molecular affects in human geographies', *Environment and Planning A*, 39 (2): 359–77.
Macherey, P. (1998) *In a Materialist Way*. trans. T. Stoltz. New York: Verso.
Malcolm X (1999) *The Autobiography of Malcolm X*. New York: Ballentine Books.
Marazzi, C. (2004) 'Who killed god Pan?', *Ephemera*, 4 (3): 181–6.
Marston, S., Jones III, J.P. and Woodward, K. (2005) 'Human geography without scale', *Transactions of the Institute of British Geographers*, 30: 416–32.
Marx, K. (1973) *Grundrisse*, trans. M. Nicolaus. New York: Penguin.
Marx, K. (1976) *Capital, vol. 1*. trans. B. Fowkes. New York: Penguin.
Marx, K. (1978) *Economic and Philosophic Manuscripts of 1844*, trans. M. Milligan, in R.C. Tucker (ed.), *The Marx–Engels Reader*. New York: W.W. Norton. pp. 66–125.
Massumi, B. (1995) 'The autonomy of affect', *Cultural Critique*, 31: 83–109.

Massumi, B. (2002) *Parables for the Virtual: Movement, Affect, Sensation*. Durham: Duke University Press.

Milburn, K. (2004) 'Return of the tortoise: Italy's anti-empire multitudes', in D. Solnit (ed.), *Globalize Liberation: How to Uproot the System and Build a Better World*. San Francisco: City Lights. pp. 469–80.

Modern Times (1936) C. Chaplin, dir. C. Chaplin, P. Goddard, perf. Warner Home Video.

Mullarkey, J. (2006) *Post-Continental Philosophy: An Outline*. New York: Continuum.

Natter, W. and Jones III, J.P. (1997) 'Identity, space, and other uncertainties', in G. Benko and U. Strohmayer (eds), *Space and Social Theory: Geographical Interpretations of Postmodernity*. Oxford: Blackwell. pp. 141–61.

Negri, A. (1991) *The Savage Anomaly*, trans. M. Hardt. Minneapolis: University of Minnesota Press.

Negri, A. (1999) 'Value and affect', trans. M. Hardt. *boundary 2*, 26 (2): 77–88.

Nietzsche, F. (1998) *On the Genealogy of Morality*. trans. M. Clark and A.J. Swensen. Indianapolis: Hackett.

Notes from Nowhere (eds) (2003) *We are Everywhere: The Irresistible Rise of Global Anticapitalism*. New York: Verso.

Philo, C. (2009) 'Society', in D. Gregory, R. Johnston, G. Pratt, M. Watts and S. Whatmore (eds), *The Dictionary of Human Geography, 5th edition*. Oxford: Blackwell. pp. 701–3.

Read, J. (2002) 'A fugitive thread: The production of subjectivity in Marx', *Pli*, 13: 125–46.

Read, J. (2003) *The Micro-politics of Capital: Marx and the Prehistory of the Present*. Albany: State University of New York Press.

Reich, W. (1973) *The Function of the Orgasm*, trans. V.R. Carfagno. New York: Farrar, Straus and Giroux.

Rose, M. and Wylie, J. (2006) 'Animating landscape', *Environment and Planning D: Society and Space*, 24: 475–9.

Saldanha, A. (2006) 'Reontologising race: the machinic geography of phenotype', *Environment and Planning D: Society and Space*, 24: 9–24.

Sedgwick, E.K. (2003) *Touching Feeling: Affect, Pedagogy, Performativity*. Durham: Duke University Press.

Sedgwick, E.K. and Frank, A. (1995) 'Shame in the cybernetic fold: Reading Sylvan Tomkins', *Critical Inquiry*, 21: 496–522.

Shiva, V. (2000) *Stolen Harvest: The Hijacking of the Global Food Supply*. Cambridge, MA: South End Press.

Shiva, V. (2002) *Water Wars: Privatization, Pollution, and Profit*. Cambridge, MA: South End Press.

Simonsen, K. (2004) 'Commentary: Networks, flows and fluids. Reimagining spatial analysis?', *Environment and Planning A*, 36: 1333–7.

Singer, P. (1995) *Animal Liberation*. London: Pimilco.

Sitrin, M. (ed.) (2006) *Horizontalism: Voices of Popular Power in Argentina*. Oakland, CA: AK Press.

Smith, D.M. (1997) 'Geography and ethics: A moral turn', *Progress in Human Geography*, 21: 596–603.

Smith, D.M. (2000) *Moral Geographies: Ethics in a World of Difference*. Edinburgh: Edinburgh University Press.

Spinoza, B. (2000) *Ethics*, trans. G.H.R. Parkinson. New York: Oxford University Press.

Szasz, T. (1988) *Pain and Pleasure: A Study of Bodily Feelings*. N.p., Syracuse University Press.

Sztybel, D. (2006) 'The rights of animal persons', *Animal Liberation Philosophy and Policy Journal*, 4 (1). <http://www.cala-online.org/Journal/Journal_Articles_download/Issue_5/sztybel.pdf>

Thien, D. (2005) 'After or beyond feeling? A consideration of affect and emotion in geography', *Area*, 37: 450–4.

Thrift, N. (2004) 'Intensities of feeling: towards a spatial politics of affect', *Geografiska Annaler B*, 86 (1): 57–78.

Tolia-Kelly, D. (2006) 'Affect: An ethnocentric encounter?: Exploring the "universalist" imperative of emotional/affective geographies', *Area*, 38: 213–7.

Tomkins, S. (1995) in E.K. Sedgwick and A. Frank (eds), *Shame and its Sisters*. Durham: Duke University Press.

Toscano, A. (2004) 'Factory, territory, metropolis, Empire', *Angelaki: Journal of the Theoretical Humanities*, 9 (2): 197–216.

Toscano, A. (2006) *Theatre of Production: Philosophy and Individuation between Kant and Deleuze*. London: Palgrave.

Toscano, A. (2007) 'Vital strategies: Maurizio Lazzarato and the metaphysics of contemporary capitalism', *Theory, Space & Society,* 24 (6): 71–91.

Trapese Collective, The (eds) (2007) *Do it Yourself: A Handbook for Changing our World.* London: Pluto Press.

Williams, C. (2007) 'Thinking the political in the wake of Spinoza: Power, affect and the imagination in the *Ethics*', *Contemporary Political Theory,* 6: 349–69.

Woodward, K. (forthcoming) 'Events, spontaneity and abrupt conditions', in B. Anderson and P. Harrison (eds), *Taking Place: Non-Representational Theories and Geography.* Hampshire: Ashgate.

Woodward, K., Jones III, J.P. and Marston, S.A. (2007) 'The eagle and the flies, a fable for the micro', *Secons: Socio-Economic of Space,* 3 (12). <http://www.giub.uni-bonn.de/grabher/downloads/Woodward.pdf >

Wylie, J. (2002) 'An essay on ascending Glastonbury Tor', *Geoforum,* 32 (4): 441–55.

Wylie, J. (2005) 'A single day's walking: Narrating self and landscape on the South West Coast Path', *Transactions of the Institute of British Geographers,* 30 (2): 234–47.

7

Assemblage Geographies

Paul Robbins and Brian Marks

THE NON-HUMANS HAVE RE-ENTERED THE SOCIAL IMAGINATION

By a landslide vote in Spring, 2000, citizens of Montana, otherwise known for their dogged dedication to private property rights, banned commercial hunting on enclosed game farms. Banning this practice, dubbed 'canned hunting' by its opponents and 'alternative agriculture' by its proponents, was a surprise outcome in that it was a practice supported by the United States Department of Agriculture, a consortium of large landowners, and a reliably powerful association of professional outfitters. The result was greeted in some quarters as a political upheaval since it represented a limitation on property rights by a convergence of diverse social interests including local working-class hunters and national animal rights groups. In the process it created a new constellation of power, re-writing ideologies of property rights.

In this sense, this case is a quintessentially *social and political geography*, a situation in which individuals and groups struggle for their interests through dynamic discursive practices and shift the location of power towards a particular result, often creating new and complex cross-scale geographic alliances in the process.

Yet this social explanation, however congruent with practices within the field of geography, tells only a fraction of the story. Much of this radical and surprising outcome was the result of the combined habits of an animal and a neural protein. As it turns out, the congregation of elk in confined areas and their transportation between states as part of a commodity market for game animals tends to increase the incidence of chronic wasting disease (CWD), a transmissible spongiform encephalopathy (TSE) and a neurological disease in wild cervids (deer, elk, etc.) related to BSE or mad cow disease. Infected animals are emaciated, have a wide stance, a lowered head, droopy ears, excessive salivation, display 'depression,' increased thirst and urination, and later paralysis and a slow and painful death.

The causes of this unpleasant outcome can be seen in immunohistochemical examination of the brainstem, which reveals countless small but fatal lesions caused by abnormal infectious *things*: prions (proteinaceous infectious particles), the 'bent' versions of naturally occurring proteins. With no associated DNA, prions are not alive in any normal sense and can persist in soil for decades and resist almost any form of cleaning or sterilization, even fire. These latent prions can re-infect new hosts, setting off a chain reaction in which exposure 'bends' naturally occurring prions, spreading the disease. This is exacerbated by the fact that elk tend to be extremely uncooperative in confinement and have a remarkable capacity for escape. Both behavioral tendencies increase the risk of the disease spreading. Elk also have neurological systems similar to most mammals, including humans, suggesting the possibility that prions can flow between species, a possibility that impinged on Montana public responses to risk in a way different from almost any other property conflict in the state's history.

Seen in this expanded light, proteins and elk were not simply the object of Montana voters, but were active in reworking the social fabric of the region. And while neither the elk nor the prions lobbied local officials, in the absence of their socio-natural and fundamentally relational condition such a radical reconfiguration of property rights would have been unlikely. In short, social and political outcomes were determined by more than humans.

Nor is this outcome unique to Montana. A burgeoning literature in social, cultural, and economic geography has recently begun to come to terms with this 'more-than-human' geographic condition (Whatmore, 2006).[1] A perusal of recent literature in cultural, social, or human-environment geography confronts the reader with many cases. Gardens are understood to *constitute* the subject status of gardeners (Power, 2005) and not simply be constituted by them. Research on conservation argues that bears *participate in* and contribute to non-governmental organizational actions (Hobson, 2007). Elm trees and tree diseases are both understood to *labor* in the American urban economy, affecting and altering capital accumulation (Perkins, 2007). Prions interact with scientists and cattle to *produce* uncertainties that impinge on processes of policy-making (Hinchliffe, 2001). Dogs make people (Haraway, 2003). Mosquitoes speak (Mitchell, 2002). In a recent frenzy of insightful 'critical animism,' non-humans have re-entered the landscape, confounding 'social' explanations of anything and everything.

On the other hand, prions, elk, gardens, bears, elm trees, mosquitoes and dogs do not exist or 'act' in the world independent of socialized knowledge, discourse, and scientific text. In each newspaper invocation, in every laboratory observation and inscription, and in all debates about the 'natural' or 'unnatural' character of technology, a host of deeply humanized and politicized representations occur. This represents a puzzle for any project that admits social geographies are more than human: confronting a world constituted by more-than-human actors, joined in a cat's cradle of physically grasping relationships, threaded through a fun house of representations.

If this were not complicated enough, further admission of this condition raises questions about 'human' geography more generally. Consider the nature of prions themselves, which constitute us, in part, as they do elk. Indeed, when seen through the lens of traveling neural tissue, it is hard to know where we leave off and the elk begin. At bottom, it raises questions not only about being social, but about being human and making claims about the world of, and lives of, humans. Certainly these challenges suggest the potential importance of shifting modes of explanation, not only to make non-humans 'matter' but to rethink the ontological status of the 'social.' So too, it represents a shift of research attention to the embodied, grounded and *material* aspects of these social relationships.

In this chapter we summarize the history of this recent rematerialization, celebrate its possibilities, and simultaneously signal caution as we proceed. In the next section, we briefly outline the recent disciplinary history of discussion on the topic of rematerializing geography, describing basic areas of agreement and ongoing debate, and conclude that most efforts to advance this mode of explanation have settled methodologically on some form of 'assemblage geography.' We next examine the varying strategic and explanatory forms these assemblage geographies take, including what we describe as symmetrical, intimate, metabolic, and genealogical assemblages. Here we suggest each form of assemblage invokes different metaphors with differing normative implications for explanation. In the process, we hint at the following further questions: To what degree do efforts in rematerialized geography embrace or eschew the epistemological lessons of power/knowledge from poststructuralism, feminism, science studies, and postcolonialism, if at all, and at what risk? What are the normative political implications, if any, of assemblage geographies? What explanatory burdens do assemblage explanations have, and what counts as reliable evidence of their effect? Together, we suggest that these questions, coupled with the ambiguity of the answers geographers have so far provided, present the puzzle of assemblage geography.

REASSEMBLING SOCIAL GEOGRAPHY: THE RETURN OF THE MATERIAL

A full survey of the 'cultural' turn in explanation and the emergence of 'social constructionism' is unnecessary as excellent surveys exist elsewhere (Hacking, 1999; Castree, 2005; Demeritt, 1994, 1998). In terms relevant to this chapter, the central elements of this shift included a stress upon discourse and meaning, resulting in a profusion of productive methods (i.e., interpretive and deconstructive approaches) and new metaphors for geographic analysis (e.g., landscape as text; see Barnes and Duncan, 1992). Secondly, the cultural shift entailed epistemologically critical ways of thinking (from poststructuralism and feminism, most notably) that sought to show how taken-for-granted and effectively naturalized truths (like race and gender) were historically and socially produced. The common goal shared with other social sciences, as Ian Hacking (1999) summarizes in the *Social Construction of What?*, was to show that many things we accept as true and inevitable actually need not have existed and may have pernicious effects.

At the same time, the *social*, as a distinctive sphere or category of reality – one capable of providing an incubator for such constructions – was to a degree enshrined as distinct and autonomous. To make these sorts of arguments, the source of these taken-for-granted truths needed necessarily not to be found in 'nature,' a material place outside of the interpretive faculties of social beings. As a result, the material, more-than-human, or non-human were to varying degrees evacuated from explanation in social geography, albeit to good effect.

The material, of course, never really left human geography.[2] Poststructural scholars went to great lengths to remind readers that all discourses were materialized in institutions and practices (Foucault, 1980b). Marxist geographers and critical realists continued to stress a dialectical relationship between humans and non-humans, constituting social reality through the labor process (Smith, 1996). Work in these areas maintained concern about how material conditions impinged on and produced opportunities for changing economic and social conditions (Henderson, 1999). So too in cultural ecology, political ecology, and risk/hazards research, there were ongoing efforts to understand non-human conditions, including soils, land cover, and flows of water, energy, and waste, with little serious break. Neither did these fields fully abandon materialist accounts of basic environmental processes (Robbins, 2004).

Nevertheless, an examination of even these geographies reveals a critical effort to hold aside the material from explanation in an attempt to *denaturalize*, as Castree (2005) puts it, what had long been problematic natural (i.e., inevitable, essential, and universal) strategies of explanation. Specifically, historically problematic tendencies and explanations that made use of 'nature' in arguments to defend the political status quo came under scrutiny, including population and other naturalized accounts of land degradation, starvation, and poverty (Blaikie and Brookfield, 1987). So, even in fields seriously dedicated to more-than-human topics, natural explanations were tempered to explore the social roots of outcomes and knowledges.

Sightings of material geographies

Sightings of the material began in earnest not long after consensus was reached on the social historical contribution or constitution of material truths. As Bakker and Bridge (2006) recently summarized in their survey of the problem, this resurgence has not been restricted to human-environment geographies. Cultural geography's embrace of the everyday and of problems of consumption has meant encountering and accounting for a world of traveling objects (Crang, 1996). Urban geography's renewed interest in city living and sustainability has meant concern for material conditions of built environments (Lees, 2002). Feminist examination of embodied experience meant an engagement with the socio-physical site of the body (Colls, 2007) and the position of the body in grounded material places (Nast and Pile, 1998). These works apply the insights of critical theory to areas historically dominated by strictly material concerns (specifically, resource geography) as well as applying the lessons of historically material geographies to areas of social geographic concern.

Interest in animal geographies and the co-evolved partner species that accompany people (Wolch and Emel, 1998; Anderson, 1997, 1998; Philo, 2000, among many others) has further propelled interest in understanding the social in an expansive and material way, including the worlds of zoo elephants, house cats, and wildlife predators on the edges of cities. These animals influence the fate of social, economic, and human development over varying times and spaces, demanding a rematerialized sort of geography to trace and explain.

A concomitant geographic concern with the nature of human experience and our co-constitution by non-humans again points to the blurring of the social and the material. These beings take diverse forms, ranging from stomach bacteria that have been with(in) humanity since its beginning to entirely novel cybernetic implants developed in laboratories in just the last few years. Referred to as 'post-humanism' by various observers,[3] an exploration of this condition is admittedly not new to geography and has long been embraced in other fields (Badmington, 2004).

These research concerns have been accompanied (whether led or followed is less clear) by the surge in examination of theoretical works that stress relational ontology and make space for all manner of material concerns. This approach is rooted in philosophical traditions that stress the relationality of things, people, and the broader world of substance and material being and experience (Deleuze, 1988). So, too, it is linked to urgent interventions in feminism that question unproblematic views of social constructions (sex/gender) that float free of never-fully-cooperative material conditions (human bodies) they seek to constrain and direct (Butler, 1993). Together these works provide the underpinnings for analysis of the co-combination and mutual constitution of what had formerly been ontologically divided: material objects and bodies, social representations and discourses, and subjective experiences, ideas, and emotions. As Giles Deleuze and Félix Guattari put it, 'there is no longer a tripartite division between a field of reality (the world) and the field of representation (the book) and the field of subjectivity (the author). Rather, an assemblage establishes connections between certain multiplicities drawn from each of these orders …' (Deleuze and Guattari, 1987: 25).

Between ongoing theoretical explorations of these problems and a burgeoning research agenda into relational, embodied, and co-constituted geographies, therefore, the stage is set for a 'materialist return,' as Whatmore (2006) puts it, one portending a 'more-than-human' geography. The tendencies in this approach, she further explains, include a stress on practice rather than discourse, affect rather than meaning, knowledge rather than identity.

In sum, there have been enough sightings of these material returns to warrant attention and to consider the sort of contribution they might make to social geography and its allied fields. Having said this, it is also clear that this cacophonous notification is made up of very different kinds of thinkers and researchers doing very different kinds of work. Amidst these sightings of the material's return, however, there are some apparent areas of consensus, at least among practitioners of cultural, social, and human/environment geographies.

Emerging consensus

The first strong apparent consensus, repeated by many researchers and theorists in this area, is that a 'resurgence' of the material, despite its occasional inconvenient designation as 'posthuman' or 'postsocial,' is not an indication of a new condition or crisis. Geographers in this field generally reject assertions by millennial thinkers that the difficulty of drawing boundaries between people and machines or other species is inherently good, bad, or new, or that it portends an upheaval in or foregrounds the end of 'humanity' (see especially Fukuyama, 2002). Rejecting apocalyptic perspectives and their short-sighted view of evolutionary and species history, geographers working at this edge of the discipline suggest instead that the world, and humans within it, have always been more than human. They reject the humanist proposition of an historical rupture, demarked by a line between social and after-social, as both unstable and dangerously conservative, and instead propose the more-than-human as a trans-historical position of political potential. As Braun suggests, 'from this emerges a different politics, no longer a celebration of transcendence, nor a politics of recovery … but a politics attuned to humans as always in the middle of multiple becomings, always an *effect* of politics, rather than that which *grounds* politics' (Braun, 2004: 1354, italics in original).

Similarly, more-than-human geographers stress that this way of thinking is by no means itself another new 'post'-ing of cultural, social, urban, or any other form of geography, meant to signal a sea-change in intellectual progress. As recounted above, the long lineage of this thinking is notable (as is hesitation to initiate or join intellectual fads). The more-than-human is neither, therefore, epochal nor necessarily 'paradigmatic' for these observers in any sense. Favoring the language of 'returns,' Whatmore explains instead that what is happening is a productive repetition: 'turning seemingly familiar matters over and over, like pebbles on the beach – rather than a product of sudden encounter or violent rupture' (Whatmore, 2006: 601).

These approaches to geography suggest, whether explicitly or tacitly, a common, basic rethinking and redefinition of the concept and sphere of the *social*. If situations and consequences are understood to be composed of many classes of actors and kinds of relationships, they can be considered social only if we change our definition from one in which the social designates a particular class of phenomena (distinct for example from cultural, physical, or economic phenomena), to one simply denoting what Latour identifies in his book *Reassembling the Social* as an 'association between entities' (2005: 64). The social does not represent a unique, distinct, or categorically different domain of reality, instead: 'it is the name of a movement, a displacement, a transformation, a translation, an enrollment' (Latour, 2005: 64–5). This more expansive definition is powerful, insofar as it allows power-laden social geographies to be the *product* of a world of interacting objects, bodies, and actors, rather than a single conceptual element, location, or thing.

To make such an expansive move represents a serious break, of course. Consider that, as a prefix for any number of apparently useful analytic terms, 'social' has long been a powerful modifying place-holder: social reproduction, social capital, social justice, to name just a few examples. Here social represents a *type* of reproduction, capital, or justice, distinct from other forms, including biological reproduction, natural capital, or environmental justice, among many others. Just as 'natural' has rightly become an unstable modifier, revealed through compelling geographical inquiry, the imperative of the social begins to retreat. Thus, more-than-human geographers share an increasing ambivalence about the social as a coherent category.

Finally, geographers who analytically engage the world as always more-than-human share an ongoing commitment to the *geography* of that condition. As Murdoch (1998) points out, some proponents of this approach in science studies, sociology, and related fields are skeptical or hostile to geography (as an analytical optic), insofar as its Euclidian form implies simple distance and proximity-dominated notions of connection, causation, and association (see for example Law, 2002).[4] But relational understandings of space, born specifically in the field of social geography and drawing on the insights of Lefebvre (1991), Harvey (1996), Massey (1994), and others, cohere convincingly with more-than-human geographies as they assert the conditional production of space itself. Thus, Murdoch argues, insofar as these approaches seek 'to analyze how social and material processes (subjects, objects, and relations) become seamlessly entwined within complex sets of associations …,' there is a necessary concomitant relevance for understanding the geography of 'network topologies' that trace 'the ways that spaces emerge as socio-material relations are arranged into orders and hierarchies' (Murdoch, 1998: 359).

In sum, the admittedly diverse rematerialization of social geography entails common elements. These include: eschewal of epochal, paradigmatic, or millennial thinking about nature and society; redefinition of the social in expansive relational terms; and insistence on the significant geographies of these relations.

Despite these common concerns, however, the heterogeneity of approaches has together proffered no single meaningful methodological map for producing knowledge in social geography. To date, most serious meditations have signaled a coherent change of mood, a cautious exploration, and a robust conceptual vocabulary, but not a way to do research. Nor is this a simple thing, since a view of socio-natural processes of this kind means charting somewhat new research and writing strategies. Admitting that the world is more than human and more than socially constructed while acknowledging and simultaneously insisting on the partial, non-universal, and historically contingent character of various natures makes defining causes and effects difficult, along with identifying explanans and explanandum, and describing why and how things happen the way they do. This is entirely fitting, in a way. Under conditions where heterogeneous human and non-human actors constitute the outcomes of the world around them, each outcome is arguably *sui generis* and requires an *ad hoc* explanatory strategy.

Nevertheless, as case materials begin to mount, examination of recent research efforts suggests that common explanatory strategies have developed. Research in this area most commonly traces what we call *assemblage geographies*.

DIVERSE METAPHORS AND METHODS OF SOCIAL ASSEMBLAGE

Assemblage, as understood and elusively identified by Deleuze and Guattari (1987), is a dynamic structure applied to semi-stable socio-natural configurations and geographies that emerge over space and time. In keeping with the imperatives of re-materialization, sensitivity in analysis to assemblages draws attention to: 1) relationships between people and things; 2) changing trajectories and rates of change, including acceleration and transmutation as well as deceleration and stabilization; and 3) spatially heterogeneous forms and effects. As Braun suggests, therefore, an emphasis on assemblage stresses 'the making of socionatures whose intricate geographies form tangled webs of different lengths, density, and duration, and whose consequences are experienced differently in different places' (Braun, 2006: 644).

To one degree or another in geography, whether identified as assemblage, network, or actor-network, this form of analysis seems to predominate in recent socio-material geography. Research projects in this vein generally involve some part of a threefold effort. First, proceeding from the proposition that the world is relational, research evaluates the relative position of various actors to one another, describing the territories, scales, and geographic configurations that result. Second, premised on the notion that 'objects are an effect of stable arrays or networks of relations' (Law, 2002: 91) rather than vice versa, analysis typically traces the way particular configurations actually make involved actors the way they are, producing the contingent character of the objects and agents involved. Third, accepting that not all configurations are the same or behave in the same way (consider Deleuze and Guattari, 1987, especially Chapter 12), assemblage geographies typically trace the implications of specific network forms in terms of their momentum and social, economic, ecological, and political outcomes.

Within this broad embrace, there are a few key approaches. From a brief (and admittedly incomplete) review of the literature, we suggest at least four such forms of assemblage: *symmetrical, intimate, metabolic, and genealogical* (outlined in Table 7.1). Though they inevitably overlap, each represents a different form of explanation and each has a different narrative style. Each, however, upends traditional social geographic explanation in one way or another by populating the field of causality with new and troubling actors.

Table 7.1 Styles and strategies of assemblage explanation

Assemblage	*Exemplary theorist*	*Mobilizing metaphors*	*Stresses*	*Explanatory principle*	*Narrative style*
Symmetrical	Latour	Quasi-objects	Purification/ translation	Nothing just sits there [1]	Paradoxical description
Intimate	Haraway	Companion species	Everyday practices of co-constitution	'Beings do not preexist their relatings' [2]	Reflexive connection
Metabolic	Marx	Circulation and metabolism	Uneven geographic processes and results; capitalism and justice	By acting on the world and changing it, people at the same time change their own nature [3]	Tragic unmasking
Genealogical	Mitchell	Epistemic things	Concentration and reorganization of expert power	'Ideas and technology ... emerged from the mixture and were manufactured in the processes themselves' [4]	Ironic revelation

Notes:

1 Paraphrased from Latour (2005: 129); see below.

2 Haraway (2003: 6).

3 Paraphrased from Marx (1967); see below.

4 Mitchell (2002: 52).

Symmetrical assemblages

> all the actors *do something* and don't just sit there (Latour 2005: 129).

Consider sewers. Nothing seems more human, more controlled, more deliberate, or more volitional than urban infrastructural development. Conceived at the drafting table, paid for and argued over in city council meetings, and laid out by engineers, the key to understanding them and their role in urban geography typically lies in understanding problems of annexation, struggles over suburban growth, historical constructions of the sanitary city, and political debates over effluent discharge in the face of economic development and rising ecological consciousness. Sewage is an inherently social phenomenon, suffused with capital, politics, and systems of meaning-making.

For Phil Jones and Neil Macdonald, however, such an understanding of the geography of cities perilously overlooks the least tractable but most efficacious of agents, unruly water itself (Jones and Macdonald, 2007). In their analysis of Glasgow's changing infrastructural strategies, they point to the way water management approaches have moved from 'hard' systems of drainage that rapidly and efficiently move water out of the city, to 'softer' approaches that make space in the city for water, attempting to reconcile and absorb it. Where this move might be seen as one emerging from capital costs, technological innovation, class struggle, or any range of ready-made social explanations, Jones and Macdonald insist the major driver is water itself.

The central goal of their explanatory strategy is to produce a symmetrical field of explanation, one in which the human and the non-human are treated in parallel. In the process, they apply a series of metaphoric theoretical terms to water that have historically been reserved for people. Specifically they suggest that water has been 'disciplined' in the explicitly Foucaultian sense (as per Foucault, 1995). More recently, they argue, a new form of governance has emerged in which 'new forms of water management are beginning to arise which attempt a more regulated, productive form of discipline attempting to work with water's more unruly characteristics rather than trying to suppress them outright' (Jones and Macdonald, 2007: 536).

Symmetrical assemblages thus follow the first rule of Latour's injunction for expansively reassembling social explanation. For him – and inherent in many understandings of assemblage geography – an effective assemblage requires that all the assembled players are active in the outcome and impinge upon the dynamics of the system. A good account 'is a narrative or a description or a proposition where all the actors *do something* and don't just sit there. Instead of merely transporting effects without transforming them, each of the points in the text may become a bifurcation, an event, or the origin of a new translation' (Latour, 2005: 128, emphasis in original).

In this sense, networks are not 'things' in and of themselves but instead indicate the desirable qualities or characteristics of texts:

> the network does not designate a thing out there that would have roughly the shape of interconnected points, much like a telephone, a freeway, or a sewage network. It is nothing more than *an indicator of the quality of a text* about the topics at hand. It qualifies its objectivity, that is, the ability of each actor to *make* other actors *do* unexpected things (Latour, 2005: 129, emphasis in original).

And this is precisely the case for Glasgow's sewage system, where it is the water that forces the issue, becomes entangled with modes of governance historically developed from other social and material interactions, and forces surprising responses from planners, decision-makers, and citizens with otherwise stubborn habits of thinking and management.

It is possible to ask what insight such an inversion of explanation provides. Ultimately, such symmetrical geographies may flirt with banality: water overflows during storms, rocks roll downhill, animals move in search of food. All of these of course impinge on pipe-makers, erosion control engineers, and wildlife managers. So what? What do we know in the wake of this explanation that we did not know before and could not have known with a more traditional social approach to explaining infrastructural change?

The answer lies again in the quality of such a text. By stressing efforts and technologies that control water and the way water responds to such forms of control, Jones and Macdonald are necessarily led to conceptual categories that might have been overlooked in other modes of explanation: specifically including ideologies of domination and the historical and material dynamics that produce and subvert them amongst planners, engineers, and people who lay cement. In such an explanation we can see that what we understand to be social ideas (domination, control, discipline) are suffused with material interactions and histories, and so we come to view them as historically contingent, indeed vulnerable to other ways of thinking and from the surprising actions and responses of material conditions. This subverts a central urge dogmatically located in the training of social scientists, which, as Latour suggests, is the desire to *denaturalize* all forms of social process and outcome: 'To become a social scientist is to realize that the inner properties of objects do not count, that they are mere receptacles for human categories' (Latour, 1993: 52).

This act of explanatory purification (parallel to that of traditional physical sciences to *desocialize* the condition of the objects of its analysis) is constantly vulnerable to cases that refuse such divisions. These limits of explanation typically follow when observers encounter objects that defy denaturalization and desocialization. These *quasi-objects* straddle nature/society binaries and subvert simple domestication. The crises in explanation that follow may lead to efforts to start explanation precisely at the site of these objects, treat them symmetrically, and come to understand the socio-material history and geography of our interaction with them (Latour, 1993). Symmetrical assemblage geographies revolve around and leverage these paradoxical objects (paradoxes only as long as we cling to asymmetrical understandings and explanations) to provide larger insights into the world.

Examining the awkwardness of quasi-objects highlights the way they are social in the sense that they are humanized resources, while also being natural in the sense that they are ultimately uncooperative and beyond volitional control. Such symmetrical explanations shed light onto the myriad locations in society (expansively defined) where habits are formed, power is codified, and long-standing hegemonic forces are eroded and reworked. At their best, symmetrical assemblages do more than subvert anthropocentrism – they paint a wider portrait of a world humans inhabit and that inhabits them.

But if these geographies inhabit us as much as we inhabit them, symmetrical assemblages are somewhat less focused on the transformations produced in such intimate interactions and inhabitations. Such intimacies are everywhere, however, and in a constant process of remaking human beings themselves. Consider the common garden.

Intimate assemblages

> Through their reaching into one another, through their 'prehensions' or graspings, beings constitute each other and themselves. Beings do not preexist their relatings (Haraway, 2003: 6).

Gardens are typically viewed as cultural artifacts of social or personal desire. Different forms of gardens, in this way of thinking, are embodied forms of traditional preference or sites for cultural contestation. Consider, for example, the Mexican house lot garden, which has been shown convincingly to be a crucial space for household reproduction, cultural exchange, and transformation of social roles (Christie, 2004). Gardens are viewed as strictly 'human achievements,' suggests Emma Power (2005), as gardeners are shown to select varieties, lay out plots, and manipulate growing conditions. Landscapes are the outward 'natural' reflection of stubbornly inward 'social' relationships.

After observing gardeners and garden landscapes, Power notes some inevitable, yet commonly overlooked, phenomena that undermine this appearance of unidirectional control. First, as gardeners observe their gardens' dynamics, they respond and order their responses, behaviors, and lives as a result. So, too, the growth conditions and morphologies of planted species tend to drive the form and conditions of the other species, creating new patterns and responses. Interactions with pests, invasives and weeds create further dynamics, forcing adaptation and reimaginings from the gardener, typically disrupting expected patterns of control and changing them as subjects of the landscape. As Power suggests, such a reverse pattern of domestication 'unsettles nature–culture frameworks by drawing people and plants into a relation of care. It also ruptures the ideal of domestication that saw plants changing in order to satisfy the needs of humans. Rather, in this garden, domestication describes a process in which the humans were equally altered' (Power, 2005: 48).

In this sense, gardeners are very much the product of the gardens and not vice versa (see also Robbins, 2007). Extending these logics into human interaction, evolution, and sociability suggests the long-term implications of the garden for social geography. As William Doolittle (2004) observes, the garden represents the adaptation of plants to the inadvertent disposal practices of ancient people, a seizing of advantage by non-humans that created landscapes to which human interactions would later adapt, only to further select and transform the species that had volunteered. The result is a condition of mutual exploitation and domestication – people made new botanical landscapes that made new kinds of people that made yet newer landscapes.

Such assemblage arguments are further mustered in contemporary animal geographies to suggest that the specific actions and adaptations of wild animals produce political effects. For example, tracing the movements and practices of wild animals as part of conservation, not merely treating them as its object, represents a departure from political ecologies that typically de-center these species in favor of the human struggles in which they are represented and invoked. Hobson writes, in her research of Moon Bear conservation in Asia, both that 'what it means to be a "Moon Bear" is being reconstituted through [political action]' and that 'the bears can be argued as subjects in the story of animal politics in East Asia' (Hobson, 2007: 262–3).

These insights from gardening and conservation (among many others) result from employing an assemblage strategy that differs somewhat from simple symmetrical arguments. Stressing the extremely intimate way individuals and species are mutually remade, intimate assemblages directly identify and trace the peculiar associations created through what Donna Haraway describes as 'significant otherness.' Crucially, Haraway insists, all of this mutual becoming is not free of coercion, inequity, accumulation, or exploitation. The history of relations within and between species thoroughly contradicts any romantic notion of interaction. Nevertheless, she maintains, the point of narration and inquiry and the motivation for sketching such assemblages is precisely to name those relationships, meditate on their contingencies, and potentially imagine other ways of becoming in the world. She reminds us that 'feminist inquiry is about understanding how things work, who is in the action, what might be possible, and how worldly actors might somehow be accountable to and love each other less violently' (Haraway, 2003: 7).

Such goals are of course congruent with the goals of most practitioners of critical and feminist social geography. The innovation here is not simply to add other species or objects and 'stir.' Instead, it is to reflexively remind us of the embodied and evolutionary character of ourselves as humans and more-than-humans. Social relations are more-than-social and more than extensions of the social into other locations.

To trace and document such graspings requires documentation of relational intimacies, evidence of mutual transformations that such relationships entail, and consideration of resulting implications for all involved. Explanation in this vein must necessarily proceed with caution, therefore. In arguments like these, the affectivity of non-humans is often evidenced not in the behavior, actions, or adaptations of non-humans themselves but instead in the behavioral, emotional, and political response of the humans with whom they are understood to interact. Thus Hobson's otherwise compelling narrative of Moon Bear conservation described above relies on the accounts of human beings to register the actions of bears. Specifically, in this account, evidence of bears as political subjects (rather than objects) rests *solely* on their perceived ability to recover from torturous previous treatment when in the care of animal welfare agencies. This ability (or *rehability* as Hobson puts it) is seen in 'the bears' playful, *seemingly* healthy and inquisitive behavior' when in recovery (Hobson, 2007: 263, our emphasis). Such attractive performances provide those agencies with the necessary cultural capital to carry on their campaigns and so, in this assemblage argument, stand in as the evidence for the bears as subjects of their own histories.

Without rejecting such an account and many excellent ones like it, it is possible to use fairly traditional deconstructive tools to ask at what point the 'experience' and behavior of bears and plants are interpreted and by whom. In politicized cases like contentious issues in wildlife conservation, moreover, it is typical for such behaviors and experiences themselves to be sites of discursive struggle, with resources of expertise (biologists) and conviction (activists) juxtaposed in ways that avail themselves of critical scrutiny. Who perceives and communicates a bear's needs and to whom does a bear's behavior *seem* to reflect one or another condition? Understanding such struggles does not necessarily require or benefit from 'assemblage thinking,' nor is the assertion of human response and action unproblematic evidence of the efficacy of those or any non-human actors.

Even so, such assemblages can and often do invoke affective acknowledgement of inter-subjectivity and mutual domination. They trace the constant blurring of boundaries between humans and non-humans and compel difficult questions about the authorship of social history and geography. As such, their mission, to produce reflexive connections in observers and readers, is a critical one. Even so, the *work* such unions and connections produce is somewhat less clear. Do such mutual constitutions produce economic and political effects as understood in social geography more traditionally? Do dogs and bears labor? Do trees?

Metabolic assemblages

> Labour is, in the first place, a process in which both man and Nature participate ... [man] opposes himself to Nature as one of her own forces ... By thus acting on the external world and changing it, he at the same time changes his own nature (Marx, 1967: 177).

Elm trees, because of their canopy structure, size, and hardiness, have become an essential planning feature in infrastructure development in cities throughout the United States, lining roads from coast to coast, producing green, grand thoroughfares of seeming opulence. As part of a broader history of urban landscaping, elm trees are an essential feature of the American capitalist city, and a resource into which significant labor and capital is invested.

The arrival of Dutch elm disease (*Ophiostoma ulmi* and *novo-ulmi* species – a family of fungal pathogens) therefore represented a cataclysmic, expensive, and nearly intractable problem for urban environmental planners. Piggybacking on elm bark beetles who themselves hopped a ride on timber shipments from northwest Europe, the disease was first seen stateside in the 1930s and became a national epidemic by the close of the 20th century. The rapid spread of the disease began to take a serious, indeed devastating, toll on the hallmark ecological investments of urban planners throughout the US. Efforts to control and eradicate Dutch elm disease included extensive tree-cutting, pesticide spraying, and street-to-street management in many cities, and extended to galvanizing US support for international phytosanitary control measures and national restrictions on wood imports that did not meet these standards (Perkins, 2007).

As traced by Harold Perkins (2007) in his effort to reconcile historical materialist theories of labor and value with a more-than-human world of actor-networks (extended from the work of Castree, 2002; Kirsch and Mitchell, 2004), an explanation of such a phenomenon must necessarily take seriously the long stability of socio-ecological assemblages as well as their fragility in the face of changes. He examines the (r)evolutionary potential of the fungus itself, which has over time come to outpace chemical controls used on it, further stressing the ability of other actors in the elm tree/urban planning/fungus system to adapt to its activities. 'Despite the ability of human actants to employ their social labors to curb the fungus, it demonstrates a remarkable ability to respond and adapt to new network configurations quickly' (Perkins, 2007: 1160).

Here, then, we have the hallmark signature of an assemblage geography: a changing urban planning situation explained in terms of a dynamic network where non-human players, their adaptation, and their integration with key features of existing systems are crucial for understanding overall outcomes. In most regards such a system recalls the explanations of symmetrical assemblage geography.

Perkins, however, amasses his evidence to make rather a different point. Stressing the way elms thrived in the pre-disease period, benefiting from plantation, care, and management by city parks departments and private individuals, while simultaneously stressing the way cities accumulated fixed capital in the built environment and ground rents (amenities, higher land values, etc.) through the tree's self-reproduction, Perkins reminds us that cities labored for the trees and trees labored for cities. These labor systems represent for Perkins an inherently metabolic relationship where reciprocal, reinforcing flows of labor circulate through the system (and transgress any human/non-human binary) to support capital accumulation:

> ... elm trees exploited via social labor for social (re)production are also the products of nonsocial labor; they performed the 'work' of growing in part by enrolling or appropriating/exploiting the labors of the afore-mentioned social actants thereby producing networks conducive to their own benefit. Elm trees and forests prior to their demise by DED were simultaneously living laborers and the products of their own past or dead forms of nonsocial labor (Perkins, 2007: 1157).

The advent of the disease, therefore, ruptures the elm/urban accumulation metabolism by preying on it and adapting to control efforts causing the devaluation of fixed capital. Though they are passive opportunists in the sense that they inadvertently arrived on globally traded commodities, fungi actively networked isolated patterns of ecological circulation. Global timber imports were suddenly connected to the fates of urban municipal economies, not directly through commodity chains, but through the rhizomatic linkages produced by uncooperative and radical agents.

> While the production of urban forests for human social reproduction may have been a localized process in the past, the expansion and integration of global commodity networks now means that urban forests are directly enrolled into new and increasingly extra-local socio-ecological configurations. In other words, the formation of human social reproductive networks within contemporary capitalism involves an increasingly global and urban political economy ... (Perkins, 2007: 1159).

In sum, using the metaphor of metabolism, Perkins writes a geography of assemblage that connects the self-organized alliances of city planners and trees to the global circulation of commodities, which in turn produced new political imperatives, new problems of planners, and new opportunities for differing species (the bark beetles and the elm disease fungus). The story is designed to show how differing capitalisms intersect as their flows of labor merge, split, and accrete. It is a symmetrical explanation insofar as it makes non-humans matter and not simply 'sit there,' being represented or used.

Such an approach owes more generally to a kind of assemblage geography that roots its understanding of human/non-human relationships specifically and universally in *Stoffwechsel* as the concept was used and understood by Marx (Marx, 1967; Foster, 2000) to describe the metabolic flow between nature and society through labor. This is an assemblage story that highlights the political (ecological) economic stakes in play in the reconfiguration of actor-networks. As such, its advantages are those shared with other materialist approaches, especially those including an important answer to the 'who cares' questions that may come from more descriptive analyses. By focusing on the asymmetrical and power-laden forces at work in capitalism, the configuration and reconfiguration of networks explains far-reaching struggles around labor processes among humans and non-humans and, more pressingly, over the *control of the labor of both and the appropriation of surplus value from that labor*.

Defined here as metabolic assemblages, such explanations mobilize the inherently biological metaphors of metabolism and circulation in order to recognize the way, as Swyngedouw puts it, 'metabolic circulation fuses together physical dynamics with the social regulatory and framing conditions set by the historically specific arrangements of the social relations of appropriation, production, and exchange – in other words, the mode of production' (Swyngedouw, 2006: 25).

These explanations, therefore, operate like many other materialist ones, seeking to unmask the hidden relationships (those of labor and exchange) that lurk within those of apparently different orders (tree photosynthesis and fungal transport). So, too, they stress the inherently exploitative and tragic results of capitalization in these relationships and the way accelerated exchange exacerbates such linkages and proceeds through ongoing cycles of creation and destruction.

At the same time, however, such an embrace of the unruly precepts of more-than-human geography ironically affects its domestication. In such accounts, anarchic and potentially indeterminate metabolic assemblages are 'framed' and 'regulated' (in Swyngedouw's own terms) by an identifiable set of socio-economic relations. These may change through time, from feudalism to capitalism for example, but they form historically specific subject positions and relations that are always already known in advance (at least 'in the last instance'): workers, owners, commodities, raw materials and first nature, appropriation, production, exchange, and so on.

For many observers, this may raise questions. Lurking behind such explanations are logics that inhere in such economies, dynamics attributable to capitalism most obviously. These logics (e.g., accumulation) exist outside of, and seemingly pre-exist, these specific relationships. Their form is inflected with the specificities of non-human influence, but the last card rests in the hand of universal and non-contingent social processes. So, too, such logics are known through the inquiries of social theorists and scientists more specifically (rather than, say, entomologists or experts on fungus development), and so arguably re-inscribe the binary social/natural divisions these analyses explicitly seek to deflate. Metabolic assemblages also reinforce the social/natural binary when the toil of non-humans is held outside the category of social labor, following from Marx's exclusion of worker bees from the proletariat and spiders from the petty bourgeoisie in *Capital* (Marx, 1967).

Class analysis of non-humans *as workers* could enrich understandings of contemporary capitalism and the political strategies and alliances possible for subaltern classes. Potent cases for this analysis could include the crisis of honeybees, time-space compression and speed-up of their work as pollinators, and colony collapse disorder (Barrionuevo, 2007), or the industrialization of the chicken and avian influenza (Boyd and Watts, 1997; Davis, 2005). Unrecognized political economic diversity may be found in some metabolic assemblages that take potentially non-capitalist trajectories, such as relations of direct appropriation (fishing, gathering and hunting), exploitation, or reciprocity (companion and working animals, crops in community and self-provisioning gardens, etc.). Following Gibson-Graham's (2006: 60, note 19) tentative inclusion of human/non-human economic transactions in their schematics on diverse economies, non-human labor processes and economic subjectivities also populate the socio-economic landscape.

These critiques are not necessarily problematic in and of themselves, at least not for observers dedicated to understanding these specific processes and configurations. Metabolic assemblage provides compelling and potentially actionable forms of explanation enhanced from the binaries of previous generations of (historical) materialist explanation. As a result, it inevitably differs from other forms of assemblage in its necessary privileging of some important, established categories of labor process and capital flow. It might be possible to argue through the application of rigorous genealogy, however, that even these ideas, concepts, and discourses are themselves results and achievements of yet other socio-natural assemblages.

Genealogical assemblages

> Ideas and technology ... emerged from the mixture and were manufactured in the processes themselves (Mitchell, 2002: 52).

Given the uncertain consequences of (nominally) planned developments in diverse fields like reproductive medicine, biotechnology, or nuclear power, and likely consequences of unintended (but hardly innocent) phenomena such as climate change, environmental toxins or invasive species, the 'precautionary principle,' which holds that in the absence of sufficient, stable, scientifically reliable information positively proving safety, new technologies or other forms of innovation should not be adopted, is gaining credence as a means of governing the deployment of assemblages such as genetically modified organisms. Steve Hinchliffe's (2001) genealogy of knowledge surrounding bovine spongiform encephalopathy (BSE), however, raises questions about the reliability of such a seemingly progressive (and reliable) way of thinking about risk.

Specifically examining the assemblage of scientific practices, political efforts, and the complex and changing condition of BSE itself, he demonstrates the way such diseases, like scrapie and other possibly prion-driven diseases (such as chronic wasting disease, described previously), entirely evade traditional experimental frameworks and narratives in disease biology and ecology. This results in the proliferation of expert opinions and burgeoning scientific conflict, despite the best efforts of experts to shut down debate and 'recapture' the disease in traditional understandings. The disease and its constituent prions cannot be simply reduced to their social, expert, scientific constructions. Neither, however, are they asocial in the sense that they were not activated and mobilized in their relation to people and other things, including cows and human neural tissue. As 'epistemic things' (following Rheinberger, 1997), prions and BSE are identifiable and put under scrutiny precisely because of the absence of knowledge about their status, their inscrutability, and their poor fit with existing ways of knowing. Given the dynamic and contingent nature of BSE and its relationships not only with cows and humans as a disease but also to science as a knowable object, precautionary approaches are insufficient and misleading, since they depend on, and reinscribe, a notion of science as a machine for producing clear answers to coherent questions.

On the contrary, Hinchliffe suggests, the more we know about 'sociability' (in the expansive definition outlined previously) of prions, the better we understand how they constitute often unforeseen conditions and connections beyond and outside themselves. 'Knowing prions is therefore a knowing of indeterminacy. … Likewise geographies of prion associations can assist in generating a greater sense of the mutability, and therefore uncertainty, of non-human identities' (Hinchliffe, 2001: 192).

The strategy that Hinchliffe's form of explanation follows might best be described as genealogical assemblage, a technique where contemporary conditions and knowledges are shown to be the product of associations that together stabilize or destabilize reliable ways of knowing. In general, such genealogies share with previous generations of Foucaultian analysis an interest in how the world is cognitively divided up into the categorical reality in which we find it, giving momentum and authority to certain kinds of expertise.

Where these assemblage explanations depart from previous strands of Foucaultian poststructural explanation is in their insistence that people (e.g., police, doctors, entomologists) and social institutions (e.g., prisons, hospitals, laboratories) are not the sole actors in producing these configurations of knowledge and expertise. Instead, a full accounting must inevitably wrestle with the many other players at work in forcing the material/discursive worlds in which we live, with all of their consequences.

All such assemblage genealogies, following Mitchell (2002), are motivated by several common critical understandings: 1) that social, technological, or scientific ideas, discourses, and expertise do not precede the encounters of objects and actors in which they are entangled; 2) that the material world is not simply a force or set of conditions that provides friction or resistance to social practices or expertise but instead constitutes these; and 3) that narrating histories as if ideas and objects and the social and material were distinct *is itself* an artifact of the historical force relations of those constitutive encounters.

As such, the narrative style of genealogical assemblage typically takes the form of ironic revelation. Such stories show the way the material interactions that underpin the power of experts, capital, development, and planning also subvert the exclusive control upon which such people and arrangements depend. In the socio-material structures upon which power rests lie the seeds of their own collapse. Thus, in describing the effort to reach a definitive understanding of prions, Hinchliffe characteristically suggests, for example, that 'indeterminacy was ironically produced at the same moment of its denial' (Hinchliffe, 2001: 199). Here he substantively and stylistically echoes Mitchell, who points to irony in his genealogy of malaria in Egypt and the array of failed techno-scientific responses to the disease: 'Technoscience had to conceal its extrascientific origins. Nowhere … was it mentioned that every one of these technologies … were themselves responses (and unsuccessful responses) to problems caused by earlier techno-scientific projects' (Mitchell, 2002: 42).

Such irony depends on describing the intervention of numerous actors outside of the powerful and hegemonic forces typically arrayed in critical analysis. Like all assemblage approaches, such narratives therefore depend on careful tracing of actor networks where many players (e.g., scientists, politicians, cows, microbes, meat consumers) are at work in constituting the outcome. As Mitchell observes, however, reconstructing histories of ideas, force relations, and political configurations through these interactions of objects/actors does not mean explanation freely assembles a limitless cast of characters, each equal in power, all equally efficacious, and all with coherent intentions. 'Rather, it means making this issue of power and agency a question, instead of an answer known in advance. It means acknowledging something of the unresolvable tension, the inseparable mixture, the impossible multiplicity, out of which intention and expertise emerge' (Mitchell, 2002: 53).

In terms of the 'so what' of assemblage geography, the 'practical' or at least policy-relevant implications of genealogy are potentially far reaching. The precautionary policy framework that emerged in the wake of BSE in Hinchliffe's story, for example, was based on a form of natural realism and 'decisionism' that sought a form of closure. This insistence on confidence and resolution, even while strained through a public 'participatory' process, was inherently undemocratic insofar as it failed to acknowledge the ongoing, processual, contingent and socio-politically indeterminate nature of the disease. In other words, a combination of material entanglements with political and expert authority led to poorly conceived policy, which may have put people at more, not less, peril, even while giving the appearance of fairness and openness. Genealogical assemblages can be tools for critical decision-making, laying bare the roots of poorly conceived policy and so making space for alternatives.

Despite the promise of assemblage approaches for reinventing and advancing social genealogical analysis and making or criticizing policy, as suggested by Hinchliffe and others, the problem of evaluating such narratives remains. Specifically, it is not altogether clear, given Mitchell's admonition that not all actors and networks are equally efficacious, how readers might evaluate competing genealogical accounts. What would count as evidence for more or less connectivity, force, or explanatory power in evaluating such an assemblage as Hinchliffe's in the face of other accounts? On what basis might we adjudicate? When material objects and ideas are co-constituted, where do we stand to evaluate the role of each in producing the others? These epistemological problems are perhaps inevitable traveling companions in a more-than-human social science, but when the stakes include deciding on plans of action in facing potentially deadly pathogens, the complexity of assemblages presents a not inconsequential challenge.

THE PUZZLE OF WRITING ASSEMBLAGES

Taken together, network, intimate, metabolic, and genealogical assemblages present remarkable heterogeneity amidst common unifying themes of more-than-human geography. The crude summary of these (Table 7.1) necessarily splits apart overlapping and concurrent themes and does a form of violence to nuanced argument. Nevertheless, a survey of assemblage geographies suggests to us that not all appropriations of the same concepts from Deleuze, Latour, Haraway, and others do identical work, nor do they harness the same strategies of explanation. Each route through the tangle of more-than-human worlds leads to different destinations and has more or less currency for differing audiences and problems.

We conclude, on balance, that all such interventions represent a welcome response to the challenges represented by rematerialized social geographies and the 'onus they place on experimentation and, by implication, on taking (and being allowed to take) risks,' as Whatmore (2006: 606) insists. This experimental mode, moreover, must inevitably lead to a proliferation of very different kinds of explanation, from which both productive avenues and dead ends will emerge. This diversity of explanations will likely be the evolutionary advantage of more-than-human thinking as a whole.

Despite their great promise, however, there are many reasons for caution. First, reflected in assemblage geographies is the Deleuzian insistence that, owing to the dynamic morphology of rhizomatic reality, 'in order to designate something exactly, anexact expressions are utterly unavoidable … anexactitude is in no way an approximation; on the contrary, it is the exact passage of that which is under way' (Deleuze and Guattari, 1987: 22). Acceptance of this unavoidable condition, while essential to powerful explanation, seems simultaneously to be a recipe for potentially egregious short cuts and half-baked ideas. Assemblage geographies as texts, presentations, and arguments will have to embrace their freeing explanatory innovations with an eye towards clarifying rather than obfuscating the points they wish to make.

Second, the dense language and descriptive modes of assemblage geography should not stand in merely as novel terminology to forward arguments that to some degree re-invent and re-present moribund work that has come before. In many cases, such efforts do not much more than re-energize discussions that might otherwise be viewed as antiquated (consider Doak and Karadimitriou, 2007, for example, in terms of structure/agency debates). As assemblage geography becomes a part of social geography's landscape, it will be important for authors and researchers to ask themselves what work their explanatory strategy does and whether such work illuminates new ideas or merely puts a shine on an already well made (or, worse, justifiably abandoned) argument.

So, too, the complexity invited in writing assemblage geographies can invite sloppiness. The Deleuzian injunction to 'begin in the middle' methodologically, which admirably embraces the reality that all actors and subjects are always already themselves in the middle, is an important one for assemblage geography, but also one ripe for abuse. Half-finished stories, endings that become beginnings, and flashbacks are all part of the arsenal of excellent authors, but they can also be the signatures of unfinished research, quick editing, and incomplete thinking.

Finally, it must be noted that assemblages are by no means the only way to imagine or re-embrace the material in geography. Some continue to insist, for example, on a dialectical examination of nature/society as distinct but mutually constitutive spheres (Hartwick, 2000), sometimes also stressing the degree to which material nature's character might make it more or less 'cooperative' with distinct socio-economic processes, including commoditization (Mann and Dickenson, 1978; Bakker, 2004; Henderson, 1999). Many extremely productive approaches to human geography that treat nature instrumentally, including critical risk/hazard geography among many others (Beck, 1999), will likely continue to provide critical insights into the world around us without adopting an assemblage strategy.

Nevertheless, taking seriously the troubling but productive breakdown of nature/society binaries over recent years necessarily entails seriously examining new geographic modes of explanation. Assemblage geographies have become a unifying strain of responses to these ontological and epistemological ruptures. Greeting them warmly as experimental and risky efforts must inevitably go hand-in-hand with critical scrutiny of their explanatory traction, their purchase on political leverage, and their ability to clarify rather than obscure the important and troubling conditions of the hybrid world around us.

NOTES

1 Similar and parallel discussions of this problem have referred to it alternatively as 'posthuman' or 'more-than-human' (Badmington, 2004; Braun, 2004), both implying a form of 'more-than-social' analysis. The differences between these designations are not insignificant but, for the purposes of our discussion here, they together represent a common challenge to traditional social geography.

2 The argument that it did may itself have been somewhat regional and subdisciplinary within the field, insofar as divisions between physical and human geography, for example, are arguably more acute in the United Kingdom than in the United States and more pronounced in climatology and cultural geography than in biogeography and cultural ecology. A blanket suggestion about the 'disappearance' of the material from human geography must be considered a significant overstatement.

3 See particularly the special issue dedicated to the topic from *Environment and Planning A*, 2004, Vol. 36.

4 Such an understanding and critical skepticism is reminiscent of Foucault's apprehensions in his interview/essay: 'Questions on geography' (1980a).

REFERENCES

Anderson, K. (1997) 'A walk on the wild side: a critical geography of domestication',

Progress in Human Geography, 21 (4): 463–85.
Anderson, K. (1998) 'Animal domestication in geographic perspective', *Society & Animals*, 6 (2): 119–35.
Badmington, N. (2004) 'Mapping posthumanism', *Environment and Planning A*, 36 (8): 1344–51.
Bakker, K. (2004) *An Uncooperative Commodity: Privatizing Water in England and Wales*. Oxford: Oxford University Press.
Bakker, K. and Bridge, G. (2006) 'Material worlds? Resource geographies and the "matter of nature"', *Progress in Human Geography*, 30 (1): 5–27.
Barnes, T.J. and Duncan, J.S. (1992) 'Introduction: writing worlds', in T.J. Barnes and J.S. Duncan (eds), *Writing Worlds: Discourse, Text, and Metaphor in the Representation of Landscape*. New York: Routledge. pp. 1–17.
Barrionuevo, A. (2007) 'Honeybees, gone with the wind, leave crops and keepers in peril', *New York Times*, February 27: A1.
Beck, U. (1999) *World Risk Society*. Oxford: Blackwell.
Blaikie, P. and Brookfield, H. (1987) *Land Degradation and Society*. London and New York: Methuen.
Boyd, W. and Watts, M. (1997) 'Agro-industrial just-in-time: the chicken industry and postwar American capitalism', in D. Goodman and M. Watts (eds), *Globalising Food: Agrarian Questions and Global Restructuring*. London: Routledge. pp.192–225.
Braun, B. (2004) 'Modalities of posthumanism', *Environment and Planning A*, 36: 1352–55.
Braun, B. (2006) 'Environmental issues: global natures in the space of assemblage', *Progress in Human Geography*, 30 (5): 644–54.
Butler, J. (1993) *Bodies that Matter: On the Discursive Limits of Sex*. New York: Routledge.
Castree, N. (2002) 'False antitheses? Marxism, nature and actor-networks', *Antipode*, 34 (1): 111–46.
Castree, N. (2005) *Nature*. New York: Routledge.
Christie, M.E. (2004) 'Kitchen space, fiestas, and cultural reproduction in Mexican houselot gardens', *Geographical Review*, 94 (3): 368–90.
Colls, R. (2007) 'Materialising bodily matter: intra-action and the embodiment of "fat"', *Geoforum*, 38 (2): 353–65.
Crang, P. (1996) 'Displacement, consumption, and identity', *Environment and Planning A*, 28 (1): 47–67.
Davis, M. (2005) *The Monster at our Door: The Global Threat of Avian Flu*. New York: New Press.
Deleuze, G. (1988) *Spinoza, Practical Philosophy*. San Francisco: City Lights Books.
Deleuze, G. and Guattari, F. (1987) *A Thousand Plateaus: Capitalism and Schizophrenia*. London: Continuum.
Demeritt, D. (1994) 'Ecology, objectivity, and critique in writings on nature and human societies', *Journal of Historical Geography*, 20: 22–37.
Demeritt, D. (1998) 'Science, social constructivism and nature', in B. Braun and N. Castree (eds), *Remaking Reality: Nature at the Millennium*. New York: Routledge. pp. 173–93.
Doak, J. and Karadimitriou, N. (2007) '(Re)development, complexity and networks: A framework for research', *Urban Studies*, 44 (2): 209–29.
Doolittle, W.E. (2004) 'Gardens are us, we are nature: Transcending antiquity and modernity', *Geographical Review*, 94 (3): 391–404.
Foster, J.B. (2000) *Marx's Ecology: Materialism and Nature*. New York: Monthly Review Press.
Foucault, M. (1980a) 'Questions on geography', in C. Gordon (ed.), *Power/Knowledge: Selected Interviews and Other Writings 1972–1977*. New York: Pantheon.
Foucault, M. (1980b) 'Two lectures', in C. Gordon (ed.), *Power/Knowledge: Selected Interviews and Other Writings 1972–1977*. New York: Pantheon.
Foucault, M. (1995) *Discipline and Punish: The Birth of the Prison*. New York: Vintage.
Fukuyama, F. (2002) *Our Posthuman Future: Consequences of the Biotechnology Revolution*. London: Profile Books. pp. 63–77.
Gibson-Graham, J.K. (2006) *A Postcapitalist Politics*. Minneapolis: University of Minnesota Press.
Hacking, I. (1999) *The Social Construction of What?* Cambridge, MA: Harvard University Press.
Haraway, D. (2003) *The Companion Species Manifesto: Dogs, People, and Significant Otherness*. Chicago: Prickly Paradigm Press.
Hartwick, E.R. (2000) 'Towards a geographical politics of consumption', *Environment and Planning A*, 32 (7): 1177–92.

Harvey, D. (1996) *Justice, Nature, and the Geography of Difference*. Cambridge, MA: Blackwell.

Henderson, G. (1999) *California and the Fictions of Capital*. New York: Oxford University Press.

Hinchliffe, S. (2001) 'Indeterminacy in-decisions – science, policy and politics in the BSE (bovine spongiform encephalopathy) crisis', *Transactions of the Institute of British Geographers*, 26 (2): 182–204.

Hobson, K. (2007) 'Political animals? On animals as subjects in an enlarged political geography', *Political Geography*, 26 (3): 250–67.

Jones, P. and Macdonald, N. (2007) 'Making space for unruly water: sustainable drainage systems and the disciplining of surface runoff', *Geoforum*, 38 (3): 534–44.

Kirsch, S. and Mitchell, D. (2004) 'The nature of things: Dead labor, nonhuman actors, and the persistence of Marxism', *Antipode*, 36 (4): 687–705.

Latour, B. (1993) *We Have Never Been Modern*. Cambridge, MA: Harvard University Press.

Latour, B. (2005) *Reassembling the Social: An Introduction to Actor-Network Theory*. Oxford: Oxford University Press.

Law, J. (2002) 'Objects and spaces', *Theory, Culture & Society*, 19 (5–6): 91–105.

Lees, L. (2002) 'Rematerializing geography: the "new" urban geography', *Progress in Human Geography*, 26 (1): 101–12.

Lefebvre, H. (1991) *The Production of Space*. New York: Blackwell.

Mann, S. and Dickenson, J. (1978) 'Obstacles to the development of a capitalist agriculture', *Journal of Peasant Studies*, 5 (4): 466–81.

Marx, K. (1967) *Capital, Volume I*. New York: International Publishers.

Massey, D. (1994) *Space, Place, and Gender*. Cambridge: Polity Press.

Mitchell, T. (2002) *Rule of Experts: Egypt, Techno-Politics, Modernity*. Berkeley: University of California Press.

Murdoch, J. (1998) 'The spaces of actor-network theory', *Geoforum*, 29 (4): 357–74.

Nast, H.J. and Pile, S. (eds), (1998) *Places through the Body*. New York: Routledge.

Perkins, H.A. (2007) 'Ecologies of actor-networks and (non)social labor within the urban political economies of nature', *Geoforum*, 38 (6): 1152–62.

Philo, C. (ed.) (2000) *Animal Spaces, Beastly Places: New Geographies of Human–Animal Relations*. New York: Routledge.

Power, E.R. (2005) 'Human–nature relations in suburban gardens', *Australian Geographer*, 36 (1): 39–53.

Rheinberger, H.-J. (1997) *Toward a History of Epistemic Things: Synthesizing Proteins in the Test Tube*. Stanford, CA: Stanford University Press.

Robbins, P. (2004) *Political Ecology: A Critical Introduction*. New York: Blackwell.

Robbins, P. (2007) *Lawn People: How Grasses, Weeds, and Chemicals Make Us Who We Are*. Philadelphia: Temple University Press.

Smith, N. (1996) 'The production of nature', in G. Robertson, M. Mash, L. Tickner, J. Bird, B. Curtis and T. Putnam (eds), *Future-Natural: Nature/Science/Culture*. New York: Routledge. pp. 35–54.

Swyngedouw, E. (2006) 'Metabolic urbanization: The making of cyborg cities', in N. Henyen, M. Kaika and E. Swyngedouw (eds), *In the Nature of Cities*. New York: Routledge. pp. 21–40.

Whatmore, S. (2006) 'Materialist returns: practising cultural geography in and for a more-than-human world', *Cultural Geographies*, 13 (4): 600–09.

Wolch, J. and Emel, J. (eds) (1998) *Animal Geographies*. London: Verso Press.

SECTION 2

Geographies and Social Economies

Edited by

Susan J. Smith

Introduction: Into the Black Box

Susan J. Smith

It is unusual for a book about social geographies to devote an entire section to questions of economy. To do so is to recognise three things. First, it has become clear in recent years that many of the concepts that economists take for granted are, in the other social sciences, themes which researchers wish to problematise. Put simply, markets, prices, value, models and money may not be what they seem. Second, there is growing intolerance for an intellectual division of labour that abstracts economy from society, as well as from place and even from space, without properly recognising that these distinctions *are* an abstraction. Finally, analysts are building on new sociological, anthropological and geographical research whose findings show that economic ideas, relations and imperatives are, above all, 'ordinary' – they are part and parcel of the myriad goings on of everyday social, cultural and, of course, political life. The five essays in this section address all these themes, as they profile what can be achieved by exposing economies, economics, and economic concepts to wide-ranging interdisciplinary scrutiny.

The chapters that follow embrace what we called earlier the 'general' vision of social economy: they are concerned with the always-present economy in society, and with the thoroughly social character, content and effects of economy. By peering into some of the 'black boxes' that these essays open up, this brief introduction draws attention to three core issues. First, there is a comment on the merits of unpacking the sociality, materiality and spatiality of economies. This is followed by a note on the relational and emotional qualities of thoroughly social and geographical economic life. Finally, there is an observation on the performative, and therefore political, character of economics and of economies.

One or two of these themes are particularly well-developed in one or another specific chapter. In spirit, however, most elements run through most of the essays. Collectively, the contributions to this section of the handbook lay the foundations for a style of social geography that is sensitive to the force of economy; that contributes to a revitalised vision of social economy, and indeed of economic geography; and that heralds a future in which debates around society, economy, politics and culture are more fully trans- or post-disciplinary (see also Lee et al., 2008).

SOCIAL, MATERIAL, CONTEXTUAL ECONOMIES

It is increasingly *de rigueur* to contrast the rational individual decision-taker, idealised as *homo economicus*, with the lived and thoroughly social realities of everyday life. The well-rehearsed argument is that 'economic person' does not exist because human life is inescapably social, relational and multiple in its logics, values and many ways of going on.

Economists, of course, are aware of this though such awareness has, of late, mainly been manifest in analysts' enthusiasm for a behavioural turn, born of an increasingly close encounter between mainstream economics and a particular style of psychology. The flourishing of behavioural economics has been powerful and productive, generating a wide array of new ideas by turning attention to preferences and behaviours which are *anchored* in ideas that may seem superficial, arbitrary or irrational, which are *framed* by experience, and which may therefore be *contextualised* by particular histories and geographies (Camerer and Leowenstein, 2004).

The relevance of behavioural approaches to economic geography has been reviewed by Strauss (2008). But captivating though this departure from classical economics is – with its attention to the psychology of price, the personality of decision-taking and so on – a key reservation for *social* geographers must nevertheless be the extent to which the behavioural tradition remains preoccupied with the (essential and essentialised) individuality of economic beliefs and behaviours.

The truth is that behavioural economics has a greater affinity with clinical and experimental psychology than with the traditions of social psychology which have, historically, inspired social geography (see Jackson and Smith, 1984; Smith, 1984). There is, indeed, a tension between the sociality of the economy, as it is portrayed in economic anthropology (for example), and the kinds of psychology that underpin the behavioural turn which has become so dominant in economics. In fact, it may not be an exaggeration to say that there is currently a *struggle* for economics, in which social geographies – as represented in the essays that follow – are plausibly staking their claim *contra* the influence of psychology.

Whether negotiating with classical or behavioural economics, an even bigger question for social geographers is whether – for a body of scholarship founded on the presumption of complexity and relationality – it is *ever* worth abstracting economic practices from the sociality they are ingrained in, for analytical or heuristic reasons. Is the project of economics ever of direct interest to the conduct of social geography? This question is raised by Roger Lee in the opening chapter of the section. His answer is that, notwithstanding the richly social fabric constituting all of human life, it is important to chart the many ways by which this life is actively econom*ised*. That is, it is crucial to recognise that social geographies are in practice shot through with economic imperatives, whose character and effects are worth teasing out and exploring. There are some parallels here with Michel Callon's (1998) idea that a key challenge for social research is to understand why and how certain parts of life are framed by economy, and experienced or operated as 'economic'.

The claim that it is possible, desirable, even imperative, for social research to show how economic entities and ideas are shaped – how, for example, markets work *as* markets – has not been uncontroversial. So much so, that the published debates are too numerous and extensive to list. What is important for the readers of this handbook, as Lee (Chapter 8) points out when setting the scene for geographers, is the argument that the variable and uneven economic framing of everyday life is worth engaging with. It must, Lee asserts, be important to understand when and why people and organisations behave *as if* they are primarily economic and rational; and it is not difficult to approach this by questioning, rather than lapsing into, the economic determinism that might otherwise be implied. To this end, the hard work of appreciating just what economists do is worthwhile (even if the compliment is not always returned). At the very least, embracing economics constitutes a position of strength from which to criticise some core assumptions. More constructively, it also provides a benchmark against which to judge the extent to which, and reasons why, particularly 'economised' ways of going on are valorised.

The social implications of conferring a particular set of economic assumptions, imperatives and responsibilities onto the conduct of individuals is starkly apparent in Paul Bennett's account of recent shifts in the character and management of financial risk and exclusion. Bennett's paper (chapter 9) provides a systematic overview of the character and effects of the different logics of risk management adopted by public and private agencies. It charts the changing geographies of financial exclusion that this jostling between sectors constitutes, and it provides a disturbing account of the spatial mediation of the financial exclusions that result. Most tellingly, it raises a suite of ethical questions for geographers interested in charting the social ramifications of economic life. Key challenges include: developing fully participatory research on these themes; understanding scales and locations of responsibility; imagining and realising what geographies of financial inclusion could look like and achieve.

Bennett's paper shows that it can be helpful (for critique, for policy, and in the interests of shaping a humane, inclusive vision for the future) to recognise, and to question, the shift of responsibility for financial wellbeing that has taken place in the neo-liberal world. There are real differences between a 'welfare ideal' steeped in visions of what states can and should do (on the one hand), and an economised conception of how markets might or must work (on the other). However, a further challenge, taken up in the coming chapters, is the need to deconstruct this sharp divide, dismantling the 'black boxes' that otherwise isolate economy, in order to re-think, even re-appropriate, the character of the mechanisms (markets, price-determination, and so on) and behaviours that lie inside.

That is, rather than think about states and markets as two distinct spheres which inherently work (or, more properly, have been made to function) in different ways, there is something to gain by beginning with an account of how the world really works and using this to question current assumptions of what, say, markets consist of, or how, say, welfare transfers might best be managed. This, as we shall later see, is a way of recognising that the mechanisms by which life chances and rewards are dispensed and distributed have to be created and instituted; they do not arise naturally, nor do they cluster immovably into sectors conventionally thought of as 'public', 'private', 'states', 'markets' and so on. These spheres have, to be sure, achieved a certain amount of 'lock-in' to their own, discrete, spaces; and this is reinforced by the materials, technologies, accounting systems and so on that have accumulated over the years and acquired a life of their own. But this can be seen as a challenge for researchers – a process to be traced and documented – rather than a pre-supposition taken for granted in their work.

This is why, Roger Lee places the project of embracing the social in the economy, as well as the economics in social life, at the heart of his contribution. In addition to setting the scene for the section as described above (pointing to the way in which – in some circumstances – societies are effectively urged to become ever more 'economic' in their workings and appearance), Lee turns attention squarely towards the sociality, materiality and contextuality (or spatiality) of every scrap of economic life. His point is that nothing that appears 'economic' can be read as such without an appreciation of the wider structures of social relations – trust, imitation, humour, concern, even care – through which the ordinary, practised, economy is constituted. Furthermore, the sociality of the economy exceeds human relations. As Knorr-Cetina and Bruegger (2000) put it, people's relationships with 'things' can be as important as their relationships with other people. Donald Mackenzie's (2009) recent work underlines this, documenting the full extent to which both economy and society are material as well as relational, sociological, affairs. Lee's paper both informs and elaborates on these ideas, showing just how and why material, contextual geographies matter for the lived, experienced, practised and thoroughly 'ordinary' economy.

Two other things follow, which are taken up in the remaining essays. First, there is the truism that economies are affective, emotional and value-laden in multiple ways (of which 'rationality' is just one). Second, there is the extent to which the economy in society is political or performative. Economies have to be made and remade through multiple acts whose outcomes can, inadvertently, through experimentation, or as a consequence of deliberate effort, be quite different tomorrow compared with what they are today.

EMOTIONAL ECONOMIES

It is curious, in light of the considerable interdisciplinary scrutiny now applied to the socio-technical and material character of economy, that rather little of this innovative literature addresses the way people *feel* about their life as economic subjects. It is perhaps an unfortunate coincidence that so much of this work is gendered in complex ways and often rooted in the male-dominated world of financial (and, to a lesser extent, property) markets. One result is that, for all their richness of texture, some of the most innovative glimpses into the engines of economy compound that sense of separation between the emotional lives of 'women at home' and the rational, calculating, lives of men at work that is the starting point of Nancy Ettlinger's important chapter. This chapter (10) on emotional economic geographies is itself a very full introduction to, and elaboration of, the importance of recognising the emotional content of economic – as of all other – transactions and interactions. Three points, however, can usefully be underlined.

First, there is the bottom line: emotions have economic effects. This, ironically, is a theme at the heart of behavioural finance – an approach which Ettlinger is wary of, largely because of her conviction that emotions are relational qualities rather than person-centred drivers of individual behaviours. The irony here is that it is thanks, in large part, to the efforts of economist Robert Shiller – a key figure inspiring the behavioural turn – that the price effects of emotional geographies have become so starkly apparent. His commentary on the dynamics of US housing and stock markets depicts geographically uneven price appreciation (price 'bubbles') as an expression of 'irrational exuberance' on the part of individuals (Shiller, 2005). The idea is that buyers, fuelled by the impulse of fear and greed, pay inflated prices for stocks and property to avoid missing out on potential investment returns. Much of this literature is illuminating and plausible; it has for example generated heated debate in housing studies on the relative contribution of economic fundamentals and individual psychology to the volatility of house prices. However, evidence from a UK study of the social geography of house price appreciation (see Bondi et al., 2000) is consistent with Ettlinger's insistence that a further layer of explanation is required.

In this Scottish study, one in three buyers paid ten per cent or more above a professional home valuation supplied immediately prior to purchase. The findings confirm that fear – that staple of behavioural finance, which propels people to invest in appreciating assets to avoid 'the sharp pain of regret' should prices continue to rise – does have price effects. However, home-seekers speak less of missing out on investment returns and more of the severing of emotional ties – of hopes dashed, dreams shattered, attachments undermined – by a spiral of rising prices that were themselves 'out of control', 'crazy' or 'wild' (Christie et al., 2008). This work points to the 'feeling rules' that drive residential search in appreciating markets; and it suggests that emotional economies are as likely to express an ecology of hope (an emotional bond between buyers and the structures of neighbourhoods, the architectures of housing and the homeliness of individual properties) as a geography of fear (Munro and Smith, 2008).

For Ettlinger, findings like this suggest that, while the emotional economy of say housing markets has demonstrable price effects, the individual psychological drivers identified in behavioural economics are only the start. Affective ties among people, and between people and things, also matter. In short, as the essays collected in Smith and Munro (2009) also show, there is a sociology of emotion infusing housing – and presumably many other – markets that testifies as much to the impulse of desperation as to the lure of speculation; and there is a sensibility among consumers that is more redolent of emotional intelligence than of irrational exuberance.

A second point follows from this, namely that the emotions comprising economy are many and varied. There are multiple 'logics' or 'rationalities' underpinning every financial 'bottom line'. These, argues Ettlinger, are not the neat multiplicities assumed in work on cognitive dissonance – there is not a sense in which one logic comes along to eclipse another in order to drive a particular outcome. Instead there is 'an *incoherent* mix of rationalities and emotions' at the centre of social life (including the life of economy within this). The emotional economy is therefore always fluid and untidy, even when it appears in the guise of one kind of rationality. There are, to be sure, powerful impulses to build an economy that appears to be economically 'rational'; there is a concerted attempt in some quarters to set up systems of calculation that are dispassionate, and which check or restrain some emotional states as if this would also suspend the emotional content of economic encounter. But this is a theoretical convenience rather than a practical possibility. And, for Ettlinger, there are good ethical as well as analytical reasons for recognising this.

One of these ethical reasons, and a third point of note around the idea of emotional economy, is the possibility that the act of regarding, experiencing and accounting for economy as an emotional geography can itself help transform that economy. This issue of transformation is taken up later, but the potential for change that Ettlinger describes has two possible realisations. On the one hand, recognising that economy – notwithstanding its usual rational apparel – is intrinsically embodied and emotional, is itself potentially empowering. The challenge is to bring these qualities to the fore, working with, rather than against, the sociological grain that already permeates the economic landscape. On the other hand, Ettlinger raises the possibility that, by placing emotional geographies quite deliberately at the centre of what currently passes for economy – by enriching the texture of an economic life that has hitherto been deliberately stripped of all depth – it may be possible to revise and redefine dominant practices and so develop a new social economy that is explicitly post-capitalist.

Paralleling Nancy Ettlinger's concern with the multiple 'logics' or rationalities infusing an economy which is thoroughly emotional, is David Clarke's account of the distinction between value and values (chapter 11). This again is an essay that points to the transformative potential of an encounter between the subject matters of social geography and the traditional sphere of economics. In an impressive sweep of a thorny, well-worn and often inconclusive set of debates, Clarke is impatient with a well-meaning tendency to pitch 'alternative values' against the hegemony of 'value' in markets. He asks instead why the very idea of value has assumed such a crucial role in modern societies. Provocatively, then, this is not just an essay on the multiplicity of values. Clarke's title refers to the 'limits to value' precisely because the concept of values is, in his view and in the end, as limited as the concept of a singular economic value. His point is that values always space, group and rank people because the whole concept implies hierarchy, of an undesirable, exclusive and therefore discriminatory kind. How, to what ends, and with what ethical consequences this might be resisted is just one of the challenges Clarke's paper opens up. Perhaps the value of value is not in ideas but, as Miller (2008) argues, in the way values are practised. More radically, for Clarke, there is the question of imagining a society *without* values;

perhaps there is a 'flat' ontology for values just as there may be for scale (Marston et al., 2005). How that would work as a moral geography, how it would measure up to the yardstick of social justice, where it would take the structures of social life, is a debate that Clarke's paper neatly introduces, but by no means exhausts.

POLITICAL ECONOMIC SOCIETIES

There is a thread through all these chapters to suggest that a key motivation for peering into the black box of economic objects is not just to lay bare the contents, but also to develop (and enact) ideas about how the socio-technical assemblage of mechanisms and devices thus exposed might, in the end, be made to work differently. That economies, markets, pricing and prices are manufactured, rather than mined, by economics, politics, sociologies and geographies is elegantly set out in a fascinating paper by Donald Mackenzie and Yuval Millo (2003). Using the example of the Black–Scholes option pricing theory, these researchers show how economic ideas have to be practised in order to work, and they illustrate how, through practice, economic models and ideas can make themselves true (see also Mackenzie, 2006). This conviction that economic 'givens' are outcomes rather than inputs, and that the results could potentially be different, is, in a nutshell, what the literature on performing economies, and indeed societies, is all about (Law and Urry, 2004; Smith et al., 2006; Thrift, 2000).

There are heated debates around precisely what is involved, but the point of this literature is to recognise first that economies (their technologies, accounting systems, mechanisms and practices) are manufactured, and secondly that – therefore – they are experiments which could always end differently. Precisely how differently is a matter of debate; my view, certainly, is that markets, for example, could work very differently with a bottom line that is geared as effectively to an ethic of care as it is to an ideal of profit-maximisation (Smith, 2005). The notion that actively experimenting with different styles of market could produce more civilising forms of economy than those that have dominated modernity has more recently been voiced by Callon (2009).

This idea that economies do not have to be the way they are – that making them so is an effort and an experiment – has a reasonably long history, even though some core ideas of what 'the' economy (as a singular set of practices) consists of may be a mid-twentieth century invention (Mitchell, 2008). Gray (1998), for example, has cogently argued that maintaining that iconic economic concept, the 'free' market, requires a huge act of political will and that this same political will could enact a different style of economic future. As he puts it:

> market institutions are social constructions, artifacts which we may not have designed, and which are for us historical inheritances, but which we may properly alter and reform so that they better contribute to human aims (1998: 74).

Tapping into this kind of reasoning is effectively what lies at the root of Clive Barnett's critique (chapter 12) of the frenzy of work by geographers of all kinds on neoliberalism. Barnett is critical of the way neoliberalism has been treated by critical geographers, not least because he sees this treatment as reinforcing rather than resisting the residualisation of 'the social' and its associated social geographies. Certainly, there is a tendency to leave unresolved the awkward truism that a world criticised for being shaped by free markets and minimal states, and animated by economised actors, actually consists of strong governments, highly regulated markets, and actors whose behaviours are thoroughly social and emotional. Of course, as is clear from the outset of this section, it is important to examine the way economic ideas, market principles and so on are infused into social life. One of Barnett's many acute observations, though, is that this is most likely to be achieved not by criticising an undifferentiated conception of 'free market economics' but rather by attending more carefully to ideas driving the processes of administrative reform, constitutional design and democratic governance that have been enacted in recent years. If social geographers are interested in the forms of democracy, rights and social justice that these processes actively deny, then they must – Barnett argues – be prepared to engage not with 'straw' concepts (such as a homogenised view of neoliberalism and its ills), but rather with those specific areas of 'liberal' thinking in which issues of rationality, motivation and agency are most fully theorised. Central among these is public choice theory, but this is just the start.

Taking up his own challenge, Barnett provides an astute, even paradigm-shifting, account of what is wrong with the theory, practice and critique of neoliberalism. He concludes, controversially, not only that theories of neoliberalism provide a rather poor account of the shape of the social landscape, but that neoliberalisation is itself an effect, rather than a cause, of broader secular changes in social formations. These much broader implications of Barnett's essay serve as something of a conclusion for the section as a whole. His message is that concepts whose power and endurance might once have been taken for granted are in fact open to change – their very character testifies to this. But in order to make things different, knowing what we wish to be critical *of* is simply the first step. More crucial is the need to develop a normative understanding of just what we are being critical *for*. This is the key to more actively creating socio-economic geographies that are democratic, just and inclusive.

REFERENCES

Bondi, L., Christie, H., Munro, M. and Smith, S.J. (2000) *The Anatomy of a Housing Boom*. ESRC End of Award Report. Available at www.esrc.ac.uk

Callon, M. (1998) 'Introduction: the embeddedness of economic markets in economics', in M. Callon (ed.), *The Laws of the Markets*. Oxford: Blackwell. pp. 1–57.

Callon, M. (2009) 'Civilizing markets: carbon trading between *in vitro* and *in vivo* experiments', *Accounting, Organizations and Society*, 34: 538–48.

Camerer, C.P. and Leowenstein, G. (2004) 'Behavioural economics: past, present, future', in C.P. Camerer, G. Leowenstein and M. Rabin (eds), *Advances in Behavioural Economics*. Princeton and Oxford: Princeton University Press. pp. 3–51.

Christie, H., Smith, S.J. and Munro, M. (2008) 'The emotional economy of housing', *Environment and Planning A*, 40: 2296–312.

Gray, J. (1998) *False Dawn*. London: Granta Books.

Jackson, P. and Smith, S.J. (1984) *Exploring Social Geography*. London: Allen & Unwin.

Knorr-Cetina, K. and Bruegger, U. (2000) 'Global microstructures: the virtual society of financial markets', *American Journal of Sociology*, 107: 905–50.

Law, J. and Urry, J. (2004) 'Enacting the social', *Economy and Society*, 33: 390–410.

Lee, R., Leyshon, A. and Smith, A. (2008) 'Rethinking economies/economic geographies', *Geoforum*, 39: 1111–15.

Mackenzie, D. (2006) *An Engine, Not a Camera. How Financial Models Shape Markets*. Boston, MA: MIT Press.

Mackenzie, D. (2009) *Material Markets: How Economic Agents are Constructed*. Oxford: Oxford University Press.

Mackenzie, D. and Millo, Y. (2003) 'Constructing a market, performing theory: the historical sociology of a financial derivatives exchange', *American Journal of Sociology*, 109: 107–45.

Marston, S., Jones, J.P. III and Woodward, K. (2005) 'Human geography without scale. *Transactions* ', *Institute of British Geographers*, 30 (4): 416–32.

Miller, D. (2008) 'The uses of value', *Geoforum*, 39: 1122–32.

Mitchell, T. (2008) 'Rethinking economy', *Geoforum*, 39: 1116–21.

Munro, M. and Smith S.J. (2008) 'Calculated affection? The complex economy of home purchase', *Housing Studies*, 23: 349–67.

Shiller, R.J. (2005) *Irrational Exuberance* (2nd edn). Princeton and Oxford: Princeton University Press.

Smith, S.J. (1984) 'Practising humanistic geography', *Annals of the Association of American Geographers*, 74: 353–74.

Smith, S.J. (2005) 'States, markets and an ethic of care', *Political Geography*, 24: 1–20.

Smith, S.J. and Munro, M. (eds) (2009) *The Microstructures of Housing Markets*. London: Routledge.

Smith, S.J., Munro, M. and Christie, H. (2006) 'Performing (housing) markets', *Urban Studies*, 43: 1–18.

Strauss, K. (2008) 'Re-engaging with rationality in economic geography: behavioural approaches and the importance of context in decision-making', *Journal of Economic Geography*, 8: 137–56.

Thrift, N. (2000) 'Performing cultures in the new economy', *Annals of the Association of American Geographers*, 90: 674–92.

8

Economic Society/ Social Geography

Roger Lee

INTRODUCTION

Context and argument

It has, of late, become fashionable – if not uncontroversial – to understand economy as embedded or entangled in, and framed by, wider social, political and environmental relations[1] and even to suggest that notions of embeddedness and entanglement imply an unacceptable duality in understanding economy (see, e.g., Lee, 2006). However, debate on the formative relationships between economy and culture and the division of academic labour between them has a long and multi-disciplinary history (see, e.g., Peck, 2005; Sayer, 2001). The connections between culture as cultivation, tending, husbandry (Williams, 1976)[2], and economy as thrift and 'the proper husbanding of resources', are close and obvious. And yet, as Timothy Mitchell (2002: 4) goes on to comment,

> [I]t is a curious fact that while critical theory has interrogated almost every leading category of modern social science, it has left perhaps the most central one untouched … the idea of the economy.

Thus

> [T]he economy always remained, tacitly, as a material ground out of which the cultural is shaped, or in relation to which it acquires its significance (Mitchell, 2002: 3).

It is not the intention here to attempt to re-establish this direction of influence. Rather, the argument is that there is not, and cannot be, a separate economic and a separate social. The apparent distinction between economy and society arises not from their separation but from a failure to recognise the diverse relations of value involved in the struggle of people to make a living. Economy necessarily involves a multiplicity of relations of value corresponding to the complexity of social life. This is, I take it, what Marx (1973: 265, emphasis added) meant when referring to the '*sum* of interrelations' that constitute social life.

To be sure, consumption, exchange and production are enabled through the construction of circuits of value – the producers and products of economic geographies (of which, more below) – but they are continuations of, not separate from, all the other practices and relations of social life.[3] Thus notions of dis/embedding or dis/entanglement which imply a prior separation are simply inappropriate. This is so no matter how sophisticated (apparently) or simple (again, apparently) economic geographies may be.

However, circuits of value are social and material imperatives. As remains all too obscenely apparent in the contemporary world, without a connection to, or the creation of, materially effective circuits of value, life itself is jeopardised. But the imperative of economy and economic geographies does not necessarily imply a foundational primacy of economy in social existence – and that, in turn, does not imply, contra David Harvey (2006: 411), 'a depoliticised geography'. Would that it were that simple: The conceptual trick in thinking economic society must be to accept economic imperatives without also accepting economic determination. It is this conundrum of economy/economic geography – imperative but not separate or socially foundational – that is addressed in this short essay. And it is by considering the multiple synchronous relations involved in thinking geographically about socio-material life that the integral nature of economic society may better be glimpsed.

This chapter explores the inseparability of economy and society in three ways. First, using the example of debates around neoliberalism, it explores how, for some, society should become economy. It then examines the mutual constitution of the material, social and developmental attributes of economy/economic geography and, finally, it explores – if only schematically – the complementarities between Simmel's (1910–11) observations on the 'soulfulness' of people within society and the vexed question of the resolution of individuals and societies, and Marx's views on the relationality of individuals and society. The concluding section links these ideas to questions of analysis and the inherence of politics in the geographical imagination. Before moving on, however, it is worth outlining a number of well-established propositions around the notion of economisation and the shaping of society by economy.

ECONOMISATION

The first proposition concerns the presumed primal autonomy of economy:

> the radical autonomisation which pure theory effects by constituting the economic sphere as a separate world ... with its own principles and its own logic – the logic of calculation, of profit, etc.

But, Pierre Bourdieu goes on,

> paradoxically, the universe of reason is rooted in a world view which, though it has the principle of reason (or, if one prefers, the principle of economy) at its centre, does not have reason as its central principle (2005: 5,6).

Thus Bourdieu insists on the economy as the conversion and reinvention of 'a long collective history, endlessly reproduced in individual histories'.

In a rather different register, Mitchell argues that during the twentieth century

> the economy became arguably the most important set of practices for organising what appears as the separation of the real world from its representations, of things from their values, of actions from intentions, of an objective world from the realm of ideas (2002: 6).

But this does not mean (Bourdieu, 2005: 5, 6, again) that these separations – 'these kinds of distinctions [– are] something foundational'. And this is especially so 'in the case of economy, because its organisation and understanding are so dependent on the distinctions in question'. Indeed, they necessitate a critical

> labour of conversion to break with the primal vision of economic practices ... the illusion of the ahistorical universality of the categories and concepts employed by [economic] science (2005: 5,6).

The autononomous and totalising economy is, then, rather less than this.

The second proposition concerns the economisation of social science, including Geography. Again, there are two opposing positions here. The first is that social scientists must take seriously the analytical framework of economics, which must be known in full and applied with rigour. Such is the problematic stance taken in some versions of network sociology (Peck, 2005). But it is also apparent in calls (e.g., Clark et al., 2000) for economic geographers to get into bed with economists – notwithstanding the fact that their advances are ignored for the most part.

The danger with this argument is that it may be read simply as a call for economic geography to become, analytically and methodologically, like economics, which is accepted unproblematically as the fount of almost all social wisdom. It takes real critical care not to fall into this trap. However – and notwithstanding the autistic nature of much economics – it is neither impossible nor undesirable to take economics seriously without simply accepting it for what it is presumed to be, although this involves very hard work (Martin and Sunley, 2001, 2006, 2007; Scott, 2006). As a way of thinking about society, economics offers not merely rigour and analytical clarity but reflects one facet of the complexity of human being and behaviour. And so the hard work may be worthwhile. The problem is precisely that, analytically at least, economics confines itself to just one facet. Thus its significance may be understood only when reconnected with all other facets.[4]

The second argument is that economics has a great deal to learn from economic geography – not least to take spatiality and the geographical imagination seriously – and that the latter should not be sacrificed on the altar of economics worship or envy (see, for example, Martin, 1999). Notwithstanding the kinds of insight of which economics is capable, it should – at least – be spatialised and transformed to reflect evolutionary and complexity thinking and the significance of institutions, for example (Martin and Sunley, 2007). But this may well require the formulation of alternative analytical approaches.[5] Simply adding space may well not only not address the problem of the inadequacies of economics but make it worse by leaving those deficiencies largely intact and so enhanced.[6] Thus the very notion of heterodox economics may itself be problematic if it leaves mainstream economics undisturbed, untroubled and so impervious to change.

The third proposition concerns the economisation of political economy. In a recent series of papers Andrew Sayer (2004; see also Lee and Smith, 2004) has developed a moral critique of economy. '[T]he moral dimension is', Sayer argues 'unavoidable. ... Economic relations ... are structured by moral-economic norms about rights, entitlements, responsibilities and appropriate behaviour ... ' (2004: 3).

This is but one example of the point made above concerning the multiplicity of social interrelations that constitute social life. Thus Sayer goes on,

> moral sentiments and norms both influence and are themselves influenced by particular forms of economic organisation ... (2004: 10).
>
> In ... capitalist societies ... what is good or right may be overridden – or instrumentalised – by considerations of what is profitable. Money becomes not merely a means to the end of production and consumption but an end in itself, pursued through production. What might otherwise be considered matters of traditional authority or public deliberation becomes treated as matters of individual market choice according to individual preferences (2004: 4).

Nevertheless,

> [E]conomic responsibilities for others are a transhistorical necessity of any economy, given our nature as vulnerable, dependent, social beings (2004: 11).

The significance of such vulnerability and its consequences for sustainability are dramatically exposed in economic geographies that allow little space for considerations of morality. Thus the neoliberal economic impact on post-socialist social geographies, for example, is severe,[7] constituting as it does nothing less than '[T]he unmaking and making of relations' (Humphrey, 2002: xvii). However, even as the economic inevitably drives the social in the sustenance of life, these examples demonstrate that the social is not subjugated by the economic:

> it is impossible for people to live without making some sense of the world around them. In fact although people may see ... processes as 'happening to them,' they themselves have been and are participants (Humphrey, 2002: xvii.).

Indeed, as will be argued later, the social relations of economy are crucial determinants of the nature and dynamics of circuits of value.[8]

All three of these propositions demonstrate the argument that economisation cannot be a one-way process. But, at the same time, they do not gainsay the significance of the economic – clearly manifest, for example, in the neoliberal restructuring of post-socialist societies. It is to the implications of a socially normative view of neoliberalism that this essay now turns.

MORAL ORDERS OF ECONOMY

In its most recent manifestation, the debate around the relationships between economy and society has centred primarily on the question of neoliberalism, which adopts a deep-seated economic view of society.[9] Its proponents insist on the need for the reformulation of the state as a means of promoting and protecting the primacy – indeed, in some readings, the exclusivity – of individualised economic relations in enabling and ensuring the 'good' society.

As such, not only is the society–economy couplet reversed (from society in economy to economy in society) but this latest moment in a long-standing debate encourages, even enforces, a rigorous policing of disciplinary (see, for example, Thrift, 2000) and even intra-disciplinary boundaries and the rejection of those beyond (e.g., Lawson, 2003). It also represents perhaps the most powerful and all-embracing set of propositions about the economic shaping of society. David Harvey puts it thus:

> Neoliberalism is in the first instance a theory of political economic practices that proposes that human well-being can best be advanced by liberating individual entrepreneurial freedoms and skills within an institutional framework characterised by strong private property rights, free markets and free trade (2005: 2).

Furthermore, and most importantly, the proponents of neoliberalism recognise the impossibility of separating economy and society. The neoliberal argument for the primacy of individualised economic relations is, as Harvey's definition recognises, founded on a view of the constitution of a moral order whilst, at the same time, not making explicit the notion that all economies are moral economies. Indeed, one of the reasons for beginning this essay with a consideration of some aspects of neoliberalism is simply that it shows immediately the power and potential range of economic influence on society.

Thus the concern and motive of those self-consciously involved in what Jamie Peck (2008) calls 'Remaking laissez faire' go well beyond the positive realm of ideas. They are concerned as much – if not more – with a normative politico-moral project to use economic relations to guard against political and social tendencies to unfreedom and totalitarianism.

Peck argues that, from its origins in the 1930s, neoliberalism was a reactive but creative project 'aimed at the contradictory problem space between the state and the market' (2008: 2, 7). It set out to derive 'a conception of the state as the guarantor of a competitive order'. As such, remaking laissez faire is, at root and more than a little ironically, a project of moral intervention. Its objective is to redesign the state as a means of promoting and sustaining competition between individuals, economically defined, and thereby to create a free society unencumbered by political power beyond that needed to sustain private property rights and the 'legitimate'[10] means of violence. The underlying assumptions here are that individualisation is a guarantor of freedom, that competitive economic relations facilitate individualisation – 'where competition can be created, it is a better way of guiding individual efforts than any other' (Friedrich Hayek, quoted in Peck, 2008: 15) – and that political relations tend towards collectivisation and the centralisation of power.

It is difficult to imagine either a more directly or thoroughly economised vision of society or a more socialised purpose for economy. Economic relations untrammelled by anything other than state-backed conditions of competition between individuals would promote the market – which would, thereby, become what Foucault called a 'kind of permanent economic tribunal' (quoted in Peck, 2008: 49) operating in every nook and cranny of social life – so ensuring the desired moral order of individual freedom. In the neoliberal project, these relations are so formative that they become reductive of society. For Ward and England, neoliberalism appears 'to have become the ubiquitous commonsense condition of recent years' (2007: 2).

Nevertheless, it is also difficult to imagine a critical sensibility that could simply accept a neoliberal reading of the relations between economy (shaper) and society (shaped). And yet, such acceptances (critical or otherwise) there are. As *The Economist* (1999: 31 July: 78) – a consistent protagonist of markets – puts it

> Liberty calls for markets because it requires, so far as possible, freedom from coercion: markets are places where people do things voluntarily. Scepticism calls for markets because a million experiments are safer than one big plan handed down by the Chief Engineer: markets weed out mistakes rather than entrenching them; their solutions to economic problems are always provisional, always adapting.

The number of questions begged in this assertion is staggering. Freedom from coercion? But what of the coercion to make a living? Why imply a political but not an economic coercion? Chief Engineer? Yes, but only if political movers and shakers are deemed always to be economically dominant and determinant – hardly likely in any geographically expansionary economy like the present phase of globalisation. Markets are voluntary? Well, yes, if voluntary starvation is acceptable. Weeding out mistakes? Fine, as long as those people and societies so weeded out can simply be ignored and disposed of. Experiments? But all markets are themselves social constructs hedged around with rules and regulations. There is no such thing as a free market. At least, however, the notion of the market as a geography – 'markets are places' – is accepted, even if that geography is simplistic and unproblematised and its implications for competition and for 'freedom' are simply ignored.

So, for geographers, there is a further irony here. The neoliberal belief in competition is entirely a-spatial – it is never exposed to the geographical imagination. And yet not only are the propositions of neoliberalism – and, indeed, its origins (Peck, 2008) – profoundly compromised by the geographies through which it takes place, but those geographies of taking place enable its differentiated emergence and shape the ways in which it is played out in different places: 'neoliberalism is made by actually existing people in actually existing spaces'[11] (England and Ward, 2007b: 261; see also Leitner et al., 2007).

At the same time, although an a-geographical perspective tends towards 'seeing similarities where none exist' (Ward and England, 2007: 21) – 'every country is different, and historical [actually geographical] analysis can reveal remarkably rich details' (Saad-Filho and Johnston, 2005: 3) – Henry Giroux (2004: xiii, 155) insists that '[U]nder neoliberalism everything is either for sale or is plundered for profit ... [it is] the age of totalitarianism lite'. Thus, in political economic terms at least, 'the overall picture is clear ... neoliberalism is a hegemonic system of enhanced exploitation of the majority' (Saad-Filho and Johnston, 2005: 3, 5).

This dialectic between global hegemony and geographical formation and differentiation is central. For Saad-Filho and Johnston 'the so-called process of globalisation ... is merely the international face of neoliberalism: a world-wide strategy of accumulation and social discipline ... ' (2005b: 2).

The geography of the 'exploitation of the majority' and the 'marginalisation of everywhere' (Lee, 2003) is, therefore, critical to this dialectic and to the sustenance and uneven development of neoliberalism. This significance reflects the relationality as well as the territoriality of geography. As Leitner et al. (2007: ix; see also Conway and Heynen, 2006) put it,

> the emergent spatiality of urbanising societies is bound up with the articulations between neoliberalism and contestation.

Clearly, in exploring the notion and nature of economic society, it is vital to take the formative geography of economy seriously.

CIRCUITS OF VALUE/ECONOMIC GEOGRAPHIES

Economic geographies are circuits of value: they are spatialised and material flows of value shaped by social relations of value (Hudson, 2005; Lee, 2002, 2006, 2007). This shaping of economy by geography works in at least three ways – through the differences and spatialities of social life, through the materialities of circuits of value that constitute economic geographies, and through the social relations of value involved in constructing and sustaining economic geographies. Each will be considered in turn. However, as is apparent in what follows, these three sets of influences are synchronous and this synchronicity may be illustrated by considering the material dynamics of development.

Spatialities

Drawing on Ed Soja's (1980) notion of the socio-spatial dialectic, Paul Plummer and Eric Sheppard (2006: 632) point to the profound significance of the spatiality of economic geographies:

> [A]cknowledgement of the possibility that the capitalist space economy is a complex dynamical system, a socio-spatial dialectic, creates considerable difficulties for analysis.

And these 'difficulties' are magnified if a desired social order – such as neoliberalism – is premised upon a lack of recognition of them. As space is uneven and dynamic (in terms of relative location, for example) and is shaped by the formative relations of the socio-spatial dialectic in which social structures shape spatial interdependencies and are, in turn, shaped by those interdependencies,

> [H]uman agency shapes structure, but broader structural changes may undermine the efficacy of agency. Individuals share interests across class and space lines ... that can result in collective action and social conflict. Markets cannot automatically arbitrate these, and market-based outcomes need not be socially beneficial (Plummer and Sheppard, 2006).

Thus the very guarantor of neoliberal freedom – competition – is immediately transformed as soon as the realities of space are included within the formulation of society. Every nook and cranny of social geographic life contains the possibility of the development of control over, or the uneven acquisition of, competitive advantage. In such circumstances 'planning *against* competition',[12] so passionately opposed by the neoliberalistes, becomes a necessity unless special interests and relations of power are allowed to usurp the market.

Paradoxically, this verity is clearly recognised by policy makers in the communist People's Republic of China who use space and difference explicitly in managing the spatially graduated introduction of market regulations (Dicken, 2007) and capitalist financial markets (Li, 2010, forthcoming). This, it might be added, is a paradox only for those whose geographical imagination is entirely undeveloped.

Materialities

The second way in which geography shapes economy is through the socio-materiality of circuits of value. Economy has always been associated with society and culture – with making a living, with creativity, with life. This is reflected, for example, in countless critiques of the capitalist labour process and, of course, it is celebrated by Karl Marx (1875: Part 1):

> In a higher phase of communist society, after the enslaving subordination of the individual to the division of labour, and therewith also the antithesis between mental and physical labour, has vanished; after labour has become not only a means of life but life's prime want; after the productive forces have also increased with the all-around development of the individual, and all the springs of co-operative wealth flow more abundantly – only

> then can the narrow horizon of bourgeois right be crossed in its entirety and society inscribe on its banners: From each according to his ability, to each according to his needs!

Here too is a moral order of economy. Indeed, the argument of this essay is that it is impossible to conceive of the materialities in economy outside their socialities. But this is a moral order based less on economic individualism than on a vision of a kind of post-economic society: post-economic in the sense that a moral order founded in cooperative wealth, rather than scarcity, becomes possible.

Circuits of value

Economy as creative life sounds fun. But economy is also more prosaic. If social life is to be sustained, materially effective and exploitative circuits of value are simply unavoidable and irreducibly necessary. Circuits of value – through which value circulates from consumption via exchange to production and further exchange to consumption and so on – are the means through which people strive to make their living. Unless they are able to create – or, more commonly, to get connected to – effective circuits of value, their lives are, literally, in jeopardy. This is the brutal simplicity of economy.

In this sense, then, resources are always scarce.[13] Indeed, given the material significance of space and time with respect to the creation and sustenance of, and access to, value, scarcity is inevitable and universal. What is at issue, however, is how this inherent scarcity is managed and for whose benefit, and how scarcity is also created as a social product deriving from production and distribution decisions in circuits of value.

Thus economics cannot merely be a science of the relation between ends and scarce means, as Lionel Robbins (1932), a leading neoliberal, defines it – although it is and must be that – but a vital socio-material practice. It must involve evaluation of material practice in circuits of value. A critical awareness of the significance and relations of evaluation is vital if a freedom more genuine and infinitely broader in scope than that proposed by the neoliberalistes is to be identified and sustained.

Evaluation

As circuits and flows of value, economic geographies must be validated (Sheppard and Barnes, 1990). They must be performed in ways deemed – by one means or another – morally acceptable and economically and environmentally efficient. Hence circuits of value are necessarily sites of political contestation, struggle and conflict over the social relations of value which define acceptable notions of efficiency and sensibility. And these conflicts must be resolved if the sustained production exchange and consumption of value to support social life are to be possible.

Once resolved – even if only by violence and imposition – evaluations of the performance of circuits of value against criteria (e.g. profitability, productivity, social justice, environmental sustainability) defined through social relations of value must be made. Of course, in many circuits of value – and especially those in which the notion of economy has a far richer meaning and significance then mere material sustenance – these evaluations are not made consciously or explicitly, or are made only in the crudest possible of ways – through life and death.

Assemblages of coordination and regulation

Crucial to these processes of evaluation are the modes and relations of coordination, exchange, regulation and evaluation which provide the links – and hence the material validation – between production and consumption in circuits of value. They are relations – facilitated by money or trust, for example – for overcoming, negotiating and enabling difference (Li, 2010, forthcoming) between capital/labour, seller/buyer, demand/supply, here/there, now/then. They operate both at the micro-scale – the level of the firm and a particular product, for example – and at the macro-scale – the level of the circuit of value considered as a whole.

Such relations of coordination and evaluation are commonly conceptualised as taking one of three forms:[14] more, or less, bureaucratic hierarchies – based, for example, on the power of politics or on a widespread belief in the endowment of magic amongst certain members of a society – to determine the appropriate relationships between consumption and production; networks through which information is exchanged directly or through various third parties to facilitate the movement of value between consumption and production; or mechanisms of exchange such as interactions through markets.

Markets

Although these three modes of coordination in circuits of value are often understood as being distinct and as operating singly – and even in opposition (e.g., markets versus bureaucracies) – they are better understood as assemblages in which all three modes work together in mutually formative, if not conflict-free, ways. Nevertheless, a feature of contemporary neoliberal capitalism has been the widespread growth in the significance of markets, and especially financial markets, as a means of coordination and evaluation in circuits of value. However, it is important to stress that that there is no such thing as the market. All markets are shaped by the assemblage of relations of coordination in circuits of value. Thus markets may be positioned along several continua of differentiation – from more to less regulated, for example.

Markets enable coordination to take place in an apparently automatic fashion. According to neoclassical theory, countless individual and autonomous decisions about production and consumption – including, crucially, those of non-participation based on constraint or choice – are constantly processed and reprocessed in the market via the price mechanism. Demand and supply schedules represent the preferences of the myriad of buyers and sellers participating or not participating (often by not getting involved or by being prevented from getting involved) in the market through a set of prices that resolve the quantity demanded or supplied at any given price. The information so generated offers criteria of judgement, of evaluation and so of validation to guide production and consumption. A market-clearing price is set at the point where demand and supply schedules intersect.

In this way, markets enable simultaneous decisions to be made on the allocation of the forces of production across a range of alternative productive activities and on the distribution of output across a population. And they do so, apparently, by simultaneously acquiring and acting upon the information that they generate. This is, indeed, a remarkable and indispensable mechanism in circuits of value. However, markets are never free. They are shaped not only by the range of regulations which constrain the freedom of their participants but by the institutions – including firms and bureaucracies – through which they are performed, by the social and political contexts – the geographies – through which they work, and by the performance by market actors of particular theoretical understandings of markets – which may, thereby, have the effect of turning theory into reality (Mackenzie, 2006; Mackenzie et al., 2007).

And, most significantly, markets can never operate outside a set of accepted or imposed social relations of value and so they are never innocent of social intent. For example, quoting Bourdieu (1998 : 2) Dennis Conway and Nik Heynen (2006: 19) argue that 'neoliberal theory is a *political project* which "aims to create the conditions under which the 'theory' can be realised and can function: *a programme of the methodological destruction of collectives*"'. Thus, for Bourdieu,

> [N]eoliberalism tends on the whole to favour severing the economy from social realities and thereby constructing, in reality, an economic system conforming to its description in pure theory, that is a sort of logical machine that presents itself as a chain of constraints regulating economic agents (1998 : 2–3).

And yet the 'social realities' are ever present in the form of social relations of value.

Thus, elemental notions like the intersection of demand and supply schedules enabling the formation of market-clearing prices and the nostrum that 'you can't buck the market' bear little relation to geographical realities. Not only is it impossible to consider competition outside the geographies and social relations through which it takes place, so too is it impossible to consider markets outside the geographies, theories and social relations that bring them into existence, and the geographies that they enable.

Markets and the (de)formation of circuits of value

So, no matter how inconvenient it may be for those who wish to promote some kind of placeless and universal 'freedom' through market-based competition, markets are – again, like money and trust – predicated on geographies of difference formed and connected through circuits of value. They are, in other words, *products* of geography. At the same time, they are *embedded* in distinctive territorial and topological geographies of environmental, social and political relations and so work in different ways in different places. But they are also *producers* of geographies. They enable the ongoing but selective creation of new geographies through the possibilities opened up by the negotiation of difference.

Thus, in linking financial supply and demand through trading for profit in risk, agents within capitalist financial markets perform them by looking backwards and forwards across as many circuits of value as they can reach. These data are then interrogated to distinguish between people, places and activities on criteria that assess risk against potential profitability. In so allocating finance across circuits of value, actors in financial markets constantly switch capital from person to person, place to place and activity to activity. They are, therefore, highly effective geographers: they gather data about economic geographies, transform them into usable information and then use this information and their understandings of it to perform markets and so to create, sustain, transform or destroy circuits of value and the economic geographies through which they take place. As such, they create their own circuits of value and the complex geographies – the hierarchical but multi-scalar networks of financial production, exchange and consumption culminating in global financial centres – through which these circuits take place.

Paradoxically, however, it is precisely their indifference to the social and material relations and particularities of these geographies that endows financial markets with transformative power within what may be called spaces of hegemony in capitalist circuits of value. Spaces of hegemony become hegemonic for at least three reasons: the sheer size of financial flows moving through financial markets; the geographical reach over which networked financial market agents can shape the trajectories of these flows; and the material and discursive influence of financial markets over, as well as their shaping by, the social relations of value brought to bear on the criteria for evaluating the effectiveness and geographies of circuits of value.

Indeed, the increasing significance of markets as the means of coordination and validation in circuits of value is both a reflection and a producer of prevailing social relations. It reflects a politics shaped by economic and philosophical discourse, semiotics and metrics, promoting reduced regulation in markets and, in some cases, the withdrawal of the state from the assemblage of exchange mechanisms that constitutes markets.

But the increasing significance of markets also serves to enable the coherence of a certain semiotics of meaning around market-driven processes. The power of markets to shape social relations in the contemporary world reflects their diversity and size, both of which have grown rapidly with the withdrawal of the state from an evaluative and regulatory role in exchange and the liberalisation of markets. Indeed, such moves are intended to 'free' markets from political distortion. A good example is the widespread removal of exchange control restrictions. This has served both to make the foreign exchange market by far the largest and one of the most dynamic markets in the world and to promote the notion that the value of a currency is revealed solely in and through exchange – that the market, rather than the state, is the means of monetary validation. This is a view supported and promoted in the UK, for example, by the decentralisation of national responsibility for managing inflation from the UK government to the Bank of England.

Of course, the material effects of markets can work in both directions. Damaging practical economic, environmental and social realities, along with effective political struggle, may challenge the coherence of a more, or less, marketised economy. A good example is the social movements around the Repeal of the Corn Laws in nineteenth-century Britain. Although landowners and the nobility had benefited from the blockades of the Napoleonic wars and so favoured the continuation of a protectionist regime in the form of the Corn Laws, merchants, manufacturers and the rapidly growing number of urban industrial workers in the UK felt the disbenefits through the high prices for grain which reduced demand and raised industrial costs. A series of struggles – some violent and bloody like the so-called Peterloo massacre in St Peter's Field, Manchester, in August 1819 – led mainly by the industrial and mercantile middle classes in the Anti Corn Law League and other movements, resulted in the Repeal of the Corn Laws in 1846. This marked a decisive shift away from the traditional power of landed capital and towards industrial and commercial capital in a mid-nineteenth-century Britain shaped increasingly by the rapidly urbanising geography of the working class in cities.

Here is an example of the (uneven and classed) benefits of markets as against state regulation. Indeed, it is all too easy, as Susan Smith (2005) has pointed out, to assume that markets – based upon individualism and hence on uneven power and the apparent 'destruction of collectives' – must always be harmful and therefore of little if any use in the promotion of social justice or an ethic of care. But if, as they must be, markets are social constructs, then they and the decentralised power that they convey may be framed in such a way as to help to achieve social goals. Thus the flow of funds through markets may be harnessed to facilitate development. An example is the proposed Tobin tax on short-term currency speculation in foreign exchange markets or, at a smaller scale, the holding – and hence re-collectivisation – of funds passing through local housing markets by institutions like *Trésors Publiques* in France. More radically, it has been argued (Smith et al., 2009) that the risk faced by individuals with lumpy and relatively immobile investments in housing may be offset by making a derivatives market in housing finance based, for example, on house price indices, especially, perhaps, across a range of differentiated housing markets.

This raises a wider question, exploration of which is beyond the scope of this essay. The growth in flows of funds through markets – such as the housing or foreign exchange markets, for example – may be used further to create and expand circuits of value, not merely via the means of credit issued by finance capital but through the securitisation of underlying assets. This process may itself allow further securitisation. Thus circuits of value may be constructed, not just around 'fictitious capital' (e.g. Harvey, 1982; Roberts, 1994) in the classic Marxian sense of credit or of claims on wealth beyond that of total surplus value in a circuit of value, but also in the derived sense of the capitalisation or securitisation of asset ownership or derived ownership. Such circuits are themselves busy inventing and producing financial instruments designed to expand themselves – through further securitisation, for example. It is, therefore, vital to consider the role of securitisation not just for finance capital but, through the diverse retail instruments created by finance capital, for investment by individuals. In such ways individuals become financialised as their own reproduction becomes, in contradictory fashion, dependent on more than just the sale of their labour power.

Socialities

If economic geographies are brutal in material terms, socially they may be even more so. Economic geographies are socially constructed. They do not arise automatically, nor can they ever be purely physical sets of flows and transactions. They are structured and directed by prevailing forms and notions of knowledge and by relations of power. Such relations may derive from within or without economy and may be negotiated or simply imposed. But they are ultimately sustained by the appropriation of value produced through economic geographies – even if such powers of appropriation are dispersed amongst, and are accepted by, the members of a social group involved in those geographies.

Social relations of value are relations of shared or imposed understandings and values around the nature, purposes and parameters of (circuits of) value and of the economic geographies through which value is consumed, exchanged and produced. They reflect prevailing relations of, and struggles over, class as well as mutuality, trust as well as regulation, control as well as spontaneity. They are the ties of understanding – including all the intense conflicts over the nature of that understanding – that bind economic geographies together or, alternatively, constantly threaten to disrupt them but, in any event, make sense of, and so legitimise – if only temporarily and vulnerably – and give direction to, circuits of value. Further, social relations of value offer a framework and criteria of evaluation and thereby constrain the ways in which people make their living and come to understand their relationship to the natural and social world. Above all, they deny the possibility of the autonomous individual who somehow comes into being independently of the society and environment on which s/he is completely dependent (e.g. Lee, 1989).

However, social relations of circuits of value are neither singular – all economic geographies operate with multiple social relations of value – nor imposed deterministically. People construct understandings of social relations of value and responses to them within an intersectional framework of meanings and relations (e.g. McDowell, 2008) such as those of gender, 'race' (notions of ethnicity, colour and whiteness), religion and status, for example, shaped by the geographies and historical geographies through which they take place. But vital here – and notwithstanding the financialisation of workers – are the predominant relations of class. Class relations are predominant in circuits of value as they shape the economically inescapable processes of material exploitation and accumulation.

At the same time, the practice and experience of circuits of value – whether, for example, they are perceived as materially successful, albeit unevenly – may promote a change in the acceptability and legitimacy of social relations and hence the possibility and desirability of the transformation or construction of new sets of social relations to guide circuits of value in a more acceptable manner. However, such change is seldom thought through or implemented in a systematic fashion. More generally, it comes about in part through social struggle, in part as unintended consequence, and in part through chance discoveries made through practice.

Economic geographies cannot, therefore, be reduced to a consideration of one static set of dominant social relations of circuits of value as such would be an impossibility. Rather, they are constituted as a dynamic hybridisation of alternative contested, complementary or competing social relations which itself may vary over the shortest stretches of time and space.

Nevertheless, social relations of value provide the bases for social communication and economic understanding and thereby establish the conditions of coherence, contradiction and conflict and for the identification of the criteria of evaluation within circuits of value. In such ways they map the limits of the possible in economic geographies and define the metric for their measurement and evaluation. They therefore delimit the economic parameters of social and environmental sustainability and the boundaries of social inclusion or exclusion in circuits of value. If, for example, the production of a surplus is a measure of success in an economic geography, then such a geography cannot be said to be sustainable unless the surplus is produced in quantities judged to be adequate by those in positions of influence to arbitrate on adequacy.

Thus social relations of value frame the very nature of circuits of value – what economic geographies are for (satisfaction of needs and wants, fulfilment of human creativity, maintenance of established power relations, accumulation, ...) – as well as shaping the bases of access to circuits of value (through self-sufficiency, as independent producers, as lords or serfs, as capital or labour, ...), the norms to which they respond, the viability of the very knowledge applied to their understanding, and the consequent trajectories that they follow.

Socio-material dynamics

Why, then, do societies develop (or not) in material terms? This question implies a social *raison d'être* but an answer requires a response to a prior and much more simple question: how do societies develop in material terms? The answer lies in increases in productivity.[15] And yet there is nothing insignificant about material development. Without it, societies would be faced with material stasis – as most people were until the last 250–300 years or so of human existence and as they still are in many parts of the global South.[16] Not only does this lead to severe deprivation but it denies the kind of choice that markets are supposed to enable as the possibility of the developmental use of a surplus is limited.[17] Redistribution of any surplus or the seizure of the means of subsistence – often driven by regressive relations of power – is all that is possible. Even then, however, as Adrian Smith and Alena Rochovská (2007 : 1168) show in the context of post-socialist transformation, it is vital to recognise that people do still make their own geographies – often in extraordinarily inventive ways in which, for example,

> domestic and non-capitalist economic relations are constitutive of the extension of the market in a reciprocal set of relationships involving the construction of value, action and a diverse range of economic practices.

But then why should productivity increase and, more particularly, why should it continue to increase over centuries? Robert Brenner (1986) argues that the answer to this question lies in the ways in which the social relations of capitalism shift social (and, it should be added, moral) norms through the inherently competitive economic relations embodied in them. In effect, capitalist development is not a choice but a necessity. The individual units of production or firms combining labour and capital are forced to operate at the highest level of competition (itself a product of the geography of circuits of value) if they are to remain in business.

Thus capital – and, more especially, labour – as well as the places that they create may readily be sacrificed so that firms may continue to exist, even if in fundamentally transformed ways and/or under quite different structures of ownership:

> Men make their own history, but they do not make it just as they please; they do not make it under circumstances chosen by themselves, but under circumstances directly encountered, given and transmitted from the past (Marx, 1852/1968: 96).

And Marx might have added that, for histories to be made, so too do geographies – circumstances may also be encountered, given and transmitted from the here and there – and that, for economic geographies, time works in both directions from past and future to present. It is with an ever more sophisticated eye to the future of present possibilities that market actors, working in spaces of hegemony, collect information about capitalist circuits of value and convert it into usable data for sale and incorporation into decisions about the switching of capital, within and across geographical space, to sustain and enhance levels of profitability and accumulation and so bring the future constantly into the present.

Thus, as Doreen Massey (2005) has pointed out, development and underdevelopment are spatial rather than temporal processes. They reflect the stretching of social relations of value across topological and territorial geographies of evaluation which differentiate spaces around notions of profitability and so (re)incorporate them within or (dis)incorporate them from capitalist circuits of value.

SOULFUL BEINGS AND THE SUM OF INTERRELATIONS IN SOCIETY

> On account of the fact that the objects of the societary synthes*is* are independent beings, psychic centres, personal unities, they resist that absolute merging in the soul of another person, to which the selflessness (*Selbstlosigkeit*) of soulless things must yield (Simmel, 1910–11: 375).

Simmel's observation elucidates the inevitability of multiple relations of value at work in economic geographies. And so, throughout this essay, I have taken seriously his geographical understanding of society as a problematic relational construct:

> a collection of men is really a unity in a much higher, more ideal sense, yet in a much lower degree than tables, chairs, sofa, carpet and mirror constitute 'the furniture of a room' or river, meadow, trees, house, 'a landscape,' or in a painting 'a picture.'

This unity is both 'lower' and 'higher' because of the simultaneous individuality and sociability of people.

Equally, I stress the inherently relational characteristics of society noted by Marx:

> Society does not consist of individuals, but expresses the sum of interrelations, the relations within which these individuals stand (1973: 265).

It was, as indicated above, precisely the attempt to begin to consider 'the *sum* of interrelations' that motivated this essay. And this is why this final section begins to raise the question of the 'selfishness' of soulful people within the sum of social interrelations.

In his brilliant historical geography of the making of neoliberalism, Jamie Peck (2008: 51) reveals how the apparent unity and simplicity of the neoliberalistes' arguments were neither unified nor simple and were as open ended as the very entity – what they considered to be an insufficiently singular and economised society and polity – that they were trying to reform. In a sense, their failure is hardly surprising. Given the concern of the neoliberalistes for the significance of political economy in a wider moral, social and political order – most particularly for notions and practices of freedom – there never could be any 'singular "essential neoliberalism"'.

This is due in part to the very complexity of the relationships with which they were concerned, but it also reflects their failure to consider geography and to think of markets and competition unproblematically in singular, even universal, rather than in differentiated and dynamic terms – especially with respect to the multiple notions of value always at play in economic relations and practices. Furthermore, it reflects a failure to deconstruct economy/economic geography as a differentiated and diverse set of relationships linking consumption, exchange and production in myriad networks across space and time. Think, for example, of Marx's overdrawn but still useful distinction between the anarchy of the market and the planned coherence – apparent at least – within the factory gates and the office doors. Think of the framing of economy by economics and the consequent performativity of much economic practice in line with applicably convincing theory. Think, too, of the commodification of personal and social relationships like caring (e.g. Smith, 1997; Smith, S.J. 2005) and child-rearing. And think, conversely, of subversive notions like shopping as love (Miller, 1998), of do-it-yourself economic geographies responding to and performing a quite different set of social relations of value and notions of value from those that characterise the mainstream (Lee et al., 2004), and of all those ordinary economic activities that do so within the mainstream (Lee, 2006).

The point here is not to provide a comprehensive checklist of the multiple relations associated with soulful beings involved in sustaining circuits of value. Rather, the intention is simply to draw attention to the sheer range of social relations of value at work in economy/economic geography and hence to the multiple continuities between economy/economic geography and society which cannot, therefore, be separated, dis/embedded or dis/entangled.

CONCLUDING COMMENTS: GEOGRAPHY AND THE POLITICS OF SELFISHNESS

People are not – indeed, cannot be – inert. But, equally, they are not agents pure and simple, adrift from their essential social and environmental conditions – their geographies – of formation and existence. How, then, can analysis cope with independence and relationality at the same time?

'We cannot', E.P. Thompson wrote (1968: 9), 'have love without lovers, nor deference without squires and labourers.' Although criticised for apparent notions of voluntarism, Thompson was, surely, far too subtle a historian (actually, historical geographer!) to fall foul of such an elementary mistake. His point is that structures and agents exist, but not independently of each other or of the historical and geographical context in which they are experienced and take on practical and active meaning.

Deference is a structural condition associated with particular kinds of social relations of value which must be understood, accepted and entered into if it is to exist in any practical sense. But it cannot exist outside, or be merely imposed upon, individuals. It is experienced by, embodied in, and practised and contested by 'real people in a real context' (Thompson, 1968: 9). And 'real' here means specific as opposed to generic, whilst 'context' is alive to the influence of collective as well as individual sources of understanding – as if they could ever be separated. People may be squires and labourers but to be so involves a process of accepting and then adopting and practising certain social relations of value across particular places and times. These social relations of value may be accepted unproblematically, or they may be resisted or celebrated. However, no matter how creative they may become in making their histories and geographies,[18] over their general conditions of existence individuals and even groups of individuals acting together may have little or no influence.

Similarly, love is not a condition that can be imposed upon people. Again, it has to be entered into and takes on life only if experienced and practised by lovers at particular times and in particular geographies. Thus, although love may appear to be a more individualised and less institutionalised social relation than deference, the particular contexts in which it is experienced are powerful influences. They shape the contours not only of meaning, understanding and practice but of the conditions and possibilities of entry and exit. Lovers are, in turn, defined through the love that they practise and they, in turn, define and modify it and the geographies through which it takes place.

Thompson's understanding of the 'sum of interrelations … within which … individuals stand' illustrates the bases of the 'selfishness' of Simmel's 'soulful' person (the converse of his 'selflessness of soulless things in society'). But it also points to the resolution of the economy–society duality – a duality which the neoliberalistes were incapable of resolving. The market, for example, is not something that is capable either of being bucked or of not being bucked. It is not something that exists outside market agents acting in and so creating and performing markets – however constrained that performance may be. And the same is true of competition: it takes on practical meaning only within specific geographical circumstances. It is not a condition universally imposed.

Economic society – certainly, it is inescapable. But economic society is never merely given, never primal. It is always made and experienced in everyday life by people actively constructing their own social and material geographies through which economies are formed. But, at the same time, economic society is never merely neutral. It is always highly political. It always involves the need for exploitation – not least self-exploitation but, more commonly, systematic social exploitation. A surplus is, simply, necessary. That is why economic society necessitates keeping 'the conditions for real politics thinkable' (Harvey, 2006: 412). It is, above all, what generates such politics.

Speaking of class, Thompson wrote

> Consciousness of class arises in the same way in different times and places, but never in just the same way. The same kinds of conditions also attach to class. ... Class is defined by men as they live their own history [and geography!] (1968: 10, 11).

The relationship of class – as with deference and love – is always embodied in real people and real places. That, of course, is the lesson of geography. It is not just that the practical experience and relations of class are different in different places but that the consciousness of class is different too. Thus 'a depoliticised geography' (Harvey, 2006: 411) – if a *geography* it truly is – is, simply, impossible and so necessitates careful and considered critique (Marxist or otherwise).

NOTES

1 In terms of contemporary debates, the starting point may be taken to be Karl Polanyi's (1944) *The great transformation*. More recent, mainly geographical, contributions to the 'economic' side of this debate include Lash and Urry (1993), Lee and Wills (1997), the *Antipode* debate (Amin and Thrift, 2000; Antipode 33, 2001), Amin and Thrift (2005), and N. Smith (2005).

2 Why 'economy' is missing from Raymond Williams's (1976) *Keywords* is, for me, a source of continuing bafflement. And, thankfully, not only for me. See, for example, Mitchell (2002: Introduction).

3 See Lee (2006) for a discussion of the diversity of social relations of value.

4 See, for example, post-autistic economics review (http://www.paecon.net/). (Fullbrook, 2005).

5 A rare example is offered by Jamie Peck (2005) (op. cit.).

6 See Timothy Mitchell's (2002) commentaries on the similar consequences of post-structural critiques.

7 See, for example, Burawoy et al (2000) on survival; Round (2006) on social capital; Smith and Rochovská (2007) on possibilities.

8 These notions of the integral nature of social relations within economy have long informed my own understandings of economy–society; see, e.g., Lee (1989, 2006) for an elaboration of such arguments.

9 There is a vast literature on neoliberalism. Some more recent, geographically sensitive accounts include: Conway and Heynen (2006); England and Ward (2007a); Leitner et al (2007); Smith and Rochovská (2007).

10 Justified not least in terms of the protection of private property.

11 These words clearly echo those of E.P. Thompson (1968), uttered almost 40 years earlier – see below.

12 Hayek, quoted in Peck (2008): 15.

13 A point which is more scarily apparent in the context of contemporary environmental transformations and reallocations of environmental goods and bads which include not merely liveable climates (as if that could ever be 'mere') but supplies of land and water.

14 Peter Dicken (2007) argues that this tripartite division is inadequate as all three modes of coordination are in fact networks.

15 But see Storper and Salais (1997), ch. 1 for a view which challenges the significance of productivity in economic development.

16 Excluding the contributions of east and south-east Asia – and especially of China and India – the share of world GDP in the global South has declined from about 25 percent to under 20 percent over the past 50 years.

17 Of course, I realize that the appropriation and use of a surplus may itself be highly regressive and may serve to sustain repressive social relations of value and class relations.

18 Smith and Rochovská (2007) offer a beautifully nuanced account of how, in making their geographies and histories, households also contribute to the making of neoliberalism.

REFERENCES

Amin, A. and Thrift, N. (2000) 'What kind of economic theory for what kind of economic geography?', *Antipode,* 32: 4–9.

Amin, A. and Thrift, N. (2005) 'What's left? Just the future', *Antipode,* 37: 220–38.

Anon (1999) 'What's progress? Economics focus', *The Economist,* 31 July: 78.

Antipode (2001) 33 (2): 147–227.

Bourdieu, P. (1998) 'The essence of neoliberalism', *Le Monde Diplomatique,* December. http://mondediplo.com/1998/12/08bourdieu (accessed 18 May 2009).

Bourdieu, P. (2005) '*The Social Structures of the Economy.* Cambridge, Malden: Polity Press.

Brenner, R. (1986) 'The social basis of economic development', chapter 2 in J. Roemer (ed.), *Analytical Marxism.* Cambridge: Cambridge University Press/Editions de la Maison des Sciences de l'Homme. pp. 23–53.

Burawoy, M, Krotov, P. and Lytkina, T. (2000) 'Involution and destitution in capitalist Russia', *Ethnography,* 1: 43–65.

Clark, G.L. Feldman, M.P. and Gertler, M.S. (eds) (2000) *The Oxford Handbook of Economic Geography.* Oxford: Oxford University Press.

Conway, D. and Heynen, N. (eds) (2006) *Globalization's Contradictions: Geographies of Discipline, Destruction and Transformation.* London and New York: Routledge.

Dicken, P. (2007) *Global Shift,* 5th edn. London: Sage.

England, K. and Ward, K. (eds) (2007a) *Neoliberalization: States, Networks, Peoples.* Malden MA, Oxford and Carlton, Victoria: Blackwell.

England, K. and Ward, K. (2007b) 'Conclusion: reflections on neoliberalizations', ch. 10 in K. England and K. Ward (eds), *Neoliberalization: States, Networks, Peoples.* Malden, MA, Oxford and Carlton, Victoria: Blackwell.

Fullbrook, E. (2005) 'Post-autistic economics', *Soundings,* Spring: 96–109.

Giroux, H.A. (2004) 'The Terror of Neoliberalism: Authoritarianism and the Eclipse of Democracy. London and Boulder, CO: Paradigm.

Harvey, D. (1982) *The Limits to Capital.* Oxford: Blackwell.

Harvey, D. (2005) *A Brief History of Neoliberalism.* Oxford: Oxford University Press.

Harvey, D. (2006) 'Editorial: The geographies of critical geography', *Transactions of the Institute of British Geographers,* 31: 409–412.

Hudson, R. (2005) *Economic Geographies: Circuits, Flows, and Spaces.* London, Thousand Oaks, CA, and New Delhi: Sage.

Humphrey, C. (2002) *The Unmaking of Soviet Life.* Ithaca and London: Cornell University Press.

Lash, S. and Urry, J. (1993) *Economies of Signs and Space.* London: Sage.

Lawson, T. (2003) *Reorienting Economics.* London: Routledge.

Lee, R. (1989) 'Social relations and the geography of material life', ch. 2.4 in D. Gregory and R. Walford (eds), *Horizons in Human Geography.* Houndmills: Macmillan. pp. 152–69.

Lee, R. (2002) '"Nice mops, shame about the theory"? Thinking geographically about the economic', *Progress in Human Geography,* 3: 333–55.

Lee, R. (2003) 'The marginalisation of everywhere? Emerging geographies of emerging markets', ch. 4 in J. Peck and H.w.-c. Yeung (eds), *Remaking the Global Economy: Economic-Geographic Perspectives.* London, Thousand Oaks, CA and New Delhi: Sage. pp. 61–82.

Lee, R. (2006) 'The ordinary economy: tangled up in values and geography', *Transactions of the Institute of British Geographers,* 31: 413–32.

Lee, R. (2007) 'Circuits of value and financial markets', in *Socio-economics, Markets and Space: Performing Markets.* Frankfurt am Main: Johann Wolfgang Goether Universität.

Lee, R. and Smith, D.M. (eds) (2004) *Geographies and Moralities.* Oxford: Blackwell.

Lee, R. and Wills, J. (1997) *Geographies of Economies.* London: Arnold.

Lee, R., Leystion, A., Aldridge, T., Tooke, J., Williams, C. and Thrift, N. (2004) 'Making histories and geographies? Constructing local circuits of value', *Environment and Planning D, Society and Space,* 22: 595–617.

Leitner, H. Peck, J. and Sheppard, E.S. (2007) 'Preface', in H. Leitner, J. Peck and E.S. Sheppard (eds), *Contesting Neoliberalism: Urban Frontiers.* New York: Guilford.

Li, Y. (forthcoming, 2010) 'Bringing it all back home? A Chinese bank global'. PhD thesis, University of London.

MacKenzie, D. (2006) *An Engine, not a Camera: How Financial Models Shape Markets.* Boston, MA: MIT Press.

MacKenzie, D. Muniesa, F. and Siu, L. (eds) (2007) *Do Economists Make Markets? On the Performativity of Economics.* Princeton, NJ: Princeton University Press.

Martin, R.L. (1999) 'The "new geographical turn" in economics: a critical survey', *Cambridge Journal of Economics,* 23: 65–91.

Martin, R. and Sunley, P. (2001) 'Rethinking the "economic" in economic geography: broadening our vision or losing our focus?', *Antipode,* 33: 148–61.

Martin, R. and Sunley, P. (2006) 'Path dependence and regional evolution', *Journal of Economic Geography,* 6: 395–437.

Martin, R. and Sunley, P. (2007) 'Complexity thinking and evolutionary economic geography', *Journal of Economic Geography*, 7: 573–601.

Marx, K. (1852/1968) 'The Eighteenth Brumaire of Louis Napoleon', in *Marx and Hegel Selected Works.* London: Lawrence and Wishart.

Marx, K. (1875/1970) *Critique of the Gotha Programme.* Moscow: Progress Publishers.

Marx, K. (1973) *Grundrisse.* Harmondsworth: Penguin Books.

Massey, D. (2005) *For Space.* London, Thousand Oaks, CA, and New Delhi: Sage.

McDowell, L. (2008) Thinking through work: complex inequalities, constructions of difference and trans-national migrants, *Progress in Human Geography*, 32: 491–507.

Miller, D. (1998) *A Theory of Shopping.* Cambridge: Polity Press, and Cornell University.

Mitchell, T. (2002) *'Rule of experts', in Egypt. Techno-politics, Modernity.* Berkeley and London: University of California Press.

Peck, J. (2005) 'Economic sociologies in space', *Economic Geography,* 81: 129–75.

Peck, J. (2008) 'Remaking laissez faire', *Progress in Human Geography,* 32: 3–43.

Plummer, P. and Sheppard, E.S. (2006) 'Geography matters: agency, structures and dynamics at the intersection of economics and geography', *Journal of Economic Geography,* 6: 619–37.

Polanyi, K. (1944) *The Great Transformation.* Boston, MA: Beacon Press.

Robbins, L. (1932) *An Essay on the Nature and Significance of Economic Science*. London: Macmillan.

Roberts, S. (1994) 'Fictitious capital, fictitious spaces: the geography of offshore financial flows', ch. 5 in S. Corbridge, R. Martin and N. Thrift (eds), *Money, Power and Space.* Oxford and Cambridge, MA: Blackwell. pp. 91–115.

Round, J. (2006) 'Marginalized for a lifetime. The everyday experiences of Gulag survivors in post-Soviet Magadan', *Geografiska Annaler,* 88B (1): 15–34.

Saad-Filho, A. and Johnston, D. (2005) 'Introduction', ch. 1 in A. Saad-Filho and D. Johnston (eds), *Neoliberalism: A Critical Reader.* London and Ann Arbor, MI: Pluto Press.

Sayer, A. (2001) 'For a critical cultural political economy', *Antipode,* 33: 687–708.

Sayer, A. (2004) *Moral Economy*. Lancaster: Department of Sociology, Lancaster University. http://www.comp.lancs.ac.uk/sociology/papers/sayer-moral-economy.pdf

Scott, A. (2006) *Geography and Economics.* Oxford: Oxford University Press.

Sheppard, E. and Barnes, T.J. (1990) *The Capitalist Space Economy. Geographical Analysis after Ricardo, Marx and Sraffa*. London: Unwin Hyman.

Simmel, G. (1910–11) 'How is society possible?', *American Journal of Sociology,* 16: 372–91.

Smith, A. and Rochovská, A. (2007) 'Domesticating neo-liberalism: Everyday lives and the geographies of post-socialist transformations', *Geoforum*, 6:1163–78.

Smith, D.M. (1997) 'Geography and ethics: a moral turn?', *Progress in Human Geography,* 21: 583–90.

Smith, N. (2005) 'What's left? Neocritical geography, or, the flat pluralist world of business class', *Antipode,* 37: 887–97.

Smith, S.J. (2005) 'States, markets and an ethics of care', *Political Geography,* 24: 1–20.

Smith, S.J., Searle, B.A. and Cook, N. (2009) 'Rethinking the risks of home ownership', *Journal of Social Policy*, 38: 83–102.

Soja, E. (1980) 'The socio-spatial dialectic', *Annals of the Association of American Geographers,* 70: 207–25.

Storper, M. and Salais, R. (1997) *Worlds of Production: The Action Frameworks of the Economy.* Cambridge, MA: Harvard University Press.

Thompson, E.P. (1968) *Making of the English Working Class.* Harmondsworth: Penguin.

Thrift, N. (2000) 'Cultural economy', in G.L. Clark, M.P. Feldman, and M.S. Gertler (eds), *The Oxford Handbook of Economic Geography.* Oxford: Oxford University Press.

Ward, K. and England, K. (2007) 'Introduction: Reading neoliberalization', ch. 1 in K. England and K. Ward (eds), *Neoliberalization: States, Networks, Peoples.* Malden, MA, Oxford and Carlton, Victoria: Blackwell.

Williams, R. (1976) *Keywords: A Vocabulary of Culture and Society*. London: Fontana.

9

Geographies of Financial Risk and Exclusion

Paul Bennett

INTRODUCTION

One of the key consequences of the well-documented retreat of the state over the last three decades is that 'many of the responsibilities and functions collected together under the banner of the welfare state are either being returned to the private sector, or are being systematically discounted in terms of their real value as governments under-invest or fail to maintain budget-to-budget the original value of those functions and entitlements' (Clark, 2000: 16). Individuals are encouraged to prepare *themselves* for the risks of unemployment, ill-health and death, as well as for their housing and age-related needs, and increasingly have no alternative but to turn to the private sector to purchase adequate provision. Even services which have traditionally been provided privately, such as mortgages and associated life insurance, have taken on a greater significance in many states as private home-ownership has been encouraged at the expense of the (socially) rented sector. The private sector, however, has a rather different logic of risk management to that of welfare states (recognising that, especially internationally, both sectors are highly diverse). The causes and consequences of this different treatment of risk is the subject of this chapter.

Giddens (1991) and Beck (1992) describe a process of individualisation in which people, faced with a loss of faith in traditional forms of expertise about risk and protection against it, must constantly decide how best to manage their own, as yet unwritten, risk biographies. Instead of assuming comprehensive support will be provided by the welfare state, individuals must (quite often literally) choose from a menu of financial products, creating a combination that they perceive best suits their own need and risk profile, given their ability to pay.

Individual responsibility and choice run into problems, however, when individuals are denied access to those financial products, resulting in financial exclusion. For Rogaly et al. (1999: 3) financial exclusion is 'exclusion from particular sources of credit, and other financial services (including insurance, bill-payment services, and accessible and appropriate deposit accounts)'. People who are financially excluded may find it difficult to access everyday financial products including mortgages and other types of credit, bank accounts, private pensions, and a wide range of insurance products (see OFT, 1999; Leyshon and Thrift, 1997; Kempson and Whyley, 1999; Burchardt and Hills, 1997; Bennett and Smith, 2007). Financial exclusion need not mean outright refusal. It can also mean higher insurance premiums, higher rates of interest and/or lower maximum loans relative to house values, all of which can result in *de facto* exclusion.

Financial exclusion may appear to be but one dimension of people's wider experience of social exclusion, and not even the most obvious or pressing one. It might be regarded as a side-effect of poverty, homelessness, unemployment, racism, health and environmental vulnerability, and other axes of exclusion and discrimination. But it is important to recognise financial exclusion is itself a key process that *produces* social exclusion, both widening existing social divides and creating new ones. It affects not only those who are already excluded in other ways, but all those deemed to be *at risk* (of defaulting on loans or making insurance claims, for instance). Financial exclusion may prevent people from accessing the credit they need to improve their long-term welfare. It may also mean exclusion from resources which protect that long-term welfare: insurances, pensions and savings, for instance. While the purchase of the latter products may not be top priority for those in poverty and may be dismissed as a middle-class concern, ensuring financial inclusion may also be seen as a preventative measure that protects people who are not yet in poverty from falling into it

Even the UK government, at the forefront of the individualisation and privatisation of welfare, felt it necessary to launch a Financial Inclusion Strategy in 2004 and recognises that there is

> growing evidence that the market has not been able to meet everyone's needs. While the majority enjoy access to an ever-increasing range of products, a small but significant minority of people are unable to access even the simplest of financial services. For these people, financial exclusion means significant additional cost and loss of opportunity (HM Treasury, 2007: 5).

There are certainly some advantages to an academic and policy agenda of tackling 'exclusion' which recognises 'the multifaceted nature of social deprivation in the advanced societies, as well as the way processes of chronic neglect and marginalisation – and not just naked exploitation and domination – have become symptoms of social injustice' (Bowring, 2000: 309). A strategy focusing on exclusion and inclusion is not without its drawbacks, however. Levitas (1998: 7) argues that it

> represents the primary significant division in society as one between an included majority and an excluded minority. ... Exclusion appears as an essentially peripheral problem, existing at the boundary of society, rather than a feature of society which characteristically delivers massive inequalities across the board and chronic deprivation for a large minority. The solution implied by a discourse of social exclusion is a minimalist one: a transition across the boundary to become an insider rather than an outsider in a society whose structural inequalities remain largely uninterrogated.

In the case of financial exclusion, the individual consumption of mainstream private financial services is normalised as the best way of providing social and economic security for all in contemporary society. Reasons for financial exclusion appear to be found in the nature of the excluded themselves. Even where financial services are themselves held to blame, problems are constructed as peripheral, the exceptions that prove the rule, that are to be corrected by voluntary codes or light-touch regulation at best. There is little sense of the structural processes in wider society that cause particular individuals, groups and areas to become viewed as high-risk, nor that risk assessment, discrimination and exclusion are inherent to decision-making in financial services.

None of this is to say that the financial inclusion/exclusion agenda should be ignored or that geographers shouldn't make a contribution to understanding exclusion and public policy; far from it. But it does mean that researchers need to have a critical awareness of both the wider causes and consequences of financial exclusion (indeed, this may be the very aim of their research) as well as the limitations of individual, well-intentioned policy measures.

In the rest of this chapter I examine three areas of research into welfare risks and financial exclusion where a geographical approach, broadly defined, has made and continues to make important contributions. First, understanding financial exclusion (at least as more than a residual problem) requires us to understand how both the scales and the structures of social responsibility for sharing risk interact with one another to make exclusion more or less likely. Second, some outcomes of financial exclusion have distinctly spatial patterns of unevenness, such as the use of redlining, predatory sub-prime lending or the pattern of bank-branch closures, and here geographers have a special contribution to make in understanding the processes that produce these particularly geographical outcomes. Third, geographers have noted that the processes within the financial services sector that lead to financial exclusion, particularly the collection and assessment of risk knowledge, also have a particular geography that has undergone significant shifts in recent decades, with implications for the nature of financial exclusion. Following this review of existing key research areas, the chapter concludes by considering potential future research directions.

THE CHANGING GEOGRAPHY OF SOCIAL AND ECONOMIC RESPONSIBILITY

How the responsibility to provide welfare and the right to receive it are constructed have important implications for people's wellbeing and their ability to deal with the financial risks that they face over their lifetime. It is also an important geographical question, because the scale at which the responsibility for meeting welfare needs is defined has implications for the possibilities of both spreading risk and redistributing resources. Those possibilities are clearly different within a single household in comparison to, say, a national population. Of course, the *probability* of risk spreading and/or redistribution occurring may be different again as a sense of a duty of care may also vary tremendously with scale: 'life would surely be better if the concerns for persons in close proximity conventionally associated with community could be transformed into a spatially extensive beneficence, in the sense of caring for more distant others in need' (Smith, 2000: 93).

The development of insurance, both by private companies and by the state, is the most significant way in which responsibility for managing one another's risks was transformed from the scale of community to national and even (through re-insurance companies) international scales. Indeed, Ewald (1991) suggests that actuarial technologies allowed societies to envisage themselves as vast systems of insurance, creating a new collective morality. The development of life tables and other actuarial tools means that risks to whole populations could be calculated and acted upon. But he also notes that 'the mutualities created by insurance have special characteristics: they are abstract mutualities, unlike the qualitative mutualities of the family, the corporation, the union, the commune' (Ewald, 1991: 203). They become institutionalised by contract: the social contract provided by the welfare state or insurance contracts made with private companies.

In fact mutuality, in an abstract sense, is but one of two key principles that underpin welfare and insurance contracts, the other being solidarity (Wilkie, 1997). The changing weight accorded to each principle has had considerable implications for people's ability to cope with the risks they face because they determine not so much the *distance* of social responsibility, but the extent to which social responsibility extends between people or groups with *different* risk profiles. Indeed, it is the main argument of this chapter that recent shifts from predominantly solidarity-based systems, in which there is cross-subsidisation between different risk groups, to mutuality-based systems, where there is no such cross-subsidisation, have made financial exclusion much more likely.

The definition of both solidarity-based and mutuality-based welfare and insurance systems is not wholly straightforward, even for ideal types, because these definitions depend on both the nature of welfare collection and on its distribution. Welfare providers may collect contributions in at least three different ways:

- contributions related to ability to pay (so that high earners pay more than low earners);
- contributions are at a fixed rate for all (as in a poll tax);
- contributions related to the risk of making a claim (so that higher risk people pay more).

Whether such contributions produce a system that is weighted towards mutuality or solidarity is also dependent upon how the welfare is then distributed:

- benefits are related to need (where 'need' may or may not be subject to financial means-testing);
- benefits are at a fixed rate for all;
- benefits are related to contributions (so that those who have paid more in get more out).

An ideal solidarity-based welfare system comprises variable contributions according to ability to pay, and variable benefits proportional to need. The National Health Service in the UK broadly fits the ideal type of a solidarity system. An ideal type of mutual-based system is composed of variable contributions related to the risk of payouts, and payouts that are related to those contributions. Commercially provided 'with profits' life insurance policies fit the ideal type of mutually structured insurance.[1] Clearly, many systems involve a combination of the two principles. Insofar as risk is spread (even if premiums are exactly proportionate to each insured's riskiness), even private insurance contains an element of solidarity. Conversely, while benefits are often related to need in national insurance systems, entitlement may also be dependent on the contributions that have been made – an element of mutuality.

In both systems, provided the government or commercial actuaries have done their calculations correctly and there are no unexpected shocks, benefits out of the system should be roughly equal to contributions in, less a little (or a lot) for the costs of bureaucracy and commercial profit, plus a little (or a lot) given any investment returns. For any individual, though, there is no guarantee *in either system* that they will get back benefits commensurate with the contributions they have made. They might stay employed until they reach retirement age, have good health and live a long life (conversely, they may lead a short life and never need to claim that pension). However, in a mutual system the *individual* expects, *on average*, to receive back the contributions that have been paid in. A mutual system implies reciprocity, in the sense of 'transactions which stipulate returns of commensurate worth or utility' (Sahlins, 1974: 194–5; Leitner and Lessenich, 2003: 329). It is mutual, in an abstract sense, because individuals are assigned to risk pools with others of assumed equal risk. Those in the pool pay the same contribution rates, knowing that while not all of them will actually claim, their risk of making a claim is roughly equal, and they are not paying for the risks of those who are less careful, or less fortunate.

In a solidarity system individuals also know that they may not get back benefits commensurate with the contributions they have made. They don't know whether the risk will happen to them. The crucial difference, however, is that there is no necessary relationship between the payments they make and the benefits expected, even 'on average'. It is a solidarity system because risks are the responsibility of the whole of society, not just those people with a similar risk profile. This system is inherently redistributive and must be supported by other values than the desire to simply spread risk. This may be altruistic, as Leitner and Lessenich (2003) imply, but it may also be pragmatic, recognising that self-interest is also served by wider social cohesion.

In the United Kingdom, the solidarity approach came under attack in the 1980s, by those emphasising the reciprocity between entitlements and obligations:

> I think we've been through a period where too many people have been given to understand that if they have a problem, it's the government's job to cope with it. 'I have a problem, I'll get a grant'. 'I'm homeless, the government must house me'. They're casting their problem on society. And, you know, there is no such thing as society. There are individual men and women, and there are families. And no government can do anything except through people, and people must look to themselves first. It's our duty to look after ourselves and then, also to look after our neighbour. People have got the entitlements too much in mind, without the obligations. There's no such thing as entitlement, unless someone has first met an obligation. (Margaret Thatcher, *Women's Own, October 31, 1987*).

Such attacks on state solidarity systems attempted to define the geography of social and economic responsibility much more narrowly by identifying and limiting the people towards whom one had responsibilities. First, they made a claim about the appropriate scale of responsibility. Individuals, families and neighbours are where welfare can best be provided and can best be exercised, not the scale of 'society'. Less extreme versions emphasised the importance of community (both in counterpoint to state and market provision) in which rights are linked to responsibilities to the wider community, and also emphasised the role of often local institutions that support people through periods of risk and uncertainty (see Etzioni, 1993). The second set of claims concerned the appropriate structure of responsibility. The reciprocity between rights and obligations (at whatever scale) was to be made more explicit, for instance in 'workfare' policies, emphasising that people are stakeholders in their own welfare (Sunley, 1999). One such obligation was an increasing expectation that it was the individual's responsibility to take precautions against the risks they faced. 'The prudential citizen was increasingly targeted by private insurance offering security against the risks of unemployment, ill-health and old-age … to replace the diminished state provision against what had been seen as collective needs' (Kemshall, 2002: 39–40; see also Association of British Insurers, 1995).

This trend towards private welfare provision has usually resulted in a shift from solidarity to mutuality. Indeed, where there is competition between providers and consumption is voluntary (as is characteristic of much market provision), solidarity in the private sector is extremely unlikely. This is because providers in competitive markets fear the risk of adverse selection. If one provider offers lower premiums for insurance (or lower interest rates for credit) to those it considers to be 'good risks', and higher prices to those it considers 'bad risks', then it is likely to attract 'good risks' from those providers who don't differentiate in this way. Those providers who fail to differentiate will end up with the bad risks (for whom they offer a comparatively good deal) who pay a rate that does not cover the costs they generate (see Bennett, 2000). Competitive markets thus drive the differentiation of premiums and the mutualisation of risk, in which good risks are charged less and poor risks are charged more (and/or face more exclusions to their potential benefits). And because some risks are charged much higher prices than others, or even refused credit or insurance altogether, mutuality and financial exclusion are intimately linked.

Interestingly, a number of geographers have investigated the role of alternatives to mainstream financial services that are often constituted at the scale of local communities in response to financial exclusion (Leyshon et al., 2003). Community credit unions, for instance, are formed at the scale of locality of residence or workplace, and allow people to access credit from pooled savings, constituting an important resource for communities that have been abandoned by the financial mainstream (see Fuller and Jonas, 2002). However, questions arise about the extent to which these institutions can tackle financial exclusion. Hayton (2001) notes that the requirement that before one can borrow, one must have savings deposited means that credit unions are unlikely to be suitable for the very poorest. Additionally, concerns have been voiced about the lack of economic self-sufficiency of credit unions, which are often dependent on outside support, including donated inputs, subsidies and grants. But the very idea that these local alternative financial institutions *should* be economically self-sustainable is itself a vote for an ethic of mutuality over solidarity, and an attempt to delimit the geography of responsibility. Requiring such institutions to be self-sustaining would reproduce the very mutualities of private finance that produce financial exclusion in the first place: there are to be no cross-subsidies between different risk groups; communities are left to their own fates. Sunley (1999: 2200) believes that the provision of welfare by stakeholding communities, while offering positive opportunities, is 'likely to produce widening local differences and a weakening sense of the desirability of a universal and equitable access to welfare services, so that accompanying policies which are more geographically redistributive are essential'.

The geography of social responsibility, of how responsibility for managing welfare risks is and should be organised and how it can lead to exclusion, is thus a complex interplay of scale (the spatial extent over which risk is shared) and structure (the rules that determine whether that sharing is done according to principles of mutuality or solidarity). In the next section I examine how that interplay can result in *spatial* financial exclusion.

SPATIAL FINANCIAL EXCLUSION

In a mutual system of providing welfare, certain people in certain 'risk pools' find themselves excluded from provision. Such pools may or may not be geographically concentrated. In some cases, such as the provision of flood insurance (in those countries where insurers are permitted to refuse cover to areas at high risk), exclusion will occur on an explicitly spatial basis as risk is related to location. However, spatial analyses of risk distributions (or even just an *a priori* perception that they are spatially concentrated) may also be used to exclude whole areas, even where the individuals therein are diverse in terms of their risk characteristics. Such instances of 'redlining', broadly defined, have historically generated the most concern, because discrimination is based on the perceived character of the area in which people just happen to live, rather than on their individual risk characteristics. This section examines the ways in which spatial financial exclusion can occur, and then considers whether actuarial objectivity and precision are appropriate standards by which to evaluate the justice of particular exclusions. That is, while the statistical overgeneralisations and pure prejudices that produce redlining are understandably condemned, does that mean 'all' we have to do to create socially just outcomes is to ensure transparent, accurate, individual risk assessments? Or, do we need to go further still and re-examine the mutual ethic upon which any risk-pricing is based?

Insurance against events that potentially affect all people in a definable area, including many natural hazards, allows the premiums of those who live in unaffected areas to compensate those in affected areas. But, as with other forms of private insurance, this inter-place cross-subsidisation is strictly limited. Risks in one place are only pooled with similar risks in other places, so that compensation is provided only by the premiums of those who had a similar chance of being affected. Ideally, in this mutual system of insurance, there should be no cross-subsidisation between places with different risk profiles. In such a system, exclusion is caused in three ways. First, because premiums are not linked to income, people on low incomes may find themselves unable to afford insurance no matter what risk pool they are in. Second, because premiums are linked to risk, more people in high-risk areas may find themselves unable to buy insurance. Third, insurance may be withheld altogether if the hazard becomes too certain (for instance, if the hazard is guaranteed to happen every other year) or if it becomes too uncertain (for instance, if environmental change means risk probabilities based on historical loss data become useless and risk-related premiums can no longer be calculated). Whatever the cause, exclusions are of particular concern in countries like the UK where flood insurance is provided entirely through the commercial sector (Priest et al., 2005). Nevertheless, insurers argue that such pricing is 'actuarially fair' – it ensures everyone (who can afford to) pays a premium commensurate with the risk they face, it creates an incentive to take action to reduce risk exposure, and it leaves the insurer solvent. But it also raises big public policy questions about what, if anything, should be done for those who cannot access insurance, and whose responsibility this is (see also Bennett and Smith, 2007, with respect to genetic risks).

The most infamous examples of spatial financial exclusion have historically been found in the practice of withholding mortgage credit (Kantor and Nystuen, 1982) and/or insurance (Squires, 2003) from particular areas of towns and cities, otherwise known as 'redlining'. Indeed, exclusions from mortgages and insurance markets are often related: given that obtaining property insurance is normally a condition of holding a mortgage, then exclusion from property insurance markets means *de facto* exclusion from obtaining a mortgage. While redlining can be a reflection of the statistical risk of defaulting on mortgage payments or claiming on insurance (aggregated for whole areas), the finding that non-white neighbourhoods in the USA were most at risk of exclusion raised the question of whether exclusion was being based on prejudice rather than an objective assessment of risk. And, even if some areas did exhibit higher risks than others, using geographic criteria as the determinant factor in lending and insuring might be regarded as a very blunt way of decision-making that is not related to individual characteristics.

Geographers' interest in redlining dates back to the 1970s in both the United States (Harvey and Chatterjee, 1974) and the United Kingdom (Boddy, 1976; Williams, 1978), and continues to be of interest in a variety of national contexts, including Canada (Harris and Forrester, 2003) and the Netherlands (Aalbers, 2005, 2007). The practice itself is usually traced back to the 1930s in the USA when the Federal Home Owners' Loan Corporation (HOLC) was asked to map variations in the risk of default to lenders in different urban areas and classify them into four categories as part of the 'City Survey Programme' in which 'almost all black neighbourhoods were classified in the fourth category (coloured red on maps – thus "redlining")' (Holloway, 1998: 254).

Like other forms of financial exclusion, redlining can have severe consequences for individuals' ability to obtain sources of financial protection and the ability to purchase a home, itself a key means of wealth accumulation, thus reinforcing existing personal inequalities (Holloway, 1998). Additionally, the spatial concentration of exclusion has wider implications for the geography of urban inequality. The areas identified by banks and insurers as no-go areas are typically already disadvantaged, but this does not mean that the whole neighbourhood is high-risk. But redlining results in the deterioration of house prices so that investments do indeed become high-risk in a self-fulfilling prophecy (Aalbers, 2005). In Tarwewijk in Rotterdam, Aalbers (2006) found that the unwillingness of banks to lend mortgages in the area meant that only 'dubious landlords' could purchase properties that were already falling in value, further contributing to a spiral of decay. Conversely, credit flows to those areas seen as more desirable which, in turn, makes them more attractive still (Holloway, 1998).

The spatiality of redlining is so objectionable because it is not related to the risk characteristics of individuals, either because it overgeneralises and ignores the wide diversity of individual characteristics or because, even as an average of risk in an area, it is a fiction. Individuals are assumed to be poor risks and excluded because of their location of residence (and the racial composition of that area) and/or their categorisation into a racial group. For Hillier (2003: 395), redlining refers to 'discrimination that bases credit decisions on the location of a property to the exclusion of characteristics of the borrower or property'. Squires (2003) notes that redlining involves practices of racial profiling and discrimination that are not based on risk. Holloway (1998) finds that the patterns of discrimination he identifies have no basis in economic statistics. At best, redlining uses an inappropriate scale of risk analysis, in which the risk of an individual is inferred from the generalised risks of whole areas or groups. At worst, redlining implies prejudice rather than statistical objectivity.

Conventional redlining, in the form of the total exclusion of areas from private credit, was typically a characteristic of the mid-20th century when mortgage credit was relatively scarce. Its illegality in many countries and growing social awareness and unacceptability from the 1960s onwards, coupled with the explosion in the availability of credit in the late 20th century, has altered the nature of geographical financial exclusion, though it has by no means ended it.

In recent decades, 'sub-prime' lending has tended to replace redlining, where people who could not previously access mainstream lending have been targeted by companies offering alternative loans ostensibly tailored to their needs. In theory, sub-prime lending allows those previously excluded from borrowing to be included, obtaining loans to purchase a home or carry out home improvements, helping to reduce inequalities. In practice, sub-prime lending has maintained and, in some cases, exacerbated social and financial exclusion through the use of substantially higher interest rates and predatory lending practices (Wyly et al., 2006). Credit may be sold to people for lucrative commissions without ensuring that they have the long-term means to make the repayments, or that they fully understand how much they will have to pay and when. Far from improving financial inclusion, such practices can end up stripping more equity from areas that are already in difficulty. The process has been driven by complex relationships in the financial services industry, in which sub-prime lenders have themselves obtained credit from major financial institutions and debts are bought and sold speculatively, providing a link between the fortunes of marginalised households and the international financial system. Eventually, when already high interest rates for sub-prime borrowers were made higher still by national rate increases, defaults spiralled and a large number of financial institutions found themselves exposed worldwide in 2007.

The redlining/sub-prime experience may suggest that financial institutions simply can't win. First they were criticised for not lending to certain groups and areas; then they were criticised for (over-)lending to 'poor risks'. Yet the shift to sub-prime lending was hardly an altruistic act or a shift to a solidarity approach in mortgage provision. The market was strictly segmented and risks were priced more highly for 'sub-prime' borrowers, with further punitive clauses around payment default. Paralleling the redlining debate, questions arise as to whether the targeting and pricing of higher interest-rate loans genuinely reflect the risk posed by the individual borrowers, or reflect only the average risk in the areas or group being targeted, or whether they are opportunistic, overpricing risk at whatever scale it is analysed and exploiting the very people who can least afford to be exploited. Leyshon et al. (2004) note that in the sub-prime 'home-collected credit' industry in the UK, pricing is based on the assumption that all borrowers will default. Wyly et al. (2006: 126) found that 'econometric models of subprime mortgage segmentation reveal persistent racial targeting and disparate impact, even after controlling for applicant income and underwriters' evaluation of borrower risks'. This suggests that many excluded from mainstream finance, often because of where they live, are being left to pay rates priced far in excess of the risk they pose.

The possibility remains, however, that some spatial financial exclusion arises indirectly from accurate risk assessments of individuals who happen to be geographically concentrated. Jones and Maclennan (1987) claim that the uneven distribution of mortgage finance in the UK was not caused by redlining but by individual assessments of risk which just happened to create apparent spatial effects. Statistical discrimination based on racial variables tends to be illegal (Squires, 2003), not least because it is such a blunt proxy for individual risks and also because the historical experience of discrimination demands a solidarity-based approach. However, discrimination based on individual assessments of creditworthiness and risk is legal and, of course, may still result in and reinforce exclusion along racial and/or spatial lines, given existing patterns of inequality. Research by Smith and Bennett (2007) into life insurance in the UK (most commonly purchased to protect a mortgage) found that neither place nor race was used as an indicator of risk in the underwriting process, which was based on the health characteristics and behaviour of the individual applicant and their family history. Nevertheless, given that people with poor health prospects may be excluded from life and health insurance, then we can expect that spatial patterns of exclusion will reflect spatial patterns of health inequalities.

If much discrimination, spatial or otherwise, is an accurate reflection of the risk posed by individuals, rather than a reflection of inappropriate spatial risk analyses or pure prejudice on the part of financial institutions, does that make such discrimination 'fair'? Certainly such discrimination tends to be legal, with major pieces of anti-discrimination legislation (such as the UK's Disability Discrimination Act) permitting insurers to discriminate if there is an actuarial basis to it. Varying from jurisdiction to jurisdiction, and between different financial products, other variables based on health, environmental hazards, crime rates, age, income, occupation, gender and genetic tests may be used legally to assess and price risks, as long as discrimination is 'transparent' and 'actuarially fair'. Yet the outcome for those who are charged higher rates or refused insurance or credit altogether can be just as problematic for individuals and individual households than if it had arisen on a more arbitrary basis. Indeed, behind this actuarially fair process, lies another arbitrary decision, one made by governments as well as individual lenders and insurers. This is the decision to prioritise an ethic of mutuality over one of solidarity. This ethic of mutuality, which effectively says that everyone should pay only for the risk they themselves pose, institutionalises discrimination into the financial system, quite legally and often without much public controversy.

THE GEOGRAPHY OF RISK KNOWLEDGE

While geographers have a clear interest in understanding spatially uneven outcomes of financial exclusion, they also have a key role to play in understanding the spatial processes that influence all sorts of financial exclusion. Central to these spatial processes is the management of information asymmetries in which 'counterparties in financial transactions always have unequal access to information about the "capability" of the other to honour their end of the deal' (Leyshon et al., 2004: 628). In the case of lending credit, banks do not have the same amount of information about the borrower's current and future ability to pay back the loan that the borrowers themselves have (irrespective of whether the borrower makes a realistic assessment of that ability). In the case of insurance, the insurer does not have the same amount of information about the insured's likelihood of making a claim in the future. This, of course, makes it difficult for financial institutions to estimate the supply costs of the products that they are selling. It also risks adverse selection. Those financial institutions that can access knowledge about their clients' risk can differentiate prices so that people pay rates commensurate with the risk they pose, ensuring both that income and expenditure match up and that products for lucrative 'good risks' are competitively priced.

The banking sector

The changing geography of knowledge acquisition and trust production has important implications for the spatial structure of the banking industry and for financial exclusion. Traditionally, banks attempted to overcome information asymmetries and ensure they could trust their customers through the use of branch networks. Bank branches were not only vital points of sale, but also of risk assessment. Leyshon and Thrift (1999) describe how applicants for credit were routinely interviewed face-to-face by their local branch manager: 'In addition to extracting relevant financial and employment details from the customer, the bank manager would also be assessing a wide range of additional tacit social and cultural signals to determine whether or not the customer would be a suitable candidate for a bank account or a loan' (Leyshon and Thrift, 1999: 441). This tacit knowledge could be sensitive to individual circumstances that allowed the context of risks to be understood and left the bank manager considerable discretion to depart from a strictly acturial risk assessment. Equally, the system was open to abuse as it left the bank manager with the discretion to practice favouritism and prejudice. The decision-making process was variable and lacked transparency. It produced mixed results, and was blamed for an increased incidence of bad debt in the 1980s (though this came when managers were under pressure to protect their market share as competition intensified). It was also slow and expensive and did not permit pooling of experience across the whole network (Leyshon and Thrift, 1999).

Today, however, trust in consumers is created in rather different ways, using differently produced risk knowledges. Leyshon et al. (1998) and Leyshon and Thrift (1999) have shown how the significance of face-to-face meetings in UK bank branches has become replaced by 'at-a-distance' means of acquiring knowledge and making decisions about the risk posed by consumers. Pollard (1996) shows how credit analysis and decision-making on standard loans in the USA has been removed from bank branches and centralised in loan centres, creating economies of scale. The most important recent development has been the growth of nationally centralised, computerised credit-scoring systems containing codified empirical knowledge about applicants (both historical data and characteristics that may indicate a future propensity to default), but stripped of the tacit knowledge held by local bank employees. While bank meetings may still take place for sales purposes and information provision (in effect to encourage the borrower to trust the lender) and for those who are not willing to apply online, the role of the bank employee in assessing risk is reduced to entering the data and then to pass back the message that the 'computer says no' (or even 'yes'). The results of credit scoring have been mixed. On the one hand, the changing nature of the knowledge used to assess applicants means that some applicants who would have been rejected under the old system can now access credit, though others who might have been accepted based on bank managers' discretion are not. For Leyshon and Thrift, credit-scoring 'may well have brought about an absolute increase in levels of financial inclusion, but they have also brought about increases in relative levels of financial exclusion; that is, financial exclusion is now a problem which overwhelmingly afflicts the poorest and most disadvantaged sections of society' (1999: 448). Automated credit-scoring, while suggesting equal treatment and precision, allows banks to exert power at-a-distance in a way that is not sensitive to individual and local circumstances.

The rise of credit-scoring, coupled with deregulation, has enabled new financial institutions to enter the marketplace, no longer requiring a network of expensive branches that was hitherto a significant barrier to entry. This increasing competition created financial pressures for traditional banks at a time when the need to maintain a large bank-branch network was becoming less apparent. Here, then, the changing geographical production of knowledge about financial risks was bound up with spatial outcomes of financial exclusion as banks withdrew from those locations where their customers were deemed to be least profitable and/or highest risk (Leyshon and Thrift, 1997; Pollard, 1996). For instance, in a study of bank-branch provision in Los Angeles, Pollard (1996) found that the number of branches halved in South Central LA between 1970 and 1990, just as the population there was increasing, and despite an increase in the number of branches in Los Angeles as a whole.

While codified systems of knowledge and decision-making from a distance have come to characterise retail banking and insurance services and exclude disadvantaged communities, this does not mean that face-to-face methods have entirely disappeared. Indeed, precisely those communities that have suffered financial abandonment have been targeted by the subprime loans sector which normally involves much more face-to-face contact. 'Home collection credit' companies, ranging from national firms to local businesses, employ field agents primarily to sell products and collect payments, but also to acquire tacit knowledge which can be used to assess the creditworthiness of those written off by automated systems (Leyshon et al., 2004). Of course, such a system is more expensive to run than computerised credit-scoring and this further increases the cost to borrowers already charged a premium for their riskiness, while sales incentives may conflict with risk assessment, leading to irresponsible lending and further exploitation of those who can least afford it.

The insurance sector

The changing geography of risk knowledge acquisition and decision-making also has implications for the changing geography of the insurance sector and exclusion from insurance. Historically, early forms of insurance also depended upon face-to-face risk assessments. Insurance of industrial capitalist enterprise was arranged through meetings in the 17th and 18th century coffee houses of London, most famously in Lloyd's Coffee House, opened in 1688, which became a key source of knowledge about the shipping industry and the place where shipowners and underwriters met to arrange insurance. Early forms of social insurance were provided by local mutual associations or philanthropically, 'where respectively one's fellow workers or one's philanthropic employer exercise their surveillance of individual expenditure, frauds and extravagances, in short the morality of the population concerned' (Defert, 1991: 219).

A combination of expanding social and economic relations, competition and changing technologies caused the scale and structure of insurance provision to change, with implications for the nature of risk assessment and control. Insurers could no longer rely on face-to-face contact with all their clients which, in any case, often proved an unreliable way of assessing risk. Varying considerably between different sectors of insurance, new technologies of risk assessment came into being. The insurance industry was often central to the development of those technologies, no more clearly so than in the role of life insurers in the development of the medical examination and population statistics (Jureidini and White, 2000). As competition and the prospect of adverse selection increased, 'it was in the economic interests of the insuring organisation to insure healthy lives as lower risks. It therefore had to maximise its information regarding health and the risks upon lives such as age, disease, occupation and residential location' (Jureidini and White, 2000: 194). Individuals became categorised by statistical life tables according to the combination of risks they posed. While they were categorised into 'mutual risk pools', these were stripped of the socio-spatial relations of earlier mutual forms of insurance which implied common responsibility towards one's fellow insured. Rather, mutual risk pools were a management tool in which insurance underwriters could assign similar, but spatially dispersed and independent insureds, to ensure that risks were balanced. For Defert (1991: 219) 'with this managerial method of insurance one simply has a hierarchy of kinds of danger, classified according to their cost'.

The routinised medical examination was an important way in which life insurance underwriters could act at a distance, ensuring that standardised information was acquired which could be interpreted centrally. Insurers could enrol networks of private (and later state-employed) doctors in their risk assessments, rather than maintaining expensive networks of their own. Insurers could also rely on self-assessment by applicants in a way that banks could not. Banks, of course, lend their money up-front and need to be sure they can get it back. Insurers, paying out after the event, have the option of withholding payment if they find out the applicant had been accidentally incorrect or deliberately untruthful in their application.

Nonetheless, while standardised, centralised, 'at-a-distance' practices of risk assessment are well established in the insurance industry, this does not mean that they are uncontroversial, nor that they are static. Economic and technological change has continued to influence insurers' production of risk knowledge. Research by Smith and Bennett (2007) into the current practices of life insurers in the UK has found an insurance market in the midst of intense competition and consolidation. Insurers are walking a tightrope between expensive, time-consuming, accurate underwriting (and a willingness to say no) on the one hand, and the need to keep costs down, make speedy decisions and write new business on the other. The routine acquisition of reports from applicants' doctors is becoming less common, as it is seen as expensive, inconsistent and unreliable, and unnecessary in most cases. Routine applications from patients declaring good health and for smaller amounts of cover (particularly where clearly linked to a mortgage) are increasingly all but signed off by computer software, apart from spot checks to deter non-disclosure. Insurers have also found it expensive to retain networks of clinically qualified medical examiners. Instead, for those applicants whose health disclosures give rise to concern and/or are applying for larger amounts of cover, health screenings by non-clinical staff in specialised outsourced health-screening companies are increasingly the norm. The need for expensive face-to-face contact is further limited to 'high-risk' cases and, even then, health data is collected by the most routinised and efficient method. Smith and Bennett (2007) have found, however, that this new trade in health risk information of individuals also seems to lead to more people being picked out as risky and refused insurance, or at least charged substantially higher rates (which may be *de facto* exclusion in many cases).

The range of risk information of interest to insurers has also continued to grow with new technological developments. Geographers, while involved in the critical assessment of such trends, are also bound up with them, as new Geographical Information Systems (GIS) technologies are employed by insurance companies to assist in the more accurate pricing of any risks that display a spatial pattern. Developments in medical technologies may also be enrolled by insurers in order to more accurately price risk. But they also worry that new medical technologies will give applicants information about the risks they face that insurers will not be party to, creating new information asymmetries. Most recently this concern has surrounded the use of new predictive genetic tests and whether insurers should be permitted to access the results of such tests, possibly creating a new group of excluded, the so-called 'healthy-ill' (Hubbard, 1993), and commodifying the smallest, most intimate pieces of information about an individual. The genetics debate allows the 'black box' of insurance underwriting to be opened up and the ethical basis of 'actuarial fairness' to be re-examined (Bennett and Smith, 2007). Bennett and Smith's Citizens' Jury found that, while the use of genetic test results was entirely consistent with the use of other sorts of health-risk information by insurers, it did not meet their requirements of care towards the most vulnerable in society. No longer able to rely on the state to provide an adequate safety net, the jury demanded that insurers ignored test results even if (or rather precisely because) they required the good risks to subsidise the bad risks. The loss of risk solidarity practised through the welfare state was accompanied by a demand that the private sector take on the responsibility to re-socialise dispersed economic relationships.

FUTURE DIRECTIONS

This chapter has reviewed three key areas where geographers have made, and continue to make, a contribution to the understanding of welfare risks and financial exclusion. There is still plenty of work to be done. In terms of understanding spatial financial exclusion, there always remains the question of whether exclusion is a genuine reflection of risks, or whether it reflects fears and prejudices by insurers and lenders that are not statistically warranted. But even if it is found that discrimination is 'actuarially fair', this is not an end to the debate, although it may change the arguments needed to tackle financial exclusion. Here it is necessary to critically evaluate the ethical basis of actuarial fairness, which is predicated on the assumption that risks should be shared according to principles of mutuality rather than those of solidarity. It is trickier to come to a definitive answer on such normative questions because they go to the heart of how society manages responsibility for dealing with risk. Neither the ethical nor the technical complexities of such debates lend themselves to research by conventional social survey techniques. Nevertheless, social geographers, well versed in participatory methodologies, are well placed to begin research into these difficult questions, using techniques that permit informed deliberation by lay-people (Bennett and Smith, 2007).

Much research has already been conducted into the impact of changing geographies of financial risk knowledge on patterns of financial exclusion. But such is the pace of technological and economic change that more research is required to keep up with changing impacts. Geographers have many new questions to deal with. What are the ethical implications of the appropriation of research elsewhere in geography, notably in GIS as well as research by physical geographers into the risk impacts of climatic change, by the financial services sector? Will national regulatory regimes be able to protect information about people's risk profiles as financial services are provided across international boundaries? Would such internationalisation of provision make it impossible to re-institutionalise solidarity? To what extent is the internet democratising risk information by making it available outside financial services institutions, and is this good or bad for processes of financial exclusion? What do immediate online applications, quotes and price-comparison sites mean for insurers' and lenders' ability to pay for risk assessment (and to risk not paying for it)?

Finally, all these areas of research into spatial financial exclusion and geographies of risk knowledge ultimately contribute to our understanding of the geography of social responsibility. Work by geographers is crucial to understanding both the advantages and the limitations of state-based, market-based and community-based strategies for tackling financial exclusion. Geographers are also well placed to critically examine how the scale at which social responsibility is delimited, and the structures by which responsibility is shared (or not) between different risk groups, interact to produce geographies of inclusion and exclusion. New interactions may throw up new alternatives, both within and without mainstream financial welfare provision. But geographers need to remain alert to the extent to which such alternatives meet the needs of those who are distant and/or different in terms of the risks that they bear.

NOTE

1 Here the term 'mutuality' is not meant to imply anything about the ownership structure of banks and insurance companies.

REFERENCES

Aalbers, M.B. (2005) 'Whose afraid of the red, yellow and green? Redlining in Rotterdam', *Geoforum*, 36: 562–80.

Aalbers, M.B. (2006) '"When the banks withdraw, slum landlords take over": the structuration of neighbourhood decline through redlining, drug dealing, speculation and immigrant exploitation', *Urban Studies*, 43 (7): 1061–86.

Aalbers, M.B. (2007) 'Place-based and race-based exclusion from mortgage loans: evidence from three cities in the Netherlands', *Journal of Urban Affairs*, 29 (1): 1–29.

Association of British Insurers (1995) *Risk, Insurance and Welfare: The Changing Balance between Public and Private Protection.* London: Association of British Insurers.

Beck, U. (1992) *Risk Society: Towards a New Modernity*. London: Sage.

Bennett, P.G. (2000) 'Anti-trust? European competition law and mutual environmental insurance', *Economic Geography*, 76: 5–67.

Bennett, P.G. and Smith, S.J. (2007) 'Genetics, insurance and participation: how a Citizens' Jury reached its verdict', *Social Science and Medicine*, 64: 2487–98.

Boddy, M. (1976) 'The structure of mortgage finance: building societies and the British social formation', *Transactions of the Institute of British Geographers*, N.S. 1: 58–71.

Bowring, F. (2000) 'Social exclusion: limitations of the debate', *Critical Social Policy*, 20 (3): 307–30.

Burchardt, T. and Hills, J. (1997) 'Private welfare insurance and social security: Pushing the boundaries', Report for the Joseph Rowntree Foundation, York.

Clark, G.L. (2000) *Pension Fund Capitalism*. Oxford: Oxford University Press.

Defert, D. (1991) '"*Popular* life" and insurance technology', in G. Burchell, C. Gordon and P. Miller (eds), *The Foucault Effect: Studies in Governmentality*. London: Harvester Wheatsheaf. pp. 211–33.

Etzioni, A. (1993) *The Spirit of Community: Rights, Responsibilities and the Communitarian Agenda*. New York: Crown.

Ewald, F. (1991) '*Insurance* and risk', in G. Burchell, C. Gordon and P. Miller (eds), *The Foucault Effect: Studies in Governmentality.* London: Harvester Wheatsheaf. pp. 197–210.

Fuller, D. and Jonas, A.E. (2002) 'Institutionalising future geographies of financial inclusion: national legitimacy *versus* local autonomy in the British credit union movement', *Antipode*, 34: 85–110.

Giddens, A. (1991) *Modernity and Self-Identity.* Cambridge: Polity Press.

Harris, R. and Forrester, D. (2003) The Suburban origins of redlining: a Canadian case study, 1953–54. *Urban Studies*, 40, 13: 2661–8.

Harvey, D. and Chatterjee, L. (1974) 'Absolute rent and the structuring of space by governmental and financial institutions', *Antipode*, 6: 22–36.

Hayton, K. (2001) 'The role of Scottish credit unions in tackling financial exclusion', *Policy and Politics*, 29 (3): 281–97.

Hillier, A.E. (2003) 'Redlining and the Home Owners' Loan Corporation', *Journal of Urban History*, 29 (4): 394–420.

HM Treasury (2007) 'Financial inclusion: The way forward', Report by HM Treasury. London: HM Treasury.

Holloway, S.R. (1998) 'Exploring the neighbourhood contingency of race discrimination in mortgage lending in Columbus, Ohio', *Annals of the Association of American Geographers*, 88: 252–76.

Hubbard, R. (1993) 'Predictive genetics and the construction of the healthy ill', *Suffolk University Law Review, 27*: 1209–24.

Jones, C. and Maclennan, D. (1987) 'Building societies and credit rationing: an empirical examination of redlining', *Urban Studies*, 24: 205–16.

Jureidini, R. and White, K. (2000) 'Life insurance, the medical examination and cultural values', *Journal of Historical Sociology*, 13 (2): 190–214.

Kantor, A.C. and Nystuen, J.D. (1982) 'De facto redlining: a geographic view', *Economic Geography*, 58 (4): 309–28.

Kempson, E. and Whyley, C. (1999) 'Kept out or opted out? Understanding and combating financial exclusion', Report for the Joseph Rowntree Foundation, York.

Kemshall, H. (2002) *Risk, Social Policy and Welfare.* Buckingham: Open University Press.

Leitner, S. and Lessenich, S. (2003) 'Assessing welfare state change: The German social insurance state between reciprocity and solidarity', *Journal of Public Policy*, 23 (3): 325–47.

Levitas, R. (1998) *The Inclusive Society? Social Exclusion and New Labour.* Basingstoke: Macmillan.

Leyshon, A. and Thrift, N. (1997) *Money/Space: Geographies of Monetary Transformation*. London: Routledge.

Leyshon, A. and Thrift, N. (1999) 'Lists come alive: electronic systems of knowledge and the rise of credit-scoring in retail banking', *Economy and Society*, 28 (1): 434–66.

Leyshon, A., Thrift, N. and Pratt, J. (1998) 'Reading financial services: texts, consumers and financial literacy', *Environment and Planning D: Society and Space,* 16: 29–55.

Leyshon, A., Lee, R. and Williams, C.C. (eds) (2003) *Alternative Economic Spaces*. London: Sage.

Leyshon, A., Burton, D., Knight, D., Alferoff, C. and Signoretta, P. (2004) 'Towards an ecology of retail financial services: understanding the persistence of door-to-door credit and insurance providers', *Environment and Planning A*, 36: 625–45.

OFT (1999) 'Vulnerable consumers and financial services'. Report of the Director General's Inquiry. London: Office of Fair Trading.

Pollard, J. (1996) 'Banking at the margins: a geography of financial exclusion in Los Angeles', *Environment and Planning A*, 28: 1209–32.

Priest, S.J., Clark, M.J. and Treby, E.J. (2005) 'Flood insurance: the challenge of the uninsured', *Area*, 37: 295–302.

Rogaly, B., Fisher, T. and Mayo, E. (eds) (1999) *Poverty, Social Exclusion and Microfinance in Britain*. Oxford: Oxfam Publishing.

Sahlins, M. (1974) *Stone Age Economics.* London: Tavistock.

Smith, D.M. (2000) *Moral Geographies: Ethics in a World of Difference*. Edinburgh: Edinburgh University Press.

Smith, S.J. and Bennett, P.G. (2007) 'Where to draw the line? The health-divide in life insurance markets'. Unpublished manuscript.

Squires, G.D. (2003) 'Racial profiling, insurance style: insurance redlining and the uneven development of metropolitan areas', *Journal of Urban Affairs,* 25 (4): 391–410.

Sunley, P. (1999) 'Stakeholder capitalism and economic geography', *Environment and Planning A*, 31: 2189–205.

Wilkie, A. (1997) 'Mutuality and solidarity: assessing risks and sharing losses', *British Actuarial Journal*, 3: 985–96.

Williams, P. (1978) 'Building societies and the inner city', *Transactions of the Institute of British Geographers*, N.S. 3: 23–34.

Wyly, E.K., Atia, M., Foxcroft, H., Hammel, D.J. and Phillips-Watts, K. (2006) 'American home: predatory mortgage capital and neighbourhood spaces of race and class exploitation in the United States', *Geografiska Annaler (B),* 88: 105–32.

10

Emotional Economic Geographies

Nancy Ettlinger

PREAMBLE: 'EMOTIONS', 'AFFECT', AND SITUATING 'EMOTIONAL ECONOMIC GEOGRAPHIES'

There is a dizzying variety of statements about 'emotions', 'affect', and their differences. And while lucid categorisations of approaches continue to appear in press (e.g. Thien, 2005; Thrift, 2004; Tolia-Kelly, 2006), the two terms are often used loosely and interchangeably. Recognising that one person's 'affect' is another's 'emotion', my purpose in this preamble is to clarify what I mean by 'emotional' as a qualifier of 'economic geographies'. My concern is less for the term I employ and more for the meaning I ascribe to it. As I discuss below, despite the usefulness of expository articles on the two terms, the ongoing evolution of thinking renders the boundaries of categories porous. In this preamble I offer an abstracted overview of different views of affect and emotion, and subsequently situate my approach to 'emotional economic geographies'. The remainder of the chapter elaborates points briefly stated in this preamble.

The conventional view of emotions is essentialist and separates emotions from other facets of life; emotions from this perspective are personal, and are often defined by way of example, in terms of love, hate, and so forth. This view is consistent with the mainstream economic view of emotions that circumscribes and locates them outside the economy – outside public space – typically confining them to the domestic sphere, which is seen as private, personal, and *feminine*. Some mainstream economists have acknowledged emotions in the economy: in behavioral finance, emotions are seen as driving for-profit investment (Shiller, 2000, 2005), and in 'the new household economics' emotions figure prominently in optimisation strategies in households (Becker, 1991). Quite distinct from more radical views concerned with the political and possibilities for transformative change, emotions in modified, mainstream perspectives are interpreted solely with reference to economic outcomes.

Feminists have countered mainstream claims in different ways. Whereas some seek to clarify that the home is a crucial site of social reproduction within the capitalist economy, others emphasise the role of emotions in formal workplaces. A more generalised perspective hinges on the conceptual link between the economy and other spheres of life, and holds that the economic, cultural, political and social are inextricably interrelated (Lee, 2006; Lee and Wills, 1997);

similarly, emotion and rationality also are inseparable (Christie et al., 2008; Ettlinger, 2003, 2004; Munro and Smith, 2008; Smith, 2004), and thus people in all spheres and power segments operate with *multiple* logics. This latter view dissolves the binary of emotions/rationality in a fluid conception of behavior, decision making, and self-perception. From a normative vantage point, feminist economists have developed the notion of a 'caring economy', whereby emotions are conceptualised as an asset to the economy, not a liability as in the mainstream view (e.g. Donath, 2000; Folbre, 2001); this view has been echoed by a number of geographers (e.g. Haylett, 2003; McDowell, 2004; Perrons, 2000; Robinson, 2006; Smith, 2005; Staehli, 2003) as well as sociologists (e.g. Hochschild, 2003), political theorists (e.g. Fraser, 1997), and cultural studies scholars (e.g. Ahmed, 2004a). At issue from this normative position is cultivating and institutionalising economies of care within capitalism.

Enter 'affect'. Nigel Thrift's (2004) discussion of four understandings of affect is a useful starting point. These include: emotions as sensual or embodied reactions to the social and physical environment; the Spinoza-based idea of the immanence of affect and affect as enabling action (i.e., an active or proactive, rather than reactive, understanding); neo-Darwinism; and psychoanalysis. Despite differences among these approaches, they all share a sense of ethics, a sense of the political; in this regard, they intersect with feminist reactions on an interdisciplinary basis to mainstream views of emotions.

Some feminists, however, have embraced the idea of '*emotional* subjects' and argued that *affective* frameworks overlook uneven power relations and issues of difference (Thien, 2005; Tolia-Kelly, 2006). Although this critique is warranted, it may nonetheless be open to question. For example, Michael Hardt and Antonio Negri's (2004) *Multitude* is, fundamentally about power relations. Their Spinoza-inspired approach to affect focuses on the role of affect in circuits of cooperation and collaboration among 'the multitude' to bring about political transformation at a global scale; Hardt and Negri's 'multitude' is constituted by 'all the diverse figures of social production' (2004: xv), especially 'immaterial labor' engaged in the production of information, knowledge, images, and so forth. According to this view, affect is immanent among the multitude; it comes 'from below' as a product of struggle, and it provides the energy to reverse the direction of biopower (top to bottom) in the age of empire to empower the multitude (the bottom) in a new world order (Hardt, 1999, 2003; Negri, 1999). The rub, however, is that although Hardt and Negri's concept of 'the multitude' recognises diversity, it does not engage difference. Power relations are engaged *between* 'the top' and 'the bottom', but not *within* either – quite a significant problem if we consider that the uneven power relations within the multitude (among diverse groups and among people within those groups) obstruct Hardt's and Negri's envisioned cohesion via a bottom-specific love.[1] Although the Spinoza-based view of affect through Hardt and Negri's (2000, 2004) popularised account engages power relations, the engagement is, however, uniscalar; it is fixed between different levels of a hierarchy, thereby missing the multiscalar dynamics revealed by the frictions of difference within these scales. At issue, then, is the way in which power relations are engaged, beyond a matter of presence or absence of attention to power relations.

Similar in some respects to Hardt and Negri, feminist geographer J.K. Gibson-Graham (2006) views affect as a catalyst towards a non- or postcapitalist politics, though there are differences with Hardt and Negri's framework. In particular, Gibson-Graham envisions a postcapitalist order at the community, not the global, scale; further, such communities may exist apart from (not in direct power relations with) capitalist communities. This view is feminist, yet it diverges from other feminist approaches that focus on uneven power relations and instead emphasises communitarian themes.

Further, the approach follows from Gibson-Graham's earlier work (1996), which represents non-waged, domestic activity *outside* the capitalist economy – a feminist view, which differs considerably from other feminist scholarship that counters neoclassical narratives by recognising unwaged work in the domestic sphere as a critical element of capitalism. Whereas the Spinoza-based view of affect dissolves conventional boundaries between emotion and rationality (though for Hardt and Negri this dissolution is restricted to the multitude), Gibson-Graham's framework implicitly draws on the binary in a separatist, rather than a relational, view of difference.

The above brief overview underscores the complexity of the conceptual terrain regarding emotion/affect. I wish to emphasise three interrelated points. First, when emotions are viewed as outside 'the political' – in economic terms only (as in mainstream economic views and variants in behavioral finance and the new household economics) – they lack transformational value and are exclusively tools of (very partial!) interpretative frameworks without critical normative content. Second, many radical approaches share a critical sense of the political while differing considerably regarding approaches to the nature of change. Third, I suggest that *how change is envisioned from the vantage point of critical theory depends on how emotion/affect is 'placed' in the economy*. Hardt and Negri (2004), for example, place affect in the economy but only 'from below'; this placement leads to a view of change that is about reversing the direction of biopower. Gibson-Graham places emotion outside the economy and her communitarian view of change is outside the capitalist system. Still another perspective represents emotions as an inseparable part of all spheres of life; the political that emerges from this view envisions a redefinition of the current system through revaluing the role of emotions.

As elaborated in this chapter, my own approach draws attention to the pervasiveness of emotions in the economy and all spheres of life. I do not confine emotions to the body; rather, towards dissolving binaries I emphasise that people carry a mélange of thoughts and feelings derived from a variety of contexts across time and space. Accordingly, I consider emotions to be inseparable from what is conventionally understood to be its antithesis, rationality. Further, every individual operates by and through a multiplicity of logics constituted by a mix of calculated rationality and emotion/affect/feeling; accordingly, what might otherwise be understood as *ir*rational represents a logic that may privilege the social, cultural, or political more than the economic in a specific context (Ettlinger, 2004). The mix of thoughts and feelings carried by each individual derives from different space/time contexts, and the multiple logics associated with these different contexts blur in the mind. My understanding of multiple logics (of which emotions/affect/feeling are a part) is relational: multiple logics constantly evolve in each individual in relation to the multidimensional experience of the contexts they traverse. And it is unpredictable when a particular logic may surface; for example, an economic logic does not necessarily surface when an individual is in a formal workplace, and similarly for political, social, cultural logics. This is because every context is itself multidimensional – political, economic, cultural, social – contrary to conventional ascriptions of particular, exclusive identities. While I recognise multiple logics in terms of reactions to the dynamics of specific contexts (as in one of the approaches to affect reviewed by Nigel Thrift), at the same time my approach has a critical normative component and embraces political transformation. But I do not view transformation in terms of the emergence of a new system, whether at a community or a global scale; rather, the type of transformation I envision entails a redefinition of the existing system by way of identifying multiple logics in all spheres of life, interpreting and proactively and strategically tapping these logics.

Despite diverse views, to date there has been little in the way of active debate about 'emotional economic geographies'. Rather, this research field in geography and across disciplines has evolved as discrete narratives regarding the meaning and significance of 'emotions' or 'affect', 'economy', and the 'place' of emotions in or outside the economy. The different geographical imaginaries of emotions, as articulated by critical theorists, suggest that the issue is far more complicated than common divides such as neoclassical/radical and global/local. The relative absence of an active debate perhaps speaks more to the relative infancy of academic attention to emotional economic geographies than to its (ir)relevance. As I elaborate below, the 'place' of emotions outside or inside but limited in capitalist space, or alternatively emotions as pervasive, requires problematisation and constitutes a crucial arena for critical discussion.

THE CONVENTIONAL PLACE OF EMOTION – OUTSIDE THE ECONOMY

By convention, the protagonist of the (neoclassical) economy is *homo economicus*, whose behavior is predictable because he operates by a singular economic rationality that defines wellbeing in terms of the efficacy of optimisation and least cost. *Homo economicus* is 'rational man'. His context also is predictable – it is economic: the workplace, the marketplace; no other context is relevant. *Homo economicus* is rational, and anyone who pursues a different logic is *ir*rational, deviant, or outside the realm of rationality altogether – emotional.

Crucially, the conventional binary of reason and emotion is underwritten by a geographical imaginary that places reason in the public sphere and emotion in the private sphere. Paralleling the geographic imaginary of reason and men in public, work space, and emotion and women in private, home space, is another geographic imaginary that genders production: men are producers whereas women are conceptualised in the home, where activity is unwaged, and therefore women are conceptualised as outside the economy – the market – altogether. This conventional reasoning bounds women and emotion alike in non-capitalist space and, by contrast, places reason, science and men firmly within scientific, capitalist, work space (Massey, 1997). Figure 10.1 illustrates the spatiality of binaries in conventional economic thinking. Significantly, the emotion/rationality divide, as well as the geographically conceived divide, between the private and public spheres, are underwritten by power relations because it is the realm of production that 'counts'.

Some neoclassical scholars, such as those in behavioral finance, recognise *homo economicus* as a myth and acknowledge the prominent role of emotions in the public sphere, as in the psychological dynamics leading to stock-market bubbles. Yet, in this insertion of emotions in the public sphere, emotions are cast as *ir*rational, that is, outside a singular economic logic, and moreover harbingers of economic disaster (Shiller, 2000, 2005). The acknowledgement of emotion in the public sphere and its interpretation as *ir*rational intersects with the conventional neoclassical view of the public sphere, specifically for 'rational man', as the *steady* workplace; from this perspective, emotions in the public sphere, in the workplace, reflect deviance. Although the field of behavioral finance is represented by its authors as radical because it engages market imperfections and reflects on the presence of non-economic logic in the public sphere, implicitly it nonetheless connects with neoclassical assumptions by

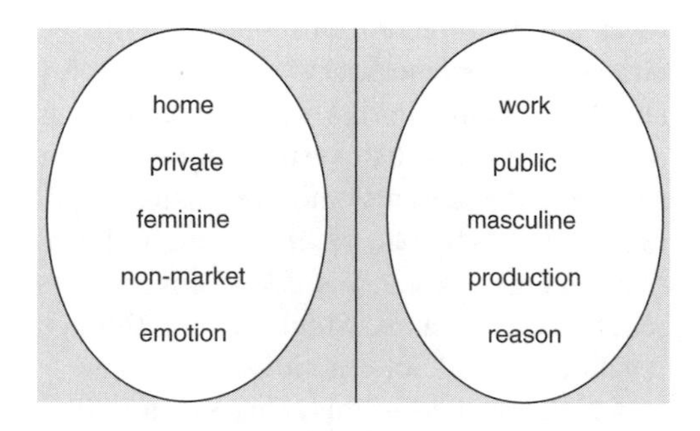

Figure 10.1 Discrete realms: the spatiality of binaries as per conventional economics.

representing emotion as *ir*rational and outside the norm. As elaborated later, the idea that a singular (economic) rationality is 'normal' is open to debate.

As in the case of modified views of emotions relative to the public sphere, there also is a modified view of emotions relative to the private sphere. Unlike most neoclassical economics, the 'new household economics' recognises the household as a *production* unit, and furthermore, it recognises feelings, notably altruism, which otherwise is understood as being absent from the market. According to this view, heads of households (men) are altruistic specifically in the home, and they develop incentives so that family members (including self-centered, spoiled kids) ultimately will act in accordance with what is optimal for the family unit (Becker, 1991).[2] Interestingly, even though emotions are acknowledged in the dynamics of the economy of the home, they nonetheless remain confined to the home. Further, emotions of men (the household heads) are understood as a positive counter to emotions of other household members that detract from optimisation; the divide, in this case, operates along the combined axes of gender and age.

RE-PLACING EMOTION IN THE (PRODUCTIVE) ECONOMY: PROBLEMATISING (AND SPATIALISING) '*LOVE'S* LABOR'

Feminists have been especially outspoken about the problems with the conventional placement of emotions outside the economy and have clarified that the emotional is economic and vice versa. In particular, feminist economists have clarified the domestic sphere as a site of production, although their argument differs considerably from the new household economics. A salient feature of feminist economics is the recognition that unwaged work is indeed 'work' that is very much part of the capitalist system.[3] From a Marxist perspective, unpaid domestic activity figures prominently as *reproductive* labor in the capitalist economy because childcare ensures a future generation of workers. Moreover, 'caring' labor adds value to commodities as, for example, purchased clothes are laundered and food is cooked. As noted in a Taiwanese context (Cheng and Hsiung, 1992), the unpaid nature of caring labor in the household and community actually frees up resources to be expended elsewhere in the economy; in contexts such as Western suburbias, unpaid women's work permits male breadwinners to earn wages by releasing them from domestic responsibilities. Further, effective unpaid care work such as nurturing children and helping them to develop their capabilities in the long run enhances formal workplaces as well as societal institutions such as social security (Folbre and Nelson, 2000). Recognising the role of women and their unpaid labor in the home and community is crucial not only in gender studies but more generally in accounts of labor markets and the economy more generally.

WOMEN (AND 'OTHERS') IN THE PAID WORK FORCE: SCALING AND NUANCING SEGREGATION

The widespread entry of Others (notably women as well as racial and ethnic minorities) into the paid workforce complicates issues of inequity. Far from an equaliser, diversity in the work force, in the absence of change at multiple scales (local and federal government, workplaces, communities, households), engenders frictions, not integration, such that tensions become expressed in deepening labor market segmentation, that is, segregation (Ettlinger, 2000). Such frictions and tensions represent an emotional geography of exclusion (Sibley, 1995). How power brokers in firms develop feelings about Others (in or outside formal work contexts) can influence who is selected for privileged tasks; indeed, there is a vocabulary for this sort of selection: 'nepotism' in the case of kin ties; 'good old boy/girl network' to clarify the social context in which selection is based on histories of friendships and favors; and 'sexism', 'racism', 'homophobism' and the like, which help clarify why less qualified people may be selected over more qualified 'Others'. How types of work become divided by, gender, for example, connects with how people feel about men, women, sexuality; conventional binaries that cast women as emotional and men as rational (Massey, 1997) figure in the relegation of women to jobs that require sensitivity, compassion, and care, while being (un)rewarded with lower wages and glass ceilings (England and Folbre, 1999; Folbre, 2001; Henderson, 1994; Robinson, 2006). The gendering[4] of occupations and, further, the segmentation of tasks within occupations, produces and is produced by feelings as to what types of people belong in different types of jobs; segregation becomes a means to ensure cognitive distance and uneven power relations (McDowell and Court, 1994).

The spatiality of segregation born of feelings of friction is far more complicated than spatially divided realms of binaries, as in Figure 10.1. Segregation plays out *within* so-called public and private spheres as discrimination is reproduced at multiple scales. While jobs and tasks become identified with particular types of workers in industries and occupations within the so-called public sphere, women nonetheless largely have retained domestic responsibilities in the so-called private sphere despite responsibilities for earning a wage – a 'double burden' (Folbre and Himmelweit, 2000); in particular contexts where women are expected to sustain unpaid community work (e.g., care for the elderly, orphans, and the like), the problem becomes a 'triple burden' (Cheng and Hsiung, 1992).

Ironically, while workplaces can be depicted as constraining (by glass ceilings) and deprecating (by the placement of women in subservient positions), many women nonetheless experience the workplace as a realm of relative security, familiarity, *home*, whereas the domestic sphere becomes a place of work (Hochschild, 1997). The sense of work as home fits the stereotype of middle-class career women, but also can characterise the feelings of women in situations of extreme exploitation. For example, sweatshop workers, while miserable in the context of abject work conditions, may nonetheless prefer the trials of work to even more grueling conditions at home; this situation is vividly depicted in the film *Mardi Gras: Made in China* (Redmon, 2006), which documents consumption practices in New Orleans during Mardi Gras as well as practices and circumstances in China where beads for Mardi Gras are produced.[5] Analogous scenarios can obtain in Western suburbias, where former housewives gain a new sense of themselves as they develop new identities and networks in waged workplaces, even if circumstances are far from ideal. The main point is that a spatial division of thought and feelings regarding home and work requires considerable qualification.

BLURRING BOUNDARIES, PRESERVING BINARIES, MULTIPLYING SEGREGATIONIST PRACTICES

While the private and public spheres require qualification as some women's feelings about home become displaced to work and vice versa, at issue is whether realms (as in private and public) become internally reconfigured, or, more radically, whether the boundaries between realms become blurred.

Consider the so-called private sphere, which has become a site of commodified care, as nannies for example, are imported from low-wage countries (Hochschild, 2003). The home becomes the public sphere for emotional labor and also a new site of class conflict as middle- and upper-class women exploit lower-class women (McDowell, 2006). And while the traditional boundary between the public and private spheres becomes blurred, nannies within households are subject to sharply demarcated private and public spaces that reflect spaces of privilege and lack thereof (Pratt, 1999).

Consider now the workplace, which traditionally has been construed as a masculinist space of work. The *process* towards profit may entail 'emotion work' on the part of an employee, such as an airline steward, towards a customer (Hochschild, 2004), or 'relational work' on the part of co-workers in collaborative activity (Fletcher, 1999). Such work in both contexts is commonly relegated to women, and although such work benefits an organisation, it nonetheless gets 'disappeared' in the sense that those doing this work are materially and discursively unrewarded for their efforts (Fletcher, 1999). The mix of so-called public/masculinist and private/feminine behavior occurs routinely in workplaces as part of the status quo,[6] while the reward system remains divided. The workplace status quo thus entails a blurring of the public/private boundary as women and 'women's work' become part of the capitalist enterprise; all the while, however, socially constructed binaries (masculinity and reason versus femininity and emotion) are preserved as part of a system of uneven power relations in which one end of the binary is materially rewarded and discursively recognised while the other is unrewarded and rendered invisible.

As the conventional public/private boundary becomes blurred in both the home and workplace, new boundaries around socially preserved binaries are constructed at finer scales to sustain uneven power relations. The social, political, cultural, and economic dividers materialise and emerge discursively along axes of difference (e.g. gender, race/ethnicity, class).[7] Paradoxically, as conventional boundaries blur, segregationist practices actually deepen across multiple scales (Ettlinger, 2009).

As elaborated below, although the blurring of conventional boundaries among different spheres of life has been recognised and researched outside neoclassical analysis, less discussed, however, is the relation of the mutual constitution of different spheres of life to emotions and their geographies; it is to this latter set of issues that I now turn.

FROM THE MUTUAL CONSTITUTION OF DIFFERENT TYPES OF RATIONALITIES TO THE MUTUAL CONSTITUTION OF RATIONALITIES AND EMOTIONS: MULTIPLE LOGICS AND LOGICS OF RESISTANCE

The landmark volume *Geographies of Economies* (Lee and Wills, 1997) clarified that interpreting the economy as a separate, bounded sphere is at best unfruitful; instead, the economic is bound up with the social, the cultural, the political (see also Lee, 2006). Based on this premise, the notion of 'rational man' makes little sense. Equally, the idea of *ir*rational man also is problematic as an expression of non-economic logic and as a sort of deviance. Apart from the 'man' issue – sexist language reflecting the gender bias of economics as a discipline – 'rational' and its antithesis, 'irrational', are problematic if we accept the interrelation of political, social, cultural, and economic rationalit*ies*. If, for example, we understand economic interactions as social relations that are laced (unevenly) with power, then we recognise not a singular rationality, but rather, multiple, imbricated rationalities (Ettlinger, 2003).

The mutual constitution of different types of rationalities (economic, political, social, cultural) challenges the models of rational and irrational man, but still leaves the relation between reason and emotion unresolved. For example, does each type of rationality – economic, political, social, cultural – constitute a different set of calculations, apart from emotions?

Conventionally, and from an essentialist perspective, reason and emotion are discrete and bounded. Reason is understood as a set of informal or formal calculations based on available information, and emotion is understood as unstructured, unplanned and exemplified by love, hate, and so forth. Although the placement of 'love' in a site of production is radical relative to the neoclassical narrative, this approach nonetheless retains an essentialised view by materialising love while overlooking feelings and the interplay of emotions with an economic rationality (see critiques by Himmelweit, 1995; Munro and Smith, 2008).[8]

Alternatively, from a non-essentialist perspective, thoughts and feelings are continuous, fluid, unbounded; accordingly, an individual's meticulous calculations about any one particular issue can influence and also be influenced by a wide range of thoughts and feelings. Far from being a private affair, emotions connect individual psyches to social relations (Ahmed, 2004a, b) in various space/time contexts. Political, economic, social, and cultural 'calculations' are inseparable from the feelings that affect and are affected by any one of a number of rationalities. And decision making based on a collage of thoughts and feelings has consequences that may be positive or negative relative to any one dimension (economic, political, social, and cultural). Indeed, while some branches of academe have been reluctant to acknowledge the prominent role of emotions in decision making, capitalist enterprises routinely have made it their business to tap people's emotions to influence consumer behavior (Goss, 1993; Voyce, 2003; Williams, 1993); analogously, fair trade non-profit organisations target the emotions of ethical consumption by developing tactics to guide people to make choices about consumption in accordance with their mission (Barnett et al., 2005).

To avoid semantic confusion, I use 'logics' not as oppositional to emotions (as in conventional usage of 'rationality'), but rather with reference to the mutual constitution of rationalities and emotions/affect – the mélange of thoughts and feelings that constitutes individuals' cognition and in part shapes social interaction and decision making. Multiple logics entail the mutual embeddedness of different types of rationalities (e.g. economic, political, cultural, social), each of which is constituted by a mix of reason and emotion. Multiple logics are likely to occur in any one context, and it is the mix, not the resolution, of logics that helps interpret the complexity of both contexts and texts of interaction. How people think, feel, and make decisions about each other and about objects of production and consumption in the workplace and consumer culture co-occurs with, but diverges from, the unilateral rationality of *homo economicus* oriented toward efficiency. The idea of multiple logics as constituted by an *incoherent* mix of rationalities and emotions (Ettlinger, 2004) counters the conventional view of 'cognitive dissonance' (Festinger, 1957) whereby one logic eclipses another, thereby resolving conflicted feelings.

The collision of multiple logics suggests that optimisation – which is always figured relative to a singular rationality – is a hypothetical matter that rarely if ever occurs. One advantage of a non-essentialist approach is that it refuses to sweep under the rug everyday behaviors and decisions that are suboptimal, as per any one type of rationality; rather, it offers a means by which to interpret behaviors and decisions relative to stated goals and, conversely, a way to evaluate stated goals relative to actual behaviors. This approach counters research in behavioral finance that interprets non-economic logic – emotion – as irrational and deviant. Thus, production strategies such as corporate restructuring, network construction, or tactical collaboration require critical evaluation relative to routine tensions between an often unidimensionally conceived mission and the multiple logics that may frustrate and possibly derail objectives (Ettlinger, 2007a). The multiplexity of housing markets (Smith, 2005; Christie et al., 2008) is also layered with multiple logics relative to different stakeholders – consumers and the various economic, social, cultural, and political architects of neighborhoods. Workplaces, markets, and other conventionally perceived 'sites' of the economy are constructed and *re*constructed as much on the basis of political, social, and cultural grounds as on economic grounds, and as much on the basis of feelings as planned calculations (Munro and Smith, 2008). Commonly, unidimensionally conceived goals are more discursive than material, and analysis might fruitfully focus on the relation between the two.[9]

Analytically, we can excavate behavior at any one time and place by tracing actors' logics to their experiences across time, over space. People's feelings about anything or anyone may be rooted in temporally and/or spatially proximate or distant contexts, and such untidy geographies affect consumer behavior and work performance in any one place and time (Ettlinger, 2004). These untidy geographies illuminate social relations in any one context by the mix of experiences that influence each actor's sensibilities, behavior, and decision making. The mix of thoughts and feelings that individuals develop over time is fluid, and crucially, while segregationist practices multiply in increasingly diverse workplaces and residential neighborhoods, the new boundaries are permeable relative to the intangible logics that people carry with them as they traverse contexts and the socially constructed boundaries around them.

An ethic of care that would diverge from segregationist practices would pivot on cooperation and collaboration *across axes of difference*,[10] and would hinge on the mix of logics within the context under consideration as well as the logics to which each individual in that context has been exposed across time and space (Ahmed, 2004a; Ettlinger, 2004). The formation of an individual's oppositional consciousnes[11] – that is, a consciousness opposed to conventionally prescribed norms – is a contingent matter relative to the interlacing of emotions and calculations in behavior across multiple spheres of life over time. Individuals risk alienation if their behavior differs from dominant patterns; whether individuals take that kind of risk depends in part on the breadth of their experience across time and space and their exposure and attachment to different tastes and values. Individualised resistance to social norms that circumscribe a person in certain work or residential spaces relative to various axes of difference (gender, race/ethnicity, class, age, and so forth) can be a matter of retaining or developing a logic that defies how one is supposed to think and feel. For example, as nannies traverse family space and women traverse male work spaces, the mix of their thoughts and feelings may or may not dovetail with their outward, prescribed demeanor. Further, men in their male work spaces may or may not think and feel as prescribed or anticipated, and similarly for persons of any majority group in majority-identified space. How logics of resistance evolve is rooted in the particular configuration of individuals' untidy geographies that challenge rather than reinforce the constraints of context-specific social norms (Ettlinger, 2004). Whereas conformity helps clarify apparent geographies of tastes and values across diverse residential and work contexts, overt or covert divergence from norms within context-specific cultural economies points to actual or potential sources of oppositional consciousness.

As Michel Foucault (2000) commented, it is important not to sacralise and thereby isolate the social by overlooking thoughts, because it is the uncovering of individuals' thoughts and (I would add) feelings[12] that holds the potential for radical criticism and social transformation. Whether a particular challenge to normalisation remains a silent performativity or becomes overt and possibly connects with others' oppositional consciousnesses is a contingent matter relative to the intersections of individuals' multiple logics across space and time. From a normative vantage point, then, at issue is how such contingencies can be tapped proactively.

NORMATIVE IMPLICATIONS, DIFFERENT AVENUES OF CRITICAL THEORY

While practices of segregation at multiple scales socially construct and preserve binaries, the blurring of conventional boundaries suggests serious problems that require critical attention and the setting of an agenda. For example, the considerable extension of women's responsibilities creates difficulty in juggling responsibilities in a variety of contexts and, moreover, contributes to a 'care deficit' at the societal scale (Hochschild, 2003). At issue is much more than transforming unpaid emotion work to paid care because this strategy alone routinely results in exploitation via low wages, or, ironically, in middle and upper-class women exploiting Other women, as in the case of the importation of nannies from low-wage countries.

A critical agenda would entail valuing emotions and care, yet there are decidedly different approaches towards this end. One avenue is to envision a new order that is different and separate from the capitalist system, while another is to acknowledge the role of emotions within capitalism and tap those emotions to constructively revise and redefine capitalist practices through a *re*valuation of emotions and recognition of their actual and potential contributions.

Approaches to a new order

Two popular exemplars of the 'new order' approach are Gibson-Graham's (2006) 'post-capitalist politics' and Hardt and Negri's (2004) 'multitude'. Critical differences between these two approaches pertain to scale, power relations, and the nature of the relation between the new order and mainstream capitalism.

Gibson-Graham envisions non- or post-capitalist economies at the scale of the community. Such communities operate on the basis of non- or post-capitalist principles, such as generosity and reciprocity, which evolve through the cultivation of the self towards a new, ethical identity. From Gibson-Graham's perspective, such communities represent 'alternative' economies (Leyshon et al., 2003)[13] that can co-exist with, but nonetheless remain separate from, capitalism. The alternativeness and separateness of such communities signify an existence *outside* and free of (that is, not dependent upon) structures and constraints of the capitalist system. Such alternative communities are distinguished from capitalism by virtue of their communitarian spirit and their constitution by ethical subjects.

Hardt and Negri (2004), on the other hand, envision a post-empire *world* order that would *reverse* power relations between the multitude and private and governmental organisations of 'empire'. Similar to Gibson-Graham (2006), affective bonds and the ethical identities through which those bonds are constructed characterise the new order exclusively. However, in Hardt and Negri's account, the 'separateness' of a new order is chronological; that is, it postdates empire by reversing power relations. This reversal rests in the first instance on immanent affective bonds of immaterial labor of the post-industrial age. Specifically, immaterial labor engenders affective bonds through the communication networks wrought of non-material work (Hardt and Negri, 2004)[14] as well as through struggle (Negri, 1999).

Although Hardt and Negri's and Gibson-Graham's visions differ regarding how the separateness of an affective economy is situated (co-existing with or post-dating capitalism), they nonetheless share common ground regarding the exclusively non-capitalist representation of affect. Ironically, despite Hardt and Negri's Spinoza-inspired framework that dissolves the emotion/reason binary, they construct their own binary *vis-à-vis* power relations and the presence/absence of ethical identities relative to "the top" and "the bottom". The binary for Gibson-Graham is explicit in her earlier work, which separates the domestic sphere from formal, capitalist workplaces (Gibson-Graham, 1996), and implicit in her later work, which represents affective economies and ethical subjects as constitutive of *non*- or *post*capitalist communities in a definition of capitalism as necessarily lacking this crucial dimension.

Re-valuation of emotion within the capitalist economy, and re-definition of capitalism

But radical pathways can recognise emotion/affect in capitalist practices across multiple spheres of life (in waged and unwaged activity in households, formal workplaces, communities, cyberspace) and emphasise a *re*valuation of emotion within capitalism towards a *re*definition of capitalist practices. Rather than accept the neoclassical discourse that marginalises, even demonises, emotion, we should look to everyday practices of "the ordinary economy" (Lee, 2006) that may well entail ruthless actions towards the achievement of efficiency, but may also entail care, reciprocity, and emotion. If we accept a multiplicity of logics, why then, should we proceed as if there is a singular logic that directs all actions? In contrast to the new-order imaginary, we can uncover emotions that conventionally are rendered invisible, and thereby recognise the prominent role of emotions in capitalist enterprise as well as the fluidity of reason and emotion. The enterprise entails clarifying profit and care as complements, not competitors, and revaluing the fluidity of reason/profit and emotion/care to produce a more democratic way of life. The agenda is an affective reinvigoration of intellectual projects towards social transformation (Butler, 2004)[15].

Issues of profit need not be abandoned because profit can permit a caring economy if the value system is reconfigured and care work is institutionalised and appropriately rewarded (Hochschild, 2003; Folbre, 2001; Fraser, 1997; Haylett, 2003; McDowell, 2004; Perrons, 2000; Robinson, 2006; Smith, 2005; Staehli, 2003). Whether a particular workplace (waged or unwaged) or a housing market, at issue is redefining the economy through a lens of ethics by interweaving, not separating, principles of efficiency and social justice (Christie et al., 2008; Ettlinger, 2007a, b; Folbre, 2001; Munro and Smith, 2008; Robinson, 2006; Smith, 2000; Smith, 2005). This type of agenda is not about reversing power relations or the spatiality of binaries – that is, displacing emotions from one sphere (e.g., the household) or from one group of actors (e.g., the multitude; ethical subjects) to other spheres (e.g., formal workplaces) or group of actors (private and governmental organisations of the mainstream economy); rather, it is about blurring boundaries while also dissolving pernicious, socially constructed binaries that result in social injustice. Resistance at a meso- or macroscale entails a collective celebration of multiple logics – a crucial prerequisite to redefining the economy by integrating profit and care. This is a difficult project for which there is no final 'arrival'. The point in setting an agenda is to delineate new principles in order to try to avoid replicating problems and to work towards new goals (Young, 2000). If we consider Nancy Folbre's (2001: 232) comment that a caring economy is deliverable only on the basis of emotionally rich relationships (not about adding care as if it were a commodity), then, from the vantage point of critical theory, at issue is how to cultivate constructive cultural economies and thwart destructive social relations.

Problematising the difference between critical agendas: inside/outside and the nature of difference

The different approaches indicated above intersect on critical normative sensibilities, notably the critique of the neoclassical narrative and an agenda that celebrates care, recognises emotion, and rethinks self, economy, place and space; yet implicitly they diverge on the conceptualisation of emotions. One view places emotions *outside* capitalism; this view is internally differentiated, as exemplified by Gibson-Graham's and Hardt and Negri's approaches. Whereas Gibson-Graham separates reason and emotion and sees emotions as the catalyst towards a *non*-capitalist, caring way of life, Hardt and Negri view affect as immanent specifically among 'the multitude', thereby enabling a reversal of power relations between the multitude and power brokers of empire. A quite different view towards a critical agenda highlights the role of emotions *in* capitalist contexts, recognises that emotions do indeed impact behavior and decision making, decries the routine undervaluation of emotions and related social injustices, and calls for changing value and reward systems by acknowledging and rendering visible the crucial interrelation of emotion and reason. Despite commonalities in rethinking place and space, one approach separates capitalist and non-capitalist places in space (Gibson-Graham, 2006) or time (Hardt and Negri, 2004), whereas the other reconstitutes places across capitalist space.

The two views towards a critical agenda are implicitly underscored by a more general issue, namely the conceptualisation of difference in separatist or relational terms. A separatist view of difference maintains boundaries. In the case of emotional economic geographies, the boundary is set spatially or temporally between capitalist and non- or post-capitalist economies as well as between reason and emotion relative to capitalist or non-capitalist actors. Alternatively, a relational approach to difference recognises actors as distinct but forming identity in relation to, and sharing common ground with, others; distinctness occurs while identities of different groups are mutually constituted and, moreover, fluid and open to continuous negotiation (Ahmed, 2004a; Butler, 2004; Connolly, 2002; Massey, 2004; Robinson, 2006; Young, 2000). A relational view of emotional economic geographies blurs the boundaries between reason and emotion, permitting interpretation of behaviors that diverge from stated missions and norms and also setting an agenda to tap the resources of capitalist trajectories by scrutinising and revaluing the relation among its constituent parts.

The larger issue of the nature of difference – separatist or relational – defines the terms of change in social, political, cultural, and economic terms, and it requires active debate. To date, interest in issues of difference in economic geography has been underscored more by similarities in perspective than by differences; both are important. The 'place' of emotions in economies – inside or outside – is a crucial frontier for deliberation.

NOTES

1 As per Hardt and Negri (2004), love is specific to the poor via struggles.

2 For a feminist critique, see feminist economist Paula England's (2003) critical overview; see also Ferber and Nelson (2003).

3 For excellent overviews of feminist critiques of mainstream economics on emotions and related issues, see Barker and Feiner (2004); Ferber and Nelson (2003).

4 One can also state the problem in terms of the racialisation of occupations. To date, economic geography has emphasised gender in issues of difference. The emphasis on gender has been in part a function of increasing numbers of women in economic eography. While in previous years gender was unattended due to the male bias of the discipline (Rose, 1993), the *color* of the discipline is increasingly at issue (Kobayashi, 2006; Kobayashi and Peake, 1994).

5 While the film *Mardi Gras: Made in China* (Redmon, 2006) is critical, evidence for preferences for work over home are routinely interpreted by business people and neoclassical researchers to justify exploitation in factories.

6 In contrast to daily routines that reinforce the status quo, some instances of strategic political activism challenge the status quo by bringing nurturing behavior (e.g., breastfeeding) that is traditionally conceptualised as private into public space (Staehli, 1996).

7 Race/ethnicity, class, and gender are well known axes of difference and are highlighted in the examples used in this paper; however, they are not intended here as a comprehensive representation of axes of difference, the range of which is considerably wider.

8 Janet Salaff's (1992) case study in Taiwan, which examines how women navigate multiple responsibilities and feelings, is an insightful empirical example of a non-essentialised approach to 'love's labor'; relatedly, see Nancy Folbre's award-winning (1994) book that examines interlocking structures of constraint on women.

9 For example, although the 'new economy' often is conceptualised in terms of both increased efficiency and an 'economy of qualities' (Callon et al., 2002), new-economy networks commonly fall short of their objectives as issues of social relations frustrate strategies to achieve efficiency, and vice versa (Ettlinger, 2008).

10 Whole work cultures can evolve around principles of cooperation and collaboration, but this commonly occurs within homogeneous groups (Ettlinger, 2000). For a critical normative framework that envisions how cooperation and collaboration might occur across axes of difference see Ettlinger (2007b, 2009).

11 See Mansbridge and Morris (2001) and Sandoval (1991) for well-known discussions of oppositional consciousness. However, these examinations are situated at the scale of a collective, that is, among actors who have already connected collectively in their oppositional consciousness. See Ettlinger (2004) on the contingency of oppositional consciousness taking root on an individual scale; see also Bosco (2006) for how oppositional consciousnesses of individuals can connect on the basis of emotional bonding.

12 One might interpret Foucault's comments in 'So is it important to think?' as pertaining to 'rationality' because of the word 'thought'; I interpret his comments broadly to pertain to the multidimensionality of an individual's mind; thus I consider Foucault's comments on 'is it important to think?' to pertain to 'multiple logics' as defined here.

13 *Alternative economic spaces,* edited by Andrew Leyshon, Roger Lee, and Colin Williams (2003), is a landmark in the burgeoning literature on diverse economies (see also Community Economies Project, 2003), yet it is important to note that the views represented are far from homogeneous. Some authors embrace the separateness of alternative life ways at the margins of capitalism in alternative spaces, even if these are difficult to sustain (Lincoln, 2003); others are cynical about the possibility of any real alternative to uneven development (Amin et al., 2003) or at least less sanguine about the prospects for separation in light of the tendency of colonisation of alternative economies by the mainstream (Crewe et al., 2003); and still others consider alternative economic spaces as very much a part of the larger economy or economies with positive transformative effects (Fuller and Jonas, 2003), or as a vehicle for organising effective and inclusive work and welfare (Williams et al., 2003). A central issue raised in this chapter for deliberation is whether the critical agenda *should* entail separation from, or reevaluation and reconfiguration of, capitalist trajectories.

14 My purpose here is to review and situate Hardt and Negri's logic, not to critique it, which would require another manuscript with a different mission. *In brief*, some of the problems with their framework include the following. First, they homogenise immaterial labor and do not account for the majority of immaterial workers in the service economy whose work does not entail communicative networks. Second, they homogenise governmental and private organisations of empire and overlook considerable ground that is contested. Third, and following from the above-stated reasons, their 'we/they' view of the world falls prey to the conceptual problems of binary thinking (despite their dissolution of another binary, namely emotion/reason). Finally, the we/they binary leads to caricatures, and absurdly casts individuals of governmental and private organisations embedded in empire to be completely lacking in affect. As in Gibson-Graham's framework, affect is exclusive despite its extensiveness among the multitude.

15 Specifically, Judith Butler (2004, p. 151) indicated a need to affectively 'reinvigorate intellectual projects of critique, of questioning, of coming to understand the difficulties and demands of cultural translation and dissent, and to create a sense of the public in which oppositional voices are not feared, degraded or dismissed, but valued for the instigation to a sensate democracy they occasionally perform'.

REFERENCES

Ahmed, S. (2004a) *The Cultural Politics of Emotion*. New York: Routledge.

Ahmed, S. (2004b) 'Affective economies', *Social Text*, 79: 117–39.

Amin, A., Cameron, A. and Lee, R. (2003) 'The alterity of the social economy', in A. Leyshon, R. Lee and C.C. Williams (eds), *Alternative Economic Spaces*. pp. 27–54. Thousand Oaks, CA: Sage.

Barker, D.K. and Feiner, S. (2004) *Liberating Economics: Feminist Perspectives on Families, Work, and Globalization*. Ann Arbor: University of Michigan Press.

Barnett, C., Cloke, P., Clarke, N. and Malpass, A. (2005) 'Consuming ethics: articulating the subjects amd spaces of ethical consumption', *Antipode*, 37: 23–45.

Becker, G.S. (1991) *A Treatise on the Family*. Cambridge, MA: Harvard University Press.

Bosco, F.J. (2006) 'The Madres de Plaza de Mayo and three decades of human rights' activism: embeddedness, emotions, and social movements', *Annals of the Association of American Geographers*, 96: 342–65.

Butler, J. (2004) *Precarious Life: the Powers of Mourning and Violence*. New York: Verso.

Callon, M., Meadel, C. and Rabeharisoa, B. (2002) 'The economy of qualities', *Economy and Society*, 31: 194–207.

Cheng, L. and Hsiung, P.-C. (1992) 'Women, export-oriented growth, and the state: the case of Taiwan', in R.P. Appelbaum and J. Henderson (eds), *States and Development in the Asian Pacific Rim*. Newbury Park, CA: Sage. pp. 233–66.

Christie, H., Smith, S.J. and Munro, M. (2008) 'The emotional economy of housing', *Environment and Planning A,* 40: 2296–312.

Community Economies Project (2003) http://communityeconomies.org/. Last accessed Jan. 4, 2007.

Connolly, W.E. (2002) *Identity/Difference: Democratic Negotiations of Political Paradox*. Minneapolis: University of Minnesota Press.

Crewe, L., Gregson, N. and Brooks, K. (2003) 'Alternative retail spaces', in A. Leyshon, R. Lee and C.C. Williams (eds), *Alternative Economic Spaces*. Thousand Oaks, CA: Sage. pp. 74–106.

Donath, S. (2000) 'The other economy: a suggestion for a distinctively feminist economics', *Feminist Economics*, 6: 115–23.

England, P. (2003) 'Separative and soluble selves: Dichotomous thinking in economics', in M.A. Ferber and J.A. Nelson (eds), *Feminist Economics Today: Beyond Economic Man*. Chicago: University of Chicago Press. pp. 33–60.

England, P. and Folbre, N. (1999) 'The cost of caring', in R.J. Steinberg and D.M. Figart (eds), *Emotional Labor in the Service Economy*. Thousand Oaks, CA: Sage. pp. 39–51. *Annals of the American Academy of Political and Social Science*, 561.

Ettlinger, N. (2000) 'Labor market and industrial change: the competitive advantage and challenge of harnessing diversity', *Competition and Change*, 4: 171–210.

Ettlinger, N. (2003) 'Cultural economic geography and a relational and microspace approach to trusts, rationalities, networks, and change in collaborative workplaces', *Journal of Economic Geography*, 3: 145–71.

Ettlinger, N. (2004) 'Towards a critical theory of untidy geographies: the spatiality of emotions in consumption and production', *Feminist Economics*, 10: 21–54.

Ettlinger, N. (2007a) 'Unchaining the micro'. SECONS, http://www.giub.unibonn.de/grabher/, track 3.

Ettlinger, N. (2007b) 'Bringing democracy home: PostKatrina New Orleans', *Antipode*, 39: 8–16.

Ettlinger, N. (2008) 'The predicament of firms in the new and old economies: a critical inquiry into traditional binaries in the study of the space-economy', *Progress in Human Geography,* 31: 45–69.

Ettlinger, N. (2009) 'Surmounting city silences: knowledge creation and the design of urban democracy in the everyday economy', *International Journal of Urban and Regional Research*, 33: 217–30.

Ferber, M.A. and Nelson, J.A. (eds) (2003) *Feminist Economics Today: Beyond Economic Man*. Chicago: University of Chicago Press.

Festinger, L. (1957) *A Theory of Cognitive Dissonance*. Stanford: Stanford University Press.

Fletcher, J.K. (1999) *Disappearing Acts: Gender, Power, and Relational Practice at Work*. Cambridge, MA: MIT Press.

Folbre, N. (1994) *Who Pays for the Kids? Gender and the Structures of Constraint*. New York: Routledge.

Folbre, N. (2001) *The Invisible Heart: Economics and Family Values*. New York: The New Press.

Folbre, N. and Himmelweit, S. (guest eds) (2000) 'A special issue on children and family policy', *Feminist Economics*, 6.

Folbre, N. and Nelson, J.A. (2000) 'For love or money – or both?', *Journal of Economic Perspectives*, 14: 123–40.

Foucault, M. (2000) 'So is it important to think?' in J.D. Faubion (ed.), R. Hurley and others (trans.), *Power/Michel Foucault*. New York: The New Press. pp.454–8. Selections from *Dits et écrits 1954–1984*, ed. D. Defert and and F. Ewald with J. Lagrange. Paris: Editions Gallimard, 1994.

Fraser, N. (1997) *Justice Interruptus: Critical Reflections on the 'Postsocialist' Condition*. New York: Routledge.

Fuller, D. and Jonas, A.E.G. (2003) 'Alternative financial spaces', in A. Leyshon, R. Lee and C.C. Williams (eds), *Alternative Economic Spaces*. Thousand Oaks, CA: Sage. pp. 55–73.

Gibson-Graham, J.K. (1996) *The End of Capitalism (As We Knew It): a Feminist Critique of Political Economy*. Cambridge, MA: Blackwell.

Gibson-Graham, J.K. (2006) *A Postcapitalist Politics*. Minneapolis: University of Minnesota Press.

Goss, J. (1993) 'The "magic of the mall": an analysis of form, function, and meaning in the contemporary built economy', *Annals of the Association of American Geographers*, 83: 18–47.

Hardt, N. (1999) 'Affective labor', *Boundary 2*, 26: 89–100.

Hardt, N. (2003) An interview with Michael Hardt, conducted by S. Budgeon and A Coläs in 2001, London. *Historical Materialism*, 11: 121–52.

Hardt, M. and Negri, A. (2000) *Empire*. Cambridge, MA: Harvard University Press.

Hardt, M. and Negri. A. (2004) *Multitude: War and Democracy in the Age of Empire*. New York: Penguin.

Haylett, C. (2003) 'Class, care, and welfare reform: reading meanings, talking feelings', *Environment and Planning A*, 35: 799–814.
Henderson, G. (1994) *Cultural Diversity in the Workplace*. Westport, CT: Quorum Books.
Himmelweit, S. (1995) 'The discovery of "unpaid work": the social consequences of the expansion of "work"', *Feminist Economics*, 1: 1–19.
Hochschild, A.R. (1997) *The Time Bind: When Work Becomes Home and Home Becomes Work*. New York: Metropolitan Books.
Hochschild, A.R. (2003) *The Commercialization of Intimate Life: Notes from Home and Work*. Berkeley: University of California Press.
Hochschild, A.R. (2004) 'Feeling management: from private to commercial uses', in A. Amin and N. Thrift (eds), *The Cultural Economy Reader*. Malden, MA: Blackwell. pp. 329–51.
Kobayashi, A. (2006) 'Why women of colour in geography?', *Gender, Place and Culture*, 13: 33–8.
Kobayashi, A. and Peake, L. (1994) 'Unnatural discourse: race and gender in geography', *Gender, Place and Culture,* 1: 225–44.
Lee, R. (2006) 'The ordinary economy: tangled up in values and geography', *Transactions of the Institute of British Geographers,* 31: 413–32.
Lee, R. and Wills, J. (eds) (1997) *Geographies of Economies*. New York: Wiley.
Leyshon, A., Lee, R. and Williams, C.C. (eds) (2003) *Alternative Economic Spaces*. Thousand Oaks, CA: Sage.
Lincoln, A. (2003) 'Alternative work spaces', in A. Leyshon, R. Lee and C.C. Williams (eds), *Alternative Economic Spaces*. Thousand Oaks, CA: Sage. pp.107–27.
McDowell, L. (2004) 'Work, workfare, work/life balance and an ethic of care', *Progress in Human Geography*, 28: 145–63.
McDowell, L. (2006) 'Reconfigurations of gender and class relations: class differences, class condescension and the changing place of class relations', *Antipode*, 38: 825–50.
McDowell, L. and Court, G. (1994) 'Missing subjects: gender, power, sexuality in merchant banking', *Economic Geography*, 70: 229–51.
Mansbridge, J. and Morris, A. (eds) (2001) *Oppositional Consciousness*. Chicago: University of Chicago Press.
Massey, D. (1997) 'Economic/non-economic', in R. Lee and J. Wills (eds), *Geographies of Economies.* New York: Wiley. pp. 27–36.
Massey, D. (guest ed.) (2004) 'The political challenge of relational space: introduction to the Vega Symposium', *Geografiska Annaler* 86B (1), special issue.
Munro, M. and Smith, S.J. (2008) 'Calculated affection? A comment on the complex economy of home purchase', *Housing Studies,* 23: 349–67.
Negri, A. (1999) 'Value and affect', trans. M. Hardt, *Boundary 2*, 26: 77–88.
Perrons, D. (2000) 'Care, paid work, and leisure: rounding the triangle?', *Feminist Economics*, 6: 105–14.
Pratt, G. (1999) 'Geographies of identity and difference: marking boundaries', in D. Massey, J. Allen and P. Sarre (eds), *Human Geography Today*. Malden, MA: Blackwell. pp. 151–67.
Redmon, D. (prod, dir., ed.) (2006) *Mardi Gras* [videorecording]: *Made in China*, Carnivalesque productions. Brooklyn, NY: Calle y Media.
Robinson, F. (2006) 'Beyond labour rights', *International Feminist Journal of Politics*, 8: 321–42.
Rose, G. (1993) *Feminism and Geography: the Limits of Geographical Knowledge*. Minneapolis: University of Minnesota Press.
Salaff, J.W. (1992) 'Women, the family, and the state in Hong Kong, Taiwan, and Singapore', in R.P. Appelbaum and J. Henderson (eds), *States and Development in the Asian Pacific Rim.* Newbury Park, CA: Sage. pp. 267–88.
Sandoval, C. (1991) 'U.S. third world feminism: the theory and method of oppositional consciousness in the postmodern world', *Genders*, 10: 1–24.
Shiller, R.J. (2000) *Irrational Exuberance*. Princeton: Princeton University Press.
Shiller, R.J. (2005) *Irrational Exuberance*, 2nd edn. Princeton: Princeton University Press.
Sibley, D. (1995) *Geographies of Exclusion: Society and Difference in the West*. New York: Routledge.
Smith, D.M. (2000) *Moral Geographies: Ethics in a World of Difference*. Edinburgh: Edinburgh University Press.
Smith, S.J. (2005) 'States, markets and an ethic of care', *Political Geography*, 24: 1–20.
Staehli, L.A. (1996) 'Publicity, privacy, and women's political action', *Environment and Planning D: Society and Space*, 14: 601–19.
Staehli, L.A. (2003) 'Women and the work of community', *Environment and Planning A*, 35: 815–31.

Thien, D. (2005) 'After or beyond feeling? A consideration of affect and emotion in geography', *Area*, 37: 450–56.
Thrift, N. (2004) 'Intensities of feeling: towards a spatial politics of affect', *Geografiska Annaler,* 86B: 57–78.
Tolia-Kelly, D.P. (2006) 'Affect – an ethnocentric encounter? Exploring the "universalist" imperative of emotional/affectual geographies', *Area*, 38: 213–17.
Voyce, M. (2003) 'The privatization of public property: the development of a shopping mall in Sydney and its implications for governance through spatial practices', *Urban Policy and Research*, 21: 249–62.
Williams, C.C., Aldridge, T. and Tooke, J. (2003) 'Alternative exchange spaces', in A. Leyshon, R. Lee and C.C. Williams (eds), *Alternative Economic Spaces*. Thousand Oaks, CA: Sage. pp. 151–67.
Williams, R. (1993) 'Advertising: the magic system', in S. During (ed.), *The Cultural Studies Reader.* New York: Routledge. pp. 320–36.
Young, I.M. (2000) *Inclusion and Democracy*. New York: Oxford University Press.

11

The Limits to Value

David B. Clarke

For we cannot analyze the question 'Value for what?' too finely. (Friedrich Nietzsche, *On the Genealogy of Morals)*

INTRODUCTION

Whatever else it may be, and however it is defined, value is a kind of conceptual virus spread by modernity. Given that the term has currency not only with respect to political economy – use-value, exchange-value, surplus-value, the law of value, etc. – but also in terms of 'the great humanist criteria of value, the whole civilisation of moral, aesthetic and practical judgement' (Baudrillard, 1993a: 9), there is always a temptation to pitch alternative values against the hegemony of market value. The old adage about those who know the price of everything and the value of nothing, for example, appeals to a broader set of values than 'economic' value alone. Critiques resting on this basis generally aim to unmask the *auri sacra fames* instilled by capitalism (Weber, 1930), revealing the essential irrationality of economic rationality (put simply: chasing after money, one loses sight of everything else). Yet such critiques, which, satisfying themselves with proposing alternative (typically more 'human') values, contribute to a general mystique in which 'All categories give way to a kind of hypersyncretism, homeostasis and indistinction' (Baudrillard, 1998: 3; cf. Baudrillard, 1993b).

> The great Nietzschean idea of the transvaluation of all values has seen itself realized in precisely the opposite way: in the involution of all values. ... For the transmutation of values we have substituted the commutation of values, for their reciprocal transfiguration we substituted their indifference to one another and their confusion. Their transdevaluation, so to speak. The contemporary conjunction, in which all values are rehabilitated and indiscriminately permutated, is the worst there has been. (Baudrillard, 1998: 2)

Just as all forms of physical energy dissipate into that state of maximal entropy portentously referred to as 'thermic death', a kind of metaphysical entropy has led everything to dissipate into the value-form, and thence to the dissipation of value itself. Rather than seeking out alternative values, therefore, it is imperative that we interrogate the nature of value as such, not least in order to disclose that which value negates, disavows, excludes or precludes.

Value is, at base, a kind of spacing in which everything is organized into 'distinctly opposed terms between which a dialectic can then be established' (Baudrillard, 2003: 15).

Aesthetic value, for example, operates in terms of an opposition between the beautiful and the ugly; moral value in terms of the opposition of good and evil; and so on. Such oppositions appear symmetrical: there would be no beauty without ugliness, no ugliness without beauty; and so forth. But this symmetry is strictly illusory. Not only is it the positive term that defines the negative term (as lacking what it possesses). The opposition is itself a product of the positively charged term. It is the positive term that asserts and controls the distinction. In fact, all value systems discriminate in order to propose an equivalence. They amount to a kind of rational construct that 'postulates the possibility of balancing out value, of finding a general equivalent for it which is capable of exhausting meanings and accounting for an exchange' (Baudrillard, 2003: 9). Value accords to a logic of equivalence, ensuring that everything can be evaluated and implying the desirability of annihilating everything that is valued negatively. Yet insofar as all such systems face an internal limit, they are destined to resolve themselves in undecidability. 'There is a kind of reversible fatality for systems,' writes Baudrillard (1993a: 91), 'because the more they go towards universality, towards their total limits, there is a kind of reversal that they themselves produce, and that destroys their own objective.' For example: as everything becomes equally important, everything becomes equally unimportant. *When everything is privileged, nothing is.* Hence the general commutation of all values that sees erstwhile distinctions collapse in on themselves. One thinks of 'heroin chic' or the spectacle of terrorism, for example. 'All that lives by difference will perish by indifference. All that lives by value will perish by equivalence. All that lives by meaning will perish by insignificance' (Baudrillard, 1998: 4).

This understanding should help to explain the proclivity of poststructuralist thought for undecidability, ambivalence and reversibility; for ways of thinking that refute an axiomatic reliance on systems of equivalence. Take life and death, for instance: 'there is in our system of values no reversibility: what is positive is on the side of life, what is negative is on the side of death; death is the end of life, its opposite' (Baudrillard, 2003: 15). Yet death can hardly be annihilated by shifting everything to the positive side of the opposition. Indeed, 'the ultimate cause of death is birth; ... life is the only truly terminal disease' (Bauman, 1992: 1). Death resolutely defies the rationality enshrined in all systems of value. 'Death is the scandal of reason' (Bauman, 1992: 1). Hence the propensity of modern society to censor death; to keep it 'hidden beneath the difficulty of living' (Baudrillard, 1990: 67). Despite modernity's best efforts at a cover-up, however, the reversibility of life and death is not so easily effaced. 'In the symbolic universe, life and death are exchanged. And, since there are no separate terms but, rather, reversibility, the idea of value is cast into question' (Baudrillard, 2003: 15). As Mauss classically observed, other societies have related to death very differently to ours, societies in which the notion of value was also virtually unknown (Mauss, 1990; Hubert and Mauss, 1964; cf. Bataille, 1988). Why is it, therefore, that value has assumed such a crucial role in modern societies? It is this question that the present chapter aims to address, considering value as a particular *form* sustained by capitalism; as 'a definite social mode of existence of human activity' (Marx, 2000: I, 46; cf. Harvey, 1982). In addition to political economy, the chapter ranges over linguistics (where the notion of value as pure form was first worked out), morality, and so on. In all cases, however, emphasis is laid on the way in which value functions as a kind of *spacing*. If social geography has traditionally seen itself as the social conscience of human geography, the present chapter envisages it more as a means of excavating the geographical unconscious underlying the social.

In line with these intentions, the next section undertakes a re-examination of the theory of value in Marx and Saussure, as a means of considering whether value does inhere purely in its form or whether there is, in fact, a substance of value. This makes way, in a second section, for a retake, drawing on De Quincey's reading of Ricardo, which ultimately develops a subjectivist understanding of value. Finally, the concluding section revisits the question of what value leaves out of the picture, assessing how the principle of ambivalence works to undermine the logic of equivalence that sustains value. It is, of course, reasonable to ask what the consequences of such an investigation might be. Suffice it to say, for now, that it is the value of value that is in question – and that this question is constantly being played out in all manner of exchanges in the world, from the most banal of conversations to the most violent of geopolitical clashes. A better understanding of the nature of value should, at the very least, allow for a better appreciation of its manifold consequences.

VALUE *SUB SPECIE SPATII*

> What is the distance between the syllable A and a table? (Marx, 2000: III, 143)

Although it typically presents itself as an intrinsic property of an object – or a word, a sentiment, a sensation, an act, an idea, etc. – value is, in fact, always *relative* in form. Value is never fully present to itself. It emanates from a system of differences. This was first proposed in the sphere of linguistics by de Saussure, who envisaged linguistics as semiotics, the 'science of signs'. Saussure's project has distinct analogies with Marx's project of a scientific study of history, historical materialism (Baudrillard, 1981; Clarke and Doel, 2000). Both Marx and Saussure began from abstractions. This is perfectly clear in Saussure's case but is often misunderstood in the case of Marx, where the proposition is sometimes regarded as insufficiently materialist. In Saussure's case, the abstraction in question is *langue* – language *as such* (rather than any particular language, such as English, Mandarin or Yaaku). On Saussure's conception, *langue* is an abstract structure that precedes any particular linguistic utterance; the ground that allows any particular utterance (*parole*) to be made. As with a jigsaw puzzle, the existence of a particular piece 'does not precede the existence of the whole, it comes neither before nor after it, for the parts do not determine the pattern, but the pattern determines the parts' (Perec, 1988: 189). Likewise, Marx saw the commodity as proceeding from a structural system. If Marx famously begins his analysis with the commodity, eschewing conceptual notions like 'value' as an appropriate starting point, we should certainly not see 'the commodity as Marx's "concrete" starting point' (Fraser, 1998: 38). Indeed, in attending to the particular *form* things take on under capitalism, Marx necessarily appeals to a general abstraction: 'Wealth, the general abstraction, takes the "form" of the commodity' under capitalist conditions (Fraser 1998: 38). As Marx himself writes:

> I do not start out from 'concepts,' hence I do not start out from 'the concept of value,' and do not have 'to divide' this in any way. What I start out from is the simplest social form in which the labour-product is presented in contemporary society, and this is the 'commodity.' I analyse it, and right from the beginning, in the *form in which it appears.* (1976: 214)

If a focus on form is common to Saussure and Marx, the differences between them hinge on the nature of value. The remainder of this section explores these differences, beginning with Saussure's contention that value is purely formal, before moving on to consider Marx's dialectical formulation.

Saussure's central insight is pitched against the view that language simply conveniently names a pre-existing reality; that language is the mirror of nature. Such a view is contradicted by the fact that different languages apprehend the world in different ways; that no universal pattern maps linguistic units (signs) onto things (referents) in the same way across different cultures. Rejecting commonsensical assumptions, Saussure (1959: 111) sought 'To prove that language [*langue*] is only a system of pure values'. Explicating this conception, Saussure proposes that 'all values are apparently governed by the same paradoxical principle. They are always composed:

1 of a *dissimilar* thing that can be *exchanged* for the thing of which the value is to be determined; and
2 of *similar* things that can be *compared* with the thing of which the value is to be determined' (1959: 115).

Saussure exemplifies this with recourse to economics. 'To determine what a five-franc piece is worth one must therefore know: (1) that it can be exchanged for a fixed quantity of a different thing, e.g. bread; and (2) that it can be compared with a similar value of the same system, e.g. a one-franc piece, or with coins of another system (a dollar, etc.)'. Despite his economic analogy, the crucial insight this imparts can best be followed with respect to language itself. Spoken words, for example, amount to particular 'sound-images' shaped by the mouth. In reciprocal fashion, these shaped sounds serve as *signifiers* of some concept or other, something that is *signified* by the particular sound. This accords with the first component of value Saussure outlines: a *sound* exchanges for an *idea* (two dissimilar materials are thereby involved). It does not, however, exhaust the matter, as it would if language simply functioned like a mirror, reflecting the world by assigning names to its various components. Accordingly, Saussure highlights the decisive role of the second, comparative component: the meaning (value) of a particular word is not pre-determined by a world that it passively reflects but is determined *by its relation to other words* (similar in kind or cut from the same cloth). Hence, as Saussure famously argued, the terms of a language are 'purely differential and defined not by their positive content but negatively by their relations with the other terms of the system. Their most precise characteristic is in being what the others are not' (1959: 117). By distinguishing language as a structural system (*langue*) from any particular linguistic utterance (*parole*), Saussure demonstrates that words operate according to – they rely upon – their potentiality (value), rather than working by pointing to referents (things) 'out there' in the world.[1] The mere *existence* in English of the term 'snow' – a term that does not exist in the same way in all languages – precedes any particular *utterance* employing that term (e.g. 'Slow down! There's snow on the road!'). Whenever I attempt to make sense, I must do so on the terms the laws of language allow; in the terms the system of language provides. 'Sense here emerges as the effect of the structure's functioning, in the animation of its component series' (Deleuze, 2004: 187).

Let us now begin to track back from linguistics to economics, to consider Marx in the light of Saussure. Note, to begin with, that it is entirely possible for language to work on the basis of written rather than verbal signifiers, marks on the page rather than spoken words. Indeed, Derrida (1976) demonstrates that writing necessarily precedes speech, that the very condition of language is its 'graphematic' quality. Language as such inheres in its capacity to be inscribed. By the same token, not just any verbal sound may count as a linguistic utterance (likewise, not just any mark etched onto a surface). Saussure insists, in fact, that 'it is impossible for sound alone, a material element, to belong to language. It is only a secondary thing, substance to be put to use. All our conventional values have the characteristic of not being confused with the tangible element which supports them' (1959: 118). The same principle also applies in the economic sphere: 'it is not the metal in a piece of money that fixes its value. A coin nominally worth five francs may contain less than half its worth of silver. Its value will vary according to its use inside or outside a political boundary.' Superficially, Marx (1954) would seem to concur with Saussure, noting, for instance, that 'The value of commodities is the very opposite of the coarse materiality of their substance, not an atom of its matter enters into its composition' (1954: 54). Yet, whilst acquiescing to the relativity of the value-form (exchange-value), Marx insists that it necessarily expresses an underlying substance. Whereas Saussure makes the substance happened upon by language (vocal chords and airwaves; paper and ink; chalk and chalkboard) more or less an incidental matter,

> One cannot forget that on the question of the relation between content and form, Marx took the standpoint of Hegel and not of Kant. Kant treated form as something external in relation to the content, and as something which adheres to the content from the outside. From the standpoint of Hegel's philosophy, the content is not in itself something to which form adheres from the outside. Rather, through its development, the content itself gives birth to the form which is already latent in the content. Form necessarily grows from the content itself. (Rubin, 1973: 117)[2]

It is notable that Saussure's casual economic analogies – implying that signifier and signified stand in the same relation to one another as exchange-value and use-value – simply assume rather than explain the existence of a money-form. From Marx's standpoint, this is a naïve assumption carrying dire consequences.

Which is heavier: a ton of lead or a ton of feathers? This old schoolyard conundrum is designed to catch out those too dull-witted to abstract from use-value. Clearly, both lead and feathers are expressed in terms of a common standard, which is set to an equivalent value (one ton). 'In the same way the exchange-values of commodities must be capable of being expressed in terms of something common to them all, of which thing they represent a greater or less[er] quantity' (Marx, 1954: 45). Which is more valuable, £5 worth of chalk or £5 worth of cheese? In *Theories of Surplus Value*, with reference to Bailey's (1931) anti-Ricardian tract – *Critical Dissertation on the Nature, Measures, and Causes of Value* – Marx riles against the tendency for the existence of a common standard of monetary value to descend into tautology.[3] It is self-evident that £5 worth of chalk = £5 worth of cheese (a self-evidence Bailey never tires of repeating, says Marx): but what determines how much chalk or cheese one gets for one's money? For Marx, the situation differs fundamentally from the amount of lead or feathers one gets to the ton. Bailey's sole contribution to political economy, in Marx's eyes, lay in doing away with a search for an invariable standard of value.[4] To this extent, the parallel with weight holds good. Thus, a (metric) tonne of lead and a tonne of feathers would express the same *relative* proportions of lead and feathers as an imperial ton. What determines the proportions of lead and feathers constituting one ton (or one tonne) is a natural law: the law of gravity. But for Marx, *contra* Bailey, what determines the amount of chalk or cheese one might obtain for £5 is a social law, the law of value – an *unnatural* rather than a natural law (Pilling, 1986; Sekine, 1980). In this case, it is not a matter of value serving as an arbitrary standard set against an invariable nature. It is a question of the abstract social labour involved in producing chalk or cheese (or bricks or diamonds or whatever) under the prevailing social and technological conditions. Accordingly, 'If we could succeed, at a small expenditure of labour, in converting carbon into diamonds, their value might fall below that of bricks' (Marx, 1954: 48).

> In general, the greater the productiveness of labour, the less is the labour-time required for the production of an article, the less is the amount of labour crystallised in that article, and the less is its value; and *vice versâ*, the less the productiveness of labour, the greater is the labour-time required for the production of an article, and the greater its value. The value of a commodity, therefore, varies directly as the quantity, and inversely as the productiveness, of the labour incorporated in it. (Marx, 1954: 48)

In Cockshott and Cottrell's (2004: 233) pithy formulation, '*The law of value states that value, understood as the labour time socially necessary to produce a commodity, is conserved in the exchange of commodities.*'[5]

For Marx, then, the *substance* of value is 'a congelation of homogeneous human labour' (1954: 46). By insisting on the purely relative character of its phenomenal *form* – exchange-value – Marx holds that the likes of Bailey adopt a kind of tunnel vision that seriously misconstrues matters. The nub of Marx's concerns become readily apparent when cast in spatial terms. Marx (2000), cites Bailey (1931: 5) as follows:

> As we cannot speak of *the distance of any object without* implying some or other object, *between which and the former this relation exists*, so we cannot speak of the value of a commodity but in reference to *another commodity compared with it*. A thing cannot be valuable in itself without reference to another thing ([In parenthesis Marx interposes:] Is social labour, to which the value of a commodity is related, not another thing?) any more than a thing can be *distant in itself* without reference to another thing. (2000: III, 143)

Proceeding to unpack this argument, Marx notes that 'If a thing is distant from another, the distance is in fact a relation between the one thing and the other', but adds that it is, at the same time, 'something different from the relation between the two things. It is a dimension of space, it is a certain length which may as well express the distance of two other things besides the things compared' (2000: III, 143). Space appears here in absolute terms. The two objects set at a distance to one another are merely contained in space. Were one to substitute the first object for another, its distance from the second object would remain unchanged. Marx then complicates this conception by invoking a relative notion of space: the possibility of a distance between the objects depends on the nature of (i.e. is relative to) the objects involved. 'If we speak of the distance as a relation between two things, we presuppose something "intrinsic", some "property" of the things themselves, which enables them to be distant from each other. What is the distance between the syllable A and a table? The question would be nonsensical'. The former conception is thereby revealed as an abstraction of the latter, demonstrating that the space to which Bailey appeals functions merely as an analogue of the measure of value. 'In speaking of the distance between two things ... we suppose both of them to be contained in space, to be points of space. Thus we equalize them as being both existences of space, and only after having them equalized *sub specie spatii* [under the aspect of space – Ed.] we distinguish them as different points in space. To belong to space is their unity' (Marx, 2000: III, 143). 'In other words', says Ilyenkov (1977: 18), 'when we wish to establish a relation of some sort between two objects, we always compare not the "specific" objects that make one object "syllable A" and the other "a table" ... but only those properties that express a "third" something, different from their existence as the things enumerated'. The situation is precisely the same as that of equalizing lead and feathers with reference to an abstract unit of measurement ('one ton'). Likewise, a triangle and a parallelogram of equal area may be equated only by abstracting from their other properties. 'If geometry, like the political economy of Mr. Bailey, contented itself with saying that the equality of the triangle and the parallelogram means that the triangle is expressed in the parallelogram, and the parallelogram in the triangle, it would be of little value', thunders Marx (2000: III, 144).

For Marx, therefore, Bailey simply resolves matters into 'a question of equation' (Marx, 2000: III, 143). Indeed, as Doel (2006: 63) says, it is the fact 'that A = B must be squared with the fact that A *is not* B' that prompted Marx's 'quest to discover the *true identity* of an *apparent non-identity*', which he allegedly finds 'in the substance of labour imparted into and valorized though commodities'. For Doel, however, Marx 'fails to appreciate ... that the ambivalence of equivalence goes all the way down, and cannot be resolved by an appeal to the substance of labour'. Even Saussure's insistence that value contains a purely differential component *and* a functional component falls foul of this misidentification. For whilst Saussure's distinction between *langue* and *parole* overcomes the problem articulated by Ilyenkov (1977: 18) – 'In what are such objects as "concept" ("idea") and "thing" related? In what special "space" can they be contrasted, compared and differentiated? Is there, in general, a "third" thing in which they are "one and the same"?' – Saussure nonetheless preserves the *shadow* of the referent in the notion of the signified. As Derrida (1982: 11) incisively notes, 'the signified concept is never present in and of itself, in a sufficient presence that would refer only to itself. ... [It] is thus no longer simply a concept, but rather the possibility of conceptuality.' What Saussure fails to recognize, in other words, is that 'It is in the "materiality" of content that form consumes its abstraction and reproduces itself as form' (Baudrillard, 1981: 145). Ironically, Marx and Saussure represent uneasy bedfellows in this regard, as one final illustration from Marx's attack on Bailey will illustrate. Marx first paraphrases, then cites, then criticizes/satirizes Bailey, thus:

> Value is nothing intrinsic and absolute ... (op. cit., p. 23).[6]
>
> 'It is impossible to *d e s i g n a t e*, or *e x p r e s s the value* of a commodity, except by *a quantity of some other commodity*' (op. cit., p. 26)
>
> (As impossible as it is to '*designate*' or '*express*' a thought except by a quantity of syllables. Hence Bailey concludes that a thought is – syllables.) (2000: III, 146)

For Saussure, however much the signifier is the determinant of the value of the sign – however much our capacity to think in certain terms is determined by the nature of the terms available in which to think – thought still involves an exchange of dissimilar substances: it is not simply a matter of moving syllables around the page. On this score, Marx and Saussure are in accord. Perhaps surprisingly, since it contradicts some famous statements to the contrary, what this means is that both are ultimately happy to fall back on a conception of the subject as constitutive rather than constituted: as the author of its own destiny (cf. Henderson, 2004, for a careful reading of Marx and an imaginative retheorization of this theme). In stark contrast to this view, however, is the radical conception that 'it is language which speaks, not the author' (Barthes, 1977: 143). Barthes's point amounts to a recognition that the subject is itself constituted through language; that the subject, which imagines itself to be fully present to itself, is an *effect* of language, not an origin. The position offered by language for the 'I' does not, and cannot, represent the presence of a subject that precedes it, but is involved in the constitution of the subject as a presence, even to the extent that it allows the subject to imagine itself as fully present, as the author of its own destiny. The danger of failing to recognize that this is an imaginary position, an instance of profound misrecognition or misidentification, is clearly brought out in the economic rhetoric of consumer sovereignty; in the ideology of personal preferences and consumer choice (Clarke, 2003).

Accordingly, the next section examines the circumstances that led to the eventual abandonment of the labour theory of value as the centrepiece of political economy, and the ascendancy of a subjectivist conception of value, which ultimately paved the way for the marginalist revolution in economic theory (Bharadwaj, 1978; Black et al., 1973). The marginalist revolution arose independently in several domains, but its principal significance lies in the importance it attached to the valuations of the individual subject. Indeed, such a conception ultimately entails that values cannot but refer back to the personal preferences of the subject. This effectively neutralizes or delegitimizes any appeal to social values, which are no longer recognizable as anything other than one preference amongst many. Removing the grounds on which such appeals might declare themselves as privileged, a subjectivist conception of value manages to disarm without disqualifying social critique, recasting the social as merely a matter of individual choice (cf. Bauman, 2001).

SATISFACTION AND ITS DISCONTENTS

> What determined the length of the race-course? (De Quincey, 1890: 35)

Is something desirable because it is valuable or valuable because it is desirable? Despite representing an epiphenomenal concern for classical political economy, this is a question with a long and venerable history, and one that was always poised to resurface given the right cultural climate. Its centrality to a radically individualized society (such as a consumer society) is not in doubt, but the particular inflexion it has received from its prolonged gestation has been sorely neglected. The central role of De Quincey is highlighted in this section, but the issue initially deserves to be cast in broader terms. For Aristotle (*Metaphysics*, 1072a29), the issue had seemed clear cut: 'We desire the object because it seems good to us, rather than the object's seeming good to us because we desire it'. However, Spinoza (1949: 136–7 [*Ethics* III, 9, scholium]) reversed the proposition: 'we neither strive for, wish, seek nor desire anything because we think it to be good, but on the contrary, we adjudge a thing good because we strive for, wish, seek or desire it'. As Wiggins (1998: 106) notes, 'Spinoza appears to have taken [Aristotle's] sentence … and deliberately negated it'. Yet Spinoza's intention, as Delahunty (1985: 227) surmises, was probably to counter 'Descartes' [1989] claim … that desire originates from the judgements of good and evil, and is inherently prospective in character (*Passions*, art. 57)':

> In seeking to deny this, Spinoza may be making a point about the causality of human action: we are not determined *a fronte*, by future goods or ills which we first see and then try to realise or avert. … Rather, we are determined *a tergo*, by desires which were themselves mechanically caused by antecedent factors, and which comprise the mechanical causes of what we do. (Delahunty, 1985: 227)

Despite appearing to stand Aristotle on his head, therefore, Spinoza 'emphatically does not believe that one can read off the goodness of a thing from the fact that it is desired, and allows that there is a standpoint from which we may judge our desires to be directed to bad and harmful objects' (Delahunty, 1985: 228–9). It is, in fact, to Kant that the idea that value is conferred on objects because they are desired is to be attributed. Whilst this standpoint finds strong advocates in contemporary Kantians such as Korsgaard (1996: 121) – 'the things that you want are good because you want them – rather than your wanting them because they are good' – it is a position with many detractors, even within the tradition of analytic philosophy. Baz (2005: 107), for instance, notes that if it seems obvious that 'there wouldn't be values, or things of value, in a world in which there were no human beings, it is wrong to argue from *this* that we *confer*, or project, value onto things, just as it is wrong to argue from the premise that our color experience depends upon our particular sensuous constitution to the claim that we confer color on things.'[7] Nonetheless, it was an essentially Kantian view that came to be enshrined within economic theory, primarily through the political-economic writings of De Quincey. If Marx's understanding of value refracted Ricardo's political economy through a Hegelian lens, De Quincey's value theory projected Ricardo through Kant.[8]

If at first blush it seems unexpected, on reflection it is unsurprising that De Quincey, a representative of English Romanticism, should have made the seminal contribution to economic thought that he did. Romanticism was ostensibly engaged in a bitter rearguard action against the economization of modern life (Connell, 2001). However, it reproduced precisely that notion of the isolated individual that Marx (1973: 83) pilloried as belonging to 'the eighteenth-century Robinsonades'. As with Defoe's *Robinson Crusoe*, the 'isolated hunter or fisherman, with whom Smith and Ricardo began' (Marx, 1973: 83), bears more than a passing resemblance to the bourgeois subject, *chez soi* in a society of free competition rather than a rude state of nature. Romanticism similarly set the autonomous subject centre stage, in union with nature but isolated from social determination (cf. Clarke, 2007). This Romantic subjectivity was bound to toe the Kantian line: value is conferred on objects because they are desired by the subject. De Quincey's role as the originator of the first truly subjectivist theory of value has, however, long been obscured by his reputation as a 'logic-chopping Ricardian' (Groenewegen, 1982: 51). De Quincey's Ricardian credentials are, in fact, far more contentious than first meets the eye. It is certainly true that De Quincey's admiration for Ricardo knew no bounds. Of the man of whom Lord Brougham declared, 'Mr. Ricardo seemed as if he had dropped from another planet' (cited in Marx, 1970: 20), De Quincey declaimed, with similar rhetorical aplomb:

> Could it be that an Englishman, and he not in academic bowers, but oppressed by mercantile and senatorial cares, had accomplished what all the Universities of Europe, and a century of thought, had failed even to advance by one hair's breadth? All other writers had been crushed and overlaid by the enormous weight of facts and documents; Mr. Ricardo had deduced, *à priori*, from the understanding itself, laws which first gave a ray of light into the unwieldy chaos of materials, and had constructed what had been but a collection of tentative discussions into a science of regular proportions, standing on an eternal basis. (1986: 100)

De Quincey (1986, 101) even credited Ricardo's work with awakening him from 'the Circean spells of opium'. Yet, despite regarding Ricardo as the man who granted economics an 'eternal basis', the successive refinements De Quincey was to apply to Ricardo's theory of value succeeded in supplanting it almost in its entirety. Referring to his initial encounter with Ricardo's (1929) *magnum opus*, De Quincey claimed that he had prophetically anticipated the arrival of his like: 'I said before finishing the first chapter, "Thou art the man!"' (1986: 100). The allusion, as Rzepka (1995: 281) notes, is to John the Baptist (John I: 29–39). If De Quincey saw himself as a fervent disciple of Ricardo, however, he was surely an inconstant disciple.

De Quincey's earliest political-economic writings certainly defend Ricardo against his detractors, seeking to explicate the logical rigour of Ricardo's argument. Marx almost admiringly identified De Quincey's (1890b) first major political-economic work, *Dialogues of Three Templars on Political Economy*, as an 'attempt at a refutation of all the attacks made on Ricardo', in which 'the inadequacies of the Ricardian view are often pointedly set forth', astutely noting that De Quincey 'does not seek to mitigate them by re-interpretation or to abandon the essential features of the problems in actual fact while retaining them in a purely formal, verbal way' (Marx, 2000: III, 123–4). Yet, without departing from his established procedure, De Quincey's second (and last) major political-economic treatise (1890c) – *The Logic of Political Economy* – did far more than merely 'mitigate' the Ricardian system. The argument it developed dealt the crucial blow that ultimately led to the abandonment of the labour theory of value and the subsequent transformation of economic thought. With the benefit of hindsight, De Quincey's (1890a) critical comments on Malthus, which figure amongst his earliest forays into political economy, reveal how early the seeds of De Quincey's divergence from Ricardo were set, even as he sought to come to Ricardo's defence.

Since Malthus had proved to be one of Ricardo's strongest critics, De Quincey endeavoured to set the record straight. De Quincey (1890a: 35) notes that Malthus, in a pamphlet of 1823, corrects his own earlier misapprehensions over the measure of value, 'and (finally, let us hope) settles it to his own satisfaction that the true measure is labour'. Yet Malthus still refused to accept Ricardo's adjudication to De Quincey's complete satisfaction. Having initially argued, *contra* Ricardo, that the true measure of value was the mean between corn and labour costs (Malthus, 2005), Malthus's belated willingness to accept labour as the sole determinant of value involved, as far as De Quincey was concerned, a further 'logical blunder'. Specifically, Malthus appealed 'not [to] the quantity of labour … which will produce X, but the quantity which X will command'.

> The question is What is the measure of value? I say … that the phrase 'measure of value' is an equivocal phrase, and, in Mr. Malthus's use of it, means indifferently that which determines value in relation to the *principium essendi* and that which determines value in relation to the *principium cognoscendi*. … I must and will express scholastic notions by scholastic phrases; but … I am then ready to descend into the arena with no other weapons than plain English can furnish. Let us therefore translate *measure of value* into *that which determines value*; and, in this shape, we shall detect the ambiguity of which I complain. For I say that the word *determines* may be taken

subjectively for what determines X in relation to our knowledge, or objectively, for what determines X in relation to itself. (De Quincey, 1890a: 35)

To make himself clearer, and displaying his penchant for vivid exemplification, De Quincey follows up with an analogous question:

> [I]f I were to ask 'What determined the length of the race-course?' and the answer were 'The convenience of the spectators, who could not have seen the horses at a greater distance' … then it is plain that by the word 'determined' I was understood to mean 'determined objectively,' *i.e.* in relation to the existence of the object; in other words, what *caused* the race-course to be this length rather than another length. But, if the answer were, 'An actual admeasurement,' it would then be plain that by the word 'determined' I had been understood to mean 'determined subjectively,' *i.e.* in relation to our knowledge, – what ascertained it? Now, in the objective sense of the phrase 'determiner of value,' the measure of value will mean *the ground of value*: in the subjective sense it will mean *the criterion of value*. (1890a: 35–6)

De Quincey is now equipped to point up the difference between Malthus's (revised) position and Ricardo's – and the inconsistency of Malthus's stance:

> [Malthus's] *labour which X commands* is opposed to Mr. Ricardo's *quantity of labour which will produce X*. Call the first A, the last B. Now, in making B the determiner of value, Mr. Ricardo means that B is the ground of value: *i.e.* that B is the answer to the question What makes this hat of more value than this pair of shoes? But, if Mr. Malthus means by A the same thing, then by his own confession he has used the term *the measure of value* in two senses: on the other hand, if he does not mean the same thing, but simply the *criterion of value*, then he has not used the word in any sense which opposes him to Mr. Ricardo. … On either ground, therefore, he is guilty of a logical error; which implies that, so far from answering his own question, he did not know what his own question was. (1890a: 36)

Whilst there is nothing but a staunch defence of Ricardo here, De Quincey's acute awareness of the subjective and objective determinants of value discloses, in latent form, what will later transmute into a vital distinction.

As the example above reveals, terminological precision is, for De Quincey, a necessary condition of logical consistency. Yet De Quincey's understanding of language maintains that there is always more at stake than mere semantics. As Heinzelman (1980: 90) avers, 'De Quincey's contention … deftly summarizes what we will hear as the battle cry of Blake, the premise of Wordsworth' – as the following passage makes clear.

> 'A mere dispute about words' is a phrase which we hear daily; and why? … [I]t is scarcely possible that a dispute on words should arise which would not also be a dispute about ideas (*i.e.* about realities). … [S]uch a plea [i.e. dismissing a dispute as merely semantic] … seeks to escape from the effort of mind necessary for the comprehending and solving of any difficulty under the colourable pretext that it is a question about shadows, and not about substances, and one therefore which it is creditable to a man's good sense to decline: a pleasant sophism this, which at the same time flatters a man's indolence and his vanity! … You fancy that between the expressions '*quantity* of producing labour' and '*value* of producing labour' there is none but a verbal difference. It follows, therefore, that the same effect ought to take place whether the value of the producing labour be altered or its quantity. (De Quincey, 1890b: 57–8)

Such an effect clearly does not take place, as De Quincey proceeds to demonstrate in painstaking detail. The different distributional consequences of changes in either the quantity or the value of labour are set out in true Ricardian fashion: 'It is Mr. Ricardo's doctrine that no variation in either profits or wages can ever affect price; if wages rise or fall, the only consequence is that profits must fall or rise by the same sum; so again, if profits rise or fall, wages must fall or rise accordingly' (1890b: 60). De Quincey's adherence to this doctrine was, however, to give way in the *Logic*, where the subjective determination of value would be recast to particularly dramatic effect. This was, in part, a reaction to the politicization of Ricardo by various post-Ricardian leftist factions of whom De Quincey wholeheartedly disapproved. However, another 'reason for this shift in the treatment of value is undoubtedly De Quincey's appreciation … of Bailey (1825), whose exposition of the causes of value seems to have exerted considerable influence on De Quincey's elaboration of this subject in the *Logic*' (Groenewegen, 1982: 54). What Groenewegen omits to mention is that Bailey first determined to undermine Ricardo's theory of value after reading De Quincey's *Dialogues* (Sackville West, 1936: 316).

The innovation that De Quincey introduces in the *Logic* is seemingly innocently framed as a comprehensive extension of Ricardo's conception of value. In the *Dialogues*, as Heinzelman (1980: 89) records, 'De Quincey noted that Ricardo had not invented new words but had hypostasized normal semantics, forcing a customarily ambivalent word such as 'value' to have one and only one economic signification'. Specifically, Ricardo had firmly distinguished between wealth ('riches') and value: 'Value ... essentially differs from riches, for value depends not on abundance, but on the difficulty or facility of production. ... Many of the errors in political economy have arisen from errors on this subject, from considering an increase in riches, and an increase in value, as meaning the same thing' (1929: 182–3). Hence, as De Quincey declares, 'Mr. Ricardo sternly insists on the *true* sense of the word Value, and (what is still more unusual to most men) insists on using it but in *one* sense' (1890b: 49). In the *Logic*, De Quincey undermines Ricardo's studious hypostasization by introducing further subdivisions into the overall schema of value.

> De Quincey divides value into two elements, value in use and value in exchange, the former being a regulative idea (like pure geometry) and the latter constitutive (the terms are derived from Kant, De Quincey's philosopher hero). Value in use he assimilates to wealth. Value in exchange, the key, is founded upon the capacity to meet a 'natural desire' and on 'difficulty of attainment' which is intended to imply costs of production. (Henderson, 1995: 104)

By distinguishing between these two components of exchange-value – 'Intrinsic utility' (U) and 'Difficulty of attainment' (D) – De Quincey effectively effaces the distinction between the subjective and objective determinants of value that he had earlier sought to maintain. In a vivid illustration, designed to indicate the different contributions of U and D to the determination of exchange-value under varying conditions, De Quincey asks the reader to assume that a 'powerful musical snuff-box' is offered for sale, in circumstances where this is the one and only chance of obtaining such an item:

> You are on Lake Superior in a steamboat, making your way to an unsettled region 800 miles ahead of civilization, and consciously with no chance at all of purchasing any luxury whatsoever ... for a space of ten years to come. ... [K]nowing from experience the power of such a toy over your own feelings, the magic with which at times it lulls your agitations of mind, you are vehemently desirous to purchase it. ... But the owner, aware of your situation not less than yourself, is determined to operate by a strain pushed to the very uttermost upon U, upon the intrinsic worth of the article in your individual estimate for your individual purposes. He will not hear of D as any controlling power or mitigating agency in the case; and, finally, although at six guineas a piece in London or Paris you might have loaded a waggon with such boxes, you pay sixty rather than lose it when the last knell of the clock has sounded which summons you to buy now or to forfeit for ever. (1890c: 138)

In this scenario, says De Quincey, 'The inertness of D allowed U to put forth its total effect. The practical compression of D being withdrawn, U springs up like water in a pump when released from the pressure of air' (1890c: 139). Costs of production are crowded out by individual desire. Unsurprisingly, Henderson (1995) sees in this example a thinly veiled translation of De Quincey's experience of opium addiction. Yet De Quincey' musical snuff-box is more powerful still – allowing him to conjure a sense of the subject as free agent from a situation in which, to all intents and purposes, the subject is given no choice whatsoever. De Quincey thus manages to position the subject as both the origin and the final arbiter of value.

De Quincey's treatment of Ricardo, refracted through Kant, was bound to resolve itself in this manner. But De Quincey's account of the subjective determination of exchange-value did not simply prefigure the future direction of economic thought. It directly influenced it. As Schumpeter notes, 'Leaning heavily on De Quincey's exposition ... [John Stuart] Mill accepted Utility and Difficulty of Attainment as conditions of exchange value.

But the energy with which he insisted on the relative character of the latter completely *annihilated* Ricardo's Real Value' (1959: 603). Granting Mill's and Edgeworth's roles as intermediaries, there is a direct line from De Quincey's *Logic* to Marshall's fully formalized supply-and-demand analysis.[9] *Contra* Aristotle and Spinoza, and entirely in line with Kant, economic discourse was, by this point, firm in its conclusion that value is *wholly and purely a subjective matter*: that desire determines value – with all the corollaries this entails. For example, on the basis that 'there's no accounting for taste' (Stigler and Becker, 1977), even the most dangerous addictions become merely a matter of choice: 'one man's [*sic*] meat is another man's poison' (Becker and Murphy, 1988). The situation in which value becomes a matter of choice translates into a situation in which, to borrow Giddens's (1994, 75) pithy phrase, 'we have no choice but to choose'. This paradox arises on the back of a conception of a fully self-conscious subject; a conception that first arose, and could only have arisen, 'in the wake of the socio-political establishment of the individual as the sole lawful owner of everything pertaining to his social identity' (Bauman, 1978: 9). That value should become the personal property of the subject is merely the logical extension of this conception. Yet De Quincey's particular role in all of this is subject to a final irony. As the author of the *Confessions*, De Quincey has often been painted as a kind of Freudian *avant la lettre*, his experience of opium making him acutely aware of the alien presence of the unconscious. Psychoanalysis has since demonstrated the pleasures of misrecognizing identity and presence. For Lacan (1979: 31), desire crosses 'the threshold imposed by the pleasure principle'. Little wonder, therefore, that De Quincey's political economy should have sought to constrain the unruly forces of desire firmly within the boundaries of the self. To this extent, De Quincey's case captures in microcosm the stratagem of value *per se*.

WORLDLY VALUES

ALL DISSENT MUST BE OF A HIGHER LOGICAL TYPE THAN THAT WITH WHICH IT IS IN CONFLICT. (Wilden, 1980: lvii)

Value is the crystallization of a general system that attempts to posit an equivalent or referent against which exchange might take place. It represents a commitment to accounting for the world in its entirety, to establishing a final resolution to the enigma of the world. 'The fact is that exchange ... grounds our morality, as does the idea that everything can be exchanged, that the only thing that exists is what can assume value' (Baudrillard, 2003: 73). Insofar as value is predicated on the resolution of opposed terms, however, it can only ever feign its status as a self-sufficient principle. By forcing that which cannot be exchanged to disappear, all systems of value are destined to see their ambition humiliated, for as they approach their own limit they become subject to a fatal reversibility. Take, for example, positing death as the end of life, as its opposite, which ensures that death is destined to haunt life. As Bauman puts it, 'Fighting death is meaningless. But fighting the causes of dying turns into the meaning of life' (1992: 7). In order to make something appear, something else must be made to disappear. Yet, unlike death, disappearance cannot be seen as a finality. Whatever is forced to disappear is not gone for good, it 'becomes an event in a cycle that may bring it back many times' (Baudrillard, 1990: 92). Appearance and disappearance are characterized by cyclical reversibility, in contrast to the finality proposed by linear time. Thus, the fundamental ambivalence of equivalence asserts itself in the superior principle of reversibility.

It is understandable that modernity should have witnessed the proliferation and ramification of means of accounting for a world that has itself been riven by division and separation. Yet such a process is self-propelling and self-defeating at one and the same time.[10] Far from overcoming the world's ambivalence, it ultimately plunges us into a kind of radical undecidability. By pinning everything on value, we force ourselves up against the limit that defines an impossible exchange. 'At some point our moral law of exchange no longer operates' and the 'reconciliation of something with its value – with the referent which gives it a meaning – can no longer be effected' (Baudrillard, 2003: 75–6). This applies to all systems. 'Everything is taking us into a world steeped in definitive uncertainty' (Baudrillard, 2003: 76). The upshot is that it is necessary to have done with value, rather than to engage in the search for more just, pleasing, and equalitarian values. This should not, however, be taken as a statement of nihilism, a situation without hope. There is, to paraphrase Easthope (1990), a kind of negative theology involved in assuming that the absence of value would necessarily be of the same nature as its former presence. Having examined the nature and consequences of value, the task that remains is to begin to envisage a world without values. It is against the principle of value that the principle of ambivalence must be redeemed.

ACKNOWLEDGEMENTS

I am grateful to Susan Smith, Roger Lee, Marcus Doel, Pyrs Gruffudd, Keith Halfacree, Nicola Piper, Kevin Rees and Richard Smith for their invaluable comments on an earlier version of this chapter.

NOTES

1 As a system of relative values, language has no difficulty in operating with words that have no referent, such as 'if', 'but', and the names of mythical entities like 'dragon', 'axion', or 'God'.

2 For differing views of the extent of Hegel's influence on Marx, see Althusser and Balibar (1970) and, especially, Coletti (1973).

3 On Bailey, see Rauner (1961).

4 'Ricardo, hankering after an "invariable standard" like weight or length, was pursuing a Will O' the Wisp', notes Robinson (1980: xiv).

5 'The advantages of this definition are that it is cast in the normal form of a scientific law, it is empirically testable, it has a precise meaning, and it emphasizes the fundamental Marxian proposition that value cannot arise in circulation' (Cockshott and Cottrell, 2004: 233). These authors develop a notion of 'commodity-bundle space' as a means of approaching the proportionality of abstract social labour and exchange-value.

6 'Marx here sums up Bailey's argument in his own words', notes the editor of *Theories of Surplus Values* (Marx, 2000: III, 146).

7 Cf. Wiggins (1998); McDowell (1998).

8 It is telling that De Quincey (1986) reports that he first set out his ideas on Ricardo in an unpublished work entitled *Prolegomenon to All Future Systems of Political Economy.*

9 Harvey (1981: 11, n. 24) notes that Marshall (1949: viii) cites von Thünen's work on the 'frontier wage' (see Dempsey, 1960) as the basis of his marginal productivity theory. Yet, as Harvey adds, Whitaker (1975: 248–9) casts doubt on Marshall's statement that his 'obligations to Thünen are greater than to any other writer excepting only Adam Smith and Ricardo'. Marginalism clearly had numerous sources but De Quincey's influence is surely amongst the most significant.

10 This is obliquely revealed in attempts to formulate 'axiology', a science capable of dealing with the 'fact of values' (Urban, 1909; Hartmann, 1967).

REFERENCES

Althusser, L. and Balibar, E. (1970) [1968] *Reading Capital* (trans. B. Brewster). London: Verso.

Bailey, S. (1931) [1825] *Critical Dissertation on the Nature, Measures, and Causes of Value; chiefly in Reference to the Writings of Mr. Ricardo and his Followers.* Reprints of Scarce Tracts in Economics and Political Science 7. London: London School of Economics and Political Science.

Barthes, R. (1977) [1967] 'The death of the author', in *Image–Music–Text* (trans. S. Heath). London: Fontana. pp. 142–48.

Bataille, G. (1988) [1967] *The Accursed Share: An Essay on General Economy. Volume I: Consumption* (trans. R. Hurley). New York: Zone Books.

Baudrillard, J. (1981) [1972] *For a Critique of the Political Economy of the Sign* (trans. C. Levin). St. Louis: Telos.

Baudrillard, J. (1990) [1987] *Cool Memories*. London: Verso.
Baudrillard, J. (1993a) [1976] *Symbolic Exchange and Death* (trans. I. Hamilton Grant). London: Sage.
Baudrillard, J. (1993b) [1990] 'Transeconomics', in *The Transparency of Evil: Essays on Extreme Phenomena* (trans. J. Benedict). London: Verso. pp. 26–35.
Baudrillard, J. (1998) [1997] 'The destiny of value', in *Paroxysm: Interviews with Philippe Petit* (trans. C. Turner). London: Verso. pp. 1–4.
Baudrillard, J. (2003) [2000] *Passwords* (trans. C. Turner). London: Verso.
Bauman, Z. (1978) *Hermeneutics and Social Science: Approaches to Understanding*. London: Hutchinson.
Bauman, Z. (1992) 'Survival as a social construct' in M. Featherstone (ed.), *Cultural Theory and Cultural Change*. London: Sage. pp. 1–36.
Bauman, Z. (2001) *The Individualized Society*. Cambridge: Polity Press.
Baz, A. (2005) 'Moral justification and the idea of an ethical position', *Philosophy*, 80: 101–23.
Becker, G.S. and Murphy, K.M. (1988) 'A theory of rational addiction', *Journal of Political Economy*, 96 (4): 675–700.
Bharadwaj, K. (1978) *Classical Political Economy and the Rise to Dominance of Supply and Demand Theories*. Calcutta: Orient Longmans.
Black, R.D.C., Coats, A.W. and Goodwin, C. (eds) (1973) *The Marginal Revolution in Economics: Interpretation and Evaluation*. Durham: Duke University Press.
Clarke, D.B. (2003) *The Consumer Society and the Postmodern City*. London: Routledge.
Clarke, D.B. (2007) '*The City of the Future* revisited or, the lost world of Patrick Keiller', *Transactions of the Institute of British Geographers*, 32 (1): 29–45.
Clarke, D.B. and Doel, M.A. (2000) 'Cultivating ambivalence: the unhinging of culture and economy' in I. Cook, D. Crouch, S. Naylor and J.R. Ryan (eds), *Cultural Turns/Geographical Turns: Perspectives on Cultural Geography*. Harlow: Pearson. pp. 214–33.
Cockshott, W.P. and Cottrell, A.F. (2004) 'Value's law, value's metric', in A. Freeman, A. Kliman and J. Wells (eds), *The New Value Controversy and the Foundations of Economics*. Cheltenham: Edward Elgar. pp. 233–40.
Coletti, L. (1973) [1969] *Marxism and Hegel* (trans. L. Gardner). London: New Left Books.
Connell, P. (2001) *Romanticism, Economics and the Question of 'Culture'*. Cambridge: Cambridge University Press.
Delahunty, R.J. (1985) *Spinoza*. London: Routledge and Kegan Paul.
Deleuze, G. (2004) [2002] *Desert Islands and Other Texts, 1953–1974*. Los Angeles: Semiotext(e).
Dempsey, B.W. (1960) *The Frontier Wage: The Economic Organization of Free Agents*. Chicago: Loyola University Press.
De Quincey, T. (1890a) [1823] 'Malthus on the measure of value', in D. Masson (ed.), *The Collected Writings of Thomas De Quincey* (Volume IX, Political Economy and Politics). Edinburgh: Adam and Charles Black. pp. 32–6.
De Quincey, T. (1890b) [1824] 'Dialogues of three Templars on political economy', in D. Masson (ed.) *The Collected Writings of Thomas De Quincey* (Volume IX, Political Economy and Politics). Edinburgh: Adam and Charles Black. pp. 37–112.
De Quincey, T. (1890c) [1844] 'The logic of political economy', in D. Masson (ed.) *The Collected Writings of Thomas De Quincey* (Volume IX, Political Economy and Politics). Edinburgh: Adam and Charles Black. pp. 118–294.
De Quincey, T. (1986) [1821] *Confessions of an English Opium Eater*. London: Penguin.
Derrida, J. (1976) [1967] *Of Grammatology* (trans. G. Spivak). London: Johns Hopkins University Press.
Derrida, J. (1982) [1972] *Margins of Philosophy* (trans. A. Bass). Brighton: Harvester Wheatsheaf.
Descartes, R. (1989) [1649] *The Passions of the Soul* (trans. S.H. Voss). Indianapolis: Hackett.
Doel, M.A. (2006) 'Dialectical materialism: stranger than friction', in N. Castree and D. Gregory (eds), *David Harvey: A Critical Reader*. Oxford: Blackwell. pp. 55–79.
Easthope, A. (1990) 'The question of literary value', *Textual Practice*, 4 (3): 376–89.

Fraser, I. (1998) *Hegel and Marx: The Concept of Need*. Edinburgh: Edinburgh University Press.

Giddens, A. (1994) 'Living in a post-traditional society', in U. Beck, A. Giddens and S. Lash (eds), *Reflexive Modernization: Politics, Tradition and Aesthetics in the Modern Social Order*. Cambridge: Polity Press. pp. 56–109.

Groenewegen, P. (1982) 'Thomas De Quincey: faithful disciple of Ricardo?', *Contributions to Political Economy*, 1: 51–58.

Hartmann, R. (1967) *The Structure of Value: The Foundations of Scientific Axiology*. London: Feffer and Simons.

Harvey, D. (1981) 'The spatial fix: Hegel, von Thünen and Marx', *Antipode*, 13 (3): 1–12.

Harvey, D. (1982) *The Limits to Capital*. Oxford: Blackwell.

Heinzelman, K. (1980) *The Economics of the Imagination*. Amherst: University of Massachusetts Press.

Henderson, G. (2004) 'Value: the many-headed hydra', *Antipode*, 36 (5): 1002–05.

Henderson, W. (1995) *Economics as Literature*. London: Routledge.

Hubert, H. and Mauss, M. (1964) [1898] *Sacrifice: Its Nature and Function* (trans. W.D. Halls). London: Cohen and West.

Ilyenkov, E.V. (1977) [1974] *Dialectical Logic: Essays on Its History and Theory* (trans. H.C. Creighton). Moscow: Progress.

Korsgaard, C. (1996) *Creating the Kingdom of Ends*. Cambridge: Cambridge University Press.

Lacan, J. (1979) [1964] *The Four Fundamental Concepts of Psycho-analysis* (trans. A. Sheridan). Harmondsworth: Penguin.

McDowell, J. (1998) *Mind, Value, and Reality*. Cambridge, MA: Harvard University Press.

Malthus, T.R. (2005) [1820] *Principles of Political Economy: Considered with a View to Their Practical Application*. Boston: Elibron Classics.

Marshall, A. (1949) [1890] *Principles of Economics: An Introductory Volume*. London: Macmillan.

Marx, K. (1954) [1887] *Capital: A Critique of Political Economy*, Volume 1 (trans. S. Moore and L. Aveling). London: Lawrence and Wishart.

Marx, K. (1970) [1859] *A Contribution to the Critique of Political Economy* (trans. S.W. Ryazanskaya; ed. M. Dobb). New York: International Publishers.

Marx, K. (1973) [1857–8] *Grundrisse: Foundations of the Critique of Political Economy* (trans. M. Nicolaus). Harmondsworth: Penguin.

Marx, K. (1976) [1879] 'Notes on Adolph Wagner', in A. Dragstedt (ed.), *Value: Studies by Marx*. London: New Park Publications.

Marx, K. (2000) [1861–3] *Theories of Surplus Value*, Books I, II and III. New York: Prometheus.

Mauss, M. (1990) [1923–4] *The Gift: The Form and Reason for Exchange in Archaic Societies*. London: Routledge.

Perec, G. (1988) [1978] *Life: A User's Manual* (trans. D. Bellos). London: Harvill.

Pilling, G. (1986) 'The law of value in Ricardo and Marx', in B. Fine (ed.), *The Value Dimension: Marx versus Ricardo and Sraffa*. London: Routledge and Kegan Paul. pp. 18–44.

Rauner, R.M. (1961) *Samuel Bailey and the Classical Theory of Value*. London: Bell and Sons.

Ricardo, D. (1929) [1817] *The Principles of Political Economy and Taxation*. London: J.M. Dent.

Robinson, J. (1980) 'Introduction', in V. Walsh and H.Gram, *Classical and Neoclassical Theories of General Equilibrium: Historical Origins and Mathematical Structure*. Oxford: Oxford University Press. pp. xi–xvi.

Rubin, I. (1973) [1928] *Essays on Marx's Theory of Value* (trans. M. Samardzija and F. Perlman). Montreal: Black Rose.

Rzepka, C.J. (1995) *Sacramental Commodities: Gift, Text and the Sublime in De Quincey*. Amherst: University of Massachusetts Press.

Sackville West, E. (1936) *A Flame in Sunlight: Thomas De Quincey*. London: Cassell.

Saussure, F. de (1959) [1916] *Course in General Linguistics* (trans. W. Baskin). London: Peter Owen.

Schumpeter, J.A. (1959) *History of Economic Analysis*. Oxford: Oxford University Press.

Sekine, T. (1980) 'The necessity of the law of value', *Science and Society*, 44 (3): 289–304.

Spinoza, B. (1949) [1675] *Ethics* (trans. G.H.R. Parkinson). New York: Haffner Press.

Stigler, G. and Becker, G.S. (1977) 'De gustibus non est disputandum', *American Economic Review*, 67: 76–90.

Urban, W.M. (1909) *Valuation: Its Nature and Laws*. London: Swan Sonnenschein.

Weber, M. (1930) [1904–5] *The Protestant Ethic and the Spirit of Capitalism* (trans. T. Parsons). London: Allen and Unwin.

Whitaker, J.K. (1975) *The Early Economic Writings of Alfred Marshall, 1867–1890* (two volumes). New York: Macmillan.

Wiggins, D. (1998) *Needs, Values, Truth*. Oxford: Blackwell.

Wilden, A. (1980) *System and Structure: Essays in Communication and Exchange*. London: Tavistock.

12

Publics and Markets: What's Wrong with Neoliberalism?

Clive Barnett

THEORIZING NEOLIBERALISM AS A POLITICAL PROJECT

Neoliberalism has become a key object of analysis in human geography in the last decade. Although the words 'neoliberal' and 'neoliberalism' have been around for a long while, it is only since the end of the 1990s that they have taken on the aura of grand theoretical terms. Neoliberalism emerges as an object of conceptual and empirical reflection in the process of restoring to view a sense of political agency to processes previously dubbed globalization (Hay, 2002).

This chapter examines the way in which neoliberalism is conceptualized in human geography. It argues that, in theorizing neoliberalism as 'a political project', critical human geographers have ended up reproducing the same problem that they ascribe to the ideas they take to be driving forces behind contemporary transformations: they reduce the social to a residual effect of more fundamental political-economic rationalities. Proponents of free markets think that people *should* act like utility-maximizing rational egoists, despite much evidence that *they don't*. Critics of neoliberalism tend to assume that increasingly people *do* act like this, but they think that they *ought not to*. For critics, this is what's wrong with neoliberalism. And it is precisely this evaluation that suggests that there is something wrong with how neoliberalism is theorized in critical human geography.

In critical human geography, neoliberalism refers in the first instance to a family of ideas associated with the revival of economic liberalism in the mid-twentieth century. This is taken to include the school of Austrian economics associated with Ludwig von Mises, Friedrich von Hayek and Joseph Schumpeter, characterized by a strong commitment to methodological individualism, an antipathy towards centralized state planning, a commitment to principles of private property, and a distinctive anti-rationalist epistemology; and the so-called Chicago School of economists, also associated with Hayek but also including leading monetarist economist Milton Friedman. David Harvey's definition of neoliberalism condenses a set of emphases that characterize accounts of this object of analysis more generally:

> Neoliberalism is in the first instance a theory of political economic practices that proposes that human well-being can best be advanced by liberating individual entrepreneurial freedoms and skills within an institutional framework characterized by strong private property rights, free markets and free trade. The role of the state is to create and preserve an institutional framework appropriate to such practices. The state has to guarantee, for example, the quality and integrity of money. It must also set up those military, defence, police and legal structures and functions required to secure private property rights and to guarantee, by force if need be, the proper functioning of markets. Furthermore, if markets do not exist (in areas such as land, water, education, health care, social security, or environmental pollution) then they must be created, by state action if necessary. But beyond these tasks the state should not venture. State interventions in markets (once created) must be kept to a bare minimum because, according to the theory, the state cannot possibly possess enough information to second-guess market signals (prices) and because powerful interest groups will inevitably distort and bias state interventions (particularly in democracies) for their own benefit. (Harvey, 2005: 2)

The ascendancy of this 'ideology' is recounted through a standardized narrative that touches on a series of focal points (Hoffmann et al., 2006): a period of economic crisis that shook the foundations of the post-Second World War, Keynesian settlement as the conjuncture in which previously marginal neoliberal economic theories were translated into real-world policy scenarios; the role of economists from the University of Chicago in Pinochet's Chile in the 1970s, Reagonomics in the USA in the 1980s, and so-called Thatcherism in the UK in the 1980s; the role of key international agencies, such as the International Monetary Fund (IMF) and World Bank as being responsible for diffusing neoliberalism globally through the so-called Washington Consensus in development and foreign aid policy; and the taken-for-granted claim that neoliberalism has, over time, been transformed from an ideology into hegemonic common sense.

Wendy Larner observes that 'the concept of neoliberalism is overwhelmingly mobilized and deployed by left-wing academics and political activists' (2006: 450). As a critics' term, neoliberalism is presented as an ideational project and political programme that seeks to supplant collective, public values with individualistic, private values of market rationality as the guiding principles of state policy, economic governance and everyday life. It should be said that there is no single critical conceptualization of neoliberalism in human geography. Neoliberalism is sometimes conceptualized as a *policy* paradigm; sometimes more broadly as a hegemonic *ideology*; and sometimes as a distinctive form of *governmentality* (Larner, 2000). Linking these three different approaches is an overwhelming emphasis on the guiding force of explicit forms of knowledge in shaping social change.

The explicit conceptual elaboration of critical theories of neoliberalism and neoliberalization has been pioneered by human geographers and spatially sensitive sociologists. *Neoliberalism* is understood as an ideology that is shaped in a few centres and then diffuses outwards, and a political project that aims to reorder the territorial framing of capital accumulation. The resulting process of *neoliberalization* is understood to be geographically uneven. The basic outlines of neoliberalism as an object of critical analysis include the following:

- Neoliberalism is understood as an ideology that encompasses various forms of free-market fundamentalism.
- Neoliberalism is diffused and translated across contexts very quickly.
- Neoliberalism is operative at various spatial scales.
- Neoliberalism displaces established models of welfare provision and state regulation through policies of privatization and deregulation.
- Neoliberalism brings off various changes in subjectivity by normalizing individualistic self-interest, entrepreneurial values, and consumerism.

In the constitution of neoliberalism as an object of critical analysis, the overwhelming emphasis is upon neoliberalism as an 'ideational project'. It is from this emphasis that the agenda for geographical research follows:

- tracking the *diffusion* of this ideology through different geographical contexts;
- mapping the variable *articulation* of this ideology with other processes in different places;
- examining the *normalization* of this ideology in spatial practices of subject formation.

If the theoretical constitution of neoliberalism as an ideological project generates an automatic agenda for geographical research, then it also constructs the task of critical analysis in a distinctive way. If neoliberalization is assumed to work through the naturalization of market rationalities and the normalization of individualistic egoism, then the critical task becomes one of exposing the various dimensions of neoliberalization as social constructs.

Critical theories of neoliberalism and neoliberalization provide a compelling moral narrative in which recent history is understood in terms of a motivated shift away from public and collective values towards private and individualistic values. Critical narratives of neoliberalism reinforce the image of there being a clear-cut divide between two sets of values – those of private, individualistic self-interest on the one hand, and those of public, collective interests on the other. There is a preconstructed normative framing of these theories around a set of conceptual and moral binaries: market versus state; public versus private; consumer versus citizen; liberty versus equality; individual utility versus collective solidarity; self-interested egoism versus other-regarding altruism.

Theories of neoliberalism go hand in hand with a standard form of criticism that bemoans the decline of public life, active citizenly virtue, and values of egalitarianism and solidarity. These theories project ahead of themselves criteria of evaluation (cf. Castree, 2008): neoliberalism reduces democracy, creates poverty and inequality, and is imposed either from the outside or by unaccountable elites. The conceptual analysis of neoliberalism is therefore always already critical, but at a cost. Critical theorists of neoliberalism are condemned to invoke their favoured positive values (e.g. the public realm, collective solidarity, equality, democracy, care, social justice) in a moralistic register without addressing normative problems of how practically to negotiate equally compelling values. And in so far as theories of neoliberalism dismiss considerations of rational action, motivation, and decentralized coordination as so much 'ideology', they remain chronically constricted in their capacity to reflect seriously on questions of institutional design, political organization and economic coordination which, one might suppose, remain an important task for any critical theory.

The next section introduces the basic outlines of conceptualizations of neoliberalism in geography and related fields. This section considers how neoliberalism and neoliberalization have been conceptualized in Marxist political economy. Neoliberalism is understood as a revival and renewal of *laissez-faire* economic liberalism, holding to principles of free markets and the minimal state. The third section looks at how Foucault's ideas about liberal governmentality are used to bolster these narratives of political economy. The fourth section argues that it is worth taking seriously the way in which public rationalities are problematized in a family of economic models of bureaucracy, welfare and democracy that attract far less attention in geography's 'neoliberalism' than the ideas of free-market liberals like Hayek and Friedman. The final section discusses some of the normative blindspots of prevailing conceptualizations of neoliberalism and, by extension, of critical human geography more broadly.

POLITICAL ECONOMIES OF NEOLIBERALISM

Neoliberalism as accumulation by dispossession

In Harvey's (2005) conceptualization, neoliberalism emerges in response to the economic crisis of the 1970s, displacing the 'embedded liberalism' represented by Keynesianism with a more voracious and transparent strategy aimed at restoring capital accumulation. Harvey's narrative focuses on the ascendancy of finance capital over the last three decades. On this analysis, neoliberalism has not been particularly successful as a means of restoring conditions for stable economic growth and capital accumulation. It has been a redistributive rather than a generative programme, driven by strategies of 'accumulation by dispossession' (Harvey, 2005: 159–63). This is a mode of accumulation which, through practices such as privatization and financialization, seeks to transfer publicly or commonly held assets and resources into private property. In Harvey's analysis, accumulation by dispossession has the effect of fragmenting and particularizing social conflicts (ibid.: 178), in contrast to strategies that sustain accumulation through transformations to the labour process based on extended wage-labour, which have a universalizing effect in so far as they render transparent their own class content.

In Harvey's account, neoliberalism is defined as a theory of free market practices, which is highly flexible and can be implemented by both liberal democratic and authoritarian regimes. Since *neoliberalization* is understood as an accumulation strategy aimed at restoring class power, *neoliberalism*, with its seductive rhetoric of freedom, has 'primarily worked as a system of justification and legitimation for whatever needed to be done to achieve this goal' (2005: 19). So it turns out that, as a 'theory', neoliberalism does not serve a very *practical* function in actually pursuing accumulation by dispossession at all. It is mainly 'a benevolent mask full of wonderful-sounding words like freedom, liberty, choice, and rights, to hide the grim realities of the restoration or reconstitution of naked class power' (ibid.: 119).

The defining claim in Marxist political economies of neoliberalism is that the ideational project represented by neoliberalism, supposedly formulated by Hayek and others, has been translated into a project of socio-economic transformation, neoliberalization, whose primary agent is 'the state': 'Neoliberalization has in effect swept across the world like a vast tidal wave of institutional reform and discursive adjustment' (Harvey, 2006: 145). Harvey's narrative explains this translation of theory into reality by invoking the Gramscian idea of hegemony, suggesting that neoliberal ideas have become incorporated into 'the common-sense way we interpret, live in and understand the world (ibid.: 145). The deployment of the term 'hegemony' in political-economic accounts of neoliberalism over-estimates the degree to which the reproduction of unequal social relations depends on winning the consent of subordinated, exploited actors. In Harvey's account, neoliberalism becomes hegemonic through a vaguely defined ideological mechanism of 'naturalization':

> For any system of thought to become hegemonic requires the articulation of fundamental concepts that become so deeply embedded in common-sense understandings that they become taken for granted and beyond question. For this to occur not any old concepts will do. A conceptual apparatus has to be constructed that appeals almost 'naturally' to our intuitions and instincts, to our values and our desires, as well as to the possibilities that seem to inhere in the social world we inhabit. (Harvey, 2006: 146)

The intuitively appealing concept that neoliberalism deploys is 'freedom', any usage of which is therefore cast under a dark cloud of suspicion. 'Social justice' on the other hand is assumed to have an obvious, unambiguous resonance.

Harvey (2005: 40-41) alludes to hegemony being secured by the changing experiential basis of everyday life under volatile capitalism. This leaves open the possibility of exploring the ways in which various modalities of rational action are framed and mobilized in the construction of hegemony. However, the analysis of neoliberalization as a redistributive rather than a generative process of accumulation by dispossession precludes the possibility that capital accumulation might be a positive-sum game, and that this could provide material grounds through which legitimation is secured. Neoliberalism ends up being legitimated 'ideologically', by manipulating the representational content that people carry around in their heads. Hegemony is presented as a cultural process of constructing common sense that is misleading, obfuscatory, and disguises real problems (Harvey, 2005). Geography's Marxism therefore attains its culturalist high point in seeking to sustain an economistic rendering of the contemporary scene.

Neoliberalization as a tendential trajectory

Theories of neoliberalism effectively abolish the recurrent problem in Marxism of 'the relative autonomy of the state' by describing neoliberalization as a political project which, at the level of theory, favours market relations over state intervention while, at the level of hegemonic practice, has successfully captured the state as the means of pursuing its objectives. Capital's internal logic, conceptually isolated through an analysis pitched at a very high level of abstraction, is found to cascade downwards until it is directly voiced by the state.

The idea that 'the state' voices the class interests of capital, and thus becomes a vehicle for its own diminution, is most clearly expressed in 'state-theoretic' accounts of neoliberalism which draw on regulation theory. These approaches emphasize processes of geographical rescaling in narrating a shift from Fordist to post-Fordist regimes of capital accumulation. Regulation theory focuses on the question of how a crisis-ridden system like capitalism establishes stable conditions for growth. It draws on intermediate concepts to explain the functional relationship between particular organizations of the labour process and systems of production (a *regime of accumulation*) and extended infrastructures for social reproduction (a *mode of regulation*). Under Fordism, so the story goes, high wages and high profits were sustained through Keynesian devices that rolled out welfare provision and state infrastructures to sustain high levels of consumption. Accumulation and regulation were both 'scaled' at the national level. The crisis of Fordism, in turn, is manifest in the reordering of these different institutional arrangements, not least in terms of the 'hollowing-out' of the national level as various regulatory functions are relocated to subnational and supra-national scales (Jessop, 2002; Peck, 2001).

From this perspective, neoliberalism is the 'tendential' trajectory from the Keynesian Welfare National State to a Schumpeterian Workfare Regime, expressed in a raft of policies for managing a new relationship between a post-Fordist regime of accumulation and a re-tooled mode of regulation. Describing neoliberalism as 'tendential' is a way of claiming that this is the leading trajectory of transformation everywhere, even though nowhere in particular accords to either of these ideal-typical models. In the regulationist account of neoliberalism, the culturalist inflection to political economy is given even freer reign than it is by Harvey. Objects of regulation, and indeed the dimensions of economic crisis itself, are understood to be constructed through narratives (Jessop, 1999). 'Globalization' functions as a master narrative of crisis, and neoliberalism provides the discursive solution to this crisis.

The reference to Schumpeter in the regulationist analysis is important for understanding the normative background to political-economy approaches to neoliberalism. Writing in the 1940s, Schumpeter (1942) presented capitalism as a vibrant system characterized by 'creative destruction', in which capitalist risk-takers pursuing their own self-interest with minimal state interference would generate investment and innovation to sustain high levels of economic growth. To secure this positive-sum outcome, capitalism should be subjected only to the regulatory tinkering of the liberal state in the interests of maximizing market efficiency.

Standing opposed to Schumpeter in the regulationist narrative of neoliberalism is the figure of Karl Polanyi. Also writing in the 1940s, Polanyi (1944) provided a compelling moral critique of the idea that human welfare could best be secured by letting free markets reign supreme. For Polanyi, free markets can create rapid growth only by undermining the conditions of human sociality upon which they depend. For him, creative destruction was more destructive than it was creative. To be sustainable, and to promote human welfare, economic relationships needed to be embedded in a fabric of regulations, institutions and social norms.

Polanyi's ideas provide both an ontological framework within which to locate the pathological consequences of free-market fundamentalism, and a normative framework in which to criticize the limitations of this ideology. Neoliberalism represents the triumph of a narrowly economizing mode of market rationality, which in turn leads to the disembedding of economic activities from a wider context of substantive social relationships, institutions and norms upon which long-term socio-economic stability depends. This in turn generates an ongoing dynamic through which neoliberalism constantly adjusts to the volatile crises it is itself responsible for.

Theories of neoliberalism therefore exploit an ambivalence in Polanyi's legacy. On the one hand, there is an argument that seems to suggest that market rationality, if left to its own devices, could actually float free from substantive relationships. On the other hand, there is an implication that even the freest of 'free markets' must be embedded in some context of norms and institutions. This ambivalence is exploited in theories of neoliberalism by appealing to the either/or sense of 'embedded' versus 'disembedded' markets to make critical judgements; while deploying the second, descriptive sense to bolster the argument that economic relationships are always functionally sustained by particular projects of social regulation overseen by the state.

Polanyi is an important source for sociologized critiques of free-market theories. In the discipline of economic sociology, it is argued that all markets, even the most 'free', are embedded in broader contexts. In institutional economics, 'institutions' are defined with reference to an expansive field of rules, routines and norms. In actor-network theory, emphasis is on the ways in which various technologies and devices frame fields of action as ones governed by market rationality, and in turn generate various unintended consequences. All three of these fields cast doubt on whether a purely 'free' market as envisaged in neoclassical economics is possible. In principle, there is scope here for considering how markets can be organized in accord with public values of care, welfare and equity (Smith, 2005; Rodríguez-Pose and Storper, 2006). But the primary lesson drawn from this work by theorists of neoliberalism is to argue that markets and other economic relationships are 'socially constructed'. This is presented as if it were a knock-down argument against the theoretical perspective of mainstream economics, which is itself taken to be nothing but an instrument of neoliberalization. In particular, it is concluded that the 'social constructedness' of markets effectively invalidates any and all concerns with the analysis of rational action by individualized actors (Peck, 2005). In geography's theories of neoliberalism and neoliberalization, the argument about the 'social construction' of markets serves only to sustain a claim about the highly orchestrated qualities of contemporary political-economic transformations.

Claims about the social construction of markets are closely related to arguments about the importance of drawing into view how neoliberalism is a 'political project'. But the regulationist approach works with a rather thin understanding of what counts as political action. The state is understood to be a political actor only in so far as it mobilizes particular types of resource (coercive mechanisms such as military power, policing, taxation; ideological resources such as education and nationalism) in pursuit of its generic function of cohering together a class-divided society. 'Political' refers in this approach to a means of acting (through the state) that is governed by a particular set of motivations (the self-interest of class actors). It is only in this sense that neoliberalism is understood to be a political product.

The notion that neoliberalism is best theorized as an 'ideational' project' has a pedigree that predates geography's detailed theorization of this topic over the last decade (e.g. Przeworski, 1992). It leads inevitably to a focus on elites as the primary agents of change (see Genev, 2005). In Peck and Tickell's (2002) account of the neoliberalization of space, this emphasis on neoliberalism as an ideational project is directly connected to a distinctive geographical programme of research on diffusion and contextual articulation. It is argued that the ideas of neoliberal thinkers cascaded through various academic and non-academic knowledge networks and gained ascendancy in the United Kingdom and the United States in the 1980s (see Plehwe et al., 2006). Neoliberalism has a heartland in the 'home spaces' of USA and UK, and then diffuses through various 'zones of extension'. This hierarchical distinction follows naturally from the emphasis placed on neoliberalism as first and foremost an ideational project. This in turn underwrites a linear model of geographical analysis, in which the 'generic' dimensions of neoliberal ideology are diffused outwards, touching ground in particular contexts where they 'articulate' with and 'hybridize' the contextual landscapes of particular cities, regions or nation-states in Latin America, Africa, Asia and Eastern Europe.

This picture of the geography of neoliberalization supports, and in turn is supported by, a distinctive understanding of the relationship between empirical analysis and theory building. Any observed variation or adaptation of neoliberal ideology to local context does not cause theorists of neoliberalization to revise the basics of their theories. It only confirms the main outlines of their narratives. Peck and Tickell argue that while neoliberalism takes on different forms in different places, the 'family resemblances' between these forms allow some essential features to be isolated: 'adequate conceptualizations must be attentive to *both* the local peculiarities *and* the generic features of neoliberalism' (2002: 388). There is a telling slippage here between a geographical characteristic ('local peculiarities') and a formal characteristic ('generic features'). The generic character of neoliberalism is located in the ideological content of a set of political philosophies, economist theorems and policy prescriptions (Peck, 2004). The claim that neoliberal ideas are enshrined in global 'rules' and circulated by a set of global regulatory agencies such as the WTO, IMF and World Bank which discipline states around the world is sustained through an entrenched vocabulary of 'discourse' and 'material practices'. The term 'discourse' has come to serve as a kind of inferential transponder that explains away how highly abstract philosophical principles (from Hobbes or Locke or Smith) and highly arcane social science theorems (from micro-economics and public choice theory) manage to bring off disciplinary effects on national governments, state agencies, and ordinary citizens.

This style of theoretical reasoning is what makes neoliberalism an exemplary geographical object of analysis. Refinements of theories of neoliberalization call for more attention to the path-dependent interaction between neoliberal programmes and context-specific institutional and social frameworks (Brenner and Theodore, 2002); more empirical work on the variability of neoliberalism as policy paradigms are transferred from place to place (Bondi and Laurie, 2005); and considerations of the disjunctures between 'liberal' and 'neoliberal' programmes and imperatives (Mitchell, 2004). In short, neoliberalism is a theoretical object that automatically generates a series of geographical enquiries:

- the analysis of the diffusion of neoliberal ideology through the political processes of neoliberalization;

- the analysis of the contextual specificity of neoliberalization, and of its articulation at different scales;
- the analysis of the hybridization of neoliberalism with other political projects (e.g. neoconservatism) and of class relations with other social relations (e.g. gender, race, ethnicity);
- the reordering of public and private spaces of work and care;
- and finally (always finally), there is plenty of scope for the analysis of social movements that arise *in response to* and in order to *resist* neoliberalism and the effects of neoliberalization.

The meta-theories of neoliberalism that generate this field of geographical enquiry remain immune to criticism. They are refined by focusing on *neoliberalization*. This is a concept that allows for the acknowledgement of neoliberalisms diverse origins and varied pathways, its uneven and incomplete character, while all the time insisting that it remains a singular 'tendential' trajectory of contemporary life (Peck, 2006). Whether it is theoretically coherent to ascribe general features to such a variable phenomenon, and whether the sorts of generalization from specific cases that these sort of claims require is coherent, is far from certain (Castree, 2006).

What remains unclear is why, if neoliberalism never appears in pure form, and when it does appear it is always compounded with other projects and processes, the outcome of any neoliberal ideational project should continue to be called 'neoliberalization'. What is it that makes the hybrid forms through which these specific ideologies make themselves felt always liable to be named 'neoliberal', if this is only one of their components? The one 'generic' feature that high-level abstractions of neoliberalism do not specify is the *parasitical* force which gives neoliberalism an asymmetrical energy in shaping the *corrosive* trajectories of future capitalist development in its own image. For critics, it is this parasitical and corrosive force, implied but never specified, that is the source of what is wrong with neoliberalism.

De-politicizing politics

In theories of neoliberalism and neoliberalization, the theoretical preference for very high levels of abstraction is associated with a tendency to make a geographical virtue out of the consistent failure to theorize the state as anything other than a functional attribute of the reproductive requirements of capital. Particular state-formations and patterns of political contention are acknowledged only as local, territorialized, contextual factors that help to explain how the universalizing trajectory of neoliberalism, orchestrated from the centre and organized through global networks, nonetheless always generates 'hybrid' assemblages of neoliberalism.

This style of theorizing makes it almost impossible to gainsay the highly generalized claims about neoliberalism as an ideology and neoliberalization as a state-led project by referring to empirical evidence that might seem to contradict these grand concepts. For example, it is almost taken for granted that the hegemony of neoliberalism is manifest in the reduction of state expenditures on welfare in the face of external pressures of neoliberal globalization. Empirical evidence for welfare-state decline is, in fact, far from conclusive. Welfare regimes have actually proved highly resilient in terms of both funding and provisioning (see Taylor-Gooby, 2001). At the same time, the extent to which open-market economies foster rather than menace high levels of national welfare provision is also hotly debated (Taylor-Gooby, 2003). In both cases, the idea of any straightforward shift from state to market seems a little simplistic (Clarke, 2003). But, from the perspective of geography's meta-theories of neoliberalization, all of this is so much grist to the contextualizing mill. Contrary evidence can be easily incorporated into these theories precisely because they lay levels of conceptual abstraction directly onto scales of contextual articulation.

Presenting differential state formation as a *contextual* variable is related to a much broader displacement of political action in general to a lower level of conceptual abstraction in theories of neoliberalism. One aspect of this is the persistent treatment of a broad range of social movement activity as primarily a secondary response to processes of neoliberalization. But, more fundamentally, Marxist political economies of neoliberalism pay almost no attention, at a conceptual level, to the causal significance of the institutional and organizational forms that shape political action (Hay, 2004). This is indicative of a broader failure to think through how distinctive forms of contemporary democratic politics shape pathways of economic development and capital accumulation. Theories of neoliberalism take for granted the capacity of states to implement particular policies in order to put in place the regulatory conditions for particular accumulation strategies. This assumption overlooks the degree to which the time-space constitution of democratic politics in liberal democracies serves as 'substantial impediments to the achievement of neo-liberal goals' (Johnston and Glasmeier, 2007: 15). Given the territorialization of party support and the territorialized organization of electoral politics, liberal democracy generates strong pressures that militate against wholly flexible and open labour markets, sustain subsidies and protectionist measures, and support the promotion of investment in particular locations. In theories of neoliberalism, processes of free market reform in the USA and UK since the 1980s are considered models of more general tendential logics. But these examples might be quite specific outcomes of the balance of political forces in those polities when compared to the patterns of welfare reform and tax policy in European countries (Prasad, 2006; see also Glyn, 2006).

Taking into account the ways in which state action is constrained by the time-space constitution of electoral, representative democracy is particularly relevant for understanding why relatively wealthy, advanced industrial economies do not conform to the tendential logic predicted by political-economy theories of neoliberalization. These same constraints might also be operative elsewhere. It is routine to suggest that neoliberalism is 'imposed' on developing economies externally, through the Washington Consensus promulgated by the IMF, World Bank and WTO. However, Stokes (2001) argues that patterns of neoliberalization in Latin America in the 1980s and 1990s can be explained in large part by analysis of the dynamics between electoral campaigning, party mobilization, mandate and accountability as they played themselves out in periods of democratic transition and consolidation. In her account of 'neoliberalism by surprise', democratic governance, party competition, electoral accountability and responsiveness to constituents' interests all play crucial roles in explaining whether, how, and why neoliberal policies are adopted.

Strictly speaking, these sorts of considerations do not need to disturb the secure conceptual vantage point offered by political-economy theorizations of neoliberalism. This paradigm is, as already suggested, internally attuned to recognize the variety and hybridity of neoliberalisms, and is able to ascribe variation to the necessary articulation of generic neoliberal ideology, circulated globally, with territorialized logics operative at 'lower' geographical scales. Whether or not one finds this type of analysis convincing comes down to a decision between different styles of theory. Political-economy approaches seek high-level abstractions in order to identify fundamental features of phenomena (the logic of capital accumulation in Harvey, the capitalist state in Jessop, neoliberal ideology in Peck and Tickell). These abstract imperatives are then mapped empirically through a kind of deductive cascade, where they bump into other phenomena such as states, or racial formations, or gender relations. Because of their distinctive ontological features (e.g. their institutional qualities, their territorial qualities, their discursive qualities and their identity-based qualities), these phenomena have never been amenable to the same sort of explanatory rationalism that allows the dynamics of capital accumulation to be defined so purely.

The effect of these theorizations of neoliberalism is to de-politicize politics. If the dominant logic of state action can always be discerned from understanding the logic of capital accumulation and the balance of class forces, then that is really all one ever really needs to know (Clarke, 2004a). This de-politicization of politics 'out there' is an effect of the inflation of the political force ascribed to the academic work of critique: analysis of politics is reduced to a matter of understanding *how* a logic already known in advance is differentially enacted, so that the critical task of such analysis can be presented as a political act of exposing naturalized forms as *social constructs*.

Despite the polite nods to ideas of 'relative autonomy', political-economy theories of neoliberalism retain coherence only by appealing in the last instance to a reductionist theory of the state. Gramscian state theory, with its 'strategic relational' view of the state, is a pretty sophisticated version of reductionism, able to acknowledge all sorts of autonomous action by state agencies and all sorts of contradictions arising from the underlying logics of capital accumulation. Nevertheless, narratives of neoliberalization hold fast to two basic assumptions about 'the state'. Firstly, the state is understood as a territorialized power container exercising sovereignty through its monopoly of violence and definitions of legality (Harvey, 2005: 159). Secondly, the state is understood as an arena in and through which conflicts defined by reference to class interests are fought out. For example, in Harvey's characterization, during Keynesian 'embedded liberalism' the state became 'a force field that internalized class relations' (ibid.: 11), and in turn neoliberalization reflects the conquest of this constituted state power in order to enact accumulation by dispossession.

Combining these two assumptions leads to an analysis in which the variable scope, extent and reach of sovereign state action is explained with reference to a changing balance of social forces. The state is understood as an object and instrument of class struggle, but not as 'an organization-for-itself' (Skocpol, 1979; Mann, 1988). In theories of neoliberalization, this concept of the state as a constituted *sovereign* actor that is also an *arena* for social conflict underwrites the claim that the state can and does now univocally express the class interests of capital. This sort of analysis continues to take for granted the sovereign capacities of 'the state' as an instrument for the forcing through of various political programmes translating ideational projects.

Neoliberalism and neoliberalization would appear somewhat differently from the 'polymorphous view of the state', premised on what Mann (1993: 52) calls 'organizational materialism'. This view focuses on the distinctive characteristics of political institutions and their relationships with other actors. Such a non-reductionist approach suggests a different view of the restructuring of state actions upon which so much analysis of neoliberalism and neoliberalization focuses. An organizational materialist view of state formation opens the way for an alternative style of analysis of the simultaneous retreat of the state from certain areas of activity and proliferation into other areas that so exercises political-economy accounts of neoliberalization. It suggests an analysis of the extent to which state actions are determined by the interactions between the dynamics of historically sedimented state imperatives and institutional frameworks, and their responses to the changing dynamics of mobilization and organization of collective actors in civil society, broadly defined (see Offe, 1996).

Taking the relational constitution of state–society interactions seriously (see Corbridge, 2008; Migdal, 2001) would allow analyses of contemporary transformations to bring into view the proactive role of a series of actors, projects and processes that get little if any attention in political-economy accounts of neoliberalization. This would include consideration of the secular dynamics of individualization and risk (Beck and Beck-Gernsheim, 2001; Taylor-Gooby et al., 1999), and how these are transforming the dynamics of collective will-formation which relationally constitute the scope and content of state action. It would include greater consideration of the complex dynamics of bureaucratic and administrative transformation (Du Gay, 2000). It would include the geographical dynamics of social reproduction which are not simply adjustments to neoliberalization (Yeates, 2002). Moreover, it would open space for appreciation of the proactive role of social movement mobilizations in emergent forms of 'non-governmental politics' (Feher, 2007). It is also a view consistent with recent work which theorizes the ways in which state activities continue to reach into the ordinary spaces of everyday life (see Corbridge et al., 2006; Painter, 2006).

As already suggested, theories of neoliberalism are remarkably flexible in the face of empirical evidence that seems to run counter to the pattern of state roll-back and market expansion predicted by the neoliberalization hypothesis. Political-economy theories approach breaking point when they have to account for the observable empirical fact that, contrary to the objective view they project onto the 'neoliberal project', it is found that states have not straightforwardly withdrawn from welfare provision or other forms of social regulation at all. Faced with this inconvenience, Peck and Tickell (2002) conjure up a neat conceptual distinction between what they call the 'roll-back' phase of neoliberalism and the 'roll-out' phase. The roll-out phase is triggered by the ongoing need of state actors to manage the crises generated by the roll-back phase. This is a selective deployment of the Polanyian theme of embedding and disembedding. It is used to suggest that contemporary processes of active state-building around issues of welfare, crime, family policy, urban order, participation and cultural inclusion are still best understood as the natural extensions of an ideology that is supposed to be based on a straightforward opposition between state and market.

This distinction between roll-back and roll-out phases makes neoliberalization look less like a 'tendential' path of development than a tendentious theoretical projection of a simplistic moral order onto a rather more complex reality. Nevertheless, this distinction inadvertently opens up room for tethering an alternative theoretical framework to the regulationist paradigm. In order to describe and explain the 'roll-out' of new welfare and regulatory regimes by putatively neoliberal states, geographers have increasingly turned to the theoretical vocabulary of 'governmentality'.

NEOLIBERAL GOVERNMENTALITY

The concept of 'governmentality' is a neologism used by Michel Foucault (1991) in his work on modern forms of political power. It is a term that combines 'government' and 'rationality', suggesting a form of political analysis that focuses on the forms of knowledge that make objects visible and available for governing. In Foucault's terms, governmentality refers to a distinctive modality for exercising power, one which is not reducible to 'the state'. Governmentality is understood to work 'at a distance' by seeking to shape 'the conduct of conduct'. This in turn implies that governmentality refers to a wide range of points of application, including fields of action not ordinarily thought of as political, such as medicine, education, religion, or popular culture.

Governmentality is a notion that develops Foucault's distinctive approach to the analysis of power relations. His work not only *relocates* power, dispersing it away from sovereign actions of centralized state agencies. It rethinks the type of *action* through which power is exercised (see Brown, 2006b). In fundamental respects, the significance of the notion of governmentality for social theory turns on the interpretation of just what sort of theory of action this notion presupposes. This section and the following explore just where this significance lies.

Lemke (2002) argues that Foucault's work on governmentality provides a means of understanding the relationships between knowledge, strategies of power and technologies of the self that can usefully augment narratives of neoliberalism. From this perspective, neoliberalism is understood as 'a political rationality that tries to render the social domain economic and to link a reduction in (welfare) state services and security systems to the increasing call for "personal responsibility" and "self-care"' (Lemke, 2001: 203). On this understanding, governmentality is a concept that augments the political-economy approaches outlined in the previous section. For example, Ong's (1999) account of the distinctive forms of governmentality deployed by 'post-developmental' states revolves around the assumption that various regulatory regimes manipulate cultural discourses to selectively mould people into certain sorts of economic subjects consistent with the objectives of particular national strategies of accumulation. Jessop (2007) has also argued that the convergence between Marxism and governmentality studies follows from the mutually supportive emphases of the two approaches:

> while Marx seeks to explain the why of capital accumulation and state power, Foucault's analyses of disciplinarity and governmentality try to explain the how of economic exploitation and political domination (2007: 40)

This formulation acknowledges Foucault's own observation that he was concerned with the 'how' of power, but assumes that this descriptive focus merely augments the explanatory project of Marxist political economy. What is elided in this move is a fundamental philosophical difference between these two approaches: the concept of governmentality implies an analysis that focuses on the description of practices *instead of* causes and explanations.

The Marxist and Foucauldian approaches are not necessarily as easily reconciled as it might appear. There are two main areas of difference between these approaches: their respective understandings of the state and of discourse (Traub-Werner, 2007: 1444–46). Political-economy approaches assume fairly static models of 'the state' and 'the market', and view their relationship in terms of contradictory movements of deregulation and reregulation; they also assume that 'discourse' is a representational concept, and focus upon how 'discourses' are theorized differentially and 'materialized' in particular contexts. In contrast, governmentality refers to modalities of power that stretch far beyond 'the state'; and 'discourse' is not a representational system so much as a distinctive concept of action, referring to the combination of technologies, means of representation and fields of possibility.

Despite the underlying philosophical differences between governmentality and Marxist political economy, Foucault's notion has become an important reference point in recent debates about neoliberalization (Larner, 2003; Barnett, 2005). If there is such a thing as a neoliberal project, then it is assumed that it must work by seeking to bring into existence lots of neoliberal subjects (cf. Barnett et al., 2008). Work on this topic assumes that extending the range of activities that are commodified, commercialized and marketized necessarily implies that people's subjectivities need to be retooled and reworked–: as active consumers, entrepreneurial subjects or empowered participants (see e.g. Bondi, 2005; Gökariksel and Mitchell, 2005; Mitchell, 2003, 2006; Sparke, 2006a; Walkerdine, 2005). In this interpretation, the dispersal of power implied by the notion of governmentality is re-centred around a *sovereign* conception of state action, now able to reach out all the more effectively into all sorts of arenas in order to secure the conditions of its own (il)legitimacy.

The reduction of governmentality to a mechanism of subjectification marks the point at which Foucault's historical, genealogical approach to issues of subject formation is subordinated to the presentist functionalism of theories of neoliberalization. This reduction follows from the ambivalence around subject formation in the formalized models of governmentality that have developed Foucault's ideas. Rose's (1999) analysis of 'advanced liberal governmentality' argues that forms of 'social' government, of which the classical Keynesian welfare state stands as the exemplar, are being supplanted by the 'de-socialization' of modes of governing. The rationalities of advanced liberal welfare reform 'take the ethical reconstruction of the welfare recipient as their central problem' (1999: 263). They seek to govern people by regulating the choices made by autonomous actors in the context of their everyday, ordinary commitments to friends, family and community. This rationality is visible in the proliferation of the registers of empowerment and improvement, through which individuals participating in welfare or development programmes are oriented towards transforming the relationships that they have with themselves as subjects (Cruickshank, 1999; Li, 2007).

In analyses of advanced liberal governmentality, these shifts in political rationality are the result of the efforts of a diverse set of actors pursuing plural ends. They do not reflect the aims of a singular, coherent neoliberal project pursued through the agency of 'the state'. This emphasis is lost in the functionalist appropriation of governmentality to bolster theories of neoliberalization. This is compounded by the tendency in this work to presume that the description of political rationalities also describes the actual accomplishment of subject effects. The vocabulary of theorists of neoliberal governmentality is replete with terms such as 'elicit', 'promote', 'foster', 'attract', 'guide', 'encourage' and so on:

> The key feature of the neo-liberal rationality is the congruence it endeavours to achieve between a responsible and moral individual and an economic-rational actor. It aspires to construct prudent subjects whose moral quality is based on the fact that they rationally assess the costs and benefits of a certain sort as opposed to other alternative acts (Lemke, 2001: 201).

The point to underscore here is the emphasis on a rationality that *endeavours* and *aspires* to bring about certain subject effects. Narratives of the emergence of neoliberal governmentality display little sense of just *whether* and *how* governmental programmes seek to get people to comply with projects of rule or identify with subject positions. This is in large part because the Foucauldian approach to neoliberalism continues to construe governmentality in terms of a 'politics of subjection' (Clarke, 2004d: 70–71). Such an assumption leads almost automatically to the conclusion that neoliberalism degrades any residual potential for public action inherent in liberal democracy (e.g. Brown, 2003).

Equipped with the concept of governmentality, this sort of presentation of neoliberalism is able to avoid any serious consideration of what sort of action can be exercised on subjects through acting on them 'at a distance'. The idea that governmentality is a distinctive mode of political rule that seeks to hail into existence its preferred subjects, which are then only left with the option of 'resistance', needs to be treated with considerable scepticism. Understood as a mechanism of subjection, governmentality is assumed to work through the operation of norms. However, Foucauldian theory is chronically unable to acknowledge the work of communicative rationalities in making any action-through-norms possible (Hacking, 2004). Theories of governmentality consistently fail to specify adequately the 'looping effects' between knowledge technologies, practices, and subject formation which are implied by the idea of 'governing at a distance' (Barnett, 2001). This failure leads to the supposition that governmentality works through representational modes of subjectification rather than through the practical ordering of fields of strategic and communicative action. At the very most, the governmentality approach implies a probabilistic relationship between regulatory rationalities of rule and the transformations of subjectivities, mediated by the rules of chance (Agrawal, 2005: 161–3). It might even imply a reorientation of analysis towards understanding the assemblage of dispersed, singular acts rather than focusing on psycho-social processes of individual subjection (Barnett et al., 2008).

The recuperation of governmentality as a theory of subject formation, modelled on Althusserian theories of interpellative hailing, overlooks the distinctive modality of action through which Foucault addresses questions of subjectivity. Whereas liberalism and neoliberalism are understood in political-economy approaches as market ideologies, from the governmentality perspective liberalism (and by extension neoliberalism) should properly refer to a particular *problematization* of governing, and in particular the problematization of the task of governing free subjects. While a free-market ideology might imply a problematization of free subjects, it does not follow that the problematization of free subjects is always and everywhere reducible to the imperatives of free-market ideologies. Ong (2007) suggests, for example, a definition of neoliberalism in which long-established technologies for administering subjects for self-mastery are only contingently articulated with projects directed at securing profitability. But this clarification still presumes that neoliberalism extends and reproduces itself primarily through a politics of subjection (see also Brown, 2006a). It might be better to suppose that the distinctive focus in governmentality studies on modes of problematization should reorient analysis to the forms of what Foucault (1988) once called practices of 'ethical problematization'. This would direct analytical attention to investigating the conditions 'for individuals to recognize themselves as particular kinds of persons and to reflect upon their conduct – to problematize it – such that they may work upon and transform themselves in certain ways and towards particular goals' (Hodges, 2002: 457).

Two things follow from this reorientation. Firstly, it presumes that subjectivity is the product of situated rationalities of practice, rather than the representational medium of interpellative recognition (Hacking, 2002). Secondly, it implies that the proposition that liberal governmentality seeks to construct self-regulating subjectivities should not be too easily reduced to the proposition that those of subjectivities are normatively self-interested egoists (Du Gay, 2005). For example, Isin (2004) argues that the distinctive style of problematizing contemporary subjects of rule is in terms of so many 'neurotic subjects' faced with various risks and hazards. One implication of this style of problematizing subjects is that state agencies continue to be the objects of demands to take responsibility for monitoring such neurotic subjects or securing them from harm.

In this section we have seen how the third of the approaches to conceptualizing neoliberalism identified by Larner (2000), which appeals to the concept of governmentality, can be more or less easily subsumed into the prevalent political-economy interpretation. The assumption that governmentality is a concept that refers to the inculcation of certain sorts of mentality into subjects is the prevalent interpretation of governmentality in geography's usage of this concept to bolster theories of neoliberalization, not least in the proliferation of work on neoliberal subjects. The marriage of political economy and governmentality therefore generates a shared space of debate that defines state-of-the-art research into neoliberalization (Barnett, 2005). Whereas, in the political-economy approach, discourses are treated as expressive of other levels of determination, in the governmentality approach political economic processes recede into the background; and whereas political-economy approaches privilege class relations over other social relations, the governmentality approach reduces the social field to a plane of subjectification. But these differences converge around a shared assumption that 'reproduction happens': that subjects live out their self-governing subjection as ascribed by governmental rationalities, or subordinate classes live out their regulatory roles as ascribed by hegemonic projects of consent (Clarke, 2004c). And so it is that 'the social' is reduced to being the repository of a mysterious force of resistance waiting to be activated by the revelatory force of academic demystification.

TRANSFORMING THE RATIONALITIES OF THE PUBLIC REALM

Emergent rationalities

A shared assumption of the political-economy and the governmentality approaches is the idea that neoliberalism dissolves established patterns of public life. From the political-economy perspective, the public realm is progressively constricted through privatization, the marketization of public services, the introduction of competitive pressures into public institutions, and the infusion of private financial arrangements into public institutions. The governmentality perspective adds to this a view of the progressive individualization of subjectivity, as the public identity of 'citizen' is replaced by proliferating discourses of consumer choice and personal responsibility.[1] Narratives of neoliberalism therefore reiterate a common refrain about the decline of public virtues, collective solidarities, caring values and common institutions.

These narratives overestimate the degree to which existing configurations of public life have been simply dissolved by neoliberal onslaught. For example, the range of organizational reforms in the public sector through which 'neoliberalism' is apparently manifest in the United Kingdom, while certainly shaped by efforts to deflate notions of a singular collective public interest, have generated split representations of public subjects. The public now appears as *taxpayers*, supporting a logic of curbing spending, curtailing entitlements and maximizing efficiency; as *consumers*, supporting agendas to maximize the responsiveness to user needs; as *citizens*, concerned with collective values of equity and fairness; or as *scroungers*, threatening to undermine public values of fair shares and equal entitlements (Clarke, 2005; Newman, 2004). In turn, a range of new agencies has proliferated, not least those focused on auditing and inspecting other agencies in the interests of 'the public'.

This might, of course, all be subsumed beneath the banner of 'roll-out' neoliberalism. But this differentiation of the public realm is not simply an effect of top-down projects to privatize and individualize the public realm meeting the residual resistance of embedded solidarities and loyalties of national-welfare cultures. It is also the product of emergent mobilizations for community participation, equality struggles and cultural representation. Changes in policy paradigms and welfare regimes are as much *ad hoc* responses to a range of secular social trends as they are a motivated top-down project of rolling back the state. These trends include (Clarke, 2004b):

- *changing consumer expectations*, involving shifts in expectations towards public entitlements that follow from the generalization of consumerism;
- *the decline of deference*, involving shifts in conventions and hierarchies of taste, trust, access and expertise;
- *the refusals of the subordinated*, referring to the emergence of anti-paternalist attitudes found in, for example, women's health movements or anti-psychiatry movements;
- the development of *the politics of difference*, involving the emergence of discourses of institutional discrimination based on gender, sexuality, race and disability.

This range of factors has disrupted the ways in which welfare agencies think about inequality, helping to generate the emergence of *contested inequalities*, in which policies aimed at addressing inequalities of class and income inequalities develop an ever more expansive dynamic of expectation according to which public services should address other kinds of inequality as well. In short, rather than a simple shift from state provision to privatized markets, welfare regimes have been reordered through redistributions of commodified and de-commodified provision and different combinations of social insurance, social assistance and taxation (Esping-Andersen, 1996). The social relations of welfare consumption have certainly been reordered in highly unequal ways in the process. But the political dynamic of this process is not well captured by a simple narrative of state retreat under neoliberal onslaught.

What from one perspective is interpreted as a motivated project of neoliberalization might be better understood as a much more broadly based populist reorientation of contemporary politics, policy and popular cultures. The possibility that what is too readily identified as 'neoliberalization' might be constituted by the mainstreaming of movement agendas is yet to be fully explored (see Larner, 2007; cf. Leitner et al. (2007). The focus on neoliberalization means that all sorts of emergent political formations remain marginalized in this set of debates. These would include environmental politics and the politics of sustainability; new forms of consumer activism oriented by an ethics of assistance and global solidarity; the identity politics of sexuality related to demands for changes in modes of health-care provision and other welfare services. These and other movements are indicative of the emergence of a 'politics of choice' that is reshaping relations between states, civil society and capital (see Norris, 1998). Much of this emergent politics focuses on issues of consumption, and is therefore easily misinterpreted as just another aspect of a neoliberalized roll-out of market rationality. But this misses the extent to which consumption is re-politicized in these movements as an entry point into transformative networks of distribution and production which are indicative of evolving new political economies of public life (Murray, 2004).

In short, theories of neoliberalism are not very good at describing or explaining the contemporary political-economic landscape. Larner and Walters (2004) and Larner et al. (2007) deploy the concept of governmentality not to explain how the functionalist requirements of neoliberal ideology are sutured through subject formation, but rather as a means of accounting for the *post facto* assemblage of a diverse range of imperatives and programmes into a mobile governmental rationality. This seems more in tune with the 'cock-up, foul-up' approach to theorizing political processes (Mann, 1993: 53) to which Foucault's genealogical approach seems well attuned. This interpretation of globalization as governmentality suggests a refinement of what is meant by referring to neoliberalism as a 'political rationality'. It suggests an interpretation of the rationalities that shape policy interventions as emergent effects of ongoing processes of interaction, involving various forms of cooperative behaviour such as bargaining or compromising. Thinking of political rationalities as emergent qualities of dynamic interactions suggests, however, a rather more pluralist theoretical imagination than critical theories of neoliberalism are willing to countenance.

What are markets good for?

The idea that we should focus on the emergent public rationalities of contemporary governmentalities, rather than presuming a top-down imposition of a largely unchanging ideology, follows from taking seriously *the type of action* that Foucault's own account of governmentality presupposes. Governmentality refers not to mechanisms of subjection, but to 'governing the conduct of conduct', that is, to efforts aimed at structuring the field of action of other actors. The analytics of governmentality rests upon a conception of interaction in terms of 'strategic games of liberty', 'in which some try to control the conduct of others, who in turn try to avoid allowing their conduct to be controlled or try to control the conduct of the others' (Foucault, 1997: 299). The 'action on the action of others' that defines governmentality as a distinctive rationality of rule is theorized by reference to actors' efforts to realize their own ends through the enrolment of the strategic capacities of other actors. Foucault differentiated between three senses of strategic relations: a fairly neutral understanding of means–ends relations; a sense of taking advantage of others; and a sense of obtaining victory in struggle (2000: 346). And he endorsed the idea that these three senses covered the whole field of power relations, where strategy was understood as 'the choice of winning solutions' (ibid.) in situations of confrontation or competition.

Foucault's notion of governmentality therefore rests on a conception in which social interaction is always modelled narrowly on strategic action (Honneth, 1991), and it has difficulty admitting the possibility of any type of normatively inflected communicative action (Hacking, 2004). Furthermore, the analytics of governmentality only admits to a one-dimensional view of strategic action as always competitive action, having difficulty in accounting for observed forms of cooperative strategic action that are the outcome of communicatively steered agreement.

To help us see the importance of thinking more carefully about issues of rational action, it is useful to consider Foucault's own foray onto the territory most favoured by theorists of neoliberalism, in his lecture course on 'the birth of biopolitics' (see Foucault, 2000: 73–9; Foucault, 2008; Lemke, 2001; Guala, 2006). Here Foucault lays out an analysis of the internal relationship between the emergence of governmentality as a distinctively modern technology of governing and 'liberalism' as a distinctively modern form of political reason concerned with the limits of government. Emphasizing that there is no single version of liberal governmentality, Foucault contrasts two traditions of post-war liberal thought: a German school of so-called Ordo-liberalism, that defined the concept of the social market; and the economic liberalism associated with the Chicago School. In Foucault's view, what is most distinctive about this second line of 'neoliberal' thinking is that it seeks 'to extend the rationalities of the market, the schemes of analysis it proposes, and the decision-making criteria it suggests to areas that are not exclusively or primarily economic. For example, the family and birth policy, or delinquency and penal policy' (2000: 79). The extension of economic rationality into all areas of social life, which Foucault identifies as a feature of Chicago School neoliberalism, is, in fact, just one aspect of a broader reinvention of 'political economy', in which the reasoning of microeconomics has been applied to all sorts of social phenomena: in the Law and Economics movement, to issues of jurisprudence; in public choice theory, to bureaucratic dynamics and constitutional design; and in so-called 'new public management', to the reconfiguration of administrative systems. This economizing of the social and of the state is not merely 'ideological': it is rooted in the methodological practices of microeconomic reasoning, decision theory and game theory, which allows various activities to be modelled on the principle that all human behaviour is shaped by economic values of self-interested utility maximization.

Foucault's attention to this emergent tradition of political economy is not 'eccentric' when compared to the ideas of Hayek or Friedman, which geographers assume to be so singularly influential (cf. Sparke, 2006b). This energies might actually throw more insight on the dynamics of state restructuring upon which theorists of neoliberalism focus their energies. The persistent focus on 'free-market fundamentalism' in geographers' theorizations of neoliberalism leads to rather tortuous formulations of the observed disjunctures between putative theory (reducing the state) and actual practice (all sorts of state intervention). This betrays a conceptual and normative investment in static idealizations of models of the 'state' and the 'market', and a preference for analysis of all relationships in terms of 'contradiction'. Foucault's focus on liberalism as a rationality of government enables him to point to the extent to which 'neoliberal' ideas do not, in theory, imply any reduction of state action. They do, however, imply a reformulation of the principles and objectives of state activities according to economistic assumptions of individual and corporate behaviour. Far from assuming that the rhetoric of market efficiency and consumer choice are always and everywhere indicative of a privatizing and deregulatory agenda, it is important to recognize the degree to which this vocabulary and an attendant set of technologies of reform provide 'new ways of managing government agencies' (Slater and Tonkiss, 2001: 141).

In short, Foucault leads us to ask what it is that markets are supposed to be good for.

What problematizations do market rationalities respond to? Hindess (2002: 134–5) suggests that for liberalism, understood as a political rationality of government, the market is the exemplary form of free interaction, the model for demonstrating how the activities of numerous individuals can be coordinated without central authority. This idealization of the market as a decentralized mechanism of government operates at two levels: firstly, in the immediate present, individuals in markets are governed by the reactions of others with whom they interact; in the longer term, this sort of interaction with others leads to the internalization of standards which individuals use to regulate their own behaviour, so that market interaction is understood to be a good way of inculcating virtues such as prudence and self-control. This set of assumptions implies a wide spectrum of governmental strategies. On the one side, these assumptions can justify interventions that seek to govern or 'make-up' subjects able to engage in this sort of interaction. On the other side, these assumptions can imply using markets as the means of actually instilling market virtues.

This is the understanding of the market as a model for coordinating the actions of dispersed subjects that leads to the distinctive understanding of advanced liberalism in Foucauldian governmentality studies. Advanced liberalism is not defined as an ideology of free markets and minimal states, but as a set of discourses that invoke the power of choice, modelled on economics, as a primary motivator of human action in fields of interacting free subjects. This is a form of discourse that 'effectively dissolves economy's outside' (Engelmann, 2005: 33). But it does not necessarily imply that activities of the state should be transferred to the market, only that state activities be reordered around systems shaped by 'market' principles. These might vary from introducing 'competition', treating users as 'customers' or 'consumers', 'decentralizing' authority, or using audit technologies to encourage a focus on 'accountability' or 'outcomes'.

Foucault's attention to the economizing of the social in Chicago-style political economy should lead to a broadening of focus when it comes to tracing the intellectual genealogy of contemporary policy paradigms. Rather than focusing overwhelmingly on free-market economists and explicit agendas for reducing state intervention, which by Marxist and regulationalist theorists' own admission can be of little help in understanding how the practices of 'neoliberalization' actually get played out, it might be better to look farther afield. One obvious focus should be on the genealogy of 'rational choice' theories in social science. In so far as these traditions are considered at all in theories of neoliberalization, they are dismissed as adjuncts of 'free market fundamentalism' and the supposed hegemony of 'orthodox economics' (Peck, 2005). But 'free-market economics' does not provide a theory of administrative reform or of the management of public services, nor of constitutional design or of democratic governance. In contrast, public choice theory does. For that reason, public choice theory has been highly significant in the rise of 'government by the market' (Self, 1993). Reading this tradition symptomatically throws light upon the reordering of the rationalities of public administration, in contrast to any simple decline or dissolution of the public realm.

So what is public choice theory? Public choice theory provides a descriptive and normative methodology for modelling a range of collective decision-making processes:

> why people join interest groups, how voters choose between parties at election time, how coalitions form in committees and legislatures, how bureaucracies make policy and how subnational governments deliver policy outputs to citizens. (Dunleavy, 1991: 2)

Public choice theory treats government officials, civil servants and elected representatives as individual actors who respond to economic incentives – it is assumed that people involved in collective action act in the same way as they do when they act in markets, as self-interested agents. This work is referred to as 'public choice' because the choices that voters make, while deploying the same motivations and rationalities as consumers in the market, are decisions and preferences about 'public' matters – the design of constitutions, the make-up of government, and so on.

Public choice theory focuses on the asymmetric distribution of information in market relations, broadly defined, which creates incentives for the party with more information to cheat the party with less. In the application of these ideas to political processes in liberal democracy, public choice theory generates a rather dismal view of modern politics – dubbed 'politics without the romance' by one leading exponent (Buchanan, 1984). Public choice theory is, however, just one strand of a broader tradition of modern social science that deploys economic concepts of rationality to social and political issues. For example, in Kenneth Arrow's impossibility theorem, which is formative of social choice theory and welfare economics, the demonstration of the dependency of any collective preference function on the medium of aggregating individual preferences seems to challenge understandings of democratic legitimacy based on popular sovereignty. In Mancur Olson's seminal account of the logic of collective action, asymmetries of information and problems of free-riding mean that it is more likely that small groups will organize and exert influence than larger ones. When applied to the analysis of welfare systems, these forms of reasoning lead to a view of bureaucracies and bureaucrats as always seeking to maximize their own advantage, through rent-seeking for example, and thereby reducing the efficiency of distributive outcomes. This leads to the stronger claim that public goods are actually under-supplied by state bureaucracies, which are prone to capture by special interest groups.

Public choice theory therefore belongs to what is a much broader tradition of 'bureau-critique'. Its development as an academic field has certainly been closely associated with a right-wing political inflection (cf. Dunleavy, 1991; Dryzek, 1992). But the broader tradition of bureau-critique stretches across the political spectrum (see Du Gay, 2000). This suggests that, when it is understood as a political rationality of contemporary governmentality, one can read public choice theory symptomatically as providing an insight into the relational fields through which policies easily labelled as 'neoliberal' are actually shaped. For starters, we might observe that the argument that neoliberal free-market ideology mobilizes an intuitive but seductive rhetoric of 'freedom' and 'choice' underestimates the degree to which contemporary governance-talk is all about 'delivery', 'participation' and 'empowerment'. This vocabulary is indicative of a problematization that revolves around the difficulty of making bureaucratic and administrative systems responsive and accountable to diverse users. In short, this is an approach to issues of public administration that treats market-based solutions not simply in terms of efficiency criteria, but as means of achieving 'democratic' objectives of accountability and responsiveness (Armbrüster, 2005).

If one understands this new tradition of political economy as one variant of a family of political rationalities of liberal governmentality, then its most pertinent feature is the methodological analysis of both market and non-market interactions as networks of principals and agents (Przeworski, 2003). Principal–agent relations are those where the 'principal' (a customer, a citizen, a service user) offers the 'agent' (a seller, a politician, a bureaucrat) a contract to work for him or her. The analysis of principal–agent relations focuses in particular upon situations where asymmetric information between principals and agents leads to problems of how to align the interests of the two parties: it is assumed that there is a problem in motivating agents to act on behalf of principals rather than to use their advantageous position to bolster their own self-interest. This problematization leads therefore to a search for incentive structures that will encourage agents to align their own self-interests with forms of action which will also be of benefit to their clients. It also recasts the role of elected officials as champions of the interests of public service users, seeking to rein in and discipline indifferent and inflexible 'producer' interests in bureaucracies and expert professions. Reading the rise of public choice theory and related fields such as 'new public management' symptomatically, then, brings back into view the constitutive role of relational fields of political action in reshaping relationships between different institutions of the state, and their interactions with each other and with other actors in civil society.

Thinking seriously about the political rationalities of liberal governmentality should lead to the recognition of how assumptions about *motivation* and *agency* help shape public policy and institutional design. For example, market reforms in social policy in the UK have been partly driven by fiscal pressures dictated by 'neoliberal' macroeconomic policies. However, just as important 'was a fundamental shift in policy-makers' perceptions concerning motivation and agency' (LeGrand, 2006: 4). LeGrand suggests a stylized distinction between two models of motivation and two models of agency.

- If it is assumed that people are wholly motivated by self-interest, they are thought of as *knaves*; if they are thought of as motivated by public-spirited altruism, they are *knights*.
- If it is assumed that people have little or no capacity for independent action, then they are thought of as *pawns*; if they are treated as active agents, they are thought of as *queens*.

This distinction helps to throw light upon how institutional reconfigurations of welfare are shaped by changing assumptions about how state agencies function, how officials are motivated, to what extent people are agents, and in particular how agential capacities of recipients can be mobilized to make public officials more knight-like. LeGrand characterizes the post-1979 period of social policy in the UK as 'the triumph of the knaves'. It involved two related shifts: towards an empirical assumption about the knavish tendencies of professionals working in public administration; and towards a normative assumption that users should be treated more like queens than pawns. The preference for 'market' reforms follows from these two assumptions:

> if it is believed that workers are primarily knaves and that consumers ought to be king, [then it follows that] the market is the way in which the pursuit of self-interest by providers can be corralled to serve the interests of consumers. (LeGrand, 2006: 9).

This suggests that the distinction between Keynesian social democracy and neoliberalism is not just a difference between abstract, substantive principles: egalitarianism (and the state as a vehicle of social justice) versus liberty (and the state as a threat to this). Just as significant is a practical difference between two sets of beliefs about motivation and agency (ibid.: 12). 'Neoliberals' tend to think of motivation in terms of self-interest and egoism, 'social democrats' in terms of knights and altruism. And 'neoliberals' tend to presume a capacity for autonomous action, whereas 'social democrats' presume this capacity is conditioned and therefore can be justifiably cultivated by state action.

This stylized characterization of the shifting 'rationalities' of social policy in the UK indicates that, far from 'the market' always being presented as an alternative realm to be favoured over 'the state', the market is seen as the source for various models of incentives, management and institutional design through which state practices are reconfigured. These assumptions are certainly open to criticism (see Bowles and Gintis, 2006; Green and Shapiro, 1994; Mansbridge, 1990; Taylor, 2006). But treating them symptomatically, as indicative of emergent political rationalities, underlines the extent to which the imperatives shaping public policy involve reconfiguring relationships between elected politicians, state bureaucracies and user groups. It also deflates policy paradigms as the primary forces driving social change, drawing into focus the ways in which policies are shaped in a broader relational context in which the meanings and content of accountability, democracy, entitlement, equality, legitimacy and rights are objects of political contention.

A symptomatic reading of the political rationalities of post-Keynesian public policy therefore throws light on the claims of public value embedded in these apparently 'neoliberal' discourses, claims that reach beyond narrow values of efficiency or personal freedom to encompass collective goods such as accountability and trust. This not only suggests that neoliberalization might be better thought of as an *effect* rather than a cause (cf. Mitchell, 1999), a response to broad secular changes in social formations. It also throws light upon the generation of new sites of political contestation. Programmes of governance also create new scenes of encounter between citizens and 'the state' (e.g. Corbridge et al., 2006; Skelcher et al., 2005; Barnes et al., 2003) and, by expanding imperatives to engage in collaboration, consultation and participation, they provide differential opportunities for actors to enact and challenge assigned forms of 'citizenly' agency.

SO WHAT IS WRONG WITH NEOLIBERALISM?

This chapter has highlighted various conceptual limitations of theories of neoliberalism and neoliberalization. These theories are characterized by static idealizations of the contradictions between 'the state' and 'the market' which actually reiterate the simplistic views they ascribe to neoliberal purists. They tend to suppose that changes in state activities are the outcome of 'ideational projects', a view sustained by invoking expressive concepts of ideology, culturalist conceptions of hegemony, and instrumental conceptions of discourse. They tend in turn to project a distinctive geographical imaginary of cascading scales and spaces of diffusion, enabling highly abstract deductions about capital accumulation to be articulated with more concrete notions of the state, gender relations, racial formations, and other 'contextual' factors. And it is assumed that social formations are reproduced functionally through various mechanisms of naturalization, whether ideological or, in the Foucauldian inflection, through processes of subjectification.

Theories of neoliberalism render 'the social' a residual aspect of more fundamental processes in three ways. Firstly, social practices are reduced to residual, more-or-less resistant effects of restructuring processes shaped by the transparent class interests of capital. This means that social relations of gender, ethnicity or race, for example, are considered as contextual factors shaping the geographically variable manifestations of general neoliberalizing tendencies. Secondly, 'the social' is also reduced to a residual effect by being considered only in so far as it is the object of state administration in the interests of economic efficiency, or to strategies of 'governmental rationality'. Thirdly, and related to this, 'the social' is construed as the more-or-less manipulable surface for ideological normalization or discursive subjectification.

This final section throws into relief the normative limitations of theories of neoliberalism. If neoliberalism is a critics' term, what are the terms of criticism invoked by these theories: *what is wrong with neoliberalism*?

The concept of neoliberalization implies that neoliberalism is both *parasitic* on and *corrosive* of other social processes, but, as already suggested, the source of this doubly destructive energy is never quite specified in these theories. The immediate objects of criticism are a range of substantive and observable social harms: rising levels of socio-economic inequality; authoritarianism; corrupt government; the concentration of wealth. But these immediate objects of criticism are seen as inevitable outcomes of a system which has encouraged the disembedding of economic relations from broader structures of normative steering. It is the imputed content of neoliberalism as a narrowly individualistic, egoistic rationality that is the source of the status ascribed to it as a 'strong discourse', at once parasitic and corrosive. It is on these grounds that neoliberalism is viewed as nothing short of 'a programme of the methodical destruction of collectives' (Bourdieu, 1998).

The view that neoliberalism unleashes pathological human tendencies otherwise properly held in check by collective conventions is a distinctive updating of Polanyi's view of market capitalism as an unnatural formation. What is at work here is a theoretical imaginary in which the extension of accumulation by market exchange is understood to necessarily undermine forms of social integration previously knitted together through the state. Theories of neoliberalism display an intense ambivalence towards 'the state'. On the one hand, they follow a classical Marxist view in which the state is a territorial sovereign systematically involved in the reproduction of capital accumulation. On the other, they hark back almost nostalgically to a social democratic view in which the state stands opposed to the market as a counterweight, representing an opposing principle of social integration and political legitimacy.

In accepting the same simplistic opposition between individual freedom and social justice presented by Hayek, but simply reversing the evaluation of the two terms, critics of neoliberalism end up presenting highly *moralistic* forms of analysis of contemporary political processes. In resisting the idealization of the market as the embodiment of public virtue, they end up embracing an equally idealized view of the forum as the alternative figure of collective life (see Elster, 1986). For example, while Harvey insists that neoliberalism is a process driven by the aim of restoring class power, he ends his analysis by arguing that it is the anti-democratic character of neoliberalism that should be the focal point of opposition (Harvey, 2005: 2: 205–6). But it is far from clear whether the theories of neoliberalism and neoliberalization developed by Marxian political economists, sometimes with the help of governmentality studies, can contribute to reconstructing a theory and practice of radical democratic justice. In Harvey's analysis, the withdrawal of the state is taken for granted, and leads to the destruction of previous solidarities, unleashing pathologies of anomie, anti-social behaviour and criminality (ibid.: 81). In turn, the vacuum created by the withdrawal of the state leads to social solidarities being reconstructed around other axes, of religion and morality, associationalism, and nationalism. What has been described as the rise of the 'movement society', expressed in the proliferation of contentious politics of rights-based struggles and identity politics, Harvey sees as just one aspect of a spread of corrosive social forms triggered by the rolling-back of states. In the wake of this rolling-back', '[e]verything from gangs and criminal cartels, narco-trafficking networks, mini-mafias and favela bosses, through community, grassroots and non-governmental organizations, to secular cults and religious sects proliferate, (ibid.: 171). These are alternative social forms 'that fill the void left behind as state powers, political parties, and other institutional forms are actively dismantled or simply wither away as centres of collective endeavour and of social bonding' (ibid., 171).

Harvey (2005) suggests his own bundle of rights as an alternative to the neoliberal regime of rights. These include 'the right to life chances', 'control over production by the direct producers', the right 'to a decent and healthy living environment', and 'to collective control of common property resources' (ibid.: 204). He provides little sense of how the inevitable tensions and trade-offs between these sorts of rights would be negotiated and decided in practice (beyond the reiteration of Marx's comment that 'Between equal rights, force decides' as if this were both a matter of fact and of principle). Harvey's preference for 'substantive' democracy and social justice is associated with a persistent denigration of procedural issues without which any meaningful practice of democracy is unimaginable. Harvey casts struggles for cultural, civil, sexual or reproductive rights since the 1960s as inevitably complicit with the 'neoliberal frame', favouring 'individual freedoms' over 'social justice' (ibid.: 41–3). Likewise the emergence of international human rights movements and the development of non-governmental politics is damned as complicit with the 'neoliberal frame' of individual rights and privatization (ibid.: 176–7). This is a travesty of complex political movements that have pioneered struggles for social justice along diverse fronts, not least when Harvey claims that these movements have not focused on developing 'substantive and open democratic governance structures' (ibid.: 176).

What's really wrong with neoliberalism, for critics who have constructed it as a coherent object of analysis, is the unleashing of destructive pathologies through the combined withdrawal of the state and the unfettered growth of market exchange. 'Individual freedom' is presented as a medium of uninhibited hedonism, which if given too much free reign undermines the ascetic virtues of self-denial upon which struggles for 'social justice' are supposed to depend.

Underwritten by simplistic moral denunciations of 'the market', these theories push aside a series of analytic, explanatory and normative questions. In the case of both the Marxist narrative of neoliberalization and the Foucauldian analysis of neoliberal governmentality, it remains unclear whether either of these traditions can provide adequate resources for thinking about the practical problems of democracy, rights and social justice. This is not helped by the systematic denigration in both lines of thought of 'liberalism', a catch-all term used with little discrimination. There is a tendency to present neoliberalism as the natural end-point or rolling-out of a longer tradition of liberal thought – an argument only sustainable through the implicit invocation of some notion of a liberal 'episteme' covering all varieties and providing a core of meaning. One of the lessons drawn by diverse strands of radical political theory from the experience of twentieth-century history is that struggles for social justice can create new forms of domination and inequality. It is this that leads to a grudging appreciation of liberalism as a potential source of insight into the politics of pluralistic associational life. The cost of the careless disregard for 'actually existing liberalisms' is to remain blind to the diverse strands of egalitarian thought about the relationships between democracy, rights and social justice that one finds in, for example: post-Rawslian political philosophy; post-Habermasian theories of democracy, including their feminist variants; various postcolonial liberalisms; the flowering of agonistic liberalisms and theories of radical democracy; and the revival of republican theories of democracy, freedom and justice. No doubt theorists of neoliberalism would see all this as hopelessly trapped within the 'neoliberal frame' of individualism, although, if one takes this argument to its logical conclusion, even Marx's critique of capitalist exploitation, dependent as it is on an ideal of self-ownership, is nothing more than a variation on Lockean individual rights.

Any serious consideration of democracy, rights and social justice cannot afford to ignore the fields of social science in which issues of rationality, motivation and agency are most fully theorized. These often turn out to be fields normally considered too 'liberal' for the tastes of critical human geographers (cf. Sayer, 1995). These fields can serve as potential sources for revised understandings of the tasks of critical theory, ones which do not fall back into ahistorical, overly sociologized criticisms of any appearance of individualism or self-interest as menacing the very grounds of public virtue and the common good. Problems of coordination, institutional design and justification are central to any normatively persuasive and empirically grounded critical theory of democracy. For example, the problem central to social choice theory – the difficulty of arriving at collective preference functions by aggregating individual preferences – is a fundamental issue in democratic theory, around which contemporary theories of deliberative democracy are increasingly focused (Goodin, 2003). Likewise, Amartya Sen's (2002) critique of public choice theory's assumption that people are 'rational fools' provides the most compelling criticism of the one-dimensional understanding of rationality, motivation and agency upon which orthodox economic and public policy depends. This critique informs the 'capabilities approach' which connects key problems in welfare economics to a theory of egalitarian rights and political democracy (Sen, 1999; Corbridge, 2002). These are just two examples of work that takes seriously the problematization of agency, motivation and rationality in 'rational choice' social science in order to move social theory beyond the consoling idea that rampant individualism can be tamed by moral injunctions of the public good and weak claims about social construction.

The ascendancy of 'neoliberalism' as a theoretical object of approbation is symptomatic of the negative interpretation of 'critical' in contemporary critical human geography. Being critical, in this view, requires that one has a clear-sighted view of an object that one is *critical of*. Theories of neoliberalism provide a compelling picture of such an object by providing an account of the displacement of socially embedded practices of reciprocity and their reconfiguration by the pathological rationalities of market exchange. This style of theorizing leads to a mode of critical analysis in which change is always interpreted in zero-sum terms, as the encroachment of neoliberal rationalities into realms of social solidarity. It is a style of analysis that makes it impossible to acknowledge diverse dynamics of change, and in turn remains blind to emergent public rationalities:

> If you believe in the implacable domination of economic forces, you cannot believe in the possibility of social movements; at the very best, you will see the movement of society as an expression of the systems' internal contradictions, or as a manifestation of objective suffering and poverty. (Touraine, 2001: 3)

Neoliberalism as an object of analysis is certainly a critics' term. The explicit formulation of neoliberalism into an object of theoretical analysis in critical human geography has been associated with the turning-in of intellectual curiosity around a very narrow space, bounded by Marxist political economy on the one side and poststructuralist political ontologies on the other. As long as this remains the horizon of normative reflection, critical human geographers will continue to always know in advance what they are expected to be *critical of* but will remain unable to articulate convincingly what they are being *critical for*.

NOTE

1 Foucault's work is a rather ambiguous reference for any critique of the dissolution of the public realm under the force of neoliberalism, in so far as it calls into question the validity of the normative vision of public rationality that is meant to be embodied in those institutional configurations menaced by neoliberalism.

REFERENCES

Agrawal, A. (2005) *Environmentality*. Durham, NC: Duke University Press.

Armbrüster, T. (2005) 'Bureaucracy and the controversy between liberal interventionism and non-interventionism', in P. Du Gay (ed.), *The Values of Bureaucracy*. Oxford: Oxford University Press. pp. 63–85.

Barnett, C. (2001) 'Culture, geography and the arts of government', *Environment and Planning D: Society and Space*, 19: 7–24.

Barnett, C. (2005) 'The consolations of 'neoliberalism'', *Geoforum*, 36: 7–12.

Barnett, C., Cloke, P., Clarke, N. and Malpass, A. (2008) 'The elusive subjects of neoliberalism', *Cultural Studies*, 22: 624–653.

Barnes, M., Newman, J., Knops, A. and Sullivan, H. (2003) 'Constituting "the public" in public participation', *Public Administration*, 81: 379–99.

Beck, U. and Beck-Gernsheim, E. (2001) *Individualization*. London: Sage.

Bondi, L. (2005) 'Working the spaces of neoliberal subjectivity', *Antipode*, 37: 497–514.

Bondi, L. and Laurie, N. (2005) 'Introduction: Working the spaces of neoliberalism: Activism, professionalisation and incorporation', *Antipode*, 37: 394–401.

Bourdieu, P. (1998) 'The essence of neoliberalism', *Le Monde Diplomatique*, December. <http://mondediplo.com/1998/12/08bourdieu>

Bowles, S. and Gintis, H. (2006) 'Social preferences, *homo economicus*, and *zoon politikon*', in R. Goodin and C. Tilly (eds), *The Oxford Handbook of Contextual Analysis*. Oxford: Oxford University Press. pp. 172–86.

Brenner, N. and Theodore, N. (2002) 'Cities and geographies of "actually existing neoliberalism"', *Antipode*, 34: 349–79.

Brown, W. (2003) 'Neo-liberalism and the end of liberal democracy', *Theory and event*, 7: 1.

Brown, W. (2006a) 'American nightmare: neoliberalism, neoconservatism, and de-democratization', *Political Theory*, 34: 690–714.

Brown, W. (2006b) 'Power after Foucault', in J. Dryzek, B. Honig and A. Phillips (eds), *The Oxford Handbook of Political Theory*. Oxford: Oxford University Press. pp. 65–84.

Buchanan, J. M. (1984) 'Politics without romance: a sketch of positive public choice and its normative implications', in J.M. Buchanan and R. Tollison (eds), *The Theory of Public Choice – II*. Ann Arbor: University of Michigan Press, pp. 11–22.

Castree, N. (2006) 'From neoliberalism to neoliberalization: consolations, confusions and necessary illusions', *Environment and Planning A*, 38: 1–6.

Castree, N. (2008) 'Neoliberalising nature 2: processes, effects and evaluations', *Environment and Planning A*, 40: 153–73.

Clarke, J. (2003) 'Turning inside out? Globalization, neo-liberalism and welfare states', *Anthropologica*, 45: 201–14.

Clarke, J. (2004a) 'Constructing citizen-consumers'. Paper prepared for the conference: *Contemporary Governance and the Question of the Social*, University of Alberta, 11–13 June 2004.

Clarke, J. (2004b) 'Dissolving the public realm? The logic and limits of neo-liberalism', *Journal of Social Policy*, 33: 27–48.

Clarke, J. (2004c) 'Subjects of doubt', Paper prepared for the CASCA (Canadian Anthropological Society) Conference, London, Ontario, 5–9 May.

Clarke, J. (2004d) *Changing Welfare, Changing States*. London: Sage.

Clarke, J. (2005) 'New Labour's citizens: activated, empowered, responsibilized, abandoned?', *Critical Social Policy*, 25: 447–63.

Corbridge, S. (2000) 'Development as freedom: the spaces of Amartya Sen', *Progress in Development Studies*, 2: 183–217.

Corbridge, S. (2008) 'State and society', in K. Cox, M. Low and J. Robinson (eds), *The Handbook of Political Geography*. London: Sage, pp. 107–122.

Corbridge, S., Williams, G., Srivastava, M. and Veron, R. (2006) *Seeing the State*. Cambridge: Cambridge University Press.

Cruickshank, B. (1999) *The Will to Empower*. Ithaca: Cornell University Press.

Dryzek, J. (1992) 'How far is it from Virginia and Rochester to Frankfurt? Public choice as critical theory', *British Journal of Political Science*, 22: 397–417.

Du Gay, P. (2000) *In Praise of Bureaucracy*. London: Sage.

Du Gay, P. (2005) 'Which is the self in self-interest?', *Sociological Review*, 53: 391–411.

Dunleavy, P. (1991) *Democracy, Bureaucracy, and Public Choice: Economic Explanations in Political Science*. London: Longman.

Elster, J. (1986) 'The market and the forum', in J. Elster and A. Hylland (eds), *Foundations of Social Choice Theory*. Cambridge: Cambridge University Press. pp. 103–32.

Engelmann, S. (2005) 'Posner, Bentham and the rule of economy', *Economy and Society*, 34: 32–50.

Esping-Andersen, G. (1996) Welfare States in Transition: National Adaptations in Global Economies. London: Sage.

Feher, M. (2007) *Nongovernmental Politics*. New York: Zone Books.

Foucault, M. (1988) *The History of Sexuality, Vol. 2*. London: Penguin Books.

Foucault, M. (1991) 'Governmentality', in G. Burchell, C. Gordon and P. Miller (eds), *The Foucault Effect: Studies in Governmentality*. London: Harvester Wheatsheaf. pp. 87–104.

Foucault, M. (1997) *Ethics*. London: Penguin Books.

Foucault, M. (2000) *Power*. London: Penguin Books.

Foucault, M. (2008) *The Birth of Biopolitics*. Basingstoke: Palgrave Macmillan.

Genev, V.I. (2005) 'The "Triumph of Neoliberalism" reconsidered: Critical remarks on ideas-centered analyses of political and economic change in post-communism', *East European Politics and Society*, 19:3: 343–78.

Glyn, A. (2006) *Capitalism Unleashed*. Oxford: Oxford University Press.

Gökariksel, B. and Mitchell, K. (2005) 'Veiling, secularism, and the neoliberal subject: national narratives and supranational desires in Turkey and France', *Global Networks*, 5 (2): 147–65.

Goodin, R. (2003) *Reflective Democracy*. Oxford: Oxford University Press.

Green, D. and Shapiro, I. (1994) *Pathologies of Rational Choice Theory*. New Haven: Yale University Press.

Guala, F. (2006) 'Review of Michel Foucault, Naissance de la biopolitique: Cours au Collège de France, 1978–1979', Economics and Philosophy, 22: 429–39.

Hacking, I. (2002) 'Making-up people', in *Historical Ontology*. Cambridge, MA: Harvard University Press. pp. 99–114.

Hacking, I. (2004) 'Between Michel Foucault and Erving Goffman: between discourse in the abstract and face-to-face interaction', *Economy and Society*, 33: 277–302.

Harvey, D. (2005) *A Brief History of Neoliberalism*. Oxford: Oxford University Press.

Harvey, D. (2006) 'Neo-liberalism as creative destruction', *Geografiska Annaler*, 88B: 145–58.

Hay, C. (2002) 'Globalization as a problem of political analysis: restoring agents to a process without a subject and politics to a logic of economic compulsion', *Cambridge Review of International Affairs*, 15:3: 379–92.

Hay, C. (2004) 'Re-stating politics, re-politicising the state: neo-liberalism, economic imperatives and the rise of the competition state', *Political Studies Quarterly*, 75:s1 38–50.

Hindess, B. (2002) 'Neo-liberal citizenship', *Citizenship Studies*, 6 (2): 127–43.

Hodges, I. (2002) 'Moving beyond words: therapeutic discourse and ethical problematization', *Discourse Studies*, 4: 455–79.

Hoffman, L., DeHart, M. and Collier, S. (2006) 'Notes on the anthropology of neoliberalism', *Anthropology News*, 47 (6): 9–10.

Honneth, A. (1991) *The Critique of Power*. Cambridge, MA: MIT Press.

Isin, E. (2004) 'The Neurotic Citizen', *Citizenship Studies*, 8: 217–35.

Jessop, B. (1999) 'Narrating the future of the national economy and the national state', in G. Steinmetz (ed.), *State/Culture*. Ithaca: Cornell University Press. pp. 378–405.

Jessop, B. (2002) *The Future of the Capitalist State*. Cambridge: Polity Press.

Jessop, B. (2007) 'From micro-powers to governmentality', *Political Geography*, 26: 34–40.

Johnston, R.J. and Glasmeier, A. (2007) 'Neo-liberalism, democracy and the state', *Space and Polity*, 11: 1–33.

Larner, W. (2000) 'Neo-liberalism: Policy, ideology, governmentality', *Studies in Political Economy*, 63: 5–26.

Larner, W. (2006) 'Review of A Brief History of Neoliberalism', *Economic Geography*, 82: 449–51.

Larner, W. (2007) 'Situating neoliberalism: geographies of a contested concept'. Paper presented at 'Neoliberalism and environmental governance' workshop, The Open University,Milton Keynes, September.

Larner, W. and Walters, W. (eds) (2004) *Global Governmentality: Governing international spaces*. London: Routledge.

Larner, W., Le Heron, R. and Lewis, N. (2007) 'Co-constituting "After neoliberalism": political projects and globalising governmentalities in Aotearoa New Zealand', in K. England and K. Ward (eds), *Neoliberalization*. Oxford: Blackwell.

Le Grand, J. (2006) *Motivation, Agency and Public Policy*. Oxford: Oxford University Press.

Leitner, H., Sheppard, E., Sziarto, K. and Maringanti, A. (2007) 'Contesting urban futures: decentering neoliberalism', in H. Leitner, J. Peck and E. Sheppard (eds), *Contesting Neoliberalism: Urban Frontiers*. New York: Guilford. pp. 1–25.

Lemke, T. (2001) 'The birth of bio-politics: Michel Foucault's lecture at the College de France on neo-liberal governmentality', *Economy and Society*, 30 (2): 190–207.

Lemke, T. (2002) 'Foucault, governmentality and critique', *Rethinking Marxism*, 14 (3): 49–64.

Li, T. (2007) *The Will to Improve*. Durham, NC: Duke University Press.

Mann, M. (1988) 'The autonomous power of the state: its origins, mechanisms and results', in *States, War and Capitalism: Studies in Political Sociology*. Oxford: Blackwell.

Mann, M. (1993) *The Sources of Social Power, Volume 2*. Cambridge: Cambridge University Press.
Mansbridge, J. (ed.) (1990) *Beyond Self-Interest*. Chicago: University of Chicago Press.
Migdal, J.S. (2001) *State in Society*. Cambridge: Cambridge University Press.
Mitchell, K. (2003) 'Educating the national citizen in neoliberal times', *Transactions of the Institute of British Geographers*, 28: 387–403.
Mitchell, K. (2004) *Crossing the Neoliberal Line*. Philadelphia: Temple University Press.
Mitchell, K (2006) 'Neoliberal governmentality in the European Union', *Environment and Planning D: Society and Space*, 24: 389–407.
Mitchell, T. (1999) 'Society, economy and the state effect', in G. Steinmetz (ed.), *State/Culture*. Ithaca: Cornell University Press. pp. 76–97.
Murray, R. (2004) 'The new political economy of public life', *Soundings*, 27: 19–32.
Newman, J. (2004) 'Managerialism and social welfare', in G. Hughes and G. Lewis (eds), *Unsettling Welfare*. London: Routledge. pp. 333–75.
Norris, P. (1998) *Democratic Phoenix*. Cambridge: Cambridge University Press.
Offe, C. (1996) 'State action and structures of collective will-formation', in C. Offe, *Modernity and the State*. Cambridge: Polity Press.
Ong, A. (1999) *Flexible Citizenship*. Durham, NC: Duke University Press.
Ong, A. (2007) 'Neoliberalism as a mobile technology', *Transactions of the Institute of British Geographers*, NS 32: 3–8.
Painter, J. (2006) 'Prosaic geographies of stateness', *Political Geography*, 25: 752–74.
Peck, J. (2001) 'Neoliberalizing states', *Progress in Human Geography*, 25: 445–55.
Peck, J. (2004) 'Geography and public policy: constructions of neoliberalism', *Progress in Human Geography*, 28: 392–405.
Peck, J. (2005) 'Economic sociologies in space', *Economic Geography*, 81: 129–76.
Peck, J. (2006) 'Response: countering neoliberalism', *Urban Geography*, 27: 729–33.
Peck, J. and Tickell, A. (2002) 'Neoliberalizing space', *Antipode*, 34: 380–404.
Plehwe, D., Walpen, B. and Neunhöffer, G. (eds) (2006) *Neoliberal Hegemony*. London: Routledge.
Polyani, K. (1944) *The Great Transformation*. London: Rhinehart.
Prasad, M. (2006) *The Politics of Free Markets*. Chicago: University of Chicago Press.
Przeworski, A. (1992) 'The neoliberal fallacy', *Journal of Democracy*, 3: 45–59.
Przeworski, A. (2003) *States and Markets*. Cambridge: Cambridge University Press.
Rodríguez-Pose, A. and Storper, M. (2006) 'Better rules or stronger communities?', *Economic Geography*, 82: 1–25.
Rose, N. (1999) *Powers of Freedom*. Cambridge: Cambridge University Press.
Sayer, A. (1995) *Radical Political Economy*. Oxford: Blackwell.
Schumpeter, J. (1942) *Capitalism, Socialism and Democracy*. London: George Allen and Unwin.
Self, P. (1993) *Government by the Market*. Basingstoke: Macmillan.
Sen, A. (1999) *Development as Freedom*. Oxford: Oxford University Press.
Sen, A. (2002) *Rationality and Freedom*. Cambridge MA: Harvard University Press.
Skelcher, C., Mathur, N. and Smith, M. (2005) 'The public governance of collaborative spaces', *Public Administration*, 83 (3): 573–96.
Skocpol, T. (1979) *States and Social Revolutions*. Cambridge: Cambridge University Press.
Slater, D. and Tonkiss, F. (2001) *Market Society*. Cambridge: Polity Press.
Smith, S.J. (2005) 'States, markets and an ethic of care', *Political Geography*, 24: 1–20.
Sparke, M. (2006a) 'A neoliberal nexus', *Political Geography*, 25: 151–80.
Sparke, M. (2006b) 'Political geographies of globalization: (2) Governance', *Progress in Human Geography*, 30: 1–16.
Stokes, S. (2001) *Mandates and Democracy: Neoliberalism by Surprise*. Cambridge: Cambridge University Press.
Taylor, M. (2006) *Rationality and the Ideology of Disconnection*. Cambridge: Cambridge University Press.
Taylor-Gooby, P. (ed.) (2001) *Welfare States Under Pressure*. London: Sage.
Taylor-Gooby, P. (2003) 'Open markets versus welfare citizenship', *Social Policy and Administration*, 37: 539–54.
Taylor-Gooby, P., Dean, H., Munro, M. and Parker, G. (1999) 'Risk and the welfare

state', *British Journal of Sociology*, 2 (1): 177–94.
Touraine, A. (2001) *Beyond Neoliberalism*. Cambridge: Polity Press.
Traub-Werner, M. (2007) 'Free trade: a governmentality approach', *Environment and Planning A*, 39: 1441–56.
Walkerdine, V. (2005) 'Freedom, psychology and the neoliberal worker', *Soundings*, 29: 35–46.
Yeates, N. (2002) 'Globalization and social policy: from neoliberal hegemony to global policy pluralism', *Global Social Policy*, 2: 69–91.

SECTION 3

Geographies of Wellbeing

Edited by

Rachel Pain and Susan J. Smith

Introduction: Geographies of Wellbeing

Rachel Pain and Susan J. Smith

Divisions of welfare have always been a core concern for social geographers. To this end, most effort has been expended – rightly – on spelling out what is wrong: on accounting for the drivers of inequality and exclusion; on identifying the factors that compromise health; on charting the contours of ill-being. For a while, it seemed complacent to think about the opposite end of the spectrum: to explore the condition of contentment, the state of wellness, or the predictors of wellbeing. But all this has changed in recent years. Partly this follows a flurry of empirical evidence which suggests that ill-being and wellbeing are not two sides of a coin: tackling crime does not necessarily allay people's fears; curing disease does not automatically promote health; removing risks may not enhance resilience; reducing homelessness does not create a sense of belonging; poverty and ill-being often go together, but wealth and well-being do not, and so on. The consensus now is that challenging the negatives in life is only a step towards enacting the positives.

There is also a conceptual argument for focussing on positive wellbeing – whilst always challenging the processes which damage human life – namely that the two co-exist; they are implied in (and to an extent can be wrested from) each other. Hopes and fears are not mutually exclusive, for example; they are co-present, propelling one another into life. Just how this works is context-dependent, but there are writings within this section and elsewhere which point to the transformative potential of hope-embedded-in-fear (Pain and S.J. Smith 2008; Wright 2008). At a different scale, Gough et al. (2007) note that while there is a broad tendency to link poverty with the global south and wellbeing with the developed world, these states are contingent on, and cannot be explained apart from, one another.

There is a policy steer too, though this can be worrying, emphasising as it does the many things individuals and communities – rather than societies and governments – can do to enhance their own state of health, body and mind. As Sointu (2005) argues, the rise of wellbeing has an inescapable politics, and this is very often tied to the neoliberal agendas of European governments who are keen to assign more responsibility for welfare to individuals. From this perspective the discourse of wellbeing demands 'changes in the character of subjectivity', and the creation of 'a social context which emphasises proactive agency and self-responsibility as meaningful and normal, with the self and the body providing particularly amenable areas for the exercise of self-responsible agency' (Sointu, 2005: 255). As Sointu so elegantly demonstrates, all catchy ideas are prone to political hijacking, and wellbeing is no exception. On the whole, however, a growing scholarly interest in wellbeing is inspired by a practical concern to locate, preserve and enhance both the material and emotional underpinnings of a 'good' life. Much of this work – like that reported in this section – is rooted in everyday experiences, contributing to definitions and understandings of wellbeing which reflect ground-up senses and belief systems. In that respect, they help resist and challenge top-down discourses, rather than allowing them to be absorbed into our academic work. Not all the chapters in this section use the label wellbeing, but all contribute in some way to an enlarged understanding of the spaces, places and circumstances which enhance or undermine human dignity. In this introduction, we provide a brief overview of the interrelated areas of material wellbeing, emotions and care that are being developed across a range of contemporary social geographies. We begin, however, by exploring the umbrella term that has increasing currency in the sub-discipline at present, wellbeing itself.

'Wellbeing' is a term that geographers and others have used as a loose descriptor for many years; as a more rounded conceptual tool, too, it has been important for some social scientists for nearly a quarter of a century (Diener, 1984). But it is only since the turn of the millennium that it has come to resonate widely across a range of public, policy, popular and academic spheres, rapidly becoming a catch-all state and a policy goal which is being articulated and deployed in different ways. It is a contested concept, whose meaning might be peculiarly specific to the English language, and which is tackled by a range of disciplines, and through very varied philosophical and methodological approaches (see Carlisle and Hanlon, 2007; Searle, 2008). In geography, however, the idea has so far mostly tied to debates around health. The 'growing but disparate focus' of wellbeing research is one which Robin Kearns and Gavin Andrews's chapter charts effectively, providing an account of the stages, shapes, sites, sounds and surrounds of wellbeing. This neatly complements Fleuret and Atkinson's (2007) concern with the way wellbeing is constituted in: spaces of capability or self-fulfilment, integrative spaces (rich networks of social associations), spaces of security from risk, and therapeutic spaces where particular aspects of place have a role in healing. Resonant with so many core themes of welfare geography, a focus on wellbeing provides a window onto the emotional, psychological, material, social, spiritual and economic aspects of being in places, of forging relationships in and with those places, and of constructing and experiencing what are now widely recognised as place, or contextual, effects.

This broad set of ideas frames this section of the Handbook, and it connects a handful of chapters that, some years ago, might have looked disparate. It is, indeed, the connective and holistic impulses of 'wellbeing' that many are now finding have purchase: the concept's value is in being integrative and joined-up; in acknowledging the right every person has to a 'fully rounded humanity' which is more than simply meeting subsistence needs (Gough et al., 2007). Given our interest in this Handbook in the connectedness of the many phenomena that shape the socio-spatial world, wellbeing is an appealing label for a condition which captures the many factors now thought to be important to health, happiness, security and quality of life; it also holds the potential to establish more broadly what it means (or should mean) to live with dignity; to be human and to be humane.

The essays in this section show how social geographers are building critical understandings of this relatively new concept, both to cast light on traditional themes and to open up new concerns in the subdiscipline. The authors draw together, and find links between, the many aspects of material and emotional wellbeing (on the one hand) and distress (on the other) which are part and parcel of everyday life. They build from the long tradition of work on spaces of fear, anxiety and disease, whilst embracing newer concerns with geographies of health, resilience and contentment, and they employ various conceptual framings that help in this task. The chapters thus explore the underpinnings of wellbeing (through an emphasis on safekeeping and health) and the risks of emotional and material harm. They are concerned with fear and victimisation, as well as with geographies of personal and community safety. They discuss the shape of health inequalities, whilst charting the emotional geographies of resilience, contentment and hope.

Some accounts of wellbeing in the wider literature, many of which stem from the enormous interest in this idea among psychologists, locate it as a condition of individuals. However, this section of the Handbook makes the case for a particularly *social* geographical notion of wellbeing: a condition that is at once collective and contextually sensitive; that incorporates understandings about the sociality of materials and of emotions and their interweaving with the lives of individuals, communities and societies. These are accounts which deal explicitly with issues of agency and empowerment, tackle themes like resilience as well as vulnerabilities, and include people's shared understandings of wellbeing – visions which can challenge the very visible co-option of the concept by powerful groups. The chapters engage, therefore, with themes of ethics and justice explored elsewhere in the handbook (see Section IV), as they explore the potential of wellbeing as a benchmark in achieving more just, more collective, societies. In short the construction of this section aims to be in line with Chambers's (1997) call for engagement with 'responsible wellbeing' in which there is a collective concern and responsibility for individuals' location, action and experience in local, national and global society.

For convenience in introducing the ideas the section covers, we consider separately the light they cast on the *material conditions* of wellbeing, the *emotional geographies* of wellbeing, and the construction of *care-full spaces*. These are not separate issues of course; they are part of a web of people, things, technologies, sentiments, symbols, strategies and power relations – that mix of emotional, physical, psychological, social and spatial affairs – which is implied in what the French sociologist Michel Callon (2007) might call the *agencement* of wellbeing. However, the danger of working with wellbeing 'in the round' is that it implies such a holistic understanding of social life that it may come to represent both everything and nothing. Integrated accounts of social life are relevant and timely, but so is the heuristic tactic of opening up their constituent parts. The chapters that follow, and the sections that introduce them, are structured precisely to try to avoid creating a new 'black box' effect (in which wellbeing explains everything but nothing explains it).

MATERIAL WELLBEING

To restate, all the chapters in this section engage in some way with the interlinked material and emotional geographies of wellbeing. Two chapters, however, draw particular attention to the material underpinnings of this condition, building both on a growing interdisciplinary interest in place and health, and on social geographers' continuing concerns with unequal divisions of welfare.

The contextual as well as social dimensions of wellbeing are set out by Robin Kearns and Gavin Andrews, who are interested in the spaces, places and environments that stage people's lives and have clear roles in shaping their wellbeing. This is not to embrace deterministic or mono-causal modes of explanation – for example: poor soil quality creates hunger – but rather to assert that places in all their complexity, containing unique constellations of different processes coinciding at points in space and time, have profound effects on wellbeing. 'Places' here may be concrete (a school, a factory) or perceptual (a neighbourhood, a community), sensory (including sights and sounds), transitory (a crowd, a meeting, a festival) or virtual/imaginary (a cyber community), but all have implications for risk, harm, health and wellbeing. In line with other recent work in geography, these authors move beyond the traditional focus on 'place effects' as they affect health – or more properly as they incubate illness – towards an interest in therapeutic and restorative environments which focuses upon positive health and wellbeing (see Conradson, 2005; Williams, 2008).

If Robin Kearns and Gavin Andrews turn attention from damaging material environments to health promoting space, Rich Mitchell's chapter is concerned with the complementary pairing of risk and resilience. This essay provides a crisp critique of the nature and incidence of different kinds of health risk, explaining how risk is measured, and accounting for a variety of individual and institutional responses to it. The chapter also introduces the concept of resilience, outlines the fascinating body of research this concept has inspired, and asks what geography, and geographers, can do to promote it. This emphasis engages with ideas developing within and beyond social geography around the multi-dimensional character of health capital, and the importance of health assets (see, for example, S.J. Smith et al., 2003; Searle et al., 2009). It also gestures to the material edge of health inequality, which has very many dimensions. S.J. Smith and Easterlow (2005), for example, argue that while the geography of health inequalities is to an extent an expression of risk and resilience, it also expresses the shape of health discrimination. This is another reminder that while the route to social wellbeing must include health promotion, disease prevention, and cures of all kinds, it also depends on accepting ill-health, or neediness more generally, as a human condition, on rejecting the 'healthism' that helps widen the health divide, and instituting a more comprehensive ethic of care (a theme taken up later in the section).

Together, the opening chapters of this section confirm that a growing interest in charting positive human, physical and emotional states does not detract from, but rather contributes to, the core concerns of social geography with social inequalities and injustice. Certainly, they show why interrogating themes of happiness or hopefulness cannot be perceived as a purely academic exercise or pursued only on the shaky ground that these geographies have not been explored much to date. Wellbeing, comfort and dignity are among the essentials of human life.

EMOTIONAL GEOGRAPHIES

As Kearns and Andrews note in their chapter, 'wellbeing involves both *being* well (i.e., having access to life's material necessities) and *feeling* well (having the capacity to act and find meaning in the world)'. Feelings have taken centre stage in the interests of social geography in recent years. As we mentioned in the introductory chapter to this book, emotions have long been an area of some interest. But the 'emotional turn', heralded by Anderson and S.J. Smith (2001), has given rise to a much more diverse body of scholarship, which insists on the place of emotions in analysis of the social, cultural, political and spatial world (see also Davidson et al., 2005; Pain and S.J. Smith, 2008; Turner and Stets, 2005). The suggestion is not just that we should focus on emotions, or view them as one way to understand social worlds – to do so would risk their depoliticisation or trivialisation. Rather, the focus is outward, demonstrating that emotions and their spatialities are fundamental to the layout and workings of society. They are, then, both social and relational (along similar lines to the geographies of wellbeing in our discussion above). That is, for social geography, emotions are not simply products of events, interactions and environments, resulting from things that are, and things that happen: emotions are in a reflexive relationship with context in its widest sense. They affect the world, consciously and unconsciously; they are used, and useful.

Two closely related bodies of scholarship are important here. First, a body of work broadly titled emotional geographies has investigated the importance of emotions to social processes and landscapes, to subjective experiences of space and place, and to the policy arenas which affect them (Anderson and S.J. Smith, 2001; Davidson and Milligan, 2004). Social geographers have emphasised the inherent relation of the subjectivity of emotions to various social inequalities (see Panelli et al., 2004; Thien, 2005) and power geometries (Tolia-Kelly, 2007, 2008). Such work is often closely influenced by feminist theory and practice, with empirical research forefronting the positionalities, relations and emotions of researchers and their subject/participants (see also Kindon in this volume).

Secondly, there is a growing interest in affective geographies. Here the focus is not so much on the mental state of feelings and thought that makes up an emotion, but on its bodily experience and the ways in which this relates to the 'more-than-human': in other words, how bodies, spaces and other objects are affectively intertwined. In human geography, this work seeks to realise the promise of 'a different kind of intelligence about the world' that centres on the biological constitution of being as a performative force, non-verbal communication and the openness of events (Thrift, 2004: 60). Affective geographies tend to be closely connected to non-representational geographies, and draw on theorists such as Spinoza and Deleuze (see Anderson and Harrison, 2006, and Woodward and Lea in this volume).

These two bodies of work clearly overlap – the former more closely relates to a holistic notion of wellbeing, where the focus is often on wider structures and relations that influence people's emotional geographies, and/or is interested in people's agency in recognising and mobilising emotions to effect change. Yet affective geographies are engaging with different layers of the political too. Affective geographies have been subject to critiques – that this approach constitutes subjects as at the whim of pre-cognitive contagion, and that it has been practised as an ethnocentric encounter that lacks space for marginalised voices (see Thien, 2005; Tolia-Kelly, 2006). Others have argued that such a position misrepresents the relation of affect to the human subject (Woodward and Lea, in this volume). For a full appraisal of emotions, we would suggest, social geographers might draw from both of these traditions, seeking theoretically informed accounts which recognise the full range of influences on people's wellbeing – and how people actively seek to shape their own wellbeing themselves, in the context of wider political constraints. As Bondi (2005) maintains in a discussion of the connections between geographies of emotion and psychotherapy, the relational and social aspects of emotional geographies are vital.

The two chapters in this section which deal with this aspect of wellbeing provide different takes on emotional geographies (and see Woodward and Lea, elsewhere in this volume, on affective geographies). Hille Koskela offers a timely overview of the many faces and experiences of fear, focusing especially on its role in the processes and practices of Othering. Fear has been a longstanding topic of interest among social geographers (Gregory and Pred, 2007; Hille Koskela, 1997; Pain, 2000; S.J. Smith, 1987; Tuan, 1979; Valentine, 1989). Hille Koskela's analysis shows that fear is at once emotional, material and political; that it is intimately entangled with processes of gendering, racialisation, globalisation and inclusion/exclusion in urban and other spaces. The chapter also points to the Other of fear itself – to the possibility, the hope-fulness, of cultivating cultures of tolerance. Thus, by its end, Hille Koskela's chapter provides a foil to recent and damaging obsessions in the west with security. In her chapter, Joyce Davidson uses the geographically rooted condition of agoraphobia to highlight the importance of everyday anxieties and to explore practices of, and possibilities for, emotional safekeeping. It is a neatly-crafted account of the (gendered) shape of agoraphobic lifeworlds, of embodied anxieties, and of the 'phobic' spaces that people think, feel and make. Agoraphobia is about a crisis of boundaries, distances and location, and this essay shows how these crises are precipitated, what effects they have and how – perhaps – they can be resolved.

Both these authors favour intensive qualitative methods, not least for the ethical sensitivity they bring to the question of how we know about emotions, what emotions mean, and how they are named and experienced across cultures (McKay, 2007). Both also draw attention to the political sensibilities surrounding what emotions practically do, perhaps pointing to the way geographers have recently argued for the place of hope in practice as well as in rhetoric (see Klinkenberg, 2007; Pain, 2009; Sparke, 2007; and Section V in this volume). What is clear is that emotions, as socially, spatially, and relationally constituted, are at last receiving the attention that they deserve. While some parts of the wider discipline may still view them with some squeamishness, the argument that they have relevance to all of the connected fields that this Handbook crosses is increasingly persuasive.

CARE-FULL SPACES AND PLACES

In recent years there has also been renewed interest in geographies of well-fare in the broadest sense. This has been prompted above all by a globalised process of welfare retrenchment in which an ideal of distributing resources according to need as well as ability to pay has been eclipsed by a drive to 'workfare' in which the goal of social policy is to lever needy people into the paid workforce (generally by withholding benefits to those who do not or cannot compete in that arena). One of the most thought-provoking pieces written on this in recent years is Chris Haylett's (2003) analysis of the US welfare-to-work strategy in Texas. She shows how welfare and work are constructed through one another in ways which make welfare into a new site for class struggle – a struggle to 'resist the collapse of modern life into one work-based economic sphere of thought and being' (2003: 174). By arguing for the detachment of welfare from work, Haylett is opening the space for establishing new practices of wellbeing (see also Boyer, 2007). These might include spaces of participation and belonging as described by Parr (2006) in her discussion of the inclusion of people with severe and enduring mental health problems in community arts projects. They might refer to the enactment of more ethical ways of relating, as outlined by Barnett (2005) in his discussion of intimacy and hospitality. More broadly however this struggle creates a space that can be shaped by an ethic of care. Haylett's first concern is for the possibility to combine working and caring in ways perhaps captured in McKie et al.'s (2002) feminist account of 'caringscapes'; but equally it turns attention to creation of physical spaces of care, for example Conradson's (2003) community drop-in centre; and to the scope to support and enhance relations of care across the whole spectrum of social life.

In this collection, the critical role of care-full geographies in securing human wellbeing and dignity is signalled in the final chapter of the section by Nicola Ansell and Fiona Smith who point to the full extent to which the geographies of the organisation of care for vulnerable members of society affect their welfare (see also Milligan, 2001; Parr, 2003; Williams and Crooks, 2008). Ansell and F. Smith, examine the case of young people, bringing a welcome perspective on the global and political context of changing issues of welfare. They argue that the concept of social reproduction helps us to understand the delivery of young people's wellbeing and care, focusing on the increasing tendency towards neoliberal regimes across the world. This concept also has value in bridging understandings of women's and children's lives, and their human rights, as carers, and cared-for. In all, the carefully drawn case studies in this chapter draw attention to the full impact of neoliberalisation on the quality, content and space available for exercising care relations in particular places.

CONCLUSION

Overall, the essays in this section provide a holistic appreciation of wellbeing, which attends to its social and spatial dimensions; its importance for theory and practice; its centrality to the conduct of social geographies. The focus of such work is both multiscalar and inter-scalar, ranging from the fearful body to the systems of care affected by global politics. This work is diverse, but connected, pointing to a more politicised notion of wellbeing grounded in local knowledges but able to 'jump scales' and speak back to national and global sources of injustice. So while there are dangers in imposing notions of wellbeing on others – a practice which politicians, healthcare delivery, the media and popular culture all tend to engage in – the case built here for defining and measuring wellbeing from ground up, working from people's own understandings, and supporting the changes they would like to see, is well made (see also Chambers, 1997).

There is also a sense in this collection – one which Chambers (1997) might once again underline – that responding to wellbeing is not just about informing and delivering policy solutions from on high. Social geographers' visions of wellbeing link the condition of individuals and social collectivities. In a hyper-connected world, wellbeing is testimony to the way we all live and behave. So we take up Chambers's challenge of engaging with responsible wellbeing: of, as he puts it, developing a pedagogy for the non-oppressed (cf. Freire, 1972), in which those who are relatively powerful and wealthy – including, perhaps, we who write the text, and many of you who read it – are the ones who have to change if a vision of wellbeing for all is at stake. The answer to that very traditional question – 'who gets what, where, and how?' (D. Smith, 1977) – is as important now as it was more than 30 years ago: to address it is to take up a political and moral imperative that could transform the doing of social geography, along with the making of the world it inhabits.

REFERENCES

Anderson, B. and Harrison, P. (2006) 'Questioning affect and emotion', *Area*, 38: 333–5.

Anderson, K. and Smith, S.J. (2001) 'Editorial: emotional geographies', *Transactions of the Institute of British Geographers*, 26 (1): 7–10.

Barnett, C. (2005) 'Ways of relating: hospitality and the acknowledgement of otherness', *Progress in Human Geography*, 29: 5–21.

Bondi, L. (2005) 'Making connections and thinking through emotions: between geography and psychotherapy', *Transactions of the Institute of British Geographers*, 30 (4): 433–48.

Boyer, K. (2007) 'At work, at home? New geographies of work and care-giving under welfare reform in the US', *Space and Polity*, 7: 75–86.

Callon, M. (2007) 'What does it mean to say that economics is performative?', in D. MacKenzie, F. Muniesa, and L. Siu, *Do Economists Make Markets?* Princeton University Press. pp. 351–57.

Carlisle, S. and Hanlon, P. (2007) 'The complex territory of well-being: contestable evidence, contentious theories and speculative conclusions', *Journal of Public Mental Health*, 6 (2): 8–13.

Chambers, R. (1997) 'Responsible wellbeing – a personal agenda for development', *World Development*, 25 (11): 1743–54.

Conradson D. (2003) 'Spaces of care in the city: the place of a community drop-in centre', *Social and Cultural Geography*, 4: 507–25.

Conradson, D. (2005) 'Landscape, care and the relational self: therapeutic encounters in rural England', *Health and Place*, 11: 337–48.

Davidson, J., Bondi, L. and Smith, M. (2005) *Emotional geographies*. Aldershot: Ashgate.

Davidson, J. and Milligan, C. (2004) 'Embodying emotion, sensing space: introducing emotional geographies', *Social and Cultural Geography*, 5 (4): 523–32.

Diener, E. (1984) 'Subjective wellbeing', *Psychological Bulletin*, 95, (3): 542–75.

Fleuret, S. and Atkinson, S. (2007) 'Wellbeing, health and geography: a critical review and research agenda', *New Zealand Geographer*, 63, 106–18.

Freire, P. (1972) *Pedagogy of the Oppressed*. Harmondsworth: Penguin.

Gough, I., McGregor, A. and Camfield, L. (2007) 'Theorising wellbeing in international development', in I. Gough and A. McGregor, *Wellbeing in Developing Countries: From Theory to Research*. Cambridge: Cambridge University Press. pp. 3–43.

Gregory, D. and Pred, A. (2007) *Violent Geographies: Fear, Terror and Political Violence*. Routledge: London.

Haylett, C. (2003) 'Remaking labour imaginaries: social reproduction and the internationalising project of welfare reform', *Political geography*, 22: 765–88.

Klinkenberg, B. (2007) 'Geospatial technologies and the geographies of hope and fear', *Annals of the Association of American Geographers*, 97 (2): 350–60.

Koskela, H. (1997) '"Bold walk and breakings": women's spatial confidence versus fear of violence', *Gender, Place and Culture*, 4 (3): 301–19.

McKay, D. (2007) '"Sending dollars shows feeling" – Emotions and economies in Filipino migration', *Mobilities*, 2 (2): 175–94.

McKie, L., Gregory, S. and Bowlby, S. (2002) 'Shadow times: the temporal and spatial frameworks and experiences of caring and working', *Sociology*, 36: 897–924.

Milligan, C. (2001) *Geographies of Care: Space, Place and the Voluntary Sector*. Aldershot: Ashgate.

Pain, R. (2000) 'Place, social relations and the fear of crime: a review', *Progress in Human Geography*, 24 (3): 365–88.

Pain, R. (2009) 'Globalized fear? Towards an emotional geopolitics', *Progress in Human Geography*.

Pain, R. and Smith, S.J. (2008) *Fear: Critical Geopolitics and Everyday Life*. Aldershot: Ashgate.

Panelli, R., Little, J. and Kraack, A. (2004) 'A community issue? Rural women's feelings of safety and fear in New Zealand', *Gender Place and Culture*, 11 (3): 445–67.

Parr, H. (2003) 'Medical geography: care and caring', *Progress in Human Geography, 27*: 212–21.

Parr, H. (2006) 'Mental health, the arts and belonging', *Transactions, Institute of British Geographers*, NS 31: 150–66.

Searle, B. (2008) *Well-being: In Search of a Good Life?*. Bristol: Policy Press.

Searle, B.A., Smith, S.J. and Cook, N. (2009) 'From housing wealth to well-being?', *Sociology of Health and Illness,* 31: 112–27.

Smith, D. (1977) *Human Geography: A Welfare Approach*. London: Edward Arnold.

Smith, S.J. (1987) 'Fear of crime: beyond a geography of deviance', *Progress in Human Geography*, 11: 1–23.

Smith, S.J. and Easterlow, D. (2005) 'The Strange Geography of Health Inequalities', *Transactions, Institute of British Geographers*, 30: 173–90.

Smith, S.J., Easterlow, D., Munro, M. and Turner, K. (2003) 'Housing as health capital. How health trajectories and housing careers are linked', *Journal of Social Issues*, 59: 512–25.

Sointu, E. (2005) 'The rise of an ideal: tracing changing discourses of wellbeing', *The Sociological Review*, 53: 255–74.

Sparke, M. (2007) 'Geopolitical fears, geoeconomic hopes, and the responsibilities of geography', *Annals of the Association of American Geographers*, 97 (2): 338–49.

Thien, D. (2005) 'After or beyond feeling? A consideration of affect and emotion in geography', *Area*, 37 (4): 450–6.

Thrift, N. (2004) 'Intensities of feeling: towards a spatial politics of affect', *Geografiska Annaler*, 86 B (1): 57–78.

Tolia-Kelly, D.P. (2006) 'Affect – an ethnocentric encounter? Exploring the "universalist" imperative of emotional/affective geographies', *Area*, 38 (2): 213–17.

Tolia-Kelly, D.P. (2007) 'Fear in paradise: The affective registers of the English Lake District landscape re-visited', *Senses and Society*, 23: 329–51.

Tolia-Kelly, D.P. (2008) 'Motion/emotion: picturing translocal landscapes in the Nurturing Ecologies Research Project', *Mobilities*, 31: 117–40.

Tuan, Y. (1979) *Landscapes of Fear*. Minneapolis: University of Minnesota Press.

Turner, J.H. and Stets, J.E. (2005) *The Sociology of Emotions*. Cambridge: Cambridge University Press.

Valentine, G. (1989) 'The geography of women's fear', *Area*, 21(4): 385–90.

Williams, A. (2008) *Therapeutic Landscapes*. Aldershot: Ashgate.

Williams, A. and Crooks, V. (2008) 'Introduction: space, place and the geographies of women's care-giving work', *Gender Place and Culture*, 15(3): 143–7.

Wright, S. (2008) 'Practising hope: learning from social movement strategies in the Philippines', I in R. Pain and S.J. Smith (eds), *Fear: Critical geopolitics and everyday life*. Aldershot: Ashgate.

13

Geographies of Wellbeing

Robin A. Kearns and Gavin J. Andrews

INTRODUCTION

Literally, wellbeing implies *being* well. It is an experienced state of being, in terms of healthiness and happiness. Drawing on Heidegger and other philosophical understandings, human existence is only possible through 'being' in the world; much contemporary critical and cultural geography considers being – and all the countless practices and experiences this involves – to be necessarily related to place (in other words to be necessarily '*emplaced*') (Crang, 1998). By extension, then, wellbeing might be thought of as a specific emplaced state of being. Wellbeing also suggests being some*where*, hence bringing geography into the equation. Based on these fundamental assumptions, this chapter explores wellbeing as a state affected by a complex array of factors, most of which we argue are anchored in the environmental and spatial contexts of everyday life.

At the outset, however, we acknowledge both the opportunities and constraints of the term wellbeing, for it has a vast set of possible interpretations. This, in itself, can limit the precision we can bring to any survey of the term and its applicability in geography. Indeed, Fleuret and Atkinson (2007, p. 1) suggest that '… despite research on wellbeing from a range of disciplines, the concept remains ill-defined and under conceptualised'. Similarly, with specific reference to human geography, Andrews (2007) suggests that the emerging disciplinary interest in wellbeing is characterised by its lack of cohesion. Indeed, few scholars talk about 'geographies of wellbeing'. Although the engagement with wellbeing is wide-ranging, it is nevertheless indirect; an understated understanding typically existing in studies that focus to some degree on aspects of happiness, contentment, or quality of life (Morrison, 2007). Reflecting these disciplinary trends, there has been a lack of explicit conceptual and theoretical development, and geographical understanding of wellbeing has progressed, for the most part, through a cumulative broadening of empirical inquiry (Andrews, 2007).

In this chapter we review the origins of thinking about wellbeing in geography, granting initial attention to the sub-field of health geography which, in recent years, has come to converge with newer concerns for emotional and sensory geographies. Next we selectively consider how wellbeing might be variably conceived across the life course. A fourth section makes links between embodiment and wellbeing. We then broaden out our attention beyond the individual to take in notions of wellbeing as they are applied to specific sites, settings and sounds. Ultimately, however, it is the most immediate surroundings that have the greatest bearing on our wellbeing, so we turn attention to neighbourhood contexts as they influence wellbeing. Not all surroundings and situations complement or enhance wellbeing, however. Our penultimate substantive section is therefore devoted to considering structural influences and, in particular, the links between poverty, food and wellbeing. Lastly we examine how non-medicalised wellbeing can be provided for through formal and informal means. We close by considering some critiques of this geographical focus and by reconsidering the tension between personal and population-based applications of this contested term.

FROM MEDICINE TO HEALTH TO WELLBEING

A fundamental tension in ideas of wellbeing is that being well (or getting well) implies a progression away from being ill or impaired. Hence wellness has been invoked as the naturalised positive outcome that medical activity is seeking to achieve. Beyond discourses of medicine, however, wellbeing is widely evoked as a condition far removed from its medicalised absence. This is especially so from the geographical vantage point. The development of health geography has added to traditional medical-geographic concerns with the pathological (e.g., disease, death), and sites of care (e.g., hospitals and other services), newer curiosity with aspects of wellness such as the influence of identity and everyday experience. Meanwhile, in other subdisciplines of human geography we might encounter terms like 'economic wellbeing' or 'community wellbeing' (Morrison, 2007). Within such usages lie an even greater connection to conventional geographical concerns for place, locality and region.

The past fifteen years has seen considerable change as geography has engaged with matters pertaining to human health. The new health geography that has emerged differs from the preceding (yet persisting) medical-geographical perspective with an increased interest in wellbeing. Broader social models of health and health care than the biomedical disease model tend to be employed. Other features of health geography are an increased awareness of the importance of places, an enhanced sensitivity to difference (especially *vis à vis* issues of gender and impairment), and a move towards more thematic concerns (for example, inequality, therapeutic landscapes). Kearns and Moon (2002) identify a number of indicators of movement from a medical to a health perspective in geography, including the 1995 launch of the journal *Health and Place* and successive editions of the *Dictionary of Human Geography* (e.g. Johnston et al., 2000). In the latter, there are entries for both 'medical geography' and for the 'geography of health and health care'. A biomedical model of health and a focus on quantitative methods is emphasised for the medical geography entry whereas *place* is the lead theme for the health and health care entry, along with a 'socio-ecological' model of health and methodological pluralism. In other words, contemporary health geography draws on developments elsewhere in geography and the wider social sciences to see place as an 'operational and living construct which "matters" as opposed to being a passive "container" in which things are simply recorded' (Kearns and Moon, 2002, p. 587). Places have been shown to matter through case studies grounded in the specifics of particular localities (reflected, for instance, in the title of Kearns and Gesler's 1998 collection *Putting Health into Place: Landscape, Identity and Wellbeing*). Indeed, notions of 'emplacement' have become critical to understanding the lived experience of disability and ill-health, as evidenced in the work of writers such as Isabel Dyck on women with multiple sclerosis (Dyck, 1995) and Robert Wilton on the 'diminishing worlds' of people living with HIV/AIDS (Wilton, 1995).

Within this emerging research stream, landscape and environment have taken on new emphases and meanings. With regard to the former, researchers have moved on from the medical-geographical understanding of landscape as a physical barrier to health service provision and utilisation, to consider the varied meanings of 'landscape' and its links to health and wellbeing. Here studies bring an enhanced awareness of the cultural importance of place, an implied incorporation of emotional terrain, and the intersection of the cultural and the political in the development of place-specific landscapes of health care and health promotion. Examples include landscapes of despair (Dear and Wolch, 1987) and therapeutic landscapes (Gesler, 1992). For health geographers the idea of 'landscape' is a metaphor for the complex layerings of history, social structure and built environment that converge to enhance or corrode human wellbeing in particular places (Kearns and Moon, 2002). Geographers have begun to explore environment more expansively, including how people perceive pollution and health differently in different places, and how different places affect and reflect behaviour related to health (Eyles, 1997; Wakefield et al., 2001; Baxter and Lee, 2004; Wakefield and McMullan, 2005). Here then, even in a former 'fortress' of positivistic inquiry, environment has taken on a much broader, socially and culturally constructed meaning, with concepts such as wellbeing moving to the fore in its analysis.

Another hallmark of contemporary health geography is its concern with social and cultural theory (Litva and Eyles, 1995). Various theoretical approaches have been offered and applied in the quest to understand health and wellbeing experience (e.g. structuralist, Foucauldian, feminist, humanistic). However, one framework that has offered a particular capacity to link some of the diverse perspectives currently in use in health geography is the structure and agency dynamic. This perspective examines the relative contribution of choice and constraint in human behaviour and experience (Dyck and Kearns, 2006). It can accommodate consideration of the broad macro-scale forces (e.g. economic opportunity, planning regulations) as well as the more micro-scale individual characteristics that influence human experience. This is helpful, as wellbeing involves both *being* well (i.e., having access to life's material necessities) and *feeling* well (having the capacity to act and find meaning in the world). This connection between the material, behavioural and affective means that the structure-agency dynamic potentially integrates elements of the local and the global, and facilitates generalisation outwards from micro-level case studies.

The present diversity of research that engages with matters of human wellbeing contrasts strongly with early medical-geographic interests which almost exclusively focused on disease ecology (and, more latterly, with disease mapping and health care provision). While wellbeing is, to an extent, implied in such work, the new geography of health, we contend, now embraces human wellness and the experience of *being* healthy in ways hitherto only hinted at. The principal means through which this embrace has occurred is through a closer relationship with the wider fields of social and cultural geography.

One important contemporary point of convergence is the interest in both wellbeing and emotions in human geography. These two domains of human experience are interconnected (i.e., *being* well generally involves *feeling* well). In general terms – and here we intentionally avoid the difficult issue of their exact definition – emotion is recognised as being the way something is felt (as a positive or negative, short or longer term response); it is effectively the psychological or affective adjustment to experience (Kleinginna and Kleinginna, 2005). Wellbeing, on the other hand, is recognised as a longer-term state-of-mind (and body, if not spirit), and is often regarded as synonymous with perceived quality of life. It is associated with the states of contentment and happiness that can change as a cumulative outcome of life's many emotional encounters (and responses) as well as broader changes in one's social, economic and biological circumstances (Kahneman et al., 1999). Importantly, the experience of wellbeing may vary not just at the collective level by location, culture and age, but also at the individual level by personality disposition (for instance, to one person the attractions of a beach may be the opportunities it presents as a social space in which to 'hang out' with others, whereas for another it may be the chance for solitude and 'oneness' with the ocean).

There is a great deal of synergy between this personal and particular dimension to the experience of perceived wellbeing and the terrain of emotions. With regard to emotions, geographical inquiry has recently peaked but is not entirely new. Research into emotional responses to, and within, places can be traced to humanistic ideas infused into human geography in the 1970s that have later re-surfaced variously in such fields as psychoanalytic geography (Pile, 1996), feminist research on crime (Valentine, 1998), maternal responsibility (Longhurst, 1997, 1998, 2000a, 2000b;) and disability (Dyck, 1995). These early studies of the place(s) of emotion are perhaps best regarded as predecessors of what has recently become a much more firmly established and dedicated field of inquiry that explores a wider range of emotions and circumstances including, amongst others, fear (Davidson, 2003; Andrews and Chen, 2006), awe (M. Smith, 2001), loss and longing (Bondi with Fewell, 2003) togetherness and love (Rose, 2004) and the many mixed emotions that can occur simultaneously in places, and through their recollection and historical presentation (Davidson et al., 2005; Andrews et al., 2006). Moreover, in comparison to wellbeing, emotion is a very different disciplinary terrain. For although this field certainly is associated with many of the distinct subdisciplinary twists and turns noted above in the case of wellbeing, it is a far more cohesive and distinct field, recognised as something 'new' (Davidson et al., 2005), and often specifically as an 'emotional turn' (Anderson and S.J. Smith, 2001; Davidson and Milligan, 2004) (evidenced in journal special issues, a recent edited collection [Davidson et al., 2005] and international conferences). Underpinning this distinctiveness is the fact that the field results from a greater attention to emotion across human geography and, in particular, in cultural geography. Hence, unlike in the case of wellbeing, the more specialist subdiscipline of health geography has not been the major subdisciplinary player. Indeed, emotion has very broad disciplinary appeal precisely because it relates to many forms and positive and negative feelings across social, economic and cultural life (see Anderson and S.J. Smith, 2001; Davidson and Milligan 2004; Davidson et al., 2005).

Attempts to articulate the character of wellbeing preceded the embracing of emotion generally and built on two traditions: from urban planning and economic geography, the interest in indicators of quality of life (frequently used to rank cities or countries, and often invoking only material aspects of life) (Ley, 1983; Morrison, 2007); and from health philosophy, the holistic ideas that emerged in the latter part of the twentieth century (e.g. Breslow, 1972) to identify dimensions of human experience such as positive relations with others, relative autonomy and environmental mastery. Our discussion draws more on the latter perspective. Indeed, we can see these elements of wellbeing as having been also identified by social psychologists (Ryff, 1989) as well as being incorporated into the classic World Health Organisation definition of health ('more than the absence of disease; a state of complete mental, physical and social wellbeing'). Interestingly, the holism of this view of wellbeing was long-preceded in the constructions of health developed by indigenous peoples such as New Zealand Maori (e.g. Durie, 1994). In this world view, culture, place and health – constructs relatively recently linked in western geographical thinking (Gesler and Kearns, 2002) – have long comprised a deep understanding of *hauora* (wellbeing). One recently popularised framework, for instance, sees *mauriora* (secure cultural identity), *waiora* (environmental protection), *toiora* (healthy lifestyles) and *te oranga* (participation in society) as crucial cornerstones in understanding the state of wellbeing pursued in health promotion (Kearns, Witten and McCreanor, 2006).

As geographers have worked on, and with, ideas of wellbeing during the past decade, they have gradually shifted priorities beyond the study of diseases and related services and towards everyday mental and physical health in a broad sense, including, for example, health and fitness cultures (Andrews et al., 2005), therapeutic places and experiences (Gesler, 1992; Williams, 1999), and holistic therapies and lifestyles (Williams, 1998; Wiles and Rosenberg, 2001). More recently, social geographers have also begun to explore wellbeing more explicitly and extensively. Their inquiries have involved investigations of common yet often neglected and trivialised psychological problems that might not be categorised strictly as mental illnesses, yet nevertheless impact significantly upon people and their wellbeing, and are themselves, at times, spatial practices. Here studies of phobia (Davidson et al., 2005) compulsive disorders (Doel and Segrott, 2004) and addiction (Wilton and DeVerteuil, 2006) have constituted directions in this research. Elsewhere, urban and economic geographers have played a perhaps unexpected role, extending their ongoing explorations of psychological and behavioural interactions with urban environments, to consider the consequences of particular environments for individual and group wellbeing (Morrison, 2007) (see our later section on the surrounds of wellbeing). Meanwhile, a more general focus on wellbeing which has occurred across human geography involves the body-mind continuum (and embodiment). Here, for example, the navigation of everyday life through impairment and disability is a core interest related to wellbeing (Butler and Parr, 1999) (see section on the shapes of wellbeing).

One characteristic of the emerging disciplinary interest in wellbeing, however, is that it is not often recognised or regarded as a cohesive movement. Geographers, for example, do not often talk about a 'wellbeing turn' or even 'geographies of wellbeing'. The reason for this might be traced to the overall engagement with wellbeing which, although wide-ranging, is still rather vague and indirect. For example, the nature of wellbeing is not usually towards the fore in published articles, despite an implicit understanding being that the study focuses to a degree on some aspect of happiness, contentment, or quality of life. Reflecting this, there has been a lack of explicit conceptual and theoretical development, and geographical understanding of wellbeing has progressed, for the most part, through an indirect and cumulative broadening of empirical inquiry.

STAGES OF WELLBEING

The 'life course' is a key construct used by health researchers to understand the changing challenges to, and experiences of, wellbeing as a human life unfolds. Geographical ideas and metaphors such as place, position and trajectories are often at least implicit in such discussions and provide useful cues for further disciplinary engagement. For now, it is useful to consider work relating to two 'ends' of the life course: childhood and older age.

While papers relating to the determinants of children's (medicalised) health have long populated the health and social care literature, recent work on children's geographical experience has highlighted their place as social actors actively contributing to their own wellbeing within the constraints imposed by an adult society (e.g., Matthews and Limb, 1999). Their role as social actors can be positive or negative, the latter for example, recently explored in studies of the 'tyrannical' spaces of bullying (Percy-Smith and Matthews, 2001; Andrews and Chen, 2006). As Mitchell et al. (2007) argue, this recognition of agency is significant given that young people are among the most regulated groups in western societies. Yet, despite experiences within public space potentially playing an important role in children's personal development, physical exploration and social growth (Kearns and Collins, 2006), there is a common perception that children are out of place in public space, especially when unaccompanied by an adult (Collins and Kearns, 2001). Trends towards privatising and supervising many aspects of children's lives run contrary to claims that children's wellbeing hinges on the need for a measure of freedom and independence within the ordinary spaces of everyday life such as residential neighbourhoods. As Mitchell et al. (2007) argue, the primary barrier that children encounter within the neighbourhood setting stems not from issues of design, or potential risks, but rather from the prevalent social construction of children as dependent, vulnerable and in need of constant adult guidance and supervision. This concern for children 'on the loose', combined with deep-seated beliefs in the health-benefits of rural settings, arguably contributed to the development of health camps (Kearns and Collins, 2000), institutional sites at which wellbeing is sought through exercise, regimented diet and respite from stressful homes settings.

At the opposite end of the life-course, many geographical studies have considered older people and ageing (see Andrews and Phillips, 2005). 'Geographical gerontology' is a broad field of research that crosscuts social and health geography and involves considerable input from other disciplines – including clinical gerontology, occupational therapy, environmental psychology, architecture and sociology – which possess either longstanding or rediscovered conceptual interests in space and place (Andrews et al., 2007). Although a focus here has long been on population ageing, migration and other macro-scale health and medical issues, an increasing number of studies have focused on housing environments and their varied connections with wellbeing. For example, crosscutting geographical scales, research on underlying policy and practice objectives such as 'aging in place' (Cutchin, 2003) considers the wellbeing benefits of spatial constancy and choice on older peoples' accommodation and care. Meanwhile, everyday life in, and identity with, specific places such as nursing homes, residential homes and supported housing and the everyday actions that shape older peoples' experiences within them (Peace et al., 2005), are important foci. Moving beyond health and social care (where wellbeing is almost always something to be protected, or at least its loss minimised), and mirroring wider social changes where older age is an extended phase of cultural life, places of positive and active ageing are a new-found interest in research. Here research has considered the positive choices older people make with regard to their identity and wellbeing in creating and frequenting 'retirement communities' (Katz, 2005), 'universities of the third age' (Katz, 1996), and indulging in mobile retirement cultures such as 'RV'ing (Blaikie, 1999, 2005) and seasonal and more permanent sun-seeking migration (King et al., 2000).

SHAPES OF WELLBEING

A key exhortation by early advocates of a reformed medical geography was greater attention to the place of the body (Dorn and Laws, 1994). As Kearns and Moon (2002) commented, geographers have since begun to address geographies of the body, with research predominantly being on psychologically or physically diseased, impaired, marginalised and disadvantaged bodies. Geographical research on the body provides a critical perspective to medical places, considering as it does the body in wards, clinics and community settings; the body in relation to diagnosis and medical power; 'othered' bodies and historical geographies of the ill body and mind (Parr, 1998). While health geographers have been slow to embrace the body, feminist geographers have been leaders in unpicking how body perceptions, experience and place interact in potent ways. Writing by geographers working at the permeable edges of health and social geography, and in the fields of disability and mental health geography, is increasingly addressing this gap (Dyck, 1995; Parr, 1998; Litva et al., 2001; Hall, 2000). It might also have been expected that emerging geographies of health would be accompanied by a decreased concern with dead and diseased bodies and greater interest in healthy bodies. Such work too is largely conducted outside health geography and, with exceptions (MacKian, 2000; Duncan and Brown, 2000), the very specific consequences for health and wellbeing of body adornment, inscription and management have not been discussed.

Within the broader expansion of research interest in embodiment in the social sciences, the leading questions have become not only how but '*where* does the body as a corporeal presence serve as a surface for the assignment of personal meaning and an organising principle for social interaction'? (Gubrium and Holstein, 1999, p. 520). Hence, the body is both a geography unto itself, and is assigned meaning through the geographies in which it dwells. The nursing home, for instance, is a common institutional basis for everyday life for many older people. Here, the body becomes a surface of signs, monitored for evidence of varied concerns for stakeholders – from the resident's own maintenance of identity to family members who retain a sense of responsibility after the placement of their loved one. Older age may be imbued with positive connections to past events, traditions and histories, all of which have strong connections to places (Hugman, 1999). This is particularly the case in indigenous cultures such as Maori (Durie, 1994). However, more frequently, older age is closely associated with physical and mental deterioration and decline of the body (for example changes in skin tone, body shape, body structure, mental capacity) and a range of places which are purposefully designed and provided to cope with such limitations. In this context, the nursing home represents, both literally and metaphorically, a site of concealment and disengagement of the body from society (Andrews and Kearns, 2005).

Elsewhere, a small number of geographical studies of sports and fitness places have emerged that articulate wellbeing as a motivating factor behind the activities and 'positive' body cultures they facilitate (van Ingen, 2003). Subjects studied include, for example, bodybuilding and gyms (Johnston, 1996; Park, 2004; Andrews et al., 2005), running and tracks (Bale, 2004), and surfing (Booth, 2004). Crosscutting this work is a realisation that not all that contributes to personal wellbeing is necessarily good for one's health in a medical sense as, in the case for example of overtraining, taking performance-enhancing drugs, bodily obsession and excessive sun exposure (Bale, 2004; Andrews et al., 2005; Collins and Kearns 2007). This work, although currently limited in volume and scope, perhaps signposts ways in which health geography can engage to a greater degree with the body, whilst perhaps reinvigorating the small subfield of sports geography.

SIGHTS/SITES OF WELLBEING

The burgeoning literature on therapeutic landscapes that developed as an outgrowth of Gesler's (1992) initial manifesto offers a prompt to consider a range of places that enhance wellbeing (Williams, 2007). While Gesler's work focused primarily on spas and sites of religious pilgrimage, applications of his work have increasingly expanded to embrace the 'natural' world (e.g., mountains [Palka, 1999]). Thus, rather than focus on the spectacular sites of either medicine (e.g., hospitals) or the contemporary quest for health ('healthism') (e.g., high-profile resorts), there is merit in examining 'ordinary' landscapes for their links to wellbeing (Wakefield and McMullen, 2005). Beaches provide an obvious example of a common site of pilgrimage for recreation, and relaxation, although in land-locked or colder-climate countries, parks, rivers or lakes might serve a similar function. Further, the act of cultivation makes gardens an especially fertile site to explore wellbeing, especially for older people (see Milligan, Gattrell and Bingley, 2004).

With respect to beaches, Collins and Kearns (2007) argue that it is all too easy to romanticise places which incorporate elements of risk and potential threats to wellbeing, such as drowning, marine predators or – more commonly – sunburn. Collins and Kearns (2007) build on Conradson's (2005) ideas in observing four ways in which beaches offer important opportunities to enhance wellbeing:

- They provide a degree of physical and psychological distance from everyday routines and domestic demands
- They offer opportunities to be closer to the natural environment that city-dwellers, especially, are accustomed to
- They offer opportunities for both solitude and social activity
- They can help shape individual and ultimately collective identity (e.g. someone may identify as a surfer, a fisher or a 'boatie')

The prominence of physical activity at beaches in countries such as New Zealand and Australia helps diffuse any temptation to essentialise the coast (or for that matter mountains, rivers as other natural features) with romantic and innate healing, health-promoting qualities. Indeed, as Collins and Kearns (2007) suggest, activity in a coastal setting endorses the observation that the therapeutic elements of the coast 'may depend less on its innate health-promoting elements, than on the qualities of the embodied engagements which occur there' (p. 5). This observation underscores Conradson's (2005: 346) suggestion that in our quest to understand wellbeing-in-place, we should be more attentive to the 'therapeutic landscape experience', and not simply to the landscape in and of itself.

Collins and Kearns (2007) suggest a fifth way in which beaches may be construed as therapeutic landscapes: they are key sites of exercise and routine physical activity for many visitors. In this respect, they argue, beaches are places in which individuals and families may (or may not) conform to public health exhortations to be active (through a range of activities, both on land and in water). In other words, settings such as beaches can be spaces of compliance (or non-compliance) with official policy discourses. Yet there are risks that accompany such physical activity, and this recognition was partly addressed by the advent of surf lifesaving clubs (Daley, 2003). Today, New Zealand surf lifesavers are expected not only to fulfil their traditional role of promoting water safety, but also to act as role models for sun-protective behaviour at beaches.

In Australia and New Zealand, time spent at the coast is strongly associated with both deliberate and unintentional exposure to ultra-violent radiation (UVR). Historically, it was not until the 1930s that a suntan was associated with good health (as opposed to manual labour), and interestingly, UVR exposure in childhood was deemed particularly valuable: children attending health camps in New Zealand were required to undertake an hour of naked sunbathing per day (Kearns and Collins, 2000). One result of the increasing popularity of tanning was a marked shift in the clothing worn at the beach, with formal styles giving way to swimwear which allowed for increased exposure (and display) of bodies. A sense of wellbeing thus shifted such that being at the beach became associated with particular forms of dress and undress. These forms of attire have fluctuated with fashion as has awareness of the risk of, and responsiveness to, messages about skin cancer. Thus, the sense of wellbeing that might be generated by the relaxing sound of the waves is more problematic in some countries when also derived from prolonged exposure to the heat of the sun.

SOUNDS OF WELLBEING

Although there has been limited geographical research on the links between sound, place and wellbeing, we believe it is an important new opportunity to acknowledge the breadth of 'sensory geographies' (Rodway, 1994) and their impact on wellbeing. We structure our brief discussion of aural geographies around three broad relational dynamics that exist between sound, wellbeing and place.

First, we consider the sound industries and the way they enhance the wellbeing of peoples and places. The music industry and musicians are undoubtedly proponents of the health and wellbeing of peoples and places. (Andrews, Kearns, Kingbury and Carr, 2009) have noted, for example, that since the 1980s the concerns of musicians related to international health and justice issues have become direct and pragmatic (notable examples include 'Bandaid' and 'Liveaid'). Musicians have emerged as powerful political and social forces initiating awareness of social and health inequality, or exerting direct influence through fund-raising, forms of boycott and direct action, often funding health-related initiatives out of their own pockets (Andrews et al 2009). Although such activities are well-meant, and undoubtedly produce results in terms of some equalisation of global health and wellbeing, there have been scathing critiques of this 'celebrity diplomacy'. One strand of criticism focuses on the nature of musicians' statements and arguments. These are thought by some to over-simplify social issues and the complexity of implementing reforms in the long term and ignore political, economic, social and cultural forces that create local health conditions and circumstances. A second strand of concern suggests that celebrity statements help to stereotype the developing world as a sad, sick and needy place. These stereotypes risk overlooking the unique social diversity and richness these countries offer and the extent to which the developing world can address its own health and welfare problems. A third strand of concern focuses on financial issues regarding celebrity arguments for cancelling developing world debt which, it is thought, may result in reduced financial investment in certain countries. A fourth concern points to the hypocrisy of tax-efficient rich celebrities demanding greater government spending, whilst a fifth concern simply points to how an interest in health can be a self-serving career move, in terms of the publicity and positive image it promotes. In this way then, musical activism can easily be more about the celebrity's own personal wellbeing, and that of other people's and places (Andrews et al 2009).

A *second* strand of thinking examines sounds that actively represent the wellbeing of people and places. Messages related to the health and wellbeing of people and places can be located in music itself, whether these messages concern the developed or developing world (Andrews et al 2009). One underlying way in which this occurs is in the lyrics themselves which might be powerfully evocative via political or descriptive statements. Another way is through the places where these messages are performed and played, ranging from performances at concert venues (which can be create a sense of momentary power and unity) to how recorded sound messages seep out into our everyday lives in neighbourhoods, workplaces, homes and through personal headphones (Valentine, 1995).

A *third* and related issue relates to 'soundscapes' (S.J. Smith, 1994) and the question of how music can not only talk about and represent place lyrically but also, although invisible, it can help change both us and the places we frequent. It can help create a mood or atmosphere in a place, where it represents an auditory backdrop to our daily lives (here there are many examples, including music in bars, shops on the street, elevators and so on). At another level, through our own interpretations, we can create places in our mind (soundscapes), perhaps take ourselves to another place or time, perhaps in momentary escape (Connell and Gibson, 2003). In these ways, music can help us with personal transition and moving through life stages. Importantly this auditory architecture, whether in the background or central in our minds, can also involve non-musical sounds, such as sounds of nature, perhaps occurring in natural places (e.g. birdsong, the sound of waves [Matless, 2005]) or reproduced artificially for relaxation and therapy (Andrews, 2004).

SURROUNDS OF WELLBEING

In this section we acknowledge that thus far we have maintained an at least implicit focus on the individual. This restricted perspective is, we believe, a necessary but not self-sufficient stage in embracing geographies of wellbeing. A collective perspective is also needed. Turning attention to healthy communities (rather than just healthy individuals) implies a shift in mindset from the conventional medical preoccupation with personal health to a concern for population health. As we discussed earlier, this shift has also underlain a movement in subdisciplinary focus and identity from medical to health geography (Kearns and Moon, 2002). To act in the interests of the wellbeing of *all* members of a place-based community implies a commitment to maintaining and sustaining a range of environments including social/cultural, political, built and 'natural' settings. In this section we therefore draw upon work relating to these domains of collective wellbeing. In so doing, we ask how commonly experienced sites and amenities can elevate the wellbeing of all.

A key attempt to advance ideas linking health and place has been the Healthy Cities movement, which arose from recognising that many of the influences shaping the health of people lie outside the formal health care system. In other words, there is a frequent disconnection between popular and professional perceptions as to the determinants of health. Those working within health care services are understandably and invariably preoccupied by the apparent importance of their activities to human health. However, when members of the public are asked what helps shape their health, the response often centres on features such as families, friends, neighbours, satisfying jobs, good housing and supportive neighbourhoods (Witten et al., 2001).

This principle of the Healthy Cities movement builds on the fact that the most important contributions to human health over the past 150 years were made by local government through improvements in such elements of the urban infrastructure as sanitation and water treatment (Davies and Kelly, 1993). According to their proponents, healthy cities are those in which wellbeing is advanced through resourcing safe and supportive environments for citizens of all ages, providing an educated and stable workforce to support economic development, and caring for people who are capable of addressing the complex contemporary urban issues.

To this extent, healthy cities ideas are a counter-discourse to a long-established view dating back to the industrial revolution that cities are bad for one's health. Metaphors such as 'the urban jungle', the 'big smoke' and 'the rat race' bear strong inference that a healthier life is to be found beyond, rather than within, city limits. The problem with these ways of framing urban life is that they tend to imply a tolerance of unhealthy environments and a broad, and often unattainable, yearning to escape to a simple healthy life in rural places where wellbeing is assured. To dispel, or at least contest, such views, the healthy cities approach incorporates a broad definition of health, including a range of aspects of people's lives (i.e., housing, education, religion, employment, nutrition, leisure and recreation, health and medical care, efficient transport, a clean and green environment, friendly people, and safe streets and parks that – in combination – help to promote a healthy city or town).

The Healthy Cities movement (along with more general programmes of community renewal) have proliferated over the last two decades, supported by evidence that physical as well as social infrastructures are critical determinants of health and wellbeing (Baum and Palmer, 2002). For instance, accessibility, which includes notions of ease of movement as well as travel times and distances, is a core principle (Barton and Tsourou, 2000). However, knowledge of *how* to enhance aspects of social infrastructure such as sense of place, participation, safety and the wellbeing of diverse groups of residents, though modifying social and physical environments, is less common.

We can, however, speculate that a supportive urban environment (e.g. places to meet; shops and services close at hand) can assist in people being resilient in times of stress and change. Indeed, positive images and experiences of neighbourhoods can help residents to feel positive about their locality and the quality of life that can be enjoyed there.

At the centre of neighbourhood wellbeing, the street is a conduit of social relations and economic activity. There is potential to develop more vibrant communities through encouraging walking through urban design. A key consideration in promoting neighbourhood wellbeing is that re-peopling the street can lead to enhanced actual and perceived safety and, ultimately, more cohesive communities. More walkable cities can also enable better access to services by those who cannot drive (i.e. children, older people and those with disabilities).

SAPPING WELLBEING

Thus far, we have arguably exalted the possibility that place can enhance wellbeing. It is salutary at this stage in our survey to ask to what extent ill-health is a consequence of unwise individual choices, or rather if it is related to the structural context of people's everyday life circumstances. To turn to the latter association, how might the corrosive and compounding effects of poverty impact upon health and wellbeing in the physiological and mental sense? These links are well-established in social epidemiology. The sum is greater than the parts in the sense that poverty can become a general malaise creating 'upstream' effects that taint the flow of everyday life. We therefore turn to consider the ways that wellbeing is undermined by assaults on the wider determinants of health, given a need to be mindful of broader geographies of life's limits and the variable life chances that prevail across and between nations. For, as Wilkinson (1996) pointed out, the links between health outcomes, and geographical location can be causal and direct. By way of example, societies that have pursued greater equality of opportunity have boasted demonstrably better outcomes for markers of life chances like infant mortality (e.g., Cuba cf. USA – see Feinsilver, 1993).

There has been a longstanding commitment by geographers to understanding the complex relations between wealth and health, as well as analysing the structural determinants of health (e.g., Curtis, 2006). By way of example and for the sake of brevity, we will draw upon the work of Cheer et al. (2002) who explore how households make daily decisions and choices regarding their health. Their contention is that while choices directly, or indirectly, bear on their health, any decisions regarding expenditure are ultimately made within, and constrained by, the structural context of everyday life.

For at least two reasons, food is central to wellbeing. *First*, the type of food consumed has significant consequences for the health of individuals (e.g. diet is clearly related to health problems, including obesity). People in receipt of low incomes run a higher risk of being overweight due to the consumption of foods high in fat, sugar and salt (Else, 2000). This risk is arguably exacerbated by the underlying structures that work to limit income (e.g., unemployment, high rental costs) rather than by human agency to control one's diet. *Second*, food has been identified as one of the main areas of spending that low-income earners discount for the sake of other expenses. These types of food tend to be chosen due to their low cost (Russell et al., 1999). As Cheer et al. (2002) argue, food is one of the easiest expenses to sacrifice when money is lacking. Although low-income earners have generally been found to be good budgeters out of necessity, even the best budgeters have trouble when the disposable money will not stretch to cover essential needs. Food is often sacrificed due to expenses such as housing. In a 1996 survey of Salvation Army foodbank clients in New Zealand, having no money left after rent was found to be the most common reason that clients were seeking help. In fact, 45.5 percent of respondents indicated housing costs as a reason for needing food (Gunby, 1996). The consequences in terms of corroding wellbeing are not just the obvious hunger; the 1997 National Nutrition Survey in New Zealand found that 3 percent of households felt stressed because they could not provide food for social occasions (Russell et al., 1999). This observation highlights the symbolic as well as physiological roles that food plays. This is a significant finding for migrant people from Pacific Island nations in New Zealand; people whose cultures value large-scale family occasions (e.g., funerals and weddings) which require large amounts of food to feed extended family and friends. As Macpherson (1997) points out, these occasions tend to reflect on the ability and status of the host(s) and the amount and quality of the food therefore becomes important.

In a recent evaluation of a healthy housing project in Auckland, the home improvement most valued by one respondent was the enlargement of the living area and the provision of a large dining table that facilitated family gatherings. In the words of a public health nurse: 'She really wanted her connection with the family and it's been a real winner … I can drive by the house now and see in pride of place, the huge dining table, through the open doors of the new deck.' (Bullen et al., 2008). Too easily, in other words, deficits in food and housing are presumed by policy makers and programme providers to be issues of hunger and shelter. As Maslow's hierarchy of needs reminds us, addressing physiological need is but the beginning of a cumulative process of addressing human wellbeing.

'PROVIDING' FOR WELLBEING

In many ways wellbeing can be experienced in, or later because of, services and facilities. Although hospitals and doctors have concerns for the wellbeing of their patients, geographical inquiry has focused on a broader range of settings and professional categories, whose function is more firmly wellbeing-oriented.

Mirroring the emergence of community and home as sites for care, over the last few years geographies of caring have emerged to articulate a range of new 'caringscapes' (Parr, 2003; Popke, 2006). Here recent inquiry has been focused primarily on care by members of the unpaid voluntary (Milligan 2001; Johnsen et al., 2005) and informal sectors (Wiles, 2003a, 2003b; Milligan, 2000, 2005). Because caring involves complex mixtures of social and health care and combines daily routines of social and private/family life, wellbeing is generally emphasised. Studies either focus on the wellbeing of those cared for, or focus on how carers assist the wellbeing of those they care for. A common theme in this research is, however, how wellbeing is difficult to achieve given considerable resource, financial, time and information limitations.

As a profession, nursing is centrally concerned with the wellbeing of patients and is closely linked to a number of sites and settings. A tradition of studying nursing geographically has been established in recent years (Andrews, 2006). Extending the previous very basic and vague notion of a 'clinical environment', geographies of nursing have provided a clear understanding of how the job category of nurse, and the numerous activities involved in the agency of nursing, are enacted in space and relate dynamically to places (Carolan et al., 2006). A range of relationships has been articulated, including how places characterise particular clinical specialities (Roush and Cox, 2000; Lock and Gibb, 2003), provide attachments, symbolism and identity for patients (Cheek, 2004; Gilmour, 2006), and impact upon professional-patient intimacies, interactions and relationships (Purkis, 1996; Peter, 2002; Malone, 2003).

Elsewhere in the broadly-defined health care arena, the growth in complementary and alternative medicine (CAM) in recent decades is associated in no small part with consumer demands for holistic treatment options that address physical and mental wellbeing needs. The origins of CAM are, however, located in traditional medicines in other times and places. Here geographical study dates back to the early medical geography concerns for the health of developing world peoples and places (e.g. Good, 1977; Gesler, 1979; Good et al., 1979; Rahman, 1980). Although the focus was often on the location and spatial integration of traditional and western medicine, more recent research has discussed more critically its cultural relocation in the developed world (Wilson and Rosenberg, 2002). Mirroring the growth in both provision and demand for contemporary CAM, recent geographical research has been concerned with the distributive features of these particular services and wellbeing opportunities through referral networks and practice catchment areas (Verheij et al., 1999; Williams, 2000; Anyinam, 1990). Building on an early agenda for research (Wiles and Rosenberg, 2001), qualitative studies have considered a range of issues including who uses CAM and why, how this differs between and across places, and how place itself shapes and is shaped by CAM. For example, studies have considered the importance of clinics (Andrews, 2004), broader localities and landscapes (Andrews, 2003) and materials, and unorthodox places such as magasines and the internet (Doel and Segrott, 2003a, 2003b). Moreover, recent research, specifically on counselling, psychotherapy and mind therapies, articulates how imaging place is a central therapeutic tool of practice: taking clients away, perhaps to a past or imagined place, for a therapeutic experience, and to ultimately improve their wellbeing (Williams, 1998; Bondi, 1999, 2003, 2005; Bondi with Fewell, 2003; Andrews, 2004).

A third, less formal, form of providing for wellbeing can be seen to occur through friendships and social connections well outside the health care system. Ideas of social capital involve the social cohesiveness of networks based, perhaps, on religion, family, neighbourhood, clubs and societies, or ethnicity, and maintain that people act together for their mutual health and wellbeing (Mohan and Mohan, 2002; McCulloch, 2003; Wakefield and Poland, 2005; Mohan et al., 2005). In terms of friendship certain 'structural' factors self-evidently promote sustained and welcomed social encounters, such as residential proximity, similarity of gender and socio-economic status, shared interests, common attitudes, and shared histories or age (Andrews et al., 2003). Nonetheless each friendship is individual, complex and dynamic, and can ebb and flow in defiance of such factors (Allan, 1996).

The significance of friendship for the emotional wellbeing of individuals is widely recognised. Friendship attachments provide a sense of security and a belonging which potentially counters isolation and loneliness. Friendships facilitate social integration through shared activity and common interests, and provide positive feedback on social competence both at work and in leisure. They provide a source of assistance in times of need, which can underpin the emotional health of individuals (Andrews et al., 2003). Researchers have also argued that those with a high level of friendship support are likely to have good physical health, relatively high resistance to stress, and are better able to deal with transitions and reversals in life (O'Connor, 1992). So a friendship relationship provides a 'haven', a place where one belongs and is wanted or, in effect, finds a psychological 'band-aid' when emotional support is needed. Finchum and Weber (2000) have likened friendship to a form of human medical insurance. Friendships might be said 'then' to allow changes to be made in a person's life and to minimise the loss and disruption that ensues (Wellman and Berkowitz, 1988).

CONCLUSION: WIDENING WELLBEING

This chapter has selectively reviewed conceptual and research themes associated with a growing but disparate focus on wellbeing in geography. This interest is encouraged by the breadth of vision encapsulated in the Alma Ata declaration in which health is seen as 'complete social, physical and mental wellbeing and not just the absence of disease …' as well as more recent socio-ecological formulations that embody holism and a future-orientation in health (Gesler and Kearns, 2002). A key problem for health geographers is that although health is increasingly conceptualised in a positive fashion, it continues to be measured in negative terms. This occurs with respect to personal health as well as population health. In its crudest manifestation, for instance, mortality rates are used as indicators of health status. Similarly, rates of high blood pressure or limiting long-standing illness only indirectly speak of how *well* people or populations feel about themselves or their lived environments. We have argued, however, that wellbeing cannot, and has not, been 'captured' by medical or even health interests. Rather its essential breadth and vitality links to a range of domains of human experience. Indeed, our survey has left gaps for others to chart (e.g. the place of spirituality in wellbeing and the role of places in the significance of spirituality).

We have argued that a focus on wellbeing brings us to a point of integrating health and emotional geographies as they are affectively and effectively experienced in place. This view finds resonance in the implied collective social geographies advocated by the Ottawa Charter of Health Promotion, which speaks of empowerment, community action, and capacity building. However, we believe that notwithstanding its powerful role in shifting thinking on the international stage, the Ottawa Charter has limitations within more localised settings where key dimensions of health and wellbeing are bound into histories of colonisation and the power politics of place. Invariably, international statements are insufficiently sensitised to cultural difference to encompass local experiences of diversity and wellbeing.

We close by reflecting on two possible critiques of geographies of wellbeing. First, the aspiration for geographies of wellbeing to move beyond negative definitions and indicators of health is surely good and appropriate. However, there remains a moral obligation for geographers to be vigilant that any 'turn' to wellbeing is not undertaken at the expense of ignoring inequalities in, and structural determinants of, health. In advocating this obligation, we are also exposing a subtle but important critique of 'wellbeing' studies: the ever-present risk of focusing on the experience of the well (resourced) while underplaying enduring geographies of disadvantage.

Second, as we stated at the outset, a key opportunity of working with wellbeing is its breadth, but the associated imprecision is a limitation. Indeed, there is a danger that the potency of arguments about wellbeing will be weakened by their wide-ranging applicability. Some may ask 'if wellbeing is found everywhere, then is it worth investigating?' Our answer is yes. For air too is nigh on ubiquitous, yet its quality is not. To elaborate, it is relatively straightforward to say what the parameters of an unhealthy community would be. For example Marmot and Wilkinson (2001) have produced a pithy summary of the major social determinants of ill-health. They cite social gradients in income, social exclusion, unemployment, lack of transport and access to services, poor nutrition, and addictions as key determinants of health status. These factors could, hypothetically, be developed into a comprehensive set of indicators and applied to communities. However questions and challenges arise. Can the application and mapping of indicators of deprivation in fact strip people of their dignity by labelling them in such a way that overlooks their choice to live in certain places? Can such indicators overlook experience of wellbeing they gain from behaviours that are otherwise vilified by the public health movement? As Fleuret and Atkinson (2007) suggest, as geographers, we need to augment our vocabulary that includes terms like *therapeutic landscapes*, and *healthy environments*, with the idea of *spaces of wellbeing*. The challenge for geographers is to rethink the issue of wellbeing by contextualising it into both personal and population-based experience of place.

REFERENCES

Adams, J. (2005) 'Exploring the interface between complementary and alternative medicine (CAM) and rural general practice: a call for research', *Health and Place*, 10: 285–7.

Allan, G. (1996) *Kinship and Friendship in Modern Britain*. Oxford: Oxford University Press.

Anderson, K. and Smith, S.J. (2001) Editorial: Emotional geographies. *Transactions, Institute of British Geographers*, NS 26: 7–10.

Andrews, G.J. (2003) 'Placing the consumption of private complementary medicine: everyday geographies of older people's use', *Health and Place*, 2003c (9): 337–49.

Andrews, G.J. (2004) '(Re)thinking the dynamic between healthcare and place: therapeutic geographies in treatment and care practices', *Area*, 36 (3): 307–18.

Andrews, G.J. (2006) 'Geographies of health in nursing', *Health and Place*, 12 (1): 110–8.

Andrews, G.J. (2007) 'Spaces of dizziness and dread: navigating acrophobia', *Geografiska Annaler Series B: Human Geography* (in press).

Andrews, G.J. and Chen, S. (2006) 'The production of tyrannical space', *Children's Geographies*, 4: 239–51.

Andrews, G.J. and Kearns, R.A. (2005) 'Everyday health histories and the making of place: the case of an English coastal town', *Social Science and Medicine,* 60: 2697–713.

Andrews, G.J. and Kearns, R.A. (2007) 'Connecting pop music and health: from celebrity diplomacy to medicinal melodies', *Complementary Therapies in Clinical Practice* (in press).

Andrews G J, Kearns R, A. Kingbury P Carr E R (2009) From celebrity diplomacy to medicinal melody: Bono, U2 and health. *Aporia* (in press)

Andrews, G.J. and Phillips, D.R. (eds) (2005) *Ageing and Place: Perspectives, policy and practice*. London: Routledge.

Andrews, G.J., Gavin, N., Begley, S., Brodie, D. (2003) 'Assisting friendships, combating loneliness?: users' views on a befriending scheme', *Ageing and Society,* 23 (3): 349–62.

Andrews, G.J., Sudwell, M. and Sparks, A. (2005) 'Towards a geography of fitness: an ethnographic case study of the gym in body-building culture', *Social Science and Medicine*, 60: 877–91.

Andrews, G.J., Cutchin, M., McCracken, K., Phillips, D.R., Wiles, J. (2007) 'Geographical gerontology: the constitution of a discipline', *Social Science and Medicine* (in press).

Anyinam, C. (1990) 'Alternative medicine in Western industrialized countries: an agenda for medical geography', *Canadian Geographer*, 34: 69–76.

Bale, D. (2004) *Running Cultures: Racing in time and space*. London: Routledge.

Barton, H. and Tsourou, C. (2000) *Healthy Urban Planning: A WHO guide to planning for people*, London: Spon Press.

Baum, F. and Palmer, C. (2002) '"Opportunity structures": urban landscape, social capital and health promotion in Australia', *Health Promotion International*, 17: 351–61.

Baxter, J. and Lee, D. (2004) 'Explaining the maintenance of low concern near a hazardous waste treatment facility', *Journal of Risk Research*, 6: 705–29.

Blaikie, A. (1999) *Ageing and Popular Culture*. Cambridge: Cambridge University Press.

Blaikie, A. (2005) 'Imagined landscapes of ageing and identity', in G.J. Andrews and D.R. Phillips, *Ageing and Place: Perspectives, policy, practice*. London: Routledge.

Bondi, L. (1999) 'Stages on journeys: some remarks about human geography and psychotherapeutic practice', *The Professional Geographer*, 51: 11–24.

Bondi, L. (2003) 'A situated practice for (re)situating selves: trainee counsellors and the promise of counselling', *Environment and Planning A*, 35: 853–70.

Bondi, L. (2005) 'Making connections and thinking through emotions: between geography

and psychotherapy', *Transactions Institute British Geographers*, 30: 433–48.
Bondi, L. with Fewell, J. (2003) '"Unlocking the cage door": the spatiality of counselling', *Social & Cultural Geography*, 4: 528–46.
Booth, D. (2004) 'Surf lifesavers and surfers: cultural and spatial conflict on the Australian Beach', in P. Vertinsky and J. Bale (eds), *Sites of sport: Space, place, experience*. London: Routledge.
Breslow, L. (1972) 'A Quantitative Approach to the World Health Organization Definition of Health: Physical, Mental and Social Well-being', *International Journal of Epidemiology*, 1: 347–55.
Brown, T. and Duncan, C. (2002). 'Placing geographies of public health', *Area*, 33:, 361–69.
Bullen, C., Kearns, R., Clinton, J., Laing, P., Mahoney, F. and McDuff, I. (2008) Bringing health home: Householder and provider perspectives on the Healthy Housing programme in Auckland, New Zealand, *Social Science & Medicine,* 66, 1185–96.
Butler, R. and Parr, R. (1999) *Mind and Body Spaces: Geographies of Illness, Impairment and Disability*. London: Routledge.
Carolan, M., Andrews, G.J. and Hodnett, E. (2006) 'Writing place: a comparison of nursing research and health geography', *Nursing Inquiry*, 13: 203–19.
Cheek, J. (2004) 'Older people and acute care: a matter of place', *Illness, Crisis and Loss*, 12: 52–62.
Cheer, T., Kearns, R.A. and Murphy, L. (2002) 'Housing policy, poverty and culture: "'discounting"' decisions among Pacific peoples in Auckland, New Zealand', *Environment and Planning C: Government and Policy*, 20: 497–516.
Collins, D.C.A. and Kearns, R.A. (2001) 'The safe journeys of an enterprising school: Negotiating landscapes of opportunity and risk', *Health & Place,* 7: 293–306.
Collins, D.C.A. and Kearns, R.A. (2007) 'Ambiguous landscapes: Sun, risk and recreation on New Zealand beaches', in A. Williams (ed.), *Therapeutic Landscapes*. Aldershot: Ashgate, pp. 15–32.
Connell, J. and Gibson, C. (2003) *Sound Tracks: Popular music identity and place*. London: Routledge.
Conradson, D. (2005) 'Landscape, care and the relational self: Therapeutic encounters in rural England', *Health and Place*, 11: 337–48.
Crang, M. (1998) *Cultural Geography*. London: Routledge.
Curtis, S.E. (2006) *Health and Inequality: Geographical Perspectives*. London: Sage.
Cutchin, M. (2003) 'The process of mediated aging-in-place: a theoretically and empirically based model', *Social Science & Medicine*, 57: 1077–90.
Daley, C. (2003) *Leisure and Pleasure: Reshaping and Revealing the New Zealand Body 1900–1960*. Auckland: University of Auckland Press.
Davidson, J. (2003) *Phobic Geographies: The Phenomenology and Spatiality of Identity*. Aldershot: Ashgate.
Davidson, J. and Milligan, C. (2004) 'Embodying emotion sensing space: introducing emotional geographies', *Social & Cultural Geography*, 5: 523–32.
Davidson, J., Bondi, L. and Smith, M. (eds) (2005) *Emotional Geographies*. Aldershot: Ashgate.
Davies, J.K. and Kelly, M.P. (1993) *Healthy Cities: Research and Practice*. London: Routledge.
Dear, M. and Wolch, J. (1987) *Landscapes of Despair: From Deinstitutionalisation to Homelessness*. Princeton, NJ: Princeton University Press.
Doel, M. and Segrott, J. (2003a) 'Self, health and gender: complementary and alternative medicine in the mass media', *Gender, Place and Culture*, 10: 131–44.
Doel, M. and Segrott, J. (2003b) 'Beyond belief: complementary medicine, lifestyle magazines and the dis-ease of everyday life', *Environment and Planning D: Society and Space*, 21 (6): 739–59.
Doel, M. and Segrott, J. (2004) 'Disturbing geography: obsessive-compulsive disorder as spatial practice', *Social and Cultural Geography,* 5: 597–614.
Dorn, M. and Laws, G. (1994) 'Social theory, body politics, and medical geography: extending Kearns' invitation', *The Professional Geographer*, 46: 106–10.
Durie, M. (1994) *WhaiOra: Maori Health Development*. Auckland: Oxford University Press.
Dyck, I. (1995) 'Hidden Geographies: the changing lifeworlds of women with multiple sclerosis', *Social Science and Medicine*, 40: 307–20.
Dyck, I. and Kearns, R.A. (2006) 'Structuration Theory: Agency, Structure and Everyday

Life', in G. Valentine and S. Aitken (eds), *Approaches to Human Geography*. Thousand Oaks: Sage, pp. 86–97.

Else, A. (2000) *Hidden Hunger: Food and low income in New Zealand*. Wellington: The New Zealand Network Against Food Poverty.

Eyles, J. (1997) 'Environmental health research: setting an agenda by spinning our wheels or climbing the mountain?', *Health and Place*, 3 (1): 1–13.

Feinsilver, J. (1993) *Healing the Masses: Cuban Health Politics at Home and Abroad*. Berkeley: University of California Press.

Finchum, T. and Weber, J.A. (2000) 'Applying continuity theory to older adult friendships', *Journal of Aging and Identity,* 5: 159–68.

Fleuret, S. and Atkinson, S. (2007) 'Wellbeing, health and geography: A critical review and research agenda', *New Zealand Geographer* 63: 106–18.

Gesler, W. (1979) 'Illness and health practitioner use in Calabar, Nigeria', *Social Science and Medicine*, 13: 23–30.

Gesler, W.M. (1992) 'Therapeutic landscapes: medical issues in light of the new cultural geography', *Social Science & Medicine*, 34: 735–46.

Gesler, W.M. and Kearns, R.A. (2002) *Culture/Place/Health*. London: Routledge.

Gilmour, J.A. (2006) 'Hybrid space: constituting the hospital as a home for patients', *Nursing Inquiry*, 13: 16–22.

Good, C. (1977) 'Traditional medicine: an agenda for medical geography', *Social Science and Medicine*, 11: 705–13.

Good, C., Hunter, J., Katz, S. and Katz, S. (1979) 'The interface of dual systems of health in the developing world: toward health policy initiatives in Africa', *Social Science and Medicine*, 13: 141–54.

Gubrium, J. and Holstein, J.A. (1999) 'The nursing home as a discursive anchor for the ageing body', *Ageing and Society*, 19: 519–38.

Gunby, J. (1996) *Housing the Hungry: The Third Report New Zealand Council of Christian Social Services*. Wellington: Salvation Army.

Hall, E.C. (2000) '"Blood, brain and bones": taking the body seriously in the geography of health and impairment', *Area*, 32: 21–9.

Hugman, R. (1999) 'Embodying old age', in E. Kenworthy-Teather (ed.), *Embodied Geographies: Spaces, bodies and rites of passage*. London: Routledge.

Johnsen, S., Cloke, P. and May, J. (2005) 'Transitory spaces of care: serving homeless people on the street', *Health and Place*, 11: 323–36.

Johnston, L. (1996) 'Flexing femininity: female body-builders refiguring '"the body"', *Gender, place and Culture*, 3: 327–40.

Johnston, R.J., Gregory, D., Pratt, G. and Watts, M. (2000) *The Dictionary of Human Geography (4th Edition)*. Blackwell: Oxford.

Kahneman, D., Diener, E., Schwarz, N. (1999) *Well-being: The Foundations of Hedonic Psychology*. New York: Russell Sage Foundation.

Katz, S. (1995) *Disciplining Old Age: The Formation of Gerontological Knowledge*. Richmond: University of Virginia Press.

Katz, S. (2005) 'Imagining the lifespan: from premodern miracles to postmodern fantasies', in M. Featherstone and A. Wernick (eds), *Images of Aging: Cultural representations of later life*. London: Routledge.

Kearns, R.A. and Collins, D.C.A. (2000) 'New Zealand Children's Health Camps: Therapeutic landscapes meet the contract state', *Social Science and Medicine,* 51: 1047–59.

Kearns, R.A. and Collins, D.C.A. (2006) 'Children in the Intensifying City – Lessons from Auckland's Walking School Buses', in B. Gleeson and N. Sipe (eds), *Creating Child Friendly Cities: Reinstating Kids in the City.* London: Routledge. pp. 105–20.

Kearns, R.A. and Gesler, W.M. (1998) *Putting Health into Place: Landscape, Identity and Well-being*. Syracuse, NY: Syracuse University Press.

Kearns, R.A. and Moon, G. (2002) 'From medical to health geography: theory, novelty and place in a decade of change', *Progress in Human Geography*, 26: 587–607.

Kearns, R.A., Witten, K. and McCreanor, T. (2006) 'Healthy communities', in M. Thompson-Fawcett and C. Freeman (eds), *Living Together: Towards inclusive Settlements in New Zealand*. Auckland: Oxford University Press. pp. 241–57.

King, R., Warnes, A.M. and Williams, A.M. (2000) *Sunset Lives: British Retirement to Southern Europe*. Oxford: Berg.

Kleinginna, A. and Kleinginna, R. (2005) 'A categorized list of emotion definitions, with suggestions for a consensual definition', *Motivation and Emotion*, 5: 345–79.

Ley, D. (1983) *A Social Geography of the City*. New York: Harper and Row.

Litva, A. and Eyles, J.D. (1995) 'Coming out: exposing social theory in medical geography', *Health and Place*, 1: 5–14.

Litva, A., Peggs, K. and Moon, G. (2001) 'The beauty of health: locating young women's health and appearance', in I. Dyck, N. Lewis and S. McLafferty (eds), *Geographies of Women's Health*. Routledge: London.

Lock, L.R. and Gibb, H.J. (2003) 'The power of place', *Midwifery*, 19: 132–39.

Longhurst, R. (1997) '(Dis)embodied geographies', *Progress in Human Geography*, 21: 486–501.

Longhurst, R. (1998) '(Re)presenting shopping centres and bodies: questions of pregnancy', in R. Ainley (ed.), *New Frontiers of Space, Bodies and Gender*. London: Routledge. pp. 20–34.

Longhurst, R. (2000a) 'Geography and gender: masculinities, male identity and men', *Progress in Human Geography*, 24: 439–44.

Longhurst, R. (2000b) '"Corporeographies" of pregnancy: "bikini babes"', *Environment and Planning D: Society and Space*, 18: 453–72.

McCulloch, A. (2003) 'An examination of social capital and social disorganization in neighbourhoods in the British household panel study', *Social Science and Medicine*, 56: 1425–38.

MacKian, S. (2000) 'Contours of coping: mapping the subject of world of long-term illness', *Health and Place*, 6: 95–104.

Macpherson, C., (1997) 'A Samoan solution to the limitations of urban housing in New Zealand', in J. Rensel and M. Rodman (eds), *Home in the Islands: Housing and Social Change in the Pacific*. Honolulu: University of Hawaii Press. pp. 151–74.

Malone, R. (2003) 'Distal nursing', *Social Science and Medicine*, 56: 2317–26.

Marmot, M. and Wilkinson, R.G. (eds) (2001) *Social Determinants of Health*. Oxford: OUP.

Matless, D. (2005) 'Sonic geographies in a nature region', *Social and Cultural Geography*, 6: 745–66.

Matthews, H. and Limb, M. (1999) 'Developing an agenda for the geography of children: review and prospect', *Progress in Human Geography*, 23: 61–90.

Milligan, C. (2000) 'Bearing the burden: towards a restructured geography of caring', *Area*, 32: 49–58.

Milligan, C (2001) *Geographies of Care: Space, place and the voluntary sector*. Aldershot: Ashgate.

Milligan, C. (2005) 'From home to "home": Situating emotions within the care-giving experience', *Environment and Planning A*, 37: 2075–270.

Milligan, C., Gatrell, A. and Bingley, A. (2004) '"Cultivating health": therapeutic landscapes and older people in northern England', *Social Science and Medicine*, 9: 1781–93.

Mitchell, H., Kearns, R.A. and Collins, D.C.A. (2007) 'Nuances of neighbourhood: Childrens perceptions of the space between home and school in Auckland, New Zealand', *Geoforum*, 38: 614–27.

Mohan, G. and Mohan, J.F. (2002) 'Placing social capital', *Progress in Human Geography*, 26: 191–210.

Mohan, J., Twigg, L., Barnard, S. and Jones, K. (2005) 'Social capital, geography and health: a small-area analysis for England', *Social Science and Medicine*, 60: 1267–83.

Morrison, P.S. (2007) 'Subjective wellbeing and the city', *Social Policy Journal of New Zealand*, 31: 74–103.

O'Connor, P. (1992) *Friendship Between Women: A Critical Review*. London: Harvester Wheatsheaf.

Palka, E. (1999) 'Accessible wilderness as therapeutic landscape: experiencing the nature of Denali National park, Alaska', in A. Williams (ed.), *Therapeutic Landscapes: The Dynamic Between Place and Wellness*. Lanham: University Press of America.

Park, R.J. (2004) 'For pleasure? Or Profit? Or personal health? College Gymnasia as contested terrain', in P. Vertinsky and J. Bale (eds), *Sites of Sport: Space, place, experience*. London: Routledge.

Parr, H. (1998) 'Mental Health, ethnography and the body', *Area*, 30: 28–37.

Parr, H. (2003) 'Medical geography: care and caring', *Progress in Human Geography*, 27: 212–21.

Peace, S., Kellaher, L. and Holland, C. (2005) *Environment and Identity in Later Life*. New York: Open University Press.

Percy-Smith, B. and Matthews, H. (2001) 'Tyrannical spaces: young people, bullying and urban neighbourhoods', *Local Environment*, 6: 49–63.

Peter E. (2002) 'The history of nursing in the home: revealing the significance of place in the expression of moral agency', *Nursing Inquiry*, 9: 65–72.

Pile, S. (1996) *The Body and the City: Psychoanalysis, Space, and Subjectivity*. London: Routledge.

Popke, J. (2006) 'Geography and ethics: everyday mediations through care and consumption', *Progress in Human Geography*, 30: 504–12.

Purkis, M.E. (1996) 'Nursing in quality space: technologies governing experiences of care', *Nursing Inquiry*, 3: 101–11.

Rahman, M. (1980) 'Urban and rural medical systems in Pakistan', *Social Science and Medicine*, 14: 283–89.

Rodaway, P. (1994) *Sensuous Geographies: Body, Sense, and Place*. London: Routledge.

Rose, G. (2004) 'Everybody's cuddled up and just looking really nice: an emotional geography of some mums and their family pictures', *Social and Cultural Geography*, 5: 549–64.

Roush, C.V. and Cox, J.E. (2000) 'The meaning of home: How it shapes the practice of home and hospice care', *Home Healthcare Nurse*, 19: 388–94.

Russell, D., Parnell, W. and Wilson, N. (1999) *NZ Food: NZ People: Key Results of the 1997 National Nutrition Survey*. Wellington, NZ: LINZ Activity and Health Research Unit, University of Otago for the Ministry of Health.

Ryff, C.D. (1989) 'Happiness is everything, or is it? Explorations on the meaning of psychological well-being', *Journal of Personality & Social Psychology*, 57: 1061–81.

Smith, M. (2001) *An Ethics of Place: Radical ecology, postmodernity and social theory*. New York: State University of New York Press.

Smith, S.J. (1994) Soundscapes, *Area*, 26: 232–40.

Valentine, G. (1995). Creating transgressive space: the music of kd lang. *Transactions of the Institute of British Geographers,* NS 20 (4) 474–485.

Valentine, G. (1998) '"Sticks and Stones May Break My Bones": A Personal Geography of Harassment', *Antipode*: 30.

van Ingen, C. (2003) 'Geographies of gender, sexuality and race: Reframing the focus on space in sport sociology', *International Review for the Sociology of Sport*, 38: 201–16.

Verheij, R., Bakker, D. and Groenewegen, P. (1999) 'Is there a geography of alternative medical treatment in the Netherlands?', *Health and Place*, 5: 83–97.

Wakefield, S. and McMullan, C. (2005) 'Healing places of decline: (re)imagining everyday landscapes in Hamilton, Ontario', *Health and Place*, 11: 299–312.

Wakefield, S.E. L. and Poland, B. (2005) 'Family, friend or foe? Critical reflections on the relevance and role of social capital in health promotion and community development', *Social Science and Medicine*, 60: 2819–32.

Wakefield, S.E.L., Elliott, S.J., Cole, D.C. and Eyles, J.D. (2001) 'Environmental risk and (re)action: air quality, health and civic involvement in an urban industrial neighbourhood', *Health and Place*, 7: 163–77.

Wellman, B. and Berkowitz, S. (eds) (1988) *Social Structures: A Network Approach*. Cambridge: Cambridge University Press.

Wiles, J. (2003a) 'Daily geographies of caregivers: mobility, routine, scale', *Social Science & Medicine*, 57: 1307–25.

Wiles, J. (2003b) 'Informal caregivers' experiences of formal support in a changing context, *Health and Social Care in the Community*, 11: 189–298.

Wiles, J. and Rosenberg, M.W. (2001) '"Gentle caring experience". Seeking alternative health care in Canada', *Health and Place*, 7: 209–24.

Wilkinson, R. (1996) *Unhealthy Societies: The Afflictions of Inequality*. London: Routledge.

Williams, A. (1998) 'Therapeutic landscapes in holistic medicine', *Social Science and Medicine*, 46: 1193–203.

Williams, A. (1999) *Therapeutic Landscapes: The Dynamic Between Place and Wellness*. New York: University Press of America.

Williams, A. (2000) 'The diffusion of alternative health care: a Canadian case study of chiropractic and naturopathic practices', *Canadian Geographer*, 44: 152–66.

Williams A. (ed.) (2007) *Therapeutic Landscapes*. Aldershot: Ashgate.

Wilson, K. and Rosenberg, M. (2002) 'Exploring the determinants of health for First Nations peoples in Canada: can existing frameworks accommodate traditional activities?', *Social Science and Medicine*, 55: 2017–31.

Wilton, R. (1995) 'Diminishing worlds: HIV/AIDS and the geography of everyday life', *Health & Place*, 2: 1–17.

Wilton, R. and DeVerteuil, G. (2006) 'Spaces of sobriety/sites of power: Examining social model alcohol recovery programs as therapeutic landscapes', *Social Science and Medicine*, 63: 649–61.

Witten, K., McCreanor, T., Kearns, R. and Ramasubramanian, L. (2001) 'The impacts of a school closure on neighbourhood social cohesion: narratives from Invercargill, New Zealand', *Health & Place*, 7: 307–17.

14

Health, Risk and Resilience

Rich Mitchell

INTRODUCTION

Not so long ago, I moved home and changed my job and my life. I moved from living in a room in a shared house in north west London, to live with my partner in a flat in Glasgow, Scotland. Overnight I changed physical location and my personal, social and financial situation. In many ways I changed 'my geography'. What does this have to do with health, risk and resilience? At the time, my job was to calculate risks of death for different groups of people in various parts of the UK. I couldn't help but notice that, overnight, I moved from a part of the UK in which the risk of death was apparently relatively low, to a part of the UK with just about the highest risk. This change in geographical location from low risk to high risk weighed on my mind, but I decided, despite the statistics I'd seen, that I would be fine.

I thought about it like this: I was (then) young. Glasgow's biggest killers of men were heart disease and cancer (Registrar General, 1999), but I knew that few people die at younger ages from these diseases. I conveniently forgot about other causes of death. I was also about to establish a cohabiting partnership and knew that partnered men have generally better health than single men (Willitts et al., 2004; Wyke and Ford, 1992). I was very happy, which I knew to be very good for mental, and perhaps physical, health (Perneger et al., 2004). Both moving north and moving in with someone would make me wealthier and wealth is one of the strongest factors in protecting health (Shaw et al., 1999b). All of these things, I decided, would offset the statistically increased risk of death which accompanies residence in Glasgow. So, although my own construction of the 'risk' to which I was exposed was partly based on evidence from the probabilistic and statistical realms, it was my own perception and construction of risk which mattered most. Of course, I, like everyone else, had no way of knowing for certain what was (or is) *really* going to happen to me; life is uncertain. That is what risk is all about.

Risk is a concept constructed to help deal with uncertainty and the fact that bad things can, and do, happen (Lupton, 1999). This chapter explores the nature of risk as it pertains to *health*, and different ways that geography matters in terms of its construction, its operation, its influence and its study. However, the chapter is also about a concept which may be less familiar: resilience. Resilience refers to situations in which people or places apparently avoid the adverse outcomes which we might expect them to suffer, given a particular perspective of the risks they face (Bartley, 2006). The chapter discusses risk first, then resilience.

WHAT IS RISK?

There is a myriad of perspectives on risk. Whilst academic geography and risk have a close association (there are many geography departments teaching courses on risk, for example) health-related risk and resilience have been focused on more by epidemiology, sociology and anthropology. Given the range of disciplines which focus on risk, it is no surprise that the literature is diverse. However, this diversity also stems from 'risk' being a homograph; it has multiple meanings. Before situating health-related risk in a geographical context, it will be helpful to identify some of the most important meanings which are attached to risk, and some of the theories and approaches which have been taken to studying and understanding it. I will make a distinction between approaches to risk that are based on probabilities and populations, and those which are focused on socio-cultural perspectives, and individuals.

PROBABILISTIC RISK

Many approaches to risk at a *population* level are based on statistical or probabilistic epistemology and methodology. Lupton refers to this approach as, and relates it to, modernity (Lupton, 1999). It is based on the notion that the probability, or chance, of an event is known, or at least knowable if we organise our investigations of the real and objective world properly. In the original probabilistic conception, risk was focused on the chance of 'something' happening. This means risk was a term which could have both positive and negative connotations (Douglas, 2007). Since it is we that place a value (good or bad) on the outcome of interest, and not the probabilistic or statistical approach *per se*, there can be a measurable risk of something good happening to you, as well as something bad. However, today risk has a largely negative connotation, especially when thinking about health. It is unusual to hear people describing the 'risk' of winning the lottery, or the 'risk' of not getting cancer, for example.

Let's conduct an experiment. Get yourself a coin. It has two faces; heads and tails. Now, find something quite heavy, like a big book, or a tin of beans. Take off your shoe. Toss the coin. If it lands on heads, drop the heavy item on your toe. If it lands on tails, there is no need to drop the heavy item … What? You didn't do the experiment? Why not!?

What was your judgement process in deciding not to drop the heavy item? I imagine that you *didn't* work out the probability of getting 'heads' and then make a decision based on that. We'll think more about how the decision might have been made a bit later in the chapter. For now, in probabilistic terms, the chance of tossing heads can be expressed as 1 in 2, or 50 per cent, or 0.5. If I had suggested using a dice, with only those who rolled a 6 needing to drop the heavy item, the risk of throwing a 6 would have been 1 in 6 (literally 1/6, or 16.7 per cent). Statistics which describe frequency with which an event might occur, represent one important approach to risk.

Rates and risk

Epidemiologists prefer to think about probabilities of a particular 'outcome' (in the example, getting 'heads' when the coin is tossed) for groups of people – groups they call *populations* (Bhopal, 2002). If, for example, 100 people tossed a coin, a statistician would estimate that about 50 of those 100 coins would land on heads. That expression of risk is called a *rate*. In health research, a rate is calculated by dividing the number of people with a particular 'health outcome' (the aspect of health which is of interest, for example having a particular disease), by the size of the population group who could have that particular outcome. To calculate the crude death rate for an area for one year for example, we would divide the number of deaths which occurred in the area, by the total population living there. If there had been 200 deaths in the last year, and the population was 200,000, the death rate was 200/200,000, or 0.001.

What does this kind of quantified risk actually mean to the residents of a particular area? As an isolated number, that kind of representation of risk is very hard to interpret or understand. However, what if the death rate in your neighbourhood is 100 per 100,000, but the death rate in a friend's neighbourhood is 500 per 100,000; that's 5 times higher! Is it time to stop visiting the friend, just in case …? The idea that death is 5 times more likely in one area than in another might be easier to understand than the rates themselves. The comparison of quantified risks is widely used in probabilistic approaches to health geography. It is common to compare rates of poor health between different social groups, countries, cities and neighbourhoods to observe which groups or places have 'more risk' than others.

Relative risk and risk factors

The expression of how a risk varies between groups and or places is called 'relative risk' and it is often used to associate risk with a particular behaviour or characteristic. For example, smokers are 10-20 times more likely to get lung cancer (depending on how much, and for how long they smoke), than non-smokers (Crispo et al., 2004). A consistent statistical association between behaviours or characteristics and particular health outcomes can lead to these characteristics or behaviours being described as *risk factors*. A risk factor is any characteristic which is associated, in probabilistic terms, with greater chances of a particular outcome. In our example, being a smoker is a risk factor for lung cancer; this means that among smokers, the statistical risk of getting lung cancer is greater than among non-smokers.

Once identified, reduction or elimination of a risk factor might, at least in theory, reduce the occurrence of its associated health outcome. Research carried out by Fleming in the late 1980s, for example, suggested that laying a baby down to sleep on its front is a risk factor for Sudden Infant Death Syndrome, commonly known as cot death (Blair et al., 2006; Wigfield et al., 1992). A campaign raised awareness of this risky behaviour and encouraged parents to stop it. The resulting reduction in cot deaths both in the pilot area, and nationally, is clearly seen in Figure 14.1.

Problems with risk factor reduction

Although the ability to influence health in this way might seem exciting and useful, there are problems with a risk factor approach to improving health (Popay et al., 1998). Some risk factors are not easily manipulated. Risk factors include the biological (a faulty BRACA1 gene is a risk factor for breast cancer for example, but we cannot control inheritance of it), the demographic (getting older increases the risk of a very numerous health problems, but ageing cannot be prevented), and the social (being poor is one of the greatest risk factors for premature mortality, but not many people actively choose to stay in poverty). A second problem is that a risk factor for one outcome might actually help to prevent another. A diet with greater amounts of meat in it lowers the risk of tuberculosis (Russell, 2003), but increases the risk of heart disease, for example. A third problem is that a risk factor approach makes an implicit assumption that the individuals or populations which exhibit the risk factor understand, believe in, and care about, the 'risk' to which they may be exposed. Consider smoking again. It is one of the most carefully studied health-related behaviours, proven to be a risk factor for a huge range of health problems to the extent that it is estimated each cigarette

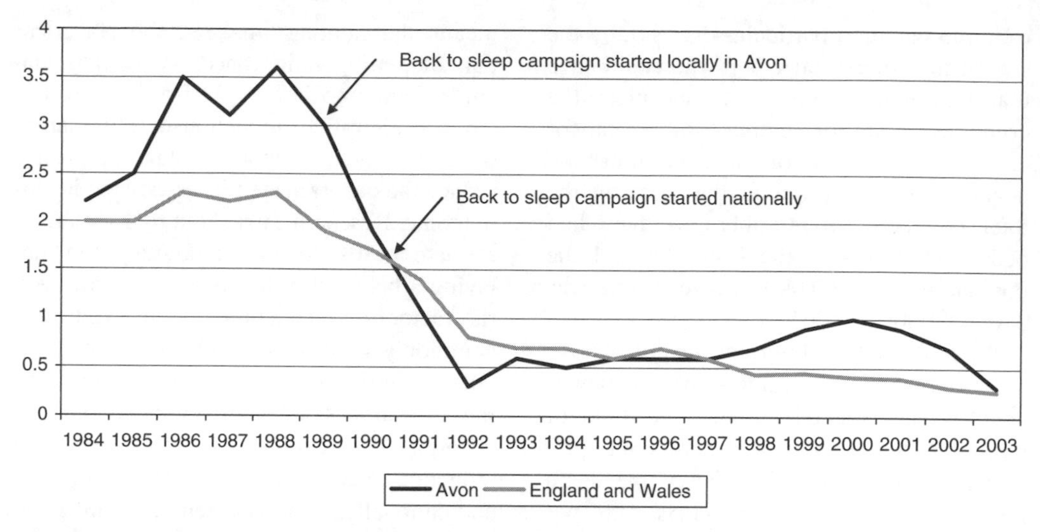

Figure 14.1 Changes in the incidence of SIDS over time in the UK.
Source: figures from Blair et al., 2006.

takes about 11 minutes off life expectancy (Shaw et al., 2000). This epidemiological knowledge has been translated into policy action; there are numerous campaigns and measures to try and reduce the numbers of people smoking, including warnings on cigarette packets which explain the risk smoking carries, yet millions of people still smoke. What does this reveal about risk? It tells us that people are not always influenced by probabilistic information about it; knowledge of high risk does not always equate to avoidance of it.

When probability and reality collide

One of the many reasons for this might be that a high statistical risk is not the same as a 'certainty'. Perhaps if people were *guaranteed* that *everyone* who undertook a 'risky' behaviour such as smoking was definitely going to become ill or die, then far fewer people would take the risk. However, that guarantee cannot not exist. The 'Uncle Norman' figure who smokes, drinks and eats all the pies, yet lives a long life in perfect health, plagues those with a professional interest in trying to convince populations to avoid 'risky' behaviours, as does the mythical 'last person', who takes plenty of exercise, eats healthily and drops dead of a heart attack at 25 years old; literally the 'last person you'd expect to die' (Davison et al., 1992; Hunt et al., 2000). Thus, people's lived experience of the relationships between risk and health in their families and neighbourhoods can often contradict the probabilistic messages from health professionals (Emslie et al., 2001).

These ideas lead us to a consideration of an alternative approach to thinking about risk; how do individuals construct and perceive it?

SOCIAL CONSTRUCTION OF RISK

Think again about the coin and toe experiment. Your decision not to take part in the experiment wasn't based on probability calculations, was it? You probably knew that there was a high chance of getting heads, you knew that the consequences of dropping the heavy object on your toe were not pleasant and that the consequences of not tossing the coin were zero. No one minded if you didn't conduct the experiment. Your judgement was not based wholly (or perhaps even partly) on a statistical assessment of probabilities, but on knowledge of the world around you. In contrast to the probabilistic approach to risk lies a variety of approaches which seek, to a greater or lesser extent, to understand these processes by which risk is perceived, understood and constructed by individuals and societies. Lupton (1999) refers to these as the socio-cultural perspectives. There are clear parallels between Lupton's perspectives on risk and some of the ways in which contemporary human geography conceptualises and considers the relationships between people and places. Lupton writes: 'Risk is never fully objective or knowable outside of belief systems and moral positions ... Social constructionists argue that humans and their social world exist in a dialectical relationship in which each creates the other' (1999: 29. This should sound familiar to all social geographers. A geographical re-write of Lupton's comment might say '[Some] geographers argue that humans and their spatial worlds exist in a dialectical relationship in which each creates the other'.

How 'real' is risk? Weak and strong constructionists

For many researchers interested in health-related risk, it is necessary to adopt a theoretical perspective which argues that there are real 'dangers' in the world. A painful death is a good example. Dying in pain is, for those who hold this perspective, a real tangible possibility and something which most people would wish to avoid. Such a perspective does not ignore or belittle the many constructions, perspectives and viewpoints around the meaning and experience of death. It states a belief that death is a real, knowable event. However, it is perfectly possible to reconcile this realist perspective with recognition that different populations and individuals may have very different understandings of and attitudes to that risk; for some people, a painful death might hold little or no fear. In this perspective, the risk is 'real'; there is an objective danger or threat, but the perceptions of these risks, their meaning and the reactions to them are constructed. Lupton calls this a 'weak constructionist' perspective (1999).

In contrast, the strong constructionist perspective is one in which 'nothing is a risk in itself' and that any perceived threats or dangers are purely constructed as such by society, and its history and government (Lupton, 1999). Weyman and Kelly summarise this perspective as follows: '... risk is inherently subjective. Risk does not exist "out there" waiting to be measured, but is an abstract concept ...' (1999: 10).

Lupton provides an example of this kind of wholly constructed 'risk'. In 1998 there was a crisis over the quality of drinking water in Sydney, Australia. Following the introduction of a new testing system, low levels of cryptosporidium and giardia (which can cause illness) had been found in the water supply. All Sydney residents were instructed to boil supplies. The combination of local government warnings and media hysteria created an apparently 'risky' situation, despite the fact that these organisms had probably been present in the water all along and were only 'discovered' by a new testing procedure, whose results were doubtful (Clancy, 2000). As Lupton comments, '[a] substance that had previously been treated as risk free – tap water – turned into a risk object' (1999: 31).

It is perhaps more useful to think of the weak and strong constructionist perspectives as defining a spectrum, rather than as alternatives. The position taken within this spectrum helps to define the way in which a particular aspect of risk is considered. It may even be that differing perspectives on risk are needed within the same research project. It is not the case that either socio-cultural perspectives or probabilistic perspectives on risk are 'more revealing' or 'more useful'. They have different epistemologies, methodologies and uses. Each perspective raises different kinds of questions about health-related risk and by bringing each perspective to bear on an issue, a more complete picture of 'risk', in all its permutations, can be achieved.

MMR – an example of differing constructions of risk

The variety of approaches needed to understand risk, constructions of risk, and their consequences can be illustrated by an example. Clinical and public responses to the risks associated with the measles, mumps and rubella (MMR) vaccine show contrasts and differences between the construction of risk by epidemiologists and by parents.

Measles, mumps and rubella are all diseases which, whilst rarely fatal in themselves, can have serious and long-term health consequences. The aim of vaccination against them is to confer 'herd-immunity' on the population (Fine, 1993). Not everyone in a population can be vaccinated (perhaps they cannot be immunised for medical reasons, or because they are too young, for example). By vaccinating the vast majority of people protection is conferred on *everyone* because it denies the diseases sufficient host humans to infect and reproduce themselves. However, if not enough people are vaccinated, the diseases can sustain themselves enough to infect vulnerable people. MMR vaccine is used in 177 countries.

In terms of a probabilistic perspective, the risks associated with these three communicable diseases are well known. It is possible to estimate the risk of infection in unvaccinated populations and to give to infected individuals numerical information on their risk of subsequent health problems. Thus, the probabilistic perspective can quantify the risk associated with *not* immunising. However, the risks associated *with* immunisation are more problematic. In 1998, a study based on just 12 children with broadly autistic symptoms suggested that, in 8 of the 12, onset of autism followed MMR vaccination (Wakefield et al., 1998). The paper stated clearly 'We did not prove an association between measles, mumps and rubella vaccine and the symptoms described' (p. 641). However, following some unguarded words at a press conference on the day of publication in the UK, a subsequent furore over the safety of the vaccine resulted in a large reduction in immunisation uptake and, subsequently, outbreaks of measles (Jansen et al., 2003).

There are studies which show, in probabilistic terms, the risk of developing autism after the MMR vaccine. At the time Wakefield et al. published their research, however, such studies were not complete, not readily available or not really paid attention to; probabilistic evidence for *adverse* consequences of MMR was essentially absent. Whilst the probabilistic evidence for the *benefits* of immunisation is vast, it was not well communicated or not trusted. The media ran stories about children who apparently developed autism subsequent to their receipt of the MMR vaccine, but not about children who have suffered serious consequences as a result of measles, mumps or rubella. Many, many parents responded by constructing the 'risk' of MMR as 'too great' and withdrawing their children from the vaccination programme. There is large literature exploring public responses to differing presentations of risk by the media and by medicine in this and other vaccination scares (see for example Bellaby, 2003; Hilton et al., 2007). What would *you* have done in that situation? How would you have constructed the risk and assessed it for your child?

Conclusion

This section has suggested that there is a variety of approaches to risk; some are based on quantifying the probability of an outcome within a population, others are concerned with understanding how people and communities think about, assess, react to, and thus construct risk. In fact, the probabilistic assessment of the risk and socio-cultural construction of risk are not so very different; in each case it is a process of *judgement*. The judgement might be the result of a rigorous scientific procedure, information from the media, the attitudes of those around us, or even just a gut feeling that we chose to follow. Essentially, both realms 'construct' risk in one way or another. In the next section we will bring 'geography' into our explorations.

RISK, SPACE AND PLACE

Geographies of risk are concerned with how risk varies across space and place. For convenience we will adopt the same distinction between probabilistic risk and socio-cultural construction of risk.

Maps, risk, context and composition

We begin with the relationship between physical location and risk, adopting a probabilistic perspective. In this perspective, the key focus is how and why quantified risk varies from space to space and place to place. When calculating the rates of illness or poor health for different populations, information is produced which can be well represented by maps. Consider the map of the risk of poor health in Figure 14.2.

Both maps in Figure 14.2 show rates of illness in UK parliamentary constituencies. The map on the right is a cartogram in which all constituencies are drawn the same size, enabling those which are physically smaller to be seen by the map reader.

Figure 14.2 is a map of risk. It represents the 'risk' to women of having a long-term illness (the map of illness risk for men is very similar). Maps like this one show that the risk of poor health in Britain is unevenly distributed across space, as it is in almost all countries in the world. There is geographical *inequality* in risk.

Yet, health happens to *people*. A place cannot have a rate of poor health or of death if it does not contain any people. The connection between people and the places in which they live is an important one for considering *explanations* for the geography of risk. When a map reveals a geographical inequality in risk, is it revealing an influence of spatial location on health? Or is it revealing a pattern produced by people with similar characteristics (and thus similar risk of poor health) tending to cluster together spatially? In other words,

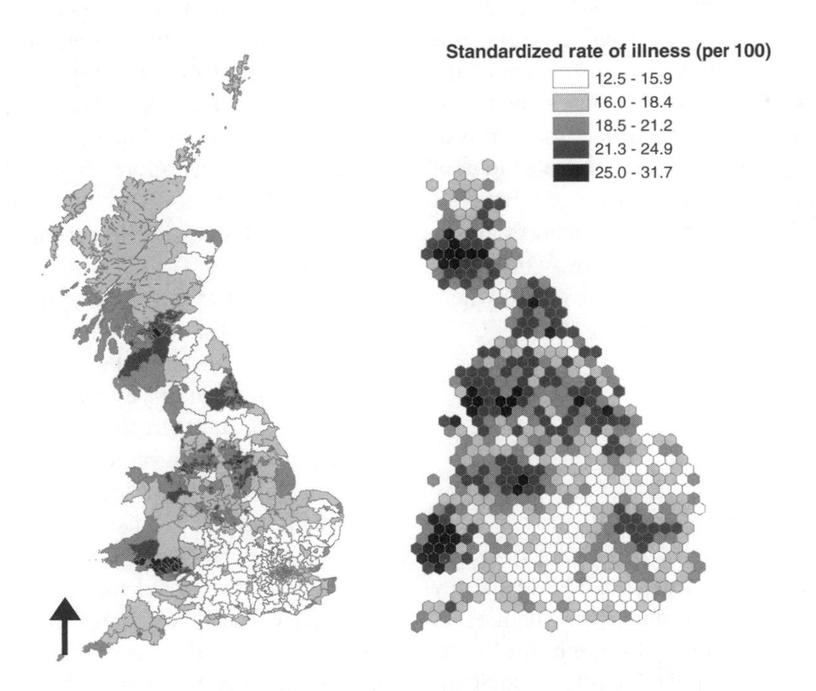

Figure 14.2 Standardized rate of limiting long-term illness, females, 2001.
Source: Data from the 2001 UK decennial census (England, Wales and Scotland).

is it the characteristics of the population (called 'composition' in the literature) or those of an area (called 'context' in the literature) which produce geographical differences in risk and health? (Macintyre et al., 1993, 2002; Shaw et al., 2002.) It would be useful to know the answer to this question because if a geography of risk is driven by individual characteristics, the individual should be the site of policy interventions to reduce and equalise that risk. If the geographies of risk are driven by characteristics of areas, then these should be the target of policies.

Many hours of research have been put into trying to separate the influence on geographies of health of the characteristics of the individuals who make up an area's population, and the characteristics of the social or physical environments which exist there. The majority of studies suggest that, in statistical terms, places which 'look risky or sick' on a map do so largely because they contain a population whose members have characteristics which make them more likely to be 'at risk' or 'sick' (Pickett and Pearl, 2001). Yet there are also small but measurable impacts of the characteristics of social or physical environments on risk, over and above the influence of the individuals who comprise the area's population (Curtis and Jones, 1998). Thus, from a probabilistic perspective, much of the geography of health-related risk is due to the geography of people, rather than of environment (though it should be noted that much of this work refers to the economically developed world, where chronic disease dominates).

Theories of place

Contributions from academic geography departments to these probabilistic studies of risk have been far less significant than one might expect. Certainly in the UK, key policy documents on geographical inequalities in health rarely cite those who might readily be identified as 'geographers' (Dorling and Shaw, 2002; Martin, 2001; Smith and Easterlow, 2005). Whatever the reason for this absence, it does have a consequence; there is a paucity of geographical theory in this body of work (Curtis and Jones, 1998; Popay et al., 1998). Social geographers understand that space is not just a passive crucible in which society 'happens'. People live where they live for a reason, and in turn the place they live in shapes their individual characteristics. Places and people are inseparable; we cannot consider the characteristics of one without considering the characteristics of the other (Harvey, 1989; Soja, 1980). Thus, trying to separate the influence of environments and individuals in determining spatial variation in risk might be considered a mistake by a geographer (Curtis and Jones, 1998; Mitchell, 2001; Popay et al., 1998; Smith and Easterlow, 2005).

Geographies of risk: place, not space

There are certainly areas on the earth in which the population-level risk of health -damaging events appears to be greater than it is in others; perhaps, at first sight, independently of any individual or population characteristics. To those with a probabilistic approach, this means that there are some places which are, in statistical terms, more 'risky' than others. Consider Figure 14.3, a map showing the deaths in Sri Lanka resulting from the Tsunami in 2004.

Most deaths occurred in the narrow coastal strip to the east and south of Sri Lanka. Those living further inland were protected from immediate harm by virtue of their geographical location. In this extreme example then, physical location seems to have conferred a higher or lower level of risk. Consider too, the geographical distribution of malaria, shown in Figure 14.4.

Much of the population in the northern hemisphere can be confident of avoiding malaria, because the environment there would not sustain the mosquito which carries the parasite. Again, physical location appears to be a determining risk.

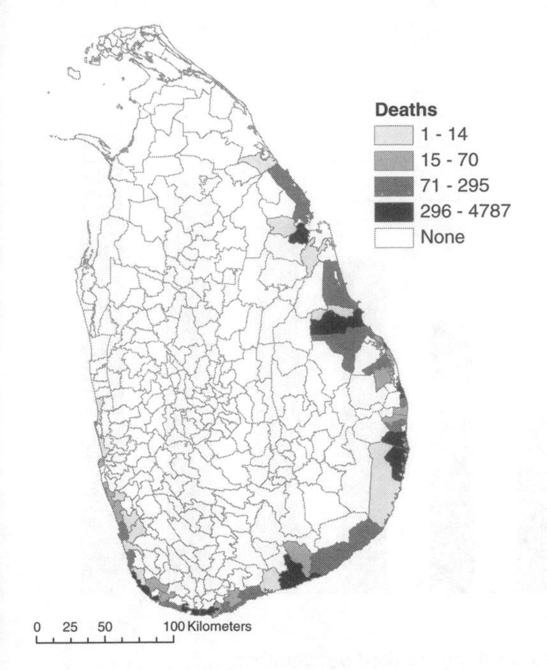

Figure 14.3 Deaths in Sri Lanka from the Tsunami, 26th December 2004.
Data source: UNDP.

However, consider the social, economic and cultural circumstances of these 'at risk areas', as well as their physical location. There were many reasons the Tsunami was so devastating to the coastal zone of Sri Lanka. Global economic status and the level of development in those areas meant that the risk of fatalities from a tsunami was high; dependence on the sea for an income, low income families living in poorly constructed housing, and neither the technical or financial ability to run a tsunami early warning system all contributed. The lack of helicopters and disaster relief systems meant many people died in the aftermath of the Tsunami, having survived the actual event. Likewise, in regions where climate may foster malarial mosquitoes, actual rates of malaria vary within and between countries because of social, economic and political variations in health care, in the provision of preventative mechanisms such as mosquito nets. Where physical location is involved in exposing people to risk of poor health, society (local and global) is involved too because social and economic processes create and locate populations and their vulnerabilities.

When location is the same, but characteristics are not

The human body is very sensitive to environment; it does not take long to become hot and sweaty in strong sunlight and warm air or to begin to shiver if the temperature drops and there is inadequate clothing. Repeated exposure to cold in the long term is known to

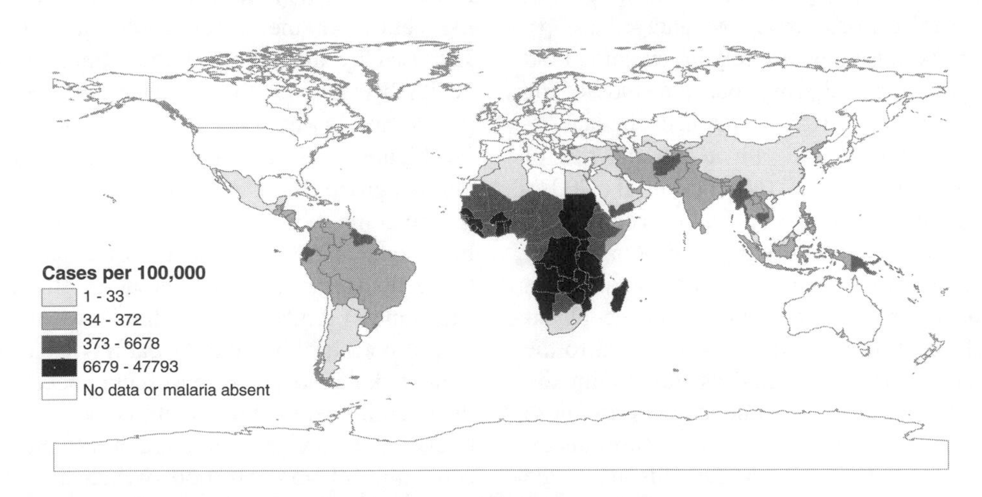

Figure 14.4 Reported cases of malaria, per 100,000 population.
Latest available data for the period 1990–2003. Data source: WHO/UNICEF.

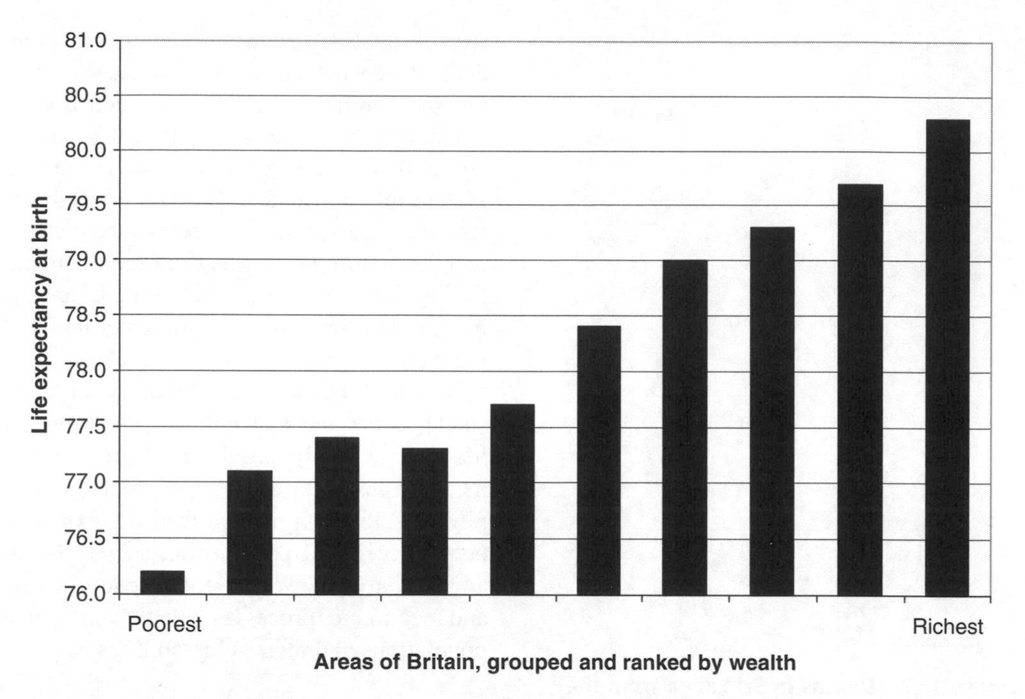

Figure 14.5 The relationship between wealth and life expectancy for areas of Britain, 2005. Data from Shaw et al., 2005.

damage the cardiovascular system, leading to greater chances of high blood pressure (Vuori, 1987).

It is generally colder in the north and west of Britain. The population is also, on average, poorer in the north and west of Britain. One aspect of poverty is that housing quality tends to be worse for less advantaged groups, often because they are relying on some kind of state or social provision. In a study of the consequences of the combined characteristics of housing and climate for the risk of high blood pressure (Mitchell et al., 2002), we found that only people who live in colder parts of Britain *and* who have poor quality housing are, statistically, at a higher risk. This means two households can be physically next to each other, and exposed to the same risk factor (in this case, cold climate), but have different vulnerabilities to those risks because of their housing circumstances. In essence, those two households are in the same space, but in a different *place* and thus at different risk.

Poverty, place and health

There is frequent mention of the connections between poverty and poor health in the examples of risk used throughout this chapter. Whilst it should be no surprise that population health is often very bad in the poorer developing nations of the world, people are often surprised by the extent of the inequality in health between relatively richer and poorer people and places within *developed* nations. For Figure 14.5, areas of Britain were divided into ten groups based on their relative wealth.

The graph shows a steep gradient such that life expectancy is markedly lower among those living in the poorer areas of Britain. This kind of graded relationship between the risk of poor health and the wealth is seen for many risk factors and diseases and underpins the overall inequality in health between relatively richer and poorer populations. Since economic relations are both written in, and produced by, spatial relations (Del Casino and Jones, 2007), place is highly significant in the experience and maintenance of poverty. Associations between poverty, place and health are therefore very important in determining geographies of risk.

Migration

Thus far I have written about the interactions between residents and their social, physical and political environments. However, we must also recognise that people *migrate* and in doing so they may shift environment and change their own characteristics (becoming employed or unemployed for example). Even from a probabilistic perspective, the ability to derive associations between individuals, their locations and environments, and their risk of poor health is challenged if we consider that those residents may not have been in that location for very long, or that their risk of poor health might be the result of contact with a different environment or place at an earlier time in their lives. There are many studies which have tried to explore the role of migration in determining, maintaining, growing or reducing geographical differences in risk (see for example Bentham, 1988; Boyle, 2004; Brimblecombe et al., 2000; Polissar, 1980). Smith and Easterlow (2005) take an alternative perspective on the relationship between migration and health, arguing that migration, and spatial inequality in health, may be partly a consequence of health status itself.

Place then, has a key role in our understanding of geographical variation in risk measured in probabilistic terms. In the next section, we consider the role of place in the social construction of risk.

PLACE AND THE CONSTRUCTION OF RISK

Where do our health-related opinions, perspectives and behaviours come from? Think about smoking for a moment. I confess that I quite liked smoking when I tried it. There was an influence of physiological reward (it's a drug after all…), the packaging, the image, and at the time, conforming to my peers. Yet, I did not pursue this pleasurable behaviour. This is partly because I believe it to be very risky for my health and this is reinforced almost daily by the evidence I see through my research (the probabilistic risk of smoking is perhaps visible to me to an unusually high degree). Perhaps more importantly, people I socialise with don't smoke, my employer prohibits smoking indoors at work and my government prohibits smoking in enclosed public spaces. My smoking behaviour is thus influenced by a complex set of factors, including my education, social position, the opinions of my family and friends and the work I do. My social and political worlds serve to reinforce and support my choice. My smoking behaviour is shaped by the *place* in which I live.

Place, risk and reward

Research into constructions of risk and reward which surround health behaviours echoes my emphasis on the significance of place (Popay et al., 2003). In seminal studies on the smoking behaviours and beliefs of working-class women, Hilary Graham makes much of the social environments in which women live and how their social, and implicitly spatial, situation effectively alters the balance of arguments for and against smoking (Graham, 1987, 1994; Graham et al., 2006). Others have been more explicit about the influence of spatial context on how the risks of smoking are perceived (Robinson and Kirkcaldy, 2007a, 2007b; Wiltshire et al., 2003). For some people, in some places, the rewards of smoking can be perceived as very great. The five minutes peace from a 'fag break', together with control of physiological and psychological withdrawal, can be a strong influence in shifting judgement on the risks of smoking from 'not worth the risk' to 'worth it' (Romer and Jamieson, 2001; Weinstein et al., 2005).

Being physically and socially surrounded by a group of people with whom one can identify, who represent 'normal' and who perhaps offer sources of advice or opinion, can also be a powerful influence on the risk perception of individuals (Hunt et al., 2000, 2001; Popay et al., 1998). To continue the smoking example, social isolation could stem from *not* smoking if smoking is the norm in a community. 'Peer-pressure' operates in adult social networks as well as those of children. Furthermore, in a place where many people smoke, and deaths from smoking-related diseases thus occur at higher levels, it is possible that the health consequences of smoking are 'normalised'; the impact of smoking-related deaths may be muted.

Community and cultural influences on risk

Space often acts to bring together people of similar ethnic or religious identity. The promotion or prohibition of particular health behaviours by religious or ethnic groups is another example of place-based influence on health-related risk. Such communities can work to create, negate, increase or decrease perceived risk (see for example Lawton et al., 2006). The prohibition or promotion of health-related behaviours (for example smoking, drinking, seeking medical attention from a doctor of the opposite sex, playing sport, etc.) by a wider community can make it much more or less likely that an individual will undertake a particular behaviour, perhaps by altering that individual's judgement process so that the behaviour appears more or less attractive, or even by altering the environment so that the risky behaviour is more difficult to put into practice. Buying alcohol in a neighbourhood whose community prohibits its consumption could be difficult, for example.

Conflicting constructions of risk

One of the biggest problems faced by health professionals in trying to exert their own particular constructions of risk on the wider population (i.e. that they judge smoking, drinking and being sedentary as risky behaviours which should be avoided) is that the places we live in can offer contradictory messages which are more powerful than the health promotion campaigns. If the probabilistic construction of the risks of smoking, drinking alcohol and being sedentary were commanding in its influence on our individual constructions of risk, none of us would undertake those 'bad' health behaviours. We do, though, and this emphasises the need for continued study as to how risk is perceived and constructed in a socio-cultural sense.

Conclusion

In probabilistic terms, then, risk varies spatially, but for risk to human health to exist it takes people. People and place are mutually constructive and apparent spatial variation in risk, in both probabilistic and socio-cultural terms, is thus the result of interactions between social and physical environmental characteristics, and individuals.

RESILIENCE

Early in the chapter I suggested that thinking about risk tends to lead to a focus on poor health and disease. However, just as there are risky behaviours or situations which may damage our health, there are also protective or salutogenic (literally, health-creating) behaviours and situations (de Chavez et al., 2005; Lindstrom and Eriksson, 2005). An approach which focuses wholly on the 'bad' can lead us to ignore the balance between risk and protective factors which may be present in a community or in an individual's world and which, when understood properly, may explain their health more completely.

Studying health, not illness

Furthermore, if our research is intended to ultimately contribute to improving health and health-related behaviour, this focus on illness seems rather odd. Why concentrate on those who are already 'sick' or 'doing the wrong things?' Surely more useful information about how to stay well could be gained from studying those who 'stay well'? An argument for a focus on salutogenesis has been a feature of many social science-based approaches to health and is claimed as a feature of the transition from medical geography to 'health geography' (Fleuret and Atkinson, 2007; Kearns and Moon, 2002).

Resilience (sometimes also called resiliency) is an emerging concept in health geography, allied to a shift away from studying illness, towards studying health and wellbeing. The key idea underpinning a resilience approach is to focus on people or places who are apparently 'doing well', 'staying healthy' or 'coping' in circumstances in which we would expect them to be 'doing badly' or 'getting sick'. It thus requires an expectation of the relationship between adversity of some kind and the risk of a 'bad' outcome. For example, if someone loses their home and ends up living on the streets, we would quite reasonably expect their health to suffer because they are exposed to much greater levels of risk through exposure to the elements and to other dangers (Shaw and Dorling, 1998; Shaw et al., 1999a). Should that person stay 'healthy', we might label them resilient. To give another example, if a neighbourhood contains a high proportion of very poor residents, we would expect the rate of poor health there to be relatively high because usually the risk of poor health increases with poverty (Shaw et al., 1999b). If the neighbourhood has relatively low levels of poor health, despite high levels of poverty, we might label it 'resilient'. Resilience thus refers to situations in which people or places are doing 'better than expected' or 'beating the odds'. The application of resilience should be clear. If we can find people and places that are resisting the expected translation of risk or adversity into a bad health outcome, and we can learn how this is achieved, we may be able to help others who face the same kinds of risk or adversity to avoid poor health.

Table 14.1 The relationships between risk and outcome

Outcome	*Level of risk faced*	
	Lower	*Higher*
Good	Easy life	Resilient
Bad	Unexpectedly bad outcome	Vulnerable

Source: Bartley, 2006.

Resilience as outcome

Table 14.1 shows one way of thinking about how relationships between risk and 'outcome' might vary. It identifies the 'high risk, good outcome' combination which, for some researchers, roughly delineates resilience.

Such expectations implicitly require a probabilistic approach to risk. They are based on a belief in the validity of 'normal' or 'average' associations between a particular risk factor and an adverse health outcome. This implies both an expectation of the normal relationship between risk and outcome, and the need for evidence that 'the odds have been beaten', in order to label someone or somewhere as resilient. Since risk is not the same as certainty, these approaches to resilience also need to ask if there is something *systematic* in the way that particular people or places seem to 'beat the odds'. Resilience is not about focusing on random variation in the relationships between risk and outcome.

Resilience as process

However, not all definitions of resilience function on the basis of achieving 'an outcome' such as 'staying healthy'. Some researchers prefer to define resilience as a *process* or as a *capability* by which risky circumstances could be coped with, rather than something which is 'achieved' or not (Luthar and Zelazo, 2003; Mitchell and Backett-Milburn, 2006). This approach avoids the need to rigidly define when 'good health' has actually been achieved. In reality, health outcomes are not often precisely 'good' or 'bad' as suggested in Table 14.1, and such categories are often actually defined by the researcher. For example, if the mortality rate in a very poor area is lower than expected, but still not *very* low, does that constitute a resilient outcome or not? We can still learn about resilience by examining the processes and practices which might foster it, even in situations where the 'outcome' is not spectacularly good health.

With this variety of approach to resilience in mind, I think that Health Canada has a particularly good definition which conveys the meaning of resilience, but which leaves its nature open to be contested:

> Resilience is the capability of individuals and systems (families, groups, and communities) to cope successfully in the face of significant adversity or risk. This capability develops and changes over time, is enhanced by protective factors within the individual/system and the environment, and contributes to the maintenance or enhancement of health. (Atlantic Health Promotion Research Centre et al., 1999: 4)

What do studies of resilience find?

Human resilience has been most thoroughly explored in psychological research on children who have had to cope with adverse and/or risky circumstances (Luthar and Zelazo, 2003). More recently however, resilience research has also focused on childhood-adulthood transitions and on adults (Netuveli et al., 2006; Schoon et al., 2003). One of the most important studies of resilience in children was carried out by Emmy Werner (Werner, 1992, 1996; Werner and Smith, 2001). She and her colleagues followed a cohort of children, born in Hawaii in 1955, from birth to adulthood. Many of these children faced multiple problems growing up (such as poverty, parental divorce, parental ill health and their own health problems stemming from birth). Facing such adversities as a child is known to increase the risk, in probabilistic terms, of problems with educational attainment and health, wealth and relationships in adulthood. About two thirds of the children who Werner identified at age 2 as being at high risk of developing serious learning or behaviour problems, indeed did so by age 10. Many then went on to have criminal records, mental health problems or teenage pregnancies by age 18, but many did not (Werner and Smith, 2001).

Werner notes a variety of factors which distinguished the resilient children from the others. These were dominated by aspects of supportive social relationship and social environment, the latter especially at significant transition times, such as moving from school to first job, or the advent of children. Good adult role models, in the family and in the family's wider social networks, helped troubled youngsters develop 'normally'. Subsequently, opportunities and support, including 'second chance' schemes such as adult education and vocational skills acquired in the military, helped almost the whole cohort to achieve stable, functional, adult lives (Werner, 1996). However, Werner's resilient children are perhaps exceptional in the extent of their adaptation to adverse circumstances. Most studies of resilience suggest that, whilst apparently resilient individuals seem to have better health than their peers, who are also exposed to adversity and risk factors, they rarely achieve the same level of good health or achievement as those who were not exposed to adversity and risk in the first place. As Bartley comments, '[e]ven the most resilient child from a poverty-stricken area, for example, will never do as well in life as a more ordinary child from a wealthy background'. (Bartley et al., 2006: 3). The definitions of a 'good outcome' are very important in judging the degree to which resilience has been shown, as are the definitions of the risks faced. One of the problems with resilience research is that there can be no standard rules which specify how adversity, risk and adaptation are to be defined; in essence, each researcher defines resilience. It is thus very hard to draw conclusions about resilience from across studies and to theorise about it because there can be no common definitions of either risk or adaptation to it (Luthar and Zelazo, 2003).

Is resilience a personal trait or something we can all have?

Most resilience researchers argue resilience is ***not*** something for which only *some* people posses a capability. Gilligan comments that

> Resilience is not some form of moral fibre randomly allocated by some mysterious process to certain fortunate people … The degree of resilience displayed by a person in a certain context may be said to be related to the extent to which that context has elements that nurture this resilience. (2004: 94).

For geographers, the use of the term 'context' might be significant, since this is a term with which the influence of place on risk has been conceptualised. In fact, the resilience literature is rich in references to place, neighbourhood and community (Adger, 2000; Gerrard et al., 2004; Luthar and Zelazo, 2003; Stewart et al., 1999).

Research on resilient places

There are a small number of studies of resilient places. These have a variety of methodological approaches and aims, from simply trying to identify resilient areas (see Doran et al., 2006, for example), to exploring the mechanisms by which resilience might be sought or attained within a community. In a project dedicated to searching for, and exploring resilience in the UK (Tunstall et al., 2007), we sought areas which had experienced prolonged and severe economic deprivation. We were able to identify a group of areas which, despite long-term poverty, had mortality rates significantly lower than their economic peers, across a range of ages, and consistently through time. The term 'lower than their economic peers' is important here. Although the resilient areas were doing well compared to others which had faced similar economic troubles, they still had mortality rates which were much worse than the UK average.

In subsequent qualitative work, we explored possible reasons for this resilience. Other studies, including those by Adger (2000) and by the Atlantic Health Promotion Research Centre (1999) have undertaken similar approaches and within this limited number of studies, the findings are remarkably alike. In its study of resilience in Canadian coastal settlements hit by collapse of the fishing industry, the Atlantic Health Promotion Research Centre noted the significance of the sense of community as a protective factor against the problems associated with industrial and economic decline: 'Participants associated the sense of connectedness with the communities' ability to survive hard times. Social support was readily available from the community at large, family and friends, and local organisations.' (1999: ii).

Tunstall et al. found that local policies to protect and improve housing quality, and to retain population in an area even when jobs were lost, were significant in fostering resilience. However, social cohesion was also important. For example, in one resilient community in Wales, which had suffered the total loss of its coal mining industry, a key informant commented that the community cohesion which had been created by a common focus on the mine, still existed and was useful in helping to keep the community together physically and socially:

> When you do … community projects, you know, it almost like rekindles, if you like, the sense of community spirit. So I think it's certainly much, much stronger than anywhere else in Wales … I mean you'll find a lot of people even when they leave home around here, they don't tend to move very far … I think generations … from families, you know, all live in the one street.

In other resilient areas, a common ethnic or religious identity, rather than a common industrial heritage, seemed to be the basis for binding the community together.

Strong social networks are not entirely unproblematic, however, and should not be left un-critiqued as a universally positive thing. A strong network, from which an individual is isolated (perhaps by virtue of a distinct ethnicity or religion), could be intimidating or damaging (Cohen, 2004; Pagel et al., 1987). A more significant critique of social networks and cohesion as the key to health-related resilience, however, concerns the *mechanisms* by which health is affected. For social cohesion to be a plausible route to resilience, it must provide a mechanism whereby the usual conversion of adversity to 'embodied poor health' is disrupted or mitigated. How can supportive social networks prevent the physiological processes which produce heart attacks and cancer? The literature does offer examples. In Werner's Hawaiian cohort, it is plausible that a 'role model uncle' who doesn't take drugs but is still 'cool' might have helped to steer an adolescent away from smoking. Friends or family assisting an older person to access health care, or keeping them mentally stimulated, might assist in protecting quality of life, if not life itself (Netuveli et al., 2006) and collective community action to defend or demand health care or social services, or protect the local environment, might be significant in protecting health at an area level. There are also plausible biological mechanisms by which social support can influence our health through reduction of stress and its physiological manifestation (Brunner, 1997; Davey Smith et al., 2005; Marmot, 1985).

Questioning what is 'risky'

A resilience approach can question what a 'risky' and a 'protective' behaviour or practice might be, challenging some conventional perspectives on risk factors. In order to deal with challenging family circumstances, for example, children sometimes truant or sleep rough (Mitchell and Backett-Milburn, 2006). Both of these things are known to carry health risks, but it is possible that the risk such behaviours carry is 'less' than that posed by the situation the child has escaped. Of course, these behaviours remain risk factors, in a probabilistic sense, for poor health and development. Sleeping rough is still incredibly risky in itself, even if it reduces the risk of abuse at home. However, the resilience perspective allows us to see the importance of context for re-evaluating the meanings and value of these risky practices and reminds us that our perceptions of risk are judgements and thus open to influence from the places and situations in which we find ourselves. Studies of resilience must be clear about what they regard as 'risky' and 'protective' circumstances, recognising that some things can be both.

Resilience as a policy tool

This part of the chapter began by raising the prospect that if we can learn how some people or places are resilient, it might help others. Resilience is a concept which has tremendous policy currency. An example comes from the 'positive deviance' approach to policy (Marsh et al., 2004). This addresses community problems by assuming that some individuals or families will already have a solution to the problem; the 'positive deviants'. Essentially, 'positive deviants' are resilient: people who face adversity and risk in a community, but have successfully adapted to avoid negative outcomes. In 1990 Save the Children (US) received an invitation from the Government of Vietnam to create a programme to enable poor villages to address the problem of childhood malnutrition (Mackintosh et al., 2002; Sternin, 2007). At that time an estimated of 60 per cent of children under the age of 5 suffered from moderate or severe malnutrition. Traditional supplemental feeding programmes were being carried out, but gains in children's nutritional status during the period of feeding were lost after the programmes ended, largely because the gains were based entirely on food resources which were no longer accessible once the aid agencies left. Yet, Save the Children saw that a small minority of poor families had children who *were* well fed; in their language, the 'positive deviants', in ours 'the resilient'. A study showed that these families avoided malnutrition by feeding their children free or inexpensive tiny shrimps and crabs found in rice paddies and by feeding their children 'a little, but often'. A carefully planned, community-led programme spread the knowledge of this practice and gave others a chance to practise it. Subsequent evaluations have shown that this new approach helped an estimated 50,000 malnourished children. More importantly, their younger siblings, many of whom were not yet born at the time this was happening, benefited from the same levels of enhanced feeding (Mackintosh et al., 2002).

However, public health problems, especially those in the economically developed world, are rarely soluble in this way. Resilience is a tantalising but problematic notion for policy makers. It seems that in many situations, the pieces and practices for resilience can be in place and yet no protection against risk is apparently conferred (Mitchell and Backett-Milburn, 2006). The very definition of resilience ('doing well against the odds') implies that it is comparatively rare, and of course, if it was easy to beat the adversity, those situations would not be considered 'risky' in the first place. We are not yet sure how and why some people and places are able to become resilient, and others are not. Certainly, loss of control over personal and social circumstances is a feature of adversity, and the accompanying loss of control over practices which might promote resilience could be one reason why it seems so hard to achieve and maintain. Furthermore, it appears that resilience is rarely so complete that all aspects of life are unaffected by the adversity. For example, children who face adversity may be resilient or cope in some facets of life, but not in others; a child of alcoholic parents might manage to do well academically at school, but not manage to achieve good social integration or friendships (Luthar and Zelazo, 2003). Lastly, resilience may be an attractive concept for policy-makers wishing to avoid costly intervention to help those in need, since if they can demonstrate that 'some people' cope with adversity and risk successfully, they may be able to imply that everyone 'should be able to cope'. In turn, this implies that people who do succumb to risk and adversity are somehow to blame for their own misfortune and not worthy of external assistance.

Conclusion

Resilience, then, is an emerging concept. It could help us learn about surviving or adapting to risky situations, and might increase our understanding of health and well-being, without a focus on disease and illness occurring. Perhaps its greatest utility for health geography is the fact that it prompts us to consider the balance between risk and protective factors for health.

FUTURES: WHAT AGENDA SHOULD BE SET FOR THE FUTURE OF RESEARCH INTO HEALTH-RELEVANT RISK AND RESILIENCE?

Clearly, compared to risk, resilience is the less developed construct, particularly in regard to its geographies. It would be excellent to see the full range of geographical methodologies brought to bear on answering the key questions, which are (as I see them) 'what fosters resilience among some people and some places?', and 'how can this knowledge be applied to help nurture resilience more generally?'.

There is still much work to do in exploring geographies of resilience, at a variety of geographic scales and settings. Personally, however, I remain somewhat sceptical as to whether a resilience approach will yield powerful new policy tools to combat the health impacts of adversity at a population level; resilience seems to be too rare, and the strength of the connections between adversity and poor health too strong, for them to be disrupted at a large scale. I am more optimistic that a resilience approach could form a useful framework for approaching the study of health, risk, and place. Approaching investigation with the question 'who does *not* succumb: how and why?' provides a fine route to alternative perspectives on, and an avenue for critical thinking about, health. Resilience offers potentially rich and unexplored ground for geographers who subscribe to qualitative and/or quantitative research methodologies, and their associated epistemologies.

There is also tremendous scope for a deeper understanding of the relationships between place and risk. There is currently a paucity of theory in work on geographical inequalities in health, especially in work which considers health at a population level. In particular, I would urge a greater engagement between social geography, epidemiology and medical sociology. A more solid basis on which to shift away from the distinction between 'context and composition'' in thinking about the role of place in creating geographical inequalities in health would be very valuable. Qualitative studies have provided some fine insights as to how neighbourhood and risk perception are related, but these insights remain somewhat trapped at the micro-scale. Understanding life in a few streets is helpful, but what can geography do to help understand and improve the health of the, literally, millions of people who are at greater risk of poor health because of the places they live or work in?

Work, in fact, also represents an avenue for research which is sorely under-explored. Almost all geographical studies of inequalities in health-related risk are concerned with area of residence. Our censuses and surveys tend to capture respondents at home. In-depth interviews are often based at, and about, our own neighbourhoods. Yet many of us spend most of our day away from home, on the way to and from, or at, work. Taking account of diurnal geographical mobility represents a major challenge to both probabilistic and socio-cultural perspectives on risk.

Lastly, my greatest ambitions for geographical approaches to risk and resilience are (i) that they be more directly pursued by geographers, working with those from disciplines who realise place matters, but who lack in-depth understanding of it and (ii) that geographers connect more strongly with policy and practice implications of this work. I concur with Ron Martin''s views:

> 'The essential motivation is to change the world not just to analyse it' (2001: 190).

Geographers should apply themselves to reducing risk and promoting resilience.

ACKNOWLEDGEMENTS

This chapter was written with support from the ESRC Priority Network on Resilience and Human Capability, grant number RES-337-25-0001, and from a University of Canterbury Erskine Fellowship. Census output is Crown copyright and is reproduced with the permission of the Controller of HMSO and the Queen's Printer for Scotland.

REFERENCES

Adger, W.N. (2000) 'Social and ecological resilience: are they related?', *Progress in Human Geography*, 24 (3): 347–64.

Atlantic Health Promotion Research Centre, in collaboration with Stewart, M., Reid, G., Buckles, L., Edgar, W., Mangham, C., Tilley, N. and Jackson, S. (1999) *A Study of Resiliency in Communities*. Ottawa: Office of Alcohol, Drug and Dependency Issues, Health Canada.

Bartley, M. (ed.) (2006) *Capability and Resilience: Beating the odds*. London: UCL.

Bellaby, P. (2003) 'Communication and miscommunication of risk: understanding UK parents' attitudes to combined MMR vaccination', *BMJ*, 327 (7417): 725–8.

Bentham, G. (1988) 'Migration and Morbidity – Implications for Geographical Studies of Disease', *Social Science and Medicine*, 26 (1): 49–54.

Bhopal, R. (2002) *Concepts of Epidemiology*. Oxford: OUP.

Blair, P.S., Sidebotham, P., Berry, P.J., Evans, M. and Fleming, P.J. (2006) 'Major epidemiological changes in sudden infant death syndrome: a 20-year population-based study in the UK', *The Lancet*, 367 (9507): 314–9.

Boyle, P. (2004) 'Population geography: migration and inequalities in mortality and morbidity', *Progress in Human Geography*, 28 (6): 767–76.

Brimblecombe, N., Dorling, D. and Shaw, M. (2000) 'Migration and geographical inequalities in health in Britain', *Social Science and Medicine*, 50 (6): 861–78.

Brunner, E. (1997) 'Socioeconomic determinants of health: Stress and the biology of inequality', *BMJ*, 314 (7092): 1472.

Clancy, J. (2000) 'Sydney's 1998 water quality crisis', *American Water Works Association Journal*, 92 (3): 55.

Cohen, S. (2004) 'Social relationships and health', *American Psychologist*, 59 (8): 676–84.

Crispo, A., Brennan, P., Jockel, K.H., Schaffrath-Rosario, A., Wichmann, H.E., Nyberg, F., Simonato, L., Merletti, F., Forastiere, F., Boffetta, P. and Darby, S. (2004) 'The cumulative risk of lung cancer among current, ex- and never-smokers in European men', *British Journal of Cancer*, 91 (7): 1280–6.

Curtis, S. and Jones, I.R. (1998) 'Is there a place for geography in the analysis of health inequality?', *Sociology of Health and Illness*, 20 (5): 645–72.

Davey Smith, G., Ben Shlomo, Y., Beswick, A., Yarnell, J., Lightman, S. and Elwood, P. (2005) 'Cortisol, Testosterone, and Coronary Heart Disease: Prospective Evidence From the Caerphilly Study', *Circulation*, 112 (3): 332–40.

Davison, C., Frankel, S. and Smith, G.D. (1992) 'The limits of lifestyle: re-assessing "fatalism" in the popular culture of illness prevention', *Social Science and Medicine*, 34 (6): 675–85.

de Chavez, A.C., Backett-Milburn, K., Parry, O. and Platt, S. (2005) 'Understanding and researching wellbeing: Its usage in different disciplines and potential for health research and health promotion', *Health Education Journal*, 64 (1): 70–87.

Del Casino, V.J. and Jones, J.P.I. (2007) 'Space for inequality researchers: A view from geography', in L. Lobao, G. Hooks and A. Tickamyer (eds)., *The Sociology of Spatial Inequality*. Albany: SUNY Press: 233–51.

Doran, T., Drever, F. and Whitehead, M. (2006) 'Health underachievement and overachievement in English local authorities', *Journal of Epidemiology and Community Health*, 60 (8): 686–93.

Dorling, D. and Shaw, M. (2002) 'Geographies of the agenda: public policy, the discipline and its (re)"turns"', *Progress in Human Geography*, 26 (5); 629–41.

Douglas, M. (2007) *Risk and Blame: Essays in cultural theory*. London: Routledge.

Emslie, C., Hunt, K. and Watt, G. (2001) '"I'd rather go with a heart attack than drag on": lay images of heart disease and the problems they present for primary and secondary prevention', *Coronary Health Care*, (5) 1: 25–32.

Fine, P.E.M. (1993) 'Herd Immunity: History, Theory, Practice', *Epidemiologic Reviews*, 15 (2): 265–302.

Fleuret, S. and Atkinson, S. (2007) 'Wellbeing, health and geography: A critical review and research agenda', *New Zealand Geographer*, 63 (2): 106–18.

Gerrard, N., Kulig, J. and Nowatzki, N. (2004) 'What doesn't kill you makes you stronger: Determinants of stress resiliency in rural people of Saskatchewan, Canada', *Journal of Rural Health*, 20 (1): 59–66.

Gilligan, R. (2004) 'Promoting resilience in child and family social work: issues for social work practice, education and policy', *Social Work Education*, 23 (1): 93–104.

Graham, H. (1987) 'Women's smoking and family health', *Social Science and Medicine*, 25 (1): 47–56.

Graham, H. (1994) 'Gender and class as dimensions of smoking behaviour in Britain: Insights from a survey of mothers', *Social Science and Medicine*, 38 (5): 691–8.

Graham, H., Inskip, H.M., Francis, B. and Harman, J. (2006) 'Pathways of disadvantage and smoking careers: evidence and policy implications', *Journal of Epidemiology and Community Health*, 60 (2): ii7–ii12.
Harvey, D. (1989) *The Urban Experience*. Baltimore: Johns Hopkins University Press.
Hilton, S., Petticrew, M. and Hunt, K. (2007) 'Parents' champions vs. vested interests: who do parents believe about MMR? A qualitative study', *BMC Public Health*, 7 (42): 42.
Hunt, K., Davison, C., Emslie, C. and Ford, G. (2000) 'Are perceptions of a family history of heart disease related to health-related attitudes and behaviour?', *Health Educ. Res.*, 15 (2): 131–43.
Hunt, K., Emslie, C. and Watt, G. (2001) 'Lay constructions of a family history of heart disease: potential for misunderstandings in the clinical encounter?', *Lancet*, 357 (9263): 1168–71.
Jansen, V.A.A., Stollenwerk, N., Jensen, H.J., Ramsay, M.E., Edmunds, W.J. and Rhodes, C.J. (2003) 'Measles Outbreaks in a Population with Declining Vaccine Uptake', *Science*, 301 (5634): 804.
Kearns, R. and Moon, G. (2002) 'From medical to health geography: novelty, place and theory after a decade of change', *Progress in Human Geography*, 26 (5): 605–25.
Lawton, J., Ahmad, N., Hanna, L., Douglas, M. and Hallowell, N. (2006) '"I can't do any serious exercise": barriers to physical activity amongst people of Pakistani and Indian origin with Type 2 diabetes', *Health Education Research*, 21 (1): 43–54.
Lindstrom, B. and Eriksson, M. (2005) 'Salutogenesis', *Journal of Epidemiology and Community Health*, 59 (6):440–42.
Lupton, D. (1999) *Risk*. London: Routledge.
Luthar, S. and Zelazo, L. (2003) 'Research on resilience: An Integrative Review', in S. Luthar (ed.), *Resilience and Vulnerability: Adaptation in context of childhood adversities*. Cambridge: CUP. pp. 510–50.
Macintyre, S., Maciver, S. and Sooman, A. (1993) 'Area, class and health – should we be focusing on places or people?', *Journal of Social Policy*, 22: 213–34.
Macintyre, S., Ellaway, A. and Cummins, S. (2002) 'Place effects on health: how can we conceptualise, operationalise and measure them?', *Social science and medicine*, 55 (1): 125–39.
Mackintosh, U.A., Marsh, D.R. and Schroeder, D.G. (2002) 'Sustained positive deviant child care practices and their effects on child growth in Viet Nam', *Food Nutr. Bull.*, 23 (4): 18–27.
Marmot, M.G. (1985) 'Psychosocial factors and blood pressure', *Prev. Med.*, 14 (4): 451-65.
Marsh, D.R., Schroeder, D.G., Dearden, K.A., Sternin, J. and Sternin, M. (2004) 'The power of positive deviance', *BMJ*, 329 (7475): 1177–79.
Martin, R. (2001) 'Geography and public policy: the case of the missing agenda', *Progress in Human Geography*, 25 (2): 189–210.
Mitchell, R. (2001) 'Multilevel modeling might not be the answer', *Environment and planning A*, 33 (8): 1357–60.
Mitchell, R. and Backett-Milburn, K. (2006) *Health and Resilience: What does a resilience approach offer health research and policy?*. Edinburgh: RUHBC, University of Edinburgh, RUHBC Findings series 11.
Mitchell, R., Blane, D. and Bartley, M. (2002) 'Elevated risk of high blood pressure: climate and the inverse housing law', *Int. J. Epidemiol.*, 31 (4): 831–8.
Netuveli, G., Wiggins, R.D., Hildon, Z., Montgomery, S.M. and Blane, D. (2006) 'Quality of life at older ages: evidence from the English longitudinal study of aging (wave 1)', *Journal of Epidemiology and Community Health*, 60 (4): 357–63.
Pagel, M.D., Erdly, W.W. and Becker, J. (1987) "Social networks – we get by with (and in spite of) a little help from our friends', *Journal of Personality and Social Psychology*, 53 (4): 793–804.
Perneger, T.V., Hudelson, P.M. and Bovier, P.A. (2004) 'Health and happiness in young Swiss adults', *Quality of Life Research*, 13 (1): 171–8.
Pickett, K.E. and Pearl, M. (2001) 'Multilevel analyses of neighbourhood socioeconomic context and health outcomes: a critical review', *Journal of Epidemiology and Community Health*, 55 (2): 111–22.
Polissar, L. (1980) 'Effect of migration on comparison of disease rates in geographic studies

in the United-States', *American Journal of Epidemiology*, 111 (2): 175–82.

Popay, J., Williams, G., Thomas, C. and Gatrell, T. (1998) 'Theorising inequalities in health: the place of lay knowledge', *Sociology of Health and Illness*, 20 (5): 619–44.

Popay, J., Thomas, C., Williams, G., Bennett, S., Gatrell, A. and Bostock, L. (2003) 'A proper place to live: health inequalities, agency and the normative dimensions of space', *Soc. Sci. Med.*, 57 (1): 55–69.

Registrar General (1999) *Annual Report of the Registrar General for Scotland*. Edinburgh: General Register Office for Scotland.

Robinson, J. and Kirkcaldy, A.J. (2007a) 'Disadvantaged mothers, young children and smoking in the home: Mothers' use of space within their homes', *Health and Place*, 13 (4): 894–903.

Robinson, J. and Kirkcaldy, A.J. (2007b) '"You think that I'm smoking and they're not": Why mothers still smoke in the home', *Social science and medicine*, 65 (4): 641–52.

Romer, D. and Jamieson, P. (2001)'Do adolescents appreciate the risks of smoking? Evidence from a national survey', *Journal of Adolescent Health*, 29 (1): 12–21.

Russell, D.G. (2003) 'Phagosomes, fatty acids and tuberculosis', *Nature Cell Biology*, 5 (9): 776–78.

Schoon, I., Sacker, A. and Bartley, M. (2003) 'Socio-economic adversity and psychosocial adjustment: a developmental-contextual perspective', *Soc. Sci. Med.*, 57 (6): 1001–15.

Shaw, M. and Dorling, D. (1998) 'Mortality among street youth in the UK', *Lancet*, 352 (9129): 743.

Shaw, M., Dorling, D. and Brimblecombe, N. (1999a) 'Life chances in Britain by housing wealth and for the homeless and vulnerably housed', *Environment and Planning A*, 31 (12): 2239–48.

Shaw, M., Dorling, D., Gordon, D. and Davey Smith, G. (1999b) *The Widening Gap: Health inequalities and policy in Britain*. Bristol: Policy Press.

Shaw, M., Mitchell, R. and Dorling, D. (2000) 'Time for a smoke? One cigarette reduces your life by 11 minutes', *British Medical Journal*, 320 (7226): 53.

Shaw, M., Dorling, D. and Mitchell, R. (2002) *Health, Place and Society*. London: Pearson.

Shaw, M., Davey, S.G. and Dorling, D. (2005) 'Health inequalities and New Labour: how the promises compare with real progress', *BMJ*, 330 (7498): 1016–21.

Smith, S.J. and Easterlow, D. (2005) 'The strange geography of health inequalities', *Transactions of the Institute of British Geographers*, 30 (2): 173–90.

Soja, E.W. (1980) 'The Socio-Spatial Dialectic', *Annals of the Association of American Geographers*, 70 (2): 207–25.

Sternin, J. (unpublished work) (2007) *Positive Deviance and Nutrition in Viet Nam*.

Stewart, M., Reid, G., Buckles, L., Edgar, W., Mangham, C., Tilley, N. and Jackson, S. (1999) *A Study of Resiliency in Communities*, Office of Alcohol, Drug and Dependency Issues, Ottawa: Health Canada.

Tunstall, H., Mitchell, R., Gibbs, J., Platt, S. and Dorling, D. (2007) 'Is economic adversity always a killer? Disadvantaged areas with relatively low mortality rates', *Journal of Epidemiology and Community Health*, 61 (4): 337–43.

Vuori, I. (1987) 'The heart and the cold', *Ann. Clin. Res.*, 19 (3): 156–62.

Wakefield, A.J., Murch, S.H., Anthony, A., Linnell, J., Casson, D.M., Malik, M., Berelowitz, M., Dhillon, A.P., Thomson, M.A., Harvey, P., Valentine, A., Davies, S.E. and Walker-Smith, J.A. (1998) 'Ileal-lymphoid-nodular hyperplasia, non-specific colitis, and pervasive developmental disorder in children', *Lancet*, 351 (9103): 637–41.

Weinstein, N.D., Marcus, S.E. and Moser, R.P. (2005) 'Smokers' unrealistic optimism about their risk', *Tobacco Control*, 14 (1): 55–9.

Werner, E.E. (1992) 'The children of Kauai: Resiliency and recovery in adolescence and adulthood', *Journal of Adolescent Health*, 13 (4): 262–8.

Werner, E.E. (1996) 'Vulnerable but invincible: High risk children from birth to adulthood', *European Child and Adolescent Psychiatry*, 5 (1): 47–51.

Werner, E.E. and Smith, R. (2001) *Journeys from Childhood to the Midlife: Risk, resilience, and recovery*. New York: Cornell University Press.

Weyman, A.K. and Kelly, C.J. (1999) *Risk Perception and Risk Communication: A review of the literature*. Health and Safety Laboratory, CRR 248/1999.

Wigfield, R.E., Fleming, P.J., Berry, P.J., Rudd, P.T. and Golding, J. (1992) 'Can the fall in Avon's sudden infant death rate be explained by changes in sleeping position?', *British Medical Journal*, 304 (6822): 282–3.

Willitts, M., Benzeval, M. and Stansfeld, S. (2004) 'Partnership history and mental health over time', *Journal of Epidemiology and Community Health*, 58 (1): 53–8.

Wiltshire, S., Bancroft, A., Parry, O. and Amos, A. (2003) '"I came back here and started smoking again": perceptions and experiences of quitting among disadvantaged smokers', *Health Education Research*, 18 (3): 292–303.

Wyke, S. and Ford, G. (1992) 'Competing explanations for associations between marital status and health', *Social Science and Medicine*, 34 (5): 523–32.

15

Young People, Care and Social Wellbeing

Nicola Ansell and Fiona Smith

The wellbeing of young people is a concern of every society. This stems in part from the fact that young people, and in particular young children, cannot secure their own welfare and therefore depend, to a greater or lesser extent, on adults. The discursive construction of children as universally dependent and vulnerable is problematic, in part because it neglects the extent of children's agency and differences related to age and other factors, as well as casting adults as fully independent. However, there are many respects in which the young do require particular investment in their wellbeing. Young children, for instance, are particularly susceptible to disease and accidents, and suffer relatively high morbidity and mortality rates. Children face real risks, which they may be ill-equipped to confront (Pain, 2006). Children are also often the first to experience adverse consequences in times of crisis, as was observed in the recent economic crisis in Argentina (Bosco, 2007), and the consequences may be more enduring than for adults if, for instance, their education is interrupted (Hilary et al., 2002).

Geographers and other social scientists have explored many aspects of young people's welfare, ranging from hunger (Bosco, 2007) and homelessness (Panter-Brick, 2004) to bullying (Andrews and Chen, 2006) and opportunities for play (Punch, 2000). Although wellbeing is multidimensional and cannot be simplistically measured (Gough and McGregor, 2007), the capacity and effectiveness of societies in delivering welfare is far from uniform. Clearly, there are immense geographical variations in children's wellbeing, along many dimensions, both within and between countries, as highlighted in numerous official reports (UNICEF, 2006, 2007). These differences need to be seen at least partly in relation to the ways in which societies care for young people. As Bosco points out, 'Questions regarding the welfare of children can be positioned in relation to geographic research that deals with care and caregiving activities – from the provision of healthcare to the family care provided by different types of caregivers even to the emotional work involved in a caregiving relationship' (2007: 56).

The significance attached to caring for young people is not, however, simply a reflection of children's dependence and vulnerability.

Children's welfare has immense symbolic significance, and this is one of the key reasons why societies, individually and collectively, dedicate such substantial resources to ensuring the material and psychosocial wellbeing of their young. Children are portrayed as 'canaries in the mine' (Bunge, 1977); because they are the first to embody the effects of adverse social change, they are viewed as indicators of the wider wellbeing of society. Societies are judged – and judge themselves – on their success in ensuring children's wellbeing.

Ensuring children's wellbeing may reflect the state of society at the present time, but perhaps more significantly it also relates to the future, and how effectively society is able to reproduce itself on a long-term as well as a daily basis. In this chapter we employ the concept of social reproduction to make sense of the changing ways in which young people's wellbeing and care is 'delivered' and how it affects them. In so doing we will explore how the global ascendancy of neoliberalism is impacting upon the care and welfare of children and young people across the world.

SOCIAL REPRODUCTION AND THE CARE OF CHILDREN

Social reproduction has been defined as: '[t]he interdependent reproduction both of the social relations within which, and the material and discursive means through which, social life is premised, sustained and transformed over time' (Lee, 2000: 760) or: 'material and social practices through which people reproduce themselves on a daily and generational basis' (Katz, 2001: 711). Both of these definitions highlight the fact that the care and wellbeing of children require particular forms of social organisation and allocation of material resources, and also that they contribute to both continuity and change in society. In any society a range of actors is involved in securing social reproduction. In order to be sustainable, a capitalist economy requires reproduction, yet does not fulfil this role alone. Much of the burden is carried by families; the state, too, is usually heavily involved; and increasingly other actors such as non-governmental organisations play a part. The roles played by these actors, and the balance and relationships between them, differ from place to place and are in constant flux. These dynamics have consequences for young people's wellbeing and are the focus of this chapter.

From a Marxist perspective, social reproduction is driven by the interests of capital. In a capitalist system, reproduction of the forces of production (labour power) must be ensured (Mitchell et al., 2003). Although capital needs social reproduction, it strives to offload the costs onto families or the state (although ideally without incurring heavy taxation). The state has long been implicated in social reproduction through provision of education and healthcare, which deliver disciplined, skilled and able-bodied workers. Social reproduction has always, however, been more than merely the reproduction of labour power (Mitchell et al., 2003), and 'welfare states', since the mid-twentieth century, have served also to secure the more general wellbeing of young people through mechanisms such as support to families with low incomes. Indeed, social reproduction is necessary for any society to be sustained, whether capitalist or not. Nonetheless, as Western states, both national and local, have come increasingly to serve the interests of the market rather than regulating it, they are progressively more concerned to promote capitalist production rather than social reproduction (N. Smith, 2002), which is offloaded onto families and other providers.

At the same time, with the decline of the male breadwinner/female caregiver family form in advanced capitalist countries, states are also increasingly having to manage what Daly and Lewis (2000) have termed the growing 'crisis of care'. They are thus being forced into taking responsibility for aspects of social reproduction, notably childcare, which enable mothers to reconcile paid employment with family life. The ways in which individual countries respond to this partly reflects 'the broader welfare regimes in which they are embedded' (Mahon, 2005: 341). Thus, while countries with a prevailing social democratic welfare system like Sweden tend to develop universal, publicly funded childcare provision, 'liberal' welfare states like Canada and the UK are more likely to favour 'demand-side supports, such as vouchers or subsidies, targeted at low-income families' (Mahon, 2005: 341). While the rate at which mothers are entering the paid labour force varies between OECD countries, what is clear is that childcare is, partly at least, being 'defamilialised' in all post-industrial economies (Lister, 1990; Esping-Anderson, 1999), leading to what Orloff (2004) has termed 'the end of maternalism'.

The work of social reproduction, particularly in capitalist societies, generally has a low status. Much of this work is unwaged or very poorly paid, takes place in the private sphere and is considered 'outside' of production.[1] Both reflecting and responsible for its low status, this work has historically been undertaken disproportionately by children and women, both in family and other settings, and by 'colonial and postcolonial subjects', including slaves and international migrants (Mitchell et al., 2003).

Although of low status, it is important to recognise that the work of social reproduction is not generally coerced (Mitchell et al., 2003). There are important ethical, psychological and emotional aspects that lead people to undertake caring responsibilities with little material reward. Parents, in particular, often feel moral commitment to care for their children personally or through family-based provision, irrespective of the financial costs (McDowell et al., 2005b). '[U]npaid family and community work involving the work of care for dependent others, is [often] productive of meanings and relations of an intimate and psychological kind, which are not reducible to the imperatives of capitalist social organisation' (Haylett, 2003: 769). In order to understand how people construct intimate and distant caring relationships through migration, it is thus necessary to recognise that they are motivated in part by non-economic considerations (Cravey, 2003).

These understandings of caring responsibilities are usually gendered in complex ways (McDowell et al., 2005a). It is for this reason, and the related fact that women are heavily implicated in securing social reproduction, both in the family and the labour market, that most social geographers writing on social reproduction have done so from a feminist perspective, and focused on women. With some important exceptions (an early paper by Bill Bunge (1977), and Cindi Katz's work in Sudan and New York (Katz, 1991), there has been less attention to social reproduction from the field of children's geographies. Yet, as Katz points out, 'A key practice of social reproduction is the socialisation and education of children' (1991: 488). Young people are the 'objects' of social reproduction, the 'recipients' of caregiving. Yet young people are also actors in social reproduction. They are actively engaged in acquiring and assimilating the shared knowledge, values and practices of social groups (Katz, 2004). They work on the production of their own futures through work in school and training, and by constructing their own identities. Importantly, many young people are also involved in securing social reproduction more widely through domestic and caring work (Ansell and van Blerk, 2004; Robson, 1996; Robson et al., 2006).

Although all societies invest in social reproduction, social stability or progressive change are not guaranteed. Under conditions where social transformation is attempted through violence, where there are dramatic changes in social practices or extreme food insecurity, social reproduction may break down. Less dramatically, political-economic change can dissolve the unity between production and social reproduction, leaving children ill-equipped for the adult lives that await them (Katz, 1991).

TRENDS IN PRACTICES OF SOCIAL REPRODUCTION AND THEIR IMPACTS ON YOUNG PEOPLE

In this chapter we consider some trends in the delivery of social reproduction over recent time. In particular, we examine the impacts of four trends associated with the ascendancy of neoliberal capitalism across the globe:

1 The progressive withdrawal of the state from direct provision of welfare
2 Pressure on mothers to participate in the labour market, resulting in commodification of reproductive work
3 Increased global interdependency in the delivery of social reproduction, enabling capital to retreat from the 'social wage'
4 Emphasis on the production of individual neoliberal subjects who will become active economic producers and consumers

All of these trends intersect with one another and with other, related or unrelated, societal trends in particular places. Each involves a change in the balance and relationship between the actors responsible for securing children's welfare and in the spatial organisation of society towards that end; and each has particular implications for children's wellbeing. The trends are discussed in turn below.

Withdrawal of the state from direct provision of welfare

Western states began to take an interest in the welfare of children as industrialisation gathered pace in the mid-nineteenth century. Legislation was enacted that prohibited children's employment in what were perceived as dangerous and unhealthy environments, and subsequently required them to attend school. While the motivations behind these measures were more complex than simply children's immediate welfare, they contributed to the emergence of an idealised notion of childhood and adolescence that persists to this day and has been exported worldwide (Ruddick, 2003). However, it was not until the early to mid-twentieth century that securing young people's welfare came to be seen as a key role of local and central government in the West (Mitchell et al., 2003). While welfare states might be criticised as a form of social control that sought to incorporate the working class and immigrants into middle-class norms (Mitchell et al., 2003), they did ensure universal provision of a minimum level of welfare for young people.

The 1970s saw a change of direction as many states shifted away from supporting the social reproduction of labour to facilitating capital investment and growth (Mitchell et al., 2003)[2]. Responsibility for social reproduction was transferred from the nation-state to lower territorial levels of government, and to charities and NGOs which were less well financed and less accountable (Mitchell et al., 2003). Public services such as education were increasingly delivered by private commercial providers, thereby reducing the cost for governments (Mitchell, 2003). Support to those on low incomes was replaced in the US and elsewhere with welfare-to-work programmes designed to cut costs to the public purse and to increase participation in the labour force (Haylett, 2003). In the US, the restrictive welfare policy labelled 'Aid to Families with Dependent Children', implemented within areas with stagnant demand for low-skilled workers, increased extreme poverty and long-term welfare dependency (Lee, 1997). In general, in Western settings, resources available to the young were eroded (Ruddick, 2003). Moreover, the types of locations and environments children spend their time in on a daily basis have been altered by changing welfare regimes. Integral to welfare redesign in most OECD states is the provision of non-parental childcare, for both pre-school and school-age children (Mahon, 2005).

Neoliberal reform of welfare was not confined to rich Western countries. Following the debt crisis of the early 1980s, structural adjustment programmes were imposed on debtor nations worldwide by the World Bank and the International Monetary Fund. These required states to cut public spending, charge for education and healthcare and remove subsidies and price controls on food. In the poorest countries, and among the poorest populations, school attendance fell (across sub-Saharan Africa, primary school enrolment declined by about 6% between 1980 and 1985 (Messkoub, 1992)) and infant and maternal mortality rates rose in some countries for the first time on record (Narman, 1995). Although by the 1990s structural adjustment programmes were tempered with 'social safety nets', designed to lessen the worst impacts on the poor, even today in places such as the state of Orissa in India, where public expenditure on health is falling, infant and child mortality rates are extremely high (Pradhan and Arokkiasamy, 2006). Older children, too, are affected: the restructuring of healthcare services in Zimbabwe disproportionately burdened children with the demands of home-based care for the sick (Robson, 2000).

The retreat of the state from welfare provision is perhaps more marked still in the 'transition states' of Eastern Europe and the former Soviet Union. Whereas the poorest countries never had well-developed welfare provision, these nations once had universal coverage. Hence the impacts of neoliberal adjustment have been particularly challenging (Pavlovskaya, 2004).

One aspect of the retreat of state provision that has particularly concerned children's geographers has been children's diminished access to high-quality public space, particularly for playing. Katz (1998) highlighted the deterioration of the urban environment in New York, and its impacts on young people's opportunities for outdoor leisure. Where play space is available to children it is increasingly provided by commercial enterprises (McKendrick et al., 2000). In the UK, much rural space is now privatised and inaccessible to rural children. Instead, out-of-school care schemes offer venues for collective play, but these commodified spaces are not available to those from families that lack the means to pay for them (Smith and Barker, 2001). Similarly, in Amsterdam, children's needs are given little consideration in the general planning of new residential areas, yet many new spaces are created specifically for children: spaces that are privatised, institutionalised and segregated from 'adult' spaces (Karsten, 2002). These processes are being compounded by increasing female labour force participation along with growing fears about children's independent use of public space, which are resulting in a boom in institutionalised childcare environments (Smith and Barker, 2004).

It is important to note that while 'the nation-state has … abandoned, reduced, or reconfigured many of its previous responsibilities for social reproduction, especially with respect to social welfare provision … it continues to exert great power through various disciplining strategies – witness US welfare reform policies that encourage marriage, advocate abstinence, and coerce work in exchange for public assistance' (Mitchell et al., 2003: 430). One of the key strategies has been to return responsibility for children's welfare (if not day-to-day care) to the family (and thus to the private sphere) (Ruddick, 2007). In indebted third-world countries, the introduction of user fees for public services was premised on a belief among the international financial institutions that families should take full responsibility for their offspring, and in former socialist countries, in particular, responsibility for children's welfare reverted from the state to the family (Ansell, 2005). In the US, 'Aid to Families with Dependent Children' was renamed 'Temporary Assistance to Needy Families', removing any sense that children had a direct claim on the state, and emphasising the temporary support for families fulfilling their responsibilities (Ruddick, 2007). Ironically, as the next section will make clear, although the state seeks to persuade parents to be fully responsible for their children, this welfare-to-work scheme often requires mothers to pass on to others responsibility for their children's care while they work. In poorer countries, the privatisation of children's welfare has meant that children's lives increasingly depend upon the survival strategies of people in their households (Messkoub, 1992) while, in the US, programmes that celebrate families, such as 'families first', are accompanied by cuts in state aid to the poorest families (Ruddick, 2007). It is not, however, every family that is celebrated. Neoliberalism intersects with neoconservativism in North America, and the notion of the 'best interests of the child' is used to argue for support of particular types of family form, specifically 'the traditional biologically constituted, patriarchal hetero-normative nuclear family' (Ruddick, 2007: 629). Families that do not conform to such arrangements are penalised and risk further impoverishment.

Mothers' labour market participation and the commodification of reproductive work

It is well documented that with the transition to service-dominated economies, combined with skills shortages triggered by ageing populations in many OECD countries, women with children are needed to participate in the paid labour market in ever-increasing numbers. All European member states, for example, have a goal of 60% female employment by 2010 (Mahon, 2005). At the same time, concern over leaving children unsupervised in public outdoor space or alone at home is growing. Thus, as mothers form an increasingly significant part of the labour force, non-parental childcare provision is 'becoming integral to social reproduction in post-industrial economies' (Mahon, 2006: 452). Growing demand from dual-earner professional households for commodified forms of domestic labour (in particular childcare) is leading to a situation where a growing number of highly paid professional women rely on poorly paid, low-skilled women and young people to provide the services that enable them to work outside the home. As Gregson and Lowe argued in 1994, '... the expansion in the professional division of labour, coupled with the growth in women's participation in service class occupations, has generated a crisis in social reproduction for middle-class households, particularly with respect to childcare' (1994: 232). More than a decade on, the continuing growth of professional women's employment, coupled with social policies to expand childcare, means that their assertion that the 'major change in the way class relates to social reproduction' which Gregson and Lowe (1994: 231) identified is still evolving.

Despite the undoubted current increase in the number of childcare workers in the UK, the lack of affordable and accessible childcare places persists in most regions (McDowell et al., 2005b). This is a serious problem for the Government because, without a sufficient supply of childcare workers, women with children may be prevented from (re)entering the paid labour market, thus jeopardising the ability of the UK economy to compete on the global stage. In order to tackle this problem the UK Government has committed to create one million new childcare places by 2010. One of the major hurdles the Government faces in terms of achieving this strategy is the lack of a trained and qualified childcare workforce. The case study in Box 15.1 highlights how the Government is dealing with this in West London.

A key outcome of the increasing importance of non-parental childcare for children is the changing location of where and how they spend their time. As Box 15.1 suggests, a growing number of children in West London, as elsewhere, spend less time within the familial home and more time in institutionalised childcare environments. The number of out-of-school clubs, for example, has increased exponentially over the last decade, altering the social geographies of children using them (Smith and Barker, 2004).

Box 15.1 Childcare training in West London

The West London area runs from the borough of Brent in the East to Hillingdon in the West and includes Hammersmith and Fulham, Hounslow, Harrow and Ealing. It has a population of nearly 1.4 million residents and is one of the most ethnically diverse regions in the UK, with almost half (49%) of all residents classifying themselves as 'Non-White' compared to a national figure of just 13% (ONS, 2003). Migrants from the EU accession countries are currently adding considerably to the West London population. Households with dependent children represent approximately 30% of all households.

West London benefits from relatively low unemployment and a number of dynamic employment sectors, many of which are suffering skills shortages. However, 'there are almost two economies extant in the area: a highly skilled, highly paid sector and a low skilled, low wage sector' (LWLSC, 2003: 7). Childcare is desperately needed in order to enable highly skilled dual-career households to participate in the waged labour market and so keep the area economically competitive (Buckingham et al., 2006). Research in West London highlights the pressure being placed upon those working in Jobcentres to 'encourage' women (particularly lone parents) and young people on benefits to undertake training courses in childcare in order to alleviate the shortage of trained childcare workers (see Smith et al., 2008).

This research clearly shows how certain aspects of social reproduction, in particular childcare, are becoming increasingly associated with young people and lone parents taking part in the 'New Deal' welfare-to-work programmes. As well as being 'encouraged' to undertake childcare training, many mothers also argue that they are choosing a childcare-related course because they need to end up working in a 'productive' job which will fit with their current 'reproductive' domestic responsibilities and which will allow them to continue caring for their own children. Ironically, these women are being trained to give professional credentials to their 'unproductive' caring work in the home which then allows them to be productive members of society by looking after other people's children in commodified childcare settings. This highlights that whilst an increasing number of women are entering the formal labour market, the responsibility for children's care (and so social reproduction) remains predominantly theirs (Jenkins, 2004; McDowell et al., 2005b). Therefore the 'choices' women with children 'are conditioned to make' (MacLeavy, 2007) regarding training and employment are heavily bounded by their identity as mothers and their primary responsibility for social reproduction.

Increased global interdependency in the delivery of social reproduction

A concern with the public/private dualism has long pervaded work on social reproduction (Mitchell et al., 2003; Ruddick, 2003). But social reproduction is also spatialised at other scales. In southern Africa, since the nineteenth century, children have been raised predominantly in rural areas where women undertake both domestic work and subsistence agriculture while men migrate to work in mines, commercial farms and factories, often crossing national borders (Murray, 1981). Employers have not needed to pay a 'social wage' that would cover the cost of reproduction by supporting an entire family. Today a similar pattern, whereby the rural subsistence sphere subsidises the urban economy, has been described in Mexico. Remittances from migrant workers, working in Mexican cities or in the US, assist families resident in rural areas. In the villages people employ natural resources and processes to support livelihoods that reproduce a workforce, subsidising the costs for urban and US employers (Klooster, 2005).

Since the late twentieth century, neoliberalism has increased the reluctance of capital to bear the costs of social reproduction. In individual countries, responsibility has been increasingly displaced from employers onto the households and communities of the poor (as seen in Box 15.2) – and especially onto women. Bezuidenhout and Fakier (2006) chart this process in South Africa, where market-based rhetoric is used to justify 'rational' restructuring of employment, with reductions in wages and heightened job insecurity. At a wider spatial scale, economic globalisation has enabled firms to reduce costs further. 'The important point about globalisation from the standpoint of children's geographies is that there is no longer a need for capital investments to be secured

Box 15.2 AIDS, social reproduction and children's wellbeing

One region in which global restructuring is leaving the reproduction of cheap labour to the families of the poor is sub-Saharan Africa. Here neoliberal economic change is complicated by an AIDS epidemic that interferes with the conventional modes through which societies are reproduced, as Janet Bujra explains:

> Now this transmission belt of new labour for old [the rural areas in which social reproduction takes place] is fraying as the hidden virus is spread to rural wives or sexual partners, incapacitating those who labour on the fields and in houses and turning the next generation of migrants into orphans and street children cast adrift even from the insurance policy of rural subsistence. (2004: 632)

If parents fall sick or die, the work of social reproduction passes to others. As family members make decisions concerning the care of AIDS-affected children, both economic and emotional considerations are significant (Ansell and van Blerk, 2005). It is recognized that while children impose a burden on households in terms of their own need for material and psychosocial care, they may also be able to undertake reproductive work themselves, caring for younger children or for sick family members. Thus children may be sent to live with needy families or with those that have resources to spare. Such practices have outcomes for children's wellbeing, both material and psychosocial. Children living with unsympathetic relatives may go hungry or be overworked, but the separation of siblings and sundering of friendships may be equally traumatic (van Blerk and Ansell, 2006).

Responsibility and care for AIDS-affected children cannot be seen in isolation from wider education and healthcare policies. Costs of school fees and availability of health services frame household decision making. The restructuring of Zimbabwe's health sector, for instance, imposed a considerable burden of work on young people, left to care for sick relatives who could not afford user fees (Robson, 2000). The AIDS pandemic and economic liberalization in combination leave children making a substantial contribution to national economies through care giving (Robson, 2004).

at particular locations' (Aitken, 2001: 123). In what Katz (2001) describes as 'vagabond capitalism', firms are able to move around the globe seeking out sources of appropriate labour, but rather than invest in the future workforce at these locations, they elect to move on and find new (cheaper) workers elsewhere.

With this spatial restructuring of social reproduction, youth and childhood are themselves being restructured (Ruddick, 2003) and rescaled (Katz, 2001). Far from increased global uniformity, an increasingly differentiated labour force is being produced (Katz, 2001). It is functional to capital that sites of purchase and expenditure of labour are separated from sites of reproduction of labour (Mitchell et al., 2003). Thus childhood becomes differentiated between places (Aitken et al., 2006): 'child workers within the global South and child consumers in the global North' (Aitken, 2001: 124). Across the globe, different 'strategies of the social reproduction of youth and children, their education and training and their acculturation carry within them imagined paths to global competitiveness (both in the "race to the top" and the "race to the bottom")' (Ruddick, 2003: 257).

It is not only capital that is increasingly mobile, globally, but also labour, and this has proved advantageous to capital seeking to cut the cost of social reproduction. As Mitchell et al. point out, 'transnational labor migrants inadvertently work to offset the costs of social reproduction for capital and national states'(2003: 437). Certain aspects of social reproduction, in particular childcare, are becoming increasingly associated with migrant women (Cox, 2000), Moreover, it is not only domestic labour that is supplied by immigrant women; many skilled migrant women are involved in other areas of social reproduction beyond the household, such as health care and education (Kofman and Raghuram, 2006).

'The participation of indigenous women in the labour force is both dependent upon and creates demand for domestic work which is [increasingly] supplied by women of migrant origin' (Kofman, 2003: 8). Many of these immigrant women, undertaking paid domestic work, leave their own children at home in the care of unpaid family members (thereby subsidising the cost of reproduction in the destination country) (Mattingly, 2001), leading to what has been termed the 'global care chain' thesis (Parrenas, 2001; Ehrenreich and Hochschild, 2002). Others take their children with them. Either way, migration can often be stressful for children and disruptive of family life (Warfa et al., 2006). Migration decisions are not driven by economic considerations alone, and care responsibilities often constrain people's willingness to engage in migration (Bailey et al., 2004). In Japan, for instance, the desire to avoid negative consequences for children often militates against women's long-distance migration (Liaw, 2003). In other situations, the desire to better provide for children is a motivator for migration (Waters, 2002). Latinos and Latinas, for instance, respond to human-centred rather than neoliberal values in constructing intimate and distant social connections, supporting their migration to the US South, although the practical effect is to facilitate the globalisation of labour markets (Cravey, 2003).

The production of neoliberal subjects

A further impact of neoliberalism on social reproduction has been a gearing of welfare policies towards the production of certain kinds of subjects. Western society has long been concerned to reproduce healthy workers. Indeed, in the late 19th and early 20th centuries, women's 'reproductive' bodies became important sites for ensuring the production of healthy 'future citisens' (Wainwright, 2003). Schools were established as sites of social reproduction, replacing the household as the locus for acquiring work-related knowledge, and designed to produce disciplined and competent workers (Bowles and Gintis, 1976; Freire, 1972). Today, with ageing populations in many OECD countries, the importance of producing productive citizens is increasing. As Esping-Anderson argues, '[f]or society, it is vital that future generations will be resourceful and productive simply because they will be numerically few, destined to shoulder huge dependent populations' (2003: 110).

Throughout the world, education continues to attract both public and private investment. Attainment of universal primary school enrolment is one of the Millennium Development Goals, and efforts toward meeting this objective by 2015 are driving policy in many Third World countries, backed by resources including heavy support from the World Bank. While governments seek to divest themselves of responsibility for the day-to-day care of children, except insofar as this frees mothers to participate in the workforce, their willingness to invest in education, and the generational reproduction it represents, reflects a belief that schooling not only reduces poverty but promotes economic growth and global competitiveness.

The World Bank has also enthusiastically supported the global expansion of 'early childhood development and care' (ECD). The Indian government's 'Integrated Child Development Services' (ICDS) operate 350,000 pre-school centres (Prochner, 2002). However, while those in charge of curriculum and training advocate learning through play, parents prefer a more formal approach to literacy and numeracy, and in most classrooms children sit in rows learning to count and recite the alphabet, which parents consider a better way of preparing for the competitive atmosphere of primary schools. India also has about 100,000 privately run 'preparatory' preschools with a focus on reading and writing, usually in English, to enable children to compete for places in private primary schools, thereby enhancing their life chances. There are even pre-nursery schools which prepare children for nursery school admission tests (Prochner, 2002). Pre-schooling, here, is clearly conceived as early preparation for a competitive labour market. Furthermore, placing children in pre-schools allows mothers to participate in the labour market (Penn, 2002).

Triggered by the looming demographic crisis of an ageing society, along with a commitment to the 'social investment' discourse of the 'Third Way' advocates in New Labour, pre-school education and childcare has also been playing an increasingly important role in UK policy. Government rhetoric surrounding the provision of good-quality pre-school services clearly links the goals of competitiveness and equality over the life-course, reflecting Esping-Anderson's argument that 'for citizens, a strong cognitive base is a pre-condition for educational attainment, subsequent earnings potential and career chances' (2003: 110). Moreover, as Adler and Adler (1994) have argued in relation to the USA, children are spending an increasing amount of time after school in institutionalised, adult-organised and supervised environments. Their contention that this provides a way for adults to reproduce the existing and dominant social structure and to socialise children with the hegemonic values of American culture can also be extended throughout most OECD countries, where the number of children spending time in this type of environment is currently increasing. The provision of both pre-school education and out-of-school childcare thus 'reflect a markedly productivist social policy orientation' (Mahon, 2005: 343). Moreover, such a 'productivist' conceptualisation of education is not confined to the 'early years'. Indeed, as the case study in Box 15.3 highlights, it extends to the education and training of young people.

Box 15.3 Success for all? Training young people to be productive citizens in the UK

Since New Labour came to power in the United Kingdom in 1997, the aim of combating social exclusion has been key to a number of high-profile and ambitious policies aimed at ensuring social cohesion and social and community regeneration. The emphasis on process (exclusion) rather than outcome (poverty) is fundamental in the UK and participation in paid work is seen as the best path towards social inclusion. New Labour has thus developed a series of 'policies to increase the "work-readiness" of currently unemployed individuals and others who are outside the labour market, and reforms of the benefit system to tie it more closely to the labour market'. (McDowell, 2004: 152). Rather than being remunerated by the state for being out of paid work, groups of unemployed individuals are being offered retraining to make them 'work ready' and to ensure that they are 'encouraged' to take responsibility for themselves and their families (McDowell, 2004). Young people in particular are being targeted by this policy through the 'New Deal for Young People'[3] as the UK government is clear that a highly skilled workforce is crucial for the development of a globally competitive 21st-century economy (Performance and Innovation Unit, 2001). Education and training opportunities are thus dually conceptualized as fundamental to the ability of individuals to (re)enter paid work within a globalized labour market (and in so doing tackle social exclusion) and key to conquering skills shortages within the UK (thus ensuring the UK economy remains globally competitive).

'Success for All' is one strategy through which the British government hopes to improve the educational outcomes and routes into higher education and employment for young people aged 14 to 19. Tied to an inclusive learning strategy for widening participation, 'Success for All' sets out the government's desire to achieve both social justice and economic success. It aims to create more accessible basic skills courses to reduce the number of young people who lack, at the very least, a level 2 qualification (equivalent to five GCSEs, grade A–C), which is considered by the government to be the 'threshold of employability' (DfES, 2006). The 'Success for All' strategy is delivered by local Learning and Skills Councils which have been charged with the task of ensuring that the learning and training they fund meets the needs of their local economies in order to maximize productivity and economic development. Learning and Skills Councils are thus involved in a process of trying to engage previously disenfranchised groups in the labour market, and in particular to target young people who are not in education, employment or training (see SEU, 1999).

While UK education policy may be premised on the idea that social exclusion can be reduced by bringing everyone into active economic participation, it is unlikely to seriously address inequality. Academic achievement is persistently low in some regions, suggesting that in practice schooling continues to reinforce inequality (Warrington, 2005). Indeed, through a variety of strategies, education systems have long served to reproduce the class structure of Western society (Bourdieu and Passeron, 1977). Moreover, in countries like the UK and USA where an economic model of childcare dominates (Smith and Barker, 2004), whereby parents have to pay market rates for commodified services which vary considerably in terms of quality, it could be argued that social inequalities will be reproduced as the opportunity to enhance 'cultural capital' (Bourdieu, 1977) also varies.

Education in Western societies is not simply about producing a skilled labour force. It is increasingly geared at moulding particular kinds of future economic actors – 'neoliberal subjects' – fully autonomous individuals (albeit autonomous largely in relation to the economy rather than other aspects of life), exercising rational choice in production and consumption and operating as engines of economic growth (Mitchell et al., 2003). If education is conceived by national governments as being about achieving competitive advantage in a global marketplace, initiatives such as the promotion of multiculturalism in education are no longer geared towards the production of tolerant and democratic national citizens but rather towards workers with the cultural capital to compete internationally (Mitchell, 2003).

Becoming globally competitive economic actors is not simply a national ambition. Securing competitive advantage for many involves seeking education elsewhere. There is now a vibrant market in the provision of education, both private and public sector, and international education is a multi-billion dollar business (Waters, 2006b). For the relatively prosperous in every society, international education is transforming the scales at which social reproduction is secured. A growing number of middle-class parents in East Asia, for instance, send their children to attend school in Canada. In 'astronaut families' the breadwinner remains at home in Asia, while his wife and children migrate to pursue education (Waters, 2002). Children's education can be a more important consideration in transnational mobility of families than the career of either parent (Hardill, 2004). Western education offers cultural capital for Asian parents as well as for their children, thereby reproducing existing class relations within Asia (Waters, 2006b). At the same time, the income generated for Canadian schools partially compensates for declining state expenditure on education under neoliberalism (Waters, 2006a). Similar processes operate in Africa, although here the brain drain of educated young people is more likely to be permanent, as cultural capital is sought to enable young people to compete for jobs in the West (Campbell, 2001). It is not only formal education that entices young people to travel the world to accumulate cultural capital. Western youth engaged in gap-year travel are involved in a similar quest to build identities that will assist them to compete in the neoliberal marketplace (Simpson, 2005). It is increasingly the case that the work of producing the neoliberal subject is the responsibility of the individual, and continues into adulthood and throughout life (Mitchell et al., 2003). Within the UK government's 'Success for All' strategy, for example, education is not conceptualised as something that stops once an individual leaves school, college or university, but 'continue[s] on even later in life' (Giddens, 2001: 125).

CONCLUSIONS

In this chapter we have examined a set of processes that are transforming children's welfare in the contemporary world. In spite of dramatic contrasts in the wellbeing of children in different parts of the world, neoliberal economic policies are having global impacts. We have focused in particular on four trends related to the global ascendancy of neoliberalism that characterise the contemporary performance of social reproduction. In relation to each, we have considered the changing balance and relationship between the actors responsible for securing children's welfare, changes in the spatial organisation of society geared towards that end, and the particular implications for children's wellbeing. There are important threads that cut across all four trends, which we summarise briefly.

In terms of the changing responsibility for children's wellbeing, there has been a clear displacement from capital and state to other actors. Non-governmental organisations and civil society have taken on elements of what was once delivered by the state, but it is the family that has been expected to become the key actor assuming responsibility for social reproduction. While the state has retreated from direct provision of welfare, however, it continues to exercise a disciplining influence, but does so largely in the interests of economic competitiveness. Thus, while responsibility for children's wellbeing is transferred to families, there is a growing expectation, at least in Western countries, that this should imply financial responsibility, and that parents should be fully engaged in the workforce. Hence it commonly becomes necessary for parents to transfer the role of social reproduction to others, either other family members or commercial providers. Furthermore, while the capitalist state may have little interest in the delivery of day-to-day childcare, it has a strong interest in the generational reproduction of the workforce and continues to invest in, and remould, education systems in order to deliver this – albeit with a growing input from private sector providers.

The displacement of responsibility for children's welfare to the family is accompanied by a spatial displacement from public to private(ised) sphere. The condition of public space – in particular space amenable to children – is in many places deteriorating, and children spend more of their out-of-school time at home or in commercially provided spaces that are often special children's environments, segregated from adult space. There are also wider global circuits through which social reproduction is spatialised. It is increasingly likely for the reproduction of labour to take place at a great distance from where it will be employed, or where the products it produces will be consumed. Employers do not need to behave in ways that encourage local investment in the workers of the future. Moreover, more and more women are migrating from poor countries to provide reproductive labour in rich countries, while the rich are sending their children around the world to be schooled.

The impacts on young people are diverse. Children of the poor in particular suffer from the deteriorating provision of welfare by the state, becoming increasingly dependent on the resources of their (increasingly impoverished) families. Where other factors such as the AIDS pandemic intervene and families' capacities to cope are stretched, children are confronted with particularly challenging situations, moved from family to family, and often bearing the brunt of their relatives' frustrations. However, it is not only orphanhood that parts children from their parents. While rendered the responsibility of their families, many children are separated from parents who are forced to work to provide for them, sometimes travelling overseas in search of adequate work. It is not only the children of the poor that are affected by these changes in the ways in which the welfare of the young is delivered. Children are increasingly removed from public environments, which are becoming more and more the preserve of adults. Moreover, their private environments are increasingly exposed to surveillance through, for instance, nanny cams and child monitors that allow absent parents a sense that they are securing their children's wellbeing from a distance

(Katz, 2006). Growing pressure is placed on children worldwide to be successful in school, and to perform particular identities and roles that will contribute most productively to building competitive nations.

Children are not simply victims of changing patterns of social reproduction, but are actively involved in these changes. Families are not simply sites where caregiving is performed for children; children themselves play a part (Ruddick, 2007). They are engaged in the work of forming themselves as neoliberal subjects. They make a direct (if delayed) contribution to society through their 'obligatory work in schools' (Qvortrup, 2005: 7), but also engage in other forms of work that contribute more immediately to social reproduction as well as furnishing them with practical and social skills that will be of value in the labour market as they grow older (Jennings et al., 2006). Children's earnings in Mexican supermarkets, for example, contribute to family survival in the face of impoverishment related to Mexico's insertion into a competitive global economic system (Jennings et al., 2006). Similarly, children in Africa make a substantial contribution to social reproduction through taking on caregiving responsibilities (Robson, 2004).

In spite of children's contributions, they are seldom able to make direct claims on the state. In the neoliberal US, 'children's rights constituted a set of protections from harm rather than access to resources' (Ruddick, 2007: 636–7). Qvortrup points out that 'nowhere have children a constitutionally-based right to receive welfare support from the state. … Even in welfare states, children are basically dependent on their parents' (2005: 10). He attributes this to 'the privatisation or familialisation of children – combined with their portrayal as incomplete, vulnerable and of no economic use' (Qvortrup, 2005: 9) and, in particular, the failure to recognise children's contributions through education. Such processes are at work today in Mexico, where '[t]raditional means of social reproduction, including children's participation from an early age in family businesses and agricultural endeavours, is giving way to oversight by federal and state government agencies' (Jennings et al., 2006: 235). The state is intervening to secure what it perceives as children's welfare – but perhaps this is to ensure social reproduction in the interests of capital, and not in the interests of children, whose views remain unrepresented.

Ruddick recently highlighted the need for increased dialogue between 'feminist geographers working on women's issues and geographers addressing children's issues' (2007: 628) who, in the past, have tended to see each as the other's limit. In this chapter we have brought together perspectives from both fields. We recognise that children's rights cannot be considered in isolation from caregivers' rights, and vice versa. We therefore support Ruddick's call, in the hope that in the future social geographers will acknowledge more explicitly the interconnections between the lives of women and children, and use concepts such as social reproduction to highlight the ways in which their geographies are inextricably linked. Only by doing so will we really begin to understand the processes that continue to reproduce social inequalities amongst children (and women), and so start to produce truly emancipatory geographies which not only explore but begin to enhance the wellbeing of children and young people.

NOTES

1 The binary distinction between production and social reproduction has been strongly critiqued from a feminist perspective (Mitchell et al., 2003).

2 It should be acknowledged that some social democratic welfare states have not conformed to this but continue to publicly fund state-provided services (Mahon, 2005). Moreover, as Peck (2001) argues, states are not simply involved in a process of 'rolling back' the welfare state, but of 'rolling out', where direct state welfare provision is replaced by 'workfare' which is heavily regulated by the state.

3 All young people (aged under 25) who have been claiming unemployment benefits for six months have to participate in the New Deal, which

'consists of a period of intense personal advice and assistance followed by one of four options linked to employment experience and training' (MacLeavy, 2007: 729).

REFERENCES

Adler, P. and Adler, P. (1994) 'Social reproduction and the corporate other: the institutionalization of afterschool activities', *Sociological Quarterly*, 35 (2): 309–28.

Aitken, S.C. (2001) 'Global crises of childhood: rights, justice and the unchildlike child', *Area*, 33 (2): 119–27.

Aitken, S., Lopez Estrada, S., Jennings, J. and Aguirre, L.M. (2006) 'Reproducing life and labor: global processes and working children in Tijuana, Mexico', *Childhood*, 13 (3): 365–87.

Andrews, G.J. and Chen, S. (2006) 'The production of tyrannical space', *Children's Geographies*, 4 (2): 239–50.

Ansell, N. (2005) *Children, Youth and Development*. London: Routledge.

Ansell, N. and van Blerk, L. (2004) 'Children's migration as a household/family strategy: coping with AIDS in Malawi and Lesotho', *Journal of Southern African Studies*, 30 (3): 673–90.

Ansell, N. and van Blerk, L. (2005) '"Where we stayed was very bad ...": migrant children's perspectives on life in informal rented accommodation in two southern African cities', *Environment and Planning A*, 37 (3): 423–40.

Bailey, A.J., Blake, M.K. and Cooke, T.J. (2004) 'Migration, care, and the linked lives of dual-earner households', *Environment and Planning A*, 36 (9): 1617–32.

Bezuidenhout, A. and Fakier, K. (2006) 'Maria's burden: contract cleaning and the crisis of social reproduction in post-apartheid South Africa', *Antipode*, 38 (3): 462–85.

Bosco, F.J. (2007) 'Hungry children and networks of aid in Argentina: thinking about geographies of responsibility and care', *Children's Geographies*, 5 (1–2): 55–76.

Bourdieu, P. (1977) 'Cultural reproduction and social reproduction', in J. Karabel and A.H. Halsey (eds), *Power and Ideology in Education, Society and Culture*. London: Sage. pp. 487–511.

Bourdieu, P. and Passeron, J. (1977) *Reproduction in Education, Society and Culture*. London: Sage.

Bowles, S. and Gintis, H. (1976) *Schooling in Capitalist America: Educational reform and the contradictions of economic life*. London: Routledge and Kegan Paul.

Buckingham, S., Marandet, E., Smith, F., Wainwright, E. and Diosi, M. (2006) 'The liminality of training spaces: places of private/public transitions', *Geoforum*, 37: 895–905.

Bujra, J. (2004) 'AIDS as a crisis in social reproduction', *Review of African Political Economy*, 102: 631–38.

Bunge, W. (1977) 'The point of reproduction: a second front', *Antipode*, 9 (2): 60–76.

Campbell, E.K. (2001) 'Preferences for emigration among skilled citizens in Botswana', *International Journal of Population Geography*, 7 (3): 151–71.

Cox, R. (2000) 'Exploring the growth of paid domestic labour: a case study of London', *Geography*, 85 (3): 241–51.

Cravey, A.J. (2003) 'Toque una ranchera, por favor', *Antipode*, 35 (3): 603–20.

Daly, M. and Lewis, J. (2000) 'The concept of social care and the analysis of contemporary welfare states', *British Journal of Sociology*, 14 (1): 281–98.

DfES (Department for Education and Science) (2006) *Further Education: Raising skills, improving life chances*. London: Stationery Office.

Ehrenreich, B. and Hochschild, A. (eds) (2002) *Global Woman: Nannies, maids, and sex workers in the new economy*. New York: Henry Holt.

Esping-Anderson, G. (1999) *The Social Foundations of Postindustrial Societies*. Oxford: Oxford University Press.

Esping-Anderson, G. (2003) 'Against social inheritance', in A. Giddens (ed.), *The Progressive Manifesto*. London: Polity.

Freire, P. (1972) *Pedagogy of the Oppressed*. Harmondsworth: Penguin.

Giddens, A. (2001) 'Introduction', in A. Giddens (ed.), *The Global Third Way*. Cambridge: Polity Press. pp. 1–21.

Gough, I. and McGregor, J.A. (eds) (2007) *Wellbeing in Developing Countries: From theory to research*. Cambridge: Cambridge University Press.

Gregson, N. and Lowe, M. (1994) *Servicing the Middle-class: Domestic labour in contemporary Britain*. London: Routledge.

Hardill, I. (2004) 'Transnational living and moving experiences: intensified mobility and dual-career households', *Population, Space and Place*, 10 (5): 375–89.

Haylett, C. (2003) 'Remaking labour imaginaries: social reproduction and the internationalising project of welfare reform', *Political Geography*, 22: 765–88.

Hilary, J., Penrose, A., King, F., Heaton, A. and Wilkinson, J. (2002) *Globalisation and Children's Rights: What role for the private sector?* London: Save the Children UK.

Jenkins, S. (2004) *Gender, Place and the Labour Market*, Aldershot. Ashgate.

Jennings, J., Aitken, S., Lopez Estrada, S. and Fernandez, A. (2006) 'Learning and earning: relational scales of children's work', *Area*, 38 (3): 231–39.

Karsten, L. (2002) 'Mapping childhood in Amsterdam: the spatial and social construction of children's domains in the city', *Tijdschrift voor Economische en Sociale Geografie*, 93 (3): 231–41.

Katz, C. (1991) 'Sow what you know: the struggle for social reproduction in rural Sudan', *Annals of the Association of American Geographers*, 81 (3): 488–514.

Katz, C. (1998) 'Disintegrating developments: global economic restructuring and the eroding of ecologies of youth', in T. Skelton and G. Valentine (eds), *Cool Places: Geographies of youth cultures*. London: Routledge.

Katz, C. (2001) 'Vagabond capitalism and the necessity of social reproduction', *Antipode*, 33 (4): 708–27.

Katz, C. (2004) *Growing up Global: Economic restructuring and children's everyday lives*. Minneapolis: University of Minnesota Press.

Katz, C. (2006) 'The terrors of hypervigilance: security and the new spatialities of childhood', *Documents d'Analisi Geografica*, 47: 15–29.

Klooster, D.J. (2005) 'Producing social nature in the Mexican countryside', *Cultural Geographies*, 12 (3): 321–44.

Kofman, E. (2003) 'Women migrants and refugees in the European Union'. Paper presented to *The Economic and Social Aspects of Migration* Conference jointly organized by the European Commission and the OECD, Brussels, 21–22 January.

Kofman, E. and Raghuram, P. (2006) 'Gender and global labour migrations: incorporating skilled workers', *Antipode*, 38 (2): 282–303

Lee, R. (2000) 'Social reproduction', in R.J. Johnston, D. Gregory, G. Pratt and M. Watts (eds), *Dictionary of Human Geography*. Oxford: Blackwell.

Lee, W. (1997) 'Poverty and welfare dependency: the case of Los Angeles County in the 1990s', *Environment and Planning A*, 29 (3): 443–58.

Liaw, K.–L. (2003) 'Distinctive features in the sex ratio of Japan's interprefectural migrants: an explanation based on the family system and spatial economy of Japan', *International Journal of Population Geography*, 9 (3): 199–214.

Lister, R. (1990) 'Women, economic dependency and citizenship', *Journal of Social Policy*, 19 (4): 445–67.

LWLSC (2003) *Needs Assessment*. London: London West Learning and Skills Council.

McDowell, L. (2004) 'Work, workfare, work/life balance and an ethic of care', *Progress in Human Geography*, 28: 145–63.

McDowell, L., Perrons, D., Fagan, C., Ray, K. and Ward, K. (2005a) 'The contradictions and intersections of class and gender in a global city: placing working women's lives on the research agenda', *Environment and Planning A*, 37: 441–61.

McDowell, L., Ray, K., Perrons, D., Fagan, C. and Ward, K. (2005b) 'Women's paid work and moral economies of care', *Social and Cultural Geography*, 6 (2): 219–35.

McKendrick, J.H., Bradford, M.G. and Fielder, A.V. (2000) 'Kid customer? Commercialization of playspace and the commodification of childhood', *Childhood*, 7 (3): 295–314.

MacLeavy, J. (2007) 'Engendering New Labour's workfarist regime: exploring the intersection of welfare stare restructuring and labour market policies in the UK', *Gender, Place and Culture*, 14 (6): 721–43.

Mahon, R. (2005) 'Rescaling social reproduction: childcare in Toronto/Canada and Stockholm/Sweden', *International Journal of Urban and Regional Research*, 29 (2): 341–57.

Mahon, R. (2006) 'Of scalar hierarchies and welfare redesign: child care in three Canadian

cities', *Transactions of the Institute of British Geographers*, NS 31: 452–66.
Mattingly, D.J. (2001) 'The home and the world: domestic service and international networks of caring labor', *Annals of the Association of American Geographers*, 91 (2): 370–86.
Messkoub, M. (1992) 'Deprivation and structural adjustment', in M. Wuyts, M. Mackintosh and T. Hewitt (eds), *Development Policy and Public Action*. Oxford: Oxford University Press/Open University. pp. 175–98.
Mitchell, K. (2003) 'Educating the national citizen in neoliberal times: from the multicultural self to the strategic cosmopolitan', *Transactions of the Institute of British Geographers*, 28 (4): 387–403.
Mitchell, K., Marston, S.A. and Katz, C. (2003) 'Introduction: Life's work: an introduction, review and critique', *Antipode*, 415–42.
Murray, C. (1981) *Families Divided: The impact of migrant labour in Lesotho*. Cambridge: Cambridge University Press.
Narman, A. (1995) 'Fighting fire with petrol: how to counter social ills in Africa with economic structural adjustment', in D. Simon, W. Van Spengen, C. Dixon and A. Narman (eds), *Structurally Adjusted Africa: Poverty, debt and basic needs*. London: Pluto. pp. 45–56.
ONS (Office for National Statistics) (2003) *Census 2001: Key statistics for wards in England and Wales*. London: Stationery Office.
Orloff, A.S. (2004) 'Farewell to maternalism? State policies and mothers' employment'. Paper presented at the Annual Meetings of RC 19, Paris, 2–4 September.
Pain, R. (2006) 'Paranoid parenting? Rematerializing risk and fear for children', *Social and Cultural Geography*, 7 (2): 221–43.
Panter-Brick, C. (2004) 'Homelessness, poverty, and risks to health: beyond at risk categorizations of street children', *Children's Geographies*, 2 (1): 83–94.
Parrenas, R. (2001) *Servants of Globalization: Women, migration and domestic work*. Stanford, CA: Stanford University Press.
Pavlovskaya, M. (2004) 'Other transitions: multiple economies of Moscow households in the 1990s', *Annals of the Association of American Geographers*, 94 (2): 329–51.
Peck, J. (2001) *Workfare States*. New York: Guilford Pres .
Penn, H. (2002) 'The World Bank's view of early childhood', *Childhood*, 9 (1): 118–32.
Performance and Innovation Unit (2001) *Modern Apprenticeships: The way to work*. DfES. London: Cassels Report.
Pradhan, J. and Arokkiasamy, P. (2006) 'High infant and child mortality rates in Orissa: an assessment of major reasons', *Population, Space and Place*, 12 (3): 187–200.
Prochner, L. (2002) 'Preschool and playway in India', *Childhood*, 9 (4): 435–53.
Punch, S. (2000) 'Children's strategies for creating playspaces: negotiating independence in rural Bolivia', in S.L. Holloway and G. Valentine (eds), *Children's Geographies: Playing, living, learning*. London: Routledge. pp. 48–62.
Qvortrup, J. (2005) 'Varieties of childhood', in J. Qvortrup (ed), *Studies in Modern Childhood: Society, agency, culture*. Basingstoke: Palgrave Macmillan. pp. 1–20.
Robson, E. (1996) 'Working girls and boys: children's contributions to household survival in West Africa', *Geography*, 81 (4): 403–07.
Robson, E. (2000) 'Invisible carers: young people in Zimbabwe's home-based healthcare', *Area*, 32 (1): 59–70.
Robson, E. (2004) 'Hidden child workers: young carers in Zimbabwe', *Antipode*, 36 (2): 227–48.
Robson, E., Ansell, N., Huber, U.S., Gould, W.T.S. and Van Blerk, L. (2006) 'Young caregivers in the context of the HIV/AIDS pandemic in sub-Saharan Africa', *Population, Space and Place*, 12 (2): 93–111.
Ruddick, S. (2003) 'The politics of aging: globalization and the restructuring of youth and childhood', *Antipode*, 35 (2): 334–62.
Ruddick, S. (2007) 'At the horizons of the subject: neo-liberalism, neo-conservatism and the rights of the child. Part Two: Parent, caregiver, state', *Gender, Place and Culture*, 14 (6): 627–40.
SEU (Social Exclusion Unit) (1999) *Bridging the Gap: New opportunities for 16–18 year olds not in education, employment or training*. London: Stationery Office.
Simpson, K. (2005) 'Dropping out or signing up? The professionalisation of youth travel', *Antipode*, 37 (3): 447–68.

Smith, F. and Barker, J. (2001) 'Commodifying the countryside: the impact of out-of-school care on rural landscapes of children's play', *Area*, 33 (2): 169–76.

Smith, F. and Barker, J. (2004) 'Inclusive environments? The expansion of out-of-school childcare in the United Kingdom' Children', *Youth and Environments*, 14 (2) http://www.colorado.edu/journals/cye/

Smith, F., Barker, J., Wainwright, E., Marandet, E. and Buckingham, S. (2008) 'A new deal for lone parents? Training lone parents for work in West London', *Area*, 40: 237–44.

Smith, N. (2002) 'New globalism, new urbanism: gentrification as global urban strategy', *Antipode*, 34 (3): 427–50.

UNICEF (2006) *The State of the World's Children 2007*. New York: UNICEF.

UNICEF (2007) *Child Poverty in Perspective: An overview on child well-being in rich countries*. Report Card 7. Florence: Innocenti Research Centre.

van Blerk, L. and Ansell, N. (2006) 'Children's experiences of migration in Southern Africa: moving in the wake of AIDS', *Environment and Planning D*, 24 (3): 449–71.

Wainwright, E.M. (2003) '"Constant medical supervision": locating reproductive bodies in Victorian and Edwardian Dundee', *Health and Place*, 9 (2): 163–74.

Warfa, N., Bhui, K., Craig, T., Curtis, S., Mohamud, S., Stansfeld, S., McCrone, P. and Thornicroft, G. (2006) 'Post-migration geographical mobility, mental health and health service utilisation among Somali refugees in the UK: a qualitative study', *Health and Place*, 12 (4): 503–15.

Warrington, M. (2005) 'Mirage in the desert? Access to educational opportunities in an area of social exclusion', *Antipode*, 37 (4): 796–816.

Waters, J.L. (2002) 'Flexible families? "Astronaut" households and the experiences of lone mothers in Vancouver, British Columbia', *Social and Cultural Geography*, 3 (2): 117–34.

Waters, J.L. (2006a) 'Emergent geographies of international education and social exclusion', *Antipode*, 38 (5): 1046–68.

Waters, J.L. (2006b) 'Geographies of cultural capital: education, international migration and family strategies between Hong Kong and Canada', *Transactions of the Institute of British Geographers*, 31 (2): 179–92.

16

Phobias and Safekeeping: Emotions, Selves and Spaces

Joyce Davidson

INTRODUCTION

Recognition of the centrality of socio-spatial anxieties and panic to contemporary life has become increasingly common beyond clinical circles and across a range of disciplinary writings. Feminist geographer Linda McDowell, for example, points out that 'anxiety is a central theme in a great deal of current work' (1996: 30), while historians Sarah Dunant and Roy Porter (1996) explore contemporary mental life in what they see as an *Age of Anxiety* (see also Wilkinson, 1999). Social theorist Jackie Orr (1990) describes panic disorders as arising in response to 'postmodern existence', and philosophers Kroker *et al.* (1989) speak of 'panic postmodernism'. Geography's recent 'emotional turn' has built on studies of phobic – among other – threats to personal safety and wellbeing, and questions of fear and anxiety are of increasing concern for social geographers today (Bondi *et al.*, 2005; Davidson and Milligan, 2004).

While safe-keeping is often conceptualized in terms of managing threats to physical safety (Brownlow, 2005; Davidson, 2003a; Day, 2000; Day *et al.*, 2003; Koskela, 1997, 1999, 2000, 2002, 2005; Koskela and Pain, 2000; Mehta and Bondi, 1999; Pain, 1991, 2000, 2006), this chapter aims to elucidate less familiar yet inherently geographical practices of *emotional* safe-keeping (Segrott and Doel, 2004). While the term itself may be unfamiliar, safe-keeping is used in preference to *safety* with the aim of emphasizing the active nature of the *process* of its achievement. A state of personal safety is never steady; it can never be accomplished or 'fixed' once and for all. Rather, the task of *keeping* ourselves safe is an ongoing procedure involving more or less continuous effort, vigilance and imagination, among other complex and relational, socio-spatial practices.

As this chapter will show, experience and management of agoraphobia is particularly – perhaps uniquely – salient for geographical understandings of emotional safe-keeping. The disorder is peculiarly well placed to provide insights into this largely taken-for-granted phenomenological *work* that safe-keeping entails, the work of wellbeing that is undertaken by all of us, each and every day of our lives. Agoraphobia is described by one of the foremost clinical researchers on the subject as 'the most common and most distressing phobic disorder seen in adult patients' (Marks, 1987: 323), and its devastating effects and frequent occurrence are perhaps responsible for the 'surge of interest' (Chambless, 1982: 1) in the condition since the late 1970s. Publications on agoraphobia and the related phenomenon of panic often begin by drawing attention to its contemporary prevalence (McNally, 1994: vii; Hallam, 1992: 114), and Rachman (1998: 115) has gone so far as to describe agoraphobia as 'the prototypical modern neurosis'. Agoraphobics are acutely aware of socio-spatial threats to the boundaries of the self, threats that most people manage rather thoughtlessly, but manage nevertheless through practices of boundary maintenance that phobic geographies throw into relief. The chapter will show how, by drawing attention to some of the more unusual ways that people manage relations with each other and with their environments, researchers have illuminated some of the ordinarily unnoticed aspects of personal geographies and practices of safe-keeping (Bankey, 2001, 2002; Davidson, 2003a; Parr, 2000). People and places are intimately interconnected, they shape and affect each other, and I argue that agoraphobia emphasizes, exaggerates, and has the potential to elucidate this dialectic.

In what follows, I review the various bodies of literature of relevance to phobias, panic and safe-keeping from a social geographical perspective. I begin with a short introductory segment that establishes a framework for my argument. The first part of the segment outlines definitions of agoraphobia, drawing particularly on clinical literature, while attempting to expand overly narrow psychological definitions through references to the social and spatial aspects of agoraphobia. The second part of this segment considers the phenomenology and embodiment of the condition, examining the various ways in which it is actually experienced by sufferers and how this experience is often marginalized in clinical accounts. I explore how theories and methods of feminist geographers have helped to rectify this failing, contributing to understandings of safe-keeping that take seriously the nature of threats to, and maintenance of, boundaries between self and space.

The remainder of the chapter is divided into four sections, followed by the conclusion. In the first of these sections I address questions of social space, relations and performance. Since agoraphobia is a spatially mediated anxiety, the problematic nature of social space is crucial to an understanding of agoraphobic experience (Carter, 2002; Milun, 2007). This section explores how sufferers' inability to engage with the social arena imposes severe restrictions on their life-worlds. The next section draws on geographical, sociological and architectural writings to consider how and why certain kinds of spaces and places are considered 'toxic'. The subsequent and concluding sections explore the disabling nature of social space and, in turn, a range of imaginative socio-spatial strategies for safe-keeping commonly employed by phobics.

In conclusion, I argue that a feminist embodiment of social geography can contribute to the production of spaces that are sensitive to the needs of those engaged in a constant struggle for safe-keeping. I consider the benefits of this research to agoraphobics as well as to social geographers seeking to further understand the emotional intersections between people and places.

INTRODUCING AGORAPHOBIC LIFE-WORLDS

- agora – Gk. Hist. An assembly; a place of assembly, esp. a market place.
- phobia – (A) fear, (a) horror, (an) aversion; esp. an abnormal and irrational fear or dread aroused by a particular object or circumstance.
- agoraphobia – [f. Gk. AGORA n. + -PHOBIA.] Irrational fear of open spaces.

(*Shorter Oxford English Dictionary*)

Contrary to popular opinion, the condition of agoraphobia actually relates to public and *social* as opposed to 'open' spaces. Although such widely held misconceptions are supported by dictionary definitions of the disorder, the *SOED* notes on the term's *origins* (above) do in fact provide substantial clues as to the realities of agoraphobia for its many sufferers. Exactly how many sufferers there are, however, is a matter of some debate, and estimates range from between 6 per 1000 (Mathews *et al.*, 1981: 12), to 6 per 100 (NIMH in McNally, 1994: 26; see also Kessler *et al.*, 2005a, b).

In Lewis Mumford's account of *The City in History*, the agora is characterized as an essential part of ancient Greek city life. It is 'the formal marketplace [... but also] the convenient open space where the elders met, big enough for the whole village to gather in' (1991: 158). It was 'laid out deliberately to serve alike as market, as place of assembly, and as festival place; and though one part of the agora was often reserved for housewives, *the agora was pre-eminently a man's precinct*' (1991: 177, emphasis added). Significantly, to this day, it is women who tend to have difficulties of a phobic nature with such public and arguably still masculine realms.[1]

The first usage of the term agoraphobia can be dated to 1871, when it was introduced by German psychiatrist Karl Otto Westphal to describe the fearful condition he found common to three of his patients. Agoraphobia was the term he chose to capture 'the impossibility of walking through certain streets or squares, or the possibility of doing so only with resultant dread of anxiety' (quoted in Marks, 1987: 323; see also Marks, 1975). In the contemporary context, the definition of agoraphobia employed in clinical practice and publication tends to be drawn from the American Psychiatric Association's *Diagnostic and Statistical Manual of Mental Disorders*. According to the *DSM (IV)*, the disorder involves 'recurrent unexpected Panic Attacks' (APA, 1994: 402–3), followed by persistent fears about future attacks and their consequences. Sufferers alter their everyday geographies in response, tending to avoid – typically crowded – places where they might be seen to be panicking and behaving strangely, and where it might be difficult to escape from; think of underground trains at rush hour or a holiday season mall and you picture an agoraphobic nightmare, an image that helps to illustrate why keeping-safe for agoraphobics involves the avoidance of such situations at almost all costs (Davidson, 2001b).

The vast majority of agoraphobia sufferers – around 89 per cent – are women (Clum and Knowles, 1991). Aside from this, however, there seem to be no other discernible predictive patterns. For example, social class or 'race', or 'types' of personality, all seem equally prone to agoraphobia (Milun, 2007: 21). The gendering of agoraphobia represents a central concern of geographical research (Bankey, 2001, 2002; Callard, 2006a, b; Davidson, 2000a, b, 2001a, 2002), and questions of why women experience more phobic threats to their safety than men will be considered in greater depth below. For those (women and men) who develop agoraphobia, the onset tends to occur between the ages of eighteen and thirty-five (Kessler *et al.*, 2005a, b; Ost, 1987), and the condition tends to be chronic (Michelson and Ascher, 1987). There is evidence that a degree of agoraphobia may remain for life (Gournay, 1989), and many sufferers will themselves attest to the fact that one can never be entirely 'cured' from agoraphobia, but must rather learn to cope with it on a continuing, daily basis (see also Chambless and Goldstein, 1982).

Clinical research on the issue of particular causes has not been entirely conclusive, but there is evidence that higher than usual levels of stress tend to be experienced prior to the onset of agoraphobia (Barlow and Cerny, 1988: 32; Michelson and Ascher, 1987: 217). While the nature of such stressors and negative life events vary between individuals, Rachman suggests, in a provocative insight taken further by geographical research, that what they may have in common is an ability to 'undermine one's sense of safety' (1998: 118).

With regard to issues of treatment of agoraphobia, reviews of recent literature suggest that the form most likely to be successful is a multi-faceted approach capable of recognizing and tackling each problematic aspect of the disorder (Rachman, 1998). Cognitive behavioural therapy (CBT) tends to be the contemporary treatment of choice, tackling patterns of thought as well as action through therapist-guided programmes of anxiety management and gradual exposure to feared situations (Barlow and Cerny, 1988: 28; see Milun, 2007: 223–51, on alternative therapies for agoraphobia).

It seems, then, that while the definitions and descriptions of agoraphobia to be found in the clinical literature acknowledge much of the disorder's complexity, its representation tends to be simplistic in certain important respects. While recognizing that agoraphobia is socially and spatially mediated, understandings of what this might *mean* for sufferers and how social and spatial theory might be of benefit are, as one might expect, limited (Davidson, 2002; Milun, 2007). In the sections that follow, I consider the ways in which some of these limitations have been at least partially rectified by geographers' *care*ful inclusion of sufferers' own voices (conspicuously absent from clinical accounts) and resolved further with reference to a sympathetic theoretical (socio-geographical, feminist and phenomenological) perspective. Such studies have worked to refine and improve existing 'definitions' of agoraphobia by offering a more spatialized and experientially influenced perspective that can better account for and understand the nature and (potentially pathological) implications of person/place relations.

In the following section, I want to begin the task of constructing a more 'intimate' picture of experience and meanings of agoraphobia by considering its implications for spaces of the self and threats to safety. I will first provide a brief clinical account of the 'defining' experience of agoraphobia – panic – before broadening the discussion to include non-clinical perspectives. While the definitive clarity of the former is not mirrored in non-clinical writings on agoraphobia, many of the latter are immensely valuable precisely because they eschew clinical precision in favour of socio-spatial and experiential significance, and cultural/historical context (de Swaan, 1981).

EMBODYING AGORAPHOBIA AND THE PHENOMENOLOGY OF PANIC

The phenomenological aspects of agoraphobia, which are of overwhelming and terrifying significance for its sufferers, clearly relate to the experience of panic. A panic attack is defined by *DSM IV* (American Psychiatric Association, 1994: 395) as being 'a discrete period of intense fear or discomfort' that involves, for example, heart palpitations and chest pain, sweating, shaking and shortness of breath, feelings of nausea, dizziness, and derealization (feelings of unreality) or depersonalization (being detached from oneself). These can be experienced in different combinations at different times, and often entail fears of dying or losing one's mind.

Social geographers, among others, have investigated the effect of these symptoms on sufferers' experience of embodiment and environment, revealing that panic radically problematizes subjects' understanding of themselves as clearly and distinctly separate from the world around them. Research has shown that the symptoms referred to above cause sufferers to question their sense of themselves and their bodily boundaries, ordinarily taken for granted, and that exploration of such phenomena is of crucial importance for understanding experience and meanings of agoraphobia. Derealization and depersonalization, for example, are commonly understood to involve strange and disturbing feelings relating to both 'inner' and 'outer' reality. During such experiences, according to Issac M. Marks, 'one feels temporarily strange, unreal, disembodied, cut off or far away from immediate surroundings' (1987: 342; see also Chambless and Goldstein, 1982).

This portrayal can be compared with the following quotation (taken from a self-help book) in which one sufferer describes personal experience of the phenomenon. The tenor of their description provides deeper insight, and puts a disturbing twist on our understanding of what it means to feel 'faint':

> [S]uddenly everything around me seemed unfamiliar, as it would in a dream. I felt panic rising inside me. ... I felt totally unreal, ... Two people came along and I almost stopped them to ask if they could see me – was I really there? (Melville, 1979: 13)

In another self-help book, Stanley N. Law communicates further the intensity of the experience.

> Suddenly, sensations stronger and stranger than any I had previously known charged through my body. ... I turned and twisted and tried to remove the devilish feelings that possessed me ... this evil thing threatened to rob me of my identity. ... Everything seemed to disintegrate. (1975: 53)

This sufferer feels that reality is 'tearing in on him', as if he were receding into an abyss, with a mighty hand trying to 'squeeze the breath, and every particle of self identity from [him]' (Law, 1975: 72). This quotation, and the one above, reveal that panic entails a horrendous sense of dissolution of self into one's environs, and a simultaneous feeling of invasion by one's surrounds. It severely disrupts our unconscious sense of ourselves, throwing the relation we have with our bodies, our selves, into profound question.

In agoraphobia, one's sense of embodied subjectivity is inescapably conspicuous, as indeed it is with many other manifestations of chronic illness and disability (Butler and Parr, 1999; Dorn, 1998; Moss and Dyck, 1999). But, given the ease with which we *normally* 'take for granted' our status as clearly defined individuals, as solid bodies which contain (and also constitute) our personalities, it comes as something of a shock to realize that, in Elizabeth Grosz's terms, we might inhabit 'volatile bodies'. For Grosz, mind and body alike are not static or impervious to our surroundings but labile and at least semi-permeable:

> [t]he limits or borders of the body image are not fixed by nature or confined to the anatomical 'container,' the skin. The body image is extremely fluid and dynamic; its borders, edges and contours are 'osmotic' – they have the remarkable power of incorporating and expelling outside and inside in an ongoing exchange. (1994: 79)

When the ability to subconsciously regulate these processes of incorporation and expulsion slip from our control, then our very existence is thrown into doubt. 'I was startled awake one day to realize that *I was almost entirely gone*. What woke me was my body, whose very being in the world suddenly shifted and changed everything' (Bordo, 1998: 80). From a phenomenological position, it is unsurprising that anxiety should manifest itself both 'bodily' and 'mentally' since theorists like Merleau-Ponty assume a model of identity which regards the body *as* the self, the 'self expressed' (Merleau-Ponty, 1962). Such phenomenological insights continue to influence feminist theory both within and beyond the discipline of philosophy, and have a significant and recurring role to play in social geographies of agoraphobia, a significance that stems precisely from the phenomenological understanding of embodiment and self-identity as being inextricably interconnected. This insight is crucial to interpreting and potentially understanding the meaning and experience of agoraphobia.

In contradistinction to the dominant cognitivism of most post-Cartesian philosophy there is something of a consensus among contemporary feminist theorists, geographers included, that the subjectivity or sense of self of each and every individual is thoroughly, absolutely, embodied. This re-emphasis on the body has drawn on numerous sources but, as Bordo (1993: 17) notes, owes as much if not more to the body-politics of second wave feminism as it does to the theorizing of Foucault. Whatever its origins, all agree that this long overdue acknowledgement of the interrelatedness of self-identity and corporeality opens new questions.

As soon as we recognize that the body and not just the mind is 'a medium of culture' (Bordo, 1993: 65; see also Reuter, 2002: 763), then the question of how women's self-identities and bodies are maintained and disciplined in and through the agency of an (often hostile) cultural environment becomes crucial. The question becomes one of the consequences for self-identity of the relative (im)permeability of that subject's boundaries to influences that are partially constitutive of, and yet potentially corrosive to, that identity. These boundaries can themselves no longer be envisaged in entirely physical or mental terms – as dependent, say, upon a 'strong constitution' or a 'weak will' – but as an inextricably complex combination of both. The question that is constantly asked of each of us is: how 'thick-skinned' can/should we be as we negotiate our daily geographies? How can we understand, and keep ourselves safe from, potential threats to our wellbeing from embodied interaction with social space?

One particularly useful sociological approach to embodiment that draws extensively on phenomenological theory is advanced by Williams and Bendelow in *The Lived Body* (1998). Like these theorists, I have found that attempts to extend and apply phenomenological understandings of embodiment to particular lived bodies in particular social contexts benefit considerably from an infusion of the sociological insights of Erving Goffman. For Williams and Bendelow, Goffman's carefully observed and empirically based 'carnal sociology' gives further practical credence to phenomenology, and his work is clearly of geographical significance, especially in its focus on the social settings in which bodily encounters occur. Goffman's work has been inspirational for geographies of agoraphobia because of his attempts to elucidate the nature of social anxieties, including stigma and embarrassment, and the tactics by which they are 'managed'.

In a statement that highlights Goffman's relevance for such projects, Williams and Bendelow write:

> For Goffman, successful passage through public space, whether it be the street, the supermarket, or a busy shopping mall, is both a practical problem and skilful accomplishment for the human agent, involving specific social rules and rituals which facilitate this passage and 'repair' disruptions to the micro-public order of social interaction. (1998: 56)

Precisely because of this focus on the largely taken-for-granted 'minutiae' of social encounters in practical(ly) 'everyday' situations – for the non-phobic at least – Goffman's work will be taken up in order to 'flesh out' geographical understandings of the phenomenal difficulties suffered by phobic selves in social space (see below).

SOCIAL SPACE, RELATIONS AND PERFORMANCE

In 'Spatializing feminism', Linda McDowell (1996: 29) emphasizes the need to perform the perhaps obvious but oft-avoided geographical task of *defining* space, and indeed Doreen Massey elsewhere (1993: 142) asserts that a discussion of this topic 'never surfaces because everyone assumes we already know what the term means'. Clearly, however, 'space' is used in geographical literature in a number of diverse and at times conflicting ways (Massey, 2005). Against this ambiguous background, McDowell begins her attempt at clarification by highlighting the importance of viewing space as 'relational and constitutive of social processes' and crucially, in her view, as inextricably connected with time (1996: 29; see also McDowell, 1999; Massey, 1992, 1993; Soja, 1989). In McDowell's sense, 'space' is not Newtonian, it is not an abstract pre-existing void, an empty container waiting to be filled by people, objects, etc. Space is something that in Lefebvre's (1994) terms is 'produced' through a (culturally mediated) dialectic between things and people.

Referring to spaces as relational need not imply that they are somehow less concrete, that they lack 'permanence' or 'solidity' and therefore cannot operate to anchor socio-cultural meanings and symbols. This is precisely why

McDowell wants to emphasize that space need not be conceived *only* as a 'set of flows' but can also be regarded as a 'set of places' which are specific locations that operate as territories, bounding and fixing these relations in socio-culturally variable ways.[2] Thus, while this characterization allows a sense of space as 'social morphology' (Lefebvre, 1994), crucially, it does not preclude discussion of 'sets' of places of potential import for understanding phobic geographies – the spaces, for example, of subjects' homes, train stations or malls – so long as the particular context is explained. For McDowell, 'spatial configurations, connections between places are significant only in the context of a specific question or investigation of specific sets of relationships' (1996: 31). Such relational articulations of space have an important role to play in social geography research, and the specific question and particular purpose of this chapter – to explore and illuminate the nature of certain socio-spatial anxieties – is facilitated by an appreciation of space that emphasizes relations between subjects (see Bondi, 2005; Jacobs and Nash, 2003).

Putting the subject centre-stage is explicit in Gillian Rose's (1999) account of 'Performing space'. Rose advances an experientially focused understanding of space that takes seriously the possibility of complex and unusual spatial experiences. Moreover, it allows for, indeed 'fits' with, agoraphobic narratives of deeply personal and confused, but evidently inter-relational and dynamic, experiences of (unsafe) space. Rose argues (1999: 248) that, as with Butler's (1990, 1993) account of gender, 'space is also a doing, that it does not pre-exist its doing, and that its doing is the articulation of relational performances'. Further:

> Space then is not an anterior actant to be filled or spanned or constructed, and to claim it is runs the risk of making a contingent spatial articulation of relationality foundational. Instead, space is practised, a matrix of play, dynamic and iterative, its forms and shapes produced through the citational performance of self–other relations. Which is not to say that space is infinitely plastic. Certain forms of space tend to recur. (Rose, 1999: 248)

The thinking and making of space is, for Rose, phantas(ma)tically complex. The processes involve emanations from and interactions (including revolts, refusals, inscriptions and investments) between three spatial modalities – the discursive, the fantasized and the embodied – and cannot be separated from the operation(s) of power. In relation to agoraphobic situations, the powerful forms of space that tend to recur are spaces infused with and reproductive of *fright*ful patriarchal ideologies and conceits. The perspectives, power and (often behind the scenes) performances of others can combine with subjective sensitivities to make space anxious and aversive, domestic, dull and drab, or oppressive and exclusive. And, for the agoraphobic subject caught up in the performance of such antagonistic space, it rarely *feels* as if she has much say in its making. Rather, she perceives herself a 'bit player', reacting against and retreating from the marginalizing performances of others (Davidson, 2003b).

This conceptualization of space as performative thus goes some way toward setting the context for addressing one question critical for this chapter: what causes certain spaces to be *felt*, by certain subjects, in a threatening way? In answering this question it is necessary to consider the role, activities, intentions – the performances – of others. These performances, combined with one's own (perhaps anxious) contribution, bring particular spaces into being; 'particular performances articulate their own spatialities' (Gregson and Rose, 2000: 441). Kathleen Kirby's view of subjective felt spatiality seems at least partially compatible with this account, and also with those of agoraphobics. She writes:

> the problem with space isn't just space;[3] it is the fact that there are other people in it – other people who are creating it, determining it, composing it … is it surprising then, that space could seem a bit hostile? (1996: 99)

This statement implies that space is charged somehow, populated with the constructions of others. However, most individuals, most of the time, are quite literally *impervious* to these unwholesome attributes of space. Space, as Elspeth Probyn points out, 'presses upon bodies differently' (1995: 83), to which it must be added that bodies, too, press differently on space (Valentine, 1996).

Clearly, it is not only feminist geographers who recognize that space is 'filled and animated by the reciprocal relations between individuals' (Vidler, 1991: 39). Opening his fascinating excursus on the damaging effect of particular (city, and thus manufactured) spaces on individual health and identity, architectural theorist Anthony Vidler makes the modest assertion that he wants to write a 'small history of modern space'. Following social and spatial theorists such as Benjamin, Simmel and Kracauer, Vidler conceives of space as 'the *expression* of social conditions' (1991: 39) and yet 'reciprocally *interdependent* with society' (1991: 32). In accordance with the feminist geographical approach introduced above, Vidler conceives of spaces and selves as mutually constitutive, affecting and at times afflicting each other. Individuals can and indeed do create, and are (at least partially re)created by, disturbing and pathological landscapes. In some respects, then, Vidler's account of self–space relations resembles that of another architectural theorist, who states that agoraphobia, 'like other urban pathologies, tells us something about the way space is constitutive of personality' (da Costa Meyer, 1996: 141).

For Vidler, space is 'of course, no more than a cultural and mental construction; for, in historical terms, like the body, or like sexuality, space is not a constant'. Rather (as Victor Burgin (1996) also notes) 'space has a history' (Vidler, 1993: 31). To produce the particular history he has in mind – a 'sociopsychological history of metropolitan space' – Vidler suggests beginning in 1871, the year that the 'essentially spatial disease' of agoraphobia was first identified (1991: 34; also see Carter, 2002; Milun, 2007). The geographical starting point for this history is situated in the pathoscapes of modernity's monstrous cities:

> The nineteenth-century city had been understood to harbor dangerous diseases, epidemics, and equally dangerous social movements; it was the breeding ground of the all-levelling masses, of frightening crowds, the unsanitary home of millions, an asphalt and stone wilderness, the opposite of nature. The metropolis carried forward all these stigmas, but added those newly identified by the mental and social sciences. It rapidly became the privileged territory of George Beard's neurasthenia, of Charcot's hysteria, of Carl Otto Westphal's and Legrand du Saulle's agoraphobia, of Benjamin Ball's claustrophobia. It sheltered a nervous and feverish population, over-excited and enervated, whose mental life as Georg Simmel had noted in 1903 was relentlessly anti-social, driven by money and haunted by the fear of touching. (Vidler, 1991: 34)

Georg Simmel was in fact crucial to the project of theorizing the mental life of modernity and the metropolis. On Vidler's reading, he:

> staged the 'sensitive and nervous modern person' in front of the backdrop of 'jostling crowdedness and motley disorder', and argued that an inner psychological barrier, a *distance* was essential for protection against despair and unbearable intrusion. The 'pathological deformation of such an inner boundary and reserve', Simmel noted, 'was called agoraphobia: the fear of coming into too close a contact with objects, a consequence of hyperaesthesia, for which every direct and energetic disturbance causes pain'. Simmel's diagnosis was at once spatial and mental: [... agoraphobia] was a product of the rapid oscillation between two characteristic moods of urban life: the over-close identification with things, and, alternately, too great a distance from them. (Vidler, 1991: 36–37)

This conception of 'distance', and the implications for subjects of its 'deformation', provide crucial insights into the subject's vulnerability when faced by crowds of others, and links with my usage of 'boundaries' in this chapter. The above account makes clear that social spaces of the city at this particular period in time were especially unsafe for 'sensitive individuals', especially given the emergence and increasing importance of 'space-conquering techniques' such as radio and railway (Schivelbusch, 1980; see also da Costa Meyer, 1996, on the connections between agoraphobia and the Industrial Revolution). Such technologies effectively *conquer* spaces *between*, robbing individuals of their comforting and insulating *distance* from others:

> For even as electricity overcame distance, it also worked to annihilate that *Denkraum* which was the zone or space of reasoning, destroying the only protection against the experience of phobia, the falling into unreason. (Vidler, 1993: 47).

The city (and its performance) thus entail a potentially disabling proximity with others, eroding 'any possibility for a stable distance of reflection' (Vidler, 1993: 46–7). When robbed of this 'distance', the invasive proximity of others is perceived by sensitive individuals to weaken their boundaries. Significantly, this proximity also creates far greater potential for objectification, the opportunity to be looked *at*, yet not engaged *with* as a subject, as in a conversational exchange. As Simmel explains, social life in the modern city

> shows a great preponderance of occasions to *see* rather than to *hear* people. ... Before the appearance of omnibuses, railroads and streetcars in the nineteenth century, men were not is [sic] a situation where for periods of minutes or hours they could or must look at each other without talking to one another'. (Simmel in Vidler, 1991: 41).

This insight, taken up more recently by Goffman (1963), is crucial to understanding the difficulties posed by social space for agoraphobics, who harbour intense fears of others' *looks* (Davidson, 2003b).

Agoraphobia, a condition inseparable from and inconceivable outwith its socio-spatial context, is clearly a source of fascination for Vidler. His account helps to situate the disorder historically and geographically in relation to the 'social estrangement that seemed to permeate the metropolitan realm', the form of alienation described by Georg Lukacs as the 'transcendental *homelessness*' of the modern world (Vidler 1991: 32). Agoraphobia was considered as proof that modern cities were in their very form *unhealthy* and, it is argued, emotionally *unsafe*. Camillo Sitte, in fact, used the disorder to justify his proposals to create 'small, protective city squares' in his native Vienna. Although he was simply mistaken in placing the problem with cities in their wide, open spaces, his recognition of the emotional importance of walls for facilitating a sense of safety was indeed most perceptive (da Costa Meyer, 1996: 145). Around the turn of the century, agoraphobia was considered, along with other newly emerging 'nervous diseases', to be 'characteristic' of city life, 'endemic to urbanism and its effects'. For the modern city's particularly female subjects, its effects were noisome and unnerving; disconcerting effects no doubt related to the fact that modernist space was 'constructed by and for men' (Deutsche, 1990).

This account recognizes that the symptoms (and performances) of agoraphobic panic have serious repercussions for individuals' perception (and creation) of the 'external' spaces of their life-worlds as well as the 'internal' spaces of their bodies (Davidson, 2000a, 2001a). Agoraphobic panic can induce a crisis in the 'boundary' between self and space that throws the *existence* of both into doubt. The dissembling, dissipative effects of agoraphobia can thus be seen to create a *garbled* geography, where that 'closest in', the body (Rich, 1986), is no longer kept safe or delimited from the outside world (see also Parr, 1999). The fearful fantasies projected and performed by agoraphobic panic create a social space corrosive to the subject's boundaries. In an extraordinarily vicious circle of performance/perception of panic, the agoraphobic subject subsumes the surrounding confusion and fears that she is 'losing her grip' on reality.

Kathleen Kirby writes similarly and insightfully of another spatial phobia, vertigo, that it involves 'a rift between subject and reality, the mobilization of the internal processes of the subject, and a new fluidity of the external realm' (1996: 99). In vertigo 'the internal/external relation breaks down, resulting in a degeneration of interior organization, and finally – one could imagine, in advanced stages – in a confusion of the external order too' (1996: 102). There are, then, other affects and effects of garbled spatial experience. Related to and perhaps arising from the problematization of bodily boundaries, is a crisis of *location*. The subject of phobic panic, whatever its 'object', evidently cannot *connect* normatively with her surroundings and feels 'out of place' in a disconcertingly alien world. Phobic accounts have shown that when panic surfaces, it threatens the dissolution of self such that the individual seems, quite literally, 'lost'. She no longer knows *where* she is, both in the sense that her surroundings have become unfamiliar and threatening and in the sense that she cannot *locate* or *delimit* her own identity; she feels 'spaced-out'. In Bordo's words:

> [e]ach of us [herself and her sisters] has suffered, each in her own way, from a certain heightened consciousness of space and place and our body's relation to them: spells of anxiety that could involve the feeling of losing one's place in space and time. (1998: 74)

Somewhat similarly, describing his own spatialized 'boundary crisis', Roger Caillois recounts a feeling of 'depersonalization by *assimilation* to space' (Caillois, 1984, quoted in Grosz, 1994: 47, emphasis added).

Clinical literature regularly includes references to, and lists of, the kinds of spaces and places that agoraphobics will tend to avoid. These, predictably, often include shops of many kinds, busy streets, restaurants and public transport, and are accompanied by statements about the *rationale* for agoraphobic avoidance. Such explanations can be summarized and paraphrased in terms of the agoraphobic's apparent fear of the consequences of panicking in such environments, that is, of being trapped and humiliated in public. I would, however, suggest that a more nuanced understanding of the nature and constitution of social space is required. There is more at stake here than subjects' anticipation of an aversive and fearful *response*. The agoraphobic's apparent *gut reaction* to social space should rather be seen as an *interaction*, as an embodied, emotional *exchange*, arising from a complexity of meanings, meetings and movements *between* particular selves and spaces. Clearly, this approach moves beyond the search for either internal (self) or external (space) explanations of agoraphobia, and is open to relational reconfiguration of both. I would suggest that by thus adopting a receptive, expansive attitude to space as 'performative', we would be better placed to conduct a sympathetic and meaningful exploration of agoraphobic landscapes, those spaces and places that partially 'produce' (and are partially 'produced' by) feelings of panic in susceptible individuals. Moreover, an approach that takes seriously the dynamic nature of self–space relations encourages analysis beyond the limitations of anxiety and exclusion. It makes room for consideration of resilience and resistance, and for exploration of agoraphobic strategies for safe-keeping in spaces felt to be 'toxic' in the extreme (Davidson, 2001b, 2003b).

CONTESTING AND COPING WITH TOXIC SPACE

This section seeks to investigate further the nature of problematic relations with social space and the difficulties agoraphobics find in its 'performance' (Freund, 1998; see also Dewsbury, 2000; Nelson, 1999 on 'performativity'). In particular, it questions why the routine activities that are hardly brought to consciousness in 'normal' experiences of social space become problematized as a source of intense anxiety for agoraphobics. As has been shown, agoraphobics fear being subjected to another's gaze, and try to avoid drawing visual attention and social intrusions to themselves. In this section, I argue that agoraphobics' fearful and avoidant behaviour can be interpreted as a 'breakdown' in their ability to utilize the 'everyday' mechanisms for safe-keeping highlighted by sociologists such as Goffman.

Goffman studies interactions between strangers, and uncovers the means by which people *manage* themselves in their relations with others. His analysis reveals a number of unspoken and largely taken-for-granted conventions, codes of conduct that govern our behaviour in the social realm and make it possible to remain comfortable in relatively close proximity with others. In Goffman's own words, '[w]hen in the presence of others, the individual is guided by a special set of rules ... called situational proprieties' (1963: 243). These conventions are intended to 'allow others their space' (Tseelon, 1995: 38), to allow the illusion that one moves in a private, protective sphere, even when firmly entrenched in the social world of strangers. Conventions of social behaviour can then be seen to dictate respectfulness towards boundaries of personal space, a respectfulness of the right 'not to be stared at or examined', that must be reciprocal if social relations are to feel safe. This allows individuals to maintain some control or 'mastery' over their immediate environs, and limit the extent of alienation that the other's presence can inflict.

Perhaps foremost among those strategies that Goffman's analysis highlights is that of 'civil inattention'. This entails:

> giv[ing] to another enough visual notice to demonstrate that one appreciates that the other is present (and that one admits openly to having seen him), while at the next moment withdrawing one's attention from him so as to express that he does not constitute a target of special curiosity or design. (1963: 84)

Civil inattention is the means by which individuals steer clear of the form of 'invasion' that is the direct gaze (Tseelon, 1995: 67), and maintain the pretence of indifference to the appearance and concerns of others.

However, to be 'one of the crowd', to not stand out and thus be subject to intense scrutiny, one needs to behave appropriately, according to certain situational rules. 'Paradoxically,' writes Goffman, 'the way in which he [sic] can give the least amount of information about himself ... is to fit in and act as persons of his kind are expected to act' (1963: 35). Of course, one needn't be aware of and intent on following explicit rules associated with particular situations. Rather, these often implicit behavioural standards and techniques of self-management are *internalized* so that we come to manage our behaviour, monitor movements and responses etc., in accordance with a tacit 'feel for the game', rather than by enacting formulaic codes.

The key to playing one's role in this 'drama' convincingly, and negotiating one's way around social space in a non-threatening, relatively inconspicuous and safe manner, is a 'disciplined management of personal appearance or "personal front"' (1963: 24) and an ability to display 'sufficient harnessing of the self' (1963: 27). One's face must be composed into an 'inscrutable mask'; indeed, we require a repertoire of faces, or masks, for a variety of situations, to maintain a comfortable degree of privacy. This principle of privacy might be defined as our ability to control the amount of information about ourselves that we display to others (Tseelon, 1995: 74). 'Putting on a face' as a tactic of social safe-keeping can be seen as one aspect of what Bauman (1993: 153) refers to as 'the art of mismeeting', a skill which *must* be mastered if one is to live among strangers (Davidson, 2003b). Bauman explains the necessity of this strategy thus:

> The overall effect of deploying the art of mismeeting is 'desocializing' the potentially social space around, or preventing the physical space in which one moves from turning into a social one. (1993: 155)

Goffman claims, via his empirical observations, to have uncovered other specifiable tactics and devices that subjects employ to *limit* their involvement in social space and their exposure to its inherent dangers. The extent to which they use these 'involvement shields' (Goffman, 1963: 40) and 'stalls' (Goffman, 1971: 56) may depend, amongst other factors, on their level of social anxiety, but they are by no means merely the preserve of 'extreme' or 'abnormally sensitive' subjects. For many, such safe-keeping strategies are in fact a familiar part of everyday social life. Perhaps one of the most obvious everyday examples of the 'involvement shield' would be that of the newspaper used by commuters in a manner that precludes social exchanges with others. Similarly, 'stalls' protect and indeed *create* private space, by 'provid[ing] external, easily visible, defendable boundaries for a spatial claim' (1971: 57). The following example is provided: 'at beaches devices such as large towels and mats can be carried along with the claimant and unrolled when convenient, thus providing a portable stall' (1963: 56). In this manner, the individual can partially stabilize and control the 'ever shifting dimensions' of personal space (1963: 58).

Alternatively, subjects can territorialize space by attempting to highlight their need to *use* it for particular purposes. 'Use space', according to Goffman, is 'the territory immediately around or in front of an individual, his [sic] claim to which is respected because of apparent instrumental needs' (1963: 58). For example, giving 'sports [people ...] the amount of elbow room they require in order to manipulate their equipment.' Clearly, however, while some strategies may successfully assert legitimacy over a given spatial domain, they will not necessarily prevent the intrusive *look* of the Other. Goffman's example of 'use space' might in fact invite and encourage audience involvement.

It seems then that the social world is rife with danger, and coping with it requires *trust* that others are practising civil inattention, that one is not constantly being stared at and invaded and thus robbed of the protective barriers of personal space. What, though, would happen were one to lose that trust in others, or be unable to trust one*self* to maintain a face or behave in a manner that invites unwelcome attention (Parr and Davidson, 2008)? Such a failure to manage social space has profound implications for the individual concerned, undermining one's ability to keep oneself safe.

> Failure or success at maintaining such norms has a very direct effect on the psychological integrity of the individual. At the same time, mere desire to abide by the norm – mere good will – is not enough, for in many cases the individual has no immediate control over his [sic] level of sustaining the norm. It is a question of the individual's condition, not his will; it is a question of conformance, not compliance. (Goffman, 1990: 152–3)

In terms of Goffman's (1969) dramaturgical analogy, agoraphobics might be regarded as suffering from a kind of 'stage-fright'. They shun 'public performances' where possible and strive to reduce their need to engage in 'impression management' to a minimum.[4] Goffman's description of how one can be 'thrown out of step' with social norms does, in fact, capture something of agoraphobic accounts of panic; in particular, experiences of depersonalization. 'When an incident occurs and spontaneous involvement is threatened, then reality is threatened ... and the participants will feel unruled, unreal and anomic' (1967: 135). This threat of breakdown is more acute in the presence of others:

> The 'strangeness' of strangers means precisely our feeling of being lost, of not knowing how to act and what to expect. ... Avoidance of contact is the sole salvation, but even a complete avoidance, were it possible, would not save us from a degree of anxiety and uneasiness caused by a situation always pregnant with the danger of false steps and costly blunders. (Bauman, 1993: 149)

Each and every agoraphobic sufferer has learned from painful experience that '[t]he surest way for a person to prevent threats to his [sic] face is to avoid contacts in which these threats are likely to occur' (Goffman, 1967: 15). However, complete avoidance of contacts is not always possible for the '[d]efence of social space is never foolproof. Boundaries cannot be hermetically sealed. There is no really infallible cure against strangers, let alone against the dread they arouse' (Bauman, 1993: 157). One might be required (for example, by pain or a strong sense of duty) to enter into social space for reasons as diverse as a trip to the dentist or an obligation to attend a family wedding (Davidson, 2003a). Failure to maintain one's 'composure' in these socially charged situations can lead to the individual having to struggle with what Goffman (1990) refers to as the 'stigma' of a 'spoiled identity'.

While the onset of agoraphobia typically entails a cessation, or at the very least, a radical curtailment of the subject's involvement in social space, the necessity of a 'face saving' front will continue even within their newly constricted life-worlds. Contact with the 'outside world' may extend no further than relations with close friends and family members, but many make massive efforts to conceal their agoraphobia even here. Once the process of putting on a face becomes a consciously felt need, then simply trying to fit in, to appear 'normal' in social space, involves a substantial effort of will. Regardless of its purpose, maintaining a pretence of this kind is exhausting, and impossible to keep up indefinitely. A place to repose, and recompose, must be found, and this often takes the shape of the subject's home.

Housebound (f)or safe-keeping?

Given the crisis state of social and spatial affairs that agoraphobia entails – of boundaries, distance and location – it is perhaps unsurprising that the sufferer should eventually become more or less temporarily house*bound*. Her boundless vulnerability means she may have no choice but to remain exclusively within the home, assuming its protective boundaries as reinforcement and extension of the psychocorporeal boundaries of the self. The agoraphobic thus *incorporates* her 'own four walls' as an essential element of her 'ontological security'.[5]

Clearly, the association of this sense of safety with the home is not a universal experience, but for some at least the home is 'a truly safe place, the container and springboard for integrated living … the foundation of an ontologically secure existence' (Marilyn K. Silverman, quoted in Bordo *et al.*, 1998: 90; compare Valentine, 1998). Agoraphobic accounts suggest a powerful contrast between meanings attaching to home spaces and the world beyond, a contrast of potential import for geographical understandings of safety. Feminist geographers have explored such issues in relation to distinctions between 'private' and 'public' spaces, arguing that the contours of this binary formation are as much a *product* as a reflection of binary constructions of gender (Bondi and Domosh, 1998; Dowling, 1998; Duncan, 1996). Perhaps, especially for the agoraphobic, whose condition 'straddles the fault line between public and private' (da Costa Meyer, 1996: 141), the boundaries between these spheres are very fluid and unfixed. This is evidenced by the fact that the home space, traditionally conceived as 'private', can itself become threatening and dangerous when, for example, relatives converge at Christmas (Davidson, 2003b). Likewise, the 'public' space of the town centre can be experienced as comfortable and safe when no one else is around. Ironically, given the common and legitimate concerns of non-phobic women for their safety, this is often when darkness provides calm and *cover* from the 'socializing' presence of others (compare Koskela and Pain, 2000; Mehta and Bondi, 1999).

The agoraphobic's experience of home can be ambiguous in other ways; for some, home becomes so 'secure' that they are rendered incapable of leaving, and it can thus simultaneously be experienced as both prison *and* asylum. But, despite the *ambivalence* of feelings, it is clearly the space of the home that is overwhelmingly perceived to be safe, and the (anti)social space beyond its confines that menaces and disturbs. The home might be regarded as a kind of 'architectural' aid to safe-keeping and reconstructing one's self-identity in the face of de(con)structive social space beyond its bounds. It thus seems relevant that, despite the achievements of feminism in expanding women's horizons, the gendered identities of women in general are *still* more likely to be enmeshed with the fabric of the home than those of men. In this context, agoraphobic women's tendency to experience home as a place of safety, of refuge, might be viewed as a retreat into a normatively feminine space where gendered boundaries are protected and potentially reinforced (Davidson, 2000a, 2001a).

In discussing emotionally difficult spaces and places, we might productively resist employing the loaded and potentially problematic distinction between public and private space (see Duncan, 1996), and better understand phobic concerns in relation to the *sociality* of space highlighted by Goffman.[6] The invasive kind of 'sociality' I have in mind tends to be encountered most consistently beyond the home, in, for example, social (and performative) spaces of consumption, where sheer numbers of others can oppress and confuse, and efforts of design are made to (over)stimulate subjects' senses (Davidson, 2001a,b; Goss, 1992, 1993; Gregson and Rose, 2000; Gregson *et al.*, 2002). Such spaces are, arguably, epitomized by large-scale shopping centres and malls, where stimulants and performances are taken to something of an extreme. These socially and sensorially overdetermined spaces 'yield both pleasure and anxiety, [such that] a "delightful experience" can quickly become a "nightmare"' (Falk and Campbell, 1997: 12). It is little wonder, then, that strategies for agoraphobic safe-keeping entail their avoidance at almost all costs, that even the ambivalent security of the home – man's castle, woman's *keep*? – is almost always preferable, by far.

Although some individuals experience panic even behind their own closed doors, it is important to recognize that the home will *still* be perceived as the safest place, because there, no-one else will *see* the sufferer panic. The experience of panic is always deeply debilitating, but if it must be endured, it is best done out of the public eye. It is also important to emphasize that agoraphobic individuals have differing abilities to cope with the everyday aspects of social and spatial life analysed in such detail by Goffman, and that there is a continuum of experiences from the 'normal' (that is, 'appropriate' and manageable) to 'abnormal' (inappropriate and unmanageable). Thus, while some sufferers retreat into the far reaches of their homes as a way of reining in the reach of panic, those who are more fortunate manage to extend the boundaries of the home outwards. Strategies for the creation of mobile senses of home-like safe-keeping are imaginative and varied, though the car is perhaps the most common and easily understood source of trans/portable (ontological) security (Davidson, 2003b). The use of the car, as with the home, to reinforce the boundaries of self-identity might be seen in terms of Arnaud Levy's concept of 'subjective space': for Levy, subjective space 'surrounds us like an envelope, like a *second skin*' (Levy, 1977, cited in Burgin, 1996: 213, emphasis added). The problem is that when the agoraphobic leaves home or gets out of her car, space ceases to be subjective. Once again she finds herself required to perform in front of those other people who create, determine and compose social space (Kirby, 1996: 99). Social space is often experienced as profoundly toxic and, one might say, *abject*, a term Julia Kristeva uses to denote that which we must 'radically exclude' from ourselves, but which is always present, threatening to invade us and causing *anxiety* (Kristeva, 1982; Sibley, 1995). In the face of such ever present (social and spatial, performative) dangers, how on earth does a phobic – or indeed *any* subject – manage to keep a sense of self safe?

Trans/portable tactics of safe-keeping

Beyond the safety of home or car, many sufferers find – unsurprisingly – that they need some kind of assistance to keep up their 'guard' and their (metaphorical and/or material) distance from others. A number of writers on agoraphobia have noted that sufferers tend to derive comfort from the use of dark glasses (e.g. Marks, 1987: 337–9). Such items can be understood to function, in Goffman's terms, as portable 'involvement shields'. Though obviously less effective than a brick wall, glasses can provide an invaluable sensation of 'cover', both in the sense of protection and of disguise. The covering of one's eyes can partially obscure one's feelings, but it can also make it more difficult for others to intrude on or 'trap' the subject by attempting to engage her in conversation or some other form of exchange. As Goffman points out, 'eye contact opens one up for face-engagement' (1963: 95), and so dark glasses shield one from involvement by literally blocking the potential for eyes to 'meet'.

The pushing of an object such as a pram can also assist ease of movement through social space, an enabling tactic frequently referred to by agoraphobics (Davidson, 2003b). In Goffman's terms, this strategy can be understood by imagining that the buggy effectively creates an area of 'use space' around the subject. It signals to others the need to keep their distance, at the same time conferring legitimacy on the subject's presence in social space. Perhaps the presence of children themselves can have something of a similar effect, blocking, or at least distracting attention from, the anxious subject and aiding the sense of safety. As Goffman emphasizes, the best defence against scrutiny is to not stand out, and performing as 'normal' (as possible) is a clear strategy for safe-keeping.

The structure and production of space *within* sufferers' homes can also reveal much about the experience of this debilitating disorder. In Goffman's (1959) terms, the walls of the home demarcate (like the face) a 'front region' from a backstage haven from social pressures. Sufferers' homes are frequently organized to minimize the fear of visual attention. Many sufferers try to construct safe space in and around their homes – 'blinds' inside, garden fences outside and so on – to work as visual aids to safety. Agoraphobic sense of spatiality is fragile, and needs to be asserted and defended more explicitly than would 'normally' be the case. Such experience of safe-keeping is peculiarly gendered even among non-phobics given that, in many contemporary Western societies at least, women are frequently more likely than men to be subjected to an intrusive and objectifying stare. This gendered phenomenon has been the focus of much feminist research, and theorists have explored visual objectification of women from many angles (Bordo, 1993; Colls, 2004; Kwan, 2002; Nash, 1996; Tseelon, 1995). One might surmise that the greater propensity for women to be stared at requires that they be adept at protective front management for safe-keeping – that women tend to have a greater need to protect themselves from visual intrusion than do men. For half of the population at least, 'doing gender' most likely involves an (ultra) awareness of the power of the Other's gaze, and this may go some way towards an explanation of the predominance of agoraphobia, as a spatially *and* socially mediated disorder, among women. After all, women are, in Goffman's (1967: 329) words, 'somewhat vulnerable in a chronic way to being hassled'.[7]

It is in this context, once we have discovered just how and why social existence can be so unnerving, that social geographical observation could be invaluable for the agoraphobic. Goffman's account, in particular, discloses those ordinarily taken-for-granted protective tactics that some sufferers must re-learn to enable (relatively) safe social engagement. Future research should aim to investigate further the practical means by which a degree of control can be reasserted over the subject's fragile social self. Many of us need to find ways to protect ourselves from the perceived peril of the public eye, but there are numerous other threats to safe-keeping that social geographers can help to reveal, and perhaps also, resist (Bondi, 2003; Bondi and Fewell, 2003; Davidson and Parr, 2008).

CONCLUSION: RE/SOLVING BOUNDARY CRISES

In its consideration of agoraphobic experience and attempts to manage social space, this chapter suggests that emotional states such as anxiety and safety are not always 'steady' or predictable, and can (be made to?) change over time. I have argued that emotions are interactive, rather than simply responsive. They come into being at the shifting interface between people and their environments, a dynamic and mutually constitutive relation that means we can at least partially influence the nature of social space and, in turn, the nature of its influence on our selves. This conclusion leads me to argue that a particular – feminist – embodiment of social geography could inform and help *perform* particular kinds of space (Rose, 1999), and thus enable more comfortable spatial engagements for those subjects continually struggling to keep themselves safe.

Agoraphobics must negotiate the least comfortable end of the spectrum between socio-spatial safety and anxiety, and while they may never become entirely *carefree*, neither must they remain confined within the four walls of their personal domestic sphere. Discussion of tactics for coping with and contesting toxic space reveals that it is possible for a path to be forged between these poles, for the agoraphobic to re-constitute herself as a relatively safely bounded individual in the face of the intrusive sociality of everyday life. Perhaps (emotionally) aided – at least initially – by 'involvement shields' such as dark glasses, the agoraphobic can come to learn that the same phenomena that previously called her safety into question can also serve to enhance and embolden her sense of embodied identity and *freedom*. Susan Bordo writes:

> Being outside, which when I was agoraphobic had left me feeling substanceless, a medium through which body, breath and world would rush, squeezing my heart and dotting my vision, now gave me definition, body, focused my gaze (Bordo et al., 1998: 83).

These metaphors, describing the shift from feeling *substanceless* in social space to having a sense of *definition*, are strongly evocative of the absence and presence of boundaries, and raise the possibility of 'translating' feelings of panic into feelings of excitement. Bordo raises the possibility that the agoraphobic might come to experience temporary loss of a 'normal' perspective as liberating. To open oneself up to excitement, to learn to endure and even enjoy the *potentiality* of panic without giving oneself over to it completely, is the phenomenal freedom to which the agoraphobic aspires. However, this process of *re-definition* is slow, often arduous and *risky*. It is usually achievable only via a process of unsafe exposure and *acclimatization* to toxic space, and the patience to persevere through almost imperceptible improvements. Very gradually, the agoraphobic's feelings of isolation and abandonment may become transformed and even replaced by a sense of freedom that is never entirely safe, but perhaps *tolerably* unstable and even welcome. Social space that challenges her boundaries and sense of safety can begin to be experienced positively, in terms of independence, as Bordo illustrates. Here, she explains how, when overcoming her agoraphobia, she began to enjoy her 'freedom', the:

> charge of leaving home, knowing that your body has been cut loose from the cycling habits of the domestic domain and is now moving unrooted across time and space, always to something new, alert to the defining gaze of strangers (Bordo et al., 1998: 81).

Emotional relations and socio-spatial interactions are obviously complex and confusing. That the stranger's gaze can be experienced as defining and not dissembling, that anxiety can be felt as intensely life-affirming rather than simply soul-destroying, reveals something crucial at the heart of socio-geographical and emotional experience. Safe-keeping and risk-taking are never clearly determined, separable or set in stone. They are inextricably connected, contentious and contestable boundary phenomena that must be continually and relationally reworked.

I want to close this chapter by suggesting that we can usefully draw on Bordo's and other feminist accounts of re-formed self-space relations, and put such embodied musings into practice for the benefit of phobic and other uncomfortably bounded women. Exposure to the look of others – an objectifying and clearly gendered phenomenon – heightens awareness of the precarious nature of self-hood and safety, and, in our defence, boundaries must be brought into being. They must be worked at and *made* to lie between us, and this is a project that ought to be undertaken inter-subjectively. Given that boundaries are negotiated in relation, the individual alone need not be held responsible for their production and maintenance. In this context, future feminist socio-geographical approaches to safe-keeping could usefully consider the role and value of women's self-help or, more appropriately, 'mutual support' groups. There is, I would argue, much potentially valuable research to be conducted in this area, given the possible benefits for emotional health of exchanges between women with similar but shifting embodied experience of boundaries (Davidson and Parr, 2008). It is perhaps in this supportive context that the possibilities for and affects of the social and spatial performance of 'boldness' (Koskela, 1997), among other assertions of feminist self-hood, spatiality, and empowered emotionality, could most productively be explored

ACKNOWLEDGMENT

'Parts of this chapter have been abridged from Davidson (2003), *Phobic Geographies*, and I would like to thank Ashgate Publishing for granting permission to reproduce this material in its current form. Thanks also to the editors of this collection and to Victoria Henderson for providing helpful feedback and editorial support in the preparation of this manuscript.'

NOTES

1 See Callard (2006a, b) and Reuter (2002, 2006) for thorough and insightful discussion of the historical gendering of agoraphobia.

2 Although perhaps McDowell (1996: 32) might sometimes be regarded as tending to replace an absolute notion of space with an abstract notion of place as an 'absolute location', as somewhere static.

3 However, for Gregson and Rose there is no 'just space'; '"stages" do not pre-exist their performances, waiting in some sense to be mapped out by their performances; rather, specific performances bring these spaces into being' (2000: 441).

4 Goffman defines 'stage confidence' as 'the capacity to withstand the dangers and opportunities of appearing before large audiences without becoming abashed, embarrassed, self-conscious, or panicky' (1969: 170).

5 This term is defined by Giddens (1997: 36) as the 'confidence or trust that the natural or social worlds are as they appear to be, including the basic existential parameters of the self and social identity'.

6 Where the term 'public' is used, I refer to spatial situations stereotypically or colloquially conceived in such terms. For example: public parks, public transport, the public eye; generally speaking references to 'public', should be read as designating 'social' space.

7 There are of course alternative gendered explanations of potential value for social geographies of phobias and safe-keeping; see Davidson (2003) for more detailed discussion.

REFERENCES

American Psychiatric Association (1994) *DSM-IV: Diagnostic and Statistical Manual of Mental disorders* (4th ed.). Washington, DC.

Bankey, R. (2001) 'La donna e mobile: Constructing the irrational woman', *Gender, Place and Culture*, 8 (1): 37–54.

Bankey, R. (2002) 'Embodying agoraphobia: rethinking geographies of women's fear', in L. Bondi, H. Avis, A. Bingley, J. Davidson, R. Duffy, V. Einagel, A.-M. Green, L. Johnston, S. Lilley, C. Listerborn, M. Marshy, S. McEwan, N. O'Connor, G. Rose, B. Vivat, and N. Wood (eds), *Subjectivities, Knowledges, and Feminist Geographies: The Subjects and Ethics of Social Research*. Lanham, MD and Boulder, CO: Rowman and Littlefield. pp. 44–56.

Barlow, D. and Cerny, J. (eds) (1988) *Psychological Treatment of Panic*. New York: Guilford Press.

Bauman, Z. (1993) 'Sociology and Postmodernity', *Sociological Review*, 36 (4): 790–813.

Bondi, L. (2003) 'Empathy and identification: conceptual resources for feminist fieldwork', *ACME: International Journal of Critical Geography*, 2: 64–76.

Bondi, L. (2005) 'Troubling space, making space, doing space', *Group Analysis*, 38 (1): 137–49.

Bondi, L. and Domosh, M. (1998) 'On the contours of public space: a tale of three women', *Antipode*, 30: 270–89.

Bondi, L. and Fewell, J. (2003) '"Unlocking the cage door": the spatiality of counselling', *Social and Cultural Geography*, 4: 527–47.

Bondi, L., Davidson, J. and Smith, M. (eds) (2005) *Emotional Geographies*. Aldershot, UK: Ashgate.

Bordo, S. (1993) *Unbearable Weight: Feminism, Western Culture, and the Body*. Berkeley: University of California Press.

Bordo, S. et al. (1998) 'Missing kitchens', in H. Nast and S. Pile (eds), *Places Through the Body*. London and New York: Routledge. pp. 72–92.

Brownlow, A. (2005) 'A geography of men's fear', *Geoforum*, 36 (5): 581–92.

Burgin, V. (1996) *In/different Spaces: Place and Memory in Visual Culture*. Berkeley, CA and London: University of California Press.

Butler, J. (1990) *Gender Trouble: Feminism and the Subversion of Identity*. London and New York: Routledge.

Butler, J. (1993) *Bodies that Matter: On the discursive limits of 'sex'.* New York and London: Routledge.

Butler, R. and Parr, H. (1999) *Mind and Body Spaces: Geographies of Illness, Impairment and Disability*. London and New York: Routledge.

Callard, F. (2006a) 'Understanding agoraphobia: Women, men, and the historical geography of urban anxiety', in C. Berkin, J.L. Pinch, and C.S. Appel (eds), *Exploring Women's Studies: Looking Forward, Looking Back*. Upper Saddle River, NJ: Prentice-Hall. pp. 201–17.

Callard, F. (2006b) "'The sensation of infinite vastness": or, the emergence of agoraphobia in the late 19th century', *Environment and Planning D: Society and Space*, 24: 873–89.

Callois, R. (1984) 'Mimicry and legendary psychasthenia', *October 31*, Winter: 17–32.

Carter, P. (2002) *Repressed Spaces: The Poetics of Agoraphobia*. London: Reaktion Books.

Chambless, D. (1982) 'Characteristics of agoraphobia', in D. Chambless and A. Goldstein (eds), *Agoraphobia: Multiple Perspectives on Theory and Treatment.* New York: John Wiley & Sons.

Chambless, D. and Goldstein, A. (eds) (1982) *Agoraphobia: Multiple Perspectives on Theory and Treatment*. New York: John Wiley & Sons.

Clum, G. and Knowles, S. (1991) 'Why do some people with panic disorder become avoidant?: A review', *Clinical Psychology Review*, 11: 295–313.

Colls, R. (2004) '"Looking alright, feeling alright": emotions, sizing and the geographies of women's experiences of clothing consumption', *Social and Cultural Geography*, 5 (4): 583–96.

da Costa Meyer, E. (1996) 'La donna e mobile: Agoraphobia, women, and urban space', in D. Agrest, P. Conway and L. Kanes Weisman (eds), *The Sex of Architecture*. New York: Harry N. Abrams.

Davidson, J. (2000a) '"... the world was getting smaller": women, agoraphobia and bodily boundaries', *Area*, 32 (1): 31–40.

Davidson, J. (2000b) 'A phenomenology of fear: Merleau-Ponty and agoraphobic life-worlds', *Sociology of Health and Illness*, 22 (5): 640–60.

Davidson, J. (2001a) 'Pregnant pauses: Agoraphobic embodiment and the limits of (im)pregnability', *Gender, Place and Culture*, 8 (3): 283–97.

Davidson, J. (2001b) 'Fear and trembling in the mall: Women, agoraphobia and body boundaries', in Isabel Dyck, Nancy Davis Lewis, and Sara McLafferty (eds), *Geographies of Women's Health*. London and New York: Routledge. pp. 213–30.

Davidson, J. (2001b) 'A phenomenology of fear: Merleau-Ponty and agoraphobic life-worlds', *Sociology of Health and Illness,* 22 (5): 640–60.

Davidson, J. (2002) 'All in the mind?: Women, agoraphobia, and the subject of self-help', in L. Bondi, H. Avis, A. Bingley, J. Davidson, R. Duffy, V. Einagel, A.-M. Green, L. Johnston, S. Lilley, C. Listerborn, M. Marshy, S. McEwan, N. O'Connor, G. Rose, B. Vivat and N. Wood (eds), *Subjectivities, Knowledges, and Feminist Geographies: The Subjects and Ethics of Social Research*. Lanham, MD and Boulder, CO: Rowman and Littlefield. pp. 15–33.

Davidson, J. (2003a) *Phobic Geographies: The Phenomenology and Spatiality of Identity.* Burlington, VT and Aldershot, UK: Ashgate.

Davidson, J. (2003b) '"'Putting on a face'": Sartre, Goffman and agoraphobic anxiety in social space', *Environment and Planning D: Society and Space*, 21 (1): 107–22.

Davidson, J. and Milligan, C. (2004) 'Embodying emotion, sensing space: Iintroducing emotional geographies', *Social and Cultural Geography*, 5: 523–32.

Davidson, J. and Parr, H. (2008) 'Anxious subjectivities and spaces of care:Therapeutic geographies of the UK National Phobics Society', in A. Williams (ed.), *Therapeutic Landscapes*. Burlington, VT and Aldershot, UK: Ashgate.

Day, K. (2000) 'The ethic of care and women's experiences of public space', *Journal of Environmental Psychology*, 20: 103–24.

Day, K., Stump, C. and Carreon, D. (2003) 'Confrontation and loss of control: masculinity and men's fear in public space', *Journal of Environmental Psychology*, 23: 311–22.

de Swaan, A. (1981) 'The politics of agoraphobia: On changes in emotional and relational management', *Theory and Society*, 10: 359–85.

Deutsche, R. (1990) 'On men in space', *Artforum*, 21–3.

Dewsbury, J. (2000) 'Performativity and the event: enacting a philosophy of difference', *Environment and Planning D: Society and Space*, 18 (4): 473–96.

Dorn, M. (1998) 'Beyond nomadism: the travel narratives of a "cripple"', in H. Nast and S. Pile (eds), *Places Through the Body*. London and New York: Routledge.

Dowling, R. (1998) 'Suburban stories, gendered lives: thinking through difference', in R. Fincher and J. Jacobs (eds), *Cities of Difference*. London and New York: Guilford Press.

Dunant, S. and Porter, R. (eds) (1996) *The Age of Anxiety*. London: Virago.

Duncan, N. (1996) 'Renegotiating gender and sexuality in public and private spaces', in N. Duncan (ed.), *BodySpace*. London and New York: Routledge.

Falk, P. and Campbell, C. (eds) (1997) *The Shopping Experience*. London: Sage.

Freund, P. (1998) 'Social performances and their discontents: The biopsychosocial aspects of dramaturgical stress', in G. Bendelow and S. Williams (eds), *Emotions in Social Life*. London and New York: Routledge.

Goffman, E. (1959) *The Presentation of Self in Everyday Life*. New York: Doubleday.

Goffman, E. (1963) *Behaviour in Public Places: Notes on the Social Organization of Gatherings*. London: Collier Macmillan. Ltd.

Goffman, E. (1967) *Interaction Ritual*. Harmondsworth: Penguin Books.

Goffman, E. (1969) *Where the Action is*. London: Allen Lane, Penguin Press.

Goffman, E. (1971) *Relations in Public: Microstudies of the Public Order*. Harmondsworth: Penguin Books.

Goffman, E. (1990) [1963] *Stigma: Notes on the Management of Spoiled Identity*. Harmondsworth: Penguin Books.

Goss, J. (1992) 'Modernity and post-modernity in the retail landscape', in K. Anderson and F. Gale (eds), *Inventing Places: Studies in Cultural Geography*. Cheshire: Longman.

Goss, J. (1993) 'The "magic of the mall": An analysis of form, function, and Meaning in the contemporary retail built environment', *Annals of the Association of American Geographers*, 83 (1): 18–47.

Gournay, K. (1989) 'Introduction: The nature of agoraphobia and contemporary issues', in K. Gournay (ed.), *Agoraphobia: Current Perspectives on Theory and Treatment*. London and New York: Routledge.

Gregson, N. and Rose, G. (2000) 'Taking Butler elsewhere: Performativities, spatialities and subjectivities', *Environment and Planning D: Society and Space*, 18: 433–52.

Gregson, N., Crewe, L. and Brooks, K. (2002) 'Shopping, space, and practice,' *Environment and Planning D: Society and Space*, 20 (5): 597–617.

Grosz, E. (1994) *Volatile Bodies: Towards a Corporeal Feminism*. Bloomington and Indianapolis: Indiana University Press.

Hallam, R. (1992) *Counselling for Anxiety Problems*. London: Sage.

Jacobs, J. and Nash, C. (2003) 'Too little, too much: cultural feminist geographies', *Gender, Place and Culture*, 10 (3): 265–79.

Kessler, R., Chiu, W.T., Demler, O. and Walters, E.E. (2005a) 'Prevalence, severity, and comorbidity of 12-month DSM-IV disorders in the national comorbidity survey replication', *Archives of General Psychiatry,* 62: 617–709.

Kessler, R., Berglund, P., Demler, O., Jin, R., Merikangas, K.R. and Walters, E.E. (2005b) 'Lifetime prevalence and age-of-onset distributions of DSM-IV disorders in the national comorbidity survey replication', *Archives of General Psychiatry,* 62: 593–602.

Kirby, K. (1996) *Indifferent Boundaries: Spatial Concepts of Human Subjectivity*. New York and London: Guilford Press.

Koskela, H. (1997) '"Bold walk and breakings": Women's spatial confidence versus fear of violence', *Gender, Place and Culture*, 4 (3): 301–20.

Koskela (1999) *Fear, Control and Space. Geographies of Gender, Fear of Violence and Video Surveillance*. Helsinki: Publications of the Department of Geography, University of Helsinki.

Koskela (2000) '"The gaze without eyes." Video surveillance and the changing nature of urban space', *Progress in Human Geography*, 24: 243–65.

Koskela (2002) 'Video surveillance, gender and the safety of public urban space. "Peeping Tom" goes high tech?', *Urban Geography*, 23: 257–78.

Koskela (2005) 'Urban space in Plural: Elastic, Tamed, Suppressed', in L. Nelson and J. Seager (eds), *A Companion to Feminist Geography*. Oxford: Blackwell.

Koskela, H. and Pain, R. (2000) 'Revisiting fear and place: women's fear of attack and the built environment', *Geoforum*, 31: 269–80.

Kristeva, J. (1992) *Powers of Horror: An Essay on Abjection*. New York: Columbia University Press.

Kroker, A., Kroker, M. and Cook, D. (1989) *Panic Encyclopedia: The Definitive Guide to the Postmodern Scene*. London: MacMillan Education Ltd.

Kwan, M.P. (2002) 'Feminist visualization: Re-envisioning GIS as a method in feminist geographic research', *Annals of the Association of American Geographers*, 92 (4): 645–61.

Law, S. (1975) *Inspired Freedom: Agoraphobia – A Battle Won*. London and New York: Regency Press.

Lefebvre, H. (1994) *The Production of Space*. Oxford: Blackwell.

Levy, A. (1977) 'Devant et derriere soi', *Nouvelle Revue de Psychanalyse*, 15 (Spring): 93–4.

McDowell, L. (1996) 'Spatializing feminism: Geographic perspectives', in Nancy Duncan (ed.), *BodySpace*. London and New York: Routledge.

McDowell, L. (1999) *Gender, Place, Identity*. Cambridge: Polity Press.

McNally, R. (1994) *Panic Disorder: A Critical Analysis*. New York and London: Guilford Press.

Marks, I. (1975) [1969] *Fears and Phobias*. London: William Heinemann Medical Books.

Marks, I. (1987) *Fears, Phobias and Rituals*. New York and Oxford: Oxford University Press.

Massey, D. (1992) 'Politics and space/time', *New Left Review*, 196: 65–84.

Massey, D. (1993) 'Power geometry and a progressive sense of place', in J. Bird, B. Curtis, G. Robertson and L. Tickner (eds), *Mapping the Futures: Local Culture, Global Change*. London and New York: Routledge.

Massey, D. (2005) *For Space*. London: Sage.

Mathews, A., Gelder, M. and Johnston, D. (1981) *Agoraphobia: Nature and Treatment*. London and New York: Tavistock.

Mehta, A. and Bondi, L. (1999) 'Embodied discourse: on gender and fear of violence', *Gender, Place and Culture*, 6 (1): 67–84.

Merleau-Ponty, M. (1962) *Phenomenology of Perception* [trans. C. Smith]. London: Routledge and Kegan Paul.

Melville, J. (1979) *Phobias*. London: Unwin Paperbacks.

Merleau-Ponty, M. (1962) *Phenomenology of Perception* (trans. C. Smith). London: Routledge and Kegan Paul.

Michelson, L. and Ascher, L. (eds) (1987) *Anxiety and Stress Disorders: Cognitive-Behavioral Assessment and Treatment*. New York: Guilford Press.

Milun, K. (2007) *Pathologies of Modern Space*. New York: Routledge.

Moss, P. and Dyck, I. (1999) 'Body, corporeal space and legitimacy. Chronic illness: women diagnosed with ME', *Antipode*, 31 (4): 372–97.

Mumford, L. (1991) *The City in History: Its Origins, its Transformations and its Prospects*. London: Penguin.

Nash, C. (1996) 'Reclaiming vision; looking at landscape and the body', *Gender, Place and Culture*, 3: 149–69.

Nelson, L. (1999) 'Bodies (and spaces) do matter: the limits of performativity', *Gender, Place and Culture*, 6 (4): 331–54.

Orr, J. (1990) 'Theory on the market: Panic, incorporating', *Social Problems*, 7 (4): 460–84.

Ost, L.G. (1987) 'Age of onset in different phobias', *Journal of Abnormal Psychology*, 96: 223–29.

Pain, R. (1991) 'Space, sexual violence and social control. Integrating geographical and feminist analyses of women's fear of crime', *Progress in Human Geography*, 15: 415–31.

Pain, R. (2000) 'Place, social relations and the fear of crime: a review', *Progress in Human Geography*, 24 (3): 365–87.

Pain, R. (2006) 'Paranoid parenting? rematerializing risk and fear for children', *Social & Cultural Geography*, 7 (2): 221–43.

Parr, H. (1999) 'Delusional geographies: the experiential worlds of people during madness/

illness', *Environment and Planning D: Society and Space*, 17: 673–90.
Parr, H. (2000) 'Interpreting the hidden social geographies of mental health: Ethnographies of inclusion and exclusion in semi-institutional places', *Health and Place*, 6: 225–37.
Parr, H. and Davidson, J. (2008) '"Virtual trust": online emotional intimacies in mental health support', in J. Brownlie, A. Greene, and A. Howson (eds), *Researching Trust and Health*. New York and London: Routledge.
Probyn, E. (1995) 'Lesbians in space. Gender, sex and the structure of missing', *Gender, Place and Culture*, 2 (1): 77–84.
Rachman, S. (1998) *Anxiety*. Sussex: Psychology Press Ltd.
Reuter, S. (2002) 'Doing agoraphobia(s): a material-discursive understanding of diseased bodies', *Sociology of Health and Illness*, 24 (6): 750–70.
Reuter, S. (2006) *Narrating Social Order: Agoraphobia and the Politics of Classification.* Toronto: University of Toronto Press.
Rich, A. (1986) *Blood, Bread and Poetry: Selected Prose, 1979–1985*. New York: Norton.
Rose, G. (1999) 'Performing space', in D. Massey, J. Allen, and P. Sarre (eds), *Human Geography Today*. Cambridge: Polity Press.
Schivelbusch, W. (1980) *The Railway Journey: Trains and Travel in the 19th Century* ([trans. A. Hollo]). Oxford: Blackwell.
Segrott, J. and Doel, M. (2004) 'Disturbing geography: obsessive-compulsive disorder as a spatial practice', *Social and Cultural Geography*, 5 (4): 597–614.
Sibley, D. (1995) *Geographies of Exclusion*. London and New York: Routledge.
Soja, E. (1989) *Postmodern Geographies: The Reassertion of Space in Critical Social Theory*. London: Verso.
Tseelon, E. (1995) *The Masque of Femininity*. London: Sage.
Valentine, G. (1996) '(Re)negotiating the "heterosexual street": Lesbian productions of space', in N. Duncan (ed.), *BodySpace*. London and New York: Routledge.
Valentine, G. (1998) '"Sticks and stones may break my bones": a personal geography of harassment', *Antipode*, 30: 305–32.
Vidler, A. (1991) 'Agoraphobia: spatial estrangement in Simmel and Kracauer', *New German Critique*, 54: 31–45.
Vidler, A. (1993) 'Bodies in space / Subjects in the city: Psychopathologies of modern urbanism', *Differences: A Journal of Feminist Cultural Studies*, 5 (3): 31–51.
Wilkinson, I. (1999) 'Where is the novelty in our current "age of anxiety"?', *European Journal of Social Theory*, 2 (4): 445–67.
Williams, S. and Bendelow, G. (1998) *The Lived Body: Sociological Themes, Embodied Issues*. London and New York: Routledge.

17

Fear and its Others

Hille Koskela

FEAR AND ITS OTHERS

Fear as a social problem has long been a field of interest. Debates around fear have been going on within urban politics, as well as in such academic disciplines as sociology, anthropology, criminology and geography. As a research topic, fear is fascinating. It brings together three standpoints in a unique way: the individual, the social and the spatial. Fear is a truly *personal* emotion which both reflects *social* relations and has influence on them. Most often, the consequences of fear take *spatial* forms. Fear has the power to modify spatial realities. Without a spatial dimension, fear would be nothing much but a feeling – a state of mind. Whenever it relates to an individual or a group of individuals 'making a move', it contributes to the *social production of space.*

As an everyday topic, fear is tricky. The more it is on the agenda, the less lonely fearful people may feel. Whenever fear is acknowledged, it becomes a legitimate issue rather than an anomaly. Public debate turns blame away from an individual and treats fear as a collective problem that relates both to those who are fearful and to those who create threat. Yet, simultaneously, the more fear is on the agenda, the more it will reproduce itself, grow, multiply and reach towards new directions. Talking about fear easily exaggerates it. Dangers are perceived as more probable, threats as common and omnipresent. *The social production of fear* does not take place through an individual's own experiences, but through the experiences of the others, circulated either in face-to-face conversations or in the media.

Despite being an individual emotion, fear is indeed, to a great extent, socially produced. For a researcher, it may take a while to reason that in very mundane daily conversations the difference between 'be careful' and 'don't be afraid' is of utmost importance. It is exactly in those minuscule, sensitive differences in the discourses we produce where the social production of fear takes place. Sentences such as 'be careful' have an unarticulated message: someone or something is or might be dangerous and it is the hearer's responsibility to avoid it.

Personally, fear can contribute to lowering one's quality of life and shrinking one's spatial realities. Being afraid easily overcomes everything. It is not just an emotional experience but also a bodily experience which freezes an individual. There is nothing much one can do about it; hardly any way to suppress it. Collectively, fear plays an important role in the process of 'Othering'. If there was no Other there would be no reason to be afraid. Fear *needs* the Other. Whether it is justified (as one can imagine in the case of a lone woman crossing a notorious park alone at night) or unjustified (as in the collective Western imagination of dangerous alien nationalities), fear is determinedly tied to the process of Othering. Being either directly or indirectly targeted towards 'someone else' – someone potentially dangerous – fear has an unholy alliance with prejudice, hate and anger. However, it was not always conceived in this way. As a topic of academic understanding, fear has a long history which deserves a closer look.

This chapter will take its reader on a journey across time, and try to grasp how fear has been conceptualized from the past decades to present times. Chronology, however, is only part of the story, because most of these traditions are still alive as parallel paradigms. I will start the journey by focusing on humanistic geography, where fear is understood as an individual emotion, as part of the sense of place, and the Others barely have a role. From there, I will continue to feminist geography, which sees fear as a form of power relation and identifies the Others who keep up fear and hence sustain control. While feminist interpretations of fear are most often connected to local settings, the next part will point to the globalization of fear. The Others in the context of global terrorism are continuously present in the collective imagination, but yet impossible to identify. This leads to widespread prejudice and territorial defense. In the last part, I will focus on urban space and examine how fear takes forms in structures and social relations. Fear has enormous effects on everyday urban realities.

TOPOPHOBIA: 'NO OTHERS'

In the academy, there has been a persistent tendency to treat 'the emotional' as the less valuable end of the rational–emotional dichotomy, and emotions have habitually been regarded as taken for granted and not worth conceptual examination (e.g. Abu-Lughod and Lutz, 1990; Nussbaum, 2001; in geography see Rose, 1993). Emotional experiences are often ambivalent or mutable by nature. There is no sound reality to be grasped, but instead multiple unstable, nebulous and unpredictable realities. Hence, emotions have been hard to conceive of by traditional scientific means. Furthermore, when emotions were first studied, they were mostly regarded as entirely subjective, without any understanding of their connections to wider social processes. The rational–emotional dichotomy, however, is an artificial academic construction which turns interest away from some essential parts of humanity. Emotions can be considered as a form of intelligence – as judgements in which people acknowledge the importance of things that they are unable to control (Nussbaum, 2001). People's spatial relations are saturated with emotions. Human relationship to places and spaces contain various feelings: attachment, excitement, love, desire, nostalgia, repulsion, aggression, curiosity – and fear.

Within the discipline of geography, emotions were first launched as an issue within humanistic geography (e.g. Tuan, 1974, 1979; Relph, 1976; Ley and Samuels, 1978; Porteous, 1990). The challenge of this field was to study the emotional connections that human beings had to physical environments. Places were then, perhaps for the first time, examined as being something beyond the simple measurable geometry of spatiality. Place, when conceptualized as 'a center of meaning constructed by experience' and 'known not only through the eyes and mind but also through the more passive and direct modes of experience', evades objectification (Tuan, 1975: 151). When talking about the humanistic conceptualization of place, it must be understood as a response to the dominating trend of positivism in the 1960s (Rose, 1993: 41). With this response, geographers managed to bring the previously excluded reasoning of emotions, feelings and the sensibilities of every day into academic discourse.

On an emotional level, individuals' relations to places are anything but straightforward. Physical environments as such, and the meaning-giving that happens when people are experiencing these environments, melt together. Buildings and activities are perceived as meaningful in various ways: they can be beautiful or ugly, useful or hindrances, enjoyable or alienating, protective or frightening, etc. (Relph, 1976). The emotional was one of the core subjects of humanistic geography because its essential concept of 'sense of place' can itself be considered as a feeling – a feeling of being an insider, of belonging somewhere.

People's experiential relationship with place is largely based on feelings and emotions. The concept of *topophilia* – described as 'a love of place', or a positive commitment attached to particular place – has been used to describe a strong sense of place or local identity (Tuan, 1974). When scholars started to pay attention to meanings and feelings attached to places, antipathy, disgust and fear were among those. As opposed to topophilia there was *topophobia*: an individual could perceive a place as unpleasant, dangerous or frightening (ibid.). While topophilia was described as the positive side of the human–place relation, often with a nostalgic tone, topophobia was seen as the unpleasant side of this relation. Sense of place can also be oppressive.

Traditional 1970s humanistic geography saw that the relationship between people and places is an essential part of living, and that fear – topophobia – will rupture this relationship. Mostly, insideness and attachment to place have been quite idealistically described as synonyms for a safe haven. For an individual to feel 'inside' a place is to feel safe and 'at home', and the experience of outsideness is the reverse of these states (e.g. Tuan, 1974; Relph, 1976). It is in outsideness where the alienating, unreal or unpleasant nature of place resides. Fear has influence on sense of place: insecurity in everyday living responds to 'an insensitivity to place' (Sparks et al., 2001: 895).

Yi-Fu Tuan (1979) also launched the idea of *landscapes of fear,* to which negative meanings were attached. These landscapes were defined by imagination of potential dangers and threats. Tuan perceived this concept as a metaphor. Rather than being interested in what constitutes fear, or how it influences everyday life, he focused on immaterial imagined constructions (see also Porteous, 1990). These landscapes were invisible rather than concrete, tying together attitudes, values and physical responses. The metaphor was used in order to enable a 'study of imaginative landscapes from children's fairy tales to the perception of natural hazards' (Gold and Revill, 2003: 33).

Giving meaning to places is a part of 'being in the world'. Perception of places plays an important role in the production of emotions: it is possible to have feelings and bonds for places similar to those established between people (González, 2005). Place relations shape individuals' identity. Positive feelings and memories build up this identity, negative ones – such as fear, frightening or threatening experiences – gnaw holes in it. Topophobia, thus, is an unwanted condition by definition. Fear of an environment will cause stress, detachment and alienation. When emotions are attached to places, they tend to be long lasting. Experiences of fear, in a certain place, are *remembered*. Place, as a theoretical concept, is 'slow and sticky'. Emotions attached to places are more or less permanent – they will stay in individuals' minds.

Humanistic geographers have pointed out that the original purpose of human dwelling was to *provide shelter*. Cities were built as fortresses which would protect the inhabitants against threat (Tuan, 1979). In that sense, it can be claimed that the history of fear is as long as the history of humanity. Providing shelter against anything threatening or dangerous would be a basic need. The history of 'defensive design' parallels the history of the evolution of urban places

(Schneider and Kitchen, 2002; Ellin, 2003; Bauman, 2005). Danger, at early times, was perceived as coming from outside and threats were mostly tied to the culture–nature dichotomy: the imminent elements were often part of nature (Tuan, 1979). Real and symbolic protective edges were to define human dwelling. Walls were erected at the boundaries of cities, citadels, castles and empires. The mythical walls and towers of Jericho and other ancient cities were 'early examples of urban target hardening in an effort to deter predators and war' (Schneider and Kitchen, 2002: 68). The walls of the Roman cities were examples of walls that represent simultaneous aggression and defense: they were built to protect the 'civilized' Roman communities from the 'barbarians' outside (Marcuse, 1997: 105). This 'premodern fear' (Robin, 2004) has parallels to contemporary emotional relations to places.

Humanistic geography provides a particular conceptualization of fear which opens up several interesting points of view. It focuses on the triangle of place, individual and fear. There are three elements that contribute to the production of fear and the disruption of a sound place relationship: phobias, experiences and memories. Phobias are deep, existential states of mind such as topophobia or agoraphobia (see Joyce Davidson's chapter – Chapter 16 – in this volume). Experiences modify relations to place, and unpleasant, frightening or violent events create fear. Memories of something unpleasant sustain fear and keep it attached to a specific place or to certain types of places.

Individuals can use various strategies in order to cope with fear. One can seek protection, try to avoid frightening places, or endeavour to overcome one's fear. Seeking protection can take a personal form of self-defense or a more collective form of building a shelter. Avoidance strategies will mean spatial restrictions, which are tighter the more widespread fear is. If, for example, fear is attached to a particular city or a part of a city, restrictions are not necessarily very constraining; but if fear is of a more general nature, it can change an individual's life profoundly. Escapism can become a strategy for life. The third strategy is more proactive. One can try to 'take risks', negotiate and overcome the fear. I will return to this topic later in this chapter.

While the understandings of providing shelter and negotiating risks do still matter, the early trends in geography can be criticized of being somewhat naive. The potential threat was presumed as being outside social relations. It was not the Other that one needed to be protected against. Rather, danger was conceptualized as something unspecified, flickering, non-personal, not power related. Later, there have been lines of thought that have challenged this view, yet still keeping fear in the centre of their focus. It has been pointed out that the threat can come from inside as well: being inside does not necessarily equate with being safe (Rose, 1993; Kern, 2005). The city walls, as well as having a role in protecting cities' goods and inhabitants, are linked to community organization, land economics and technological changes (Schneider and Kitchen, 2002). Further, boundaries have 'different meanings for different people, and even for the same people' (Marcuse, 1997: 112). It is not necessarily the actual boundary that matters; but the meanings of boundaries, both physical and symbolic ones, lie in the *act of 'drawing'*: in dividing people onto two different sides.

Since the material and the social fields of action are fundamentally intertwined, the geography of fear should not be explained as just a combination of frightening physical structures and social situations. Fear is to be conceptualized through the emotion-related and power-related production of space. Space and social characteristics are seen as mutually modifying, interacting dimensions which deeply affect the nature and shape of fear. Hence, insecurity should be regarded as a problem that relates to inequality and polarization in societies. Fear and crime are part of a larger problem and the main focus of debate should be expanded to cover social power relations.

(FEMINIST) GEOGRAPHY OF FEAR: 'LOCAL OTHERS'

While humanistic geography headed towards comprehending the relationship to place and what role threat plays in the formation of frightening places, feminist geography – as it developed since the 1980s – had a different focus. It tried to identify the everyday practices which produce fear or undermine it, and to understand the (often gendered) social power relations behind fear. Scholars endeavoured to take into account symbolic connotations embedded in space – symbols of danger or threat – and the gendered or other social relations which contribute to changing the nature of space. Space was seen to be produced in the ostensibly private and personal but simultaneously power-related elbowroom negotiations, route decisions and mobilities.

In other words, there was a paradigmatic shift from using the concept of *place* to developing the concept of *space*. This did not mean that feminist geographers neglected emotions. Rather, space was perceived as becoming 'meaningful through experience and interpretation' (Rose, 1993: 146). Nevertheless, the issues surrounding fear and one's environments were no longer explained as an (unwanted) form of individual experience or a disruption in the human–place relationship, but as a form of collective social production of things. In this shift, fear was *politicized*. Concepts such as fear and danger were no longer seen as unavoidable, detached matters, but socially produced conditions. In this politicization of fear resides the Other.

When emotions are politicized, understanding of the experiencing, sensitive and sentimental 'individual' changes. It became clear that there is no such thing as sole, isolated individuals, but that personal identities – and feelings – are constructed through and in power relations (e.g. Rose, 1993; Massey, 1994; Nussbaum, 2001). The 'pure' individual experience of place, which was the main research topic of humanistic geography, was 'contaminated' with those social relations in which space is produced.

Discourse of fear – the communication of threats and the symbolic awareness and expectation of danger and risk – is an essential part of everyday life. The social production of fear takes place in manifold formal and informal arenas: in parental and spousal warnings, in other daily conversations and rumors, in the media, in crime-prevention advice and so on (Valentine, 1992; Furedi, 2002; Banks, 2005; Altheide, 2006). These all foster imaginations of threats and avoidance strategies as well as dangerous and safe spaces. What is acceptable in a particular time and place varies. What might be a perfectly acceptable behaviour for women during the day may be regarded as reckless at night (Koskela, 2003). What might be tolerated behaviour for the young people on a school yard may be interpreted as threatening in the city centre (Pain, 2003; Thomas, 2005). What might be accepted behaviour among sexual minorities in semi-public 'pink' space is regulated by (often unarticulated) social norms in public 'heterosexual space' (Duncan, 1996). The norms vary according to gender, sexuality, age and so on.

Danger is learned in *childhood*: 'children are taught to "say no, run and tell" if approached by a stranger' (Stanko, 1996: 57). For children, the warnings and restrictions imposed by parents are the main source of information about danger. At present, young people have experienced greater socialization into fear, having grown up in times when fear has been one of the leading guidelines of parenting (Pain, 2001; Furedi, 2002). Knowledge about danger is accumulated and carried into adult life. Fear is part of *women's* socialization. While it is evident that research on gendered fear has not focused on women solely, and that men's fear is worth interpretation of its own (see for example Brownlow, 2005), the focus on women's fear is justified here by claiming that this literature has been a pioneer in the research on fear, and by stating that women's fear is able to reveal structures and patterns that also apply to the parallel fears of other (somehow subordinate) groups.

As Gillian Rose (1993: 143) argues, 'fear is partly about being defined as a woman'. Beliefs about vulnerability and dangerousness are central to conceptions of gender and are constructed and transmitted through conversation (Hollander, 2001). Women are expected to act as if they were (potential) victims and interpret men's behaviour as potentially dangerous (Stanko, 1996). The social production of fear is often based on stereotypical images about what is criminal and who is more likely to commit crime (Madriz, 1997). Fear is often constructed from a perspective that reinforces prejudice. Women's race prejudice and race fear are shaped and reflected in their moving habits (Day, 1999).

Fear is connected to feelings of vulnerability and women's subordinate position (Smith, 1987; see also Pantazis, 2000). Women's fear is of specific interest because it is common and widespread. There is more to this, however: women's fear differs from men's because of its nature and its effects on women's lives (Pain, 1991). Women are more likely to restrict their (spatial) behaviour because of fear (Valentine, 1989). The gender-specific experiences that arouse fear range from minor forms of sexual harassment to rape (Gardner, 1995). Gendered fear is power-related: women's images of fearful spaces are not only a product of how they individually perceive their environment but also of the way space is controlled by different groups. Ideas about gender and its relationship to vulnerability and danger are pervasive in talk about violence, and this talk is further marked by ideas about age, race, social class and sexual identity (Hollander, 2001).

In early times of feminist geographies of fear, one task was to challenge the so-called *fear paradox*. The idea of a paradox described the simplistic notion that the only justified reason for fear would be the one that is drawn from crime statistics. This reasoning lead to a conclusion – later labelled as 'notorious' (Pain, 2001) – that the fear of crime felt by women and the elderly is 'irrational' because, according to the statistics, they were less likely to be victimized than, for example, young men. Women, however, are more likely to assess their risk of personal violence, including in relation to domestic violence, and feel more able to admit vulnerability (Stanko, 1996). Further, women do not always report crime – even serious ones such as rape – and hence these experiences often remain outside statistics (Stanko, 1990). It must also be acknowledged that all types of crime are not equal: rape – which women are most afraid of – is perceived to be extremely serious, changing one's life for ever. As Rachel Pain (1991: 421) has argued, sexual harassment 'evokes fear of more severe sexual attack through routinely creating a state of insecurity and unease amongst women'.

It is the *power of uncertainty* that keeps women meek, not the calculated risks. Intuition and learned knowledge can be contradictory, and feelings are often based on both (Koskela, 1997: 304). Disapproving feelings can lead to sensible strategies of being in space and moving around. Even when the origins of fear appear irrational and internally contradictory, the resulting reactions can be comprehensible. Emotions and feelings can never be conceived as a mathematical function of actual risks. Rather, they are complicated products of personal experiences, memories and social relations which surround the individual.

The critique of the fear paradox helped to develop the understanding that fear of women, the elderly and members of ethnic minority groups is 'linked to their subordinate social, economic and political status' (Pain, 2001: 900). Fear can thus reflect systematic structural violence rather than actual attacks. Fear has a connection to social inequality, and some types of crime – namely, hate crimes, genderbashing and gaybashing – specifically target minority groups (Namaste, 1996; Perry, 2001; Mason, 2005). It has been pointed out that sexist, racist, homophobic and ageist harassment, which is not necessarily considered as criminal, also extends fear of crime.

These types of experience are often disparaged and invalidated. Sexual harassment and minor violent attacks are easily described with a phrase 'nothing really happened' because women tend combine the experiences with a more serious imagined possibility of 'how much worse it could have been' (Kelly and Radford, 1996).

Women's decisions concerning the routes they choose and places they go to are modified by the threat of violence. Public space can be considered as a territory from which women are often excluded by harassment and fear of male violence, because men hold greater rights to it than women (Gardner, 1995; Macmillan et al., 2000). Violent attacks and sexual harassment constantly remind women that they are not meant to be in certain spaces. Fear produces 'a sense of space as something tricky, something to be negotiated, a hazardous arena' (Rose, 1993: 146). Women commonly aim to distance themselves – in both space and time – from potential attackers (Valentine, 1992). Women's fear is not an isolated private matter, but their spatial constraints are intertwined with unequal social relations.

In the late 1980s, Gill Valentine (1989) argued that women's fear of violence is *a spatial expression of patriarchy*. Later, the argument became more sophisticated: space is produced in the gendered practices of everyday life. This process is only partly conscious, and is deeply connected to larger structures in which both women and men reproduce culturally defined spatial structures. Neither gender passively experiences space: they actively produce, define and reclaim it, negotiate threats, and read the signs of danger (Koskela, 1997). Feelings of fear are simultaneously a consequence of women's subordinate position and their own contributions to the perpetuation of gendered power in relation to space. Women's decisions not to go out in the street are producing a different kind of space than their decisions to go out. If women stay indoors for fear of violent attack, their oppressors gain more control of space. By restricting their mobility because of fear, women unwittingly reproduce masculine domination over space. With violence – and with a threat of violence – city streets are kept as male-dominated, heterosexual spaces (Rose, 1993).

Women are not to be regarded as a unique and homogenous group (e.g. Madriz, 1997; Day, 1999; Hollander, 2001; Pain, 2001). Not all women are equally fearful. The recognition of *diversity and difference*, and paying attention to the intersections of gender, age, race, ethnicity, sexuality, class, income, able-bodiedness and area of residence, are essential. The 'embodied discourses' of fear take place in multiple subject positions (Bondi and Mehta, 1999). It is important to acknowledge that women are active agents, not just passive victims: many women are confident and well able to cope with their environments and to take possession of space (Koskela, 1997). Gender relations are to be understood as 'non-personalized' reciprocal and complex power relations that always include the possibility of resistance. As Rose argues, '[s]kin colour, class and gender are all social attributes which are inscribed onto bodies; and part of women's sense of oppression, of confinement, is their awareness of that process' (1993: 145). When gender, age, race and class are perceived as 'interlocking systems' (Day, 1999), or 'pliable positions' (Pain, 2003), it becomes superficial to detach them.

Nevertheless, fear is connected to the formulation of social control. Previously, the control of women had a moral basis and society was structured by norms on what is 'suitable' for women. In contemporary societies, *fear has taken the place of moral norms*. The question of 'what is suitable' has been replaced by the question of 'what is safe'. Hence, the social production of fear contributes profoundly in the definition and formation of social gender relations. The idea of women being endangered in public space is part of the construction of power. In addition, similar kinds of modes of thinking restrict the mobility of children and the elderly and, at least in some parts of the world, also of people of colour. Fear should thus simply not be approached as just an individual feeling. It is always a matter of power.

The approach of feminist geography made an essential difference to humanistic geography and expanded understanding of fear. After the discussions that took place in the 1980s and 1990s, fear was perceived as a socially produced phenomenon which needs collective political solutions rather than individual deeds. However, the threat, while being politicized, was not yet globalized. The feminist approach was most influential in focusing on the 'micro scale': individual mobilities, cities and detailed forms of urban space. The causes of fear were local rather than global.

POST-9/11 FEAR: 'GLOBAL OTHERS'

In the late 1990s and early 2000s, a new approach to fear developed. While this approach can be described as multidisciplinary, space had a crucial role in its conceptualizations – perhaps as a result of the 'spatial turn' which touched most of the social sciences at that time. The connection between the terrorist attack on New York's World Trade Center on 11th September 2001 (and other terrorist attacks in Madrid, London and elsewhere since then) and changes in societies is not obvious, and it is hard to say whether there really was 'a rupture'. There is no point in glorifying '9/11' by presenting it as a beginning of a completely new era, but it must be acknowledged that it made a difference to how fear was conceptualized. The local threats, which were connected to gender relations, ageism and the construction of youth as dangerous, were replaced by – or at least combined with – global threats. Furthermore, many of the theories and explanations of fear, which originally had been developed before the attack, suddenly became extremely popular and were used in explaining both why the attack took place and what happened after it (Davis, 1990; Ellin, 1997; Young, 1999; Bauman, 2000; Presdee, 2000; Garland, 2001; and Furedi, 2002, the first edition of which was published in 1997).

It seems clear that the troubles and insecurities people face are more difficult to grasp than before, and the boundaries between worries about crime and other, vaguer kinds of anxiety and concern are blurring (Sparks et al., 2001: 896). Zygmund Bauman (2006: 130) talks about 'security obsession'. There are more and more connections between fear as a situated experience and fear as a transformation of culture and economy. Fear is set as assemblages (Pain and Smith, 2008). New forms of vulnerability appear to be combined with moral ascendancy and fear of the Other which easily leads to different forms of exclusion of people regarded as outsiders. People draw borders between 'us' and various kinds of 'them'. Caution, mistrust and tense social relations form a new condition of living: the 'culture of fear' (Furedi, 2002).

As Frank Furedi, in the opening of his latest book, states: 'The politics of fear appear to dominate public life in Western societies. We have become very good at scaring one another and appearing scary' (2006: 1). The conceptualization of fear underwent a change which can be described as a move from micro-scale to macro-scale. Rather than being part of the everyday spatialities one habitually negotiates, fear became an omnipresent, all-pervading state of living. As Bauman accurately points out, '[f]ear takes root in our motives and purposes, settles in our actions and saturates our daily routines' (2006: 133). It no longer has a tangible set of targets as previously – such as a potential male rapist in a dark park – but people are just collectively 'shaken' and generally fearful. On the one hand, fear is enigmatic and ubiquitous and danger seems to be everywhere. On the other hand, since danger has become more widespread, it has become more difficult to identify and avoid. Global tensions and local insecurities are no longer seen as separate but have become intertwined in a fundamental way, local Others being replaced by global Others. Fear needs to be rethought in this new *globalized context*.

Typical for the social relations of this time is 'the continuous reformulation of ordinary experience as dangerous' (Furedi, 2002: 113). In the culture of fear 'caution has become institutionalized to cover every aspect of life' (ibid.: 108). Threats are seen as 'normal', unpleasant but unavoidable parts of life. This leads to a situation where individuals do not aim to reduce threats but to *protect* themselves and their families. Fear provides a justification for behaving in a self-centred and family-oriented way: for defending one's own. As I argued before, since the beginning of the history of fear, one of the central elements of it has been to protect territories, to defend against incursion which is most often perceived as coming 'from outside'.

Now, this attitude has been exaggerated. As Jock Young (1999: 67) puts it, '[y]ou want above all to avoid trouble rather than understand it'. When the expectation of presumed 'full security' is not fulfilled, there is increasing frustration which 'channels anxiety into a desire to locate and punish the culprits' (Bauman, 2006: 130). People believe that they should defend themselves against 'dangerous enemies' rather than be concerned about their welfare and prospects for rehabilitation (Garland, 2001). Instead of being devoted to supporting the welfare state and taking care of others, people are committed to sustaining social control and spatial exclusion.

The meaning of the concept 'terrorism' is socially constructed and highly contested, and there is a growing tendency to label almost any unwanted activist coalitions as terrorist groups (see e.g. Wekerle and Jackson, 2005). Nevertheless, it clearly has influences in everyday life: the fear of terrorism is associated and equated with the fear of the Other. The most important qualities of contemporary terrorism are its randomness and its ability to target a whole society: these keep up fear. Fear of terrorism is a combination of collective experience, political rhetoric and public commemoration. Fear now links more and more to questions of inclusion and exclusion, blaming and boundary drawing, justice and welfare, social conflicts and spatial divisions. The individual experiences and emotions reflect global events, national reactions and media representations of the time.

The focus of research has been changing accordingly. Globalized fear requires explanations that were not used before. The picture has become more complicated. Patriarchal power is by no means the only form of power that contributes to the production of fear, but it seems to be just one structure among others. Gender relations are not less meaningful than before, but they are often combined with or overpowered by a vague fear of the Other, which is defined in terms of race, colour of skin, religion, culture or country of origin. The connectedness of global geopolitical fears and local everyday fears has become more palpable than before, and this has effects on how research questions are formulated (Pain and Smith, 2008). Globalized fear has challenged meanings of place and forced a rethink of the concepts of space, boundaries and scale (Williams, 2003). Cultural, political, economic and religious relations and structures all contribute to the social production of fear. It has become less obvious who is 'in power' or how power works: the conventionally powerful Western cultures (and people) feel threats coming from the conventionally less powerful cultures (and people). As Sparks and colleagues point out: 'traditions of research that treat "fear of crime" as a separate and discrete object of social enquiry and policy intervention are exhausted' (Sparks et al., 2001: 895). Instead of either individual emotions or international relations, fear is situated in a complicated setting which includes 'rescaling and reterritorialization of security as both a concept and a practice' (Coaffee & Murakami Wood, 2006: 504). Global fears are grounded in local settings (Pain and Smith, 2008).

Securitization – the formulation of various things as questions of security – has become pervasive. The language of security permeates every sphere of life, which is markedly apparent in the increasing emphasis placed on aspects of 'risk' and 'security' across social life (Jayasuriya, 2007). Securitization emphasizes extreme politicization and heightened attempts at governmental control and undermines trust, communication and small-scale actions. The rhetoric of terrorism and threat is used in order to gain political consensus. One of the aims of the political agenda of securitization has been to attempt to blur the boundaries between dissent and what are defined as acts of terrorism: the repression of progressive movements has been normalized by the 'anti-terrorist frame' (Wekerle and Jackson, 2005). Further, fear is used as a means of manipulation: beliefs are constituted and manipulated by those who seek to benefit (Altheide, 2006). It is clearly possible to exaggerate fear and articulate it for particular political purposes (Coleman, 2004). As Furedi argues, '[i]n the name of personal health and safety, many of us are willing to accept the kind of structures that would seem intrusive or moralistic if they came from a traditional figure of authority' (2002: 153). Fear is used as a *political tool* – both on the part of the Western regimes and on the Others. Fear is 'a fundamental and often mortally powerful motor of politics' (Sparks et al., 2001: 885). While 'as a social problem, fear of crime has been widely used for political ends' (Pain, 2001: 901), since the terrorist attacks, the mobilization of fear for political purposes has become more intense than before (Robin, 2004).

Potential 'real' risks are accompanied by *security talk*. Indeed, 'fear is constituted through interaction and meaning with others' (Altheide, 2006: 24). In a saturated media environment this talk and the images presented – the semiotics of danger – have become extremely important. Any terrorist act is, among other things, a *spectacle* of terror in which wide audience and global attention are essential (Kellner, 2004). Terrorism is partly 'a war of signs', which can be mobilized for different interests or politics (Luke, 2003). This does not only apply to terrorist groups, but in the politics of the spectacle both 'sides' employ media events to promote their agendas. Successful political projects – whether they are acts of terror or conventional political strategies – are based on carefully planned and executed media strategies. As Douglas Kellner points out, 'politics are increasingly mediated and constituted by the production of spectacular media events and the political agendas of their producers' (2004: 59). Any actual acts are followed by a particular narrativization with competing interpretations of its meaning and significance (Bird, 2003). The vagueness of the 'enemy' – the absence of an apparent target for reprisals – has contributed to the construction of symbolic enemies (Altheide, 2006: 100). The media discourses exaggerate the binary opposition between good and evil and generate 'a highly dichotomous opposition, undermining democratic communication and consensus' (Kellner, 2004: 47).

The use of the discourses of terrorism has become both politicized and anchored in global and national policies. It has caused tension in international relations as well as a shift in Western foreign policies, emphasizing national strategies for protecting territory (e.g. Graham, 2004). Western governments easily approach the rest of the world with a biased, prejudiced attitude with an emphasis on fundamentalism. Fear is at the core of the new racism. It has increased tensions in racial- and religion-related relations. There has been a rise of intolerance, anti-semitism and Islamophobia. Many ethnic and minority groups now face routine harassment as well as racial and religious profiling (Wekerle and Jackson, 2005; Hopkins, 2007). At worst, they are deemed to pose a threat to national security.

The management of risk is dealt with at the level of population rather than of individuals: it is the *movement* of people which is posed as a security risk (Jayasuriya, 2007, italics added; see also Willams, 2003). The contemporary geopolitical forces are propelling the rise of a new authoritarianism, heightened border anxieties, hostility towards refugees and the legitimization of violence towards the Other (Papastergiadis, 2006). The more eagerly people seek to protect their own and gain security, the more tight becomes the national border control (Bigo, 2006). This will change our concept of both the dynamics of present global flows and that of belonging (Papastergiadis, 2006). Being able to move freely and being entitled to a positive sense of place have become privileges.

Furthermore, fear has led to an upswelling of nationalism. Patriotism has become a synonym of endless 'war on terrorism' (Altheide, 2004). The 9/11 attack itself was 'local' in some sense, but was presented – specifically in the United States – as a national disaster (and yet, had effects which are truly global). Both the victims (of the attack) and the 'new enemy' were quickly nationalized (Smith, 2002: 99). This attack has been widely interpreted in an American context – as shaking American values, and being the most significant act of terror in the country (e.g. Savitch, 2003; Eisinger, 2004). There are obvious parallels between the anti-Communist and cold-war rhetoric and this crisis, which emphasized the importance of security in both national and international politics (Jayasuriya, 2007).

However, both the '11-M' bombing in Madrid in 2004 and the '7/7' attack in London in 2005 were also followed by a rhetoric which promoted national security and a shift towards a security state. Fortification of space increased (Coaffee, 2004) and there were racialized interpretations in which young Muslim men were associated with terrorism (Hopkins, 2007). Fear has become the leading paradigm throughout the Western world (Marcuse, 2004). This is apparent, even in the Scandinavian countries, where terrorism has hardly played any concrete role. Policing strategies target terrorism and pose it as one of the main national threats. Furthermore, fear plays an important role in the former communist countries, where former 'fear of the state' has been transformed into fear of crime which has, paradoxically, led to a longing for a stronger state (Los, 2002). The communist regime caused worries because of the unpredictability of its actions (Bauman, 2006). This has now been replaced by 'capitalist freedom' which carries with it both sensational media and fear of crime. The processes of protection and Othering have come along with it.

There has also been a trend towards urban-based fear. Interests across the political spectrum have sought to discursively frame terrorist threats to cities and to redefine what it means to have urban security (Wekerle and Jackson, 2005). Public security, order and protection have become central issues for cities, leading to the diffusion of fear as a specifically urban phenomenon which has impacts on the use of urban space. Fear is an important element in contemporary urban conflicts. It stimulates and fuels hostilities between different groups of people. Hostile reactions can be traced to a complex interplay between old phobias and new fantasies (Papastergiadis, 2006). Fear provokes both open and hidden expressions of racialization and sexualization. This, at its worst, can lead to a vicious circle of violence and cumulative fear. There are examples around Europe of how various forms of injustice, such as poor housing conditions, increasing unemployment, ethnic discrimination and police brutality, can cause unrest and urban violence (see e.g. Body-Gendrot, 2000). At the same time, cities face new responsibilities in relation to civic protection and security. As Jon Coaffee and David Murakami Wood (2006) cleverly phrase it:'security is coming home': the previously international security discourses and procedures are applied in the lower levels of governance, yet with the threats being positioned as global.

Popular culture and mass media depictions of fear and victimization have contributed to the transformation of the meaning of terrorism 'from a strategy to a condition' (Altheide, 2004). Citizens' exaggerated concerns about terrorism lead to high security expenses (West and Orr, 2005). The 'capital of fear can be turned to any kind of profit – commercial or political' (Bauman, 2005: 162). The popular media contribute in linking 'defence against global threats through "homeland security" right down to personal safety as one continuous spectrum of security' (Coaffee and Murakami Wood, 2006: 515). Fear of terrorism has supported consumption as a way to sustain national identity. Perhaps the best example of the contemporary social production of fear is the traffic light-like terror alert system on US television (e.g. Marcuse, 2004; Altheide, 2006). Rather than being interpreted as a fundamental change in a society, this should be interpreted as truly a socially produced reality which brings the atmosphere of fear to the everyday realities of private living rooms.

NEW URBAN REALITIES

The changed nature of fear has had manifold consequences for social life and urban structures. These can quite literally be seen in how contemporary cities are designed, how urban space is controlled and regulated, and how everyday life in cities has changed. As Ali Madanipour has pointed out, 'whenever political and economic developments have led to the segregation of social groups, spatial development has followed this trend and has contributed to that segregation' (1996: 145). Spatial constraints are increasingly important in understanding present urbanities.

Some scholars have presented rather pessimistic images of the urban condition. Mike Davis (1990) was one of the first to enunciate critical and polemic notions on 'the urban fortress model' where safety is guaranteed by exclusionary design. In its extreme forms, the defense mentality leads to paranoia, protectionism and lack of common interest (see also Flusty, 1994; Mitchell, 1995; Soja, 1996; Ellin, 1997). The fortress model creates divided and polarized urban space in which some areas are transformed into controlled, guarded zones that are privately owned and maintained, whereas other places are neglected and left to deteriorate. Fear has caused social groups to flee from each other into isolated homogenous enclaves. Segregation, social polarization and inequality have become visible in urban form.

The political and normative dynamics within the socio-spatial order raises questions concerning the processes relating to disobedience and exclusion in urban space. While these tendencies were already predicted in the early 1990s, the trend has intensified ever since. Concurrently, urban space is increasingly becoming a means of *exclusion* rather than supporting diversity and the positive notion of urbanity. In the name of fear, 'public space is becoming increasingly structured in favor of a narrowly defined social order' (Hubbard, 2000: 257). Unwanted behaviour is excluded, not tolerated. It is '[t]he widening gap between social strata' (previously local or national, now ever more often global) which is associated with 'the rising fear of crime and concerns about safety in cities' (Madanipour, 1996: 146).

The new meanings of insecurity – and security – have arrived with a *neoliberal order*. The neoliberal rule has been extremely efficient in defining 'dangerous' spaces, activities, groups or individuals. It has brought with it various programmes and models of action. Some of them – such as safer cities initiatives and zero tolerance campaigns – are directly linked to security; others – such as urban regeneration projects, public–private partnership projects in 'cleaning' the streets, and city branding campaigns – have only indirect links to fear. This neoliberal order, which aims to erase the 'traces' of inequality (Coleman, 2004: 227), is labelled by risk-based social control which is allied to the powerful and used to 'promote particular political visions' (ibid.: 14). Social integration and solidarity are replaced by segregation and zero tolerance. Security has become 'the justification for measures that threaten the core of urban social and political life' (Marcuse, 2004: 275).

It is somewhat paradoxical that space is being designed and regulated as exclusionary, rather than more open, in the name of safety. The question of safety should not be regarded as independent of critical evaluation of the changing notions of planning, legislation and policy making. Fear plays an important role in the purification and homogenization of urban space. Open and democratic public spaces have increasingly been replaced by 'single-minded, sanitised spaces in which certain groups and individuals are seen to be "out of place"' (Hubbard, 2000: 255). Nevertheless, these trends should not be approached as indisputable developments without alternatives. Wherever new forms of control and suppression rise, new forms of resistance and alternative values are created. Protective norms are opposed by proactive strategies. Activities which generate 'looseness of space' – diversity, change and risk – can be matters of leisure, entertainment, self-expression or political expression (Franck and Stevens, 2007). They foster spontaneity, flexibility, ability to surprise, and creative disorder.

However, it is not only public urban space that has been changing. Nan Ellin (2003) identifies three new trends in housing – traditionalism, escapism and retribalization – and sees that these are reactions to fear. Insecurity gives 'rise to nostalgia'. (Miles, 2003: 44). People escape from the areas they perceive as dangerous and seek the company of new 'tribes' – people they find similar enough not to be threatening. Urban regeneration projects are modest examples of these trends; gated communities are extreme examples. Isolation is 'cumulative': it creates passive individuals who do not wish to have an influence on their environment but rather choose to isolate themselves in voluntary ghettos and exclude problems outside (Blakely and Snyder, 1997). Polarization, which is both income- and race-related, is followed by 'a barricading of segregated spaces' (Marcuse, 2004: 271). As David Garland has pointed out, the development of gated communities 'is part of a broader shift towards security-oriented architecture and planning' in which the 'primary concern is to manage space and to separate out different "types" of people' (2001: 162). Protective design is problematic because it may create a vicious circle of fear. If a city is designed to look dangerous, then danger will be embedded in people's imaginations although originally there may have been no reason for it. In these kinds of environments people are, instead of experiencing victimisation, 'experiencing the omnipresent *probability* of victimisation' (Lianos with Douglas, 2000: 114).

Control of urban space – public and private policing, access control and surveillance – aims to *'normalize'* it. The social norms that contribute to controlling behaviour have been amplified, and the 'orderly, controlled vision of public space is squeezing out other ways of imagining public spaces' (Mitchell, 1995: 125). Ensuring the exclusion of delinquency or deviance has become an important aim for all parties across the political scale (Furedi, 2006). It reflects fears about populations regarded as different. What Phil Hubbard refers to as 'the exclusionary urge' is the way that 'groups and individuals whose lifestyles are viewed as incompatible with so-called "normal" ways of behaving have had their access to urban space limited' (2000: 248). Whether these 'deviants' are committing crime 'is a matter of secondary importance to those parts of society that define what deviance is, a matter to be dealt within the social and geographical spaces where the deviants are concentrated' (Lianos with Douglas, 2000: 104).

Fear has exaggerated the conflicts that different groups have over the use of urban space (Sparks et al., 2001). Minorities may appear 'only as objects of oppression' (Miles, 2003: 50). The conflict, which was once called 'a cold war on the streets' (Davis, 1990: 234), has been expanded to legal battles. The regulation of urban space contributes to the process of Othering. Public order acts, city bylaws, and other laws and forms of regulation contribute in defining not only what but also *who* is acceptable – who is considered as respectable and who is excluded, who has the right to (be in) what space. Discussions about fear are turned into discussions about 'geographical exclusion' (Sibley, 1995) and 'right to urban space' (Mitchell, 2003).

In urban planning, regulation and politics, fear has had various nefarious consequences which are often unarticulated and would not necessarily gain wide agreement if they were stated outright. In crime prevention, there has been a shift from focusing on the offender towards focusing on the victim and the environment and, hence, 'place-based' strategies have replaced those focusing on crime as a problem that relates to social wellbeing and equality (Garland, 2001). Insecurity is used as a justification for place-based crime prevention issues and principles such as territoriality, surveillance, access control, activity support and maintenance (Oc and Tiesdell, 1997; Schneider and Kitchen, 2002; Coaffee, 2004). Inclusive ideas about the local prevention of crime have turned into an exclusive politics of public safety (van Swaaningen, 2005). Participation has turned into protection.

In the name of security, societies also face widespread *surveillance*. Highly sophisticated electronic means are increasingly replacing informal social control. In this 'cam era', surveillance cameras and other monitoring systems follow people literally everywhere (Koskela, 2003). In cities, surveillance covers private premises and places of consumption as well as urban space, but the 'surveillance society' spreads beyond that, towards border control and consumer behaviour monitoring. Surveillance is getting more intense, as well as increasingly automatized, integrated and globalized (Lyon, 2003). Surveillance is a 'powerful tool in managing and enforcing exclusion' (Norris, 2002: 267). The practices of surveillance are not inclusive by nature but, rather, 'inflate stereotypes' (Lyon, 2001: 63). Since surveillance is widely used to monitor those who are perceived as deviant – suspicious youth, people of colour, the homeless, activists, sexual minorities and so on – it contributes to the process of Othering. A particular 'normative space-time ecology' (Graham, 1998: 491) is being created. Surveillance definitely contributes to reinforcing existing power relations rather than challenging them.

Widespread surveillance has strengthened the link between fear and the security business. This is apparent in the marketing of various security equipment and private policing services. The marketing of both is presently directed not only at private companies and governments but also to housing areas. Safety has become a vital selling point and the security business has expanded (Marcuse, 2004). Security apparatuses and the ability to respond to threats have become extremely important marketing strategies for cities and urban regions, and key issues for companies that wish to relocate their posts (Coaffee and Murakami Wood, 2006). Those who can afford it will fortify themselves (Bauman, 2005). The main problem of the security business is that it is ethically highly problematic. If a field of business is structured so that the profit will be bigger if people are more afraid – and hence feel they need more protection – it will be unethical.

One further consequence of insecurity – especially of fear of terrorism – is that the power of the *mass media* has increased immensely. As Maria Balshaw and Liam Kennedy argue, '[t]elevisual space may or may not be the visual space of our urban futures, but it is an increasingly powerful mode of representation of the urban present' (2000: 11). The 9/11 attacks literally showed that how to be seen – not to hide – is what makes criminal acts meaningful and thrilling for the criminal (see Presdee, 2000; Weibel, 2002). These types of dramatized representation in the media have a 'hypnotic fascination' (Miles, 2003: 52). The mass media have become a 'symbolic battleground'. This is important also because it 'provides legitimacy to security responses, and normalizes the event' (Miles, 2003: 48). News coverage sustains fear as 'self-propelling and self-intensifying' (Bauman, 2006: 132). In and through images, *crime becomes a commodity*. In news production and reality TV programmes, fighting crime can make 'an excellent, exciting, eminently watchable show' (Bauman, 2000: 215). The higher 'the fetish character' of an image, the more valuable it is 'as a good' (Weibel, 2002: 211). The audience is provided with an impression that it is able to both verify and participate in what is happening in the world of crime. With a pretext of control, people are able to peep into the field of criminal action, and to moralise on it. As Mike Presdee accurately argues, 'we all participate in the creation of crime as we consume the filming of the carnival of chase, becoming part of the process of production of real crime and real violence' (2000: 65). Crime, and fear of crime, become tied to the consumer society by the production and consumption of programmes and products whose fascination is based on crime and fear.

Nevertheless, the media also create a forum for alternative presentations. People are actively involved in both the production and the interpretation of stories and this carries with it an emancipatory potential. While the commercial media clearly have the most powerful role, many alternative ways of 'presenting reality' are increasingly accessible for the public, for example, via the internet. The economy of attention is structured around the pair activism versus consumerism. Revealing things that are not conventionally shown, either in the new media or in public urban space, can be conceptualized as a political act, as celebrating difference. As Bauman states, '[i]t is the *exposure of difference* that in time becomes the major factor of happy cohabitation through causing the urban roots of fear to wilt and fade' (2005: 167). The erosion of marginality is never permanent.

CONCLUSIONS: TOWARDS A CULTURE OF TOLERANCE

Fear is something no-one wants. Safety and security are something everyone wants – and deserves. There is a solid consensus. This consensus, however, as beautiful it seems at the first sight, is problematic in many ways. When the aim for maximum security is perceived as incontrovertible, people's own judgement and sense of proportion will weaken. Compulsive attempts to ensure safety are easily moralistic and intolerant. Those regarded as 'deviant' are interpreted as 'potentially dangerous' rather than simply as *different*. When security becomes an obsession, tolerance becomes difficult. In the name of security, people and societies produce a culture of prejudice and hate. The unholy alliance of fear and hate makes the issue quite complex. Hate gives fuel to intimidation.

To increase the security of some groups means decreasing security for others. Those who can afford will 'buy' a high level of security; others are left with less. The architecture that aims to maximize security is often alienating and exclusive. Paradoxically, the very design that has aimed to increase security, has produced environments that signal danger. Fear, and the control that aims to guarantee security, stiffen social interaction. The social production of fear leads to a condition where people believe in threats. Both fear and forms of control, such as surveillance, create mutual distrust. The ones who are dangerous, you don't trust. Fear is the opposite of trust. Without trust, there is no interaction. Negligence stands by fear's side.

Fear is more and more connected to other emotions: anger, hate, disgust, shame and envy – as well as (often lack of) trust and respect. Its reaches far beyond individual strategies. Fear's consequences take spatial forms, indeed, but these forms have been multiplied. Fear changes social relations and interaction. It directs legislation and trends of regulation and control of public space. Fear leads and modifies the objectives of urban planning. And it is has the power to change consumer culture and media literacy.

All this should not be perceived as deterministic. There should be a new view which would not completely undermine the arguments that sustain the fear and insecurity people face, but would provide a richer perspective. Life, indeed, is simultaneously dangerous and fascinating, hostile and inviting, orderly and disorderly, confusing and attractive. Urban space teems with unpredictable encounters, miscellaneous experiences and ambivalent emotions. The vision of a completely orderly, perfectly safe city based on pure rationalism is only one utopia among others. It could be replaced by a utopia of diversity and tolerance. Maybe, the way out of fear is not to be more careful but to avoid Othering, gating and segregation, and to promote mutual respect, sustainable solidarity – the culture of fear turned into a culture of tolerance.

REFERENCES

Abu-Lughod, L. and Lutz, C.A. (eds) (1990) *Language and the Politics of Emotion*. Cambridge: Cambridge University Press.

Altheide, D.L. (2004) 'Consuming terrorism', *Symbolic Interaction*, 27: 289–308.

Altheide, D.L. (2006) *Terrorism and the Politics of Fear*. Oxford: AltaMira Press.

Balshaw, M. and Kennedy, L. (2000) 'Introduction: Urban space and representation', in: M. Balshaw and L. Kennedy (eds), *Urban Space and Representation*. London: Pluto Press. pp. 1–21.

Banks, M. (2005) 'Spaces of (in)security. Media and fear of crime in a local context', *Crime, Media, Culture*, 1: 169–87.

Bauman, Z. (2000) 'Social issues of law and order', *British Journal of Criminology*, 40: 205–21.

Bauman, Z. (2005) 'Seeking shelter in Pandora's box. Or: fear, security and the city', *City*, 9: 161–68.

Bauman, Z. (2006) *Liquid Fear*. Cambridge: Polity Press.

Bigo, D. (2006) 'Security, exception, ban and surveillance', in D. Lyon (ed.), *Theorizing Surveillance. The Panopticon and Beyond.* Cullompton: Willan. pp. 46–68.

Bird, J. (2003) 'The mote in God's eye: 9/11, then and now', *Journal of Visual Culture*, 2: 83–97.

Blakely, E.J. and Snyder, M.G. (1997) *Fortress America. Gated Communities in the United States*. Washington, DC: Brookings Institution Press.

Body-Gendrot, S. (2000) *The Social Control of Cities. A Comparative Perspective*. Oxford: Blackwell.

Bondi, L. and Mehta, A. (1999) 'Embodied discourse: on gender and fear of violence', *Gender, Place and Culture: A Journal of Feminist Geography*, 6: 67–84.

Brownlow, A. (2005) 'A geography of men's fear', *Geoforum*, 36: 581–92.

Coaffee, J. (2004) 'Rings of steel, rings of concrete and rings of confidence: designing out terrorism in central London pre and post September 11th', *International Journal of Urban and Regional Research*, 28: 201–11.

Coaffee, J. and Murakami Wood, D. (2006) 'Security is coming home: rethinking scale and constructing resilience in the global urban response to terrorist risk', *International Relations*, 20: 503–17.

Coleman, R. (2004) *Reclaiming the Streets. Surveillance, Social Control and the City*. Cullompton: Willan.

Davis, M. (1990) *The City of Quartz. Excavating the Future in Los Angeles.* New York: Vintage.

Day, K. (1999) 'Embassies and sanctuaries: women's experiences of race and fear in public space', *Environment and Planning D: Society and Space,* 17: 307–28.

Duncan, N. (1996) 'Renegotiating gender and sexuality in public and private spaces', in N. Duncan (ed.), *BodySpace: Destabilizing Geographies of Gender and Sexuality.* London: Routledge. pp. 127–45.

Eisinger, P. (2004) 'The American city in the age of terror. A preliminary assessment of the effects of September 11', *Urban Affairs Review*, 40: 115–30.

Ellin, N. (1997) 'Shelter from the storm or form follows fear and vice versa', in N. Ellin (ed.), *Architecture of Fear*. New York: Princeton Architectural Press. pp. 13–45.

Ellin, N. (2003) 'Fear and city building', *The Hedgehog Review*, 5: 43–61.

Flusty, S. (1994) *Building Paranoia. The Proliferation of Interdictory Space and the Erosion of Spatial Justice.* Los Angeles: Los Angeles Forum for Architecture and Urban Design.

Franck, K.A. and Stevens, Q. (2007) 'Tying down loose space', in K.A. Franck and Q. Stevens (eds), *Loose Space. Possibility and Diversity in Urban Life*. London: Routledge. pp. 1–33.

Furedi, F. (2002) *Culture of Fear. Risk-taking and the Morality of Low Expectation.* London: Continuum.

Furedi, F. (2006) *Politics of Fear. Beyond Left and Right*. London: Continuum.

Gardner, C.B. (1995) *Passing by. Gender and Public Harassment*. Berkeley: University of California Press.

Garland, D. (2001) *The Culture of Control. Crime and Social Order in Contemporary Society*. Oxford: Oxford University Press.

Gold, J.R. and Revill, G. (2003) 'Exploring landscapes of fear: marginality, spectacle and surveillance', *Capital and Class*, 80: 27–50.

González, B.M. (2005) 'Topophilia and topophobia – the home as an evocative place of contradictory emotions', *Space and Culture*, 8: 193–213.

Graham, S. (1998) 'Spaces of surveillant simulation: new technologies, digital representations, and material geographies', *Environment and Planning D: Society and Space*, 16: 483–504.

Graham, S. (ed.) (2004) *Cities, War, and Terrorism: Towards an Urban Geopolitics*. Malden, MA: Blackwell.

Hollander, J.A. (2001) 'Vulnerability and dangerousness. The construction of gender through conversation about violence', *Gender & Society*, 15: 83–109.

Hopkins, P.E. (2007) 'Young people, masculinities, religion and race: new social geographies', *Progress in Human Geography*, 31: 163–77.

Hubbard, P. (2000) 'Policing the public realm: community action and the exclusion of street prostitution', in J.R. Gold and G. Revill (eds), *Landscapes of Defence*. Harlow: Pearson Education. pp. 246–62.

Jayasuriya, K. (2007) '9/11 and the new "anti-politics" of "security"', *Social Science Research Council Internet Pages*. After September 11 archive: http://www.ssrc.org/sept11/essays/

Kellner, D. (2004). '9/11, spectacles of terror, and media manipulation', *Critical Discourse Studies*, 1: 41–64.

Kelly, L. and Radford, J. (1996) '"Nothing really happened": the invalidation of women's experiences of sexual violence', in M. Hester, L. Kelly and J. Radford (eds), *Women, Violence and Male Power*. Buckingham: Open University Press. pp. 19–33.

Kern, L. (2005) 'In place and at home in the city: connecting privilege, safety and belonging for women in Toronto', *Gender, Place and Culture*, 12: 357–77.

Koskela, H. (1997) '"Bold walk and breakings": women's spatial confidence versus fear of violence', *Gender, Place and Culture*, 4: 301–19.

Koskela, H. (2003) '"Cam Era" – the contemporary urban Panopticon, *Surveillance and Society*, 1: 292–313. www.surveillance-and-society.org/articles1(3)/camera.pdf

Ley, D. and Samuels, S. (eds) (1978) *Humanistic Geography. Prospects and Problems*. London: Croom Helm.

Lianos, M. with Douglas, M. (2000) 'Dangerization and the end of deviance. The institutional environment', in D. Garland and R. Sparks (eds), *Criminology and Social Theory*. Oxford: Oxford University Press. pp. 103–25.

Los, M. (2002) 'Post-communist fear of crime and the commercialization of security', *Theoretical Criminology*, 6: 165–88.

Luke, T.W. (2003) *Postmodern Geopolitics in the 21st Century: Lessons from the 9.11.01 Terrorist Attacks*. Center for Unconventional Security Affairs. Occasional Paper Series 2.

Lyon, D. (2001) *Surveillance Society. Monitoring Everyday Life*. Buckingham: Open University Press.

Lyon, D. (2003) *Surveillance after September 11*. Oxford: Blackwell Publishing.

Macmillan, R., Nierobisz, A. and Welsh, S. (2000) 'Experiencing the streets. Harassment and perceptions of safety among women', *Journal of Research in Crime and Delinquency*, 37: 306–22.

Madanipour, A. (1996) *Design of Urban Space: An Inquiry into a Socio-spatial Process*. Chichester: Wiley.

Madriz, E.I. (1997) 'Images of criminals and victims: a study on women's fear and social control', *Gender and Society*, 11: 342–56.

Marcuse, P. (1997) 'Walls of fear and walls of support', in N. Ellin (ed.), *Architecture of Fear*. New York: Princeton Architectural Press. pp. 101–14.

Marcuse, P. (2004) 'The "war on terrorism" and life in cities after September 11, 2001', in S. Graham (ed.), *Cities, War, and Terrorism: Towards an Urban Geopolitics*. Malden, MA: Blackwell. pp. 263–75.

Mason, G. (2005) 'Hate crime and the image of the stranger', *British Journal of Criminology*, 45: 837–59.

Massey, D. (1994) *Space, Place and Gender*. Cambridge: Polity Press.

Miles, M. (2003) 'Strange days', in M. Miles and T. Hall (eds), *Urban Futures. Critical Commentaries on Shaping the City*. London: Routledge. pp. 44–59.

Mitchell, D. (1995) 'The end of public space? People's Park, definitions of the public, and democracy', *Annals of the Association of American Geographers*, 85: 108–33.

Mitchell, D. (2003) *The Right to the City. Social Justice and the Fight for Public Space.* New York: Guilford Press.

Namaste, K. (1996) 'Genderbashing: sexuality, gender and the regulation of public space', *Environment and Planning D: Society and Space*, 14: 221–40.

Norris, C. (2002) 'From personal to digital: CCTV, the Panopticon, and the technological mediation of suspicion and social control', in D. Lyon (ed.), *Surveillance as Social Sorting: Privacy, Risk and Digital Discrimination*. London: Routledge. pp. 249–81.

Nussbaum, M.C. (2001) *Upheavals of Thought: The Intelligence of Emotions*. Cambridge: Cambridge University Press.

Oc, T. and Tiesdell, S. (eds) (1997) *Safer City Centres. Reviving the Public Realm.* London: Paul Chapman.

Pain, R. (1991) 'Space, sexual violence and social control: integrating geographical and feminist analyses of women's fear of crime', *Progress in Human Geography*, 15: 415–31.

Pain, R. (2001) 'Gender, race, age and fear in the city', *Urban Studies*, 38: 899–913.

Pain, R. (2003) 'Youth, age and the representation of fear', *Capital and Class*, 80: 151–71.

Pain, R. and Smith, S.J. (2008) 'Fear: critical geopolitics of everyday life', in R. Pain and S.J. Smith (eds), *Fear: Critical Geopolitics and Everyday Life*. Aldershot: Ashgate. pp. 1–19.

Pantazis, C. (2000) '"Fear of crime", vulnerability and poverty', *British Journal of Criminology*, 40: 414–36.

Papastergiadis, N. (2006) 'The invasion complex: the abject other and spaces of violence', *Geografiska Annaler, Series B: Human Geography* 88: 429–442.

Perry, B. (2001) *In the Name of Hate: Understanding Hate Crimes*. London: Routledge.

Porteous, J.D. (1990) *Landscapes of the Mind. Worlds of Sense and Metaphor*. Toronto: University of Toronto Press.

Presdee, M. (2000) *Cultural Criminology and the Carnival of Crime*. London: Routledge.

Relph, E. (1976) *Place and Placelessness*. London: Pion Books.

Robin, C. (2004) *Fear. The History of a Political Idea.* Oxford University Press.

Rose, G. (1993) *Feminism and Geography. The Limits of Geographical Knowledge*. Minneapolis: University of Minnesota Press.

Savitch, H.V. (2003) 'Does 9-11 portend a new paradigm for cities?', *Urban Affairs Review*, 39: 103–27.

Schneider, R.H. and Kitchen, T. (2002) *Planning for Crime Prevention. A TransAtlantic Perspective*. London: Routledge.

Sibley, D. (1995) *Geographies of Exclusion. Society and Difference in the West*. London: Routledge.

Smith, N. (2002) 'Scales of terror. The manufacturing of nationalism and the war for US globalism', in M. Sorkin and S. Zukin (eds), *After the World Trade Center: Rethinking New York City*. New York: Routledge. pp. 97–109.

Smith, S.J. (1987) 'Fear of crime: beyond a geography of deviance', *Progress in Human Geography*, 11: 1–23.

Soja, E.W. (1996) *Thirdspace. Journeys to Los Angeles and Other Real-and-Imagined Places.* Cambridge, MA: Blackwell.

Sparks, R., Girling, E. and Loader, I. (2001) 'Fear and everyday urban lives', *Urban Studies*, 38: 885–98.

Stanko, E. (1990) *Everyday Violence. Women's and Men's Experience of Personal Danger*. London: Pandora Press.

Stanko, E. (1996) 'Reading danger: sexual harassment, anticipation and self-protection', in M. Hester, L. Kelly and J. Radford (eds), *Women, Violence and Male Power*. Buckingham: Open University Press. pp. 50–62.

Swaaningen van, R. (2005) 'Public safety and the management of fear', *Theoretical Criminology* 9, 289–305.

Thomas, M.E. (2005) 'Girls, consumption and the contradictions of hanging out in the city', *Social and Cultural Geography*, 6: 587–605.

Tuan, Y. (1974). *Topophilia. A Study of Environmental Perception, Attitudes and Values*. Englewood Cliffs, NJ: Prentice-Hall.

Tuan, Y. (1975). 'Place: an experiential perspective', *The Geographical Review*, 65: 151–65.

Tuan, Y. (1979) *Landscapes of Fear*. Oxford: Blackwell.

Valentine, G. (1989) 'The geography of women's fear', *Area*, 21: 385–90.

Valentine, G. (1992) 'Images of danger: women's sources of information about the spatial distribution of male violence', *Area*, 24: 22–29.

van Swaaningen, R. (2005) 'Public safety and the management of fear', *Theoretical Criminology*, 9(3): 289–305.

Weibel, P. (2002) 'Pleasure and the panoptic principle', in: T.Y. Levin, U. Frohne and P. Weibel (eds), *CTRL[SPACE]: Rhetorics of Surveillance from Bentham to Big Brother*. Karlsruhe: ZKM Centre for Art and Media. pp. 206–23.

Wekerle, G.R. and Jackson, P.S.B. (2005) 'Urbanizing the security agenda', *City*, 9: 33–49.

West, D.M. and Orr, M. (2005) 'Managing citizen fears. Public attitudes toward urban terrorism', *Urban Affairs Review*, 41: 93–105.

Williams, R.W. (2003) 'Terrorism, anti-terrorism and the normative boundaries of the US polity. The spatiality of politics after 11 September 2001', *Space and Polity*, 7: 273–92.

Young, J. (1999) *The Exclusive Society. Social Exclusion, Crime and Difference in Late Modernity*. London: Sage.

SECTION 4

Geographies of Social Justice

Edited by
Sallie A. Marston

Introduction: Geographies of Social Justice

Sallie A. Marston

While the substantive linking of social justice and geography can be seen to be a disciplinary project set firmly in the mid-twentieth century, particularly through the original scholarship of geographers such as James Blaut, David Harvey and David Smith, the history of social justice concerns in the discipline is far more complicated and older. Unlike certain subfields, such as political geography or biogeography, that have a largely coherent and relatively consistent developmental trajectory, social justice as an organizing framework for geographic concerns has followed a much more ephemeral and sometimes indiscernible path. In its (arguably) earliest appearance in the nineteenth century,[1] social justice concerns – that is, the distribution of resources within society and over space, and the processes that shape that distribution – were the preoccupation of isolated individuals who wrote voluminously and passionately on the topic but who never entrained a 'school' that followed in their wake. In the early to mid-twentieth century, ethical concerns with the destructive and exploitative impacts of development were also voiced but did not, at the time, coalesce into a body of theory or practice that could be recognized as social justice but might more appropriately be seen as social critique. Despite their evanescent nature, these precursors to our contemporary engagement with social justice in geography have since become significant and influential in different ways and it is thus a matter of importance to consider both their historical context and their current value and consequence especially for post-structuralist and radical ecological theory. Such a consideration provides a constructive framework for appreciating the five chapters that constitute this section of the Handbook and link it to the other sections of the Handbooks, where some of these same individuals, and their intellectual and activist commitments mentioned here, reverberate.

While they appear to have had very little influence on mainstream scholarship in European geography at the time, it would be imprudent to ignore the important contributions to issues of justice made by the nineteenth-century geographers, scientific explorers and classical anarchists Élisée Reclus (1830–1905) and Peter Kropotkin (1842–1921). Both, in their own ways, were fierce champions of social justice and produced large bodies of work that articulated their own notions of geography and justice within the larger structure of anarchist thought (for a comprehensive biography, bibliography, collected works of and commentary on both Reclus and Kropotkin, consult the web-based Anarchist Archives, 2008). What is perhaps most impressive about both Reclus and Kropotkin is that although their publications circulated widely in the mid-late nineteenth century and into the early twentieth, their ideas have only recently come to exert a strong influence on geography and geographers. Reclus' anarchism, as Clark and Martin have shown, is a 'sweeping one with universalistic dimensions, but it encompasses a social and ecological ethic that is based on a concern for the self-realization of all beings, in their uniqueness and particularity, and a practice of love and care for those beings' (2004: p. 3). Kropotkin, friend and collaborator of Reclus, followed a somewhat similar path in joining geography to anarchism and developed important concepts that prefigure our contemporary ideas about social justice. Through the idea of mutual aid (in contrast to social Darwinism), Kropotkin meant to signal the interdependent and communitarian nature of human society (and human-nature interaction). And while Reclus based his understanding of a just and ethical world on human emotion – love, care, sympathy – Kropotkin believed in the evolutionary development of the species as the source of the instinct for justice. He wrote:

> It is a feeling infinitely wider than love or personal sympathy – an instinct that has been slowly developed among animals and men in the course of an extremely long evolution, and which has taught animals and men alike the force they can borrow from the practice of mutual aid and support, and the joys they can find in social life ... It is the unconscious recognition of the force that is borrowed by each man from the practice of mutual aid; of the close dependency of every one's happiness upon the happiness of all; and of the sense of justice, or equity, which brings the individual to consider the rights of every other individual as equal to his own. (1902, paragraphs 9 and 10)

Although premising their ideas about social justice, as we now call it, on rather different foundations, the extensive writings of both Reclus and Kropotkin locate classical anarchist thought as an important antecedent to our current formulations of social justice at the same time that they have come to exert a significant influence on contemporary theory and practice.

It took several more decades for concern with issues of justice to reemerge within the discipline, and again, a few lone figures stand out as significant. While there are others who might have been highlighted here, I have chosen Carl O. Sauer, Keith Buchanan and William Bunge, because they serve as archetypes of a new sensibility and political commitment that would gain full expression by the 1970s. Each of these three geographers was traditionally trained and in their earlier careers pursued non-political kinds of research. But their experiences in the field (and perhaps their personal biographies as well) seem to have influenced them greatly, though in different ways, such that they were vociferous about the destructive impact of modernization and development on cultural ecologies (Sauer) and highly critical of the inequities of colonization and the dislocations of decolonization (Buchanan) and were able to see injustice and inequality within 'modern' and 'developed' regions (Bunge). Because they were at the vanguard as critics of these processes, I include them in this brief intellectual history.

In the years before the relevance turn in geography, Sauer's concern over the destruction of cultural landscapes – particularly the effect of the Green Revolution in Mexico – caused him to challenge the Rockefeller Foundation's interfering with local ecologies in order to reproduce American-style agriculture (Perkins, 1990). In a letter to J. H. Willits, an officer at the Foundation, Sauer wrote:

> A good aggressive bunch of American agronomists and plant breeders could ruin the native

> resources for good and all by pushing their American commercial stocks ... The example of Iowa is about the most dangerous of all for Mexico. Unless the Americans understand that, they'd better keep out of this country entirely. This thing must be approached from an appreciation of the native economies as being basically sound. (From Perkins, 1990; Sauer, 1941)

Although it would be misleading to credit Sauer as a social or ecological justice crusader based on the contents of this letter to the Rockefeller Foundation as well as his public criticism of modernization projects in poor countries, the mistake of ignoring him would be to miss one of the first calls within the discipline in the twentieth century for defending local populations against the vicissitudes of development. The larger point is that as most of the discipline of geography in the United States might have been seen to be indifferent to issues of justice until the 1960s, there were voices like Sauer's and later Buchanan's and Bunge's that were unambiguous in their calls to reconsider the negative impacts of colonialism and modernization on local populations. Buchanan's anti-colonialism, anti-modernization and his ethical concern for subordinated peoples have recently been assessed in a piece by Marcus Power and James Sidaway (2004) on the emergence of tropical geography – from the ashes of imperial and colonial geography – and its ultimate eclipse by the more recent conceptual framework of development geography. What Power and Sidaway argue is that Buchanan was at the leading edge of the Anglo-American radical geography movement and made substantial contributions to it well before it coalesced in the 1960s and 1970s around publications like *Antipode*.

> In the late 1940s and early 1950s, amid publications derived from his work in Birmingham, such as agricultural geographies of the English Midlands (Buchanan 1948), are early critical papers on the status of 'coloureds' and 'Indians' in South Africa (Buchanan 1950), on 'internal colonialism' in Nigeria (1953), followed, in the 1960s, by a steady flow of papers, reviews, and essays on China, Southeast Asia, revolution, development, and environment, amid occasional works elaborating the framework of internal colonialism with regard to the status of Britain's 'Celtic Fringe.' As the 1960 moved on and revolutionary pressures in the South accelerated (epitomized by the insurgencies in Vietnam and the Portuguese colonies and the lurch into Mao's Cultural Revolution in China) Buchanan embraced them [1963a, 1963b], some years before development geography (or indeed wider human geography) was recast as radical. (Power and Sidaway, 2004: 591–92)

Buchanan's radical position was premised on a rejection of the racism of modernization and tropical geography and the disregard of its practitioners for the impact of modernization on the livelihoods and well-being of local people. Although Buchanan is highlighted here because of his early concerns with the uneven distribution of resources and life chances, it should not be assumed that he operated as a lone figure for very long. Certainly, by the 1960s we can point to the work of Bunge as an indicator of the accelerating emergence of radical geography and its concern with questions of justice and environmental degradation. Bunge's work, especially *The Atlas of Love and Hate* (1969), *The First Years of the Detroit Geographical Expedition* (1969), and *Fitzgerald: Geography of a Revolution* (1971) are significant because they demanded that Western geographers redirect their empirical gaze away from the exceptional, exotic, and 'out there', to confront the existence of urban poverty and inequality of access to the basics of a decent life at home. *Fitzgerald* (1971), for instance, is in many ways a classic Sauerian cultural landscape study, but it supersedes that genre in its explicit attention to the growing urbanization of the American population, particularly poor, racialized people, and the social injustices they were experiencing in urban spaces. This focus was a direct response not only to domestic deprivation and inequality but also to the urban civil unrest that exploded because of it and forced Western graduate students and faculty to take notice of the world that existed just beyond their own, comfortable, middle-class one.

Carl Sauer, Keith Buchanan and Bill Bunge stand as key markers of the parameters of a radical geography and its concern with social justice that became fully established by the mid-1970s. Their varying interests in cultural ecologies, in colonial and postcolonial human-environmental contexts, and in urban decay and poverty suggest that no aspects of human geography were left unaffected by social justice concerns. In addition to including the range of human geographies that could be explored through a social justice perspective, the theoretical foundation of social justice concerns was also being rapidly developed and consolidated through the work of an extensive group of radical geographers whose ranks swelled over the years as they were joined by feminists, anti-racists, queer geographers, geographers concerned with questions of ethics and participatory frameworks, and many others. Central to the growth and development of these social justice concerns in geography was the emergence of welfare geography, most closely associated with David Smith's *The Geography of Social Well-being in the United States* (1973), and radical geography which was foreshadowed by David Harvey's *Social Justice and the City* (1973). Finally, in addition to the many articles and books that soon began to appear that critiqued injustice, inequity, environmental degradation and decay, the launching of *Antipode: A Journal of Radical Geography* (founding date 1969) helped to more securely consolidate a group of scholars and students who began to understand their academic and political identities as radical and to promote social justice concerns, particularly with respect to anti-colonialism, anti-war, anti-poverty, and anti-capitalism, most generally. The radicalism of the 1970s grew and developed for another decade and, since the new century, has been reshaped for many scholars, by post-modern, post-structural and political-ecological concerns that are both theoretical and methodological in nature.

The present moment is a particularly exciting one because social justice concerns, wrapped up as they were in radical geography, have reemerged after a decade of relative quiescence (Pain, 2003, 2004, 2006). This section and the Handbook itself, is testimony to the revitalized interest in justice and equity in geography that characterizes this first decade of the new century. The chapters that constitute this section of the Handbook explore social and spatial justice, argue for the reassessment of personal practices with respect to justice, insist on the relevance of the environmental justice, and promote the importance of academic engagement with communities struggling for better lives. They investigate multiple facets of justice and how geographic understandings of justice contribute to wider concerns with it both inside and outside of the discipline. Drawing from geographic colleagues as well as from activists, philosophers, and other social science scholars, the treatment of issues of justice produced here exposes the ways justice works, or does not work, geographically. More specifically, they explore the multiple ways space is materially implicated in the production and reproduction of justice and inequalities with respect to difference in both humans and the environment.

The opening chapter by Marvin Waterstone argues for a reconnection to an ontology that recognizes human beings as deeply social beings; not autonomous entities, but beings connected to other beings through complex and extensive relationships. Establishing the social in human nature is critical to his argument because he makes a strong claim for justice based upon the fundamental relationality of human existence that requires an ethic of care and responsibility for others. In his four-part essay he examines the concept of justice and unfolds the ways justice is always social and always socially contingent. Thus, there is no one justice that is universally applicable but many justices that are derived from the social context in which they are required and produced. Because of the social geographical contingency of justice, Waterstone also explores the connections between geography and justice, the latter of which must be understood not only as a site of knowledge production (the discipline) but also as the location of practice (its manifestation in space and place). Having established these critical aspects of the relationality of geography and justice, Waterstone lays out an argument about how the discipline and its practitioners must, ethically, respond to the call for engagement in issues of justice and rights in the classroom, the field, and in our daily lives outside of the academy. He makes his strongest claim with respect to the impossibility of universality with respect to issues of justice because, by its very nature, justice is a social process and product and is dependent upon the diverse and complex ways that the categories of identity and subjectivity are formed and re-formed in and through geographies that are also open and changing. He writes: 'If our very existence as beings is relational, then we are dependent rather than independent, connected rather than autonomous, collectively rather than self-made, and within and a part of history rather than apart from history' (this volume, Chapter 19).

Jeff Popke's Chapter provides an excellent companion piece to Waterstone's as it extends and deepens the latter's consideration of social justice by describing the ways that ethical and moral questions intersect with justice and how there can be no social justice without recognizing the geographical foundations of ideals of fairness and equity. Popke's project is to bring socio-ethical investigations to the forefront of geographical concern by exploring the complex ways the ethical and the moral come together to shape our understanding of the 'social' in social geography. He provides a helpful distinction between morality and ethics, two critical terms that are often elided in discussions of justice; morality describing what is good and ethics being about our responsibilities toward others (human and non-human). Popke enables us to appreciate the deep connections between the two that produce social geographies constituted through a geographically particular understanding about what is good or proper (morality) and our obligations and responsibilities toward various others both near and far (ethics). As such moral and ethical geographies are produced and Popke seeks to interrogate how it is that moral geographies are the result of performance and contestation within particular geographical contexts and how ethical geographies are the result of the ways the nature and extent of these responsibilities are understood both empirically and theoretically. Significantly, Popke recognizes that the distinction between moral and ethical questions – between individual conduct and social responsibilities – is generated out of complex cultural and political struggles and compromises and is never fully settled or unanimous. One of the chief aims of his chapter is lay out a 'project to reclaim the social as a site of collective ethical responsibility, to expose the ways in which contemporary social institutions and political-economic relations militate against our dispositions to act on that responsibility, and thereby to facilitate a more generalized expression of solidarity and regard' (this volume, Chapter 19).

Richie Howitt and Michael Hillman's chapter focuses on how questions of justice are central to the regulation and management of environmental relations, amplifying and extending the ethical foundation of our social responsibilities toward non-human as well as human others. They are concerned particularly with how neo-liberal governance systems are dislocating common property resources through a new era of 'globalized', commercially based resource extraction – what they term a new era of primitive accumulation – that involves water, forests, fisheries and conservation reserves. They too argue for a strong commitment to a geographically centered understanding of social justice; one that fully comprehends its environmental implications, particularly with respect to indigenous peoples. Their position echoes something of both Waterstone and Popke as it engages directly with the heterogeneity that is manifested when we attempt to recognize and act upon the situatedness of environmental justice formulations and practices. But it is also conceptually and practically distinct in that they insist on the co-constitution of social and environmental justice, particularly in cases where the indigenous governance of common pool resources is undermined by globalized commercially based governance systems. They insist that 'in addressing the injustices that arise from contemporary primitive accumulation, environmental justice needs to be conceptualised as foundational to sustainable social geographies rather than secondary to questions of economic and social justice' (this volume, Chapter 20, p. 456). Using Nancy Fraser's (1995, 1997) redistribution-recognition binary, they demonstrate how strategies for securing social justice through environmental sustainability might be achieved. Thinking about the inextricability of economy, culture and environment, Howitt and Hillman point to the need to balance economic justice and cultural justice through a complex appreciation of social justice that works to redistribute resources at the same time that it embraces difference instead of seeking universals; difference in ecologies as well as in cultural notions of justice, rights, morality and ethics.

As the key tropes in the title – 'governance of crime' and the 're-moralization of city spaces' – indicate, Nicholas Fyfe's chapter addresses one of the classic areas of social geography: urban crime. What makes the chapter unique and relevant to questions of justice and geography today is that he orients his discussion not on the *where* of crime but on how the neo-liberal culture of regulation, control and punishment with respect to urban crime is premised on new understandings of citizen rights and responsibilities that produce new partnerships and policing communities. Following criminologist David Garland's analysis of the way that public safety is secured in cities through new regimes of state practice and community 'responsibilization', Fyfe provides a thorough discussion of how new regimes of governance around crime and safety are drawing upon a discourse of rights – such as the right to security and safety – that is premised on a substantive 're-moralization' of the urban landscape. Fyfe's chapter extends the previous three by demonstrating the ways that the state has seized upon the discourse of justice and rights in order to reconfigure urban space to produce a new moral landscape. It is through state practices of social control and punishment by way of 'expulsion and exclusion', as well as more community oriented strategies, that stress prevention and partnership and where communities are encouraged to police themselves, that new notions of 'the good' are produced with the aim of stabilizing commercial activity and encouraging the formation of new urban residential subjects. Fyfe writes: 'The impacts of the different interventions that flow from these two agendas are ... distributed unevenly over the city and the search for safety has significant implications for people's experiences of and rights to use the city' (this volume, p. 484). Significantly, this chapter provides a telling contrast to the others by describing how rights discourses have been captured by powerful institutions and redeployed, not with the purpose of enabling complex forms of justice for the wide range of different subjects and collectivities but to support new forms of residential and consumption spaces that are exclusionary and thus produce new social geographies of the city that perpetuate uneven experiences of security, safety and access.

The final chapter in this section, by Amy Ross, tackles the idea and the concept of human rights, particularly the emergence of state and activist sponsored universal human rights discourses and connects these to social geographers' commitment to an explicitly located understanding of human rights. She writes: '... the idea of human rights as situated in particular times/places helps illuminate the power-relations wrapped up in the concept of human rights; the failure to recognize human rights as situated and contingent disguises the intense power-relations that determine what counts as a human right and who makes that designation' (this volume, Chapter 22, p. 489). Ross first provides an institutional history of human rights as they emerged out of military rules of engagement and the proper treatment of prisoners to the more recent construction of a moral narrative of human rights that locates their importance at the apogee of contemporary global political concerns.

Using the concept of human rights abuse to better understand what counts as a human right, Ross describes the problem with separating out rights and abuses from acts of war and legally sanctioned violence and how social movement organizations have pushed states to reconsider state sponsored violence in new terms that called for the creation of new institutions – national, international, and transnational – to define and protect human rights as well as prosecute human rights abuses. Hers is an investigation that charts the emergence and formalization of a universal human rights narrative over the course of Western legal history and the challenges that narrative has confronted by activist organizations and truth-seeking tribunals. Ross makes clear that, although we are immersed in a 'human rights era', the geographical unevenness of the establishment of human rights protections and the prosecution of abuses deeply problematizes the idea of difference that is central to the other chapters in this section. It suggests that we are a long way yet from balancing a sensitivity to difference that acknowledges the impossibility of universal human rights at the same time that it recognizes a need for fundamental benchmarks upon which particular applications of human rights protections and the prosecution of abuses must be based.

The section provides the reader with a range of approaches to the problems of justice, rights, security, safety, morality and ethics being undertaken in geography today. It explores social geography's engagement with inequality as something which is made rather than pre-given, and how things should and could be different. The five chapters in this section direct our attention to the idea and practice of a more inclusive, just, ethical, caring society and the ways social geographers have been involved in understanding and attempting to forge that society. Traversing the history and contemporary terrain of social justice in geography as well as recognizing the many different ways in which the justice has been problematized and deployed (through social considerations, environmental ones, ethics and morality), we find social geography's concerns with justice have a resonance and relevance far beyond the boundaries of the discipline. These explorations of justice- and rights-based struggles for the capacity to become and act and to have equal access to the economic, political, social, cultural, and environmental resources that constitute worlds raise issues that are likely to occupy our imagination, research, and activist efforts for a long time to come.

NOTE

1 Eighteenth-century geographer and naturalist Alexander von Humboldt could also be included in this group of early influences on our understanding of contemporary social justice. His approach was very much more oriented to natural systems and is being treated in the 'Social Nature' section.

REFERENCES

Anarchist Archives, An Online Research Center on the History and Theory of Anarchism: Elisée Reclus (http://dwardmac.pitzer.edu/Anarchist_Archives/bright/reclus/reclus.html) accessed 29 February 2008.

Anarchist Archives, An Online Research Center on the History and Theory of Anarchism: Peter Kropotkin (http://dwardmac.pitzer.edu/Anarchist_Archives/kropotkin/Kropotkinarchive.html) accessed 29 February 2008.

Buchanan, K.M. (1948) 'Modern farming in the Vale of Evesham', *Economic Geography*, 24 (4): 235–50.

Buchanan, K.M. (1950) 'The "coloured" community in the Union of South Africa', *The Geographical Review*, 40 (3): 97–414.

Buchanan, K.M. (1953) 'Internal colonization in Nigeria', *The Geographical Review*, 43 (3): 416–18.

Buchanan, K.M. (1963a) 'The third world: its emergence and contours', *New Left Review*, 18 (1): 5–23.

Buchanan, K.M. (1963b) 'Bingo or UNO? Further comments on the affluent and proletarian nations', *New Left Review*, 21 (1): 21–9.

Clark, J.P. and Martin, C. (eds) (2004) *Anarchy, Geography, Modernity: The Radical Social Thought of Elisée Reclus*. Lanham and Oxford: Lexington Books.

Fraser, N. (1995) 'From redistribution to recognition? Dilemmas of justice in a "post-socialist" age', *New Left Review*, 212: 68–93.

Fraser, N. (1997) *Justice Interruptus: Critical Reflections on the 'Postsocialist' Condition*. New York and London: Routledge.

Garland, D. (2001) *The Culture of Control*. Oxford: Oxford University Press.

Harvey, D. (1973) *Social Justice and the City*. Baltimore; London: Edward Arnold.

Kropotkin, P. (1902) *Mutual Aid: A Factor of Evolution* (The Project Etext of *Mutual Aid*) (http://www.gutenberg.org/dirs/etext03/mtlad10.txt) accessed 29 February 2008.

Pain, R. (2003) 'Social geography: on action-orientated research', *Progress in Human Geography*, 27, 677–85.

Pain, R. (2004) 'Social geography: participatory research', *Progress in Human Geography*, 28, 1–12.

Pain, R. (2006) 'Social geography: seven deadly myths in policy research', *Progress in Human Geography*, 30, 250–9.

Perkins, John H. (1990) 'The Rockefeller Foundation and the Green Revolution, 1941–1956' *Agriculture and Human Values*, 7 (3/4): 6–18.

Power, M. and Sidaway, J.D. (2004) 'The degeneration of tropical geography', *Annals of the Association of American Geographers*, 94 (3): 585–601.

Sauer, C.O. (1941) Correspondence to [J.H. Willits], [Feb (?)], Rockefeller Foundation Archives, RG 1.2, Series 323, Box 10, Folder 63.

Smith, D. (1973) *The Geography of Social Well-being in the United States*. London: McGraw-Hill.

18

Geography and Social Justice

Marv Waterstone

TWENTY-FIRST CENTURY VIGNETTES

It's the 19th hour of my third 20-hour shift in a row this week, sewing the same pocket on the same designer jeans. I'm so tired that I can't even think clearly about whether my wages, if I'm paid (a very big if), will allow me to buy the few liters of water from the private water company so that my baby girl can get enough nourishment to overcome her premature birth weight, her diarrhea, and survive. I also try to think about the people buying these jeans. Surely they must know what I'm going through. How could they not know? Are they so pressed to save a few dollars? Do they think it's fair?

It's my 10th trick of the night. As I lie beneath this tourist, I remember (vaguely) life on our family's farm before my mother died of malnutrition and my father committed suicide. We worked hard, morning till night, but at least we never starved. I wandered into Mumbai, my wife six weeks pregnant, and nowhere to go. Now I wonder, 'if I'm not beaten will I survive my AIDS to support my wife and raise my son? And for what? What kind of life can they possibly have?' I also try to think about the man on top of me. Surely he must know what I'm going through. How can he not know? Am I that good an actor? Does he think this is fair? Does he care?

God it stinks! Once again, I'm literally wading through shit to get to my 'home.' I've been rummaging through the garbage heaps to find a few scraps of food for myself, my wife, and my eight children. I know this food will probably make us sick again, but what is the choice? Die slowly from disease or more quickly from starvation? I think about those whose refuse I now live off. Surely they must know what we are going through. How can they not know? Can they possibly think it is just that they have so much that others should survive on what they discard?

Last night was my 60th birthday, and I threw myself a little bash. I rented the 35,000 square foot Park Avenue Armory. The papers are saying that it cost me about $3 million (and possibly as much as $15 million), but I'll never tell. It does cost a bit to get entertainment these days, and as Liz Smith (2007) reported: 'there was a veritable bombardment of entertainment – marching bands … military cadets ... men from Yale singing "The Whiffenpoof Song" ... the Abyssinian Baptist choir ... comic Marty Short ... Marvin Hamlisch leading a group from "A Chorus Line,"... Patti LaBelle ... and, finally, the million-dollar singer and comeback kid,

Rod Stewart.' I also had to reproduce the décor from the living room in my $40 million co-op. But I deserved it, I think. After all, just a couple of days ago, I closed the biggest buyout deal in the world ($39 billion). It only seems fair that I can let off a little steam.

INTRODUCTION

In John Rawls's (1971) famous thought experiment for designing a system of justice, he invokes the notion of a 'veil of ignorance' to help insure as equitable a distribution system for life's good and bads as possible. Rawls suggests that if the designers have no idea (that is, they are ignorant) of where they will be positioned in the resultant system, it will be in the designers' interests to fashion a system that would be to the advantage of the least well off (since the designers themselves might well end up there). Right now, at the beginning of the 21st century, most of us in the 'first' world are operating behind a veil, not only of ignorance, but of incredible apathy regarding the injustices and inequities faced by most of the rest of the people with whom we share this planet. Given the lucky accidents of our own births, how do we live with ourselves, other than by willful ignorance or apathy (what Hannah Arendt refers to as the 'banality of evil'), and how can we tolerate our own (mostly unmerited) relative luxury and the utter immiseration of much of the world's population? Is it possible to imagine, in any of the contexts above (except the last), how people go on day after day or why? When do these billions of fellow human beings ever have a moment that could be considered a life? Are they really so distant (in every sense that matters) that they are beyond our consideration? What is our responsibility, as geographers and as human beings, in such pressing matters?

This chapter will take up the following questions explicitly: 1) what is justice; 2) in what ways is justice always social and contingent; 3) what are the connections between justice and geography (as a discipline, and as space and place); and 4) what are the implications for geography and geographers of a sustained engagement with issues of justice? Along the way, the discussion will also consider the relationships among justice, ethics and rights, as well as matters of identity and subjectivity. Before turning to these questions directly, however, I want to spend a moment thinking about the notion of the social, since this will permeate all of the discussion that follows.

WE AND ME: AN ONGOING CONTEST

In her influential 1990 book *Justice and the Politics of Difference*, Iris Marion Young constructs a useful explication of the nature of social groups. She begins this way because she is interested in oppression and injustice as systemic, structural phenomena rather than as mechanisms simply affecting individuals *per se*. She distinguishes social groups immediately from both aggregates and associations. The basis for these distinctions is manifold. The first is ontological, and suggests that most characterizations of the latter two categories assume that identity precedes affiliation, and that such identity is individuated, atomistic, whole, and centered. In *aggregates*, membership is imposed upon whole individuals according to various characteristics that members of the aggregate are presumed to share. These characteristics might include, to use some of Young's examples, eye color or street of residence, but can clearly be thought of as both somewhat arbitrary, and more importantly as not necessarily salient to one's self-identity or social position. A second distinction assumes that affiliation, again by whole individuals, with *associations* is voluntary. One chooses to be associated with other whole individuals who share some important interests, practices or intentions. Clearly, some important elements of self-identity may be bound up in the kinds of associational relations encountered in such interactions.

What Young is interested in, however, are groups with high social salience, to which people are assigned arbitrarily, and through which identities and subjectivities are defined relationally (rather than as ontologically prior to assignment to the group). In order to advance this concept she draws upon Heidegger's (1962) notion of 'thrownness.' Young takes this to mean:

> ... one *finds oneself* as a member of a group, which one experiences as always already having been. For our identities are defined in relation to how others identify us, and they do so in terms of groups which are always already associated with the specific attributes, stereotypes, and norms. (1990: 46, emphasis in original)

Two insights emerge from this orientation that are critical for the discussion below. The first is the ontological assertion that identities and subjectivities are relational rather than individuated. Each of us exists as always already situated with respect to 'others.' This position has important implications for notions of justice, morality and ethics. The second key point is the arbitrary (particularly, as I will elaborate momentarily, from a moral perspective) nature of our assignment to potent social groups that are differentially inflected with respect to matters of (in)justice.

Anticipating some of my later remarks, the argument about the relational nature of identity can logically be extended to assert that these necessary relationships carry with them certain obligations and duties to the 'others' with whom we are always and ineluctably entangled. If our very existence as beings is relational, then we are dependent rather than independent, connected rather than autonomous, collectively rather than self-made, and within and a part of history rather than apart from history.

Of course, this ontological position, and its concomitant normative, moral and ethical commitments, is itself a site of intense intellectual and political struggle. In fact, the necessity of re-asserting the social in the present *Handbook*, is the result of ongoing cultural work (in a variety of venues and through multiple mechanisms) to construct our notion of the world otherwise, that is, as based on an individuated social ontology. To argue for such an ontology is to argue simultaneously for a diminishing of our social entanglements and responsibilities to others; it is to argue for the dystopic, Thatcherite worldview that there is no such thing as society. It is the perspective of all against all, the competitive self-serving atom, whose only interests are his/her own. I will return to a number of these comments in the subsequent discussion. For now, I want to use Young's/Heidegger's other key insight, 'thrownness,' to begin a more systematic examination of justice.

WHAT IS JUSTICE? OR WHAT'S FAIR IS FAIR

One critical dimension of Heidegger's notion of 'thrownness' is its arbitrary nature. The term itself connotes the uncontrollability of our initial position (and endowments) in life. Not only are original positions serendipitous, but more to the point they are also morally arbitrary, and this is the key link to notions of justice. If we begin this exploration of justice with the notion of moral arbitrariness, it immediately makes clear that we neither deserve (merit) disproportionate shares of life's benefits nor should we be blamed for a disproportionate share of life's burdens.

David Smith presents a concise, and spatialized, starting definition of justice as 'who gets what, where, when and how' (1994: 26). Because of the moral arbitrariness of initial benefits and burdens, Smith (along with many other moral philosophers) argues for equality as both the logical definition of justice, as well as the ideal normative intent for an appropriate system of justice. Smith's formulation implies a distribution (of life's benefits and burdens), and provokes questions about what, precisely, is to be distributed. As we will see presently, others suggest that the notion of justice goes far beyond simply matters of distribution.

The conception of morally arbitrary starting positions also carries several other important implications for our notions of justice. Because no one has control over the circumstances (temporal, geographic, familial, socio-economic, gender, race, biological, etc.) of his/her birth, or the potential or actual uneven life chances that such accidents of birth entail, many moral philosophers argue that systems of justice should be aimed at reducing these disparities. That is, systems of justice should be pointing to equality as an ideal. From this position, it follows that competing theories of justice (those that compete with egalitarian theories of justice), therefore, are aimed at justifying (or at least explaining) inequality. Such theories ask: on what bases can inequality be justified? Smith (1994) provides a useful overview of several such competing theories (utilitarianism, libertarianism, contractarianism, communitarianism, feminism and Marxism), and works through their rationalizations of unequal treatment of persons, as well as provides a cogent critique of their relative conceptual and practical strengths and weaknesses. Essentially all of these approaches maintain equality as an ideal, but push forward either pragmatic or normative explanations for deviations from this ideal. But the notion of justice as equality is itself quite problematic in several respects.

First, as already noted, is the issue of what is to be equalized? This is both a conceptual matter as well as a practical consideration. Does justice demand an equalization of life's goods and bads, *per se* (raising, of course, the specter of differing definitions of goods and bads), or an equalization of opportunity for accessing these outcomes (attempting to even out all of those disparities produced by the morally arbitrary circumstances of birth)? What about accounting for all of those contingent factors that might intervene between opportunity and outcome? Does justice demand attention to these matters as well? In what ways do these concerns ramify across space and over time? What is the spatial and temporal jurisdiction of justice, and what can equality mean within such considerations?

A second concern, tied very closely to these matters, is the typical connection between justice as equalization and the notion of justice as a matter of distribution. For many moral philosophers, this conflation is itself a problem. As we shall see below, many argue that such a connection immediately implies a flattened, monolithic view of justice (as universal), thereby denying legitimate calls for recognition of difference and competing notions of the good. It also tends to reduce justice to a set of tangible goods, services, and positionalities that are argued to be too limiting for personal actualization and growth.

DIFFERING NOTIONS OF JUSTICE

James O'Connor draws an important distinction between the kinds of distributive justice just described, and what he terms 'productive justice,' and argues that:

> In bourgeois thought, 'justice' refers to the equitable distribution of things, not the equitable *production* of things, for example, the equal application of the law to all, not the equal production of the law by all (in fact, law is produced by elites). Bourgeois justice is thus 'distributive justice,' not 'productive justice.' More, distributive justice pertains, first and foremost, to individual rights/claims not to social rights/claims. (1998: 338, emphasis in original)

A number of important insights emerge from this formulation. Firstly, it makes clear that (in)justice precedes and permeates distributions, and plays a critical role in their nature and content. Second, it repositions various actors relative to issues of (in)justice and begins to take account of the unevenness of power and its role in determining both life chances and outcomes. Third, this perspective opens up the concept of justice beyond an assumed universal form and content, to allow difference its due. And finally, O'Connor's orientation takes the notion of justice beyond the allocation (fair or unfair) of material things. In this regard, O'Connor's formulation also differs from the notion of procedural justice, which speaks to the fairness of mechanisms of distribution and not necessarily to their construction.

All of these elements resonate quite closely with Young's (1990) refiguring of justice as the reduction (at least) or elimination (when/where possible) of oppression. In thinking about justice this way, Young is attempting both to specify as clearly as possible the important elements of (in)justice, as well as to move the concept beyond simply distribution. She couches her formulation as comprising five faces of oppression: exploitation, marginalization, powerlessness, cultural imperialism, and violence. She conceives of each of these as structural and systemic, rather than as the result of individuated practices.

The need to better understand the nature of oppression stems from Young's expanded notion of justice, and her commitment to furthering the emancipatory goals of social movement groups. Her assessment is worth examining in some detail. As in O'Connor's formulation, in Young's work the concept of justice moves beyond the equitable distribution of life's necessities, comforts, luxuries, and burdens, to include the potential for people to participate fully in the conditions, situations and decision processes that give rise to particular distributions in the first place. As Young makes clear, fair and equitable distribution of life's benefits and burdens is inevitably a key component of justice, but for some groups to be always and only (that is, systemically) on the receiving end of these distributional processes (even if equitable) is itself an injustice.

As Young elaborates, the first three faces of oppression (exploitation, marginalization and powerlessness) emerge from the social division of labor and the unequal power relations embedded in that division. Groups burdened with these forms of oppression clearly face obstacles in their material lives as well as in their ability to control and deploy their own creative and other capabilities. Young's use of the notion of exploitation is a fairly straightforward Marxian interpretation:

> this oppression occurs through a steady process of the transfer of the results of the labor of one social group to benefit another. The injustice of class division does not consist only in the distributive fact that some people have great wealth while most people have little ... Exploitation enacts a structural relation between social groups. Social rules about what work is, who does what for whom, how work is compensated, and the social process by which the results of work are appropriated operate to enact relations of power and inequality. These relations are produced and reproduced through a systematic process in which the energies of the have-nots are continuously expended to maintain and augment the power, status and wealth of the haves. (1990: 49–50)

Though Young acknowledges critiques of this Marxist notion of exploitation as somewhat narrow in its typical focus on class relations, her discussion goes on to elaborate how this form of oppression (and injustice) can be tied conceptually to gendered and racialized notions of inequity as well. These linkages are intimated in the definition of exploitation above; that is, exploitation occurs whenever there is the transfer of energies (labor power) from one group to another to produce unequal distributions. This diagnostic evaluation of exploitation also leads Young to conclude that this form of injustice cannot be remedied through simple redistribution. As she states:

> as long as [unjust] institutionalized practices and structural relations [of exploitation] remain unaltered, the process of transfer will re-create an unequal distribution of benefits [and burdens]. Bringing about justice where there is exploitation requires reorganization of institutions and practices of decisionmaking, alteration of the division of labor, and similar measures of institutional, structural and cultural change. (1990: 53)

Marginalization, Young's second face of oppression, affects those members of societies whom the labor system cannot or will not use. In addition to those subjected to the capricious vicissitudes of mobile capital (both within and across societies), other social groups are oppressed through processes of marginalization: the young, the elderly, those who are differently abled (physically or mentally), or those precluded from the labor system by other exigencies (for example, single mothers without access to childcare). By definition then, these people are constrained in obtaining material security, but for Young marginalization as oppression goes beyond such matters of distribution. To some extent material deprivation can be alleviated through redistribution schemes (the most common liberal form being welfare provision), but this does not address two additional elements of oppression that occur as a result of being marginalized: the dehumanizing aspects of being dependent in advanced capitalist societies, and the lack of self-respect and usefulness that full participation in society both brings and valorizes. Those who are marginalized, though perhaps not materially deprived, might still be subjected to these affronts to personal dignity and diminished participation in social life. One avenue for redressing the injustice of marginalization, then, is to recalibrate the relationship between socially meaningful 'work' (as comprising only paid work in sanctioned arenas of production) and access to means of consumption and full social participation.

Young's conception of powerlessness, the third face of oppression, emerges from her assessment of the nature of contemporary class-based social divisions of labor within advanced capitalist societies. Here Young differentiates 'middle' and 'working' classes and professionals from non-professionals. While all may be labor (as opposed to capital), not all are equal in the social division of labor. Young characterizes non-professionals as being doubly oppressed by both their exploitation (see above) as well as their relative powerlessness:

> The powerless are those who lack authority or power ... those over whom power is exercised without their exercising it; the powerless are situated so that they must take orders and rarely have the right to give them.... The powerless have little or no work autonomy, exercise little creativity or judgment in their work, have no technical expertise or authority .... This powerless status is perhaps best described negatively: the powerless lack the authority, status, and sense of self that professionals tend to have. (1990: 56–7)

As with other faces of oppression, powerlessness brings both unjust distributional material effects, as well as broader social forms of injustice. For Young, these additional inequities stem from the lack of social respect with which those in non-professional dimensions of the social division of labor are treated. Professionalization usually carries with it expanded expertise, authority (for example, over non-professionals), and concomitant privileges beyond the workplace. It is through this combination of characteristics that professionals gain status and respectability in society, and the lack of this respectability produces injustice and oppression for those not similarly endowed. For Young these injustices include 'inhibition in the development of one's capacities, lack of decision-making power in one's working life, and exposure to disrespectful treatment because of the status one occupies' (1990: 58).

The two additional faces of oppression (cultural imperialism and violence), Young argues, operate in a somewhat different manner from these previous three (all of which are tied to the social division of labor). Young uses the notion of cultural imperialism (her fourth face of oppression) to describe the systematic and structural ways in which a dominant group constructs a social hierarchy of difference, with their own experiences and cultural products as superior, and those of all other groups as subordinate. The worldview of the dominant group is taken as the norm and all other viewpoints as not only different, but inferior. In Young's argument cultural imperialism is the principal mechanism through which a dominant group's perspectives become taken for granted, universalized, and naturalized as not only the way things are (descriptively), but also as the way things should be (normatively and prescriptively). Of course, these are never settled matters, but are sites for intense struggle. Young argues that cultural imperialism produces a kind of paradoxical doubled oppression through which subordinated groups are both stereotyped and devalued, while simultaneously erased and stripped of effectivity. (In)justice itself becomes a matter of dominant articulations, and competing, differentiated views are made invisible and silent. This form of oppression and injustice has resonance within geography with much of the life-long work of the late Jim Blaut (1970, 1975, 1994, 2000).

Finally, Young is concerned with systematic (as opposed to 'random') violence as a form of direct oppression and injustice. While the notion of violence is reasonably self-evident, the potential connections between violence and the other faces of oppression need elaboration. To do so it is useful to draw on Antonio Gramsci's (1971) notions of hegemony and coercion. By and large, the four other faces of oppression work very much in accordance with Gramsci's formulation of hegemony as domination, largely (though not completely or evenly) with the consent of the dominated. Under hegemonic conditions, the interests of subordinated groups are made to seem, through various apparatuses (the media and the educational system to name just two), congruent with those of dominant groups or elites. Those in dominant positions are seen to hold those positions legitimately since they are presumably acting in the interest of all. As long as the hegemony holds, domination produces little resistance or opposition. It is when hegemony begins to break down, when the legitimacy and credibility of those in dominant positions begins to be questioned, that other means of social control become necessary to maintain the status quo. One of these other means is systemic violence.

One crucial intersection between the other faces of oppression and violence, and the dimension that makes it systemic rather than individuated, and therefore a matter of (in) justice, is the social context produced by exploitation, marginalization, powerlessness and cultural imperialism in which some groups are significantly devalued and delegitimized relative to others. These processes not only mark out differences from the dominant 'norm,' but hierarchize such differences in a social pecking order, establishing a set of cultural and societal patterns that make violence against members of such groups both 'possible and acceptable' according to Young (1990: 61–2).

It is worth reiterating that Young's careful dissection of oppression and injustice in these ways has quite profound implications for political coalition and movements for justice. To the extent that oppressions can be shown to be variously produced, but systemic nonetheless, it might be possible to reduce internecine claims that some oppressions are more fundamental (or authentic or worthy) than others, and that differing bases for calls for justice can be used to join struggles together.

A way into this matter is to examine some of the work of another justice scholar, Nancy Fraser, who in much of her work takes up similar questions to those of Young, and for quite similar reasons.[1] Fraser, like Young, is vitally concerned with matters of social justice, and seeks to understand it in ways that go beyond the typical and traditional focus on (re)distribution. She constructs her analysis along two important axes of claims for justice, neither of which, she argues, is reducible to the other: 1) *redistribution*, understood as redress for existing maldistributions of benefits and burdens; and 2) *recognition*, understood as redress for cultural domination and impositions of dominant culture as the norm. As Fraser (1997a) describes, her interest in these intersecting dimensions of justice grew out of empirical observations that the rise of post-socialist political culture and of identity politics seemed to put these two bases for claims for justice into conflict or competition. Much of her recent work is an attempt to reconcile these appeals for justice and to demonstrate their fundamental compatibility within the realms of both analysis and politics.

In many respects, the work of Fraser and the work of Young is quite similar. Fraser combines Young's first three faces of oppression (exploitation, marginalization and powerlessness) into the axis of redistribution, and equates Young's notion of cultural imperialism (and by extension, Young's category of violence) with the axis of recognition. Her argument is that both maldistribution and misrecognition are distinct categories of injustice, that they arise through different mechanisms, and that they require different forms of remedy and redress. Although there are some similarities in intention and approach,

Fraser's explicit focus on the issue of recognition allows us to examine several critical components of justice in more detail.

A useful route into this examination is a brief discussion of a debate between Fraser and Young over the course of the 1990s (Fraser, 1989, 1995, 1997a, 1997b, 1999; Young, 1990, 1997). Though there are many interesting elements to this debate, here I single out one main theme for its salience to the present discussion: the question of the relationships among oppression, liberation, and justice. Young and Fraser are in substantial agreement on these matters when thinking about justice as fair distribution of material goods and bads (that is, those elements of both schemas that relate directly to the political economy and the division of labor; Young's first three faces of oppression and Fraser's axis of distribution). Where they diverge is over the matter of recognition (Fraser) and cultural imperialism and violence (Young). The nub of the argument is that Young sees recognition (or the redress for cultural imperialism and violence) as a means (one among several) to the end of a just distribution, while Fraser seems to see recognition primarily as an end itself. Two critical questions arise from this element of the debate. First, what is the metric to be used to assess justice? Put another way, how do we know when oppression (in Young's terms) or misrecognition (in Fraser's terms) have been eliminated or reduced? Young's answer is when distributions are more equitable and remaining inequalities can be explained not as the result of invidious comparisons among stereotyped groups, but rather due largely to the arbitrariness of life's lottery. (Incidentally, it is precisely in this sense that not all inequality is injustice.)

Fraser's analysis provides no clear answer to this question. It is somewhat difficult to see how remedies of misrecognition could be assessed meaningfully except as they result in more equitable distributions. Indeed, elsewhere Fraser herself recognizes that such is the case. In a more recent piece, Fraser wonders why so many contemporary conflicts take the form of claims to recognition. Her conclusion:

> To pose this question is also to note the relative decline in claims for egalitarian redistribution. Once the hegemonic grammar of political contestation, the language of distribution is less salient today. The movements that not long ago boldly demanded an equitable share of resources and wealth have not, to be sure, wholly disappeared. But thanks to the sustained neoliberal rhetorical assault on egalitarianism, to the absence of any credible model of 'feasible socialism' and to widespread doubts about the viability of state-Keynesian social democracy in the face of globalization, their role has been greatly reduced .... In this context, questions of recognition are serving less to supplement, complicate and enrich redistributive struggles than to marginalize, eclipse and displace them. (Fraser, 2000: 107–108)

In other words, failing to achieve more parity in distributional terms, misrecognition remedies take the form of symbolic compromises. As Fraser goes on to note in this vein 'insofar as the politics of recognition displaces the politics of redistribution, it may actually promote economic inequality' (2000: 108).

The foregoing then leads to the second question, and perhaps this question helps to resolve the dilemma: what is to be included in the notion of distribution? It is clear that Young's conception of justice goes beyond fair distribution of material goods and includes some control over the decision processes that govern distributions. Fraser's position here is similar and is made explicit with her concept of 'parity of participation.' As described above, O'Connor (1998: 338) construes this as a distinction between productive and distributive justice. For O'Connor, productive justice operates in precisely the spheres of decision making, capacity enablement, communication, and participation that concern Young and Fraser. Productive justice includes real (as opposed to merely token) involvement in the processes that help determine life chances for oneself and others. Are there ways, in this light, to think about distribution as including more than material goods and bads? Productive justice (or Young's expanded notion of justice, or Fraser's parity of participation) is about control over one's own decisions and choices.

But to what end? Ideally, to the fair distribution of all of life's goods and bads, including material as well as such non-material goods as respect, security from harm, and the elimination (or at least reduction) of hierarchies of difference and associated systemic violence.

This formulation is responsive to Young's critique of Fraser and helps to resolve the dilemma that Fraser presents. By thinking about recognition as a necessary, though often insufficient, step toward fair distribution, and by thinking about distribution in this expanded way, it is possible to reconcile these two axes of justice, and accord them their due status in both theoretical and political spheres.

Before turning to the specific connections between justice and geography, I want to spend a moment discussing the linkages (multiple and complex) among justice, ethics and rights. As the discussion thus far should make quite clear, I view all of these as relational and contingent matters. Our notions of justice (fairness), ethics (the good), and rights (our entitlements or just deserts) are bound up with other elements of our acculturation and socialization in particular times and places. The fact that some elements of these matters appear (or have been made to appear) to be timeless and universal through wide practice should not blind us to their essential, contingent nature. Nor should normative arguments that particular notions of justice, ethics or rights *should* obtain universally sway us overmuch. Such assertions should be seen for the power plays they are, and should keep us alert to the fact that the content of justice, rights and ethics are important and ongoing sites of struggle and contestation.

Justice, ethics and rights, for all of their contingency, are held in a mutually reinforcing ontological embrace. It is only because we have some notion of the good (albeit constructed and dynamic over time and space, and always subject to interpretation and contest) that we can recognize injustice at all (that is, as a lack of the good for some, or its overabundance for others). Equally importantly, such a sense of the good must constitute the basis for appeal when competing and conflicting claims for just treatment require adjudication, rather than resolution through pure power politics. Likewise, reflection upon matters of (in)justice (and fair or unfair treatment) and actions seeking redress (e.g., through the invocation of existing or new rights) may call up new or revised notions of the good. Rights, in this conception, represent particular (and often transitory or merely rhetorical) instantiations of the good or the just at particular moments and in specific places. Drawing upon notions of the good and/or the just, victims of oppression and injustice (as described above) can call for legitimized redress by appealing to existing rights regimes, or can demand (as citizens, humans, or other 'identities') that rights regimes be expanded to fit new conditions of injustice. As Mitchell (1997) argues, rights are often problematic (not least because they often validate the legitimacy and power of the rights-granting authority), but are worth pursuing nonetheless. Without pursuing those matters further, suffice to say here, that rights (as summoning up obligatory relations with 'others,' rather than as 'things' we possess), call into focus the nature of the good and the just, as well as the identities for whom those matter.

GEOGRAPHY AND JUSTICE

With the foregoing understanding of justice (and ethics and rights) in hand, I now want to turn to the connections between these matters and geography. In this section I mean geography in two senses of the word: geography as places and spaces (material and discursive) that people inhabit, and geography as discipline, including its intellectual and political commitments, personnel and practices.

The discussion above has already signaled the two principal ways in which (in)justice is connected to places and spaces. The first is the geographic unevenness with which life's material and social resources are distributed around the planet conjoined with the arbitrariness (the 'thrownness') of the circumstances of human birth. Where (in physical and social space) and when we appear in the world has a great deal to do with our subsequent life chances. The second, and closely associated, connection to geography in this sense is the fact that we are also arbitrarily 'thrown' into an uneven moral and ethical landscape at birth, which inflects and calibrates the material and social circumstances (including our own personal attributes) of our entry into the world, as well as our sense of what is just and unjust.

Here, at the beginning of the 21st century, these spatial disparities (and consequent injustices) could not be more apparent. For example, according to Mike Davis (2006), somewhat more than one in six people (over 1 billion of our fellow beings) now live in the burgeoning slums that surround the major urban areas of the global south. Also, according to a recent report of the World Bank, even in the midst of abundance for a small minority of the world's population, 1.2 billion people live on less than US$1/day and almost 3 billion on less than US$2/day.[2] The 'household per capita income differential between a rich city like Seattle [Washington, USA] and a very poor city like Ibadan [Nigeria] is as great as *739 to 1* – an incredible inequality' (Davis, 2006: 25–7, emphasis in original). These stark spatial disparities in wealth and development that have characterized 'centers' and 'peripheries' (and more latterly, the so-called 'first' and 'third' worlds) for the past several centuries are likely to become even more dramatic as competition for the planet's remaining scarce resources (principally oil and water) intensifies over the next two decades, in what Michael Klare (2001) terms the impending 'resource wars,' and David Harvey (2003) calls 'the new imperialism.' Declining availability of relatively cheap energy [the so-called 'global oil peak' described by, among many others, Kunstler (2005)] will produce wrenching changes within and across many societies, and like the antecedent conditions onto which these new calamities will be imposed, the outcomes for particular places and people are far from uniform. It is unclear, at the moment, whether these changes, at least over the long term, might narrow the gap between haves and have nots (by virtue of many more people joining the ranks of the have nots). In the lead-up to the loss of these resources, however, and in any transition to a new status quo, it seems quite likely that diminishing vital resources will simply exacerbate existing inequalities and injustices.

The second connection between justice and geography (as space and place) concerns the disparate notions of ethics (and consequently, justice) that exist within and across societies. Many geographers have explored these linkages (including Sack, 1999; and D. Smith, 1994, 2000), but the one I want to concentrate on here is Kenneth Olwig's close examination of the relationship between landscape and justice.[3] In his 1996 paper 'Recovering the substantive nature of landscape' Olwig provides a detailed history and rehabilitation of the long-standing geographic concept of landscape. Through both an etymological excavation and a philosophical recovery project, Olwig re-articulates a set of linkages between place and identity, including the links (non-deterministic to be sure) between the particularities embedded in the struggles over such geographic phenomena as landscapes, communities, and territories and the specific knowledges built through those struggles. As Olwig puts it: Landscape ... need not be understood as being either territory or scenery; it can also be conceived as a nexus of community, justice, nature, and environmental equity, a contested territory that is as pertinent today as it was when the term entered the modern English language at the end of the sixteenth century (1996: 630–1).

Olwig points to the important intersections between people and the places they inhabit. Through his analysis of landscape (in its various interpretations), we come to see how places and people are mutually constituted. *Where* one is in the world plays a crucial role in *how* and *what* one is in the world. The kinds of relationships and networks exemplified by Fraser's new social movements and Young's social groups, actually exist in particular times and places, and these material dimensions of their existence, as Olwig argues, matter a great deal to their make-up and to the acculturating effects they exert on their inhabitants. Knowing one's place means more than a knowledge of the physical landscape, and clearly implies knowing one's position in social, cultural, political, and power landscapes as well. Such knowledges are built in particular times and places through the performance of everyday practices in interaction with others, and such practices vary over time and among and between places. In his own words, again, Olwig draws on evidence from Northern European landscape art of the late 1400s and early 1500s:

> [The subject of the art] is clearly *Landschaft* in the full sense of the word. It was much more than 'beautiful natural scenery.' It was imbued with meanings, etched by custom in the land, that were at the heart of the major political, legal, and cultural issues of the time. It was at the center of the process by which members of the non-noble estates of emerging national bodies sought to establish cultural identities as active, politically engaged, and patriotic citizenries. (1996: 634–635)

As Olwig makes clear, it is in places that we develop significant aspects of our identities including notions of justice, ethics and morality, for good or ill. And, it is to the issue of identity, and its connections both to geography (now as both space/place and discipline) and to justice that I wish to turn in the final sections of this chapter. I want to approach these matters through some of the recent work of Sarah Whatmore (and through her Donna Haraway, 1991 and Bruno Latour, 1993, among others).

An influential paper by Whatmore (1997): 'Dissecting the autonomous self: hybrid cartographies for a relational ethics,' opens up key questions about identity, the ethical subject and the spatial relations of ethics, morality and justice. Whatmore develops three key arguments in her paper: 1) in a discussion that draws upon recent work in feminist scholarship, and that resonates with major elements of parts of this chapter, she reframes and deepens our understanding of people as always constructed in relation to others, rather than as autonomous; 2) drawing upon work in environmental ethics, she makes an argument for extending moral considerability beyond the human; and 3) she considers the spatial implications for justice considered in these relational ways. The thread that ties the three arguments together is the possibility of expanding the notion of ethical community, and for extending the purview of justice. In making such arguments, Whatmore is assessing both the conceptual matters themselves, as well as their implications for the practice of geographic scholarship and activism.

Whatmore's first argument seeks to problematize the notion of the autonomous, independent self. The adherence to individualized notions of self and other, inherited from early enlightenment thinkers (for instance, Locke) erects boundaries that prohibit the extension of moral considerability. Such formulations, Whatmore argues, contribute directly to a geography of proximity and homogeneity (that is, a bounded 'us' at a variety of scales: individual, neighborhood, nation) where care and justice obtain (though often quite unevenly), and a sharply demarcated, heterogeneous outside, where such considerations apply much less consistently, if at all. Taken to its logical extreme this orientation eventuates in the Thatcherite individuation decried at the outset of the chapter. If, in contradistinction, the boundaries between self and other can be seen as always artificial, blurry, and dialectical, then one's obligations and sense of caring and justice might more readily be extended to an always, already co-present 'we.'

The second argument, drawing directly on evolving scholarship in environmental ethics, makes an analagous case for extending the boundary of moral considerability to the other entities (both human and non-human) with which we share the planet. By identifying the parallels based on the interconnectedness of human beings in relation to networks of other living, and non-living 'things,' Whatmore's argument attempts to avoid the dilemmas that environmental ethicists have faced when trying to extend human-centered moral considerability to non-humans and the environment. These difficulties arise precisely from the same foundational concepts of autonomy and separateness that are typically encountered in extending care (morality, ethics, justice) to human 'others.' Whatmore argues that these problems are eased considerably when we are no longer able to postulate our identities (our subjecthood or self) in isolation from the networks in which we are always embedded. Just as we are always relationally defined by interaction with other people, we are materially (corporeally) immersed in the complicated relationships that comprise the biosphere. Understanding the always, already nature of these relationships both constrains us from thinking ourselves separately and enables the extension of moral considerability to other organisms and inanimate 'nature.'

Whatmore's final set of comments seeks to make all of this explicitly spatial. She is interested, here, in thinking through the possibilities of extending what feminist scholars (e.g., Gilligan, 1982) have called an 'ethic of care.' If notions of autonomy and independence allow for moral considerability largely on the basis of proximity (whether materially or affectively), Whatmore argues that notions of the self dialectically and continuously in relation to 'others,' should help us rethink our concepts of 'nearness' and 'distance.' In drawing on Latour's (1993) notion of hybridity as networks of animate, mechanical and discursive actants, Whatmore suggests that this orientation is a way to break through an impasse of 'individualist ethics' at a number of points:

> First, it [Latour's hybridity] releases 'nature' and non-human beings from their relegation to the status of objects with no ethical standing in the human pursuit of individual self-interest, *without* resorting to the extension of this liberal conception of ethical agency to other animals. Second, it substantiates an intersubjective understanding of ethical agency and community by which the corporeal connectivities between differently constituted actants can be traced in particular material circumstances and specified cases. And finally, it liberates the geographical imaginary of ethical community from the terriorialised spaces of the embodied individual, the local neighborhood, and the nation-state, to trace the threads of ethical considerability through more dynamic, unstable, and performed spatial orderings of flow, mobility and synthesis. (1997: 47–9, emphasis in original)

What Whatmore is articulating in these arguments, I would suggest, is an alternative topology of justice. Though she uses the terms cartography and topography in her formulations, I believe her argument moves beyond the mapping and study implied by this vocabulary. Rather, I think her arguments (as do those of Latour and Haraway) move us into actually rethinking the ontologies of situated actors and the situations (sites and conditions) that they both create and act within. For such a topology, we need an alternative metric. Linear distance can no longer be the measure of near or far 'others' who always co-habit the networks we share. Perhaps such metrics as density and intensity of connections, necessity and frequency of reciprocity, or stability or emphemerality of affinities, could serve as the new measures that would allow us to construct and negotiate these alternative imaginaries of geographic justice and morality.

JUSTICE AND THE PRACTICE OF GEOGRAPHY

These final concerns of Whatmore's lead me into a brief discussion of the implications of a commitment to social justice for geography as a discipline, and for the practices of 'good' geographers. In modern geography a concern with social justice can be noted in the work of the anarchists (e.g., Kropotkin, Reclus) in the late 1800s. It was not until the late 1960s, however, that the field (like many others in the social sciences and humanities) took a decisive 'normative' turn from which there is now no possible retreat, though 'progress' is never assured or even. The phrase 'normative turn' has taken on various meanings over time, but here I take it to signify several inter-related dimensions. First, and foremost, it means that (for those who take the critiques of the normative turn seriously), geographical scholarship must be concerned not only with description and explanation of what the world *is*, but must equally be concerned with questions of what the world *should be*. Second, it has meant, and continues to mean, coming to grips with such questions as what is scholarship, who is authorized to produce it, under what circumstances, and for what purposes? This normative turn consisted of both a negative critique of existing responses to such questions within geography (and in academia more generally), and a positive critique that offered alternative questions, methods and purposes. Though the calls during this period were, in part at least, for relevance for the field, it was a particular kind of relevance that was being advocated. It is clear that the kinds of geographic scholarship that preceded this normative turn could also put forward legitimate claims to relevance, but on very different grounds; grounds that were quite strenuously critiqued by the new vanguard in the discipline (see Staeheli and Mitchell, 2005, for some related observations).

At this point, a number of geographers, responding both to conditions within the field and to material and intellectual circumstances in society more generally, grew quite restive with many facets of the discipline. These scholars were becoming more aware of (and more responsive to) a number of important social movements that were beginning to coalesce around key issues of the time, including: 1) rising opposition to the Vietnam War (and its characterization as part of ongoing imperialist and neo-colonialist projects against the global south by the global north); 2) the early stirrings of so-called 'second wave' feminism and mounting resistance to the structures and strictures of patriarchy (and by extension, other forms of traditionally constituted 'normativity'); 3) an ongoing struggle for the expansion of civil rights to a variety of minorities who saw themselves excluded from the post-World War II prosperity that had lifted many other segments of the US society; and 4) a newly energized environmental movement given its impetus by overt signs of an environment polluted and overburdened to the point of crisis.

An important early piece by David Harvey (1972) both encapsulated the nature of the critique, and issued a (rather shrill some said at the time) clarion call to a new kind of geographic scholarship. In 'Revolutionary and counter-revolutionary theory in geography and the problem of ghetto formation' Harvey articulates the incipient concerns of the 'normative' turn, formulates a cogent critique of the then-current state of geographic scholarship from this normative perspective, and describes (by means of both argument and an abbreviated case study) what he himself was then groping toward as a more engaged, productive and progressive form of such scholarship.

In Harvey's view, evolving at the time, Marxism provided a useful corrective for one prominent aspect of status quo geography, an issue fundamental to the 'normative' turn. As he states, following Marx directly, 'positivism simply seeks to understand the world, whereas Marxism seeks to change it' (1972: 7). In pursuing this orientation, Harvey argued strongly that not only is status quo (and even more extremely, counter-revolutionary) theorizing unlikely to lead to progressive change, it actually contributes to oppressive conditions. It accomplishes this important legitimizing function by supplying support, if only tacitly, to existing circumstances. The kind of evidentiary work being carried out at the time by most mainstream geographers (and other social scientists), even when working on crucial social issues, in Harvey's view, provided a sense that 'bleeding heart liberals' (1972: 10) were contributing to solutions when, in fact, they were merely perpetuating the problems themselves. Since the underlying causes of these problems reside in the capitalist system itself, and since that system was never a subject of analysis, Harvey argues that mainstream scholars were constantly doomed to treating symptoms and missing the underlying issues entirely.

Finally, Harvey argues in the piece for a new role for geographers and other scholars, as intellectuals and academics. This new role consists in developing arguments of such persuasive strength that 'all opposition to that system of thought looks ridiculous' (1972: 11). And he includes the caution that academics, in such matters, are often 'our own worst opponents.' Here Harvey is clearly referring to the difficulty of challenging the taken-for-granted categories of thought and scholarly practice that often constrain the shift to new paradigms, particularly those that also challenge the political status quo within which academics do their work. This, as Harvey concludes, becomes especially difficult when the intersections between theory and practice are also a part of the changing mix. He lays down a gauntlet in advocating the need for 'real' as opposed to 'merely liberal' commitment to social change, and in the taunt that it is 'indeed very comfortable to be a mere liberal' (1972: 11).

What Harvey (and others writing at the time) begins to open up in this piece is the complex and continuous inter-relationships among the various elements that together construct scholarly/intellectual thought, and highlights the then-emerging contentions within geography over knowledge, politics, personnel, and practices and methods. These formative statements continue to resonate strongly within the discipline to this day. The piece puts into sharp relief some of the questions raised above: what is scholarship and what should it be? who/what is it for? who can/should produce it? how is it to be pursued? As noted, once asked in this way, these questions are difficult to un-ask.

Consequently, over the last 35 years or so significant elements of the discipline have been concerned with the inevitable political and social contexts within which scholarship is produced. This concern has included assessments of geography's connections (and often complicity) with class exploitation, colonialism and imperialism in both their classical and neo-forms [from Blaut's early work up through recent contributions from Neil Smith (2003) and David Harvey (2003/2005)], as well as other systems of oppression and injustice, including patriarchy (see e.g., Foord and Gregson, 1986; Bowlby et al., 1989); heteronormativity (Bell et al., 1994); and racism (e.g., Bonnett, 1997).

This work has also focused on 'personnel' matters within the discipline, including an expanded notion of who counts in the production of knowledge (from early feminist work such as Hayford, 1973; Tivers, 1978; Monk and Hanson, 1982; up through recent queer geographies of Binnie, 1997; and Valentine, 1993), and other matters of justice in the practice of geography (the make-up and functioning of academic departments, including the multiple roles of students, the corporatization of the academy (Castree and Sparke, 2000) and the concomitant downsizing and casualization of the academic workforce, and the role and stance of our professional organizations and journals). Many of these concerns have also forced a continual reflection on the complex relationships between scholarship and activism both within and 'outside' of the academy (Castree, 2000, 2002; Peck, 1999; Waterstone, 2002, 2004).

Following the 'normative' turn, it has also become much more important (in fact, unavoidable) to consider quite carefully the various ways in which different knowledges and scholarship are produced. What are the range of methods and routes to understanding? How is knowledge to be produced or co-produced with the 'others' with whom we are always and ineluctably entangled? Such questions were much more easily elided under the mantle of apparent objectivity that accompanied geography's (and many other disciplines) long romance with positivism and the (again apparent) rigid tenets of *the* scientific method. The normative turn sensitized geography and geographers to the profound critiques embodied in the standpoint epistemologies of feminists and the important ontological and epistemological challenges of post-structuralism and post-modernism, and the implications of these trenchant critiques for the practices and purposes of scholarly work.

The contemporary concern of geography with social justice illustrates the ways in which engaged scholarship evolves and does its 'work' in society. The kinds of questions just articulated, which would surely have struck most of our disciplinary forebears as recently as 1965 as inappropriate at best and apostasy at worst, are now thoroughly and irretrievably (though unevenly) woven into the fabric of modern geographic theory and practice. For many geographers, asking questions about, and being committed to furtherance of, social justice, now makes as much sense as did the precise elaboration of distance decay functions and von Thünen rings a generation ago. Of course, contests over the meaning of social justice and its role within the discipline must continue to be fought, but the fact that these are legitimate struggles within the discipline is no longer a matter for much serious debate. An incremental step, perhaps, but we should be thankful for the justice of that!

NOTES

1 This discussion draws upon and paraphrases a similar examination that appears in Henderson and Waterstone (2009).

2 The figures are from the G8 Okinawa Summit *Global Poverty Report*, July 2000, available at www.worldbank.org/html/extdr/extme/G8_poverty2000.pdf, accessed 2 March 2007.

3 Again, this discussion draws upon a similar treatment in Henderson and Waterstone (2009).

REFERENCES

Bell, D., Binnie, J., Cream, J., Valentine, G. (1994) 'All hyped up and no place to go', *Gender, Place and Culture*, 1: 31–48.

Binnie, J. (1997) 'Coming out of geography: towards a queer epistemology?' *Enivironment and Planning D: Society and Space*, 15: 223–37.

Blaut, J.M. (1970) 'Geographic models of imperialism', *Antipode*, 2: 65–85.

Blaut, J.M. (1975) 'Imperialism: the Marxist theory and its evolution', *Antipode*, 7: 1–19.

Blaut, J.M. (1994) *The Colonizer's Model of the World*. London: Guilford.

Blaut, J.M. (2000) *Eight Eurocentric Historians*. New York: Guilford.

Bonnett, A. (1997) 'Geography, "race" and whiteness: invisible traditions and current challenges', *Area*, 29: 193–9.

Bowlby, S., Lewis, J., McDowell, L., Foord, J. (1989) 'The geography of gender', in R. Peet and N. Thrift (eds), *New Models in Geography*, Volume 2. London: Unwin Hyman.

Castree, N. (2000) 'What kind of critical geography for what kind of politics'? *Environment and Planning* A, 32: 2091–5.

Castree, N. (2002) 'Border geography', *Area*, 34: 103–12.

Castree, N. and Sparke, M. (2000) 'Introduction: professional geography and the corporatization of the university: experiences, evaluation and engagements', *Antipode*, 32 (3): 222–9.

Davis, M. (2006) *Planet of Slums*. New York: Verso.

Foord, J. and Gregson, N. (1986) 'Patriarchy: towards a reconceptualization', *Antipode*, 18: 186–211.

Fraser, N. (1989) *Unruly Practices: Power, Discourse and Gender in Contemporary Social Theory*. Minneapolis: University of Minnesota Press.

Fraser, N. (1995) 'From redistribution to recognition? Dilemmas of justice in a "postsocialist" age', *New Left Review*, 212: 68–93.

Fraser, N. (1997a) *Justice Interruptus: Critical Reflections on the 'Postsocialist' Condition*. London: Routledge.

Fraser, N. (1997b) 'A rejoinder to Iris Young', *New Left Review*, 223: 126–9.

Fraser, N. (1999) 'Social justice in the age of identity politics: redistribution, recognition, and participation', in L. Ray and A. Sayer (eds), *Culture and Economy After the Cultural Turn*. London: Sage.

Fraser, N. (2000) 'Rethinking recognition', *New Left Review*, 3: 107–20.

Gilligan, C. (1982) *In a Different Voice*. Cambridge: Harvard University Press.

Gramsci, A. (1971) *Selections from the Prison Notebooks*. New York: International Publishers.

Haraway, D. (1991) *Simians, Cyborgs and Women: The Reinvention of Nature*. London: Free Association Books.

Harvey, D. (1972) 'Revolutionary and counter-revolutionary theory in geography and the problem of ghetto formation', *Antipode*, 4 (2): 1–13.
Harvey, D. [2005 (2003)] *The New Imperialism*. Oxford: Oxford University Press.
Hayford, A. (1973) 'The geography of women: an historical introduction', *Antipode*, 5: 26–33.
Heidegger, M. (1962) *Being and Time*. New York: Harper and Row.
Henderson, G. and Waterstone, M. (2009) *Geographic Thought: A Praxis Perspective*. London and New York: Routledge.
Klare, M. (2001) *Resource Wars*. New York: Metropolitan Books.
Kunstler, J. (2005) *The Long Emergency: Surviving the Converging Catastrophes of the 21st Century*. New York: Atlantic Monthly Press.
Latour, B. (1993) *We Have Never Been Modern*. Brighton: Harvester Wheatsheaf.
Mitchell, D. (1997) 'State restructuring and the importance of "rights talk"', in L. Staeheli, J. Kodras, and C. Flint (eds), *State Devolution in America: Implications for a Diverse Society*. Thousand Oaks, CA: Sage Publications.
Monk, J. and Hanson, S. (1982) 'On not excluding half of the human in human geography', *Professional Geographer*, 34 (1): 11–23.
O'Connor, J. (1998) *Natural Causes: Essays in Ecological Marxism*. New York: The Guilford Press.
Olwig, K. (1996) 'Recovering the substantive nature of landscape', *Annals of the Association of American Geographers*, 86 (4): 630–53.
Peck, J. (1999) 'Grey geography'?, *Transactions of the Institute of British Geographers*, New Series, 24: 131–5.
Rawls, J. (1971) *A Theory of Justice*. Cambridge: Harvard University Press.
Sack, R. (1999) 'A sketch of a geographic theory of morality', *Annals of the Association of American Geographers*, 89 (1): 26–44.
Smith, D.M. (1994) *Geography and Social Justice*. Oxford and New York: Blackwell.
Smith, D.M. (2000) 'Moral progress in human geography: transcending the place of good fortune', *Progress in Human Geography*, 24 (1): 1–18.
Smith, L. (2007) 'Bash makes history', *New York Post*, 16 February.
Smith, N. (2003) *American Empire: Roosevelt's Geographer and the Prelude to Globalization*. Berkeley: University of California Press.
Staeheli, L. and Mitchell, D. (2005) 'The complex politics of relevance in geography', *Annals of the Association of American Geographers*, 95 (2): 357–72.
Tivers, J. (1978) 'How the other half lives: the geographical study of women', *Area*, 10: 302–6.
Valentine, G. (1993) '(Hetero)sexing space: lesbian perceptions and experiences of everyday spaces', *Environment & Planning D: Society & Space*, 11: 395–413.
Whatmore, S. (1997) 'Dissecting the autonomous self: hybrid cartographies for a relational ethics', *Environment and Planning D: Society and Space*, 15: 37–53.
Waterstone, M. (2002) 'Antipode: a radical journal of geography or a journal of radical geography?' *Antipode*, 34 (4): 662–6.
Waterstone, M. (2004) 'T(r)opes: geographicus interruptus,' *Environment and Planning A*, 36 (3): 481–9.
Young, I.M. (1990) *Justice and the Politics of Difference*. Princeton: Princeton University Press.
Young, I.M. (1997) 'Unruly categories: a critique of Nancy Fraser's dual systems theory', *New Left Review*, 222: 147–60.

19

Ethical Spaces of Being In-common

Jeff Popke

Social life – that is, *we*, not *I* – is the normal form of life. *It is life itself* … In that constant, everpresent identification of the unit with the whole, lies the origin of all ethics, the germ out of which all the subsequent conceptions of *justice*, and the still higher conceptions of *morality*, evolved. (Petr Kropotkin 1968: 60–1)

That Being is being-with, absolutely, this is what we must think. (Jean-Luc Nancy 2000: 61)

INTRODUCTION

Over the past decade or so, the discipline of geography has gone through something of an 'ethical turn'. It is now commonplace to find mention of ethics in a wide range of geographical discussions, from environmental issues to geopolitics, from what we buy to what we eat. It is difficult to say whether this trend has developed out of an increased societal concern for the well-being of others, or because of mounting evidence that such concern is decidedly lacking. In either case, it would appear that our troubled twenty-first century world can use all the help it can get, and that a geographically-attuned ethical sensibility is something that is in need of cultivation. Indeed, David Smith goes so far as to suggest that it may be vital: 'The interface with ethics is one of the final disciplinary frontiers inviting geographical exploration, the outcome of which could be crucial to the wisdom required to address issues on which the very survival of a decent and sustainable form of human life on Earth may depend' (Smith, 2004: 197). Central to this project is a more careful consideration of just what a 'decent form of life' can and should look like, and how we might collectively organize our communities, our institutions, and our political forms in such a way as to bring it about. Here is perhaps where ethical concerns intersect most saliently with the tasks of social geography.

Chris Philo has suggested that 'the story of social geography is very much the story of changing (and arguably enlarging and enriching) conceptions of "the social" being drawn into human geography more generally' (Philo, 1991: 4). If this is so, then it will also be a story about how 'the social' itself is conceptualized, how it is lived and negotiated in various contexts, and how it may sustain, enhance or inhibit forms of human solidarity and mutual regard. To state the matter in this fashion is to paint social geography with a fairly broad brush, and indeed in what follows I take an expansive view – both conceptually and historically – of the field.

Among geographers, concepts such as morality, ethics and justice are open to a significant degree of interpretation, and there is a good deal of overlap in their definitions and usage. Although I make no attempt in this chapter to adhere to strict definitions, the following comments may be useful to set the stage. I take *justice* to be an evaluative frame for considering the extent to which socioeconomic, political, and/or environmental relations and institutions can be said to be fair or just, conventionally underpinned by an aspiration toward greater social equality and respect. 'Geographies of justice', therefore, would concern the extent to which our territorial arrangements approach the ideals of fairness or equity, as well as the movements and struggles to achieve these ideals by marginalized or disadvantaged groups in specific locales. Because this topic is covered in a separate chapter in this volume, I will have relatively less to say about justice, and will instead focus attention on moral and ethical geographies.

I use *morality* to describe commonsense conventions about what is good, virtuous, suitable or proper, especially in describing conduct or behavior. To speak of 'moral geographies' then, is to inquire about the emergence of such notions, and the ways that they are variously performed, policed and contested in particular geographical contexts. The idea of a 'moral landscape' may be used to indicate how particular moral or normative understandings both influence and reflect the meanings that we ascribe both to natural landscapes and the built environment.

By *ethics*, I understand a field of inquiry opened up by concerns about the nature of our interactions with, and responsibilities toward, both human and non-human others. To speak of ethical geographies, then, is to consider the nature and extent of these responsibilities, both empirically and theoretically, as well as the ways in which our actions and dispositions toward others tend to fulfill or abrogate them within particular contexts or institutional arrangements.

Clearly, each of these concepts bears an intimate relation to our understanding of the social. The premise of this chapter is that our notions about what society is, as well as the ways in which the social is constituted and enacted within particular spatial contexts, are underpinned by a complex set of understandings about what is good or proper (morality), and about the nature, scope and geographical scale of our obligations and responsibilities toward various others (ethics). Note that this distinction – between a moral sphere of individual conduct and an ethical realm of responsibility and solidarity – is itself an ethical matter, and the outcome of cultural and political negotiation. Indeed, we might view the history of thinking on the social to consist in a kind of tug-of-war between individual and collective notions of responsibility, and the associated ideals of liberty and equality, and of independence and interdependence, with which they are implicated. If contemporary neoliberal discourse has tended to champion the former at the expense of the latter, this is all the more reason to insist upon a view of the social in which moral and ethical matters are foregrounded. At the intersection of ethics and social geography, then, lies a project to reclaim the social as a site of collective ethical responsibility, to expose the ways in which contemporary social institutions and political-economic relations militate against our dispositions to act on that responsibility, and thereby to facilitate a more generalized expression of solidarity and regard.

As we will see, many currents of contemporary geographic theory are making a contribution toward this aim. Before surveying the field, however, I turn to examine some of the ways that moral or ethical questions have figured in the historical development of social geography.

GEOGRAPHY'S EARLY VIEWS ON THE ETHICAL

Geography's engagement with questions of an ethical or moral nature extends at least as far back as Kant, who considered 'moral geography' to be one of five discrete branches of the discipline. For Kant, however, moral geography was little more than a descriptive anthropology, consisting of an empirical catalogue of 'the diverse customs and characteristics of people in different regions' (quoted in May, 1970: 263). As David Harvey (2000) has pointed out, such descriptions were suffused with racialized stereotypes and folk myths in ways that blunt the force of Kant's broader philosophical ethics.

By the turn of the twentieth century, Kant's empirical-descriptive legacy was filtered through the explanatory framework of environmental determinism, and in particular what Livingstone (1991) has called the 'moral discourse of climate'. Under the sway of essentially evolutionary understandings, it was a short step from geographical descriptions of 'customs and characteristics' to more or less normative pronouncements about spatial patterns of moral degeneracy caused by environmental controls. Thus, Ellsworth Huntington could proclaim that 'the hard conditions of climate have steadily forced the Arabs to frame a moral code which condones violence' (Huntington, 1925: 122) and Ellen Churchill Semple could meditate upon the relationships between ethics and geographical isolation: 'The morals of the [Kentucky] mountain people lend strong evidence for the development theory of ethics … the same conditions that have kept their ethnic type pure have kept the social phenomena primitive, with their natural concomitants of primitive ethics and primitive modes of social control' (Semple, 1901: 616).

This kind of thinking, of course, helped to legitimate colonialism as a 'civilizing enterprise' (Peet, 1985). It also advanced an essentially descriptive view of ethics as a set of locally- and culturally-specific customs or norms as opposed to a more abstract set of normative principles or an overarching philosophy. Interestingly, however, a very different sense of ethics was being articulated around the same time, by anarchist geographers such as Petr Kropotkin and Elysée Reclus. Both Kropotkin and Reclus sought to transcend the local particularities of cultural and ethnic difference, by articulating a larger moral vision of humanity. In so doing, they anticipated some of the more important contemporary currents of thought regarding the socio-ethical.

The anarchist vision was influenced by Kropotkin's theory of mutual aid, which he viewed as a driving motor of evolution. In contrast to prevailing social Darwinist interpretations, Kropotkin emphasized the importance of cooperation over competition in the maintenance of both human and animal communities. 'The social instinct', he argued, 'is the common source out of which all morality originates' (Kropotkin, 1968: 37). For both Kropotkin and Reclus, this cooperative social instinct is expressed materially in collective labor, a notion that is also fundamental to Karl Marx's early philosophical writings. In describing the development of cities and towns, for example, Kropotkin notes that 'the civilization of the town, its industry, its special characteristics, have slowly grown and ripened through the cooperation of generations of its inhabitants before it could become what it is today …' (Kropotkin, 1972: 44). This legacy of accumulated, cooperative labor instantiates the social as an essentially collective achievement, and provides the grounds for a critique of existing inequalities: 'There is not even a thought, or an invention, which is not common property, born of the past and the present. … By what right then can any one whatever appropriate the least morsel of this immense whole and say: This is mine, not yours?' (Kropotkin, 1972: 44, 46).

In addition to this historical perspective, anarchist thought also sought to promote a more spatially expansive view of the social, and an essentially global vision for social geography. 'The essence of human progress,' argued Reclus, 'consists of the discovery of the totality of interests and wills common to all peoples; it is identical with solidarity' (in Clark and Martin, 2004: 239). For Reclus in particular, this solidarity extended even beyond the human community, to encompass a broader responsibility toward the natural world. Indeed, Reclus was a staunch vegetarian, and was one of the first commentators to critique the inhumane treatment of domesticated animals used for food (Clark and Martin, 2004).

It is noteworthy, I think, that both men saw the advancement of geographical knowledge as a means to cultivate the kind of solidarity they were calling for. In an essay entitled 'What geography ought to be', Kropotkin argued forcefully that an understanding of geography was crucial to the development of a wider sense of collective responsibility. 'Geography ... must teach us, from our earliest childhood, that we are all brethren, whatever our nationality' he argued, '[it] must be ... a means of dissipating ... prejudices and of creating other feelings more worthy of humanity' (1996: 141).

Ethics and morality, then, were not for Kropotkin or Reclus cultural features to be described, but rather part and parcel of a project to be realized, through the advancement of knowledge that would instill a commitment to solidarity, mutual respect and harmonious relationships with nature. As Kropotkin put it, '[if man] desires to have a life in which all his forces, physical, intellectual, and emotional, may find a full exercise, he must once and for ever abandon the idea that such a life is attainable on the path of disregard for others' (Kropotkin, 1968: 25). Instead, anarchist geographers sought to cultivate what Reclus called an 'anarchist morality': 'we must ... act in ways that respect the rights and interests of our comrades. Only then can one become a truly moral being and awaken to a feeling of responsibility' (in Clark and Martin, 2004: 138).

Above all, then, anarchist geographers proposed a theory of ethics that was also a theory of society, one which emphasized the inherent, even necessary, sensibilities of cooperation, mutual regard and collective responsibility: 'Social life – that is, *we*, not *I* – is the normal form of life', wrote Kropotkin, '*It is life itself* ... In that constant, everpresent identification of the unit with the whole, lies the origin of all ethics, the germ out of which all the subsequent conceptions of *justice*, and the still higher conceptions of *morality*, evolved' (Kropotkin, 1968: 60–1).

Although this kind of communal and socialist sensibility could vie for political space in the latter decades of the nineteenth century, it would wane significantly into the twentieth. Instead, conceptions of social ethics moved increasingly toward the individual as the site of agency and responsibility, a view fostered by both the ascendancy of liberal individualism and the more objective quantitative epistemology that eventually took hold within the social sciences. A century later, as I will suggest below, the anarchist legacy, and the social ethics they sought to develop, are worth revisiting.

THE DEVELOPMENT OF SOCIAL GEOGRAPHY

Prior to the 1960s, the term social geography was used chiefly as a synonym for human regional geography. It was considered to be, in the words of Wreford Watson (1951: 482), 'the regional differentiation of social characteristics'. This process generally entailed the empirical description of things like population and settlement, communications and public services, and sometimes cultural features such as language, religion and customs in specific regions. Discussion of these latter features at times included consideration of moral or ethical norms, and although most authors had by now jettisoned the more unpalatable aspects of environmental determinism, the broad evolutionary perspective that underlay it remained.

By the 1960s, this approach to social geography withered under the more general critique of regional geography put forward by advocates of a more scientific and nomothetic form of geographic inquiry. As much of the discipline turned toward a more positivist 'science of space', the banner of social geography was taken up by human geographers working in the tradition of human ecology, articulated earlier by Barrows (1923) and subsequently developed within the so-called Chicago School of urban sociology. Such work examined urban residential patterns through the ecological metaphor of 'natural areas', formed through processes such as competition, dominance, invasion and succession (Park, 1936). The city was viewed as a mosaic of 'different cultural areas representing different mores, attitudes, and degrees of civic interest' (McKenzie, 1924: 301).

As with the earlier regional studies, the existence of localized cultural differences lent themselves to a descriptive moral geography, but now of urban neighborhoods rather than regions. Urban communities, wrote Wreford Watson, 'are bounded by no other frontiers than by those where their particular association of daily interactions comes to an end. The spatial pattern is, in the last instance, a reflection of the moral order' (1951: 475). This Chicago School legacy laid the foundations for a generation of urban-based investigation that largely supplanted region-based inquiries in claiming the mantle of 'social geography'. Textbooks and edited collections focused on topics such as residential mobility, housing, social deviance, welfare, collective consumption, poverty and ageing. Many of these investigations brought on board the prevailing interest in quantitative methods, and for the most part ethical concerns remained in the background.

This focus began to change in the 1970s, as US and British geographers reacted against a series of social and political crises, as well as to the perceived inability of quantitative methodologies to effectively address them. The decade of the 1960s had brought with it in the United States the Civil Rights movement, the Vietnam War, and urban unrest within a number of cities. For many who trained their eye on the subject matter of social geography, it became increasingly clear that 'the social' was strained if not downright broken (Smith, 1971; Peet, 1980). 'What shall it profit a profession,' asked Gilbert White in 1972, 'if it fabricate a nifty discipline about the world while that world and the human spirit are degraded?' (White, 1972: 104).

The responses to this question came from two different directions, each of which made contributions to geographical understandings of ethics. The humanist response attempted to develop an enhanced understanding of, and appreciation for, the human spirit of which White spoke. Drawing upon a diverse range of philosophical traditions, particularly phenomenology, humanist geographers focused attention on the social as lived and experienced by people, and on 'the importance of place as a center of meaning' (Entrikin, 1976: 626). Against the objectivist epistemology favored by spatial science, humanists promoted a view that emphasized human agency and social interactions in the construction of meaning. For David Ley, the neglect of human agency in positivist approaches was a 'moral error', in which 'ethical and moral issues are themselves appropriated into the domain of the technical' (Ley, 1996: 208). Ley called instead for an approach emphasizing 'intersubjectivity … [as] the basis for a social model of man' (Ley 1977: 509).

Although ethics was seldom an explicit element, these discussions pointed toward the ways in which social life is dependent upon empathy and regard toward others, and laid the groundwork for contemporary examinations of affect and emotion. Yi Fu Tuan, for example, examined the ways in which 'human beings establish fields of care, networks of interpersonal concern, in a physical setting' (1996: 451, also Tuan, 1989). And Anne Buttimer, in similar fashion, suggested that a phenomenology of the lifeworld could help to develop a deeper appreciation of human experience, and 'could elicit a heightened self-awareness and identity and enable one to empathize with the worlds of other people' (Buttimer, 1976: 281).

If the disaffection sparked by both disciplinary and societal changes led humanists to advocate more introspective approaches, others reacted to the same events with calls for a more activist stance. Radical geographers, many drawing explicitly from Marxist theory, called for not only a rethinking of geography's aims and methods, but also a more explicit concern with ethical issues than had previously been the case. As David Harvey recalls: 'it seemed absurd to be writing when the world was collapsing in chaos around me and cities were going up in flames … I felt a crying need to retool myself again, to take up … moral and ethical questions … and try to bring them closer to the ground of everyday political life' (Harvey, 2002: 168).

The founding of *Antipode* in 1969 reflected the growing sense that geography was lacking in ethical commitment, and much of the content of the journal's early issues reflected a specific concern with social geography. Research focused on topics such as inner city poverty and crime, 'black ghettos' and racial inequality, housing and other service provision, and the causes of hunger. The watchword for much of this work was what Harvey termed 'territorial distributive justice' (1973) or, as David Smith once put it, 'who gets what, *where*' (1974; also Smith, 1994). As attention was increasingly drawn to social-geographic inequalities, so too did radical geographers call for a rethinking of geographic inquiry. William Bunge's urban expeditions, in particular, served as a model for activist research (Merrifield, 1995), as well as the ethical commitment to work against racism and inequality, or what David Harvey referred to as 'the moral obligation of geographers' (Harvey, 1974: 23).

In seeking to expand geography's moral imagination, a number of radical geographers found inspiration in the earlier tradition of anarchist geography (*Antipode*, 1978–79). Richard Peet, for one, described anarchist principles as a 'politics of human liberation', emphasizing decentralization, collective decision-making, and a new form of ethics. Such an ethics, he argued, 'must come from the deepest source, which is the necessary way we relate to each other and the earth' (Peet, 1978–79: 129).

Despite this and other attempts to engage with Marxist and anarchist theory, the most salient ethical legacy of the radical intervention is really its insistent reminder to consider the social and political relevance of our work (Stoddart, 1981; Mitchell and Draper, 1982). Debates about such issues continue into the present, and the need to address our most pressing social issues is clearly a motivating factor for many who express a concern with ethics. Nevertheless, and despite radical geography's welcome sense of outrage, its ethical orientation was never made explicit. If there was a need, as Peet suggested, to 'relate to each other and the earth' in new and different ways, there was as yet little attempt to think through the precise nature of our ethical responsibilities, or to theorize the social as a site of collective ethical responsibility.

Theorizing the social: the postmodern challenge

The implicit ethical stance of the 1970s began to change with geography's increasing engagement with broader debates within philosophy and social theory beginning in the 1980s, and in particular what Dear (1988) labeled 'the postmodern challenge' (also Dear and Flusty, 2002). Among the widespread changes induced by these debates, two are worth noting here in particular.

First, the influence of social theory altered the traditional subject matter of social geography. The turn to postmodern theory led to a new, more open, epistemology of society and space, one that placed increasing emphasis on social difference and the nature of socio-spatial exclusion. Second, and related to this, there was a rethinking of the nature of power and resistance, with greater attention paid to the ways in which social and cultural meanings become normalized and contested in and through space. These insights led in turn to a reexamination of political agency and strategy. The righteous indignation of earlier Marxist approaches gave way to more hopeful strategies of prizing open the social to cultivate moments of resistance, of recovering lost or subaltern voices, and of fostering a plurality of transformative projects in lieu of a singular vision of social change.

These theoretical developments provided the resources for a richer conception of, and a more robust conversation about, social and geographical ethics (see Kobayashi and Proctor, 2003; Smith, 2003). A few early interventions set the stage for this exploration, including Buttimer's (1974) exploration of values in geography, Susan Smith's (1984) discussion of pragmatism and Gordon Clark's (1986) consideration of John Rawls' theory of justice. But it wasn't until the mid-1990s that geography underwent what Andrew Sayer and Michael Storper called a 'reawakening of normative theory' (1997: 14). In large measure, this reawakening is due to the work of David Smith. Beginning with his groundbreaking writings on territorial justice in the 1970s, Smith has championed the need to consider the ethical implication of both the work that geographers do and the geographical patterns and institutions that form our subject matter. Smith's work has staged a series of conversations between the traditional concerns of geographic theory – territoriality, development, landscape, place and community – and theories of ethics and morality. Most prominent among these have been a series of interventions in the journal *Progress in Human Geography* (Smith 1998, 2000a) culminating in Smith's definitive *Moral Geographies* (2000b). Sparked by the pioneering work of Smith and others, the last decade or so has witnessed a proliferation of work at the intersection of moral or ethical theory and a broadly conceived social geography (Birdsall, 1996; Proctor, 1998; Proctor and Smith, 1999; Lee and Smith, 2004).

If recent commentators agree on the importance of normative theory, however, they are far from agreement on the best way to get there (see Bridge, 2000). Even as the postmodern turn offered resources for a rethinking of ethics, it also prompted its critics to clarify their own normative commitments and assumptions. David Harvey, for one, has argued that the postmodern condition inhibits our ability to make moral or ethical judgments: 'The experience of time and space has changed, the confidence in the association between scientific and moral judgments has collapsed, aesthetics has triumphed over ethics as a prime focus of social and intellectual concern … [and] ephemerality and fragmentation take precedence over eternal truths and unified politics' (1989: 328)

Stuart Corbridge and David Smith have agued similarly. Thus Corbridge (1994: 97) defends a revitalized Marxist approach against 'an amoral politics of indifference' and Smith calls for what he calls a 'context sensitive universalism' (2004: 201) that might provide a 'way out of the postmodern moral maze' (Smith, 2000c: 1160). 'There are natural facts about human sameness,' David Smith avers, 'from which moral conclusions can be drawn' (Smith, 2000c: 1160).

On the other side of the fence stand those, like David Slater (1997) and Sarah Whatmore (1997), who have attempted to describe a more contingent, relational or intersubjective form of ethics. I have previously advocated this kind of position as well (Popke, 2003, 2004). Indeed, my own engagement with ethical thought was spurred by a desire to develop a theoretically grounded defense of poststructuralist epistemology, not in order to deny any form of human commonality, but rather to suggest that the contours of political or ethical responsibility cannot be predetermined.

Despite my prior intervention into these debates, I do not attempt in what follows to police the boundaries of ethical thinking, and while I believe that some critics paint a highly misleading picture of postmodern thought, my sense is that the positions are in fact not as far apart as they sometimes appear. Without wishing to diminish important differences in philosophical approach, then, I want to suggest a set of common projects around which we might focus our investigations at the intersection of ethics and social geography.

CONTEMPORARY ETHICS AND SOCIAL GEOGRAPHY: THINKING THROUGH THE IN-COMMON

Let us begin with the social, for one of the incontrovertible 'facts of human sameness' (in Smith's words) is that all humans exist in society, and therefore in community with others. This proposition has been a central tenet of various strands of socialist thought, and has more recently figured prominently in the philosophy of Jean-Luc Nancy. For Nancy, the essence of Being should be regarded as 'being-with', the sharing of being with co-present others in space and time. This being-in-common is more than a banal empirical observation, it represents what Nancy calls 'an originary or ontological sociality' (1991a: 28). If our collective being-together can be accepted as an ontological proposition, however, this does not tell us much about the ways in which our sociality is constituted or experienced. What we deem to be 'the social' should thus be seen as an agonistic space of negotiation over the very meaning and contours of the in-common.

Here, then, we can identify a set of investigations that we might place under the banner of social geography. First, how do we understand the construction of the in-common as a spatial or geographical phenomenon, what Nancy calls 'the taking-place of the in-common' (Nancy, 1991b: 11)? And second, how is the space of the in-common figured as a site of ethical responsibility? Here, I would follow Antonio Negri's simple assertion that 'ethics is the responsibility for the common' (2003: 183). If this is so, then it should lead us to consider how our field of collective responsibility is variously enlarged or circumscribed in ways that bear upon the construction of the in-common.

This is, on the one hand, a theoretical or philosophical project, aimed at better understanding the space of the in-common as a site of ethical engagement and regard. But it is also, I would argue, an urgent political one, to defend – and where possible expand – our collective responsibilities in the face of contemporary political and economic restructuring. As we know, one of the hallmarks of neoliberal discourse has been the enshrinement of the autonomous individual subject as the site of responsibility, as suggested by Margaret Thatcher's famous quip that 'there is no such thing as society'. Indeed, one might say that within neoliberalism, the truly ethical subject is one who opts out from society, who manages to disregard the ontological condition of being-together in favor of individual self-cultivation, such that she or he makes no claims to be an object of responsibility for anyone else. One of social geography's major contributions to ethical thinking would be to challenge this narrowing of ethical responsibility, and to reclaim the kind of broad and expansive view of the social that was in evidence more than a century ago in anarchist thought.

With this vision in hand, then, I want to consider in the remainder of this chapter some contemporary perspectives on the relationship between ethics and social space. I want to explore two kinds of questions, in particular. First, how do we understand the nature of community, and the attendant responsibilities that it might entail? And second, how do we broaden our conception of that community across space, and thereby extend our responsibilities to both distant and different others?

Constructing and enlarging community

One task of social geography, then, is to understand the nature and scope of our responsibilities toward those human and non-human others with whom we must share our worlds. This kind of project would suggest the need to investigate the construction and maintenance of our sense of community or fraternity, and the processes of inclusion and exclusion through which social alterity is produced and regulated.

In some ways, these kinds of questions were addressed in the early work of urban social ecologists who, as we have seen, tended to view various neighborhood communities as 'moral orders' through which social and cultural norms were maintained and reproduced across generations. Recent scholarship, though, has gone further to suggest some of the specific mechanisms through which such norms, in both urban and rural settings, retain their performative force. In the urban arena, as Felix Driver (1988) has shown, attention to the city's moral geographies dates back to the Victorian era, and reflected societal concerns about improper urban conduct, such as delinquency, drunkenness, crime and pauperism, concerns that have resonated throughout the traditions of urban planning and design (Smith, 2001). Assumptions about the proper moral order, in other words, have tended to reflect a modern penchant to order and control the social and spatial contours of the city as much as any direct concern with specific behaviors and activities. Rural areas, too, have been examined as moral landscapes, reflecting societal norms about human interactions with land and nature, and the particular aesthetics and practices constitutive of the rural (Matless, 1994; Enticott, 2003; Setten, 2004).

What is notable about this work for thinking about ethics and responsibility is that conceptions of moral space often rely upon the discursive constitution of community in and through space, such that the in-common of the 'we' is maintained against various spatialized 'others'. This in turn can be related to notions about who 'belongs' in particular spaces, and who is 'out of place' (Cresswell, 1996). Thus, social geographers have been concerned to examine the ways in which the other has been subject to discourses of spatial exclusion based upon a wide range of socio-cultural identifiers, particularly race (Anderson, 2000; Dwyer and Jones, 2000) and sexuality (Hubbard, 2000).

Psychoanalytic approaches have added an important dimension to this work, showing how discourses about racialized or sexualized others can be viewed not only as attempts to order or purify urban spaces, but also a means of maintaining a stable subject position within a social order. Thus, for example, common concerns about hygiene, sanitation and disease were frequently projected onto defiled or abject nonwhite bodies and spaces, thus symbolically rendering 'our' spaces and subject positions pure and secure (Sibley, 1995; Wilton, 1998; Craddock, 2000). This is an important insight for thinking about ethics, for it suggests that our attempts to expand our sense of responsibility must come to grips with the ways in which the social may be riven by unconscious fears and desires, such that the recognition and acknowledgement of our intersubjectivity, and the extension of ethical regard that might follow from it, may be an unsettling proposition.

If investigations of moral geographies generally examine the delimitation of our field of concern, a different body of work focuses on how this concern is articulated and, at least potentially, widened in scope. Perhaps the most influential entry point for such work has been the notion of care. Derived largely from feminist scholarship, discussions of care within geography have highlighted the diverse social sites, motivations and emotions that are implicated in our everyday caring activities and relationships (see Popke, 2006). More than simply a landscape of institutions and familial practices, care has also been theorized as a particular form of social ethics, one based in a collective concern for the well-being of others. As Victoria Lawson has put it, 'care ethics begins with a social ontology of connection, foregrounding social relationships of mutuality and trust' (Lawson, 2007: 3).

Care is, in this sense, what we might call a communal project. It is also, as a number of commentators have argued, an important political one for reasons I have already discussed. Thus, a number of social geographers have called on us to question a political economy that produces the need for extensive care, and also to challenge the contemporary neoliberal move in the industrialized West to privatize carework while undermining networks of collective welfare and security (Haylett, 2003; Smith, 2005).

Affect and the in-common

The mundane, day-to-day activities involved in care should alert us to the fact that the nature of our responsibilities toward others is often unacknowledged or implicit. Even so, concern or regard for others nevertheless shapes our daily practices in quite significant ways. Consumption provides a widely discussed example (Barnett et al., 2005a). Thus, Barnett and colleagues have considered what they call the 'ordinary ethics' of consumption. 'Ordinary consumption,' they insist, 'is already shaped in all sorts of ways by values of caring for other people, and sometimes by quite explicit moral values' (Barnett et al., 2005b: 3). This understanding of ethics as an everyday or mundane disposition suggests that we should pay attention to the ways in which our commonplace inclinations toward empathy or concern may be mobilized, for example, in attempts by charitable organizations to instill a sense of generosity or guilt in order to elicit donations (Cloke et al., 2005).

More generally, there is an important role here for a consideration of emotion, affect and spirituality, and the manner in which they help to structure our relations of care and obligation. In this regard, Anderson and Smith's call for 'a geographical agenda sensitive to the emotional dimensions of living in the world' (Anderson and Smith, 2001: 8), has been at least partially answered. In recent accounts, emotion has been depicted as a relational and intersubjective accomplishment (Conradson, 2003; Colls, 2004; Bondi, 2005), one that is tied to our experiences of particular places (Davidson and Milligan, 2004). Although this work is not explicitly concerned with ethics, it has much to contribute to 'the goal … of discovering an emotional, connected and committed sense for the other' (Cloke, 2002: 594).

Additional resources for thinking through the ethics of the social are provided by so-called non-representational theory, a label used to describe a diverse set of approaches united by their broad concern with what we might call the 'actuality' of the social, and the way it is embodied, performed and lived through practical daily experience. As Lorimer describes it, 'the focus falls on how life takes shape and gains expression in shared experiences, everyday routines, fleeting encounters, embodied movements, precognitive triggers, practical skills, affective intensities, enduring urges, unexceptional interactions and sensuous dispositions' (2005: 84).

The question of ethics within this kind of approach is less about diagnosing or proscribing (which in any case reflects a certain hubris on the part of social science) than it is about creating new kinds of affective experience. As McCormack (2003: 502) puts it, 'if one begins attending to and through affect, one also shifts the burden of the ethical away from the effort to do justice to individual subjects, and towards a commitment to develop a *fidelity to the event* as that through which new spaces of thinking and moving may come into being'. This commitment to develop 'new spaces of thinking and moving' also draws attention to new kinds of performance and experimentation, such as dance or music, which may be capable of producing new kinds of encounter, of heightening our sense of the possible, by 'being open to the eventhood of the world' (Dewsbury, 2003: 1930).

What remains at issue in this work, I think, is the extent to which such spaces of encounter may be considered a collective project. There is a latent individualism in some non-representational depictions of social space, and my inclination would be to move the considerable insights of this work in the direction of thinking about how to heighten those sensibilities and affective orientations that construct and maintain the in-common as a collective ethical project. Nigel Thrift, one of the most vocal advocates of the non-representational approach, offers some suggestive hints of what this kind of approach might look like. As a political project, he proposes, non-representational theory asks us to rethink our notions about the kind of encounter that counts as knowledge. We need 'to search for modes of disclosure of, intervention in, and extension of what we are capable of that are *co-produced* … it requires practices and ethics of listening, talking, metaphorising and contemplating which can produce a feeling of being in a situation together' (2004: 84). These 'everyday moments of encounter,' he proposes, 'can be cultivated to build an ethics of generosity' (2004: 93) or to 'inject more kindness and compassion into everyday interaction' (Thrift, 2005: 144). There is much to admire in such a stance, but the ethical question remains how to move from a sense of the co-produced to a broader responsibility toward our collective *being-in-common*, in a way that expands the net of ethical agency beyond the immediacy of individual experience.

Materiality, autonomy and cooperative labor

I want to change tack here slightly, and approach the in-common from the essential materiality of collective life, to consider the social as a site not only of affective encounters, but also, in a Marxist or anarchist sense, of material production and cooperative labor. The work of Michael Hardt and Antonio Negri is extremely productive in this regard. Drawing from Marx, Hardt and Negri have developed a materialist philosophy grounded in the human transformation of the world through cooperative living labor. As Negri puts it, 'the theme proposed by Marx is that of the all-expansive creativity of living labor. Living labor constitutes the world, by creatively modeling, *ex novo*, the materials that it touches' (Negri, 1999: 326). Importantly, this labor, for Hardt and Negri as for Marx, is collective and cooperative. It constructs our being-in-common, and is thus also the basis for a sense of solidarity and responsibility: 'labor immediately involves social interaction and cooperation … in the expression of its own creative energies, immaterial labor thus seems to provide the potential for a kind of spontaneous and elementary communism' (Hardt and Negri, 2000: 294).

Hardt and Negri, then, picture the social through a kind of spontaneous materialism, in which the construction of, and responsibility for, the common emerges through the cooperative activity of social subjects. I find this a productive line of thinking for social geography, but I also wish to register a concern about Hardt and Negri's approach. Although I share their basic sense of collective agency, I am less certain about their somewhat passive optimism about the 'spontaneous' nature of the construction of community. Here I would suggest that it is important not only to theorize the *existence* of ethics and cooperation, but to try to *cultivate* them, through representational strategies aimed at making visible the social relations and connections through which ethical responsibility might flow.

Within geography, this kind of project is best exemplified by the recent work of J.K. Gibson-Graham (2006), who endeavors to highlight the specific ways in which our collective labors create the economic as a field of ethical interdependence and decision. Through their writing, and in a series of 'action research projects', Gibson-Graham attempts to bring into being what they call the 'community economy', in which ethical decisions and orientations of care are foregrounded. Their aim is to highlight what they call, following Nancy, our 'economic being-in-common' and to reinscribe the economy as an essentially social space, within which new collective subjectivities and solidarities might emerge: 'resocializing (and repoliticizing) the economy involves making explicit the sociality that is always present, and thus constituting the various forms and practices of interdependence as matters for reflection, discussion, negotiation and action' (2006: 88).

A similar kind of sentiment, and commitment to practice, is evident in recent geographical discussions of autonomous geographies (Pickerill and Chatterton, 2006). The concept of autonomy has many diverse antecedents, including the anarchist tradition and Antonio Negri's early writings arising from the Italian Marxist tradition. What these and other intellectual currents share is an open-ended sense of experimentation and engagement with others to build collective projects of solidarity and resistance. They entail, in this sense, 'an obligation to recognize co-existence, negotiations and conflict' which must inevitably characterize our attempts to construct and expand the affective and material spaces of the in-common (Pickerill and Chatterton, 2006: 736). The ethical stakes at issue in all of this work is what Gibson-Graham describes as 'a truly salient distinction, between whether interdependence is recognized and acted upon or whether it is obscured or perhaps denied' (2006: 84).

EXTENDING THE SCOPE OF CONCERN

Attempts to theorize the social as an ethical space of interdependence, affect and care beg crucial, and fundamentally geographical, questions regarding the spatial extent of ethical responsibility, or what David Smith (1998) has so eloquently called 'the spatial scope of beneficence'. In addition to thinking through the social geographies comprising the in-common of community, then, social geography can also play a role in widening our geographical and ethical horizons in order to develop a wider ambit of responsibility.

Such a project was undertaken, of course, by none other than Immanuel Kant. Even while Kant was depicting a geographical landscape of locally variant moral norms, he was also putting forth a much wider form of cosmopolitan ethics, necessitated by the increasing interconnection, through trade and exploration (and, it should be said, conquest) of the different regions on the world. Kant hinted at the ways in which our ethical responsibilities transcend distance, noting that 'the growing prevalence of a (narrower or wider) community among the peoples of the earth has reached a point at which the violation of right at any *one* place on the earth is felt in *all* places' (Kant, 2006: 84).

If Kant could envision a cosmopolitan ethos in the late eighteenth century, we are undoubtedly even more aware of its urgent need in a world in which the suffering of others is so evidently visible. But the availability to our senses of the pain and distress of others is not in and of itself a motivation for ethical action, nor does it provide a guide toward what such action should entail in any particular circumstance. The geographical question, then, is how to think the in-common in more ethically expansive and cosmopolitan ways (see Popke, 2007). How, in other words, can we rethink the social as a space of cosmopolitan responsibility?

Most commentators on cosmopolitan ethics take the city as their object of inquiry, for it is the urban that most clearly illustrates the diversity and interconnection characteristic of our contemporary global condition. In the words of Ash Amin (2006: 1012), 'the "being-together" of life in urban space has to be recognized, demanding attendance to the politics of living together'. The social-geographic questions at stake in this have to do with the spatial extent and negotiation of the in-common, including the hospitality (or lack thereof) offered to foreigners, migrants and refugees, as well as ethical determinations about whether such 'outsiders' have what Henri Lefebvre once called a 'right to the city' (Mitchell, 2003; Purcell, 2003). It also means, as Doreen Massey has so elegantly argued, that we need to re-imagine our sense of place in a more open and relational way, to pay heed to the existence of spatial interconnections as a precursor to cultivating a more 'global sense of place' (see Massey, 1997, 2004; Amin, 2004).

If an ethic of hospitality can be said to foster an inclusive and open conception of community, however, it remains a rather passive means of conceptualizing responsibility at a distance, and questions remain about the ways in which we can conceptualize a sense of obligation toward distant others with whom we may never interact. Putting it somewhat simply, we can identify two different perspectives on this question. The first is a theoretical argument, suggesting that the nature of our engagement and responsibility transcends context and is something universal, either an outcome of mutually-agreed upon norms, or else an essential feature of what it means to be human. The latter view is perhaps best exemplified by the philosophy of Emmanuel Levinas, for whom ethical responsibility for a singular other is an unconditional injunction irrespective of specific historical or geographical circumstances, a demand that would appear difficult to enact in practice (Barnett, 2005).

Another kind of theoretical argument, championed by David Smith, begins from the inherent 'randomness' or contingency involved in our geographical location. Because our life chances are to a great extend determined by what Smith calls 'the place of good fortune', there is no justification for the existence of the massive material inequalities that exist from place to place. In common parlance, this kind of perspective is perhaps best exemplified by the exhortation to 'put yourself in someone else's shoes' or the saying 'there but for the grace of God go I' (Smith, 2000c; also Corbridge, 1993).

Again, however, such theoretical motivations may be difficult to put into practice. There may very well be a generalizable human capacity for empathy and concern that transcends distance, but that does not ensure that it is translated into ethical action. There are questions here about how our dispositions to care about distant others are mobilized through appeals, charitable campaigns, media images, and the like, concerns which obviously link up with the affective and emotional geographies discussed above (Silk, 1998).

But another concern may be added here as well, for the obverse is equally, if not more, ethically important, particularly in the age of 'the war of terror': how is it that some human or non-human subjects are made to exist *outside of* the ambit of responsibility, in what we can call, following Agamben (2005), 'spaces of exception'? How is it, in other words, that some lives may be made to matter less than others, or in certain cases, not to matter at all (see Pratt, 2005; Gregory, 2006)?

Our entanglements with distant others

Beyond these more abstract theorizations, there is also an empirical claim to be made, that our late modern globalizing world has multiplied the webs of connection between ourselves and distant others, with implications for thinking about both the social and the nature of responsibility. Beck and Sznaider, for example, have argued that contemporary sociological investigation must account for a new cosmopolitan condition arising from our increased sense of global interconnection: 'Under conditions of an interdependent global world ... every act of production and consumption and every act of everyday life links actors to millions of unseen others ... it creates the moral horizon for a newly conceived form of at times banal, and, at times, moral cosmopolitanism' (Beck and Sznaider, 2006: 22).

This changing reality, suggests Beck, requires nothing less than a new cosmopolitan social science capable of coming to grips with the nature of our transnational connections and experiences (Beck, 2006).

A different kind of methodology of connection is represented by actor-network theory (ANT), which has gained significant influence within geography. ANT describes the world from a relational ontology of actor-networks, composed of heterogeneous associations of things and materials. As Murdoch explains it, 'actor-network theorists seek to investigate ... the means by which associations come into existence and how the roles and functions of subjects and objects, actors and intermediaries, humans and nonhumans are attributed and stabilized' (Murdoch, 1997: 331).

It is not possible here to do justice to the full complexity of ANT, but two points are worth emphasizing. The first is that, within the network ontology of ANT, nonhuman actants are granted the possibility of agency. Not only is the social, then, refigured as an effect of relational networks, but the very boundaries of the social are expanded to encompass a broader materiality, one that is attentive to what Whatmore calls 'the more heterogenous company of the "non-human"' (2005: 845). Second, this suggests in turn a broader relational notion of ethical responsibility, one that 'emphasizes the affective relationships between heterogeneous actants' and thereby extends 'the promise of a more than human ethical praxis' (Whatmore, 2002: 160).

To date, this is a promise that remains largely unfulfilled, and I believe that a more extensive engagement between actor-network theory and geographical conceptions of ethics is warranted. If actor network perspectives are to assist in making sense of our responsibilities toward the in-common, however, they will need to overcome a kind of radical empiricism, or epistemological agnosticism, that abjures strong forms of judgment. As Kirsch and Mitchell have argued, questions of power – and, I would add, of justice and responsibility – are often underplayed in ANT analyses. Ethically, then, we need to view the heterogeneous associations that comprise the social as also sites of actual or potential collective responsibility, to recognize, as Kirsch and Mitchell put it, that 'some actor-networks are more equal than others' (2004: 690).

A relational understanding of contemporary forms of global interconnection, in other words, should work to highlight the specific linkages or networks within which we are embedded in ways that can engender a greater sense of responsibility. If we are, as Beck contends, linked to millions of unseen others, then this suggest that we may be, in quite concrete and specific ways, culpable for the fate of distant strangers. This argument has been made forcefully by Stuart Corbridge, who reasons as follows: 'to the extent that we can show that our lives are radically entwined with the lives of distant strangers – through studies of colonialism, of flows of capital and commodities, of modern telecommunications, and so on – we can argue more powerfully for change within the global system' (1994: 105). Cloke suggests something similar in deploying Hannah Arendt's notion of 'trespass' as a form of what Cloke calls a 'more *ordinary evil* ... the lack of thought about the unanticipated/invisible/distant effects our actions may have on others' (2002: 598).

We can usefully return here to the realm of consumption, because it is perhaps the most visible and widely studied practice that illustrates our geographical entanglements with distant peoples and places (see Popke, 2006). The unmasking of these entanglements can in one sense be viewed as an updated version of Marx's theory of commodity fetishism, that is, an attempt to reclaim the inherent sociality of the labor that went into making the commodity (Miller, 2003). But the more germane question for the current discussion is, as Noel Castree asks, '*where* ... does the unseen sociality of commodities actually lie?' (2001: 1522). At least partial answers to this question can be found in recent work on commodity chains and circuits of ethical consumption, which has illustrated through empirical case studies the ways in which our consumption habits, as well as various codes and standards for so-called fair-trade goods, impact directly upon the lives of distant producers (Goodman, 2004; Hughes, 2005).

An exclusive focus on trade and commodity chains, however, has its limits, for it tends to put forth a view of the social that separates the location of production from that of consumption, in order to highlight the essential inequalities between the global North and South. Although such a project is vital for cultivating a greater sense of responsibility across distance, we might also do well to theorize forms of connection and interaction that are more collective, even cooperative. That is, we might benefit from thinking responsibility to the in-common as a global project constituted through trans-boundary networks of labor, communication, affect and practice.

This, in essence, is Hardt and Negri's argument in proposing 'the multitude' as the new revolutionary subject within contemporary forms of global capitalism and empire (2000, 2004). Linked together by transnational circuits of cooperation, interaction and movement, the multitude actively creates the in-common as a global phenomenon, and thereby extends the skein of responsibility. As Hardt and Negri put it, 'the spatial dimension of ontology today is demonstrated through the multitude's concrete processes of the globalization, or really the making common, of the desire for human community' (2000: 362). In the multitude, then, we have a theory of the social writ large, a sense of community and solidarity that transcends borders, and thus perhaps a sense of ethics that is appropriate for these global and neoliberal times.

Postcolonial ethics and social geography

Rather than leave the final word to the multitude, however, I want to close with a reminder about the importance of taking account of history and power in thinking through the nature of our global ethical responsibility. For what Hardt and Negri refer to as the 'making common' of the social can easily become a kind of epistemological violence if it seeks to promulgate as universal a particular, Occidental conception of the social and of the kind of ethics that might logically follow. Indeed, the articulation of a particular conception of the social was central to the project of European colonization, and continues to be a central pillar of contemporary neoliberal interventions in places such as Afghanistan and Iraq (Gregory, 2004). This suggests that our views of the social – and of the specific modalities of responsibility and obligation that that are constitutive of it – are born of a material history toward which our debts are not yet settled.

There is an important role here for what could be termed postcolonial ethics, or what Deborah Bird Rose (2004) has called an 'ethics for decolonisation'. The aim of such an ethics would be to reinscribe the social as a site of plurality and difference, to develop a subaltern sense of space and community, and to learn from the very different conceptions of the social that exist within the world's diverse cultural and spiritual traditions. We must be attentive to the rich and creative variations in how the in-common is enacted and maintained in everyday spaces of community, and the ways in which ethical responsibility is lived and narrated. This may also mean continuing to rethink the boundaries between the social and the natural, in order to grant agency to the non-human, and to widen the scope of the in-common to encompass both material and spiritual worlds. 'Indigenous ethics speaks to a world of sentient living beings whose passion for life is sustained in connection,' says Rose, 'a dialogical approach to connection impels one to work to realize the well-being of others' (Rose, 1999: 185).

The good news is that this kind of sentiment is increasingly in evidence across a wide range of social experiments and ethical projects. From the diverse forms of resistance embodied in the so-called anti-globalization movement to the more local autonomous practice perhaps best exemplified by the Zaptista movement in Mexico, communities are being constructed around the social geographies of being-in-common, and in ways that respect local difference and autonomy. The goal for the twenty-first century, perhaps, is to provide the space for the expansion of such projects, and to support the proliferation of new ones, not in order to decide in advance the contours of the in-common, but rather to construct, in the well-known phrase of Subcomandante Marcos, 'a world where many worlds will fit'.

CONCLUSION

> To want to say 'we' is not at all sentimental, not at all familial or 'communitarian'. It is existence reclaiming its due or its condition: coexistence (Jean-Luc Nancy 2000: 42).

I have tried in this chapter to suggest some of the dimensions of social geography's ethical project. It is a project that has been underway for nearly a century, at least since Petr Kropotkin's exhortation that 'social life – that is, *we*, not *I* – is the normal form of life'. In the intervening decades, geographers have made significant contributions to better understanding the nature of this collective social life and its spatial manifestations. From inquiries into territorial social justice to explorations of our intersubjective lifeworlds, geographical scholarship has illuminated the social as a site of political negotiation, contested meaning, and collective praxis. What unites these disparate approaches in my view, and what has characterized much recent geographical inquiry, is a concern to theorize the social as a space of responsibility, within which we contribute in our own small ways to weaving and tending the bonds of our being-together. In the face of continuing neoliberal attempts to evacuate the social, this notion is worthy of our defense.

Contemporary explorations of ethics and social geography are assisting in this defense, by drawing attention to our entanglements with others in a wide variety of contexts, and by shedding light on our dispositions toward care and concern, our affective and embodied encounters, and our historical and material geographies of assemblage and interconnection. Ethics, as Negri reminds us, is the responsibility for the common. It is also, he notes elsewhere, 'the terrain of possibility, of action, of hope' (1996: 170; also Anderson, 2006). And in a world beset by ethical lapses and failures of responsibility, this too is worth defending. If the future trajectory of social geography remains faithful to its past, geographical scholarship will have much to contribute.

REFERENCES

Agamben, G. (2005) *State of Exception*. Chicago: University of Chicago Press.

Amin, A. (2004) 'Regions unbound: towards a new politics of place', *Geografiska Annaler,* 86 B: 33–44.

Amin, A. (2006) 'The good city', *Urban Studies* 43 (5/6): 1009–23.

Anderson, B. (2006) '"Transcending without transcendence": utopianism and an ethos of hope', *Antipode*, 38 (4): 691–710.

Anderson, K. (2000) '"The beast within": race, humanity and animality', *Environment and Planning D: Society and Space,* 18: 301–20.

Anderson, K. and Smith, S. (2001) 'Emotional geographies', *Transactions of the Institute of British Geographers,* NS 26: 7–10.

Antipode (1978–79) Special issue on social anarchism. Volumes 10 (3) and 11 (1).

Barnett, C. (2005) 'Ways of relating: hospitality and the acknowledgment of otherness', *Progress in Human Geography,* 29 (1): 5–21.

Barnett, C., Cafaro, P. and Newholm, T. (2005a) 'Philosophy and ethical consumption', in R. Harrison, T. Newholm and D. Shaw (eds), *The Ethical Consumer*. London: Sage. pp. 11–24.

Barnett, C., Clarke, N., Cloke, P. and Malpass, A. (2005b) 'The political ethics of consumerism', *Consumer Policy Review*, 15 (2): 2–8.

Barrows, H. (1923) 'Geography as human ecology', *Annals of the Association of American Geographers*, 13 (1): 1–14.

Beck, U. (2006) *The Cosmopolitan Vision*. Malden, MA: Polity Press.

Beck, U. and Sznaider, N. (2006) 'Unpacking cosmopolitanism for the social sciences: a research agenda', *The British Journal of Sociology*, 57 (1): 1–23.

Birdsall, S. (1996) 'Regard, respect, and responsibility: sketches for a moral geography of the everyday', *Annals of the Association of American Geographers,* 86 (4): 619–29.

Bondi, L. (2005) 'Making connections and thinking through emotions: between geography and psychotherapy', *Transactions of the Institute of British Geographers,* NS 30: 433–48.

Bridge, G. (2000) 'Rationality, ethics, and space: on situated universalism and the self-interested acknowledgment of "difference"', *Environment and Planning D: Society and Space,* 18: 519–35.

Buttimer, A. (1974) *Values in Geography*. Commission on College Geography, Resource Paper No. 24. Washington, DC: Association of American Geographers.

Buttimer, A. (1976) 'Grasping the dynamism of the lifeworld', *Annals of the Association of American Geographers,* 66 (2): 277–92.

Castree, N. (2001) 'Commodity fetishism, geographical imaginations and imaginative geographies', *Environment and Planning A,* 33: 1519–25.

Clark, G. (1986) 'Making moral landscapes: John Rawls' original position', *Political Geography Quarterly*, 5 (4): S147–S162.

Clark, J. and Martin, C. (eds) (2004) *Anarchy, Geography, Modernity: The Radical Social Thought of Elisée Reclus*. Lanham, MD: Lexington Books.

Cloke, P. (2002) 'Deliver us from evil? Prospects for living ethically and acting politically in human geography', *Progress in Human Geography*, 26 (5): 587–604.

Cloke, P., Johnson, S. and May, J. (2005) 'Exploring ethos? Discourses of "charity" in the provision of emergency services for homeless people', *Environment and Planning A*, 37: 385–402.

Colls, R. (2004) '"Looking alright, feeling alright": emotions, sizing and the geographies of women's experiences of clothing consumption', *Social and Cultural Geography*, 5 (4): 583–96.

Conradson, D. (2003) 'Doing organizational space: practices of voluntary welfare in the city', *Environment and Planning A*, 35: 1975–92.

Corbridge, S. (1993) 'Marxism, modernities, and moralities: development praxis and the claims of distant strangers', *Environment and Planning D: Society and Space*, 11: 449–72.

Corbridge, S. (1994) 'Post-Marxism and post-colonialism: the needs and rights of distant strangers', in D. Booth (ed.), *Rethinking Social Development: Theory, Research and Practice*. Essex: Longman. pp. 90–117.

Craddock, S. (2000) *City of Plagues: Disease, Poverty, and Deviance in San Francisco*. Minneapolis: University of Minnesota Press.

Cresswell, T. (1996) *In Place/Out of Place: Geography, Ideology and Transgression*. Minneapolis: University of Minnesota Press.

Davidson, J. and Milligan, C. (2004) 'Embodying emotion sensing space: introducing emotional geographies', *Social and Cultural Geography*, 5 (4): 523–32.

Dear, M. (1988) 'The postmodern challenge: reconstructing human geography', *Transactions of the Institute of British Geographers*, NS 13: 262–74.

Dear, M. and Flusty, S. (eds) (2002) *The Spaces of Postmodernity: Readings in Human Geography*. Malden, MA: Blackwell.

Dewsbury, J.-D. (2003) 'Witnessing space: "knowledge without contemplation"', *Environment and Planning A*, 35: 1907–32.

Driver, F. (1988) 'Moral geographies: social science and the urban environment in mid-nineteenth century England', *Transactions of the Institute of British Geographers* NS, 13: 275–87.

Dwyer, O. and Jones, J.P. (2000) 'White socio-spatial epistemology', *Social and Cultural Geography*, 1 (2): 209–22.

Enticott, G. (2003) 'Risking the rural: nature, morality and the consumption of unpasteurised milk', *Journal of Rural Studies*, 19: 411–24.

Entrikin, J.N. (1976) 'Contemporary humanism in geography', *Annals of the Association of American Geographers*, 66 (4): 615–32.

Gibson-Graham, J.K. (2006) *A Postcapitalist Politics*. Minneapolis: University of Minnesota Press.

Goodman, M. (2004) 'Reading fair trade: political ecological imaginary and the moral economy of fair trade foods', *Political Geography*, 23: 891–915.

Gregory, D. (2004) *The Colonial Present: Afghanistan, Palestine, Iraq*. London: Blackwell.

Gregory, D. (2006) 'The death of the civilian?', *Environment and Planning D: Society and Space*, 24: 633–8.

Hardt, M. and Negri, A. (2000) *Empire*. Cambridge: Harvard University Press.

Hardt, M. and Negri, A. (2004) *Multitude: War and Democracy in the Age of Empire*. New York: Penguin Press.

Harvey, D. (1973) *Social Justice and the City*. Baltimore: The Johns Hopkins University Press.

Harvey, D. (1974) 'What kind of geography for what kind of public policy?', *Transactions of the Institute of British Geographers*, 63: 18–24.

Harvey, D. (1989) *The Condition of Postmodernity*. Cambridge, MA: Basil Blackwell.

Harvey, D. (2000) 'Cosmopolitanism and the banality of geographical evils', *Public Culture*, 12 (2): 529–64.

Harvey, D. (2002) 'Memories and desires', in P. Gould and F. Pitts (eds), *Geographical Voices*. Syracuse: Syracuse University Press. pp. 149–88.

Haylet, C. (2003) 'Class, care, and welfare reform: reading meanings, talking feelings', *Environment and Planning A*, 35: 799–814.

Hubbard, P. (2000) 'Desire/disgust: mapping the moral contours of hetersexuality', *Progress in Human Geography,* 24 (2): 191–217.

Hughes, A. (2005) 'Corporate strategy and the management of ethical trade: the case of the UK food and clothing retailers', *Environment and Planning A,* 37: 1145–63.

Huntington, E. (1925) *The Character of Races*. London: Charles Scribner's Sons.

Kant, I. (2006) *Toward Perpetual Peace and Other Writings on Politics, Peace, and History*. New Haven: Yale University Press.

Kirsch, S. and Mitchell, D. (2004) 'The nature of things: dead labor, nonhuman actors, and the persistence of Marxism', *Antipode*, 36 (4): 687–705.

Kobayashi, A. and Proctor, J. (2003) 'Values, ethics, and justice', in G. Gaile and C. Willmott (eds), *Geography in America at the Dawn of the 21st Century*. Oxford: Oxford University Press.

Kropotkin, P. (1968) *Ethics: Origin and Development*. New York: Benjamin Blom.

Kropotkin, P. (1972) *The Conquest of Bread*. New York: New York University Press.

Kropotkin, P. (1996) 'What geography ought to be', in J. Agnew, D. Livingstone and A. Rogers (eds), *Human Geography: An Essential Anthology*. Malden, MA: Blackwell. pp. 139–54.

Lawson, V. (2007) 'Geographies of care and responsibility', *Annals of the Association of American Geographers,* 97 (1): 1–11.

Lee, R. and Smith, D. (eds) (2004) *Geographies and Moralities: International Perspectives on Development, Justice and Place*. Malden, MA: Blackwell.

Levinas, E. (1986) 'Bad consciousness and the inexorable', in R. Cohen (ed.), *Face to Face with Levinas*. Albany: State University of New York Press. pp. 35–40.

Ley, D. (1977) 'Social geography and the taken-for-granted world', *Transactions of the Institute of British Geographers,* NS 2(4): 498–512.

Ley, D. (1996) 'Geography without human agency: a humanistic critique', in J. Agnew, D. Livingstone and A. Rogers (eds), *Human Geography: An Essential Anthology*. Malden, MA: Blackwell. pp. 192–210.

Livingstone, D. (1991) 'The moral discourse of climate: historical considerations on race, place and virtue', *Journal of Historical Geography*, 17 (4): 413–34.

Lorimer, H. (2005) 'Cultural geography: the busy-ness of being more-than-representational', *Progress in Human Geography,* 29 (1): 83–94.

Massey, D. (1997) 'A global sense of place', in T. Barnes and D. Gregory (eds), *Reading Human Geography: The Poetics and Politics of Inquiry*. London: Arnold. pp. 315–23.

Massey, D. (2004) 'Geographies of responsibility', *Geografiska Annaler*, 86 B (1): 5–18.

Matless, D. (1994) 'Moral geography in broad-land', *Ecumene* 1 (2): 127–55.

May, J. (1970) *Kant's Concept of Geography and its Relation to Recent Geographical Thought*. Toronto: University of Toronto Press.

McCormack, D. (2003) 'An event of geographical ethics in spaces of affect', *Transactions of the Institute of British Geographers,* NS 28 (4): 488–507.

McKenzie, R.D. (1924) 'The ecological approach to the study of the human community', *The American Journal of Sociology*, 30 (3): 287–301.

Merrifield, A. (1995) 'Situated knowledge through exploration: reflections on Bunge's "geographical expeditions"', *Antipode*, 27 (1): 49–70.

Miller, D. (2003) 'Could the internet defetishise the commodity?', *Environment and Planning D: Society and Space,* 21: 359–72.

Mitchell, B. and Draper, D. (1982) *Relevance and Ethics in Geography*. London: Longman.

Mitchell, D. (2003) *The Right to the City: Social Justice and the Fight for Public Space*. New York: Guilford.

Murdoch, J. (1997) 'Towards a geography of heterogeneous associations', *Progress in Human Geography*, 21 (3): 321–37.

Nancy, J.-L. (1991a) *The Inoperative Community*. Minneapolis: University of Minnesota Press.

Nancy, J.-L. (1991b) 'Of being-in-common', in Miami Theory Collective (ed.), *Community at Loose Ends*. Minneapolis: University of Minnesota Press.

Nancy, J.-L. (2000) *Being Singular Plural*. Stanford: Stanford University Press.

Negri, A. (1996) 'Twenty theses on Marx: interpretation of the class situation today', in S. Makdisi, C. Cassarino and R. Karl (eds), *Marxism Beyond Marxism*. London: Routledge. pp. 149–80.

Negri, A. (1999) *Insurgencies: Constituent Power and the Modern State*. Minneapolis: University of Minnesota Press.

Negri, A. (2003) *Time for Revolution*. London: Continuum.

Park, R. (1936) 'Human ecology', *The American Journal of Sociology*, 42 (1): 1–15.

Peet, R. (1978–79) 'The geography of human liberation', *Antipode*, 10 (3) and 11 (1): 119–34.

Peet, R. (ed.) (1980) *Radical Geography: Alternative Viewpoints on Contemporary Social Issues*. Chicago: Maaroufa Press.

Peet, R. (1985) 'The social origins of environmental determinism', *Annals of the Association of American Geographers,* 75 (3): 309–33.

Philo, C. (1991) 'Introduction, acknowledgements and brief thoughts on older words and older worlds', in C. Philo (compiler) *New Words, New Worlds: Reconceptualizing Social and Cultural Geography*. Lampeter: Department of Geography, St. David's University College. pp. 1–13.

Pickerill, J. and Chatterton, P. (2006) 'Notes towards autonomous geographies: creation, resistance and self-management as survival tactics', *Progress in Human Geography*, 30 (6): 730–46.

Popke, E.J. (2003) 'Poststructuralist ethics: subjectivity, responsibility and the space of community', *Progress in Human Geography*, 27 (3): 298–316.

Popke, E.J. (2004) 'The face of the other: Zapatismo, responsibility and the ethics of deconstruction', *Social and Cultural Geography*, 5 (2): 301–17.

Popke, J. (2006) 'Geography and ethics: everyday mediations through care and consumption', *Progress in Human Geography*, 30 (4): 504–12.

Popke, J. (2007) 'Geography and ethics: spaces of cosmopolitan responsibility', *Progress in Human Geography,* 31 (4): 509–518.

Popke, J. (2009) 'Geography and ethics: non-representational encounters, collective responsibility and economic difference', *Progress in Human Geography*, 33 (1): 81–90.

Pratt, G. (2005) 'Abandoned women and spaces of the exception', *Antipode*, 37 (5): 1052–78.

Proctor, J. (1998) 'Ethics in geography: giving moral form to the geographical imagination', *Area*, 30 (1): 8–18.

Proctor, J. and Smith, D. (eds) (1999) *Geography and Ethics: Journeys in a Moral Terrain*. London: Routledge.

Purcell, M. (2003) 'Citizenship and the right to the global city: reimagining the capitalist world order', *International Journal of Urban and Regional Research*, 27 (3): 564–90.

Rose, D.B. (1999) 'Indigenous ecologies and an ethics of connection', in N. Low (ed.), *Global Ethics and Environment*. London: Routledge. pp. 175–87.

Rose, D.B. (2004) *Reports From a Wild Country: Ethics for Decolonisation*. Sydney: University of New South Wales Press.

Sayer, A. and Storper, M. (1997) 'Ethics unbound: for a normative turn in social theory', *Environment and Planning D: Society and Space,* 15: 1–17.

Semple, E.C. (1901) 'The Anglo-Saxons of the Kentucky mountains: a study in anthropogeography', *The Geographical Journal*, 17 (6): 588–623.

Setten, G. (2004) 'The habitus, the rule and the moral landscape', *Cultural Geographies,* 11: 389–415.

Sibley, D. (1995) *Geographies of Exclusion: Society and Difference in the West*. London: Routledge.

Silk, J. (1998) 'Caring at a distance', *Ethics, Place and Environment*, 1 (2): 165–82.

Slater, D. (1997) 'Spatialities of power and postmodern ethics – rethinking geopolitical encounters', *Environment and Planning D: Society and Space,* 15: 55–72.

Smith, D. (1971) 'Radical geography – the next revolution?', *Area*, 3 (3): 153–57.

Smith, D. (1974) 'Who gets what *where*, and how: a welfare focus for human geography', *Geography*, 59: 289–97.

Smith, D. (1994) *Geography and Social Justice*. Cambridge, MA: Blackwell.

Smith, D. (1998) 'How far should we care? On the spatial scope of beneficence', *Progress in Human Geography*, 22 (1): 15–38.

Smith, D. (2000a) 'Moral progress in human geography: transcending the place of good fortune', *Progress in Human Geography,* 24 (1): 1–18.

Smith, D. (2000b) *Moral Geographies: Ethics in a World of Difference*. Edinburgh: Edinburgh University Press.

Smith, D. (2000c) 'Social justice revisited', *Environment and Planning A,* 32: 1149–62.

Smith, D. (2003) 'Geographers, ethics and social concern', in R. Johnston and M. Williams (eds), *A Century of British Geography*. Oxford: Oxford University Press. pp. 625–41.

Smith, D. (2004) 'Morality, ethics and social justice', in P. Cloke, P. Crang and M. Goodwin (eds), *Envisioning Human Geographies*. London: Arnold. pp. 195–209.

Smith, M. (2001) 'Repetition and difference: Lefebvre, Le Cobusier and modernity's (im) moral landscape', *Ethics, Place and Environment*, 4 (1): 31–44.

Smith, S. (1984) 'Practicing humanistic geography', *Annals of the Association of American Geographers,* 74 (3): 353–74.

Smith, S. (2005) 'States, markets and an ethic of care', *Political Geography*, 24: 1–10.

Stoddart, D. (ed.) (1981) *Geography, Ideology and Social Concern*. Totowa, NJ: Barnes and Noble Books.

Thrift, N. (2004) 'Summoning life', in P. Cloke, P. Crang and M. Goodwin (eds), *Envisioning Human Geographies*. London: Arnold. pp. 81–103.

Thrift, N. (2005) 'But malice aforethought: cities and the natural history of hatred', *Transactions of the Institute of British Geographers,* NS 30: 133–50.

Tuan, Y-F. (1989) *Morality and Imagination: Paradoxes of Progress*. Madison: University of Wisconsin Press.

Tuan, Y.-F. (1996) 'Space and place: humanistic perspective', in J. Agnew, D. Livingstone and A. Rogers (eds), *Human Geography: An Essential Anthology*. Malden, MA: Blackwell. pp. 445–57.

Whatmore, S. (1997) 'Dissecting the autonomous self: hybrid cartographies for a relational ethics', *Environment and Planning D: Society and Space,* 15: 37–53.

Whatmore, S. (2002) *Hybrid Geographies: Natures, Cultures, Spaces*. London: Sage.

Whatmore, S. (2005) '*Hybrid Geographies:* author's responses and reflections', *Antipode*, 37 (4): 842–45.

White, G. (1972) 'Geography and public policy', *The Professional Geographer*, 24 (2): 101–4.

Wilton, R. (1998) 'The constitution of difference: space and psyche in landscapes of exclusion', *Geoforum*, 29 (2): 173–85.

Wreford Watson, J.W. (1951) 'The sociological aspects of geography', in G. Taylor, (ed.), *Geography in the Twentieth Century*. London: Methuen. pp. 463–99.

20

Environmental Justice and the Commons

Richard Howitt and Michael Hillman

INTRODUCTION

Overlapping concerns for social and environmental justice within social geography often emerge 'as a response to perceived injustice, as judged through observations of unreasonable inequality in outcome and lack of fair treatment for, in particular, people and social groups that are already marginalised and disadvantaged' (Walker and Bulkeley, 2006: 656). Integrative, holistic approaches to place, community and nation acknowledge that environmental, socio-cultural and political-economic dimensions of justice necessarily co-constitute its complex landscapes. As a result, questions of justice are central not only to the relationship between states and populations – both citizens and people denied citizenship – but also in the regulation and management of environmental relations. State claims on public and common-pool resources, therefore, raise urgent questions about environmental governance, sustainability and the challenges of managing specific environmental resources as diverse as water, forests, fisheries and conservation reserves. In the new scale politics of globalization, citizenship and identity, contestation of states' claims about just and sustainable management of common property inevitably pose new and urgent questions about the place of environmental justice in the work of social geography.

Many indigenous and local resource and environmental management systems are constituted through high context social and environmental relations – where people have close connections over long periods of time. As with high context cultures (Hall, 1981), these are situations where social and environmental relations are deeply co-embedded and understood by the people involved without need for explanation or analysis. Indeed, such relations have long been central to human interaction with common-pool resources. In the colonial phases of the geographical expansion of market capitalism, it was enclosure of the Commons and displacement of the societies whose sustenance depended on sustainable management of Commons and common-pool resources, that provided both a pool of labor and substantial environmental capital that became available for ownership and exploitation through the processes Marx (1954), also Luxembourg (1963), referred to as primitive accumulation – a process that was fundamental to the expansion of wealth and power that underpinned growth. More recently, globalizing neo-liberal values of economic developmentalism, and the institutionalization of these values through worldwide trading systems and enforceable systems of governance and accountability, have often produced precisely the sorts of perceived injustices that Walker and Bulkeley (2006) refer to. In this chapter we argue that such circumstances, where local and indigenous governance of common pool resources is overtaken by demands from external commercial and globalized governance systems, often produce contemporary processes of primitive accumulation with social implications for environmental justice. We further argue that in addressing the injustices that arise from contemporary primitive accumulation, environmental justice needs to be conceptualized as foundational to sustainable social geographies rather than secondary to questions of economic and social justice.

In many environmental governance systems post-colonial legacies of inclusion and exclusion constitute the structures of accumulation and appropriation of environmental, social and economic capital that in turn underpin current social geographies of injustice. Contemporary debates over 'just sustainability' (Agyeman and Evans, 2003) mirror, but also extend, the tensions identified in Fraser's benchmark analysis (1997) of the paradoxical tension between strategies for social justice that target redistribution of resources to achieve economic justice, and strategies targeting recognition and acceptance of difference to achieve cultural justice. Fraser's focus on notions of social justice that are disengaged from environmental settings sets up the didactic binary system that she relies on to explore the paradoxical challenges of developing political strategies to secure social justice. Recognizing environmental justice as both the context for and constitutive of the social and economic dimensions of justice reframes one's approach to geographies of justice.

Reframing social geography in terms of the shifting and scaled relationships between environment, economy and culture is a powerful tool for pursuing sustainable futures that accommodate, rather than require the erasure of cultural and ecological diversity by market processes. Such reframing demands refocusing on elements of social geography which might otherwise be assigned marginal importance as merely contextual. In foregrounding, for example, the people – environmental relations that structure key environmental decision-making processes in a local society, this approach effectively recontextualizes the possibilities of geographical engagement with environmental decisions.

Acknowledging the inherently *scaled* nature of the politics that are played out around issues of environmental justice in various complex, plural and diverse social and ecological settings (that is, across complex societies and habitats), provides us with important tools for situating and engaging with questions of *environmental* justice in *social* geography. While universal declarations and conventions frame the content and nature of justice, rights and good by providing important benchmarks for thinking about justice, it is through the struggle for environmental justice, typically waged in the highly contextualized setting of people's everyday lives, where specific local social, cultural, economic, political and environmental circumstances set boundaries and constraints on what is possible; what is meaningful; what is sought. Relational views of scale provide a way of bridging the institutional gaps between global governance frameworks and local sites of conflict and livelihood (see, e.g., Howitt, 2003; Howitt and Suchet-Pearson, 2003). In short, scaled analysis opens up the interplay across sites, between values and governance systems, and across time in ways that allow for action to address injustice at different scales and sites.

Socio-spatial and scale literate analysis unsettles various singular, binary, reductionist and categorical generalizations that reinforce the legitimacy of primitive accumulation as the pre-history of the state and its authoritative position in systems of justice and resource allocation. They do this by identifying as integral to systems' construction and operation, elements that more conventional approaches render as external, marginal or unimportant for consideration in analysis that emphasizes profit, production or science over engagement with the messy overlaps of coexisting relationships that actually constitute both the resources and the systems that manage them. Legitimizing the state against Indigenous and local systems of authority and environmental management, including management of common-pool resource systems, inhibits the progressive impact of struggles against unjust or unsustainable regimes of appropriation, regulation and accumulation, and restricts the exploration, development and advocacy of just and sustainable alternatives. In short, socio-spatial literacy is needed to avoid universalizing prescriptions for environmental governance that rely on the imposition of a singular common sense which is not shared across different cultural groups or spatial and temporal scales. Whether these forms of governance are framed in terms of economic efficiency, social justice or environmental protection, their pursuit as self-evidently good is naive and threatening to many social and ecological communities affected by them.

In common property systems, for example, there is often a mismatch between the scales at which people – environment relations operate, and the scale of the institutional frameworks that manage these relationships with the resource. It is often this mismatch that constitutes the problem. Similarly, overlaps between externally-oriented commercial exchange systems and locally-oriented use systems that rely on the same places (if not the same materials) often construct geographies of injustice. In the processes of primitive accumulation, the mobilization of various materials that embody environmental capital for commercial gain are always supported by a scaled institutional arrangement in which some people are privileged over others. In this sense, the scale politics of common property and environmental services is inescapably constituted as involving both environmental and social justice as well as both local and wider scale social geographies of justice.

REVISITING THE 'TRAGEDY OF THE COMMONS'

> Hardin's 'tragedy of the Commons' (1968) and Ehrlich's 'population bomb' (1968) succeeded so phenomenally well not because they oversimplified reality (which they did), nor even because they supported the entrenched power of political-economic elites (which they also did): they succeeded in large measure because they were good stories that effectively communicated a powerful idea. (Walker, 2006: 385)

Identifying and responding to the new and enduring forms of postcolonial appropriation and accumulation of common-pool resources and common property require a situated and holistic analysis, one which avoids the reductionist and binary frames that typify both Hardin's influential formulation of the so-called 'Tragedy of the Commons' (1968) and many related critiques from both the right and left. In this section, the substance and main critiques of Hardin's thesis are briefly dealt with as a basis for later discussion.

In the terms framed by Hardin, key questions of environmental governance, appropriation and degradation relate substantially to what are now generally referred to as common-pool resources, defined by Dietz et al. (2002) as a natural or human-made resource where excluding access is difficult (although possible), and where use by one individual or group subtracts from the amount available to others. This definition primarily aims to differentiate common-pool resources from private goods, which are excludable and subtractable, as well as from public goods, which are neither excludable nor subtractable (Connor and Dovers, 2002; McInnes, 2004). Other terms have been used to describe the same phenomenon but are now generally seen as conflating the characteristics of the resource itself with the property system that governs its application and use (Connor and Dovers, 2002). Common-pool resources can be managed under a number of property regimes, usually categorized as:

- *Open access*: absence of property rights, unregulated access, free to all;
- *Common property*: access/use regulated by local community/ies either autonomously or within legal or political parameters set by broader authority;
- *State regulation*: use and access rights are directly held by government authority; or
- *Private property*: individual or corporations have a right to specific use or access that excludes others and is usually marketable (Dolsak and Ostrom, 2003).

Hardin's intention with respect to common-pool resources was to critique Adam Smith's foundational assumption that the sum of decisions reached individually about management of common-pool resources would also be the best decision for an entire society. His thesis emphasized the link between population growth, environmental degradation and resource scarcity:

> Each man is locked into a system that compels him to increase his herd without limit – in a world that is limited. Ruin is the destination toward which all men rush. Each pursuing his own best interest in a society that believes in the freedom of the Commons. Freedom in a Commons brings ruin to all. (Hardin, 1968: 7)

Hardin argued that 'the tragedy of the food basket is averted by private property, or something formally like it' (Hardin, 1968: 8). However, since 'airs and waters' cannot be fenced, the problem of common-pool resources must also be met with 'coercive laws or taxing devices', a point he added almost as an afterthought (Hardin, 1968: 8; Hardin, 1998). As Bryan (2004) points out, Hardin's formulation of 'mutually agreed coercion' suggests a range of social and institutional arrangements that is broader than top-down command and control regimes. In practice, however, his 'solution' has been seen as a choice between privatization and free market environmentalism (Anderson and Leal, 1991; Vanderheiden, 2005) and state regulation, a binary which bedevils contemporary policy in areas such as global climate change, land and water conservation, fisheries and intellectual property.

Responses and critiques

Hardin's original thesis has been widely criticized on a number of grounds, particularly over its historical inaccuracy and partiality. Specific critiques include observations that management of the Commons was usually multifaceted rather than driven simply by economic rationalism and that common-pool resources often involve multiple rather than single use-values, producing a failure of single-use models to recognize the diversity of individual motivations. In a similar vein, the liberal assumption of rational self-interest is seen as ignoring the importance of social interaction and human-nature dialogue and of failing to recognize the wide range of socio-cultural institutional arrangements and motivations for regulating the Commons, as argued by Berkes and Feeny:

> Resource managers don't always understand that communal property systems are not guided strictly by optimality objectives. Social and cultural objectives such as the education and socialization of the young may be just as important as the procurement of game in native community-based resource use systems. (1990: 49)

A third type of criticism goes to the conflating of common-pool resources with the form of governance, hence failing to distinguish between common property and open access regimes (Ostrom, 1990; Feeny et al., 1990; Syme et al., 1999; McCay, 2002; Bryan, 2004). Others have commented more generally on the fuzzy distinctions that occur in practice between the various property regimes, arguing that these categories are both theoretically and empirically inadequate to provide a basis for analyzing environmental governance (Chander and Sunder, 2004; Paavola, 2007).[1] Degradation of common-pool resources results not from the sharing of property rights, but rather from the absence, lack of understanding or expression of such rights. Nor is over-exploitation essentially driven by internal dynamics or human nature as Hardin initially argued, but is rather contingent upon the breakdown of pre-existing common systems due to both social and biophysical external disruption and disturbance (Berkes, 1989). Neither privatization nor regulation may avert this outcome, and in many instances are more likely to be the drivers of environmental degradation and loss of cultural identity.

In response to the critics, Hardin (1994) later regretted the important omission of the word 'unmanaged' [Commons] from his original title, and acknowledged the partiality of his approach and its relevance to (post) colonial appropriation:

> What I have realized from reading numerous criticisms of the theory of the Commons is that both Lloyd and I were analyzing a subset of Commons – those where 'help yourself' or 'feel free' attitudes prevail. This was the message European pioneers in North America thought they had been given by the land they chose to perceive as unpeopled. (Hardin, 1998: 683)

Hardin continued to maintain, however, the duality of state regulation and privatization when he wrote: 'In correcting this omission, one can generalize the practical conclusion in this way: A "managed Commons" describes either socialism or the privatism of free enterprise' (Hardin, 1998: 683).

Critics of Hardin frequently proceed via a consideration of the wide range of models available for managing resources (McKean, 1992), challenging the state–private property binary and emphasizing active agency by detailing 'how communities and individuals fashion different ways of governing the Commons' (Ostrom, 1990: 2). Ostrom's work is just one of many subsequent attempts to set out the characteristics of equitable and sustainable regimes or institutions of environmental governance at various levels of generality (e.g. Ostrom, 1992; Low and Gleeson, 1998; Dovers, 2001; Agyeman and Evans, 2003; Chander and Sunder, 2004; Trawick, 2003; Bryan, 2004). Martin and Verbeek (2002) emphasize the embodiment of behavioral characteristics in private property regimes, whilst Berkes (1989) takes a more ecosystem-based approach, pointing to the capacity for adaptation, resilience and equity in a well-functioning common property regime. Acheson (2003) and Bakker and Bridge (2006) emphasize the value of an understanding of, and relationship with, the material characteristics of the resource itself. Williams and Mawdsley argue for recognition of the differing socio-spatial contexts of governance, property rights and the role and contribution of the environment in people's everyday lives: 'western environmental justice research needs to fully contextualize southern environmental actors rather than using them as ciphers and symbols of distant "others"' (Williams and Mawdsley, 2006: 662). Most, if not all, of this literature argues strongly for the importance of *both* biophysical and social geography in contextualizing and situating resource management.

Environmental governance approaches

Castree views the enclosure of the Commons one of the 'cutting edge environmental issues' (2003: 83) within which the development of a distinct human geography perspective is, or should be, core business. Attention to institutional structure and human agency, and on context and material conditions, mean that responding to Commons issues is contingent upon a place-specific understanding of environmental characteristics, cultural identity and decision-making processes. The contribution of social geography, therefore, must go beyond a partial view of the capacity of particular modes of governance, whether based on private property, state regulation or even co-managed or community-based management regimes, to solve Commons issues. It needs to also engage in both site-specific and cross-scale and multi-site work that addresses the messy overlaps and institutional mechanisms that constitute and constrain environmental injustices.

The rapid emergence of discourses of global environmental governance in the 1990s, most significantly perhaps out of the Brundtland Report (WCED, 1987) and the 1992 Rio Earth Summit, shifted the scale at which the solution to various environmental crises was proposed. As a result, the scaling of governance affects not only different institutional concerns, but also goes to the nature of the resource itself, in particular whether a resource is in fact 'excludable' (use can be restricted albeit with difficulty) or 'subtractable' (use reduces the amount available to others) at a range of scales from local to global.[2] New global institutions were endorsed as having a capacity to address ostensibly global crises – even though these same institutions were often distant (both geographically and culturally) from the systems and problems they sought to influence. More recent reflection has advocated a multifaceted approach of commissions, networks and inter-agency protocols (Streck, 2002) rather than singular, macro-level institutional solutions to environmental governance. Similarly, the development of national and regional environmental agencies has come under increasing pressure to respond to and engage with the complex realities of both cultural and biophysical diversity – with a predictable need to produce institutional reform that accommodates rather than annihilates diversity (Hillman and Howitt, 2008). Calls for a 'Global Environment Organisation' with powers to match the World Trade Organization are often supplemented with recognition of much less centralized models of cooperation and governance (Speth, 2002) and realistic sustainability assessment of governance processes (Hales and Prescott-Allen, 2002).

In this context, several brief examples, below, provide a series of place-based discussions to highlight the significance of scale politics, the diverse forms of appropriation (Glassman, 2006) and the negative impacts of one-dimensional characterizations of multifaceted concepts such as environment and justice in many settings. In dealing with common-pool resources, the continued pressure for commercial and technical governance systems to effect alienation of resources from traditional governance systems is notable – and is more typically a portent of primitive accumulation than good environmental governance and environmental justice. As Glassman has argued:

> Primitive accumulation has myriad forms, virtually all of which Marx had already identified in his writings on the topic, but each of these forms also has new twists, as with the development of new forms of environmental governance that allow private appropriation of the conditions of production or privatization of public goods produced through previous rounds of social struggle. (Glassman, 2006: 622)

WHALING: A GLOBAL COMMONS?

Despite a trend over decades towards neoliberal, market-based forms of marine environmental governance (Mansfield, 2004), whaling continues to be framed in the tradition of Western sea-going nations as a single-scale 'global Commons' to be regulated by international treaties and authorities, in particular the International Whaling Commission (IWC). Recent attention, however, has turned to the distributive impacts of such regulation, along with an increased focus on the politics of inclusion and exclusion and the links between whaling and cultural identity. These shifts are one manifestation of the emergence and broadening of the environmental justice movement (Debbane and Keil, 2004; Walker and Bulkeley, 2006) and more generally of a pragmatic, differentiated new environmental movement, both of which have emerged in part as a response to a monolithic and modernist global sustainable development discourse (McGregor, 2004). These changes, in turn, have led to a more nuanced appraisal of the scaled politics of a whaling moratorium and criticism of the legitimacy of the IWC itself. Osherenko (2005) sees the cultural dominance of Western developed nations within the centralized IWC as an example of both distributive and procedural injustice and as a continuation of postcolonial practices when she writes:

> Ironically, the moratorium on commercial whaling that the IWC adopted in 1982 and put into effect in 1985 does not represent an end to that racist and imperialist past. Rather, the moratorium perpetuates patterns of domination in which hegemonic nations impose their values, preferences, and worldviews on less powerful as well as racially, culturally, and ethnically different nations. (Osherenko, 2005: 224)

Scheiber (1998) argues that the global scaling of whaling governance and regulation unfairly conflates traditional subsistence harvesting by Indigenous Peoples such as the Inuit with the claims of developed coastal countries such as Japan and Norway to industrial whaling rights. In this sense the normalized 'solution' to the tension between environmental sustainability and social justice is in reality complex, scaled and contentious both economically and culturally. Whilst the beneficiaries of a blanket moratorium are arguably environmental NGOs and global agribusiness, the economic losers are local communities where whaling has traditionally been a core activity. Other perceived elements of injustice, cultural dominance and moral hypocrisy by the developed nations are the focus on banning hunting in the face of the continuation of other whale-harming practices such as the use of naval sonar and increasing ocean pollution (Parsons et al., 2000; Nowacek et al., 2004).

More broadly, the dominant approach to whaling, based on human/non-human separation, ignores the mutually dependent material and cultural relations of Indigenous Peoples and cetaceans as part of the natural world, including shared knowledge of appropriate hunting habitats and practices (Simmonds et al., 2002; Awatere, 2005). A similar point is made by Natcher et al. (2005: 246) regarding the relational problems of co-management where fish catch and release programs are seen by some First Nation peoples as breaching shared moral grounds between humans and non-humans and as threatening the inter-species 'relational sustainability' that underpins culture and livelihood. Likewise, differing versions of resource management and environmental justice set up non-humans either as victims of human acts or as sentient, culturally aware and co-dependent beings. This binary is place and scale specific – it is easier to maintain the human/nature boundary in the face of a global undifferentiated and monolithic activity labeled as whaling. The notion of 'ecological justice' towards nature as a dynamic, diverse and scaled entity has been put forward as an additional element required to balance these anthropocentric and categorical perspectives in resource management and within the environmental justice movement itself. Conventional neoliberal versions of justice applied to environmental issues fail to recognize the complexity, variability and stochastic character of natural ecosystems. This ecologically oriented view of justice must be met with an understanding of the complexity of nature itself, and of our relationship with nature, rather than simply trying to extrapolate from anthropocentric, linear or restorative approaches to justice (Swyngedouw and Heynen, 2003)

Alternative models of the regulation of whaling do exist at smaller scales, sometimes formalized in reaction to the perceived problems of global regulation. For example, Huntington et al. (2002) argues that the Alaska Beluga Whale Committee (ABWC) was set up to maintain the viability of traditional subsistence harvests in the face of concern over the possible extension of the IWC into this region. The ABWC has historically drawn on cooperative and interdisciplinary research between government and community; literally, between scientists and hunters. The success of the ABWC is attributed in no small part to a dual continuity of personnel and process, promoting the formation of 'epistemic communities' (Michaels and Laituri, 1999: 60) of values, commitment and practice. A similar point has been made in relation to other sustainable harvesting of common-pool marine resources (e.g. Acheson, 2003). As Natcher et al. (2005) argue, co-management is about managing relationships rather than a narrow view of resource management as the production of economic goods and formal access. Such relationships are part of broader processes rather than reducible to single material outcomes or manifestations. Attempts to construct global regulatory regimes typically fail to address this point or find a means to enact it.

PRIVATIZING THE COMMONS: CORPORATE AND MARKET STRATEGIES TOWARDS WATER MANAGEMENT

> A truly Commons approach to common-pool resources may promote both equity and sustainability where privatization may fail to achieve one or both of these objectives. (Toly, 2005: 28)

> It seems that, with regard to water, Hardin (1968) got it backwards, confusing causes with solutions to a problem that immediately changes character once the history of the region is known (Trawick, 2003: 978).

Hardin argued for privatization as one response to the over-exploitation of the Commons. In the era of neo-liberal economics, privatization of water resources has been a widespread phenomenon, either directly through full privatization as in the United Kingdom (Gearey and Jeffrey, 2006) or through hybridized strategies of corporatization, where state ownership is mixed with private sector philosophy. These are both key forms of primitive accumulation, or 'accumulation by dispossession' (Swyngedouw, 2004: 82). Such market models provide politically attractive responses to complex problems of environmental degradation but fail to incorporate local practices, knowledge and values (Rohde, et al., 2006). Commodification that incorporates decision-making mechanisms such as cost-benefit analysis may be restricted to the short-term profitable enterprises, whilst long-term infrastructural and environmental considerations are either ignored or re-socialized.

Rahm et al. (2006) make this point in relation to Tribal Grazing Lands Policy in Botswana, where increasing private control of boreholes has led to an expansion of cattle into former wildlife areas, resulting in loss of water quality, delays in the provision of water to local communities, and reduced the monitoring of water use. Far from providing a 'free market' regime, privatization has led to the dominance of large global transnational companies in the water sector, particularly but not exclusively in developing countries (Hoekstra, 2006). South America is another prominent example, where World Bank sponsored water privatization strategy has been based on the example of Pinochet's Chile in the 1980s. It is important to point out that there has been strong resistance in many cases to water privatization (Swyngedouw, 2004), for instance the 2000 'siege of Cochabamba' in Bolivia, where a blockade of city entrances led to a roll-back of privatization plans and the imposition of conditions by the Inter-American Development Bank (Warner, 2006).

Trawick (2003) argues for a solution to water scarcity based upon the choices of either private or communal governance by local communities and that takes account of both human and physical geographical commonalities and differences. Without underestimating the importance of human agency in responding to appropriation of water rights, an authentic political ecology approach, one emphasizing difference (Escobar, 2006), would also recognize what Debbane and Keil (2004: 210) refer to as the 'materiality' of water – its 'reluctance' to be subdued to 'immaterial abstractions' in the sense of marketization, commodification and privatization (Swyngedouw, 2004). Part of this materiality hinges upon the variability and multiple use-values of water at a range of spatial and temporal scales (Sneddon et al., 2002) which we usually construct as both an ontological and epistemic singularity – a dominant use-value such as irrigation or navigation, a particular reach of a river viewed in isolation from the catchment, or a narrow disciplinary perspective on water management. Emphasis on the material character of water (Castree, 2003), such as variability, mutability and the identity and difference of 'resources', represents an emerging strand within social geography and addresses an often overlooked characteristic of the 'environment' in environmental justice discourse itself (Castree and Braun, 2001; Hillman, 2006).

INTERNAL AND EXTERNAL 'REGULATION' OF THE COMMONS: BIOPROSPECTING AND BIOPIRACY

In contemporary capitalism, and most notably in postcolonial societies, common resources have been seen as a cheap, abundant and accessible source of material for commercial exploitation and a new enclosure of the Commons. Intellectual property, copyright legislation and global treaties such as the Trade Related Aspects of Intellectual Property Rights (TRIPS) Agreement, whilst ostensibly providing a 'level playing field' to protect initiative and discovery, in reality promote the interests of Western bioprospecting. At issue is the diversity of knowledge systems and their relationship to property regimes, in particular the 'external', globalized and legalistic intellectual property regime of developed countries and the 'internal', localized and evolved common property regimes of Indigenous Peoples. The interaction of these regimes produces many instances of social, environmental and ecological injustice.

Robinson (2006) provides examples of bioprospecting in Thailand, including the appropriation of plant genetic resources in Jasmine rice, a product that comprises about 25% of Thai rice exports. In this instance, a North American company took out trademark rights on a name ('Jasmati', suggesting a relationship to Jasmine rice) and the patent on a product with Jasmine characteristics, created by cross-breeding and irradiation, for growing by American farmers, intended to compete with Thai imports. Whilst complex, this case was widely seen in Thailand as not only concerned with issues of economic loss but also about the misappropriation of traditional knowledge that had been developed and improved over many generations through communal practice and experience. Rice growing is an important part of Thai culture as well as an economic livelihood, so that misappropriation occurs across social, economic and environmental dimensions. In this sense, what is at stake is not only the just distribution of economic benefits accruing from intellectual property, but also the potential damage to identity and social networks that make up village and community.

The damage to economic livelihood and cultural identity, however, are closely related. The globalized patent system recognizes and protects economic gain accruing from short-term high-technology modifications rather than the inter-generational customs and gradual improvements which form the platform for such windfall profits to occur. One form of 'regulation' of the Commons through long-term collaborative knowledge-sharing is replaced by a centralized regime vested in private ownership of intellectual property directed towards improved exchange-value (at the expense of long-standing multiple use-values) through the use of 'high' technology and 'enclosure' of the material and intellectual Commons (Shiva, 1997; Toly, 2005). In the development and operation of these globalized intellectual property regimes, there is lack of legal recognition of the transparency and adequacy of the patent process (where any serious oversight relies on NGOs), whilst the differing social and cultural impacts of resource use are generally not accorded significance.

The multiple scales and dimensions at which the appropriation of traditional knowledge occurs further emphasizes the danger of categorizing justice as environmental, social or ecological, and of positioning institutional/state regulation against market-based mechanisms. In practice, these Hardin-style solutions can appear in tandem, producing inequitable outcomes, exclusion from decision-making and consent mechanisms, disruption of social identity and long-standing connections with ecosystems, and ultimately loss of livelihoods. A share in the financial proceeds of patenting, whilst providing a measure of distributive justice, will not compensate for such disruption to socio-cultural practices. Grand universal discourses and binaries promote and support regimes that ultimately prove disruptive to both social and environmental systems. The emphasis on economic equity (important though it is) and the positioning of intellectual property against'romantic discourses of the public domain' (Chander and Sunder, 2004: 1335) rather serves to legitimate and mask the exploitation of traditional knowledge and acts against local struggles to prevent such exploitation.

JUSTICE, IDENTITY AND SUSTAINABILITY

Directly addressing arbitrary, categorical or binary distinctions, particularly in the construction of resources and between humans and the environment, is a pre-requisite for a broadening of the environmental justice movement, and for an effective *geographic* application of the idea of justice. In this section, some of the case materials discussed above are drawn on to explore more theoretical implications and to develop the argument that taking the biophysical domain seriously changes the notion of geographies of justice. The section critiques reification of environment (and environmental services). It explores one-dimensional, anthropocentric and bi-polar econocentric representations of justice in terms of the politics of identity or redistribution (further developing Fraser's work). On this basis, it seeks to accommodate geography and place-based ecological-social relations and diverse views of nature and the negotiation of those relationships in cross-scale systems of trade and governance – e.g. Forest Stewardship Council, ICCM, Bio-banking in different guises, human-nature and mutuality models of inter-species justice, etc.

TENSIONS IN THE DISCOURSE OF SUSTAINABILITY AND JUSTICE

> There has been a myriad [sic] Interventions to improve resource use in the pursuit of sustainability. These include traditional regulation, through real-market interventions like subsidies or preferred purchasing schemes, to complex artificial market interventions like the creation of credit schemes, cap and trade programs, or property rights in water or other fugitive resources. (Martin and Verbeek, 2002: 74)

In principle, a close association between the discourses of sustainability and environmental justice should be apparent, given the origins of the environmental justice movement itself in the articulation of the links between economic, social and environmental disadvantage (Kidd, 1999). Articulating this nexus of disadvantage should also have potential for the formation of political alliances and coalitions between social groups that have often been at odds over conflicting anthropocentric and eco-centric views of the world (Cannan, 2000). For many writing from a broad justice perspective, however, sustainable development is viewed in practice as little more than ecological modernization (e.g. Young, 2000) under existing neo-liberal capitalist economic systems with a lack of consideration of questions of equity (Harvey, 1996; Davies, 2006; Luke, 2006). Conversely, critiques by social geographers and others have focused on the absence within the mainstream environmental justice movement of a broad understanding of the social and ecological dimensions of justice (Moore and Bache, 1997; Low and Gleeson, 1998; Debbane and Keil, 2004; Williams and Mawdsley, 2006; Walker and Bulkeley, 2006) This latter position argues that a reductionist emphasis on justice as economic (re)allocation occurs at the expense of an understanding of the complex social and ecological processes that underpin distribution and of the everyday dynamics of injustice that arise within and across scales and species. This approach has arguably failed to link justice and the environment in any coherent or meaningful way to develop what Bosselmann (1999: 30) refers to as a 'general theory' of environmental justice.

Institutions and norms involved in the governance of common-pool resources and the associated distribution of environmental hazards and goods will inevitably be drawn into the dynamics of these changing environmental conditions and social characteristics. Such institutions need to be open-ended and place- and process-focused. In pursuit of this flexibility, a disjuncture emerges between the application of generic global models (either of state regulation or privatization strategies) and the diversity of biophysical and cultural landscapes. In policy terms, differing and contested notions of environmental health and principles of justice complicate planning and implementation of program of sustainable management, creating 'wicked' problems involving multiple goals and limited resources (Lachapelle et al., 2003) and the need for attention to differing criteria for the equitable distribution of environmental costs and benefits (Low and Gleeson, 1998: Michaels and Laituri, 1999). It is also likely that cultural differences will make different elements of justice more important for different groups and societies (Conner, 2003). It has become apparent that different social and physical geographies produce contrasting versions of environmental justice (Harvey, 1996; Debbane and Keil, 2004) and that place-specific explanations of environmental inequality are required (Pellow, 2004). For example, the correlation of environmental and racial disadvantage in the United States has proved less significant than socio-economic factors in countries with limited large-scale ethnic segregation (Agyeman et al., 2002). The risk of embedding a neo-liberal justice framework with little applicability to postcolonial societies has also been noted (Williams and Mawdsley, 2006). Understanding differing ideas of fairness in environmental decision-making is therefore a key to effective policy (Nancarrow and Syme, 2001). Institutional responses to these challenges have often been reactive, ad hoc, and have taken little account of environmental or cultural diversity (Connell et al., 2005).

The tensions between justice and sustainability have been articulated in various ways. Benjaminsen et al., 2006: 524 provides a critique of a technocratic notion of carrying capacity, which 'gives privilege to environmental sustainability and to one particular perception of the ideal landscape at the expense of livelihood security and poverty alleviation'. Agyeman and Evans (2003) argue for a stronger, more eco-centric approach to sustainability:

> True sustainability with a full regard to environmental justice would be best reached by advancing sustainability ideals toward hard/strong sustainability or eco-centric theories while highlighting environmental justice theories that incorporate intergenerational, intragenerational, international, and interspecies equity, and supporting economic reforms that value community economic development with redistributive values and policies. (2003: 3–4).

Moore and Bache (1997) assert that we need both a human-centred and a biospheric focus to achieve a complete notion of environmental justice. From this perspective, decisions must be based both on equity, that is our relations with other humans, and on natural ethics, our relationships with nature (Rayner et al., 1999). This includes who gets to define the environment (Agyeman et al., 2002) and recognition of the multiplicity of knowledge and resource management systems that operate with respect to it (Mailhot, 1994). Low and Gleeson argue that in the pursuit of the dual goals of sustainability and justice, or of redistribution and recognition, a key distinction can be made between environmental justice – the distribution of environmental quality among people – and ecological justice – a concern for 'responsible relationships between humans and the non-human natural world' (Low and Gleeson, 1998: 2; Low and Gleeson, 1999). A failure in this sphere will perpetuate the deep and enduring colonial legacy of appropriation of common-pool resources and fail to address the discontinuity and disjuncture apparent between old and new forms of regulation through community-based knowledge and practice, through state-based centralization and through privatized market-based regimes. These alleged shortcomings reflect the lack of a political-ecological perspective within such discourses. That is, environmental justice lacks an ecological perspective, whilst sustainability lacks a political (justice) perspective.

With respect to the various forms of dispossession and alienation identified in the previous section, an exclusive emphasis on economic costs and benefits tends to reduce both sustainability and justice to economic equity and (re)distribution at the expense of what Escobar (2006) refers to as 'cultural distribution', along with due attention to the procedural, relational and ecological underpinnings of distribution itself. This privileging of allocation also carries with it a narrow focus on environmental exchange-values rather than use-values, a trade-off of outcome for process, place and identity, and resulting loss of awareness of the human-nature connection, particularly (but by no means exclusively) in Indigenous communities. These issues are now further considered through the work of Nancy Fraser on redistribution and recognition.

FRASER'S BINARIZED VIEW OF JUSTICE

The paradoxical tension between different 'dimensions' of justice was the focus of Nancy Fraser's attention in her seminal work on social justice (1995, 1997). Fraser identifies two interpenetrating political imaginaries, one rooted in materialist socialism, the other in a new cultural politics which she labels 'post-socialist'. In these two political imaginaries, 'justice' has quite different orientations. In materialist socialist positions, Fraser suggests, struggles against material inequality and liberation from economic exploitation are prioritized. She summarizes the strategic focus of these economically focused struggles as 'redistribution'. In 'post-socialist' cultural politics, struggles for recognition and liberation from cultural domination, struggles around racial or gender inequality and the politics of difference have been given greater prominence. Fraser summarizes the strategic focus of these identity-focused struggles as 'recognition'. While noting that such distinctions are an analytical convenience rather than categorical reality, Fraser identifies the 'redistribution-recognition dilemma' as one of the 'central political dilemmas of our age' (1997: 13). Missing in Fraser's typology, however – and from the work of many of Fraser's critics – is any reference to environmental justice (Howitt, 2001: 92). Integrating an environmental justice dimension into Fraser's bi-focal typology disrupts its binarizing simplicity, pushing one away from any simple gravity model of competing weights at each (environmental, social, economic) node, and towards a more integrative notion of just and sustainable economic, social *and* environmental outcomes.

This more integrative approach is evident in the thinking of many Aboriginal groups, for whom relationships between people, place and cosmos that are glossed as 'Country' (see e.g. Rose, 1996) encompass specific social, economic and environmental relations including:

- people-to-people relationships that constitute the particular culture, law and tradition of a group of people and are closely woven into individual and collective identities;
- people-to-place relationships that establish and codify the rights and responsibilities at the core of their social and economic activity;
- the relationships between people (individuals and groups), specific elements of the landscape (wildlife, sites, biophysical forces and processes) and the cosmos through their mythic representations;
- relationships between non-human elements of the landscape; and
- various relationships with non-Indigenous interests and institutions, including governments, industries and individuals.

In this context, a binarized orientation to justice which focuses on economic and cultural dimensions but excludes environmental dimensions of justice (and injustice) simply fails to capture the practical dilemmas of Indigenous Peoples' struggles to secure just and sustainable futures. The Indigenous Peoples' movement generally pursues strategies that simultaneously target securing recognition, improved material conditions *and* sustainable environmental relations.

It is also possible that within the overall struggle for recognition of Indigenous rights (including not only cultural rights but also economic and environmental rights), different historical circumstances will require different priorities to be set or different issues to be targeted for different groups. In this sense, the notion of a master narrative of social change – a blueprint designed as a 'top-down' guide for specific actions and interventions in environmental justice struggles – must be rejected. So, in Indigenous politics, this challenge is an everyday reality. It does not sit comfortably with Fraser's characterization of the'postsocialist' condition, which she sees as requiring a 'critical approach (that) must be "bi-valent", ... integrating the social and the cultural, the economic and the discursive' (1997: 5).

Rejection of a singular Indigenous political project not only draws us to consideration of the property rights, cultural and social practices and environmental relationships that characterize the particular material conditions of Indigenous Peoples' struggles for justice. It also draws us to both discursive and material engagement with 'difference' and 'otherness' – both social and environmental. In other words, the material circumstances of Indigenous Peoples' struggles make it necessary for geographers to deal not only with historically specific social, economic and environmental relations, but also with the discursive construction of social reality in critical social theory, and the discursive construction of environmental knowledge and understanding that underpins institutions of environmental governance through science and politics. In other words, we need to be conscious of the deep colonizing nature of both science and politics in dealing with difference. We need to recognize that colonial discourses conflate differences of many sorts (class, race, gender, language and so on) in order to contrast it to an imagined singular and privileged colonizing subject. In the politics of environmental justice it is necessary to avoid privileging an authoritative 'environmentalist' position that brooks no questioning, no challenge. A situated engagement (Suchet, 1999) with Indigenous and environmental otherness, then, will require both a theory and practice that recognizes the co-consitutiveness of socio-cultural, political-economic and environmental dimensions of just and sustainable geographies.

NEGOTIATING GEOGRAPHIES OF JUSTICE

> Although ecological justice is a highly situational ethic, this moral imperative is subject to abstraction and efficiency and given to governance by the market (which, as Polanyi, 1944, asserted, is an attempt to extract the economic from all social and natural context), in that the primacy of the economic over the political is a fundamental element of realistic politics (Ellul, 1997b, p. 56). (Toly, 2005: 29)

The social contextualization of environmental and ecological justice is critical to an authentic geographical approach to the governance of common-pool resources. However, in providing an alternative Commons narrative that meets the goals of sustainability, justice and identity, we need to be careful not to 'localize' or romanticize community-based management of common-pool resources. Fundamentalist appeals to the 'local' and to the principle of subsidiarity (e.g. in Local Agenda 21) may in practice be used to support more community participation *or* privatization (Mostert, 2003). Simplistic stereotypes of isolated, small, stable, and homogeneous groups sharing the same interests and traditional norms for preserving local resources often fit poorly with the complexity of how diverse local and external actors struggle to make and break rules about exploiting and replenishing resources that may be mobile and interconnect broad areas (Bruns, 2005: 13-1–13-13). Recognizing the 'transformative potential' of differing forms of environmental governance rather than simply adding another stake or participation point within existing frameworks is therefore critical.

Understanding how primitive accumulation of common-pool resources is legitimized and how economic, cultural and political mechanisms are used in environmental decision-making and resource allocation is also critical to effective responses (Martin and Verbeek, 2002; Swyngedouw, 2004). Connor and Dovers (2002: 120) argue that the rise of property rights instruments (PRIs) –'entitlements to resource use that have been endowed with characteristics of property interests, such as the ability to trade them in a market and capture changes in their value' – have been coincident with the rise of the sustainability discourse, but have been more than a policy tool, often changing the distribution of and access to the resource itself (and we would argue the decision-making process and the perception of the resource). The result is that the construction of resource justice itself is up for negotiation. Such negotiation is diverse and pluralist rather than singular and reductionist, encompassing multiple 'spheres of justice' (Paavola, 2007) – social, economic, cultural and environmental – in both human and non-human terms.

The impact of over-consumption and misappropriation of the world's resources has been met by regimes and strategies that have in the main exacerbated the problems, reducing rather than promoting social and environmental justice and equity. A richer and more geographic response to new forms of primitive accumulation entails re-focusing on genuine triple bottom line, robust and just forms of sustainability. It involves simultaneously giving the environment a voice and acknowledging biophysical and cultural diversity is a key component of environmental and ecological justice; engaging with what Powell (2006: 130) calls 'technologies of existence', that articulate cultural values along with the business of economic equity; and ensuring ongoing economic viability of the systems of governance and social reproduction that are generated. Ultimately, negotiating justice requires analysis of the 'connections between these disparate faces of capitalist alienation' (Glassman, 2006: 616). Environmental governance that will ultimately go beyond neo-liberal or top-down command and control responses to governing the Commons will therefore negotiate across multiple, scaled and contextualized physical and cultural landscapes.

The contribution of social geographers to this endeavor will largely depend on the discipline's capacity to integrate political-economic, socio-cultural and biophysical perspectives on justice, place and scale. Social geographies which insist on isolated consideration of engagement with the 'social' risk marginalizing the discipline and underselling its integrative and synthesizing capacities. In particular, reductionist and categorical views of scale which relegate scaled analysis to the margins of site-based or systemic analyses undermine the discipline's capacity to analyze and respond to the volatile politics of justice across scales and across cultural, political and ecological divides. Similarly, physical and bio-geographical approaches that dismiss the social, institutional and economic context of the systems they investigate risk entrenching environmental injustices in ways that threaten management systems that sustain inequality, poor representation, inequity and injustice. The challenge is to bring our understandings of social, economic and environmental justice together in ways that allow us to pursue more integrated and sustainable ways of coexisting with diverse human and non-human others in governance systems that value and nurture diversity rather than insist on its erasure.

NOTES

1 A similar problem of categorization exists for the defining properties of CPRs: both excludability and subtractability are clearly contingent upon scale and place for the same resource. This emphasizes the importance of a geographical approach and of the need for a contextualized understanding of both the Commons and of justice.

2 Such distinctions may be ontological impossibilities – quite literally unthinkable – in many cases/ societies – here we are thinking of various notions such as the Australian Aboriginal English term 'country' (Rose, 1999).

REFERENCES

Acheson, J. (2003) *Capturing the Commons: Devising institutions to Manage the Maine Lobster Industry*. Hanover, NH: University Press of New England.

Agyeman, J., Bullard, R. and Evans, B. (2002) 'Exploring the nexus: bringing together sustainability, environmental justice and equity', *Space and Polity,* 6 (1): 77–90.

Agyeman, J. and Evans, T. (2003) 'Toward just sustainability in urban communities: building equity rights with sustainable solutions', *Annals of the American Academy,* 590: 35–53.

Anderson, T. and Leal, D. (1991) *Free Market Environmentalism*. Boulder, CO: Westview Press.

Awatere, S. (2005) 'The influence of cultural identity on willingness to pay values in contingent valuation surveys', Contributed paper to the *NZARES Conference*, Nelson, New Zealand.

Bakker, K. and Bridge, G. (2006) 'Material worlds? Resource geographies and the "matter of nature"', *Progress in Human Geography*, 30 (1): 5–27.

Benjaminsen, T.A., Rohde, R., Sjaastad, E., Wisborg, P. and Lebert, T. (2006) 'Land reform, range ecology, and carrying capacities in Namaqualand, South Africa', *Annals of the Association of American Geographers*, 96 (3): 524–40.

Berkes, F. (1989) 'Cooperation from the perspectives of hyuman ecology', in F. Berkes (ed.) *Common Property Resources: Ecology and Community-based Sustainable Development*. London: Belhaven Press. pp.70–88.

Berkes, F. and Feeny, D. (1990) 'Paradigms lost: changing views on the use of common property resources', *Alternatives*, 17 (2): 48–55.

Bosselmann, K. (1999) 'Justice and the environment: building blocks for a theory on ecological justice', in K. Bosselmann and B.J. Richardson (eds), *Environmental Justice and Market Mechanisms*. The Hague: Kluwer Law International. pp. 30–57.

Bruns, B. (2005) 'Community-based principles for negotiating water rights: some conjectures on assumptions and priorities'. International workshop on *'African Water Laws: Plural Legislative Frameworks for Rural Water Management in Africa'*, 26–28 January 2005. Johannesburg, South Africa: 13-1–13-13.

Bryan, T.A. (2004) 'Tragedy averted: the promise of collaboration', *Society and Natural Resources*, 17: 881–96.

Buck, S.J. (1985) 'No tragedy on the Commons', *Environmental Ethics*, 7 (Spring): 49–61. Reprinted in K. Conca, M. Alberty, G.D. Dabelko, (eds), *Green Planet Blues. Environmental Politics from Stockholm to Rio*. Boulder, CO: HarperCollins. pp. 46–52.

Byrne, J. and Glover, L. (2002) 'A common future or towards a future Commons: Globalization and sustainable development since UNCED', *International Review for Environmental Strategies*, 3 (1): 5–25.

Cannan, C. (2000) 'The environmental crisis, greens and community development', *Community Development Journal*, 35 (4): 365–76.

Carlsson, L. and Berkes, F. (2005) 'Co-management: concepts and methodological implications', *Journal of Environmental Management*, 75: 65–76.

Castree, N. (2003) 'A post-environmental ethics?', *Ethics, Place and Environment*, 6 (1): 3–12.

Castree, N. (2004) 'Environmental issues: signals in the noise?', *Progress in Human Geography*, 28 (1): 79–90.

Castree, N. and Braun, B. (eds) (2001) *Social Nature: Theory, Practice, and Politics*. Malden, MA: Blackwell.

Chander, A. and Sunder, M. (2004) 'The romance of the public domain', *California Law Review*, 92: 1331–74.

Conner, D.S. (2003) 'Socially appraising justice: a cross-cultural perspective', *Social Justice Research*, 16 (1): 29–39.

Connor, R. and Dovers, S. (2002) 'Property rights instruments: transformative policy options', *Property: Rights and Responsibilities. Current Australian Thinking*. Canberra: Land and Water Australia. pp. 119–36.

Connell, D.S., Dovers, S. and Grafton R.Q. (2005) 'A critical analysis of the National Water Initiative', *Australasian Journal of Natural Resources Law and Policy,* 10: 81–107.

Davies, A.R. (2006) 'Environmental justice as subtext or omission: Examining discourses of anti-incineration campaigning in Ireland', *Geoforum*, 37: 708–24.

Debbane, A.-M. and Keil, R. (2004) 'Multiple disconnections: environmental justice and urban water in Canada and South Africa', *Space and Polity*, 8 (2): 209–25.

Dietz, T., Dolsak, N., Ostrom, E. and Stern, P.C. (2002) 'The drama of the Commons', in E. Ostrom, T. Dietz, N. Dolsak, P.C. Stern, S. Stonich, and E.U. Weber (eds), *The drama of the Commons*. Washington, DC: National Academy Press. pp. 3–35.

Dietz, T., Ostrom, E. and Stern, P.C. (2003) 'The struggle to govern the Commons', *Science*, 302, 1907–12.

Dolsak, N and Ostrom, E. (2003) 'The challenges of the Commons', in N. Dolsak and E. Ostrom (eds), *The Commons in the New Millennium: Challenges and Adaptation*. Cambridge, MA: MIT Press. pp.3–34.

Dovers, S. (2001) 'Institutions for sustainability', *Tela*. 7.

Escobar, A. (1999) 'After nature: Steps to an antiessentialist political ecology', *Current Anthropology*, 40 (1): 1–30.

Escobar, A. (2006) 'Difference and conflict in the struggle over natural resources: outline of a political ecology framework', *Development*, 49: 6–13.

Feeny, D., Berkes, F., McCay, B.J. and Acheson, J.M. (1990) 'The tragedy of the Commons: twenty-two years later', *Human Ecology*, 18 (1): 1–19.

Fraser, N. (1995) 'From redistribution to recognition? Dilemmas of justice in a "post-socialist" age', *New Left Review*, 212: 68–93.

Fraser, N. (1997) *Justice Interruptus: critical reflections on the 'postsocialist' condition*. New York and London: Routledge.

Gearey, G. and Jeffrey, P. (2006) 'Concepts of legitimacy within the context of adaptive water management strategies', *Ecological Economics*, 60: 320–37.

Glantz, M. (2002) *Water, Climate, and Development Issues in the Amudarya Basin*. Report of Informal Planning Meeting held 18–19 June 2002 in Philadelphia, Pennsylvania. Boulder, CO: Environmental and Societal Impacts Group, NCAR.

Glassman, J. (2006) 'Primitive accumulation, accumulation by dispossession, accumulation by "extra-economic" means', *Progress in Human Geography*, 30 (5): 608–25.

Hales, D. and Prescott-Allen, R. (2002) 'Flying blind: assessing progress toward sustainability', in D.C. Esty and M.H. Ivaniva (eds), *Global Environmental Governance: Options and Opportunities*. New Haven CT: Yale School of Forestry and Environmental Studies. pp. 31–52.

Hall, E.T. (1981) *Beyond Culture*. New York: Anchor Books.

Hardin, G. (1968) 'The tragedy of the Commons', *Science*, 162, 1243–8.

Hardin, G. (1994) 'The tragedy of the unmanaged Commons', *Trends in Ecology and Evolution*, 9: 199.

Hardin, G. (1998) 'Extensions of "The Tragedy of the Commons"', *Science*, 280 (5364): 682–3.

Harvey, D. (1996) *Justice, Nature and the Geography of Difference*. Oxford: Blackwell.

Hillman, M. (2006) 'Situated justice in environmental decision-making: Lessons from river management in Southeastern Australia', *Geoforum*, 37, 695–707.

Hillman, M. and Howitt, R. (2008). 'Institutional change and transition in natural resource management: Lessons for social and environmental justice from experience in New South Wales, Australia: sustaining capacity and justice. *Local Environment,* 13 (1): 55–66.

Hoekstra, A.Y. (2006) *The Global Dimension of Water Governance: Nine Reasons for Global Arrangements in Order to Cope with Local Water Problems*. Delft: UNESCO-IHE Institute for Water Education.

Howitt, R. (2001) *Rethinking Resource Management: Justice, Sustainability and Indigenous Peoples*. London: Routledge.

Howitt, R. (2003) 'Scale', in J. Agnew, K. Mitchell and G. Toal (eds), *A Companion to Political Geography*. Oxford, Blackwell. pp. 138–57.

Howitt, R. and Suchet-Pearson, S. (2003) 'Ontological pluralism', in K. Anderson, M. Domosh, S. Pile and N. Thrift (eds), *Contested Cultural Landscapes. Handbook of Cultural Geography*. London: Sage. pp. 557–69.

Huntington, H.P., Brown-Schwalenberg, P.K. Frost, K.J. Fernandez-Gimenez, M.E. and Norton, D.W. (2002) 'Improving communication between holders of traditional and scientific knowledge', *Environmental Management*, 30 (6): 778–92.

Kidd, M. (1999) 'The pursuit of environmental justice in South Africa', in K. Bosselmann and B. J. Richardson (eds), *Environmental Justice and Market Mechanisms*. The Hague: Kluver Law International. pp. 324–36.

Klug, H. (2002) 'Straining the law: conficting legal premises and the governance of aquatic resources', *Society and Natural Resources*, 15: 693–707.

Lachapelle, P.R., McCool, S.F. and Patterson, M.A. (2003) 'Barriers to effective natural resource planning in a "messy" world', *Society and Natural Resources*, 16: 473–90.

Low, N. and Gleeson, B. (1998) 'Situating justice in the environment: the case of BHP at the OK Tedi copper mine', *Antipode*, 30 (3): 201–26.

Low, N. and Gleeson, B. (1999) 'One earth: social and environmental justice', *TELA: Social and Environmental Justice*, 2.

Luke, T.W. (2006) 'The system of sustainable degradation', *Capitalism Nature Socialism*, 17 (1): 99–112.

Luxembourg, R. (1963) *The Accumulation of Capital*. London: Routledge Keagan Paul.

Mailhot, J. (1994) *Traditional Ecological Knowledge: The Diversity of Knowledge Systems and Their Study*. Great Whale Environmental Assessment Background Paper No. 4. Montreal: Great Whale Public Review Support Office.

Mansfield, B. (2004) 'Neoliberalism in the oceans: ''rationalization,'' property rights, and the Commons question', *Geoforum*, 35: 313–26.

Marston, S.A., J.P.J. III and Woodward, K. (2005) 'Human geography without scale', *Transactions of the Institute of British Geographers*, 30 (4): 416–32.

Martin, P. and Verbeek, M. (2002) 'Rights, institutions and sustainability. How can we make it work?', *2002 Fenner Conference on the Environment: Agriculture for the Australian Environment*: 68–94.

Marx, K. (1954) *Capital, Volume I*. Moscow: Progress Publishers.

McCay, B.J. (2002) 'Emergence of institutions for the commons: Contexts, situations, and events', in E. Ostrom, T. Dietz, N. Dolsak, P. Stern, P. Stonich, S. Stonich and E.V. Weber (eds), *The Drama of the Commons*. Nation Research Council, Washington, D.C.: National Academy Press. 361–402.

McGregor, A. (2004) 'Sustainable development and "warm fuzzy feelings": discourse and nature within Australian environmental imaginaries', *Geoforum*, 35: 593–606.

McInnes, R. (2004) *Lord Howe Island: Customary Law, Corporations and the State*. Paper presented to Ecopolitics XV Conference, Macquarie University, Sydney, November 2004.

McKay, J. and Bjornlund, H. (2001) 'Recent Australian market mechanisms as a component of an environmental policy that can make choices between sustainability and social justice', *Social Justice Research*, 14 (4): 387–403.

McKean, M.A. (1992) 'Success on the Commons', *Journal of Theoretical Politics*, 4 (3): 247–81.

Michaels, S. and Laituri, M. (1999) 'Exogenous and indigenous influences on sustainable management', *Sustainable Development*, 7: 77–86.

Moore, S. and Renton, S. (2002) 'Remnant vegetation, landholders' values and information needs: An exploratory study in the West Australian wheatbelt', *Ecological Management and Restoration*, 3 (3); 179–87.

Moore, S.A. and Bache, S. (1997) *Spatial scale and environmental justice in Australian environmental dispute resolution: does it matter and to whom?* Paper presented to Environmental Justice: Global Ethics for the 21st Century, University of Melbourne.

Mostert, E. (2003) 'The challenge of public participation', *Water Policy*, 5: 179–97.

Nancarrow, B.E. and Syme, G. (2001) 'Challenges in implementing justice research in the allocation of natural resources', *Social Justice Research*, 14 (4): 441–52.

Natcher, D.C., Davis, S. and Hickey, C.G. (2005) 'Co-management: managing relationships, not resources', *Human Organization*, 64 (3): 240–50.

Nowacek, D.P., Johnson, M.P. and Tyack, P.L. (2004) 'North Atlantic right whales (*Eubalaen glacialis*) ignore ships but respond to alerting stimuli'. *Proceedings of the Royal Society, Biological Sciences*, 271 (1536): 227–31.

Osherenko, G. (2005) 'Environmental justice and the International Whaling Commission: Moby-Dick Revisited', *Journal of International Wildlife Law and Policy*, 8: 221–39.

Ostrom, E. (1990) *Governing the Commons: The Evolution of Institutions For Collective Action*. Cambridge: Cambridge University Press.

Ostrom, E. (1992) 'The rudiments of a theory of the origins, survivals, and performance of common property institutions', in D.W. Bromley (ed.), *Making the Commons Work: Theory, Practice and Policy*. San Francisco: ICS Press. pp. 293–318.

Paavola, J. (2007) 'Institutions and environmental governance: A reconceptualization', *Ecological Economics*, 63 (1): 93–103.

Parsons, E.C.M., Birks, I., Evans, P.G.H., Gordon, J.G., Shrimpton, J.H. and Pooley, S. (2000) 'The possible impacts of military activity on cetaceans in West Scotland', *European Reşearch on Cetaceans*, 14: 185–90.

Pellow, D.N. (2004) 'The politics of illegal dumping: an environmental justice framework', *Qualitative Sociology*, 27 (4): 511–25.

Powell, D.E. (2006) 'Technologies of existence: The indigenous environmental justice movement', *Development*, 49 (3): 125–32.

Rahm, D., Swatuk, L. and Matheny, E. (2006) 'Water resource management in Botswana: balancing sustainability and economic development', *Environment, Development and Sustainability*, 8: 157–83.

Rayner, S., Malone, E.L. and Thompson, M. (1999) 'Equity issues and integrated assessment', in F.L. Toth, (ed.), *Fair Weather: Equity Concerns in Climate Change*. London: Earthscan Publications: 11–43.

Robinson, D.F. (2006) *Governance and Micropolitics of Traditional Knowledge, Biodiversity and Intellectual Property in Thailand. Research Report*. Bangkok, National Human Rights Commission of Thailand, University of New South Wales and University of Sydney.

Rohde, R.F., Moleele, N.M, Mphale, M., Allsopp, N., Changa, R., Hoffman, M.T., Magole L. and Young, E. (2006) 'Dynamics of grazing policy and practice: environmental and social impacts in three communal areas of southern Africa', *Environmental Science and Policy*, 9: 302–16.

Rose, D.B. (1996) *Nourishing Terrains: Australian Aboriginal Views of Landscape and Wilderness*. Canberra: Australian Heritage Commission.

Rose, D.B. (1999) 'Indigenous ecologies and an ethic of connection', *Global Ethics and Environment*. N. Low. London, Routledge: 175–187.

Scheiber, H.N. (1998) 'Historical memories, cultural claims, and environmental ethics in the jurisprudence of whaling regulation', *Ocean and Coastal Management*, 38: 5–40.

Shiva, V. (1997) *Biopiracy: The Plunder of Nature and Knowledge*. Boston: South End Press.

Simmonds, M.P., Johnston, P.A. and Troisi, G.M. (2002) 'A note concerning "novel pollutants" and cetaceans', *Journal of Cetacean Research and Management*, 4 (supplement): 311–12.

Sneddon, C. (2002) 'Water conflicts and river basins: the contradictions of comanagement and scale in northeast Thailand', *Society and Natural Resources*, 15: 725–41.

Sneddon, C., Harris, L., Dimitrov R. and Ozesmi, U. (2002) 'Contested waters: conflict, scale, and sustainability in aquatic socioecological systems', *Society and Natural Resources*, 15: 663–75.

Speth, J.G. (2002) 'The global environment agenda: origins and prospects', in D.C. Esty and M.H. Ivaniva (eds), *Global Environmental Governance: Options and Opportunities*. New Haven, CT: Yale School of Forestry and Environmental Studies. pp. 11–30.

Streck, C. (2002) 'Global public policy networks as coalitions for change', in D.C. Esty and M.H. Ivaniva (eds), *Global Environmental Governance: Options and Opportunities*. New Haven, CT: Yale School of Forestry and Environmental Studies. pp. 121–39.

Suchet, S. (1999) 'Situated engagement: a critique of wildlife management and postcolonial discourse', PhD Dissertation, Department of Human Geography, Macquarie University.

Swyngedouw, E. (2004) 'Dispossessing H_2O: the contested terrain of water privatization', *Capitalism Nature Socialism*, 16 (1): 81–98.

Swyngedouw, E. and Heynen, N.C. (2003) 'Urban political ecology, justice and the politics of scale', *Antipode* (Special issue 2003): 898–918.

Syme, G., Nancarrow, B.E. and McCreddin, J.A. (1999) 'Defining the components of fairness in the allocation of water to environmental and human uses', *Journal of Environmental Management*, 57 (1): 51–70.

Taylor, D. (2000) 'The rise of the environmental justice paradigm: injustice framing and the social construction of environmental discourse', *American Behavioral Scientist*, 43 (4): 508–80.

Toly, N.J. (2005) 'A tale of two regimes: instrumentality and Commons access', *Bulletin of Science, Technology and Society*, 25 (1): 26–36.

Trawick, P. (2003) 'Against the privatization of water: an indigenous model for improving existing laws and successfully governing the Commons', *World Development*, 31 (6): 977–96.

Vanderheiden, S. (2005) 'Missing the forest for the trees: Justice and environmental economics', *Critical Review of International Social and Political Philosophy*, 8 (1): 51–69.

Walker, G. and Bulkeley, H. (2006) 'Geographies of environmental justice', *Geoforum*, 37 (5): 655–9.

Walker, P.A. (2006) 'Political ecology: where is the policy?', *Progress in Human Geography*, 30 (3): 382–95.

Warner, J.F. (2006) 'More sustainable participation? Multi-stakeholder platforms for integrated catchment management', *Water Resources Development*, 22 (1): 15–35.

WCED (World Commission on Environment and Development) (1987) *Our Common Future*. New York: United Nations.

Williams, G. and Mawdsley, E. (2006) 'Postcolonial environmental justice: Government and governance in India', *Geoforum*, 37: 660–70.

Young, S.C. (ed.) (2000) *The Emergence of Ecological Modernism*. London: Routledge.

21

Crime and the 'Re-moralization of City Spaces'

Nicholas R. Fyfe

INTRODUCTION: THE GOVERNANCE OF CRIME AND SAFETY IN THE NEO-LIBERAL CITY

In J.G. Ballard's thriller *Super-Cannes* about life in Eden-Olympia, a gated community and high-tech business park in the hills above Cannes in the south of France, residents and employees no longer have to worry about crime. Safety in this 'suburb of paradise' is ensured by a combination of the presence of a private police force, closed circuit television (CCTV) surveillance system, security gates and perimeter fencing. But, as this exchange between a new resident and one of the architects of community life at Eden-Olympia illustrates, the absence of crime also derives from self-policing on the part of residents:

> 'What about crime?', I asked. 'It looks as if security might be a problem'....
> 'Forget about crime. The important thing is that residents of Eden-Olympia think they're policing themselves.'
> 'They aren't but the illusion pays off.'
> 'Exactly'
> (Ballard, 2001: 19–20)

Although a fictional community, Eden-Olympia nevertheless captures important elements of changing approaches to the governance of safety in contemporary societies. The presence of the world's leading multi-national companies within Eden-Olympia is illustrative of how in neo-liberal cities, 'the provision of reassurance and security are regarded as prerequisites for attracting people and capital to move to, invest in, or remain in, certain urban locations' (Crawford, 2006: 219). At another level, Eden-Olympia draws attention to the changing modes of governance with respect to crime and safety in neo-liberal cities. As the criminologist David Garland observes: 'Today's most visible crime control strategies may work by expulsion and exclusion but they are accompanied by patient, on-going, low-key efforts to build up the internal controls of neighbourhoods and encourage communities to police themselves' (Garland, 2001: 17). Garland's analysis of 'the culture of control' is significant because it specifically highlights how the right to safety in neo-liberal cities involves a complex interplay between traditional 'sovereign state' strategies with their emphasis on the state's role in delivering enhanced social control and expressive punishment via 'expulsion and exclusion', and the emergence of strategies of 'responsibilization' that stress prevention and partnership, encouraging 'communities to police themselves' (Garland, 2000: 348). For social geographers, these concerns with the governance of crime and safety represent relatively new territory. Traditional geographies of crime maintained a narrow focus on mapping patterns of offences and the contours of 'delinquency areas' rather than considering broader questions relating to the effects of crime and crime control. Increasingly, however, geographical research on fear and the impacts and implications of different forms of policing has not only forged important connections with wider debates in social and political geography but has also provided the basis for significant contributions by geographers to public policy in the fields of crime and community safety.

Against this background, this chapter begins with a brief sketch of the changing contours of geographical interest in issues of crime and safety before considering in more detail the two distinct but overlapping strategies of crime control ('sovereign state' and 'responsibilization') identified by Garland as dominating the public policy agenda in late modern societies. The remainder of the chapter then examines different interventions based on these strategies and how these interventions affect (and are affected by) the social geography of the city. Focusing first on the streets of downtown city centre areas, it considers the importance of high visibility, zero tolerance policing (ZTP) strategies and the use of closed circuit television (CCTV) surveillance as exemplars of the sovereign state and responsibilization strategies respectively. Both ZTP and CCTV are part of wider attempts to revive the fortunes of city centres given concerns that these spaces are 'insecure … both economically and socially, for business and consumers alike' (Coleman, 2004: 76) and both have significant implications for urban social geography. Indeed, both ZTP and CCTV surveillance illustrate how government and private sector investment in 'a vernacular of "safety" in urban centres is linked to 'a moral recovery of space for the propertied and "respectable"' (Coleman, 2004: 66) and are part of a wider agenda to inculcate 'acceptable patterns of behaviour commensurate with the free flow of commerce and the new urban aesthetics' (Macleod, 2002: 605). In the next part of the chapter I consider how responsibilization and sovereign state approaches are also deployed in residential areas of the city by examining the significance of gated communities and strategies for tackling anti-social behaviour. Just as in urban centres, there is a policy perception that neighbourhood regeneration strategies are at risk unless security can be provided and anti-social behaviour tackled. As Crawford (2006: 219) observes, 'There is a growing connection made in urban and housing policy between community safety and urban renewal, with security forming the bedrock on which community life flourishes and without which communities will tip into spirals of decline and decay'. Furthermore, just as in urban centres, the strategies for creating safe residential environments hinge on the re-moralization of space via the codes of conduct which residents of gated communities must observe and the disciplinary role of Anti-Social Behaviour Orders (ASBOs) in areas of social housing.

THE CHANGING CONTOURS OF GEOGRAPHICAL RESEARCH ON CRIME AND THE CITY

The foundations of geographical interest in the interplay between crime, space and society date back to the mid-nineteenth century when European 'cartographic criminologists' sought to link regional patterns of crime and offender residence to aspects of the social and physical environment (Fyfe, 2000). At this time, too, the city was becoming firmly connected in the popular imagination with notions of danger and threat, captured most vividly in Henry Mayhew's ethnography of London's underworld. This urban focus to the geography of crime was sustained in the 1920s through the work of the Chicago School and its meticulous mapping of juvenile delinquent residence in the city. This work revealed both spatial regularities and temporal stability in the pattern of delinquency residence, patterns which the Chicago School sought to explain in terms of the social disorganization thesis focused on the inter-relations between economic deprivation, deterioration in the physical environment, high population turnover and cultural fragmentation. Paralleling this concern with offender residence, geographers have also had a keen interest in the spatiality of offences. Initially such studies relied heavily on 'official' (i.e. police-recorded) offence statistics despite the recognized limitations of this data as an index of crime because of differential public reporting and police recording practices (Herbert, 1982). With the development of crime surveys in the 1970s, however, greater precision has been possible in mapping the contours of crime. Based on asking samples of the public directly about their experiences of victimization, crime surveys avoid the vagaries of public reporting and police recording practices and geographers have made extensive use of this data (Smith, 1986). At the local level, such surveys consistently reveal marked intra-urban variations in crime risk with high risk neighbourhoods found in inner city locations and on the poorest public housing schemes in both inner city and peripheral areas and low risk neighbourhoods located in affluent suburbs and retirement areas (Fyfe, 1997). Geographical information systems technology has allowed further advances in crime pattern analysis, helping identify so-called crime 'hot spots', such as particular street intersections, retails outlets or residential dwellings that generate a disproportionate number of calls for police attention (Ashby and Craglia, 2007).

While this research on the geography of crime has been of theoretical significance as well as practical importance, the overwhelming focus on the spatiality of offences and offender residence has tended to marginalize consideration of the wider social and political landscapes within which the problems of crime are experienced and addressed. The last twenty years, however, have witnessed significant geographical contributions to a much more critical analysis of the effects of crime on victims and other social groups as well as examination of how changes in law and order policy impact on practices of crime control. An important stimulus to shifting the centre of geographical attention away from traditional geographies of deviance focused on offences and offenders and towards victims has been the use of crime surveys. These provide a rich source of information on the effects of crime and the importance of perceptions of fear and safety. Pioneering work by Susan Smith (1986, 1987) followed by significant contributions by, among others, Gill Valentine (1989, 1992) and Rachel Pain (1992, 2001) has directly engaged with the experiences of victims and other social groups to explore the importance of fear in inhibiting spatial mobility and exacerbating social exclusion. Feminist research in particular has emphasized the extent to which many women live under a self-imposed curfew, often avoiding going out alone at night, not walking down particular streets, and relying on private rather than public transport. In addition, this work has highlighted a 'spatial paradox', with women typically fearing attacks by strangers in public spaces despite being most vulnerable to people they know in private spaces.

A second key advance has been with respect to a growing geographical interest in the nature and effects of 'law and order' policy and, more specifically, crime control in cities. Initially this focused on the work of the public police and attempts to understand the spatialities of police work (Fyfe, 1991, 1992; Herbert, 1997) but attention has increasingly shifted from 'the police' to 'policing' as a result of the plethora of research carried out on the nature of urban restructuring in the 1990s. Amidst the various claims and counter claims that contemporary urban restructuring had spawned a new form of urbanism – the postmodern city – the issue of policing has loomed large in the vivid descriptions of the gated communities, fortified buildings and the intensely surveilled public spaces, shopping malls and theme parks, which are viewed as crucial components of postmodern urban structure (Ellin, 1996). Reinforcing the findings of postmodernists, those approaching urban restructuring from the perspective of neo-liberal urbanism have also made much of how the economic vitality of downtown areas is highly dependent on a costly system of surveillance performed through a blend of architectural design, private security, a technological infrastructure of CCTV cameras as well as the presence of the public police (Fyfe and Bannister 1996; Fyfe, 2004). Indeed, reflecting more general trends in neo-liberal forms of governance, geographers and others have increasingly come to understand the policing of cities under advanced capitalism in terms of complex 'security networks', comprising the public police, municipal policing (provided by local urban authorities), civilian or voluntary policing (such as membership of neighbourhood watch or block watch schemes) and the rapid expansion of commercial or private policing (Newburn, 2001).

From a relatively narrow sub-discipline focused on where criminals live and where crimes occur, the geography of crime has now clearly forged much broader connections with debates in social and political geography about fear, safety and social control. The remainder of this chapter exemplifies this more wide-ranging research agenda by illustrating the contributions of geographers and others to understanding the social impact and implications of key innovations in crime control and community safety in the contemporary city. In order to understand fully the policy context in which these innovations have emerged, however, it is necessary to return briefly to the key features of the 'culture of control' alluded to in the introduction and which now characterize late-modern societies.

CRIME CONTROL AND COMMUNITY SAFETY IN THE NEO-LIBERAL CITY

According to Garland's highly influential analysis, public policy with respect to crime control and community safety in neo-liberal societies is dominated by a sovereign state strategy emphasizing robust control and punishment and a responsibilization strategy centring on prevention and partnership. The reasons behind this new combination of approaches are rooted in the complex social, economic and political changes associated with late modernity. These include fiscal pressures on the state, a neo-liberal emphasis on partnership working between public, private and voluntary sectors, and a 'new collective experience of crime and insecurity' in which high crime rates have become a 'normal social fact' (Garland, 2000: 354). The normality of high crime rates has meant that governments increasingly argue that they cannot by themselves succeed in controlling crime and that there must be a process of relocating and redefining responsibilities for crime control 'beyond the state'. This position has resulted in the 'responsibilization' strategy in which 'the state works *through* civil society, and not *upon* it' (Garland, 2001: 140, original emphasis). This same analysis is echoed in the work of Hughes (2002) who has highlighted the emergence of a new politics of public safety in the UK which rests on an appeal to 'community' and 'partnership' in policies of crime control:

> [T]he promotion of crime control *in* and *by* the community, and by means of multi-agency partnerships of the agencies of both state and civil

> society, represents a major shift in how we think about the governance of crime specifically and social order more generally. With 'partnership' now inscribed as the primary symbolic and organizational means of delivering community safety politics, a broader rearticulation of the responsibilities between national and local government, public and private agencies and groups in local communities has begun to occur. (Hughes, 2002: 3)

Evidence of this approach to public safety can be found in a variety of initiatives, from the continuing commitment to forms of community policing and the proliferation of neighbourhood or block watch schemes in affluent suburbs, to the rapid spread of CCTV surveillance in towns and cities and the encouragement given to the 'fortress impulse' in architecture and urban design, evident in the increasing number of gated communities.

At certain times, however, and with respect to specific offences and offenders, governments reactivate 'the old myth of the sovereign state', insisting that via strategies of more intensive forms of policing, harsher sentencing and greater use of imprisonment, they can 'win the war against crime' and uphold the rights of citizens to protection from 'criminal depredations'. As Garland observes, there is now a long list of measures that provide compelling evidence of the importance of 'symbolic gestures of sovereign might' on the part of governments: '"three strikes" and mandatory minimum sentencing laws … the revival of chain gangs and corporal punishment; boot camps and supermax prisons … community notification laws and paedophile registers; zero tolerance policies and Anti-Social behaviour Orders' (Garland, 2001: 142).

SAFETY AND THE 'ORDERLY STREET': FROM ZTP TO CCTV

Within the context of neo-liberal urbanism, attempts to revive the economic fortunes of city centres have become fused with strategies of crime control and community safety (Fyfe, 2004; Macleod, 2002; Pain and Townsend, 2002). Increasingly, securing an urban renaissance is viewed in terms of tackling obstacles to economic consumption in the city and in particular those 'nuisances' or incivilities which might subject shoppers 'to behaviour which causes them distress' (Beck and Willis, 1995: 31). Of these strategies one of the most high profile (and most controversial) has been the introduction of zero tolerance policing (ZTP) in several major cities in the US and UK. Exemplifying the sovereign state approach to crime control and community safety, and first introduced in New York City in the mid-1990s as an attempt to combat 'the sense that the entire public environment is a threatening place' (New York City Police Department, 1994: 5), ZTP has been presented in policy discourse as a significant defence of people's right to safety in the city by reclaiming 'the streets for the law-abiding citizen' (Bowling, 1999: 532). Its distinctiveness lies in the targeting of 'quality of life' offences, including drunkenness, public urination, begging, vandalism, graffiti, and other activities labelled as 'anti-social behaviour', offences which, the police contend, restrict the use of public space. The rationale for the focus on these 'quality of life offences' is that ZTP will reduce fear and encourage greater use of the public realm, which in turn will help prevent more serious types of crime and disorder from occurring. Such reasoning has been given academic credibility by the 'broken windows thesis' (Wilson and Kelling, 1982). Relatively minor signs of disorder (such as broken windows), it is argued, engender a sense of fear among local people which, if unchecked, leads to a general retreat from public interaction and thus a decrease in informal mechanisms of surveillance, allowing more serious forms of disorder to increase.

Advocates and critics of ZTP alike agree that it has a considerable impact on the social geography of the city. Supporters claim significant reductions in crime and improvements in feelings of safety in public space as a direct result of this form of high visibility policing. According to the NYPD, ZTP contributed to falls in the recorded crime rate of more than a third in the three years after it was introduced and, more generally, has helped 'reclaim the streets for respectable law-abiding people and ... overcome the "culture of fear" ... characteristic of late modern urban environments' (Hughes, 1998: 112). Critics, however, not only question the simple 'cause and effect' logic on which such claims are based but also point to the wider, negative implications of ZTP for social life and social justice in the city. Some depict ZTP as a 'Robocop version of beat policing [which] could quite easily destroy the "ballet of the street" and the "benign disorder" that are so crucial to a vital street life' (McLaughlin and Muncie, 2000: 130), crushing any 'street spontaneity and vibrancy' (Merrifield, 2000: 485). For others ZTP signals 'the advent of a *fin de siecle* American revanchism in the urban landscape ... a visceral identification of the culprits, the enemies who had stolen from the white middle class a city that members of the latter assumed to be their birth right' (Smith, 1999: 187). For critics, then, ZTP exemplifies what Young (1999: 46) has called an oppressive 'criminology of intolerance' intent on excluding anyone who might 'disrupt the smooth running of the system' or who is perceived as 'degrading the urban aesthetic' (Coleman, 2004: 81).

The difficulty with the arguments of supporters and critics of ZTP is that both make exaggerated claims for its significance. In terms of crime reduction, evidence of the impact of ZTP is quite equivocal given that in many US cities which have not adopted ZTP tactics, crime rates fell during the mid-1990s at a rate comparable to those in New York City (Body-Gendrot, 2000). From the perspective of the re-moralization of city spaces, the revanchist, radical totalitarian reading of ZTP by its critics relies heavily on caricature. ZTP has rarely meant '24 hours, 7 days a week, perpetual enforcement of quality of life offences' (Silverman and Della-Giustina, 2001: 954) and often involves improved community – police interaction, the cultivation of informants and information-based police action rather than aggressive enforcement (Johnston, 2000: 67). In terms of social justice, too, the readiness to only see danger in 'the zero tolerance gospel' (Shapiro, 1997) risks underestimating the significance that the cumulative impact of minor incivilities present. Those working with the victims of domestic and racial violence have long argued that this kind of serious crime is typically the end point of a continuum of aggressive behaviour that might begin with relative minor offences. It is important therefore to recognize the ambivalence surrounding ZTP policing tactics. When used sensitively (say, in relation to the abuses suffered by women, black and ethnic minorities and other vulnerable social groups) it may enhance the confidence of these groups in using city centres; used insensitively as 'the zealous pursuit of all quality of life offences' it may contribute to the punitive social exclusion of individuals and social groups (Fyfe, 2004).

A second key strategy aimed at reviving the fortunes of city centre public spaces is the introduction of CCTV surveillance. Exemplifying the responsibilization approach to crime control and community safety (given the involvement of both the private sector and local authorities working in partnership with the police to establish and run camera networks), advocates of this form of surveillance have long asserted that it contributes to dramatically falling crime rates and to reassuring town and city centre users that they are safer (Home Office, 1994: 14). A plethora of 'Before' and 'After' studies of the impact of CCTV on the incidence of crime as well as opinion surveys examining the effect of cameras on the use of urban space, have highlighted how this technology 'increases public freedom, enhancing opportunities for people to enjoy public spaces' (Arlidge, 1994: 22). But these positive outcomes for the social geography of the city are questioned by critics. Doubts have been cast over the methodological rigour and robustness of the evaluations of the impact of CCTV on crime research and concerns expressed that CCTV systems simply displace crime to areas not covered by cameras and which may be less able to cope with the problems of crime. Furthermore, in terms of its contribution to feelings of safety, CCTV may also be less significant than supporters of CCTV claim. For women, who typically express the greatest fears with respect to using public space in city centres, the introduction of CCTV has not, according to Brown (1998), prompted significant changes in patterns of mobility. This is partly because CCTV is perceived as reinforcing a sense of 'male policing', which for women is itself problematic, but also because CCTV is unable to relate to or address the ways in which women are made to feel insecure in public spaces in the form of 'general intimidation, verbal harassment, staring, and drunken rowdiness amongst groups of men' (218). It is this 'culture of masculinity' which most constrains women's movements within the city and CCTV is unlikely to change this.

More generally, the use of CCTV surveillance technology has been at the centre of wider debates about the re-moralization of city centre spaces. Echoing concerns that were articulated in relation to ZTP, CCTV has been viewed as an instrument to preserve 'the public spaces of our town centres … for the consumer citizen, while those whose spending power is low … are effectively excluded' (Williams et al., 2000: 184). A study of the city of Liverpool concluded, for example, that CCTV surveillance is targeted at anyone or any activity which is viewed as a risk to 'orderly regeneration', from the sellers of homeless magazines, to young people, ethnic minorities and street traders (Coleman, 2004). From this perspective, the fusion of urban regeneration and community safety agendas is seen as contributing to 'a strategy of socio-spatial transformation that is fostering the cultivation of urban subjectivities around particular groups and individuals that raises questions over their right to the city' (Coleman, 2004: 189). As with ZTP, the urban entrepreneurial agenda of creating safe public spaces as part of wider regeneration initiatives means that CCTV surveillance may in fact do little in terms of promoting equality of access to city space and risks reinforcing existing social divisions.

SAFETY AND BEHAVIOUR IN RESIDENTIAL SPACE: 'NEIGHBOURS FROM HEAVEN' TO 'NEIGHBOURS FROM HELL'

The vernacular of 'safety' is not confined to debates over entrepreneurial urbanism and city centre public spaces. Within residential areas too, neo-liberal urban policy places increasing emphasis on the links between security, renewal and community development. Moreover, just as in city centre spaces, a complex mix of sovereign state and responsibilization interventions are being deployed to address the safety concerns of local residents. Perhaps few environments better illustrate an almost aggressive assertion of a right to safety than the increasing prevalence of gated communities found in affluent, private housing neighbourhoods. Their built forms use gates, walls, fencing and controlled entrances to restrict public access and 'prevent penetration by non-residents' (Blakely and Snyder, 1997: 2). Exemplifying the responsibilization approach to the governance of safety, gated communities are also distinguished by distinctive socio-legal environments that require residents to take collective responsibility for the management of the community (such as maintaining common services) and ties residents to codes of conduct. Within what is perceived as an increasingly dangerous urban environment, gated communities therefore appear to offer 'the promise of a sanitised residential cocoon' (Blandy: 2006: 239) of 'neighbours from heaven' in which crime and conflict are rare.

To what extent, however, does living within a gated community yield a heightened sense of safety? Much research suggests that anxieties about crime persist for gated community residents and that any sense of greater security is illusory. In a comparison of perceived safety and actual crime rates between gated and non-gated communities in high-income neighbourhoods and public housing projects in California, no significant differences were found (Wilson-Doenges, 2000). According to the resident of one residential development, interviewed as part of a study of gated communities in the US: 'There's a perception of safety among residents that may not be real and could potentially leave one more vulnerable if there was ever an attack' (Low, 2004: 8). Moreover, many of the respondents in this study also talk of how, after moving into a gated community, they feel much less safe when they need to leave the development to go downtown. This heightened sense of the dangers of non-gated areas may be particularly important with respect to children being brought up in gated communities. As Low observes,

> Are the children growing up in gated communities more afraid of people who live outside the gates and of being hurt by a random act of violence than other kids are? Are they more vulnerable to drug problems, suicide, or violence partly because of their racial and social separation from other children, especially blacks and Latinos, who become exoticized and whose imagined lifestyles are mimicked in a stereotypical and potentially dangerous way? (2004: 109)

There are important echoes here of Richard Sennett's concerns about how the purification of disorder and difference from space has important psychological and behavioural consequences. '[D]isorderly, painful events' in the city are worth encountering, he argues, because they force us to engage with 'otherness', to go beyond one's own defined boundaries of self, and are thus central to civilized and civilizing social life (Sennett, 1996: 131–2). Living in the presence of difference and engaging with uncertainty are viewed as necessary experiences for individual and social development. From this perspective, the search for safety by residents of gated communities may have significant unintended consequences for those living within these communities.

Related to these concerns about the experience of living within gated developments are a set of wider questions about the implications for gated communities for the moral geographies of the city. Writing within a UK context, Atkinson and Blandy have raised concerns about the impact of the 'ghettoisation of the affluent' on those outside these new enclaves: 'The choice of the relatively few gated dwellers is part of a wider socio-spatial contract which may, if not balanced, lead to a downward spiral of urban social relations. … [T]he locational choices made by affluent households affect the outcomes for the poor in terms of city sustainability, security and social segregation' (2005: 179). Of particular concern is the extent to which residents of gated communities attempt to disengage with particular urban problems and responsibilities – both fiscal and social – in order to insulate themselves from the wider context of the urban environment. As Mike Davis notes, gated communities are emblematic of 'Fortress America' in which cities are 'brutally divided between "fortified cells" of affluent society and "places of terror" where the police battle the criminalised poor' (Davis, 1990: 244). But, as with the discussion of ZTP and CCTV, critics of gated communities may risk over-stating their negative impact on social life within the city. Gated communities are not exclusively restricted to affluent homeowners. Analysis of the 2001 American Housing Survey found a prevalence of low-income, racial minority, renters living in gated communities (Atkinson and Blandy, 2005: 181). In the UK, too, there are examples of gating being used in low income areas to enhance the security of residents. The 'alley-gating' programme gives local authorities the power to close off rights of way in deprived areas in order to reduce the opportunities for criminal activity. Indeed, such programmes would appear to resonate with the aspirations of the UK Labour Government, which declared that 'if gated communities were to be established in deprived areas, this would "make available to the many what is currently available to the few"' (Blunkett, 2004, cited in Blandy, 2006). The socially divisive character of gated communities has also been questioned by those who have studied so-called 'citadel gentrification' where gated communities designed for affluent residents have been built within more deprived neighbourhoods, thus creating more mixed communities. Drawing on case-study evidence from

London, Manzi and Smith-Bowers (2005) have shown how two gated communities built in deprived parts of the city have helped reduce residential segregation by offering opportunities for social mixing in areas that would otherwise have been exclusively the preserve of households experiencing multiple-deprivation.

If gated communities appear to offer the prospect of living with 'neighbours from heaven', the introduction of Anti-Social Behaviour Orders (ASBOs) by the UK government in the late 1990s provides a vivid example of how to deal with 'neighbours from hell'. Described as 'an almost hysterical form of a sovereign attempt at crime control' (Carr and Cowan, 2006: 75) in areas affected by a range of problems linked to inter-personal conflict (such as intimidation and harassment), social disorder (including street drinking and begging) and environmental incivilities (such as graffiti and vandalism), the government has passed a series of pieces of legislation to tackle anti-social behaviour. According to *The Economist* (5 February 2005), this legislation gives the state 'new powers to deal with minor offences and other crime which are scarcely less draconian than those to deal with suspected terrorism'. Government concern with anti-social behaviour has been triggered by evidence that many poor neighbourhoods are plagued by 'persistent bad behaviour on lower edge of criminality' (Burney, 2005: 2) and the ASBO is viewed as 'a powerful tool to make [such] communities safe' by placing specific prohibitions on individuals from going to certain places and/or carrying out specified acts 'likely to cause harassment, alarm or distress'. The ASBO (originally termed a Community Safety Order) was introduced in the Crime and Disorder Act 1988, but, to the frustration of the UK government, there was resistance among criminal justice and welfare agencies to using this new tool. This resistance was partly for reasons of cost and a perception that the process of obtaining an order was time-consuming but also because of a fear of conflict with the European Convention on Human Rights (ECHR) given the concern had already been expressed in the UK Parliament that the term anti-social behaviour was 'unacceptably vague' (Burney, 2005: 35). The response of the government was simply to make the process of obtaining an ASBO simpler and to extend the powers of the police with respect to anti-social behaviour. The Anti-Social Behaviour Act 2003 included powers to disperse groups of two or more people if anti-social behaviour is prevalent in designated areas and to impose curfews on children under 16, while the Serious Organised Crime and Police Act 2005 extended the range of organizations who can apply for ASBOs to include parish councils and neighbourhood watch schemes. For the UK government this legislation had the desired effect: over 3,500 ASBOs were issued between January 2003 and December 2004, compared with fewer than 1,000 in the previous three years (Flint and Nixon, 2006).

As a strategy for the governance of safety, the use of ASBOs overlaps in important ways with other approaches discussed in this chapter. First, the UK government's determination to tackle anti-social behaviour is underpinned by the same 'broken windows' theoretical framework that provided the justification for ZTP in New York City and elsewhere. As a government report, *Respect and Responsibility – Taking a Stand against Anti-Social Behaviour* explains:

> The anti-social behaviour of a few damages the lives of the many. We should never underestimate its impact. We have seen the way communities spiral downwards once windows get broken and are not fixed, graffiti spreads and stays there, cars are left abandoned, streets get grimier and dirtier, youths hang around street corners intimidating the elderly. The result: crime increases, fear goes up and people feel trapped. (Home Office, 2003)

Second, although the UK government's punitive approach adopted to deal with anti-social behaviour via the use of ASBOs and extending police powers has all the hallmarks of a sovereign state strategy for community safety, there are also strong influences from the responsibilization agenda. As Flint and

Nixon (2006) observe, 'ASBOs provide a means by which communities are encouraged to take an active part in the surveillance and regulation of conduct and self-governing individuals are urged to "take a stand" against those who do not conform to accepted norms of conduct by collecting evidence, acting as witnesses and helping enforce breaches of the order' (943). From this perspective, the governance of safety has therefore involved transferring some disciplinary power to groups that operate outside the criminal justice state, including neighbourhood, street and city wardens, housing officers and housing associations. Third, the effort to tackle anti-social behaviour, like the use of ZTP, CCTV surveillance and the development of gated communities, is bound up with the re-moralization of city spaces. The empowerment of individuals and organizations with respect to anti-social activities is framed within a strongly moral discourse about the existence of 'outsider' groups or individuals whose conduct is constructed as being inconsistent with 'conventional norms and values posited to exist in the majority of … "ordinary people"' (Flint, 2006: 4). Exemplifying this moral discourse are the 'naming and shaming strategies' whereby local groups use the media to publish details of individuals subject to ASBOs.

From the perspective of wider issues about social life and social justice in the city, the UK government's approach to the governance of anti-social behaviour raises several overlapping concerns. Critics draw attention to the lack of precision in defining anti-social behaviour, noting that the all-encompassing approach used in legislation is justified in terms of 'the need to protect the self-governing, law-abiding citizen from the dangerous, uncivilized "other"' (Nixon and Parr, 2006). Significantly, however, this imprecision blurs the boundary between criminal and non-criminal conduct and extends the range of behaviours that are subject to surveillance and intervention in the city. Furthermore, although anti-social behaviour is something which affects many areas of cities, from night-time entertainment districts to shopping streets, it is poorer residential areas that are the focus of policy concerns and, in particular, areas of social housing which have become a spatial synonym for anti-social behaviour (Atkinson, 2006). However, it is important to recognize that one significant reason lying behind the concentration of anti-social behaviour in these areas has been the social residualization within the public housing sector. As a result of earlier UK government initiatives, such as the right of tenants to buy their council houses, social renting not only became increasingly stigmatized but concentrated tenants dependent on welfare in areas of social rented housing. A final concern within current policy discourse is that anti-social behaviour is constructed as being partly the fault of local communities themselves and that if these communities were more socially cohesive then tolerance of anti-social behaviour would decline. As Atkinson observes, 'These areas and their communities have been cast as normatively different, even deficient, in their judgement of acceptable behaviour' (2006: 105) and that as a result residents of these areas experience a 'compounded form of citizenship' in which they have 'to work much harder to attain a sense of normality or reduction in local social problems'. In other words, residents of areas with high levels of ASB increasingly find themselves in a situation where their rights are diminished (via curfews and increased levels of surveillance) but their responsibilities (in terms of participation in partnerships and applying for and monitoring ASBOs) are accentuated.

CONCLUSIONS

The search for safety in the neo-liberal city increasingly depends on interventions that flow from the sovereign state and responsibilization agendas. On the one hand, the state continues to insist that it can ensure safe environments via investment in policing or by passing new laws, such as those to tackle anti-social behaviour. On the other hand, the state also insists that tackling crime and maintaining safety are the responsibilities of individuals, private organizations and communities outside the criminal justice system.

The impacts of the different interventions that flow from these two agendas are, as this chapter has shown, distributed unevenly over the city and the search for safety has significant implications for people's experiences of and rights to use the city. ZTP and CCTV target individuals and groups in the public spaces of the city whose presence is perceived to conflict with the aspirations of urban entrepreneurialism and the 'moral recovery' of space for the consumer citizen, contributing to the purification of 'the public sphere of disorder and difference through the spatial exclusion of those social groups who are judged to be deviant, imperfect and marginal' (Toon, 2000: 141). Gated communities offer the promise of a safe haven within the city for affluent homeowners but typically leave residents feeling no less fearful about crime and may heighten their anxieties when outside this 'sanitised cocoon'. The introduction of ASBOs is meant to empower the poorest communities in relation to the surveillance and disciplining of individuals who engage in anti-social activities but risks criminalizing behaviour that at worst might be undesirable and in some cases might be entirely innocent.

Is there evidence that people in late modern societies feel any safer as a result of these and other interventions? In the UK, observers have highlighted a 'reassurance paradox' (Crawford, 2006: 222) because, despite falling crime rates, and record numbers of police officers, 'public insecurity and fear of crime remain stubbornly high'. More recently, however, evidence from the British Crime Survey (a nationally representative, household victimization survey of over 45,000 people) has revealed that the proportion of people feeling very unsafe walking alone after dark in their local area is at its lowest since the British Crime Survey first asked the question in 1984, and the proportion of people feeling very unsafe in their own home alone at night is also at its lowest since this question was introduced in 1988 (Home Office, 2006). In addition, significant decreases have been recorded in the proportion of respondents perceiving anti-social behaviour to be a very or fairly big problem and nearly two-thirds of respondents stated that anti-social behaviour did not have a bad effect on them (Wood, 2004).

While such evidence about people's perceptions of safety is welcome, it also needs to be interpreted with caution. This is partly because such headline findings mask the persistence of significant social and spatial variations in feelings of safety. In 2004/5, women were over four times more likely than men to feel very unsafe walking alone in their home area after dark; Black people were one and half times more likely to feel unsafe than White people; those in poor health were more than three times more likely to feel unsafe than those in good health; and people living in the social-rented sector were more than three times more likely than those living in the private-rented sector to feel unsafe (Home Office, 2006: 28). Another reason for caution is that it is not possible to establish the extent to which the types of intervention discussed in this chapter might have specifically contributed to these reported declines in people's worries about their safety. Indeed, it might be that ZTP, CCTV surveillance, gated communities and ASBOs are ultimately counter-productive in attempting to offer reassurance. As the urbanist Richard Sennett (1996) cogently argues in *The Uses of Disorder*, communities often express a strong desire to 'purify experience' and shield themselves from disruptive influences, but this, he contends, only offers a short-term solution. In the long term, this disengagement with 'others' might actually accentuate fear by inhibiting the creation of mutual trust and solidarity, thereby increasing paranoia and distrust among people (Bannister et al., 2006: 933). For Sennett there is real value in engaging with the 'otherness' that the city contains because learning to confront disorder and uncertainty, while at the same time having the maturity to handle its consequences, are central components of urban social life. This is a view echoed by Robins

(1995: 49) who argues that 'At its best, urban culture involves some kind of accommodation between provocation and stimulation, on the one hand, and security and stability on the other'. The potential danger associated with the interventions considered in this chapter is that in the long term this accommodation breaks down. As Sennett (1996: 44–5), observes, in contexts where individuals and communities have 'little tolerance of disorder in their own lives … the eruption of social tension becomes a situation in which the ultimate methods of aggression, violent force and reprisal, seem to become not only justified, but life preserving'.

Intriguingly, these points return us to Ballard's examination of life in the gated community, Eden-Olympia, with which this chapter began. Reflecting on the experience of living in this purified, secure urban space, one of the residents notes that initially he thought Eden-Olympia was 'the anteroom to paradise', a place where 'All the old urban nightmares [of street crime and traffic congestion] had been dispelled at a stroke' (Ballard, 2001: 254). But, over time, his perception changes. He observes how residents' sense of morality begins to wither as they live and work in an environment where they no longer need to make 'a single decision about right and wrong' (255). One consequence of the absence of that moral calculus is that many of the wealthy inhabitants of Eden-Olympia begin to engage in acts of random violence in neighbouring communities, in the form of vigilante activities, road-rage, thefts and robberies. As one of the residents of Eden-Olympia observes, 'Societies that dispense with the challenged conscience are more vulnerable than they realize' (256).

REFERENCES

Arlidge, J. (1994) 'Welcome Big Brother', *The Independent*, 2 November, p. 22.

Ashby, D. and Craglia, M. (2007) 'Profiling places: geodemographics and GIS', in T. Newburn, T. Williamson and A. Wright (eds), *Handbook of Criminal Investigation*. Cullompton: Willan Publishing. pp. 517–46.

Atkinson, R. (2006) 'Spaces of discipline and control: the compounded citizenship of social renting', in J. Flint (ed.), *Housing, Urban Governance and Anti-Social Behaviour*. Bristol: The Policy Press. pp. 99–115.

Atkinson, R. and Blandy, S. (2005) 'The new enclavism and the contractual neighbourhood: The search for security and the rise of gated communities', *Housing Studies*, 20 (2), 177–86.

Ballard, J.G. (2001) *Super-Cannes*. London: Flamingo.

Bannister, J., Fyfe, N. and Kearns, A. (2006) 'Respectable or respectful? (In)civility and the city', *Urban Studies*, 43 (5/6): 919–38.

Beck, A. and Willis, A. (1995) *Crime and Insecurity: Managing the Risk to Safe Shopping*. Leicester: Perpetuity Press.

Blakely, E. and Snyder, M. (1997) *Fortress America: Gated Communities in the United States*. Washington: Brookings Institute.

Blandy, S. (2006) 'Gated communities: a response to, or remedy for, anti-social behaviour' in J. Flint (ed.), *Housing, Urban Governance and Anti-Social Behaviour*. Bristol: The Policy Press. pp. 239–55.

Blunkett, D. (2004) Speech to New Local Network Annual Conference, 22 January.

Body-Gendrot, S. (2000) *The Social Control of Cities: A comparative perspective*. Oxford: Blackwell.

Bowling, B. (1999) 'The rise and fall of New York murder: zero tolerance or crack's decline', *British Journal of Criminology*, 39: 531–54.

Brown, S. (1998) 'What's the problem girls? CCTV and the gendering of public safety', in C. Norris, J. Moran and G. Armstrong (eds) *Surveillance, Closed Circuit Television and Social Control*. London: Ashgate, pp. 207–20.

Burney, E. (2005) *Making People Behave: Anti-social behaviour, politics and policy*. Cullompton: Willan Publishing.

Carr, H. and Cowan, D. (2006) 'Labelling: constructing definition of anti-social behaviour?', in J. Flint (ed.), *Housing, Urban Governance and Anti-Social Behaviour*. Bristol: The Policy Press. pp. 57–78.

Coleman, R. (2004) *Reclaiming the Streets: Surveillance, social control and the city*. Cullompton: Willan Publishing.

Crawford, A. (2006) 'Policing and community safety in residential areas: the mixed economy of visible patrols', in J. Flint (ed.), *Housing, Urban Governance and Anti-Social Behaviour.* Bristol: The Policy Press. pp. 219–38.

Davis, M. (1990) *City of Quartz.* London: Verso.

Ellin, N. (1996) *Postmodern Urbanism.* Oxford: Blackwell.

Flint, J. (2006) 'Introduction', in J. Flint (ed.), *Housing, Urban Governance and Anti-Social Behaviour.* Bristol: The Policy Press. pp. 1–15.

Flint, J. and Nixon, J. (2006) 'Governing neighbours: Anti-social behaviour orders and new forms of regulating conduct in the UK', *Urban Studies,* 43 (5/6): 939–56.

Fyfe, N.R. (1991) 'The police, space and society: the geography of policing', *Progress in Human Geography*, 15: 249–67.

Fyfe, N.R. (1992) 'Space, time and policing: towards a contextual understanding of police work', *Environment and Planning D: Society and Space*, 10: 469–86.

Fyfe, N.R. (1997) 'Crime', in M. Pacione (ed.), *Britain's Cities Geographies of Division in Urban Britain.* London: Routledge. pp. 244–61.

Fyfe, N.R. (2000) 'Crime, geography of', in R. Johnston, D. Gregory, G. Pratt, D. Smith and M. Watts (eds), *The Dictionary of Human Geography.* Oxford: Blackwell. pp. 120–3.

Fyfe, N.R. (2004) 'Zero tolerance, maximum surveillance? Deviance, difference and crime control in the late modern city', in L. Lees (ed.), *The Emancipatory City: Paradoxes and Possibilities.* London: Sage. pp. 40–56.

Fyfe, N.R. and Bannister, J. (1996) 'City watching: closed circuit television surveillance and the city', *Area*, 28: 37–46.

Garland, D. (2000) 'The culture of high crime societies: some preconditions of recent "law and order" policies', *British Journal of Criminology*, 40: 347–75.

Garland, D. (2001) *The Culture of Control.* Oxford: Oxford University Press.

Herbert, D.T. (1982) *The Geography of Urban Crime.* Harlow: Longman.

Herbert, S. (1997) *Policing Space: Territoriality and the Los Angeles Police Department.* Minneapolis: University of Minnesota Press.

Home Office (1994) *CCTV: Looking Out for You*. London: Home Office.

Home Office (2003) *Respect and Responsibility: Taking a Stand Against Anti-social Behaviour.* London: Home Office.

Home Office (2006) *Worry about Crime in England and Wales: Findings from the 2003/04 and 2004/05 British Crime Survey.* London: Home Office.

Hughes, G. (1998) *Understanding Crime Prevention: Social control, risk and late modernity.* Buckingham: Open University Press.

Hughes, G. (2002) 'The shifting sands of crime prevention and community safety', in G. Hughes, E. McLaughlin and J. Munice, (eds), *Crime Prevention and Community Safety: New Directions.* London: Sage. pp.1–10.

Johnston, L. (2000) *Policing Britain: Risk, Security and Governance*. Harlow: Longman.

Low, S. (2004) *Behind the Gates: Life, Security and the Pursuit of Happiness in Fortress America.* London: Routledge.

Macleod, G. (2002) 'From urban entrepreneurialism to a revanchist city? On the spatial injustices of Glasgow's renaissance', *Antipode*, 34 (3): 602–24.

Manzi, T. and Smith-Bowers, B. (2005) 'Gated communities as club goods: Segregation or social cohesion?', *Housing Studies*, 29 (2): 345–59.

McLaughlin, E. and Muncie, J. (2000) 'Walled cities: surveillance, regulation and segregation', in S. Pile et al. (eds), *Unruly Cities.* London: Routledge, pp.103–48.

Merrifield, A. (2000) 'The dialectics of dystopia: disorder and zero tolerance in the city', *International Journal of Urban and Regional Research*, 24: 473–88.

Newburn, T. (2001) 'The commodification of policing: security networks in the late modern city', *Urban Studies*, 38: 829–48.

New York City Police Department (1994) *Strategy Number 5: Reclaiming the Public Spaces of New York.* New York: City of New York.

Nixon, J. and Parr, S. (2006) 'Anti-social behaviour: voices from the frontline', in J. Flint (ed.) *Housing, Urban Governance and Anti-Social Behaviour.* Bristol: The Policy Press. pp. 79–98.

Pain, R. (1992) 'Space, sexual violence and social control: integrating geographical and feminist analyses of women's fear of crime', *Progress in Human Geography*, 15: 415–31.

Pain, R. (2001) 'Gender, race, age and fear in the city', *Urban Studies*, 38: 899–913.

Pain, R. and Townsend, T. (2002) A safer city centre for all? Senses of 'community safety' in Newcastle upon Tyne, *Geoforum,* 33 (1): 105–19.

Robbins, K. (1995) 'Collective emotion and urban culture', in P. Healey, S. Cameron and S. Davoudi (eds), *Managing Cities: the New Urban Context.* Chichester: John Wiley. pp. 45–62.

Sennett, R. (1996) *The Uses of Disorder: Personal Identity and City Life.* London: Faber and Faber.

Shapiro, B. (1997) 'Zero tolerance gospel', *Index on Censorship*, 4: 17–23.

Silverman, E. and Della-Giustina, J-A. (2001) 'Urban policing and the fear of crime', *Urban Studies*, 38: 941–58.

Smith, N. (1999) 'Which new urbanism: New York City and the revanchist 1990s', in R. Beauregard and S. Body-Gendrot (eds), *The Urban Moment: Cosmopolitan Essays on the late 20th century city*. Thousand Oaks: Sage. pp. 185–208.

Smith, S.J. (1986) *Crime, Space and Society.* Cambridge: Cambridge University Press.

Smith, S.J. (1987) 'Fear of crime: beyond a geography of deviance', *Progress in Human Geography*, 11: 1–23.

Toon, I. (2000) 'Finding a place in the street: CCTV surveillance and young people's use of public space', in D. Bell and A. Haddour (eds), *City Visions.* Harlow: Longman. pp. 141–65.

Williams, K., Johnstone, C. and Goodwin, M. (2000) 'CCTV surveillance in urban Britain: beyond the rhetoric of crime prevention', in J.R. Gold and G. Revill (eds), *Landscapes of Defence*. London: Prentice Hall. pp. 168–87.

Wilson-Doenges, G. (2000) 'An explanation of sense of community and fear of crime in gated communities', *Environment and Behaviour*, 32 (5), 597–611.

Wilson, J.Q. and Kelling, G.L. (1982) 'Broke Windows', *Atlantic Monthly*, March, pp. 29–38.

Young, J. (1999) *The Exclusive Society: Social Exclusion, Crime and Difference in Late Modernity*. London: Sage.

Valentine, G. (1989) 'The geography of women's fear', *Area*, 21: 385–90.

Valentine, G. (1992) 'Images of danger: women's sources of information about the spatial distribution of male violence', *Area*, 24: 22–9.

Wood, M. (2004) *Perceptions and Experience of Anti-social Behaviour: Findings from the 2003/04 British Crime Survey.* London: Home Office.

22

A Social Geography of Human Rights

Amy Ross

INTRODUCTION: THE HUMAN RIGHTS UNIVERSE[1]

Developments in law and society have elevated the topic of human rights to '… the dominant moral narrative for thinking about world affairs …' (Reiff, 1999: 36). Former United Nations Secretary General Kofi Annan has called human rights 'the yardstick by which we measure human progress' (Ignatieff, 1999: 58). Especially in the period following the Second World War, human rights have become a significant feature of global, national and local landscapes. In particular, national and international social movements organized around issues associated with human rights have proliferated. Individually, these social movements have made human rights visible in specific places. In addition to the impact in the locale, social organizations and movements associated with human rights have created remarkable networks (see especially Keck and Sikkink, 1998). The networks that have emerged between and among human rights actors, social movements and organizations have created a web across the globe, linking peoples and places in new and complicated geographies. Indeed, social movements have come to represent, symbolize and make material what many have called the 'human rights era'.

Yet, while scholars and policy analysts concur on the growth, importance and stature of human rights in society (as manifested in legal developments and social movements), it is also apparent that the violation of human rights is widespread. To refer to human rights is, in many instances, to refer to human rights violations. Human rights abuses occur everywhere. Although differing patterns have been identified, it is also clear that all types of bodies are subjected to abuses. It is a popular assertion that the present era is among the most violent, qualitatively and quantitatively, in recorded human history. That seems a difficult, and perhaps specious, case to prove. The shifting notion of what constitutes a 'human right' and therefore what constitutes a 'human rights violation' makes it difficult to assess whether the contemporary period has seen an escalation of such violence. Regardless of whether the present era is exceptionally violent (in relation to human history), what is most relevant is the need to unpack and interrogate the social perceptions of what *counts* as a human right (and therefore what *counts* as a human rights violation) and how these perceptions influence human security and well-being.

This chapter seeks to critically examine the *idea* of human rights, as well as its dialectical relationship to geography. By analyzing human rights as an idea situated in particular spaces at particular times, this essay uses social geography to illuminate the uneven development of human rights. A social geography of human rights reveals what *counts* as a human right, and a human rights violation across space, rather than reifying the already-existing, taken-for-granted, assumptions of what human rights 'are'. Rethinking the idea of human rights as situated in particular times/places helps illuminate the power-relations wrapped up in the concept of human rights; the failure to recognize human rights as situated and contingent disguises the intense power-relations that determine what counts as a human right and who makes that designation. Central to the analysis is the dialectical relationship between geographies and human rights. In this approach, geography is more than just a 'backdrop' to events of human society. Rather, places and spaces influence social practices and ideas, as social movements and organizations transform places and spaces.

The discussion that follows is organized into three parts. The first provides a genealogy of human rights. I locate the most significant historical precedents within centuries of social history concerning the laws of war and international law, and the nineteenth-century development of international humanitarian law. My purpose here is to highlight that acts of violence are in no way self-evidently 'abuses,' but that the interpretation of violence as either an act of war or a human rights abuse is variably situated throughout time and space, constructed and always contentious. The second part focuses on the post-Second World War period as the key moment in the transformation of developments in law and society (concerning power and rights) into the discursive field of human rights, with associated material consequences. This section focuses on the proliferation of human rights social movements and organizations. The third part discusses power-relations between and among social movement actors, national governments and international institutions, using the International Criminal Court (ICC) as an example. In this discussion, the ICC and other human rights instruments (conventions, organizations, social movements, etc.) are understood less as examples of a 'progressive' development of human rights, than portals through which to view the nexus of power/knowledge that produces particular ideas and practices of human rights.

The chapter concludes with a discussion of the uneven development of human rights, and future directions in geographic theory. The uneven development of human rights recasts the 'puzzle' of the human rights story: its coincidental successes and failures, rather than existing in opposition, exist together in a system of uneven development. The unevenness of the landscapes of the human rights universe is less an accident than an element of its design. By way of metaphor: a fish net consists of many materials, but the holes are as essential to its purpose as the twine. In the human rights universe, the violations are as integral to the landscape(s) as the conventions, declarations and other manifestations of human rights' promotion.

EARLY FOUNDATIONS OF HUMAN RIGHTS

Contemporary understandings of human rights have philosophical and material roots in centuries-old bodies of law and political practice. Broadly, the laws of war and the development of international law contributed to the establishment of *international humanitarian law* in the mid-nineteenth century, laying the foundation for human rights as a legal, political and social phenomena of the

20th century. Understanding the background of the laws of war and international law is essential to understanding contemporary human rights, which are an outgrowth of these histories.

Codes of conduct for soldiers, the prescriptions concerning who could be the legitimate target of warfare, and agreements about the treatment of civilians are as old as the oldest civilizations and persist into the present (Neier, 1998). Ancient societies in Egypt and India banned certain types of warfare and the English courts codified 'rules of chivalry' to regulate warfare between medieval knights (Beigbeder, 1999; Ignatieff, 1997). Ignatieff (1997) stresses the importance of this body of norms – which he calls 'the warrior's honor' – with respect to the concepts and practices that legitimized warfare. War had to be differentiated from mere barbarism in order to achieve social and political legitimacy. These codes of conduct – the warrior's honor – were rules to restrict war to a competition between strong, honorable men fighting other, strong, honorable men. Chivalry and these rules of war were alleged to elevate the battlefield into a realm of legitimacy so that the violence occurring there would be (somehow) distinguished from pure barbarity or mere slaughter.

A war fought in compliance with standards and rules permits massive intentional killing and destruction that, absent a war, would violate fundamental social norms. Hence these 'rules of war' create a divide between the brutality and destruction that is permitted, or privileged, and that which is illegal and subject to sanction. The ability to declare violence as legitimate and heroic (an act of war) rather than 'unjust' – for instance a crime of war – is extremely important, and demonstrates the force of particular powers. The creation and perpetuation of laws of war have had the effect of legalizing certain acts of violence as war and regulating war rather than outlawing the practice.

International law is '… a complex mix of multilateral treaties, customary law, State practice, UN Security Council resolutions, judicial decisions, the work of advisory commissions and legal experts, and "general principles of law"' (Dorsey, 1999: 386). International law is constantly being contested and reworked, influenced by notions of 'rights' and the power of the nation-State. Like the laws of war, 'international law' in its pre-Second World War form, served to shore-up State sovereignty rather than subvert it in principle and the practice. International law was born from the advent and development of the modern State in the mid-seventeenth century. The Peace of Westphalia (1648), with the consequential agreement to regulate conduct between States, is generally seen as launching international law (Steiner and Alston, 1996) precisely because the need to protect States (and State sovereignty) rested on the establishment of an international order. As these States formed, they increasingly sought codes, agreements and regulations for their dealings with one another. In particular, the Western tradition of international law co-evolved with the competition among European States for the imperial conquest of much of the world. Most scholars locate the genesis of international criminal law in States' efforts to contain piracy on the high seas during the era of global merchant capitalism (Rosenbaum, 1993). For the imperialist European powers, it was essential that trade proceeded smoothly, under the appropriate flag and with the established rules of exchange. Pirates on the high seas threatened this order. The common interests of nations lay in protecting navigation. By common agreement, States established 'international' laws so as to criminalize the threat to exchange. These laws had the effect of establishing the concept of *universal jurisdiction*, and the early foundations for the principle that certain crimes were so serious as to be of concern to an international community beyond the borders and interests of a particular nation State.

In general, though, and certainly before the Second World War, States expressed little concern for what another State did to its own people. States attended to what occurred inside another State only when these actions affected their political-economic interests (Henkin, 1989; Ratner, 1998). Sovereignty served as a shield and international law reflected those political relations between States. International law in its early stages of development correspondingly addressed the relations *between* States and only rarely addressed what another State could do to human bodies (i.e. pirates, diplomats) and failed to encompass the rights and welfare of human beings more generally. Statehood, and the principle of sovereignty, was a cloak that served to protect a State against the intervention of other States.

Prior to the 20th century, the rights of individual humans were linked to the relationship between man[2] as citizen and the sovereign (Beigbeder, 1999; Neier, 1998). For example, during the Enlightenment in Europe, philosophers debated the responsibilities of the prince toward the populace. These notions of 'rights' influenced the debates during the drafting of the Universal Declaration of Human Rights (discussed below). Prior to the Second World War, the concept of 'rights of man' tended to influence the status of citizens *within* specific nations, rather than the international political and legal system.[3]

These developments of international law (agreements between States) and the laws of war converged in the mid-19th century into a body of law called international humanitarian law. International humanitarian law is expressly concerned with the laws of war, the correct conduct of States and armies during war, and the treatment of civilians, particularly the sick, the wounded, prisoners, shipwrecked persons, women, and children; that is, those other than the 'strong men' considered the appropriate target of violence during legitimate battle (Weschler, 1999). The emergence of international humanitarian law is generally pegged to the Declaration of St. Petersburg in 1868, a treaty signed by the main governments of Europe. These governments agreed to 'the technical limits at which the necessities of war ought to yield to the requirements of humanity'; that is, to prohibit weapons that result in unnecessary suffering beyond the legitimate goal of war. The Declaration of St. Petersburg stated that 'the only legitimate object which States should endeavor to accomplish during war is to weaken the military forces of the enemy' (Rosenbaum, 1993: 28; see also Weschler, 1999; Ignatieff, 1997).

Contemporary international humanitarian law departs from the early norms and ideologies concerning warfare in two critical ways. First, international humanitarian law attempts to limit the damage a State can inflict during war – even if that war is considered a just war. As such, international humanitarian law impinges on sovereignty in precisely the way that earlier aspects of international law reinforced the autonomy of States. Second, early international humanitarian law recognizes and codifies distinct human identities, with violence against certain bodies considered abhorrent, even within the practice of a just war. Initially, international humanitarian law addressed the treatment of wounded and captured soldiers, and later, addressed the treatment for the protection of those bodies identified as 'civilian'. Hence these developments in international humanitarian law reflect and create evolving tensions between the body of the individual and the actions of nations.[4]

A further stimulus to the development of international humanitarian law was the growing concern for the fate of bodies. By the late 19th century, public awareness concerning the treatment of sick and wounded bodies of soldiers contributed to legal social movements and the emergence of legal regulations. Why the increasing concern for the welfare of debilitated soldiers and soldiers' corpses? Many scholars attribute this new development to the advent of the war correspondent in the U.S. Civil War (Neier, 1998; Gutman and Reiff, 1999). For Americans, the Civil War enabled, simultaneously, a more visible and more savage war. With the invention of Morse Code and technological advances in photography, war correspondents generated war reports. Previously, reports from the battlefields were submitted by the general, who tended to report on heroism and glory. The dead rarely had the opportunity to share their stories. The war correspondent shifted this equation slightly, and the public reacted. In response to this new public exposure to the horrors of the battlefield, President Abraham Lincoln passed legislation, the Lieber Code for Armies in the Field, in 1863, governing the conduct of soldiers and their treatment by the enemy when captured (Neier, 1998: 14).

In addition to the governmental responses in terms of laws and treaties, social movements formed to exert pressure for the protection of the victims of war. The establishment of the International Committee of the Red Cross is an example of a social organization formed in response to a humanitarian concern for the fate of bodies in war. Jean-Henri Dunant, a wealthy Swiss national, witnessed the Battle of Solferino in 1859. Although the rest of Europe was celebrating the battle, Dunant was obsessed with the images he had seen of the war dead and wounded. In *A Memory of Solferino* (1862), he described the horrors of the battlefield, the ground dark with blood, severed body parts, splintered bone fragments, wounded men desperately flailing about, and local peasants harvesting the corpses for boots and other plunder. Dunant lobbied for an international convention that would allow for first-aid societies to care for the wounded (from both sides) in battle. The Red Cross (so named due to the association with the Swiss flag) was soon formed in Geneva. In 1901 Dunant, the founder of the (then renamed) International Committee of the Red Cross, was awarded the first Nobel Peace Prize. Geneva, and later The Hague in the Netherlands, became the centers of a series of initiatives that greatly amplified international humanitarian law. The first 'Geneva Convention' (1864) was the product of a meeting of representatives from sixteen countries, including the United States, to discuss ways to improve medical services on the battlefield. A series of agreements followed ('the Geneva Conventions').

The Geneva Conventions, the Hague Conventions (1899, 1907) and other elements of international humanitarian law, sought to impose constraints on warfare without outlawing war itself. These agreements hold the force of 'customary international law', which means that they are recognized as binding due to the '... general and consistent practice followed by States from a sense of legal obligation' (Roht-Arriaza, 1995: 24). All civilized peoples were to recognize these conventions as valid; as such these laws dictated membership in a civilized community. International humanitarian law attempted to universalize crimes of war (Steiner and Alston, 1996), and in doing so contributed to an evolving space of an international community. Despite these initiatives of international humanitarian law, the new scale of destruction of World War One was a grim reminder as to the limits of law and the brutality of battle.

In sum, the laws of war, international law and international humanitarian law established the foundations for the concept of 'human rights' that emerges in the 20th century. Over time, certain bodies were considered appropriate targets of violence, and others prohibited. The invention of the notion of the 'innocent civilian' influenced the practices of warfare and in turn the practices of war influenced the identity and often, the fate of particular bodies.

POST-WORLD WAR TWO AND HUMAN RIGHTS: SOCIAL MOVEMENTS AND ACTIVIST NETWORKS

The conclusion of the Second World War stimulated the growth of human rights law, social movements concerned with such rights, and more broadly the emergence of a global human rights regime. The extent of the Holocaust 'shook the complacency of a

Western culture that had overestimated the depth of its civilized qualities ...' (Davidson, 1966: 7) and generated the discourse of 'Never Again'. The world community was shocked by the concentration camps. The dramatic impact of the revelations[5] of the brutal and methodical murder of at least six million people contributed to the political support for the establishment of the State of Israel (Segev, 1993). Moreover, the prosecution of defeated Germans in Nuremberg marked a further significant development in the formation of international human rights law. The Nuremberg trials were innovative on two counts. First, individuals were to be held accountable for actions taken as officials of the State. Second, individuals were judged guilty for 'crimes against humanity' for actions against citizens of their own State. Whereas 'war crimes' addressed actions between combatants, 'crimes against humanity' concerned the actions of civilians (including leaders of State) against citizen/civilians.

The Nuremberg trials were critiqued as 'victors' justice', in reference to the notion that the trials were an example of justice as an execution of authority. Critics contend that the post-Second World War trials represent 'victors' justice' rather than a more neutral justice due to: 1) the lack of trials for Allied officials for war crimes, and; 2) the fact that the Nazis were tried for *ex post facto* crimes, that is crimes that were established in law, after the activities of these particular individuals. In this context, the Nuremberg and the Tokyo trials are merely the result of a victorious alliance of armies imposing its will on a defeated people, in order to demonstrate its victory/authority/power to the world community.[6]

Despite the caveats and complaints regarding this form of 'victor's justice', what is clear is that these trials represented a shift: the security of 'humanity' (existing everywhere) was the domain and concern of 'international' law (again, existing everywhere). The Charter of the United Nations (1945) established that certain crimes relating to war would be crimes of international concern. Aggression (crimes against peace) was outlawed except in self-defense. These initiatives were a departure from international law that had previously avoided addressing such concerns in deference to the power of State sovereignty; 'Human-rights law . . . touches governments at their most sensitive point: how they exercise power over their own citizens. Never before have States agreed to accept so many restrictions on their domestic behavior or to submit to international scrutiny' (Manasian, 1998: 5).

The Universal Declaration of Human Rights originated during this frenzy of international enthusiasm and consensus. Yet quickly, the drafting of the text of the Declaration was subjected to polarized notions of 'rights'. The fundamental conflict – between concepts of 'individual' versus 'community' rights – was grounded in century-old philosophical debates regarding 'liberalism' and 'socialism'. The struggle over the text was defined by the growing hostility between the Soviet Union and the United States that would evolve into the five-decade long Cold War. It is important to note in this regard that observers have pointed out that the Universal Declaration of Human Rights was consciously more of a wish-list than a statement of existing laws/practices as both the Soviet Union and the United States had a tempered tolerance for proclamations of 'rights' in the first place. Ignatieff writes:

> Everyone had something to be ashamed of – the Americans their Jim Crow legislation in the South, the Canadians and their treatment of native peoples, the Soviets and the Red Terror. The embarrassing State of the 'is' kept all eyes firmly focused on the 'ought.' Agreement on high principles was also made easier by leaving the matter of their enforcement entirely unresolved ... Instead, the drafters put their hopes in the idea that by declaring rights as moral universes, they could foster a global rights consciousness among those they called 'the common people'. (1999: 58)

The approval (1948) and entry into force (1951) of the Convention on the Prevention and Punishment of the Crime of Genocide further asserted the supremacy of international law over domestic law and

State sovereignty. The Genocide Convention established that perpetrators of such a crime could be held accountable under international law, even in the absence of applicable domestic law. The Genocide Convention further detailed that an individual acting in his/her role as head of State would be accountable under international law. Perhaps most significantly, the Genocide Convention required States to take action to prevent genocide, provoking intense debate about international trespass on States' individual sovereignty (see Power, 2003).

A series of treaties and conventions followed in the next several decades. The Geneva Conventions were upgraded and extended, and the Universal Declaration of Human Rights was divided into two parts (1952) reflecting the growing ideological divide between the United States and the Soviet Union. The resulting two documents, the International Covenant on Civil and Political Rights and the International Covenant on Economic, Social and Cultural Rights were not approved until 1966, and it took another decade for the two Covenants to get the number of States needed for their entry into force. The United Nations served as the place where such initiatives were developed. Donnelly (1993) adopts a 'supply and demand' analysis for assessing the emergence of the human rights regime, arguing that it arises from the 'demand' generated from the Holocaust, with international laws and norms, and specifically, the Universal Declaration of Human Rights and the Genocide Convention, created to 'supply' a response to these demands. The international instruments and local social movements organized around human rights have become powerful and extensive, launching a 'revolution' in international law (Manasian, 1998).

This revolutionary development has occurred within the modern incarnation of globalization. Waters (1995) insists that a critical transformation occurs within the political landscape in the aftermath of the Second World War. He credits this transformation to the emergence of a social recognition of what he calls 'planetary problems'. Widespread and globally extensive problems such as *human rights, the environment, development and inequality*, and *peace* (1995: 101) called for the submission of individual nation-States to a multilateral order. The fact that all inhabitants of the planet were threatened by these problems necessitated a global response. These shared planetary problems demanded attention beyond the private treaties between States, and were deemed too serious to be left to the 'dubious intentions of any one hegemonic power' (i.e. the United States – 1995: 101).

The central result of the post-Second World War (re)conceptualizations of these widespread problems, Waters argues, was a weakening of the sovereignty of individual nation-States (to various degrees). Waters observed three ways in which the redefinition of social problems as global problems undermines State sovereignty. First, political preferences are reshaped in light of these problems. Second, the nation-State is increasingly de-legitimatized as a problem solver, since these planetary problems are considered beyond the realm of any single State to address. Finally, social and political energies are redirected toward global mechanisms (such as international non-government organizations) as solutions for these problems.

This transformation/weakening of individual State sovereignty has resulted in a system of 'global governance' emerging with its own policy development and administrative systems which further curtails State powers. In order to understand this emergence it is important to recognize that globalization occurs alongside transformations in the particular powers of individual nation-States, rather than existing in a zero-sum relationship. Instead of 'more' globalization resulting in 'less' State sovereignty, the geographical transformations are complex. Often globalization can increase certain States' power, while other States feel an impingement. Waters argues that the key development in the contemporary process of globalization is 'the institutionalization of the view that individual human beings have rights *qua* humans that can be sustained against the sovereignty of the State' (1995: 102). The subject of human rights has been 'internationalized beyond all expectations' (Buergenthal, 1995: 20) and the protection of human rights has been elevated to a central feature of the discourse of individual nations, international organizations and a large network of other organizations, especially the United Nations, which established a communicative and normative framework, where the human rights movement found a home.

Further, the post-Second World War period witnessed the growth of a web of human rights related non-governmental organizations (NGOs). (Some estimates place the number at more than a quarter million organizations associated with social change/human welfare, broadly defined (Herb, 2005)). Individually, such organizations may cover as few as two national societies, but in their operations together they create what scholars have termed a 'global network' (Keck and Sikkink, 1998). NGOs can be 'particularly unruly' (Waters, 1995: 101) as their capacity to link diverse people in relation to common causes and interests can undermine the meaning and power of the State.

The example of the international human rights group Amnesty International illustrates the experience of a human rights organization's impact on local, national and global landscapes. Founded in 1961, Amnesty International originated with a newspaper appeal by a British lawyer, Peter Benenson, entitled 'The Forgotten Prisoners'.[7] An initial 1,000-plus responses launched a campaign under the rubric of the international support for human rights, everywhere. That first year, Amnesty International investigated 210 cases and operated on a budget of less than $10,000. The organization grew quickly, drawing membership from more than 100 countries and conducting investigations throughout the world. Local human rights movements were stimulated by the existence of the international organization, which (sometimes) provided effective protection and support.

As an international NGO, Amnesty International was in a position to lobby the United Nations, based on cases from particular locales, and directly impact particular nation-States. The UN Human Rights Commission experienced difficulty 'naming' Argentina as a human rights offender because certain UN members were reluctant to establish a precedent, lest they be subjected to the same sanctions. Amnesty International persisted with the presentation of information about two Argentineans who had been 'disappeared', forcing the United Nations to address the problem in some manner (Guest, 1990). The United Nations sought to establish a mechanism to get around a 'country specific' inquiry, and therefore established the 'thematic' mechanism of the UN Working Group on Disappearances. During this period, Argentina attempted to block Amnesty International's presentation of information on the disappeared, but the UN Human Rights Commission ruled that NGOs could submit such materials. As such, local human rights issues gained access to a global audience.

Increasingly, social movements found material benefits through association demands based on human rights. For example, in Latin America, the efforts to combat disappearances, extra-judicial assassinations, and other forms of State terrorism, spawned social movements organized around demands of *habeas corpus*. In its specific legal usage, *habeas corpus* refers to a writ requiring that a detained person be brought before a court at a stated time and place to decide the legality of his/her detention or imprisonment. These social movements, such as the *Madres de la Plaza de Mayo* in Argentina, provided a vehicle for protest, and importantly, drew international attention to the occurrence and extent of the atrocities.

Although the overt demands were for information regarding the bodies of missing loved ones, the implicit social objectives were for political and judicial accountability, and in some cases, a complete regime change from the military rule associated with the violent practices, to a (theoretically) democratically elected civilian government accountable to national society and potentially the evolving global civil society. While repressive regimes (such as the Argentine juntas) attempted to dismiss popular resistance as the work of violent guerrillas (frequent pejoratives included 'terrorist' or 'communist'), the face of these social movements – oftentimes grandmothers marching with pictures of children and grandchildren – diminished the plausibility of these representations. In many instances, the local organization of marching grandmothers gained prestige, power and protection from association with international human rights organizations.

As the human rights movement gained traction, more issues and organizations sought its umbrella-protection. Increasingly, issues beyond State-sponsored political violence have entered the human rights fold. Once considered 'environmental' or associated with poverty/development, human welfare concerns also find a home in the human rights universe. As what 'counts' as a human right has expanded to include more infractions, more threatened persons fall, theoretically, under the protection of such rights.

The development of human rights has transformed geographies, and in turn geographies have transformed human rights. By the end of the 20th century, it had become clear that the process known as 'globalization' has been both product and producer of 'human rights'. The human rights universe that emerged in the 20th century contributed to the growth and character of a global civil society and the (imagined) international community. In turn, these geographical transformations hosted the development of features of the human rights universe. The power of human rights activism and organization launched many of the ideas central to global consciousness – evidence of 'crimes against humanity' provoked consciousness concerning the existence of a *humanity* capable of being concerned with rights everywhere. Additionally, global networks and transnational activists (e.g. Activists Beyond Borders) have transformed local, national and regional politics. In short, rather than existing in opposition to State sovereignty, globalization can coincide with the strength of the State (Giddens, 2000); '... it is not absolutely necessary to demonstrate that the nation-State is in decline in order to support a case for political globalization.... Indeed, the emergence of the nation-State is itself a part of the globalization process ...' (Waters, 1995: 98).

The human rights regime can be understood to exist locally, nationally and internationally, and operates in all of these spaces at once. Local, national and international space(s), rather than constituting distinct levels, exist in simultaneous relation to each other. Eagleton (1999: 270), critiques the false dichotomy between a 'global level' and a 'local level', complaining about the slogan: 'think global, act local – what else can we ever do?' All human activity happens *somewhere* (the local) and yet potentially has implications in national politics and international fora. Even violence that is formally denied (i.e., attempts to 'disappear' persons) can potentially set off national and international movements. In turn, the development of international infrastructure, norms and political arrangements increasingly affect the body in its locale.

HUMAN RIGHTS IN THE 21ST CENTURY: THE INTERNATIONAL CRIMINAL COURT AND THE UNEVEN GEOGRAPHIES OF JUSTICE

The violence of a 'human rights abuse' happens 'locally' (i.e. to a particular body). Yet these acts and experiences of violence reverberate in national and international politics. As the (above) discussion of the development of the human rights universe suggests, these local, situated social practices and national politics, shape an international space as well, which in turn influences local developments in the human rights arena.[8] As Roht-Arriaza (2005) demonstrates, the confluence of domestic factors with international influences shapes the course that justice will take. As she points out, the 'transnational' process of establishing a case against Chilean General Augusto Pinochet proved more effective than the Chilean national judiciary, or international law, in isolation. The jurisdiction of a given body of law is often highly contested, as is the reification of distinct (and discreet) scales of space.

Contemporary and future issues associated with human rights will likely exhibit complex, overlapping and intertwined geographies. International institutions are proliferating, but local and national politics and social movements remain intense; rather than 'overshadowed' by the international, local and regional practices seem fully engaged and inflamed. The example of the gestation and infancy of the International Criminal Court illustrate the complicated social, political and legal landscapes of human rights, and particularly the unevenness of human rights.

The establishment of the International Criminal Court (ICC) in 2002 was the result of decades of advocacy and campaigning by human rights professionals. The hope attached to the ICC was that a permanent court, capable of prosecuting the most powerful perpetrators on the planet, would be able to protect the weak from the violence of the powerful. The international arena was seen as one way to combat the prevalence of impunity in the national context (Ross, 2001). The (so-called) international community was imagined to be a superior space for justice and human rights, as local and national politics appeared repeatedly to protect the powerful. In activity that has been described as scale-jumping, local victims would link-up with international activists and by-pass the impunity at the national level. After numerous attempts at prosecuting international crimes (genocide, crimes against humanity and war crimes) in national courts under the principle of universal jurisdiction, the ICC was seen as the embodiment of a global force for justice (see Sewall and Kaysen, 2000).

Interest in a permanent international body devoted to prosecuting war crimes has been expressed at various points in history (Bass, 2001). During the political polarization of the Cold War period, neither superpower was overly eager to relinquish the domain of righteousness to an independent international institution. As the Cold War moved towards its closure (1989–1991), interest returned in the form of a proposal to prosecute drug-trafficking in the Caribbean as an international crime. Although the proposal drifted at the outbreak of violence in the former Yugoslavia, the idea of international courts remained popular. There are several features that potentially can give a crime 'international' status. One criterion recognizes violence within a State as having international impacts, such as the disruption caused by refugee/displaced peoples as well as charges of cross-border interference. Under its Chapter Seven mandate to protect international peace and security, the UN Security Council established the International Criminal Tribunal for the former Yugoslavia (ICTY) in 1993. More broadly, over time, certain crimes are considered to be so heinous as to be of 'international concern'. The so-called 'crimes of international concern' are genocide, crimes against humanity and grave-breaches of the laws and violations of war (also known as 'war crimes'). In 1994, the Security Council again acted to establish an international court to prosecute crimes of international concern committed in Rwanda.

Still, certain powerful sectors remained averse to a permanent international court that would have jurisdiction over every potential perpetrator on the planet. Among those objecting were the likely subjects – the notoriously violent dictators and despots who had every reason to resist judicial accountability. Indeed, this class of thug-cum-political leader had managed to do so in their home country for years. Objections also came from the US government, which expressed fears that submission to the jurisdiction of an international court would undermine US sovereignty and its potential for global military activity. While the US had supported 'international justice' for the peoples of Rwanda and the former

Yugoslavia (and later for Sierra Leone and Cambodia), it was far less willing to consider such courts for its own nationals. Despite US objections, the Rome Statute was drafted in 1998, and by 2002 the Statute had garnered the requisite State ratifications to bring the ICC into existence. International social movements were essential to the creation and promotion of the International Criminal Court; a group of more than 800 NGOs established the Coalition for the International Criminal Court and participated at unprecedented levels in the drafting of the Statute, the lobbying of State parties, and the hard, grass-roots work of bringing diverse national constitutions in line with international aspirations regarding human rights norms.

Although 120 States in Rome voted for the ICC Statute, seven voted against – including the United States. When the ICC got started in 2002–2003, its staff was extremely conscious of its vulnerability. At the ICC's first major press conference in July 2003, the chief prosecutor sought to explain how the fledgling court was going to proceed among a universe of possible crimes. Extreme violence was everywhere … but what to count as legitimate warfare, and what to declare a crime against humanity? The ICC, in its initial statements, stuck to careful ground, narrowly interpreting its jurisdiction and stressing the limits of its resources. In June 2003, the ICC announced that it would take special interest in the violence in Ituri, a province in the Northeast of the Democratic Republic of the Congo (the DRC). The violence in Ituri had resulted in millions of civilian casualties, many within the temporal jurisdiction of the ICC. The case was also indisputably atrocious. For the ICC, Ituri presented the additional 'advantage' in that pursuing the militia leaders in the Congo and Great Lakes region (probably) would fail to disrupt major power geopolitical interests.

Uganda appeared next and probably took the ICC a bit by surprise. In January 2004 the ICC announced that the government of Uganda had referred the situation of the Lord's Resistance Army (the LRA) in Northern Uganda to the International Criminal Court. For the ICC, Ugandan President Museveni's invitation, a so-called 'State-party referral' was seen as the best means for the ICC to take action, much preferred to the 'trigger' mechanism by which the prosecutors would move on his own (*proprio motu*). For the newly established ICC, conscious of its critics (including the US administration), acting at the invitation of a government was far preferable to being seen as intervening in the internal affairs of a sovereign State.

The ICC's involvement in Northern Uganda has been problematic and suggest the limits of the institution's ability to fulfill its stated mission. While the extreme violence and suffering in Northern Uganda present a crisis of enormous magnitude,[9] the scale and nature of the atrocities in the ICC's jurisdiction[10] also defy easy solutions. After all, investigating and prosecuting genocide, crimes against humanity, and grave breaches of the laws and customs of war is an inherently difficult task. The Chief Prosecutor, Luis Moreno-Ocampo, has stated that the ICC will be a 'success' if it fails to hold a single trial. What he means by this is that the greatest effect of the ICC would be to deter genocide, crimes against humanity, and war crimes. Although the ICC's intervention was initially greeted positively among international human rights enthusiasts, internally its entry into the conflict in Northern Uganda was met with apprehension, confusion, and outright objections by civil society. By accepting Musevini's invitation to investigate the LRA (announced in London at a press conference where the ICC's Chief Prosecutor Luis Moreno-Ocampo and President Museveni stood side by side), Moreno-Ocampo appeared to the people in Northern Uganda as having taken Museveni's side in the two-decades old conflict. As such, the ICC became viewed locally as a protagonist in the conflict rather than a promoter of peace.

During the first years following the referral, local community leaders in Northern Uganda articulated sharp disapproval with the ICC's intervention in their region, and asked for the ICC to suspend its activities.

A respected coalition of NGOs and representatives of civil society directly asked the ICC to refrain from issuing indictments, in order to give the peace process more viability. But just months later in October 2005, the ICC issued its first arrests warrants for Joseph Kony and four other LRA commanders.[11]

Many might have expected that the ICC's enemies would come from the sector most concerned with the personal threat of prosecution (the protagonists in the armed conflict that might have committed war crimes, crimes against humanity and/or genocide and therefore might have reason to fear the ICC). But instead of the generals, in Uganda, in one of its first cases, the first and most vocal voices against the ICC came from local leaders and representatives of civil society in Northern Uganda, especially those sectors that claimed to represent the plight of the victims of the violence.

While weathering the storm of criticism from local and international organizations in civil society, the ICC has insisted that it is acting impartially and according to the parameters of its statute. Whereas the ICC might see itself as beginning a 'new' presence or process in Uganda, from the standpoint of historical memory the ICC fits into a long trajectory of international interventions. These interventions sought to classify local norms concerning punishment and rehabilitation as 'sorcery' or witchcraft, and replace these (newly classified) taboos with an outside form of authority (Behrend, 1999). Of special interest is that the colonialists failed to distinguish between the victim and perpetrator, in that the 'witch' was punished even though she/he was a victim. This has left a local legacy of perceiving outside attempts to sanction and/or classify wrongdoers as flawed. The spirits describe/interpret the problems as being a failure to 'cleanse' returning soldiers after battle, such that these soldiers take up arms again and the violence continues. Therefore indictments from The Hague (especially communicated through President Museveni's State-controlled press) are seen as retaliation, or a continuation to the conflict, rather than the cleansing that would allow soldiers (and the bad 'sen' – vengeful spirit of someone who has died a bad death) to give up the fight.

A sense of revenge, based on historical animosities, has fueled new fighting. Specifically, this has meant that the 'losers' of armed groups find themselves joining new armed rebellions, because of a failure to reintegrate combatants into society. The concern in contemporary Uganda (shored up by a history of armed insurrections) is that if the LRA fighters find themselves punished/prosecuted or otherwise excluded from the benefits of society, these ex-combatants would be more likely to take up arms again. This history-repeating cycle of violence is described in Northern Uganda in terms of the existence of spirits, or bad 'sen'. Bad 'sen' (bad spirits), are spirits that died improperly, or were not adequately cleansed. While this may sound far fetched, pre-modern, or mystical, the world of the spirits and the material world are interconnected. Moreover, without the reconstruction and resettlement, the returning combatants are going to be left without options, and therefore more likely to engage in armed, lucrative activities. That violence can justify further violence is obviously a phenomenon beyond Northern Uganda, but especially relevant when one considers the ICC's temporal jurisdiction. The point here is that from the standpoint of the role of spirits in the battle, the failure to cleanse leads to more violence. The ICC's activities are not being presented and interpreted as cleansing, but rather another strike in the longer conflict.

The International Criminal Court, established in 2002, was lauded as the culmination of millennial aspirations for justice and the future protection of human rights. Yet, at the time of this writing, the 'international' court has indicted only African warlords and militia leaders. Granted, although these suspects are accused of heinous violence (rape, child abduction, forcing family members to kill each other) documented in detail by reputable human rights watchdog organizations, the impact of their violence is arguably less than that of the State, which happen to be the same authority that cooperates with the ICC. In the case of Uganda, the Prosecutor has investigated and indicted the bizarre, reclusive, and quite possibly insane Joseph Kony of the Lord's Resistance Army, but has (to date) ignored the violations committed by the Ugandan State. As such, its activities illustrate the 'unevenness' of the pursuit of justice and accountability.

CONCLUSION: WHAT'S WRONG WITH RIGHTS

The social geography of the idea of human rights illuminates their uneven development. As mentioned above, the popular narrative of the progressive evolution of human rights depicts a history of unerring forward 'progress' toward greater respect for human rights, and accounts for massive atrocity as 'accidents' 'aberrations' or States of exception (Nyers, 2006; Agamben, 2005). From the perspective of geographically uneven development, with certain acts considered human rights violations and other violence considered acceptable, Ahrundati Roy observes that:

> It is becoming more than clear that violating human rights is an inherent and necessary part of the process of implementing a coercive and unjust political and economic structure on the world. Without the violation of human rights on an enormous scale, the neo-liberal project would remain in the dreamy realm of policy. But increasingly Human Rights violations are being portrayed as the unfortunate, almost accidental fallout of an otherwise acceptable political and economic system. (2004: 2)

What constitutes a human rights abuse and what constitutes business as usual? Does Joseph Kony (the leader of the Ugandan Lord's Resistance Army) become 'international' when he: 1) camps across the border in Sudan, or more recently in the Eastern DRC; 2) is indicted by the International Criminal Court, and/or 3) kills, rapes and kidnaps civilians (particularly children) in a 'wide-spread and systematic' fashion?

When is a specific, local act of violence granted the status of a human rights abuse, as opposed to business as usual? How is a horribly deadly situation such as extreme poverty constructed such that it passes as 'acceptable'?

The laws of war developed (over centuries) as a way to regulate, rather than outlaw, war and violence. International law has its roots in protecting and contributing to principles of State sovereignty, rather than superseding States with a higher, supra-authority. Like these intellectual predecessors, modern human rights are about regulating violence and State power rather than abolishing either. The uneven development of human rights illustrates the situated-ness of such rights; in certain contexts violence is considered criminal, while in other contexts violence is considered appropriate. How are certain acts of violence deemed to be 'human rights violations' whereas others are considered business as usual? Considering the case of rape analyzed in Catharine MacKinnon's *Are Women Human?* (2006), how does the violated subject produce a conception of the nature of the violence? In turn, who has the power to declare that a right is a 'human' right, and accuse others of their violation? How does the act of classifying certain activities as criminal, serve to sanctify others? For example, historically, at the conclusion of the Second World War the Nazis' concentration camps were declared a 'crime against humanity' whereas the dropping of atomic bombs was scripted as heroic, the bomb 'saved lives' as it ended the war. How does the identification (and in some cases the prosecution) of certain acts as human rights violations serve to legitimize other acts of violence?

Geographers have not been especially active in studying human rights, possibly because the disciplines of political science and international relations have dominated the discussion and cast a State-centric shadow across the field of debates. Geographers may interrogate that premise through empirical and theoretical explorations into the evolving role of space and power in the human rights universe. Political science, in particular, has treated geography as fixed and/or static, a mere backdrop to the otherwise dynamic activities of human society. Geography is much more than the stage that hosts the performance of war, violence, and human rights abuses. Colin Flint (2005) has debunked the notion that geography's relationship to war has to do with the 'fixedness' or 'permanency' of geography. Restricting geography's role to its 'physicality,' argues Flint, '... provides a limited understanding of geography' (2005: 5) and therefore fails to illuminate the nature of human activity.

The links between geography and human rights appear in approaches to the relationship between violence and territory. Michael Watts invokes Edward Said's observation that violence is 'struggles over geography' in order to discuss violent struggles in Nigeria (Watts, 2000: 2). David Delaney has more broadly argued that the power to declare one 'inside' or 'outside' specific territory, often violently, confirms William Connolly's (1996) suggestion that 'To occupy a territory is to receive sustenance and to exercise violence. Territory is land occupied by violence' (quoted in Delaney, 2005: 14). Others, such as Joesph Nevins (2005) and Carl Dahlman (2005) have addressed the '... nexus of territory, identity and power – issues which repeatedly play a central role in contexts of mass violence' (O'Lear et al., forthcoming).

One of the richest areas of geographical inquiry concerns the focus on the body. Feminist scholarship on the relationship between power, subjectivities, and the violence inflicted on particular bodies (Butler, 1993) have informed geopolitics and political geography (see, especially, Hyndman, 2000, 2007, and Hyndman and Mountz, 2007). Hyndman's geographies of placement and displacement, and Melissa Wright's tracking of the fate of women's bodies in Cuidad Juarez, Mexico, demonstrate the productive lens geography provides for situating knowledge about abuses. Allan Pred's insistence that 'situated ignorance' (2007) is an essential component for terror and the associated violence relies on geographical imaginaries (Gregory and Pred, 2007) with material consequences.

David Harvey reminds us as well that human rights is a rich topic of study for geographers, particularly with respect to the relationship between bodies and global discourses and practices. Harvey notes (2000: 15) that '... globalization is the most "macro" of all discourses, whereas that of "the body" is the most micro – these two discursive regimes – globalization and the body – operate at opposite ends of the spectrum ... but little or no attempt has been made to integrate "body talk" with globalization talk. ... The only strong connections to have emerged in recent years concern individual and human rights'. Future social geographies may take up the challenge to further these connections.

NOTES

1 Several terms exist that attempt to describe human rights and the associated laws, organizations, social movements, politics, etc: 'human rights regime,' and 'human rights movement' are among the most popular.

2 'Man' is used here (rather than human) because most of the documents and treaties that comprise the intellectual development of 'rights' use the word man, and refer to men. Even which men had rights was restricted by race and class.

3 An exception concerned debates regarding slavery. During the early stages of global colonization and expansion, a Spanish Dominican missionary, Bartolome de las Casas, became one of the first to call for the abolition of the slavery of indigenous Americans by Europeans, citing the rights of the indigenous people as humans (bodies with souls). Over the course of several centuries, national policies outlawed the international trade of slaves, and treaties were established to outlaw the practice.

4 For a more detailed discussion of the invention of 'civilians,' and the relationship between identities and the politics of violence, see Ross, 2008. For a detailed historical survey and analysis of the development of notions of innocents in war, see McKeogh, 2002.

5 'Revelations' refers to the widespread awareness and attention to the Holocaust, rather than the 'discovery.' At least some of the extermination activities being conducted by the Nazis were known by Allied leaders, the Vatican, and the International Red Cross (Beigbeder, 1999: 31, see also Lipset, 1986).

6 The central problem associated with victors' justice is that it takes a 'victory'; increasingly, since the end of the Cold War, conflicts are being resolved through negotiated settlements, without one clear victor. Hence Nuremberg fails as a contemporary model, as 'victors' and 'victories' are increasingly rare. A further problem ascribed to victors' justice is that it is imposed from an outside authority (from 'above') and hence fails to resonant with the local community associated with the crimes.

7 For Amnesty International's own account of its origins, see www.amnesty.org.

8 Sally Engle Merry describes the overlapping local, national and transnational legal orders, arguing that these systems are also 'mutually constitutive' (1992: 358). She demonstrates this point in a case study of Hawaii (Merry, 1997), in which she describes the way in which 'traditional' (indigenous Hawaiian) norms of justice absorb and incorporate international laws to create a hybrid body of law to address the particular needs of the culture in the era of hypermodernity.

9 At the time of this writing, the United Nations estimates that more than 1,000 persons a week die from violence, malnutrition and disease – an 'excess mortality' that places Northern Uganda among the worse crises of the 21st century. The violence is linked to an almost 20-year-old conflict between the Lord's Resistance Army (the LRA) and the Ugandan government, but is most often visible on the bodies of civilians through disfigurement, death, and mass dislocation. Children are especially vulnerable as the targets for abduction and other abuses. An estimated 1.4–1.6 million – more than 90% of the population – 'internally displaced persons' live in crammed camp conditions (IDP camps) without adequate food, water and security. In a recent (and rare) survey of residents in the region, human rights experts found that 45% of the respondents had witnessed the killing of a family member (Pham et al., 2005).

10 The ICC has jurisdiction over the so-called 'crimes of international concern': genocide, crimes against humanity and war crimes, all over which are defined in detail in the Rome Statute. A fourth category, the crime of aggression, will be defined and adopted by 2009. See Schabas, 2004.

11 In addition to Joseph Kony, other indictees are: Vincent Otti, Okot Ojiambo, Dominic Ongwen, and Rask Lukwiya – the last was reported killed in 2006 by Ugandan government forces. In October 2007 news reports indicated that Otti had been murdered on Kony's orders.

REFERENCES

Agamben, G. (2005) *State of Exception.* Chicago: University of Chicago Press.

Andreopoulos, G., Kabasakal Arat, Z.F. and Juviler, P. (eds) (2006) *Non-State Actors in the Human Rights Universe*. Bloomfield, CT: Kumarian Press, Inc.

Bass, J.G. (2001) *Stay the Hand of Vengeance: The Politics of War Crimes Tribunals.* Princeton: Princeton University Press.

Behrend, H. (1999) *Alice Lakwena & the Holy Spirits; War in Northern Uganda 1986–97.* Athens, Ohio: Ohio University Press.

Beigbeder, Y. (1999) *Judging War Criminals: The Politics of International Justice.* New York: St Martin's Press.

Buergenthal, T. (1995) *International Human Rights in a Nutshell.* St. Paul, MN: West Publishing Co.

Butler, Judith. (1993) *Bodies That Matter: On the Discursive Limits of 'Sex.'* New York; Routledge.

Clausewitz, C. (1968) *On War.* London: Penguin Books. (1st edn, 1832).

Connolly, W. (1996) 'Tocqueville, territory and v', in M. Shapiro and H. Alker (eds). *Challenging Boundaries; Global Flows, Territorial Identities.* Minneapolis: University of Minnesota Press. pp. 141–64.

Dahlman, C. (2005) 'Geographies of Genocide and Ethnic Cleansing: The Lessons of Bosnia-Herzegovina', in C. Flint (ed.), *The Geography of War and Peace: From Death Camps to Diplomats.* New York: Oxford University Press.

Davidson, E. (1966) *The Trial of the Germans.* New York: Colliers Book.

Delaney, D. (2005) *Territory: A short introduction.* Oxford: Blackwell Publishing.

Donnelly, J. (1993) *International Human Rights.* Boulder: Westview Press.

Dorsey, A. (1999) 'Note on the law and legal terms', in R. Gutman and D. Reiff (eds), *Crimes of War.* New York: W.W. Norton & Company. p. 386.

Eagleton, T. (1999) 'Local and global', in O. Savic (ed.), *The Politics of Human Rights.* New York: Verso. pp. 262–71.

Fanon, Frantz (1963) 'Concerning violence,' from *The Wretched of the Earth,* in *The Geopolitics Reader,* Tuathail, Dalby and Routledge (eds). New York: Routledge, 1998.

Flint, C. (ed.) (2005) *The Geography of War and Peace: From Death Camps to Diplomats.* Oxford: Oxford University Press.

Foucault, M. (1979) *Discipline and Punish; the Birth of the Prison.* New York: Vintage Books.

Giddens, A. (2000) *Runaway World: How Globalization is Reshaping Our Lives.* New York: Routledge.

Gregory, D. (2007) 'Introduction', in D. Gregory, and A. Pred, *Violent Geographies: Fear, Terror and Political Violence.* New York: Routledge. pp. 1–6.

Guest, I. (1990) *Behind the Disappearances: Argentina's Dirty War Against Human Rights and the United Nations.* Philadelphia: University of Penn Press.

Gutman, R. and Reiff, D. (eds) (1999) *Crimes of War: What the Public Should Know.* New York: W.W. Norton & Company.

Harvey, D. (2000) *Spaces of Hope*. Edinburgh: Edinburgh University Press.

Henkin, L. (1989) 'International law: politics, values and functions', Excerpt reprinted in H. Steiner and P. Alston (eds) (2000), *International Human Rights in Context; Law, Politics, Morals.* Oxford: Oxford University Press. pp. 127–30.

Herb, G.H. (2005) 'The geography of peace movements', in C. Flint (ed.) *The Geography of War and Peace: From Death Camps to Diplomats*. Oxford: Oxford University Press. pp. 347–68.

Hyndman, J. (2000) *Managing Displacement: Refugees and the Politics of Humanitarianism.* Minneapolis: Minnesota University Press.

Hyndman, J. (2007) 'Feminist geopolitics revisited: body counts in Iraq', *The Professional Geographer*, 59 (1): 35–46.

Hyndman, J. and Mountz, A. (2007) 'Refuge or refusal: geography of exclusion', in D. Gregory and A. Pred (eds), *Inhuman Geographies/spaces of political violence*. New York: Routledge. pp. 77–92.

Ignatieff, M. (1997) *The Warrior's Honor: Ethnic War and the Modern Consciousness.* New York: Henry Holt and Co.

Ignatieff, M. (1999) 'Human rights: the midlife crisis', *The New York Review of Books.* Vol. XLVI, No. 9: 58–62.

Keck, M. and Sikkink, K. (1998) *Activists Beyond Borders: Transnational Advocacy Networks in International Politics.* Ithaca: Cornell University Press.

Lauren, P.G. (2003) *The Evolution of International Human Rights.* Philadelphia: University of Pennsylvania Press.

Lipset, D. (1986) *Beyond Belief*. New York: Free Press.

MacKinnon, C. (2006) *Are Women Human?* Boston: Harvard University Press.

Manasian, D. (1998) 'Survey-Human Rights Law', *The Economist*, December 5th, pp. 5–12.

McKeogh, C. (2002) *Innocent Civilians: The Morality of Killing in War.* New York: Palgrave.

Merry, S.E. (1992) 'Anthropology, law and transnational processes'. *Annual Review of Anthropology*, 21: 357–79.

Merry, S.E. (1997) 'Legal pluralism and transnational culture: The Ka Ho'okolokolonui Kanaka Maoli Tribunal, Hawaii, 1993', in R. Wilson (ed.), *Human Rights, Culture and Context: Anthropological Perspectives*. London: Pluto Press. pp. 28–48.

Neier, A. (1998) *War Crimes: Brutality, Genocide, Terror, and the Struggle for Justice.* New York: Times Books.

Nevins, J. (2005) *A Not-So-Distant Horror: Mass Violence in East Timor.* Ithaca: Cornell University Press.

Nyers, P. (2006) *Rethinking Refugees: Beyond States of Emergency.* New York: Routledge.

O'Lear, S., Egbert, S. and Montgomery-Anderson, E. (draft manuscript 2007, forthcoming) 'Introduction: Theme Issue on Geography of Genocide', *Space and Polity*.

Pham, P., Vinck, P., Wierda, M., Stover, E. and di Giovanni, A., (2005) *Forgotten Voices: A Population-Based Survey of Attitudes about Peace and Justice in Northern Uganda*. New York: International Center for Transitional Justice and Berkeley: Human Rights Center.

Power, S. (2003) *'A Problem from Hell': America in the Age of Genocide.* Boston: Basic Books.

Pred, A. (2007) 'Situated ignorance and state terrorism', in D. Gregory, and A. Pred, *Violent Geographies: Fear, Terror and Political Violence.* New York: Routledge. pp. 363–85.

Ratner, S.R. (1998) 'The schizophrenias of international criminal law', *Texas International Law Journal*, 33: 237–45.

Reiff, D. (1999) 'The precarious triumph of human rights', *The New York Times Magazine*, August 8: 36–41.

Roht-Arriaza, N. (ed.) (1995) *Impunity and Human Rights in International Law and Practice*. Oxford: Oxford University Press.

Roht-Arriaza, N. (2005) *The Pinochet Effect: Transnational Justice in the Age of Human Rights*. Philadelphia: University of Pennsylvania Press.

Rosenbaum, A. (1993) *Prosecuting Nazi War Criminals*. Boulder: Westview Press.

Ross, A. (2001) 'Geographies of justice: international law, national sovereignty and human rights', *Finnish Yearbook of International Law*, Vol. XII: 7–16.

Ross, A. (2008) 'The body counts: Civilian casualties and the crisis of human rights', in A. Bullard (ed.), *Human Rights in Crisis*. Boston: Ashgate.

Roy, A. (2004) 'Speech upon accepting the Sydney Peace Prize'. Nov 4 2004, http://www.smh.com.au/news/Opinion/Roys-full-speech/2004/11/04/1099362264349.html

Savic, O. (ed.) (1999) *The Politics of Human Rights*. New York: Verso.

Schabas, W. (2004) *Introduction to the International Criminal Court*. Cambridge: Cambridge University Press.

Segev, T. (1993) *The Seventh Million: The Israelis and the Holocaust*. New York: Hill and Wang.

Sewall, S. and Kaysen, C. (eds) (2000) *The United States and the International Criminal Court: National Security and International Law*. New York: Rowman and Littlefield.

Steiner, H.J. and Alston, P. (eds) (1996) *International Human Rights in Context: Law, Politics, Morals*. Oxford: Clarendon Press.

UNICEF (2005) 'Suffering in silence, a study of sexual and gender-based violence (SGBV)' in Pabbo Camp. Kampala.

Waters, M. (1995) *Globalization*. New York: Routledge.

Watts, Michael J. (2000) 'Geographies of violence and the narcissism of minor difference', in *Struggles over Geography: Violence, freedom and development at the millennium*. Department of Geography, University of Heidelberg.

Weschler, L. (1999) 'International humanitarian law: an overview', in R. Gutman and D. Reiff (eds), *Crimes of War*. New York: W.W. Norton & Company.

Wright, M. (2006) *Disposable Women and Other Myths of Global Capitalism*. New York: Routledge.

SECTION 5

Doing Social Geographies

Edited by
Rachel Pain

Introduction: Doing Social Geographies

Rachel Pain

KNOWING AND DOING

In any book outlining any sub-disciplinary field, the inclusion of issues dedicated to the process of knowledge production is always appropriate. Epistemological and methodological concerns are sometimes viewed as just another worthy parcel of information – a set of philosophies and techniques to be studied, usually early in our research careers; dusted off for the often brief periods that we spend 'in the field'; sometimes developed or debated, but rarely a concern that has equivalence with the more important concerns of detailing and theorising our substantive research topics.

But the practices and politics of research are always fundamentally connected to the shape of knowledge. This is the case whether we are people-people, numbers-people, library-people or all three; whether we direct a flotilla of assistants or roll up our own sleeves and do research; whether our research interactions are fleeting, over in days or weeks, or are sustained collaborative engagements. And neither research practice nor knowledge outputs exist in isolation from the wider landscapes of professional research and wider society – the institutional and political frameworks in which we are all located in some way shape what becomes 'social geographies', more than perhaps we ever acknowledge. And whatever our position, and however we do research, we're also bound in complex and delicate sociocultural relations with others, raising big issues of ethics, morality and care. So while the 'doing' of social geographies is dealt with in a sustained way in this final section of the book, all of the themes we raise in this introduction and the chapters that follow echo and connect with what has been discussed about the 'knowing' this far. Moreover, some of the most recent contributions to methodological and epistemological debate in social geographies are suggesting the severe limits to our knowledge as well as our empirical practice.

For social geographies, the connections between knowing and doing feel particularly strong. Intellectually and politically, this should not be the case any more than for other subfields of the discipline. But, perhaps because of the type of researchers and research the subdiscipline is increasingly made of, we tend to be more explicit, more exploratory and more reflective on issues of practice, politics and method, giving them a more central place in our intellectual concerns. Because social geographies often involve research on the most marginalised people and places, political and personal dilemmas feel closer to the surface. Researchers are more likely to use qualitative techniques that bring issues of relationality, ethics and care to the fore (Limb and Dwyer, 2001; and see Besio, Chapter 25, in this volume), or to forge collaborative research relationships with communities and activist organisations that both complicate and bring closer to home issues of positionality and politics (see Pratt, 2007; and Chapter 23 by Kindon and Chapter 27 by Browne in this volume).

BEYOND METHOD

The chapters here all mention different methods – and there is now an exciting array for social geographers to choose from (see Crang, 2003; Cope and Elwood, forthcoming; Flowerdew and Martin, 2005; Kindon et al., 2007; Kesby and van Blerk, 2008; Pink, 2006) – but this is not the central concern of the commentaries provided here. Instead, their focus reflects a recent, tangible and significant shift; the focus of conversations about doing research has moved outwards from methods to epistemology, and to wider issues of ethics, accountability, care, politics, participation, relevance and justice in relation to research in social geographies. While the critical appraisal and development of research techniques is vital work, methods are pliable and as effective as research contexts, approaches, overall goals and relationships between researcher and researched allow them to be (Kesby 2007). For example, as Mei-Po Kwan argues here, quantitative research techniques have been mistakenly linked with widely (though not entirely fairly) discredited positivist research approaches. Quantitiative methods for social geographies thus fell out of favour and fashion during the 1980s and 1990s, but are resurfacing in new forms, offering specific benefits in analysing the social geographical world and in identifying and challenging social injustices. As her chapter demonstrates, debates about 'quantitative' versus 'qualitative' have been superseded – partly as mixed techniques are now providing exciting new avenues for data gathering, representation and impact (see Elwood, forthcoming); partly through discussions about what Brown and Knopp (2008) call the productive tensions of colliding epistemologies; and partly because discussions about the wider implications of the politics and ethics of research are gathering pace.

Such issues, of course, are not specific to *social* geographies, but this is where debate and practice are amongst the most innovative and challenging at present. In particular, this is the case with the issue of the role of research in social change. This concern has a long-standing heritage, especially from two quarters: left radical geographies, which have questioned notions of relevance and informed geographers' efforts to engage as or with activists (Bunge, 1977; Chatterton et al., 2007; Fuller and Kitchin, 2004; and see Marston (Introduction to Section Four) in this volume), and feminist theory and method, which has informed and inspired qualitative practice and participatory research in geography, as in other disciplines (Limb and Dwyer, 2001; mrs kinpaisby, 2008; Women and Geography Study Group, 1997; and see Kindon, Chapter 23 in this volume). These two approaches to transformative knowledge production are currently prominent (in Anglo-American geography at least), and are closely related. Problematically, there has also been a persistent 'the feminist and the rest' dualism to these approaches that mirrors gendered schisms that appear elsewhere in the discipline. However, the gendering of research practices as loud/public/active/immediate/attention-seeking versus quiet/private/collaborative/long term/caring, is a too-easy characterisation that is starting to be transcended in the current wave of interest in social change (see Fuller and Askins, 2007; Kindon et al., 2007; Pratt, 1998).

Now, social geographers are connecting backwards and projecting forwards with greater and growing senses of consolidation and reflection, drawing on developments in other disciplines and returning insights about the roles of space, scale and social justice in research. The result has been a welcome growth in writing to draw on which develops and inspires on the subject of doing research. Some of the most exciting recent writers have been asked to comment on these developments here, to close this collection and give a sense of the future.

THE CHAPTERS: CONNECTING BACK, AND PROJECTING FORWARDS

The chapters in this section address five overlapping themes that are often encountered in the doing and thinking of social geographies. All involve longstanding concerns that have recently resurfaced and are being thought out and practised in quite different ways, prompted by the sharpening of concerns about social and spatial equality and justice in the early years of the twenty-first century. Set against this backdrop, Sara Kindon offers a critical overview of participatory social geographical research. Lynn Staeheli and Don Mitchell then address the question of research relevance, an issue that has re-emerged loudly in recent years, but is frequently ill-conceived. Kathryn Besio explores the ethics and politics of research interactions through a very personal account of her research. Mei-Po Kwan goes on to make a powerful argument for the role of quantification in social geographical research. Finally, connecting back around to issues of participation, Kath Browne embarks on a novel reappraisal of positionality, seeking to understand better how relational social and political positions affect research processes and outcomes.

The authors are engaged in very different research topics and approaches. They have been asked to provide some overview without standing back from their own research experiences. Rather than further summarise the 'doing' issues they explore here, in the rest of this introduction I pick up on some key 'knowing' issues from earlier sections of the book, in order to highlight the connections between what have often been practised – but can no longer be sustained – as two separate spheres of activity. Appropriately for a book on social geographies, these issues are fundamentally about the connections and relations that come with being human – to our respondents and participants, to each other, and to our wider local, national and global communities.

DIFFERENCE AND DIVERSITY

The issues raised in Section 1 of the book on 'Geographies of difference' are also pertinent to thinking about research practice. A key question is how we can research and understand diverse populations, when as academics, professional researchers and students most of us are privileged by some or all of our class, race, nationality and gender. The histories and cultures we are embedded in creep into all of our thinking and encounters, despite the efforts we make to resist or rework them. Feminist researchers are largely responsible for highlighting issues of cultural, economic, social and political difference between academics/research subjects and the profound effect that this has on the production and shape of knowledge (see Madge et al., 1997; Moss, 2001). Anglo-American work initially focused on the stark gendering of knowledge production that was most evident to Western feminist scholars (see Oakley, 1981; Stanley and Wise, 1983), but black feminists went on to theorise issues connected to race and indigeneity in research (hooks, 1984; Kobayashi, 1994) and, more recently, a host of other salient issues such as nationality, (dis)ability, class, age and sexuality have been subject of social geographers' concern (e.g. Binnie, 2007; Kitchin, 1999; and see Peake, and Pain and Hopkins, in this volume). As Linda Peake commented in

Section 1, our very knowledges about difference are products of particular times, cultures and spaces and this, too, is where social geographers have particular contributions to make to understanding research relations and politics.

The question of what to do with difference has been a thorny one. For many, reflexivity and positionality offer practical means to situate knowledge, embracing difference and writing ourselves into situate research accounts (England, 1994; Laurie et al., 1999; Rose, 1997). However the potential for over-reflexivity to reinscribe lines of power has been remarked on more recently (Kobayashi, 2003; Sultana, 2007; and Browne in this volume). Peter Hopkins (2008) is one of those who advocates positions of betweenness. Often, we are neither clearly insiders or outsiders in research, but negotiating points of similarity as well as difference can provide a more hopeful view. For Gerry Pratt et al. (2007), this is also a transformative position: there is productivity in working through difference itself, via discussion, developing trust and shared understandings, and collaborating in struggles for justice and autonomy.

Kath Browne's chapter here addresses these issues directly, and offers further suggestions for working with and through them. As the key academic researcher on a collaborative research project about marginalisation within a lesbian, gay, bisexual and transgendered community, she was relatively privileged. But positionalities are not fixed; rather, they shift radically across different spaces and times of the research process. Working through these complex and challenging issues, Kath Browne engages with reflections on the research encounters from her research partners, Leela Bakshi and Arthur Law. She suggests that we rethink positionalities in a way that involves neither cavalier abandonment of reflexivity nor self-aggrandising self-absorption, both of which can substantiate hegemonic (albeit slippery and mobile) power relations. Difference and the paradoxes and conflicts it raises can not be resolved, but they can be navigated through engaging the perspectives of others.

THE SOCIAL ECONOMIES OF ACADEMIC KNOWLEDGE PRODUCTION

Many of the concerns in Section 2 of this book, around the social/economic nexus, creeping neoliberalisation and the marketisation of social life, have direct bearing on discussions geographers have had recently about the 'economic' aspects of their research. Although a fraught and contested term (see Castree, 2006; Barnett in this volume), 'neoliberalism' has been applied heavily to critiques of Higher Education by left geographers, especially the effects of incorporating market values into research and the 'motivated shift away from public and collective values towards private and individualistic values' (Barnett in this volume). The neoliberal academy encourages certain types of practice and not others (Castree and Sparke, 2000; Fuller and Askins, 2007; mrs kinpaisby, 2008; Short, 2002; Sidaway, 1997). Vexing issues for doing social geographies include how and what research is funded; how its quality is assessed; the value and rewards that different activities and outputs are given; and to whom and on what terms geographers are accountable. And, following the argument made in Section Two, these issues may have seemed in the past to be beyond the remit of 'social' geographies, but they not only provide a context that has a fundamental effect on our research, they are indivisible from the particular forms of social life that academics pursue and perform.

As Barnett's chapter suggests, the theoretical thrust and general timbre of left academic critiques of neoliberalism tend to preclude people's capacity for resistance and change. But it can be seen very clearly in the doing of research: while many social geographers do occlude with hegemonic expectations, many others resist the pressures they entail.

As Sara Kindon has reflected elsewhere (for example, see her chapter in this volume), growing disenchantment with the political-economic structures of Higher Education explains the current growth of alternative modes of research and pedagogy:

> In a strange kind of way I'm grateful for the impositions [from neoliberalisation] that we've all suffered within our universities, because they've made us actually question what it means to be an academic ... I'm concerned that our current regimes seem to demand that as soon as we go into our offices suddenly all we do is work from our neck up ... I think what a lot of us are interested in doing is saying 'well actually, all of the stuff that happens outside of my office, is what I care about'. And so, how can I find a way of working that honours that, that respects me as a whole being, and that comes back to issues around relationality, what does it mean to be human? For me, it's about having relationships with places, with people, with ideas ... it recognises that we don't stop being members of our communities, various, diverse, geographically local or distant, once we close our office door. (mrs kinpaisby, 2008: 294–5)

WELL-BEING, CARE AND EMOTIONS

The issues of well-being, care and holism raised by the quote above connect directly with the concerns of Section 3 of the book, and they have further practical implications for the doing of research. These surround the relationships formed in social geographical research, which usually involve various sorts of first-hand encounters with other people. First, issues of caring for others and caring for ourselves in and through research have not routinely been considered or discussed, given that research is usually seen as part of 'work' rather than that separate emotional part of us that we locate in the 'domestic'. But the growing articulation of an 'ethic of care' as research focus (e.g. Smith, 2005), along with calls for more explicit consideration with moral, ethical and political choices in geographical research (Cloke, 2002; Pain, 2003), have led to a sense that relations of care are also embedded in processes of knowledge production (e.g. Adams and Moore, 2007; Lawson, 2007; Pratt, 2007; and see Oakley, 1981). In Kathryn Besio's chapter, this volume, she describes the networks of care relations she was enmeshed in during ethnographic research, and their complication by the wider political relations between her country of residence (the United States) and this part of Pakistan (these themes also emerge, in different ways, in the chapters by Browne and Kindon).

Secondly, with the explosion of interest in emotional geographies as a research focus (see Pain and Smith in this volume), we can no longer ignore how emotions inform the research process, or pretend that as researchers we are not emotionally involved with and affected (sometimes even sustained) by our research topics and subjects (see Bondi, 2005; Widdowfield, 2000). Intensive qualitative research often involves emotional labour to different degrees, though it is rarely discussed publicly; and especially where contact is sustained, this labour may be undertaken by both researchers and 'researched' (see Besio in this volume). Moreover, research can have a powerful impact on the emotional states of those outside the process, and social geographers have begun to mobilise this potential of representation. For example, one argument for using quantitative data and presenting them in novel visual ways is its capacity to affect those in power (see Kwan in this volume). Policy-makers are more likely to respond to findings and representations of research that make an emotional pull as well as a 'rational' argument. Further, emotions are not simply captured by or reflected in research processes; they drive, develop and change them. They are harnessed and mobilised in activist and participatory action research to drive social change outcomes (Cahill, 2004; Chatterton et al., 2007); in this context, research using media such as drama, art and video can connect directly with audiences and has 'affect with effect' (see Kindon in this volume).

SOCIAL JUSTICE AND ETHICS

Finally, as Section 4 of the book makes clear, social geographies have always been about seeking social justice as well as describing it: using research to document inequalities and injustices, identify pathways to social justice and, increasingly, having some role in effecting change. As Lynn Staeheli and Don Mitchell argue in their Chapter 24, 'relevant' research could in theory apply to anything, and does not automatically equate with any particular political sense. The term has, however, been colonised by geographers who claim to pursue goals of social justice through their research. Staeheli and Mitchell question what it really means, to what and whom we want to be relevant; they point out the impact of institutional constructions of relevance, and some of the dangers of pursuing research whose primary motivation is relevance.

As Jeff Popke outlined in Section 4, geography's 'ethical turn' is closely connected to the growing concern of social justice. Longstanding attention in social geography to the ethics and politics of particular bounded research encounters has broadened out to encompass the institutions and structures which contain and constrain research. In particular, more widespread formal institutional ethical review has caused increasing difficulties for those whose priorities in 'ethical' research (to protect and promote research participants' interests) conflict with the primary discourse of the former (to protect institutions from liability) (see Elwood, 2007; Martin, 2007). As Sara Kindon's chapter makes clear, participatory research is founded in a particular conception of ethics which is relational, as researchers' ethical frames are negotiated with those of participants (see also Cahill, 2007a). There are complex, multi-layered geographies to ethical encounters in research, too. Kathryn Besio's chapter demonstrates the co-existence of ethical and political issues at the scales of the personal, institutional and international, drawing out the ways in which these interplay and how, through small as well as larger interactions, the commanding patterns of socio-political relations that are involved might be resisted and rebuilt.

CONNECTING WORLDS AND THINKING THE FUTURE: MOVING BEYOND WESTERN EPISTEMOLOGIES?

I end this introduction on an overarching theme that connects the first and last offerings (from Sara Kindon and Kath Browne) in this Section: this theme takes us back to the connectedness of doing and knowing social geographies that was my starting point. Participation in research does not simply draw a wider circle of others into academic worlds; it also more firmly relates us, as social geographers, to the worlds that we are already a part of. Participatory geographies – the growing practice of working with research 'subjects' as collaborators in defining questions, selecting methods, analysing data and disseminating findings, with the goal of pursuing social justice and change directly – have seen an explosion of interest in recent years (see Pain, 2004; Kindon et al., 2007; mrs kinpaisby, 2008; and Kindon in this volume). In terms of doing research, it has been an energising but fraught term and set of practices: as Sara Kindon outlines here, 'participation' at once offers possibilities for radical change (of the world outside, but also within our institutions and ourselves) and dangers. It collapses the persistent relationship of practice (doing) and theory (knowing), as working alongside community researchers and opening up the academy to their perspectives and direction makes for more robust and surprising theory (see Cahill, 2007b; mrs kinpaisby, 2008). Indeed, as Reason and Bradbury (2006: 10) have outlined, participation is a theory of knowledge itself. Yet participation also implies partialness, and while it should entail a meeting in the middle, Western academics have had a hard time relinquishing the control that is so germane to our training and ways of being (see Cooke and Kothari, 2001). Sara Kindon's chapter is a critical and careful appraisal that highlights some of the most inspiring participatory work in social geography at present.

I also raised at the start of this introduction the often unspoken relationship between research approaches, methods and the shape of knowledge. Just how limited and partial this knowledge might be is highlighted perhaps most clearly in the emerging recognition of the fundamental challenges to Western research practice that indigenous methodologies and knowledges present (see Kobayashi and de Leeuw in this volume; Panelli, 2008; Shaw et al., 2006; Smith, 1999). In Anglo-American social geographies in particular, encounters with difference largely remain limited and bounded, and attempts to transcend our colonial past (Howitt and Jackson, 2004) among white scholars are few and far between. But the implications of indigenous perspectives and methodologies should cause a profound rethinking of the frameworks of understanding widely taken for granted (see Howitt and Suchet-Pearson, 2006; Louis, 2007; Panelli, 2008; Smith, 1999). The possibilities of collaborative cross-cultural research may work with but do not erase difference (see Kindon in this volume). Indigenous perspectives hold profound lessons for first-world social geographers about our enduring approach to research, about difference (as Peake in this volume also notes) and our culturally constrained view of the social geographies of the world (Panelli, 2008).

As the Maori scholar Linda Tuhiwai Smith explains:

> When [the word 'research'] mentioned in many indigenous contexts, it stirs up silence, it conjures up bad memories, it raises a smile that is knowing and distrustful. [...] The ways in which scientific research is implicated in the worst excesses of colonialism remains a powerful remembered history for many of the world's colonised peoples. It is a history that still offends the deepest sense of our humanity. (Smith, 1999: 1)

In her chapter here, as a Western researcher Kathryn Besio directly addresses some of the issues of trust and care that are implicated in this worldview, stating her own aim to 'decolonise and destabilise the binaries of colonialism, while remaining attentive to colonialism's violence and violent legacies, and to write and work against their perpetuation in the colonial present' (p. x). Otherwise, we have been 'stirring up silence' (Smith, 1999: 1): but do we know it, and how can we know it? Rather than thinking, as in previous decades, that doing research well means pursuing better techniques of data collection to break down silences, social geographers are now attending to more respectful research relations that involve decentring ourselves and Western social geographies. If social equality, social justice and social geographies are to be more than just subjects for our intellectual stimulation, then some of the key questions for the future include: What approaches can we pursue to understand and change social geographies? How do we interact, exchange with, and open up to knowledge systems other than our own? Can we learn not just to listen, but to move aside?

Then, what will social geographies look like and what will they do?

REFERENCES

Adams, M. and Moore, G. (2007) 'Participatory action research and researcher safety', in S. Kindon, R. Pain and M. Kesby (eds), *Connecting People, Participation and Place: Participatory Action Research Approaches and Methods*. London: Routledge. pp. 41–8.

Binnie, J. (2007) 'Sexuality, the erotic and geography: methodology, epistemology and pedagogy', in K. Browne, J. Lim and G. Brown (eds), *Geographies of Sexualities Theory, Practices and Politics.* Aldershot: Ashgate.

Bondi, L. (2005) 'The place of emotions in research: from partitioning emotion and reason to the emotional dynamics of research relationships', in J. Davidson, L. Bondi and

M. Smith (eds), *Emotional Geographies*. Aldershot: Ashgate.

Bunge, W. (1977) 'The first years of the Detroit Geographical Expedition: a personal report', in R. Peet (ed.) (1977), *Radical Geography*. London: Methuen. pp. 31–9.

Brown, M. and Knopp, L. (2008) 'Queering the map: the productive tensions of colliding epistemologies', *Annals of the Association of American Geographers*, 98: 1–19.

Cahill, C. (2004) `Defying gravity? raising consciousness through collective research', *Children's Geographies*, 2 (2): 273–86.

Cahill, C. (2007a) 'Repositioning ethical commitments: Participatory action research as a relational praxis of social change', *An International E-Journal for Critical Geographies*, 6 (3): 360–73.

Cahill, C. (2007b) 'The personal is political: developing new subjectivities in a participatory action research process', *Gender, Place, and Culture*, 14 (3): 267–92.

Castree, N. (2006) 'From neoliberalism to neoliberalisation: consolations, confusions, and necessary illusions', *Environment and Planning A*, 38: 1–6.

Castree, N. and Sparke, M. (2003) 'Professional geography and the corporatization of the University: experiences, evaluations, and engagements', *Antipode*, 32 (3): 222–9.

Chatterton, P. Routledge, P. and Fuller, D. (2007) 'Relating action to activism: theoretical and methodological reflections', in S. Kindon, R. Pain and M. Kesby (eds), *Connecting People, Participation and Place: Participatory Action Research Approaches and Methods*. London: Routledge. pp. 216–23.

Cloke, P. (2002) 'Deliver us from evil? Prospects for living ethically and acting politically in human geography', *Progress in Human Geography*, 26 (5): 587–604.

Cooke, B. and Kothari, U. (eds) (2001) *Participation: The New Tyranny?* London: Zed Books.

Cope, M. and Elwood, S. (eds), (forthcoming) *Qualitative GIS: A Mixed Methods Approach*. Sage Publications.

Crang, M. (2003) 'Qualitative methods: touchy, feely, look-see?', *Progress in Human Geography*, 27 (4): 494–504.

Elwood, S. (2007) 'Negotiating participatory ethics in the midst of institutional ethics', *ACME: an International E-Journal for Critical Geographies*. 6 (3): 329–38.

Elwood, S. (forthcoming) 'Mixed methods: thinking, doing, and asking in multiple ways', in D. DeLyser, S. Aitken, M. Crang, S. Herbert and L. McDowell (eds), *Handbook of Qualitative Methods in Human Geography*. London: Sage.

England, K. (1994) 'Getting personal: reflexivity, positionality, and feminist research', *Professional Geographer*. 46 (1): 80–9.

Flowerdew, R. and Martin, D. (2005) *Methods in Human Geography*. London: Pearson.

Fuller, D. and Askins, K. (2007) `The discomforting rise of "public geographies": a "public" conversation', *Antipode*, 39 (4): 579–601.

Fuller, D. and Kitchin, R. (eds) (2004) *Radical Theory, Critical Praxis: Making a Difference Beyond the Academy?* Praxis e-book series, available at http://www.praxis-epress.org/rtcp/fpages.pdf

hooks, b. (1984) *Feminist Theory: From Margin to Center*. Boston, MA: South End Press.

Hopkins, P. (2008) 'Women, men, positionalities and emotion: doing feminist geographies of religion', *ACME: An International E-Journal for Critical Geographies*.

Howitt, R. and Jackson, S. (2004) 'Some things do change: indigenous rights, geographers and geography in Australia', *Australian Geographer*, 29 (2): 155–73.

Howitt, R. and Suchet-Pearson, S. (2006) 'Changing country, telling stories: research ethics, methods and empowerment – working with Aboriginal women', in K. Lahiri-Dutt (ed.) *Fluid Bonds: Gender and Water*. Calcutta: Stree.

Kesby, M. (2007) 'Methodological insights on and from children's geographies', *Children's Geographies*, 5 (3): 193–205.

Kesby, M. and van Blerk, L. (2008) *Doing Children's Geographies*. London: Routledge.

Kindon, S. Pain, R. and Kesby, M. (2007) Participatory Action Research Approaches and Methods: Connecting People, Participation and Place. London: Routledge.

Kitchin, R. (1999) 'Morals and ethics in geographical studies of disability', in J.D. Proctor and D.M. Smith (ed), *Geography and Ethics: Journeys in a Moral Terrain*. London: Routledge. pp. 223–36.

Kobayashi, A. (1994) 'Colouring the field: gender, "race", and the politics of fieldwork', *Professional Geographer*, 46 (1): 73–80.

Kobayashi, A. (2003) 'Gender, place and culture ten years on: is self-reflexivity

enough?', *Gender, Place and Culture,* 10 (4): 345–49.
Laurie, N., Dwyer, C., Holloway, S. and Smith, F. (1999) *Geographies of New Femininities.* London: Longman.
Lawson, V. (2007) 'Geographies of care and responsibility', *Annals of the Association of American Geographers*, 97 (1): 1–11.
Limb, M. and Dwyer, C. (2001) *Qualitative Methodologies for Geographers: Issues and Debates*. London: Hodder Arnold.
Louis, R.P. (2007) 'Can you hear us now? Voices from the margin: using indigenous methodologies in geographic research', *Geographical Research,* 45: 130–9.
Madge, C., Raghuram, P., Skelton, T., Willis, K. and Williams, J. (1997) 'Methods and methodologies in feminist geographies: politics, practice and power', in Women and Geography Study Group (eds), *Feminist Geographies: Explorations in Diversity and Difference*. Harlow: Addison Wesley Longman.
Martin, D. (2007) 'Bureacratizing ethics: institutional review boards and participatory research', *ACME: An E-Journal for Critical Geographies*, 6 (3): 319–28.
Moss, P. (2001) *Feminist Geography in Practice: Research and Methods*. London: Wiley.
mrs kinpaisby (2008) 'Taking stock of participatory geographies: envisioning the communiversity', *Transactions of the Institute of British Geographers*, 33: 292–99.
Oakley, A. (1981) 'Interviewing women: a contradiction in terms', in H. Roberts (ed.), *Doing Feminist Research*. London: Routledge and Kegan Paul. pp. 30–61.
Pain, R. (2003) `Social geography: on action-orientated research', *Progress in Human Geography*, 27 (5): 677–85.
Pain, R. (2004) 'Social geography: participatory research', *Progress in Human Geography,* 28 (5): 652–63.
Pain, R. (2006) 'Social geography: seven deadly myths in policy research', *Progress in Human Geography,* 30: 250–59.
Panelli, R. (2008) 'Reorienting social geographies: encounters with indigenous and more-than-White/Anglo geographies', *Progress in Human Geography*. London: Sage.
Pink, S. (2006) *Doing Visual Ethnography*. London: Sage. London: Sage.
Pratt, G. (1998) `Comments on activism, in Lost and found in the posts: addressing critical human geography', *Environment and Planning D: Society and Space*, 16 (3): 264–5.
Pratt, G. in collaboration with the Philippine Women Centre of B.C. and Ugnayan ng Kabataang Pilipino sa Canada/Filipino-Canadian Youth Alliance (2007) Working with Migrant Communities: Collaborating with the Kalayaan Centre in Vancouver, Canada, in S. Kindon, R. Pain, and M. Kesby, (eds), *Participatory Action Research Approaches and Methods: Connecting People, Participation and Place*. London: Routledge.
Reason, P. and Bradbury, H. (2006) *The Handbook of Action Research*. London: Sage.
Rose, G. (1997) 'Situating knowledges; positionality, reflexivities and other tactics', *Progress in Human Geography,* 21: 305–20.
Shaw, W.S., Herman, R.D.K., Dobbs, G.R. (2006) 'Encountering indigeneity: re-imagining and decolonizing geography', *Geografiska Annaler.* 88B: 267–76.
Short, J.R. (2002) 'The disturbing case of the concentration of power in human geography', *Area*, 34 (3): 323–4.
Sidaway, J.D. (1997) 'The production of British geography', *Transactions of the Institute of British Geographers*, 22: 488–504.
Smith, L.T. (1999) *Decolonizing Methodologies: Research and Indigenous Peoples.* London: Zed Books.
Smith, S.J. (2005) 'States, markets and an ethic of care', *Political Geography,* 24 (1): 1–20.
Stanley, L. and Wise, S. (1983) *Breaking Out: Feminist Consciousness and Feminist Research*. London: Routledge, Kegan and Paul.
Sultana, F. (2007) 'Reflexivity, positionality and participatory ethics: negotiating fieldwork dilemmas in international research', *ACME: an E-Journal for Critical Geographies,* 6 (3): 374–85.
Widdowfield, R. (2000) 'The place of emotions in academic research', *Area*, 32 (2): 199–208.
Women and Geography Study Group (1997) *Feminist Geographies: Explorations in Diversity and Difference*. Harlow: Addison Wesley Longman.

23

Participation

Sara Kindon

INTRODUCTION

As I write, participation is both in vogue and in crisis. The interest in participation and use of participatory approaches within social geography has been growing enthusiastically (Kindon et al., 2007; Pain and Kindon, 2007; Pain, 2004). This enthusiasm has been spurred on by academics concerned with the crisis of representation, questions about the 'relevance' of Geography and growing unease about the corporatisation of higher education under neoliberalism (Castree and Sparke, 2000; Staeheli and Mitchell, 2005 and in this volume). It has also been a response to feminist, indigenous and community level critiques arguing for greater democratisation of the research process, and calls to widen participation of non-mainstream epistemes within the academy (Kuokkanen, 2004; Rose, 1993; Tuhiwai-Smith, 1999). The use of participation in research can also be connected to various shifts in 'best teaching practice' that have emphasised community research-based teaching (see Kindon and Elwood, forthcoming, for a wider discussion; Savin-Baden and Wimpenny, 2007). And lastly, changes in priorities for research funding have stressed the importance of participation for the formation of collaborative partnerships and the production of policy and end-user driven research (Cottrell and Parpart, 2006; Taylor and Fransman, 2003).

At the same time, since the late 1990s, concern has been mounting about how the newfound status of participation may effectively mask business as usual; strengthening hierarchical and elite forms of knowledge production rather than achieving its aim of opening them up to wider community priorities and accountability. At the centre of ongoing tensions about participation is the concern that it has been de-radicalised through its incorporation into mainstream research and practice, and its ascendance to hegemonic status within policy circles. Moreover, there is disquiet about how the particular techniques often used within participatory work may actually produce the particular forms of knowledge desired by those in control of their use (Sanderson and Kindon, 2004), and result in a kind of tyranny frequently replicating or worsening the very inequalities they sought to challenge (Cooke and Kothari, 2001).

There have been various moves to recuperate the benefits of participation and to acknowledge that participation – as a practice of power – can have both negative and positive effects (see, for example, Hickey and Mohan, 2004; Kesby, 2007a). How and where participation is performed, and by whom with what effects, constitute important geographies worthy of consideration (Pain and Kindon, 2007). Further, in an effort to reclaim participation, geographer Giles Mohan (2001) and others (see, for example, Cameron and Gibson, 2005; Chatterton et al., 2007; Kapoor, 2005; Kindon et al., 2007) propose a need to re-engage Participatory Action Research (PAR). PAR is a radical, yet still marginal approach to research, which has conscientisation and positive change at its core (Fals-Borda, 2006a). It goes far beyond the application of participatory techniques (Kesby et al., 2005).

So what exactly is participation and why has it generated so much interest within social geography? If we work with a simple definition of participation as ways of:

> effectively and ethically engaging people in processes, structures, spaces, and decisions that affect their lives, and working with them to achieve equitable and sustainable outcomes on their own terms

then, there is an immediate connection with social geography's focus on 'the recognition and critique of social difference and the power relations that this involves' (Panelli, 2004: xiii). Participation offers a vehicle for not just studying difference, power and inequality, but for contesting normal modes of academic enquiry and involving us – in Ghandi's famous words – in being the change we wish to see (Chatterton et al., 2007).

Participation therefore offers exciting and promising means through which social geographers can deepen understandings of the social relations informing and being constituted by spatial difference, and simultaneously contribute to social action aimed at increasing social justice and well-being (see Box 23.1).

In this chapter, I critically appraise participation's relationship to social geography. In what follows, I review the recent rise and 'fall' of participation – particularly in majority world 'development' contexts – and some of their implications for the practice of participation within academic research. I then explore various ways in which participation (in the form of PAR) and social geography may inform, enrich and repoliticise each other. In a sense, I aim to chart a course for social

Box 23.1 The value/use of participatory research and development

Participation ideally seeks to facilitate 'people in the processes of learning about their needs and opportunities, and in the *action* required to address them' (emphasis in the original) (*pla notes*, 2003: i).

Specifically, it seeks to:

a) make research and data collection more people-centred and democratic through negotiation, reciprocity and the development of research capacity and common goals;
b) lessen hierarchies between researchers/facilitators and participants by fostering collaborative and emotional relationships to occur;
c) provide accurate and reliable data using ethical and inclusive approaches (as opposed to 'traditional' extractive approaches to social science and anthropological research);
d) develop processes through which people can more easily and equitably influence the agenda and outcomes of social research and development (Beazley and Ennew, 2006); and
e) facilitate the expression and negotiation of social difference (between researchers/facilitators and participants, between and among participants, and between participants and other members of society or institutions).

This way of working usually takes place through the use of innovative visual and projective methods, and lots of talking! The benefits of such an approach include effecting meaningful change at a rate and scale that those involved can support through:

- the retrieval and sharing of social histories and personal stories normally absent from mainstream media and archives;
- the challenging of stereotypes (of identity and of places); and
- the generation of possibilities for alternative or self-representation (by increasing people's narrative authority);
- the use of these alternative representations to mobilize for change and a redistribution of resources.

geography's future engagements with and desire for making a difference to the workings of power/knowledge, the negotiation of difference, and the transformation of inequalities at a range of scales.

PARTICIPATION'S RISE

> The concept of participation points [...] both to new forms of engagement with [...] projects and to new benefits from such projects (Jupp, 2007: 2832–3).

Participation in research and development projects, versus participatory research and development

Within the field of international development, where the issue of participation first rose to prominence, much confusion exists about what the term means, how it is best practised and whether it is a means towards an end, or should be an end in itself (Chambers, 1994c; Williams, 2004b). In a helpful review, Rosemary McGee (2002) differentiates between *participation in* development and *participatory* development. In simple terms, these can be viewed as 'top-down' versus 'ground-up' participation. In both participation in development and participatory development, participation may be sporadic, piecemeal and reinforce social hierarchies. Equally, and perhaps somewhat paradoxically, participation may promote new forms of social organisation, democratise decision-making and resource allocation, and mobilise people across personal differences and spatial scales.

People's *participation in* government and donor agency development plans and schemes is not new. There are many examples of large-scale schemes within the colonial era associated with land-reform, education and taxation for example, which involved institutionalised processes of participation aimed at mobilising people's labour and resources to achieve the political aims of ruling elites (Chambers, 2005). Currently, governments all over the world are seeking greater participation of citizens, partly out of a desire to deliver development more efficiently, and partly in response to calls from civil society for greater accountability and transparency (Gaventa, 2004). Processes such as participatory appraisal, stakeholder analysis and community forums are a common feature of attempts by local and regional government to engage their 'clients' and 'end-users' in policy and planning decisions that will affect their lives, and are often a requirement of international aid funding regimes. This form of participation is also most evident within programmes administered by the World Bank and Food and Agriculture Organisation of the United Nations, as well as other major donor organisations.

More radical ideas about participation as *participatory development* have been in circulation since the 1960s, arising out of ground-up political and social movements in both majority and minority worlds associated with feminism, environmentalism, anti-US imperialism, anti-racism, and post-colonialism. Within these more radical contexts, participation has been about people's conscious efforts to seek solutions to their own problems in locally appropriate ways (Miller, 2008, pers. comm.). Increasingly, through non-governmental organisations and alliances with academic researchers, participation is closely aligned with advocacy and human rights agendas seeking social well-being and economic justice. Here processes tend to be more organic, even haphazard. They rely on dialogue, alliance-building and other forms of solidarity, and activist-oriented change (Chatterton et al., 2007). It is this understanding of participation that I have sought to work with in my own practice as a social geographer since 1990, growing out of and informing my collaborative research in Costa Rica (see Box 23.2), Indonesia (see Box 23.3) and Aotearoa New Zealand (see Box 23.6).

By the early 1980s, participatory development involved a number of approaches developed by some Indian and African non-governmental organisations. Drawing on applied anthropology, agricultural extension and Participatory Action Research, approaches such as Rapid/Relaxed Rural Appraisal (RRA), then Participatory Rural Appraisal (PRA) and Participatory Urban Appraisal (PUA) were developed. These approaches – under their combined acronym PLA (Participatory Learning and Action) – now commonly involve a sequence of applied research techniques such as interviewing, participatory mapping, participatory diagramming, ranking and scoring chosen from a wide 'tool-kit' (see, for example, Kumar, 2002). These techniques are used to explore community development issues with participants so that they can develop a plan of action to address them. The techniques emphasise shared knowledge, shared learning, and flexible yet structured collaborative analysis (*pla notes,* 2003) and, in theory, are adapted to the specific geographical and cultural contexts in which they are being used.

Within social geography research, these participatory techniques have been used in both minority and majority worlds to support groups traditionally marginalised by: disability (Chouinard, 2000; Kitchin, 2001), class (Fuller et al., 2003), violence (Moser and McIlwaine, 1999), gender and sexuality (Cieri, 2003; Kesby, 2000a), age and ethnicity (Cahill, 2004; Cahill et al., 2004), housing status (Pain and Francis, 2003) and indigeneity (Kindon, 2003; Smith, 2003). And, as Mike Kesby (2000b: 432) has argued, the wider adoption of participatory techniques in research is highly appropriate because of their scientific rigour and ability to 'facilitate *in practice* participants' own deconstruction/ reconstruction of the categories and meanings that structure their lives' (emphasis in original).

In many respects, the use of these techniques has furthered the goals of social geography by providing new and exciting ways to build on the work of geographers such as Richard Peet (1969, 1977) and David Harvey (1972, 1973, 1974). Forty years ago, they argued for geographers to draw on radical theories and politics rooted in anarchism, Marxism, and other critical movements to help solve social problems rather than just studying them (see also Berry, 1972; White, 1972; and see Marston in this volume).

In addition, social geographers have begun to draw on and experiment with the long tradition of Participatory Action Research (PAR) because, as Mike Kesby, Rachel Pain and I caution elsewhere (Kesby et al., 2005), the adoption of *participatory techniques* does not in itself constitute *participatory research.* Increasingly, participatory techniques are added into research which otherwise constitutes 'business as usual'. Yet, without the participatory epistemology offered by PAR, they are unlikely to meet social geography's interests in increasing social well-being and social justice, and may actively further the depoliticisation of participation mentioned previously.

Participatory (Action) Research

Participatory Action Research (PAR) aims to be valuable to, and result in positive change for, those involved (Cameron and Gibson, 2005; Cooke, 2001; Pratt, 2000). Put simply, it involves academic researchers in research, education and socio-political action with members of community groups as co-researchers and decision makers in their own right (Hall, 1981; McTaggart, 1997; Thomas-Slayter, 1995). This is because participatory action researchers believe people who have been systemically excluded, oppressed or marginalised have particular and invaluable insights and understandings about unjust social arrangements (Fine, 2008). It is an approach which values the process as much as the product, so that the 'success' of PAR rests not only on the quality of information generated, but also on the extent to which skills, knowledge and participants' capacities are developed (Cornwall and Jewkes, 1995; Kesby et al., 2005; Maguire, 1997). In short, PAR is not conducted *on* a group, but *with them* to achieve change that *they* desire (Pratt, 2000).

There are many variants of PAR. They have evolved in different places at different times since the 1940s, and they all share an emphasis on dialogue, collaborative knowledge production and iterative cycles of action and reflection (Kindon, 2005; Parkes and Panelli, 2001). There are also many interpretations of PAR's origins and history (Brydon-Miller, 2001; Brydon-Miller et al., 2003; Brydon-Miller et al., 2004; Fals-Borda, 2006a, 2006b; Hall, 2005; Kindon et al., 2007; McTaggart, 1997; Park et al., 1993). And, at the risk of over-simplifying here, it seems that there are two key strands in the development of PAR, which have become woven together in different ways over time.

First, Action Research, which was coined by Kurt Lewin in the post-war USA (Lewin, 1946) to describe a research process in which 'theory would be developed and tested by practical interventions and action; [where] there would be consistency between project means and desired ends; and that ends and means [would be] grounded in guidelines established by the host community' (Stull and Schensul, 1987, cited in Fox, 2003: 88). Lewin argued that the best way to know about something was to try and change it. Thus, action research involves the systematic collection and analysis of information on a specific topic for the purposes of social change and action (Barnsley and Ellis, 1992). It may not necessarily be participatory in terms of involving marginalised others, and is frequently used as a form of practitioner-based research to inform and improve professional practice. Its orientation reflects its evolution within a positivistic research paradigm, and it is sometimes viewed as a scientific method (Shani and Basuray, 1988 cited in Gatenby and Humphries, 1996).

Second, ten to twenty years later in the majority world, a number of approaches emerged which came to be known loosely as Participatory Research. These approaches sought to find alternatives to the ongoing legacies of colonisation, the post-war imperialism of the USA, and the newly emerging international division of labour associated with export-oriented production, the anti-Vietnam war protest, and the failures of development and scientific academic research (Miller, pers comm).

In Brazil, educator Paulo Freire (1972) worked with poor and marginalised groups to facilitate a process of conscientisation (conscientisacao) about the forces informing their lives, which could inform political action for change (Reason, 1994 in Gatenby and Humphries, 2000).[1] A similar process was founded in Colombia with sociologist Orlando Fals-Borda, which sought to decolonise and democratise research and orient it towards locally relevant emancipatory action and social change (Lykes, 2001). In Tanzania, Canadian adult educators and Tanzanian development professionals developed what they called 'participatory research' processes in their efforts to integrate the knowledge and expertise of community members into development projects (Hall, 2005). In India, scholars like Rajesh Tandon developed a similar approach he called 'Community-based Research' (Hall, 1997; see also Brown and Tandon, 1983). Within the USA, Sol Tax and William Foote Whyte experimented with 'action anthropology', which enabled local people in the USA to voice their concerns without the influence or mediation of a so-called outside expert (Grillo, 2002). And, John Gaventa, Peter Park and others worked closely with impoverished communities on aspects of land tenure in Appalachia through the Highlander Research Center (Park et al., 1993).

Participatory research in its various forms demonstrated a commitment to liberationist movements (Reason, 1994), which assumed that participants 'can [...] learn and theorise from concrete experiences in their everyday lives [and are] autonomous, responsible agents who participate actively in making their own histories and conditions of life' (Gatenby and Humphries, 1996: 79). It therefore reflected more humanistic and critical epistemological orientations than action research. Further, within the USA, Whyte (1991) argued that participatory research, unlike action research, did not have to result in any external action towards change. For others, the emphasis has been most definitely upon change through the active involvement of participants in collective and democratic investigation and analysis (Participatory Research Network 1982 in Gatenby and Humphries, 1996). Consequently, there has been something of a debate about the place of 'action' within participatory research, and Orlando Fals-Borda (2006a) has argued that Participatory (Action) Research is perhaps a more appropriate label which can signify that Participatory Research is already inherently action-oriented through its central commitment to dialogue and conscientisation.

While these subtle differences in terminology and orientation persist, action and participatory research approaches tend to inform one another and are often blurred within the umbrella term Participatory Action Research (Kindon et al., 2007). Through their dialogic processes and other discursive practices, these discourses of participation aim to enable people to critically reflect on their lives and then work towards change on their own terms.

Participation and social geography

Given that there is wide alliance amongst social geographers with many of the aspects outlined in Box 23.1, it is somewhat surprising that geographers have been slow to pick up on the methodological developments discussed above (Breitbart, 2003; Kindon, 2003; Kindon et al., 2007; Pain, 2004; Pain and Kindon, 2007). Only in the last ten years have a more visible body of geographers begun to use and adapt participatory approaches and methods within their work (see disciplinary progress reports by Pain, 2003, 2004, 2006).[2] So noticeable has this trend been that Duncan Fuller and Rob Kitchin (2004) suggested we are witnessing a 'participatory turn' in human geography, which seeks in part to rematerialise geography after the impact of the earlier cultural turn (Naylor et al., 2000).

In particular, social geographers working with young people and children have responded enthusiastically to calls to make research more inclusive and useful (Smith, 2004) and have seen the benefits that participatory techniques can bring to the immediacy and creative play required when working with children (Aitken, 2001; see also Van Blerk and Kesby, 2008). Working through schools, youth groups, community centres, as well as out on the streets, geographers have engaged participatory approaches and techniques to explore young people's relationships to, and experiences of, particular spaces, services and communities. Most energy has focused on children and young people's engagements with urban spaces, particularly in the minority world (for example, Cahill, 2004; Cahill et al., 2004; Cahill, 2007c; Cope, forthcoming; Cope and Halfhill, 2003; Hart, 1997; Fuller et al., 2003; Herman and Mattingley, 1999; Leavitt et al., 1998; Nairn et al., 2003; Young, 2003; Young and Barrett, 2001). However, rural spaces and children's experiences of rurality have also received attention (Leyshon, 2002; McCormack, 2000; Matthews et al., 2000; Nairn et al., 2003; Panelli et al., 2007; Punch, 2001).

For many social geographers, a motivation for using participatory approaches has been to address current inequalities and to effect positive change within children's and young people's lives. As a result, their work has focused on young people's participation in, or exclusion from, social services (Matthews, 1995; Pain, 2003), their experiences and negotiation of crime and violence (Gaskell, 2002; McIntyre, 2003; Pain, 2003; Pain and Francis, 2003), their experiences of economic change (Cahill, 2007c) and adult-organised groups (Juckes Maxey, 2004).

Within these approaches, a range of participatory techniques has been adapted to enable children and young people to tell their own stories and represent their experiences as they 'see' them. In particular, drawing (Pain et al., 2008; Young and Barrett, 2001), mapping

(Young and Barrett, 2001, Pain 2003), craft (Cope, forthcoming), photography (Aitken and Wingate, 1993; McIntyre, 2000; Young and Barrett, 2001) and video (Matthews et al., 2000) have been used to stimulate interest and participation, as well as to effect change. Frequently, the geographers engaged in these processes comment upon the ability of these techniques to 'reveal' the multiple childhoods that exist in any locale, and the implications that these have if the planning and provision of services are to be effective and equitable. They have also highlighted the agency of children and young people in negotiating their life-worlds and adult-imposed structures, as well as producing meaning from their own lived experiences.

To date, most of this work has focused on documenting and reflecting upon the role that participatory methods play in destabilising hierarchies in research relationships. While children may participate in data generation in collaborative and creative ways, they are not always involved in designing the research, choosing what methods to use, or in the analysis, dissemination and actions that might result from the research (Kesby, 2007b). As such, much of this work reflects what I might call children's 'participation in research' rather than 'participatory research with, by and for children' (drawing on the earlier discussion from McGee, 2002 about development). Such work is valuable, but may not result in the longer-term or deeper changes that might be needed if children's or young people's voices, power and influence are to be increased in decisions that intimately affect their lives.[3]

Participatory approaches have also been popular with feminist social geographers. The work of Patricia Maguire (1987) and Maria Mies (1983) raised questions about the masculinist bias of much participatory research, as well as recognition of the need for greater attention to the gendered nature of research processes and outcomes. These ideas have reverberated within feminist geography (Hanson and Monk, 1982; Rose, 1993). Working in majority world contexts, feminist geographers have employed participatory approaches as a means of valuing gendered forms of knowledge and experience, and of supporting more gender-informed development interventions. Their work has involved attention to: agricultural practices and ecological justice (Rocheleau, 1991, 1994, 1995; Rocheleau and Ross, 1995; Rocheleau and Edmunds, 1997); sustainable development planning (Kindon, 1993, 1998, and see Box 23.3; Momsen, 2003); the negotiation of urban violence (Moser and McIlwaine, 2001); responses to domestic violence and reproductive health (Peake, 2000); livelihood strategies of rainforest settlers (Townsend et al., 1995); sexual health and the impacts of HIV/AIDS (Kesby, 2000); popular theatre as a community development strategy (Farrow, 1995); environmental education programmes (Shaw, 1995); and alternative conceptions and practices of economic development (Robinson et al. ????).

Through this work, feminist geographers have highlighted the range and diversity of women's agency within unequal gendered relations at different scales, and raised questions about the current theorisation of and practices associated with international development and economic change. For example, in my own work with a women's cooperative in Costa Rica in 1990, my colleague and I used a feminist participatory research approach to inform locally appropriate change and to speak back to unrealistic conceptions of women, in women in development theory and policy (Box 23.2).

Important work has also been carried out with women and communities in the minority world contending with rapid social and economic change (Gibson-Graham, 1994; Cameron and Gibson, 2005; Reed, 2000), facing adjustment to a new culture as a result of migration (Pratt, 1998; Pratt et al., 2007; Kobayashi, 2002; Mountz et al., 2008), and changing labour practices and rights (Moss, 1995). Jan Monk and colleagues (Monk et al., 2003) have also bridged majority and minority worlds through a participatory project involving university academics, women's

Box 23.2 Feminist participatory research in Costa Rica

For four months in early 1990, Carol Odell and I lived and worked with the Women's Association of Acosta in central Costa Rica. A national women's animator who knew the group facilitated our entry and relationship with the President and Vice-President because she wished to support their efforts in providing employment for women in the production of jam and fruit-drinks.

Through our work we adopted Maria Mies' (1983) approach of conscious partiality (rather than objective neutrality), a commitment to supporting an ongoing movement, and a process of research as conscientization (also see Friere, 1972). Practically, this meant living and working with the women who asked us to carry out a survey of all 52 members, which could act as a planning tool and help them to establish more income-generating enterprises. We worked with the 40 or so unemployed members to develop key ideas to inform the interview-survey before visiting every member to apply it. We then presented and checked findings through a participatory workshop to which all members were invited and produced a report in cartoon-format that could be read by those women with low literacy. We also brought the national women's animator back to run capacity building workshops designed to support their ongoing efforts.

For the unemployed members in the organization, our approach worked well. It provided a vehicle for their histories with the association, their concerns, needs, and their aspirations. For those already in positions of power within the organization, however, it was a different story. Our approach, while endorsed and supported, produced an analysis that was very threatening to them because it raised critical questions about power relations in the organization. We had to negotiate our position very carefully before leaving! (Kindon and Cupples, 2003) The findings also called into question common assumptions at the time about women's roles in development and the assumption that women would 'naturally' work cooperatively together.

and non-governmental organisations in the USA and Mexico.

In addition to the rising interest in participatory approaches within social geography, there has also been some interest in the effectiveness of arts and participatory communication initiatives for supporting social justice objectives. Participatory communication involves situations where people are not just recipients and consumers of messages, but also creators and transmitters of their own messages to one another (Mda, 1993). With the advancement of communication technologies, media liberalisation and the proliferation of various forms of technologies (newspapers, community radio and TV, popular theatre, public or community art, small format video, disposable cameras, the Internet, ICTs and so forth) over the last thirty years, attention has focused also on how arts and communications technologies can facilitate people's participation in decisions and plans affecting their lives (Boeren, 1994; White et al., 1994).

For example, social geographers have explored the effects of popular theatre (Pratt and Kirby, 2003; Shaw, 1995), community art (Rose, 1997b) in community development and activist initiatives. Increasingly geographers employing these techniques as part of their own research agendas (see Askins and Pain, 2008; Nelson, 2007; Tolia-Kelly, 2007 for public art; Cieri and McCauley, 2007; Herman and Mattingley, 1999; Mattingley, 2001 for popular theatre; Aitken and Wingate, 1993; Krieg and Roberts, 2007; Leavitt et al., 1998; Leyshon, 2002; McIntyre, 2000; Young and Barrett, 2001 for (auto)photography). Elsewhere, social geographers have adapted Geographic Information Systems (GIS) technologies to be more participatory in both majority and minority world contexts (Elwood, 2004; Stocks, 2003; Williams and Dunn, 2003) and in some cases GIS have been combined with other tools from arts and popular culture to create multi-layered cognitive maps reflecting the experiences of usually marginalised groups (see Cieri, 2003).

Video is also increasingly used to raise awareness of social difference or inequality, or to challenge social injustice: Hester Parr (2007) worked with users of mental health services in Scotland to produce a video for public education and advocacy, and Caitlin Cahill (Cahill, 2008) has been facilitating a participatory research video documentary project with young people from Salt Lake City in the USA on undocumented students' experiences of racism at high school. Kaye Haw

(Haw, 2008) in the United Kingdom has explored how participatory video can provide an alternative voice on youth risk and resilience associated with crime. In the Caribbean, Pamela Richardson (2008) has been using participatory video to understand more about sugar and agribusiness networks, and in Uganda Louise Waite and Cath Conn (Waite and Conn, 2008) have been using PV in their work with young women around issues of sexual health. In Western Australia, Guy Singleton and his colleagues from the Ngalia Aboriginal people are exploring the role of PV and other ICT to develop effective cultural heritage management strategies to protect their sacred places/sites and develop sustainable livelihood options for their community (Singleton, pers. comm. 2007). And my own work with Geoff Hume-Cook and members of Te Iwi o Ngaati Hauiti has explored aspects of indigenous self-representation and community-building (Hume-Cook et al., 2007; Kindon, 2000, 2003, 2008a, 2008b; Kindon and Latham, 2002; Kindon et al., 2005 – see also Box 23.6).

While the fascination with and creative deployment of participatory approaches and techniques continues, geographers have begun to think more broadly about the implications of doing participation geographically (Cahill, 2007d; Kesby, 2005, 2007a; Kindon and Pain, 2006). They are grappling with the unique contributions that geography might make to theorising participatory practice (see Cahill, 2007a; the special issue edited by Pain and Kindon, 2007; Mohan, 2007), and how a commitment to a participatory epistemology may inform all our professional practices and not be confined to our field research (for example, see Kindon, 2008a; mrs kinpaisby, 2008). I return to some of these ideas in Sections IV and V of this chapter.

Summary

By creating spaces for alternative values, knowledges and relationships, participation and its various techniques challenge the traditional values of development, media and academic research practices (Bery, 2003). They involve a commitment to breaking down hierarchical practices of elite knowledge producers through collaboration at every stage of the research process, including dissemination and action. In particular, they enable a shift from an insistence on quantifiable, objective knowledge as a means of accessing 'the truth', to a more subtle and nuanced engagement with shifting subjectivities and multiple truths (Guidi, 2003). This engagement, its advocates hope, will enable greater social justice outcomes for those involved. Hence, the recent growing interest in participatory research and methods within social geography.

PARTICIPATION'S 'FALL': UNAVOIDABLE QUESTIONS OF POWER

Participation is also not without its critics.

> This is the trouble with participation – it can be passive, consultative, bought, interactive or mobilising. It depends on what we want from a situation. Most professional agencies would probably like to keep things at the consultative ends of the spectrum, as it means controlling power. (Pretty, 2003: 171)

Participation as the new tyranny

The first main criticism of participation concerns its representation as a benevolent process full of liberatory potential, capable of reversing biases in development and research practice (see, for example, Chambers, 1983, 1994a). With greater time and reflection, however, it has become clear that despite the best of intentions the dominant way in which participation is conceived and practised still configures power and value systems in ways that end up being exclusionary (Guijt and Shah, 1998; Kapoor, 2002; Mosse, 1994).

The second main criticism is that while current forms of participation frequently claim to be radical, they continue to exemplify a liberal populist approach which favours local and singular projects and frequently fails to address wider inequalities or the negative impacts of macroeconomic structures (Mohan and Stokke, 2000). In both development and research contexts, it has proven challenging to situate and connect locally specific projects within multi-sited, networked approaches to enable local agency to be adequately supported by wider structural changes (Greenwood, 2007).

For some development practitioners like Irene Guijt (2003: 85), there is a concern that power as a concept and area of theoretical understanding does not inform participatory practice enough 'to enable the meaningful discussion of discrimination, oppression and difference'. For others, most notably development studies academics engaging Foucauldian critiques, participation operates as a new form of tyranny subjecting people to particular disciplinary forces – facilitation, participatory and visual methods and group analysis in public spaces – often reproducing the very power relations it was supposed to subvert (Cooke and Kothari, 2001). These tyrannies are worth further discussion here given social geographers' interest in epistemology and methodology, and our tendency to carry out research with groups of people (Panelli, 2004).

Facilitators

The first tyranny concerns the role of facilitators. Participatory development and participatory research emphasise the need for facilitator/researchers to relinquish their power and control by adopting attitudes and behaviours such as transparency, honesty, humility, respect and patience (Kapoor, 2005). These, it is thought, will enable them to 'step out of their "expert" role and become co-learners in projects' (White, 2003: 45), 'hand over the stick' to collaborators (Chambers, 1994b: 1253, 1256), and promote participants to carry out their own research, analysis and action (Freire, 1972; Pretty et al., 1995, Wadsworth, 2001).

Yet, facilitators/researchers manage almost every part of a participatory process, from calling the initial meeting to facilitating the final action. Their apparent desire to be neutral and benevolent may be nothing more than a morally acceptable smokescreen, 'hiding' their desire and ability to exert influence and control (Kapoor, 2005). Further, facilitation's emphasis upon building rapport as a basis for collaborative analysis does not necessarily ensure that understanding occurs. Rather it may represent a form of manipulation (some have called it 'facipulation') aimed at making 'the researcher feel good' (Lyons, 2000: 5). Such complicity may be compounded by the rhetoric of equality and empowerment inherent within participatory research and development (Cornwall and Brock, 2005). This rhetoric overlooks the fact that subjects/participants frequently have their own understandings of what research or development involves, and what performances or appropriate subject positions they should adopt to secure benefits (Henkel and Stirrat, 2001; Lyons, 2000).

A challenging and potentially risky situation therefore exists (White, 2003). As development practitioner Jules Pretty observes (2003: 171), 'Making participation really work means giving up personal and institutional power, and we all know that this is very difficult indeed'. How much power or control to exert ultimately depends upon the particular context within which participatory research or development is taking place (Sense, 2006). Sometimes, particularly where co-researchers' or participants' time and resources are limited, it may be appropriate for a facilitator/researcher to initiate, mobilise and educate (Maguire, 1993; Park et al., 1993; Smith et al., 1997). At others, it may be vital that co-researchers and participants assume these roles. Such a state of affairs connects us to ideas about subjectivity, reflexivity, positionality and ethics prevalent in social geography – aspects I return to in Section IV.

Methods

Within the current budgetary and time constraints of many research and development projects, participatory practice tends to privilege the reasonably 'quick and dirty' use of techniques such as participatory mapping, diagramming and ranking for data collection (Leurs, 1996). In many ways, such privileging is understandable as these techniques/methods are very effective at engaging people on their own terms and can result in effective short-term action. Unfortunately, they are frequently applied in ways that subject participants to formulaic sequences rather than engage them in longer-term dialogue, negotiation and collaborative action. This standardisation of what was originally conceived to be diverse and locally constituted practices means that while participation is becoming increasingly popular, not all researchers or development facilitators are doing it well or effectively (Kaul Shah, 2003; Parnwell, 2003). In many instances, hierarchies between researcher/researched are reinforced and standard sequences of methods become 'tyrannically' applied (Cooke and Kothari, 2001; Parkes and Panelli, 2001; Wadsworth, 1998),

The popularity of participatory techniques and methods and the desire to create, invent and discuss innovative approaches has also resulted in what Cooke and Kothari (2001) have called 'methodological fetishism'. This process has tended to exclude or devalue other complementary (more traditional) social research methods – such as participant observation and ethnography – and overlook wider epistemological issues associated with power and the construction of knowledge.

For example, development anthropologist David Mosse (1994) reflected on what he perceived to be participation's failure to address gender inequalities in projects in India. There he was concerned because project staff didn't carry out deeper social analyses of the gendered power relations and structures informing their participatory work and this limited the possibilities for the gender-equitable participation and outcomes they were ultimately seeking. I came to a similar conclusion in my own work in Bali, Indonesia as I discuss in Box 23.3.

Many others have since argued for the need to complement participatory techniques with more in-depth social (and where appropriate economic or ecological) research (Guijt and Cornwall, 1995; Guijt and Shah, 1998; Kesby, 2000; Lennie, 1999). This growing awareness is good news for social geographers interested in participation. Their usually high awareness of epistemology and its impact on methodology and their interests in the interplay of social and spatial relationships and structures (Panelli, 2004) can strengthen participation's practice and its ability to contribute to meaningful theory-building – a point I return to in Section IV. In particular, informed by recent insights from post-structuralist conceptions of power and discourse, social geographers are in a better position to avoid the inherent dangers of empiricism associated with participation, which assume that participants speak for themselves and produce maps and diagrams that can be treated uncritically as factual truths. Rather they can bring useful skills to inquire about the contexts and discourses informing the production of these particular products (Cameron and Gibson, 2005).

A related point on methodological tyranny is that while there has been an explosion of creative engagements with visual processes which seek to democratise the production of knowledge, these practices can exclude forms of knowledge that are more difficult to codify in this way (Mosse, 1994), for example emotional violence inhibiting women's participation in community or income generation activities (Odell and Kindon, 1990), or dimensions of spirituality informing voluntary work (Sanderson, 2007). Not all knowledge can be represented visually. Further, local knowledge is frequently haptic rather than visual, produced through embedded practices and lived experiences (Katz, 2004, Mohan, 2001) or it is articulated orally and linguistically through songs, proverbs and myths. Indeed Mosse (1994: 520), drawing on the work of Bloch (1991), cautions us that, 'knowledge

Box 23.3 Reflections on using participatory rural appraisal techniques to advance gender equitable outcomes in Bali

In 1991–92, I was employed by the Bali Sustainable Development Project (BSDP) – a Canadian International Development Agency (CIDA) funded research consortium involving one Canadian and two Indonesian universities – to provide the gender dimensions of a sustainable development strategy for Bali.

Over the 14 months 'in the field', I worked with a Balinese counterpart – Putu Hermawati – using PRA techniques with disaggregated groups of women and men in six temple communities (banjar) from two villages which represented two of the island's key agricultural zones. Through a series of participatory workshops with each group, we explored gender roles, relationships and needs within development. Our aims were to facilitate an empowering research process, challenge gender myths and assumptions and develop appropriate recommendations to improve gender equity informed by grassroots analysis. The findings and priority needs when communicated via presentations and reports resulted in the provision of technical training, funding for road improvements and the construction of a community health clinic (see Kindon, 1993, 1995, 1998 for more details).

At the time of doing this research and for a few years afterwards, I was an enthusiastic and largely uncritical proponent of PRA and its techniques. I was proud that a number of practical gender needs (Moser, 1989) were met as a result of our work and that participants' perspectives were taken seriously by government decision makers. With time, and after two return visits to some of the communities with whom we worked, however, I became aware that there had been little or no change in the structures of gendered power and resource allocation as a result of people's participation.

This realization was sobering, for without those deeper shifts in power relations, none of the gendered myths and assumptions, let alone their material manifestations, had been transformed (see also Mosse, 1994). The spaces opened up through our workshops for women to analyse their lives; the dialogues which had taken place for the first time between women and men about their gendered division of labour; and the joint action planning to address women's and men's priorities, had come to little.

I began to question the political effects of PRA within the context of short-term gender and development interventions, where decisions on timing, funding and outputs were pre-determined. I now consider my work in Bali to be a classic example of 'participation in development' (McGee, 2002) rather than the participatory development I was aiming for.

which readily presents itself as explicit or codified should be treated especially cautiously, in that it suggests the workings of particularly powerful interests' (cited in Jupp, 2007: 2838).

Finally, and a point that relates to the second criticism above about localism, is that so much energy has been focused on participatory methods that the larger and longer-term participatory processes (Kaul Shah, 2003) needed to upscale and affect changes 'in economic structures, or reformed institutions, or access to resources' (Pretty, 2003: 172) have been overlooked.

Groups

The third tyranny associated with participation is the emphasis on group work and analysis, which, particularly within development contexts, tends to take place in public spaces. According to feminist academic Patti Lather (1985, cited in Reinharz, 1992), the most effective emancipatory approaches are interactive, involving self-disclosure (of facilitators/researchers and participants), multiple interviews, group work and the negotiation of the interpretation of information generated. Similar processes are evident within participatory research and development and generally involve 'entire' communities, or smaller sub-groups thought to represent particular interests such as women, youth, homeless people and so forth. Depending upon the development or research agenda (and funding), these groups may meet for a few hours or a few days, or work together over the course of several weeks and months. Initially, they may be invited to form by external facilitators or researchers, or can replicate or build upon existing associations. Most participatory research takes place in groups because of a belief that group membership motivates individuals, enables the relatively quick production of solutions to problems and enables more effective learning for individuals than if they were working alone (Cooke, 2001).

There are several concerns here. First, a person's inclusion in a group or their invitation to participate is always already imbued with existing power relations. Development anthropologist Andrea Cornwall (2004) identifies the difference between what she calls 'invited' spaces and 'popular' or 'autonomous' spaces in terms of the power relations at work informing people's participation in groups. Often groups invited to participate by outsiders reinforce existing hierarchies and exclusions, and can impose foreign structures, which inhibit, constrain or domesticate people's participation. Sometimes it can be more effective to provide spaces within which people create their own vehicles for connection and representation (Williams, 2004a); although no space is beyond the reach of power (Kesby, 2007a).

Second, rather primitivist notions of 'the local' as being constituted by harmonious communities are often reflected in the ways in which participatory research and development promotes consensus within group work (Mohan, 1999). Further, these ideas of harmony and consensus reflect tendencies to romanticise poor and rural communities, and to overlook their diversity and frequently hierarchical and gendered power relations (Guijt and Shah, 1998; Mosse, 1994). Such notions can clearly limit the representativeness and sustainability of interventions that aim at social change, as I discussed in Box 23.3.

Third, once in groups, development management academic Bill Cooke (2001) identifies four aspects of group dysfunction which can limit the effectiveness of participatory activities:

(a) individuals may be inclined to take more risks when in a group decision-making context than when alone, often persuaded by a charismatic or dominant individual or sub-group;
(b) individuals may fail to communicate accurately their needs and desires, or may do the opposite because of certain fears or risk averse behaviours, leading to a collective misperception of group needs and desires followed by anxiety, frustration, anger and blame;
(c) individuals may experience a strong collective identity in opposition to another external group, which is rationalised through stereotyping, self-censorship and internal pressure to conform; and
(d) individuals may be convinced (some argue 'brain-washed') that the current situation they or their community face is no longer tolerable or sustainable and that there is no alternative but to change at an individual and collective level.

When combined, these aspects of group dysfunction can result in group-think and limit the possibility for independent critique or the negotiation and accommodation of difference.

A fourth and allied point is that much group work (at least in the majority world) takes place in public spaces. This spatial aspect of participatory work informs who is able to participate and therefore what knowledge is constructed (Brockington and Sullivan, 2003; Cooke, 2003; Mosse, 1994; Sanderson and Kindon, 2004). As a result, this knowledge tends to reflect dominant societal power relations (Kothari, 2001; Mohan 1999). This is most evident in the frequently limited participation of women or children, indigenous groups, the landless and sexual minorities within public participation initiatives. Alternatively, in a desire to present a harmonious image of their 'community', group members may involve a wide range of people and feign consensus, thereby concealing conflicts and disagreements, which resurface later.

Finally, and despite the limitations expressed here, group work does generate useful information and can often be the catalyst for action. However, as social geographer Mike Kesby (2005) has reflected, it is often very difficult to extend the empowering effects of participatory work into other spaces and arenas in an effort to sustain change. While longer-term participatory projects may suspend 'normal' social relations enabling new subjectivities to emerge (see also Cahill, 2007a; Cameron and Gibson, 2005), the empowering effects of participation frequently remain embedded in place, and often require the identification of additional resources if their effects are to be 'distanciated' over time and space (Kesby et al., 2007).

Summary

Participation's 'fall' from grace – mostly within the literature rather than in actual practice – represents a growing awareness of 'the politics and manipulations of power that exist beneath [its] veneer' (McKinnon, 2007: 776). Common to the above criticisms is the concern that participation represents a mode of governance which may be linked to specific policy or research agendas, and which inevitably constitutes knowledge and citizenship in particular, usually quite conservative, ways (see also Jupp, 2007). Increasingly this mode of governance – associated with ideas about devolution, user pays and local control and autonomy – perpetuates neoliberal agendas and reinforces existing power inequalities (see Box 23.4). It frequently represents a depoliticisation of participation's once radical ideals.

Yet, as development geographer Katharine McKinnon (2007) reminds us, participatory discourse (whether within research or development contexts) is always incomplete and imperfect, and represents but one intervention within a field of competing ideological formations. It is therefore important not to see participation as an endpoint within our research or development agendas, but rather as part of an ongoing process of negotiation and politics. When viewed in this light, recent work within social geography offers possibilities to retheorise participation in helpful ways and to open up spaces for the transformation of oppressive and less self-reflexive forms of power. Simultaneously, social geography can benefit from further consideration of recent debates and practices within the fields of participatory research and development discussed here in its efforts to contribute to greater social equity and justice.

REPOLITICISING PARTICIPATION AND SOCIAL GEOGRAPHY

> Participation is about power relations. It is about much else, as well; but power relations are pervasive: they are always there, and they affect the quality of process and experience. (Chambers, 2005: 113)

Within the recent critical discussions reviewed in previous sections – particularly pertaining to the use of participatory techniques and the implementation of participatory development – Participatory Action Research (PAR) has been heralded as a strategy for participation's repoliticisation (Kapoor, 2005; Hickey and Mohan, 2004). PAR emphasises dialogue and critical literacy, rather than techniques, and frequently involves a longer-term commitment to change at a range of scales – personal, interpersonal, group and society.

As I hinted in Section III, however, PAR is no panacea. It is still a marginal approach within academic and development institutions

Box 23.4 Some negative power effects of participatory approaches

- De-legitimization of research methods that are *not* participatory.
- Production of participants as subjects *requiring* 'research'/'development'.
- Production of suitably disciplined subjects as *participants* expected to perform appropriately within participatory processes.
- Retention of researchers' control whilst presenting them as benign arbiters of neutral or benevolent processes.
- Re-authorization of researchers as experts *in* participatory approaches.
- Romanticization or marginalization of local knowledge produced through participatory processes.
- Reinforcement of pre-existing power hierarchies among participating communities.
- Legitimization of elite local knowledge simply *because* it is produced through participatory processes.
- Legitimization of neoliberal programmes and institutions (such as the World Bank) that also deploy participatory approaches and/or techniques.

Source: Kesby et al. (2007): 21, emphasis in original.

Box 23.5 Ongoing institutional challenges facing participatory action research

Last year, I applied for some funding to carry out a PAR-based social geography project with refugee-background youth in Wellington, New Zealand. I wanted to work with them to explore their hopes and fears as part of a wider project involving young people in urban and rural settings in New Zealand and the United Kingdom (Pain et al., forthcoming). Funding was denied: according to the University research committee, my methodology 'lacked specificity'.

I had conformed to participatory discourse's calls to relinquish control and had specified that the project would adopt a PAR process and therefore that the precise number and types of participants would be determined collectively with my community partners, as would the methodology to be adopted and the outputs to be generated. The funding body wanted to know exact numbers and the precise demographic characteristics of my 'sample' as well as the specific methods that would be used to generate and analyse information so that I might be able to *measure* the outcomes and *predict* the publishable *outputs*. In other words, I was being asked to conform to discourses of standard positivistic research and be in control of both the process and the knowledge to be produced (see also Fine, 2008).

for a number of reasons. First, it challenges the bases of various forms of positivist research, which remain hegemonic (Greenwood, 2007). Second, PAR's collaboratively negotiated process, which is labour, resource and time intensive, means that neo-liberal managerial agendas frequently regard it as 'woolly' and/or risky, inefficient and not sufficiently output oriented (see Box 23.5).

Yet, when combined with recent understandings from social geography – particularly its engagements with feminist, post-structuralist and postcolonial epistemologies – I would argue that PAR has the potential to result in shifts of power that make a difference to those involved and to others at wider scales within both theory and practice (Chambers and Pettit, 2004); and that these shifts matter for the practice of our discipline and for the future relevance of 'the University' (see also mrs kinpaisby, 2008).

In this section, I reconnect to two of this book's main aims: the desire to forge connections and the wish to make a difference. I do so in order to discuss some of the ways in which social geography can contribute to theories and practices of participation to enhance its repoliticisation, and to explore the ways which participation may support social geographers' own activism. To ground these discussions, I touch on the recent trends in social geography addressed in this book: engagements with the non-human world; the inseparability of society and economy; reflections on the role of emotions and affect within social well-being and the persistent desire to contribute to social justice.

Retheorising and practising participation from within social geography

Partly in response to the perceived overemphasis on textual analysis associated with the cultural turn, social geography has recently 're-focused attention on the materialities of objects within particular cultures and landscapes' (Pain et al., 2007: 28). As contributors to Section 1 of this book discuss, many ideas about categories and identities of social difference have been unsettled in the past 40 years with the advent of postmodernism and poststructuralist theories. In addition, newer divides associated with technological advances, genetic engineering and biotechnologies, and the place of 'nature' and animals in human-non-human relations have both reproduced and challenged older inequalities based on gender, race and 'class' (see Section 1 of this volume).

The unsettling of these categories and identities, along with the ongoing concern with inequality, provide avenues through which social geography can refine participation's ability to engage effectively with difference, both within and beyond the researcher-researched relationship. Indigenous perspectives (see also Kobayishi and de Leeuw in this volume) are also important here as they provide insights into different cosmologies and understandings of human-non-human relations, which can inform both social geography and participation – a point I return to later.

In addition, social geography's engagement with concepts and practices of reflexivity and positionality provide helpful ways to think through and inform how power is practised in participatory arenas (for example, see Nagar et al., 2003). While some are ambivalent about the value, or even the possibility, of reflexivity (Rose, 1997a; Kapoor, 2005), others propose that the iterative practice of reflexivity can support more resilient and participatory research (Mendis-Millard and Reed, 2007; Reed and Peters, 2004). This is particularly the case if collaborators and participants are able to reflect and negotiate their own positions and subjectivities, and if these new understandings are incorporated into the process of intersubjective analysis (see Browne, this volume; Cahill, 2007a; Cameron and Gibson, 2005).

The importance of working productively with difference in this way, and of engaging aspects of *both* researchers' and participants/co-researchers' shifting positionalities and subjectivities can also mitigate against some of the concerns about tyrannical facilitation common within the participation literature. As sociologist Yoland Wadsworth (2001: 420) reflects, if all who are relevant or who have an interest are able to participate then facilitation becomes 'a more collective undertaking shaped by the micro action of all participants'. Further, by acknowledging and actively fostering the co-construction of knowledge we are more able to acknowledge the uncertainty/contingency of all research encounters and see this as productive.

Epistemologically then, social geography can contribute to participation's repoliticisation through its acknowledgement of 'the open-endedness of what is said and done in the research event and the multiplicity of sometimes incommensurable "truths" that it admits' (Whatmore, 2003: 99, drawing on the work of Isabelle Stengers). In addition, social geographers' experiments with non-verbal methods (Crang, 2003), and their rising interest in emotions, embodiment, non-representational theory and affect (see, for example, Bondi et al., 2005; Longhurst, 2001; 2008; Thrift, 2008; Tolia-Kelly, 2006), provide opportunities to challenge the methodological parochialism currently apparent within much participatory discourse and practice (Cooke and Kothari, 2001) and to broaden the range of participatory interventions. In a sense I would argue that social geographers working with participatory approaches are moving slowly towards a means of being able to engage *affect with effect* and that through their methodological innovations, they are becoming better able to spread and sustain the effects of participatory enquiry (see also Kindon et al., 2007).

Related to this issue are social geography's theorisations about how people's involvement in the different processes that shape their identities, lives and societies, enables them to cross social and spatial differences to act on certain issues (Pratt, 1998). Social geographers like Mike Kesby (2004) and Ellie Jupp (2007) have emphasised the need to pay attention not only to *who* participates, but also to *where* they participate and *how*. Where and how PAR takes place provide the opportunities for and constraints on 'what is deemed to constitute possible knowledge at that moment in time and space' (Sanderson and Kindon, 2004: 125). Yet, there has been a tendency to take for granted the narrative authority of knowledge generated by participants within the spaces constructed by projects (see also Mosse, 1994). This tendency represents a form of naive empiricism, which has excluded an analysis of the symbolic economy within which knowledge is being produced, represented and consumed (Mattingley, 2001).

It is more helpful, therefore, to see the spaces of participatory research as part of a continuum of spaces where people are asked to self-represent and articulate (Jupp, 2007), so that we can pay attention to the interdiscursive realms informing participation. It is critical that these aspects are acknowledged and explored if PAR is to be able to open up possibilities for alternative readings and representations of local community development (Cameron and Gibson, 2005) and if it is to enrich understandings of social action and transformative change (Panelli, 2004).

Finally, participation's tendency to overlook the wider symbolic economy and its place within a continuum of spaces and interdiscursive realms has resulted in a preponderance of attention on the producers and products of their knowledge. This is particularly the case in rapid participatory interventions. It has led to criticisms about participation's localism and its inability to effect wider structural change (Kapoor, 2005; Mohan, 1999). How the actors and their new subjectivities or the products of participatory work actually travel, and the spaces and audiences within which they are received or consumed, have been largely overlooked (Kindon, 2008b). Yet, clearly the contexts in which voices are heard and representations are engaged matter enormously (Mattingley, 2001). In sum, social geography's rising attention to the materiality of things;[4] its growing recognition of the inseparability of economy and society; its interest in aspects of consumption; and its longstanding interest in the spaces of social action, may productively engage interspatial and interscalar relations to enable participation's repoliticisation (see also the special journal issue edited by Pain and Kindon, 2007).

Rethinking the theory and practice of social geography from a participatory perspective

An engagement with the history and philosophies informing participation, as well as the various approaches to PAR, are also important if social geography is to remain a vital arena of academic inquiry that actually makes a difference. It is through participation, I would argue, that social geographers can enrich their understanding of social and spatial difference, and promote effective ways to address and enhance social equity and justice. To illustrate this point, I provide a reflective look at my ongoing work with members of Te Iwi o Ngaati Hauiti in Aotearoa, New Zealand, in Box 23.6, and then discuss key aspects of PAR within the remainder of this section.

First, participatory techniques when applied within a participatory epistemology embody the process of transformative reflexivity in which both researcher and participants reflect on their (mis)understandings and negotiate the meanings of the information generated together (see Crang, 2003: 497). This process can also be demonstrated in the final (textual) products, which reflect the diversity of participants' analyses and communicate 'a narrative "between" the perspectives of participants and those of researchers' – itself a form of positioned objectivity (Kesby, 2000: 432). In addition, because knowledge is co-produced through iterative cycles of action and reflection within participatory research, our collaborators' and participants' lived realities can inform and challenge the conceptual and theoretical understandings of research. This increases the rigour and value of our work, and opens up the hold that academics usually have on knowledge production.

Second, as a result of the intersubjective and dynamic context within which social research takes place, participatory approaches can help us to engage more effectively the subtle performances of identity, and the negotiations of difference and power at work, as people go about their daily lives or work together towards social action. They provide opportunities to rethink or 'trouble' our research practice and to perhaps more effectively navigate the gap between articulated knowledge (through participatory techniques for example) and knowledge in practice or tacit knowledge gained through sharing experiences alongside people in less structured ways (Jupp, 2007). They also provide a means of practising a more politicised form of representation in our work through the inclusion of people's voices and representa-

Box 23.6 Reflections on using participatory action research with members of Te Iwi o Ngaati Hauiti, Aotearoa, New Zealand

Since 1998, I have been involved in a participatory research partnership with members of Te Iwi o Ngaati Hauiti – a Maaori tribe – in the central north island of Aotearoa New Zealand. Along with my life partner and a video producer – Geoff Hume-Cook – we have been exploring aspects of place, identity and social cohesion and helping to build the iwi's capacity in video production.

I have written in more detail elsewhere about the development of this project and the ethical and cultural negotiations of its responsibility structure and research orientation (Kindon, 2003; Kindon and Latham, 2002). However, it is worth reiterating here that the process of these negotiations took place over eight months and that a great deal of energy went into establishing an appropriate orientation, frame and foundation for the subsequent partnership, training and empirical research. Such an investment, of course, is not possible within most PRA projects, which typically last about three weeks in total.

At the time of doing this research, I was still in thrall to ideas and techniques within participatory development discourse. These informed my early attempts at facilitation and participatory workshops. While various mapping and diagramming exercises were 'OK', it was sometimes hard to know exactly what or whom the information generated represented, or how to use it in an evolving research context. Many of the techniques that had worked well in Bali, because we focused on developing specific action plans within each community, seemed forced and somewhat artificial with Ngaati Hauiti where there was no immediate 'issue' or 'problem' to solve; just lots of questions to explore and skills to develop. Ngaati Hauiti also comprised a far more fluid and complex 'community' than those in Costa Rica and Bali (see Box 23.2 and Box 23.3). Participating members were also more educated, informed and politicized.

The process that emerged involved less PRA techniques and was more typical of participatory action research, informed by ideas and values from Maaori research and our collective engagement and interest in participatory video (see Hume-Cook et al., 2007). It involved us in almost continual negotiations about our understandings as new skills were developed and practised, and as new information was generated through interviews, training videos and reflections on video recordings of our workshops and discussions. As such, it was highly reflexive, dialogic and, at times, emotional. It privileged process and relationships over 'results'. It afforded insights into the multiple and shifting aspects of our identities and subjectivities over the spaces and times of our collaboration. And it provided a hopeful way of working within a decolonizing context like New Zealand. Finally, while the politics of our process were paramount, several iwi members have developed stronger research and video skills and we have collaboratively shared our experiences at conferences, written a book chapter and edited a documentary. It has been a demanding way to do research, and the most rewarding in my experience to date.

tions on their own terms (see Cahill and Torre, 2007; mrs c kinpaisby-hill, 2008).

Third, because participation is, in and of itself, a practice of hope, participatory approaches engage people's emotions. They often rely on people's emotional commitment to sustain their involvement and contribution over time. Moreover, enabling people to critically reflect on their identities and experiences of place, and the power relations that construct these, is often highly emotional as people bring into consciousness deeply held values and beliefs, feelings, connections and passions. This emotionality (hope, passion, anger, outrage, grief, love) when blended with rationality (analysis, strategy, planning) can – and is often required to – produce effective action and change (see also Cahill, 2007b). Participation can therefore enrich social geography's understandings of the role that emotions place in social life and people's negotiations of spatial difference and social well-being. For social geographers, this has to be an exciting development, which can only serve to enrich our scholarship and enhance the relevance of our work.

Fourth, because participation is relational, emotional and potentially confrontational, a great deal of attention has been paid to the understanding and practice of ethics, from initial inception of a research project through to the production and dissemination of its outputs (Cahill et al., 2007; Manzo and Brightbill, 2007). Current definitions and expectations of institutional review boards or university human ethics committees often fall short of the ethical requirements needed for participatory research. However, indigenous and aboriginal methodologies can provide useful guidance – particularly within settler societies – and can encourage us to think beyond data collection into relationships with research participants, their ancestors, their lands and their knowledges. Here the primacy of interpersonal relationships, the notion of an ethic of care and concern for social responsiveness, agency and accountability all point towards research which not only does no harm, but actively seeks to do some good through engaged and sustained engagement (Manzo and Brightbill, 2007; Tuhiwai-Smith 1999). In addition, indigenous researchers remind that all research happens within a context informed by history and the legacies of colonial and unequal power relations. Working to recognise these legacies and search for alternatives can provide important challenges to social geographers concerned with social equity and justice.

Finally, engaging participation within social geography provides opportunities for us to practise activism within our work, both within and beyond our universities (Kindon, 2008a; mrs kinspaisby, 2008). This activism can take place within our classrooms through the teaching and practice of PAR (Kindon and Elwood, forthcoming), through our research collaborations with communities and groups beyond the university and, perhaps most importantly, through participatory interventions into administrative decisions associated with timetabling, funding, leave, tenure and promotion (Kindon, 2008a). And, while the rise of participatory geographies is encouraging in this respect, we need to guard against participation's incorporation and deradicalisation within current neoliberal regimes. Participation potentially offers a new lens through which to view debates about what constitutes 'good' research practice, efficient bureaucratic structures and policies, and successful funding regimes based on academic publications (mrs kinpaisby, 2008), but it must be nurtured and protected if it is to avoid some of the dilemmas now facing participation within the international development arena.

CONCLUSION

Social geographers with social justice and activist agendas seem to be those most interested in participation (Pain and Francis, 2003). They tend to emphasise its value in ethical terms (Cahill et al., 2007) or its ability to bring about desired change more successfully than 'normal' ('traditional') social science research methods (Brockington and Sullivan, 2003). According to Kesby (2000), this may be because it offers a tangible way of being able to put the aims and principles of social geography into practice and to work for change, equity and justice (see also Kesby et al., 2005, Pain, 2003, 2004; Parkes and Panelli, 2001).

For many, embracing participation means specifically addressing issues of racism, ableism, sexism, heterosexism, and imperialism and how these manifest through people's unequal access to and control over resources, or in their positions within inequitable social relationships. Others suggest that people's participation in their own research may challenge prevailing biases and preconceptions about their knowledge by others in positions of power (Sanderson and Kindon, 2004), and that this can, in and of itself, transform unequal power relations. They talk of participation as enabling the practice of social justice through its emphasis on the mobilisation for social change by marginalised groups of participants that can happen through acts of solidarity and resistance (Chatterton et al., 2007). However, as White (2003: 46) notes, 'participation brings with it red flags that signal the need for caution and care in the many aspects of its catalytic action'. This chapter has sought to exercise this caution and care, by critically reflecting on both the value and dangers inherent in participation to argue that there is a role for social geography in the repoliticisation of participation, and a role for participation in revitalising social geography.

For, if we accept that we have an opportunity and an obligation to co-construct responsible geographies (McLean et al., 1997) then participation – in the form of participatory action research – offers us an exciting means of undertaking relevant, change-oriented social geography. And, while the academy does necessarily reward such activism, the central role of space in many people's oppression (Ruddick, 2004) means that social geographers are uniquely positioned to adopt more participatory ways of researching which build collaborative communities of inquiry and foster social equity and justice.

NOTES

1 Processes of conscientisation 'lead to people's awareness of structural causes of poverty and help build consensus and action based on individual creativity and knowledge' (Thomas-Slayter, 1995: 11). Freire's work was revolutionary at the time because of the links it made between participation, knowledge and power, and because of its emphasis on working with people who research their own lives as the starting point for political action and social change (Tandon, 1980).

2 The first conference sessions discussing participatory approaches within geographic research took place at the International Geographical Congress (IGC) Conference in Glasgow in 2004 and the Association of American Geographers Conference in 2005. In 2006, the Canadian Association of Geographers Conference and International Geographical Union (IGU) in Brisbane incorporated a number of sessions on participatory research in geography. Since then all major conferences have included participatory geography sessions. In 2008, the inaugural international conference of participatory geographies was held at Durham University, UK, involving delegates from Europe, USA, Canada, Africa, Australia and New Zealand. Also in 2008, the Participatory Geographies Working Group (established in 2005) achieved Research Group status within the Royal Geographical Society/Institute of British Geographers in the UK. The establishment of an RGS/IBG research group is seen by many as marking the arrival of a vibrant sub-discipline in the field.

3 Although see the work of Caitlin Cahill and the Fed Up Honeys for an excellent example of longer term participatory research with young women of colour in New York (Cahill et al., 2004, 2008).

4 These points echo Marcus Banks' (2001) call for researchers to read through and behind images to understand the social relations of their construction, but take it further to consider the relationships and power effects of inter-discursive spaces upon the reception and consumption of PAR products in different contexts.

5 mrs kinpaisby is a collective *nom de guerre* for Sara Kindon (VUW), Rachel Pain (Durham, UK) and Mike Kesby (St. Andrews, UK).

6 mrs c kinpaisby-hill is a collective *nomme de guerre* for Sara Kindon, Rachel Pain, Mike Kesby and Caitlin Cahill.

REFERENCES

Aitken, S. (2001) 'Playing with children: Immediacy was their cry', *The Geographical Review*, 91 (1–2): 496–508.

Aitken, S. and Wingate, J. (1993) 'A preliminary study of the self-directed photography of middle-class, homeless, and mobility impaired children', *The Professional Geographer*, 45 (1): 65–72.

Askins, K. and Pain, R. (2008) 'Art for art's sake? Materiality, participation and the messiness of interaction'. Paper presented to the *Association of American Geographers Conference*, Boston, April.

Bailey, C., Convery, I., Mort, M. and Baxter, J. (2004) 'Different public health geographies of the 2001 foot and mouth disease epidemic: "citizen" versus "professional" epidemiology'. Unpublished paper available from the authors.

Banks, M. (2001) *Visual Methods in Social Research*. London: Sage.

Barnsley, J. and Ellis, D. (1992) *Research for Change: Participatory Action Research for Community Groups*. Vancouver: Women's Research Centre.

Beazley, H. and Ennew, J. (2006) 'Participatory methods and approaches: Tackling the two tyrannies', in V. Desai and R. Potter (eds) *Doing Development Research*. London: Sage. pp. 189–99.

Berry, B. (1972) 'More relevance and policy analysis', *Area*, 4: 77–80.

Bery, R. (2003) 'Participatory video that empowers', in S. White (ed.), *Participatory Video: Images that Transform and Empower*. London: Sage. pp. 102–21.

Bloch, M. (1991) 'Language, anthropology and cognitive science', Man (New Series), 26: 183–98.

Boeren, A. (1994) *In Other Words ... The Cultural Dimension of Communication for Development*. Centre for the Study of Education in Developing Countries, The Hague.

Bondi, L., Davidson, J. and Smith, M. (eds) (2005) *Emotional Geographies*. Aldershot: Ashgate.

Breitbart, M. (2003) 'Participatory research methods', in N. Clifford and G. Valentine (eds), *Key Methods in Geography*. London: Sage. pp. 161–78.

Brockington, D. and Sullivan, S. (2003) 'Qualitative research', in R. Scheyvans and D. Storey (eds), *Development Fieldwork: A Practical Guide*. London: Sage. pp. 57–76.

Brown, D. and Tandon, R. (1983) 'Ideology and political economy in inquiry: Action research and participatory research', *The Journal of Applied Behavioral Science*, 19 (3): 277–94.

Brydon-Miller, M. (2001) 'Education, research and action: theory and methods of Participatory Action Research', in D. Tolman and M. Brydon-Miller (eds), *From Subjects to Subjectivities: A handbook of participatory and interpretive methods*. New York: New York University Press. pp. 76–94.

Brydon-Miller, M., Greenwood, D. and Maguire, P. (2003) 'Why action research?' *Action Research*, 1 (9): 1–28.

Brydon-Miller, M., Maguire, P. and McIntyre, A. (eds) (2004) *Traveling Companions: Feminism, Teaching and Action Research*. Westport: Praeger.

Cahill, C. (2004) 'Defying gravity: raising consciousness through collective research', *Children's Geographies*, 2 (2): 273–86.

Cahill, C. (2007a) 'The personal is the political: Developing new subjectivities in a participatory action research process', *Gender, Place and Culture*, 14 (3): 267–92.

Cahill, C. (2007b) 'Doing research with young people: Participatory research and the rituals of collective work', *Children's Geographies*, 5 (3): 297–312.

Cahill, C. (2007c) 'Negotiating grit and glamour: Young women of color and the gentrification of the Lower East Side', *City and Society*, 19 (2): 202–31.

Cahill, C. (2007d) 'Afterward: Well positioned? locating participation in theory and practice, theme issue: participatory geographies', *Environment and Planning A*, 39 (12): 2861–5.

Cahill, C. (2008) 'Participatory action research, positionality and whiteness'. Paper presented to the *Inaugural International Conference of Participatory Geographies*, Durham, University of Durham, January.

Cahill, C., Arenas, E., Contreras, J., Jiang, N., Rios-Moore, I. and Threatts, T. (2004) 'Speaking back: Voices of young urban women of color using Participatory Action Research to challenge and complicate representations of young women', in A. Harris (ed.), *All About the Girl: Power, Culture and Identity*. New York: Routledge. pp. 233–44.

Cahill, C., Sultana, F. and Pain, R. (2007) 'Participatory ethics: politics, practices and institutions', *ACME: E-Journal of Critical Geographies*, 6 (3): 304–18.

Cahill, C. and Torre, M. (2007) 'Beyond the journal article: representations, audience and the presentation of Participatory Action Research', in S. Kindon, R. Pain and Kesby M. (eds), *Participatory Action Research Approaches and Methods: Connecting People, Participation and Place*. London: Routledge. pp. 196–205.

Cahill, C., Rios-Moore, I. and Threatts, T. (2008) 'Different eyes/open eyes: Community-based Participatory Action Research', in J. Cammarota and M. Fine (eds), *Revolutionizing Education: Youth Participatory Action Research in Motion*. New York: Routledge.

Cameron, J. and Gibson, K. (2005) 'Participatory action research in a poststructuralist vein', *Geoforum*, 36 (3): 315–31.

Cammarota, J. and Fine, M. (eds) (2008) *Revolutionizing Education: Youth Participatory Action Research*. London: Routledge.

Castree, N. and Sparke, M. (2000) 'Professional geography and the corporatization of the university: experiences, evaluations and engagements', *Antipode*, 32 (3): 222–9.

Chambers, R. (1983) *Rural Development: Putting the Last First*. Harlow: Longman.

Chambers, R. (1994a) The origins and practice of participatory rural appraisal', *World Development*, 22 (9): 953–69.

Chambers, R. (1994b) 'Participatory Rural Appraisal (PRA): Analysis and experience', *World Development*, 22 (9): 1253–68.

Chambers, R. (1994c) 'Participatory Rural Appraisal (PRA): Challenges, potentials and paradigms', *World Development*, 22 (10): 1437–54.

Chambers, R. (2005) *Ideas for Development*. London: Earthscan Publications.

Chambers, R. and Pettit, J. (2004) 'Shifting power to make a difference', in L. Groves and R. Hinton (eds), *Inclusive Aid: Changing Power and Relationships in International Development*. London: Earthscan. pp. 137–62.

Chatterton, P., Fuller, D. and Routledge, P. (2007) 'Relating action to activism: Theoretical and methodological reflections', in S. Kindon, R. Pain and M. Kesby (eds), *Participatory Action Research Approaches and Methods: Connecting People, Participation and Place*. London: Routledge. pp. 216–22.

Chouinard, V. (2000) 'Getting ethical: for inclusive and engaged geographies of disability', *Ethics, Place and Environment*, 3 (1): 70–80.

Cieri, M. (2003) 'Between being and looking: queer tourism promotion and lesbian social space in Greater Philadelphia', *ACME: International E-Journal of Critical Geographies*, 2 (2): 147–66.

Cieri, M. and McCauley, R. (2007) 'Participatory theatre: "Creating a source for staging an example" in the USA', in S. Kindon, R. Pain and M. Kesby (eds), *Participatory Action Research Approaches and Methods: Connecting People, Participation and Place*. London: Routledge. pp. 141–9.

Cooke, B. (2003) 'A new continuity with colonial administration: participation in development management', *Third World Quarterly*, 24 (1): 47–61.

Cooke, B. and Kothari, U. (eds) (2001) *Participation: The New Tyranny?*. London: Zed Books.

Cooke, U. (2001) 'Power, knowledge and social control in participatory development', in B. Cooke and U. Kothari (eds), *Participation: The New Tyranny?* London: Zed Books. pp. 139–52.

Cope, M. (forthcoming) 'Challenging adult perspectives on children's geographies through participatory research methods: Insights from a service-learning course', *Journal of Geography in Higher Education*.

Cope, M. and Halfhill, J. (2003) 'Progress report: Buffalo kids' space project', Buffalo, State University of New York. Paper available from authors.

Cornwall, A. (2004) 'Spaces for transformation? Reflections on issues of power and difference in participation in development', in S. Hickey and G. Mohan (eds), *Participation: From Tyranny to Transformation*, London: Zed Books. pp. 75–91.

Cornwall, A. and Brock, K. (2005) 'What do buzzwords do for development policy? A critical look at "participation", "empowerment" and "poverty reduction"', *Third World Quarterly*, 26 (7): 1043–76.

Cornwall, A. and Jewkes, R. (1995) 'What is participatory research?' *Social Science and Medicine*, 41 (12): 1667–76.

Cottrell, B. and Parpart, J. (2006) 'Academic-community collaboration, gender research, and development pitfalls and possibilities', *Development in Practice*, 16 (1): 15–26.

Crang, M. (2003) 'Qualitative methods: Touchy, feely, look-see', *Progress in Human Geography*, 27 (4): 494–504.

Elwood, S. (2004) 'Experiential learning, spatial practice and critical urban geographies', *Journal of Geography*, 103 (2): 55–63.

Fals-Borda, O. (2006a) 'Participatory (action) research in social theory: origins and challenges', in P. Reason and H. Bradbury (eds), *Handbook of Action Research*. London: Sage. pp. 27–37.

Fals-Borda, O. (2006b) 'The north-south convergence: a 30-year first-person assessment of PAR', *Action Research*, 4 (3): 351–8.

Farrow, H. (1995) 'Researching popular theatre in Southern Africa: Comments on a methodological implementation', *Antipode*, 27 (1): 75–81.

Fine, M. (2008) 'An epilogue of sorts …', in J. Cammarota and M. Fine (eds), *Revolutionalizing Education: Youth Participatory Action Research in Motion*. London: Routledge. pp. 213–34.

Fox, N. (2003) 'Practice-based evidence: Towards collaborative and transgressive research', *Sociology*, 37 (1): 81–102.

Freire, P. (1972) *Pedagogy of the Oppressed*. Harmondsworth: Penguin Books.

Fuller, D. and Kitchin, R. (2004) 'Radical theory/critical praxis: academic geography beyond the academy?', in D. Fuller and R. Kitchin (eds), *Radical Theory, Critical Praxis: Making a Difference Beyond the Academy?* ACME e-book series, 1–20.

Fuller, D, O'Brien, K. and Hope, R. (2003) *Exploring Solutions to 'Graffiti' in Newcastle Upon Tyne*. Newcastle Upon Tyne: University of Northumbria.

Gaskell, C. (2002) 'Active youth citizenship: a response to street crime and violence'. London: Queen Mary University of London. Paper available from author.

Gatenby, B. and Humphries, M. (1996) 'Feminist commitments in organizational communication: Participatory action research as feminist praxis', *Australian Journal of Communication*, 23 (2): 73–87.

Gatenby, B. and Humphries, M. (2000) 'Feminist participatory action research: Methodological and ethical issues', *Women's Studies International Forum*, 23 (1): 89–105.

Gaventa, J. (2004) 'Towards participatory governance: assessing the transformative possibilities', in S. Hickey and G. Mohan (eds), *Participation: From Tyranny to Transformation? Exploring New Approaches to Participation in Development*. London: Zed Books. pp. 25–41.

Gibson-Graham, J.K. (1994) 'Stuffed if I know! Reflections on postmodern feminist social research', *Gender, Place and Culture*, 1 (2): 205–24.

Greenwood, D. (2007) 'Teaching/learning action research requires fundamental reforms in public higher education', *Action Research*, 5: 249–64.

Grillo, R. (2002) 'Anthropologists and development', in V. Desai and R. Potter (eds), *The Companion to Development Studies*. London: Arnold. pp. 54–8.

Guidi, P. (2003) 'Guatemalan Mayan women and participatory visual media', in S. White (ed.), *Participatory Video: Images that Transform and Empower*. London: Sage. pp. 252–70.

Guijt, I. (2003) 'Intrigued and frustrated, enthusiastic and critical: reflections on PRA', in A. Cornwall and G. Pratt (eds), *Pathways to Participation: Reflections on PRA*. London: ITDG. pp. 82–7.

Guijt, I. and Cornwall, A. (1995) 'Editorial: Critical reflections on the practice of PRA', *PLA NOTES*, 24: 2–7.

Guijt, I. and Shah, M. (1998) *The Myth of Community: Gender Issues in Participatory Development*. London: Intermediate Technology Publications Ltd.

Hall, B. (1981) 'Participatory research, popular knowledge and power: a personal reflection', *Convergence*, 14 (3): 6–17.

Hall, B. (1997) 'Preface', in S. Smith, D. Williams and N. Johnson (eds), *Nurtured by Knowledge: Learning to do participatory action research*. New York: Apex Press. pp. xiii–xv.

Hall, B. (2005) 'In from the cold? Reflections on participatory research from 1970-2005', *Convergence*, 38 (1): 5–24.

Hart, R. (1997) *Children's Participation: The theory and practice of involving young citizens in community development and environmental care*. New York: UNICEF.

Harvey, D. (1972) 'Revolutionary and counter-revolutionary theory in geography and the problem of ghetto formation', *Antipode*, 4 (2): 1–2.

Harvey, D. (1973) *Social Justice and the City*. Baltimore, MD: Johns Hopkins University Press.

Harvey, D. (1974) 'What kind of geography for what kind of public policy?', *Transactions of the Institute of British Geographers*, 63 (Nov): 18–24.

Haw, K. (2008) 'The ordinary and extraordinary everyday lives of young people living in a high crime area'. Paper presented to the *Association of American Geographers Conference*, Boston, April.

Henkel, H. and Stirrat, R. (2001) 'Participation as spiritual duty; empowerment as secular subjection', in B. Cook and U. Kothari (eds), *Participation: The New Tyranny?*. London: Zed. pp. 168–84.

Herman, T. and Mattingley, D. (1999) 'Community, justice and the ethics of research: negotiating reciprocal research relations', in J. Proctor and D Smith (eds), *Geography and Ethics: journeys into a moral terrain*. London: Routledge. pp. 209–22.

Hickey, S. and Mohan, G. (eds) (2004) *Participation: From Tyranny to Transformation*. London: Zed Books.

Hume-Cook, G., Curtis, T., Woods, K., Tangaroa Potaka, J., Wagner, A. and Kindon, S. (2007) 'Uniting people with place using participatory video in Aotearoa/New Zealand', in S. Kindon, R. Pain and M. Kesby (eds), *Participatory Action Research Approaches and Methods: Connecting People, Participation and Place*. London: Routledge. pp. 160–9.

Juckes Maxey, L. (2004) 'The participation of younger people within intentional communities: evidence from two case studies', *Children's Geographies*, 2 (1): 29–48.

Jupp, E. (2007) 'Participation, local knowledge and empowerment: researching public space with young people', *Environment and Planning A*, 39: 2832–44.

Kapoor, I. (2002) 'The devil's in the theory: a critical assessment of Robert Chambers' work on participatory development', *Third World Quarterly*, 23 (1): 101–17.

Kapoor, I. (2005) 'Participatory development, complicity and desire', *Third World Quarterly*, 26 (8): 1203–20.

Katz, C. (2004) *Growing Up Global: Economic Restructuring and Children's Everyday Lives*. Minneapolis: University of Minnesota Press.

Kaul Shah, M. (2003) 'The road from Lathodara: some reflections on PRA', in A. Cornwall and G. Pratt (eds), *Pathways to Participation: Reflections on PRA*. London: ITDG. pp. 189–95.

Kesby, M. (2000a) 'Participatory diagramming as a means to improve communication about sex in rural Zimbabwe: a pilot study', *Social Science and Medicine*, 50 (12): 1723–41.

Kesby, M. (2000b) 'Participatory diagramming: deploying qualitative methods through an action research epistemology', *Area*, 32 (4): 423–35.

Kesby, M. (2004) 'Participatory diagramming and the ethical and practical challenges of helping Africans themselves to move HIV work "beyond epidemiology"', in E. Kalipeni, S. Craddock, J. Oppong and J. Ghosh (eds), *HIV/AIDS in Africa: Beyond Epidemiology*. Oxford: Blackwell. pp. 217–28.

Kesby, M. (2005) 'Retheorizing empowerment-through-participation as performance in space: Beyond tyranny to transformation', *Signs: Journal of Women in Culture and Society*, 30 (4): 2037–65.

Kesby, M. (2007a) 'Spatialising participatory approaches: The contribution of geography to a mature debate', *Environment and Planning A*, 39 (12): 2813–31.

Kesby, M. (2007b) 'Methodological insights on and from children's geographies', *Children's Geographies*, 5 (3): 193–205.

Kesby, M., Kindon, S. and Pain, R. (2005) 'Participatory approaches and diagramming techniques', in R. Flowerdew and D. Martin (eds), *Methods in Human Geography: A guide for students doing a research project*. London: Pearson Prentice Hall. pp. 144–66.

Kesby, M. Kindon, S. and Pain, R. (2007) Participation as a form of power: retheorising empowerment and spatialising Participatory Action Research, in Kindon, S. Pain, R. and M. Kesby (eds), *Participatory Action Research Approaches and Methods: Connecting People, Participation and Place*. London: Routledge, pp. 19–25.

Kindon, S. (1993) *From Tea Makers to Decision Makers: Applying Participatory Rural Appraisal to Gender and Development in Rural Bali, Indonesia*. Toronto: University Consortium on the Environment Student Paper Series. Paper #16. 206 pages.

Kindon, S. (1995) 'Dynamics of difference: exploring empowerment methodologies with women and men in Bali', *New Zealand Geographer*, 51 (2): 10–12.

Kindon, S. (1998) 'Of mothers and men: questioning gender and community myths in Bali', in R. Slocum, L. Wichart, D. Rocheleau and B. Thomas-Slayter (eds), *Power, Process and Participation: Tools for Social and Environmental Changes*. London: Intermediate Technology Publications Ltd. pp. 105–9.

Kindon, S. (2000) '(Re)framing and (re)presenting: participatory community video in geographic research', in M. Roche, M. McKenna and P. Hesp (eds), *Proceedings of the Twentieth New Zealand Geography Conference*, 5–8 July 1999, Palmerston North, Massey University. pp. 175–8.

Kindon, S. (2003) 'Participatory video in geographic research: a feminist practice of looking?' *Area*, 35 (2): 142–53.

Kindon, S. (2005) 'Participatory action research', in I. Hay (ed.), *Qualitative Methods in Human Geography*. Melbourne: Oxford University Press. pp. 207–20.

Kindon, S. (2008a) 'Creating participatory spaces for the sharing of knowledge: engaged pedagogy, participatory action research and the neoliberal university'. Keynote Address to the *Inaugural International Conference of Participatory Geographies*, Durham, University of Durham, January.

Kindon, S. (2008b) *'But that's not how it was!' – Participatory video products, audiences and space*. Research seminar presentation to Department of Geography, Glasgow, University of Glasgow: January.

Kindon, S. and Latham, A. (2002) 'From mitigation to negotiation: ethics and the geographical imagination in Aotearoa/New Zealand', *New Zealand Geographer*, 58 (1): 14–22.

Kindon, S. and Cupples, J. (2003) 'Leaving the field', in R. Scheyvans and D. Storey (eds), *Development Fieldwork: A Practical Guide*. London: Sage. pp. 197–216.

Kindon, S. and Elwood, S. (2009) 'Introduction: More than methods – reflections on participatory action research in geographic teaching, learning and research', *Journal of Geography in Higher Education*, 33 (1): 19–32.

Kindon, S. and Pain, R. (2006) 'Doing participation geographically'. Unpublished paper, available from the authors.

Kindon, S., Pain, R. and Kesby, M. (eds) (2007) *Participatory Action Research Approaches and Methods: Connecting People, Participation and Place*. London: Routledge.

Kindon, S., Hume-Cook, G., Woods, K., Curtis, T. and Potaka, J. (2005) 'What does participatory video have to offer Maori? Reflections from a small space on shifting ground'. Paper presented to the *Indigenous Knowledges Conference: Reconciling Academic Priorities with Indigenous Realities*, Wellington, Victoria University of Wellington, June.

Kitchin, R. (2001) 'Using participatory action research approaches in geographical studies of disability: some reflections', *Disability Studies Quarterly*, 21 (4): 61–9.

Kobayashi, A. (2002) 'Migration as a negotiation of gender: Recent Japanese immigrant women in Canada', in L. Hirabayashi, J. Hirabayashi and A. Kikumura Yano (eds), *New World Lives: Globalization and People of Japanese Ancestry in the Americas and from Latin America in Japan*. Stanford: Stanford University Press. pp. 205–20.

Kothari, U. (2001) 'Power, knowledge and social control in participatory development', in B. Cooke and U. Kothari (eds), *Participation: The New Tyranny*?. London: Zed. pp. 139–52.

Krieg, B. and Roberts, L. (2007) 'Photovoice: Insights into marginalisation through a "community lens" in Saskatchewan, Canada', in S. Kindon, R. Pain and M. Kesby (eds), *Participatory Action Research Approaches and Methods: Connecting People, Participation and Place*. London: Routledge. pp. 150–9.

Kuokkanen, R. (2004) 'Towards the hospitality of the academy: the (im)possible gift of indigenous epistemes'. Unpublished PhD thesis, Vancouver, University of British Columbia.

Kumar, S. (2002) *Methods for Community Participation: A complete guide for practitioners*. London: ITDG Publishers.

Leavitt, J., Lingafelter, T. and Morello, C. (1998) 'Through their eyes: Young girls look at their Los Angeles neighbourhood', in R. Ainley (ed.), *New Frontiers of Space, Bodies and Gender*. London: Routledge. pp. 76–87.

Lennie, J. (1999) 'Deconstructing gendered power relations in participatory planning: towards an empowering feminist framework of participation and action', *Women's Studies International Forum*, 22 (1): 97–112.

Leurs, R. (1996) 'Current challenges facing participatory rural appraisal', *Public Administration and Development*, 16 (1): 57–72.

Lewin, K. (1946) 'Action research and minority problems', *Journal of Social Issues*, 1–2: 34–6.

Leyshon, M. (2002) 'On being "in the field": practice, progress and problems in research with young people in rural areas', *Journal of Rural Studies*, 18 (2): 179–91.

Longhurst, R. (2001) *Bodies: Exploring Fluid Boundaries*, London: Routledge.

Longhurst, R. (2008) *Maternities: Gender, Bodies and Space*. London: Routledge.

Lykes, M. (2001) 'Activist participatory research and the arts with rural Mayan women: interculturality and situated meaning making', in D. Tolman and M. Brydon-Miller (eds), *From Subjects to Subjectivities: A handbook of participatory and interpretive methods*. New York: State of New York University Press. pp. 183–99.

Lyons, L. (2000) '(De)Constructing the interview: A critique of the participatory model', *Resources for Feminist Research*, Fall-Winter, 28 (1–2): 33–45.

McCormack, J. (2000) 'Children's lived experiences in rural New Zealand', *Childrenz Issues*, 4 (2): 13–18.

McClean, R. Berg, L. and Roche, M. (1997) 'Responsible geographies: co-creating knowledge in Aotearoa /New Zealand', *New Zealand Geographer*, 53 (2): 9–15.

McGee, R. (2002) 'Participating in development', in U. Kothari and M. Minogue (eds), *Development Theory and Practice: Critical Perspectives*. London: Macmillan. pp. 92–116.

McIntyre, A. (2003) 'Through the eyes of women: photovoice and participatory research as tools for reimagining place', *Gender, Place and Culture*, 10 (1): 47–66.

McKinnon, K. (2007) 'Postdevelopment, professionalism and the politics of participation', *Annals of the American Association of Geographers*, 97 (4): 772–85.

McTaggart, R. (ed.) (1997) *Participatory Action Research: International Contexts and Consequences*. New York: State of New York University Press.

Maguire, P. (1993) 'Challenges, contradictions and celebrations: Attempting participatory research as doctoral student', in P. Park, M. Brydon-Miller, B. Hall and T. Jackson (eds),

Voices of Change: Participatory Research in the US and Canada, Toronto: OISE Press.

Maguire, P. (1997) *Doing Participatory Research: A Feminist Approach*. Amherst, MA: Centre for International Education.

Manzo, L. and Brightbill, N. (2007) 'Towards a participatory ethics', in S. Kindon, R. Pain and M. Kesby (eds) *Participatory Action Research Approaches and Methods: Connecting People, Participation, and Place*. London: Routledge. pp. 33–40.

Matthews, H. (1995) 'Living on the edge: children as outsiders', *Tijdschrift voor Economishche en Sociale Geografie*, 86 (5): 456–66.

Matthews, H., Taylor, M., Sherwood, K., Tucker, F. and Limb, M. (2000) 'Growing-up in the countryside: children and the rural idyll, *Journal of Rural Studies*, 16 (2): 141–53.

Mattingley, D. (2001) 'Place, teenagers and representations: lessons from a community theatre project', *Social and Cultural Geography*, 2 (4): 445–59.

Mda, Z. (1993) *When People Play People: Development Communication Through Theatre*. New Jersey: Zed Books.

Mendis-Millard, S. and Reed, M. (2007) 'Understanding community capacity using adaptive and reflexive research practices: lessons from two Canadian biosphere reserves', *Society and Natural Resources*, 20 (6): 543–59.

Merrett, C. (2000) 'Teaching social justice: reviving geography's neglected tradition', *Journal of Geography*, 99 (5): 207–18.

Mies, M. (1983) 'Towards a methodology for feminist research', in G. Bowles and R. Duelli Klein (eds), *Theories of Women's Studies*. London: Routledge. pp. 117–39.

Miller, V. (2008) Personal Communication, March 17.

Mohan, G. (1999) 'Not so distant, not so strange: the personal and the political in participatory research', *Ethics, Place and Environment*, 2 (1): 41–54.

Mohan, G. (2001) 'Beyond participation: Strategies for deeper empowerment', in B. Cooke and U. Kothari (eds), *Participation: The New Tyranny?* London: Zed Books. pp. 153–67.

Mohan, G. (2007) 'Participatory development: from epistemological reversals to active citizenship', *Geography Compass*, 1 (4): 1–18.

Mohan, G. and Stokke, K. (2000) 'Participatory development and empowerment: the dangers of localism', *Third World Quarterly*, 21 (2): 2347–68.

Momsen, J. (2003) 'Participatory development and indigenous communities in the Mexican Caribbean', in J. Pugh and R. Potter (eds), *Participatory Planning in the Caribbean: Lessons from Practice*. Aldershot: Ashgate. pp. 155–72.

Monk, J. and Hansen, S. (1982) 'On not excluding half of the human in human geography', *Professional Geographer*, 34 (7): 11–23.

Monk, J., Manning, P. and Denman, C. (2003) 'Working together: feminist perspectives on collaborative research and action', *ACME: International E-Journal of Critical Geographies*, 2 (7): 91–106.

Moser, C. (1989) 'Gender planning in the third world: meeting practical and strategic gender needs', *World Development*, 17 (11): 1799–1825.

Moser, C. and McIlwaine, C. (1999) 'Participatory urban appraisal and its application for research on violence', *Environment and Urbanization*, 11 (2): 203–26.

Moser, C. and McIlwaine, C. (2001) 'Violence and social capital in urban poor communities: Perspectives from Colombia and Guatemala', *Journal of International Development*, 13 (7): 965–84.

Moss, P. (1995) 'Reflections on the "gap" as part of the politics of research design', *Antipode*, 27 (1): 82–90.

Mosse, D. (1994) 'Authority, gender and knowledge: theoretical reflection on the practice of participatory rural appraisal', *Development and Change*, 25 (3): 497–526.

Mountz, A., Moore, E.B. and Brown, L. (2008) 'Participatory Action Research as pedagogy: boundaries in Syracuse', *ACME: An International E-Journal for Critical Geographies.*

mrs kinpaisby (2008) 'Taking stock of participatory geographies: envisioning the communiversity', *Transactions of the Institute of British Geographers* , 33 (3): 292–9.

mrs c kinpaisby-hill (2008) 'Publishing from participatory research', in A. Blunt (ed.), *Publishing in Geography: A Guide for New Researchers*, London: Wiley-Blackwell. pp. 45–7.

Nairn, K., Panelli, R. and McCormack, J. (2003) 'Destabilizing dualisms: young people's experiences of rural and urban environments', *Childhood*, 10 (1): 9–42.

Nagar, R. in consultation with F. Ali and *Sangatin* women's collective, Sitapur, Uttar Pradesh, India (2003) 'Collaboration across borders: Moving beyond positionality',

Singapore Journal of Tropical Geography, 24 (3): 356–72.

Naylor, S., Ryan, J., Cook, I. and Crouch, D. (2000) *Cultural Turns/Geographical Turns, Perspectives on Cultural Geography*. Harlow: Prentice Hall.

Nelson, A. (2007) '"Listen: We and the River have Stories to Tell" – community muralism as participatory geography discourse and discovery'. Unpublished PhD Thesis, Davis: University of California Davis.

Odell, C. and Kindon, S. (1990) 'Mejores unidas para solas (Better united than alone)'. Unpublished report for the Association de Mujeres de Acosta, Costa Rica.

Pain, R. (2003) 'Social geography: action-oriented research', *Progress in Human Geography*, 27 (5): 649–57.

Pain, R. (2004) 'Social geography: participatory research', *Progress in Human Geography*, 28 (5): 1–12.

Pain, R. (2006) 'Social geography: seven deadly myths in policy research', *Progress in Human Geography*, 30 (2): 250–60.

Pain, R. and Francis, P. (2003) 'Reflections on participatory research', *Area*, 35 (1): 46–54.

Pain, R. and Kindon, S. (2007) 'Participatory geographies, guest editorial of special issue', *Environment and Planning A*, 39 (12): 2807–12.

Pain, R., Kindon, S. and Kesby, M. (2007) 'Participatory Action Research: making a difference to theory, practice and action', in S. Kindon, R. Pain and M. Kesby (eds), *Participatory Action Research Approaches and Methods: Connecting People, Participation and Place*. London: Routledge. pp. 26–32.

Pain, R., Panelli, R., Kindon, S. and J. (forthcoming) 'Little moments in everyday/distant geopolitics: young people's fears and hopes', *Geoforum*.

Panelli, R. (2004) *Social Geography*. London: Sage.

Panelli, R., Pain, R., Kindon, S. and Little, J. (2007) *Moments in everyday/distant geopolitics of hope and fear*. RGS/IBG Conference, London, August.

Park, P., Brydon-Miller, M., Hall, B. and Jackson, T. (eds) (1993) *Voices of Change: Participatory Research in the US and Canada*. Toronto: OISE Press.

Parkes and Panelli, R. (2001) 'Integrating catchment ecosystems and community health: the value of participatory action research', *Ecosystem Health*, 7 (2): 85–106.

Parnwell, M. (2003) 'Consulting the poor in Thailand: enlightenment or delusion?', *Progress in Development Studies*, 3 (2): 99–112.

Parr, H. (2007) 'Collaborative film-making as process, method and text in mental health research,' *Cultural Geographies*, 14 (1): 114–38.

Peake, L. (2000) *Women Research Women: Methodology Report and Research Projects on the Study of Domestic Violence and Women's Reproductive Health in Guyana*, on behalf of Red Thread Women's Development Programme, Georgetown, Guyana, Inter-American Development Bank.

Peet, R. (1969) 'A new left geography', *Antipode*, 1 (1): 3–5.

Peet, R. (1977) 'The development of radical geography in the United States', in R. Peet (ed.), *Radical Geography: Alternative Viewpoints on Contemporary Social Issues*. London: Methuen. pp. 1–30.

pla notes (2003) *Editorial Statement*, December, London: International Institute of Environment and Development. Available www.iied.org/NR/agbioliv/pla_notes/pla_backissues/48.html (Accessed 31 May 2007).

Pratt, G. (1998) 'Grids of difference', in R. Fincher and J. Jacobs (eds), *Cities of Difference*. London: Guilford Press. pp. 26–48.

Pratt, G. (2000) 'Participatory action research', in R. Johnston, D. Gregory, G. Pratt and M. Watts (eds), *The Dictionary of Human Geography*, 4th edn. Oxford: Blackwell. p. 574.

Pratt, G. and Kirby, E. (2003) 'Performing nursing: the BC Nurses Union Theatre Project', *ACME: An International E-Journal for Critical Geographies*, 2 (1): 14–32.

Pratt, G. in collaboration with the Philippine Women Centre of BC and Ugnayan ng Kabataang Pilipino sa Canada/Filipino-Canadian Youth Alliance (2007) 'Working with migrant communities: Collaborating with the Kalayaan Centre in Vancouver, Canada', in S. Kindon, R. Pain and M. Kesby (eds), *Participatory Action Research Approaches and Methods: Connecting People, Participation and Place*. London: Routledge. pp. 95–103.

Pretty, J. (2003) 'What have we learned about participatory methods? Some thoughts on the personal and professional', in A. Cornwall and G. Pratt (eds), *Pathways to Participation: Reflections on PRA*. London: ITDG. pp. 170–6.

Pretty, J., Guijt, I., Thompson, J. and Scoones, I. (eds), (1995) *Participatory Learning and*

Action: A Trainer's Guide. London: International Institute for Environment and Development.

Punch, S. (2001) 'Multiple methods and research relations with children in rural Bolivia', in M. Limb and C. Dwyer (eds), *Qualitative Methodologies for Geographers: Issues and Debates*. London: Arnold. pp. 165–80.

Reason, P. (1994) 'Three approaches to participatory inquiry', in N. Denzin and Y. Lincoln (eds), *Handbook of Qualitative Research*. Thousand Oaks, CA: Sage. pp. 324–39.

Reason, P. and Bradbury, H. (eds), (2001) *Handbook of Action Research: Participative Inquiry and Practice*. London/Thousand Oaks, CA: Sage.

Reed, M. (2000) 'Taking stands: a feminist perspective on "other" women's activism in forestry communities of Northern Vancouver Island', *Gender, Place and Culture*, 7 (4): 363–87.

Reed, M. and Peters, E. (2004) 'Using ecological metaphors to build adaptive and resilient research practices', *ACME: An International E-Journal for Critical Geographies*, 31 (1): 18–40.

Reinharz, S. with assistance of Davidman, L. (1992) *Feminist Methods in Social Research*. New York: Oxford University Press.

Richardson, P. (2008) 'Ethical engagements with participatory video in the Caribbean'. Paper presented to the *Association of American Geographers Conference*, Boston, April.

Robinson, K., Gibson, K., McKay, D. and McWilliam, A. (2004) 'Negotiating alternative economic strategies for regional development', *Development Bulletin*, 65: 46–50.

Rocheleau, D. (1991) 'Participatory research in agroforestry: Learning from experience and expanding our repertoire', *Agroforestry Systems*, 12 (2): 111–37.

Rocheleau, D. (1994) 'Participatory research and the race to save the planet: Questions, critique and lessons from the field', *Agriculture and Human Values*, 11 (2-3): 4–25.

Rocheleau, D. (1995) 'Maps, numbers, text and context: Mixing methods in feminist political ecology, *Professional Geographer*, 47 (4): 458–67.

Rocheleau, D. and Ross, L. (1995) 'Trees as tools, trees as text: Struggles over resources in Zambrana-Chacuey, Dominican Republic', *Antipode*, 27 (4): 407–28.

Rocheleau, D. and Edmunds, D. (1997) 'Women, men and trees: Gender, power and property in forest and agrarian landscapes', *World Development*, 25 (8): 1351–71.

Rose, G. (1993) *Feminism and Geography: The Limits of Geographical Knowledge*. Cambridge: Polity Press.

Rose, R. (1997a) 'Situated knowledges: positionality, reflexivities and other tactics', *Progress in Human Geography*, 21 (3): 305–20.

Rose, R. (1997b) 'Performing inoperative community: the space and resistance of some community arts projects', in S. Pyle and M. Keith (eds), *Geographies of Resistance*. London: Routledge. pp. 184–202.

Ruddick, S. (2004) 'Activist geographies: building possible worlds', in P. Cloke, P. Crang and M. Goodwin (eds), *Envisioning Human Geographies*. London: Arnold. pp. 229–41.

Sanderson, E. (2007) 'Cartographies of development space: Embodying development and spirituality. Unpublished PhD thesis, Wellington, Victoria University of Wellington.

Sanderson, E. and Kindon, S. (2004) 'Progress in participatory development: opening up the possibilities of knowledge through progressive participation', *Progress in Development Studies*, 4 (2): 114–26.

Savin-Baden, M. and Wimpenny, K. (2007) 'Exploring and implementing participatory action research', *Journal of Geography in Higher Education*, 31 (2): 331–43.

Sense, A. (2006) 'Driving from the rear passenger seat: Control dilemmas in participative action research', *International Journal of Social Research Methodology*, 9 (1): 1–13.

Shaw, B. (1995) 'Contradictions between action and theory: Feminist participatory research in Goa, India', *Antipode*, 27 (1): 91–9.

Singleton, G. (2007) Personal communication, October 22.

Smith, D. (2003) 'Participatory mapping of community lands and hunting yields among the Bugle of Western Panama', *Human Organization*, 62 (4): 332–43.

Smith, F. (2004) 'Is there a place for children's geographers in the policy arena?' *Children's Geographies*, 2 (1): 157–61.

Smith, S., Williams, D. and Johnson, N. (eds) (1997) *Nurtured by Knowledge: Learning to do Participatory Action Research*. New York/Ottawa: The Apex Press.

Staeheli, L. and Mitchell, D. (2005) 'The complex politics of relevance in geography', *Annals of the Association of American Geographers*, 95 (2): 357–72.

Stocks, R. (2003) 'Mapping dreams in Nicaragua's Bosawas Reserve', *Human Organization*, 62 (4): 344–56.

Tandon, R. (1980) *Participatory Research in Asia*. Canberra: Centre for Continuing Education, Australian National University.

Taylor, P. and Fransman, J. (2003) 'Learning and teaching participation in institutions of higher learning: an overview', *PLA NOTES*, 48: 5–9.

Thomas-Slayter, B. (1995) 'A brief history of participatory methodologies', in R. Slocum, L. Wichhart, D. Rocheleau and B. Thomas-Slayter (eds), *Power, Process and Participation: Tools for Social and Environmental Change*. London: Intermediate Technology Press Ltd. pp. 9–16.

Thrift, N. (2008) *Non-representational Theory: Space, Politics, Affect*. London: Routledge.

Tolia-Kelly, D. (2006) 'Affect – an ethnocentric encounter?: Exploring the "universalist" imperative of emotional/affectual geographies', *Area*, 38 (2): 213–17.

Tolia-Kelly, D. (2007) 'Participatory art: Capturing spatial vocabularies in a collaborative visual methodology with Melanie Carvalho and South Asian women in London, UK', in S. Kindon, R. Pain and M. Kesby (eds), *Participatory Action Research Approaches and Methods: Connecting People, Participation and Place*. London: Routledge. pp. 132–40.

Tolman, D. and Brydon-Miller, M. (eds) (2001) *From Subjects to Subjectivities: A Handbook of Interpretive and Participatory Methods*. New York: New York University Press.

Townsend, J. with Arrevillaga, U., Bain, J., Cancino, S., Frenk, S., Pacheo, S. and Crez, E. (1995) *Women's Voices from the Rainforest*. London: Routledge.

Tuhiwai-Smith, L. (1999) *Decolonizing Methodologies: Research and Indigenous Peoples*. London: Zed Books.

Van Blerk, L. and Kesby, M. (eds) (2008) *Doing Children's Geographies*. London: Routledge.

Wadsworth, Y. (1998) 'What is participatory action research?' *Action Research International*. Paper 2. Available at www.scu.edu.au/schools/gcm/ar/ari/p-ywadsworth98.html (Accessed 25 March 2007).

Wadsworth, Y. (2001) 'The Mirror, the Magnifying Glass, the Compass and the Map: Facilitating Participatory Action Research', in P. Reason and H. Bradbury (eds), *Handbook of Action Research*. London: Sage. pp. 420–32.

Waite, L. and Conn, C. (2008) 'Participatory video: How to see without gazing?' Paper presented to *Association of American Geographers Conference*, Boston, April.

Whatmore, S. (2003) 'Generating materials', in M. Pryke, G. Rose and S. Whatmore (eds), *Using Social Theory*. London: Sage. pp. 89–104.

White, G. (1972) 'Geography and public policy', *The Professional Geographer*, 24 (May): 101–4.

White, S. (ed.) (2003) *Participatory Video: Images that Transform and Empower*. London: Sage.

White, S., Nair, K. and Ashcroft, J. (eds) (1994) *Participatory Communication: Working for Change and Development*. New Delhi: Sage.

Whyte, W. (ed.) (1991) *Participatory Action Research*. London: Sage.

Williams, G. (2004a) 'Towards a repoliticization of participatory development: political capabilities and spaces of empowerment', in S. Hickey and G. Mohan (eds), *Participation: From Tyranny to Transformation? Exploring New Approaches to Participation in Development.* London: Zed Books. pp. 92–108.

Williams, G. (2004b) 'Evaluating participatory development: tyranny, power and (re)politicisation', *Third World Quarterly*, 25 (3): 557–78.

Williams, C. and Dunn, C. (2003) 'GIS in participatory research: assessing the impact of landmines on communities in north-west Cambodia', *Transactions in GIS*, 7 (3): 393–410.

Young, T. (2003) '"It's strange kids coming in": young people and belonging in a community undergoing residential restructuring'. Paper presented to the *Association of American Geographers Conference*, New Orleans, April.

Young, L. and Barrett, H. (2001) 'Adapting visual methods: action research with Kampala stress children', *Area*, 34 (2): 141–52.

24

Relevance

Lynn A. Staeheli and Don Mitchell

RELEVANCE

In the spring of 2000, we began our interviews for a project funded by the National Science Foundation on relevance and the sociology of knowledge related to research on public space. We had boldly promised in our proposal that we would develop a model to track the ways that knowledge developed within the academy, that it circulated amongst scholars and students, and that it was transported beyond the academy. We wanted to understand the pathways by which knowledge was developed and modified through its use by a variety of people, including scholars, students, practitioners, and the general public. We argued that by conducting this research on one empirical topic, we could provide an approach that could be applicable to other fields of study or to research on other empirical topics. We expected the research would be relevant in several ways: its focus was relevance, there were lively debates about relevance in the discipline of geography, and governmental funding agencies and research councils were demanding it. Finally, the empirical topic of public space was one for which the contentious nature of debates surrounding the spaces meant that research by geographers potentially *could* be relevant. And since public space research draws the attention of critical geographers, who express a desire to remake the social geographies of our cities and our world, we expected that public space research *should* be relevant. And so we began our research.

Our project involved reading all of the Anglophone literature on public space published by geographers or in geography journals and books. We interviewed people who had written those articles. And we went into 'the field', interviewing people who were directly involved in public space controversies. From each source of 'data', we tried to assess the relevance of research. In the literature, we looked at whether the article discussed how the author wanted information to be used or the significance of the argument. In the interviews with researchers, we asked the same questions, but also asked questions about the audience for the research, or for whom they wanted the research to be relevant. In the interviews with practitioners, we asked about the importance of public space, but also whether they used the work of academics, and academic geographers more particularly.

Relevance was everywhere. Articles were justified by it; researchers wanted it; practitioners thought public space was important to the quality and character of life in cities and for democracy. But there was a problem. Not an unanticipated problem, but one that was startling in its absoluteness. After over sixty interviews with practitioners in five cities, only three people actually used academic research in their work on public space – and two were themselves academics. The work of academics seemed irrelevant to the practitioners and activists we interviewed. One person even said he did not know what academics did with their time, as it took so long for them to make research available to the public. What was going on? Researchers wanted their work to be relevant. Academic institutions and disciplines encouraged it. Practitioners wanted it. But the research of geographers seemed not to be relevant. Could it be that research in human geography is *ir*relevant, despite the intentions of researchers? In answering this question, we will try to unravel why it often seems that research is irrelevant. In so doing, however, we will argue that the blanket categories 'relevant' and 'irrelevant' mask a much more complex set of processes and relationships. We will argue that relevance always needs to be qualified, asking the following: relevance *for whom?* under what circumstances? for what ends? for which political purposes? As these questions imply, relevance is complex, and there is some sentiment that the term should be discarded (e.g., Pain, 2006). We use the term, however, to focus attention on the inherently political nature of social geography, and in particular, of social geography that takes a goal of being useful, of making changes in society, of being relevant. We do so, however, without proscribing the means by which relevance is to be achieved or the particular political goals of researchers.

In this chapter, we explore the debates over relevance in human geography, but with a specific focus on social geography. First, based on interviews and an analysis of the literature we conducted for the research project introduced above, we undertake a consideration of whether relevance is even a goal for geographers. We then provide a working definition of relevance that highlights its multifaceted and inherently political nature. In the third section, we examine the political contexts of research as they shape the possibilities for making research relevant. This is followed by an examination of the institutional contexts in which academic geographers labour and discuss the ways this conditions the relevance of research. Finally, we turn the tables and explore whether all the calls for relevant research risk subverting scholarship itself. With the caveats of this section in mind, we conclude the chapter with what might almost be thought of as a manifesto for relevant research, following Rachel Pain's (2006) reminder that, as academics, we are not victims and our hands are not completely tied. As such, we move away from the barriers to relevant research and consider the *opportunities* for it.

DO GEOGRAPHERS *WANT* TO BE RELEVANT?

In 2001 and 2002, a lively – some might say heated – debate was published in *Progress in Human Geography* over geography's relative absence from public policy discussions and the misinterpretation of what geographical research was used. In her article 'Geography on the agenda', Doreen Massey (2001) lamented the fact that geographers' work was not recognized or incorporated into regional regeneration and development policy in the United Kingdom. She argued that geographers needed to do a better job of demonstrating the importance of approaching the regional problem with a geographical imagination that highlights the ways in which multiple stories and experiences occur in the same place, and that highlights multiplicity and simultaneity, rather than stories that prioritize and wipe away other experiences and other imaginations. She wanted geographers to think about space in ways that highlight how seemingly contradictory experiences occur together, and in fact, are dependent on each other. She wanted them, further, to base those geographical imaginations on experiences and events on the ground and to work with activist campaigns, with community organizations, with political parties, and with government policy makers in order to infuse debates over regional regeneration with a geographical imagination. In an article in the next issue of *Progress*, Ron Martin (2001) bemoaned the lack of involvement of geographers in economic policy making, noting that the current moment presented a real opportunity to make geographic research more visible, more engaged by policy makers, more relevant. In a later commentary (Martin, 2002), he worried that a perceived dilettantism in geography limited its effectiveness and utility in policy circles. These articles were followed by a stinging response by Danny Dorling and Mary Shaw (2002) that excoriated critical geographers generally, and Massey in particular, for confusing better conceptualization with real engagement; they argued that if geography was to be relevant, then geographers needed to engage with data, with the needs of policy makers rather than the imperatives of social theory, and perhaps to shed their identity as geographers and just get down to business.

This debate was curious, in some ways, as it seemed to rest on a premise that most geographers did not want their work to be relevant, that relevance was *ir*relevant to them. While this was a subtle strand in Massey's argument (why else would we need to be implored to put geography on the agenda?), it was blatant in Dorling and Shaw's argument. It was a strand that has run through many of the addresses and newsletter columns that came from leaders of the Association of American Geographers around the same time, thereby demonstrating this was not just some problem with British geography. Yet this is puzzling, since we assumed most people would want their research to be used. And, indeed, of the public space researchers we interviewed, all but one wanted their work to be relevant in some way. So what is the basis of the implication that geographers – and human geographers in particular – are unconcerned with relevance?

Perhaps this sense that geography as a whole was not interested in relevance can be traced to the geographical literature itself. As part of our larger study, we read 218 articles, books, and book chapters that we believed was comprehensive of the Anglophone geographic literature on public space through 1998. In reading, we coded the articles for whether or not the authors explicitly wrote about the way they *wanted* their work to be relevant. We also coded different ways that the research *could* be relevant, even if the authors were not explicit about it. We did this by looking at the conclusions of the article where authors typically try to summarize the importance or significance of their work.

Table 24.1 Relevance in public space books, chapters and articles

	Number of articles	*% of articles*
Relevance made explicit		
Yes	92	42
No	126	58
Total	218	
How Could Articles be Relevant?*		
Improve quality of life in city	75	34
Resolve theoretical issues	75	34
Enhance conceptual clarity	59	27
More inclusive society	31	14
Help achieve social justice	31	14
Affect policy	27	12
Empowerment	25	11
Improve access to public space	18	8
Improve safety of public space	14	6
Prediction	3	1

* Articles could be relevant in more than one way.

As can be seen in Table 24.1, fewer than half of the articles had an explicit statement about the relevance of the research. Authors' statements about why the work was important were most frequently declarations as to the necessity of improved public spaces for a better quality of life in the city or were statements about the importance of resolving theoretical issues; alongside theoretical development was the importance of advancing conceptual clarity. Promoting social justice, an inclusive society and empowerment were also ways that authors hoped the research could potentially be useful. Policy as such was relatively infrequently mentioned.

The assertion of theoretical and conceptual importance of published work may be one reason that critics might argue that the work is, in fact, *ir*relevant. Several commentators have complained that social geographers – and those relying on critical social theory, in particular – are more concerned with clever theoretical arguments than with addressing real problems or with conveying information in a usable fashion. Certainly this was at the crux of Dorling and Shaw's (2002: 634) argument, when they wrote:

> It is possible that geographers are being ignored because people can neither hear nor understand them ... Regardless of what they have been saying, the language and expression of 'reconceptualizing geographers' has often become an elitist jargon. We often wonder whether people writing in this way actually want to be taken seriously (indeed if they really wish to be understood) outside their small peer group.

While we would not jump to the conclusion that theoretical work is necessarily irrelevant or of interest only to a small, elitist peer group, we do note that the primary audience for most of the material we read – again, as noted in the authors' statements about why the work was important – was other scholars; this was the case with over 70% of the articles. Public officials and policy makers seemed to be intended as an audience in only 14% of the articles.

It is possible, and indeed likely, that this assessment of relevance reflects the fact that we read *academic* literature, and that there is a division of labour within the academy that emphasizes the production of theory.[1] In such a context, theoretical development *is* relevant. But rather than resolving the puzzle of why geographers' research seems to be irrelevant, this answer only raises another question.

WHAT IS RELEVANCE, ANYWAY?

For us, what emerged from the exchanges on the pages of *Progress* was a sense that the authors were talking about very different things, and that they held quite different understandings of the nature of relevance and of the public geographers should serve. The debate continues, and not just in the pages of one journal; it has been raised in multiple arenas and by multiple authors (cf., Castree, 2006; Dear, 1999; Fuller and Kitchen, 2004; Harman, 2003; Murphy, 2006; Murphy et al., 2005; Staeheli and Mitchell, 2005; Turner, 2005; Ward, 2005). The sense that we may be meaning different things, but using the same term 'relevance', continues, however.

If we step back from the heat of the debate in the pages of *Progress* and in disciplinary associations, it is possible to clarify what is meant by 'relevance', to understand the different meanings and audiences that people intend when talking about it.[2] Michael Dear (1999) identified three conceptualizations of the term: as pertinence, as commitment, and as application. When research is relevant because it is *pertinent*, it means that the research addresses a timely issue. In 2007, pertinent issues in social geography might include the integration of immigrants and religious minorities into national societies, neoliberal welfare reform, or the ways that certain groups – such as teenagers – are vilified and thereby made 'dangerous'. Relevance as *commitment* implies a commitment to action and to social change, to the solution of social issues. Research that displays this form of relevance would be designed to bring about immediate changes that reflect the political goals of the researcher, goals that are perhaps developed in concert with community groups or campaign organizations. Commitment is motivated by normative values and is often devoted to political projects that involve working with people outside the academy to design, conduct, and act upon research (see Kindon, this volume). Finally, Dear argues that research can be thought of as relevant in cases where it can be *applied*, as when research feeds into policies or decisions by groups that may not have been directly involved in the research.

In a later article (Staeheli and Mitchell, 2005), we supplemented Dear's definition with two more elements of relevance. The first was relevance as *centrality*. This is an understanding of relevance that has often been promoted by disciplinary leaders who wish to highlight the way that geography is integrative by nature, and therefore should be at the heart of interdisciplinary endeavours. By acting on and drawing attention to geography's centrality, the argument goes, we can build better understandings of the social world and also enhance geography's standing amongst its cognate disciplines. There is a way in which this understanding of relevance emphasizes the relevance of geography as a discipline as an end in and of itself, rather than drawing attention to the social problems that relevant research – in the senses of commitment and applicability – might address. Finally, we noted that an important aspect of relevance is often for *teaching*. When we can use our research to help students draw connections between broad structural relationships and the social patterns and interactions they see in their daily lives, research has a certain kind of relevance that may have long-term implications, even if those implications are difficult to trace in the short term.

Politics is woven through each of these senses of relevance, whether it is in the intention to use research in policy and public debate, in the underlying norms and values that shape a commitment to social change, or in helping students understand how they might intervene in the social issues that they confront in their daily lives. But as Massey (2002) argues, it is precisely the failure to recognize the politics of relevance that limits our abilities to intervene in the venues that might achieve the kinds of changes we desire. It is not an easy matter to become a 'public intellectual' and Kevin Ward (2006) notes that geographers are rarely amongst the scholars holding that label. And while geographers often are called upon to testify or contribute their research findings to government hearings and to policy makers (see Turner, 2005), only a small fraction of our research is used in this way. For example, in 2001 the Home Office in the UK invited commentary from academics on a White Paper on asylum seekers. None of those commentaries or research results seem to have been published or considered by the government, forcing researchers to find other outlets. Those outlets might reach a particular audience, but it is not clear that it found its way back to the Home Office and to government ministers (see Yuval-Davis et al., 2005). Furthermore, a great deal of research – and we suspect that the majority of social geography – involves working with community groups or marginalized populations and is motivated by a desire and a political intention to make a difference. As Massey (2002: 646) argues, relevant research is not simply about producing technically correct answers; it also involves interventions to help create the political will to address social problems. More than talking about *policies*, she argues that we need to talk about *politics* when thinking about relevance. In this situation, our concern as researchers – and as critical social geographers – might be better thought of as 'counter-policy' research, rather than as policy relevant (Pain, 2006).

POLITICAL CONTEXT OF RELEVANCE IN SOCIAL RESEARCH

We cannot simply will our research into being relevant in the ways we wish. If we could, it is quite likely we would see that all research has some obvious element of relevance. For instance, in the study we described in the introduction, we asked public space researchers whether they wanted their work to be relevant in some way. All but one of the respondents said that they most certainly did want it to be. But most of the researchers were frustrated by structural conditions that both defined and limited the relevance of their research. In this section of the chapter, we discuss some elements of the political context that conditions what 'counts' or what appears to be relevant. We note that the practices embedded in these contexts all seem to deny the inherently political nature of social problems, of attempts to redress them, and attempts to intervene in them through research; in that denial, an ethic of value-neutrality is often projected. Yet through the social practices of governing, certain kinds of topics are deemed relevant for policy or for discussion, certain ways of debating and discussing issues are validated, and certain kinds of researchers and political agents are granted access to the venues in which social issues are debated. These political contexts condition the relevance of social research, irrespective of researchers' intents. We briefly address four elements of this context: institutional cultures of policy-making, access to social policy debates, the social relations embedded in research, and science policy.

Institutional cultures of policy-making

One of the first issues that researchers attempting to work with policy confront is the fact that most institutions do not work like universities; a lack of familiarity with the institutional cultures of policy-making may make doing research on policy or doing research in support of policy difficult to accomplish. There are many ways that these cultures are manifested, but we focus here on issues surrounding language and critique, as these may most directly affect the ways in which geographers are motivated by commitment to do relevant work.

Policy-makers (sometimes also known as 'government bureaucrats') have developed their own, specialized languages to facilitate their work. Sometimes these languages enter the general parlance, as with ASBOs in the UK[3], but sometimes they are highly specific, technical, and opaque to those outside the bureaucracy. Languages to describe specific building or neighbourhood land use regulations or that are used to regulate child protection, education, and minority-majority relations can be very difficult to penetrate. One could say that this is simply a matter of learning the language, and that such learning is appropriate if one is serious about intervening in or contributing to policy debates. But it is not so simple.

Languages are not simply collections of words, but rather, they also construct systems of meaning and interpretation. As such, language is deeply involved in what we know about the world, how we know it, and what we think is possible. The language of policy itself, therefore, is implicated in what we know about a problem, and more importantly, what we *can* know and do about it. Jürgen Habermas (1970) has argued that policy discourse rests on a particular way of discussing problems – a particular language – that is rational and technical. Ways of speaking, languages, and the ideas that cannot be conveyed in those languages or modes of address that do not conform to the technical rationality of the bureaucracy may not be capable of being accommodated within bureaucratic discourse. Ideas, people, and values may thereby be excluded from policy debates by virtue of the languages spoken, even if the process of debate and deliberation seems otherwise to be open. Consider, for instance, how the voices and words of children can be included in policy debates about a 'child friendly city'. Children will lack both the specialized knowledge and the presumption of being a rational, knowledgeable participant in those discussions (see Simpson, 1997). While it might be possible to 'translate' their words, it is likely that meanings, ideals, and aspirations will be changed as the words are filtered through adult and bureaucratic languages and rationalities. Similarly, bringing the voices of immigrants and those for whom English is not their first language into public hearings is not a trivial matter (e.g., Pulido, 1994). Translators have to be arranged – and paid – but even so, the full meanings and emotions behind people's words are not easily conveyed. And it is not just the language of children and non-English speakers that may not be easily accommodated. It is not clear that certain motivations and values – such as love and compassion – can be incorporated into a technical, rational language. These issues may well be intractable, as the dispassionate language of planning can mask the realities of systematic exclusion, marginalization, and injustice in our cities (Healy, 1992).

Access to social policy debates

It is not enough to *want* to intervene in policy debates; one has to have *access* in some way. Return to Massey's (2001) arguments about intervention and putting geography on the agenda. Her ability to contribute to policy debates stems from a long engagement with community and activist groups, as well as her involvement with the Greater London Council in the 1970s and with ministers and other officials in government and in the Labour Party. Such engagement reflects great commitment, dedication, and we suspect, persistence. But it is also a *long* engagement with people in the place where she lives. How can we build that engagement with people and debates that may be far from where we live? Or when we are just starting an academic career? Or when we may be forced to be an 'astronaut', dropping in and out of debates and activism given where we are in life and career courses? It is simply not the case that government agencies and community organizations welcome researchers – their questions, their research, or their 'answers' – with open arms. For instance, as we write this chapter in 2007, many British citizens and government ministers believe that the relationship between minority communities, religious communities, and British society is one of the most important issues for the nation. What could be more relevant, in the sense of pertinent, than research on Muslim and immigrant communities and community organizations? Yet many Muslim organizations and community centres are wary of the increased scrutiny and attention, fearing that it will only expose them to greater risk and possible harassment from police and 'domestic terrorism' initiatives (see Staeheli and Nagel, 2008). Working with governments may be no easier, as agencies can limit access to data or can constrain the kinds of questions that are addressed in government-funded research and consultancies. And, of course, there is no guarantee that governments or political officials will listen, as Massey's dismay at regional policy in the UK attests.

It might seem that persistence and couching our arguments in the right language is all that is required to enter policy debates, but the experiences of the public space researchers we interviewed suggest otherwise. Several of our respondents gave talks or provided advice to community groups and government officials. Many tried to present their ideas in ways that would be engaging to a broad public, and several published in presses for an educated lay public. Many worked with community and activist groups. And almost all of them used their research in teaching. Yet few felt they had reached the illusive goals of being a public intellectual or of influencing policy or attitudes on particular public space debates. One issue in this regard is almost certainly that academic researchers often ask different questions than either community groups or governments. This is important, according to one of our respondents, because one way that research can become relevant is by bringing important issues to the surface. But if researchers miss that mark or if the context is not right for the issue to be taken up, issues are likely to remain just below the surface, and research therefore may not enter political debates. Access is about timing and the context in which issues are raised, not just about persistence and the open doors of government and communities. In other words, serendipity may be as crucial as positioning and the intrinsic importance of our research.

The social relations of research

A closely related issue that shapes the ways in which relevant research is conducted concerns social relations, positionality, and the possibility of critique.[4] As noted, many social geographers are motivated by a feeling that there is injustice in our world, and they want their work to be useful in addressing – and redressing – those injustices. Those who choose to work with either political parties or governments – to work on the 'inside' – have to negotiate relationships that are social, as well as political. We often work with organizations at their sufferance, not because our presence is an unqualified benefit to the organization or because they are convinced we will do what they want done. This is as true when working with community organizations as it is when working with bureaucracies. Our ability to do our research – to be relevant – is dependent on them granting access; it depends on a form of social capital. For instance, Alison Mountz conducted an institutional ethnography of Citizenship and Immigration Canada (CIC) that was motivated by a feminist politics of inclusion and a desire to intervene in the ways that states construct some migrants as 'illegal' (Mountz, 2002). At various times, however, she was silenced by her tenuous position within the agency and her need to maintain a presence within it; at one point, CIC withdrew its permission for her to conduct research in the agency precisely because she was asking questions that were sensitive and critical – in other words, because she was doing what researchers are *supposed* to do. In other cases, it may be difficult to engage in critique of the community organizations and individuals with whom researchers work. Richa Nagar (1997; Nagar and Ali, 2003) has confronted this in several situations as she works with women and women's organizations that confront violence, sexism, class, and caste in Tanzania and India. While supporting these efforts, she has also been critical of some practices of women and women's organizations. The difficulty of critiquing projects and people that she supports is compounded by her own positionality with respect to gender, caste and class, as well as her position as an Indian woman based in an American university. Even as she works toward a postcolonial and transnational feminist praxis, she may sometimes be limited in her ability to engage in critique because this might risk the collaboration that is the basis of her scholarly work. There are no easy or enduring answers to these issues. The numerous calls for relevant research from other academics and from government funding councils do not provide guidance or assistance, as we argue in the next section.

Science policy

As researchers, many of us operate within institutional contexts that are publicly subsidized, whether by direct government subsidy, by laws that exempt universities from paying property taxes, by other laws that allow deduction of tuition from income taxes, and through national, regional, and local support for research. To better understand this element of the context of research, we turn to a description of science policy in the US.[5]

David Demeritt (2000) argues that American science policy after the Second World War initially enshrined science as a public good and shielded it from market pressures. Science was viewed as a public good in and of itself, and a boundary (albeit a permeable boundary) was drawn between the public good of science and the future applications of that science in the marketplace. This understanding of the public nature of science was never fully achieved, of course, as Cold War politics quickly created a very thin membrane between government and industry – at least with regard to military applications of scientific research (Kleinman, 1995). Science also became an ingredient in economic development policy, as research and development functions propelled growth in certain sectors of the US economy and regions of the country. Over time, other conceptualizations of the public nature of science gained prominence. Beginning in the 1960s, critics of government spending on research and science focused on what was perceived to be a lack of accountability in the use of federal funds, and on seemingly obscure, inconsequential, or even silly research. Social sciences came under particular attack in the 1990s for their perceived irrelevance, or perhaps worse, for relevant research that reflected a liberal bias. More recently, Senator Kay Bailey Hutchison recommended that the National Science Foundation (NSF) stop funding social science research, or at least discontinue the Sociology and Political Science programs (Mervis, 2006).[6] As Demeritt (2000: 313) argues, the politics of science funding now emphasize public accountability by making '… accountability synonymous with cost-effectiveness, public needs with the demands of paying customers, and public relevance with wealth generation and the research needs of policy making'. Social critique, exposition of new forms of inequality, marginalization and oppression, and capacity building for community groups do not appear on the new agenda. Instead, a market-based logic is applied in allocating resources for research.

One marker in the transition to the new model of science is in the NSF's mandate to researchers that they demonstrate the broader relevance of their research beyond the intellectual contributions of basic science. It is not clear that NSF administrators themselves wanted this change, but the policy of the Foundation now is that each proposal must clearly identify the broader impacts of proposed research at key places. The broader impacts are to be discussed in the following terms:

- How well does the activity advance discovery and understanding while promoting teaching, training and learning?
- How well does the proposed activity broaden the participation of underrepresented groups?
- To what extent will it enhance the infrastructure for research and education, such as facilities, instrumentation, networks and partnerships?
- Will the results be disseminated broadly to enhance scientific and technological understanding?
- What may be the benefits of the proposed activity to society? (NSF, nd: 1)

The first three 'broader impacts' are in fact impacts on the contexts of research and education in the US, focusing on enhancing education, infrastructure, and so-called 'pipeline' issues. The third item suggests that broader networking impacts might also be important, but the explanatory text only mentions networks between universities, government institutions, and other research and development institutions (including businesses). The fourth impact addresses dissemination of research, but again, the explanatory text emphasizes dissemination to educational institutions (including museums, K-12 educators, and libraries) and the ever-so-vague 'broad audience' and 'broad context'. Looking at the specific examples, the public for whom research is supposed to be relevant seems not to be expansive and inclusive, but instead seems to represent a narrow range of positions allied with the conduct of government in some form.

The last impact identified by the NSF addresses the benefits to society. Surely this is where the social, political, ethical, or perhaps moral value of the research could be addressed. The background material provided by the NSF is rather different, however, suggesting only that research 'may contribute to understanding the environment, commercial technology, public policy, health or safety and other aspects of the public welfare'. Examples of these benefits include the potential applications of the research, partnering with staff in federal agencies and the private sector, analyses that are accessible to non-scientists, or that 'provide information for policy formulation by Federal, State, or local agencies' (NSF, nd: 4-5). Nowhere – and understandably so, given the scepticism with which the social sciences are viewed by the US Congress – does the document ascribe a value to assisting community organizations build their capacity, to providing the ability for citizens to participate in policy discussions, to generating evidence that communities might use to challenge government or corporate decisions affecting their localities, or to bringing marginalized groups more fully into the public.

THE RELEVANCE – AND IMPORTANCE – OF SCHOLARSHIP

The NSF and the Economic and Social Research Council (ESRC) were originally established to support 'basic research' – research whose immediate applicability, or even pertinence, might not be readily obvious. In recent years, however, instrumental relevance is expected in research and they require that every proposal address the ways in which the project will have 'broader impacts'. While there is nothing inherently wrong with such demands (in fact there might be much that is good in them), we cannot help but wonder whether the ongoing push for 'relevant research', no less than the constant calls for greater relevancy in and for geography, forgets something important: that sometimes the greatest value of research is its mere existence. That is to ask, does the push for *relevance* threaten to forget the need for *knowledge*? Sometimes, the best way to be relevant might be to ignore immediate relevance altogether and to engage in those things academics are good at and for which a special place in the division of labour has been reserved: reading, thinking, theorizing, writing.[7]

Speaking of progressive, or 'leftist', scholarship, but in an argument of wider applicability, Castree (2000: 960) has asserted that 'research can itself be "active" – rather than simply academic – when it discloses hitherto unknown things or makes concrete recommendations for change on the basis of new evidence'. In other words, it is sometimes just the hard slog of research itself that creates relevance, more so than the effort to directly link research to particular political projects or certain communities of interest (policy makers, civic organizations seeking to 'build capacity', and so forth). This is not to argue that relevance as we have so far been discussing it is irrelevant; pertinence, commitment, application, centrality and teaching remain important values in any research endeavour. But it is to argue that the single-minded pursuit of such values can often interrupt research itself, thereby limiting its worth. The goal of immediate applicability, for example, may so foreshorten research timelines that the ability to delve deeply into a problem, theory, or body of knowledge is constrained. The result can include a closing off of the possibility to do the sort of long-term, basic research that provides the knowledge upon which new ideas, new activisms, new inventions, and so forth, are founded.

A related problem that all of us who work and learn in the contemporary academy know very well is an increasing pressure, both internally and externally applied, to shift teaching and learning from a pursuit of knowledge to an exercise in training. Consider all those 'methodology' classes that spend so much time on the best ways to transcribe an interview, to prepare an assay, or to negotiate an ethics review board that no time is left at all to raise questions about questions: questions about what is to be known and why it is important to know it. Knowing how to prepare an assay or to prepare a statement about research ethics are vital, indispensable skills, but the learning of them often crowds out the more basic learning that allows for advances in knowledge. As Peter Gould (1985) warned more than twenty years ago, the growing emphasis on *training* in universities threatens to undermine *thinking* in them. He argued that training is the antithesis of thinking; training is learning to do something without having to think about it. As such, an emphasis on training may transform what a university is and what it is for, and thereby, the kind of knowledge production that is possible. To put this in stark terms, one of the values of the university is that it provides a space in which apparently 'useless' thinking – thinking that is not directly or immediately pertinent or applicable – can take place. Thinking is, and often must be, literally *useless* in an instrumental sense and will not (cannot, should not) provide immediate returns (see Mitchell, 2004a: 765).

We often forget that as scholars, theorists, and, indeed experts, our involvement in community organizations, activist groups, policy circles, or as commentators in the media is not only sought because of what we *do*, but also because of what we *know*. And what we know is a function of the ability to absent ourselves from these arenas and engage in pursuits that often feel like the antithesis of relevant work: reading, checking over data, debating with colleagues and students, engaging in 'jargon'-filled discourse, and writing for other academics – the very activities that make knowledge possible. The trick for those of us who wish to engage in relevant research is to find ways to preserve the space for the sort of basic scholarship that creates knowledge that (just possibly) might *become* relevant. To engage in relevant scholarship, one must first engage in scholarship.[8]

FOR RELEVANT RESEARCH

The point of the previous sections is to suggest that our position as scholars – our position high up in the ivory tower – is not only, or always, an obstacle to relevant research, but is also often an opportunity. But it is only an opportunity to the degree that we remember the complexity of relevancy. As Pain (2006: 250) has argued, the term "relevance" has become overused – indeed subject to almost wholesale alliance within critical geography (itself subject to almost wholesale alliance in human geography) – so that it is no longer very useful'. We need, then, to think of relevance as something more than a slogan, something more than a special pleading for the 'obvious' importance of geography. Recognizing the complexity of relevance – its different facets, the complex ways in which research is and is not taken up by activists, scholars, policy makers, students, and others, and the possible disconnection between the effects intended by researchers and the actual use to which research is put – allows for a more realistic assessment of what makes research in social geography relevant and the many ways in which geographers can – and cannot – intervene in policy debates, social action, and public knowledge (cf. Castree, 2006; Fuller and Kitchen, 2004; Murphy, 2006; Murphy et al., 2005; Ward, 2005, 2006).

Such a recognition also requires a realistic assessment of the constraints that academics face in their work and other lives – the pressures of tenure, the rising teaching and service workloads, the increasing pressure to secure external money from corporations, foundations, or state funding bodies,[9] together with the ways these pressures shape family and social opportunities – while also recognizing that we are not simply victims. As Rachel Pain (2006: 255, citing Castree, 2002) argues: 'we are responsible too – for being part of unhelpful working cultures, for bureaucracy, for failing to subvert assessment exercises'. But, Pain (2006: 256) continues 'many social geographers are finding creative ways around this in seemingly unsupportive institutions, and becoming more willing, not less, to find new ways to engage with policy' (and, we would add, other forms of relevancy). The challenge, therefore, is to find ways to take fuller control of the social processes that make work relevant. As such, we suggest focused action around the following points as possible avenues forward:

1 Support for more 'relevant' research in social and other geographies should begin not from an assessment of geography's instrumentality for particular groups (business, government, community organizations, activists, and so forth), as important as that may be, but rather in reaffirming a commitment to – and a reinforcement of the institutional structures that promote – geographical *scholarship*. Without a commitment to scholarship as scholarship, geography might well purchase an immediate

pertinence and instrumental applicability at the cost of a longer-term commitment to the development of theories, debates, ideas, and so forth, that will strengthen the *centrality* of geographic research not only to social problems, but to emerging intellectual and political currents and debates.

2 Support for scholarship must understand that 'relevance' is multifaceted, and always politically conditioned. Debate needs to be fostered on the multiple meanings of relevance and how best to address the fact that promotion of one kind of relevance can limit the possibilities for relevance of other kinds. It is equally important to recognize that relevance is determined at least as much after the fact – by the users of research and ideas, by research's actual application – more than its intended *applicability* or by intention. Relevance is a social practice, and debate needs to centre less on bringing pressure on the intentions of researchers, and more on the structures that constrain and/or open up possibilities for research to be *made* relevant.

3 The discipline – and its governing bodies such as the RGS/IBG, AAG, CAG, IGU – needs to take the role of *teaching* as a form of relevance more seriously than it has, for it is in our role as teachers that most of us most consistently and readily 'make a difference' (see Staeheli and Mitchell, 2005). We have thought too little – as a discipline – about how teaching makes research relevant. We need, among other things, to engage in a disciplinary assessment of the ways in which teaching is and is not valued in hiring, tenure, promotion, and merit raise decisions and determine if or how colleges and universities should reform the tenure and promotion process.[10]

4 We need to better recognize that there are different audiences for our scholarship and that our writing and presentations will reflect our assessment of these audiences. Such a recognition brings with it the further recognition that writing for lay audiences, policy makers, and the like, is difficult and time-consuming (and something that not every one is suited for). Thus, appropriate structures to promote and reward such writing – without allowing it to crowd out writing of other kinds – need to be established. These include: a re-evaluation of how popular writing is valued in the tenure and promotion process; the establishment of postdoctoral or other fellowships that provide the time and resources to engage in the work of popularization and that provide legitimacy for scholars that do so; and other structural changes. Such a recognition requires institutional support for fledgling 'public geographies' projects such as those housed in the School of Geography at the University of Birmingham or the Public Humanities Program being developed by Katharyne Mitchell at the University of Washington.

5 Finally, efforts to promote directly applicable, pertinent, and popular geographic research should not be diminished. But pertinence, applicability and popularization should be understood clearly as only facets of relevance, facets that might conflict with relevance as centrality, for teaching, and especially as commitment. Thus, not only the *politics of relevance* needs to be debated. Also crucial is the *relevance of politics* to relevance; we need to always ask, for *whom* should our research be relevant, and under what conditions?

None of this will guarantee that social geography will be more relevant, but as social geographers and our counterparts in other parts of the field research and debate these points in all their complexity, we might be able to begin to develop programmes and projects that both are sensitive to, and seek to shape, the multiple, sometimes contradictory, routes by which geography is made relevant.

NOTES

1 See the post-script to Staeheli and Mitchell (2008) and Ward (2006).

2 This discussion draws from Staeheli and Mitchell (2005).

3 Even when languages enter the public vocabulary of a place, it does not mean they will be understood outside that place. ASBO stands for 'anti-social behaviour ordinance'. People are given 'ASBOs' when they violate the ordinances by loitering, being raucous, tagging walls, not maintaining gardens (or yards), and so forth. Teenagers are particular targets for ASBOs in many British cities.

4 See Kindon in this volume for a more in-depth discussion of these issues.

5 We focus on US science policy as an example, but do not imply it represents or provides a model for the science policy of all countries. A similar analysis, for instance, could be done on British research councils, such as ESRC and the Natural Environment Research Council (NERC).

6 In the end, the Senate reached a compromise that preserved the Social, Behavioral, and Economic Sciences Directorate of the NSF, and even increased funding to it by the same percentage the rest of the Foundation received.

7 This section is based, in part, on Mitchell (2004b).

8 Our point here is not to promote the construction of 'high theory' over 'low practice'; Pain (2006) is correct that this is a false dualism. It needs to be recognized that 'basic research' is quite often the dull, painstaking, or just plain tiring work of parsing data (however defined), checking facts, and so forth, and not at all 'sexy' theory construction (to use Dorling and Shaw's (2002) phrase). Rather, our point is that just this sort of work, which we often forget to think about clearly in our normative arguments about what social geography should be, is indispensable to both theoretical claims and relevance.

9 According to the guidance sent to one of us as part of a promotion at one university, for example, candidates are to be assessed on 'Criteria in respect of applied research and development, evidence of research exploitation, enterprise and innovation:

- transfer of intellectual property into the wider economy;
- translation of research findings into clinical solutions;
- development of innovation;
- research and consulting relationships with other organizations;
- influence on the formulation of policy;
- enrichment of the wider culture through creativity in the social sciences, humanities and the visual and performing arts'.

10 Continuing with the promotion criteria mentioned above, nowhere in the section on 'knowledge transfer' is teaching mentioned. Nor does the section on teaching and learning really give much confidence that administrators understand that teaching is more a form of collaboration between faculty and students than a simple matter of 'delivery' of 'taught programmes' such that there are 'satisfactory student outcomes and good levels of student satisfaction'.

REFERENCES

Castree, Noel (2000) 'Professionalisation, activism and the university: whither "critical geography"?' *Environment and Planning A*, 32 (6): 955–70.

Castree, Noel (2002) 'Border geography', *Area*, 34 (1): 81–6.

Castree, Noel (2006) 'Geography's new public intellectuals', *Antipode*, 38 (2): 396–412.

Dear, Michael (1999) 'The relevance of post-modernism', *Scottish Geographical Magazine*, 115 (2): 143–50.

Demeritt, David (2000) 'The new social contract for science: accountability, relevance, and value in the US and UK science and research policy', *Antipode*, 32 (3): 308–29.

Dorling, Danny and Shaw, Mary (2002) 'Geographies of the agenda: public policy, the discipline and its (re)turns', *Progress in Human Geography*, 26 (5): 629–41.

Fuller, Duncan and Kitchen, Rob (eds) (2004) *Radical Theory/Critical Praxis: Making a Difference Beyond the Academy.* Vancouver, BC: Praxis E-Books.

Gould, Peter (1985) *The Geographer at Work.* Oxford: Blackwell.

Habermas, Jürgen (1970) *Toward a Rational Society: Student Protest, Science, and Politics.* Boston, MA: Beacon Press.

Harman, Jay (2003) 'Wither geography?' *The Professional Geographer*, 55 (4): 415–21.

Healy, Pasty. (1992) 'A planner's day: knowledge and action in communicative practice', *Journal of the American Planning Association*, 58: 9–20.

Kleinman, David (1995) *Politics on the Endless Frontier: Postwar Research Policy in the United States.* Durham, NC: Duke University Press.

Martin, Ron (2001) 'Geography and public policy: the case of the missing agenda', *Progress in Human Geography*, 25 (2): 189–209.

Martin, Ron (2002) 'A geography for policy, or a policy for geography? A response to Dorling and Shaw', *Progress in Human Geography*, 26 (5): 642–44.

Massey, Doreen (2001) 'Geography on the agenda', *Progress in Human Geography*, 25 (1): 5–17.

Massey, Doreen (2002) 'Geography, policy and politics: response to Dorling and Shaw', *Progress in Human Geography*, 26 (5): 645–46.

Mervis, Jeffrey. (2006) 'Senate panel chair asks why NSF funds social sciences', *Science*, 213 (12 May): 829.

Mitchell, Don (2004a) 'Geography in an age of extremes: a blueprint for a geography of justice,' *Annals of the Association of American Geographers,* 94: 764–70.

Mitchell, Don (2004b) 'Radical scholarship: a polemic on making a difference outside the academy', in Duncan Fuller and Rob Kitchen (eds), *Radical Theory/Critical Praxis: Making a Difference Beyond the Academy*. Vancouver, BC: Praxis E-Books. pp. 21–31.

Mountz, Alison (2002) 'Feminist politics, immigration, and academic identities', *Gender, Place and Culture*, 9 (2): 187–94.

Murphy, Alexander (2006) 'Enhancing geography's role in public debate', *Annals of the Association of American Geographers,* 96 (1): 1–13.

Murphy, Alexander, Gregory, Derek, DeBlij, Harm and Gilmore, Ruth (2005), 'The role of geography in public debate', *Progress in Human Geography,* 29 (2): 165–93.

Nagar, Richa (1997) 'Exploring methodological borderlands through oral narratives', in J.P. Jones, H. Nast, and S. Roberts (eds), *Thresholds in Feminist Geography*. Oxford: Roman and Littlefield.

Nagar, Richa and Ali, Farah (2003) 'Collaboration across borders: moving beyond positionality', *Singapore Journal of Tropical Geography*, 24 (3): 356–72.

National Science Foundation (no date) 'Merit review broader impacts criterion: representative activities', http://www.nsf.gov/pubs/gpg/broaderimpacts.pdf. Last viewed 22 February 2006.

Pain, Rachel (2006) 'Social geography: seven deadly myths in policy research', *Progress in Human Geography*, 30 (2): 250–59.

Pulido, Laura (1994) 'Restructuring and the contraction and expansion of environmental rights in the United States', *Environment and Planning A*, 26 (6): 915–36.

Simpson, S. (1997) 'Toward the participation lof children and young people in urban planning and design', *Urban Studies*, 34 (5/6): 907–25.

Staeheli, Lynn A. and Mitchell, Don (2005) 'The complex politics of relevance in geography', *Annals of the Association of American Geographers*, 95 (2): 357–72.

Staeheli, Lynn A. and Mitchell, Don (2008) *The People's Property? Power, Politics, and the Public*. New York: Routledge.

Staeheli, Lynn A. and Nagel, Caroline R. (2008) 'Rethinking security: perspectives from Arab-American and British Arab activists', *Antipode*, 40 (5): 765–86.

Turner, Billie Lee (2005) 'Geography's profile in public debate "inside the Beltway" and the national academies', *The Professional Geographer*, 57 (3): 462–67.

Ward, Kevin (2005) 'Geography and public policy: a recent history of "policy relevance"', *Progress in Human Geography*, 19, 310–21.

Ward, Kevin (2006) 'Geography and public policy: towards public geographies', *Progress in Human Geography*, 30 (4): 495–503.

Yuval-Davis, Nira, Anthias, Floya and Kofman, Eleonore (2005) 'Secure borders and safe haven and the gendered politics of belonging: beyond social cohesion', *Ethnic and Racial Studies*, 28 (3): 513–35.

25

The Politics and Ethics of Trust in Geographic Research

Kathryn Besio

The sun was dipping behind the valley walls, and the sky lilting into the long twilight. Soon it would start to cool down for the day. It's nice out walking in the fallow fields late at this time of the afternoon. In November, the fields are empty of workers. On some of my walks, I may come upon an old man fixing a fence, dragging thorny brush to the edge of the fields, and then piling them on the rock walls. Or, sometimes a boy is tracking down one of his yak, wandering the fields. Perhaps even a dazed military guy, sucking in all this low-elevation air, walking back down from the Baltoro Glacier. But, no tourists. They've all gone home for the year.

I've run into no one today. It's just time to collect my thoughts and soak in the peaks.

My walks are short. People already think it's kind of strange that I disappear on a regular basis, but they seem to comprehend my loneliness and needs in their terms. Many of the women encourage me to go home so I can see my mother. 'Do you miss her?' they ask. Yes. It's true that I miss those I love, but my loneliness is not only for the faces and people I want to see. It's a longing to understand without the burden of my impatience. There's layer upon layer of translation to every question and every gesture. I want something more like transparency.

Time to wander back to the village. I take the most obscure paths I can find. I tell myself that if I take the path by Haji's house, it will allow me to steal into 'my' room unseen, thief that I am. As if it were a possibility to slip by the small rooftop sentries, I hug the wall between the two houses and make my way to the house. I fool myself into thinking that I can dodge detection by taking this less-used route.

It's quiet, and I can't see anyone on the roof. I walk through the outside door into the entry level and towards my room by the latrine. Ah, I have made it. I fiddle with the key hung around my neck and unlock my door. I walk in.

There, standing in the middle of my room, is a small goat. Chewing quietly, he looks at me but doesn't move.

Ever vigilant, the sentries were watching. They stole out into the opaque coolness of the afternoon, while I stole in, all of us with mysteries in our wakes.

INTRODUCTION

First, a disclaimer: this chapter will not tell you how a goat ended up in my room or provide a definitive reason why. Some mysteries are best left unsolved, although I will speculate. I use the story of the goat to introduce one of what I would call a grounded or situated ethical dilemma that I experienced while undertaking ethnographic research in northern Pakistan in the late 1990s (Besio, 2005; Besio and Butz, 2004; Butz and Besio, 2004; Besio, 2007). The story of the goat is an uneasy one for me. Yet I elaborate on the goat story because the event it describes became an ethical dilemma for me: given the context of my research site, I did not know how to respond to what, on the surface, appears to be a rather ordinary violation of 'private' space. While this may seem inconsequential, even a non-event constituting an ethical dilemma, it nevertheless raised a host of concerns for me. As I will lay out below, my response and other researchers' responses to situations such as the one I describe, are embedded in a much broader social and historical context, which may render something as mundane as an unwanted entry a point of ethical concern.

Like the event itself, I have thought about the story and my representation of the goat over the last ten years and wondered what to do with it. The story and its subject matter did not really 'fit in' as a research finding *per se*, because what it describes is often considered 'background' to the research and just a fieldwork interaction; it is also a story. It was not until I began writing this chapter that the goat again re-entered my thoughts as an entrée into discussing the nesting of ethics *and* politics in geographic research. Until now, I have left ethical dilemmas to the sidelines, concentrating instead on the politics of representation, effectively overlooking the ways that ethical relations in the field may have influenced my representational politics.

My decision has been to leave the story moldering in the unpublished sections of my dissertation and recount it only in presentations as an example of using stories to write geographies, which I did at an Association of American Geographers meeting in 2006. The story's resurfacing as part of this chapter has to do with a comment made at that same AAG meeting, but at a different session from the one in which I read parts of my goat story and very far from 'my' ostensible field and its goats in northern Pakistan (Katz, 1994). In that session, Liz Bondi made a brief remark about trust and the ethics of geographic research that struck me at the time as relevant to my field research experiences, and which I had not heard mentioned before in discussions about research ethics. In brief, she said that 'trust' could be a more positive way to frame ethical behavior than that of 'doing less harm.' Harm reduction often informs the institutional codes of ethics that researchers subscribe to, particularly those set out by academic human subject committees and ethics review boards.

With Bondi's permission, I have drawn upon her comments here, although my thoughts about trust are directed less towards institutional review boards and their recommendations, and directed more at ethical interactions at the goat-level, although the two are certainly related. It seems worthwhile to examine trust and ethics further, especially as a way to think about the gaps between what ethic review boards *prescribe* to researchers and what we *do* in field research settings. In short, I want to suggest that thinking about trust early in the research process rather than years later, seems particularly relevant to the aims of researchers who face situated, relational ethical dilemmas that may seem to sit askew to the purview of institutional review boards.

Trust is something unequally given and gained in research settings, is not necessarily reciprocal, and in a constant state of negotiation. In the example I describe, trust is contextualized by specific colonial and patriarchal relations of care and, as such, ethics, care, and representation sit together, albeit uncomfortably. It is this nesting of ethics, care and representation that I reflect upon in this chapter as one example that may assist other researchers in thinking through their own situated ethical dilemmas. I do not set out a 'how to' chapter, as if that were possible with situated ethical concerns. Instead, I offer my critical reflections as a place from which to think about social geographers' ethical commitments. As David Butz notes (2008, 254).

> If the purpose of critical reflexivity is to help researchers understand how our situatedeness (institutionally, personally, and in terms of historically structured power relations) vis-à-vis the social worlds we study influences the knowledge we produce and the implications of our research practice 'on the ground,' then the research ethics procedures we employ and their underlying ideologies are important objects of critical reflection.

Drawing from my ethnographic research experiences in Pakistan, I reflect on the ways that trust and day-to-day relations of care were central to research and in the negotiation over research ethics. I examine the ways that the ethical decisions I made (and I assume that other geographers might face) were emplaced in particular spaces of care which, in turn, influenced other research decisions, such as how to ultimately represent research relations and projects.

Relations of care for and by researchers are found in all geographic research, although these research relations of care are often ignored. As researchers, we all eat, sleep and have a range of material needs that we must meet *for* others – family members, other researchers, research subjects, etc. – and that are met *by* others during the research process. Depending on the situation, our care needs are filled by various people, some of whom are paid to care for us, although many times partners and family members may provide unremunerated care. Yet, as in all social relations, research care relations take place within specific historical and social contexts that are very much a part of geographic research, although these relations often remain a silent background to more prominent concerns in researcher-researched relations.

Geographers have spent a lot of time discussing the establishment of mutually beneficial research projects through more participatory research projects, particularly in feminist research practices (see Kindon this volume), proposing greater reflectivity and writing more reflexively. Researchers' expression of positionality (see Browne this volume) and their reflexivity/reflectivity about their emplacement in research projects, have come to be important ways to contextualize research findings (England, 1994; Gilmartin, 2003; Cahill, 2007; Rose, 1997; Hopkins, 2007; Sultana, 2007). Writing about positionality provides a kind of 'critical reflectivity,' which makes more apparent authorial privileges and other privileges that researchers have because of class, status, race, and gender. Recently, critiques of critical reflexivity have become more focused and more prominent (Raju, 2002; Kobayashi, 2003) and I am grateful for authors' contributions towards more 'fully reflexive research' (Al-Hindi, 2002). What I hope to demonstrate in this reflection of my situated ethical dilemma is that a researcher's positionality is always within *specific* social-historical contexts that matter very much to all aspects of our research. As researchers, we must remain attentive and vigilant to the ways we are situated by and how we situate others, particularly around issues as contentious as trust and as intimate as relations of care. Perhaps one reason geographers may have skirted around the issues of care relations and how these are experienced in the activities of research, is because they are grounded in the day-to-day messiness of research interactions, which somehow are understood to fall outside of the research process (though there are exceptions, and see Sultana, 2007 and Hopkins, 2007 for recent examples).

Relevant to these issues of positionality, reflectivity and care relations, trust reflects relations of power in a number of ways: in terms of the day-to-day politics of research, in the politics of representation, and in the types of research projects undertaken (see Smith, 1999). To say that researchers 'trust' those with whom they research and that they trust researchers, has often been a rather one-sided definition of trust, with feminist and participatory researchers challenging these notions most notably. In many instances, and especially under colonial relations of research, research subjects' trust has been widely abused (Smith, 1999). Given these past-histories of abuse, trust is, indeed, a charged issue that deserves researchers' careful consideration. Yet, as Bondi points out, a salient benefit in embracing trust as an ethical starting point is that by beginning research from an attitude of building trust with others, we frame research ethics positively, proactively embracing the uncertainties of human interactions, such as those embedded in care relations and respecting the agency of those research.

It is curious that as much time as geographers have spent discussing ethics, writing about ethics, and worrying over research ethics, some of the ethical dilemmas we face in the field are never published. These discussions remain as widely remarked upon backdrops to the social and spatial relations we describe in our publications (see *ACME*'s 2007 special issue on participatory ethics for notable exceptions, especially Sultana, 2007).[1] As Popke suggests, this could be due to the fact that 'the presumed audience' for published writings on ethics are institutions, organizations and those interested in public policy (2006: 504). He notes that there is a growing interest amongst geographers 'to expand the realm of the social that is normally subject to moral or ethical judgment' (2006: 505). One way that he sees this occurring is in the growing interest in the 'moral geographies of caringscapes,' especially those in the realms of social reproduction (2006: 505).

Following Conradson (2003: 508), I define care relations as 'the proactive interest of one person in the well-being of another and as the articulation of that interest (or affective stance) in practical ways. Care may thus be present in everyday encounters between individuals who are attentive to each other's situations ...' As I look back on the care relations in my research situation, they were inseparable from all aspects of 'my' research, which include resolution of ethical dilemmas and, ultimately, the politics of representation.

In what follows, I first situate my ethnographic research in its historical and geographic context, addressing why the Northern Areas of Pakistan's colonial history is important to consider in terms of the care relations and the situated ethical dilemmas I encountered. Using the goat story to explain my ensuing dilemma, I then explain how the contextualized relations of care influenced my reconciliation of ethical dilemmas about goats in my room, which, in turn, influenced my representational politics.

PENNING THE GOAT: DESCRIBING THE SITE

Ethnographic research formed a key portion of my dissertation research data, and was part of a larger, multi-researcher project that analyzed portering relations in northern Pakistan (Butz and MacDonald, 2001; MacDonald, 1998; Besio, 2005; Besio, 2007; MacDonald and Butz, 1998). Portering – carrying loads for pay – in northern Pakistan has a long history, dating back to the British Raj, and differs from portering in other parts of the Hindu-Kush-Karakoram-Himalaya in that it is work for males – women do not porter – and is government regulated, unlike portering in Nepal, for instance. In the Northern Areas of Pakistan, portering is paid employment that males undertake for mountaineering expeditions and tourist treks (hikes or tramps), whereby men may earn cash incomes amongst other less-tangible benefits, such as learning to speak other languages, expanding social networks, interacting with people from other parts of the world, etc. My research within the larger research project was specifically to analyze how portering embedded itself within daily life in the village, discursively and materially, with a focus on understanding household relations (Besio, 2007). How I came to do research in the Northern Areas of Pakistan and the site itself has its own history and research genealogy, as do all research projects.[2] Yet my role was to do the 'gender work' for the project, interviewing and living with household members, to provide a more holistic picture of portering in one village of the Karakoram.

Ethnographic research made me keenly aware of the lived world of portering, and provided me with some understanding of the ways that postcolonial relations sediment in the village's daily activities and in its power relations. During the months I spent in the village, I lived in two households, both of which affiliate with one of the village's main clans, significantly, the hereditary headman's clan. In both households, I was provided with a room and cooked meals, and treated effectively as a household guest, and everyone knew I was there to do research or 'write a book,' which was the common description of what I did on a daily basis. As a researcher/guest, I had no responsibilities for the household's daily maintenance, except to reciprocate with a cash payment at the end of my stay. The responsibilities for my care fell largely to the women and girls of the household, who added feeding me to their daily tasks. My theoretical leanings are poststructuralist-postcolonialist. In my care relations I was mindful that: a) my female gender definition differed from those I lived with and in some respects I was more masculine than feminine; b) I was a white woman, cared for by brown women; and c) that my 'whiteness' positioned me more along the colonizer end of the colonized-colonizer continuum in this particular place.

Historical and contemporary relations of colonialism – British Raj, Pakistani colonialism, and American imperialism – figured prominently into my understanding of my positionality as a researcher and in the negotiation of my position as a guest in the household (Besio, 2003; Besio, 2007). While colonial legacies contextualized my positionality, they also intersected with issues of gender, class, and status in various, unpredictable ways. For example, the effects of my postcolonial positioning often manifested in my ongoing concerns about how to behave in the field in ways that were consistent with my anti-colonial politics, especially in server/served relations, and which were complicated by the localized patriarchal relations.

It is too sweeping a statement to say that just because a researcher is 'white' and of Euro-American descent, she or he is colonial, sharing similar desires and designs to researchers of the past, who were also a heterogeneous group with a range of desires and practices. Increasingly, geographers are mindful of their colonial legacies (Jacobs, 1994; Jacobs, 1996; Robinson, 2003; Sidaway, 2000; Godlewska and Smith, 1994; Crush, 1994). Linda Tuhiwai Smith is often quoted as saying that 'the term, "research" is inextricably linked to European imperialism and colonialism' and that the word 'researcher' is amongst the 'dirtiest words in the indigenous world's vocabulary' (Smith, 1999, 1). In Smith's 1999 landmark book, *Decolonizing Methodologies*, she describes in detail the experiences of Maori in Aotearoa and the antipathy felt towards western researchers, as well as towards representations that depicted Maori as less than human. She also suggests how the research process must be changed and indigenized if it is to move beyond its colonial legacy. She outlines what she calls 'decolonizing methodologies,' which are powerful to read but often difficult for non-indigenous and anti-colonial researchers to deploy, situated as we are on the other side of the indigenous fence in her rather dualistic model.

I agree with Smith that research practices must be decolonized. Researchers who are non-indigenous and who wish to work against colonial practices seek to develop anti-colonial research practices that complement the aims of indigenous researchers. As an anti-colonial researcher who is not an indigenous person, I want to find ways to do research that decolonize and destabilize the binaries of colonialism, while remaining attentive to colonialisms' violence and violent legacies, and to write and work against their perpetuation in the colonial present.

One way of engaging with Smith's compelling critique is to attend to the inherent inequalities of power in the transcultural relations that take place during fieldwork. I draw from Mary Louise Pratt's conceptualization of colonialism as one in which unequal interactions occur but where there is a dynamic negotiation of the texts of colonialism (Pratt, 1992). To my mind, this is a powerful model of colonial relations because it emphasizes the creative agency of those who may be written out, and is suggestive of the ways that researchers may better engage with the projects and desires of those they research. It acknowledges the significant contributions of indigenous knowledges to what we misguidedly call 'western knowledge.' Pratt focuses squarely upon the ways that those with power represent their colonized subjects and how colonized subjects represent their *own* interests autoethnographically, through texts and other practices. As researchers, we may want to strive in developing research methods that heighten awareness of moments in the research process where those we research are exercising their voice, desires and intentions, in ways that may not be consistent with researchers' agendas. In my research representation, I wanted it to be clear that in as much as I was relaying my interpretations, I was also attempting to remain attentive to how information had been made known to me by those who were allowing me – implicitly if not explicitly trusting in me – to research and represent their community. Thinking from an 'autoethnographic sensibility' (Butz, 2001; Butz and Besio, 2004) has helped me reexamine the ways that researchers and researched subjects negotiate their site-specific relations of power, sometimes performatively through, for instance, acts of everyday resistance (Scott, 1990; Scott, 1985), perhaps, like entering into the researcher's room when she or he is not there.

Upon rereading my stories, I have been able to reflect on the transcultural nature of the research process, as well as on why I represented field relations in the way that I did (see Besio, 2005). For example, when I wrote the story about the goat, I used the word 'thief' to describe how I 'stole' back to my room, in order to draw attention to the politics of colonial legacies in places like northern Pakistan, where, as in many places, people's stories, photos and lives had been the fodder for explorers' writings (Butz and MacDonald, 2001). In northern Pakistan, many of these colonial era representations are unfavorable, and explorers' tales are some of the only 'authoritative texts' to have been written about the region. Their narratives continue to circulate and contribute to perceptions about the region. To complicate matters, this history of exploration in the Karakoram provided me with some of the few archival sources with which to familiarize myself with the region, providing a source of historical data. Problematic as the representations are, explorers' tales remain references from which to draw. Thus, in as much as I used these as data, I also tried to write against them.

However, what I now re-read in the goat story is an elision of the ethical dilemma that frames the story. In the story, I refer to myself negatively as a 'thief' to allude to a colonial legacy from which I did not wish to disentangle fully in order to make it clear that reflexively, I knew where I was positioned closer to the colonizer end of the continuum because of my 'whiteness', if not my politics, place of birth, etc. I assumed that my use of the word 'thief' in the goat story would be ambiguous, and readers would ask themselves about who had left a goat in my room and why, wondering if there was more than one thief in the story. I hoped that tension would creep out in between the lines, leaving readers with questions about the mutuality of unwanted entry, as it were. This uncertainty would appear as a crack in the representational surface, which would then muddy interpretation of 'my data,' keeping the problematic of authority and representation in the foreground.

Unfortunately, by embedding the ambiguity of multiple thieves in the story, I also pushed the situated ethical dilemmas and their context into the background. My original intention in writing the story was to allude to the situation, and it was not to elaborate upon it. While the story drew attention to my positionality as someone perhaps closer to colonizer than colonized, there is something clearly missing from the story. I effectively erased the months of ethical unease from the research process, as well as the intricacies of the social relations of care that contextualized this dilemma.

POST-GOATS AND ETHICAL RELATIONS

Many geographers enter into field research with theoretical stances to which they are committed and that informs their attempts to dismantle unjust social relations and make their research relevant (see Staeheli and Mitchell, this volume). As noted, my baggage included feminism, poststructuralism and postcolonialism, which led me to research social reproduction under the conditions of postcolonialism in the portering industry. However, theory is only part of the process; it is also significant that in addition to the theoretical frameworks researchers use, our projects are contextualized by the contemporary demands of institutional ethics review, which were instituted, in part, to address research abuses that occurred if not during colonial rule, then during a time when research was becoming more regulated.[3] My main understanding of the ethical dilemmas and expectations I would face were framed by the demands of institutional review, and what I had gleaned from various courses and readings.

Iain Hay (2003: 37) states quite simply that 'to behave ethically in geographical research requires that you and I act in accordance with notions of right and wrong – that we conduct ourselves morally. Ethical research is carried out by thoughtful, informed and reflexive geographers who act honorably because it is the 'right' thing to do, not because someone is making them do it.' Certainly, this is the ideal, and there is a wide range of practices and ideals employed towards meeting them. One of the main roles of ethics review boards is that they inform applicants as to how to meet the minimum demands of ethical research practices. In meeting ethical demands, review boards and human subjects committee have established ethical frameworks for researchers that make researchers more keenly aware of some but not all of the ethical situations they may face. Given that ethics review boards oversee a wide range of research with human subjects, from biomedical research to geographic research, review boards are necessarily operating at a scale of review far removed from the day-to-day situations that many researchers encounter. Thus, ethics review boards simply cannot direct researchers about the wide range of ethical eventualities they may encounter, and conversations about relational ethics and ethics based on trust are significant ones that augment the omissions that necessarily exist in the frameworks set out by review boards.

Hay (2003: 41) provides a good synopsis of the aims and principles of ethics review boards, stating that three main principles – justice, beneficence/non-maleficence, and respect – drive the evaluation and review of research proposals. Three criticisms of institutional review are noteworthy and relevant to my discussion, and I take up the last critique in more detail in the following section, because it pertains to the colonial context of research.

First, ethical review boards protect institutions, as well as those people who are researched, leading to a difficult task of assessing risks for parties who may have mutually exclusive interests. One important remit for ethical review boards is to keep institutions away from costly lawsuits and settlements and 'bad' publicity from research gone astray. Thus, 'doing less harm' to subjects may be more about 'mitigating risk' for institutions. Engendering trust in research is far more difficult to operationalize because it is proactive more than reactive, and is relational.

Engendering trust does not follow as readily from the frameworks commonly employed, although this is not to say that engendering trust is at odds with doing less harm. Yet there is a significant difference in the actions of 'engendering with' versus 'doing less,' with leads me to my second concern.

As Deborah Martin notes, ethical review boards conceptualize research as something *done* to people, not as a participatory project between researchers and research subjects (Martin, 2007). For many critical geographers, specifically feminist, indigenous and anti-colonial researchers, research is conceptualized as a participatory project that, in as much as possible, is done *with* subjects. From my transcultural framework, I conceptualized research as negotiated, although my project was not explicitly framed as participatory. As much as I could, I attempted to be responsive and participatory, although according the parameters of participatory research, I cannot say my project would meet the criteria. Martin notes that the difference between research *with* and research *on* subjects raises additional questions about participation and politics in research. That is, participatory research projects may intentionally critique the institutions that grant research approvals, putting review boards in a difficult gate-keeper position. Following from Martin's critique, engendering trust in research cannot be done to someone, but is worked out *between* subjects and researchers.

Third, and important to my own project, ethics review boards have a limited purview and originate from an individualistic worldview (Smith, 1999). Hay explicitly acknowledges the difficulties of a 'one-size-fits-all kind of ethics,' and those who sit on research ethics review boards may understand that different ethical epistemologies exist in all research, although they cannot fully address them (2003). For example, review boards cannot regulate ethics embedded in day-to-day life across the range of places across the world; it is simply too complex. Importantly, for many geographers working in colonial/postcolonial settings, review boards may reflect colonial epistemologies that run contrary to local epistemologies, and through the ethical exercise reproduce those colonial thinking (see Smith: 118). Smith (1999) specifically cites epistemological differences in understanding informed consent. She uses the example of collective versus individualistic notions of self, producing different understandings of what constitutes consent. While review boards alert researchers to particular institutional ethical concerns, they cannot address many of the context-specific ethical dilemmas that arise. It is to this last critique that I turn in detail, because I want to suggest that by engendering trust, researchers may open themselves to more responsive and dynamic ways of framing ethical interactions in specific places, especially those embedded in the day-to-day relations of care.

TRUSTED GOATS AND GROUNDED ETHICS

Prior to doing my ethnographic research, I had given a lot of thought to the ethical research issues I *thought* I would face, particularly the ones I now distinguish as 'institutional' issues, such as informed consent, confidentiality, anonymity, etc. I assumed that the best I could do was plan carefully and attempt to comply with the recommendations set out by my institution's human subjects committee. My preparations for research included application to and approval from the committee for the review of research with human subjects, producing consent forms, thinking about issues of oral consent, etc. Like many researchers who use participant-observation as a method, I assumed I would be faced with the problems of gaining consent from people who had very little experience with social science research and could not read or write, making forms of oral and written consent of dubious legitimacy. I was especially concerned about the ethics of participant-observation, wherein I would be constantly interacting with people from whom I would not be able to receive informed consent.

However, what I had not considered prior to my fieldwork were the situated ethical dilemmas of day-to-day life that seemed to be at every turn, especially those that were a part of my care relations. These dilemmas included but are not limited to, how I should respond when it was a busy woman's task to cook me meals, when she had many other things to do? What was my role in terms of household maintenance as a live-in guest? And, as the goat story illustrates, how should I respond when I perceived that people had 'violated' the privacy of a room that they had been generous enough to allow me to live in for months on end? Was I right to think that the room I had been allowed to stay in should be subjected to my codes of privacy and ownership? If so, should I have then attempted to enforce my ethical codes of trespass, although within the power structures of the family and village I resided in, if only temporarily? In the end, it was up to me to figure out my ethical responsibilities to those whose hospitality allowed me to conduct this research and who cared for my daily needs, providing me with food, a place to sleep, and, most importantly, a kind of companionship in a place where I was far from family and friends.

I struggled with my various ethical dilemmas for months, but it was the goat that I thought about the most, because it was one situation I thought I had most control over. I could not change that women would cook me meals, make my tea, or act companionably with me, although I thought I could maintain a locked door. At various times, I interpreted the comings and goings in my room as youthful curiosity, everyday resistance to research, and, as a minor violation to my space and belongings, with the latter option being the most difficult for me to accept. I felt hurt that someone was going through my things in my absence (Widdowfield, 2000), and I tried to simply shrug it off. I eventually settled on an interpretation that I had not lost anything of value in the rummaging through my belongings, and that I should overlook these entries because they were understandable to me, given what were gross differences in material circumstances between me and those I researched. I could always find a way to justify these events, even if they made me uncomfortable and sad.

Here comes the part where I speculate. Another important reason why I was inclined to overlook the entries was because the person who I knew had the spare key to the room was the person who took care of me: she and her eldest daughter cooked most of my meals, talked with me, laughed with me, took me with her to the fields, and asked about my moods. I did not want to do anything to change what was one of the most satisfying relationships I had at my field site. Moreover, I told myself, it could easily have been her younger daughters who used her keys to get in and out my room. This woman was not hired help like a research assistant, but the headwoman of the household in which I lived, and her family would eventually receive payment. Thus, she was fulfilling her obligations as head female of the household to care for her household's guest, but she did much more than that, too. This was a kind of care-relationship that was unlike anything I had ever experienced, and which was complicated by the transcultural and postcolonial nature of this particular care/service relationship. As I wrangled with my feelings and ethical choices, it was her relations of care and the context in which they took place, that most influenced how I eventually resolved the dilemma: by remaining silent. By calling attention to what I perceived to be trespasses upon my room, I felt I would risk destroying whatever trust she had in me and I hoped that my silence would produce greater trust between us.

My desire to engender trust was at least twofold. First, as an individual, I wanted the women and girls in the village to have confidence in me and to know that I would keep their secrets if necessary. Secondly, I wanted to differentiate myself from the legacies of colonial mistrust, although in retrospect and upon further analysis, I greatly oversimplified my reading and perhaps theirs of colonial relations. Certainly, this specific case was complicated by relations of server and served and its colonial overtones, yet gender relations complicated the situation as much as the former. My care-giver looked after me because she was serving her household, and thus embedded in the patriarchal relations that girded the village's power structures. Moreover, from the comments I heard and my understanding of this household's power structure, I was not sure how her husband – the village headman and head of household – would react to my questions about who had been entering my room. I was convinced he would punish the women and girls in the household even if they were not the ones who had entered – it certainly could have been the headman, too – and although my care-giver and her daughters were my 'prime suspects,' I did not want to find out what would happen if I spoke out. I wanted them to trust me, and, with no small bit of colonial and patriarchal irony, I wanted to protect them.

Certainly, this sounds a lot like the prescriptions of ethical research for 'doing less harm.' Cynically, it also could be argued that I continued to benefit by the relations of care that were being offered to me because by remaining silent, I did nothing to upset those who were providing me with a place to live and to do 'my' research. At the time, my theoretical background in feminist/postcolonial research framed my response to this situated dilemma. In my ethical reasoning, remaining silent made me feel that I was working against the specific colonial and patriarchal relations of 'server and served' that this care-relationship was embedded within. I could not overlook the care relations I was embedded within, and my ethical decision rested, rightly or wrongly, on my attempts to engender and reciprocate trust.

CONCLUDING THOUGHTS TO CHEW ON

In the end, silence seemed the best resolution to the dilemma, although as the goat story attests, I have never felt the issue to be completely resolved nor have I been completely silent. I may have opted not to mention the entries into the room to the 'authorities' in the village, but I did 'squeal' when it came time to write about my field experiences, sort of. In calling attention to unwanted goats in my bedroom through the story, readers might have had questions about the event itself. Some of these questions may have been practical: did I just shoo the goat out and carry on? Yes. That is all that I did, although I looked high and low for someone in the vicinity. Other questions may have been more like the ones that occupied my long hours of solitude: was the goat a calling card and ultimately a test to see whether this time I would finally ask who had been coming in and out of my room for months? Or was it just an innocent prank? I have never found the answers to these queries.

In the end, my representational decision to write a story about the event was influenced both by the uncertainty of this situation, and what may be described as my representational politics, that included a critique of the transparency of academic 'truths,' stemming from what has come to be known as the 'crisis of representation' (Clifford, 1988; Clifford and Marcus, 1986; Geertz, 1973; Pratt, 1986; Rabinow, 1986). In this story and in other parts of my writing, I found that I could not adequately address the complexity of representing what went on in the field, which included the ethical dilemmas that are a key part of this story except obliquely and as a mystery of sorts. The story allowed this, while also functioning as a kind of metaphor for the research process itself: that as much as we might like to determine the results of our research, ultimately, there will always be unexplained and unexplainable human interactions that retain a dynamic indeterminacy.

As I have described in this chapter, the ethical principles set out by my institutions human subjects committee certainly helped me in considering some but not all of the issues I faced during research. And, as many researchers note, ethics guidelines are just that, meant to guide, and are riddled with contradictions and problems, particularly for researchers who employ qualitative methods (Butz, 2008). For many researchers, ethics guidelines are cumbersome and unresponsive to many situations, and particularly so for researchers who seek to work with populations for whom an individuated self is a problematic construction. Perhaps the most striking irony is that the researchers most encumbered by 'one-size fits all' ethics guidelines are those who actively work against the colonial legacies that necessitate stringent ethical review.

For geographers concerned with issues of social justice, trust and reciprocity are not secondary concerns. As I have described my project here, I felt compelled to reciprocate the trust that I had been given by being allowed to live and work in the community I did, negotiating to the best of my ability the dilemmas I faced. I had limited means to reciprocate my care and the research space I had been granted; I could not have engaged in the ethnographic research that I did, had I not begun with an a priori assumption that those I researched trusted me enough to grant me permission to be there, and later to represent them and their lives in good faith. For my part, I attempted to reciprocate their trust in every way that I could, with that reciprocity responsive to the social relations that developed in this specific transcultural context. As in all human relationships, the trust of this research relationship was in a constant state of negotiation, as the presence of unwanted goats in my room attests.

What I hope my reflections in this chapter point to is further engagement with the growing body of literature on relational ethics (Hay, 2003; Popke, 2003, 2006, Smith, 1999; Valentine, 2003, 2004, 2005; Whatmore, 2002). Ethical research practices sit at the core of developing more mutually beneficial research projects. I hope that my ruminations on ethical and representational/political dilemmas – naive as I may have been as a doctoral student researcher (Israel and Hay, 2006) – may provide social and cultural geographers with something to chew on as we continue to grapple with the complexities of geographic research in specific places.

NOTES

1 I'd like to thank Tina Mangieri for the insights she describes about spaces of care in her ethnographic research, which she voiced at the session 'Stereotypical Geographies/Iconoclastic Ethnographies,' San Francisco, CA, April 2007.

2 See Besio, 2003 for a more detailed description of the research genealogy of this site. Some of the points I raise in this chapter I intend as responses to some of the very astute critiques I received after publication of that piece.

3 Mark Israel and Iain Hay (2006: 24) provide a useful timeline of the key moments in the development of ethical codes of conduct. Their timeline begins in 1945, about the time of rapid decolonization, and while colonial examples are absent from their timeline, colonial 'research' should nevertheless remain a significant referent for researchers in places that may be called 'postcolonial.'

REFERENCES

Al-Hindi, K.F.A.H.K. (2002) 'Toward a more fully reflexive feminist geography', in P. Moss (ed.), *Feminist Geography in Practice.* Oxford: Blackwell.

Besio, K. (2003) 'Stepping in it: postcoloniality in northern Pakistan', *Area*, 35: 24–33.

Besio, K. (2005) 'Telling stories to hear autoethnography: Researching women's lives in Northern Pakistan', *Gender Place and Culture*, 12: 317–32.

Besio, K. (2007) 'Depth of fields: Travel photography and spatializing modernities in northern Pakistan', *Environment and Planning D: Society and Space*, 25: 53–74.

Besio, K. and Butz, D. (2004) 'Autoethnography: A limited endorsement', *The Professional Geographer*, 56: 432–8.

Butz, D. (2001) 'Autobiography, autoethnography and intersubjectivity', *Analyzing Communication in Northern Pakistan*, in P. Moss (ed.), *Placing Autobiography in Geogography.* Syracuse: University Press.

Butz, D. (2008) 'Sidelined by the guidelines: reflections on the limitations of standard informed consent procedures for the conduct of ethical research', *ACME: An International e-Journal for Critical Geographies*, 7 (2): 239–59.

Butz, D. and Besio, K. (2004) 'The value of ethnography for field research in transcultural settings', *The Professional Geographer*, 56: 350–60.

Butz, D. and Macdonald, K.I. (2001) 'Serving sahibs with pony and pen: the discursive uses of "Native Authenticity"'. *Environment and Planning D: Society and Space*, 19: 179–201.

Cahill, C. (2007) 'Repositioning ethical commitments: participatory action research as a relational praxis of social change', *ACME: An International e-Journal for Critical Geographies*, 6 (3): 360–73.

Cahill, C., Farhana Sultana and Rachel Pain (2007) 'Participatory ethics: politics, practices, institutions', *ACME: an International e-Journal for Critical Geographies*, 6: 304–18.

Clifford, J. (1988) *The Predicament of Culture.* Cambridge: Harvard University Press.

Clifford, J. and Marcus, G. (1986) *Writing Culture: The Poetics and Politics of Ethnography.* Berkeley: UC Press.

Conradson, D. (2003) 'Spaces of care in the city: the place of a community drop-in centre', *Social and Cultural Geography*, 4 (4): 507–25.

Crush, J. (1994) 'Postcolonialism, decolonization and geography, in A. Godlewska, and N. Smith, (eds), *Geography and Empire.* Oxford: Blackwell.

England, K. (1994) 'Getting personal: reflexivity, positionality and feminist research', *The Professional Geographer*, 46: 80–9.

Geertz, C. (1973) 'Thick description: Towards an interpretive theory of culture', *The Interpretation of Cultures.* New York: Basic Books.

Gilmartin, M. (2003) 'Making space for personal journeys', in P. Moss (ed.), *Feminist Geographies in Practice.* Malden, MA: Blackwell Publishers, Ltd.

Godlewska, A. and Smith, N. (eds) (1994) *Geography and Empire,* Oxford: Blackwell.

Hay, I. (2003) 'Ethical practice in geographical research', in N.J.A.G.V. Clifford (ed.), *Key Methods in Geography.* Thousand Oaks, CA: Sage Publications.

Hopkins, P. (2007) 'Positionalities and knowledge: Negotiating ethics in practice', *ACME*, 6: 386–94.

Israel, M. and Hay, I. (2006) *Research Ethics for Social Scientists.* Thousand Oaks, CA: Sage Publications.

Jacobs, J. (1994) 'Earth honouring: Western desires and indigenous knowledges', in A. Blunt and G. Rose (eds), *Writing Women and Space: Colonial and Postcolonial Geographers.* London: Routledge.

Jacobs, J. (1996) *Edge of Empire.* London: Routledge.

Katz, C. (1994) 'Playing the field: Questions of fieldwork in ethnography', *The Professional Geographer*, 46: 67–72.

Kobayashi, A. (2003) 'GPC ten years on: Is self-reflexivity enough?' *Gender, Place and Culture*, 10: 345–49.

Macdonald, K.I. (1998) 'Push and Shove: Spatial history and the construction of a portering economy in northern Pakistan', *Comparative Studies in Society and History*, 40: 287–317.

Macdonald, K.I. and Butz, D. (1998) 'Investigating portering relations as a locus for transcultural interaction in the Karakorum region of northern Pakistan', *Mountain Research and Development*, 18: 333–43.

Martin, D. (2007) 'Bureacratization of Ethics: Institutional review boards and participatory research', *ACME: an International e-Journal for Critical Geographies*, 6: 319–28.

Popke, J. (2003) 'Poststructuralist ethics: subjectivity, responsibility and the space of community', *Progress in Human Geography*, 27: 298–316.

Popke, J. (2006) 'Geography and ethics: everyday mediations through care and consumption', *Progress in Human Geography*, 30: 504–12.

Pratt, M.-L. (1992) *Imperial Eyes: Travel Writing and Transculturation.* London: Routledge.

Pratt, M.-L. (1986) 'Fieldwork in common places', in J. Clifford and G.E. Marcus (eds), *Writing Culture: The Poetics and Politics of Ethnography.* Berkeley, CA: University of CA Press.

Rabinow, P. (1986) 'Representations are social facts', in J. Clifford and G.E. Marcus (eds), *Writing Cultures.* Berkeley: UC Press.

Raju, S. (2002) 'We are different, but can we talk?' *Gender, Place and Culture*, 9: 173–7.

Robinson, J. (2003) 'Postcolonising geography: tactics and pitfalls', *Singapore Journal of Tropical Geography*, 24: 273–89.
Rose, G. (1997) 'Situation knowledges: Positionality, reflexivities and other tactics', *Progress in Human Geography*, 21: 305–20.
Scott, J.C. (1985) *Weapons of the Weak: Everyday Forms of Peasant Resistance.* New Haven: Yale University Press.
Scott, J.C. (1990) *Domination and the Arts of Resistance.* New Haven: Yale University Press.
Sidaway, J.D. (2000) 'Postcolonial geographies: An exploratory essay', *Progress in Human Geography*, 24: 591–612.
Smith, T.L. (1999) *Decolonizing Methodologies: Research and Indigenous Peoples.* London and New York: Zed Press.
Sultana, F. (2007) 'Reflexivity, positionality and participatory ethics: negotiating fieldwork dilemmas in international research', *ACME: An International e-Journal for Critical Geographies*, 6 (3): 374–85.
Valentine, G. (2003) 'Geography and ethics: in pursuit of social justice – ethics and emotions in geographies of health and disability', *Progress in Human Geography*, 27: 375–80.
Valentine, G. (2004) 'Geography and Ethics: questions of considerability and activism in environmental ethics', *Progress in Human Geography*, 28: 258–63.
Valentine, G. (2005) 'Geography and ethics: moral geographies? Ethical commitment in research and teaching', *Progress in Human Geography*, 29: 483–87.
Whatmore, S. (2002) *Hybrid Geographies: Natures, Cultures, Spaces.* Thousand Oaks, CA: Sage Publications.
Widdowfield, R. (2000) 'The place of emotions in academic research', *Area*, 32: 199–208.

26

Quantification

Mei-Po Kwan

INTRODUCTION

Attentive to the importance of space in social life and issues of social inequality, social geography has a strongly empirical tradition (Jackson, 2000). Quantitative approaches have played an important role in empirical research in social geography, especially from the late 1960s when geographers were heavily influenced by the spatial science tradition. Quantitative approaches were often used at that time to analyze the spatial structures of cities and to understand the underlying social processes (e.g., analysis of the spatial patterns of housing). As quantification was criticized in subsequent rounds of reflection, its value was questioned as an approach in geography. Paradigms continued to shift, and social geographers increasingly turned to other perspectives (e.g., humanist, Marxist, feminist, poststructuralist, postcolonial and queer perspectives). As many have questioned the adequacy of quantitative methods for addressing the issues at the heart of social geography, such as social justice and inequality, these approaches have become a rather marginal pursuit in social geographic research today. However, as many geographers have recently argued, this need not be the case (e.g., McLafferty, 1995; Plummer and Sheppard, 2001; Sheppard, 2001; Kwan, 2004a): quantification can potentially make rich contributions to understanding and challenging these issues.

In this chapter I suggest that critiques of the spatial science tradition and its epistemological foundation should not prevent social geographers from fruitfully applying quantitative approaches. In fact, quantitative approaches are very effective for addressing certain issues of social inequalities. They are appropriate in certain research contexts and can provide sound alternatives to qualitative approaches for certain research questions. For instance, quantitative methods may be the only way to investigate some topics when time or financial resources limit the possibility to collect qualitative data. They enable us to identify broad geographical patterns in social issues that call for urgent attention and provide us a powerful means to influence policy makers – which other approaches cannot always easily accomplish. Further, contrary to conventional thinking about the nature of geographical methods, quantitative and qualitative methods should not be understood in terms of 'counter-positional, A/not-A binaries' (Massey, 2001: 13; see also Kwan, 2004a). This kind of thinking seems to have hampered consideration of mixed methods until recently. However, as quantitative and qualitative methods are increasingly used in combination in social geographic research, it is increasingly apparent that quantitative approaches have much to offer social geography. We should not consider quantification as irreconcilable or incompatible with critical social geography. We just need to approach quantification critically and sensitively, paying particular attention to when, where and for which questions quantitative methods are appropriate.

Quantification not only involves the use of numbers such as official statistics. It includes the entire process in which data are collected, assembled, turned into numbers (coded), and analyzed using mathematical or statistical means. Social geographic research that relies mainly on quantitative methods can use a variety of methods to explore or analyze the data. These range from simple measures such as frequency counts and percentages, to complex techniques such as multilevel models or geographically weighted regression. The results of quantitative analysis can be presented in the form of summary statistics, test statistics, statistical tables, and graphs. They can also be represented in complex cartographic or three-dimensional forms with the assistance of GIS (Geographical Information Systems). This variety of analytical and representational means renders quantitative approaches especially useful for addressing certain social and public policy issues.

Recent developments in quantitative geography have also addressed many of the limitations of conventional quantitative approaches, whose primary objective was often taken to be the establishment of law-like generalizations (Fotheringham, 2006). The application of local forms of spatial analysis (e.g., local statistics), for instance, has facilitated the analysis of relationships between local contexts and people's everyday lives. Instead of making sweeping generalizations of an entire study area or population, these methods were developed to reveal the effect of local context on social processes and their spatial outcomes. The recent development of GIS-based geocomputational and geovisualization methods has shown how the complexities of people's everyday lives and the urban environment can be taken into account to a certain extent (Kwan and Weber, 2003; Kwan, 2004b). Such recent developments are particularly relevant and valuable to social geographic research.

As recent debate in geography suggests, it is important to avoid the binary that considers quantitative and qualitative approaches as two separate and irreconcilable domains, and quantitative approaches may still be fruitfully used in contemporary social geographic research (e.g., Sheppard, 2001; Kwan, 2004a). In what follows, I revisit the limitations and value of quantitative methods and consider when, where and for which questions quantitative methods are appropriate. I examine the role and benefits of quantification in contemporary social geography. I map out a critical agenda concerning the use of quantitative methods in social geographic research, using my recent work as an example.

CRITIQUES OF QUANTIFICATION

Quantitative geographic methods were developed during a period now commonly referred to as the 'quantitative revolution' in geography. These methods were developed with the intention of making geography a scientific discipline not unlike physics, where validity of the knowledge generated was justified according to positivist principles. Part of this development was associated with what was called 'social physics,' which drew directly upon theories in physics to derive mathematical relations for analyzing human socio-spatial interaction. An early example of this kind of work was the gravity model, which drew upon Newton's Law of Gravitation and postulated that the interaction between places (such as migration) is directly proportional to the product of their masses (often measured by population size) and inversely proportional to some function of the distance between them. With a positivist epistemology, the purpose of geographic research was to seek universally applicable generalizations. The researcher was considered a detached observer capable of acquiring objective knowledge of the world through discovering empirical regularity in social, economic or spatial phenomena.

As geographers inspired by alternative perspectives began to question the relevance and value of spatial science in the early 1970s, social geography using quantitative approaches was criticized as positivist and empiricist because it was based upon the principles of scientific objectivity, value neutrality, and the search for universally applicable generalizations. In particular, many social geographers used quantitative methods to identify the socio-spatial structure of cities and its relationships with underlying social processes, and adopted quantitative approaches, as critics argued, in order to turn geography into a 'science.' While their work illuminated certain aspects of social inequalities such as housing and crime, their studies tended to be considered empiricist as they privileged claims to knowledge based primarily upon observable 'facts.' Feminist geographers have further argued that 'truths' often put forward as universally applicable were valid only for men of a particular culture, class, or race (WGSG, 1997). They are also critical of the tendency to derive analyses of universal causality from inferential statistics.

Quantitative methods were also criticized for other reasons. For instance, since quantitative methods depend on some quantifiable attributes of the phenomena under study, they are not capable of representing complex human experiences and social realities. This is a serious limitation, since a substantial portion of people's experiences cannot be expressed through numbers and is therefore not quantifiable. Further, the 'live connections' with research subjects are often lost through the use of quantitative data, making it difficult to convey a sense of people's feelings and their interactions with others. This in turn makes it difficult to obtain a contextualized and holistic understanding of the complex processes involved in their everyday experiences. Quantitative data and methods are therefore 'disembodied', as abstracted and decontextualized information is used in the process (WGSG, 1997). Feminist geographers have also argued that these methods make the identity and masculinist biases of the researcher invisible, thus obfuscating his or her positionality relative to the research and those being studied (see Chapter 27 by Browne in this section).

Quantitative social geography was also criticized for assigning any specific individual's experience into hard-and-fast categories in the collection and analysis of quantitative data, whether these categories are predefined by the researcher or according to official criteria (Jayaratne and Stewart, 1991). The rigid nature of the categories and variables used not only imposes a structure that hinders our understanding of socio-spatial processes, it also fails to reflect the complexities of people's lived experiences. Very different phenomena may be lumped together in the statistics as if they were the same thing, and the statistics may have a problematic connection with the life they claim to represent (Pugh, 1990). Further, since pre-existing categories and official statistics are often based on the lives of men and other dominant group(s) in society, using them without extreme caution in social geographic research can be problematic. They may actually make it more difficult, if not impossible, to reveal the processes underlying the inequality that women and other marginalized groups experience (e.g. Perrons, 1999). For instance, official statistics are often found to be unreliable and even useless for studying women's labor force participation or contribution to the economy, because many forms of women's unpaid work are omitted in official definitions of 'work' (Samarasinghe, 1997). Another example is Pugh's (1990: 107) study on homelessness, where she concluded that 'life will always be more complex and ambiguous than any possible usable system of coding and classification.' Further, using pre-determined categories makes it difficult for research to be open to change or surprise during the research process. This in turn means that it becomes more difficult for the researcher to be responsive to the input or influence of respondents in the research design and process, thus seriously limiting the practice of the researcher's reflexivity,

APPROACHING QUANTIFICATION IN SOCIAL GEOGRAPHY

As I suggested in the introduction to this chapter, quantitative methods still have value in addressing certain types of questions in social geography. However, there are several important issues to consider if we are to use quantitative methods in ways which are critical, valid and valuable in contemporary social geography. These include epistemological considerations, the qualitative/quantitative binary, issues of representing complex socio-spatial processes and patterns, and measurement and analytical issues in quantitative methods. I address each of these issues in turn below.

Epistemological considerations

Revisiting the relation between epistemology and method in geography sheds new light on the value of quantification in social geography. As many recollections indicate (e.g., Morrill, 1993), an important but often ignored aspect of the quantitative revolution is that its epistemological justification came years after quantitative methods had been advocated and practiced (e.g., Billinge et al., 1984). As Barnes (2000) argues, when geographers turned to positivism, it was actually an ex-post rationalization of quantification. Careful historical examination therefore reveals that epistemological justification of quantification was subsequent to the intent to create a new kind of geographic practice, and there is no necessary connection between positivism and the use of quantitative methods in geographic research.

Given that the relationship between a particular epistemology and a particular type of methods is not a one-to-one relation (Bennett, 1985), a geographer's epistemological stance cannot be read off directly from the method(s) used. There can be nonpositivist use of quantitative methods, and there can be positivist use of qualitative methods (McDowell, 1992; Suchan and Brewer, 2000; Sheppard, 2001). Once this is recognized, it becomes apparent that the choice between quantification and other approaches is a false one (Wyly, 2004). Perhaps we have fallen into the trap of conflating method and epistemology, and our collective memory left by decades of contestations and binarized discourses has hampered our ability to imagine creative connections between social geography and quantitative geography (Kwan, 2004a).

In fact, not long ago scientific methods were typically conceived as a means for progressive social change rather than an instrument of oppression, and recent critique of science 'does not necessarily render irrelevant the positive uses to which scientific research can be put' (Hannah and Strohmayer, 2001: 396). Further, the feminist critique of science by Haraway (1991) also emphasizes the idea of reclaiming the power of modern techno-science for emancipatory purposes (Kwan, 2002). This suggests that the apparent technical/scientific characteristics of quantitative geography should not preclude the possibility of its use in social geography. An important task in the process is to identify alternative, critical practices of quantitative methods that can, at least to a certain extent, address the criticisms of quantification.

The qualitative/quantitative binary

Another important point is that criticisms of quantitative methods, as a reaction to positivism and empiricism, can lead to an unfruitful oppositional stance that holds qualitative methods as the preferable alternative to quantitative methods (Harding, 1989). This not only perpetuates dualist thinking through reproducing a qualitative/quantitative binarism that characterizes masculinist thinking, but also ignores the possibility of post-positivist, critical quantitative methods that are consistent with epistemologies and politics inspired by various critical perspectives (Sheppard, 2001). It is perhaps more helpful to think of quantitative methods as one of many possible geographic methods that can be used together with other methods. As the analysis of quantitative data can be complemented by a contextualized understanding of people's everyday lives provided by qualitative data, and the interpretation of qualitative data can be assisted by the broad picture provided by quantitative methods, using multiple methods in a single study may provide a more complete understanding of the questions at hand. This strategy of 'triangulation' has advantages because the weaknesses of each single method may be compensated by the counter-balancing strengths of another (Rose, 1993).

In the practice of social geographic research, it is important to recognize the limitations and strengths of quantitative methods. Quantitative methods simply cannot provide the kind of rich and contextualized account of people's experiences obtained through qualitative methods (Jayarante and Stewart, 1995). They are therefore more suitable for answering certain questions and are less appropriate for addressing others. Social geographers need to determine the appropriateness of quantitative methods and their combined use with other methods for a given research question. It is also important to identify the research question based on substantive social geographic concerns and/or theories before deciding which method(s) one will use in a particular study. The primary issue is what data are needed and which methods are appropriate for addressing the research question.

Issues of representing complex socio-spatial processes and patterns

There are other concerns about the practice of quantification in social geographic research. Quantitative data can come from secondary data sources, such as official statistics. They can also come from primary data collection through surveys. The counting procedures or classification schemes used to collect official data, however, often ignore significant aspects of the lives and experiences of socially marginalized groups. For instance, official statistics are not reliable sources of accurate data on anti-Muslim hate crimes (including attacks on Muslim properties) in the U.S., because in police reports of crimes, mosques are not included in the categories of places where crimes happened (but churches and temples are). Collecting primary quantitative data may therefore be a better strategy than relying on official statistics for many issues of interest to social geographers. A good example is a study discussed in Reinharz (1992: 82) by two law students, who collected data from a judge and police chiefs to show the prevalence of wife battering in the local area.

Another issue is that great care is needed when developing a coding scheme, because rigid categorization is a major weakness of quantitative methods. For example, based on the important notion of intersectionality (Valentine, 2007), social differentiation and identities should be defined by using many dimensions, such as gender, race, ethnicity, class, sexuality, and religion. The use of more refined coding schemes for classifying individuals into social groups would yield better understanding of significant differences between individuals than one based upon any single criterion such as gender. The use of advanced categorical data analysis techniques that can consider several differentiating dimensions at the same time is also preferable to those that are based on a single dimension at a time. Further, presentation of quantitative data should be accompanied by a description of the ambiguity or problems of the classification scheme. Any reservations about the results because of this should also be provided. An evaluation of the sensitivity of the results to different classification schemes will be even more helpful to the audience.

Measurement and analytical issues

Another important issue concerns the quantification process and the analysis of quantitative data. Before quantitative data can be collected, concepts central to the research question need to be *operationalized*. This means that the researcher has to determine how various phenomena are to be measured and how the required data are to be collected. Turning concepts such as 'class' or 'discrimination' into quantifiable measures is far from straightforward. Social geographers therefore need to deal with all operational issues with care. For example, how should one measure women's 'household responsibility?' One commonly used measure is the number of children in the household, which is unlikely to be a good measure because it may not have a consistent relationship with the amount and type of domestic tasks women perform. The extent to which a spouse shares domestic duties will also play a significant role in influencing the amount of household responsibility a woman shoulders. Further, as existing quantitative measures may have serious biases, it is important to critically reassess all existing measures and look for any such bias before using them. It may be necessary to develop one's own method of counting or measurement for the research question.

It is also important to note that some researchers have argued against the use of inferential statistics in social and geographic research, where only non-parametric and descriptive statistics are considered appropriate. Social geographers therefore need to understand the concepts of statistical inference and significance, and to situate these techniques in the context of critical epistemologies in geography. Although all statistical inferences, including non-parametric statistics, assume some notion of 'typicality' in circumscribed populations, using inferential statistics does not necessarily mean making totalizing generalizations or asserting universal causality (Pratt, 1989). Inferential statistics are based upon our understanding of the likelihood of occurrence of certain events. They can provide a basis to determine whether the phenomenon observed is typical or not for the population subgroups being studied (without arguing that the relationship observed is also true for the larger population). If there are wide variations in what individuals experience in a sample, it is difficult to argue that it is shared by members of the group. If differences among various subgroups of individuals are statistically significant, such differences are unlikely to be caused by chance alone and therefore deserve a closer look. Inferential statistics can therefore be used in social geographic research in a non-generalizing, non-totalizing manner.

THE ROLE OF QUANTIFICATION IN CRITICAL SOCIAL GEOGRAPHY

Since the strengths of quantitative methods are in describing and analyzing complex patterns of social, economic and geographic phenomena of interest to social geographers, they are invaluable for certain purposes. First, quantitative methods are useful for describing the measurable aspects of social life and analyzing complex spatial relations between geographical phenomena. They are particularly helpful for providing a broad picture of the social, spatial or temporal inequalities experienced by individuals of different social groups. As McLafferty (1995: 438) has argued, quantitative methods can reveal 'the broad contours of difference and similarity that vary not only with gender but also with race, ethnicity, class and place.' Quantitative methods are therefore especially valuable when there is an urgent need to have a broad view of people's current situations (e.g., to reveal the geographical concentration of certain health problems) but where detailed individual-level data are not readily available or the limited resources at hand prevent the collection of qualitative data. They also help to highlight the shared experiences of many similarly situated individuals such as domestic violence and sexual discrimination (Moss, 1995), thus enabling the researcher to make some generalizations about these shared experiences. But all such generalizations should be made with respect only to the particular social group(s) or individuals being studied, and we should be careful not to extrapolate the results to other social groups or contexts. Bearing this caveat in mind, generalization can be an important benefit of quantitative methods.

A good example is the research by McLafferty and Preston (1992) which used aggregate census data to analyze the complex relationships between gender, race, ethnicity, occupational status and commuting distance. Their studies showed that the well-known gender differences in the length of the commute trip varied considerably among race and ethnic groups. Although the categories employed in their quantitative analysis can be questioned (e.g. gender or ethnicity), and the data they used did not give a contextualized understanding of the lives of the people they studied, their research indicates the distinctive value of quantitative methods.

Another way in which quantitative methods are useful in social geography is that the presentation of quantitative data or results of quantitative analysis can often be more forceful in public policy domains. 'Hard' data obtained using quantitative techniques are sometimes viewed as more valid, rigorous, reliable and convincing than 'soft' qualitative data. Surveys may have the power to change public opinion in ways that a limited number of in-depth interviews may not. For instance, Seager and Olson (1986) documented the extent to which women were unequal and subordinate to men throughout the world using official statistics. They concluded that women are worse off than men everywhere – they have less autonomy, less power, less money, but more work and responsibility. Several studies had already shown that women in general have more spatially restricted lives than men – they work closer to home and travel less – and are often employed in female-dominated occupations and earn less than men (e.g. Tivers, 1985; Hanson and Pratt, 1995). Descriptive data like these effectively present the unequal power and gender relations within the household and the economy at large. In describing certain measurable aspects of people's lives, quantitative data can help to reveal the social and political processes that perpetuate the inequality and oppression they experience.

Further, quantitative data and methods can also be used in empowering research approaches such as participatory research. A good example is Public Participation GIS (PPGIS), where quantitative data and methods can be used critically to empower local community organizations in the planning process (e.g. Elwood, 2006). In light of this, quantitative data and methods may be a powerful instrument for initiating progressive social and political change, and reduce the oppression of marginalized social groups. They may be potentially helpful for critical theorization of social injustice and oppression when used in the appropriate contexts. While geographers tend to think that qualitative research is much more capable of addressing ethical issues in research, quantitative research does not necessarily preclude the possibility for the researcher to practice Vicky Lawson's (2007) 'care ethics' or Paul Cloke's (2002) 'living ethically and acting politically.' Although currently underused, quantitative methods can play a highly positive role in critical social geography.

Closely related to this point is that the analysis of quantitative data may stimulate questions about the wider social processes that are beyond its reach. This may help reveal research areas that urgently require attention and indicate directions for more in-depth and qualitatively-oriented research. For example, in a study by McLafferty and Tempalski (1995), quantitative analysis helped identify the lower-middle income neighborhoods in New York City where the problem of low birthweight is serious. With these results, healthcare and social work professionals can undertake in-depth qualitative research in these areas to obtain a better understanding of the problem. Quantitative methods can also be used to reveal and challenge the gender or racial bias in existing geographical concepts and methods. For example, in my research on conventional measures of accessibility, I found that all conventional accessibility measures failed to take women's need to undertake multipurpose trips and their space-time constraints into account and therefore suffered from a serious male bias. This led me to formulate and implement space-time measures of individual accessibility that can better reflect women's individual access to urban opportunities (Kwan, 1998, 1999a).

Further, quantitative research can be emergent in that it is open to surprise during the research process and may raise issues and questions that the researcher had not previously thought of. In my recent study examining the relationships between women's employment status and journey to work (discussed in detail in the next section), I observed that women employed full-time travel longer to work than men, but they experience a higher level of fixity constraint than men. For the subjects in the study, fixity constraint arose mainly from the need to undertake activities associated with household needs (such as picking up a child from day-care center). This is surprising in light of the high occupational status and high level of access to private cars of these women. It contradicts the postulates of the convergence hypothesis, which suggests that women's improved occupational status would 'naturally' lead to more equitable gender division of domestic labor and lower level of fixity constraint. This unexpected result led me to undertake further quantitative analyses in order to unravel the complex interactions among gender, employment status, journey to work and space-time constraints (Kwan, 2007).

GENDER, OCCUPATIONAL STATUS AND THE JOURNEY TO WORK

In this section I use one of my recent research projects to illustrate some of the arguments I have put forward so far. It concerns the complex relationships between women's employment status, journey to work and space-time constraints. It built upon earlier research on women's labor market position (occupational segregation) and commuting by feminist geographers who used quantitative methods or combined both quantitative and qualitative methods in their research (e.g., Hanson and Pratt, 1995; England, 1993; Johnston-Anumonwo, 1995, 1997; McLafferty and Preston, 1996, 1997).

I formulated my research questions in light of two important trends in women's participation in the labor force and the gender division of social and domestic labor. First, as more and more women participate in the labor force, some of them have been able to achieve relatively high occupational status and income. Second, as the proportion of women who can use their own automobile to commute increases, many women now have better spatial mobility to work farther from home than before. Many researchers believe that these two trends together will enable certain groups of women to take up high-status jobs farther from home, and this in turn will lead to a decrease in their shares of domestic responsibilities within a household. Smaller shares of women's household responsibilities, according to this view, imply that men will take up larger proportions of household responsibilities. These changes in the position of women in the local labor market and in the gender division of domestic labor in turn will likely lead to more equitable gender relations within the household and society at large (Gershuny and Robinson, 1988).

My study examined the claims of this so-called convergence hypothesis, which argues that women's improved occupational status would 'naturally' lead to progressive change in the gendered division of social and domestic labor. It explored whether these two trends would lead to changes in the shares of household responsibilities between the male and female heads of a household. I also examined whether the constraints associated with women's need to perform domestic responsibilities are still important in determining their employment status and commuting distance.

The main theoretical constructs I used were a set of time-geographic concepts employed in earlier research on the geographies of women's everyday lives (e.g. Tivers, 1985). The concept most relevant to the study is 'space-time constraints,' which impact upon women's daily lives in significant ways and stem from two main sources. The first source is the limited time available for a person to perform various activities in a particular day – commonly referred to as the time budget constraint. The second source, referred to as the fixity constraint, arises from the fact that activities that need to be performed at fixed location or time (e.g. child-care drop-off) restrict what a person can do for the rest of the day. Past studies observed that space-time constraints significantly affect women's job location, occupational status, and activity patterns (e.g. Pratt and Hanson, 1991).

I adopted a quantitative approach when I conceived the project. In relation to the specific research questions that I sought to answer, however, the main reason for choosing a quantitative approach was that the literature on women's labor market position and commuting I drew upon is largely quantitative, and the primary intention of my study was to overcome some of the limitations found in this literature. For instance, no previous studies had attempted to quantitatively measure the space-time constraint associated with the performance of various daily activities and evaluate the extent to which they affect women's employment status and commuting distance. In addition, the focus was often exclusively on the distance (or travel time) between home and work place and its relationships with women's employment status, while little attention was paid to the location of non-employment activities relative to a person's home and work sites. As many of these non-employment activities are associated with the performance of specific household responsibilities and can affect job and residential choice in significant ways, I argued that an explicit focus on these activities might reveal important gender differences within a household. Such an approach would also have considerable potential to shed light on the factors that influence women's occupational and employment status.

An important purpose of the study was therefore to bring back into the analysis some significant but missing elements that mediate the home-work link (Kwan, 1999b). To address the complex relationships between women's domestic responsibilities, employment status, journey to work and space-time constraints, I decided to collect quantitative data from a sample of working women in Columbus (Ohio, USA), using activity-travel diaries and to utilize statistical techniques (e.g. structural equations model) to analyze the data.

I had to resolve several operational issues about how to turn the notion of space-time constraints into something measurable before collecting the data. Based upon previous work on this area, I decided to solicit information about the space-time fixity of each activity a person performed through an activity-travel diary survey. The diary recorded details of all activities and trips made by the respondent in two designated travel days. I included four specially designed questions in the diary to obtain information about the spatial and temporal fixity of each activity (see Kwan, 2000). Using answers to these four questions, I designated three types of fixity: (a) spatially fixed activities; (b) temporally fixed activities; and (c) activities which are both spatially and temporally fixed.

Another operational issue involved identifying the purpose of each activity performed by the respondent. A common approach in past studies comprised categorizing activity purposes and then coding the written description provided by the respondent. One major difficulty of this approach is that the primary purpose of an activity may not be reflected from the written description of the activity given by the respondent. For example, an activity can be performed for different purposes by the same person (e.g., grocery shopping may be undertaken for meeting household needs or for social purposes), and the same activity may be performed for different purposes by different individuals. To overcome this problem,

I included a question in the activity diary to record the primary and secondary purpose of an activity according to the respondent's subjective evaluation. Five activity purposes were initially provided to the respondent as guidelines, but they can also provide their own answers in an open-ended question.

I developed the survey instrument after resolving these operational issues. It includes two main parts: a household questionnaire and a two-day activity-travel diary. Using this survey instrument, I collected an activity-travel diary data set from a sample of adults (over 18 years of age) in households with one or more employed members in the study area in 1995. The household questionnaire collected information about the socio-economic characteristics and transport resources of all household members. The two-day activity-travel diary collected detailed information about the activities and trips of the respondent for two designated days. Data collected included street address, travel mode used, car availability, routes taken, the primary purpose of each activity, a subjective fixity rating for each activity, and other individuals present when performing each activity.

Because the small number of ethnic minorities in the sample does not allow for meaningful statistical analysis, they were excluded from the analysis (this would not have been the case if qualitative information had been collected). The final subsample consists of three groups of white people: 28 full-time employed females, 13 part-time employed females (who work less than 35 hours a week), and 31 full-time employed males. I analyzed the differences in fixity constraint experienced by individuals in these three groups using simple descriptive statistics and analysis of variance (Kwan, 2000). The results show that women employed part-time encounter more fixed activities in their daily lives than the other two groups. Many of these fixed activities are associated with household needs that have a strong restrictive effect on the locations of their out-of-home activities and job location (such as picking up a child from day-care center). Further, despite the fact that women employed full-time travel longer to work than men, they experience a higher level of fixity constraint than men. This result is surprising, considering the high occupational status and high level of access to private cars of the full-time employment women in the subsample. It is in contrast to the postulates of the convergence hypothesis, which suggests that women's improved occupational status would lead to more equitable gender division of domestic labor and lower level of fixity constraint.

In light of these unexpected results, further in-depth causal analysis of the activity diary data using statistical methods seemed necessary. To analyze the complex interrelations among women's day-time fixity constraint, non-employment activities, household responsibilities and employment status, I estimated a nonrecursive structural equation model with latent variables for the women in the subsample (Kwan, 1999b). I found that household responsibilities, besides exerting a direct effect on women's employment status, has an indirect impact on it through the mediating effect of day-time fixity constraint and the number of out-of-home non-employment activities. An increase in women's day-time non-employment activities due to part-time employment tends to increase the level of fixity constraint as measured in this study, as part-time employed women have the time and flexibility to undertake more fixed activities during the day. These results confirm that fixity constraint has a significant impact on women's employment status (where women with higher levels of fixity constraint are more likely to work part-time).

Overall, the findings of the study call into question the belief that increasing female participation in the labor force will lead to significant change in women's gender roles and space-time constraints. The results also suggest that the situation of women may not change much without first changing the gender relations and redressing the division of domestic labor within the household. Despite the belief that recent trends in the increasing number of women with higher occupational status and improvement in their access to private means of transportation will lead to changes in traditional gender roles, the results of my study suggest otherwise.

CONCLUSION

In this chapter I suggested that critiques of quantification should be revisited, and that they should not prevent the use of quantitative approaches in social geography. I argued that quantitative approaches are very effective for addressing certain issues of social inequalities. They are appropriate in certain research contexts and can be sound alternatives to qualitative approaches for certain research questions. They allow us to identify broad geographical patterns in social issues that call for urgent attention and provide us a powerful means to influence policy makers. This makes them particularly useful in research that seeks to empower marginalized social groups and address the inequality and oppression they experience. In this light, quantitative research can also be mobilized for critical, ethical social geography research that makes a difference to the world.

Further, I suggested that a geographer's epistemological stance cannot be read off directly from the method(s) used, and the binarized discourses that consider quantitative and qualitative approaches as polar opposites have hampered our ability to imagine creative connections between social geography and quantitative approaches, as well as consideration of mixed methods, until recently. As quantitative and qualitative methods are increasingly used in combination in social geographic research, it is increasingly apparent that quantitative approaches have much to offer social geography. We should not consider quantification as irreconcilable or incompatible with critical social geography. We just need to approach quantification critically and sensitively, paying particular attention to when, where and for which questions quantitative methods are appropriate.

Lastly, I emphasized that the apparent technical/scientific characteristics of quantitative geography should not preclude the possibility of its use in social geography. An important task in the process is to identify alternative, critical practices of quantitative methods that can, at least to a certain extent, address the criticisms and limitations of quantification. Recent developments in quantitative geography have addressed many limitations of conventional quantitative approaches, and quantitative social geographic research can benefit greatly from these developments. These developments include exploratory spatial data analysis, geographically weighted regression, spatially autoregressive models, multilevel models, local analysis that is more sensitive to local context, geocomputation and GIS-based geovisualization (which is a more open-ended mode of data analysis, unlike conventional GIS-based data analysis; see also discussion in Kwan, 2007). With these new methods, certain complexities of people's everyday life and the urban environment may be taken into account. These recent changes have rendered quantitative methods more congenial to social geographic research than before.

REFERENCES

Barnes, T.J. (2000) 'Quantitative revolution', in R.J. Johnston, D. Gregory, G. Pratt and M. Watt (eds), *The Dictionary of Human Geography*. Oxford: Blackwell. pp. 664–7.

Bennett, R.J. (1985) 'Quantification and relevance', in R.J. Johnston (ed.), *The Future of Geography*. London: Methuen. pp. 211–24.

Billinge, M., Gregory, D. and Martin, R. (1984) 'Reconstructions', in M. Billinge, D. Gregory and R. Martin (eds), *Recollections of a Revolution: Geography as Spatial Science*. London: Macmillian, pp. 1–24.

Cloke, P. (2002) 'Deliver us from evil? Prospects for living ethically and acting politically in human geography', *Progress in Human Geography*, 26 (5): 587–604.

Elwood, S. (2006) 'Negotiating knowledge production: the everyday inclusions, exclusions,

and contradictions of participatory GIS research', *The Professional Geographer*, 58 (2): 197–208.
England, K. (1993) 'Suburban pink collar ghettos: the spatial entrapment of women?' *Annals of the Association of American Geographers*, 83: 225–42.
Fotheringham, A.S. (2006) 'Quantification, evidence and positivism', in S. Aitken and G. Valentine (eds), *Approaches to Human Geography*. London: Sage. pp. 237–50.
Fotheringham, A.S., Brunsdon, C. and Charlton, M. (2002) *Geographically Weighted Regression: The Analysis of Spatially Varying Relationships*. West Sussex: John Wiley and Sons.
Gershuny, J. and Robinson, J.P. (1988) 'Historical shifts in the household division of labor', *Demography*, 25: 537–53.
Hannah, M.G. and Strohmayer, U. (2001) 'Anatomy of debate in human geography', *Political Geography*, 20: 381–404.
Hanson, S. and Pratt, G. (1995) *Gender, Work, and Space*. London: Routledge.
Haraway, D. (1991) *Simians, Cyborgs, and Women: The Reinvention of Nature*. New York: Routledge.
Harding, S. (1989) 'Is there a feminist method?' in N. Tuana (ed.), *Feminism and Science*. Bloomington: Indiana University Press. pp. 17–32.
Jackson, P. (2000) 'Social geography', in R.J. Johnston, D. Gregory, G. Pratt and M. Watt (eds), *The Dictionary of Human Geography*. Oxford: Blackwell. pp. 753–54.
Jayaratne, T.E. (1983) 'The value of quantitative methodology for feminist research', in G. Bowles and R.D. Klein (eds), *Theories of Women's Studies*. London: Routledge and Kegan Paul. pp. 140–61.
Jayaratne, T.E. and Stewart, A.J. (1991) 'Quantitative and qualitative methods in the social sciences: current feminist issues and practical strategies', in M.M. Fonow and J.A. Cook (eds), *Beyond Methodology: Feminist Scholarship as Lived Research.* Bloomington, IN: Indiana University Press. pp. 85–106.
Johnston-Anumonwo, I. (1995) 'Racial differences in commuting behavior of women in Buffalo, 1980–1990', *Urban Geography*, 16: 23–45.
Johnston-Anumonwo, I. (1997) 'Race, gender, and constrained work trips in Buffalo, NY, 1990', *Professional Geographer*, 49: 306–17.
Kwan, M.-P. (1998) 'Space-time and integral measures of individual accessibility: a comparative analysis using a point-based framework', *Geographical Analysis*, 30 (3): 91–216.
Kwan, M.-P. (1999a) 'Gender and individual access to urban opportunities: a study using space-time measures', *Professional Geographer*, 51 (2): 210–27.
Kwan, M.-P. (1999b) 'Gender, the home-work link, and space-time patterns of nonemployment activities', *Economic Geography*, 75 (4): 370–94.
Kwan, M.-P. (2000b) 'Gender differences in space-time constraints', *Area*, 32 (2): 145–56.
Kwan, M.-P. (2002) 'Feminist visualization: Re-envisioning GIS as a method in feminist geographic research', *Annals of the Association of American Geographers*, 92 (4): 645–61.
Kwan, M.-P. (2004a) 'Beyond difference: From canonical geography to hybrid geographies', *Annals of the Association of American Geographers*, 94 (4): 756–63.
Kwan, M.-P. (2004b) 'GIS methods in time-geographic research: Geocomputation and geovisualization of human activity patterns', *Geografiska Annaler B*, 86 (4): 267–80.
Kwan, M.-P. (2007) 'Hybrid GIS and cultural economic geography', in A. Tickell, E. Sheppard, J. Peck and T. Barnes (eds), *Politics and Practice in Economic Geography*. London: Sage. pp. 165–75.
Kwan, M.-P. and Weber, J. (2003) 'Individual accessibility revisited: Implications for geographical analysis in the twentieth century', *Geographical Analysis*, 35 (4): 341–53.
Lawson, V. (2007) 'Geographies of care and responsibility', *Annals of the Association of American Geographers*, 97 (1): 1–11.
Massey, D. (2001) 'Geography on the agenda', *Progress in Human Geography*, 25 (1): 5–17.
McDowell, L. (1992) 'Valid games? A response to Erica Schoenberger', *The Professional Geographer*, 44 (2): 212–15.
McLafferty, S. (1995) 'Counting for women', *Professional Geographer*, 47 (4): 436–42.
McLafferty, S. and Preston, V. (1992) 'Spatial mismatch and labor market segmentation for African American and Latino women', *Economic Geography*, 68 (4), 406–31.
McLafferty, S. and Preston, V. (1996) 'Spatial mismatch and employment in a decade of

restructuring', *Professional Geographer*, 48: 420–31.
McLafferty, S. and Preston, V. (1997) 'Gender, race, and the determinants of commuting: New York in 1990', *Urban Geography*, 18 (3): 192–212.
McLafferty, S. and Tempalski, B. (1995) 'Restructuring and women's reproductive health: Implications for low birthweight in New York City', *Geoforum,* 26: 309–23.
Morrill, R. (1993) 'Geography, spatial analysis, and social science', *Urban Geography*, 14 (5): 442–6.
Moss, P. (1995) 'Embeddedness in practice, numbers in context: The politics of knowing and doing', *The Professional Geographer*, 47: 442–9.
Perrons, D. (1999) 'Missing subjects? Searching for gender in official statistics', in D. Dorling and S. Simpson (eds), *Statistics in Society: The Arithmatic of Politics*. London: Arnold. pp. 105–14.
Plummer, P. and Sheppard, G. (2001) 'Must emancipatory economic geography be qualitative?' *Antipode*, 33 (2): 194–99.
Pratt, G. (1989) 'Quantitative techniques and humanistic-historical materialist perspectives', in A. Kobayashi and S. Mackenzie (eds), *Remaking Human Geography*. Boston: Unwin Hyman. pp. 101–15.
Pratt, G. and Hanson, S. (1991) 'Time, space, and the occupational segregation of women: A critique of human capital theory', *Geoforum*, 22 (2): 149–57.
Pugh, A. (1990) 'My statistics and feminism – a true story', in L. Stanley (ed.), *Feminist Praxis: Research, Theory and Epistemology in Feminist Sociology*. London: Routledge. pp. 103–12.
Reinharz, S. (1992) *Feminist Methods in Social Research*. Oxford: Oxford University Press.
Rose, D. (1993) 'On feminism, method and methods in human geography: an idiosyncratic overview', *The Canadian Geographer*, 37 (1): 57–60.
Rosenbloom, S. and Burns, E. (1994) 'Why working women drive alone: implications for travel reduction programs', *Transportation Research Record*, 1459: 39–45.
Samarasinghe, V. (1997) 'Counting women's work: the intersection of time and space', in J.P. Jones III, H.J. Nast and S.M. Roberts (eds), *Threshold in Feminist Geography: Difference, Methodology, Representation*. New York: Rowman and Littlefield. pp. 129–44.
Seager, J. and Olson, S. (1986) *Women in the World: An International Atlas*. London: Pluto.
Sheppard, E. (2001) 'Quantitative geography: representations, practices and possibilities', *Environment and Planning D,* 19: 535–54.
Suchan, T.A. and Brewer, C.A. (2000) 'Qualitative methods for research on mapmaking and map use', *The Professional Geographer*, 52 (1): 145–54.
Tivers, J. (1985) *Women Attached: The Daily Lives of Women with Young Children*. London: Croom Helm.
Valentine, G. (2007) 'Theorizing and researching intersectionality: A challenge for feminist geography', *The Professional Geographer*, 59 (1): 10–21.
Women and Geography Study Group (WGSG), the Institute of the British Geographers. (1997) *Feminist Geographies: Explorations in Diversity and Difference*. Harlow, Essex: Longman.
Wyly, E.K. (2004) 'Geographies of the United States in the year 2004', *The Professional Geographer*, 56 (1): 91–5.

27

Positionalities: It's not About Them and Us, It's About Us

Kath Browne, with Leela Bakshi and Arthur Law

INTRODUCTION

Positionalities can be understood as how research is created through the interactions and relationships between researchers and those being researched. The title is derived from a phrase Arthur uses 'it's not about them and us, it's about us', and focuses attention on the mutual construction of research and research relationships that move beyond objective them/us segregations. At times positionalities can be reduced to the effects of personal backgrounds on research and addressed using simplistic lists of social differences (gender, age, sexuality, ethnicity, dis/ability). In social geography research contexts, the practices of reflecting on, analysing and critiquing researchers' positions in relation to those being researched is termed reflexivity (or more accurately reflectivity; see Falconer-Al-Hindi and Kawabuta, 2002: 104). These processes are to be encouraged in assessing and possibly addressing issues of exploitation and inequitable power relations. More than this, as Haraway (1991) contends, despite the 'god trick' some researchers engage in, whereby they assume a neutral, objective and unengaged position in relation to the research and particularly in its written 'conclusion', all researchers create their research field and data. It is important, then, to explore how we are implicated in these (re)creations, and particularly our interactions. It should be noted at this stage that positionalities, although most often discussed in relation to primary data collection, are not limited to social research contexts. They relate to all acts of researchers' engagements and writings. Nonetheless, for the purposes of this chapter I[1] will be focusing on research interactions.

Feminist social researchers in geography were amongst the first to argue for researchers to position themselves when discussing their research projects. In doing this, they sought to highlight how research is constructed in part by who we are. However, positionalities and reflective thinking are encouraged throughout the research process to explore different ways of working with participants. From the conceptualisation of the project, through the research collection to the write-up critically assessing interactions, relationships, preconceptions and positions of power enable researchers to engage practically with issues of power. On the one hand, for those working with vulnerable groups and those who are disenfranchised, these engagements are seen as crucial to addressing current social injustices (and potentially address disempowering research practices that further marginalise individuals and groups). In addition, these practices can offer certain forms of reciprocity to the group, as rather than enacting an 'objective', 'distant' or 'neutral' researcher role, there is the potential to engage with these groups on a personal level. On the other hand, the practices of engaging in and writing about positionalities can also highlight researchers' vulnerability and the limits to researcher/writer power (see Browne, 2004). Thus the practices of positioning oneself and relational engagements with participants do not necessarily fall into the paradigm of powerful researcher/powerless researched. Close attention to these nuanced engagements can reveal not only the construction of the data but also offer further insights into the phenomenon under investigation.

The aim of this chapter is to examine how positionalities are (re)created throughout the research process, beyond celebratory narratives of becoming an 'insider', and recognising the fluidity of positions of power and privilege. I will do this drawing on a participatory action research project that at the time of writing was at the analysis stage. It seeks to address assumptions that power operates solely around or in relation to the identity categories of male,[2] heterosexual and white by exploring issues of power beyond these categorisations and the fluidities of research relationships beyond individual researchers.

The first part of the chapter outlines debates and issues within discussions of positionalities, addressing the creation of knowledge, reflective practices and the potential impasse of current debates. The chapter then moves on to discuss participatory action research (PAR)[3] and positionalities, before moving on to the specific example of Count Me In Too, a PAR project that looks at lesbian, gay, bisexual and trans-marginalisations and need in Brighton & Hove, southern England (see www.countmeintoo.co.uk for a full account of the research and the findings reports). This section uses three accounts written by the co-researchers (Kath Browne, academic researcher, Leela Bakshi, Spectrum[4] trustee and Arthur Law, Spectrum co-ordinator) to further explore diverse research positionalities and address issues of knowledge creation, power and marginalisations.

CREATING KNOWLEDGES-POSITIONINGS

Writing oneself into research products has quite an extensive history within the discipline of geography, particularly within feminist geographies. Previously, those operating within positivist (social) science frameworks had striven to construct research accounts and undertaken neutral and objective research free from the 'bias' of their involvement. The principle underlying such approaches has been that research can be undertaken in a rational manner, where the researcher is distanced from 'irrational' personal or emotional involvement with or affected by those s/he is researching. This rational/irrational dichotomy, it has been argued, suggested that the 'neutral, objective' researcher was assumed to be white, middle class, male and heterosexual (Rose, 1993). These men (in most cases) appeared to believe they were able to undertake research without biasing the results with their own opinions, agendas and actions. In contrast, it is contended that such a 'view from nowhere' does not exist (Longino, 1993: 137). All knowledge is produced in particular contexts and it matters profoundly by whom, how, where and why this knowledge is formed (Harding, 1987; Stanley and Wise, 1983). If all knowledge is seen to be situated, then who constructs this knowledge is central to what is produced (Haraway, 1991).

The contextualisation of knowledge, it has been argued, is achieved by openly and honestly reflecting on the research process and the position of the researcher in relation to participants (England, 1994; Kleinmann and Copp, 1993; Lohan, 2000; Morris et al., 1998; Twyman et al., 1999). In this way the researcher can become a research tool, offering further insights into the accounts formed (Falconer Al-Hindi and Kawabuta, 2002). This is because identifying the researcher's role in the construction of knowledge provides more insights into the knowledge produced. It is contended that *all* research is produced subjectively, and that excluding consideration of the researcher from the research process or write-up perpetuates the myth of objectivity without addressing the underlying 'biases' inherent to all research. Thus, critically reflecting on the positioning of the researcher, both during the research and through writing oneself into the 'findings', challenges the neutrality and presumed objectivity of the research process (Cook and Fonow, 1990; Harding, 1987; Hirsh and Fox Keller, 1994; Jones III et al., 1997; Maynard, 1994; McCormack, 1987; Morris et al., 1998; Oakley, 1998; Price-Chalita, 1994). Harding (1993) asserts that using these processes in politically guided research places the researcher on the same plane as the researched and produces 'better' (more valid) knowledge.

Reflexive practices

The positionality of the researcher is usually attained through reflexive practices. These see researchers and writers reflect on their creation of knowledge and the specificity of their identities and interactions in this process. Where identities are seen as fixed and stable, positioning oneself can occur in order to 'bracket' oneself out of the research process, identifying specific prejudices and identities that may 'bias' the research. Breakwell (1995: 239), for example, contends that 'the characteristics of a researcher (for example, demeanour, accent, dress, gender, age, etc.) will influence the respondents' willingness to participate and to answer accurately'. He admits that 'interviewer effects' cannot be eliminated but he suggests that steps can and should be taken to control such effects. In this understanding of identities and embodiments, interactions are not seen as productive of identities, rather identities are essential, stable and fixed. There are obvious dangers of reifying positions in this way and even authors who do not wish to 'bracket' themselves out of the research can engage in practices of listing identities. Consequently, even where authors theoretically engage with the conceptualisation of identities as constructed, lists of researcher 'characteristics' such as ethnicity, gender and sexuality, are used to position researchers (see for example Hubbard et al., 2002). This does not connect with, or account for, the interrelationships that re-construct research and writing.

Alternative conceptualisations of identities and embodiments have used performativities to argue that identities are not fixed, but are instead (re)created through reiterated acts and interactions between people, places and things (Butler, 1990; Rose, 1999; Gregson and Rose, 2000). Thus, it has been contended that our positionalities are not located in reified categories, rather they are relational and often reiterated performativities (Kobayashi, 1994; England, 1994). This challenges notions that fixed or essentialised categories (such as gender, age, ethnicity, sexuality) can be used to 'position' oneself in relation to the research or the participants (or other academics through the writing and reviewing process, conference interactions, interviews, etc.). Relations of power are not fixed and, as Kobayashi (1994) noted, researchers' positionalities can vary over the course of the research project, creating a plethora of 'researcher' identities. In contextualising research interactions and resulting researcher positionalities it has long been argued that we do not relate homogenously to each other and this is also the case in research contexts. Valentine (2002) has contended that assumptions of sameness on the basis of sexuality is problematic; rather the focus should be on specific interactions and research relationships. Similarly, research that seeks to develop relationships with participants relies on a dynamic relationship between researchers and participants that often rests on allowing researchers 'in' to a particular group or context. It is this dynamism that contests the fixity of positionalities within specific essentialist frames.

In exploring how research relations are created, contested and reiterated over the course of research and the resulting production (and consumption) of knowledge, it may be possible to examine a more fluid research context. Crang (2003: 497) warns against writings of positionality that narrate an 'unchanging research project conducted by a singular researcher with one stable essential identity, both between locations and over time, and suggests the latter is also true of the researched'. Therefore, I am arguing for a conscious exploration of the continual negotiations that create research. Nevertheless, there is an excess of what we can consciously know and represent in texts. As we can never fully know ourselves or the interactions we have with others, reflecting on the research process and our position in constructing this is seen as partial and selective (Rose, 1995, 1997; Haraway, 1991).

Recent debates in geographies regarding reflexivity and positionality have begun to interrogate the (re)creation of hegemonies resulting from how authors write themselves into accounts of research (see Crang, 2003; Domosh, 2003; Murphy, 2002; Vanderbeck, 2005). This attempt to critically interrogate the creation of celebratory, self-serving and researcher-focused accounts is welcome, yet must consider the fluidity and contextually based power relations that (in)form research fields and writings.

Power

Those who are interested in critically addressing issues of power in research see reflecting upon and attempting to address issues of power imbalances as central to creating ethical research. In these cases, identities and interactions can be reflected upon in order to contest the traditional structures of power relations in research which contends that researchers are in positions of power over their research 'subjects' (Browne, 2003; McDowell, 1992; Moss, 1993, 2002). Here, 'bias' is not a central consideration, rather discussions of power address researcher exploitation and the importance of negotiation throughout the research process. In this section I will critically consider issues of power and positionalities.

We carefully choose what we write, selecting aspects of identities or particular interactions that in part exemplify and in part conceal aspects of the research process. Binnie (1997) and Knopp (1999) have noted the dangers of 'coming out' as gay men in print in geographies and the implications that acts of positioning can have in terms of career progressions and employment.[5] The choice of which 'pieces' of oneself to reflect upon in the research write-up is not straightforward and is instead imbued with relations of power that are not solely located in 'the field' (see also Vanderbeck, 2005). In what continues to be a masculinist and heterosexist discipline (see Berg, 2002; Dias and Blecha, 2007; Browne, 2008), the power relations within institutions and the broader discipline continue to play a part in research writings. These influence what we consciously choose to include in writing up research accounts.

Recently, there has been some debate about the problems of positioning oneself and whether this act necessarily contests hegemonic power relations. Robert Vanderbeck (2005) demonstrates through his use of anthropological research studies, how 'male superethnographers' (p. 395) reclaim a particular hegemonic masculinity and heterosexuality through writing themselves into the fieldwork context. These, he argues, often read as 'autobiographical versions of job recommendation letters' (p. 398), resting on a particular narrative that is based on the outsider/insider dichotomy. These writings position the ethnographer/anthropologist initially as an outsider to the group who then gains a certain amount of acceptance in order to research and engage with those being researched (Lewin and Leap, 1996). This 'insider' status allows for the production of 'real' knowledge and addresses the fluidity of identities and research relationships.

Hegemonic heterosexual masculinities are rarely questioned in these narratives; in contrast they are often reclaimed and celebrated (see Vanderbeck, 2005 for examples). There is also a more subtle form of dominance reiterated through the 'positioning' of oneself as 'white, heterosexual, male and middle class' in order to argue that your position is selective and partial. Vanderbeck points to the irony of this move in a geographical context which historically has celebrated these identities. He also points to the question of reinforcing particular power relations by locating oneself on the more credible sides of these binaries.

Vanderbeck's fear is that in gendered research it is the 'uncomfortable details' of non-hegemonic lives that are called for in discussions of positionality. He points to the dangers of writing about being the 'other' in a heterosexist masculine discipline, and this has yet to be fully interrogated.

Where now?

Vanderbeck (2005: 399) calls for a 'broader stocktaking of the writing practices that these calls have helped to authorise' and appears to be critical or at least wary of any further written (public) examination of researcher positionalities. However, in contrast to the studies Vanderbeck highlights, David Butz's and Lawrence Berg's (2002) discussion of 'duppy feminism' serves to contest masculine dominance or at least overtly explore the privileges of masculinities. Arguing that masculine privilege is in part how they, and other senior men in academia, have 'succeeded', they contest the individualisation and celebration of academic achievements as solely reliant on individual effort and 'brilliance' (although they recognise that these factors are also important). This deconstruction of the often unacknowledged power positionalities within academia illustrates the potential vulnerabilities of naming such privileges. I want to consider how reflective writing practices could be done differently, contesting fixed and essentialised categories.

Not only am I mindful that I am sidestepping Vanderbeck's important challenge, I am also aware of Domosh's (2003) concern that the focus on researchers' positionalities is becoming rather narcissistic where discussions of positionalities emphasise the researcher. However, following Lohan (2000) I want to argue for a 'responsible reflexivity', one that places knowledge 'in the context of interactions between knower and known' (p. 110). Although this has a number of strands, bearing in mind that, in this context, positionality is regarded in terms of interactions, here I will address the (re)creation of hegemonic subject positions and how these interactions are varied and fluid.

Whilst I agree with Vanderbeck (2005) that there is a danger in positioning oneself as hegemonic and anti-hegemonic, the original call for researchers to include themselves was to contest a disembodied voice of knowledge/authority that was often assumed to be male, heterosexual and white. I agree that those who fit within specific hegemonies could potentially reinforce these hegemonies by the act of naming, yet they can also be deconstructed and challenged by acts of writing. Critical reflexive writing should explore and problematise embodied performances, as well as potential and solidifying hegemonies and privileges within and beyond the fieldwork context. This could potentially move us beyond locating power within the subject position of white, heterosexual, middle class and male paradigm, to a conceptualisation of power that can both empower and disempower.

In examining hegemonies and positionalities it is important to contextualise rather than universalise hegemonies, identities or positionalities. Calls for practices and writings that examine research interactions as fluid performativities, need to recognise that power relations within geographical academic writing may be quite different from those in the field. In the context of this chapter – although geography continues to be a heterosexual (and often heterosexist/homophobic) discipline – in the fieldwork I will describe, this was not the case. However, protecting oneself from the heterosexuality of the discipline is only one way of engaging with these modes of power. If we take the call to discuss privilege as well as disenfranchisement seriously then the positive aspects of power, privilege and difference can also be addressed and included, not only in a conquering of 'difference' and a celebration of 'overcoming obstacles' but also in a consideration of the use of power to advance progressive social change.

ENOUGH ABOUT ME, LET'S TALK ABOUT YOU – WHAT DO YOU THINK OF ME?: PARTICIPATORY ACTION RESEARCH AND NEGOTIATED POSITIONALITIES

Having outlined some of the key issues regarding positionalities, I now want to move to the particularities of participatory action research in relation to positionalities, before moving on to a discussion of positionalities in the project Count Me In Too. This chapter could be accused of overly self-reflective focusing as it does on the researchers (see Domosh, 2003), but the difference here is that this chapter engages researchers beyond the 'academy' and seeks to contest the researcher/participant binary. There is some precedent for this (see for example Falconer-Al-Hindi and Kawabata, 2002), yet there is a dearth of debate or discussion which explores researchers' identities in PAR research, beyond fixed essentialised categories (for an exception to this see Cahill, 2007).

It is rare to engage non-academic researchers in reflecting on how the research was undertaken and their role in constructing it. This situation is perhaps unsurprising given that the focus of PAR research is on the relational process of empowering and sharing. In 'giving back' and encouraging democratic participation, the emphasis is on those who participated and the processes that enable such participation. In foregrounding participants' and co-researchers' needs and outcomes, the researcher's role (when it is included) is often written in terms of facilitation, rather than constructing/creating the research. In this way the researchers' positionality is understandably placed in the background. Despite this, where the researcher engages in democratic decision-making processes as well as processes of empowerment, they are implicated in the creation of the research. There is a danger in these narratives that the researcher exists as a benign presence and/or is placed as distant to (and distinct from) the process of constructing the research. If we are to argue that research is created through interactions and relations then it is important to address even these 'background' roles and responsibilities, particularly when the researcher is engaging with academic structures such as writing chapters for books! It is not only the research that is constituted through these processes; as Cahill (2007) argues, her own fractured and fluid positionalities were recreated through her research. She intricately weaves a discussion of poststructural identity formations with a critique of PAR's often authenticating and essentialising practices based on specific models of social justice.

Conversely, PAR presents new challenges to the consideration of positionalities. To only assess and explore the academic researcher's role would be to deny the power and engagements of the co-researchers and participants in designing and facilitating the project. PAR often contests simplistic boundaries between researcher/participants, and this has implications for discussions of positionalities. Converting PAR research into academically 'valid' and 'valued' research can be problematic (see Kindon et al., 2007), and explorations of positionalities are no different in this endeavour.

Those undertaking community roles who are facilitating social change or resisting oppressive regimes can see the possibilities of research in furthering their goals. Yet to ask them to reflect on their role in the creation of such research can challenge their view of the research itself. Certainly, when I sought to involve Arthur Law and Leela Bakshi in the writing of this chapter, the task of explaining positionality and its relevance was not easy or straightforward. They both agreed to participate but their reservations highlighted (amongst many other things!) that there is still a need in particular situations to represent research as much as possible as 'neutral' and 'objective'. In this context, to reflect on one's place in the construction of research is risky. For them (as well as other stakeholders in the research) distance is still valued, respected and expected.

This is an interesting dilemma in exploring the intersection of positionalities and participatory action research. In the Brighton & Hove context, one advantage of university branding on a research project is the value placed on 'academic' research in order to influence policies and those in power (see also Kwan, in this volume, on the uses of quantitative approaches for the same reason). This chapter offers a very different reading and use of academic research. It shows the negotiation of the 'powerful' position of not just the 'researcher' but also the contextualisation of the researcher within an institution such as a university. Whereas in writing this chapter I am potentially marginalising myself and risking specific forms of discrimination (in relation to the hegemonic academic geographies), for Arthur and Leela their carefully chosen words (and what was not included) were read in relation to the potential damage to Spectrum (see below) and the power of Count Me In Too to advance social change for LGBT people in Brighton & Hove. I will now outline the Count Me In Too project before moving to the three accounts produced by myself, Leela and Arthur.

COUNT ME IN TOO

Count Me In Too seeks to explore and address issues of marginalisation within and between the lesbian, gay, bisexual and trans (LGBT) collective in Brighton & Hove. From an academic perspective, it engages with the power relations between those who identify as LGBT and explores power relations beyond heteronormativity, including those that can be loosely conceptualised as homonormative.[6] The project seeks to engage with the margins of these normalisations and particularly engage those who are disenfranchised and marginalised. It began in September 2005 and it is a PAR project that was designed and led in collaboration with 'community partners', Spectrum, and LGBT individuals. The project was initiated through CUPP (the community university partnership project at the University of Brighton) and is funded by Brighton and Sussex Community Knowledge Exchange (BSCKE), Brighton & Hove Primary Care Trust (National Health Service) and the Brighton & Hove City Council.

Count Me In Too followed Spectrum's lead in seeking to facilitate community involvement in the project. This initially involved creating a steering group (October 2005–October 2006) that consisted of twelve LGBT people from minority groups. This group made key decisions regarding research design and conceptualisation. They helped to come up with a list of over thirty groups that may have been disenfranchised within the LGBT community and under-represented in large-scale questionnaires. They then designed the questions for the focus groups (there were 21 focus groups undertaken with 69 participants). A large-scale questionnaire was also designed with questions submitted by mainstream and LGBT statutory and voluntary services, local LGBT groups and individuals. However, the steering group decided from the 400+ questions submitted which questions would be included in the questionnaire. The steering group worked on designing questions and engaging people in completing the questionnaire and attending focus groups. The action group was then established to guide the analysis of research to the initial findings reports and event (November 2006–June 2007). With an acknowledgement of the workload of voluntary workers and organisations, and the time restrictions, the project was designed such that Arthur Law and I would take on the main workload but that we would liaise with and be guided by the steering and action groups. This has meant that busy volunteers have been involved in shaping the project.

The action group consists of LGBT people who are charged with highlighting the key findings for the stakeholders in the research (LGBT groups and organisations, the project funders, statutory and voluntary services). Following this, a series of dissemination events have been undertaken around specific identities and areas of need, enabling the rich findings to be interrogated by diverse groups and agencies (see www.countmeintoo.co.uk for full reports). Dissemination events were co-hosted by Spectrum and partner groups and organisations to ensure that the research engages the services it sought to influence and those whom it is supposedly representing. The Count Me In Too findings informed each event.

The project also reports to a 'monitoring group' which was a condition of funding by BSCKE. This group meets quarterly and although Arthur Law and I feed back to this group, it does not have any decision-making powers.

KATH'S MOMENTS

As a lesbian researcher, in the initial stages of the project I felt 'homonormative' and privileged in the context of this project. However, as the project developed, my positionality became one of 'focus group attendee' and in this way simultaneously 'marginal' and 'expert'. This part of the chapter will examine the implications of these diverse positionalities, not as a linear trajectory of inclusion, but as an example of dynamic research relationships that are (re)created through research events and the paradoxical positioning of power and powerlessness in the research process. This section will focus on three events. Firstly, my initial 'placing' in the context of a paper I wrote for a presentation in Leeds; secondly, on participating in the last focus group of the project; and finally, my reflections with the community partners (and co-researchers) in this project. Through these reflective moments, I seek to suggest that hegemonic and marginalised positionalities are fluid and recreated through diverse research relations.

Moment 1: Leeds Conference presentation: Too normal to be queer, April 2006[7]

I am not 'marginalised' in the way the steering group have categorised marginalisation. I am actively engaged in the LGBT scene, use the scene regularly, I am well networked with a good support system. I have a steady income, am white, able bodied and sit on in a desirable trustee position on the board of Pride. When I began this project I was painfully aware of this positionality. I was/am acutely conscious that I may be part of the problem in terms of lesbian and gay homonormativity. I buy into (literally) things that many find oppressive, alienating, and exclusionary. This I thought placed me in the realm of straight identified researchers who studied lesbian and gay communities. I am aware of discussions such as those provided in England's (1994) account of her failed attempt to undertake sexuality research as a straight identified woman or in Hubbard's (1999) case as an 'outsider'. However, by virtue of our 'sameness' around sexuality I am somewhat accepted. It has been mentioned by the members of the steering group that they would not have been involved had I attempted this project as a straight identified person. Yet, I was uneasy of taking on this project, wary of exploitation and appropriation of difference for the sake of academic research. I feel had this not been a participatory action project I would not have taken it on.

Kitchin (2000) suggests that researchers should lend their skills and expertise to facilitate changes for excluded individuals and groups allowing them to engage in the research process. My position as the Count Me In Too researcher has to date been very much as a mediator, someone who is identifiably a gay woman but not necessarily an 'insider'. I have simultaneously been positioned as 'the expert'. This (re)constitutes me in relation to academic hierarchies as well as local knowledges. I have tried to emphasise the role of the steering group and their need for ownership of the project. I reveal the limits of my knowledge, admitting my lack of information of the intricate histories of the Brighton & Hove communities, networks, personalities and events. I try to cast myself as 'helping' this project to occur but not pretending to know how people would like to be spoken to, addressed by whom and in what contexts. I rely heavily on Arthur whose research skills and experiences with previous research regarding LGBT need in the city are invaluable. We both rely on the steering group who are keen to point out how they would like to be addressed and the potential pitfalls in order to engage meaningfully with those we are to speak to. I rarely feel 'powerful' in a steering group meetings and I now realise that the most intense critique that I am likely to be subjected to is in the pages of LGBT magasines and at LGBT community meetings.

In contrast to my lack of knowledge, what facilitates my acceptance as well is in part my anonymity. I am not well known within the LGBT community of Brighton & Hove and I have not developed a history by which I could be judged. Nevertheless, my position as a Pride trustee could be contentious. Pride is seen as a powerful organisation in the LGBT city and financially supports voluntary and community groups through grants for their events in winter and summer Pride weeks. As I am part of the decision making process in awarding grants, I have to negotiate my Pride trustee positionality and my role as the researcher on Count Me In Too. As a Pride trustee I am often associated with the persona of the (then) chair of Pride who is often perceived as one of 'the white gay men' who are read as controlling 'gay Brighton'.

My complex positionality regarding this research is such that I continually negotiate my sexuality and marginalisation questioning my positions of power. This means the practices of creating action orientated knowledge are not reduced to simplistic discourses of either helping or being part of the powerful elite. Instead it recognises the differential power relations that are involved, these are fluid and negotiated throughout the research. Power then is not simply contained within centre/margin, bad/good binaries.

Moment 2: Moving towards 'marginalisation'? December 2006

As I outlined above, at the outset of the research I was quite unaware of certain LGBT issues in Brighton & Hove; however, over the course of the research I have become informed of structures, engagements and negotiations that occur throughout the city. I, in some ways, was able to engage with who had 'the power in LGBT Brighton & Hove' because I was being invited to meetings and had witnessed first hand their interactions and engagements with the city's power bases, as well as those who had positions of power within the city. However, the last focus group that was held for Count Me In Too was entitled 'first generation immigrants'. I participated in this group, having been asked to do so by Leela (see below) and because I fitted the category having emigrated from Ireland. In keeping with the Count Me In Too ethos, I felt that I should engage how the steering group saw fit rather than stick with academic conventions of distance and neutrality. These are unique (and multiple) positionalities. By participating in the focus group the notion of researcher objectivity could be questioned. I am also not anonymous to the action group, the steering group or Arthur (or now the readers of this chapter!).

In contrast to the celebratory narratives of some anthropologists, crossing the boundaries of 'marginalisation' and becoming the 'same' is often imbued with an understanding of inherent 'difference'. Objective research has often been posited as distant and disengaged, with participatory action research operating in a seemingly contrasting paradigm. In the PAR context researchers are encouraged to 'get close to' and engage with the research. Previously investigated 'subjects' can (and some would argue should) become researchers in the process of PAR, the blurring of researcher/participant boundaries are apparent in different ways here. If participatory action research is to be empowering then 'researchers' in the broadest sense would not be distanced. Perhaps where appropriate, useful and invited researchers could engage in ways that challenge participant/researcher boundaries? As I will address in the next section, this can put the researcher at risk in ways that are not apparent in detached researcher paradigms.

Moment 3: Doing a Count Me In Too Researcher Identity – January 2007

Although I have been involved in the research as a participant, I continue to occupy the positionalities of 'the Count Me In Too researcher'. One aspect of this is as Spectrum develops consultations with a number of service agencies through the promise of evidence based research, I am often requested at meetings to represent 'the project'. This is clearly an 'expert' role and one that I am expected to play more and more regularly as anticipation heightens for the findings of the research project. However, my position as Pride trustee is also noted in some of these meetings. In this way I am positioned as both a 'researcher' and part of LGBT communities with specific 'vested interests'. I have multiple and potentially 'conflicting' identities. These in part relate to the desire for researchers to be 'neutral' and unbiased and represent the standards that Arthur describes below. This remains despite describing how the research was guided and developed by community-led groups. Doing the 'interviews' with Arthur and Leela allowed me to reflect on my own positionalities as they questioned me on particular issues and highlighted the importance of my positionalities in relation to theirs and the processes undertaken in Count Me In Too. This final moment outlines some of the issues in these conversations.

In my discussions with Leela it became clear that there is a real lack of understanding or provision within the university (academic?) settings of an ethic of care for researchers. She equated me with a front-line worker, similar to Arthur who receives monthly external supervision. We had an interesting dialogue around connection, empathy and care for self:

Leela: I don't know how you operate in this. I just can't understand it but you don't have supervision, you don't have any sort of therapy session to go back to so where do you go with all this pain and anguish and hurt and suffering?

Kath: I don't know. It's interesting that you say that because I think I distance myself from it. The way I distance myself from it is by saying that I am not as marginalised as the people in this. It's like taking that empathetic role but not feeling it as my own pain. I suppose that's how I've dealt with it.

Leela: Well, does it not ring bells for you? To me the way you listen to the stories to me feels like a level of engagement and if you really hear what people are telling you then my personal belief is, it is because you are able to empathise and empathise means feeling it.

Kath: I think I do but I feel it for them rather than for me. I think I still have that degree of separation. This hadn't ever really occurred to me because I have never really spoken about it, but yeah, I think that was around not feeling this multiple marginalisation.

Throughout this dialogue and my considerations of research, it is clear that I have adopted a separation from multiple marginalisations and my personal experiences. Perhaps distance and 'objectivity' are important in academic settings where researchers remain unsupported. In this way building 'rapport' and 'empathy' at a distance is a safer strategy than engaging with issues that could put the researcher at risk. Leela addressed this in her response to the first reading of this chapter:

Early on in the project, I was impressed by Kath's commitment to participants directing the project, flexibility about timelines in order to accommodate process led by participants, and tranquillity about incorporating suggestions from participants when these seemed to me at odds with these researchy ways of doing things.

It seems a common view that being a researcher demands that you are to some degree disconnected from your subjects, in order to achieve 'objectivity'. But can subjects fully engage and communicate when the researcher takes this stance, and if the researcher drops personal responses, experiences and opinions, then can they understand and capture what they are researching? In my opinion this demand for connection transforms researchers into 'front-line workers'. In order to carry out their role effectively over time, I think researchers in this role would require supervision and support to respond to and process the emotions of participants, and their own emotional responses. Do they choose the safer strategy of remaining distant because this support is not available? Do researchers use a number of researchy/academic common practices in order to avoid connection, including things like timelines, deadlines and scientific method, in addition to not recognising that they are in effect 'front-line workers'?

Discussions with Leela also pointed to the problems with categories in identifying marginalisations (see below) and we discussed my feelings of not being marginalised despite being part of a focus group. Throughout this research I moved into and out of categories of 'marginalisation', both in terms of my perceptions and the perceptions of others. Therefore when 'positioning' oneself in the research context there are problems of fixing 'self' and 'other' that reflexive analyses usually entail. Koyabashi (1994) discussed the possibilities of her position as 'insider' and her movement to 'outsider' as a result of her research. I appear to have a more complex trajectory moving between 'outsider' and 'insider' in relation to sexuality and marginalisation. These positionalities are unstable, and unsettling, yet they are key to how the research as a process unfolds and refolds.

LEELA: DOES MARGINALISATION COME IN DIFFERENT FLAVOURS?

Leela became involved in Count Me In Too as the link trustee from Spectrum. She was involved in the steering group and set up the action group, applying for money from the council. I interviewed Leela and then wrote an account of this. Having read a draft of this chapter she then wrote a response to it and her interview. Both are combined to create what follows.

Does marginalisation come in different flavours?

At a meeting early in the project (which I didn't attend), the steering group listed identities which potentially led to individuals experiencing marginalisation. While I understood why it was necessary to 'recruit' identified identities to focus groups, and that 'themed' focus groups insights would be gained from them, I felt really uncomfortable about this 37 flavours of marginalisation approach. I don't like my cultural heritage and family history being lumped under the term 'BME' – I think that many researchers and planners who use the term 'BME' do so not recognising the complexity of BME identity. Also, I don't like my experience of marginalisation being attributed to my skin colour/ethnic origin when there are multiple ways/identities that contribute to my experience of marginalisation – and these other ways weren't, and perhaps can't be, listed. At that time I felt that the steering group, by not acknowledging aspects of my marginalisation, was marginalising me.

I didn't feel that way when I started attending steering group meetings. We were a group of people who, I'm talking for myself here, might usually feel the bottom of the pile in terms of marginalisation. You come to the steering group and you think 'oh, I am not the most marginalised person in the room any more'. That was a very new experience. Just being in a space where we all had our needs met and all got listened to and all got equally valued was very, very novel.

I assumed that feeling marginalised was an experience common not only to the diverse group of people who came together as the steering group of participants guiding the research, but also experienced by other marginalisation-aware LGBT people connected with the project. Sameness meant there wasn't the need to struggle to build a core that there usually is, particularly meetings with straight people where the incidental conversation is often alienating, marginalising. We didn't need to do that rapport building because we were already speaking the same language. It works really well because we can have conversations without getting lost in not quite understanding what each other is saying. We have talked about our background-in-common (LGBT identity) as something that facilitated effective work together, and I understood this to be common positionality. I've come to realise that people who potentially shared LGBT identities, had different positionality to me, relating to *marginalisation*. I sometimes felt like I was being cast as a marginalised person by non-marginalised people. I didn't feel comfortable with it. It feels like another experience of marginalisation and contrasts with talking about my experiences of marginalisation with other marginalised people, which feels more empowering.

Kath: What about the focus groups?

I saw the focus groups as an opportunity to explore multiple marginalisation and I was really happy that this was acknowledged through encouraging people to attend multiple focus groups if that felt appropriate (e.g. trans and bi). It was really, really important for me. For me it felt like it was the first time I was invited into a space where I can tell my stories. It was a really important experience for me to have my stories and opinions heard *and* conveyed outside of the marginalised minority communities that I am part of. Sharing experiences with insiders feels like withdrawing from the arena of harm to 'lick our wounds': it's empowering and healing, but doesn't feel like it will tackle exclusion and marginalisation.

What is hard about telling those stories is that they are very, very painful. I think the focus group questions elicit honesty and stories that people don't tell anywhere else and hearing those things explicitly for the first time is hard. I guess for me listening to people talking about all sorts of stuff it touches on stuff in my own life. It's really emotional reading them. I think because a lot of it relates to stuff I have experienced. It's very empowering to see other people describe it and give voice to things that perhaps I felt but haven't really been able to express yet, haven't been able to express verbally. This contrasts my experience of listening to stories with connections and your (Kath's) experience of listening with separation (see Kath's Moment 3 above). Perhaps this is why I thought it might be important for you to receive that sort of supervision, projecting from my own responses.

Power and processes

For me, researchers moving away from scientific method in order to accommodate human behaviour have increased my confidence and participation in the project. I realised that it wasn't just about asking people and then researchers doing their own thing. It was about the steering group really influencing. I felt questions went into the questionnaire that probably you (Kath) as a researcher didn't particularly think were very good but you put them in because that's what the steering group wanted, and that seemed to me to be at odds with researchy ways of doing things. One that we cut out was put forward by somebody outside the circle – it was put it in by a funder but somebody who is not part of the steering group. That sort of lined up, I guess the politics of who's in charge of this. The people who were paying don't get what they want out of the steering group, and those who are very disempowered actually are the ones who get the important power.

I worry that researchers have more power because they are researchers and people listen to researchers who have university status. They have got universities behind them with money. They've got time and capacity. I guess that's what I mean being an unpaid volunteer that my power is diminished by the fact that I don't have a lot of time or office or even an email system that works properly to influence things.

Kath: In what ways [do the university researchers have power?]

I mean it's just like having information at your [university researchers] fingertips. You know like you can say to Andrew [Church] 'how much money is in the budget?' In theory he has a whole lot of minions who are adding up how much is in the budget and can tell him. There isn't the same support structure in Spectrum and that is quite disempowering. Even being able to host a meeting, it does actually give you a lot of power to be able to have a meeting on your territory. You know we can't really do that at Spectrum.

As the project has progressed, I noticed different distributions of power. In spite of my personal opinion that all LGBT people involved in the project have experience of marginalisation, and the success of the project in involving marginalised LGBT people in project design and data analysis, 'outsiders' still hold significant power. I feel that people who identify as marginalised are less represented in the bodies that have most influence over the design of the project and the messages it conveys through dissemination (see Figure 27.1).

The action group, in my head, is about having steering group meetings in a nicer environment so we value the people who are attending, because I felt we weren't valuing them properly. We weren't looking after them. It meant a lot to me when an action group member said to me or us all 'it's great to come here and have a free lunch. A free lunch means a lot to me'. That is sort of recognising who it is we are engaging with. I guess it's a bit of me offloading my own feeling that I'm an oppressor because of the ways I'm empowered by having a lot of money and respect at work, so I am empowered to talk over people who perhaps aren't in a place in their life where they can do that to me.

I think that the experiences that lead to 'marginalisation' can compromise our confidence and capacity to engage in more time consuming and complex tasks, and alienation from the bodies that hold power. I do believe I have this confidence and capacity but this makes me wonder whether I am actually marginalised – whether I can legitimately claim this identity. From the outset, I was clear that I *felt* marginalised, but looking at academics' descriptions of positionality, many reasons to identify as 'not-marginalised' apply to me, including income, education, professional position, position in community – and the list goes on. I feel I've achieved these things in spite of my experiences of racism, sexism and homophobia, as well as other prejudices and exclusions that I don't know names for. I think I'm marginalised because of a mosaic of factors and experiences that I choose to recognise and connect with. Possibly, when significantly marginalised individuals become empowered enough to become part of the research establishment, and disconnected enough to choose objective scientific research over passionate service provision, their identity as 'marginalised' may be compromised. As they become part of the power structures that carry out research, they become 'coconut' (brown skin on the outside, white thinking inside).

Challenging 'outsiders' to enter marginalisation

The term 'marginalised' suggests we're on the edge of the rest of society – maybe we are the outsiders. But as marginalised people working together in the context of PAR, we are the 'insiders' to our experience of marginalisation, and people who don't share that identity are 'outsiders'. I felt that within this project, marginalised came to mean *different* rather than *excluded*: 'not part of the prevailing culture', so it included groups like 'LGBT

Most power, smaller proportion of marginalized people

↑

Action group and monitoring group (Commissioners, Funders, and Board of Trustees of community partner)
Steering group
Participants in focus groups/people who completed questionnaires

↓

Least power, greater proportion of marginalized people

Figure 27.1 Flows of power in Count Me in Too.

people who have pets', and 'women who don't use mixed spaces'. This felt good to me as someone labelled marginalised, because my identities give rise to pleasant and unpleasant, empowering and oppressing, joyful and painful and not-very-significant experiences, not just exclusion. It also made me think that everyone has experiences of marginalisation that they can tap into, so potentially we all experience being 'insiders'. Because of this I think polarised identities (male-female, white-BME, straight-LGBT or Queer) are not useful in defining position in relation to each other, because our positionalities are fluid and complex. Assumptions about power/disempowerment based on these identities are not reliably true. We all have experiences of being excluded and marginalised – privileged straight white men and everyone else.

I think we all have the opportunity to use our own experiences to connect with those of the 'others' that we make the subjects of our research. I took part as a participant not a facilitator in the BME focus groups. Facilitating would have put me in a position of holding back from contributing. I was initially unsure about facilitating the first generation immigrants group, but agreed to do it because I have some understanding of issues around being an immigrant from my family's experiences of immigration. So I didn't fully feel like an outsider. I think facilitators need to work hard to connect when working with groups and identities that they are not familiar with.

I recognise that part of the motivation for me to set up a first generation immigrants' focus group was that it would cast as marginalised people in power connected with the project. I perceived this as offering something 'empowering' rather than 'challenging' to people I was friendly with. I felt frustrated that people told me that they don't identify as marginalised by this aspect of their identity, and two of them didn't think it was appropriate for them to take part in a focus group because of this. I felt disappointed that people who I perceived as marginalisation-aware and powerful didn't choose to explore their own experiences of marginalisation, or perhaps felt that doing this would not be consistent with their position of power. I've since come to realise that it was important to me not only because it would place these people in the same 'marginalised' space as me, but also because I think we'll do better research if we all connect with our own experiences of marginalisation.

If the researcher is an 'outsider' to the experience of marginalisation, then as individuals they will face a challenge to hear from the people that they exclude, and their interactions with 'the marginalised' may be marginalising. I think empathy is expressed when listeners respond with sadness that it happened and warm support for person telling their story, and that empathy comes from self-awareness: connecting with their own experiences of marginalisation. I try to offer that to others when they talk about marginalisation that I haven't experienced. I am very committed to people's stories being heard, that's right there down in the core for me. That's why I'm a speech therapist and it's also to do with personal experience and my family's history of stories not being heard, and how much pain and mess that creates.

I think researchers should help those who exclude those groups and individuals to hear from the people that they exclude. As a participant in focus groups, I felt that Kath connected with our stories in order to prompt us to elaborate and explain the stories, so that experiences were examined and recorded. The researcher acted as a conduit to ensure that story is heard by others who perhaps would not engage and hear if told the story first-hand. It made me feel heard and present and gave me a sense of connecting that counteracts feeling marginalised.

ARTHUR: IT'S NOT ABOUT THEM AND US, IT'S ABOUT US

Arthur worked on the original Count Me In and became involved in Count Me In Too as the Spectrum coordinator where he and the Spectrum trustees pushed for community engagement with the project from the outset. These are Arthur's words, except where 'Kath' is indicated, summarised from a taped discussion with Kath.

It's not about them and us, it's about us

I start from a position of not feeling included. 'It's not my scene' was my opening sentence when I arrived in Brighton. I am not a proper one of what I am supposed to be, and that was a liberation. Although people put me on a pedestal, that is not where I see myself. I am me with my own exclusions and marginalisation, working with other people, who have experienced similar but different forms of marginalisation but they are not this other set of people. That's my kind of point of entry *it's not about them and us, it's about us.* I am part of the us, not one of them or those people over there or those poor unfortunate people we have never spoken to in the next room and we are not talking to them. That's not where I start from, that's not where Spectrum starts from.

I was the activist and my activism has always been based up until now, and still is, with having one foot in policy and strategic stuff and another ear on the ground listening to what's actually happening. So all my activism, which people think is me being gobby, Arthur speaking for everybody else, was from spending hours on the phone, hearing people. I was passionate, passion is a big thing for me, about connecting all of these fragments into a whole and people had a set of needs. Spectrum, which I helped to set up, was how to do it, how to make it all cohere. I came back a couple of years ago in this role [as Spectrum coordinator]. I am not afraid of authority. It is still very much part of who I am now that I work with people who wouldn't work with me for 15 years, who characterised me as a gay terrorist. I am still passionate and I get paid for what I have always done and aren't I lucky?

My vision hasn't changed about this place [Brighton & Hove] and if it can't happen here, where can it happen? And we deserve it. I see my job as being about keeping everything safe for everybody as we go on this is journey of a roller coaster ride to heaven. I am not interested in private salvation on a yacht going to some gay paradise out on a magic island somewhere. I don't want it [Brighton & Hove] to be some gay mecca or gay capital or whatever. I want it to be what it can be – which is a home for us, whoever us is – and that's really exciting to me. I want to inspire, persuade, cajole or arm twist other people to believe in that possibility and it is happening. Count Me In Too is part of the very strong sense of politics that I have. I don't believe in it because it is in my job description.

Count Me In Too

Kath: What do you see as your role in Count Me In Too?

It's about being an advocate for people who don't have a voice, commonly. Through my kind of extensive experience historically of people not having power, coming together and having the voice and expressing themselves in various ways, to me it's no different to that really. I also know from years and years of work the power of testimony as a way to influence change so I actually think the voice of people's own lives is much better than rafts of statistics or whatever. I think Count Me In Too is captured both, it's being able to quantify scale of various problems but also to allow those voices to sing through which I think we'll move people and change things quite dramatically.

All I want to do is to bring the gap between the providers up there and the people with the stories over there nearer together through this process. Things are a bit scary at the moment because things are speeded up so much, but once we've got the vision actually getting there is quite easy. It becomes an invitation rather than a challenge. That is all that needs to happen is that they talk to each other – when they are talking things happen. When they are hearing each other things happen. It's when they're not listening to each other, when it's not worth saying anything because we are going to do this anyway or we don't do that because that's what we are told to do by the government, you know that's when it doesn't happen. This process is bringing people nearer together around a table where they can do business hopefully. If it's not doing that then it's failing.

Kath: Who are we encouraging to come to the table by this process do you think?

I would think our passions, yes, and I am using the word passion deliberately, that a kind of quality and energy about what you want to do has communicated itself through the networks of people who they also trust and who have been caught with that passion, to make a difference. Some have come and spoken because they trust the process and they also trust the process because it can extend immediately to a process that will deliver change. I think there are some people who just need to tell their story without a sense of what was going to happen to it. There were with other people who came with a very deep and lasting need for the world to stop treading on them so painfully and wanted things to happen. They knew because of those people who fronted the project and maybe also the connection that Spectrum can deliver and will make the difference. They also wanted to be part of that inclusive model as well.

The painful bit is carrying people's hopes and it is actually quite a sad process. It's about cutting down the richness into a serving suggestion that are really complex and rich sets of stories and each of those is somebody's life. It's not just a census form. It's actually about some lives which are incredible stories in their own right. I know we didn't set out to do that but the process of paring it down means that some particular stories get lost or the uniqueness of that experience. So, it's a privilege to have access to all of it but quite forbidding in that trying to make something, we lose something in the process. You can't say everything or make every point that people have made to us in all of the hours and days that people gave us.

Kath: It's quite a privileged position for us to be in, isn't it, as well as a very difficult …

And quite vulnerable in some senses because people want things to be written in capital letters in the findings that 'I need this' and it may be that it doesn't get there.

Kath: How was it for you being part of a focus group?

As Spectrum co-ordinator, helping to facilitate it's quite difficult because obviously I know lots of people. I am a bit concerned that my presence influenced in some way what people said and also because I work for one of the services in a different job, that that might have kind of somehow influence what people said. So that's partly why I didn't want to become engaged too much with focus groups. However, the model which I helped to shape was important because the idea of just simply bringing people to tell their stories is (a) both empowering to those people and (b) allows them to discover things that they haven't understood about their experiences and have a voice to say and be heard and other people have the same thing and for it to be of permanent value is really important.

Kath: I think you have a different role as well. I remember when we had that discussion around who wanted access to the data and you said 'it's my role to protect these people who have given us access to their lives'.

But that is Spectrum's role. It's about trust and trust actually means about respect and honouring what people have told you. It's not just about confidentiality. It's about protecting thugs coming in and stealing all the goodies and ignoring the bits they don't want to deal with.

'Experts/expertise?'

Kath: When you say it's Spectrum's role to do that how much of Spectrum is your role to do it?

Spectrum is an organisation I work for and lone workers have become the spirit of an organisation. That's tough, that comes with the territory, but you know I'm it and I can't avoid that. Spectrum means I don't have a private life as such. I can't go somewhere as me. I am always Spectrum. But in the same way that I carry people's hopes and expectations and means of an organisation, so do you. I think what you bring to the equation, you and the university is a status. This isn't just a wish list from a load of disenfranchised people who want to come and have a whinge. It's going to be academically sound and pass the test of all those people who are going to go 'that's not right, that was a leading question, or whatever'. As far as I'm concerned we have passed all our responsibility – for those kinds of issues and it standing up as a piece of research as a tool for future work – to the university. It is being carried with the name of the university.

Kath: I think I strategically deployed the name of the university but I also would distance it from the university in a sense in trying to engage the community. If it was just seen as an academic piece of research, I don't think people would have engaged with it the way they have.

Of course it's not. It is just part of the life and soul of being, hands on, dirty activist, which is what I am really, because I'm immersed in stuff. In terms of the research that's quite different. My understanding is that researchers are 'supposed to be' aloof and not to be contaminated in the evidence and come out from a different world and stand with white clipboards. You've brought down from the Tower of Babel, the university, into dirty politics of horse trading around questions. In that process but you have been helped by having other people with some experience of those processes.

The journey doesn't end here ...

There aren't beginnings and endings, it's all about middles. I don't believe in ends. It's all about the process and it's all about engaging. If we can help that then we are succeeding. If we are getting in the way of it then we are failing. It's as simple as that.

I want to encourage people to listen to each other and it's a two way process. But we exist over there as well as over there. I think the hardest thing is being those of us who sit on both sides of the fence. We are providers. We are part of the evil machine that is shitting on people's lives and we know that it is happening. We work with these authorities that are doing this and that and our sense of collusion with the evil machine is quite difficult. There are people who bring to the table a very different journey, of privilege, around their own sexuality and around other identities. They are having to learn that no, not everybody had that journey. That is difficult for them and is true for all of us.

CONCLUSION

I will finish with an academic conclusion after what I find to be powerful and moving words from Leela and Arthur. The accounts from Arthur, Leela and myself illustrate that positionalities are continually and relationally (re)created throughout research processes in social geographies. Although we can give accounts of our positionalities in write-ups of research, researchers are continually (re)positioning themselves. Those who are engaging in this process can seek to explore the possibilities and problems of the power relations that are inherent not just to research, but also to the critical processes of addressing marginalisations, disenfranchisements and exclusions. In this chapter I move beyond positionalities that rely on the categorisations of researchers' identities and associated assumptions of power. I follow Cahill (2007) in exploring (shifting) positionalities and their relational construction, in this context between researchers, partners and participants. These do not only alter temporally, they are created beyond the 'tower' of the universities and 'researchy ways' between the spaces of participation, activism and everyday lives. They are also risky, as the politics of emotions and the ethics of care for researchers, as front line workers, have yet to be substantially addressed.

This chapter illustrates that in participatory action research projects the place of the researchers as co-constructors of the research is relevant to understanding how PAR research is created. There are dangers in reflecting on positionalities. Vanderbeck (2005), as well as pointing to the dangers of 'coming out' with powerful positionalities that are not questioned, queried or undermined, argues that lives and careers can be negatively affected by coming out as other to these hegemonies. Yet, not to explore or acknowledge positionalities renders the researcher invisible, and thus is problematic for the construction of social geographical knowledge. If knowledge is formed then in order to understand its creation, including its successes, possibilities and limitations, we need to contextualise data and research processes. In the example outlined here, the synergies between 'us' as researchers/participants and our diverse practices and readings, offer important insights into how Count Me In Too was created.

Positionalities in PAR contexts are complex, and could perhaps be undertaken even more critically than we have done. However, this poses a number of problems. Professionally, public critique has the potential to undermine the project and challenge the important relationships that have been created (not just between the researchers but also with stakeholders, funders and others who have a 'stake' in the project – particularly those for whom research can improve their lives). In addition, the performance of academic critique even in the pages of an academic book has personal consequences, where the friendships and relationships are meaningful beyond the research and its products – such as this chapter. It is certain critiques and silences that will always be the excess of the accounts I (and others) will give of Count Me In Too. This is not limited to this research project; suffice to note that it is not always 'knowability' (Rose, 1995) that creates excesses to research accounts; it is also (perhaps justifiable) political and personal decisions. These require careful negotiation.

The accounts here demonstrate that considerations of positionalities do not operate solely around, or in relation to, identity categories of male, heterosexual, white. If hegemonies are diversely (and spatially) recreated, one can be hegemonic even when not conforming to the 'white, middle class, heterosexual, male' category. This is not to say that white, heterosexual males should not critically interrogate their 'journey of privilege'. Rather that 'hegemony' and 'privilege' may also apply to those who 'fail' to do our sexuality/gender within particular hegemonic frames. This chapter has shown that relations of power within and between the LGBT communities (as well as other marginalised identities) need critical attention in addressing the permeability of privilege and the fluidity of power, especially in Arthur's words where 'we sit on both sides of the fence' and we are 'part of the evil machine that is shitting on people's lives'.

Ending one of her powerful pieces of writing, Gillian Rose (1996: 73) states: 'I turn to you as my audience [...] and, as I can't hear your reactions, end this chapter with the recognition that without you, I am nothing'. Similarly, I want to turn to the diversity of this audience/you, and many other audiences beyond you, to recognise your multiplicity and diversity. Those who deviate from hegemonic norms within the (geographical) academy are not only read by those who reiterate them. It may be empowering for those of us who do not 'fit' to understand and engage with 'failed', 'other' and 'different' research identities, interactions and relationships.

Moreover, reflecting Leela's thoughts on marginalisations, discussions of research practices and critical engagements with power relations could perhaps make 'white, middle class, heterosexual males' vulnerable, or encourage them to connect with and question their marginalisations and privileges. Positionalities, then, are not simplistic acknowledgements of privilege, power or marginalisations within pre-defined powerful/powerless categories: they are engagements with relations of power which understand that 'without you, I am nothing'. It's not about them and us, it's about us.

NOTES

1 I is used here to refer to Kath Browne, except where otherwise indicated.

2 In using 'male', I am referring to performances of hegemonic masculinities (see Vanderbeck, 2005; Van Hoven and Horschelmann, 2005)

3 For the purposes of this chapter and the Count Me In Too research project, participatory action research is understood as research that is co-constructed in order to change lives in socially progressive ways (see Kindon, this volume, for a full account of PAR).

4 Spectrum was the 'community partner' for this research project. It was formed after the Count Me In survey in 2000 highlighted (amongst many other things) the need for ongoing LGBT community engagement with statutory services. Spectrum is continually evolving with that broad remit but currently sees itself as an evidence based organisation and will use Count Me In Too to further their work with the LGBT communities and statutory services in Brighton & Hove.

5 There is a developing literature that explores coming out in the research process and write-up that is beyond the scope of this chapter, but starting points would include Binnie, 1997; Lewin and Leap, 1996; Knopp, 1999; Skelton, 1997; Valentine, 2002.

6 Homonormativity is understood here as the privilege associated with normalising particular forms of lesbian and gay sexualities. It is a contested concept and one I use tentatively in this chapter for the purpose of exploring privilege and power beyond heteronormativity. See Ahmed, 2004; Browne, 2006; Browne et al., 2007; Halberstam, 2005 for further discussions of this concept.

7 Postgraduate symposium on researching citizenship and belonging, University of Leeds, 14th March 2006. Keynote (http://www.geog.leeds.ac.uk/conferences/pscb/)

REFERENCES

Ahmed, S. (2004) *The Cultural Politics of Emotion*. Edinburgh: Edinburgh University Press.

Bell, D. (1997) 'Sex lives and audiotape: geography, sexuality and undergraduate dissertations', *Arena Symposium: Teaching Sexual Geographies*: 411–17.

Berg, L. (2002) 'Gender equity as "boundary object": ... or the same old sex and power in geography all over again?', *The Canadian Geographer*, 46 (3): 248–54.

Binnie, J. (1997) 'Coming out of geography: towards a queer epistemology?', *Environment and Planning D: Society and Space*, 15: 223–37.

Breakwell, G.M. (1995) 'Interviewing', in, G.M. Breakwell, S. Hammond and C. Fife-Schaw (eds), *Research Methods in Psychology*. London: Sage.

Browne, K. (2003) 'Negotiations and fieldworkings: Friendship and feminist research', ACME: *An International E-Journal for Critical Geographers*, 2 (2): 132–46.

Browne, K. (2006) 'Challenging "queer" geographies', *Antipode* , 38 (5): 885–93.

Browne, K. (2008) `Power and privilege: (re) making feminist geographies,' in. P. Moss and K. Falconer-Al-Hindi (eds), *Feminisms in Geography: Rethinking Space, Place and Knowledges*. Plymouth: Rowman and Littlefield, pp. 140–9.

Browne, K., Lim, J. and Brown, G. (2007) *Geographies of Sexualities: Theories, practices and politics*. London: Ashgate.

Butler, J. (1990) *Gender Trouble*. London: Routledge.

Butz, D. and Berg, L. (2002) 'Paradoxical space: geography, men, and duppy feminism', in P. Moss (ed.), *Feminist Geography in Practice*. Oxford: Blackwell. pp. 87–102.

Cahill, C. (2007) 'The personal is political: Developing new subjectivities through participatory action research', *Gender, Place and Culture*, 14 (3): 262–92.

Cook, J.A. and Fonow, M.M. (1990) 'Knowledge and women's interest: issues of epistemology and methodology in feminist sociological research', in J. McCarl Nielson (ed.), *Feminist Research Methods: Exemplary Readings in the Social Sciences*. London: Westview Press. pp. 69–91.

Crang, M. (2003) 'Qualitative methods: touchy, feely, look-see?', *Progress in Human Geography*, 27 (4): 494–504.

Dias, K. and Blecha, J. (2007) 'Feminism and social theory in geography: An introduction', *The Professional Geographer*, 59 (1): 1–9.

Domosh, M. (2003) 'Toward a more fully reciprocal feminist inquiry', *ACME: An International E-Journal for Critical Geographers*, 2 (1): 107–11.

England, K. (1994) 'Getting personal: reflexivity, positionality, and feminist research', *Professional Geographer*, 46 (1): 80–9.

Falconer-Al-Hindi, K. and Kawabata, H. (2002) 'Toward a more fully reflexive feminist geography', in P. Moss (ed.), *Feminist Geographies in Practice*. Oxford: Blackwell. pp. 103–15.

Gregson, N. and Rose, G. (2000) 'Taking Butler elsewhere: performativities, spatialities and subjectivities', *Environment and Planning D-Society & Space*, 18: 433–52.

Halberstam, J. (2005) *In a Queer Time and Place: Transgender Bodies, Subcultural Lives*. New York: New York University Press.

Haraway, D. (1991) *Simians, Cyborgs and Women: The Reinvention of Nature*. London. FA.

Harding, S. (1987) *Feminism and Methodology*. Milton Keynes: Open University Press.

Harding, S. (1993) 'Rethinking standpoint epistemology: what is strong objectivity?' in L. Alcoff and E. Potter (eds), *Feminist Epistemologies*. London: Routledge. pp. 49–82.

Hirsh, M. and Fox Keller, E. (1994) *Conflicts in Feminism*. London: Routledge.

Hubbard, P. (1999) 'Researching female sex work: reflections on geographical exclusion, critical methodologies and "useful" knowledge', *Area*, 31 (1): 229–37.

Hubbard, P., Kitchin, R., Bartley, B. and Fuller, D. (2002) *Thinking Geographically: Space, Theory and Contemporary Human Geography*. London: Continuum.

Jones III, J.P., Nast, H.J. and Roberts, S.M. (1997) 'Thresholds in feminist geography: difference, methodology, representation', in J.P. Jones III, H.J. Nast and S.M. Roberts (eds), *Thresholds in Feminist Geography: Difference, Methodology, Representation*. Oxford: Rowman & Littlefield Publishers. pp. xxi–xxxix.

Kindon, S., Pain, R. and Kesby, M. (2007) *Participatory Action Research Approaches and Methods: Connecting People, Participation and Place*. London: Routledge.

Kitchin, R. (2000) 'The researched opinions on research: disabled people and disability research', *Disability and Society*, 15 (1): 25–47.

Kleinmann, S. and Copp, M.A. (1993) *Emotions and Fieldwork*. London: Sage.

Knopp, L. (1999) 'Out in academia: the queer politics of one geographer's sexualisation', *Journal of Geography in Higher Education*, 23 (1): 116–23.

Kobayashi, A. (1994) 'Coloring the field: gender, race, and the politics of fieldwork', *Professional Geographer*, 46 (1): 73–80.

Lewin, E. and Leap, W. (1996) *Out in the Field: Reflections of Lesbian and Gay Anthropologists*. Chicago: University of Illinois Press.

Lohan, M. (2000) 'Come back public/private (almost) all is forgiven: using feminist methodologies in communication technologies', *Women's Studies International Forum*, 23 (1): 107–17.

Longino, H.E. (1993) 'Subjects, power, and knowledge: description and prescription in feminist philosophies of science', in L. Alcoff and E. Potter (eds), *Feminist Epistemologies*. London: Routledge, pp. 101–20.

Maynard, M. (1994) 'Methods, practice and epistemology: the debate about feminism and research', in M. Maynard and J. Purvis (eds), *Researching Women's Lives from a Feminist Perspective*. London: Taylor & Francis. pp. 10–26.

McCormack, T. (1987) 'Feminism and the new crisis in methodology', in W. Tomm (ed.), *The Effects of Feminist Approaches on Research Methodologies*. Calgary: Winfrid Laurier University Press. pp. 13–30.

Morris, K., Woodward, D. and Peters, E. (1998) '"Whose side are you on?" Dilemmas in conducting feminist ethnographic research with young women', *Social Research Methodology*, 1 (3): 217–30.

Moss, P. (1993) 'Focus: feminism as a method', *The Canadian Geographer*, 37 (1): 48–9.

Moss, P. (2002) 'Taking on, thinking about and doing feminist research in geography', in P. Moss (ed.), *Feminist Geographies in Practice*. Oxford: Blackwell. pp. 1–20.

Murphy, P. (2002) 'The anthropologist's son (or living and learning in the field)", *Qualitative Inquiry*, 8 (2): 246–61.

Oakley, A. (1998) 'Gender, methodology and people's way of knowing: some problems with feminism and paradigm debate in social science', *Sociology*, 32 (4): 707–34.
Price-Chalita, P. (1994) 'Spatial metaphor and the politics of empowerment: mapping a place for feminism and postmodernism and geography?', *Antipode*, 26 (3): 236–54.
Rose, G. (1993) *Feminism & Geography: The Limits of Geographical Knowledge*. Cambridge: Polity Press.
Rose, G. (1995) `Distance, surface, elsewhere: a feminist critique of the space of phallocentric self/knowledge,' *Environment and Planning D*, 13: 761–81.
Rose, G. (1996) 'As if the mirrors had bled: masculine dwelling, masculine theory and the feminist masquerade', in N. Duncan (ed.), *Bodyspace: Destablising Geographies of Gender and Sexuality*. London: Routledge. pp. 56–74.
Rose, G. (1997) `Situating knowledges: positionality, reflexivities and other tactics,' *Progress in Human Geography*, 2 (3): 307–20.
Rose, G. (1999) 'Performing space', in D. Massey, J. Allen, and P. Sarre (eds), *Human Geography Today*. Cambridge: Polity Press. pp. 257–59.
Skelton, T. (1997) 'Issues of sexuality in the teaching space', *Journal of Geography in Higher Education*, 21 (3): 424–31.
Stanley, L. and Wise, S. (1983) *Breaking Out*. London: Routledge.
Twyman, C., Morrison, J. and Sporton, D. (1999) 'The final fifth: autobiography, reflexivity, and interpretation in cross-cultural research', *Area*, 31 (4): 313–25.
Valentine, G. (2002) 'People like us: negotiating sameness and difference in the research process', in P. Moss (ed.), *Feminist Geography in Practice*. Oxford: Blackwell. pp. 116–26.
Van Hoven, B. and Horschelmann, K. (2005) *Spaces of Masculinities*. London: Routledge.
Vanderbeck, R. (2005) 'Masculinities and fieldwork: widening the discussion', *Gender, Place and Culture*, 12 (4): 387–402.

Index